Writers'
& Artists'
YEARBOOK
2022

Other Writers' and Artists' titles

Writers' & Artists' Guides to . . . Series

Self-publishing
Writing for Children and YA by Linda Strachan
Getting Published by Alysoun Owen
How to Hook an Agent by James Rennoldson
How to Write by William Ryan

The Organised Writer: How to stay on top of all your projects and never miss a deadline by Antony Johnston
    'Antony has uncovered a secret I wish I'd learned twenty years ago;
    writing benefits way less from inspiration than from sound process.'
                    Merlin Mann

'I'm a messy-brained writer. *The Organised Writer* helped me to tidy-up, and improved my working life on a daily basis.' *Kieron Gillen*

The Right Word: A Writer's Toolkit of Grammar, Vocabularly and Literary Terms

NEW in July 2021
Children's Writers' & Artists' Yearbook 2022
    'It's rare to find a book that's as useful as it is inspiring . . . essential
                reading.' *M. G. Leonard*

You can buy copies of all these titles from your local bookseller or online at www.writersandartists.co.uk/shop

Writers' & Artists' YEARBOOK 2022

ONE HUNDRED AND FIFTEENTH EDITION

THE ESSENTIAL GUIDE TO THE MEDIA AND PUBLISHING INDUSTRIES

The perfect companion for writers of fiction and non-fiction, poets, playwrights, journalists, and commercial artists

BLOOMSBURY

LONDON · OXFORD · NEW YORK · NEW DELHI · SYDNEY

BLOOMSBURY YEARBOOKS
Bloomsbury Publishing Plc
50 Bedford Square, London, WC1B 3DP, UK
29 Earlsfort Terrace, Dublin 2, Ireland

BLOOMSBURY YEARBOOKS, WRITERS' & ARTISTS' and the Diana logo
are trademarks of Bloomsbury Publishing Plc

First published in Great Britain 1906
This edition published 2021

A catalogue record for this book is available from the British Library

ISBN: PB: 978-1-4729-8283-4; eBook: 978-1-4729-8282-7

2 4 6 8 10 9 7 5 3 1

Typeset by DLxml, a division of RefineCatch Limited, Bungay, Suffolk
Printed and bound in Great Britain by CPI Group (UK) Ltd, Croydon, CR0 4YY

MIX
Paper from
responsible sources
FSC® C020471

To find out more about our authors and books visit www.bloomsbury.com and sign up for our
newsletters.

Writers' & Artists' team
Editor Alysoun Owen
Assistant editor Eden Phillips Harrington
Articles copy-editor Virginia Klein
Listings editors Lisa Carden, Rebecca Collins, Eden Phillips Harrington
Editorial assistance Lauren MacGowan; Sophia Blackwell (poetry)
Production controller Ben Chisnall

A note from the Editor

The Editor welcomes readers to this edition of the *Writers' & Artists' Yearbook*

There is some good news for booklovers, and publishers, from the last year: in 2020 we saw a very significant rise in sales (units and revenue) of consumer or general interest digital and audiobooks, and some more modest increase in print sales too. At times of unexpected incarceration it seems people took solace in the written word. All genres of books, fiction and non-fiction for all ages, sold in greater numbers than in the previous few years. The trend looks set to continue in the immediate term, as Tom Tivnan's article *News, views and trends: review of the publishing year* (page 102) indicates.

Having readers with an appetite for stories is good news for writers, and this *Yearbook* brings advice from successfully published authors to encourage you as you craft your own narratives. It provides testimonies that span from the very established and international bestselling writer at the top of his game, Peter James (see *Becoming a bestselling author: my writing story* on page 230), to the debut writer Femi Kayode, whose article *Shelf space: a debut writer's journey to claim his space* on page 246 charts how the first in his series of novels came to be published. Are you unsure whether your idea is ripe for a novel or for other treatment? In *Audio dramatist or novelist?* (page 365), award-winning writer of novels, film scripts and radio dramas, Jonathan Myerson helps you decide. Ingrid Persaud illustrates how winning a literary prize can help get you and your work noticed (see *The winning touch: the impact of winning a prize* on page 250) and Sam Missingham, in *Building your author brand* (page 626), provides tips on how else you might get attention from readers, particularly if you are trying to self-publish.

If finding an agent to represent you is what you are hoping for, then take a look at what Sallyanne Sweeney says in *What a debut novelist should expect from an agent* (page 405). Carina Martin, in *Becoming a successful copywriter* on page 301, suggests how else you might employ your professional creative skills and Ed Needham proves that it is possible to be ambitious and successful in his *Setting up and editing a new magazine* on page 11. Ed's magazine, *Strong Words,* is a must for all bibliophiles and, as Cathy Rentzenbrink eloquently reminds us in her essay *Reading as a writer* (on page 241), the best writers are readers first.

It is helpful to learn about how the publishing industry operates; sales manager David Wightman provides his insights into selling books in *Getting books to market: how books are sold* on page 110. If you need support with the financial and legal aspects of being a writer or artist, turn to the last two sections of this *Yearbook*. We have a new piece on *Author-Publisher contracts* on page 710, a completely rewritten article on *National Insurance contributions* by Sarah Bradford (page 732) and comprehensive guidance from Jonathan and Louise Ford on *Managing your finances: a guide for writers* (page 721).

Alongside all these news articles are a wide range of updated essays, collectively offering practical advice for poets, novelists, screenwriters, dramatists, and authors of non-fiction books and magazine articles. Whether you seek a publisher or literary agent or want to take the do-it-yourself route, the entries across each section of this book list who you need to contact.

Happy writing, happy book buying and happy reading.

Alysoun Owen
Editor

All articles, listings and other material in this yearbook are reviewed and updated every year in consultation with the bodies, organisations, companies and individuals that we select for inclusion. To the best of our knowledge the websites, emails and other contact details are correct at the time of going to press.

Short story competition

The annual *Writers' & Artists' Yearbook* Short Story Competition offers published and aspiring writers the chance to win a place on an Arvon residential writing course (worth £850). In addition, the winner's story will be published on the Writers & Artists website.

To enter the competition, submit a short story (for adults) of no more than 2,000 words, on any theme by 11 February 2022 to waybcompetitions@bloomsbury.com. For full details, terms and conditions, and to find out more about how to submit your entry, visit www.writersandartists.co.uk/competitions.

ARVON runs creative writing courses and retreats from three writing houses in the UK, each in a beautiful rural location. Published writers lead week-long or short residential courses. Covering a diverse range of genres, from poetry and fiction to screenwriting and non-fiction, Arvon courses have provided inspiration to thousands of people at all stages of their writing lives. You can find out more and book a course online at www.arvon.org.

More than a book

The Writers & Artists **website** (www.writersandartists.co.uk) has relaunched. It offers more free content and resources than ever before.

Here you will find hundreds of **articles** on the writing and publishing process, regular **writing competitions**, and a **community** space to share your work or ask questions about the entire creative process. Brand new features, such as being able to annotate and book-mark pages, can be accessed by creating your **free user account.** As a registered member of the Writers & Artists community, you will receive – straight to your dashboard – exclusive discounts on books, events and editing services and regular content to match your particular interests.

You can find details of our range of **editing services** as well as our **writing courses** and **workshops** (face-to-face and online), including **Manuscript Submission** Masterclasses and one-day **How to Get Published** events.

Our **Listings subscription** offers you access to the entire database of contacts in the latest edition this *Yearbook*, as well as hundreds of additional online-only entries.

Whatever your needs, we hope that Writers & Artists resources, whether delivered in an ebook, print, online or at our events, will provide you with the information, advice and inspiration you are looking for.

Contents

A note from the Editor v
More than a book vii

Newspapers and magazines
Getting started 1
Writing for online and print – Suzanne Elliott 2
Life's a pitch: how to get your ideas into print
– Mike Unwin 7
Setting up and editing a new magazine
– Ed Needham 11

Listings
National newspapers UK and Ireland 15
Regional newspapers UK and Ireland 24
Magazines UK and Ireland 36
Syndicates, news and press agencies 96

Books

The publishing process
How to get published 99
News, views and trends: review of the
publishing year – Tom Tivnan 102
The mathematics of publishing – Scott Pack 107
Getting books to market: how books are sold
– David Wightman 110
Crowdfunding your novel – Alice Jolly 114
Managing a successful writing career
– Tony Bradman 117
Debut success with an indie publisher
– Wyl Menmuir 121
Defining genre fiction – Maxim Jakubowski 124
On mentoring – Jill Dawson 127

Listings
Book publishers UK and Ireland 130
Book publishers overseas 198
Audio publishers 223
Book packagers 226

Inspiring writers
Becoming a bestselling author: my writing story
– Peter James 230
First chapters: how to grab your reader's
attention – Emma Flint 233
Keeping the writing dream alive – S.J. Watson 237
Advice to a new writer – Rachel Joyce 239
Reading as a writer – Cathy Rentzenbrink 241
Real people write books – Samantha Shannon 244
Shelf space: a debut writer's journey to claim his
place – Femi Kayode 246
The winning touch: the impact of winning an
award – Ingrid Persaud 250

The 'how to' of writing how-to books
– Kate Harrison 253
Finding my agent – Martina Cole 257
Notes from a successful children's author
– J.K. Rowling 259

Writing advice
Changing lanes: writing across genres and
forms – Mark Illis 262
Turning to crime: writing thrillers
– Kimberley Chambers 265
Writing character-led novels – Kerry Hudson 268
Writing romantic fiction – Raffaella Barker 271
Ever wanted to write a saga? – Di Redmond 274
Writing speculative fiction – Claire North 277
Breaking into comics – Antony Johnston 280
Writing a romcom – Rachel Winters 284
Writing historical fiction: lessons learned
– Tim Pears 288
Writing popular history books – Tom Holland 292
Blurring facts with fiction: memoir and
biography – Nell Stevens 295
Ghostwriting – Gillian Stern 298
Becoming a successful copywriter
– Carina Martin 301
Making facts your mission: the pleasure of
writing non-fiction – Jane Robinson 305
How to become a travel writer – Jonathan Lorie 309
Writing about science for the general reader
– Suzanne O'Sullivan 314
So you want to write about nature ...
– Melissa Harrison 317
Writing for the health and wellness market
– Anita Bean 320
Writing sports books – Frances Jessop 324

Poetry
How to become a poet – Andrew McMillan 329
Poems for the page and on stage
– Raymond Antrobus 332
Notes from a passionate poet
– Benjamin Zephaniah 334
Getting your poetry out there – Neil Astley 336

Listings
Poetry organisations 342

Screen and audio
Successful screenwriting – Anna Symon 351
Adapting books for stage and screen
– Ana Garanito 354
Writing series for television – Russell Lewis 357
Podcasting: how to get creative and make
money – Sam Delaney 361

Audio dramatist or novelist?
– Jonathan Myerson   365
Should I make an audiobook? – James Peak   369
Writing for videogames: a guide for the curious
– Chris Bateman   373

Listings
Television and radio   377

Theatre
How to get your play published and performed
– Temi Wilkey   385
Writing about theatre: reviews, interviews and
more – Mark Fisher   389

Listings
Theatre producers   393

Literary agents
What a debut novelist should expect from an
agent – Sallyanne Sweeney   405
What does a literary agent do?
– James Rennoldson   408
Putting together your submission
– Hellie Ogden   410
Advice from an 'accidental' agent
– Clare Grist Taylor   415
Cross-format representation: what a literary
agent can do for you – Sarah Such   419
How to submit a non-fiction proposal
– Andrew Lownie   423
A day in the life of a literary agent
– Charlotte Seymour   427

Listings
Literary agents UK and Ireland   430
Literary agents overseas   461

Art and illustration
Freelancing for beginners – Fig Taylor   475
Illustrating non-fiction books – Frances Moffatt   483
How to make a living: money matters
– Alison Branagan   488

Listings
Art agents and commercial art studios   492
Card and stationery publishers that accept
illustrations and photographs   497

Societies, prizes and festivals
Festival fun: your guide to why, how and what
– Adam Hamdy   501
Developing talent: support and opportunities
for writers – Helen Chaloner   505

Listings
Society of Authors   509
WGGB (Writers' Guild of Great Britain)   512
Alliance of Independent Authors   515
Societies, associations and clubs   516

Prizes and awards   556
Opportunities for under-represented writers   592
Prize winners   595
Festivals and conferences for writers, artists and
readers   596

Self-publishing
Self-publishing online: the emerging template
for sales success – Harry Bingham   607
Going solo: self-publishing in the digital age
– Dean Crawford   611
Getting your book stocked in a high-street
bookshop – Sheila O'Reilly   614
What do self-publishing providers offer?
– Jeremy Thompson   618
In praise of fanfic – Hari Patience   621
Building your author brand – Sam Missingham   626
Making waves online – Simon Appleby   630

Listings
Book sites, blogs and podcasts   635
Editorial services and self-publishing providers   640

Resources for writers
Editing your work   651
Writing an award-winning blog – Julia Mitchell   658
Indexing – Society of Indexers   660
ISBNs: what you need to know   662
Public Lending Right   665
A matter of style: A mini A-Z of literary terms   670
Who's who in publishing   673
Glossary of publishing terms   675
Software for writers   680

Listings
Libraries   682
Writers' retreats and creative writing courses   691

Law and copyright
UK copyright law and publishing rights
– Lynette Owen   703
A legal lexicon   709
Author-Publisher contracts   710
Copyright Licensing Agency Ltd   713
Authors' Licensing and Collecting Society   715
DACS (Design and Artists Copyright Society)   717
Publishers' Licensing Services   719

Money, tax and benefits
Managing your finances: a guide for writers
– Jonathan and Louise Ford   721
National Insurance contributions
– Sarah Bradford   732

Indexes
Subject indexes   742
General index   777
Listings index   781

During the preparation of this edition of the *Yearbook*, the impacts of the 2020-21 coronavirus were still being felt. Some of the articles allude to this. The lockdowns and associated social distancing and uncertainties have necessarily impacted on live events such as literary festivals, award ceremonies, poetry and theatre performances, face-to-face creative writing courses, and much more besides. We have included updated listings for these as we do every year in consultation with the companies and organisations themselves, though are aware that many will not be going ahead in their usual form. Please do check online for the different ways organisations, societies and other groups will be supporting writers and illustrators over the coming months and be aware that some of the information in this year's *Yearbook* will be subject to greater change than usual.

Newspapers and magazines
Getting started

Most of the titles included in the newspapers and magazines section of this *Yearbook* offer opportunities to the writer. To help you get started, see the guidelines below.

Study the market

• It is an editor's job to know what readers want, and to see that they get it. Thus, freelance contributions must be tailored to fit a specific market; subject, theme, treatment, length must meet the editor's requirements.

• Before sending in a pitch, an article or feature, always look at the editorial requirements of the magazine: the subjects covered by the publication as well as the approach, treatment, style and typical length of pieces.

Check with the editor first

• Before submitting material to any newspaper or magazine it is advisable to first contact the relevant editor. A quick telephone call or email will establish the name of the relevant commissioning editor.

• It is not advisable to send illustrations 'on spec'; check with the editor first.

Understand how the market works

• It is worth considering using an agent to syndicate material. Most agents operate on an international basis and are aware of current market requirements. See page 96.

• The larger newspapers and magazines buy many of their stories, and the smaller papers buy general articles, through well-known syndicates.

• For the supply of news, most of the larger UK and overseas newspapers depend on their own staff and press agencies. The most important overseas newspapers have permanent representatives in the UK who keep them supplied with news and articles. While many overseas newspapers and magazines have a London office, it is usual for freelance contributions to be submitted to the headquarters' editorial office overseas.

Payment

• Many newspapers and magazines are reluctant to state a standard rate, since the value of a contribution may be dependent not upon length but upon the standing of the writer or the information supplied. Many other periodicals prefer to state 'by negotiation' or 'by arrangement', rather than giving precise payment information.

Writing for online and print

Experienced freelance journalist Suzanne Elliott has sound advice on how to work successfully as a writer across different platforms in the age of fake news, social media and new technology.

Not long ago journalists were split into digital or print specialists, with a certain snottiness reserved for the online usurpers. But that attitude has changed and writing for online is no longer considered the poor cousin of print journalism. There is now far more content and staff crossover. Magazines, in particular, have embraced a more fluid relationship between the two platforms, with many pulling everything under a single 'content' umbrella.

Having worked in print and online, in newsrooms, for fashion magazines, creative agencies and press agencies, I've ridden the wave of a shifting media world over the last 20 years. Having lived through the eye of the storm, it's been fascinating watching the shift, as the internet changed how we consumed news and, as a consequence, how journalists write.

While this changing environment has proved challenging for traditional news outlets, it does provide exciting opportunities for freelancers and I hope these tips I've picked up in my time as a freelance journalist will make it easier for newcomers to exploit.

News writing

Despite the changing landscape, the *'when, where, who, what, why'* formula still applies – whether you are writing for online or print, newspaper or magazine.

The inverted triangle method puts the most important detail – the five 'Ws' – in the first one or two sentences. The reader should be able to stop reading at this point and still have grasped the main points of the story. This journalism 101 may have been around since the printing press but, in a world where people consume news at a rapid pace, it has never been more appropriate. For example:

Two people have died after their car was involved in a collision with a lorry on the M25 near Leatherhead.

After this initial scene setting, you move on to the middle section that fleshes out the story, identifying victims, giving their ages, explaining how the accident happened.

The final third will include other relevant background information, quotes and perhaps a reference to a similar story.

Writing for online *v* print

While the foundations of journalism apply across all formats, there are some differences between writing for online and print. Online articles traditionally follow several other formats: news pieces; listicles (also popular in magazines); picture-led galleries (usually reserved for fashion, beauty and celebrity content); and short, blog-like articles.

Until recently, the emphasis had been to keep online articles short and, while that rule still applies to a lot of online content, more traditional long-form pieces of between 1,000 and 20,000 words are gaining popularity with publishers and readers.

Many of the regular, daily-updated and news-focused articles will be written in-house, so you will find that focusing on evergreen articles (content that is always relevant and does not date like news stories) can be a more successful route to catching an editor's eye.

Comment or opinion (op-ed) pieces are common in both print and digital. Timely pieces differ from news articles as they enable a writer to express their own, often provocative or controversial, opinion on a topical subject. They are usually personal and conversational and, unlike a news piece, they entertain as well as stimulate conversation.

What is fake news?

An article no longer has to be a comment or opinion piece to merit discussion. The internet enables readers to give immediate feedback on features and news stories, not all of it positive.

Increasingly, the term 'fake news' has become an accusation aimed at journalists by people who don't like what has been reported. It is also an increasing frustration for journalists trying to unearth the truth in a world full of false chatter. Fake news is nothing new, but in a 'post-truth' world, fuelled by social media and with some powerful politicians fixated on it, fake news has become a mainstream problem. Its impact on journalism is not to be underestimated. As it gains traction, fake news makes it difficult for journalists to cover high-profile news stories and undermines reports from reputable publications. Put simply, when we're telling the truth the world is not listening. A study by Buzzfeed found the top 20 fake news stories about the 2016 US presidential election received more engagement on Facebook than the top 20 *real* news stories from 19 major media outlets.

Never assume anything that appears on social media – or even other news outlets – is true until you have verified the source yourself. After the Manchester Arena bombing in May 2017, several posts of fake victims went viral within hours of the attack. One of the photos used in a montage was of Jayden Parkinson who was murdered in 2013, while another showed a picture of a young boy who had been used as a model for a fashion line several years before. Following the Grenfell Tower fire, a story of a baby being thrown from a window and caught was published in many newspapers and websites, but a BBC investigation discovered that the incident probably never happened.

Journalists need to play their part in fighting fake news, not fuelling it. Real news will always take a while to filter through, even in a world where everything is so immediate. Taking time to fact-check in the middle of a frantic breaking news story requires confidence and conviction. But it's better to be slow than to be wrong.

Style, accuracy and sources

Every publication has its own house style to ensure stylistic consistency and tone of voice. An editor may give you guidelines in the commission, but the best way to get a clear idea of style is to read the magazine, newspaper or website thoroughly.

Fact-check meticulously and don't be tempted to fudge facts. Choose your words carefully – simply replacing one word for another can alter the meaning of a sentence completely.

Record all interviews and ensure your sources are reliable and trustworthy. Many a journalist has been tripped up by failing to check the credibility of a too-good-to-be-true scoop. In 2004, Piers Morgan was sacked as editor of the *Daily Mirror* after printing fake photos of British soldiers abusing an Iraqi, claiming he had fallen victim to a 'calculated and malicious hoax'.

A working knowledge of **libel laws** is an absolute necessity for any journalist. Writing anything potentially libellous can, at best, end with the publication having to print an apology, and, at worse, land them and you in court.

The Defamation Act was updated in 2013 to include social media. You can defame someone by publishing material:

- in newspapers, magazines and other printed media;
- in radio and TV broadcasts;
- on the internet, including online forums, social media and blogs;
- by email.

Spreading 'false' news, through sloppiness and errors of judgement, is only going to further discredit journalism and fuel accusations of fake news in the mainstream media.

The rise of the internet has given a voice to citizen, or public, journalism. American journalist Courtney Radsch, author of *Cyberactivism and Citizen Journalism in Egypt: Digital Dissidence and Political Change* (Palgrave Macmillan 2016) defines it as an 'activist form of news gathering' that is 'driven by different objectives and ideals and relies on alternative sources of legitimacy than traditional or mainstream journalism.'

Technology, including smart phones and social media, have enabled members of the public to report a breaking news story more quickly than journalists, particularly in countries where foreign media access is limited. Citizen journalism played a key role in the 2010 Arab Spring, the war in Syria – especially during the battle of Aleppo – and in the 2018 economic protests in Iran.

While citizen journalism plays a significant role in unfolding news stories, a degree of caution should be applied to reports from non-professional journalists, as citizen journalism by its very nature is subjective. This doesn't devalue its worth, but its objectives and reference points should always be understood before taking it as verbatim.

Online journalism – the ins and outs

Flexibility and an open mind are important when working as a freelance journalist across different platforms. Working online involves embracing technology and usually means going beyond a traditional journalist's job description. It is common to be asked to picture edit, sub-edit, promote articles on social channels such as Twitter and Facebook and, increasingly, video edit. A grasp of content management systems (CMS) is essential if you work online. No two systems are the same, but they are increasingly user-friendly.

Online headlines have to work extra hard. They not only have to grab a reader's attention, they must contain the right *keywords* to make it more visible to a search engine. Most search queries are two to four words long and consist of proper names and keywords. Ensuring that your headline and copy are SEO or search engine optimisation-friendly without compromising the quality of your writing is an important skill for online journalists. The journalistic maxim 'man bites dog' – used to describe how unusual events are more likely to be reported as news – would need to be rewritten for online purposes using keywords and proper names to make it SEO-friendly, for example: '*Hampshire man, 39, bites golden retriever on leg at Center Parcs*'.

How to find a story

- Social media and news wires can be great sources of breaking news and a way of monitoring popular campaigns (e.g. #MeToo or the ice bucket challenge), but you certainly won't have been the only journalist to have spotted a trending topic – so don't rely too heavily on these.
- Social media can be helpful in other ways. Got a story and need case studies? Twitter and Facebook can be excellent ways to find people, under the hashtag #journorequest.

• Online journalist communities also offer excellent resources for freelancers to broaden their network, ask for contacts and stay up-to-date with the latest media news and jobs. Try JournoAnswers (www.facebook.com/groups/JournoAnwers) or the online reporters and editors group on LinkedIn (www.linkedin.com/groups/75711).

• Have something (a pen, a smartphone) to jot down any light-bulb story ideas. A seemingly irrelevant observation or off-hand remark can be the first germ of a far bigger idea.

• Sometimes a more interesting story is hidden *within* the story you are going after, or hidden within a seemingly unexceptional press release.

• Think locally – read the local papers, talk to local people. Big news stories can be buried in bin collection disputes or fundraising efforts.

• Be curious and ask questions. People love talking about themselves, especially about something they are passionate about.

Pitching

While print and digital formats are more symbiotic that ever, they often still exist and are structured as two separate publications within an organisation. In a row with the *Guardian* in 2017 over commentator Katie Hopkins, *Daily Mail* editor Paul Dacre distanced himself from MailOnline, declaring in an editorial that the online version was 'a totally separate entity that has its own publisher, its own readership, different content and a very different world view'. It's therefore important to find out who the editor, or section editor, is within each platform.

Do not approach publications with a one-size-fits-all pitch. Think about how you consume articles online and pitch those ideas accordingly.

Tips for starting out

1. Start a blog

A blog can be an effective way to promote yourself and your writing. It is particularly useful if you're a freelance journalist just starting out, as it allows you to establish yourself as an authority, on a subject and as a writer. A well-managed blog can help create writing opportunities and at the same time demonstrate your initiative and interests. It's a great way to help find your voice as a writer and to sharpen your CMS and SEO skills.

The dos and don'ts of pitching

DO include your pitch within an email. No busy editor will want to download and then open a Word document, or equivalent.

DO explain who you are and why the piece you are pitching is relevant to the publication.

DO read the site you are pitching to thoroughly. Don't skim through the home page and assume you've seen everything. How often do they publish? What kind of article formats do they publish (galleries, long-form, etc)? Look at the word count for each one.

DON'T send a pitch email on a Friday afternoon or first thing on a Monday.

DON'T jump on the news bandwagon assuming you're the first person to think of a pitch.

DO flag up time-sensitive features and include a deadline if it is a news–related piece.

DON'T be precious about being edited. Even the most hard-nosed and experienced of journalists can bristle at an edit, but learning not to is an important skill.

DO get the tone of the publication right in the pitch. Pitching to a music website aimed at people in their 20s is different to pitching a long-form piece to a gardening print magazine with readers over 60.

DO keep the pitch short. Avoid going beyond four paragraphs; start with a brief sentence introducing yourself; then a sentence or two on the topic, why you want to write it, who you plan to interview, your suggested word count and any possible leads; finish with why you are the person to write it.

DO follow up the email within a few days if you have not heard back.

2. Have a social media presence

A Twitter profile will not only give you visibility; used well, it can also give you credibility. Use your full name (not a cheeky nickname from school) for your handle. In your bio, include your email address, your job title, publications you've written for and any speciality areas you work in. Tweet regular, appropriate updates that signpost your interests, and don't be afraid to let your personality come through.

And don't ignore LinkedIn. As well as being an excellent resource for journalists looking for scoops and jobs, by showing an up-to-date CV and a list of your skills and areas of expertise, LinkedIn makes it easier for editors who are looking for freelancers to find you.

3. Explore other writing opportunities

Content marketing, writing for a brand who want to behave like publishers, is a path increasingly open to journalists and writers. While it may not fit with your dreams of being the next Bob Woodward and Carl Bernstein, the essence of good editorial remains the same. Journalists know how to tell a good story; they know how to hook a reader with quality writing and present clear, compelling content – skills much in demand by brands.

4. Build relationships

One of the best pieces of advice I was given when I went freelance was to 'batter my contacts'. Do not be shy to approach people you have a connection with – whether it's a former colleague, someone you studied with, or an editor you met fleetingly at a party.

Do not assume they remember you, and keep your contact email formal, but people are far more likely to commission you if there is a trusted link there. Remember you are often a solution to someone's fix – you are looking for the work and they need someone to do it.

The essential bookshelf for the budding journalist

As Stephen King says: 'If you don't have time to read, you don't have the time (or the tools) to write.' Reading great journalists and writers can inspire, educate and galvanise.

• *How to write* – George Orwell, in *Politics and the English Language* (Horizon 1946)

Orwell's advice to 'Never use a long word when a short one will do' rings in my head whenever I write.

• *Bliss to be alive: the collected writings of Gavin Hills* (Penguin 2000)

Hills was what the *Independent* described as one of the 'serious boys of the Loaded generation'. His hugely engaging and vital pieces covered everything from civil war to football violence.

• *On Writing: a memoir of the craft* – Stephen King (New English Library 2001)

Read this and you'll never look at an adverb the same way again.

• *Scoop* – Evelyn Waugh (Chapman & Hall 1938)

While journalism has changed a great deal since William Boot, the *Daily Beast*'s timid nature correspondent, was sent to cover a socialist insurrection in (fictional) Ishmaelia, so much of this biting satire still rings true.

• *The Journalist and the Murderer* – Janet Malcolm (Knopf 1990)

A fascinating exploration of journalism ethics and the strange relationship between a reporter and their subject – in this case a man accused of murdering his wife and daughters.

Suzanne Elliott is a freelance journalist who has worked for ITV News, Vogue International, RedBull.com, EuroNews, *Men's Fitness, Shortlist, Huffington Post, Glamour, Marie Claire, Konfekt* and the *National* and has written editorial for companies including Iris Worldwide, Flash Pack, Global Radio, EE and Debenhams. For more information see https://muckrack.com/suzanne-elliott-7/portfolio or https://theviewfromtheuppercircle.com. Follow her on Twitter @CakeSuzette.

Life's a pitch: how to get your ideas into print

Mike Unwin has lots of valuable advice for would-be freelance writers keen to see their work in print, and explains what magazine and newspaper editors are looking for in a pitch.

Dear Editor

I'm desperate to write for you. Please let me. I'm not yet sure what to write – and I hesitate to share my ideas, in case you don't like them. But if you could just explain what you're looking for I'm sure I could do the job. I know you've never heard of me, but I'm a great writer – all my friends say so – and I could certainly match what you usually publish. Other editors haven't yet recognised my talent but you can change all that. Commission me and you won't regret it.
What do you say?

Kind regards
A.D. Luded-Freelance

How does an aspiring freelance get into print? The answer, short of blackmail or nepotism, is via the 'pitch'. This is a written proposal to a commissioning editor. Get it right and it can bag you a commission, complete with brief, fee and deadline. Get it wrong, and the first impression you make may well be your last.

Pitching is a notoriously tricky art. With editors' inboxes already groaning, the odds are stacked against freelances, especially first-timers. The example above may be ridiculous but it nonetheless expresses the frustration felt by many freelances. How on earth do you break through?

Every freelance has a subjective take on this dilemma, depending on their field. Mine is travel and wildlife, so my advice is drawn from experience in this particular part of the industry. But the challenges are likely to be pretty similar whatever you write about. If there is a foolproof formula for success, I've yet to find it. What follows reflects 15 years of trial and error.

'Some pitches are good, most are OK, but many are dire,' says freelance commissioning editor Sue Bryant. You may never learn why your pitch succeeds or fails, but you *can* ensure that it always falls into the first of those three categories. The rest may just come down to luck.

Do your homework

First, before you write a word, familiarise yourself with your target publication. Trawl the website – or splash out on a paper copy. Establish how often it comes out: pitching a story about an imminent one-off event to a quarterly whose next edition won't appear for three months is wasting the editor's time. And check that nothing similar has already appeared. 'My bugbear is when people pitch something we've recently covered,' says Andrew Purvis, commissioning editor at *Telegraph Travel*.

Second, consider the readership. 'This is where people most often go wrong,' says Lyn Hughes, publisher of travel magazine *Wanderlust*. 'It's vitally important that you understand who the readers are and what interests them.' You don't need demographics: the ads and letters pages speak volumes. Hughes describes how *Wanderlust* has received pitches for articles on golf – utterly irrelevant to readers interested in adventure travel and the natural world. Ignorance shows. 'You can always tell if they've not thought about the magazine and the target audience,' confirms Laura Griffiths-Jones of *Travel Africa* magazine, who would never entrust a fact-finding commission to a writer who can't even be bothered to research the magazine.

Don't cut corners. An all-purpose pitch to several publications simultaneously may save you time but will seldom get past the editor, who has a nose for the mail shot. Mistakes can be excruciating. 'We see a lot of cut-and-pasting,' says Hughes. 'The giveaway is the different font.'

Finally, address your pitch to the right person. Larger publications may have different commissioning editors for different sections, including their website, and a misdirected pitch may disappear without trace. Heed protocol: copying in the commissioning editors of rival publications in your address line – a common mistake, according to Griffiths-Jones – will *not* endear you to the editor you're addressing. And don't pull rank. 'Never go over the editor's head and talk to the publisher,' warns Bryant. 'That used to make me furious.'

Most commissioning editors would rather not receive a pitch by phone: it can feel confrontational – and they will, in any case, seldom be able to say yes or no without investigating further. Social media is also seen by many as too throw-away for the initial pitch – although, if you establish a relationship, it may become useful further down the line.

Get to the point

Once you've worked out where to direct your pitch, your challenge is to make it stand out from all the others. First comes the subject line, which must convey the gist in as few words as possible. 'You've almost got to put in as much effort on the subject line as in the pitch,' stresses Hughes. Bear in mind that longer lines may half disappear on the screen of a smartphone. Thus 'New snow leopard safari to Ladakh' is more effective than 'Proposal to write a travel feature about visiting the Himalayas in search of snow leopards'.

If the editor takes the bait, the pitch that follows must flesh out that subject line succinctly. 'Ideally one paragraph, explaining what the story is,' recommends Griffiths-Jones. I aim for one paragraph of no more than 100 words, sometimes adding a few brief supplementary details (see example opposite). It can help to think of your pitch as being like a 'standfirst': the introductory paragraph that a magazine often places above an article.

Your 'angle' is critical. In travel journalism this might be a new means of experiencing an old destination or a topical hook, such as a forthcoming movie. In reality, your angle may not be very original – in travel, as elsewhere, subjects are revisited and dusted down on rotation – but your job is to make it sound novel and convince the editor that you are the one to write it. 'If I think: "So what? I could write that from my desk," then it's a non-starter,' warns Bryant.

A scattergun approach suggests lack of focus, so don't cram too many ideas into one story and certainly don't bundle several stories into one pitch. Settling on one idea can be difficult: in travel writing, almost any trip could yield multiple stories and it can feel risky to cram all your eggs into one basket. But editors are commissioning a story, not a destination. If torn, one compromise is to lead with a main angle but allow a little room for manoeuvre by including two or three brief subsidiary points that might suggest other angles should the main idea not appeal. Here's an example:

New snow leopard safari to Ladakh

In January I join a new tour to Ladakh, India, in search of snow leopards. This endangered big cat recently starred on BBC's *Planet Earth* and is one of the world's most sought-after wildlife sightings. Confined to the high Himalayas, it has long been off the tourist agenda. This pioneering venture (www.snowleopardsafaris.com) now offers snow leopard tracking for the first time. Accommodation is in community home-stays, from where expert local trackers guide small groups in to the mountains. Tourism revenue helps fund community-based conservation. Highlights include:
– Tracking snow leopards
– Wolves, ibex, eagles and other wildlife
– Trekking in the high Himalayas
– The ancient Ladakh capital of Leh (3,500m)
– Buddhist culture: monasteries, festivals, village home-stays
– Snow leopard conservation project
Peak season Jan–April; could file story from end January.

If the editor doesn't know you, some brief credentials might help: a simple sentence at the end explaining who you are, plus a sample or two of your work. Keep any attached files small: the editor won't want PDFs clogging up their inbox. Any weblinks should be to articles relevant to your pitch. 'Don't just say "visit my website",' warns Bryant. 'It sounds really arrogant and I haven't got time.'

Mind your language

Even the most perfectly structured pitch can founder on the detail. Typos happen, but this is one place where they mustn't. Hughes describes how *Wanderlust* regularly receives pitches for stories about 'Equador' and 'Columbia'. Remember, you are trying to persuade an editor to trust your ability with words. What will they think if you stumble at the first hurdle? Editors work to tight budgets and schedules so the last thing they want is more work. 'If it's riddled with errors, and they can't construct a sentence or a paragraph correctly,' asks Purvis, 'why would I waste all that time – and budget – sorting it out?'

So double-check your pitch before sending. If in doubt, print it out: research shows that we all spot errors more easily on the printed page. To guard against embarrassing disasters, never insert the recipient's address in your email until you're ready to press 'Send'.

Style is important too. In general, less is more: the pitch is not a place for purple prose. And try to avoid journalistic faux pas, such as opening with long subordinate clauses or overusing the passive voice. And avoid cluttering your pitch with clichés: 'land of contrasts' and 'best-kept secret' are travel industry horrors that spring to mind. Editors are writers too. It doesn't take much for them to sniff out a weakness.

Me, me, me ...

Perhaps the worst error in pitching your story is to make yourself its subject. 'Don't make the pitch about you,' insists Bryant, 'unless you're really famous or really funny.' A travel editor is not generally looking for a Bruce Chatwin or Bill Bryson; they have no use for your hilarious anecdotes or journey of discovery. They want your writing to sell an experience that their readers can go out and buy. 'We're not interested in you,' confirms Hughes. 'We're interested in our readers.' That's why any travel article will have at the end a fact box 'call to action', with all the details that the reader will need in order to replicate your experience.

Any hint of neediness is an instant deterrent. Your needs are not important, so don't suggest that by publishing your work the editor will be helping launch your career. A particular bugbear for travel editors is 'blagging': securing a commission in order to get yourself a free trip. 'I was recently offered a place on an Amazon River trip, but couldn't find a sponsor for the flights to Lima,' began one pitch that Bryant instantly rejected. Whilst a commission is a part of the equation that enables freelance travel writers to travel, the publication in question does not generally want to be caught up in the mechanics. You're a freelance; that's *your* lookout.

And beware how you present yourself. Editors talk to one another and reputations are quickly acquired. Social media can be a minefield: Bryant recalls discovering a long rant on Twitter from a writer she was considering commissioning that threatened to have a PR fired because the writer had not received a flight upgrade. 'When you're on the road on a commission,' she stresses, 'you are representing the publication and our advertisers.'

Editor empathies

If in doubt, try placing yourself in the shoes of the commissioning editor. Invariably they will be overburdened, against deadline and quite possibly battling some cost-cutting edict from on high. The last thing they're looking for, usually, is unsolicited pitches from writers that they've never heard of. 'Editors can be lazy,' admits Bryant. 'They don't like surprises.'

What's more, an editor's job is not to showcase your writing but to publish material that trumps the competition. Ultimately all editorial decisions are commercial. 'You're going to be held accountable for spending the money,' points out Purvis. Your job is to make their life easier by offering something that meets their needs.

Remember, too, that it was you who made the approach. An editor is under no obligation to justify their decision. Indeed – common courtesy aside – they are not even obliged to reply. The frustrating reality for freelances is that responses may be very slow and, at times, non-existent. Your pitch may never reach the front of the queue.

If you don't hear back, do send a gentle reminder. I usually leave it a couple of weeks and if I still hear nothing after that, I drop it. But never express your frustration; swallow it and look elsewhere. Who knows? Your name or idea may have struck a chord. The editor may get back to you months later, when you least expect it. It has happened to me. Don't burn your bridges.

And never give up. Somewhere out there is an article with your byline on it.

Mike Unwin is a freelance writer, editor and photographer who specialises in travel and wildlife. He worked for 14 years in book publishing before leaving to pursue a freelance career. Today he writes for a variety of newspapers and magazines, including the *Telegraph*, the *Independent*, *BBC Wildlife*, *Wanderlust* and *Travel Africa*. Among his 35 published books for both adults and children are *Migration* (Bloomsbury 2018), *The Enigma of the Owl* (Yale 2016), *Swaziland* (Bradt Travel Guides 2012) and *Endangered Species* (Aladdin Books 2000). His awards include BBC Wildlife Nature Travel writer of the year 2000, the British Guild of Travel Writers' UK Travel Writer of the Year 2013 and Latin American Travel's Newspaper Feature of the Year 2018. He was a finalist in the 2020 GTMA Global Travel Writer Award.

Setting up and editing a new magazine

Ed Needham shares his experience and outlines the essential steps, decisions and realities involved in publishing a new magazine as a solo operation, and gives practical advice on how to turn your concept into a successful venture in today's changing digital industry.

I have spent much of my adult life working as a journalist and editor in magazines. I edited *FHM* in its million-selling heyday in the '90s, and launched and edited that magazine in the United States. Also in the USA, I was the managing editor at *Rolling Stone* and editor-in-chief at *Maxim*, then the biggest men's magazine in the world. I've established a successful online publishing and marketing company, and developed magazines for other companies. But, over the last decade or so, the magazine as a fact of life – a glossy, portable, affordable luxury, object of desire and trusted source of guidance – has fallen badly out of fashion, evicted from so many of the gaps it used to fill in people's lives by the mobile phone. That one gadget has changed the fortunes of the industry calamitously. Readers and advertising have wandered off. Titles have closed. And by 2017 I found myself looking for a job, in a market where positions for top editors had become reserved for candidates with far more modest salary expectations than mine.

But a couple of interesting developments also emerged from the magazine industry's change of life: 1) many of the special skills and physical processes that used to require an army of talent had been replaced by affordable software; 2) while legacy magazine publishers were struggling for sustenance at a diminishing waterhole, there was still plenty of margin for people operating in niche markets and who didn't have a heavy payroll or central London floorspace to maintain. Perhaps I could publish my own magazine? And to keep the costs really low, perhaps I could do the whole thing on my own?

I found an envelope and did a few sums on the back of it. I produced a dummy – a trial issue – to see whether one person could write and edit an entire magazine (and then another one in short order – the revelation that Issue Two comes hard on the heels of Issue One routinely comes as a shock to people 'having a go' at magazines). I had it printed to see what it would look like, liked it, and in 2018 launched *Strong Words*, a magazine about books. It appears nine times a year, and each issue has reviews of over 100 titles, as well as interviews and features that send readers into an ecstasy of book-buying, trying authors, genres and categories of books they wouldn't previously have dreamt of dabbling in. And it does so entertainingly – people like to be informed and amused by reviews, not lectured gravely on how important something is. There is no sad head-shaking nor acts of critical violence; if I find a book disappointing, I don't cover it, but I think the days of the snooty, disdainful review to showcase the critic's cleverness are nearly over. *Strong Words* is for people who want to read more, not less. So why waste valuable space urging people not to buy a book? Even though it requires my attention all seven days of the week, I've proved it can be done. At time of writing, I've just sent Issue 26 to the printer. And here are some of the things I've learned, if you'd like to have a go yourself.

1. Do some initial thought experiments

I was taught that the first question to ask when embarking on a new magazine project was 'Who's it for?' But the people asking that question used to be big magazine companies whose starting point was identifying which market to shove themselves into next. Now I think you need to answer two different questions first: 1) 'Why am I doing it?' and 2) 'Where's the money coming from?' If you can answer those two questions honestly, rather than as a delusional pipe dream, you'll have sketched a foundation for your project. My answer to 1) was that I needed to earn a living – but with a view to eventually also applying my model to established magazines that might benefit from my approach to costs. My answer to 2) was initially the Bank of Ed Needham and then through subscriptions. Not advertising – at first, that's another cost. But until you can answer those questions with confidence, you can't go to the next square.

2. Who's it for?

Identify your market. Why does anyone need your magazine? Bear in mind that the younger consumers can easily imagine reaching the end of their lives without ever once touching one. I chose a print product because I understand them, and they have a credibility that online doesn't; it's like the difference between a house and a picture of a house. Neither did I have the time to do print *and* online to an acceptable standard. I chose to write about books because the UK is the world's bookiest nation (no other country publishes as many books per capita), yet there is no consistently reliable source for book buyers to find out what's new.

There are the highbrow journals and the broadsheets, but all too often they make books feel like homework, whereas most people buy books for pleasure. The internet is a formidable marketing machine, but it rarely leaves a person thinking, 'That's the book for me.' If anyone is going to appreciate the special magic of ink on paper, it's book buyers. Books are a great untapped reservoir of the new and the useful, the funny and the gossipy, endless revelation about just how dysfunctional our planet and its population is. And that is the stuff of life – something people have a gluttonous appetite for.

3. The practicalities

If you haven't made a magazine before, familiarise yourself with InDesign, the universal page-making software from Adobe, for which you pay a license fee. Work out how many pages you want – it should be a multiple of eight, plus four more for the cover. Make a flatplan, i.e. decide, before you start, what is going on every page and in what order. The only bit of the process I can't do is design, so my original concept for *Strong Words* was to pay a designer friend to establish a template, which I could re-use with different content each issue, thus keeping design costs low. But I do still need a designer for a couple of weeks each issue.

You're going to need content, which – unless you know people keen to work for nothing – you either have to produce yourself or pay for. And you're going to need pictures, which you also either have to produce yourself or pay for. Helping yourself from the internet is not advisable. You might get away with it, or you might end up in court. I get my stock pictures from Shutterstock (www.shutterstock.com), more specific images such as archive news images from Alamy (www.alamy.com), and I use press-approved images from the books I write about, where possible.

As for copy, I produce it all myself – it amounts to reading the equivalent of *War and Peace* each week (about 1,500 pages) and writing the equivalent of *The Great Gatsby* each issue (about 45,000 words). I cut the copy to fit, write the headlines, write the display copy (the various other bits, like captions) check the spellings and punctuation and prices. You need a cover – traditionally known as the most important page in a magazine. If you're selling your publication in shops, you need a bar code; these are easy to buy (see www.axicon.com), but before that you need an ISSN number. ... If I can get one, you can.

You may want to trademark your name; do it yourself at www.gov.uk/how-to-register-a-trade-mark/apply (apply in class 09 for digital, class 16 for print). Don't pay a third party. And ignore the avalanche of scam letters that follow straight after.

4. Print it

I'd always thought this was the big barrier to a solo operation. You used to have to order the paper, and well in advance. If you wanted special paper, even more in advance. You usually had to buy quite a lot of it. It required middlemen. Now you can print a single copy. This was where I began to see what was possible: someone mentioned a business called Newspaper Club (www.newspaperclub.com) who print on newsprint, and so the first three issues of *Strong Words* came as a newspaper. You just upload your files, choose your paper quality, and pay.

My original marketing plan was to print loads and give them away ... then everyone would faint with delight and subscribe on the spot. When I discovered that news-stands couldn't cope with a tabloid newsprint magazine, because it didn't fit their racks, I switched to a conventional A4 format, and used a company called Mixam (https://mixam.co.uk). NB: if you're sending your magazine out by post, you need to know how much it's going to weigh before you print it. Postage costs are brutal, so you want to keep them down but still ensure a decent paper stock. Printers' websites enable you to calculate the weight of an issue. This is a nasty shock to any budget (... keep smelling salts handy). And don't forget to factor in the weight of the envelope. Mixam provided great quality, but I needed specific delivery dates so now I use The Magazine Printing Company (magprint.co.uk), who also give stunning quality and invaluable customer service. Upload the files, approve them, send. It is mind-blowingly easy.

5. Distribution

I thought this would be a big barrier too, but no. I use a third-party company called Webscribe (www.webscribe.co.uk) to run the subscription fulfilment, so they take the money and send the issues out – I don't have to handle credit cards and customer data, all that tricky stuff. If you want to sell in shops, third-party companies will look after that too; I used one called MMS (www.mmslondon.co.uk) and sold in independents and in WHSmith travel outlets at railways and airports (you have to pay an annual fee per outlet). When travel fell out of favour during lockdown, I switched to subscription only, and the poor Smith's staff weren't always sure where to rack *Strong Words*, so I'd sometimes find it shoved somewhere inappropriate like Gardening, so I'm not sure I'd go back.

And now for some difficult news. Congratulations for getting this far, but you have only reached the foot of the mountain, because the biggest challenge is ...

6. Marketing

I think you can divide people into two groups: people who make things and people who sell things. Few excel at both. Persuading someone to buy your product is not a skill that emerges naturally from learning how to produce magazines. This is the main reason why people have business partners – to overcome this skill set schism. But those magazines aren't going to sell themselves and, having made such a thing of beauty, it's heartbreaking to see them not find new homes.

I wish I could reveal the golden key to marketing serenity, but it hasn't been revealed to me yet. This is what I think I know. There are two steps: 1) make people aware of the magazine; 2) persuade them to subscribe. The tools at your disposal are: social media; conventional media (I find the former better for step one, the latter for step two); newsletters, podcasts, events, influential people (someone once recommended focusing on your 1,000 most influential customers first, rather than scatter-gunning your efforts in a frantic marketing orgy). Make sure everyone you have ever met knows what you are doing. Somehow make yourself a topic of conversation. Explain how your product helps people. Trade favours. Most of all, get on with it and find out what works for you, and spend as much time on selling as on making.

Your project may be an act of supreme folly or it may transform the media landscape, but if you don't give it your everything, it WILL fail, and you will never find out. Looking forward to seeing you all on my subscription list soon. Good luck.

Ed Needham is an editor and journalist, and publisher of *Strong Words* magazine which he launched in 2018, published by his own company De Pentonville Media Ltd. His former roles include Editor, then Editor-in-Chief, of *FHM* in the UK and USA, 1997–2002, Managing Editor of *Rolling Stone*, 2002–04, Editor-in-Chief of *Maxim*, 2004–06, and founder and Editor-in-Chief of *Coach* magazine, 2015–16. For more information see www.strong-words.co.uk. Follow him on Twitter @Needham014.

National newspapers UK and Ireland

This section includes listings for national newspapers available in print, in both print and online, and as online-only news websites.

BBC News

email haveyoursay@bbc.co.uk
website www.bbc.co.uk/news
Facebook www.facebook.com/bbcnews
Twitter @BBCNews
Director of BBC News Fran Unsworth

Online only. The website contains international and regional news coverage as well as entertainment, sport, science and political news. Founded 1997.

City AM Ltd

3rd Floor, Fountain House, 130 Fenchurch Street, London EC3M 5DJ
tel 020-3201 8900
website www.cityam.com
Facebook www.facebook.com/cityam
Twitter @cityam
Editor Andy Silvester
Mon–Fri Free

Financial and business newspaper. Covers the latest economic, political and business news as well as comment, sport and lifestyle features. Founded 2006.
    Comment & Features Editor Sascha O'Sullivan
    Lifestyle Editor Steve Dinneen
    Sports Editor Frank Dalleres

The Conservation

Shropshire House (4th Floor), Capper Street, London WC1E 6JA
email uk-editorial@theconversation.com
website www.theconversation.com
Facebook www.facebook.com/theconservation
Twitter @ConversationUK
Executive Editor Stephen Khan

An online-only independent source of news and views, sourced from the academic and research community and delivered direct to the public. Founded 2011.
    Business & Economy Editor Stephen Vass
    Cities, Education & Young People Editor Grace Allen
    Environment & Energy Editor Jack Marley
    Health & Medicine Editor Clint Witchalls
    Investigates Editor Josephine Lethbridge
    News Editor Stephen Harris
    Politics Editor Laura Hood
    Science Editor Miriam Frankel
    Science & Tech Editor Abigail Beall
    Society & Arts Editor Kuba Shand-Baptiste
    Special Projects Editor Holly Squire

Daily Express

One Canada Square, Canary Wharf, London E14 5AP
tel 020-8612 7000
email news.desk@express.co.uk
website www.express.co.uk
Facebook www.facebook.com/DailyExpress
Twitter @Daily_Express
Editor-in-Chief Gary Jones
Daily Mon–Fri 75p, Sat £1.20
Supplements **Daily Express Saturday**

Exclusive news; striking photos. Leader page articles (600 words); facts preferred to opinions. Payment: according to value. Founded 1900.
    Deputy Editor Collette Harrison
    Environment Editor John Ingham
    Features Editor Fran Goodman
    Head of Lifestyle Mernie Gilmore
    News Editor Geoff Maynard
    Online Editor Geoff Marsh
    Political Editor Macer Hall
    Sports Editor Mike Allen
    Travel Editor Jane Memmler

Daily Express Saturday Magazine
Editor Mel Brodie
Free with paper

Daily Mail

Northcliffe House, 2 Derry Street, London W8 5TT
tel 020-7938 6000
email news@dailymail.co.uk
website www.dailymail.co.uk
Facebook www.facebook.com/DailyMail
Twitter @MailOnline
Editor Geordie Greig
Daily Mon–Fri 70p, Sat £1.10
Supplements **Weekend**

Founded 1896.
    Deputy Editors Tobyn Andreae, Gerard Greaves
    City Editor Alex Brummer
    Diary Editor Sebastian Shakespeare
    Education Correspondent Eleanor Harding
    Executive Editor of Features Leaf Kalfayan
    Executive News Editor Ben Taylor
    Good Health Editor Justine Hancock
    Head of Sport Steven Fletcher
    Literary Editor Sandra Parsons
    Moneymail Editor Victoria Bischoff
    Picture Editor Paul Bennett
    Political Editor Jason Groves
    Travel Editor Mark Palmer

MailOnline
tel 020-7938-6000
email tips@dailymail.com
Editor Danny Groom
The online platform for the *Daily Mail*.
Founded 2003.

Daily Mirror

One Canada Square, Canary Wharf, London E14 5AP
tel 020-7293 3000
email mirrornews@mirror.co.uk
website www.mirror.co.uk
Facebook www.facebook.com/DailyMirror
Twitter @DailyMirror
Editor Alison Phillips
Daily Mon–Fri 90p, Sat £1.50
Supplements **We Love TV**

Top payment for exclusive news and news pictures.
Freelance articles used, and ideas bought: send
synopsis only. Unusual pictures and those giving a
new angle on the news are welcomed; also cartoons.
Founded 1903.
   Associate Picture Editor Derek Momodu
   Business Editor Graham Hiscott
   Mirror Online Editorial Director Ben Rankin
   News Editor Dominic Herbert
   Political Editor Pippa Crerar
   Sports Editor David Walker

Daily Record

1 Central Quay, Glasgow G3 8DA
tel 0141 309 3000
email reporters@dailyrecord.co.uk
website www.dailyrecord.co.uk
Facebook www.facebook.com/
TheScottishDailyRecord
Twitter @Daily_Record
Editor David Dick
Daily Mon–Fri 90p, Sat £1.20
Supplements **Saturday, Seven Days, Living, TV
Record, Road Record, Recruitment Record, The
Brief**

Topical articles, from 300–700 words; exclusive
stories of Scottish interest and exclusive colour
photos. Founded 1895.
   Assistant Editor & Head of News Kevin Mansi
   Assistant Editor & Head of Sports Austin Barrett
   Assistant News Editor Vivienne Aitken
   Digital Editor Graeme Thomson
   Political Editor David Clegg

Saturday
Free with paper
Lifestyle magazine and entertainment guide. Reviews,
travel features, shopping, personalities, colour
illustrations. Payment: by arrangement.

Daily Star

One Canada Square, London E14 5AP
tel 020-8293 3000
email news@dailystar.co.uk
website www.dailystar.co.uk
Facebook www.facebook.com/thedailystar
Twitter @Daily_Star
Editor Jon Clark
Daily Mon–Fri 55p, Sat 75p
Supplements **Hot TV, Seriously Football**

Hard news exclusives, commanding substantial
payment. Major interviews with big-star personalities;
short features; series based on people rather than
things; picture features. Illustrations: line, half-tone.
Payment: by negotiation. Founded 1978.
   Daily Star Online Editor Jon Livesey
   Deputy Sports Editor Dan Gibbs
   Digital Showbiz & TV Editor Samantha Bartlett
   News Editor Steve Hughes

Daily Star Sunday

Express Newspapers, The Northern & Shell Building,
10 Lower Thames Street, London EC3R 6EN
tel 020-8293 3000
website www.dailystar.co.uk/sunday
Editor Denis Mann
Sun 95p
Supplements **OK! Extra**

Opportunities for freelancers. Founded 2002.

Daily Telegraph

111 Buckingham Palace Road, London SW1W 0DT
tel 020-7931 2000
email dtnews@telegraph.co.uk
website www.telegraph.co.uk
Facebook www.facebook.com/telegraph.co.uk
Twitter @Telegraph
Editor Chris Evans
Daily Mon–Fri £2.50, Sat £3
Supplements **Gardening, Cars, Property, Culture,
Sport, Telegraph Magazine, Travel, Your Money**

Articles on a wide range of subjects of topical interest
considered. Preliminary letter and synopsis required.
Length: 700–1,000 words. Payment: by arrangement.
Founded 1855.
   Deputy News Editor Bill Gardner
   Fashion Editor Lisa Armstrong
   Health Editor Laura Donnelly
   News Editor Mark Hughes
   Associate Editor Gordon Rayner

Telegraph Magazine
Editor Marianne Jones
Free with Sat paper
Short profiles (about 1,600 words); articles of topical
interest. Preliminary study of the magazine essential.
Illustrations: all types. Payment: by arrangement.
Founded 1964.

Telegraph Online
email dtnews@telegraph.co.uk
website www.telegraph.co.uk
Readers need to set up a monthly subscription after
30 days free access to view full articles. Founded 1994.

Digital Director Kate Day
Head of Digital Production Ian Douglas
Head of Technology (editorial) Ellie Zolfagharifard

Financial Times

Bracken House, 1 Friday Street, London EC4M 9BT
tel 020-7873 3000
email ean@ft.com
website www.ft.com
Facebook www.facebook.com/financialtimes
Twitter @FinancialTimes
Editor Roula Khalaf
Daily Mon–Fri £2.70, Sat £4
Supplements **Companies, FTfm, FT Special Reports, FT Executive Appointments, FT Weekend Magazine, House and Home, FT Money, How To Spend It, FT Wealth, Life & Arts**

One of the world's leading business news organisations, the FT provides premium and essential news, commentary and analysis. Founded 1888.
   Deputy Editor Patrick Jenkins
   Chief Economics Commentator Martin Wolf
   FT Weekend Editor Alec Russell
   House & Home Editor Nathan Brooker
   International Business Editor Peggy Hollinger
   Managing Editor Tobias Buck
   Markets Editor Katie Martin
   News Editor Matthew Garrahan
   Political Editor George Parker
   UK Editor-at-Large Robert Shrimsley

The Guardian

Kings Place, 90 York Way, London N1 9GU
tel 020-3353 2000
email national@theguardian.com
website www.theguardian.com
Facebook www.facebook.com/theguardian
Twitter @guardian
Editor Katharine Viner
Daily Mon–Fri £2.20, Sat £3.20
Supplements **Sport, G2, Film & Music, The Guide, Weekend, Review, Money, Work & Careers, Travel, Family, Cook**

Few articles are taken from outside contributors except on feature and specialist pages. Illustrations: news and features photos. Payment: apply for rates. See contributors guidelines on website. Founded 1821.
   Deputy Editor Owen Gibson
   Business Editor Julia Finch
   Chief Books Editor Lisa Allardice
   Deputy Opinion Editors Joseph Harker
   Economics Editor Larry Elliott
   Education Editor Richard Adams
   Fashion Editor Hannah Marriott
   Head of National News Fay Schlesinger
   Head of Travel Andy Pietrasik
   Music Editor Ben Beaumont-Thomas
   Opinion Editor David Shariatmadari
   Society Editor Alison Benjamin

Weekend
Free with Sat paper
Features on world affairs, major profiles, food and drink, home life, the arts, travel and leisure. Also good reportage on social and political subjects. Illustrations: photos, line drawings and cartoons. Payment: apply for rates.

theguardian.com/uk
website www.theguardian.com/uk
Free website where the *Guardian* and the *Observer* publish all their current and archived content. Currently gives access to over three million stories. Although the service is free, readers are invited to make a donation. There are also US and Australian editions of the website. Founded 2013.

Herald

Herald & Times Group, 125 Fullarton Drive, Glasgow East Investment Park, Glasgow G32 8FG
tel 0141 302 7000
email news@theherald.co.uk
English office Loudwater Mill, Station Road, High Wycombe, Bucks HP10 9TY
tel (01932) 821212
website www.heraldscotland.com
Editor Donald Martin
Fri £1.60, Sat £2

Articles up to 1,000 words. Founded 1783.
   Arts Editor Keith Bruce
   Business Editor Ian McConnell
   Foreign Affairs Editor David Pratt
   Holyrood Political Editor Tom Gordon
   UK Political Editor Mike Settle
   Sports Editor Matthew Johnston
   Multimedia Editor Craig Alexander

Herald on Sunday

Herald & Times Group, 125 Fullarton Drive, Glasgow East Investment Park, Glasgow G32 8FG
tel 0141 302 7000
email news@theherald.co.uk
website www.heraldscotland.com
Sun £2.20
Supplements **Sport, Scottish Life Magazine**

News and stories about Scotland, the UK and the world. Opportunities for freelancers with quality contacts. Founded 2018.
   Editor Donald Martin
   Features Editor Garry Scott
   Foreign Editor David Pratt
   Opinion Editor Andrew Clark

i

2 Derry Street, London W8 5TT
tel 020-3615 0000
email newsdesk@inews.co.uk
website https://inews.co.uk/
Editor Oly Duff
Mon–Fri 65p

Originally sister paper to the *Independent* which is now online only. Founded 2010.

  Deputy Editor Andy Webster
  Managing Editor Tal Gottesman
  Acting Digital Editor Luke Bailey
  Acting Head of Digital Daisy Wyatt
  Art Director Tim Alden
  Assistant Editor (News) Andrew Johnson
  Assistant Editor (Production) Siobhan Norton
  Business Editor Chris Newlands
  Comment Editor Barbara Speed
  Foreign Editor Michael Day
  Picture Editor Sophie Batterbury
  Scotland Editor Chris Green
  Sports Editor Ally McKay

i Weekend

2 Derry Street, London W8 5TT
tel 020-7361 5678
email i@inews.co.uk
website https://inews.co.uk/
Editor Oly Duff
Sat £1.20

Weekend newspaper of the weekly i. Founded 2012.

Independent

Northcliffe House, 2 Derry Street, London W8 5HF
tel 020-7005 2000
email newseditor@independent.co.uk
website www.independent.co.uk
Facebook www.facebook.com/TheIndependentOnline
Twitter @independent
Acting Editor David Marley

Online only. Occasional freelance contributions; preliminary letter advisable. Payment: by arrangement. Founded 1986.

  Assistant Editor Lucy McInerney
  Culture Editor Patrick Smith
  Executive Editor Chloe Hubbard
  Head of Travel Cathy Adams
  International Desk Gemma Fox
  Lifestyle Editor Harriet Hall
  News Editor Olivia Alabaster
  Sports Editor Ben Burrows

Irish Examiner

Linn Dubh, Assumption Road, Blackpool, Cork T23 RCH6, Republic of Ireland
tel +353 (0)21 4272722 (newsroom)
email news@examiner.ie
website www.irishexaminer.com
Editor Tom Fitzpatrick
Daily Mon–Fri €2.30, Sat €3.20

Features. Material mostly commissioned. Length: 1,000 words. Payment: by arrangement. Founded 1841.

  News & Digital Editor Dolan O'Hagan
  Features Editor Vickie Maye
  Visual Media Manager Jim Coughlan
  Sport Tony Leen

Irish Independent

Independent House, 27–32 Talbot Street, Dublin D01 X2E1, Republic of Ireland
tel +353 (0)17 055333
email contact@independent.ie
website www.independent.ie
Facebook www.facebook.com/independent.ie
Twitter @Independent_ie
Editor Cormac Bourke
Daily Mon–Fri €2.20, Sat €3

Special articles on topical or general subjects. Length: 700–1,000 words. Payment: editor's estimate of value. Founded 1905.

  Irish Editor Fionnán Sheahan
  Group Head of News Kevin Doyle

The Irish Times

The Irish Times Building, PO Box 74, 24–28 Tara Street, Dublin D02 CX89, Republic of Ireland
tel +353 (0)16 758000
email newsdesk@irishtimes.com
website www.irishtimes.com
Facebook www.facebook.com/irishtimes
Twitter @IrishTimes
Editor Paul O'Neill
Daily Mon–Fri €2.30, Sat €3.50
Supplements **The Irish Times Magazine, The Ticket (Sat), Health + Family (Tue), Business (Daily), Sport (Mon, Wed, Sat)**

Mainly staff-written. Specialist contributions (800–2,000 words) by commission on basis of ideas submitted. Illustrations: photos and line drawings. Payment: at editor's valuation. Founded 1859.

  Arts & Culture Editor Hugh Linehan
  Business Editor Ciaran Hancock
  Digital Editor Paddy Logue
  Education Editor Carl O'Brien
  Features Weekend Review Conor Goodman
  Foreign Editor Chris Dooley
  Literary Editor Martin Doyle
  Magazine Editor Rachel Collins
  News Editor Mark Hennessy
  Opinion Editor John McManus
  Political Editor Pat Leahy
  Picture Editor Brenda Fitzsimons
  Social Media Editor David Cochrane
  Sports Editor Malachy Logan

BreakingNews.ie

website www.breakingnews.ie

Online platform for news for *The Irish Times*.

Mail on Sunday

Northcliffe House, 2 Derry Street, London W8 5TT
tel 020-7938 6000
email news@mailonsunday.co.uk
website www.mailonsunday.co.uk
Editor Ted Verity

Sun £1.80
Supplements **You, EVENT**

Articles. Illustrations: line, half-tone; cartoons. Payment: by arrangement. Founded 1982.
   Arts Editor Dominic Connolly
   Business Editor Ruth Sutherland
   Deputy Features Editor Kate Mansey
   Executive Editor David Dillon
   Literary Editor Susanna Gross
   Political Editor Jason Groves
   Sports Editor Alison Kervin

Financial Mail on Sunday
tel 020-7938 6984
Part of main paper

City, industry, business and personal finance. News stories up to 1,500 words. Full colour illustrations and photography commissioned. Payment: by arrangement.

EVENT
Editor Andrew Davies
Free with paper

Fresh and exclusive take on celebrity, film, music, TV and radio, books, theatre, comedy, food, technology and cars. Founded 2013.

You
Editor Jo Elvin
Free with paper

Women's interest features. Length: 500–2,500 words. Illustrations: full colour and b&w drawings commissioned; also colour photos. Payment: by arrangement.

Morning Star
People's Press Printing Society Ltd,
William Rust House, 52 Beachy Road,
London E3 2NS
tel 020-8510 0815
email enquiries@peoples-press.com
website www.morningstaronline.co.uk
Editor Ben Chacko
Daily Mon–Fri £1.20, Sat–Sun £1.50

Newspaper for the Labour movement. Articles of general interest. Illustrations: photos, cartoons, drawings. Founded 1930.
   Assistant Editor Ros Sitwell
   News Editor Will Stone

The National
125 Fullarton Drive, Glasgow G32 8FG
tel 0141 302 7000
email reporters@thenational.scot
website www.thenational.scot
Facebook www.facebook.com/thenationalnewspaperscotland
Twitter @ScotNational
Editor Callum Baird
Mon–Sat £1

Scottish daily newspaper owned by Newsquest and the first daily newspaper in Scotland to support Scottish independence. Founded 2014.

The New European
Archant, Prospect House, Norwich NR1 1RE
tel (01603) 772682
email theneweuropean@archant.co.uk
website www.theneweuropean.co.uk
Facebook www.facebook.com/theneweuropean
Twitter @TheNewEuropean
Editor Jasper Copping
Weekly Thurs £3

A pro-EU weekly newspaper. Writers include Alastair Campbell, Michael White, Bonnie Greer, Hardeep Singh-Kohli, Yasmin Alibhai-Brown and A.C. Grayling. Founded 2016.

The Observer
Kings Place, 90 York Way, London N1 9GU
tel 020-3353 2000
email observer.news@observer.co.uk
website www.theguardian.com/observer
Editor Paul Webster
Sun £3.20
Supplements **Observer Magazine, New Review, Sport, Observer Food Monthly**

Some articles and illustrations commissioned. Payment: by arrangement. Founded 1791.
   Assistant Editor & Comment Editor Robert Yates
   Assistant Editor (National & International News) Steve Bloomfield
   Arts Editor/Deputy Editor, the New Review Sarah Donaldson
   Books Editor/Deputy Editor, the New Review Ursula Kenny
   Deputy News Editor Lisa Bachelor
   Design Director Lynsey Irvine
   Fashion Editor Jo Jones
   Menswear Fashion Editor Helen Seamons
   New Review Editor Jane Ferguson
   Observer Food Monthly Editor Allan Jenkins
   Picture Editor Jim Powell
   Political Editor Toby Helm
   Readers' Editor Elisabeth Ribbans
   Sports Editor Matthew Hancock

Observer Magazine
tel 020-3353 2000
email magazine@observer.co.uk
Editor Harriet Green
Free with paper
Commissioned features. Length: 2,000–3,000 words. Illustrations: first-class colour and b&w photos. Payment: NUJ rates; see website for details.

The Poke
email info@thepoke.co.uk
website www.thepoke.co.uk
Facebook www.facebook.com/PokeHQ

Twitter @ThePoke

Online only. A satirical and topical news source. Founded 2002.

politics.co.uk

Senate Media Ltd, 4 Croxted Mews, Croxted Road, London SE24 9DA
tel 020-3758 9407
email editorial@politics.co.uk
website www.politics.co.uk
Facebook www.facebook.com/politicscoukofficial/
Twitter @politics_co_uk
Editor Ian Dunt

Online only. See website for details on how to submit articles.

Scotland on Sunday

Orchard Brae House, 30 Queensferry Road, Edinburgh EH4 2HS
tel 0131 311 7311
email reception@scotsman.com
website www.scotsman.com
Editor Euan McGrory
Sun £2

Features on all subjects, not necessarily Scottish. Payment: varies. Founded 1988.
    Arts & Books Editor Roger Cox
    Sports Editor Graham Bean

Spectrum Magazine
Editor Alison Gray
Free with paper

Scotsman

Orchard Brae House, 30 Queensferry Road, Edinburgh EH4 2HS
tel 0131 311 7311
email reception@scotsman.com
website www.scotsman.com
Facebook www.facebook.com/
TheScotsmanNewspaper
Twitter @TheScotsman
Editor Neil McIntosh
Daily Mon–Fri £1.50, Sat £1.95
Supplements **Saturday Magazine, Critique, Property, Motoring, Recruitment**

Considers articles on political, economic and general themes which add substantially to current information. Prepared to commission topical and controversial series from proved authorities. Length: 800–1,000 words. Illustrations: outstanding news pictures, cartoons. Payment: by arrangement. Founded 1817.
    Arts & Books Editor Roger Cox
    Head of Content Alan Young
    Picture Editor Kayt Turner
    Sports Editor Graham Bean

Scottish Sun

News International Newspapers Scotland Ltd, 6th Floor, Guildhall, 57 Queen Street, Glasgow G1 3EN
tel 0141 420 5200
email scottishsunletters@the-sun.co.uk
website www.thescottishsun.co.uk
Facebook www.facebook.com/thescottishsun
Twitter @ScottishSun
Editor Alan Muir
Daily Mon–Fri 50p, Sat 70p, Sun £1
Supplements **Fabulous**

Scottish edition of the *Sun*. Illustrations: transparencies, colour and b&w prints, colour cartoons. Payment: by arrangement. Founded 1985.

Socialist Worker

PO Box 74955, London E16 9EJ
tel 020-7840 5656
email reports@socialistworker.co.uk
website https://socialistworker.co.uk/
Facebook www.facebook.com/SocialistWorkerBritain
Twitter @socialistworker
Editor Charlie Kimber
Weekly £1

A revolutionary socialist newspaper produced by the Socialist Workers Party. Founded 1968.

Sun

1 London Bridge Street, London SE1 9GF
tel 020-7782 4100
email exclusive@the-sun.co.uk
website www.thesun.co.uk
Facebook www.facebook.com/thesun
Twitter @TheSun
Editor Victoria Newton
Daily Mon–Fri 30p, Sat 85p
Supplements **Cashflow, TV Magazine**

Takes freelance material, including cartoons. Payment: by negotiation. Founded 1969.
    Deputy Editor Simon Cosyns
    Bizarre Editor Simon Boyle
    Business Editor Tracey Boles
    Political Editor Harry Cole
    Showbiz Editor Amy Brookbanks
    Deputy Head of Sport Martin Lipton
    Travel Editor Lisa Minot
    TV Editor Andy Halls

Sun on Sunday

1 London Bridge Street, London SE1 9GF
tel 020-7782 4100
email exclusive@the-sun.co.uk
website www.thesun.co.uk
Editor Victoria Newton
Sun £1.20
Supplements **Fabulous**

Takes freelance material. Founded 2012.

Sunday Business Post

Second Floor, Block B, The Merrion Centre,
Merrion Road, Dublin D04 H2H4,
Republic of Ireland
tel +353 (0)16 026000
email editor@businesspost.ie
website www.businesspost.ie
Editor Richie Oakley
Sun €3.20

Features on financial, economic and political topics;
also lifestyle, media and science articles. Illustrations:
colour and b&w photos, graphics, cartoons. Payment:
by negotiation. Founded 1989.
  Deputy Editor Susan Mitchell
  Managing Editor Gillian Neilis
  Books & Arts Editor Nadine O'Regan
  Political Editor Michael Brennan

Sunday Express

Northern & Shell Building, 10 Lower Thames Street,
London EC4R 6EN
tel 020-8612 7000
email sundaynews@express.co.uk
website www.express.co.uk/news/sunday
Editor Gary Jones
Sun £1.40
Supplements **'S', Property, Review, Sport, Travel,
Finance**

Exclusive news stories, photos, personality profiles
and features of controversial or lively interest. Length:
800–1,000 words. Payment: top rates. Founded 1918.
  Finance Editor Geoff Ho
  Health Editor Amy Packer
  Literary Editor Charlotte Heathcote
  Political Editor David Maddox
  Sports Editor Scott Wilson
  Television Editor David Stephenson

'S'

tel 020-8612 7257
email sundaymag@express.co.uk
Editor Margaret Hussey
Free with paper

Sunday Independent

27–32 Talbot Street, Dublin D01 X2E1,
Republic of Ireland
tel +353 (0)17 055333
email info@independent.ie
website www.independent.ie
Editor Alan English
Sun €3.70

Special articles. Length: according to subject.
Illustrations: topical or general interest, cartoons.
Payment: at editor's valuation. Founded 1905.

Sunday Mail

1 Central Quay, Glasgow G3 8DA
tel 0141 309 3000

email reporters@sundaymail.co.uk
London office One Canada Square, Canary Wharf,
London E14 5AP
website www.dailyrecord.co.uk
Editor Lorna Hughes
Sun £1.90
Supplements **Entertainment, Fun on Sunday,
Jobsplus!, 7-Days, Right at Home**

Exclusive stories and pictures of national and Scottish
interest; also cartoons. Payment: above average.
Founded 1982.
  Deputy Editor Steven Hendry
  News Editor Derek Alexander
  Sports Editor Allan Bryce

Sunday Mirror

One Canada Square, Canary Wharf, London E14 5AP
tel 020-7293 3000
email scoops@sundaymirror.co.uk
website www.mirror.co.uk
Editor Alison Phillips
Sun £1.50
Supplements **Notebook, Holidays & Getaways**

Concentrates on human interest news features, social
documentaries, dramatic news and feature photos.
Ideas, as well as articles, bought. Payment: high,
especially for exclusives. Founded 1963.
  Deputy Editors Tom Carlin, Gemma Aldridge
  Political Editor Nigel Nelson
  Head of News Angela Wormald

Sunday National

125 Fullarton Drive, Glasgow G32 8FG
tel 0141 302 7000
email reporters@thenational.scot
website www.thenational.scot
Facebook www.facebook.com/
thenationalnewspaperscotland
Twitter @ScotNational
Editor Richard Walker
Sun £2

Scottish Sunday newspaper owned by Newsquest.
Replaced the Sunday Herald. Sister paper of the first
daily newspaper in Scotland to support Scottish
independence. Founded 2018.

Sunday People

One Canada Square, Canary Wharf, London E14 5AP
tel 020-7293 3842
email feedback@people.co.uk
website www.mirror.co.uk/all-about/sunday-people
Editor Alison Phillips
Sun £1.60
Supplements **Take it Easy**

Exclusive news and feature stories needed.
Investigative and campaigning issues. Features and
human interest stories as speciality. Strong sports
following. Payment: rates high, even for tips that lead
to published news stories. Founded 1881.

Arts Director Adele Jennings
Political Editor Nigel Nelson

Take it Easy
Editor Samantha Cope
Free with paper

Sunday Post

Spiers View, 50 High Craighall Road,
Glasgow G4 9UD
tel (01382) 223131
email mail@sundaypost.com
website www.sundaypost.com
Editor Jim Wilson
Sun £1.70
Supplements **Travel & Homes, TV & Entertainment**

Human interest, topical, domestic and humorous
articles, and exclusive news. Payment: on acceptance.
Founded 1914.

in10 magazine
tel (01382) 223131
Head of Content Dawn Donaghey
Monthly Free with paper

General interest articles. Length: 1,000–2,000 words.
Illustrations: colour transparencies. Payment: varies.
Founded 1988.

Sunday Telegraph

111 Buckingham Palace Road, London SW1W 0DT
tel 020-7931 2000
email stnews@telegraph.co.uk
website www.telegraph.co.uk
Editor Allister Heath
Sun £2.50
Supplements **Business Reporter, Life, It's Your
Money, Sport, Stella, Discover**

Occasional freelance material accepted.
Founded 1961.
   Film Editor Ross Jones
   Group Business Editor James Quinn
   Picture Editor Mike Spillard

Stella
tel 020-7931 2000
email stella@telegraph.co.uk
Editor Marianne Jones
Free with paper
All material is commissioned. Founded 1995.

The Sunday Times

The News Building, 1 London Bridge Street,
London SE1 9GF
tel 020-7782 5000
email newsdesk@sunday-times.co.uk
website www.thetimes.co.uk
Facebook www.facebook.com/timesandsundaytimes
Twitter @thesundaytimes
Editor Emma Tucket
Sun £2.90

Supplements **Appointments, Business, Culture,
Driving, Home, Money, News Review, Sport, Style,
The Sunday Times Magazine, Travel**

Special articles by authoritative writers on politics,
literature, art, drama, music, finance, science and
topical matters. Payment: top rate for exclusive
features. Founded 1822.
   Deputy Editor Ben Taylor
   Arts Commissioning Editor Nancy Durrant
   Economics Editor David Smith
   Literary Editor Andrew Holgate
   Political Editor Tim Shipman
   Social Affairs Editor Greg Hurst
   Sports Editor Alex Butler

The Sunday Times Magazine
tel 020-7782 5000
Free with paper
Articles and pictures. Illustrations: colour and b&w
photos. Payment: by negotiation.

TES (The Times Educational Supplement)

26 Red Lion Square, London WC1R 4HQ
tel 020-3194 3000
email newsdesk@tes.com
email features@tes.com
website www.tes.com
Twitter @tes
Editor Jon Severs
Weekly £30 per quarter print and digital; £15 per
quarter digital only

Education magazine and website. Articles on
education written with special knowledge or
experience; news items; features; book reviews.
Outlines of feature ideas should be emailed.
Illustrations: suitable photos and drawings of
educational interest, cartoons. Payment: by
arrangement. Founded 1910.

TESS (The Times Educational Supplement Scotland)

email scoted@tesglobal.com
website www.tes.com
Twitter @TESScotland
Contact Henry Hepburn
Weekly £3.50

Education newspaper. Articles on education,
preferably 800–1,000 words, written with special
knowledge or experience. News items about Scottish
educational affairs. Illustrations: by arrangement.
Payment: by arrangement. Founded 1965.

THE (Times Higher Education)

26 Red Lion Square, London WC1R 4HQ
email john.gill@timeshighereducation.com
website www.timeshighereducation.co.uk
Facebook www.facebook.com/timeshighereducation
Twitter @timeshighered

Editor John Gill
Weekly £4.50

Articles on higher education written with special knowledge or experience, or articles dealing with academic topics. Also news items. Illustrations: suitable photos and drawings of educational interest. Payment: by arrangement. Founded 1971.

The Times

The News Building, 1 London Bridge Street, London SE1 9GF
tel 020-7782 5000
email home.news@thetimes.co.uk
website www.thetimes.co.uk
Facebook www.facebook.com/timesandsundaytimes
Twitter @thetimes
Editor John Witherow
Daily Mon–Fri £2.20, Sat £2.70
Supplements **Books, Crème, Football Handbook, The Game, The Knowledge, Money, Times 2, Times Law, The Times Magazine, Times Sport, Travel, Arts and Entertainment, Fashion, Saturday Review, Technology, Weekend**

Outside contributions considered from experts in subjects of current interest and writers who can make first-hand experience or reflection come readably alive. Phone appropriate section editor. Length: up to 1,200 words. Founded 1785.

Deputy Editor Tony Gallagher
Business Editor Richard Fletcher
Foreign Editor Roland Watson
Head of Sport Les Snowdon
Health Editor Andrew Gregory
Literary Editor Robbie Millen
News Editor Wesley Rock
Political Editor Francis Elliott
Travel Editor Duncan Craig

The Times Magazine
Free with Sat paper
Features. Illustrated.

Timesonline
website www.thetimes.co.uk
Editor Alan Hunter
Subscription website containing news from *The Times* and the *Sunday Times*. Founded 1999.

TLS (The Times Literary Supplement)

1 London Bridge Street, London SE1 9GF
tel 020-7782 4985
email queries@the-tls.co.uk
website www.the-tls.co.uk
Editor Martin Ivens

Weekly £3.95

Will consider poems for publication, literary discoveries and articles on literary and cultural affairs. Payment: by arrangement. Founded 1902.

Tortoise

website www.tortoisemedia.com
Facebook www.facebook.com/agathathetortoise
Twitter @tortoise
Editor & Founder James Harding

Online only British news service dedicated to being selective and deliberative in the news it reports. Founded 2019.

The Voice

236 Elephant and Castle Shopping Centre, London SE1 6TE
tel 020-7510 0340
email newsdesk@gvmedia.co.uk
website www.voice-online.co.uk
Facebook www.facebook.com/voicenews
Twitter @TheVoiceNews
Managing Director & Editor George Ruddock
Weekly £1

Weekly newspaper for black Britons. Includes news, features, arts, sport and a comprehensive jobs and business section. Illustrations: colour and b&w photos. Open to ideas for news and features on sports, business, community events and the arts. Founded 1982.

Lifestyle, Arts & Entertainment Editor Joel Campbell
News Editor Vic Motune
Sports & Features Editor Rodney Hinds

Wales on Sunday

6 Park Street, Cardiff CF10 1XR
tel 029-2024 3604
email newsdesk@walesonline.co.uk
website www.walesonline.co.uk
Facebook www.facebook.com/WalesOnline
Twitter @walesonline
Editor Paul Rowland
Sun £1.60
Supplements **Life on Sunday, Sport on Sunday**

National Sunday newspaper of Wales offering comprehensive news, features and entertainment coverage at the weekend, with a particular focus on events in Wales. Accepts general interest articles, preferably with a Welsh connection. Founded 1989.

Political Editor David Williamson
Head of Sport Paul Abbandonato

Regional newspapers UK and Ireland

Regional newspapers are listed in alphabetical order under region. The list is not exhaustive. Over recent years, it has become increasingly difficult for freelance writers to have pitches accepted or commissions requested by regional news companies. The below listing includes those papers that may still be accepting work from freelance writers. Some will accept and pay for brief fillers and gossip paragraphs, as well as puzzles and quizzes.

BELFAST

Belfast Telegraph
Belfast Telegraph House, 33 Clarendon Road,
Clarendon Dock, Belfast BT1 3BG
tel 028-9026 4000
email newseditor@belfasttelegraph.co.uk
website www.belfasttelegraph.co.uk
Facebook www.facebook.com/belfasttelegraph
Twitter @beltel
Editor Eoin Brannigan
Group Managing Editor Edward McCann
Daily Mon–Sat £1.30

An Independent News & Media publication. Any material relating to Northern Ireland. Payment: by negotiation. Founded 1870.

Irish News
113–117 Donegall Street, Belfast BT1 2GE
tel 028-9032 2226
email newsdesk@irishnews.com
website www.irishnews.com
Facebook www.facebook.com/IrishNewsLtd
Twitter @irish_news
Editor Noel Doran
Daily Mon–Sat £1.20

Founded 1855.

News Letter
Suites 302–303, Glandore, Arthur House,
41 Arthur Street, Belfast BT1 4GB
tel 028-3839 5577
email newsdesk@newsletter.co.uk
website www.newsletter.co.uk/news
Facebook www.facebook.com/belfastnewsletter
Twitter @News_Letter
Editor Alastair Bushe
Daily Mon–Sat £1.35

Pro-Union. Founded 1737.

Sunday Life
Belfast Telegraph House, 33 Clarendon Road,
Clarendon Dock, Belfast BT1 3BG
tel 028-9026 4000
email sinews@sundaylife.co.uk
website www.belfasttelegraph.co.uk/sunday-life
Editor Eoin Brannigan

Sun £1.90

Items of interest to Northern Ireland Sunday tabloid readers. Illustrations: colour and b&w pictures and graphics. Payment: by arrangement. Founded 1988.

CHANNEL ISLANDS

Jersey Evening Post
PO Box 582, Five Oaks, St Saviour, Jersey JE4 8XQ
tel (01534) 611611
email news@jerseyeveningpost.com
website https://jerseyeveningpost.com/
Facebook www.facebook.com/jerseyeveningpost
Twitter @jepnews
Editor Richard Heath
Daily Mon–Sat 90p

News and features with a Channel Islands angle. Length: 1,000 words (articles/features), 300 words (news). Illustrations: colour and b&w. Payment: £110 per 1,000 words. Founded 1890.

CORK

Evening Echo
Linn Dubh, Assumption Road, Blackpool,
Cork T23 RCH6, Republic of Ireland
tel +353 (0)21 4272722
email news@eecho.ie
website www.eveningecho.ie
Facebook www.facebook.com/echolivecork
Twitter @echolivecork
Editor Maurice Gubbins
Daily Mon–Sat €1.50

Articles, features and news for the area. Illustrations: colour prints. Founded 1892.

DUBLIN

Herald
Independent House, 27–32 Talbot Street,
Dublin D01 X2E1, Republic of Ireland
tel +353 (0)17 055722
email hnews@independent.ie
website www.herald.ie
Facebook www.facebook.com/Herald.ie

Twitter @HeraldNewsdesk
Editor Stephen Rae
Daily Mon–Sat €1.30

Articles. Illustrations: line, half-tone, cartoons.
Payment: by arrangement. Founded 1783.

EAST ANGLIA

Cambridge News
Building 100, Cambridge Research Park,
Waterbeach CB25 9PD
tel (01223) 632293
email newsdesk@cambridge-news.co.uk
website www.cambridge-news.co.uk
Facebook www.facebook.com/cambridgeshirelive
Twitter @CambsLive
Editor Richard Duggan
Daily Mon–Sat 95p

The voice of the Cambridge region – news, views and
sport. Illustrations: colour prints, b&w and colour
graphics. Payment: by negotiation. Founded 1888.

East Anglian Daily Times
1 Bath Street, Ipswich IP2 8SD
tel (01473) 230023
email newsroom@archant.co.uk
website www.eadt.co.uk
Facebook www.facebook.com/eadt24
Twitter @eadt24
Editor Brad Jones
Daily Mon–Fri 95p, Sat £1.80

Features of East Anglian interest, preferably with
pictures. Length: 500 words. Illustrations: NUJ rates.
Payment: negotiable. Founded 1874.

Eastern Daily Press
Prospect House, Rouen Road, Norwich NR1 1RE
tel (01603) 628311
website www.edp24.co.uk
Facebook www.facebook.com/edp24
Twitter @edp24
Editor David Powles
Daily Mon–Fri £1, Saturday £1.90

Limited market for articles of East Anglian interest
not exceeding 650 words. Founded 1870.

Ipswich Star
1 Bath Street, Ipswich IP2 8SD
tel (01473) 230023
website www.ipswichstar.co.uk
Facebook www.facebook.com/ipswichstar24
Twitter @ipswichstar24
Editor Brad Jones
Daily Mon–Fri 95p

Founded 1885.

Norwich Evening News
Prospect House, Rouen Road, Norwich NR1 1RE
tel (01603) 628311
website www.eveningnews24.co.uk
Facebook www.facebook.com/NorwichEveningNews
Twitter @EveningNews
Editor David Powles
Daily Mon–Sat 85p

Interested in local news-based features. Length: up to
650 words. Payment: Agreed rates. Founded 1882.

EAST MIDLANDS

Burton Mail
2 Siddals Road, Derby DE1 2PB
tel (01283) 245000
email editorial@burtonmail.co.uk
website www.burtonmail.co.uk
Facebook www.facebook.com/BurtonNews
Twitter @BurtonMailNews
Editor Julie Crouch
Daily Mon–Sat 85p

Features, news and articles of interest to Burton and
south Derbyshire readers. Length: 400–500 words.
Illustrations: colour and b&w. Payment: by
negotiation. Founded 1898.

Chronicle & Echo, Northampton
Northamptonshire Newspapers Ltd,
400 Pavilion Drive, Northampton NN4 7PA
tel (01604) 467032
email editor@northantsnews.co.uk
website www.northamptonchron.co.uk
Facebook www.facebook.com/northamptonchron
Twitter @ChronandEcho
Editor David Summers
Weekly Thurs £1.85

Articles, features and news – mostly commissioned –
of interest to the Northampton area. Length: varies.
Payment: by negotiation. Founded 1931.

Derby Telegraph
2 Siddals Road, Derby DE1 2PB
tel (01332) 411888
website www.derbytelegraph.co.uk
Facebook www.facebook.com/derbyshirelive
Twitter @Derbyshire_live
Editor Julie Bayley
Daily Mon–Sat 70p

Articles and news of local interest. Payment: by
negotiation. Founded 1879.

Leicester Mercury
16 New Walk, Leicester LE1 6TF
tel 0116 366 5218
website www.leicestermercury.co.uk
Facebook www.facebook.com/leicestershirelive

Twitter @LeicsLive
Editor Adam Moss
Daily Mon–Fri 80p, Sat 90p

Occasional articles, features and news; submit ideas to editor first. Length/payment: by negotiation. Founded 1874.

Nottingham Post

3rd Floor, City Gate, Tollhouse Hill,
Nottingham NG1 5FS
tel 0115 948 2000
email newsdesk@nottinghampostgroup.co.uk
website www.nottinghampost.com
Facebook www.facebook.com/Nottinghamshirelive
Twitter @NottsLive
Editor Natalie Fahy
Daily Mon–Sat 85p

Material on local issues considered. Founded 1878.

Peterborough Telegraph

c/o Brightfields Business Hub, Bakewell Road,
Peterborough PE2 6XU
tel (01733) 555111
email news@peterboroughtoday.co.uk
website www.peterboroughtoday.co.uk
Facebook www.facebook.com/peterboroughtoday
Twitter @peterboroughtel
Editor Mark Edwards
Weekly Thurs £1.45

Founded 1948.

LONDON

London Evening Standard

2 Derry Street, London W8 5TT
tel 020-3367 7000
email news@standard.co.uk
website www.standard.co.uk
Facebook www.facebook.com/eveningstandard
Twitter @standardnews
Editor Emily Sheffield
Daily Mon–Fri Free

Founded 1827.

ES-Magazine

Editor Laura Weir
Weekly Free with paper on Thurs, Fri
Feature ideas, exclusively about London. Illustrations: all types. Payment: by negotiation.

Homes & Property

email homesandproperty@standard.co.uk
Editor Prudence Ivey
Weekly Free with paper on Wed
UK property. Payment: by negotiation.

This Is London

website www.standard.co.uk
Online news website for *London Evening Standard*.

NORTH EAST

Berwick Advertiser

c/o Orchard Brae House, 30 Queensway Road,
Edinburgh EH4 2HS
tel (01289) 334686
email advertisernews@tweeddalepress.co.uk
website www.berwick-advertiser.co.uk
Facebook www.facebook.com/BAdvertiser
Twitter @BAdvertiser
Editor Paul Larkin
Daily Mon–Fri £1.35

Articles, features and news. Founded 1830.

The Chronicle

Eldon Square, Percy Street,
Newcastle upon Tyne NE1 7JB
tel 0191 232 7500
email ec.news@ncjmedia.co.uk
website www.chroniclelive.co.uk
Facebook www.facebook.com/NewcastleChronicle
Twitter @ChronicleLive
Editor Helen Dalby
Daily Mon–Sat 65p

News, photos and features covering almost every subject of interest to readers in Tyne & Wear, Northumberland and Durham. Payment: by prior arrangement. Founded 1858.

Darlington and Stockton Times

PO Box 14, Priestgate, Darlington DL1 1NF
tel (01325) 381313
email newsdesk@nne.co.uk
website www.darlingtonandstocktontimes.co.uk
Facebook www.facebook.com/darlingtonstocktontimes
Twitter @DAndSTimes
Editor Hannah Chapman
Weekly Fri £1.30

Founded 1847.

Durham Advertiser

PO Box 14, Priestgate, Darlington DL1 1NF
tel 0191 384 4600
email newsdesk@nne.co.uk
website www.durhamadvertiser.co.uk
Facebook www.facebook.com/durhamadvertiser
Editor Hannah Chapman
Weekly Fri 30p

Founded 1814.

The Gazette

Ground Floor, Hudson Quay, The Halyard,
Middlehaven, Middlesbrough TS3 6RT
tel (01642) 245401
email news@gazettemedia.co.uk
website www.gazettelive.co.uk
Facebook www.facebook.com/Teessidelive
Twitter @TeessideLive
Editor Helen Dalby
Daily Mon–Sat 80p

News, topical and lifestyle features. Length: 600–800 words. Illustrations: line, half-tone, colour, graphics, cartoons. Payment: £75 per 1,000 words; scale rate or by agreement for illustrations. Founded 1869.

Hartlepool Mail

North East Business and Innovation Centre, Westfield, Enterprise Park East, Sunderland SR5 2TA
tel (01429) 225644
email mail.news@northeast-press.co.uk
website www.hartlepoolmail.co.uk
Facebook www.facebook.com/hartlepoolmailnews
Twitter @HPoolMail
Editor Joy Yates
Daily Mon–Sat 75p

Features of local interest. Length: 500 words. Illustrations: colour, b&w photos, line. Payment: by negotiation. Founded 1877.

The Journal

Eldon Court, Percy Street,
Newcastle upon Tyne NE1 7JB
tel 0191 201 6446
email ec.news@ncjmedia.co.uk
website www.chroniclelive.co.uk
Facebook www.facebook.com/NewcastleChronicle
Twitter @TheJournalNews
Editor Helen Dalby
Daily Mon–Fri 80p, Sat £1.30

News, sport items and features of topical interest considered. Payment: by arrangement.

The Northern Echo

Newsquest North, Priestgate, Darlington DL1 1NF
tel (01325) 381313
email newsdesk@nee.co.uk
website www.thenorthernecho.co.uk
Facebook www.facebook.com/thenorthernecho
Twitter @TheNorthernEcho
Editor Karl Holbrook
Daily Mon–Fri 92p, Sat £1.30

Articles of interest to North-East and North Yorkshire; all material commissioned. Preliminary study of newspaper advisable. Length: 800–1,000 words. Illustrations: line, half-tone, colour – mostly commissioned. Payment: by negotiation. Founded 1870.

The Shields Gazette

North East Business and Innovation Centre, Wearfield, Enterprise Park East, Sunderland SR5 2TA
tel 0191 501 7326
website www.shieldsgazette.com
Facebook www.facebook.com/shieldsgazette
Twitter @shieldsgazette
Editor Joy Yates
Daily Mon–Sat 88p

Founded 1855.

The Sunday Sun

Eldon Court, Percy Street,
Newcastle upon Tyne NE1 7JB
tel 0191 201 6201
email scoop.sundaysun@ncjmedia.co.uk
website www.chroniclelive.co.uk/all-about/sunday-sun
Editor Matt McKenzie
Weekly Sun £1.90

Looking for topical and human interest articles on current problems. Particularly welcomed are special features of family appeal and news stories of special interest to the North of England. Length: 200–700 words. Illustrations: photos. Payment: normal lineage rates, or by arrangement. Founded 1919.

Sunderland Echo

JPI Media, 1st Floor, North East BIC, Wearfield, Enterprise Park East, Sunderland SR5 2TA
tel 0191 501 5800
email echo.news@northeast-press.co.uk
website www.sunderlandecho.com
Facebook www.facebook.com/sunderlandechoonline
Twitter @SunderlandEcho
Editorial Director Joy Yates
Daily Mon–Sat 83p

Local news, features and articles. Length: 500 words. Illustrations: colour and b&w photos, line, cartoons. Payment: by negotiation. Founded 1875.

NORTH WEST

Blackpool Gazette

15 Olympic Court, Boardmans Way, Whitehills Business Park, Blackpool FY4 5GU
tel (01253) 400888
email editorial@blackpoolgazette.co.uk
website www.blackpoolgazette.co.uk
Facebook www.facebook.com/blackpoolgazette
Twitter @the_gazette
Editor Gillian Parkinson
Daily Mon–Sat £1

Local news and articles of general interest, with photos if appropriate. Length: varies. Payment: on merit. Founded 1929.

Bolton News

Newsquest Lancashire and Greater Manchester, The Wellsprings, Civic Centre, Victoria Square, Bolton BL1 1AR
tel (01204) 522345
email newsdesk@nqw.co.uk
website www.theboltonnews.co.uk
Facebook www.facebook.com/theboltonnews
Twitter @TheBoltonNews
Editor Steve Thompson
Daily Mon–Sat 75p

Founded 1867.

Carlisle News and Star

CN Group, Newspaper House, Dalston Road,
Carlisle CA2 5UA
tel (01228) 612600
website www.newsandstar.co.uk
Facebook www.facebook.com/newsandstar
Twitter @newsandstar
Associate Editor Vanessa Simms
Daily Mon–Sat 65p

Founded 1910.

The Chester Chronicle

Maple House, Park West, Sealand Road,
Chester CH1 4RN
tel (01244) 606455
email newsroom@cheshirenews.co.uk
website www.chesterchronicle.co.uk
Facebook www.facebook.com/CheshireLive
Twitter @CheshireLive
Editor Frances Barrett
Weekly Thurs £1.60

Local news and features. Founded 1775.

Lancashire Post

Stuart House, 89 Caxton Road, Fulwood,
Preston PR2 9ZB
tel (01772) 838134
email lep.newsdesk@lep.co.uk
website www.lep.co.uk
Facebook www.facebook.com/lancashireeveningpost
Twitter @leponline
Editor Gillian Parkinson
Daily Mon–Sat 95p

Topical articles on all subjects. Area of interest:
Wigan to Lake District, Lancs. and coast. Length:
600–900 words. Illustrations: colour and b&w photos,
cartoons. Payment: by arrangement. Founded 1886.

Lancashire Telegraph

c/o The Wellsprings, Civic Centre, Bolton BL1 1AR
tel (01254) 678678
email lancsnews@nqnw.co.uk
website www.lancashiretelegraph.co.uk
Facebook www.facebook.com/lancashiretelegraph
Twitter @lancstelegraph
Editor Steven Thompson
Daily Mon–Sat 73p

Will consider general news items from East
Lancashire. Payment: by arrangement. Founded 1886.

Liverpool Echo

5 St Paul's Square, Liverpool LS3 9SJ
tel 0151 472 2453
website www.liverpoolecho.co.uk
Facebook www.facebook.com/theliverpoolecho
Twitter @LivEchonews
Editor Maria Breslin
Daily Mon–Fri 95p, Sat £1.35, Sun £1.10

Articles of up to 600–800 words of local or topical
interest; also cartoons. Payment: according to merit;
special rates for exceptional material. Connected
with, but independent of, the *Liverpool Post*: articles
not interchangeable. Founded 1879.

The Mail

Newspaper House, 1 Wainwrights Yard,
Kendal LA9 4DP
tel (01229) 840150
email news.em@newsquest.co.uk
website www.nwemail.co.uk
Facebook www.facebook.com/northwesteveningmail
Editor Vanessa Sims
Daily Mon–Fri 70p, Sat 80p

Articles, features and news. Length: 500 words.
Covering the whole of South Cumbria. Illustrations:
colour photos and occasional artwork. Founded 1898.

Manchester Evening News

Mitchell Henry House, Hollinwood Avenue,
Chadderton OL9 8EF
tel 0161 832 7200 (editorial)
email newsdesk@men-news.co.uk
website www.manchestereveningnews.co.uk
Facebook www.facebook.com/
ManchesterEveningNews
Twitter @MENNewsdesk
Editor Darren Thwaites
Daily Mon–Sat 95p

Feature articles of up to 1,000 words, topical or
general interest and illustrated where appropriate,
should be addressed to the Features Editor. Payment:
on acceptance. Founded 1868.

Southport Reporter

4A Post Office Avenue, Southport PR9 0US
tel 08463 244195
email news24@southportreporter.com
website www.southportreporter.com
Facebook www.facebook.com/SouthportReporter
Twitter @SouthportReport
Editor Patrick Trollope

Online only. An independent news and information
online newspaper. Founded 1999.

SCOTLAND

The Courier

D.C. Thomson & Co. Ltd, 2 Albert Square,
Dundee DD1 1DD
tel (01382) 575291
London office 185 Fleet Street, London EC4A 2HS
tel 020-7400 1030
website www.thecourier.co.uk
Facebook www.facebook.com/thecourieruk
Twitter @thecourieruk
Editor David Clegg
Daily Mon–Fri £1.10, Sat £1.30

Supplements **Motoring, House & Home, What's On, Menu, Weekend, Beautiful Homes, Perfect Weddings, Farming, Business, Sport**

One of Britain's biggest regional morning newspapers and an established title in cast central Scotland. Publishes four daily editions and covers local news for Perthshire, Fife, Angus and The Mearns and Dundee. Founded 1810.

Dundee Evening Telegraph and Post

D.C. Thomson & Co. Ltd, 2 Albert Square, Dundee DD1 1DD
tel (01382) 575452
email newsdesk@eveningtelegraph.co.uk
London office 185 Fleet Street, London EC4A 2HS
tel 020-7400 1030
website www.eveningtelegraph.co.uk
Facebook www.facebook.com/eveningtele
Twitter @Evening_Tele
Editor Dave Lord
Daily Mon–Sat 80p

Founded 1877.

Evening Express (Aberdeen)

Aberdeen Journals Ltd, 1 Marischal Square, Broad Street, Aberdeen AB10 1BL
tel (01224) 343033
email ee.news@ajl.co.uk
website www.eveningexpress.co.uk
Facebook www.facebook.com/EveningExpressAberdeen
Twitter @eveningexpress
Editor Craig Walker
Daily Mon–Sat 90p

Lively evening paper. Illustrations: colour and b&w. Payment: by arrangement. Founded 1879.

Evening News (Edinburgh)

Orchard Brae House, 30 Queensferry Road, Edinburgh EH4 2HS
tel 0131 311 7311
email reception@scotsman.com
website www.edinburghnews.scotsman.com
Facebook www.facebook.com/edinburgh.evening.news
Twitter @edinburghpaper
Editor Euan McGrory
Daily Mon–Sat 83p

Features on current affairs, preferably in relation to the circulation area. Women's talking points; local historical articles; subjects of general interest; health, beauty and fashion. Founded 1873.

Glasgow Evening Times

Herald & Times Group, 125 Fullarton Drive, Glasgow East Investment Park, Glasgow G32 8FG
tel 0141 302 7000
website www.glasgowtimes.co.uk
Facebook www.facebook.com/glasgowtimes

Twitter @TheEveningTimes
Editor Donald Martin
Daily Mon–Sat 80p

Founded 1876.

Greenock Telegraph

2 Crawfurd Street, Greenock PA15 1LH
tel (01475) 558904
email editorial@greenocktelegraph.co.uk
website www.greenocktelegraph.co.uk
Facebook www.facebook.com/greenocktelegraph
Twitter @greenocktele
Editor Brian Hossack
Daily Mon–Sat 65p

News and features from the area in and around Greenock. Founded 1857.

Inverness Courier

New Century House, Stadium Road, Inverness IV1 1FG
tel (01463) 246575
email newsdesk@hnmedia.co.uk
website www.inverness-courier.co.uk
Facebook www.facebook.com/invernesscourier
Twitter @InvCourier
Editor Andrew Dixon
Biweekly Tue £1.20, Fri £1.50

Articles of Highland interest only. Unsolicited material accepted. Illustrations: colour and b&w photos. Payment: by arrangement. Founded 1817.

Paisley Daily Express

Scottish and Universal Newspapers Ltd, 14 New Street, Paisley PA1 1YA
tel 0141 309 3555
email pde@reachplc.com
website www.dailyrecord.co.uk/all-about/paisley
Facebook www.facebook.com/paisleydailyexpress
Twitter @PDEofficial
Editor Gavin McInally
Daily Mon–Sat 55p

Articles of Paisley interest only. Considers unsolicited material. Founded 1874.

Press and Journal

5th Floor, 1 Marischal Square, Broad Street, Aberdeen AB10 1BL
tel (01224) 343311
email pj.newsdesk@ajl.co.uk
website www.pressandjournal.co.uk
Facebook www.facebook.com/ThePressandJournal
Twitter @pressjournal
Editor Richard Neville
Daily Mon–Fri £1.30, Sat £1.40

Contributions of Scottish interest. Illustrations: half-tone. Payment: by arrangement. Founded 1747.

SOUTH EAST

The Argus
Dolphin House, 2–5 Manchester Street,
Brighton BN2 1TF
tel (01273) 021400
email editor@theargus.co.uk
website www.theargus.co.uk
Facebook www.facebook.com/brightonargus
Twitter @brightonargus
Editor Aaron Hendy
Daily Mon–Fri 70p, Sat 85p

Founded 1880.

Banbury Guardian
c/o Regus Milton Keynes, Atterbury Lakes,
Fairburn Drive, Atterbury MK10 9RG
tel (01295) 817674
email editorial@banburyguardian.co.uk
website www.banburyguardian.co.uk
Facebook www.facebook.com/banburyguardian
Twitter @banburynews
Editor David Summers
Daily Mon–Sat £1.25

Local news and features. Founded 1838.

Echo
Echo House, Howard Chase, Basildon SS14 3BE
tel (01268) 522792
email echonews@nqe.com
website www.echo-news.co.uk
Facebook www.facebook.com/echo.essex
Twitter @Essex_Echo
Editor Victoria Birch
Daily Mon–Fri 70p

Mostly staff-written. Only interested in local material.
Payment: by arrangement. Founded 1969.

Essex Chronicle
Kestrel House, Hedgerows Business Park,
Chelmsford Business Park, Chelmsford CM2 5PF
tel (01245) 602730
email newsdesk@essexlive.news
website www.essexlive.news/news
Twitter @essexlive
Editor Alan Woods
Weekly Thurs £1.50

Local news and features for Essex. Founded 1764.

Hampshire Chronicle
5 Upper Brook St, Winchester SO23 8AL
tel (01962) 860836
email news@hampshirechronicle.co.uk
website www.hampshirechronicle.co.uk
Facebook www.facebook.com/hampshire.chronicle
Twitter @hantschronicle
Editor Bill Browne
Weekly Thurs £1.15

Founded 1772.

Isle of Wight County Press
Brannon House, 123 Pyle Street, Newport,
Isle of Wight PO30 1ST
tel (01983) 259003
email editor@iwcp.co.uk
website www.iwcp.co.uk
Facebook www.facebook.com/iwcponline
Twitter @iwcponline
Editor Emily Pearce
Weekly Fri 90p

Articles and news of local interest. Founded 1884.

Kent and Sussex Courier
Courier House, 80–84 Calverley Road,
Tunbridge Wells TN1 2UN
tel (01892) 239042
email kentlivenewsdesk@reachplc.com
website www.kentlive.news
Facebook www.facebook.com/kentlivenews
Twitter @kentlivenews
Editor Luke Jacobs
Weekly Fri £1

Local news, articles and features. Founded 1872.

Medway Messenger
Medway House, Ginsbury Close,
Sir Thomas Longley Road, Medway City Estate,
Strood, Kent ME2 4DU
tel (01634) 227800
email medwaymessenger@thekmgroup.co.uk
website www.kentonline.co.uk
Facebook www.facebook.com/MedwayMessenger
Twitter @MedwayMessenger
Editor Matt Ramsden
Biweekly Mon 90p, Fri £1.60

Emphasis on news and sport from the Medway
Towns. Illustrations: line, half-tone. Founded 1855.

The News, Portsmouth
100 Lakeside, North Harbour, Portsmouth PO6 3EN
tel 023-9262 2118
email newsdesk@thenews.co.uk
website www.portsmouth.co.uk
Facebook www.facebook.com/portsmouthnews
Twitter @portsmouthnews
Editor Mark Waldron
Daily Mon–Fri 83p, Sat 90p

Articles of relevance to South-East Hampshire and
West Sussex. Payment: by arrangement.
Founded 1873.

Oxford Mail
Newspaper House, Osney Mead, Oxford OX2 0EJ
tel (01865) 425262
email news@nqo.com
website www.oxfordmail.co.uk
Facebook www.facebook.com/oxfordmail
Twitter @TheOxfordMail

Editor Pete Gavan
Daily 78p

Founded 1928.

The Oxford Times

Newspaper House, Osney Mead, Oxford OX2 0EJ
tel (01865) 425262
email news@nqo.com
website www.oxfordtimes.co.uk
Facebook www.facebook.com/TheOxfordTimes
Twitter @oxfordtimes
Editor Pete Gavan
Weekly Thurs £1.40

Local weekly newspaper for Oxford. The team is also responsible for the daily *Oxford Mail* and weeklies *Bicester Advertiser*, *Witney Gazette* and the *Herald* series. Founded 1862.

Reading Chronicle

2–10 Bridge Street, Reading RG1 2LU
tel 0118 955 3333
email news@readingchronicle.co.uk
website www.readingchronicle.co.uk
Facebook www.facebook.com/readingchronicle
Twitter @rdgchronicle
Group Editor Andrew Colley
Weekly Thurs 90p

Southern Daily Echo

Newspaper House, Test Lane, Redbridge, Southampton SO16 9JX
tel 023-8042 4777
email ncwsdcsk@dailyecho.co.uk
website www.dailyecho.co.uk
Facebook www.facebook.com/dailyecho
Twitter @dailyecho
Editor Gordon Sutter
Daily Mon–Sat 68p

News, articles, features, sport. Length: varies. Illustrations: line, half-tone, colour, cartoons. Payment: NUJ rates. Founded 1888.

Swindon Advertiser

Richmond House, Unit 1 and 2, Edison Park, Swindon SN3 3RB
tel (01793) 528144
email newsdesk@swindonadvertiser.co.uk
website www.swindonadvertiser.co.uk
Facebook www.facebook.com/swindonadvertiser
Twitter @swindonadver
Editor Pete Gavan
Daily Mon–Sat 75p

News and information relating to Swindon and Wiltshire only. Considers unsolicited material. Founded 1854.

SOUTH WEST

Bournemouth Echo

Richmond Hill, Bournemouth BH2 6HH
tel (01202) 554601
email newsdesk@bournemouthecho.co.uk
website www.bournemouthecho.co.uk
Facebook www.facebook.com/bournemouthdailyecho
Twitter @bournemouthecho
Editor Gordon Sutter
Daily Mon–Fri 68p, Sat 85p

Founded 1900.

Cornish Guardian

3rd Floor, Studio 5–11, Milbay Road, Plymouth PL1 3LF
tel (01872) 271451
email cgedit@c-dm.co.uk
website www.cornishguardian.co.uk
Facebook www.facebook.com/cornwalllivenews
Twitter @CornwallLive
Editor Jeff Reines
Weekly Wed £1.20

Items of interest for Cornwall. Founded 1901.

Cornishman

Harmsworth House, Lemon's Quay, Truro TR1 2LP
tel (01872) 271451
email wbnews@c-dm.co.uk
website www.cornishman.co.uk
Facebook www.facebook.com/cornwalllivenews
Twitter @cornishmanpaper
Editor Jacqui Walls
Weekly Thurs £1.20

Local news and features. Founded 1878.

Dorset Echo

Fleet House, Hampshire Road, Weymouth DT4 9XD
tel (01305) 830930
email newsdesk@dorsetecho.co.uk
website www.dorsetecho.co.uk
Facebook www.facebook.com/dorsetecho
Twitter @Dorsetecho
Editor Diarmuid MacDonagh
Daily Mon–Fri 65p, Sat 70p

News and occasional features, length: 1,000–2,000 words. Illustrations: b&w photos. Payment: by negotiation. Founded 1921.

Express & Echo

3rd Floor, Studio 5–11, Millbay Road, Plymouth PL1 3LF
tel (01392) 346763
email newsdesk@devonlive.co.uk
website www.exeterexpressandecho.com
Facebook www.facebook.com/devonlivenews
Twitter @DevonLiveNews
Editor Scott Harrison
Weekly Thurs 50p

Features and news of local interest. Length: 500–800 words (features), up to 400 words (news). Illustrations: colour. Payment: lineage rates; illustrations: by negotiation. Founded 1904.

Gloucester Citizen

Reach PLC, Suite 121C, 1st floor, Gloucester Quays, St Ann Way, Gloucester GL1 5SH
tel (01452) 689320
email gloslivenews@reachplc.com
website www.gloucestershirelive.co.uk
Facebook www.facebook.com/GlosLiveOnline
Twitter @GlosLiveOnline
Editor Jenni Phillips
Weekly Thurs £1.50

Local news, business, entertainment, property, motors and sport for Gloucester, Stroud and the Forest of Dean. Founded 1876.

Gloucestershire Echo

Reach PLC, Suite 121C, 1st floor, Gloucester Quays, St Ann Way, Gloucester GL1 5SH
tel (01242) 689320
email gloslivenews@reachplc.com
website www.gloucestershirelive.co.uk
Facebook www.facebook.com/GlosLiveOnline
Twitter @GlosLiveOnline
Editor Rachel Sugden
Weekly Thurs £1.80

Local news, business, entertainment, property, motors and sport for Cheltenham, Cotswolds and Tewkesbury. Founded 1873.

The Herald

3rd Floor, Studio 5–11, Millbay Road, Plymouth PL1 3LF
tel (01752) 765500
email news@plymouthherald.co.uk
website www.plymouthherald.co.uk
Facebook www.facebook.com/plymouthlive
Twitter @plymouth_live
Editor Edd Moore
Daily Mon–Fri 55p, Sat 60p

Local news, articles and features. Will consider unsolicited material. Welcomes ideas for articles and features. Illustrations: colour and b&w prints. Founded 1895.

Herald Express

Harmsworth House, Barton Hill Road, Torquay, Devon TQ2 8JN
tel (01752) 293084
website www.devonlive.com
Editor Jim Parker
Weekly Thurs £1

Founded 1925.

Hereford Times

Stirling House, Unit 23, 1st floor, Centenary Park, Skylon Central, Hereford HR2 6FJ
tel (01432) 845873
email news@herefordtimes.com
website www.herefordtimes.com
Facebook www.facebook.com/herefordtimes
Twitter @HerefordTimes
Editor John Wilson
Weekly Thurs £1.35

Local news and sports. Correspondence by email only to this address: news@herefordtimes.com. No phone calls or postal submissions. Founded 1832.

Independent

Indy House, Lighterage Hill, Truro TR1 2XR
tel (01872) 613163
email newsdesk@sundayindependent.co.uk
website www.indyonline.co.uk
Facebook www.facebook.com/sundayindependent
Twitter @thesundayindy
Editor John Collings
Weekly Sun £1.50

Sport and news features on West Country topics; features/articles with a nostalgic theme; short, quirky news briefs (must be original). Length: 600 words (features/articles), 300 words (news). Illustrations: colour, b&w. Payment: by arrangement. Founded 1808.

Post

Temple Way, Bristol BS2 0BU
tel 0117 934 3000
email bristolpostnews@localworld.co.uk
website www.bristolpost.co.uk
Facebook www.facebook.com/bristolpost
Twitter @BristolLive
Editor Mike Norton
Daily Mon–Thurs 90p, Fri £1

Takes freelance news and articles. Payment: by arrangement. Founded 1932.

Western Daily Press

Yeovil Innovation Centre, Barracks Close, Copse Road, Yeovil BA22 8RN
tel (01935) 709735
website www.westerndailypress.co.uk
Facebook www.facebook.com/WesternDaily
Twitter @SomersetLive
Editor Gavin Thompson
Daily Mon–Fri £1.10, Sat £2.10

National, international or West Country topics for features or news items, from established journalists, with or without illustrations. Payment: by negotiation. Founded 1858.

Western Morning News

3rd Floor, Studio 5–11, Plymouth PL1 3LF
tel (01392) 346763
website www.devonlive.com
Facebook www.facebook.com/devonlivenews
Twitter @Devonlivesnews

Editor Philip Bowern
Daily Mon–Fri £1.10, Sat £2.10

Articles plus illustrations considered on West Country subjects. Founded 1860.

WALES

Cambrian News
7 Science Park, Aberystwyth SY23 3AH
tel (01970) 615000
email edit@cambrian-news.co.uk
website www.cambrian-news.co.uk
Facebook www.facebook.com/CambrianNews
Twitter @CambrianNews
Editor Natalie Lawson
Weekly Wed £1

Wales' biggest-selling weekly newspaper. Payment for freelance articles and pictures by arrangement. Founded 1860.

Daily Post
Bryn Eirias, Colwyn Bay LL29 8BF
tel (01492) 584321
email welshnews@dailypost.co.uk
website www.dailypost.co.uk
Facebook www.facebook.com/northwaleslive/
Twitter @northwaleslive
Editor Dion Jones
Daily Mon–Sat 85p

Founded 1855.

The Leader
NWN Media Ltd, Mold Business Park,
Wrexham Road, Mold CH7 1XY
tel (01352) 707707
website www.leaderlive.co.uk
Facebook www.facebook.com/LeaderLive
Twitter @leaderlive
Editor Susan Perry
Mon–Fri 75p

Founded 1973.

South Wales Argus
Cardiff Road, Maesglas, Newport NP20 3QN
tel (01633) 810000
email newsdesk@gwent-wales.co.uk
website www.southwalesargus.co.uk
Facebook www.facebook.com/southwalesargus
Twitter @southwalesargus
Editor Gavin Thompson
Daily Mon–Sat 75p

News and features of relevance to Gwent. Length: 500–600 words (features); 350 words (news). Illustrations: colour prints and transparencies. Founded 1892.

South Wales Echo
6 Park Street, Cardiff CF10 1XR
tel (02920) 243600

email newsdesk@walesonline.co.uk
website www.walesonline.co.uk
Twitter @walesonline
Editor Tryst Williams
Daily Mon–Fri 90p, Sat £1.20

Evening paper: news, sport, features, showbiz, news features, personality interviews. Length: up to 700 words. Illustrations: photos, cartoons. Payment: by negotiation. Founded 1884.

South Wales Evening Post
South Wales Evening Post, Urban Village,
High Street, Swansea SA1 1NW
tel (01792) 555520
email postnews@mediawales.co.uk
website www.walesonline.co.uk
Twitter @WalesOnline
Editor Jonathan Roberts
Daily Mon–Sat 80p

Founded 1893.

WEST MIDLANDS

The Asian Today
6A Olton Wharf, Richmond Road, Solihull B92 7RN
tel 0121 314 2892
email editorial@theasiantoday.com
website www.theasiantoday.com
Facebook www.facebook.com/theasiantoday
Twitter @theasiantoday
Editor Anita Chumber

A free fortnightly community newspaper published and distributed in the Midlands providing the region's south-Asian community access to important news stories, current events and encouraging community interaction and dialogue as well as provoking debate and discussion. Found 2002.

Coventry Telegraph
Corporation Street, Coventry CV1 1FP
tel 024-7663 3633
email news@coventrytelegraph.net
website www.coventrytelegraph.net
Facebook www.facebook.com/livecoventry
Twitter @live_coventry
Editor Adam Moss
Daily Mon–Sat 90p

Topical, illustrated articles with a Coventry or Warwickshire interest. Length: up to 600 words. Payment: by arrangement. Founded 1891.

Express & Star
51–53 Queen Street, Wolverhampton WV1 1ES
tel (01902) 313131
email newsdesk@expressandstar.co.uk
website www.expressandstar.com
Facebook www.facebook.com/expressandstar
Twitter @expressandstar

Editor-in-Chief Martin Wright
Daily Mon–Fri 75p, Sat 90p

Founded 1874.

Sentinel

Staffordshire Sentinel News & Media Ltd,
Sentinel House, Bethesda Street, Hanley,
Stoke-on-Trent ST1 3GN
tel (01782) 864100
email newsdesk@thesentinel.co.uk
website www.stokesentinel.co.uk
Facebook www.facebook.com/stokeontrentlive
Twitter @SotLive
Editor Marc Waddington
Daily Mon–Sat 85p

Articles and features of topical interest to the north
Staffordshire and south Cheshire area. Illustrations:
colour and b&w. Payment: by arrangement.
Founded 1873.

Shropshire Star

Waterloo Road, Ketley, Telford TF1 5HU
tel (01952) 242424
website www.shropshirestar.com
Facebook www.facebook.com/ShropshireStar
Twitter @ShropshireStar
Editor Martin Wright
Daily Mon–Fri 75p, Sat 90p

News and features. No unsolicited material; write to
Features Editor with outline of ideas. Payment: by
arrangement. Founded 1964.

The Shuttle

Second Floor, Copthall House, 1 New Road,
Stourbridge DY8 1PH
tel (01384) 358050
website www.kidderminstershuttle.co.uk
Facebook www.facebook.com/kidderminstershuttle
Twitter @ksshuttle
Editor Stephanie Preece
Thurs weekly

Formerly the *Kidderminster Shuttle*, the *Shuttle* is a
free weekly newspaper available in the Wyre Forest
area in Worcestershire. Founded 1870.

Sunday Mercury

60 Church Street, Birmingham B3 2DJ
tel 0121 234 5000
website www.birminghamlive.co.uk
Print Editor Paul Cole
Sun £1.70

News specials or features of Midland interest.
Illustrations: colour, b&w. Payment: special rates for
special matter. Founded 1918.

Worcester News

Berrows House, Hylton Road, Worcester WR2 5JX
tel (01905) 742397
website www.worcesternews.co.uk
Facebook www.facebook.com/theworcesternews

Twitter @worcesternews
Editor Michael Purton
Daily Mon–Sat 70p

Local and national news, sport and features. Will
consider unsolicited material. Welcomes ideas for
articles and features. Length: 800 words (features),
300 words (news). Illustrations: colour jpg files.
Payment: by negotiation.

YORKSHIRE/HUMBERSIDE

Grimsby Telegraph

First Floor, Heritage House, Fisherman's Wharf,
Grimsby DN31 1SY
tel (01472) 808444
email newsdesk@grimsbytelegraph.co.uk
website www.thisisgrimsby.co.uk
Facebook www.facebook.com/grimsbylive
Twitter @GrimsbyLive
Editor Neil Hodgkinson
Daily Mon–Sat 55p

Considers general interest articles. Illustrations: line,
half-tone, colour, cartoons. Payment: by
arrangement. Founded 1897.

Halifax Courier

The Fire Station, Dean Clough Mills,
Halifax HX3 5AX
tel (01422) 260208
email editor@halifaxcourier.co.uk
website www.halifaxcourier.co.uk
Facebook www.facebook.com/HalifaxCourier
Twitter @HXCourier
Editor John Kenealy
Weekly Fri £1.55

Huddersfield Daily Examiner

Pennine Business Park, Longbow Close,
Bradley Road, Huddersfield HD2 1GQ
tel (01484) 430000
email editorial@examiner.co.uk
website www.examiner.co.uk
Twitter @YorkshireLive
Editor Wayne Ankers
Daily Examiner 80p, *Weekend Examiner* 90p

No contributions required at present. Founded 1851.

Hull Daily Mail

Blundell's Corner, Beverley Road, Hull HU3 1XS
tel (01482) 315016
email news@hulldailymail.co.uk
website www.hulldailymail.co.uk
Facebook www.facebook.com/hulllive
Twitter @hulllive
Editor Neil Hodgkinson
Daily Mon–Sat 65p

Lincolnshire Echo

Lincolnshire Live, Suite 4, The Regatta, Henley Way,
Doddington Road, Lincoln LN6 3QR

tel (01522) 804300
website www.lincolnshirelive.co.uk
Facebook www.facebook.com/LincsLive
Twitter @LincsLive
Editor Adam Moss
Weekly Thurs £1.10

The Press

Newsquest York, PO Box 29, 84–86 Walmgate,
York YO1 9YN
tel (01904) 567131
email newsdesk@thepress.co.uk
website www.yorkpress.co.uk
Facebook www.facebook.com/thepressyork
Twitter @yorkpress
Editor Nigel Burton
Daily Mon–Sat 60p

Articles of North and East Yorkshire interest. Length:
500–1,000 words. Illustrations: line, half-tone.
Payment: by arrangement. Founded 1882.

Scarborough News

Newchase Court, Hopper Hill Road,
Scarborough YO11 3YS
tel (01723) 860161
email newsdesk@jpress.co.uk
website www.thescarboroughnews.co.uk
Facebook www.facebook.com/thescarboroughnews
Twitter @TheScarboroNews
Editor Jean MacQuarrie
Weekly £1.45

Scunthorpe Telegraph

4–5 Park Square, Scunthorpe DN15 6JH
tel (01724) 709067

email newsdesk@scunthorpetelegraph.co.uk
website www.scunthorpetelegraph.co.uk
Facebook www.facebook.com/scunthorpelive
Twitter @ScunthorpeLive
Editor Jamie Macaskill
Weekly Thurs £1.20

Local news and features. Founded 1937.

Telegraph & Argus

Hall Ings, Bradford BD1 1JR
tel (01274) 729511
email newsdesk@telegraphandargus.co.uk
website www.thetelegraphandargus.co.uk
Facebook www.facebook.com/tclegraphandargus
Twitter @Bradford_TandA
Editor Nigel Barton
Daily Mon–Sat 65p

Daily paper: news, articles and features relevant to or
about the people of West Yorkshire. Length: up to
1,000 words. Illustrations: line, half-tone, colour.
Payment by negotiation. Founded 1868.

Yorkshire Post

No1 Leeds, 26 Whitehall Road, Leeds LS12 1BE
tel 0113 243 2701
website www.yorkshirepost.co.uk
Facebook www.facebook.com/
yorkshirepost.newspaper
Twitter @yorkshirepost
Editor James Mitchinson
Daily Mon–Fri £1.25, Sat £2.50
Supplements **Yorkshire Post Magazine**

Authoritative and well-written articles on topical
subjects of general, literary or industrial interests.
Founded 1754.

Magazines UK and Ireland

Listings for regional newspapers start on page 24 and listings for national newspapers start on page 15. For quick reference, magazines are listed by subject area starting on page 742. If you do have a piece placed with a magazine or journal, read any contract or licence document carefully: retaining copyright over your own writing is important and you should understand what you are agreeing to. Contact the Society of Authors (www.societyofauthors.org) for further information.

Accountancy Age
Contentive, 1 Hammersmith Broadway,
London W6 9DL
tel 020-8080 9513
website www.accountancyage.com
Twitter @AccountancyAge
Editor Michael McCaw
Online

Articles of accounting, financial and business interest. Freelance assignments commissioned. Payment: by arrangement. Founded 1969.

Accountancy Daily
Croner-i, 240 Blackfriars Road, London SE1 8BU
tel 020-3965 2410
email accountancynews@croneri.co.uk
website https://www.accountancydaily.co/
Editor Sara White
Monthly £99 p.a. (premium)

Articles on accounting, taxation, audit, financial, tax law and regulatory compliance targeted at accountants, tax advisers and finance professionals in practice or industry. All feature ideas to be submitted by email in the form of a brief, bullet-pointed synopsis. Founded 1889.

Accounting & Business
Association of Chartered Certified Accountants,
The Adelphi, 1–11 John Adam Street,
London WC2N 6AU
tel 020-7059 5000
email info@accaglobal.com
website https://abmagazine.accaglobal.com/uk/en.html
Editor-in-Chief Jo Malvern
Online only, accessible to all

Journal of the Association of Chartered Certified Accountants. Features accountancy, finance and business topics of relevance to accountants and finance directors. Illustrated. Founded 1998.

Acumen Literary Journal
6 The Mount, Higher Furzeham, Brixham,
South Devon TQ5 8QY
tel (01803) 851098
email patriciaoxley6@gmail.com
website www.acumen-poetry.co.uk
Editor Patricia Oxley
3 p.a. £5.50 or £15.50 p.a.

Poetry, literary and critical articles, reviews, literary memoirs, etc. Send sae with submissions; online submissions also accepted (see website for guidelines). Please send books for review to Glyn Pursglove, 25 St Albans Road, Brynmill, Swansea SA2 0BP. Payment: small. Founded 1985.

Aeroplane Monthly
Key Publishing Group, Units 1–4,
Gwash Way Industrial Estate, Ryhall Road,
Stamford, Lincs. PE9 1XP
email ben.dunnell@keypublishing.com
website www.aeroplanemonthly.com
Editor Ben Dunnell
Monthly £5.49

Articles and photos relating to historical aviation and aircraft preservation. Length: up to 5,000 words. Illustrations: line, colour. Payment: £100 per 1,000 words, payable on publication; photos £25 or more depending on size. Founded 1973.

Aesthetica Magazine
21 New Street, York YO1 8RA
tel (01904) 629137
email info@aestheticamagazine.com
website www.aestheticamagazine.com
Twitter @AestheticaMag
Instagram @aestheticamag
Editor Cherie Federico
Bi-monthly £5.95

Worldwide destination for art and culture. In-depth features foreground today's most innovative practitioners, both established and emerging, across art, design, photography, architecture, music and film. Also hosts the annual Aesthetica Art Prize, Creative Writing Award and the Aesthetica Film Festival for international practitioners. Founded 2002.

Africa: St Patrick's Missions
St Patrick's Missionary Society, Kiltegan,
Co. Wicklow W91 Y022, Republic of Ireland
tel +353 (0)59 6473600
email africa@spms.ie
website www.spms.org
Facebook www.facebook.com/AfricaMagazineKiltegan
Editor Rev. Seán Deegan
9 p.a. €15 p.a.

Articles of missionary and topical religious interest. Length: up to 1,000 words. Illustrations: colour.

Africa Confidential
37 John's Mews, London WC1N 2NS
email andrew@africa-confidential.com
website www.africa-confidential.com
Twitter @Africa_Conf
Deputy Editor Andrew Weir
Fortnightly £907 p.a. (print and online), £779 p.a. (online only)

News and analysis of political and economic developments in Africa. Unsolicited contributions welcomed, but must be exclusive and not published elsewhere. Length: 1,200-word features, 500-word pointers. No illustrations. Payment: from £300 per 1,000 words. Founded 1960.

African Business
IC Publications Ltd, 7 Coldbath Square, London EC1R 4LQ
tel 020-7841 3210
email editorial@icpublications.com
website www.africanbusiness.com
Monthly £4 or from £22.99 p.a.

Articles on business, economic and financial topics of interest to businessmen, ministers and officials concerned with African affairs. Length: 1,000–1,400 words; shorter coverage 500 words. Illustrations: line, half-tone, cartoons. Payment: £90–£100 per 1,000 words; £1 per column cm for illustrations. Founded 1978.

Agenda
Harts Cottage, Stonehurst Lane, Five Ashes, Mayfield, East Sussex TN20 6LL
tel (01825) 831994
email editor@agendapoetry.co.uk
website www.agendapoetry.co.uk
Twitter @agendapoetry
Editor Patricia McCarthy
£28 p.a. (individuals), £22 p.a. (concessions), £35 p.a. libraries and institutions

Poetry and criticism. Study the journal and visit the website for submission details before submitting via email (submissions@agendapoetry.co.uk). Young poets and artists (from age 15 to mid/late 30s) are invited to submit work for the online publication *Broadsheet*. Detailed criticism of poems available to subscribers.

AIR International
Key Publishing Ltd, PO Box 100, Stamford, Lincs. PE9 1XQ
tel (01780) 755131
email airint@keypublishing.com
website www.airinternational.com
Monthly £5.30

Technical articles on aircraft; features on topical aviation subjects – civil and military. Length: up to 3,000 words. Illustrations: colour transparencies/prints, b&w prints/line drawings. Payment: £50 per 1,000 words or by negotiation; £20 colour, £10 b&w. Founded 1971.

Allegro Poetry
email allegropoetry@gmail.com
website www.allegropoetry.org
Editor Sally Long
2 p.a. Free

Online journal of contemporary poetry. Published twice a year, in March (general issue) and September (themed issue) respectively. See website for information on forthcoming submission windows and full details. Previously published work is not accepted. Payment: none.

Amateur Gardening
Future plc, Pinehurst 2, Pinehurst Road, Farnborough Business Park, Farnborough, Hants GU14 7BF
tel (01202) 555138
email amateurgardening@futurenet.com
website www.amateurgardening.com
Group Editor Garry Coward-Williams
Weekly £1.99

No longer accepts any form of unsolicited material. Founded 1884.

Amateur Photographer
(incorporating Photo Technique)
Kelsey Publishing Ltd, The Granary, Downs Court, Yalding Hill, Yalding, Maidstone, Kent ME18 6AL
email ap.ed@kelsey.co.uk
website www.amateurphotographer.co.uk
Facebook www.facebook.com/amateur.photographer.magazine
Twitter @AP_Magazine
Group Editor Nigel Atherton
Weekly £3.49

Unsolicited editorial submissions are not encouraged. Founded 1884.

Ambit
Staithe House, Main Road, Brancaster Staithe, Norfolk PE31 8BP (correspondence)
tel 07715 233221
email contact@ambitmagazine.co.uk
website www.ambitmagazine.co.uk
Twitter @ambitmagazine
Editor Briony Bax, Kirsty Allison (from 1 August 2021)
Quarterly £29.99 p.a. (UK)

Literary magazine. Publishes poetry, fiction, flash fiction and art in a full-colour quarterly magazine. Accepts submissions via online portal (see website for details). Contributors may send up to five poems in one document or a story of up to 5,000 words; flash fiction no more than 1,000 words. Payment: see website. Founded 1959 by Dr Martin Bax.

Angling Times

Bauer Media Group, Media House, Lynch Wood, Peterborough Business Park, Peterborough PE2 6EA
tel (01733) 395097
email steve.fitzpatrick@bauermedia.co.uk
website www.gofishing.co.uk/Angling-Times
Twitter @AnglingTimesEd
Editor-in-Chief Steve Fitzpatrick
Weekly £2.40

Articles, pictures, news stories, on all forms of angling. Illustrations: line, half-tone, colour. Payment: by arrangement. Founded 1953.

Apollo

22 Old Queen Street, London SW1H 9HP
tel 020-7961 0150
email editorial@apollomag.com
website www.apollo-magazine.com
Editor Thomas Marks
Monthly £7.95

Scholarly and topical articles of c. 2,000–3,000 words on art, architecture, ceramics, photography, furniture, armour, glass, sculpture and any subject connected with art, museums and collecting. Interviews with collectors, leading international artists and cultural leaders. Exhibition and book reviews, articles on current developments in the culture sector, regular columns on the art market. Illustrations: colour. Payment: by arrangement. Founded 1925.

The Architects' Journal

EMAP, Telephone House, 69–77 Paul Street, London EC2A 4NW
tel 020-3953 2600
website www.architectsjournal.co.uk
Twitter @ArchitectsJrnal
Editor Emily Booth
Monthly £15

Articles (mainly technical) on architecture, planning and building, accepted only with prior agreement of synopsis. Illustrations: photos and drawings. Payment: by arrangement. Founded 1895.

Architectural Design

John Wiley & Sons, 25 John Street, London WC1N 2BS
tel 020-8326 3800
website https://onlinelibrary.wiley.com/journal/15542769
Editor Neil Spiller
6 issues p.a. £146 p.a. (print, individual; other rates available)

International architectural publication comprising an extensively illustrated thematic profile and magazine back section, *AD Plus*. Uncommissioned articles not

accepted. Each issue has a guest editor. Payment: by arrangement. Founded 1930.

The Architectural Review

EMAP, Telephone House, 69–77 Paul Street, London EC2A 4NW
tel 020-3033 2741
email editorial@architectural-review.com
website www.architectural-review.com
Editor Manon Mollard
Monthly £17.50

Articles on architecture and the allied arts (urbanism, design, theory, history, technology). Writers must be thoroughly qualified. Length: up to 3,000 words. Illustrations: photos, drawings, etc. Payment: by arrangement. Founded 1896.

Architecture Today

34 Pentonville Road, London N1 9HF
tel 020-7837 0143
email editorial@architecturetoday.co.uk
website www.architecturetoday.co.uk
Twitter @Arch_Today
Editor Isabel Allen
10 p.a. Circulated free of charge to architects; subscription options available

Mostly commissioned articles and features on today's European architecture. Length: 200–800 words. Illustrations: colour. Payment: by negotiation. Founded 1989.

Art + Framing Today

Unit 2, Wye House, 6 Enterprise Way, London SW18 1FZ
tel 020-7381 6616
email info@fineart.co.uk
website www.fineart.co.uk/art_and_framing_today.aspx
Editor Lynn Jones
5 p.a. £8

Distributed to the fine art and framing industry. Covers essential information on new products and technology, artist and gallery news, market trends and business analysis. Length: 800–1,600 words. Illustrations: colour photos, cartoons. Payment: by arrangement. Founded 1905.

Art Monthly

12 Carlton House Terrace, London SW1Y 5AH
tel 020-7240 0389
email info@artmonthly.co.uk
website www.artmonthly.co.uk
Twitter @ArtMonthly
Editor Patricia Bickers
10 p.a. £7.50 (inc. p&p)

Features on modern and contemporary visual artists and art history, art theory and art-related issues; exhibition and book reviews. All material commissioned. Length: 750–1,500 words.

Illustrations: b&w photos. Payment: features £100–£200; none for photos. Founded 1976.

The Art Newspaper
17 Hanover Square, London W1S 1BN
tel 020-3586 8054
email info@theartnewspaper.com
website www.theartnewspaper.com
Editor Alison Cole
11 p.a. From £94 p.a. (print and digital subscription)

International coverage of visual art, news, politics, law, exhibitions with some feature pages. Length: 200–1,000 words. Illustrations: colour and b&w photos. Payment: £350+ per 1,000 words. Founded 1990.

Art Quarterly
Art Fund, 2 Granary Square, London N1C 4BH
tel 020-7225 4800
email artquarterly@artfund.org
website www.artfund.org
Editor Helen Sumpter
Quarterly Free to Art Fund members with National Art Pass

Magazine of Art Fund, the national charity for art, which supports museums and galleries across the UK. Features information about what's on in UK galleries and museums. Also includes in-depth features, interviews and conversations about art and artists, exhibition previews and reviews, opinion by writers, critics, commentators and experts in the field, and updates on the impact of Art Fund's charitable programme.

ArtReview and ArtReview Asia
1 Honduras Street, London EC1Y 0TH
tel 020-7490 8138
email office@artreview.com
website www.artreview.com
Facebook www.facebook.com/ArtReview.Magazine
Twitter @ArtReview_
Editor Mark Rappolt
ArtReview 9 p.a. £35 p.a. (print and online);
ArtReviewAsia 4 p.a. £24 p.a. (print and online)

Contemporary art features and reviews. Proposals welcome. Illustrations: colour. Payment: £350 per 1,000 words. Founded 1949.

ARTEMISpoetry
3 Springfield Close, East Preston,
West Sussex BN16 2SZ
email admin@secondlightlive.co.uk
website www.secondlightlive.co.uk/artemis.shtml
Contact Dilys Wood
2 p.a. £6, £12 p.a. or free to members of Second Light Network

Bi-annual journal of women's poetry and writing about poetry. Published in May and November each year by the Second Light, membership of which is open to female poets over the age of 40 (associate membership if under 40). Submissions should be hitherto unpublished work by women authors. See website for full details and specific information on forthcoming issues.

The Artist
The Artists' Publishing Co. Ltd, Caxton House, 63–65 High Street, Tenterden, Kent TN30 6BD
tel (01580) 763673
email info@tapc.co.uk
website www.painters-online.co.uk
Editor Sally Bulgin
13 p.a. (issues published every four weeks) £4.80

Practical, instructional articles on painting for all amateur and professional artists. Illustrations: line, half-tone, colour. Payment: by arrangement. Founded 1931.

Artists & Illustrators
Jubilee House, 2 Jubilee Place, London SW3 3TQ
tel 020-7349 3700
email info@artistsandillustrators.co.uk
website www.artistsandillustrators.co.uk
Twitter @AandImagazine
Editor Steve Pill
13 p.a £4.75

Practical and inspirational articles for amateur and semi-professional artists. Length: 500–1,500 words. Illustrations: hi-res digital images, hand-drawn illustrations. Payment: variable. Founded 1986.

Ash Tales
email ryan@ashtales.com
website www.ashtales.com/submit
Twitter @Ash_Tales
Editor Ryan Law
Monthly Free

Independent online literary journal focusing on short stories (up to 2,000 words) and flash fiction in the apocalyptic, post-apocalyptic and dystopian sub-genres. Welcomes submissions from new and established authors. Online submissions only (see website for guidelines). Payment: none, but work will be promoted via monthly digital magazine, social media channels and the Ash Tales podcast.

Astronomy Now
Pole Star Publications, PO Box 175, Tonbridge, Kent TN10 4ZY
tel (01732) 446110
email editorial2021@astronomynow.com
website https://astronomynow.com/
Facebook www.facebook.com/astronomynow
Twitter @astronomynow
Editor Keith Cooper
Monthly £5.50

Specialises in translating exciting astronomy research into articles for the lay reader. Also covers amateur astronomy with equipment reviews and observing notes. Please submit article pitches to the editorial email address. Length: 800–2,000 words. Payment: 15p per word; from £10 per photo. Founded 1987.

Asylum

c/o PCCS Books, Wyastone Business Park, Wyastone Leys, Monmouth NP25 3SR
tel (01600) 891509
email editors@asylummagazine.org
website https://asylummagazine.org/
Twitter @AsylumMagUK
Editor Volunteer editorial group
Quarterly From £12 p.a.

A forum for debate about critical, radical and alternative perspectives on mental health, psychiatry and related professions. Especially welcomes contributions from service users, ex-users or survivors, carers, activists and frontline psychiatric or mental health workers. Founded 1986.

Athletics Weekly

21six Sport Ltd, The Barn, Calcot Mount, Calcot Lane, Curdridge, Hants SO32 2BN
email jason.henderson@athleticsweekly.com
website www.athleticsweekly.com
Facebook www.facebook.com/athleticsweekly
Twitter @athleticsweekly
Instagram @athletics.weekly
Editor Jason Henderson
Monthly £5.95

News and features on track and field athletics, road running, cross country, fell running and race walking. Material mostly commissioned. Length: 300–1,500 words. Illustrations: colour and b&w action and head/shoulder photos, line. Payment: varies. Founded 1945.

Attitude

Stream Publishing Limited, The Cowshed, Ladycross Farm, Hollow Lane, Dormansland, Surrey RH7 6PB
email attitude@attitude.co.uk
website www.attitude.co.uk
Twitter @AttitudeMag
Editor-in-Chief Cliff Joannou
13 p.a. £5.25

Men's style magazine aimed primarily, but not exclusively, at gay men. Covers style/fashion, interviews, reviews, celebrities, humour. Illustrations: colour transparencies, b&w prints. Payment: £150 per 1,000 words; £100 per full-page illustration. Founded 1994.

The Author

24 Bedford Row, London WC1R 4EH
tel 020-7373 6642
email theauthor@societyofauthors.org
website www.societyofauthors.org/author
Editor James McConnachie

Quarterly £17 or free to members of the Society of Authors

Commissioned articles from 800–1,500 words on any subject related to the craft, legal, commercial or technical side of authorship. Little scope for the freelance writer: preliminary letter advisable. Artwork and illustrations accepted (full colour, CMYK). Payment: by arrangement. Founded 1890.

Auto Express

Dennis Publishing Ltd, 31–32 Alfred Place, London WC1E 7DP
tel 020-3890 3890
email editorial@autoexpress.co.uk
website www.autoexpress.co.uk
Twitter @AutoExpress
Editor-in-Chief Steve Fowler
Weekly £3.50

News stories and general interest features about drivers as well as cars. Illustrations: colour photos. Payment: varies. Founded 1988.

Aviation News

Key Publishing Group, Units 1–4, Gwash Way Industrial Estate, Ryhall Road, Stamford, Lincs. PE9 1XP
tel (01780) 755131
email dino.carrara@keypublishing.com
website www.aviation-news.co.uk
Twitter @AvNewsMag
Editor Dino Carrara
Monthly £4.49

Covers all aspects of aviation. Many articles commissioned. Payment: by arrangement.

BackTrack

Pendragon Publishing, PO Box 3, Easingwold, York YO61 3YS
tel (01347) 824397
email pendragonpublishing@btinternet.com
website www.pendragonpublishing.co.uk
Editor Michael Blakemore
Monthly £4.85

British railway history from 1820s to 1980s. Welcomes ideas from writers and photographers. Articles must be well researched, authoritative and accompanied by illustrations. Length: 3,000–5,000 words (main features), 500–3,000 words (articles). Illustrations: colour and b&w. Payment: £30 per 1,000 words, £18.50 colour, £10 b&w. Founded 1986.

Bandit Fiction

email banditfiction@gmail.com
website https://banditfiction.co.uk
Facebook www.facebook.com/banditfiction/
Twitter @BanditFiction
Instagram @BanditFiction
Editor-in-Chief Alisdair Hodgson

Online literary journal. Actively looking for: flash fiction (250 to 1,000 words); short stories (1,000 to 3,5000 words); narrative non-fiction (1,000 to 3,500 words); and poems (50 lines or less). Submissions accepted all year around via website.

Banipal

1 Gough Square, London EC4A 3DE
tel 07979 540594
email editor@banipal.co.uk
website www.banipal.co.uk
Editor-in-Chief Samuel Shimon, *Publisher* Margaret Obank
3 p.a. £11 per issue; digital and print subscription options available

Showcases contemporary Arab authors in English translation. Welcomes inquiries from authors and translators; see website for full submission guidelines. Features prose and poetry. Complete archive now available online for digital subscribers.

The Banker

FT Specialist, Bracken House, 1 Friday Street, London EC4M 9BT
tel 020-7873 3000
email joy.macknight@ft.com
website www.thebanker.com
Editor Joy McKnight
Monthly From £95 per month

Global coverage of retail banking, corporate banking, banking technology, transactions services, investment banking and capital markets, regulation and top 1,000 bank rankings.

Baptist Times

129 Broadway, Didcot, Oxon OX11 8RT
tel (01235) 517677
email editor@baptisttimes.co.uk
website www.baptisttimes.co.uk
Twitter @baptisttimes
Editor Paul Hobson
Website only.

Religious or social affairs, news, features and reviews. Founded 1855.

BBC Countryfile Magazine

Immediate Media Co. Ltd, Eagle House, Colston Avenue, Bristol BS1 1EN
tel 0117 927 9009
email editor@countryfile.com
website www.countryfile.com
Twitter @BBCCountryfile
Editor Fergus Collins
Monthly £4.75

Articles and features on making the most of the UK's countryside, and the lives of its rural communities.

BBC Gardeners' World Magazine

Immediate Media Co. Ltd, Vineyard House, 44 Brook Green, London W6 7BT
tel 020-7150 5770
email magazine@gardenersworld.com
website www.gardenersworld.com
Twitter @GWmag
Editor Lucy Hall, *Deputy Editor* Kevin Smith, *Features Editor* Catherine Mansley
Monthly £5.25

Advice, support and features for gardeners of all levels of expertise. Fully illustrated. Does not accept speculative features.

BBC Good Food

Immediate Media Co. Ltd, Vineyard House, 44 Brook Green, London W6 7BT
email enquiries@bbcgoodfoodmagazine.com
website www.bbcgoodfood.com
Twitter @bbcgoodfood
Editor-in-Chief Christine Hayes
Monthly £5.25

Inspiration for everyday, weekend and seasonal cooking for cooks of all levels. Features recipes from many BBC TV chefs as well as other leading food writers, along with an extensive range of hints, tips and features.

BBC History Magazine

Immediate Media Co. Ltd, Eagle House, Colston Avenue, Bristol BS1 1EN
email historymagazine@historyextra.com
website www.historyextra.com
Facebook www.facebook.com/historyextra
Twitter @historyextra
Editor Rob Attar
Monthly £5.50

Popular history writing on a wide range of topics, from Ancient Egypt to the Second World War. Contents include feature spreads, book reviews, opinion and news. Contributors include Mary Beard, Tracy Borman, Dan Snow and Michael Wood. Illustrated. Founded 2000.

BBC Music Magazine

Immediate Media Co. Ltd, Eagle House, Colston Avenue, Bristol BS1 1EN
email music@classical-music.com
website www.classical-music.com
Twitter @MusicMagazine
Editor Oliver Condy
Monthly £5.99

Reviews and articles on all aspects of classical music. Also interviews with leading practitioners, information on technical equipment and forthcoming tours. Free CD with every issue.

BBC Science Focus

Immediate Media Co. Ltd, Eagle House, Colston Avenue, Bristol BS1 1EN

tel 0117 314 8779
email daniel.bennett@immediate.co.uk
website www.sciencefocus.com
Twitter @sciencefocus
Editor Daniel Bennett
Monthly £5.20

Science and technology magazine featuring articles
from popular scientists and leading academics, as well
as news. Submissions accepted for articles only from
experienced and previously published science writers:
send 2–8pp overview along with feature pitch form
provided on the website to
jason.goodyer@immediate.co.uk. Photography and
illustration submissions also accepted: see website for
full specifications.

BBC Sky at Night Magazine
Immediate Media Co. Bristol Ltd, Eagle House,
Colston Avenue, Bristol BS1 1ST
email contactus@skyatnightmagazine.com
website www.skyatnightmagazine.com
Twitter @skyatnightmag
Editor Chris Bramley
Monthly £5.99

Aimed at both experienced amateur astronomers and
those new to the subject. The magazine's main focus
is on practical astronomy, both visual and
photographic: the best sights to observe and image in
the night sky each month; the telescopes, cameras
and accessories to do that with; and how to put these
to best use. Also covers news in all branches of space
science, in particular cosmology and exoplanets; dark
skies travel, both in the UK and internationally; and
the history of astronomy. Founded 2005.

BBC Top Gear
Immediate Media Co. Ltd, Vineyard House,
44 Brook Green, London W6 7BT
tel 020-7150 5559
email charlie.turner@bbctopgearmagazine.co.uk
website www.topgear.com
Twitter @BBC_TopGear
Editor-in-Chief Charlie Turner
13 p.a. £4.90

Articles and photographic features on motoring,
lifestyle and cars.

BBC Wildlife Magazine
Immediate Media Co. Ltd, Eagle House,
Colston Avenue, Bristol BS1 1EN
email wildlifemagazine@immediate.co.uk
website www.discoverwildlife.com
Twitter @WildlifeMag
Editor Paul McGuinness
Monthly £4.50

Consumer natural history magazine. Expert-written
articles and features, along with award-winning
photography.

Bella
H. Bauer Publishing, Academic House,
24–28 Oval Road, London NW1 7DT
tel 020-7241 8000
website www.bellamagazine.co.uk
Editor-in-Chief Julia Davis
Weekly £1.20

Women's magazine with celebrity interviews,
exclusive photos, real-life stories, high-street fashion,
diet advice, health, food and travel. Payment: by
arrangement. Founded 1987.

Best
Hearst UK, House of Hearst, 30 Panton Street,
London SW1Y 4AJ
tel 020-7339 4500
email siobhan.wykes@hearst.co.uk
Twitter @BestMagOfficial
Executive Editor Siobhan Wykes
Weekly £1.99

Unsolicited work not accepted, but always willing to
look at ideas/outlines. Payment: by agreement.
Founded 1987.

BFS Horizons
The British Fantasy Society, The Apex,
2 Sheriffs Orchard, Coventry CP1 3PP
email bfshorizons@britishfantasysociety.org
email poetry@britishfantasysociety.org
website www.britishfantasysociety.org
Fiction Editors Shona Kinsella, Tim Major, *Poetry
Editor* Ian Hunter

Official publication of the British Fantasy Society,
focusing on fiction and poetry across a broad fantasy
genre, including weird fiction, horror and science
fiction. Length: stories of up to 5,000 words (ideally);
poems of no more than 36 lines. See website for full
guidelines and house style guide. Payment: none.

BFS Journal
The British Fantasy Society, The Apex,
2 Sheriffs Orchard, Coventry CV1 3PP
email bfsjournal@britishfantasysociety.org
website www.britishfantasysociety.org/bfs-journal/
Editor Sean Wilcock

Official publication of the British Fantasy Society,
focusing on features, non-fiction and academic
articles, including interviews, opinion pieces and
biographies. Contact editor with outline first. Length:
preferably 2,500-6,000 words. Payment: none. Letters
to the Editor also welcomed.

The Big Issue
43 Bath Street, Glasgow G2 1HW (editorial office)
tel 0141 352 7260
email editorial@thebigissue.com
website www.bigissue.com
Editor Paul McNamee
Weekly £3

Features, current affairs, reviews, interviews – of general interest and on social issues. Length: 1,000 words (features). No short stories or poetry. Illustrations: colour and b&w photos and line. Payment: £160 per 1,000 words. Founded 1991.

Bike

Bauer Media Group, Media House, Lynch Wood, Peterborough Business Park, Peterborough PE2 6EA
tel (01733) 468181
email bike@bauermedia.com
website www.bikemagazine.co.uk
Editor Hugo Wilson
Monthly £4.50

Motorcycle magazine. Interested in articles, features, news. Length: articles/features 1,000–3,000 words. Illustrations: colour and b&w photos. Payment: £140 per 1,000 words; photos per size/position. Founded 1971.

Bird Watching

Bauer Media Group, Media House, Lynch Wood, Peterborough Business Park, Peterborough PE2 6EA
tel (01733) 468201
email birdwatching@bauermedia.co.uk
website www.birdwatching.co.uk
Twitter @BirdWatchingMag
Editor Matthew Merritt
13 p.a. £4.50

Broad range of bird-related features and photography, particularly looking at bird behaviour, bird news, reviews and UK birdwatching sites. Limited amount of overseas features. Emphasis on providing accurate information in entertaining ways. Send synopsis first. Length: up to 1,200 words. Illustrations: emailed jpgs and photo images on CD, bird identification artwork. Payment: by negotiation. Founded 1986.

Birdwatch

Warners Group Publications Plc, Studio 2, 3rd Floor, 40 Cumberland Road, London N22 7SG
tel 020-8881 0550
email editorial@birdwatch.co.uk
website www.birdguides.com
Editor Rebecca Armstrong
Monthly £4.99

Topical articles on all aspects of British and Irish birds and birding, including conservation, identification, sites and habitats and equipment, as well as overseas destinations. Length: 700–1,500 words. Illustrations: hi-res jpgs (300 dpi at 1,500 pixels min. width) of wild British and European birds considered; submit on CD/DVD or full size via email or file-sharing site. Artwork: by negotiation. Payment: by negotiation. Founded 1991.

Black Beauty & Hair

Hawker Publications, Lombard Business Park, 12 Deer Park Road, Wimbledon, London SW19 3TL
tel 020-3746 2626
email info@blackbeautyandhair.com
website www.blackbeautyandhair.com
Twitter @BlackBeautyMag
Instagram @blackbeautymag
Editor-in-Chief Irene Shelley
Bi-monthly £3.75

Beauty and style articles relating specifically to women of colour; celebrity features. True-life stories and salon features. Length: approx. 1,000 words. Illustrations: colour and b&w photos. Payment: by arrangement. Founded 1982.

Black Static

TTA Press, 5 Martins Lane, Witcham, Ely, Cambs. CB6 2LB
website www.ttapress.com
Twitter @TTApress
Editor Andy Cox
Bi-monthly £7 or £12 double issue

New horror and dark fantasy stories. Also features interviews with, and profiles of, authors and filmmakers. Send sae with all submissions. Considers unsolicited material and welcomes ideas for articles and features. Length: 3,000–4,000 words (articles and features), short stories unrestricted. Illustrations: send samples and portfolios. Payment: by arrangement. Founded 1994.

Blithe Spirit

email ed.blithespirit@gmail.com
website www.britishhaikusociety.org.uk
Editor Caroline Skanne
Quarterly Free to members

80pp journal of the British Haiku Society. Includes original poems (from Society members only), articles and reviews. Four submission windows (see website for up-to-date details); poems must not have appeared, or be under consideration, elsewhere.

Boat International

41–47 Hartfield Road, London SW19 3RQ
tel 020-8545 9330
email stewart.campbell@boatinternationalmedia.com
website www.boatinternational.com
Twitter @boatint
Editor Stewart Campbell
12 p.a. £7

News and features on superyachts and the lifestyles of those who own them. Also yacht listings in a brokerage section and reviews.

The Book Collector

(incorporating Bibliographical Notes and Queries)
PO Box 1163, St Albans AL1 9WS

email editor@thebookcollector.co.uk
website www.thebookcollector.co.uk
Editor James Fleming
Online £60 p.a. (UK), €70 (Europe), US$80 (RoW)

Articles, biographical and bibliographical, on the collection and study of printed books and MSS. Payment: for reviews only. Founded 1952.

Books Ireland

Unit 9, 78 Furze Road, Dublin D18 C6V6, Republic of Ireland
tel +353 (0)1 2933568
email ruth@wordwell.ie
website www.booksirelandmagazine.com
Twitter @booksirelandmag
Online

Reviews of Irish-interest and Irish-author books, as well as articles of interest to librarians, booksellers and readers. Length: 800–1,400 words. Founded 1976 (print); fully digital as of 2019.

The Bookseller

Floor 10, Westminster Tower,
3 Albert Embankment, London SE1 7SP
tel 020-3358 0369
email katie.mansfield@thebookseller.com
website www.thebookseller.com
Twitter @thebookseller
Editor Philip Jones
Weekly £5.95

Long-established magazine of the UK book industry magazine, featuring news, analysis, bestseller charts, interviews, previews of forthcoming titles and jobs in the industry, as well as in-depth coverage of international book fairs including Frankfurt, Bologna and Beijing. While outside contributions are welcomed, most of the journal's contents are commissioned. Length: about 1,000–1,500 words. Payment: by arrangement. Founded 1858.

Bowls International

Oyster Media Group Ltd, 31 The Heights, Whitstable, Kent CT5 4PT
tel 07791 696718
email editor@bowlsinternational.com
website https://bowlsinternational.keypublishing.com
Facebook www.facebook.com/BowlsInternational
Twitter @BowlsInt
Editor Sian Honnor
Monthly £4.20

Sport and news items and features; occasional, bowls-oriented short stories. Illustrations: colour transparencies, b&w photos, occasional line, cartoons. Payment: by arrangement. Founded 1981.

Breathe

GMC Publications Ltd, 86 High Street, Lewes BN7 1XN
tel (01273) 477374

email hello@breathemagazine.com
website www.breathemagazine.com
Publisher Jonathan Grogan
9 p.a. £5.99

Mindfulness magazine aiming to help readers achieve a healthier life across five key areas: wellbeing, living, creativity, mindfulness and escape. Submissions welcomed from experienced or new writers, and from illustrators. See www.breathemagazine.com/submissions for specific requirements for each type of potential contributor.

British Birds

tel (01424) 755155
email editor@britishbirds.co.uk
website www.britishbirds.co.uk
Twitter @britishbirds
Editor Dr Roger Riddington
Monthly From £63 p.a. (print, UK)

Publishes major papers on identification, behaviour, conservation, distribution, ecology, movements, status and taxonomy with official reports on: rare breeding birds, scarce migrants and rare birds in Britain. Payment: token. Founded 1907.

British Chess Magazine

Albany House, Shute End, Wokingham, Berks. RG40 1BJ
email editor@britishchessmagazine.co.uk
website www.britishchessmagazine.co.uk
Monthly £5.50

Authoritative reports and commentary on the UK and overseas chess world. Payment: by arrangement. Founded 1881.

British Journal of Photography

Studio 8, Trampery on the Gantry, Broadcast Centre, Here East, 1 Waterden Rd, London E15 2HB
email editorial@bjphoto.co.uk
website www.1854.photography/journal/
Editor Izabela Radwanska Zhang
Monthly £9.99

Focus on all aspects of contemporary photography: articles on fine art, commercial, fashion, documentary and editorial, alongside trend reports and technical reviews. Founded 1854.

British Journalism Review

SAGE Publications, 1 Oliver's Yard, 55 City Road, London EC1Y 1SP
tel 020-7324 8500
email editor@bjr.org.uk
website www.bjr.org.uk
Twitter @TheBJReview
Editor Kim Fletcher
Quarterly £49 p.a. for individuals (print only; institutional rates also available)

Comment, criticism and review of matters published by, or of interest to, the media. Length: 1,500–3,000 words. Illustrations: b&w photos. Payment: by arrangement. Founded 1989.

British Medical Journal

BMJ Publishing Group, BMA House,
Tavistock Square, London WC1H 9JR
tel 020-7387 4410
email fgodlee@bmj.com
website www.bmj.com/thebmj
Editor-in-Chief Dr Fiona Godlee
Weekly Free to members of BMA; for subscription details see website

Medical and related articles. Payment: by arrangement. Founded 1840.

Brittle Star

Diversity House, 72 Nottingham Road, Arnold,
Nottingham NG5 6LF
email brittlestarmag@gmail.com
website www.brittlestar.org.uk
Twitter @brittlestarmag
Editors Jacqueline Gabbitas, Martin Parker
2 p.a. £15 p.a. (UK), £25 p.a. (RoW)

Not-for-profit literary magazine run by volunteers. Seeks high-quality contemporary literature for adults, including all forms of poetry as well as literary short fiction. Send submissions by post, having first read a copy of the magazine, along with a covering letter and an sae (see website for further details and up-to-date postal address). Submitted work should not be under consideration elsewhere.

Broadcast

Media Business Insight, Cally Yard, Unit 4D,
445 Caledonian Road, London N7 9BG
tel 020-8102 0900
email chris.curtis@broadcastnow.co.uk
website www.broadcastnow.co.uk
Editor Chris Curtis
Weekly From £322 p.a. + VAT

For people working or interested in the UK and international broadcast industry. News, features, analysis and opinions across a variety of platforms. Covers the latest developments in programming, commissioning, digital, technology and post-production.

Building

Assemble Media Group, 81 Rivington Street,
London EC2A 3AY
email chloe.mcculloch@building.co.uk
website www.building.co.uk
Editor Chloë McCulloch
49 p.a. From £160 p.a. (digital only; premium subscriptions, including print, are also available)

Covers all aspects of the construction industry and built environment, from architecture to property development. Sectors include housing, commercial property, education and health buildings, and

infrastructure. Will consider articles on the built environment in the UK and abroad; including news, comment, analysis and photos. Payment: by arrangement. Founded 1843.

Building Design

Assemble Media Group, 81 Rivington St,
London EC2A 3AY
email elizabeth.hopkirk@bdonline.co.uk
website www.bdonline.co.uk
Facebook www.facebook.com/BDmagazine
Twitter @BDonline
Editorial Director Chloë McCulloch
Annual subscriptions from £60 p.a.

Daily online newspaper and magazine. News and features on all aspects of architecture and urban design. Plus annual World Architecture WA100 printed magazine, the authoritative survey of world's biggest architects. Founded 1970.

The Burlington Magazine

14–16 Duke's Road, London WC1H 9SZ
tel 020-7388 8157
email editorial@burlington.org.uk
website www.burlington.org.uk
website https://contemporary.burlington.org.uk/journal
Editor Michael Hall
12 p.a. £28.50

Academic journal dealing with the history and criticism of art; book and exhibition reviews; publishes free-access online journal on contemporary art, 'Burlington Contemporary', with reviews of exhibitions and books. Submissions must offer new research; potential contributors must have specialist knowledge of the subjects treated. Length: 500–5,000 words. Illustrations: colour images. Payment: up to £150 (exhibition reviews in print magazine only). Founded 1903.

Buses

Key Publishing Ltd, Foundry Road, Stamford,
Lincs. PE9 2PP
tel (01780) 755131
Editor Alan Millar, PO Box 14644, Leven KY9 1WX
tel (01333) 340637
email alan.millar@keypublishing.com
website www.busesmag.com
Monthly £4.49

Articles of interest to both road passenger transport operators and bus enthusiasts. Preliminary enquiry essential. Illustrations: digital (first preference), colour transparencies, half-tone, line maps. Payment: on application. Founded 1949.

Business Traveller

41 Maddox Street, London W1S 2PD
tel 020-7821 2700

email editorial@businesstraveller.com
website www.businesstraveller.com
Editorial Director Tom Otley
10 p.a. £3.95

Articles, features and news on consumer travel aimed at individual frequent international business travellers. Submit ideas with recent clippings/links and a CV. Length: varies. Illustrations: colour for destinations features. Payment: on application. Founded 1976.

Butcher's Dog

1 Jackson Street, North Shields NE30 2JA
email editor@butchersdogmagazine.co.uk
website www.butchersdogmagazine.co.uk
Facebook www.facebook.com/butchersdogmagazine/
Twitter @ButchersDogMag
Instagram @butchersdogmag
Managing Editor Dr Jo Clement
2 p.a. £5.99

Bi-annual poetry magazine founded and published in North-East England. Aims to print outstanding poems by diverse writers with distinctive voices from across the UK and ROI, regardless of their career stage. Submissions accepted during open calls digitally via the homepage. Unpublished and original work only, although translations are welcome as long as the author's permission has been granted in advance. Payment: none, but contributors receive free copies. Tip-jar option. Founded 2012.

Campaign

Haymarket Ltd, Bridge House, 69 London Road, Twickenham TW1 3SP
tel 020-8267 8032
email maisie.mccabe@haymarket.com
website www.campaignlive.co.uk
UK Editor Maisie McCabe
Monthly From £33 per month

News and articles covering the whole of the mass communications field, particularly advertising in all its forms, marketing and the media. Features should not exceed 2,000 words. News items also welcome. Payment: by arrangement.

Candis

Newhall Publications Ltd, Newhall Lane, Hoylake, Wirral CH47 4BQ
tel 0151 632 3232
email helen@candis.co.uk
website www.candis.co.uk
Twitter @candismagazine
Editor Helen Etheridge
Monthly Subscription only

Commissions one 2,500-word short story each month by a well-known published author. Unsolicited material is no longer received and will be returned unread. Writers willing to share a personal life story or experience for real lives feature may send

a synopsis to the email address above. Also covers health, news, celebrity interviews, family issues, fashion and beauty.

Car

Bauer Media Group, Media House, Lynch Wood, Peterborough Business Park, Peterborough PE2 6EA
tel (01733) 468379
email car@bauermedia.co.uk
website www.carmagazine.co.uk
Editor-in-Chief Phil McNamara, *Editor* Ben Miller
Monthly £4.99

Top-grade journalistic features on car driving, car people and cars. Length: 1,000–2,500 words. Illustrations: b&w and colour photos to professional standards. Payment: minimum £350 per 1,000 words. Founded 1962.

Car Mechanics

Kelsey Publishing Ltd., The Granary, Downs Court, Yalding Hill, Yalding, Maidstone, Kent ME18 6AL
email cm.ed@kelsey.co.uk
website www.carmechanicsmag.co.uk
Facebook www.facebook.com/Car-Mechanics-123672554385156/
Twitter @CarMechanics
Monthly £4.70

Practical articles on maintaining, repairing and uprating modern cars for DIY plus the motor trade. Always interested in finding new talent for this rather specialised market, but study a recent copy before submitting ideas or features. Email outlining feature recommended. Illustrations: line drawings, colour prints, digital images. Supply package of text and pictures. Payment: by arrangement. Founded 1958.

Caravan Magazine

Warners Group Publications Plc, The Maltings, West Street, Bourne, Lincs. PE10 9PH
tel (01778) 391000
website www.caravanmagazine.co.uk
Monthly £4.99

Lively articles based on real experience of touring caravanning, especially if well illustrated by photos provided by the author or from regional Tourist Boards, attractions etc. Payment: by arrangement. Founded 1933.

The Caterer

Jacobs Media Group, 52 Grosvenor Gardens, London SW1W 0AU
tel 020-7881 4803
email info@caterer.com
website www.thecaterer.com
Editor James Stagg, *Assistant Editor (Acting)* Caroline Baldwin, *News Editor* Katherine Price
Weekly From £61.78 p.a. (digital; other subscription packages are available, and some content remains free)

Multimedia brand for the UK hospitality industry. In print and online, offers content, job news and a digital platform for hotel, restaurant, food service, and pub and bar operators across the country. Article length: up to 1,500 words. Illustrations: line, half-tone, colour. Payment: by arrangement. Founded 1878.

The Catholic Herald
Herald House, Lamb's Passage, Bunhill Row, London EC1Y 8TQ
tel 020-7448 3603
email features@catholicherald.co.uk
website www.catholicherald.co.uk
Facebook www.facebook.com/CatholicHeraldMagazine/
Twitter @CatholicHerald
Editor Christopher R. Altieri
Weekly From £43 p.a.

Independent magazine covering national and international affairs from a Catholic/Christian viewpoint as well as church news. Length: articles 800–1,200 words. Illustrations: photos of Catholic and Christian interest. Payment: by arrangement.

Catholic Pictorial
3 & 4 Pacific Chambers, 11–13 Victoria Street, Liverpool L2 5QQ
tel 0151 522 1007
email p.heneghan@rcaol.co.uk
website www.catholicpic.co.uk
Editor Peter Heneghan
Monthly Free

News and photo features (maximum 450 words plus illustration) on Merseyside, regional and national Catholic interest only. Payment: by arrangement. Founded 1961.

The Catholic Universe
Oakland House, 76 Talbot Road, Manchester M16 0PQ
tel 0161 820 5722
email pool@thecatholicuniverse.com
website www.thecatholicuniverse.com
Twitter @ukcatholicpress
Contact Joe Kelly
Weekly £99 p.a. (print), £55 p.a. (digital)

Catholic Sunday newspaper. News stories, features and photos on all aspects of Catholic life required; also cartoons. Send sae with MSS. Payment: by arrangement. Founded 1860.

Ceramic Review
63 Great Russell Street, London WC1B 3BF
tel 020-7183 5583
email editorial@ceramicreview.com
website www.ceramicreview.com/
Facebook www.facebook.com/ceramicreview
Twitter @ceramicreview

Instagram @ceramicreview
Editor Karen Bray, *Assistant Editor* Annie Le Santo
6 p.a. £9.90

International magazine containing critical features, reviews and practical information on all forms of ceramics and clay art and craft. It also looks at the role of ceramics within contemporary culture. Welcomes article proposals – critical, profile, technical, historical or experiential. Feature articles run from 800 to 1,500 words and must include large, hi-res images. Payment: offered at current rates on publication.

Chat
Future plc, 161 Marsh Wall, London E14 9AP
tel 020-3148 5000
email kate.williams@futurenet.com
website www.lifedeathprizes.com
Facebook www.facebook.com/ChatMagazine
Twitter @ChatMagazine
Weekly £1.10

Tabloid weekly for women. Includes readers' letters, tips and true-life features. Payment: by arrangement. Founded 1985.

Church of England Newspaper
Religious Intelligence Ltd, 14 Great College Street, London SW1P 3RX
tel 020-7878 1001
email cen@churchnewspaper.com
website www.churchnewspaper.com
Twitter @churchnewspaper
Weekly £75 p.a. (print and digital)

Anglican news and articles relating the Christian faith to everyday life. Evangelical basis; almost exclusively commissioned articles. Prior study of paper desirable. Length: up to 1,000 words. Illustrations: photos, line drawings, cartoons. Payment: c. £40 per 1,000 words; photos £22, line by arrangement. Founded 1828.

Church Times
3rd Floor, Invicta House, 108–114 Golden Lane, London EC1Y 0TG
tel 020-7776 1060
email editor@churchtimes.co.uk
website www.churchtimes.co.uk
Twitter @ChurchTimes
Editor Paul Handley
Weekly £2.95

Articles on religious topics are considered. No verse or fiction. Length: up to 1,000 words. Illustrations: news photos, sent promptly. Payment: £100 per 1,000 words. Negotiated rates for illustrations. Founded 1863.

Classic Boat Magazine
The Chelsea Magazine Company, Jubilee House, 2 Jubilee Place, London SW3 3TQ
tel 020-7349 3755

email cb@chelseamagazines.com
website www.classicboat.co.uk
Group Editor Rob Peake
Monthly £4.95

Cruising and technical features, restorations, events, new boat reviews, practical guides, maritime history and news. Study of magazine essential: read three to four back issues and send for contributors' guidelines. Length: 500–2,000 words. Illustrations: colour and b&w photos; line drawings of hulls. Payment: £75–£100 per published page. Founded 1987.

Classic Cars

H. Bauer Publishing, Media House, Lynch Wood, Peterborough Business Park, Peterborough PE2 6EA
tel (01733) 468000
email classic.cars@bauermedia.co.uk
website www.classiccarsmagazine.co.uk
Facebook www.facebook.com/classiccarsmagazine
Editor Phil Bell
Monthly From £4

Specialist articles on older cars and related events. Length: from 150–4,000 words (subject to prior contract). Photography: classic car event photography on spec; feature photography on commission basis. Payment: by negotiation. Founded 1973.

Classical Music

St Jude's Church, Dulwich Road, London SE24 0PB
tel 020-7338 5454
email editor@classical-music.uk
website www.classical-music.uk
Twitter @ClassicalMusic_
Editor Lucy Thraves
Monthly From £55 p.a.

News, opinion, features on the classical music business. All material commissioned. Illustrations: colour photos and line; colour covers. Payment: minimum £130 per 1,000 words. Founded 1976.

Climber

email info@climber.co.uk
website www.climber.co.uk
Twitter @climbermagazine
6 p.a. From £24 p.a. (print)

Articles on all aspects of rock climbing/mountaineering in Great Britain and abroad, and on related subjects. Study of magazine essential. Length: 1,500–2,000 words. Illustrations: colour transparencies. Payment: according to merit. Founded 1962.

Closer

Bauer Media, 24–28 Oval Road, London NW1 7DT
email closer@closermag.co.uk
website www.closeronline.co.uk
Editor Lisa Burrow
Weekly £1.90

Women's celebrity weekly magazine with real-life stories, lifestyle, fashion, beauty and TV entertainment and listings sections. Payment by negotiation.

Coin News

Token Publishing Ltd, 40 Southernhay East, Exeter, Devon EX1 1PE
tel (01404) 46972
email info@tokenpublishing.com
website www.tokenpublishing.com
Editor John W. Mussell
Monthly £4.20

Articles of high standard on coins, tokens, paper money. Send text in digital form. Length: up to 2,000 words. Payment: by arrangement. Founded 1983.

Commercial Motor

6th Floor, Chancery House, St Nicholas Way, Sutton, Surrey SM1 1JB
tel 020-8912 2163
email george.barrow@roadtransport.com
website www.commercialmotor.com
Twitter @Comm_Motor
Editor George Barrow
Weekly £3.30

Technical and road transport articles only. Length: up to 1,500 words. Illustrations: drawings and photos. Payment: varies. Founded 1905.

Community Care

St Jude's Church, Dulwich Road, Herne Hill, London SE24 0PB
tel 020-3915 9444
email communitycare@markallen.com
website www.communitycare.co.uk
Editor Mithran Samuel

Online magazine site with articles, features and news covering the Social Services sector.

Computer Weekly

25 Christopher Street, London EC2A 2BS
email cw-news@computerweekly.com
website www.computerweekly.com
Facebook www.facebook.com/computerweekly
Twitter @computerweekly
Editor Bryan Glick
Weekly Free to registered subscribers

Feature articles on IT-related topics for business/industry users. Length: 1,200 words. Illustrations: colour photos. Payment: £250 per 1,000 words. Founded 1966.

Computeractive

Dennis Publishing Ltd, 31–32 Alfred Place, London WC1E 7DP
website www.dennis.co.uk/brands/technology/computer-active/
Group Editor Daniel Booth

Fortnightly £2.40

Computing magazine offering plain-English advice for PCs, tablets, phones and the internet, as well as product reviews and technology news.

Condé Nast Traveller

The Condé Nast Publications Ltd, Vogue House, 1–2 Hanover Square, London W1S 1JU
Katharine.Sohn@condenast.co.uk
website www.cntraveller.com
Editor-in-Chief Melinda Stevens
Monthly £4.95

Lavishly photographed articles on all aspects of travel, featuring exotic destinations and those close to home. Specialist pieces include food and wine, motoring, health, foreign correspondents, travel news, hotels. Illustrations: colour. Payment: by arrangement. Founded 1997.

Cosmopolitan

Hearst UK, House of Hearst, 30 Panton Street, London SW1Y 4AJ
tel 020-7439 5000
website www.cosmopolitan.co.uk
Twitter @CosmopolitanUK
Editor-in-Chief Claire Hodgson
Monthly £2

Commissioned material only. Payment: by arrangement. Illustrated. Founded 1972.

Cotswold Life

Cumberland House, Oriel Road, Cheltenham, Glos. GL50 1BB
tel (01242) 216050
email candia.mckormack@archant.co.uk
website www.cotswoldlife.co.uk
Facebook www.facebook.com/cotswoldlife/
Twitter @cotswoldlife
Editor Candia McKormack
Monthly £4.50

Articles on the Cotswolds, including places of interest, high-profile personalities, local events, arts, history, interiors, fashion and food. Founded 1967.

Country Homes and Interiors

Future plc, 161 Marsh Wall, London E14 9AP
tel 020-3148 5000
email countryhomes@futuremedia.com
website www.housetohome.co.uk/
countryhomesandinteriors
Facebook www.facebook.com/
countryhomesandinteriors
Twitter @countryhomesmag
Editorial Director Rhoda Parry
Monthly £4.80

Articles on country homes and gardens, interiors, food, lifestyle. Payment: from £250 per 1,000 words. Founded 1986.

Country Life

Future plc, Pinehurst 2, Pinehurst Road, Farnborough Business Park, Farnborough, Hants GU14 7BF
tel (01252) 555062
website www.countrylife.co.uk
Twitter @Countrylifemag
Editor Mark Hedges, *Deputy Editor* Kate Green
Weekly £4.25

Illustrated journal chiefly concerned with British country life, social history, architecture and the fine arts, natural history, agriculture, gardening and sport. Length: about 1,000 or 1,300 words (articles). Illustrations: mainly colour photos. Payment: according to merit. Print editorial team can be contacted via the email address above. Founded 1897.

Country Living

Hearst UK, House of Hearst, 30 Panton Street, London SW1Y 4AJ
tel 020-7439 5000
email country.living@hearst.co.uk
website www.countryliving.co.uk
Twitter @countrylivinguk
Content Director Louise Pearce
Monthly £4.99

Up-market home-interest magazine with a country lifestyle theme, covering interiors, gardens, crafts, food, wildlife, rural and green issues. Unsolicited material not accepted. Illustrations: line, half-tone, colour. Payment: by arrangement. Founded 1985.

Country Smallholding

Archant SW, Unit 3, Old Station Road, Barnstaple EX32 8PB
tel 07725 829575
email editorial.csh@archant.co.uk
website www.countrysmallholding.com
Editor Julie Harding
Monthly £3.99

The magazine for smallholders in the UK. Practical, how-to articles and seasonal features on organic farming, small-scale poultry and livestock keeping, country crafts, cookery and general subjects of interest to smallholders or those interested in finding out more about that lifestyle. Approach the Editor by email with ideas. Length: up to 1,500 words. Payment: on application. Founded 1975 as *Practical Self-Sufficiency*.

Country Walking

Bauer Consumer Media, Media House, Lynch Wood, Peterborough Business Park, Peterborough PE2 6EA
tel (01733) 468205
website www.livefortheoutdoors.com/countrywalking
Editor Guy Procter
13 p.a. From £44 p.a.

Features. Length: 1,000 words on average.

Illustrations: digital images. Payment: by arrangement. Founded 1987.

The Countryman

Dalesman Publishing, The Gatehouse, Skipton Castle, Skipton, North Yorkshire BD23 1AL
tel (01756) 701381
email editorial@thecountryman.co.uk
website www.countrymanmagazine.co.uk
Twitter @Countrymaned
Editor Mark Whitley
Monthly £3.99

Features rural life, wildlife and natural history, country people, traditions, crafts, covering whole of UK. Positive view of countryside and rural issues. Non-political, and no bloodsports. Unusual or quirky topics welcomed. Copy must be well written and accurate, for well-informed readership who are generally 40+ with strong affection for countryside. Articles between 600–1,000 words. Illustrations: good-quality digital images. Study magazine before submitting ideas. Send detailed outline first. Payment: by agreement. Founded 1927.

Crafts Magazine

44A Pentonville Road, London N1 9BY
tel 020-7806 2538
email crafts@craftscouncil.org.uk
website www.craftsmagazine.org.uk
Bi-monthly £8.50

Magazine for contemporary art, craft and design, published by the Crafts Council and The River Group. Its content spans specialist features, craft news and reviews, covering a global range of makers, artists and designers. Submissions for review should include pictures and applicants should be mindful of the lead times associated with a bi-monthly schedule.

Crannóg

email editor@crannogmagazine.com
website www.crannogmagazine.com
website www.crannogmagazine.com/submissions
Editors Sandra Bunting, Tony O'Dwyer, Ger Burke, Jarlath Fahy
2 p.a. €8.00

Literary magazine bringing together the best poetry and fiction from Irish and international contributors. Published bi-annually in March and September: submission windows are the month of November for the March issue and the month of May for the September issue. See website for further information. Contributor's fee paid. Founded 2002.

The Critic

Carlyle House, 235–237 Vauxhall Bridge Road, London SW1V 1EJ
email editorial@thecritic.co.uk
website https://thecritic.co.uk
Twitter @thecriticmag

Co-Editors Michael Mosbacher, Christopher Montgomery
10 times p.a. (monthly, with July/August and January/February double issues) £5.95

Essays, non-fiction, reportage, reviews and arts reflections. Pitch ideas before submitting and study magazine before pitching. Poetry and cartoon submissions welcome. Length: dependent on type of piece; individual pieces range from 800–4,500 words. Payment: by arrangement. Founded 2019.

Critical Quarterly

email cs-journals@wiley.com
website https://onlinelibrary.wiley.com/journal/10.1111/(ISSN)1467-8705
Editor Colin MacCabe
Quarterly £46 p.a. (individual, print and online)

Fiction, poems, literary criticism. Length: 2,000–5,000 words. Study magazine before submitting MSS. Payment: by arrangement. Founded 1959.

Crystal Magazine

3 Bowness Avenue, Prenton, Birkenhead CH43 0SD
tel 0151 608 9736
email christinecrystal@hotmail.com
website www.christinecrystal.blogspot.com
Editor Christine Carr
6 p.a. £21 p.a. (UK), £25 p.a. (overseas)

Poems, stories (true and fiction), articles. Also: Wordsmithing, a humorous and informative look into the world of writers and writing; letters; news; and competitions (open to all writers). Free gift. Founded 2001.

Cumbria Magazine

Dalesman Publications Ltd, The Gatehouse, Skipton Castle, Skipton, North Yorkshire BD23 1AL
tel (01756) 701381
email johnm@dalesman.co.uk
website www.cumbriamagazine.co.uk
Editor Jon Stokoe
Monthly £3.20

Articles of rural interest concerning the people and landscapes of the Lake District and surrounding county of Cumbria. Short length preferred; articles should be of a journalistic nature and no more than 1,200 words. Illustrations: first-class photos, illustrations. Payment: £70 per 1,000 words. Pictures extra. Founded 1947, New Series 1951.

Custom Car

Kelsey Media, The Granary, Downs Court, Yalding Hill, Yalding, Kent ME18 6AL
tel (01959) 541444
email cc.ed@kelsey.co.uk
website www.customcarmag.co.uk
Editor David Biggadyke
Four-weekly £4.99

Hot rods, customs and drag racing. Length: by

arrangement. Payment: by arrangement. Founded 1970.

Custom PC

Raspberry Pi Trading, Maurice Wilkes Building, St John's Innovation Park, Cowley Road, Cambridge CB4 0DS
email ben.hardwidge@raspberrypi.com
email edward.chester@raspberrypi.com
website https://custompc.co.uk
Facebook www.facebook.com/cpcmagazine
Twitter @CustomPCMag
Editor Ben Hardwidge, *Features Editor* Edward Chester
Monthly £5.99

Magazine covering performance PC hardware, technology and games with full-page and DPS single-product reviews, group tests, and practical and technical features.

Cycling Weekly

Future plc, Pinehurst 2, Pinehurst Road, Farnborough Business Park, Farnborough, Hants GU14 7BF
tel (01252) 555100
email cycling@futurenet.com
website www.cyclingweekly.com
Facebook www.facebook.com/CyclingWeekly
Twitter @cyclingweekly
Editor Simon Richardson
Weekly £3.25

Racing, fitness, features and technical reviews. Illustrations: topical cycling racing photos considered; cartoons. Length: not exceeding 2,000 words. Payment: by arrangement. Founded 1891.

Cyphers

3 Selskar Terrace, Ranelagh, Dublin D06 DW66, Republic of Ireland
tel +353 (0)1 4978866
website www.cyphers.ie
Editor Eiléan Ní Chuilleanáin
3 p.a. €21 p.a.

Poems, fiction, translations. Submissions cannot be returned unless accompanied by postage (Irish stamps or International Reply Coupons). Payment: €35 to 50 per page. Founded 1975.

Dalesman

Country Publications Limited, The Gatehouse, Skipton Castle, Skipton, North Yorkshire, BD23 1AL
tel (01756) 693479
email editorial@dalesman.co.uk
website www.dalesman.co.uk
Facebook www.facebook.com/yorkshire.dalesman
Twitter @The_Dalesman
Editor Jon Stokoe
Monthly £3.30

Articles and stories of genuine interest concerning Yorkshire (1,000 to 1,200 words). Payment: £70 per 1,000 words plus extra for useable photos/illustrations. Founded 1939.

Dancing Times

36 Battersea Square, London SW11 3RA
tel 020-7250 3006
email editorial@dancing-times.co.uk
website www.dancing-times.co.uk
Editor Jonathan Gray
Monthly £3.95

Ballet, ballroom, Latin, contemporary dance and all forms of stage and social dancing from general, historical, critical and technical angles. Well-informed freelance articles used occasionally, but only after preliminary arrangements. Illustrations: occasional line, action photos preferred; colour welcome. Payment: by arrangement. Founded 1910.

Dare

The River Group, 16 Connaught Place, London W2 2ES
tel 020-7420 7000
website www.therivergroup.co.uk
website www.superdrug.com/dare
Free

Superdrug magazine. Predominantly features aspirational yet affordable beauty and fashion.

Darts World

email info@dartsworld.com
website www.dartsworld.com/
Twitter @Darts_World
Monthly £3.99

Articles and stories with darts theme. Illustrations: half-tone, cartoons. Payment: £40–£50 per 1,000 words; illustrations by arrangement. Founded 1972.

The Dawntreader

24 Forest Houses, Cookworthy Moor, Halwill, Beaworthy, Devon EX21 5UU
email dawnidp@indigodreams.co.uk
website www.indigodreams.co.uk
Facebook www.facebook.com/indigodreamspublishing
Twitter @IndigoDreamsPub
Editor Dawn Bauling
Quarterly £4.50, £17 p.a.

Poetry, short stories and articles up to 1,000 words encompassing themes of the mystic, myth, legend, landscape, nature and love. New writers welcome. Lively feedback pages. No payment. Email submission preferred. Founded 2007.

Decanter

Future plc, 161 Marsh Wall, London E14 9AP
tel 020-3148 5000
email editor@decanter.com
website www.decanter.com
Editor Amy Wislocki

Monthly £5.50

Articles and features on wines, wine travel and food-related topics. Welcomes ideas for articles and features. Length: 1,000–1,800 words. Illustrations: colour. Payment: £275 per 1,000 words. Founded 1975.

delicious.

Axe & Bottle Court, 3rd Floor, 70 Newcomen Street, London SE1 1YT
tel 020-7803 4115
email readers@deliciousmagazine.co.uk
website www.deliciousmagazine.co.uk
Twitter @deliciousmag
Instagram @deliciousmag
Editor Karen Barnes
Monthly £6.49

Articles on food, recipes, skills, trends, chefs, sustainability, food waste, producers, food issues, humour, wine and ingredients. Founded 2003.

Derbyshire Life

Derbyshire Life, 61 Friar Gate, Derby DE1 1DJ
tel (01332) 227851
email nathan.fearn@archant.co.uk
website www.greatbritishlife.co.uk
Editor Nathan Fearn
Monthly £3.99

Articles, preferably illustrated, about Derbyshire life, people, places and history. Length: up to 1,200 words. Some short stories set in Derbyshire accepted; no verse. Illustrations: photos of Derbyshire subjects. Payment: according to nature and quality of contribution. Founded 1931.

Descent

Wild Places Publishing, PO Box 100, Abergavenny NP7 9WY
tel (01873) 737707
email descent@wildplaces.co.uk
website www.wildplaces.co.uk
Editor Chris Howes
Bi-monthly £6.75

Articles, features and news on all aspects of cave and mine sport exploration, including history (coalmines, active mining or showcaves are not included). Submissions must match magazine style. Length: up to 2,000 words (articles/features), up to 1,000 words (news). Illustrations: colour. Payment: on consideration of material based on area filled. Founded 1969.

Devon Life

Archant South West, Newbery House, Fair Oak Close, Exeter Airport Business Park, Clyst Honiton, Exeter, Devon EX5 2UL
tel (01392) 888423
email andy.cooper@archant.co.uk
website www.devonlife.co.uk
Editor Andy Cooper
Monthly £4.50

Articles on all aspects of Devon, including inspiring people, fascinating places, beautiful walks, local events, arts, history and food. Some articles online, plus a lively community of Devon bloggers. Unsolicited ideas welcome: 'ideal' articles comprise a main section of 650–700 words alongside two sections of associated facts/points of interest on the subject material. Founded 1963.

The Dickensian

The Dickens Fellowship,
The Charles Dickens Museum, 48 Doughty Street, London WC1N 2LX
email E.J.L.Bell@leeds.ac.uk
website www.dickensfellowship.org/dickensian
Editor Dr Emily Bell, 9.2.10 Cavendish Road, School of English, University of Leeds, Leeds LS2 9JT
3 p.a. £19 p.a. (UK individuals), £29 p.a. (UK institutions); £21 p.a. (overseas individuals), £32 p.a. (overseas institutions); reduced rate for Dickens Fellowship members

Welcomes articles (max. 5,000 words) on all aspects of Dickens's life, works and character. Send contributions by email attachment to the Editor. See website for house-style conventions and specifications for any photographic material. Payment: none.

Digital Camera

Future plc, Quay House, The Ambury, Bath BA1 1UA
tel (01225) 442244
email digitalcamera@futurenet.com
website www.digitalcameraworld.com
Editor Niall Hampton
Monthly £5.60

Practical guide to creating best-ever photographs. Each issue contains inspirational images, expert techniques and essential tips for capturing great photos, plus how to perfect them on a computer. Also includes reviews of the latest cameras, accessories and image-editing software.

Director

SevenC3 Publishing, 3–7 Herbal Hill, London EC1R 5EJ
email directormagazine@seven.co.uk
website www.director.co.uk
6 p.a. Free to Institute of Directors members; £20 p.a. for UK non-members (print)

Authoritative business-related articles. Send synopsis of proposed article and examples of printed work. Length: 500–2,000 words. Payment: by arrangement. Illustrations: colour. Founded 1947.

Diva

Twin Media Group, Room 32, Spectrum House, 32–34 Gordon House Road, London NW5 1LP

tel 020-3735 7873
email editorial@divamag.co.uk
website www.divamag.co.uk
Editor Carrie Lyell
Monthly £4.50

Lesbian and bisexual women's lifestyle and culture: articles and features. Length: 200–2,000 words. Illustrations: colour. Payment: £15 per 100 words; variable per photo; variable per illustration. Founded 1994.

Diver

Suite B, 74 Oldfield Road, Hampton,
Middlesex TW12 2HR
tel 020-8941 8152
email enquiries@divermag.co.uk
website www.divernet.com
Publisher and Editor-in-Chief Nigel Eaton, *Editor*
Steve Weinman
Monthly £4.40

Articles on recreational scuba-diving and related developments. Length: 1,500–2,000 words. Illustrations: colour. Payment: by arrangement. Founded 1963.

Dogs Today

The Old Print House, 62 High Street, Chobham,
Surrey GU24 8AA
tel (01276) 858880
email enquiries@dogstodaymagazine.co.uk
website www.dogstodaymagazine.co.uk
Publisher Beverley Cuddy
Monthly £4.75

Study of magazine essential before submitting ideas. Interested in human interest dog stories, celebrity interviews, holiday features and anything unusual – all must be entertaining and informative and accompanied by illustrations. Length: 800–1,200 words. Illustrations: colour, preferably digital. Payment: negotiable. Founded 1990.

Dorset Life – The Dorset Magazine

3 Rempstone Barns, Corfe Castle, Wareham,
Dorset BH20 5DT
tel (01929) 551264
email editor@dorsetlife.co.uk
website www.dorsetlife.co.uk
Supervising Editor John Newth
Monthly £2.95

Articles (c. 1,000 or 1,500 words), photos (colour) with a specifically Dorset theme. Payment: for text, on publication and by agreement with the editor; for photos, dependent on size used. Founded 1968.

Drapers

EMAP, Telephone House, 69–77 Paul Street,
London EC2A 4NQ
tel 020-3033 2770
email kirsty.mcgregor@emap.com
website www.drapersonline.com
Facebook www.facebook.com/Drapersonline
Twitter @Drapers
Editor Kirsty McGregor
From £194 p.a.

Online only. Business editorial aimed at fashion retailers, large and small, and all who supply them. Illustrations: colour and b&w photos. Payment: by negotiation. Founded 1887.

Dream Catcher

Stairwell Books, 161 Lowther Street, York YO31 7LZ
tel (01904) 733767
email rose@stairwellbooks.com
website www.dreamcatchermagazine.co.uk
Editor Hannah Stone
2 p.a. £8, £15 p.a.

International literary and arts journal. Welcomes poetry, short stories (optimum length of 2,000 words), artwork, interviews and reviews. Each issue features a selected artist whose work is reproduced on the cover and inside. Promotes reading and workshops across the UK. Founded 1996 by Paul Sutherland.

The Dublin Review

PO Box 7948, Dublin 1, Republic of Ireland
tel +353 (0)1 6788627
email enquiry@thedublinreview.com
website www.thedublinreview.com
Editor Brendan Barrington
Quarterly €11.25 (UK)

Essays, memoir, reportage and fiction for the intelligent general reader. Payment: by arrangement. Founded 2000.

Early Music

Faculty of Music, University of Cambridge,
11 West Road, Cambridge CB3 9DP
email earlymusic@oxfordjournals.org
website https://em.oxfordjournals.org/
Twitter @EarlyMus
Editors Helen Deeming, Alan Howard, Stephen Rose
Quarterly £86 p.a. (individual, print)

Lively, informative and scholarly articles on aspects of medieval, renaissance, baroque and classical music. Payment: £20 per 1,000 words. Illustrations: line, half-tone, colour. Founded 1973.

East Lothian Life

1 Beveridge Row, Belhaven, Dunbar,
East Lothian EH42 1TP
tel (01368) 863593
website www.eastlothianlife.co.uk
Twitter @eastlothianlife
Editor Pauline Jaffray
Quarterly £3

Articles and features with an East Lothian slant.

Length: up to 1,000 words. Illustrations: b&w photos, line. Payment: negotiable. Founded 1989.

Eastern Art Report

EAPGROUP International Media, PO Box 13666, London SW14 8WF
tel 020-8392 1122
email ear@eapgroup.com
website www.easternartreport.net
website www.eapgroup.com
Twitter @easterneap
Publisher/Editor-in-Chief Sajid Rizvi, *Emeritus Editor* Shirley Joseph
Quarterly £14.95

Original, well-researched articles on all aspects of the visual and performing arts, cinema and digital media – Asian and diasporic, Buddhist, Islamic, Judaic, Indian, Chinese and Japanese; reviews. Length of articles: minimum 1,500 words. Illustrations: colour or b&w, hi-res digital format. No responsibility accepted for unsolicited material. Payment: by arrangement. Founded 1989.

Economica

STICERD, London School of Economics, Houghton Street, London WC2A 2AE
tel 020-7955 7855
website https://onlinelibrary.wiley.com/journal/10.1111/(ISSN)1468-0335
Editors Nava Ashraf, Tim Besley, Francesco Caselli, Maitreesh Ghatak, Stephen Machin, Henry Overman and Noam Yuchtman
Quarterly From £58 p.a. (other subscription rates on application)

Learned journal covering the fields of economics, economic history and statistics. Payment: none. Founded 1921; New series 1934.

The Economist

1–11 John Adam Street, London WC2N 6HT
tel 020-7576 8000
website www.economist.com
Facebook www.facebook.com/TheEconomist
Twitter @TheEconomist
Editor Zanny Minton Beddoes
Weekly £5.99

Articles staff-written. Founded 1843.

Educate

National Education Union, Hamilton House, Mabledon Place, London WC1H 9BD
tel 020-7380 4708
email educate@neu.org.uk
website https://neu.org.uk/educate
Editor Max Watson
6 p.a. Free to NEU members

Articles, features and news of interest to all those involved in the education sector. Email outline in the first instance. Length: 500 words (single page), 1,000 (double page). Payment: NUJ rates to NUJ members.

Electrical Review

SJP Business Media Ltd, 2nd Floor, 123 Cannon Street, London EC4N 5AU
tel 020-7062 2526
email clairef@datacentrereview.com
website www.electricalreview.co.uk
Twitter @elecreviewmag
Editor Claire Fletcher
Monthly Free (restricted qualification; see website for details) or £232 p.a. (print and digital subscription)

Technical and business articles on electrical and control engineering; outside contributions considered. Good quality imagery an advantage. Electrical news welcomed. Payment: according to merit. Founded 1872.

ELLE (UK)

Hearst UK, House of Hearst, 30 Panton Street, London SW1Y 4AJ
tel 020-7150 7000
website www.elleuk.com
Facebook www.facebook.com/Ellemagazine
Twitter @Ellemagazine
Editor-in-Chief Farrah Storr
Monthly £4.80

Commissioned material only. Illustrations: colour. Payment: by arrangement. Founded 1985.

Embroidery

The Embroiderers' Guild, c/o Bucks County Museum, Church Street, Aylesbury, Bucks. HP20 2QP
mobile 07742 601501
email johalleditor@gmail.com
website www.embroderersguild.com/embroidery
Twitter @johalleditor
Instagram @johalleditor
Editor Joanne Hall
6 p.a. £6.50

News and illustrated features on all aspects of embroidery and contemporary textiles in art, design, craft, illustration, fashion, interiors and world textiles. Features on internationally renowned artists, makers and designers working with modern textiles, stitch and embroidery. News covering exhibitions, books and products, plus event listings, book and exhibition reviews and opportunities. Length of articles accepted: exhibition reviews 500 words; book reviews 250 words; profile features/interviews 1,000 words. Published every two months from January each year. Founded 1932.

Empire

Endeavour House, 189 Shaftesbury Avenue, London WC2H 8JG
tel 020-7295 6700
website www.empireonline.com
Facebook www.facebook.com/empiremagazine
Twitter @empiremagazine

Editor-in-Chief Terri White
13 p.a. £4.99

Guide to film on all its platforms: articles, features, news. Length: various. Illustrations: colour and b&w photos. Payment: approx. £300 per 1,000 words; varies for illustrations. Founded 1989.

Energy Engineering
Media Culture Ltd, Pure Offices, Plato Close, Leamington Spa, Warks. CV34 6WE
tel (01926) 671338
email info@energyengineering.co.uk
website https://energyengineering.co.uk
Managing Editor Steve Welch
6 p.a. £65 p.a.

Features and news for those engaged in technology, manufacturing and management. Contributions considered on all aspects of engineering. Illustrations: colour. Founded 1866.

The Engineer
Mark Allen Group, St Jude's Church, Dulwich Road, London SE24 0PB
tel 020-7970 4437
email jon.excell@markallengroup.com
website www.theengineer.co.uk
Twitter @TheEngineerUK
Editor Jon Excell
Monthly Price on application (free in some instances)

Features and news on innovation and technology, including profiles, analysis. Length: up to 800 words (news), 1,000 words (features). Illustrations: colour transparencies or prints, artwork, line diagrams, graphs. Payment: by negotiation. Founded 1856.

Engineering in Miniature
Warners Group Publications Plc, The Maltings, West Street, Bourne, Lincs. PE10 9PH
tel (01778) 391000
website www.world-of-railways.co.uk
Publisher (Railways) Steve Cole
Monthly £4.50

Articles containing descriptions and information on all aspects of model engineering. Articles welcome but technical articles preferred. Payment dependent on pages published. Founded 1979.

The English Garden
Jubilee House, 2 Jubilee Place, London SW3 3TQ
tel (020)-7349 3700
email theenglishgarden@chelseamagazines.com
website www.theenglishgarden.co.uk
Facebook www.facebook.com/theenglishgardenmagazine
Twitter @TEGmagazine
Editor Clare Foggett
13 p.a. £4.95

Features on gardens in the UK and Ireland, plants, practical gardening advice and garden design. Length:

800–1,200 words. Illustrations: colour photos and botanical artwork. Payment: variable. Founded 1997.

Erotic Review
120 New Kings Road, London SW6 4LZ
email editorial@ermagazine.org
website https://eroticreviewmagazine.com/
Twitter @EroticReviewMag
Editor Jamie Maclean
Online

Online literary eZine with fiction, reviews and sophisticated erotic lifestyle for sensualists, libertarians and libertines. Commissions features (500–2,500 words) and short fiction (1,000–5,000 words). Information on submissions can be found online in the contributor guidelines section of the website. Founded 1995.

Esquire
Hearst UK, House of Hearst, 30 Panton Street, London SW1Y 4AJ
tel 020-7439 5601
website www.esquire.co.uk
Editor-in-Chief Alex Bilmes
6 p.a. £8

Quality men's general interest magazine – articles, features. No unsolicited material or short stories. Length: various. Illustrations: colour and b&w photos, line. Payment: by arrangement. Founded 1991.

Essex Life
Portman House, 120 Princes Street, Ipswich IP1 1RS
tel 07834 101686
email julian.read@archant.co.uk
website www.greatbritishlife.co.uk/
Editor Julian Read
Monthly £4.50

No unsolicited material. Founded 1952.

Evergreen
185 Fleet Street, London EC4A 2HS
tel 020-7400 1083
email editor@evergreenmagazine.co.uk
website www.evergreenmagazine.co.uk
Features Editor Isobel King
Quarterly £6.49

Articles about Great Britain's heritage, culture, countryside, people and places. Length 250–3,000 words. Illustrations: digital only. Payment: £15 per 500 words, £10 poems (8–24 lines). Founded 1985.

The Face
email hello@theface.com
website https://theface.com
Twitter @TheFaceMagazine
Instagram @thefacemagazine
Editor Matthew Whitehouse
Quarterly £9.95

Iconic magazine in a new guise, covering style, music, culture and society. Founded 1980; relaunched 2019.

Family Law journal

LexisNexis, 30 Farringdon Street, London EC4A 4HH
tel 0330 161 1234
email editor@familylaw.co.uk
website www.familylaw.co.uk
Facebook www.facebook.com/JordansFamilyLaw
Twitter @JPFamilyLaw
Editor Elsa Booth
Monthly £430 p.a.

Practitioner journal, aimed at helping family law professionals keep abreast of latest developments in the field and their impact. Each issue includes news on legislative change, case reports, articles and news items. Length between 2,000 and 3,000 words, no illustrations. Founded 1971.

Family Tree

Warners Group Publications Plc, The Maltings, West Street, Bourne, Lincs. PE10 9PH
tel (01778) 395050
email editorial@family-tree.co.uk
website www.family-tree.co.uk
Facebook www.facebook.com/familytreemaguk
Twitter @familytreemaguk
Editor Helen Tovey
Every 4 weeks £5.25, £48 p.a. Digital issues also available.

Features on family history, genealogy and related topics. Payment: by arrangement. Founded 1984.

Farmers Weekly

Quadrant House, The Quadrant, Sutton, Surrey SM2 5AS
tel 020-8652 4911
email farmersweekly@markallengroup.com
website www.fwi.co.uk
Editorial Director Karl Schneider, *Editor* Andrew Meredith
Weekly From £30 p.a.

Commissions freelance contributors to write articles; willing to consider pitches. Founded 1934.

Feminist Review

SAGE Publications Ltd, 1 Oliver's Yard, 55 City Road, London EC1Y 1SP
tel 020-7324 8517
website https://uk.sagepub.com/en-gb/eur/feminist-review/journal203522
Twitter @FeministReview_
Edited by a Collective
3 p.a. Subscriptions from £57 p.a. (digital) and £62 p.a. (print)

Peer-reviewed, interdisciplinary journal that aims to set new agendas for feminism. Feminist Review invites critical reflection on the relationship between materiality and representation, theory and practice,

subjectivity and communities, contemporary and historical formations. Publishes academic articles, experimental pieces, visual and textual media and political interventions, including, for example, interviews, short stories, poems and photographic essays. Founded 1979.

Fenland Poetry Journal

email fenlandpoetryjournal@gmail.com
website www.fenlandpoetryjournal.co.uk
Facebook www.facebook.com/fenlandpoetryjournal/
Twitter @FenlandJ
Editor Elisabeth Sennitt Clough
Bi-annual £6 per issue, or £10 p.a.

Poetry and art magazine. Accepts new and previously published work as well as simultaneous submissions, but see website for full details. Poets with a connection to the Fenland area are encouraged to submit their work, but contributions from other areas, national and international, are welcomed too. Payment: none, but contributors will receive a free copy of the edition featuring their work.

The Field

Future plc, Pinehurst 2, Pinehurst Road, Farnborough Business Park, Farnborough, Hants GU14 7BF
tel (01252) 555000
email field.secretary@futurenet.com
website www.thefield.co.uk
Facebook www.facebook.com/TheFieldMagazine
Twitter @TheFieldmag
Editor Jonathan Young
Monthly £5.95

Specific, topical and informed features on the British countryside and country pursuits, including natural history, field sports, gardening and rural conservation. Overseas subjects considered but opportunities for such articles are limited. No fiction or children's material. Articles of 800–2,000 words by outside contributors considered; also topical 'shorts' of 200–300 words on all countryside matters. Illustrations: colour photos of a high standard. Payment: on merit. Founded 1853.

Financial Adviser

Financial Times Business, 1 Southwark Bridge, London SE1 9HL
tel 020-7775 3000
email dan.jones@ft.com
website www.ftadviser.com
Editor-in-Chief Dan Jones
Weekly Free (after registering)

Topical personal finance news and features. Length: variable. Payment: by arrangement. Founded 1987.

FIRE

Blue Sky Offices, 25 Cecil Pashley Way, Shoreham-by-Sea BN43 5FF

tel (01273) 434943
email andrew.lynch@fireknowledge.co.uk
website www.fire-magazine.com
Editor and Publisher Andrew Lynch
Monthly £86.50 p.a.

Articles on firefighting and fire prevention from acknowledged experts only. Length: 1,500 words. No unsolicited contributions. Illustrations: dramatic firefighting or fire brigade rescue colour photos. Payment: by arrangement. Founded 1908.

Firewords

email info@firewords.co.uk
website https://firewords.co.uk
Twitter @FirewordsMag
Editors Dan Burgess, Jen Scott
2 p.a. £9 inc. delivery

Literary magazine with high design and production standards. Accepts submissions for fiction, short stories and poetry: issues are (loosely) themed, so check website for forthcoming themes and specifications. Original work preferred, but previously published pieces may be considered: prospective authors should indicate if their material has appeared elsewhere. Payment: none. Founded 2014.

Fishing News

Kelsey Media, The Granary, Downs Court, Yalding Hill, Yalding, Kent ME18 6AL
tel (01434) 607375
email dave@linkie.co.uk
website www.fishingnews.co.uk
Twitter @YourFishingNews
Editor Dave Linkie
Weekly £122 p.a.

News and features on all aspects of the commercial fishing industry. Length: up to 1,000 words (features), up to 500 words (news). Illustrations: colour and b&w photos. Payment: negotiable. Founded 1913.

Flash: The International Short-Short Story Magazine

Department of English, University of Chester, Parkgate Road, Chester CH1 4BJ
tel (01244) 513152
email flash.magazine@chester.ac.uk
website www1.chester.ac.uk/flash-magazine
Editors Dr Peter Blair, Dr Ashley Chantler
Bi-annual £6, £11 p.a. Subscription includes membership of International Flash Fiction Association (IFFA)

Quality stories of up to 360 words (title included); see website for submission guidelines. Suggestions for reviews and articles considered. Payment: complimentary copy. Founded 2008.

Flora

4–5 Kinnerton Place South, Belgravia, London, SW1X 8EH
tel 020-7235 6235
email editor@judithblacklock.com
website www.flora-magazine.co.uk
Facebook www.facebook.com/FloraInternationalMagazine/
Editor Judith Blackstock
Bi-monthly £4.75

Magazine for flower arranging and floristry; also features flower-related crafts and flower arrangers' gardens. Unsolicited enquiries and suggestions welcome on any of these subjects. Send brief synopsis together with sample illustrations. Payment: by arrangement. Founded 1974.

Fly Fishing & Fly Tying

Rolling River Publications, The Locus Centre, The Square, Aberfeldy, Perthshire PH15 2DD
tel (01887) 829868
email MarkB.ffft@btinternet.com
website www.flyfishing-and-flytying.co.uk
Editor Mark Bowler
12 p.a. £3.99

Fly-fishing and fly-tying articles, fishery features, limited short stories, fishing travel. Length: 800–2,000 words. Illustrations: colour photos. Payment: by arrangement. Founded 1990.

Fortean Times

Dennis Publishing Ltd, 31–32 Alfred Place, London WC1E 7DP
tel 020-3890 3890
email drsutton@forteantimes.com
website www.forteantimes.com
Twitter @forteantimes
Editor David Sutton
13 p.a. £4.60

Journal of strange phenomena, experiences, related subjects and philosophies. Includes articles, features, news, reviews. Length: 500–5,000 words; longer by arrangement. Illustrations: colour photos, line and tone art, cartoons. Payment: by negotiation. Founded 1973.

FourFourTwo

Future Publishing Ltd, 3 Queensbridge, The Lakes, Northampton NN4 7BF
email fourfourtwo@futurenet.com
website www.fourfourtwo.magazine.co.uk
Editor James Andrew
Monthly £5.99

Football magazine with interviews, in-depth features, issues pieces, odd and witty material. Length: 2,000–3,000 (features), 100–1,500 words (Up Front pieces). Illustrations: colour transparencies and artwork, b&w prints. Payment: £200 per 1,000 words. Founded 1994.

France

Cumberland House, Oriel Road, Cheltenham, Glos. GL50 1BB
tel (01242) 216050
email editorial@francemag.com
website www.completefrance.com
Group Editor Karen Tait
Monthly £4.50

Informed quality features and articles on the real France, ranging from cuisine to culture to holidays exploring hidden France. Length: 800–2,000 words. Payment: £100 per 1,000 words; £50 per page/pro rata for illustrations. Founded 1989.

The Friend

173 Euston Road, London NW1 2BJ
tel 020-7663 1010
email editorial@thefriend.org
website www.thefriend.org
Editor Joseph Jones
Weekly From £74 p.a. online or £95 p.a. print

Material of interest to Quakers and like-minded people; spiritual, political, social, economic, environmental or cultural, considered from outside contributors. Length: up to 1,200 words. Illustrations: b&w or colour photographs and line drawings by email preferred. Payment: not usually but will negotiate a small fee with professional writers. Founded 1843.

Frieze

1 Surrey Street, London WC2R 2ND
tel 020-3372 6111
email infolondon@frieze.com
website www.frieze.com
8 p.a. £9.95 (back issues £15)

Magazine of European contemporary art and culture including essays, reviews, columns and listings. Frieze Art Fair is held every October in Regent's Park, London, featuring over 150 of the most exciting contemporary art galleries in the world. Founded 1991.

The Frogmore Papers

21 Mildmay Road, Lewes, East Sussex BN7 1PJ
email frogmorepress@gmail.com
website www.frogmorepress.co.uk/submission-guidelines/
Editor Jeremy Page
2 p.a. £5

Long-established poetry and prose magazine. Two submission windows per year: 1–31 October for the March issue and 1–30 April for the October issue. Submissions from UK-based writers should be made by post to the address above, but overseas writers may contribute via email. Send no more than four to six poems at one time; short stories should be no more than 2,000 words. Familiarity with the magazine advised; also see website for further guidance.

The Furrow

St Patrick's College, Maynooth, Co. Kildare W23 TW77, Republic of Ireland
tel +353 (0)1 7083741
email editor.furrow@spcm.ie
website www.thefurrow.ie
Editor Rev. Pádraig Corkery
Monthly €4.87

Religious, pastoral, theological and social articles. Length: up to 3,500 words. Articles are available through JSTOR and from the Secretary at *The Furrow* office. Illustrations: line, half-tone. Payment: average €20 per page (450 words). Founded 1950.

gal-dem

email info@gal-dem.com
website https://gal-dem.com/about/#pitch
Twitter @galdemzine
Ceo Mariel Richards
Online

Focuses on the stories of people of colour from marginalised genders and their communities. Accepts material across five sections (First Person, Life, Politics, Culture, Music): article formats include comment pieces, essays, profile interviews and multi-interview features. Pitches must be made via an online form (see website address above); potential contributors should familiarise themselves with the magazine to check their contribution has not been covered previously.

Garden Answers

Bauer Media Group, Media House, Lynch Wood, Peterborough Business Park, Peterborough PE2 6EA
tel (01733) 468000
email gardenanswers@bauermedia.co.uk
website www.gardenanswersmagazine.co.uk
Twitter @GardenAnswers
Editor Liz Potter
Monthly £4.35

Some commissioned features and articles on all aspects of gardening. Reader garden photo and interview packages considered. Study of magazine essential. Approach by email with examples of published work. Length: approx. 750 words. Illustrations: digital images and artwork. Payment: by negotiation. Founded 1982.

Garden News

Bauer Media Group, Media House, Lynch Wood, Peterborough Business Park, Peterborough PE2 6EA
tel (01733) 468000
email gn.letters@bauermedia.co.uk
website www.gardennewsmagazine.co.uk
Facebook www.facebook.com/GardenNewsOfficial
Twitter @GardenNewsMag

Weekly £1.99

Up-to-date information on everything to do with plants, growing and gardening. Payment: by negotiation. Founded 1958.

Gay Times

Room 2.03, 133 Whitechapel High St, London E1 7QA
tel 020-7424 7400
email edit@gaytimes.co.uk
website www.gaytimes.co.uk
Twitter @gaytimesmag
Instagram @gaytimesmag
Editorial Director Lewis Corner
13 p.a. £8.95

Features diverse LGBTQI talent. Includes features and interviews on celebrity, gay lifestyle, health, parenting, music, film, technology, current affairs, opinion, culture, art, style and grooming. Length: up to 2,000 words. Payment: by arrangement. Founded 1984.

Geographical

3.16 QWest, 1100 Great West Road, London TW8 0GP
tel 020-8332 8444
email magazine@geographical.co.uk
website www.geographical.co.uk
Facebook www.facebook.com/GeographicalMagazine
Twitter @Geographicalmag
Editor Katie Burton
Monthly £4.99

Magazine of the Royal Geographical Society (with the Institute of British Geographers). Covers culture, wildlife, environment, science and travel. Illustrations: top-quality hi-res digital files, vintage material. Payment: by negotiation. Founded 1935.

The Geographical Journal

Royal Geographical Society (with the Institute of British Geographers), 1 Kensington Gore, London SW7 2AR
tel 020-7591 3026
email journals@rgs.org
website https://rgs-ibg.onlinelibrary.wiley.com/journal/14754959
Editors Darren Smith, Ben Anderson, Parvati Raghuram, Rob Wilby
4 p.a. Subscriptions from £294 p.a. (institutional rate available only)

Papers range across the entire subject of geography, with particular reference to public debates, policy-oriented agendas and notions of 'relevance'. Illustrations: photos, maps, diagrams. Founded 1893.

Gibbons Stamp Monthly

Stanley Gibbons Ltd, 7 Parkside, Ringwood, Hants BH24 3SH
tel (01425) 481042

email dshepherd@stanleygibbons.co.uk
website www.stanleygibbons.co.uk
Editor Dean Shepherd
Monthly £4.75

Articles on philatelic topics. Contact the Editor first. Length: 500–2,500 words. Illustrations: photos, line, stamps or covers. Payment: by arrangement, £60 or more per 1,000 words.

Glamour

The Condé Nast Publications Ltd, The Adelphi, 1–11 John Adam Street, London WC2N 6HT
email glamoureditorialmagazine@condenast.co.uk
website www.glamourmagazine.co.uk
Principally online but bi-annual print editions £2

Lifestyle magazine containing fashion, beauty, real-life features and celebrity news aimed at women aged 18–34. Feature ideas welcome; approach with brief outline. Length: 500–800 words. Payment: by arrangement. Founded 2001.

Golf Monthly

Future plc, Pinehurst 2, Pinehurst Road, Farnborough Business Park, Farnborough, Hants GU14 7BF
tel (01252) 555197
email golfmonthly@futurenet.com
website www.golf-monthly.co.uk
Editor Michael Harris
Monthly £4.99

Original articles on golf considered (not reports), golf clinics, handy hints. Illustrations: half-tone, colour, cartoons. Payment: by arrangement. Founded 1911.

Good Housekeeping

Hearst UK, House of Hearst, 30 Panton Street, London SW1Y 4AJ
tel 020-7439 5590 (editorial enquiries)
email goodh.mail@hearst.co.uk
website www.goodhousekeeping.com/uk
Editor-in-Chief Gaby Huddart
Monthly £4.99

Articles on topics of interest to women. No unsolicited features or stories accepted. Homes, fashion, beauty and food covered by staff writers. Illustrations: commissioned. Payment: magazine standards. Founded 1922.

Governance and Compliance

Institute of Chartered Secretaries and Administrators, Saffron House, 6–10 Kirby Street, London EC1N 8TS
tel 020-7580 4741
website www.govcompmag.com
Editor Sonia Sharma
Monthly £185 p.a. (full rate; free to members)

Published by ICSA: The Governance Institute. Offers news, views and practical advice on the latest developments in governance and compliance.

GQ

The Condé Nast Publications, The Adelphi,
1–11 John Adam Street, London WC2N 6HT
tel 020-7851 1800
website www.gq-magazine.co.uk
Editor Dylan Jones (until August 21)
Monthly £4.99

Style, fashion and general interest magazine for men.
Illustrations: b&w and colour photos, line drawings,
cartoons. Payment: by arrangement. Founded 1988.

Granta

12 Addison Avenue, London W11 4QR
tel 020-7605 1360
website www.granta.com
Twitter @GrantaMag
Editor Sigrid Rausing
Quarterly £34 p.a.

Original literary fiction, poetry, non-fiction, memoir,
reportage and photography. Study magazine before
submitting work. No academic essays or reviews.
Note that submissions are accepted only via online
submissions system (https://granta.submittable.com/
submit). Length: determined by content. Illustrations:
photos and original artwork. Payment: by
arrangement. Founded 1889; reconceived 1979.

Grazia

Bauer Consumer Media, Academic House,
24–28 Oval Road, London NW1 7DT
email graziadaily@graziamagazine.co.uk
website https://graziadaily.co.uk/
Twitter @graziauk
Editor Hattie Brett
Weekly £2.75

Women's magazine with the latest trends, gossip,
fashion and news in bite-size pieces.

Greetings Today

(formerly Greetings Magazine)
Lema Publishing, 1 Churchgates, The Wilderness,
Berkhamsted, Herts. HP4 2AZ
tel (01442) 289930
email tracey@lemapublishing.co.uk
website www.greetingstoday.media/
Monthly Controlled circulation

Trade magazine with articles, features and news
related to the greeting card industry. Mainly written
in-house; some material taken from outside. Length:
varies. Illustrations: line, colour and b&w photos.
Payment: by arrangement.

The Grocer

William Reed Publishing Ltd, Broadfield Park,
Crawley, West Sussex RH11 9RT
tel (01293) 613400
website www.thegrocer.co.uk
Facebook www.facebook.com/TheGrocer
Twitter @TheGrocer

Group Editor Adam Leyland, *Editor of thegrocer.co.uk*
Carina Perkins
Weekly From £224 p.a. (digital; other rates are
available)

Trade journal: articles, news or illustrations of general
interest to the grocery and provision trades. Payment:
by arrangement. Founded 1861.

Grow Your Own

25 Phoenix Court, Hawkins Road,
Colchester CO2 8JY
tel (01206) 505979
email laura.hillier@aceville.co.uk
website www.growfruitandveg.co.uk
Editor Laura Hillier
Monthly £4.99

Magazine for kitchen gardeners of all levels of
expertise. Will consider unsolicited material.
Welcomes ideas for articles and features. Length:
1,000 words (articles), 1,500 words (features), 200
words (news). Illustrations: transparencies, colour
prints and digital images. Payment: varies.

Guitarist

Future plc, Quay House, The Ambury,
Bath BA1 1UA
tel (01225) 442244
website www.musicradar.com/guitarist
Editor Jamie Dickson
13 p.a. £7.49

Aims to improve readers' knowledge of the
instrument, help them make the right buying choices
and assist them in becoming a better player. Ideas for
articles welcome. Founded 1984.

Gutter

0/2, 258 Kenmure Street, Glasgow G41 2QY
email contactguttermagazine@gmail.com
website www.guttermag.co.uk
Twitter @Gutter_Magazine
Instagram @Gutter_Magazine
Managing Editor Kate MacLeary
Bi-annual From £14 p.a.

Award-winning print journal featuring new Scottish
and international poetry and prose. Invites
submissions of up to 3,000 words of fiction or 120
lines of poetry, and seeks provocative work that
challenges, reimagines or undermines the individual
or collective status quo. See website for more
information. No longer offering editorial review.

H&E naturist

Hawk Editorial Ltd, PO Box 545, Hull HU9 9JF
tel (01482) 342000
email editor@henaturist.net
website www.henaturist.net
Editor Sam Hawcroft
Monthly £4.99

Articles on naturist travel, clubs, beaches and naturist

lifestyle experiences from the UK and beyond. Length: 800–1,200 words. Illustrations: digital images featuring naturists in natural settings; also cartoons, humorous fillers and features with naturist themes. Payment: by negotiation but guidelines for contributors and basic payment rates available on request.

Harper's Bazaar

Hearst UK, House of Hearst, 30 Panton Street, London SW1Y 4AJ
tel 020-7439 5000
website www.harpersbazaar.co.uk
Editor-in-Chief Lydia Slater
Monthly £5.20

Features, fashion, beauty, art, theatre, films, travel, interior decoration – some commissioned. Founded 1867.

HCM

Leisure Media Company Ltd, Portmill House, Portmill Lane, Hitchin, Herts. SG5 1DJ
tel (01462) 431385
email healthclub@leisuremedia.com
website www.healthclubmanagement.co.uk
Editorial Contact Steph Eaves
11 p.a. From £67 p.a.

Europe's leading publication for the health and fitness industry, covering the latest news, interviews, new openings and trends across the public and private health and fitness sectors. Print and digital editions of the magazine are available, as is *Health Club Management Handbook*, an annual reference book for buyers and decision-makers in the health and fitness sector. Founded 1995 as *Health Club Management*.

Healthy

The River Group, Garden Floor, 16 Connaught Place, London W2 2ES
tel 020-7420 7000
email healthy@therivergroup.co.uk
website www.healthy-magazine.co.uk
Twitter @healthymag
Editorial Director Ellie Hughes
8 p.a. From £23.90 p.a.

Holland & Barrett magazine. Health and nutrition information, features, tips, news and recipes, all from a holistic health angle. Ideas from freelancers welcome, with a view to commissioning. It does not do product reviews, will not mention products not available in Holland & Barrett and cannot cite any brand names in the copy. Email ideas in first instance. Payment: by negotiation. Founded 1996.

Heat

Bauer Consumer Media, Academic House, 24–28 Oval Road, London NW1 7DT
email hcatEd@heatmag.com
website www.heatworld.com
Editor-in-Chief Julia Davis
Weekly £1.99

Features and news on entertainment and popular media. Founded 1999.

hedgerow: a journal of small poems

email hedgerowsubmission@gmail.com
website https://hedgerowhaiku.com
Editor Caroline Skanne
Quarterly £11 inc. postage (UK and US), £14 inc. postage (Europe and Canada), £17 (RoW)

Short-poetry journal dedicated to publishing an eclectic mix of new and established voices across the spectrum of the short poem, with particular attention to the constantly evolving forms of English-language haiku, senryu and tanka. Includes original poems & artwork. Four submission windows (see website for up-to-date details).

Two sections are available to read for free online: hedgerow: young voices (haiku and related short poems by poets under 16); hedgerow: vines (collaborative poems, sequences, linked forms & articles).

Hello!

Wellington House, 69–71 Upper Ground, London SE1 9PQ
tel 020-7667 8700
website www.hellomagazine.com
Twitter @hellomag
Editor-in-Chief Rosie Nixon
Weekly £2.50

News-based features – showbusiness, celebrity, royalty; exclusive interviews. Illustrated. Payment: by arrangement. Founded 1988.

Here Comes Everyone

email raef@hcemagazine.com
website www.hcemagazine.com
Facebook HCEmagazine
Twitter @HereComesEvery1
Editors Mairnan Barton, Raef Boylan
Triannual £5

Original prose, poetry, non-fiction and art written to fit a theme. Submissions are accepted via online submissions form on the website (see above; submissions guidelines available here too). Current and past issues can be purchased in print and digital forms, and an archive of older issues can also be previewed online.

Hi-Fi News

MyTime Media Ltd, Enterprise House, Enterprise Way, Edenbridge, Kent TN8 6HF
tel 0844 848 8822
email paul.miller@hifinews.com
website www.hifinews.com

Editor Paul Miller
Monthly From £32 p.a. (digital), £45.75 (print)

Articles on all aspects of high-quality sound recording and reproduction; also extensive record review section and supporting musical feature articles. Audio matter is essentially technical, but should be presented in a manner suitable for music lovers interested in the nature of sound. Length: 2,000–3,000 words. Illustrations: line, half-tone. Payment: by arrangement. Founded 1956.

High Life

Cedar Communications Ltd, 9th Floor, Bankside 3, 90-100 Southwark Street, London SE1 0SW
tel 020-7550 8000
email high.life@cedarcom.co.uk
website www.cedarcom.co.uk
Global Content Director Gina Roughan
Bi-monthly

Inflight consumer magazine for British Airways passengers. Articles on entertainment, travel, fashion, business, sport and lifestyle. Founded 1973.

History Today

2nd Floor, 9 Staple Inn, London WC1V 7QH
tel 020-3219 7810
email admin@historytoday.com
website www.historytoday.com
Editor Paul Lay
Monthly £6.50

History in the widest sense – political, economic, social, biography, relating past to present; world history as well as British. Length: 3,500–4,000 words (feature articles); 1,300–2,200 words (mid-length features); 600–1,000 words (news/views). Do not send original material until publication is agreed. Accepts freelance contributions dealing with genuinely new historical and archaeological research. Payment: by arrangement. Founded 1951.

Homes & Gardens

Future plc, 161 Marsh Wall, London E14 9AP
tel 020-3148 5000
email HomesAndGardens@futurenet.com
website www.homesandgardens.com
Twitter @homesandgardens
Editorial Director Sarah Spiteri
Monthly £4.99

Articles on home interest or design, particularly well-designed British interiors (snapshots should be submitted). Length: 900–1,000 words (articles). Illustrations: all types. Payment: generous, but exceptional work required; varies. Founded 1919.

Horla

email horlamagazine@hotmail.com
website www.horla.org
Editor Matthew G. Rees

Online literary journal, which describes itself as 'the home of intelligent horror'. Accepts flash fiction and short stories of between 1,000 and 4,500 words. See website for full submission details, including authors Horla regards as relevant to its genre. Word documents only are accepted.

Horse & Hound

Future plc, Pinehurst 2, Pinehurst Road, Farnborough Business Park, Farnborough, Hants GU14 7BF
email pippa.roome@futurenet.com
website www.horseandhound.co.uk
Editor-in-Chief Sarah Jenkins, *Magazine Editor* Pippa Roome, *Website Editor* Carol Phillips
Weekly £2.99

News, reports, features and opinion, covering all areas of equestrianism, particularly the Olympic disciplines of eventing, showjumping and dressage, plus showing and hunting. Payment: by negotiation.

Horse & Rider

DJ Murphy Publishers Ltd, Olive Studio, Grange Road, Tilford, Farnham, Surrey GU10 2DQ
tel (01428) 601020
email editor@djmurphy.co.uk
website www.horseandrideruk.com
Twitter @HorseandRiderUK
Content Editor Louise Kittle
Monthly £4.25

Covers all forms of equestrian activity at home and abroad. Good writing and technical accuracy essential. Length: 1,500–2,000 words. Illustrations: photos and drawings, the latter usually commissioned. Payment: by arrangement. Founded 1959.

Hortus

Bryan's Ground, Stapleton, Nr Presteigne, Herefordshire LD8 2LP
tel (01544) 260001
email all@hortus.co.uk
email d.a.wheeler@hotmail.com
website www.hortus.co.uk
Editor David Wheeler
Quarterly £38 plus postage

Articles on decorative horticulture: plants, gardens, history, design, literature, people; book reviews. Length: 1,500–5,000 words, longer by arrangement. Illustrations: line, half-tone and wood-engravings. Payment: by arrangement. Founded 1987.

Hot Press

100 Capel Street, Dublin 1, Republic of Ireland
tel +353 (0)1 2411500
email info@hotpress.ie
website www.hotpress.com
Twitter @hotpress
Editor Niall Stokes
Fortnightly €5.95

High-quality, investigative stories, or punchily written offbeat pieces, of interest to 16–39 year-olds, including politics, music, sport, sex, and religion. Length: varies. Illustrations: colour with some b&w. Payment: by negotiation. Founded 1977.

House & Garden

The Condé Nast Publications Ltd, Vogue House, Hanover Square, London W1S 1JU
email houseandgarden@condenast.co.uk
website www.houseandgarden.co.uk
Editor Hatta Byng
Monthly £4.90

Articles (always commissioned), on subjects relating to domestic architecture, interior decorating, furnishing, gardens and gardening, exhibitions, travel, food and wine.

House Beautiful

Hearst UK, House of Hearst, 30 Panton Street, London SW1Y 4AJ
tel 020-7439 5000
email house.beautiful@hearst.co.uk
website www.housebeautiful.com/uk/
Group Editorial Director Gaby Huddart
Monthly £4.75

Specialist features for the homes of today. Unsolicited submissions are not accepted. Illustrated. Founded 1989.

Housebuilder

27 Broadwall, London SE1 9PL
tel 020-7960 1630
email info@house-builder.co.uk
website www.house-builder.co.uk
Twitter @housebuildermag
Publishing Director Ben Roskrow
10 p.a. Free to read online

Official Journal of the Home Builders Federation published in association with the National House-Building Council. Technical articles on design, construction and equipment of dwellings, estate planning and development, and technical aspects of house-building, aimed at those engaged in house and flat construction and the development of housing estates. Preliminary letter advisable. Length: articles from 500 words, preferably with illustrations. Illustrations: photos, plans, construction details, cartoons. Payment: by arrangement.

Icon Magazine

Media 10, Crown House, 151 High Road, Loughton, Essex IG10 4LF
tel 020-3235 5200
email icon@icon-magazine.co.uk
website www.iconeye.com
Editor Francesca Perry
Monthly From £27.99 p.a.

Articles on new buildings, interiors, innovative design and designers. Payment by negotiation. Founded 2003.

Ideal Home

Future plc, 161 Marsh Wall, London E14 9AP
tel 020-3148 5000
email ideal_home@futurenet.com
website www.idealhome.co.uk
Twitter @idealhome
Editorial Director Rhoda Parry
Monthly £4.75

Lifestyle magazine, articles usually commissioned. Contributors advised to study editorial content before submitting material. Illustrations: usually commissioned. Payment: according to material. Founded 1920.

The Idler

Great Western Studios, Unit 7, 65 Alfred Road, London W2 5EU
tel 020-3176 7907
email mail@idler.co.uk
email art@idler.co.uk
website www.idler.co.uk
Founder Tom Hodgkinson, *Programming Director* Victoria Hull, *Art Director* Alice Smith
Bi-monthly £9

Magazine dedicated to 'the art of living'. Includes a range of features and articles on topics from film to music, business and eating out, as well as readers' letters and diary pieces. Also runs online courses and stages live events in London. Unsolicited material rarely commissioned, but ideas may be emailed to the Editor. Illustrators may send their portfolio to the Art Director via the second email address given above.

Improve Your Coarse Fishing

Bauer Media Group, Media House, Lynch Wood, Peterborough Business Park, Peterborough PE2 6EA
tel (01733) 395104
email james.furness@bauermedia.co.uk
website www.anglingtimes.co.uk/magazines/improve-your-coarse-fishing/
Editor James Furness
13 p.a. £3.99

Articles on technique and equipment, the best venues, news and features. Ideas welcome by email. Founded 1991.

The Independent Publishing Magazine

website www.theindependentpublishingmagazine.com
Facebook www.facebook.com/TheIndependentPublishingMagazine
Twitter @theindiepubmag
Editor-in-Chief Mick Rooney

Online magazine for writers and publishers with a focus on providing essential information, news, resources, reviews of publishing service providers and an overview of the changing landscape of the publishing industry. Provides a regularly updated publishing service index. Guest posts welcome, but see website for full guidelines. Also offers one-on-one online consultancy services: see website for details. Founded 2007.

Index on Censorship

Fourth Floor Rear, Autograph, 1 Rivington Place, London EC2A 3BA
email info@indexoncensorship.org
website www.indexoncensorship.org
Twitter @IndexCensorship
Head of Content Jemimah Steinfeld
Quarterly £35 p.a. (print), £18 p.a. (digital)

Articles of up to 3,000 words dealing with all aspects of free speech and political censorship. Illustrations: b&w, cartoons. Payment: £200 per 1,000 words. Founded 1972.

Ink Sweat & Tears

website www.inksweatandtears.co.uk
Facebook www.facebook.com/InkSweatandTears
Twitter @InkSweatTears
Instagram @insta.inksweatandtears
Editor Helen Ivory, *Publisher* Kate Birch
Online

Poetry, short prose and word and image webzine. Accepts previously unpublished submissions of up to 750 words. Publishes something new every day. Has a paid editing internship programme for writers from the Black, Asian, Latinx, Mixed and other minority ethnic communities and a 'Pick of the Month' feature voted for by readers.

Publishes both new and more established writers and welcomes submissions of well-written reviews. The IS&T Commission Competition is open every two to three years, to write a pamphlet of poems published by IS&T Press; 2014 co-winner Jay Bernard's 'The Red and Yellow Nothing' was shortlisted for the 2016 Ted Hughes Award. 2017 winners Jo Young ('Firing Pins') and Gail McConnell ('Fothermather') were shortlisted for the 2020 Saboteur and Michael Marks awards, respectively.

Inside Soap

Hearst UK, House of Hearst, 30 Panton Street, London SW1Y 4AJ
tel 020-7439 5000
email editor@insidesoap.co.uk
website www.insidesoap.co.uk
Facebook www.facebook.com/insidesoap
Twitter @InsideSoapMag
Editor Steven Murphy
Weekly £2.20

Gossip and celebrity interviews with soap and popular TV characters on terrestrial and satellite channels. Submit ideas by email in first instance. Payment: by negotiation.

Inspire Magazine

CPO, Garcia Estate, Canterbury Road, Worthing, West Sussex BN13 1BW
tel (01903) 264556
email editor@inspiremagazine.org.uk
website www.inspiremagazine.org.uk
Twitter @inspirestories
Editor Russ Bravo
8–10 p.a. Free/donation; available in churches

Magazine with 'good news' stories of Christian faith in action and personal testimonies. Length: 400–700 words (features). Freelance articles used rarely. Payment: by arrangement.

Insurance Age

InfoPro Digital Services, 133 Houndsditch, London EC3A 7BX
tel 020-7316 9458
email sian.barton@infopro-digital.com
website www.insuranceage.co.uk
Editor Siân Barton, *News Editor* Ida Axling
10 p.a. £150 p.a. (free to FCA registered brokers)

News and features on general insurance and the broker market, personal, commercial, health and Lloyd's of London. Payment: by negotiation. Founded 1979.

Insurance Post

InfoPro Digital Services, 133 Houndsditch, London EC3A 7BX
tel 020-7316 9000
email postonline@infopro-digital.com
website www.postonline.co.uk
Editor Stephanie Denton
Weekly From £1,195 p.a.

Commissioned specialist articles on topics of interest to insurance professionals in the UK, Europe and Asia; news. Illustrations: colour photos and illustrations, colour cartoons and line drawings. Payment: by negotiation. Founded 1840.

InterMedia

International Institute of Communications, Highlands House, 165 Broadway, London SW19 1NE
email enquiries@iicom.org
website www.iicom.org
Editor Sophie Kowald
Quarterly Free to IIC members

International journal concerned with policies, events, trends and research in the field of communications, broadcasting, telecommunications and associated issues, particularly cultural and social. Founded 1970.

International Affairs

The Royal Institute of International Affairs, Chatham House, 10 St James's Square, London SW1Y 4LE
tel 020-7957 5728

email adorman@chathamhouse.org
website www.chathamhouse.org/publications/ia
Twitter @ChathamHouse
Editor Professor Andrew Dorman
6 issues p.a. From £42 p.a. (individuals), or from
£637 p.a. (institutions)

Peer-reviewed academic articles on international
affairs; up to 50 books reviewed in each issue.
Unsolicited articles welcome; submissions on
ScholarOne: mc.manuscriptcentral.com/inta. Article
length: 7,000-10,000 words. Illustrations: none.
Payment: by arrangement. Founded 1922.

The Interpreter's House
6/12 Commercial Wharf, Edinburgh EH6 6LF
email interpretershousesubmissions@gmail.com
website https://theinterpretershouse.org
Twitter @theinterpreter6
Editor Georgi Gill, *Assistant Editor* Andrew Wells,
Poetry Editor Louise Peterkin, *Fiction Editors* Annie
Rutherford, Lizzie Fowler
2 p.a. (April/October) online

Poetry, short stories, flash fiction and reviews. Online
only. Send sae with submissions; online submissions
preferred (however, see website for guidelines and
submission windows). Payment: none for
contributors currently but their work will be
promoted via social media channels.

Interzone
TTA Press, 5 Martins Lane, Ely, Cambs. CB6 2LB
website www.ttapress.com
Twitter @TTAPress
Bi-monthly £4.99

Science fiction and fantasy short stories, articles,
interviews and reviews. Read magazine before
submitting. Length: 2,000–6,000 words. Illustrations:
colour. Payment: by arrangement. Founded 1982.

Investors Chronicle
Bracken House, 1 Friday Street, London EC4M 9BT
tel 020-7873 3000
email ic.cs@ft.com
website www.investorschronicle.co.uk
Editor John Hughman
Weekly £155 p.a.

Journal covering investment and personal finance.
Occasional outside contributions for features are
accepted. Payment: by negotiation.

Ireland's Own
Channing House, Upper Rowe Street,
Wexford Y35 TH2A, Republic of Ireland
tel +353 (0)53 9140140
email info@irelandsown.ie
website www.irelandsown.ie
Editor Seán Nolan, *Assistant Editor* Shea Tomkins
Weekly €1.90, Monthly specials €3.10

Short stories: non-experimental, traditional with an
Irish orientation (1,800–2,000 words); articles of
interest to Irish readers at home and abroad (750–800
words); general and literary articles (750–800 words).
Monthly special bumper editions, each devoted to a
particular seasonal topic. Suggestions for new features
considered. Payment: varies according to quality and
length. Founded 1902.

Irish Arts Review
Tower 3, Fumbally Court, Fumbally Lane,
Dublin DO8 TXY8, Republic of Ireland
tel +353 (0)1 6766711
email news@irishartsreview.com
website www.irishartsreview.com
Twitter @IrishArtsReview
Editor Brigid Mulcahy
Quarterly €75 p.a. (UK and Europe), €80 p.a. (US),
€90 p.a. (RoW)

Magazine committed to promoting Irish art and
heritage around the world with reviews of Irish
painting, design, heritage, sculpture, architecture,
photography and decorative arts. To submit info on
Irish Art Exhibitions overseas, email:
production@irishartsreview.com

Irish Farmers Journal
Irish Farm Centre, Bluebell, Dublin D12 YXW5,
Republic of Ireland
tel +353 (0)1 4199530
email edit@farmersjournal.ie
website www.farmersjournal.ie
Editor Justin McCarthy
Weekly From €9.99 per month

Readable, technical articles on any aspect of farming.
Length: 700–1,000 words. Payment: £100–£150 per
article. Illustrated. Founded 1948.

Irish Journal of Medical Science
Royal Academy of Medicine in Ireland,
Setanta House, 2nd Floor, Setanta Place, Dublin 2,
Republic of Ireland
tel +353 (0)1 6334820
email selene.carey@springernature.com
website www.springer.com/journal/11845
Editor William P. Tormey
Quarterly £69 p.a. (individual, online)

Official publication of the Royal Academy of
Medicine in Ireland. Original contributions in
medicine, surgery, midwifery, public health, etc;
reviews of professional books, reports of medical
societies, etc. Illustrations: line, half-tone, colour.

Irish Medical Times
23 Fitzwilliam Street Upper, Dublin 2, D02 DF75,
Republic of Ireland
tel +353 (0)1 8176300
email editor@imt.ie
website www.imt.ie
Editor Terence Cosgrave

Weekly Free to medical professionals, otherwise €298 p.a. (Republic of Ireland), €434 p.a. (UK)

Medical articles. Opinion column length: 850–1,000 words.

Irish Pages: A Journal of Contemporary Writing

129 Ormeau Road, Belfast BT7 1SH
tel 028-9043 4800
email editor@irishpages.org
website www.irishpages.org
Twitter @irishpages
Editors Chris Agee, Kathleen Jamie, Cathal Ó Searcaigh, Meg Bateman
Bi-annual £20 p.a.

Poetry, short fiction, essays, creative non-fiction, memoir, essay reviews, nature writing, translated work, literary journalism, and other autobiographical, historical and scientific writing of literary distinction. Publishes in equal measure writing from Ireland and abroad. Accepts unsolicited submissions by post only. Payment: pays only for certain commissions and occasional serial rights. Founded 2002.

The Irish Post

88 Fenchurch Street, London EC3M 4BY
tel 020-8900 4137
email editor@irishpost.co.uk
website www.irishpost.co.uk
Twitter @theirishpost
Managing Editor Fiona Audley
Weekly £1.50

Coverage of all political, social and sporting events relevant to the Irish community in Britain. Also contains a guide to Irish entertainment in Britain. Annual events include The Irish Post Awards. The Post also has links to some of the biggest Irish festivals and events in Britain, including the Mayor of London St Patrick's Day Festival and the GAA All-Britain Competition. Among The Irish Post's annual magazines are *Building Britain*, which promotes the Irish construction industry; *Companies100*, a guide to the top one hundred Irish companies in Britain; and *In Business*, an informative list of Irish business leaders across Britain. Founded 1970.

Irish Tatler

Irish Studio Media Publishing Ltd,
Drumcliffe House, 47 Stephens Place, Dublin 2,
D02 NX78
website www.irishtatler.com
Twitter @irishtatler
Editor Sarah Macken
Monthly From €149 p.a.

General interest women's magazine: fashion, beauty, interiors, cookery, current affairs, reportage and celebrity interviews. Length: 2,000–4,000 words. In association with ivenus.com. Payment: by arrangement.

Jane's Defence Weekly

Sentinel House, 163 Brighton Road, Coulsdon, Surrey CR5 2YH
tel 020-3253 2100
website www.janes.com
Editor Peter Felstead
Weekly From £395 p.a.

International defence news; military equipment; budget analysis, industry, military technology, business, political, defence market intelligence. Illustrations: colour. Payment: minimum £200 per 1,000 words used. Founded 1984.

Jewish Chronicle

915 High Rd, London N12 8QJ
tel 020-7415 1500
email editor@thejc.com
website www.thejc.com
Twitter @JewishChron
Editor Stephen Pollard
Weekly £159 p.a. (print and digital)

Authentic and exclusive news stories and articles of Jewish interest from 500–1,500 words are considered. Includes a lively arts and leisure section and regular travel pages. Illustrations: of Jewish interest, either topical or feature. Payment: by arrangement. Founded 1841.

Jewish Telegraph

Telegraph House, 11 Park Hill, Bury Old Road, Prestwich, Manchester M25 0HH
tel 0161 740 9321
email manchester@jewishtelegraph.com
The Galehouse Business Centre, Chapel Allerton, Leeds LS7 4RF
tel 0113 295 6000
email leeds@jewishtelegraph.com
120 Childwall Road, Liverpool L15 6WU
tel 0151 475 6666
email liverpool@jewishtelegraph.com
May Terrace, Giffnock, Glasgow G46 6LD
tel 0141 621 4422
email glasgow@jewishtelegraph.com
website www.jewishtelegraph.com
Facebook www.facebook.com/jewishtelegraph/
Twitter @JewishTelegraph
Editor Paul Harris
Weekly Price varies per location

Non-fiction articles of Jewish interest, especially humour. Exclusive Jewish news stories and pictures, international, national and local. Length: 1,000–1,500 words. Illustrations: line, half-tone, cartoons. Payment: by arrangement. Founded 1950.

Kent Life

c/o Sussex Life, 28 Teville Road, Worthing BN11 1UG
tel (01903) 703730

email anna.lambert@archant.co.uk
website www.kent-life.co.uk/home
Facebook www.facebook.com/kentlife
Twitter @kentlife
Editor Anna Lambert
Monthly £3.99

Local lifestyle magazine, celebrating the best of county life. Features local people, entertainment, Kent towns, walks, history and heritage. Welcomes ideas for articles and features, length: 1,000 words. Illustrations: hi-res jpgs. Payment: contact editor. Founded 1962.

Kerrang!

Wasted Talent, 90–92 Pentonville Road, London N1 9HS
email feedback@kerrang.com
website www.kerrang.com
Twitter @KerrangMagazine
Editor Sam Coare
Weekly £3.50

News, reviews and interviews; music with attitude. All material commissioned. Illustrations: colour. Payment: by arrangement. Founded 1981.

Kitchen Garden

Mortons Media Group Ltd, Media Centre, Morton Way, Horncastle, Lincs. LN9 6JR
tel (01507) 529396
email sott@mortons.co.uk
website www.kitchengarden.co.uk
Editor Steve Ott
Monthly £5.99

Magazine for people with a passion for growing their own vegetables, fruit and herbs. Includes practical tips and inspirational ideas. Specially commissions most material. Welcomes ideas for articles and features. Length: 700–2,000 (articles/features). Illustrations: colour transparencies, jpgs, prints and artwork; all commissioned. Payment: varies. Founded 1997.

The Lady

The Kinetic Business Centre, Theobald Street, Borehamwood WD6 4PJ
tel 020-7379 4717
email editors@lady.co.uk
website www.lady.co.uk
Facebook www.facebook.com/TheLadyMagazine
Twitter @TheLadyMagazine
Editor Maxine Frith
Fortnightly £5.75

Features, interviews, comment, columns, arts and book reviews, fashion, beauty, interiors, cookery, health, travel and pets. Plus classified ads, holiday cottages and pages of puzzles. Brief pitches by email preferably. Founded 1885.

The Lancet

125 London Wall, London EC2Y 5AS
tel 020-7424 4922
email editorial@lancet.com
website www.thelancet.com
Twitter @TheLancet
Editor Dr Richard Horton
Weekly From £181 p.a.

Research papers, review articles, editorials, correspondence and commentaries on international medicine, medical research and policy. Material may be submitted directly through a dedicated online system. Founded 1823.

LandScape Magazine

Bauer Media, Media House, Lynchwood, Peterborough PE2 6EA
tel (01733) 468000
email landscape@bauermedia.co.uk
website www.landscapemagazine.co.uk
Editor Rachel Hawkins
Monthly £4.60

Seasonal content covering gardening, cookery, history and heritage, craft, travel, walks and country matters.

The Lawyer

79 Wells Street, London W1T 3QN
tel 020-7970 4000
email editorial@thelawyer.com
website www.thelawyer.com
Editor Catrin Griffiths
Weekly From £549 p.a.

News, articles, features and views relevant to the legal profession. Length: 600–900 words. Illustrations: as agreed. Payment: £125–£150 per 1,000 words. Founded 1987.

Legal Week

18 King William St, Candlewick, London EC4N 7BP
tel 020-3875 0662
website www.law.com/international-edition/region/uk-legal-week/
Editor-in-Chief Paul Hodkinson
Online From £455

News and features aimed at business lawyers. Length: 750–1,000 words (features), 300 words (news). Considers unsolicited material and welcomes ideas for articles and features. Founded 1999.

Leisure Painter

Caxton House, 63–65 High Street, Tenterden, Kent TN30 6BD
tel (01580) 763315
email ingrid@tapc.co.uk
website www.painters-online.co.uk
Editor Ingrid Lyon
Every four weeks £4.80

Instructional articles on painting and fine art.

Payment: £75 per 1,000 words. Illustrations: line, half-tone, colour, original artwork. Founded 1967.

LGC (Local Government Chronicle)
EMAP, Telephone House, 69–77 Paul Street, London EC2A 4NW
tel 020-3033 2787
email lgcnews@emap.com
website www.lgcplus.com
Editor Nick Golding
Weekly From £290 p.a.

Aimed at senior managers in local government. Covers politics, management issues, social services, education, regeneration, industrial relations and personnel, plus public sector finance and Scottish and Welsh local government. Length: 1,000 words (features). Illustrations: b&w and colour, cartoons. Payment: by arrangement. Founded 1855.

Life and Work: The Magazine of the Church of Scotland
121 George Street, Edinburgh EH2 4YN
tel 0131 225 5722
email magazine@lifeandwork.org
website www.lifeandwork.org
Editor Lynne McNeil
Monthly £3 (print), £1.99 (digital download)

Articles not exceeding 1,200 words and news; occasional stories and poetry. Study the magazine and contact the Editor first. Illustrations: photos and colour illustrations. Payment: by arrangement.

Lighthouse Literary Journal
71 Rosary Road, Norwich NR1 1SZ
email submissions@lighthouse.gatehousepress.com
website www.gatehousepress.com/lighthouse
Poetry Editors Andrew McDonnell, Julia Webb, Meirion Jordan, Jo Surzyn, Adam Warne; *Prose Editors* Anna De Vaul, Helen Rye, James Smart; *Art Editor* Natty Peterkin
Quarterly £28 p.a. plus postage

Publishes poetry, short fiction and artwork from new writers/artists from within the UK and beyond. Submissions by email only; see website for details. Payment: none at present, but all published receive a free copy of the journal and are able to purchase more at a discounted rate. Founded 2012.

Lincolnshire Life
County House, 9 Checkpoint Court, Sadler Road, Lincoln LN6 3PW
tel (01522) 527127
email studio@lincolnshirelife.co.uk
website www.lincolnshirelife.co.uk
Monthly

Articles and news of county interest. Approach in writing. Length: up to 1,500 words. Illustrations: colour photos and line drawings. Payment: varies. Founded 1961.

The Linguist
The Chartered Institute of Linguists, 7th Floor, 167 Fleet Street, London EC4A 2EA
tel 020-7940 3100
email linguist.editor@ciol.org.uk
website www.ciol.org.uk
Twitter @Linguist_CIOL
Editor Miranda Moore
Bi-monthly Free online to CIOL members or from £55 p.a.

Articles of interest to professional linguists in translating, interpreting and teaching fields. Most contributors have special knowledge of the subjects with which they deal. Articles usually contributed, but payment by arrangement. Length: 800–2,000 words.

Literary Review
44 Lexington Street, London W1F 0LW
tel 020-7437 9392
email editorial@literaryreview.co.uk
website www.literaryreview.co.uk
Facebook www.facebook.com/LiteraryReviewLondon
Twitter @lit_review
Editor Nancy Sladek
Monthly (double issue December/January) £4.99

Reviews, articles of cultural interest, interviews and profiles. Material mostly commissioned. Length: articles and reviews 800–1,500 words. Illustrations: line and b&w photos. Payment: by arrangement; none for illustrations. Founded 1979.

Litro
90 York Way, London N1 9AG
email info@litro.co.uk
website www.litro.co.uk
Publisher and Editor-in-Chief Eric Akoto
Monthly £44 p.a.

Literary magazine featuring fiction, non-fiction, reviews, articles of cultural interest, interviews, profiles and a monthly short story competition. Length: short stories, 2,500 words; articles and reviews, 800–1,500 words. Illustrations: line and b&w photos. Founded 2006.

Little White Lies
TCO London, 71A Leonard Street, London EC2A 4QS
tel 020-7729 3675
email hello@tcolondon.com
website https://lwlies.com/
Editor David Jenkins
5 p.a. From £27 p.a.

Independent movie magazine that features cutting-edge writing, illustration and photography to get under the skin of cinema. Also explores the worlds of music, art, politics and pop culture as part of its mission to reshape the debate across the movie landscape. Length: various. Illustrations and photography. Payment: varies for illustration, articles and reviews. Founded 2005.

Living Plantfully

email editor@livingplantfully.co.uk
website www.livingplantfully.co.uk
Facebook www.facebook.com/livemoreplantfully
Twitter @LivePlantfully
Editor Lindsey Harrod

Online magazine embracing food, nutrition, health and wellness, growing and gardening, sustainability and eco issues, focusing on a holistic plant-centred lifestyle. Guest contributions and collaborations are welcome; contact the editor for guidelines.

The London Magazine: A Review of Literature and the Arts

Administration 11 Queen's Gate, London SW7 5EL
email info@thelondonmagazine.org
website www.thelondonmagazine.org
Editors Steven O'Brien, Matthew Scott
Bi-monthly £6.95

The UK's oldest literary magazine. Poems, stories (2,000–5,000 words), memoirs, critical articles, features on art, photography, theatre, music, architecture, etc. Submission guidelines available online. Founded 1732.

London Review of Books

28 Little Russell Street, London WC1A 2HN
tel 020-7209 1101
email edit@lrb.co.uk
website www.lrb.co.uk
Twitter @LRB
Editors Jean McNicol and Alice Spawls, *Consulting Editor* Mary-Kay Wilmers
Fortnightly £4.75

Features, essays, poems. Payment: by arrangement.

Long Poem Magazine

20 Spencer Rise, London NW5 1AP
email longpoemmagazine@gmail.com
website www.longpoemmagazine.org.uk
Facebook www.facebook.com/groups/longpoemmagazine
Twitter @LongPoemMag
Editor Linda Black, *Deputy Editor* Claire Crowther
2 p.a. £10.50 (UK, inc. p&p), £18 (RoW, inc. p&p)

Published in May and October each year. Offers a wide range of poetry, including sequences and translations, plus one essay per issue on an aspect of the long poem. Also publishes online reviews. See website for up-to-date details of current submission windows. Send no more than two original, unpublished poems of at least 75 lines each inside the dates indicated, by email only. Simultaneous submissions not accepted. Contributors should familiarise themselves with the magazine before sending in material. Founded 2008.

Lothian Life

4/8 Downfield Place, Edinburgh EH11 2EW
tel 07905 614402
email office@lothianlife.co.uk
website www.lothianlife.co.uk
Twitter @LothianLife
Editor Anne Hamilton
Online publication only

Articles, profiles, etc with a Lothians angle. Length: 500–2,000 words. Payment terms can be found on the website. Founded 1995.

The Mace

Unit 3 & 4 Croxted Mews, 286–288 Croxted Road, London SE24 9DA
email editor@macemagazine.com
website https://macemagazine.com/contact
Twitter @MaceMagazine
Editor-in-Chief William Cash, *Deputy Editor* Emilia Wild, *Digital Editor* Ferdie Rous
Online and quarterly print Digital access free, digital + print £39.95 p.a.

Politics and public affairs magazine. Sets out to take a 'cross-party view on the Business of Politics'. Founded 2020.

Magma Poetry

23 Pine Walk, Carshalton SM5 4ES
email info@magmapoetry.com
website https://magmapoetry.com
website https://magmapoetry.submittable.com/submit
Twitter @magmapoetry
Chair Lisa Kelly
3 p.a. £8.50 (inc. p&p), £22 p.a. (inc. p&p)

Magazine of contemporary poetry and writing about poetry including reviews, each issue of which has a different editor and theme (see website for details). Features new and established writers: recent contributors include Simon Armitage, Jackie Kay, Mona Arshi, Leo Boix, Jen Hadfield, Kathryn Maris and Andrew McMillan. Previously unpublished poems are welcome via Submittable (see above) or (from UK writers only) by post, but potential contributors should check the website first for calls for submission and any specific requirements.

Management Today

Bridge House, 69 London Road, Twickenham, TW1 3SP
email adam.gale@haymarket.com
email kate.bassett@haymarket.com
website www.managementtoday.co.uk
Editor Adam Gale
Online From £23 per month

Company profiles and analysis, features up to 3,000 words. Payment: £350 per 1,000 words. Founded 1966.

Maritime Journal

Mercator Media Ltd, Spinnaker House,
Waterside Gardens, Fareham, Hants PO16 8SD
tel (01329) 825335
email editor@maritimejournal.com
website www.maritimejournal.com
Editor Jake Frith
Monthly £85 p.a.

Industry information and news for the European
commercial marine business. Also reviews products
and services. Founded 1987.

Marketing Week

Wells Point, 79 Wells Street, London W1T 3QN
tel 020-7970 4000
email mw.editorial@centaur.co.uk
website www.marketingweek.co.uk
Editor Russell Parsons
Weekly From £395 p.a.

Aimed at marketing management. Accepts occasional
features and analysis, but no bylined pieces. Length:
1,000–2,000 words. Payment: by arrangement.
Founded 1978.

MBUK (Mountain Biking UK)

Immediate Media Co., Tower House, Fairfax Street,
Bristol BS1 3BN
tel 0117 927 9009
email mbuk@immediate.co.uk
website www.mbuk.com
Editor James Costley-White
Every 4 weeks £5.99

Magazine for mountain bike enthusiasts with
features, reviews, news and world and domestic
racing coverage.

MCN (Motor Cycle News)

Bauer Media Group, Media House, Lynch Wood,
Peterborough Business Park, Peterborough PE2 6EA
tel 01733 468000
email mcn@motorcyclenews.com
website www.motorcyclenews.com
Editor Richard Newland
Weekly £2.75

Leading authority on all things motorbike – both in
print and online – from riding the latest models to
in-depth news investigations, up-to-the-minute
sports news and insight. Adheres to strict modern
journalism standards, with full fact-checking and
unique angles on all stories sourced and developed
through an extensive network of industry contacts
and biking community relationships. Founded 1955.

Medal News

Token Publishing Ltd, 40 Southernhay East, Exeter,
Devon EX1 1PE
tel (01404) 46972
email info@tokenpublishing.com
website www.tokenpublishing.com

Editor John Mussell
10 p.a. £4.20

Well-researched articles on military history with a
bias towards medals. Send text in digital form.
Length: up to 2,000 words. Illustrations: if possible.
Payment: by arrangement; none for illustrations.
Founded 1989.

Men's Fitness

Kelsey Media, The Granary, Downs Court,
Yalding Hill, Yalding, Kent ME18 6AL
email reception@kelsey.co.uk
website https://mensfitness.co.uk/
Twitter @MensFitnessMag
Editor Isaac Williams
Monthly £4.40

Magazine for men who want to get more out of their
lives, focusing on an upbeat, optimistic, proactive
lifestyle. Focuses on both mental and emotional
fitness.

Men's Health

Hearst UK, House of Hearst, 30 Panton Street,
London SW1Y 4AJ
email contact@menshealth.co.uk
website www.menshealth.co.uk
Editor-in-Chief Toby Wiseman
10 p.a. £4.30

Active pursuits, grooming, fitness, fashion, sex, career
and general men's interest issues. Length 1,000–4,000
words. Ideas welcome. No unsolicited MSS. Payment:
by arrangement. Founded 1994.

Methodist Recorder

1 Merchant Street, London E3 4LY
tel 020-7793 0033
email editorial@methodistrecorder.co.uk
website www.methodistrecorder.co.uk
Twitter @MethRecorder
Weekly £3.75

Methodist newspaper; ecumenically involved.
Limited opportunities for freelance contributors.
Preliminary contact advised. Founded 1861.

Mixmag

Wasted Talent, 90–92 Pentonville Road,
London N1 9HS
tel 020-7078 8400
email mixmag@mixmag.net
website www.mixmag.net
Twitter @Mixmag
Global Editorial Director Nick DeCosemo
Monthly £5.80

Dance music and clubbing magazine. No unsolicited
material. Illustrations: colour and b&w. Payment:
£200 per 1,000 words. Founded 1983.

MMM (The Motorhomers' Magazine)

Warners Group Publications Plc, The Maltings,
West Street, Bourne, Lincs. PE10 9PH

tel (01778) 391154
email danielattwood@warnersgroup.co.uk
website www.outandaboutlive.co.uk
Head of Content and Managing Editor Daniel Attwood
Every four weeks £5.25

Articles including motorcaravan travel, owner reports and DIY. Length: up to 2,500 words. Illustrations: line, half-tone, colour prints and transparencies, high-quality digital. Payment: by arrangement. Founded 1966 as *Motor Caravan and Camping*.

Model Boats

MyTime Media Ltd, Suite 25, Enterprise House, Enterprise Way, Edenbridge, Kent TN8 6HF
tel (01689) 869840
email editor@modelboats.co.uk
website www.modelboats.co.uk
Editor Lindsey Amrani
Monthly £5.85

Founded 1964.

Model Engineer

MyTime Media Ltd, Enterprise House, Enterprise Way, Edenbridge, Kent TN8 6HF
tel (01689) 869840
email mrevans@cantab.net
website www.model-engineer.co.uk
Editor Martin Evans
Fortnightly £4.20

Detailed description of the construction of engineering models, small workshop equipment, machine tools and small electrical and mechanical devices; articles on small power engineering, mechanics, electricity, workshop methods, clocks and experiments. Relevant event reporting and visits. Illustrations: line, half-tone, colour. Payment: up to £50 per page. Founded 1898.

Modern Language Review

Modern Humanities Research Association, Salisbury House, Station Road, Cambridge CB1 2LA
email mail@mhra.org.uk
email d.f.connon@swansea.ac.uk
website www.mhra.org.uk/journals/MLR
General Editor Professor Derek Connon
Quarterly

Articles and reviews of a scholarly or specialist character on English, Romance, Germanic and Slavonic languages, literatures and cultures. Payment: none, but electronic offprints are given. Founded 1905.

Modern Poetry in Translation

The Queen's College, Oxford OX1 4AW
email editor@mptmagazine.com
website www.modernpoetryintranslation.com
Twitter @mptmagazine
Editor Clare Pollard
3 p.a. £23 p.a.

Features the work of established and emerging poets and translators from around the world. Welcomes translated work that has not been published previously; contemporary pieces preferred. Up to six poems may be submitted. Potential contributors should familiarise themselves with the magazine before sending their work. See website to submit, for full guidelines and to keep up to date with open calls.

Mojo

Bauer Media Group, Endeavour House, 189 Shaftesbury Avenue, London WC2H 8JG
tel 020-7208 3443
email mojo@bauermedia.co.uk
email danny.eccleston@bauermedia.co.uk
website www.mojo4music.com
Editor-in-Chief John Mulvey, *Senior Editor* Danny Eccleston
Monthly £5.95

Serious rock music magazine: interviews, news and reviews of books, live shows and albums. Send pitches to the senior editor (address given above). Length: up to 10,000 words. Illustrations: colour and b&w photos, colour caricatures. Payment: £250 per 1,000 words; £200–£400 illustrations. Founded 1993.

MoneyWeek

Dennis Publishing, 31–32 Alfred Place, London WC1E 7DP
email editor@moneyweek.com
website www.moneyweek.com
Twitter @MoneyWeek
Editor-in-Chief Merryn Somerset Webb
Weekly £4.50

Economic analysis, investment recommendations and market tips, as well as in-depth looks at national and international politics. Founded 2000.

The Moth

Ardan Grange, Milltown, Belturbet, Co. Cavan, Republic of Ireland
tel +353 (0)8 72657251
email editor@themothmagazine.com
website www.themothmagazine.com
Facebook www.facebook.com/themothmagazine
Twitter @themothmagazine
Founders Rebecca O'Connor, Will Govan, *Editor* Rebecca O'Connor
Quarterly €7

Original poetry, short fiction and interviews alongside full-colour artwork. Submissions welcome, although potential contributors should familiarise themselves with the magazine first. Send no more than six poems and two short stories (max. 3,000 words) by email or post (with sae). Annual Moth Poetry Prize (€10,000 for a single unpublished poem, plus three runner-up prizes of €1,000), *Moth* Short Story Prize (first prize, €3,000; second prize, week-long retreat at Circle of Misse plus €250 stipend; and third prize, €1,000); the *Moth* Art Prize (€1,000 plus a two-week stay at The Moth Retreat); and the *Moth* Nature Writing Prize (€1,000 plus a week-long stay at The Moth Retreat). Also runs an artists' and writers' retreat and publishes a junior version, *The Caterpillar*. Founded 2010.

Motor Boat and Yachting

Future plc, Pinehurst 2, Farnborough Business Park, Farnborough, Hants GU14 7BF
tel (01252) 555159
email hugo.andreae@futurenet.com
website www.mby.com
Editor Hugo Andreae
Monthly £48.49 p.a.

General interest as well as specialist motor boating material welcomed. Features up to 2,000 words considered on all sea-going aspects. Payment: varies. Illustrations: hi-res photos. Founded 1904.

The Motorship

Mercator Media Ltd, Spinnaker House, Waterside Gardens, Fareham, Hants PO16 8SD
tel (01329) 825335
email editor@motorship.com
website www.motorship.com
Twitter @Motorship
Editor Nick Edström
11 p.a. £173 p.a.

News, information and insight for marine technology professionals.

Mslexia

PO Box 656, Newcastle upon Tyne NE99 1PZ
tel 0191 204 8860
email postbag@mslexia.co.uk
website www.mslexia.co.uk
Twitter @Mslexia
Editorial Director Debbie Taylor, *Books Editor* Danuta Kean
Quarterly £8.95

Magazine for women writers which combines features and advice about writing with new fiction and poetry by women. Considers unsolicited material within specific submission slots. Length: up to two short stories of no more than 2,200 words, up to four poems of no more than 40 lines each, in any style, or up to two short scripts of no more than 1,000 words, which must relate to current themes (or adhere to poetry or short story competition rules). Also accepts submissions for other areas of the magazine, including Mslexia Moths, Bedtime Stories, Poet Laureate, etc., variously themed and unthemed. Articles/features by negotiation. Illustrations: by commission only; email submissions welcome. Payment: by negotiation. Founded 1998.

Music Teacher

MA Education, St Jude's Church, Dulwich Road, London SE24 0PB

email harriet.clifford@markallengroup.com
website https://musicteachermagazine.co.uk/
Twitter @MusicTeacherMag
Editor Harriet Clifford
Monthly From £67 p.a.

Information and articles for both school and private instrumental teachers, including reviews of books, music, software and other music-education resources. Articles and illustrations must both have a teaching, as well as a musical, interest. Length: articles 600–1,700 words. Payment: by arrangement. Founded 1908.

Music Week

Future Publishing Ltd, 1–10 Praed Mews, London W2 1QY
tel 0330 390 6751
email mark.sutherland@futurenet.com
website www.musicweek.com
Weekly £179 p.a. (print)

News and features on all aspects of producing, manufacturing, marketing and retailing music, plus the live music business and all other aspects of the music industry. Payment: by negotiation. Founded 1959.

Musical Opinion

1 Exford Road, London SE12 9HD
tel 020-8857 1582
email musicalopinion@hotmail.co.uk
website www.musicalopinion.com
Editor Robert Matthew-Walker
Bi-monthly £28 p.a.

Suggestions for contributions of musical interest, scholastic, educational, anniversaries and ethnic. DVD, CD, opera, festival, book, music reviews. Illustrations: colour photos. Founded 1877.

Musical Times

7 Brunswick Mews, Hove, East Sussex BN3 1HD
email mted@gotadsl.co.uk
website http://themusicaltimes.blogspot.co.uk
Editor Antony Bye
4 p.a. £8.99

Musical articles, reviews, 500–6,000 words. All material commissioned; no unsolicited material. Check website to see if submissions are being considered. Illustrations: music. Founded 1844.

My Weekly

D.C. Thomson & Co. Ltd, 2 Albert Square, Dundee DD1 1DD
tel (01382) 223131
email myweekly@dcthomson.co.uk
website www.myweekly.co.uk
Twitter @My_Weekly
Editor Stuart Johnstone, *Assistant Editor* Sally Rodger, *Features Editor* Alison Graves, *Health Editor* Moira Chisholm, *Celebrity Editor* Susan Anderson, *Fiction Editor* Karen Byrom, *Digital Editor* Allison Hay

Weekly £1.40

Modern women's magazine aimed at 50+ age group. No unsolicited MSS considered. Send ideas or pitches to relevant department editor. Illustrations: colour. Payment by negotiation. Founded 1910.

The National Trust Magazine

The National Trust, Heelis, Kemble Drive, Swindon SN2 2NA
tel (01793) 817716
email magazine@nationaltrust.org.uk
website www.nationaltrust.org.uk
Editor Sally Palmer
3 p.a. Free to members

Lifestyle title with focus on the National Trust, encompassing interiors, gardens, food, UK travel, wildlife, environment, topical features and celebrity content. No unsolicited articles. Length: 1,000 words (features), 200 words (news). Illustrations: colour transparencies and artwork. Payment: by arrangement; picture library rates. Founded 1932.

Nature

Springer Nature, The Macmillan Building, 4 Crinan Street, London N1 9XW
tel 020-7833 4000
email nature@nature.com
website www.nature.com/nature
Editor-in-Chief Dr Magdalena Skipper
Weekly £199 p.a.

Devoted to scientific matters and to their bearing upon public affairs. All contributors of articles have specialised knowledge of the subjects with which they deal. Illustrations: full colour. Founded 1869.

NB magazine

c/o Agile Ideas, Studio 10, Glove Factory Studios, Brook Lane, Holt, Wilts. BA14 6RL
tel (01225) 302266
email info@nbmagazine.co.uk
website https://nbmagazine.co.uk
Managing Director Alistair Giles, *Managing Editor* Jade Craddock
4 p.a., from £34.99 (UK, including p&p)

Aimed at book lovers and book clubs. Includes extracts from new books, poems, original short stories and articles and features about and by authors, publishers, booksellers, reviewers, bloggers, librarians and more. A diverse range of genres are covered within the magazine, and readers voices and opinions are represented. Also covers news from the book world, including updates on awards and prizes. Alongside the basic magazine subscription, bespoke book subscription packages are also available.

Neon

email info@neonmagazine.co.uk
website www.neonmagazine.co.uk
Twitter @Neon_Lit_Mag

Editor Krishan Coupland
Bi-annual £6

Independent literary magazine publishing fiction, poetry, comics and photography. Print and digital editions. Slight speculative/sci-fi leanings. Prose: 400–5,000 words. Poetry: 10–60 lines. Illustrations: photographs. Payment: 1p/word for prose, 10p/line for poetry, £3.50 per image or comic page. Submissions are welcomed, but see website for up-to-date guidelines, as alternate issues are themed. Supporters of the magazine receive personalised feedback on submissions.

New Humanist

The Green House, 244–254 Cambridge Heath Road, London E2 9DA
tel 020-3633 4633
email editor@newhumanist.org.uk
website https://newhumanist.org.uk
Editor Samira Shackle
Quarterly £27 p.a. (print), £10 p.a. (digital)

Articles on current affairs, philosophy, science, the arts, literature, religion and humanism. Length: 750–4,000 words. Illustrations: colour photos. Payment: 10–20p per word. Founded 1885.

New Internationalist

The Old Music Hall, 106–108 Cowley Road, Oxford OX4 1JE
tel (01865) 403345
email ni@newint.org
website https://newint.org
Twitter @newint
Co-editors Hazel Healy, Dinyar Godrej, Amy Hall, Husna Rizvi
Bi-monthly £7.45

World issues, ranging from food to feminism to peace and the environment; one subject examined in each issue. Length: up to 2,000 words. Illustrations: line, half-tone, colour, cartoons. Payment: £250 per 1,000 words. Founded 1973.

New Law Journal

LexisNexis Butterworths, Lexis House, 30 Farringdon Street, London EC4A 4HH
tel 020-7400 2500
email newlaw.journal@lexisnexis.co.uk
website www.newlawjournal.co.uk
Twitter @newlawjournal
Editor Jan Miller
48 p.a. £442 p.a.

Articles and news on all aspects of civil litigation and dispute resolution. Length: up to 1,900 words. Payment: by arrangement.

New Scientist

25 Bedford Street, London WC2 9ES
tel 020-7611 1202

email enquiries@newscientist.com
website www.newscientist.com
Editor Emily Wilson
Weekly £4.50

Authoritative articles of topical importance on all aspects of science and technology. Potential contributors should study recent copies of the magazine and initially send only a 200-word synopsis of their idea. Illustrations: all styles, cartoons; contact art dept.

New Statesman

(formerly New Statesman & Society)
12–13 Essex Street, London WC2R 3AA
tel 020-7936 6400
email editorial@newstatesman.co.uk
website www.newstatesman.co.uk
Editor-in-Chief Jason Cowley, *Deputy Editor* Tom Gatti
Weekly £4.75

Interested in news, reportage and analysis of current political and social issues at home and overseas, plus book reviews, general articles and coverage of the arts, environment and science seen from the perspective of the British Left but written in a stylish, witty and unpredictable way. Length: strictly according to the value of the piece. Illustrations: commissioned for specific articles, although artists' samples considered for future reference; occasional cartoons. Payment: by agreement. Founded 1913.

New Welsh Reader

(formerly New Welsh Review)
PO Box 170, Aberystwyth, Ceredigion SY23 1WZ
tel (01970) 628410
email submissions@newwelshreview.com
website www.newwelshreview.com
Editor Gwen Davis
3 p.a. From £14.99 p.a.

Literary – critical articles, creative non-fiction, short stories, poems, book reviews and profiles. Especially, but not exclusively, concerned with Welsh writing in English. Length: up to 3,000 words (articles). Send by email or hard copy with a sae for return of material. Decisions within three months of submission. See website for information on New Welsh Writing Awards and *New Welsh Rarebyte* (ePub). Illustrations: colour. Payment: £68 per 1,000 words (articles); £28 per poem; £100 per short story; £47 per review. Founded 1988.

NME (New Musical Express)

(incorporating Melody Maker)
email editors@nme.com
website www.nme.com
website https://bandlabtechnologies.com/
Facebook www.facebook.com/nmemagazine
Twitter @nme
Online only

The latest music news, the best new bands, world exclusive features and new album reviews every week. Length: by arrangement. Preliminary letter or phone call desirable. Illustrations: action photos with strong news angle of recording personalities, cartoons. Payment: by arrangement. Founded 1952.

The North

email office@poetrybusiness.co.uk
website https://poetrybusiness.co.uk/about/submissions
Twitter @poetrybusiness
Editors Ann Sansom, Peter Sansom, Suzannah Evans
2 p.a. £10

Contemporary poetry from new and established writers, as well as book reviews, critical articles and a range of features. Up to six poems may be submitted online only; full information on submission windows given on the website.

Nursery World

MA Education, St Jude's Church, Dulwich Road, London SE24 0PB
tel 020-8501 6693
email liz.roberts@markallengroup.com
website www.nurseryworld.co.uk
Editor Liz Roberts
Fortnightly From £119 p.a.

For all grades of primary school, nursery and childcare staff, nannies, foster parents and all concerned with the care of expectant mothers, babies and young children. Authoritative and informative articles, 800 or 1,300 words, and photos on all aspects of child welfare and early education, from 0–8 years, in the UK. Practical ideas, policy news and career advice. No short stories. Illustrations: by arrangement. Payment: by arrangement.

Nursing Times

EMAP, Telephone House, 69–77 Paul Street, London EC2A 4NQ
tel 020-3953 2707
email steve.ford@emap.com
website www.nursingtimes.net
Twitter @nursingtimes
Twitter @nursingtimesed
Editor Steve Ford
Monthly From £23 + VAT per quarter

Articles of clinical interest, nursing education and nursing policy. Illustrated articles not longer than 2,000 words. Press day: first or last Friday of the month. Illustrations: photos, line. Payment: NUJ rates; by arrangement for illustrations. Founded 1905.

OK!

Northern & Shell Building, 10 Lower Thames Street, London EC3R 6EN
email kirsty.tyler@ok.co.uk
website www.ok.co.uk/home
Editor-in-Chief Caroline Waterston
Weekly £2.40

Exclusive celebrity interviews and photographs. Submit ideas in writing. Length: 1,000 words. Illustrations: colour. Payment: £150–£200 per feature. Founded 1993.

The Oldie

Moray House, 23–31 Great Titchfield Street, London W1W 7PA
tel 020-7436 8801
email editorial@theoldie.co.uk
website www.theoldie.co.uk
Editor Harry Mount
Monthly £4.75

General interest magazine reflecting attitudes of older people but aimed at a wider audience. Features (600–1,000 words) on all subjects, as well as articles for specific sections. Potential contributors should familiarise themselves with the magazine prior to submitting work. See website for further guidelines. Enclose sae for reply/return of MSS. No poetry. Illustrations: welcomes b&w and colour cartoons. Payment: approx. £250 per 850 words; £100 for cartoons. Founded 1992.

Olive

Immediate Media Co. Ltd, Vineyard House, 44 Brook Green, London W6 7BT
tel 020-7150 5000
website www.olivemagazine.com
Monthly £4.90

Upmarket food magazine which aims to encourage readers to cook, eat and explore. Each edition includes a range of recipes for both everyday and weekend cooking, as well as information on techniques, trends and tips; restaurant recommendations across the UK; and foodie-inspired travel ideas from around the world.

Opera

36 Black Lion Lane, London W6 9BE
tel 020-8563 8893
email editor@opera.co.uk
website www.opera.co.uk
Editor John Allison
13 p.a. From £54.99 p.a.

Reviews of opera from the UK and around the world, including profiles of opera's greatest performers and a comprehensive calendar of productions and events. Length: up to 2,000 words. Illustrations: photos. Payment: by arrangement.

Opera Now

Mark Allen Group, St Jude's Church, Dulwich Road, London SE24 0PB
tel 020-7333 1701
email opera.now@markallengroup.com
website www.rhinegold.co.uk/rhinegold-publishing/magazines/opera-now/

Editor-in-Chief Ashutosh Khandekar
Monthly From £35

Articles, news, reviews on opera. All material commissioned only. Length: 150–1,500 words. Illustrations: colour and b&w photos, line, cartoons. Founded 1989.

Orbis International Literary Journal

17 Greenhow Avenue, West Kirby, Wirral CH48 5EL
tel 0151 625 1446
email carolebaldock@hotmail.com
website www.orbisjournal.com
Editor Carole Baldock
Quarterly £5.50, £19 p.a. (UK), £43 p.a. (RoW). Introductory offer: 4 issues as pdfs, plus one print back copy of magazine for £12 (UK).

Literary magazine; provides feedback with proofs. Publishes poetry, fiction (1,000 words maximum), flash fiction, non-fiction, and translations. UK submissions: four poems; include C5-sized sae. Overseas: two submissions via email. Readers' Award: £50, plus £50 split between four runners-up. Subscribers also receive the Xtra Kudos Newsletter. Founded 1969.

Our Dogs

Northwood House, Greenwood Business Park, Regent Road, Salford M5 4QH
tel 0844 504 9001
email editor@ourdogs.co.uk
website www.ourdogs.co.uk
Facebook www.facebook.com/www.ourdogs.co.uk/
Twitter @OURDOGSNEWS
Editor Alison Smith
Weekly From £74.95 p.a.

Articles and news on the breeding and showing of pedigree dogs. Illustrations: b&w photos. Payment: by negotiation; £10 per photo. Founded 1895.

Oxford Poetry

Magdalen College, Oxford OX1 4AU
email editors@oxfordpoetry.co.uk
website www.oxfordpoetry.co.uk
Twitter @OxfordPoetry
Editor Luke Allan, *Managing Editor* Vala Thorodds
2 p.a. £23.23 (inc. p&p)

Previously unpublished poems (in English) and translations, both unsolicited and commissioned; also interviews, articles and reviews. Submissions via the website only. Published by Partus Press. Founded 1910.

PC Pro

Dennis Publishing Ltd, 31–32 Alfred Place, London WC1E 7DP
tel 020-3890 3890
email tim@dantonmedia.com
website www.dennis.co.uk/brands/technology/pc-pro/
Facebook www.facebook.com/pcpro

Twitter @pcpro
Editor-in-Chief Tim Danton
Monthly £5.99

Expert advice and insights from IT professionals, plus in-depth reviews and group tests, aimed at IT pros and enthusiasts. Email feature pitches to editor@pcpro.co.uk but only after reading the magazine first. Founded 1994.

Peace News

5 Caledonian Road, London N1 9DY
tel 020-7278 3344
email editorial@peacenews.info
website www.peacenews.info
Editor Milan Rai
6 p.a. From £10 p.a.

Political articles based on nonviolence in every aspect of human life. Illustrations: line, half-tone. No payment. Founded 1936.

People Management

Haymarket Ltd, Bridge House, 69 London Road, Twickenham TW1 3SP
tel 020-8267 5013
email PMeditorial@haymarket.com
website www.peoplemanagement.co.uk
Twitter @PeopleMgt
10 p.a. Free to CIPD members

Magazine of the Chartered Institute of Personnel and Development. News items and feature articles on recruitment and selection, training and development; pay and performance management; industrial psychology; employee relations; employment law; working practices and new practical ideas in personnel management in industry and commerce. Length: up to 2,500 words. Illustrations: contact art editor. Payment: by arrangement.

The People's Friend

D.C. Thomson & Co. Ltd, 2 Albert Square, Dundee DD1 1DD
tel (01382) 223131
email peoplesfriend@dcthomson.co.uk
website www.thepeoplesfriend.co.uk
Facebook www.facebook.com/PeoplesFriendMagazine
Twitter @TheFriendMag
Editor Angela Gilchrist
Weekly £1.60

Fiction magazine for women of all ages. Serials (60,000–70,000 words) and complete stories (1,000–4,000 words) of strong romantic and emotional appeal. Includes knitting and cookery. No preliminary letter required; send material for the attention of the Editor. Illustrations: colour. Payment: on acceptance. Founded 1869.

Period Living

Future plc, Quay House, The Ambury, Bath BA1 1UA

email period.living@futurenet.com
website www.homesandgardens.com/periodliving
Twitter @PeriodLivingMag
Editor Melanie Griffiths
Monthly £4.50

Articles and features on decoration, furnishings, renovation of period homes; gardens, crafts, decorating in a period style. Illustrated. Payment: varies, according to work required. Founded 1990.

The Photographer

BIPP, The Artistry House, 16 Winckley Square, Preston PR1 3JJ
tel (01772) 367 968
email editor@bipp.com
website www.bipp.com
Quarterly £50 p.a. (UK residents); free to all members of British Institute of Professional Photography

Journal of the British Institute of Professional Photography. Authoritative reviews, news, views and high-quality photographs.

Picture Postcard Collecting

16 Heron Road, Twickenham TW1 1PQ
tel 020-8892 5712
email mpgoldsmith@blueyonder.co.uk
Editor Michael Goldsmith
10 p.a. £4.50; subscriptions also available

Illustrated magazine for collectors of picture postcards. Regular features on auctions, ebay, postcard fairs, clubs and postcard activity in other countries. Topics covered in recent editions include: the 1919 Tin Town Riots in Surrey; the history of pantomime; British cruise ships, Max Kracke's cinema postcards and the Building of The Elan Valley Dams in Wales. Founded 2020.

Planet: The Welsh Internationalist

PO Box 44, Aberystwyth, Ceredigion SY23 3ZZ
tel (01970) 611255
email planet.enquiries@planetmagazine.org.uk
website www.planetmagazine.org.uk
Twitter @Planet_TWI
Editor Emily Trahair
Quarterly From £40 p.a.

Articles on culture, society, Welsh current affairs and international politics, as well as short fiction, poetry, photo essays and review articles. Article length: 1,500–2,500 words. Payment: £45 per 1,000 words, £30 per poem. Submissions by post or email, preferably by email. For articles, email enquiry in first instance. Founded 1970.

PN Review

(formerly Poetry Nation)
Carcanet Press Ltd, 4th Floor, Alliance House, 30 Cross Street, Manchester M2 7AQ
tel 0161 834 8730

Newspapers and magazines

email info@carcanet.co.uk
website www.pnreview.co.uk
Editor Michael Schmidt
6 p.a. £39.50 p.a. UK (print and digital; other subscription rates are available)

Poems, essays, reviews, translations. Submissions by post only. Payment: by arrangement. Founded 1973.

Poetry Ireland Review/Iris Éigse Éireann

11 Parnell Square East, Dublin 1 D01 ND60, Republic of Ireland
tel +353 (0)1 6789815
email publications@poetryireland.ie
website www.poetryireland.ie
Editor Colette Bryce, *Irish-language Editor* Aifric Mac Aodha
3 p.a. €12, €38 p.a. (Republic of Ireland and Northern Ireland), €43 p.a. (RoW)

Poetry. Features and articles by arrangement. Payment: €40 per contribution; €100 reviews. Founded 1981.

Poetry London

Goldsmiths, University of London, New Cross, London SE14 6NW
tel 020-8228 5707
email admin@poetrylondon.co.uk
website www.poetrylondon.co.uk
Facebook www.facebook.com/poetrylondon
Twitter @Poetry_London
Editors André Naffis-Sahel (poetry), Dai George (reviews)
3 p.a. plus digital access £30 p.a.

Poems of the highest standard, articles/reviews on any aspect of contemporary poetry. Contributors must be knowledgeable about contemporary poetry. Payment: £30 minimum. Founded 1988.

The Poetry Review

The Poetry Society, 22 Betterton Street, London WC2H 9BX
tel 020-7420 9880
email poetryreview@poetrysociety.org.uk
website https://poetrysociety.org.uk/publications-section/the-poetry-review/submissions-guidelines/
Editor Emily Berry
Quarterly From £24.99 p.a.

Poems, features and reviews. Send no more than six poems with sae. Preliminary study of magazine essential. Payment: £50+ per poem.

Poetry Wales

Suite 6, 4 Derwen Road, Bridgend CF31 1LH
tel (01656) 663018
email info@poetrywales.co.uk
website www.poetrywales.co.uk
Editor Jonathan Edwards
3 p.a. £27 p.a. (print, UK), £42 p.a. (Europe), £55 p.a. (RoW)

National poetry magazine of Wales, publishing contemporary poetry, features and reviews. Payment: £20/page for poems. Founded 1965.

The Police Journal: Theory, Practice and Principles

SAGE Publications, 1 Oliver's Yard, 55 City Road, London EC1Y 1SP
tel 020-7324 8500
website https://uk.sagepub.com/en-gb/eur/journal/police-journal
Editor-in-Chief Jason Roach
Quarterly From £68 p.a. for individual print issues; see website for further details

Articles of technical or professional interest to the Police Service throughout the world. Illustrations: line drawings. Payment: none. Founded 1928.

The Political Quarterly

Wiley-Blackwell, 9600 Garsington Road, Oxford OX4 2DQ
tel (01865) 776868
website www.politicalquarterly.org.uk
Twitter @po_qu
Editors Deborah Mabbett, Ben Jackson
4 p.a. From £11 p.a. for personal online subscription; see website for full list

Topical aspects of national and international politics and public administration; takes a progressive, but not a party, point of view. See website for submissions information. Length: average 5,000 words. Payment: about £125 per article. Founded 1930.

Popshot Quarterly

Jubilee House, 2 Jubilee Place, London SW3 3TQ
tel 020-7349 3700
email hello@popshotpopshot.com
website www.popshotpopshot.com
Twitter @popshotmag
Group Editor Steve Pill, *Editor* Matilda Battersby
4 p.a. From £20 p.a., including digital access to previous editions

Original short stories, flash fiction and poetry paired with bespoke illustrations. Study magazine before submitting work. Each issue is themed and submissions should be tailored accordingly: see the website for latest details. Length: maximum 3,000 words, shorter is preferable. Illustrations: send portfolios to illustration@popshotpopshot.com. Founded 2009.

Poultry World

website www.poultryworld.net/UK
Twitter @PoultryWorld
Editor-in-Chief Fabian Brockötter
10 p.a.

Articles on poultry breeding, production, marketing and packaging. News of international poultry interest.

Payment: by arrangement. As of late 2018, owned by Dutch media company Doorakkeren BV.

PR Week

Haymarket Ltd, Bridge House, 69 London Road, Twickenham TW1 3SP
tel 020-8267 5000
email arvind.hickman@haymarket.com
website www.prweek.com
Twitter @prweekuknews
UK Editor John Harrington, *News Editor* Arvind Hickman
Bi-monthly From £28 per month

News and features on public relations. Length: approx. 800–3,000 words. Payment: by arrangement. Send pitches to the news editor, on the email address above. Founded 1984.

Practical Boat Owner

Future plc, Pinehurst 2, Pinehurst Road, Farnborough Business Park, Farnborough, Hants GU14 7BF
tel 0330 390 6467
email pbo@futurenet.com
website www.pbo.co.uk
Facebook www.facebook.com/practicalboatownermag
Twitter @p_b_o
Editor Rob Melotti
Monthly £4.85

Boating magazine: sail and power. Hints, tips and practical articles for cruising skippers. Send full text and high-res images: see pbo.co.uk/submission_guide for details. Illustrations: photos or drawings. Payment: by negotiation. Founded 1967.

Practical Caravan

Future plc, Quay House, The Ambury, Bath BA1 1UA
email practical.caravan@futurenet.com
website www.practicalcaravan.com
Twitter @pcaravan
Editor-in-Chief Sarah Wakely
Every four weeks £4.99

Caravan-related travelogues, caravan site reviews; travel writing for existing regular series; technical and DIY matters. Illustrations: colour. Payment negotiable. Founded 1967.

Practical Fishkeeping

Warners Publishing, The Maltings, West Street, Bourne, PE10 9PH
tel (01778) 391194
website www.practicalfishkeeping.co.uk
Twitter @PFKmagazine
13 p.a. £4.75

Practical fishkeeping in tropical and coldwater aquaria and ponds. Heavy emphasis on inspiration and involvement. Good colour photography always needed, and used. No verse or humour, no personal biographical accounts of fishkeeping unless practical. Payment: by worth. Founded 1966.

Practical Wireless

Warners Group Publications Plc, The Maltings, West Street, Bourne, Lincs. PE10 9PH
tel (01778) 391000
email practicalwireless@warnersgroup.co.uk
website www.radioenthusiast.co.uk
Twitter @REnthusiasts
Editor Don Field
Monthly £4.99

Articles on the practical and theoretical aspects of amateur radio and communications. Constructional projects. Telephone or email for advice and essential *PW* author's guide. Illustrations: by arrangement. Payment: by arrangement. Founded 1932.

The Practising Midwife

Saturn House, Mercury Rise, Altham Industrial Park, Altham, Lancs. BB5 5BY
email claire@all4maternity.com
website www.all4maternity.com/about-us/tpm-writing-for-us/
Twitter @TPM_Journal
Editor Claire Feeley
Monthly From £42 p.a.

Disseminates evidence-based material to a wide professional audience. Research and review papers, viewpoints and news items pertaining to midwifery, maternity care, women's health and neonatal health with both a national and an international perspective. All articles submitted are peer-reviewed anonymously. See website for full submissions details. Illustrations: hi-res jpgs. Payment: by arrangement. Founded 1997.

The Practitioner

tel 020-8677 3508
email editor@thepractitioner.co.uk
website www.thepractitioner.co.uk
Editor Corinne Short
Monthly From £70 p.a. (online), from £75 p.a. (print)

Clinical journal for GPs. The articles, on advances in evidence-based medicine, are written by hospital consultants who are specialists in their field. The articles are independently commissioned. Unsolicited material, placed copy or suggestions from third parties not accepted. Founded 1868.

Press Gazette

40 Hatton Garden, London EC1N 8EB
tel 020-7936 6433
email pged@pressgazette.co.uk
website www.pressgazette.co.uk
Twitter @pressgazette
Editor-in-Chief Dominic Ponsford
Weekly Online only

News and features of interest to journalists and others working in the media. Length: 1,200 words (features), 300 words (news). Payment: approx. £230 (features), news stories negotiable. Founded 1965.

Pride

1 Garratt Lane, London SW18 4AQ
tel 020-8870 3755
email editor@pridemagazine.com
website https://pridemagazine.com
Twitter @Pridemag
Publisher CJ Cushnie, *Fashion and Beauty Editor* Shevelle Rhule
Monthly £24.99 p.a. (digital), £30 p.a. (print)

Lifestyle magazine incorporating fashion and beauty, travel, food and entertaining articles for the woman of colour. Length: 1,000–3,000 words. Illustrations: by arrangement. Payment: by arrangement. Founded 1991; relaunched 1997.

Prima

Hearst UK, House of Hearst, 30 Panton Street, London SW1Y 4AJ
tel 020-7312 3815
email prima@hearst.co.uk
website www.prima.co.uk
Facebook www.facebook.com/primamagazine
Twitter @Primauk
Instagram @primamag
Editor Jo Checkley
Monthly £4.25

Articles on fashion, home, crafts, health and beauty, cookery; features. Founded 1986.

Private Eye

6 Carlisle Street, London W1D 3BN
tel 020-7437 4017
email strobes@private-eye.co.uk
website www.private-eye.co.uk
Twitter @PrivateEyeNews
Editor Ian Hislop
Fortnightly £2

News and current affairs. Satire. Illustrations and cartoons: colour or b&w. Payment: by arrangement. Founded 1961.

Prole

15 Maes-y-Dre, Abergele, Conwy LL22 7HW
email admin@prolebooks.co.uk
website www.prolebooks.co.uk
Twitter @Prolebooks
Editors Brett Evans, Phil Robertson
3 p.a. (April/August/December) £6.82

Submissions of poetry, short fiction and creative non-fiction (7,500 words max) and photographic cover art welcome (see website for submission guidelines). Annual poetry competition. Payment: profit share. Founded: 2010.

Prospect Magazine

5th Floor, 23 Savile Row, London W1S 2ET
tel 020-7255 1281
email editorial@prospect-magazine.co.uk
email webdesk@prospect-magazine.co.uk
website www.prospectmagazine.co.uk
Twitter @prospect_uk
Editor Tom Clark
Monthly From £52 p.a.

Political and cultural monthly magazine. Essays, features, special reports, reviews, short stories, opinions/analysis. Length: 3,000–6,000 words (essays, special reports, short stories), 1,000 words (opinions). Illustrations: by arrangement. Payment: by negotiation. See website for full submission information. Founded 1995.

Psychologies

Kelsey Media, The Granary, Downs Court, Yalding Hill, Yalding, Kent ME18 6AL
tel (01959) 541444
email suzy.walker@psychologies.co.uk
website www.psychologies.co.uk
Editor-in-Chief Suzy Walker
Monthly £4.20

Women's magazine with a focus on how to flourish, improving mental health and helping readers create the life they want on their terms. Features cover relationships, family and parenting, personality behaviour, health, wellbeing, beauty, society and social trends, travel, spirituality and sex. Welcomes new ideas by email which fit into one of these areas, and suggestions should offer a combination of psychological insight and practical advice.

Pulse

Cogora, 140 London Wall, London EC2Y 5DN
tel 020-7214 0500
email feedback@pulsetoday.co.uk
website www.pulsetoday.co.uk
Twitter @pulsetoday
Editor Jaimie Kaffash
Weekly Free on request

Articles and photos of direct interest to GPs. Purely clinical material can be accepted only from medically qualified authors. Length: 600–1,200 words. Illustrations: b&w and colour photos. Payment: £150 average. Founded 1959.

Pushing Out the Boat

email info@pushingouttheboat.co.uk
website www.pushingouttheboat.co.uk
Facebook www.facebook.com/pushingouttheboat
Twitter @POTBmag
Biennial £5

North-East Scotland's magazine of new writing and visual arts. Features new prose, poetry and art from both the local area and the wider world, all selected (anonymously) from online submissions. The full-colour A4 print magazine (also available to view online) is run as a not-for-profit charity by volunteers. POTB's costs are met by sales revenue, plus events.

RA Magazine

Royal Academy of Arts, Burlington House, Piccadilly, London W1J 0BD
tel 020-7300 5820
email ramagazine@royalacademy.org.uk
website www.royalacademy.org.uk/ra-magazine
Twitter @RA_Mag
Editor Sam Phillips
Quarterly £5.95 (£24 p.a.)

Visual arts and culture articles relating to the Royal Academy of Arts and the wider British and international arts scene. Length: 150–1,800 words. Illustrations: consult the Editor. Payment: average £250 per 1,000 words; illustrations by negotiation. Founded 1983.

Racing Post

Floor 7, Vivo Building, South Bank Central, 30 Stamford Street, London SE1 9LS
email editor@racingpost.co.uk
website www.racingpost.com
Editor Tom Kerr
Mon–Fri, plus Weekender edition (Wednesday to Sunday) From £19.95 per month

News on horseracing, greyhound racing and sports betting. Founded 1986.

Radio Times

Immediate Media Co. Ltd, Vineyard House, 44 Brook Green, London W6 7BT
tel 020-7150 5429
email feedback@radiotimes.com
website www.radiotimes.com
Editors Tom Loxley, Shem Law
Weekly £3.50

Articles and interviews that preview the week's programmes on British TV and radio as well as on-demand programming. All articles are specially commissioned – ideas and synopses are welcomed but not unsolicited MSS. Length: 600–2,500 words. Illustrations: mostly in colour; photos, graphic designs or drawings. Payment: by arrangement.

RAIL

Bauer Media Group, Media House, Lynch Wood, Peterborough Business Park, Peterborough PE2 6EA
tel (01733) 468000
email rail@bauermedia.co.uk
website www.railmagazine.com
Facebook www.facebook.com/Railmagazine
Twitter @RAIL
Managing Editor Nigel Harris
Fortnightly From £88 p.a.

News and in-depth features on current UK railway

operations. Length: 1,000–3,000 words (features), 250–400 words (news). Illustrations: colour and b&w photos and artwork. Payment: £75 per 1,000 words; £15–£40 per photo except cover (£100). Founded 1981.

Railway Gazette International

1st Floor, Chancery House, St Nicholas Way, Sutton, Surrey SM1 4JB
tel 020-8652 5200
email editor@railwaygazette.com
website www.railwaygazette.com
Twitter @railwaygazette
Editor Chris Jackson
Monthly £110 p.a.

Deals with management, engineering, operation and finance of railway, metro and light rail transport worldwide. Articles of business interest on these subjects are considered and paid for if accepted. No 'enthusiast'- or heritage-oriented articles. Phone or email to discuss proposals. Illustrated articles, of 1,000–2,000 words, are preferred.

The Railway Magazine

Media Centre, Morton Way, Horncastle, Lincs. LN9 6JR
tel (01507) 529589
email railway@mortons.co.uk
website www.railwaymagazine.co.uk
Editor Paul Bickerdyke
Monthly £4.70

Illustrated magazine dealing with all railway subjects; no fiction or verse. Articles from 1,500–2,500 words accompanied by photos. Preliminary email or letter desirable. Illustrations: digital; b&w and colour transparencies. Payment: by arrangement. Founded 1897.

Reach Poetry

Indigo Dreams Publishing Ltd, 24 Forest Houses, Cookworthy Moor, Halwill, Beaworthy, Devon EX21 5UU
email publishing@indigodreams.co.uk
website www.indigodreams.co.uk
Twitter @IndigoDreamsPub
Editor Ronnie Goodyer
Monthly £4.50, £51.00 p.a.

Unpublished and original poetry. Submit up to three poems for consideration by post (include sae for reply) or email (preferred). New poets encouraged. Features lively subscribers' letters and votes pages. No payment, but competition winners have their subscriptions increased through a readers' vote. The editors were recipients of the Ted Slade Award for Services to Poetry 2015; Indigo Dreams won the Most Innovative Publisher Award (Saboteur Awards for Literature 2017). Founded 1998.

Reader's Digest

Reader's Digest, Fourth Floor, Highlight House, 57 Margaret Street, London W1W 8SJ

tel 0330 333 2220
email info@readersdigest.co.uk
website www.readersdigest.co.uk
Monthly £3.99

Original anecdotes, short stories, letters to the editor and jokes may be submitted online for consideration. Founded 1922.

Real People

Hearst UK, House of Hearst, 30 Panton Street, London SW1Y 4AJ
tel 020-7339 4570
website www.realpeoplemag.co.uk
Editor Karen Bryans
Weekly 85p

Magazine for women with real-life tales of ordinary people coping with extraordinary events, plus puzzles section.

Reality

St Joseph's Monastery, St Alphonsus Road, Dundalk, Co. Louth A91 F3FC, Republic of Ireland
tel +353 (0)1 492248
email info@redcoms.org
website www.redcoms.org
Monthly €2.50

Illustrated magazine for Christian living. Articles on all aspects of modern life, including family, youth, religion, leisure. Length: 1,000–1,500 words. Payment: by arrangement; average £50 per 1,000 words. Founded 1936.

Record Collector

7th Floor, Vantage London, Great West Road, London TW8 9AG
email rc.editorial@metropolis.co.uk
website www.recordcollectormag.com
Twitter @RecCollMag
Editor Paul Lester
Monthly £6.25

Covers all areas of music, with the focus on collectable releases and the reissues market. Specially commissions most material but will consider unsolicited material. Welcomes ideas for articles and features. Length: 2,000 words for articles/features; 200 words for news. Illustrations: transparencies, colour and b&w prints, scans of rare records; all commissioned. Payment: negotiable. Founded 1980.

Red

House of Hearst, 30 Panton Street, Leicester Square, London SW1Y 4AJ
tel 020-7150 7600
email red@redmagazine.co.uk
website www.redonline.co.uk
Twitter @RedMagDaily
Executive Editor Sarah Tomczak
Monthly £4.99

High-quality articles on topics of interest to women

aged 25–45: humour, memoirs, interviews and well-researched investigative features. Approach with ideas in writing in first instance. Length: 900 words upwards. Illustrations: by arrangement. Payment: NUJ rates minimum. Founded 1998.

Red Pepper

44–48 Shepherdess Walk, London N1 7JP
website www.redpepper.org.uk
website www.redpepper.org.uk/get-involved/write-for-us/
Facebook www.facebook.com/redpeppermagazine
Twitter @redppermag
Bi-monthly From £2 per month

Independent radical magazine run by an editorial collective: news and features on politics, culture and everyday life of interest to the Left and Greens. Material mostly commissioned. Length: news/news features 200–800 words, other features 800–2,000 words. Illustrations: by arrangement. Payment: for investigations, otherwise only exceptionally. See website for full information for editorial contact details, which varies per subject/topic. Founded 1994.

Reform

(published by United Reformed Church)
86 Tavistock Place, London WC1H 9RT
tel 020-7916 8630
email reform@urc.org.uk
website www.reform-magazine.co.uk
Twitter @Reform_Mag
Editor Stephen Tomkins
10 p.a. £4 (£2.95 for subscribers), £29.50 p.a.

Explores theology, ethics, personal spirituality and Christian perspectives on social and current affairs. Offers articles about Christian ideas from a range of viewpoints, as well as interviews and reviews. Published by the United Reformed Church but has readers from all Christian denominations, as well as readers from other faiths and from no faith tradition. Illustrations: graphic artists/illustrators. Payment: by arrangement. Founded 1972.

Resurgence & Ecologist

The Resurgence Trust, The Resurgence Centre, Hartland, Bideford, Devon EX39 6AB
tel (01237) 441293
email editorial@resurgence.org
website www.resurgence.org
Editor Marianne Brown
6 p.a. £5.95

Interested in environment and social justice investigations and features, green living advice and ideas, grassroots activism projects, artist profiles and reviews. Proposal first in most cases. Payment: various. See website for further guidance.

Retail Week

Ascential Information Services Ltd, 20 Air Street, London W1B 5AN

tel 020-3033 4220
email content@retail-week.com
website www.retail-week.com
Twitter @retailweek
Executive Editor George MacDonald
Weekly From £499 p.a.

Features and news stories on all aspects of retail management. Length: up to 1,400 words. Illustrations: colour photos. Payment: by arrangement. Founded 1988.

The Rialto

c/o 74 Britannia Road, Norwich NR1 4HS
email info@therialto.co.uk
website www.therialto.co.uk
Editors Michael Mackmin, Degna Stone, Edward Doegar, Will Harris
3 p.a. £9, £25 p.a.

62pp A4 magazine, mainly poetry but with occasional prose pieces. Prose is commissioned, poetry submissions are very welcome: up to six poems may be submitted either by post (sae essential) or online via Submittable. See website for details of submission windows. Payment: by arrangement. Founded 1984.

Riggwelter

email riggwelterpress@gmail.com
website https://riggwelterpress.wordpress.com/
Founding Editor Jonathan Kinsman
Online

Online journal of creative arts. Accepts submissions of fiction, poetry, visual art, essays and reviews. No submissions windows: as soon as one issue is filled, potential submissions are considered for the next. Note that essays and reviews appear on the website only. Poetry: send one to five poems as an attachment (ideally), indicating poetry submission in the title of your message; fiction: send one to five pieces, each of 1,500 words max., indicating fiction submission in the title of your message. Previously unpublished work preferred. See website for further specifications for submissions of visual art, scripts, essays, reviews and experimental/mixed media. Payment: none currently. Founded 2017.

Riptide Journal

The Editors, Riptide Journal,
The Department of English,
The University of Exeter, Queen's Building,
Queen's Drive, Exeter EX4 6QH
email editors@riptidejournal.co.uk
website www.riptidejournal.co.uk
Twitter @RiptideJournal
Editors Dr Virginia Baily, Dr Sally Flint
2 p.a. £6.95 (some free material online also)

Anthologies of short fiction by established and emerging writers. Also accepts poetry. Submissions should be original, unpublished work. See website for information on submission windows and deadlines

for forthcoming editions. Fiction pieces should typically be no more than 5,000 words and poems no longer than 40 lines (although up to five pieces can be sent at once). All submissions should be accompanied by a biographical note of 50 words max.

Royal National Institute of Blind People (RNIB)

105 Judd Street, London WC1H 9NE
tel 0303 123 9999
email helpline@rnib.org.uk
website www.rnib.org.uk
Twitter @RNIB

RNIB publishes a variety of titles in a range of formats (including audio, large print, braille and Daisy) for adults and young people who have sight loss.

Rugby World

Future plc, 161 Marsh Wall, London E14 9AP
tel 0330 390 6479
email sarah.mockford@futurenet.com
website www.rugbyworld.com
Twitter @Rugbyworldmag
Editor Sarah Mockford
Monthly £5.50

Features and exclusive news stories on rugby. Length: approx. 1,200 words. Illustrations: colour photos, cartoons. Payment: £120. Founded 1960.

Runner's World

Hearst UK, House of Hearst, 30 Panton Street, London SW1Y 4AJ
tel 020-7339 4400
email editor@runnersworld.co.uk
website www.runnersworld.com/uk
Facebook www.facebook.com/runnersworlduk
Twitter @runnersworlduk
Editor-in-Chief Andy Dixon, *Deputy Editor* Joe Mackie
Monthly £4.80

Articles on running, health and fitness, and nutrition. Payment: by arrangement. Founded 1979.

RUSI Journal

Whitehall, London SW1A 2ET
tel 020-7747 2600
email publications@rusi.org
website https://rusi.org/publication/rusi-journal
Editor Emma De Angelis
Bi-monthly; available as part of RUSI membership (see website for full list; concessions available) or a subscription in conjunction with RUSI Whitehall Papers.

Journal of the Royal United Services Institute for Defence and Security Studies. Articles on international security, military science, defence technology and procurement, and military history;

also book reviews and correspondence. Length: 3,000–3,500 words. Illustrations: colour photos, maps and diagrams.

Saga Magazine

Saga Publishing Ltd, The Saga Building, Enbrook Park, Sandgate, Folkestone, Kent CT20 3SE
tel (01303) 771523
website www.saga.co.uk/magazine
Monthly From £12 p.a. (special rate; normal rates may be higher)

General interest magazine aimed at the intelligent, literate 50+ reader. Wide range of articles from human interest, real-life stories, intriguing overseas interest (not travel), some natural history, celebrity interviews, photographic book extracts – all subjects are considered in this general interest title. Articles mostly commissioned or written in-house, but genuine exclusives welcome. Illustrations: colour, digital media; mainly commissioned but top-quality photo feature suggestions sometimes accepted. Payment: competitive rate, by negotiation. Founded 1984.

Sainsbury's Magazine

SevenC3, 3–7 Herbal Hill, London EC1R 5EJ
tel 020-7775 7775
email feedback@sainsburysmagazine.co.uk
website www.sainsburysmagazine.co.uk
website www.seven.co.uk/
Editor-in-Chief Helena Lang
Monthly £3

Features: general, food and drink, health, beauty, homes; all material commissioned. Length: up to 1,500 words. Illustrations: colour and b&w photos and line illustrations. Payment: varies. Founded 1993.

Sarasvati

24 Forest Houses, Cookworthy Moor, Halwill, Beaworthy, Devon EX21 5UU
email dawnidp@indigodreams.co.uk
website www.indigodreams.co.uk
Facebook www.facebook.com/ronniegoodyeridp
Twitter @IndigoDreamsPub
Editor Dawn Bauling
Quarterly £4.50, £17 for 4 issues

International poetry and short story magazine. New writers/poets encouraged. Lively feedback pages. Several pages given to each subscriber. Prose length: 1,000 words or under. Email submissions only. Founded 2008.

The School Librarian

School Library Association, 1 Pine Court, Kembrey Park, Swindon SN2 8AD
tel (01793) 530166
email sleditor@sla.org.uk
website www.sla.org.uk
Features Editor Barbara Band, *Reviews Editor* Joy Court

Quarterly Free to SLA members, £125 p.a. to others

Official journal of the School Library Association. Articles on school library management, best practice, use and skills, literacy, publishing, developing reading, research skills and information literacy. Reviews of books, websites and other library resources from preschool to adult. Length: 1,200–1,800 words (articles). Payment: by arrangement. Founded 1937

School Libraries in View

School Libraries Group,
CILIP: The Library and Information Association, 7 Ridgmount Street, London WC1E 7AE
email info@barbaraband.com
website www.cilip.org.uk

Articles on school librarianship, library management, information and digital skills, authors and illustrators, literacy and reading. News about books, education and resources.

Scientific Computing World

4 Signet Court, Cambridge CB5 8LA
tel (01223) 275464
email editor.scw@europascience.com
website www.scientific-computing.com
Editor Robert Roe
6 p.a. Free to qualifying subscribers, other subscription rates apply (see website)

Features on hardware and software developments for the scientific community, plus news articles and reviews. Length: 800–2,000 words. Illustrations: colour transparencies, photos, electronic graphics. Payment: by negotiation. Founded 1994.

The Scots Magazine

D.C. Thomson & Co. Ltd, 2 Albert Square, Dundee DD1 1DD
tel (01382) 223131
email mail@scotsmagazine.com
website www.scotsmagazine.com
Twitter @ScotsMagazine
Editor Robert Wight
Monthly From £26 p.a.

Articles on all subjects of Scottish interest, but authors must also be Scottish. Illustrations: colour and b&w photos. Unsolicited material considered but preliminary enquiries advised. Payment: on acceptance. Founded 1739.

The Scottish Farmer

Newsquest Scotland, 125 Fullerton Drive, Glasgow G32 8FG
tel 0141 302 7732
email ken.fletcher@thescottishfarmer.co.uk
website www.thescottishfarmer.co.uk
Editor Ken Fletcher
Weekly £3.50

Articles on agricultural subjects. Length: 1,000–1,500

words. Illustrations: line, half-tone, colour. Payment: £90 per 1,000 words. Founded 1893.

Scottish Field

Fettes Park, 496 Ferry Road, Edinburgh EH5 2DL
tel 0131 551 1000
email editor@scottishfield.co.uk
website www.scottishfield.co.uk
Facebook www.facebook.com/scottishfield/
Twitter @scottishfield
Editor Richard Bath
Monthly £4.75

Scottish lifestyle magazine: interiors, food, travel, wildlife, heritage, general lifestyle. Length of article accepted: 1,200 words. Founded 1903.

Screen International

Media Business Insight, Cally Yard, Unit 4D, 445 Caledonian Road, London N7 9BG
tel 020-8102 0900
email matt.mueller@screendaily.com
website www.screendaily.com
Editor Matt Mueller
Monthly From £175

International news and features on the international film business. No unsolicited material. Length: variable. Payment: by arrangement.

Sea Angler

Kelsey Publishing Ltd, The Granary, Downs Court, Yalding Hill, Yalding, Maidstone, Kent ME18 6AL
website www.seaangler.co.uk
Facebook www.facebook.com/seaanglermag/
Twitter @TheSeaAngler
Monthly £3.90

Topical articles on all aspects of sea-fishing around the British Isles. Illustrations: colour. Payment: by arrangement. Founded 1972.

Sea Breezes

Media House, Cronkbourne, Tromode, Douglas, Isle of Man IM4 4SB
tel (01624) 696573
website www.seabreezes.co.im
Editor Captain Peter Corrin
Monthly £6.20

Factual articles on ships and the sea past and present, preferably illustrated. Length: up to 4,000 words. Illustrations: by arrangement. Payment: by arrangement. Founded 1919.

Seen and Heard

Nagalro, PO Box 264, Esher, Surrey KT10 0WA
tel (01372) 818504
email mail@rodneynoon.co.uk
website www.nagalro.com/seen-and-heard-journal/seen-and-heard.aspx
Editor Rodney Noon
Quarterly £35 p.a.

Professional journal of Nagalro, the professional association of children's guardians, family court advisers and independent social workers. Publishes high-quality articles and academic papers on issues relating to the professional practice of child-protection social workers, child abuse and protection, adoption and the law relating to children. Potential contributors are advised to contact the editor initially with proposals. Payment: on publication, ranging from £50 to £100.

SelfBuild & Design

151 Station Street, Burton on Trent, Staffs. DE14 1BG
tel (01584) 841417
email ross.stokes@sbdonline.co.uk
website www.selfbuildanddesign.com
Editor Ross Stokes
Monthly £4.99

Articles on design and construction for individual builders. Welcomes ideas for articles. Illustrations: digital. Payment: negotiable.

The Sewing Directory

11A Tedders Close, Hemyock, Cullompton, Devon EX15 3XD
tel (01823) 680588
email julie@thesewingdirectory.net
website www.thesewingdirectory.co.uk
Facebook www.facebook.com/thesewingdirectory
Twitter @sewingdirectory
Content Editor Julie Briggs

Online directory of UK sewing business – sewing courses, fabric shops and sewing groups. Plus free sewing projects and technique guides. Payment: by arrangement. Founded 2010.

SFX Magazine

Future plc, Quay House, The Ambury, Bath BA1 1UA
tel (01225) 442244
email sfx@futurenet.com
website www.gamesradar.com/sfx
Facebook www.facebook.com/SFXmagazine
Twitter @SFXmagazine
Every 4 weeks (13 p.a.) £4.99

Sci-fi and fantasy magazine covering TV, films, DVDs, books, comics, games and collectables. Founded 1995.

Ships Monthly

Kelsey Media, The Granary, Downs Court, Yalding Hill, Yalding, Kent ME18 6AL
tel (01959) 541444
email ships.monthly@btinternet.com
website www.shipsmonthly.com
Editor Nicholas Leach
Monthly £4.80

Illustrated articles of shipping and maritime interest – both mercantile and naval, preferably of 20th- and

21st-century ships. Well-researched, factual material only. No short stories or poetry. 'Notes for contributors' available. Mainly commissioned material; preliminary letter or email essential. Illustrations: half-tone and line, colour transparencies, prints and digital images via email, DVD or CD. Payment: by arrangement. Founded 1966.

Shooter Literary Magazine
98 Muswell Hill Road, London N10 3JR
email shooterlitmag@gmail.com
website www.shooterlitmag.com
Facebook www.facebook.com/shooterliterarymagazine
Twitter @ShooterLitMag
Editor Melanie White
2 p.a. £19.99 p.a.

Submissions of short fiction and non-fiction (2,000–6,000 words) and poetry welcome. Annual story and poetry competitions. Editing services available. Please visit the website for guidelines, current theme and deadline information. Payment: £25 for prose, £5 for poetry, plus complimentary issue. Founded 2015.

Shooting Times and Country Magazine
Future plc, Pinehurst 2, Pinehurst Road, Farnborough Business Park, Farnborough, Hants GU14 7BF
tel (01252) 555000
email patrick.galbraith@futurenet.com
website www.shootingtimes.co.uk
Editor Patrick Galbraith
Weekly £2.75

Articles on fieldsports, especially shooting, and on related natural history and countryside topics. Unsolicited MSS not encouraged. Length: up to 1,400 words. Illustrations: photos, drawings, colour transparencies. Payment: by arrangement. Founded 1882.

Shoreline of Infinity
email contact@shorelineofinfinity.com
website www.shorelineofinfinity.com
Twitter @shoreinf
Editor Noel Chidwick
2 p.a. £7.50 (print); monthly £2.50 (digital)

Science fiction and fantasy science fiction stories, poetry, author interviews, articles and reviews. Based in Edinburgh, Scotland, but with a worldwide readership and contributor base. Invites submissions of short stories and poetry, both originals and translations into English, specifically: original and previously unpublished fiction of up to 6,000 words; up to six original and previously unpublished poems per issue. Contributors should indicate any translation rights issues in their cover note. Payment: £10/1,000 words for stories and articles, contributor's copy for poems plus any additional copies at discount

rates. Check website for submission window openings. Founded 2014.

Sight and Sound
BFI, 21 Stephen Street, London W1T 1LN
tel 020-7255 1444
email kieron.corless@bfi.org.uk
website www.bfi.org.uk/sightandsound
Twitter @SightSoundmag
Editor-in-Chief Mike Williams, *Deputy Editor* Kieron Corless
Monthly £5.95

Topical and critical articles on world cinema; reviews of every film theatrically released in the UK; book reviews; DVD reviews; festival reports. Length: 1,000–5,000 words. Contact Deputy Editor in the first instance. Illustrations: by arrangement. Payment: by arrangement. Founded 1932.

Skier and Snowboarder Magazine
The Lodge, Ashgrove Road, Sevenoaks TN13 1ST
tel 07768 670158
email frank.baldwin@skierandsnowboarder.co.uk
website www.skierandsnowboarder.com
Editor Frank Baldwin
5 p.a. Free

Ski features, based around a good story. Length: 800–1,000 words. Illustrations: colour action ski photos. Payment: by negotiation. Founded 1984.

Slightly Foxed
53 Hoxton Square, London N1 6PB
tel 020-7033 0258
email office@foxedquarterly.com
website www.foxedquarterly.com
Facebook www.facebook.com/foxedquarterly
Twitter @foxedquarterly
Publisher/Co-editor Gail Pirkis
Quarterly Single issue £12.50 (UK and Republic of Ireland), £14.50 (RoW); annual subscription £48 p.a. (UK and Ireland), £56 p.a. (Overseas)

Independent-minded quarterly magazine that introduces its readers to books that are no longer new and fashionable but have enduring appeal. Each issue contains 96pp of recommendations for books of lasting interest, old and new, both fiction and non-fiction. Unsolicited submissions are welcome; see website for guidelines.

Slimming World Magazine
Clover Nook Road, Alfreton, Derbyshire DE55 4SW
tel (01773) 546071
email editorial@slimmingworld.com
website www.slimmingworld.co.uk/magazine
Editor Sara Ward
7 p.a. £3.45

Magazine about healthy eating, fitness and feeling good with real-life stories of how Slimming World members have changed their lives, as well as recipes and menu plans, health advice, beauty and fitness tips, features, competitions and fashion.

The Songwriter

International Songwriters Association, PO Box 46, Limerick City, Republic of Ireland
tel +353 (0)61 228837
email internationalsongwriters@gmail.com
website www.songwriter.co.uk
Editor James D. Liddane
Quarterly

Articles on songwriting and interviews with songwriters, music publishers and recording company executives. Length: 1,000–10,000 words. Illustrations: photos. Payment: by arrangement. Founded 1967.

Songwriting and Composing

Prospect Business Park, West Wing, Leadgate, Consett, Co. Durham DH8 7PW
tel 0330 2020 760
email gisc@songwriters-guild.co.uk
website www.songwriters-guild.co.uk
Editor Colin Eade
Quarterly Free to members

Magazine of the Guild of International Songwriters and Composers. Profiles/stories, articles, contacts relating to songwriting, music publishing, recording and the music industry. Illustrations: collaboration register. Payment: £65 per year. Founded 1986.

SOUTH Poetry Magazine

PO Box 9338, Wimborne BH21 9JA
email south@southpoetry.org
website www.southpoetry.org
Facebook www.facebook.com/SOUTHpoetry
Contacts Anne Peterson, Penny Dale, Peter Keeble, Chrissie Williams and Pauline Howard
2 p.a. £7.50, £12 p.a.

Poetry magazine featuring previously unpublished poems written in English. Poems featured in the magazine are chosen by a selection panel which changes for every issue. Up to three poems (two copies required) may be submitted for each issue, but see website for full details, including annual deadlines. Potential contributors are advised to study the magazine prior to sending in their work.

Spear's Magazine

John Carpenter House, John Carpenter Street, London EC4Y 0AN
tel 020-7936 6445
email alec.marsh@spearwms.com
website www.spearsmagazine.com
Twitter @SpearsMagazine
Editor Edwin Smith
4 p.a. From £18 p.a.

Guide to wealth management, business and culture. Topics covered include wealth management, the law,

art, philanthropy, luxury, food and wine and global affairs. Readership includes ultra-high-net-worths, private bankers, top lawyers, philanthropists etc. Standard length of articles 850–1,300 words (features). Illustrations: colour and b&w. Payment: by arrangement. Founded 2003.

Speciality Food

Aceville Publications, 21–23 Hawkins Road, Colchester CO2 8JY
email holly.shackleton@aceville.co.uk
website www.specialityfoodmagazine.com
Editor Holly Shackleton
9 p.a. £3.25

Trade magazine for the fine food industry, combining expert insight, product recommendations and independent retail-focused features with the sector's latest news and opinion.

The Spectator

22 Old Queen Street, London SW1H 9HP
tel 020-7961 0200
email editor@spectator.co.uk
website www.spectator.co.uk
Editor Fraser Nelson
Weekly £4.95

Articles on current affairs, politics, the arts; book reviews. Illustrations: colour and b&w, cartoons. Payment: on merit. Founded 1828.

square mile

Square Up Media, 5 Tun Yard, Peardon Street, London SW8 3HT
tel 020-7819 9999
website https://squaremile.com
Twitter @SQUAREMILE_COM
Editor Mark Hedley
Monthly Free

Luxury lifestyle magazine aimed at men working and living in the City of London.

The Stage

Stage House, 47 Bermondsey Street, London SE1 3XT
tel 020-7403 1818
email alistair@thestage.co.uk
website www.thestage.co.uk
Editor Alistair Smith, *Features Editor* Nick Clark, *Reviews Editor* Natasha Tripney, *News Editor* Matthew Hemley
Weekly From £64.50 p.a.

Original and interesting articles on the theatre and performing arts industry may be sent for the Editor's consideration. Features range in length from 800 to 3,000 words. Payment: £100 per 1,000 words. Founded 1880.

Stamp Magazine

MyTime Media Ltd, Enterprise House, Enterprise Way, Edenbridge, Kent TN8 6HF

tel 0844 848 88 22
email Guy.Thomas@mytimemedia.com
website www.stampmagazine.co.uk
Editor Guy Thomas
13 p.a. £4.99

Informative articles and exclusive news items on stamp collecting and postal history. Preliminary letter. Payment: by arrangement. Illustrations: by arrangement. Founded 1934.

Stand Magazine

School of English, University of Leeds, Leeds LS2 9JT
tel 0113 233 4794
email engstand@standmagazine.org
website www.standmagazine.org/
Managing Editor John Whale, *Editors* Hannah Copley, Kathryn Jenner, Ian Fairley
From £15 p.a. (online), £30 p.a. (print)

Poetry, short stories, translations, literary criticism. Send sae for return for UK submissions, or include email address for overseas submissions. Will consider only original, previously unpublished material; potential contributors should familiarise themselves with the magazine first. Poetry submissions should be of four to six poems max; fiction should be no more than 3,000 words. Founded 1952.

The Strad

Newsquest Specialist Media, 4th Floor, 120 Leman Street, London E1 8EU
tel 020-7618 3095
email thestrad@thestrad.com
website www.thestrad.com
Twitter @TheStradMag
Editor Charlotte Smith
12 p.a. plus occasional supplements £5.95

Features, news and reviews for stringed instrument players, teachers, makers and enthusiasts – both professional and amateur. Specially commissions most material but will consider unsolicited material. Welcomes ideas for articles and features. Length: 1,000–2,250 (articles/features), 100–150 (news). Illustrations: by arrangement. Payment: £150–£350 (articles/features), varies for news. Founded 1890.

Strong Words

PO Box 116, 33 Parkway, London NW1 7PN
email info@strong-words.co.uk
website www.strong-words.co.uk
Twitter @strongwordsmag
Instagram @strongwordsmag
Editor Ed Needham
9 p.a. £60 p.a.

Reviews of new books, interviews with authors and features on new books, trends, great backlist titles and tips on how to write in various genres. Very limited options for outside contributions, but any pitches and information about new books for possible review can be sent via the email address. No academic essays or reviews. For a sample of an issue, see website.

Structo

email editor@structomagazine.co.uk
website www.structomagazine.co.uk
Facebook www.facebook.com/structomagazine
Twitter @structomagazine
Editor Euan Monaghan
2 p.a. £15 p.a.

Fiction, poetry, author interviews and essays. Nominally based in the UK, but with a worldwide staff, readership and contributor base. Invites submissions of short stories and poetry, both originals and translations into English, specifically: original and previously unpublished fiction of up to 3,000 words; up to three original and previously unpublished poems per issue. Payment: issues, plus any additional copies at cost. Founded 2008. The first book from Structo Press was published in 2019.

Stuff

Kelsey Media, Office 111, Blackfriars Foundry, 154–156 Blackfriars Road, London SE1 8EN
email stuff@kelsey.co.uk
website www.stuff-magazine.co.uk
Twitter @StuffTV
Editor-in-Chief James Day
Monthly From £51 p.a.

Articles on technology, games, films, lifestyle, news and reviews. Payment by negotiation. Founded 1999.

Style at Home

Future plc, 161 Marsh Wall, London E14 9AP
email styleathome@futurenet.com
website www.housetohome.co.uk/styleathome
Facebook www.facebook.com/StyleAtHomeMag
Twitter @styleathomemag
Editorial Director Vanessa Richmond
Monthly £1.99

Interiors magazine aimed at woman interested in updating, styling and decorating their home. With an emphasis on achievable, affordable home make-overs, the magazine has regular articles showing transformed rooms as well as step-by-step projects, shopping ideas and a recipe section for keen cooks.

Stylist

Shortlist Media, 26–34 Emerald Street, London WC1N 3QA
tel 020-7611 9700
email stories@stylist.co.uk
website www.stylist.co.uk
Twitter @StylistMagazine
Editor-in-Chief Lisa Smosarski
12 p.a. £16 p.a.

Women's interest magazine that covers topics from fashion and beauty to books, travel, money and women in the news. Email synopses of feature ideas to the address above. Also extensive online presence.

Suffolk Norfolk Life

Today Magazines Ltd, The Publishing House,
Station Road, Framlingham, Suffolk IP13 9EE
tel (01728) 622030
email editor@suffolknorfolklife.com
website www.suffolknorfolklife.com
Editor Kevin Davis
Monthly £3

Articles relevant to Suffolk and Norfolk – current
topics plus historical items, art, leisure, etc. Considers
unsolicited material and welcomes ideas for articles
and features. Send via email. Length: 900–1,500
words. Illustrations: transparencies, digital colour and
b&w prints, b&w artwork and cartoons. Payment:
£60–£80 per article. Founded 1989.

Surrey Life

tel (01903) 703730
email editor@surreylife.co.uk
website www.surreylife.co.uk
Facebook www.facebook.com/SurreyLife
Twitter @SurreyLife
Editor Jane Thynne
Monthly £3.99

Articles on Surrey, including places of interest, high-
profile personalities, local events, arts, history, food,
homes, gardens and more. Founded 1970.

The Tablet

1 King Street Cloisters, Clifton Walk,
London W6 0GY
tel 020-8748 8484
email thetablet@thetablet.co.uk
website www.thetablet.co.uk
Twitter @The_Tablet
Editor Brendan Walsh
Weekly £3.90

Catholic weekly: religion, philosophy, politics,
society, books and arts. International coverage.
Freelance work commissioned: do not send
unsolicited material. Length: various. Illustrations:
cartoons and photos. Payment: by arrangement.
Founded 1840.

Take a Break

H. Bauer Publishing Ltd, Academic House,
24–28 Oval Road, London NW1 7DT
tel 020-7241 8000
email tab.features@bauer.co.uk
website www.takeabreak.co.uk
Weekly £1.10

Lively, illustrated tabloid women's weekly. True-life
features, health and beauty, family; lots of puzzles.
Payment: by arrangement. Founded 1990.

Take a Break's Take a Puzzle

H. Bauer Publishing Ltd, Academic House,
24–28 Oval Road, London NW1 7DT
email take.puzzle@bauer.co.uk
website www.puzzlemagazines.co.uk/takeapuzzle

Editor Babetta Mann
Monthly £2.90

Puzzles. Fresh ideas always welcome. Illustrations:
colour transparencies and b&w prints and artwork.
Payment: from £25 per puzzle, £30–£90 for picture
puzzles and for illustrations not an integral part of a
puzzle. Founded 1991.

TATE ETC

Tate, Millbank, London SW1P 4RG
tel 020-7887 8724
email tateetc@tate.org.uk
website www.tate.org.uk/tate-etc
Twitter @TateEtcMag
Editor Simon Grant
3 p.a. £21 p.a. (UK)

Independent visual arts magazine: features,
interviews, previews and opinion pieces. Length: up
to 3,000 words but always commissioned.
Illustrations: colour and b&w photos. Payment:
negotiable.

Tatler

The Condé Nast Publications Ltd, Vogue House,
1 Hanover Square, London W1S 1JU
website www.tatler.com
Twitter @Tatlermagazine
Editor Richard Dennen
Monthly £4.95

Smart society magazine favouring sharp articles,
profiles, fashion and the arts. Illustrations: colour,
b&w, but all commissioned. Founded 1709.

Taxation

Quadrant House, The Quadrant, Sutton SM2 5AS
tel 020-8212 1949
email taxation@lexisnexis.co.uk
website www.taxation.co.uk
Twitter @Taxation
Editor-in-Chief Andrew Hubbard, *Editor* Richard
Curtis
48 issues p.a. £465 p.a.

Updating and advice concerning UK tax law and
practice for accountants and tax experts. All articles
written by professionals. Length: 2,000 words
(articles). Founded 1927.

Tears in the Fence

Flats, Durweston Mill, Mill Lane, Durweston,
Blandford Forum, Dorset DT11 0QD
email tearsinthefence@gmail.com
website https://tearsinthefence.com
Twitter @TearsInTheFence
Editor David Caddy
Monthly £10, or £25 for three issues

Socially aware literary magazine with an international
outlook and author base. Includes regular columnists
as well as critical reviews of recent books and essays
on English and American poets, flash fiction,

translations and interviews. See website for up-to-date information on forthcoming submission windows. Submissions of original, unpublished work should be made by email to the address above in the body of the message and as an attachment.

Television

RTS, 3 Dorset Rise, London EC4Y 8EH
tel 020-7822 2810
email publications@rts.org.uk
website www.rts.org.uk
Editor Steve Clarke
Monthly

Articles on all aspects of TV and related content sectors including the people, programmes, politics and media policy. Coverage of RTS events. Payment: by arrangement. Founded 1928.

Tempo

Cambridge University Press,
The Edinburgh Building, Shaftesbury Road,
Cambridge CB2 8RU
email tempoeditor@cambridge.org
website https://www.cambridge.org/core/journals/tempo
Editor Professor Christopher Fox
Quarterly From £166 p.a.

Authoritative articles on contemporary music. Length: 2,000–4,000 words. Illustrations: music type, occasional photographic or musical supplements. Payment: by arrangement.

TGO (The Great Outdoors) Magazine

Kelsey Media, The Granary, Downs Court,
Yalding Hill, Yalding, Kent ME18 6AL
tel (01959) 541444
email emily.rodway@tgomagazine.co.uk
website www.tgomagazine.co.uk
Twitter @TGOmagazine
Editor Carey Davies
13 p.a. From £29.95 p.a.

Articles on walking or lightweight camping in specific areas, mainly in the UK, preferably illustrated with photography. Apply for guidelines. Length: 700–2,000 words. Illustrations: colour. Payment: by arrangement. Founded 1978.

that's life!

H. Bauer Publishing Ltd, Academic House,
24–28 Oval Road, London NW1 7DT
tel 020-7241 8000
email stories@thatslife.co.uk
website www.thatslife.co.uk
Editor-in-Chief Sophie Hearsey
Weekly 85p

Dramatic true-life stories about women. Length: average 1,000 words. Illustrations: colour photos and cartoons. Payment: up to £2,000. Founded 1995.

This England

185 Fleet Street, London EC4A 2HS
tel 020-7400 1083
email editor@thisengland.co.uk
website www.thisengland.co.uk
Quarterly £7.49

Articles about England's traditions, customs and places of interest. Regular features on towns, villages, the English countryside, notable men and women, and readers' recollections. Length 250–3,000 words. Illustrations: digital; colour transparencies accepted only when accompanying articles. Payment: £25 per 1,000 words, £10 poems (12–24 lines). Founded 1968.

Time Out London

Time Out Group Ltd, 77 Wicklow Street,
London WC1X 9JY
tel 020-7813 3000
email hello@timeout.com
website www.timeout.com
Facebook www.facebook.com/TimeOutLondon/
Twitter @timeoutlondon
Instagram @timeoutlondon
Global Editor-in-Chief Caroline McGinn, *Time Out London Editor* Joe Mackertich
Weekly Free

Initially a magazine to help people discover the exciting new urban cultures that had started up all over the city, but now a digital and physical presence that comprises websites, mobile, magazines, live events and Time Out Market. Its curated content – written by professional journalists – covers the best food, drink, culture, entertainment and travel across 327 cities in 58 countries. Founded 1968.

Today's Golfer

Bauer Media Group, Media House, Lynch Wood,
Peterborough Business Park, Peterborough PE2 6EA
tel (01733) 468000
email chris.jones@bauermedia.co.uk
website www.todaysgolfer.co.uk
Facebook https://en-gb.facebook.com/TodaysGolferBauer/
Twitter @TheTodaysGolfer
Editor Chris Jones
13 p.a. From £40 p.a.

Specialist features and articles on golf instruction, equipment and courses. Founded 1988.

Top Santé

Kelsey Media, Welbeck Way,
Peterborough PE2 7WH
tel (01959) 541444
website www.topsante.co.uk
Twitter @topsanteuk
Editor Katy Louise Sunnassee
13 p.a. £3.99

Features and news on all aspects of health, wellbeing, fitness and beauty. Ideas welcome. Founded 1993.

Total Film

Future Publishing Ltd, 1–10 Praed Mews,
London W2 1QY
tel 020-7042 4831
email jane.crowther@futurenet.com
website www.gamesradar.com/totalfilm
Editor-in-Chief Jane Crowther
Monthly £4.99

Movie magazine covering all aspects of film. Email
ideas before submitting material. Length: 400 words
(news items); 1,000 words (funny features). Payment:
20p per word. Founded 1996.

Trail

Bauer Consumer Media, Media House,
Lynch Wood, Peterborough Business Park,
Peterborough PE2 6EA
tel (01733) 468363
website www.livefortheoutdoors.com
Editor Oli Reed
Monthly £4.80

Outdoor activity magazine focusing mainly on high
level walking with some scrambling and climbing.
Some opportunities for freelancers. Good ideas
welcome.

Trout & Salmon

Bauer Consumer Media, Media House,
Lynch Wood, Peterborough Business Park,
Peterborough PE2 6EA
tel (01733) 468000
email troutandsalmon@bauermedia.co.uk
website www.troutandsalmon.com
Editor Russell Hill
13 p.a. From £32 p.a.

Articles of good quality with strong trout or salmon
angling interest. Length: 400–2,000 words,
accompanied if possible by good quality colour
photographs. Illustrations: line, colour transparencies
and prints, cartoons. Payment: by arrangement.
Founded 1955.

Truck & Driver

DVV Media International Ltd,
Road Transport Media Ltd, First Floor,
Chancery House, St Nicholas Way, Sutton,
Surrey SM1 1JB
tel 020-8912 2131
email dougie.rankine@roadtransport.com
website www.truckanddriver.co.uk
Twitter @TRUCKNDRIVER
Editor Dougie Rankine
Monthly £3.99

News, articles on trucks, personalities and features of
interest to truck drivers. Words and picture packages
preferred. Preferred feature length: 500-1,500 words.
Payment: negotiable. Founded 1984.

Trucking

Kelsey Media, The Granary, Downs Court,
Yalding Hill, Yalding, Kent ME18 6AL
tel (01733) 347559
email trucking.ed@kelsey.co.uk
website www.truckingmag.co.uk
Twitter @truckingmag
Editor Andy Stewart
Monthly £4.20

For truck drivers, owner–drivers and operators: news,
articles, features and technical advice. Length:
750–2,500 words. Illustrations: mostly 35mm digital.
Payment: by negotiation. Founded 1983.

TV Times Magazine

Future plc, 161 Marsh Wall, London E14 9AP
tel 020-3148 5615
email colin.tough@futurenet.com
website www.whatsontv.co.uk/tv-times
Weekly £2.20

Features with an affinity to ITV, BBC1, BBC2,
Channels 4 and 5, satellite and radio personalities and
TV generally. Length: by arrangement. Photographs:
commissioned only. Payment: by arrangement.

25 Beautiful Homes

Future plc, 161 Marsh Wall, London E14 9AP
email 25beautifulhomes@futurenet.com
website www.idealhome.co.uk/25-beautiful-homes
Twitter @25BHomesMag
Editorial Director Sarah Spiteri
Monthly £4.80

Interiors magazine aiming to inspire affluent readers
in their love for their homes. Each edition shows a
selection of properties in the UK and Europe that
have been renovated or built to a high standard. The
magazine also features a selection of best buys in
decorative accessories to help make beautiful homes
achievable.

Vanity Fair

The Condé Nast Publications Ltd, The Adelphi,
1–11 John Adam Street, London WC2N 6HT
tel 020-7851 1800
website www.vanityfair.com
Twitter @VanityFair
Editor-in-Chief Radhika Jones
Monthly £4.99

Media, glamour and politics for grown-up readers.
No unsolicited material. Payment: by arrangement.
Illustrated.

The Vegan

The Vegan Society, Donald Watson House,
34–35 Ludgate Hill, Birmingham B3 1EH
tel 0121 523 1730
email editor@vegansociety.com
website www.vegansociety.com
Editor Elena Orde

Quarterly £3, free to members

Articles on health, nutrition, cookery, vegan lifestyles, land use, climate change, animal rights. Length: approx. 1,000 words. Illustrations: photos, cartoons, line drawings – foods, animals, livestock systems, crops, people, events; colour for cover. Payment: contributions are voluntary. Founded 1944.

Vegan Food & Living

Anthem Publishing, Suite 6, Piccadilly House, London Road, Bath BA1 6PL
tel (01225) 489984
email sally.fitzgerald@anthem.co.uk
website www.veganfoodandliving.com/contact
Facebook www.facebook.com/veganfoodandliving
Twitter @veganfoodliving
Instagram @veganfoodandliving/
Publisher Sally Fitzgerald
Monthly £4.99

Plant-based recipes (75 per month), along with features on new trends and cooking techniques. Also nutrition advice, and guides for gourmet travellers. Founded 2015.

Vegan Life

Prime Impact, 1 Nags Corner, Wiston Road, Nayland CO6 4LT
tel (01787) 224040
email Gemma.Tadman@primeimpact.co.uk
website www.veganlifemag.com
Editor Gemma Tadman
Monthly £4.99

Lifestyle magazine covering all things vegan. Interested in: vegan news; recipes; food and drink; celebrities, athletes, and artists; compassion pieces and animal rescue stories; restaurant reviews and vegan chefs; travel and leisure; health and nutrition; and in-depth features on the food industry, animal agriculture and exploitation, vegan advocacy etc. Length: generally 1,000–2,000 words, but flexible according to value of the article/feature. Images: writers and contributors should try to source their own large, hi-res images wherever possible. Payment: all contributions are voluntary. Writers credited for their pieces and bylines offered on request.

Viz

Dennis Publishing Ltd, 31–32 Alfred Place, London WC1E 7DP
tel 020-3890 3890
email viz@viz.co.uk
website www.viz.co.uk
Twitter @vizcomic
10 p.a. £3.90

Cartoons, spoof tabloid articles, spoof advertisements. Illustrations: half-tone, line, cartoons. Payment: £300 per page (cartoons). Founded 1979.

Vogue

The Condé Nast Publications Ltd, The Adelphi, 1–11 John Adam Street, London WC2N 6HT
website www.vogue.co.uk
Twitter @BritishVogue
Editor Edward Enninful
Monthly £3.99

Fashion, beauty, health, decorating, art, theatre, films, literature, music, travel, food and wine. Length: articles from 1,000 words. Illustrated.

Waitrose Food

John Brown Media, 10 Triton Street, Regents Place, London NW1 3BF
tel 020-7565 3236
email waitrosefood@waitrose.co.uk
Editor Jessica Gunn
Monthly £3 (free to MyWaitrose members)

In-house magazine of the Waitrose Group. Features seasonal recipes, menu ideas, interviews and travel.

walk

The Ramblers, 2nd Floor, Camelford House, 87–90 Albert Embankment, London SE1 7TW
tel 020-3961 3141
email walkmag@ramblers.org.uk
website www.ramblers.org.uk/news/walk-magazine
Twitter @WalkMagazine
Quarterly Free to members

Magazine of the Ramblers, Britain's walking charity. Articles on walking, access to countryside and related issues, and interviews. Material mostly commissioned. Length: up to 1,500 words. Illustrations: colour photos, preferably hi-res, digitally supplied. Payment: by agreement. Founded 1935.

Wallpaper*

Future plc, 161 Marsh Wall, London E14 9AP
website www.wallpaper.com
Twitter @wallpapermag
Instagram @wallpapermag
Editor-in-Chief Sarah Douglas
12 p.a. £10

International media brand covering architecture, design, art, travel, entertaining, beauty and grooming, transport, technology, fashion, and watches and jewellery. Brand extensions include an in-house creative agency, an interior design service, a series of city guides, and an annual exhibition during Milan Design Week. Founded 1996.

Wanderlust

Capital House, 25 Chapel Street, London NW1 5DH
email submissions@wanderlust.co.uk
website www.wanderlust.co.uk
Editor-in-Chief George Kipouros
8 p.a. £5.50

Features on independent, adventure and special-interest travel. See website for contributor guidelines. Length: up to 2,500 words. Illustrations: hi-res digital. Payment: by arrangement. Founded 1993.

The War Cry

The Salvation Army, 101 Newington Causeway, London SE1 6BN
tel 020-7367 4900
email warcry@salvationarmy.org.uk
website www.salvationarmy.org.uk/warcry
Facebook www.facebook.com/TheWarCryUK
Twitter @TheWarCryUK
Editor Andrew Stone
Weekly 20p

Voluntary contributions: Human interest stories of personal Christian faith. Founded 1879.

Wasafiri

School of English and Drama,
Queen Mary University of London, Mile End Road, London E1 4NS
email wasafiri@qmul.ac.uk
website www.wasafiri.org
Editor and Publishing Director Malachi McIntosh
4 p.a. £11

International contemporary literature. Accepts submissions for fiction, poetry, articles and interviews; see website for details. Founded 1984.

Waterways World

Waterways World Ltd, 151 Station Street, Burton-on-Trent DE14 1BG
tel (01283) 742950
email editorial@waterwaysworld.com
website www.waterwaysworld.com
Twitter @waterwaysworld
Editor Bobby Cowling
Monthly £4.99

Feature articles on all aspects of inland waterways in Britain and abroad, including historical material; factual and technical articles preferred. No short stories or poetry. See website for notes for potential contributors (under the contact section). Illustrations: by arrangement. Payment: by arrangement. Founded 1972.

The Week

Dennis Publishing, 31–32 Alfred Place, London WC1E 7DP
tel 020-3890 3890
email editorialadmin@theweek.co.uk
website www.theweek.co.uk
Editor-in-Chief Jeremy O'Grady
Weekly £3.99

Magazine that distils the best from the British and foreign press into 44pp, including news, art, science, business, property and leisure. Founded 1995.

The Weekly News

D.C. Thomson & Co. Ltd, 2 Albert Square, Dundee DD1 1DD
tel (01382) 575850
email weeklynews@dctmedia.co.uk
Weekly £1.40

Send fiction submissions to weeklynewsfiction@dctmedia.co.uk.

What Car?

Haymarket Motoring Magazines Ltd, Bridge House, 69 London Road, Twickenham TW1 3SP
tel 020-8267 5688
email editorial@whatcar.com
website www.whatcar.com
Editor Steve Huntingford
Monthly £5.99

Road tests, buying guide, consumer stories and used car features. No unsolicited material. Illustrations: colour and b&w photos, line drawings. Payment: by negotiation. Founded 1973.

What's On TV

Future plc, 161 Marsh Wall, London E14 9AP
tel 020-3148 5573
email kim.palfrey@futurenet.com
website www.whatsontv.co.uk
Weekly 75p

Features on TV programmes and personalities. All material commissioned. Length: up to 250 words. Illustrations: colour and b&w photos. Payment: by agreement. Founded 1991.

The White Review

A.104 Fuel Tank, 8–12 Creekside, London SE8 3DX
website www.thewhitereview.org
Twitter @TheWhiteReview
Editor Francesca Wade
Quarterly £12.99

Contemporary arts and literature journal. Welcomes submissions of fiction, poetry, essays and interviews. See website for full submission details, but briefly: all fiction and non-fiction submissions should be in English, not have been published elsewhere and (poetry excepted) be at least 1,500 words long. Interview pitches also accepted, but see previous editions for style and tone. Email no more than three poems to poetry@thewhitereview.org; all other submissions should be sent to submissions@thewhitereview.org. Founded 2011.

WI Life

(formerly WI Home & Country)
104 New King's Road, London SW6 4LY
tel 020-7731 5777
email wilife@nfwi.org.uk
website www.thewi.org.uk/wie-and-wi-life
Twitter @WILifemagazine
Editor Sarah Drew Jones
8 p.a. as part of the WI subscription

Journal of the National Federation of Women's Institutes for England and Wales. Publishes material related to the Federation's and members' activities with articles of interest to active women engaged in their communities and campaigns, mainly written in-house and by WI members but some freelance opportunities. Illustrations: colour photos. Payment: all commissions are paid; rates on request.

Woman

Future plc, 161 Marsh Wall, London E14 9AP
tel 020-3148 5000
email woman@futurenet.com
website www.womanmagazine.co.uk
Weekly £1.40

News, celebrity and real-life features, of no more than 1,000 words. Particular interest in celebrity and diet exclusives. Digital images only. Read magazine prior to submission. Fiction not published. Payment: by negotiation. Founded 1937.

Woman Alive

(formerly Christian Woman)
Premier Christian Communications Ltd,
22 Chapter Street, London SW1P 4NP
email womanalive@premier.org.uk
website www.womanalive.co.uk
Facebook www.facebook.com/womanalivemagazine
Twitter @WomanAliveUK
Monthly From £35 p.a.

Aimed at women aged 35 upwards. Celebrity interviews, topical features. Explores modern issues facing women within the context of Christian faith, profiles of women in interesting occupations, Christian testimonies and real-life stories, fashion, beauty, travel, health, crafts. All feature articles should be illustrated. Length: 700–1500 words. Payment £55–£160. Founded 1982.

woman&home

Future plc, 161 Marsh Wall, London E14 9AP
tel 020-3148 5000
email woman&home@futurenet.com
website www.womanandhome.com
Editor Miranda McMinn
Monthly £4.99

Centres on the personal and home interests of the lively minded mature, modern woman. Articles dealing with fashion, beauty, leisure pursuits, gardening, home style; features on topical issues, people and places. Fiction: complete stories from 3,000–4,500 words in length. Illustrations: commissioned colour photos and sketches. Non-commissioned work is not accepted and cannot be returned. Founded 1926.

Woman's Own

Future plc, 161 Marsh Wall, London E14 9AP
tel 020-3148 5000

email womansown@futurenet.com
website www.womansown.co.uk
Weekly £1.40

Modern women's magazine aimed at the 35–50 age group. No unsolicited features. Address work to relevant department editor. Payment: by arrangement.

Woman's Way

Harmonia Ltd, Rosemount House, Dundrum Road, Dublin D14 P924, Republic of Ireland
tel +353 (0)1 2405318
website www.womansway.ie
Twitter @Womans_Way
Weekly €1.69

Human interest, personality interviews, features on fashion, beauty, celebrities and investigations. Founded 1963.

Woman's Weekly

Future plc, 161 Marsh Wall, London E14 9AP
tel 020-3148 5000
email geoffrey.palmer@futurenet.com
website www.womansweekly.com
Facebook www.facebook.com/WomansWeekly
Editor Geoffrey Williams
Weekly £1.40

Lively, family-interest magazine. Unsolicited short stories currently not accepted. Celebrity and strong human interest features, health, finance and consumer features, plus beauty, diet, travel, homes, craft, knitting, gardening and cookery; also inspirational and entertaining personal stories. Illustrations: full colour fiction illustrations, small sketches and photos. Payment: by arrangement. Founded 1911.

Women Together

(formerly Scottish Home and Country)
email magazine@theswi.org.uk
website www.theswi.org.uk/
Editor Pauline Burnett
Monthly £2

Articles on crafts, cookery, travel, personal experience, rural interest, women's interest, health, books. Length: up to 1,000 words, preferably illustrated. Illustrations: hi-res jpg/tif files, prints, cartoons and drawings. Payment: by arrangement. Founded 1924.

The Woodworker

MyTime Media Ltd, Enterprise House, Enterprise Way, Edenbridge, Kent TN8 6HF
tel 0844 848 8822
website www.getwoodworking.com
Editor Tegan Foley
Monthly £4.99

For the craft and professional woodworker. Practical illustrated articles on cabinet work, carpentry, polishing, wood turning, wood carving, rural crafts, craft history, antique and period furniture; also wooden toys and models, musical instruments; timber procurement, conditioning, seasoning; tools, machinery and equipment reviews. Illustrations: line drawings and digital photos. Payment: by arrangement. Founded 1901.

World Fishing & Aquaculture

Spinnaker House, Waterside Gardens, Fareham PO16 8SD
tel (01329) 825335
email editor@worldfishing.net
website www.worldfishing.net
Editor Quentin Bates
10 p.a. £141 p.a.

International journal of commercial fishing. Technical and management emphasis on catching, processing and marketing of fish and related products; fishery operations and vessels covered worldwide. Length: 500–1,500 words. Illustrations: photos and diagrams for litho reproduction. Payment: by arrangement. Founded 1952.

The World of Interiors

The Condé Nast Publications Ltd, The Adelphi, 1–11 John Adam Street, London WC2N 6HT
tel 020-7851 1800
website www.worldofinteriors.co.uk
Twitter @wofinteriors
Monthly £4.99

All material commissioned: send photographs/synopsis for article ideas. Length: 1,000–1,500 words. Illustrations: colour photos. Founded 1981.

World Soccer

Kelsey Media, The Granary, Downs Court, Yalding Hill, Yalding ME18 6AL
tel (01959) 541444
email WOS.ed@kelsey.co.uk
website www.worldsoccer.com
Editor Stephen Fishlock
Monthly £5.99

Articles, features, news concerning football, its personalities and worldwide development. Length: 600–2,000 words. Payment: by arrangement. Founded 1960.

The World Today

Chatham House, 10 St James's Square, London SW1Y 4LE
tel 020-7957 5712
email aphilps@chathamhouse.org.uk
website www.chathamhouse.org/publications/twt
Editor Alan Philps
6 p.a. The most recent edition is free online, but subscribe for archive articles from £33 p.a.

Analysis of international issues and current events by journalists, diplomats, politicians and academics.

Length: 1,200–1,500 words. Payment: nominal. Founded 1945.

Writing Magazine

Warners Group Publications Plc, 5th Floor, 31–32 Park Row, Leeds LS1 5JD
tel 0113 200 2929
email jonathant@warnersgroup.co.uk
website www.writers-online.co.uk
Facebook www.facebook.com/writingmagazine
Twitter @writingmagazine
Editor Jonathan Telfer
Monthly £4.25, £39.90 p.a. by Direct Debit; £45 p.a. otherwise. (Includes *Writers' News*.)

Articles on all aspects of writing. Length: 800–2,000 words. Payment: by arrangement. Founded 1992. In addition, *Writers' News* (now part of *Writing Magazine*) features news, competitions and market information. Length: up to 350 words. Payment: by arrangement. Founded 1989.

Yachting Monthly

Future plc, Pinehurst 2, Pinehurst Road, Farnborough Business Park, Farnborough, Hants GU14 7BF
tel (0330) 390 3933
email yachting.monthly@futurenet.com
website www.yachtingmonthly.com
Editor Theo Stocker
Monthly £4.99

Articles on all aspects of seamanship, navigation, the handling of sailing craft, and their design, construction and equipment. Well-written narrative accounts of cruises in yachts. Please read the magazine to understand where your submission might fit before contacting the editorial team, who can advise on what any requirements will be. Illustrations: colour photos. Payment: quoted on acceptance. Founded 1906.

Yachting World

Future plc, Pinehurst 2, Pinehurst Road, Farnborough Business Park, Farnborough, Hants GU14 7BF
tel (01252) 555000
email yachting.world@futurenet.com
website www.yachtingworld.com
Editor Helen Fretter
Monthly £4.99

Practical articles of an original nature, dealing with sailing and boats. Length: 1,500–2,000 words. Illustrations: digital files, drawings, cartoons. Payment: varies. Founded 1894.

Yachts and Yachting

The Chelsea Magazine Company, Jubilee House, 2 Jubilee Place, London SW3 3TQ
website www.yachtsandyachting.co.uk
Group Editor Steve Peake, *Editor* Georgie Corlett-Pitt
Monthly £4.75

Technical sailing and related lifestyle articles. Illustrations: line, half-tone, colour. Payment: by arrangement. Founded 1947.

Yorkshire Life

The Barn, Elms Farm, Hobb Lane, Daresbury, Warrington WA4 5LS
kathryn.armstrong@archant.co.uk
website www.greatbritishlife.co.uk
Editor Kathryn Armstrong
Monthly £4.49

Articles on Yorkshire, including places of interest, high-profile personalities, local events, arts, history and food. Unsolicited ideas welcome. Founded 1946.

Your Cat Magazine

Warners Group Publications Plc, The Maltings, West Street, Bourne, Lincs. PE10 9PH
email editorial@yourcat.co.uk
website www.yourcat.co.uk
Facebook www.facebook.com/yourcatmagazine
Editor Michael Hallam
Monthly £4.50

Practical advice on the care of cats and kittens, general interest items and news on cats, and true-life tales and fiction (commission ideas welcome, please email). Length: 800–1,500 words (articles), 200–300 words (news), up to 1,000 words (short stories). Illustrations: hi-res digital, colour transparencies and prints. Founded 1994.

Your Dog Magazine

Warners Group Publications Plc, The Maltings, West Street, Bourne, Lincs. PE10 9PH
email editorial@yourdog.co.uk
website www.yourdog.co.uk
Facebook www.facebook.com/yourdogmagazine
Twitter @yourdog
Editor Sarah Wright
Monthly £4.25

Articles and information of interest to dog lovers; features on all aspects of pet dogs. Length: approx. 800–1,500 words. Payment: £140 per 1,000 words. Founded 1994.

Your Horse Magazine

Kelsey Media Ltd, The Granary, Downs Court, Yalding Hill, Yalding, Maidstone, Kent ME18 6AL

email yh.ed@kelsey.co.uk
website www.yourhorse.co.uk
Facebook www.facebook.com/YourHorse
Editor Aimi Clark
13 issues p.a. £4.40

Practical horse care, riding advice and inspirational interviews, features and real-life articles for riders, owners and horse lovers to enjoy. Send feature ideas with examples of previous published writing. Welcomes ideas for articles and features. Length: 1,500 words. Payment: £140 per 1,000 words. Founded 1983.

Yours

Bauer Media, Media House, Lynch Wood, Peterborough Business Park, Peterborough PE2 6EA
tel (01733) 468000
email yours@bauermedia.co.uk
website www.yours.co.uk
Facebook www.facebook.com/Yoursmagazine
Twitter @yoursmagazine
Fortnightly £1.62

Features and news about and/or of interest to the over-50s age group, including nostalgia and short stories. Study of magazine essential. Length: articles up to 300 words, short stories up to 1,200 words. Payment: at the Editor's discretion. Founded 1973.

Yours Fiction

Bauer Media, Media House, Lynch Wood, Peterborough Business Park, Peterborough PE2 6EA
email yours@bauermedia.co.uk
website https://www.yours.co.uk/
4 p.a. £2.25

Short story magazine and sister title to the women's lifestyle magazine, *Yours*. Features a selection of short stories in every issue as well as features for book lovers.

Accepts short story submissions from 500–3,000 words across a variety of genres including murder mystery, crime, historical fiction, comedy and romance. All published writers are paid for their submission, which should be emailed to the address above with 'Yours Fiction' clearly marked in the subject line. Postal submissions are also accepted (see above).

Syndicates, news and press agencies

Before submitting material, you are strongly advised to make preliminary enquiries and to ascertain terms of work. Strictly speaking, syndication is the selling and reselling of previously published work although some news and press agencies handle original material.

Academic File Information Services

EAPGROUP International Media, PO Box 13666, London SW14 8WF
tel 020-8392 1122
email afis@eapgroup.com
email main@eapgroup.com
website www.eapgroup.com
Twitter @eapgroupnews
Commissioning Editor Sajid Rizvi

Feature and photo syndication with special reference to the developing-world diasporic and migrant and immigrant communities in the West. Founded 1985.

Brainwarp

23 Chatsworth Avenue, Culcheth, Warrington, Cheshire WA3 4LD
tel (01925) 765878
email sarah@brainwarp.com
website www.brainwarp.com
Contacts Trixie Roberts, Tony Roberts, Sarah Simmons

Writes and supplies original crosswords, brainteasers, wordsearches, quizzes and word games to editors for the printed page. Does not accept work from external sources. Standard fees for syndicated puzzles. Customised work negotiable. Founded 1987.

Bulls Presstjänst AB

Augustendalsvägen 51, 131 52 Nacka Strand, Sweden
tel +46 8-55520600
website www.bullspress.com

Market: newspapers, magazines, weeklies and advertising agencies across Northern Europe. Syndicates human-interest picture stories; topical and well-illustrated background articles and series; photographic features dealing with science, people, personalities, glamour; genre pictures for advertising; condensations and serialisations of bestselling fiction and non-fiction; cartoons, comic strips, film and TV rights, merchandising and newspaper graphics online.

DMG Media Licensing

Northcliffe House, 2 Derry Street, London W8 5TT
tel 020-7566 0360
website www.solosyndication.co.uk
Director of Licensing & Syndication William Gardiner

Worldwide syndication of newspaper features, photos, cartoons, puzzles and strips. Represents the international syndication of Associated Newspapers Ltd (*Daily Mail*, *Mail on Sunday*, the *i* newspaper,

Mail Online, *Metro*), Andrews McMeel Syndication (US) and Creators Syndicate (US) in Great Britain and Ireland, Africa and the Middle East. Formerly Solo Syndication.

Europress Features (UK)

18 St Chad's Road, Didsbury, Nr Manchester M20 4WH
tel 0161 445 2945
email europressmedia@yahoo.com

Representation of newspapers and magazines in Europe, Australia, USA. Syndication of top-flight features with exclusive illustrations – human interest stories – showbusiness personalities. 30–35% commission on sales of material successfully accepted; 40% on exclusive illustrations.

Foresight News

Centaur Media Plc, 10 York Road, London SE1 7ND
tel 020-7970 4299
email enquiries@foresightnews.co.uk
website www.foresightnews.com
Twitter @ForesightNewsUK
Publisher Nicole Wilkins

Offers a vast, fully searchable database featuring thousands of forthcoming events and news from across the UK and around the world, spanning a variety of sectors including politics, business, crime and home affairs, health, entertainment and sport.

Guardian Syndication

Kings Place, 90 York Way, London N1 9GU
tel 020-3353 2539
email permissions.syndication@guardian.co.uk
website https://syndication.theguardian.com/
Head of Licensing Ross Paterson

International syndication services of news and features from the *Guardian*, the *Observer* and theguardian.com. Unable to syndicate content which has not been published in its own titles. All permission requests to be submitted via online form.

Hayters Teamwork

47 Dean Street, London W1D 5BE
tel 020-7183 6727
email sport@hayters.com
website www.hayters.com
Contacts Nick Callow, Gerry Cox

Sports news, features and data supplied to all branches of the media. Commission: negotiable according to merit. Founded 1955.

Headliners

49–51 East Road, London N1 6AH
tel 020-7749 9360
email enquiries@headliners.org
website www.headliners.org
Twitter @HeadlinersUK
Chief Executive Ali Talbot

UK-wide journalism and multi-media charity. Offers young people aged 8–18 the opportunity to write on issues of importance to them, for newspapers, radio and TV. Founded 1995.

Independent Radio News (IRN)

Academic House, 24–28 Oval Road,
London NW1 7DJ
tel 020-3227 4044
email news@irn.co.uk
website www.irn.co.uk
Twitter @IRNRadioNews
Managing Director Tim Molloy

National and international news.

Knight Features Ltd

Trident Business Centre, 89 Bickersteth Road,
London SW17 9SH
tel 020-3051 5650
email info@knightfeatures.co.uk
website www.knightfeatures.com
Contacts Gaby Martin, Andrew Knight, Sam Ferris

Worldwide selling of puzzles, strip cartoons, crosswords, horoscopes and serialisations for print and digital media. Agent in the UK and Republic of Ireland for Creators Syndicate, Tribune Content Agency. Founded 1985.

Neil Bradley Studio

Linden House, Ripley, Derbyshire DE5 8JF
tel 07814 526808
email enquire@neilbradleystudio.co.uk
Director Neil Bradley

Supplies cartoons to national and regional press; emphasis placed on variety and topicality with work based on current media listings. Daily single frame and strip cartoons. Founded 1981.

New Blitz Literary and Editorial TV Agency

Via del Fossaccio, 19, 01010 Marta, Italy
email blitzgacs@inwind.it
Manager Giovanni A.S. Congiu

Syndicates worldwide: cartoons, comic strips, humorous books with drawings, feature material, topical. Average rates of commission 60/40%, monthly report of sales, payment 60 days after the date of sale.

PA Media

website https://pa.media/
website https://pamediagroup.com/contact-page/
Twitter @PA

Chief Executive Clive Marshall, *Managing Director* Polly Curtis

Provider of multimedia content and services, and the national news agency for the UK and Ireland. Has offices in several key locations (see above). Customers include major national, regional and international media and digital brands, as well as businesses and public sector organisations. Services include: news wire and digital ready-to-publish articles, pictures; video; data APIs; hosted live blogs; graphics; listings pages; social media curation; and page production. Part of the PA Media Group of specialist media companies. Founded 1868.

The Puzzle House

Ivy Cottage, Battlesea Green, Stradbroke,
Suffolk IP21 5NE
tel (01379) 384656
email enquiries@thepuzzlehouse.co.uk
website www.thepuzzlehouse.co.uk
Partners Roy Preston & Sue Preston

Supply original crosswords, quizzes and puzzles of all types. Commissions taken on any topic, with all age ranges catered for. Wide selection of puzzles available for one-off usage. Founded 1988.

Rann Media

120 Molesworth Street, North Adelaide,
SA 5006 Australia
tel + (61) 418 832 512
website www.rann.com.au
Managing Director Chris Rann

Professional PR, press releases, special newsletters, commercial and political intelligence, media monitoring. Welcomes approaches from organisations requiring PR representation or press release distribution. Founded 1982.

Sirius Media Services Ltd

37 Lower Brook Street, Ipswich IP4 1AQ
tel (01449) 833834
email info@siriusmedia.co.uk
website www.siriusmedia.co.uk

Crosswords, puzzles and quizzes, and Zygolex.

The Telegraph – Content Licensing & Syndication

Telegraph Media Group,
111 Buckingham Palace Road, London SW1W 0DT
tel 020-7931 1010
email syndication@telegraph.co.uk
website www.telegraph.co.uk/syndication/

News, features, photography and graphics, video, worldwide distribution and representation. Content licensing packages available for print or online use.

WENN

78 York Street, London W1H 1DP
tel 020-7607 2757

email enquiries@wenn.com
website www.wenn.com
Editorial Director Kevin Lewin

Provides the world's media with up-to-the-minute entertainment news and photos. Founded 1989.

Wessex News, Features and Photos Agency

Little Mead, Lower Green, Inkpen, Berks. RG17 9DW

tel (01488) 668308
email news@britishnews.co.uk
website www.britishnews.co.uk
Editor Jim Hardy

Freelance press agency with a network of writers and photographers across the UK. Providing real-life news stories and features for national and international newspapers and magazines. Founded 1981.

Books
How to get published

The combined wisdom of the writers of the articles in this *Yearbook* provide some of the best practical advice you will need to negotiate your way through the world of publishing. Whether you opt for the traditional route via an agent or the self-publishing model, there are key things it would be useful to consider before you begin.

How can you give yourself the best chance of success whichever route you take?

1. Know your market
• Is there a readership for your book? Explore the intended market so you are sure that your publishing idea is of potential interest to an agent, publisher or reader.
• Know your competition and keep up to date with the latest publishing trends: look in bookshops, at ebook stores, at online book sites, take an interest in publishing stories in the media and, above all, *read*.

2. Agent, publisher or self-publishing?
• First decide if you want to try and get signed by a literary agent and be published by an established publisher. Self-publishing in print and digital can be a viable alternative to the traditional approach.
• If you opt for the agent/publisher route, note that many publishers, particularly of fiction, will only consider material submitted through a literary agent. See *What a debut novelist should expect from an agent* on page 405 and *Advice from an 'accidental' agent* on page 415
• For information about self-publishing, consult *What do self-publishing providers offer?* on page 618 and *Self-publishing online: the emerging template for sales success* on page 607.

3. Choose the right publisher, agent or self-publishing provider
• Study the entries in this *Yearbook*, examine publishers' lists and their websites, and look in the relevant sections in libraries and bookshops for the names of publishers which might be interested in your material.
• Consult the *Children's Writers' & Artists' Yearbook 2022* (Bloomsbury 2021) for in-depth coverage of writing and publishing for the children's and young adult markets.
• Familiarise yourself with the diagram on the next page that outlines the different stages that make up the publishing process.
• Authors should not pay publishers for the publication of their work. There are many companies that can help you self-publish your book; see *Editorial services and self-publishing providers* on page 640. Make sure you know what it is the company will actually do and agree any fees in advance.
• Crowdfunding is becoming a viable option for some (see page 196).

4. Prepare your material well
• Presentation is important. If your material is submitted in the most appropriate electronic format an agent or publisher will be more inclined to give it attention.

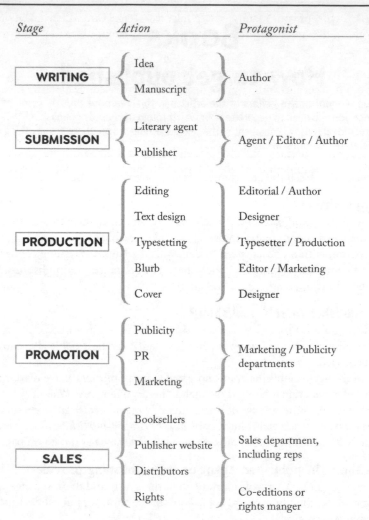

Stage	Action	Protagonist
WRITING	Idea Manuscript	Author
SUBMISSION	Literary agent Publisher	Agent / Editor / Author
PRODUCTION	Editing Text design Typesetting Blurb Cover	Editorial / Author Designer Typesetter / Production Editor / Marketing Designer
PROMOTION	Publicity PR Marketing	Marketing / Publicity departments
SALES	Booksellers Publisher website Distributors Rights	Sales department, including reps Co-editions or rights manger

Typical stages in the publishing process

• It is understandable that writers, in their eagerness to get their work published, will send their manuscript out in a raw state. Do not send your manuscript to a literary agent or publisher and do not self-publish your script until it is *ready* to be seen. Wait until you are confident that your work is as good as it can be. Have as your mantra: edit, review, revise and then edit again. See *Editing your work* on page 651.

5. Approach a publisher or literary agent in the way they prefer

• Submit your work to the right person within the publishing company or literary agency. Look at the listings in this *Yearbook* for more details. See listings starting on page 130 and page 430. Most agents will expect to see a synopsis and up to three sample chapters or the complete manuscript. Most publishers' and literary agents' websites give guidance on how to submit material.

• Always keep a copy of your manuscript. Whilst reasonable care will be taken of material in the possession of a publisher or agent, responsibility cannot be accepted if material is lost or damaged.

6. Write a convincing cover letter or email

• It will be your first contact with an agent or publisher and needs to make them take notice of your book for the right reasons.

• What is the USP (unique selling point) of the material you are submitting? You may have an original authorial 'voice', or you may have come up with an amazingly brilliant idea for a series. If, after checking out the marketplace, you think you have something truly original to offer, be confident in what you have written and be convincing when you offer it around.

7. Network

• Talk to others who write in the same genre or share a similar readership. You can meet them at literature festivals, conferences and book or writers' groups. Consider doing a course – see *Writers' retreats and creative writing courses* on page 691.

• Go to a festival and be inspired. There are numerous literature festivals held throughout the year at which authors appear (see *Festival fun: your guide to why, how and what* on page 501).

• Join one of the numerous online communities, book review and manuscript share sites; see *Book sites, blogs and podcasts* on page 635.

8. Don't give up!

• Be prepared to wait for a decision on your work. Editors and agents are very busy people so be patient when waiting for a response. Don't pester them too soon.

• Publishing is big business and it is more competitive than ever. Even after an editor has read your work, there are many other people involved before a manuscript is acquired for publication. People from the sales, marketing, publicity, rights and other departments all have to be convinced that the book is right for their list and will sell.

• The harsh reality of submitting a manuscript to a publisher or literary agent is that you have to be prepared for rejection. But many successful authors have received such rejections at some time so you are in good company.

• Have patience and persevere. If the conventional route doesn't produce the results you were hoping for, consider the self-publishing route as a viable alternative.

  Good luck!

News, views and trends: review of the publishing year

Tom Tivnan looks back on a year in which the huge disruption brought about by Covid-19 nevertheless produced a record year for the UK book trade, with a huge spike in reading and sales. He examines the changes in both retail and consumer behaviour brought about by the pandemic, noting the biggest winners and losers, and how physical retail chains suffered while there was encouraging growth in the more flexible independent sector.

It is not hyperbolic to say that the last 12 months have been the most disruptive period for the UK's book trade since the Luftwaffe was raining bombs down upon the land. Covid-19 changed working practices, smashed publication schedules, altered how estivals operated and saw the main conduit of books to readers (bricks-and-mortar shops) go dark for months. The comparison to the Second World War may actually underplay the far-reaching effects of the pandemic. WW2 was obviously a trying time for publishers and booksellers, but few of the changes wrought by the war were long-lasting, whereas many of the alterations brought on by the coronavirus look as if they will become permanent fixtures of the trade's ecosystem.

And yet. And yet. Whisper this, but for all the pain and worry of the past year many in the trade had a pretty darn good time of it. Indeed, there is an argument that few industries had better pandemics – excepting maybe face mask manufacturers – as the books world had a record year. Industry sales monitor Nielsen Book reported that 375 million units were sold across all formats (print, ebooks, audio downloads) in the UK in 2020 – a 6% year-on-year jump and the highest number ever recorded. Value sales leapt 7% to £2.65bn, also a record figure. It should be emphasised that those are top-line figures and not everyone benefited. The clear winners of the year were the big boys, as almost all the multinational publishers had an embarrassment of riches. A typical example is the world's largest trade publisher Penguin Random House, whose global revenues increased slightly by 3% to €3.8bn (£3.2bn) but its profit ballooned by a whopping 24% to €691m (£590m).

The bigger publishers prospered because of their relationship with by far the biggest coronavirus winner: Amazon. By dint of its essential retailer status, Amazon was able to operate during Britain's lockdowns to become almost the only bookseller in town for about half a year. It is difficult to gauge how much of the pie Amazon carved out during this period (even in normal times, the e-tailer is about as open with information as the Kremlin) but, factoring in the fact that pre-pandemic Amazon already had a near-monopoly on ebooks and audio, it is not outrageous to assume that at the height of the crisis nine out of every ten books sold in the UK were supplied by Amazon.

The big get bigger

An inconvenient truth for the big publishers is that essentially only dealing with one retailer, and a ruthlessly efficient one like Amazon, meant a far better bottom line. Plus, Amazon being the main conduit for books meant that consumers flocked more than ever to the bestsellers, brand authors and celebrities – of which the bigger publishers have the lion's share. One of the myths of Amazon is its 'long tail': the idea that, since readers can get any book in print from it, they will spend hours delving into its endless digital shelves. That, it turns out, is a load of hooey. Online shoppers rarely venture past category landing sites or go beyond one or two pages, even if they type in a search term. Publishers appreciate bricks-and-mortar shops with large ranges, like Waterstones, because they emphasise serendipitous browsing and there is, counterintuitively, more discoverability in a physical store than in an online retailer.

But, in a year when Amazon was the main player, customers 'shopped chart'; they went with the familiar and looked to what was already selling. This helped many big authors to monster years, such as children's stars Julia Donaldson, David Walliams and J.K. Rowling, lifestyle mega-brands Jamie Oliver and the Pinch of Nom (Bluebird 2018) duo Kay Featherstone and Kate Allinson, and crime kings James Patterson and Lee Child. It also enabled titles to stick in the charts longer. The exemplar is Charlie Mackesy's *The Boy, the Mole, the Fox and the Horse* (Ebury). Mackesy's illustrated fable was originally published in October 2019 and was a Christmas hit that year. But it excelled during the pandemic – it was the hardback non-fiction number one 19 times during 2020, including the first eight weeks of the Lockdown 1.0 and was the bestselling title of that year – the first time a book released in a previous year has topped an annual chart in its original format.

Bricks-and-mortar booksellers suffered most. Waterstones had a very bad pandemic, with the permanent closure (at this writing) of five shops and a deep cull of head office staff, plus further redundancies across the estate. WHSmith was damaged, too – no surprise as its money-making engine is the Travel division (shops in airports and train stations); WHS's loss for the year was around £75m, leading to a massive restructure and 1,500 job cuts.

Wonderfully, independent bookshops weathered the storm. The early fear was that the sector would be decimated by lockdown – fears exacerbated by Covid-19 bringing about the collapse of Bertram Books, the UK's second biggest books distributor and a key supplier to indies. But, perhaps because they are nimbler than the big chains, indies were able to pivot almost overnight, building transactional websites and finding ways to work within lockdowns, like delivering books by hand to locals. The UK launch in the autumn of Bookshop.org, a US import that offers an indie-friendly alternative to Amazon, helped. Bookshop.org's model is that if you buy a book from their online store, a portion of the proceeds go to an independent shop of your choosing; at the time of writing it has given back £1.2m to UK shops. Incredibly, the indie sector actually grew; although 44 shops closed, 50 new indies opened their doors in 2020.

UK: islands into stream

The book world also benefited from changing consumer behaviour during the pandemic. Study after study showed a huge spike in reading; for example, Nielsen Book reported that reading time doubled in the UK during lockdown (to about six hours a week). We were also watching more. Ofcom noted a 31% rise in TV and online content viewing in 2020, with the average Briton in front of their screens a somewhat alarming six hours and 25 minutes a day (egad, more time per day than Nielsen says we read per week!).

But our lockdown Netflix fix often dovetailed nicely with books, and some of the bestsellers of the year were streaming-service adaptations. Sally Rooney was one of 2020's first bookish beneficiaries as the BBC3/Hulu adaptation of her second novel, *Normal People*

Books

(Faber 2018), was the smash of Lockdown 1.0. Rooney was already Ireland's literary rock star, but the TV series pushed her to the stratosphere, with *Normal People* hitting the overall number one spot in the UK book charts two years after it was originally published.

The Christmas lockdown brought what was unarguably a streaming service's biggest books hit, *Bridgerton*, based on the series of Regency romance novels by Julia Quinn. The show struck a nerve with its blend of diverse casting, dishy light-hearted fun and, let's be honest, its stars Regé-Jean Page and Phoebe Dynevor's superhuman good looks and rather … ah … vigorous commitment to their sex scenes. At the end of January 2021, Netflix announced that it was its biggest success ever, with 82 million viewers spread across the globe. This resulted in a UK sales surge. While Quinn regularly hits the bestseller list in her native USA, her books have been unspectacularly solid in Britain – with all-time sales of just over 260,000 units sold in the past 20 years from nearly 40 titles. But with her publisher Little, Brown rushing out a new series look to tap into *Bridgerton* mania, Quinn scored her first-ever UK top 10 in February 2021.

Say hi to hybrid

One of the biggest adjustments publishers and authors had to make during the year was in how books were publicised and marketed. Even though digital plays a huge part in book promotion, a lot of the work is still done the old-fashioned way, with outdoor advertising and author events. A good traditional case study was the much-anticipated third volume in Hilary Mantel's Thomas Cromwell novels, *The Mirror and the Light* (4th Estate). As it was one of 2020's publishing events, it got the all-signing, all-dancing treatment including a massive billboard campaign, a series of marquee book-signings, and even the Tower of London being lit up with a projection of the book's cover. It worked a treat, with *The Mirror and the Light* shifting 95,000 hardbacks in its first week, an eye-popping number for a 900-page literary novel.

Mantel's book was the last big pre-lockdown title, then almost overnight all of publishers' carefully orchestrated publicity and marketing plans – some that had been in train for months – went up in smoke. Publicists, marketers and authors scrambled to go online. Take Maggie O'Farrell's *Hamnet* which was launched just after lockdown, with publisher Headline scrapping 37 live appearances and moving to virtual events – no mean feat, for this was in the early days of Zoom when people were still figuring out how best to use video conferencing. *Hamnet*'s new normal of publicity worked as well as Mantel's traditional model, helping O'Farrell to sell 210,000 units and win the Women's Prize for Fiction.

While virtual events may lack intimacy (you don't get a free glass of wine if you're sitting at home in your PJs for an online book launch, do you?), they proved effective during the pandemic and have some advantages over 'IRL' (in real-life) occasions; the costs for hosting are minimal, the size of an audience is only limited by bandwidth, anyone the world over can attend, and an author doesn't have to be physically in town to appear. There are drawbacks – even now it is hard to monetise tickets to a virtual festival – but the added engagement means that, even when pandemic restrictions are completely lifted, most festivals, book prizes and events programmers are saying a hybrid live/virtual model will be the norm.

Tired of London, excited by life

The pandemic may also, perhaps, have permanently altered the trade's day-to-day working life. Like many across the world, publishers and agents began working from home *en masse* in March 2020 and found that, through the wonders of technology, they could do so effectively. Offices reopening in 2021 will bear little resemblance to pre-pandemic versions, as many staff, finding that more time at home improved productivity (at least when they didn't have to home-school the kids) will move to a (… that word again) hybrid home/office model. Big firms like Hachette, Quarto and Bonnier are responding to staff wishes, and announced they would be greatly consolidating their office space, as the new way of working means far fewer bums on seats at their London HQs. The publishers' arms were not twisted. Yes, there are some costs to more home working, mostly in IT, but there will be huge savings on exorbitant London rents.

A very positive sidelight to pandemic remote-working is that it has shown conclusively how agents and publishers needn't be confined to the London bubble. And it has accelerated plans for many publishers to open regional hubs, such as HarperCollins' Manchester-based HarperNorth division and Hachette's new outposts in Edinburgh, Manchester, Bristol, Newcastle and Sheffield. In the end this will be beneficial to authors, as it will boost networking and commissioning in regions which are – to use the euphemistic phrase bandied about in the trade – 'currently under-represented' (translation: ignored).

Daunting for debuts

If the big-brand authors were the winners of the pandemic, it was not such a fun time for midlist, emerging and debut writers. Partially, this was due to the havoc played on the publishing schedules. With shops closing, publishers ducked and dived, pushing books further down in 2020 or to the next year. In fact, book production went way down, plummeting by 14% to just under 184,000 titles released in 2020, the lowest total in 11 years. Even with the decline in production, fewer books were brought out during lockdowns so there were bottleneck periods. One of those was 3 September, which was 2020's Super Thursday, a day in the year when the greatest amount of books are released. Normally, publishers use Super Thursday to wheel out the big Christmas guns, like celeb memoirs or cookery books. But, owing to the paucity of titles in the usually quieter spring periods, a lot of midlist and debut publications were shunted into Super Thursday. Their worried authors fretted that, deprived of the publicity oxygen they would have had if they stuck to original publication dates, their books would be Super Thursday casualties; there was even a Twitter 'support group', #3rdSeptembers.

Some debuts did A-OK. In fact, the biggest fiction title of the year was a first outing – Richard Osman's cosy crime tale, *The Thursday Murder Club* (Viking 2020), which sold a whopping 600,000 copies throughout the year. This is an outlier, though, as his publisher essentially treated the telly star as an established brand, with a huge, unmissable marketing and publicity blitz. Viking paid over seven figures in signing Osman (in a deal orchestrated by uber-agent Juliet Mushens) so he was going to be given all the oxygen he needed. The next two biggest debuts also had a platform: Douglas Stuart's *Shuggie Bain* (Picador 2020) won the Booker Prize, while *Ghosts* (Fig Tree 2020) was from the well-known journalist, influencer and podcaster Dolly Alderton. So there were few 'organic' hit debuts, apart from the likes of Naoise Dolan's *Exciting Times* (Weidenfeld & Nicolson 2020) or Bolu Babalola's *Love in Colour* (Headline 2020). It is difficult to say definitively that this was due to the stresses of 2020 – some years a lot of debuts simply don't land – but the pandemic did not help.

Books

The biggest non-pandemic story of the last year was the Black Lives Matter movement, which had a profound effect on the book trade. The protests on both sides of the Atlantic after George Floyd's murder saw anti-racist books and titles by black authors shooting up the bestseller lists, most notably Reni Eddo-Lodge's *Why I'm No Longer Talking to White People About Race* (Bloomsbury 2017) which topped the UK charts for several weeks, three years after it was originally published. Eddo-Lodge and other authors and publishers who benefited from the BLM protests were quick to acknowledge how desperately sad it was that a tragic event kick-started their sales boosts. But it did get the trade thinking more deeply about diversity and inclusion – an issue it has been wrestling with for some time – and not just in terms of the authors it publishes but the makeup of its staff.

One of the things about the pandemic is that it has pushed many things that would normally have been hot-button issues to the side. Brexit, for example, has fully begun and has been an unmitigated disaster for many publishers selling books into the EU. We are seeing a period of intense corporate conglomeration – a deep worry to authors and agents – including HarperCollins buying children's publisher Egmont and Houghton Mifflin Harcourt, and Penguin Random House's proposed acquisition of Simon & Schuster. But those feel like issues for down the road, as there are still many questions to answer from the last year: Will the bricks-and-mortar chains come back? Has Amazon's increased share made it too powerful? And on and on … But on the whole there is guarded optimism for the trade, as it is coming out of what could have been a debilitating period on a very solid footing.

Tom Tivnan is managing editor of *The Bookseller*. Tom was a freelance writer and his work has appeared in the *Glasgow Herald*, the *Independent*, the *Daily Telegraph* and the *Times Literary Supplement*. Before joining *The Bookseller* in 2007 he worked as a bookseller for Blackwell's in the UK and for Barnes & Noble in the US. He wrote the text for *Tattoed by the Family Business* (Pavilion 2010) and his debut novel is *The Esquimaux* (Silvertail 2017). Follow him on Twitter @tomtivnan.

The mathematics of publishing

Scott Pack reveals the numbers underlying the publishing business and spells out the important, surprising and sobering figures – for publisher and author alike – to be considered when publishing a book, even a bestseller.

When you think about the world of writing and publishing you probably picture an industry built upon words. And rightly so. The book world would be nothing without the written word. But numbers play a crucial part too, and some of the numbers that crunch away behind the scenes of publishing may surprise you.

How many copies does a book need to sell to become a bestseller?

100,000? 50,000? 10,000? Each week the *Sunday Times* publishes four separate book charts: top tens in Hardback Fiction, Hardback Non-fiction, Paperback Fiction and Paperback Non-fiction. For a book to be able to feature the three magic words 'Sunday Times Bestseller' on the cover, it needs to have appeared in one of these charts for at least one week.

To sit at the top of these charts, especially Paperback Fiction, you generally need to sell thousands of copies. But pick a quiet time of year, perhaps February or March, and you could sneak in at number 10 in the Hardback Non-Fiction chart by selling around 500 copies, a somewhat less daunting figure.

Let's put that in perspective. There are close to 5,000 book outlets in the UK. A book could sell one copy in just 10% of these locations in any given week and hit the bestseller chart. 90% of shops wouldn't need to have sold any at all, and you'd still have a bestseller on your hands.

Things are very different at the top of the charts, of course. The bestselling paperback novel in the UK would typically have to sell well into five figures, although that could be anywhere between 10,000 and 90,000 depending on the time of year and what books are out that week.

And things get more interesting when you start to delve into the chart data a bit more. The *Sunday Times* top tens are taken from a much larger sales report generated by Nielsen Bookscan. They create a Top 5,000 chart each week that is distributed widely within the book trade, with retailers and publishers poring over the figures in some detail.

Let's say the bestselling book in the country sold 25,000 copies in a week. That's a lot of books, but not many titles can deliver that level of sales. In the same week it is likely that the tenth bestselling book sold around 7,000 copies – still a lot, but quite a drop-off. The book at number 100 in the charts will have sold 1,500 or so. The book at 500 may actually have sold 500 copies, and you can often get into the bottom regions of the Top 5,000 by selling 50 or so copies in a week.

So how does this pan out across an entire year? In a very good year, the bestselling book in the UK can sell close to a million copies, but it would more often be about half that number. The tenth bestseller may have sold half that again. The book at number 500 might have sold around 50,000, and you could have the 5,000th bestselling book of the year by selling 5,000 copies – or just one copy in every bookshop in the land.

It is important to stress that with the many tens of thousands of books published every year, and the hundreds of thousands already in circulation, the vast majority of books never even get close to the top 5,000 at all.

Books

How much does it cost to publish a book?

These sales figures are all well and good, and may prove fascinating, but you cannot sell a single book until it is printed and distributed to shops, and that can prove to be a costly exercise.

Different types of books have different budgets – a big, illustrated, coffee-table book will usually cost several times more to produce than a fairly straightforward paperback – but for this example we are going to look at the costs for a standard novel with no fancy design elements or illustrations.

To get the manuscript ready for publication, with a developmental edit, copy edit, typesetting and proofread, you are rarely going to have much change from £2,500. A designer will charge around £750 to create a cover. Printing costs vary depending on the size of the print run, but 75p per copy is not untypical. So, to produce and print 3,000 copies of a paperback novel will cost a publisher in the region of £5,500. Of course, the major publishing houses manage a lot of these services in-house, but most medium- and small-sized publishers will be paying freelancers to do much of this work.

And that £5,500 is without spending any money on warehousing, distribution, sales, marketing or publicity, the combined costs of which could easily bring the total outlay to £10,000.

Example P&L

Sales
Book RRP
£7.99

Book sales
3,000

Discount
55%
NET BOOK SALES £10,787

Production costs
Editorial
£1,750

Typesetting
£750

Cover design
£750

Printing costs
Print costs
£2,700

Sales and marketing costs
Sales and distribution
£2,500

Marketing and publicity
£1,500
TOTAL COSTS £9,950

Other deductions
Returns @ 20%
£2,157

Royalties @ 7.5%
£1,800
Total costs + deductions £13,907

TOTAL PROFIT: -£3,120

How much money does a publisher make from a book?

So, a publisher has spent £10,000 to produce, sell, distribute and promote 3,000 copies of a new novel. Let's assume all 3,000 copies sell to bookshops, a rare feat but one that makes our maths a little easier, and that it has an RRP (recommended retail price) of £7.99.

Book retailers receive discount from publishers which can be anywhere from 30% to 70%, depending on the size of the retailer, how many copies they are ordering and whether or not the book goes into a big promotion – but let's use 55% as an average. That means that for every copy sold to bookshops the publisher receives just over £3.59. Across 3,000 copies that comes to £10,787 of revenue.

Cast your eye back a few paragraphs and you'll be reminded that it cost around £10,000 to produce these books in the first place, so even by selling the whole of the first print run, the publisher is only just breaking even. But wait! We forgot returns. In the UK, most books are sold to retailers on a sale-or-return basis. This means that shops can return unsold stock and typically 15-20% of all books sold to retailers are sent back. So that £10,787 mentioned above may end up being more like £8,630 once the returns are accounted for.

So how do publishers make any money from their books? Well, the truth is that many do not. They are often reliant on one or two books selling in excess of 10,000 copies, and ideally lots more than that, in order to generate the income needed to fund the other books on the list that sell below 3,000. Over time, they can build up a backlist of older titles that tick over, generating ongoing revenue. And ebooks can help too; they are cheaper to sell, as there are no warehouse costs and no returns, and many a book these days moves into profit on the back of healthy digital sales.

And how much money can an author make?

You probably know the score when it comes to royalties: for every copy of a book that sells, the author receives a percentage of the revenue. There are many variations on the basic deal but, if we continue with our example of a paperback novel, typically an author will receive 7.5% of the RRP for each copy that sells. On our £7.99 paperback that would be just under 60p – but I am feeling generous so will round it up.

Again, sticking with our example, if we sell 3,000 copies then the author will have made just under £1,800 in royalties. Hardly a life-changing amount, but not to be sniffed at either.

But let's not focus on such tiny numbers. Instead, let's be ambitious and bold and go back to the bestsellers that we discussed earlier. Remember that bestselling book that sold 25,000 copies in a week, taking it to the top of the charts? Assuming it was a £7.99 paperback, that book will have earned its author £15,000 in just one week. The book at number 10, selling 7,000, will have generated £4,200. And even the number 500 book will have made £300, which isn't bad for one week's work. Although don't forget that the agent will take 15% of that!

What does this all add up to?

It is important that authors understand the numbers behind the publishing world. If a book becomes a bestseller, then it is possible for both author and publisher to make a lot of money, and even a moderate seller can, over time, generate some decent income. However, the majority of books published will only make a small amount of money for their authors.

For most of us, this is not a get-rich-quick industry. Does that matter? Only you can answer that, but if you have decided to write a book in order to make your fortune, you are probably going to be disappointed. If, however, you are writing a book because you want to share your story, and you value a connection with readers above all else, then great fortune may await – it just may not be a financial one.

Scott Pack is a writer, freelance editor and publisher. He was formerly head of buying for Waterstones and spent many years at HarperCollins. He is now editor-at-large for Eye & Lightning Books and writes specialist subject questions for the BBC quiz show, *Mastermind*. His latest book is *Tips From a Publisher: A Guide to Writing, Editing, Submitting and Publishing Your Book* (Eye Books 2020). For more information see https://reedsy.com/scott-pack.

Books

Getting books to market: how books are sold

Sales manager David Wightman describes the various parts, people and processes, skills and systems within the world of book sales that interlink to bring a book from publisher to customer, and what makes this a fascinating, challenging and satisfying area of work.

I've always been excited about sales and wanted to set up a company where the focus is on maximising the sales of every book that we represent. My company, Global Book Sales, has the distribution network in place to be able to supply books to any customer in the world, and we have skilled and passionate sales teams persuading booksellers that they should stock our publishers' books.

Who sells to whom, how and where?

Selling a book globally is a complicated process, but most publishers have excellent systems in place to ensure they maximise the sales of each book in every country. The process starts

Definitions

• Distribution

All publishers of print books have a distribution facility. This is a **warehouse** where the publisher stores the books they have published. From this warehouse, the books are sent out to customers. The distributor is also responsible for invoicing the customer for their book order and collecting the money. An example of a large book distributor in the UK is Macmillan Distribution (MDL). They distribute their own books published by Macmillan imprints, as well as distributing for third parties such as Bloomsbury and many other publishers.

• Key accounts

These are the main customers for books, including chain booksellers, wholesalers, online retailers and supermarkets. UK examples of key accounts are WHSmith, Waterstones, Blackwell, Gardners, Amazon and Tesco. Key accounts generally expect to buy new books six to nine months prior to publication.

• Sales rep/representative

A sales representative is a member of the publisher's sales team. They visit independent bookshops and other accounts, such as museums and galleries, to sell new titles. Reps tend to sell a book three to five months prior to publication. In most cases, they sell a large selection of different new titles across a range of genres. They sell to customers using either AIs (advance information sheets), printed catalogues, or glossy brochures known as *blads*.

• Stock control/inventory management

Bookshops want to have stock of a selection of books that they think they can sell during a given time period, and many bookshops have automated systems that generate re-orders when a book is sold. Distributors and wholesalers have developed sophisticated warehouse and delivery systems that enable them to process orders and get books out to shops very quickly; this reduces the need for a bookshop to hold significant levels of stock of any one title.

• Wholesaler

A wholesaler is similar to a distributor but it handles books from lots of different publishers. Gardners is the biggest wholesaler in the UK and they claim to have over 500,000 different titles in stock at any one time. The benefit of a wholesaler is that any bookshop or retailer that wants to sell books can easily source all the titles it needs from one place, rather than having to contact a variety of different distributors. This obviously cuts out a lot of administration and is more efficient for the customer.

with setting up *metadata* for a new title; this includes information such as ISBN, title, author, format, price, publication date, number of pages, etc. This metadata is then added to databases owned by bibliographic agencies, such as Nielsen in the UK, who are then responsible for disseminating that information to customers globally.

Once the metadata is available, the publisher's sales teams kick into action. Key account managers and sales representatives (**Definitions** box on page 110) will pre-sell new titles to their customers three to nine months prior to publication. This is a long *sell-in* period, but during that time the distributor will be recording any orders that come in for each book. These orders are known in the UK as *dues* and in the USA as *backorders*. The number of dues a new title has will help to determine how many copies the publisher will print in the initial run.

The aim of the publisher's sales team is to make sure the book is available for the consumer to buy on the date the book is published. This may mean that there are copies in stock at an independent bookshop or a branch of Waterstones, or that it is available to order easily through an online bookseller. When the book is published (or in the run-up to publication) then a publisher's publicity team and the author take over, to alert the consumer that the book is available to buy and persuade them that it's worth reading.

Day-to-day activity of a sales manager
Working with sales partners, distributors and agents
Global Book Sales has partnerships in place for book distribution with Macmillan Distribution (MDL) in the UK and Ingram Publishers Services LLC in the USA. Stock of our publishers' books are stored in both locations and this gives us the capability of supplying any customer quickly and cost-efficiently with any book they want to order, wherever they are located across the world.

We also have a network of sales agents across the world that sells new titles to customers in different countries. Each territory may have a slightly different way of working but the principles of the 'sell in' remain the same. To successfully sell a book in advance, the sales agent or representative needs accurate metadata, strong visual sales material, good information on what the book is about and who its audience is, and finally to know why this book stands out above the many thousands of other books that will publish at the same time.

The opportunities
The traditional high-street book trade is still important for book sales, but it has declined in recent years, with some independent bookshops closing down and smaller bookshop chains either closing or being swallowed up by larger rivals. However, there is now a huge range of online booksellers, museums, galleries, gift shops, clothes retailers, music shops and toy shops that all want to sell books as part of their range. Publishers are becoming very strategic in what they publish, and they are increasingly expanding into non-book items such as games and toys to increase their overall customer base.

These opportunities to sell outside of the traditional bookshops are also evident in a number of export markets. Concept stores in Scandinavia are now selling many books and this is also happening in China, Hong Kong, Singapore, Korea and Taiwan where demand for quality books, particularly in areas such as art, photography and design, are very strong. Marketing and publicising new books using social media is now both easy and relatively cheap to do. Authors who have a large number of followers on Twitter can alert potential readers that their book is now available to buy. This can have a huge impact on book sales.

The challenges

One of the biggest challenges publishers face at the moment is shipping books between countries quickly and cost-efficiently. The pandemic has significantly reduced the number of commercial flights, and this has driven up the price of moving books by air, almost to the point that it's not profitable to do so anymore. Shipping times for sea-freight have also increased. The UK leaving the European Union has added to the cost of sending books to Europe and the price of paper is also increasing, which puts further pressure on publisher's margins.

Finances, margins, discounting and terms

In the UK, books are mostly sold at a trade discount off the RRP (recommended retail price). Each publisher will set its own discount in agreement with their customers. The range of trade discounts can vary significantly, from around 25% to 60%, depending on the type of book. Academic and education books tend to be sold at lower discounts than more consumer, mass-market titles. The average discount for more general titles would be from 45% to 50%.

Sale-or-return, and how it works

In the UK, books are sold on a sale-or-return basis. This means that any trade customer (not individuals) can buy books from a publisher and return them if they don't sell them. This means that the risk of publishing and paying to print a book rests with the publisher. For export markets, books are still sold on a sale-or-return basis but, in practice, returns are low from export customers. These customers tend to buy in a less speculative way because they are also responsible for paying the cost of shipping these books from the UK, plus any additional import taxes and duties. Publishers will often have return allowances for export customers but this allowance is rarely fully used.

In the UK, the book and publishing industry have agreed some rules which means that a customer cannot return a book within three months of buying it and not after 15 months. The books should also be returned in a saleable condition. These restrictions don't apply in other countries, in particular the USA, where there are no such restrictions.

EPOS

EPOS (electronic point of sale) is system that allows bookshops to keep track of the books they sell. It's linked to their tills and will automatically generate a stock replenishment report suggesting to the buyer which books they should re-order.

How do publishers know how well their books are selling?

Publishers can subscribe to Nielsen BookScan (https://online.nielsenbookscan.net) which records sales of books through the tills of a range of UK booksellers. Alternatively, a publisher can check to see on a daily basis how many copies of a book are being sent out by their warehouse. With these sales figures, you do need to factor in any potential returns – whereas the Nielsen figures record firm sales.

Working with marketing

Marketing departments are responsible for providing the sales team with what they need to sell a book to a buyer. They also provide regular updates of any marketing and publicity that may be happening to promote a particular title. This information can then be passed on by the sales team to their individual buyers.

Marketing departments produce *AIs* (advance information sheets) for individual new books; some will produce six-monthly catalogues featuring the publisher's spring and autumn new books, and for lead titles they often provide bound proofs and *blads* (promotional samples). The typical 'lead time' for a book is five to six months; it takes this time for the various sales teams around the world to be briefed about the book, provided with the information to sell the book, and then to contact their customers in order to sell the book to them.

The pleasure of sales

I still get a thrill from seeing a book selling a lot of copies or from discovering a new customer for books. A recent example was when a Korean website that was selling Scandinavian-designed furniture was persuaded to add a range of books with a Scandinavian interest – something that resulted in some significant sales for one of our publishers.

David Wightman is Managing Director of Global Book Sales (www.globalbooksales.co.uk), an independent sales and distribution company that works with publishers to sell their titles across the world. He was previously Group International Sales Director at Bloomsbury Publishing, Sales, Marketing and Rights Director at A&C Black Publishers, and UK Academic Sales Manager at Oxford University Press.

See also...
● *Getting your book stocked in a high-street bookshop*, page 614

Books

Crowdfunding your novel

Alice Jolly discusses why she turned to crowdfunding to publish her memoir and subsequent novels, how the system works, its place as an alternative to mainstream and self-publishing, and the pros and cons of this new publication option.

It is April 2014. I am in a bar in Soho, talking to John Mitchinson, one of the founders of the crowdfunding publisher Unbound. He is interested in publishing a memoir I have written called *Dead Babies and Seaside Towns*. Our conversations about the book itself are straightforward but the wider purpose of our meeting is more problematic. He is thinking – *she is not the ideal person to crowdfund a book*. And I would have to agree with his unspoken assessment.

I'm a country mum, a quiet, academic type, who doesn't attend literary events. I have never used social media. On top of that, mainstream publishers have already told me that, no matter how good my memoir is, there is simply no market for it. Yet, despite these inauspicious omens, John has already decided he wants the book. And I agree to the crowdfunding idea because I am absolutely determined to get my memoir published.

Cut to June 2016 and I'm standing on a platform being awarded the Pen/Ackerley prize for that same memoir. John is in the audience and I catch his eye. Neither of us need to say – *well, that's stuck it to them!* It turns out that my book *did* need to be published … and that crowdfunding was as good a way to publish it as any other.

On the basis of this experience, you might assume that I am something of an expert on crowdfunded publishing and that I would unreservedly recommend it to other writers. But the reality is more complicated. Although I have subsequently crowdfunded another two books with Unbound (both novels), I only really know about what *I* have done – and not much more; and although crowdfunding has been a good choice for me, that does not mean I would suggest every other writer should go down the same road.

The crowdfunding process

So how does a writer decide if crowdfunding might be a good choice for them? First, let me give a quick summary of how it works. The process starts with the writer submitting his or her idea (or book) to a crowdfunder. Unbound are 'curated' crowdfunders and so (like any mainstream gate-keeping publisher) they decide whether or not they want that book. The important difference from a mainstream publisher is that the company is run by three people who are writers themselves. If one of them wants to publish a certain book, then it will happen. This means that you won't be told: '*The editors loved your book but unfortunately the Sales and Marketing team just couldn't . . .*'

If Unbound agree to work with you, then they help you to put together a page on their website which will include a biography and an extract from your book. A short film will also be made which explains the book. This web page then becomes the tool which you will use to bring in pledges or – to put it more simply – to pre-sell copies of the book. This idea is far from new. It is actually the same as 'publishing by subscription', which was how many books were published in the 19th century.

If you chose Unbound's digital option, then you might need to raise £3,000 or £4,000. If you are going to be producing a hard-copy book, then the cost rises to £10,000 or £12,000, depending on length, illustrations, etc. The budget is something you discuss with Unbound and it can be adjusted. Once all of this has been agreed, then you have to bring in the pledges. Unbound have a well-developed social media presence and a huge mailing list, so that helps spread the word but, fundamentally, it is down to you, as the writer, to raise that money. That process is tough – very tough. You need thick skin, persistence and confidence in what you are doing. You will suffer many dark moments – but you will also regularly be amazed by the random generosity of people you have never even met.

Writers have a hundred different crowdfunding strategies. Some authors are highly professional and imaginative; others, like me, shamble through the whole thing, relying on the support of family and friends, slowly and painfully spreading the word by doing readings, and events and workshops.

Once the money is raised, Unbound operate in just the same way as any other publisher. They do the editing, proofreading, cover design, publicity and distribution. When the book is published, the writer does not get royalties as such but they receive a profit share of 50% (obviously much higher than the usual 10% royalty). Unbound have a distribution agreement with independent sales force PGUK.

From my own experience, I know that Unbound can publicise and distribute a book widely. But, of course, the experience of one writer may be wildly different from that of another. How often have you actually heard a writer say how pleased they were by the publicity for their new book? More or less never, I would bet. As a breed, we tend to be naturally ungrateful and disappointed, even when we don't really have a reason to be so. All the same, we know that it is not the case that big publisher equals big publicity and small publisher equals small publicity. It all depends on the type of book, the timing, the status of the author, and the personnel in the publicity department. A junior and inexperienced book publicist in a small publishing house can sometimes achieve great things if they have a passion for a particular title.

Comparisons with self-publishing

Of course, I am regularly asked – why don't you self-publish? I know that the potential financial gains are much greater. Those who do self-publish also tell me that the Unbound £10,000 budget is too high. But I've looked into it (comparing the cost with quality self-publishing) and I rather doubt that. If you want a beautiful book then the process is long, slow and expensive. Book production values are a matter of personal choice but, as ever, if you want quality you have to pay for it. Personally I don't necessarily expect my books to sell thousands of copies but I would be desperately disappointed if they looked shoddy.

Although I know that self-publishing has worked well for some genre writers, there is little evidence that it works for more literary books. There is also the intractable question of time. I don't have IT or marketing skills and I don't particularly want to acquire them. I struggle to find time for my writing – there is no chance that I'd manage to be a publisher as well. At a more fundamental level, I also want to be part of a collaborative process. Writing is a horribly lonely business. I need some people to celebrate with when it goes well, and to down a consoling glass with when it does not. Mainstream publishers, in general, seem to take a 'divide and rule' attitude to writers (. . . *For God's sake don't get more than two of them in a room together or they'll whinge incessantly*). Unbound, by contrast, have created an online forum for their authors. There are some challenging discussions, but there is also a huge amount of camaraderie, consolation and support, plus

Books

many examples of writers clubbing together to promote each other's books and organise readings and events.

A developing role for crowdfunding

I've described my experience with Unbound, but what other crowdfunding options are available? There are many online organisations who offer crowdfunding to novelists, although none (as far as I know) are 'curated' crowdfunders. Kickstarter is a platform which anyone can use to raise money, but that still leaves the writer with all the book production work. Might this approach be the worst of both worlds? I'm not qualified to judge. But do remember – publishing is not the same as printing.

So far Unbound have done well – their books have won major prizes, reached the bestseller lists and, perhaps most importantly, fuelled important debate, meaning that there are real benefits to being published by them. For me personally, being published by Unbound has continued to be a great success, with my novel *Mary Ann Sate, Imbecile* being runner up for the Rathbones Folio Prize 2019 plus being longlisted for the Ondaatje Prize and becoming a Walter Scott recommended novel for 2019.

But what are the limits of this approach? Well, sadly, I don't think it can do much to improve diversity in publishing. It does return more money to the author than the mainstream model. And that's important given that the median earnings for a professional writer is approximately £10,500 (according to ALCS figures from 2017), far below the £17,900 which the Joseph Rowntree Foundation suggests is needed for a single person to reach the minimum income standard.

In addition, Unbound bravely publish anthologies which look at issues of social justice (notably *Common People: An Anthology of Working Class Writers*, edited by Kit de Waal, 2019, *The Good Immigrant*, edited by Nikesh Shukla, 2016 and *Trans Britain*, edited by Christine Burns, 2018). However, the crowdfunding model itself will tend to favour those who already have a name, a reputation, a network.

Although a 2017 Arts Council report (*Literature in the 21st Century: Understanding Models of Support for Literary Fiction*) suggests that crowdfunding may be able to play a role in addressing the difficulties in publishing literary fiction, despite my own successes, I remain less than certain how much can be achieved. But the reality is that, if a book is going to be hard to sell, it will usually to be hard to crowdfund as well.

Unbound have made it possible for some of those challenging, difficult, eccentric books to be published which would otherwise languish in a box under a writer's bed. That matters to me. I passionately believe in a world where all the voices are heard, a world we need now more than ever. I've always preferred the 'out-crowd' to the in-crowd.

Novelist and playwright **Alice Jolly's** memoir *Dead Babies and Seaside Towns* (Unbound 2015) won the 2015 Pen/Ackerley Prize. Her short story *Ray the Rottweiler* won the V.S. Pritchett Memorial Prize in 2014. Her novel *Mary Ann Sate, Imbecile* (Unbound 2018) was runner-up for the Rathbones Folio Prize, was longlisted for the Ondaatje Prize and was a Walter Scott Prize recommended novel in 2019. Her latest novel is *Between the Regions of Kindness* (Unbound 2019). Alice teaches Creative Writing at Oxford University. Her website is http://alicejolly.com/wp. Follow her on Twitter @JollyAlice.

Managing a successful writing career

Tony Bradman shares the five guiding principles that have helped him successfully sustain the writing career he has always wanted and worked to achieve, stressing the importance of bolstering talent with market knowledge, all-round professionalism and some much-needed resilience.

I was probably about 15 when I decided I wanted to be a writer. Like most writers, I had become an obsessive bookworm at an early age and, after years of spending all my pocket money on books as well as borrowing them from the local library, I had begun to think it would be marvellous to write some of my own. Imagine having your name on the cover of a book you had written yourself! I couldn't think of anything more amazing, and from that moment on I never seriously considered any other kind of career.

Of course, I had a sneaking feeling it might not be all that easy to get published. But I was convinced I would manage it and that, once I'd written a few books, everything would fall into place. As I explained to my girlfriend at university ('She Who Is Now My Wife'), apparently there were these payments called *royalties*. Each book I published would keep earning money, so that after a while we could just sit back and watch the cash roll in.

I wasn't entirely stupid. I did realise that my writing (which mostly consisted of a few notebooks crammed with unfinished and very mediocre poems) might not be all that attractive to publishers – not yet, anyway. So I applied for jobs in journalism, with the idea that my employer would help me improve my writing and pay me into the bargain – I never doubted that I had talent. The plan seemed to work, too. I was employed by several magazines, and after a while I even began to do a bit of freelancing on the side.

Eventually I found myself working for *Parents*, a magazine about young family life. By then I was a parent myself, and I was surprised the magazine didn't review children's books, even though we were sent lots of review copies. I therefore persuaded the editor to let me write about them, and I started a regular column. Pretty soon I got to know the publicity people at most of the children's book publishers, and I also began to meet editors at book launches and other events. By then I was starting to think that I wanted to write for children myself, so when an editor asked me if I had any ideas for a children's book I seized the opportunity and sent her some rhymes I'd written for my daughters.

Those rhymes became the basis for my first picture book, and the rest, as they say, is history. More commissions followed, and my books sold well in the UK and abroad (this was the mid-1980s, the heyday of 'co-editions' in children's books). The royalties really did flow, and before long I was able to give up my job and become a full-time freelancer. That was over 30 years ago, and I've managed to make a pretty good living as a writer ever since. It turned out not to be quite as easy as I had expected – far from it, in fact. But it can be done, and I offer you here the five principles on which I've based my career.

1. Cultivate your talent

I believe there is such a thing as talent. Some people are just better at certain things; you can see that in any artistic pursuit – writing, music, art, acting. And, to be brutal, if you haven't got talent then you're unlikely ever to achieve a career as a professional in any of those fields. Yes, I know from time to time we all read books, or watch plays or TV shows or films, that appear to have been written by someone with no talent whatsoever. But trust me, it would be very hard to sustain a long-term career without any talent at all.

Books

So let's assume you have talent. The question is, what kind of talent do you have? I could have spent years trying to write poetry for grown-ups and not got anywhere at all. In my mid-20s I began to realise I wasn't ever going to be the next Seamus Heaney or Ted Hughes, but by then I'd also started to get interested in children's books. I wrote verse for my daughters, then picture book texts (which often depend on a poet-like ability to use language creatively). After that I steadily moved up the age range with my children, and discovered I had a talent for writing well-plotted stories that kept readers gripped.

I didn't leave it there though. I thought about what I was doing and tried to build on the things that worked, my aim being simply to get better. Back in the 1980s there weren't anywhere near as many creative writing courses, but there were plenty of books about the art and craft of writing, and I read as many as I could. I listened to my editors too, and tried to learn from them, and from anyone else who might give me insight into what makes good writing. I edited anthologies of short stories, which meant I often had to tell writers exactly why I didn't think their stories worked – and that was invaluable experience.

I believe this approach is the foundation of any writing career. Understanding your talent will help to make you a good writer. But you can always make yourself into a better one.

2. Know the market

This is the section of my piece that will be anathema to the purists, those who believe that writing shouldn't ever be about 'satisfying the needs of the market'. Some people believe that great writers simply write what they need to and that it will find its own way to a readership or an audience. Well, good luck with that if you want to make a living as a writer. Of course, your 1,000-page surrealist fantasy written without using the letter 'e' might well become a runaway bestseller and make you a fortune. But what if it doesn't?

I think it's perfectly possible to combine Art and Commerce as a writer; satisfying the needs of the market doesn't mean 'selling out'. If you want a good example, what about the greatest writer of all time – Shakespeare himself? It's clear from his plays that he wrote very consciously for 'the market' in theatre as it was then. But he also managed to produce the most sublime literary art. Awareness of what the market is interested in can often be very stimulating creatively – it may well give you plenty of ideas on what to write.

So how do you study the market? That's easy and fun. Simply read widely, or watch plays, films and TV shows in the areas you find interesting. Find out as much about them as possible – who's hot in your chosen field, and what's doing well. The more you know, the better. Networking is part of this, especially if you see it as something that will help you learn about the business of being a writer. Go on courses, join writing groups; editors and agents sometimes give talks at these, and they're the people you want to meet. Keep it up after you get published – opportunities will usually arise from the contacts you make. You will also be a better prospect for agents and editors if they feel you know the market.

3. Be professional (part one)

… or to put it another way, 'Don't Be Desperate or Grateful'. Begging for a commission won't get you anywhere and, if you are offered an opportunity, there's no need to be thankful. You should always be professional – and that means thinking of what you're doing as a job, the way you earn your living. It's the person who is commissioning you or buying your work who should be grateful. Your editor almost certainly has a target, a number of books to publish in a year, and you're the means of getting that done. *You* are the solution.

Being professional also means making sure you always keep up a high standard as far as your performance is concerned. You should follow the brief, hit the word count, and deliver a clean manuscript that's as good as you can make it, by the deadline you've been given. If you can't deliver on time for whatever reason (it had better be a good one!), you should let your editor know, and agree a revised delivery date. If you're asked to do edits or revisions (and they're an essential part of being a writer), you should take it as positive criticism that aims to help make your writing better. If you disagree, say so – but be courteous.

The purpose is to present yourself as someone who is good to work with, 'a safe pair of hands' who can be trusted. With that kind of reputation, you will always get work.

4. Be professional (part two)

Being professional also means taking care of business, and that's something you should make a priority. The hard truth is that few writers earn a great deal from their writing, but if you want to make sure you can make a living, then you need to think about money. I've always thought of myself as the owner of a small business, so right from the beginning I took on an accountant, made sure I kept scrupulous records, and paid my taxes.

I've also always tried to think strategically in the way that good businesses have to. I keep track of what I'm earning and think about cashflow, as well as what I'm likely to earn over the next year (for a freelance it's hard to look much further than that). I then make judgements about what kind of work I'm going to do: if it's looking like a good year, I might think about doing something more speculative, maybe that story I've always wanted to write … if it's not looking good, then I start trying to drum up new commissions before I run out of money. I do a variety of things too – books, editing, reviews, bits of consultancy and teaching, school visits and festivals – the 'Many-Eggs-In-Many-Baskets' approach.

Having an agent helps, and the commission is tax-deductible. If your books are likely to be in libraries, you should sign up for Public Lending Right (PLR; see page 665), which will pay you for loans of your books. You should also become a member of the Authors' Licensing and Collecting Society (ALCS; see page 715), which collects money for secondary uses of our work such as photocopying, foreign PLR, cable re-transmission and so on. It all adds up, and even a small payment can come at a very useful time. You should also join a union, such as the Writers' Guild of Great Britain (WGGB; page 512), or the Society of Authors (page 509). They're great sources of support, information and networking for writers - you'll find details of all these organisations elsewhere in this excellent book – itself an essential tool for the professional.

5. Be resilient

Last but not least – you should bear in mind that there will be times when everything goes wrong. Books will be rejected or sell poorly, commissions will be hard to come by, favourite editors will move on, your particular area of experience will become unfashionable, royalties that once seemed secure will dry up. I've been through all of those things, and I've had my share of struggles with the usual demons we writers have to deal with – self-doubt, worry, periods of real stress.

Books

But I kept going, through the bad times and the good, and I have my natural resilience (my 'bounce-back-ability') to thank for that. I might get knocked down, but I get up again, and if you don't think you can manage that, well, the life of a professional writer isn't for you. But if you do, and you're prepared to work hard, and have some talent to offer, you'll be fine.

I wish you the best of luck.

Tony Bradman has written for children of all ages, from babies to teenagers. His most recent book is *Daisy and the Unknown Warrior* (Barrington Stoke 2020). He has edited many anthologies of short stories and poetry, and reviews children's fiction for the *Guardian*. Tony is chair of the Authors' Licensing and Collecting Society (ALCS). Find him at www.tonybradman.com.

See also...
- *Public Lending Right*, page 665
- *Developing talent: support and opportunities for writers*, page 505
- *Society of Authors*, page 509
- *WGGB (Writers Guild of Great Britain)*, page 512
- *Authors' Licensing and Collecting Society*, page 715

Debut success with an indie publisher

Wyl Menmuir describes the long, often uncertain and obscure path that led to his debut novel being written, and the encouragement, support and belief of others that helped him reach completion and success.

To say I achieved unexpected success with my debut novel is serious understatement. When I started to write *The Many*, I knew I would finish it and that was all. I would finish it – if only to prove to myself that I could. But a novel that would appear on bookshop shelves? A novel that people might buy? That was still the same vague dream I'd had since I first visited the library as a child.

Depending on which article you read, my first novel took me between two and three years to write. The truth is, I probably started three years earlier than that. I just didn't realise that was what I was doing when I was writing the stack of impenetrable short stories and novel openings on which I cut my fictional teeth (stories, incidentally, that remain locked in a drawer where they belong). It wasn't until something clicked, while I was on an Arvon 'Starting to Write' residential week (see page 691), that I worked out what I should really be working on. One of the tutors, Nikita Lalwani, challenged me to write the story that was at the back of my head, bugging me to be written, the one I thought that I could not write. How she knew it was there still mystifies me but, of the tens of thousands of words I discarded as I wrote the novel, the thousand-word story I wrote that afternoon sits at the heart of *The Many*, pretty much as I wrote it. When I got home though, when the rush of the course dissipated, I realised I had no idea where I was going with it, or how to take those first few words and turn them into the novel I wanted it to be.

There's a vastly overused but useful metaphor which suggests that writing a novel is like going into the woods; it looks like a great idea from a distance, the canopy gleaming in the sunlight. At that point, there seem to be endless possibilities for taking your reader on a journey through those woods and leading them blinking into the sunlight at the other side, bemused and enlightened by the journey they've just taken. As a writer, what actually happens when you get to the edge of these literary woods is that there's no sign of a path at all. Or if there is a path, it's so well-worn – a fictional hollow-way trodden by too many before – that there's no point in following it. You discount the hollow-way but start to worry that you're going to lose your way immediately. Or step on a snake. Or get caught in the brambles. When I started, I had no idea of my destination. I had my thousand words from my week at Arvon but, aside from that, I felt I was picking my way through increasingly dense forest. For me at least, the novel-writing process is one in which I have to feel my way and most days I have no idea what I will write next.

My practice consisted of walking around Cornwall's coast out of season and spending hours in the small fishing villages I used as inspiration for the novel's setting. I skulked around fishing boats, watched the changing sea, took countless photographs and talked to obliging fishermen, and by the time I was back at my desk the next scene was ready to be uncovered. That's the part of the process with which no one can help you. As for everything else, I say take as much help as you can get.

Once I realised I had a novel on my hands, I signed up for an MA in Creative Writing at Manchester Metropolitan University. The course gave me much-needed deadlines and the support of a community of writers, all of whom were finding their way through their own literary woods. I signed up for an early version of the tracking and productivity app, Write Track (https://writetrack.it); some writers might roll their eyes at the idea, but it worked for me, and I'm currently tracking my second novel in the same way). A novel happens in increments, in an incalculable number of changes so small it's often impossible to see the progress. That's where tracking my writing comes in. I have a marvellous capacity for self-deception, but the app made me accountable for getting words on the page. I set myself a modest target – 500 words a day – and over the weeks and months it helped me not only to see the progress I'd made but to keep going, which is invaluable when you're ready to throw the whole thing out of the window (a more common state than many writers would like to admit). As novelist and friend Liz Jenson so eloquently put it to me when I was despairing recently, 'We may lose hope, but we can still keep our appointment with the manuscript.' Anything that helps you to keep your appointment with the manuscript is worth its weight.

By the time you come to rewrites and editing, everything changes. You don't have to know what your novel is when you start, but by the time you're at the end you'd better be unambiguous about it. You have to be able to look back through the woods and see the wrong turns and dead ends as clearly as you do the path you want your reader to follow. After I'd written my first draft, I asked the author Steve Voake for his advice on editing and rewriting and he suggested I should summarise the novel in a single sentence, pin it up, and ask myself continually whether or not each scene moves the reader towards an understanding of this central statement. I was still looking at that note ten or eleven drafts in.

When I was close to finishing, my MA tutor, Nicholas Royle, suggested that Salt Publishing, for whom he is a commissioning editor, would be interested in publishing my novel. Choosing a publisher, like choosing an agent, is a matter of trust. You've spent possibly years crafting your novel, so you have to trust that your editor and publisher will care for it, that they will lift it further and help it to find the readers it deserves. It wasn't a hard choice. I already loved Salt's fiction list, in particular the work of Alice Thompson and Alison Moore. I had worked with Nicholas on the novel already through my MA; he understood the book I wanted to write and I trusted his judgement. Then there was the question about going with a small, independent publisher. At its best, small and independent means nimble and risk-taking. It means committed. Knowing Nicholas and the novels I'd read of theirs, I felt that Salt was all of the above. And whether or not a larger publisher would have put the novel up for the Man Booker Prize over the other titles on their list, I'll never know. What I do know is that Salt did. They believed in my strange, short novel.

The day before the Man Booker longlist came out in 2016, I wrote my predictions in the margin of the *Guardian*. My novel wasn't on the list I wrote, and it didn't even cross my mind that it might be. It seemed too far removed, the domain of Kazuo Ishiguro, Hilary Mantel and Graham Swift, writers who occupied another plane of existence. Only then it wasn't. When the longlist was announced, I wasn't even listening out for it. I ignored my phone when it rang. 'You realise this changes everything?' my publisher asked me when I finally answered. I didn't. But it did. It continues to change everything. It has meant a huge boost in confidence, readers in far greater numbers than I could have hoped for, festival appearances, articles and another novel on the way. I wrote the novel I needed to write, the one that was nagging at the back of my head and wouldn't leave me be until it was down on paper, not the one I thought I ought to write. And that (to paraphrase a prince of the woodland metaphor) has made all the difference.

Shortly after I started writing, I stuck a Post-it® above my desk repeating Neil Gaiman's singularly useful piece of advice: 'Finish what you start'. It sounds prosaic, but I need that advice so much that I now have it carved into the surface of my desk as a constant reminder. It took me three, four, or seven years (take your pick), eleven drafts and countless incremental changes to finish *The Many*. And I'd like to pass Gaiman's sage words on to you. However long it takes – however many drafts, wrong turns, dead ends and backtracking it takes to get there – finish what you start. You never know where it might take you.

Wyl Menmuir is a novelist, short story writer and essayist. He is the author of two novels – *The Many* (Salt 2016) and *Fox Fires* (Salt 2021) – the first of which was nominated for the Man Booker Prize and was an *Observer* Best Fiction of the Year pick. His short fiction has appeared in *Best British Short Stories* and has been published by Nightjar Press and the National Trust. Wyl teaches creative writing at Falmouth University and the Cornish writing centre, The Writer's Block, and works as a freelance editorial and literary consultant. His website is www.wylmenmuir.co.uk. Follow him on Twitter @Wylmenmuir.

Books

Defining genre fiction

Maxim Jakubowski leads us through the web of genres, sub-genres and mini-genres that are to be found within the world of popular fiction, and encourages today's writer to seek out or create their very own niche.

So you want to write popular fiction? Let's start by getting our definitions (or intentions) clear, shall we?

I will take it for granted that every writer basically wants his or her fiction to become popular, so what exactly are we talking about here? Popular fiction is a broad term that refers, for good or bad, to the set of categories which both the book trade and reader perception would see the book fitting into. As much as we feel that, in an ideal world, all books should spring freely from the writer's pen (or word processor) unencumbered by such mercantile considerations, one cannot ignore the commercial realities of the book business. Both *The Bookseller* and *Publishers Weekly*, the established, indispensable British and US trade publications, divide their advance review sections of forthcoming titles into the following categories: literary titles (also referred to by some as 'mainstream'), crime and thriller, historical, science fiction and fantasy, romance and erotica, with poetry, graphic novels and comics and non-fiction also listed separately.

It is true to say there are some titles which prove damn awkward to fit into any of these categories and which straddle genres with gay abandon. On occasion, because they are sufficiently bold and *sui generis*, such titles can become unexpected bestsellers, but sadly it's more likely they will sink fast because chain and supermarket buyers – although less often bookshop purchasers, or even readers – don't quite know where to place or locate them on the shelves. These are the books that fall between stools, and I speak from personal experience as a writer whose lax commercial discipline has seen him mix genres rather freely – resulting in personal satisfaction but reduced sales and reach (an ironic admission for someone who has worked most of his life in a commercial publishing environment!).

Crime, mystery and thriller fiction

First let's look at crime and mystery fiction as a genre. Is it enough for the author to begin with a body, bring an investigator in – whether a police officer (in which case the result could be termed a police procedural) or a private eye or amateur sleuth – and let the plot unfold? But where exactly will the book fit in the various subgenres? Will it prove to be generic crime, with the puzzle of the culprit's actual identity unfolding, as in Agatha Christie or Colin Dexter's *Inspector Morse* books? That would make it a whodunit. But then, what about whydunits (Patricia Highsmith, Ruth Rendell), where the psychology leading up to the crime happens to be the key element of the book? Or howdunits, where the killer is often known but the method of crime is the actual mystery (John Dickson Carr, the inimitable king of the impossible crime novel)? Or a more recent and highly popular strand of psychological thriller, where the reader has to juggle with one or more unreliable narrators, preferably female (Gillian Flynn's *Gone Girl*, *The Girl on the Train*, etc)? Add the occasional whatdunit to the mix and you find a plethora of subcategories, which makes it plain that writing in the mystery genre is not as straightforward as it first appears.

Then you have what is generally referred to as the thriller. This can range from hardy action adventures (Alastair McLean, Gerald Seymour, Jack Higgins, etc) to plots specifically involved with espionage and spies (Graham Greene, John le Carré and so many others), or even crime novels in which the sprawling world on display blends many of the aforesaid subcategories together but in which, generally speaking, the mystery element takes a back seat to the action, psychology and worldview (Don Winslow, Nick Stone, James Ellroy). And let us not forget the increasingly popular world of the historical mystery, spurred into existence by Umberto Eco's *The Name of the Rose* and Ellis Peters' *Brother Cadfael* novels, in which many of the preceding subcategories can happily co-exist.

The more you delve into the thriving world of crime and thriller fiction, the more branches of the tree reveal themselves, with themes within themes: romantic suspense, women in peril, female sleuths, regional crime and so on and so on. Like anyone who has taught creative writing, I can only advise you to read what is available and find the niche that comes instinctively to you; I'm confident that your book will, by hook or by crook, satisfyingly fit into one of these categories and find its slot in the marketplace. Indeed, even if at first sight many of the subcategories or mini-genres might initially appear restrictive, I can confirm, as a judge and Chair for the past six years of the Crime Writers' Association John Creasey New Blood Dagger award, given to the best first novel of the year, that by and large new writers are constantly innovating and coming up with wondrous new twists, and allowing their books (and their publishers) to assign categories after the fact. So, where to classify your crime and thriller novel should never be your main consideration. Just write the damn thing. Right now!

Science fiction and fantasy

What about the other categories the book trade likes to place titles into? Science fiction and fantasy sadly does not always garner the same critical attention as crime and thrillers and, as a category, can prove equally divided. We are actually talking of three separate categories in their own right, each with a prestigious past, traditions and roots: actual science fiction, fantasy and (less often mentioned) horror. Some authors move across these genres, but that's infrequent. And once again, we face a dilemma: is your science fiction hard and scientific or softer and more speculative? Are you writing about outer space or the inner space, once so well advocated by J.G. Ballard? How reliant on actual science is your novel (à la Arthur C. Clarke) or are you perhaps more concerned about sociological considerations (à la Ursula K. Le Guin)? Are you interested in utopias or dystopias (the latter genre having been much in vogue in recent years and attracting pens from the mainstream, like Margaret Atwood and Naomi Alderman)? Yet again, there is an embarrassment of choices and possibilities, all of which will easily fit into what is generally classed as science fiction. And don't assume that science is essential to a science fiction book; there are excellent titles in which it plays no or little part (e.g. Dave Hutchinson's *Europe* series), just as it is possible to come across crime, mystery or thriller titles in which there are no crimes or bodies.

J.R.R. Tolkien, of course, dominates the fantasy landscape – with George R.R. Martin now hot on his heels, thanks to *Game of Thrones* – but it's not always about quests and battles, wizards and dragons. Legends and myths from all continents and civilisations keep on feeding a very active field of writing which remains highly popular in all its manifestations. And, of course, horror, dominated by big names like Stephen King, James Herbert and Dean R. Koontz, has never gone away – although its appeal goes in cycles and, on many occasions, overlaps particularly well with science fiction and fantasy. Never to be neglected, either, is the rich field of unsullied historical fiction, which in some instances can even cross over with both crime and romance to satisfying effect and doesn't necessarily necessitate overwhelming research (although you're best sticking to the facts you studied at school or gleaned from authoritative non-fiction).

Romance

You don't believe your imagination is fertile enough to pen crime or science fiction, and you'd rather write about everyday life, albeit without high falutin' literary ambitions? Not to worry – the field of romance, one of the most misunderstood areas of popular fiction, awaits you with open arms.

What is romance basically? It's about people, love, the heart, sex, the way we live. Can there be a broader canvas to write about? So banish thoughts about Mills & Boon clichés, sultans and dippy heroines, doctors and nurses, and Barbara Cartland. There is life beyond, and generations of new romance writers have understood this, viz Jilly Cooper, Jenny Colgan, Cecilia Ahern, Jojo Moyes, David Nicholls, etc. Once again we are presented with so many alternatives to straight contemporary romance, from historical settings to cross-over possibilities, with crime and mystery and even science fiction and fantasy too. As long as you have characters who have the talent to fall in love and emote, you have a work of romance. It can be serious, humorous, tragic, explicit (in which case it becomes erotica, which should not be confused with the sort of erotic romance represented by E.L. James' *Fifty Shades of Grey* which has now cast an unfortunate shadow on that particular genre), allusive, but most of all optimistic in nature. And, in the present societal mood, where years after the phenomenon of chick lit and so-called bonkbusters, a welcome trend is the success and demand amongst publishers for what is now being called 'up lit', i.e. fiction of an uplifting nature typified by Gail Honeyman's *Eleanor Oliphant is Completely Fine* and novels by Maria Semple (which is bad news for yours truly, who has always preferred downbeat endings to his books!). Add to the romantic mix the family and historical saga categories which still find a major audience today, from the days of Catherine Cookson to Nadine Dorries right now, and you get an idea of the complexity of the subgenres which actually reflects, I would guess, those of human nature and the power of love and complexity of relationships.

One could be pernickety or pedantic, and endlessly explore further branches of the confusing trees of popular fiction but, in essence, the categories mentioned above should provide you with a good guide if you want to work in any of those genres. And if you should come up with a variation which has not been mentioned in passing here, well – you could be on to a winner. So boot up that word-processing programme, get writing and surprise us!

Maxim Jakubowski is a writer, editor, translator and critic. He has published nearly 100 books in a variety of genres, particularly crime, erotica and science fiction. His latest novel is *The Piper's Dance* (Telos 2021). A regular broadcaster on TV and radio, Maxim also contributes to *The Times*, *The Bookseller* and the *Evening Standard*, and was for 12 years the *Guardian* crime reviewer and prior to that for *Time Out*. He is the former literary director of the Crime Scene Film and Book Festival and is currently Chair of the Crime Writers' Association. For more information, visit www.maximjakubowski.co.uk.

On mentoring

Bestselling author Jill Dawson explains just how valuable personal mentoring from a successful author can be in bringing out the best from a new or aspiring writer. She provides information and advice on current mentoring schemes.

In the early '90s, when writing my first novel, *Trick of the Light* (Sceptre 1996), I longed to have some feedback. Popular wisdom is that writing workshops or writers' groups are the way new writers learn. So I tried a couple of workshops at the City Lit and immediately discovered they weren't for me. I was shy. I hated groups. And I have a sort of permeable self, which – though very useful in a novelist – means I take in *everything* from everybody else and can't fend it off. Even more problematically, I realised belatedly that the very reason I *wanted* to write was to connect with this self more securely: how could I do this when inundated by the cacophony of critical voices and jostling egos of the other writers in the group?

Writing fiction was a negotiation between the joys of being hidden and the potential disaster of never being found. I do understand that writing groups and courses are the way forward for many people who want to write – please don't think I'm dismissing their value. I've taught many over the years and I try to make them a space where individual voices can be heard and where a group consensus doesn't develop. But I also know I'm not alone in finding workshops too exposing and agitating to be helpful.

What I needed was *one* trusted person, someone whose writing I admired, someone who knew what they were doing and would somehow know what I was trying to do and help me to do it better (my fantasy was Margaret Atwood, but how on earth to get hold of Margaret Atwood or ask her to read my novel?).

At that point in my life I'd never met any published writers. I was on the dole, a single parent of a toddler and living in a council flat in Hackney. What I longed for was an opportunity to meet and learn from those I thought of as 'real' writers: published authors with a body of work, and to discover if I could count myself among them. There seemed to be no way to find that, so I signed up for an MA in writing anyway, aware that a novelist I admired (Jane Rogers) ran it, and hoping for her input, or that of the esteemed poet who also taught on the course, E.A. Markham. I wasn't aware of it, but I think I was trying to see if a writer was *someone like me*. Could I imagine myself into their shoes?

It sounds obvious, but for those of us who don't have the luck of Martin Amis – to grow up in a home where books, writing, and intellectual questions were discussed at the kitchen table, and publishers and agents and other writers were real people who lived upstairs or came for dinner – it's hard to downplay how audacious it felt, to try to imagine myself a writer. Jane Rogers helped with that, with her quiet, affirming manner. She helped me too with a crucial question: what was the hook in my novel; why would a reader want to read on? In response to my uncertainty about the early chapters of my novel – should they be in another tense? should I change to the third person? – she read the extract I'd submitted and simply said: 'No, leave it as it is. The first person present tense is working fine.'

I felt that the MA didn't offer me nearly enough of Jane's time and input and I would have paid the entire fee of the course (£4,000 sterling back then) to have her all to myself.

Books

I have to be frank and say I found the group workshop element as hard to manage as ever. However, as guests, the course had other writers (Pat Barker, James Kelman) and, thrillingly, I got to hear them talk about their work. The diagram Jane drew of how she'd structured the seven voices in her novel *Mr Wroe's Virgins* (Overlook Press 1999) provided the most extraordinary insight into how a successful novelist tackles structure. So meeting writers was part of the answer, but also receiving the detailed insider discussion of process and practice that I couldn't get from listening to workshop members who, like me, hadn't really done it yet.

That's how I dreamed up the idea of Gold Dust Mentoring. Gold Dust offers 16 hours of input from an established author of at least five books, often many more, who has taught or been a professor or course director on one of the best writing courses and won, been shortlisted for or judged major prizes, such as the Booker, Costa, Women's Prize, etc. It's a selective scheme and the applicant has to submit a sample of their writing, which is read by the writer they hope might be their mentor. The mentoring usually takes the form of eight meetings spread over eight months to a year, plus eight hours of the mentor reading the work in progress. Gold Dust has had lots of successes so far, despite being small. On our website (www.gold-dust.org.uk) we name with pride some of those who have gone on to publish or to win prizes: Guinevere Glasfurd, Stephanie Scott (both mentored by Louise Doughty), Kathleen Whyman, Alex Hourston, Rosalind Stopps (mentored by me), Eleanor Anstruther and Emma Claire Sweeney (mentored by Sally Cline), Sarah Aspinall, mentored by Jane Rogers.

During lockdown, the mentoring was all done via Zoom – the need for another, more experienced writer to offer guidance, support and encouragement felt more essential than ever. As well as providing feedback on the work in progress, a mentor is well placed to offer the professional advice that most new writers crave. Approaching an agent can be a bewildering task and a mentor can demystify that world. Sarah Dunnakey, author of *The Companion* (Orion 2017) said: 'Towards the end of my time on Gold Dust, Jill helped me to draw up a list of prospective agents using her knowledge of what type of submissions they wanted. She was happy for me to mention that she recommended my writing to them. This helped to make the process far less daunting.' (We also used the good old *Writers' & Artists' Yearbook*, of course).

A high profile scheme like Gold Dust can help you be taken seriously by the publishing world once you start approaching agents and editors. (Something else to consider when choosing a mentoring scheme. The Womentoring Project – offering free mentoring for women only (https://womentoringproject.co.uk; you need a WordPress account to access the site). The Literary Consultancy (https://literaryconsultancy.co.uk) offers six sessions of online mentoring with a professional editor. There are also the high-profile Rathbones Folio Mentorships (see www.rathbonesfolioprize.com/mentorship). Word Factory offers mentoring for short story writers (https://thewordfactory.tv) and there are others which might be closer to you, such as the Oxford Literary Consultancy (www.oxfordwriters.com), Adventures in Fiction (http://adventuresinfiction.co.uk) and the National Centre for Writing (https://nationalcentreforwriting.org.uk), as well as the service offered by Writers & Artists (www.writersandartists.co.uk/editing-services/bespoke-mentoring).

Formal schemes aren't the only way to find a mentor. You might be lucky enough to know a writer you could ask for feedback or professional advice. But beware: published writers get asked an awful lot to read the novels of aspiring writers, friends, and sometimes sons, daughters and brothers-in-law of friends. Authors also get sent books to review and requests for quotes for book jackets on a weekly basis. Then they have their writer friends who have just published, and perhaps their student's work to read, and that's before we even mention reading for research or pleasure! So that casual question, 'Would you mind just reading my novel?' is perhaps a bigger ask than many realise and should be approached with caution (… or you could wait to be invited).

Mentoring can be beneficial at any point in a writing career – not just the early years (although once published, of course, we have an agent and editor and meet other writers at festivals and book events, so are probably not at such a loss to find insider industry advice). Many of us remain grateful to those who have helped us in our writing lives. I know that Andrew Miller credits Angela Carter with tutoring him on an Arvon course (see page 691), and Ian McEwan says that his time on the University of East Anglia's Creative Writing MA (see page 699) mainly consisted of him discussing his work with Malcolm Bradbury, as McEwan was the only student that first year.

There has always been informal mentoring in the past – some of it rather hidden: Virginia Woolf had Anne Thackeray (although she wouldn't have admitted it); George Eliot was having salons with Henry James; Gertrude Stein took lots of male writers under her wing. Perhaps there is a danger of influence, or of the 'mentee' developing too great a dependence on the mentor, but with formal schemes like the ones mentioned above there are clear boundaries and usually a signed contract which helps to guard against this. It's satisfying to have dreamed up and created the scheme I wanted to find myself, years ago. No need to go it alone in an attic then … unless of course you really want to. But for many of us, as Emerson put it, 'Our chief want in life is somebody who will make us do what we can.'

Jill Dawson is the author of ten novels, editor of six anthologies and founder of Gold Dust Mentoring Scheme (www.gold-dust.org.uk). Her books, all published by Sceptre, include *Watch Me Disappear* (2006), *The Great Lover* (2009), *The Tell-Tale Heart* (2014) and *The Crime Writer* (2016). Her most recent novel, *The Language of Birds*, was published by Sceptre in 2019. She has an honorary doctorate from Anglia Ruskin University and is a Fellow of the Royal Society of Literature. For more information visit https://jilldawson.co.uk.

See also...
- *Developing talent: support and opportunities for writers*, page 505
- *Managing a successful writing career*, page 117

Books

Book publishers UK and Ireland

There are changes to listings in this section every year. We aim to provide a comprehensive list of publishing imprints, the name or brand under which a specific set of titles are sold by a publisher. Any one publisher might have several imprints, for example Bloomsbury publishes cookery books under the Absolute Press imprint and nautical books under Adlard Coles. The imprint usually appears on the spine of a book. Imprints are included either under a publisher's main entry or in some cases as entries themselves. Information is provided in a way that is of most use to a reader. The subject indexes which start on p742, list publishers and imprints for different genres and forms of writing. The listings that follow are updated by the *Writers' & Artists'* editors based on information supplied by those listed.

*Member of the Publishers Association or Publishing Scotland
†Member of the Irish Book Publishers' Association
‡Member of the Independent Publishers Guild
sae = self-addressed envelope
MS = manuscript (MSS = manuscripts)

AA Publishing
AA Media Ltd, Fanum House, Basing View, Basingstoke, Hants RG21 4EA
tel (01256) 491524
email aapublish@theaa.com
website www.theaa.com/bookshop
Twitter @theaa_lifestyle

Atlases, maps, leisure interests, travel including City Packs and AA Guides. Founded 1910.

Abacus – see Little, Brown Book Group

Academic Press – see Elsevier Ltd

ACC Art Books Ltd
Sandy Lane, Old Martlesham, Woodbridge, Suffolk IP12 4SD
tel (01394) 389950
email uksales@accartbooks.com
website www.accartbooks.com/uk
Facebook www.facebook.com/ACCArtBooks
Twitter @ACCArtBooks
Instagram @accartbooks
Publisher James Smith

Publisher and distributor of books on art, photography, decorative arts, fashion, gardening, design and architecture. Founded 1966.

Ad Hoc Fiction
6 Old Tarnwell, Stanton Drew, Bristol BS39 4EA
email jude@adhocfiction.com
website www.adhocfiction.com
Director Jude Higgins

Award-winning small independent publisher specialising in short-short ficiton. Closely associated with the Bath Flash Fiction Award, produces micro-fiction from their thrice-yearly awards. Also prodces novellas-in-flash from their yearly Novella-in-Flash Award and anthologies of stories from participants of the Flash Fiction Festival UK. Founded 2015.

Ad Lib Publishers
email info@adlibpublishers.com
website www.adlibpublishers.com
Facebook www.facebook.com/adlibpublishers
Twitter @adlibpublishers
Publisher John Blake, *Editorial Director* Rob Nichols

Non-fiction publisher of true crime and celebrity memoir. Founded 2020.

Mardle Books
email jo@mardlebooks.com
Contact Jo Sollis

Commercial, mass-market books for adults.

Agora Books‡
55 New Oxford Street, London WC1A 1BS
tel 020-7344 1000
email hello@agorabooks.co
website www.agorabooks.co
Facebook www.facebook.com/agorabooksLDN
Twitter @AgoraBooksLDN
Instagram @AgoraBooksLDN
Publisher Samantha Brace

A digital-first publisher with a diverse list of fiction. Agora Books is part of Peters Fraser + Dunlop, one of the longest established literary and talent agencies in London. Accepts fiction submissions from agented and unagented writers at the following email address: submissions@agorabooks.co. Founded 2015.

Airlife Publishing – see The Crowood Press

Ian Allan Publishing Ltd
Terminal House, Station Approach, Shepperton,
Surrey TW17 8AS
tel (01932) 834959
email sales@lewismasonic.co.uk
website www.lewismasonic.co.uk
General Manager Martin Faulks

Lewis Masonic is the oldest Masonic imprint in the
world. The company has been part of Ian Allan
Publishing since 1973 and continues to produce
Masonic books and rituals as well as the quarterly
magazine *The Square*. Founded 1886.

J.A. Allen
The Crowood Press Ltd, The Stable Block,
Crowood Lane, Ramsbury, Wilts. SN8 2HR
tel (01672) 520320
email enquiries@crowood.com
website www.crowood.com

Horse care and equestrianism including breeding,
racing, polo, jumping, eventing, dressage,
management, carriage driving, breeds, horse industry
training, veterinary and farriery. Books usually
commissioned but willing to consider any serious,
specialist MSS on the horse and related subjects.
Imprint of The Crowood Press (page 144).
Founded 1926.

Allison & Busby Ltd‡
11 Wardour Mews, London W1F 8AN
tel 020-3950 7834
email susie@allisonandbusby.com
website www.allisonandbusby.com
Facebook www.facebook.com/allisonandbusbybooks
Twitter @allisonandbusby
Publishing Director Susie Dunlop, *Publishing Manager*
Lesley Crooks, *Head of Sales* Daniel Scott

Fiction, general non-fiction, young adult and
preschool. No unsolicited MSS. Founded 1967.

Allyn & Bacon – see Pearson UK

Alma Books
Thornton House, Thornton Road,
London SW19 4NG
tel 020-8405 6406
website www.almabooks.com, www.almaclassics.com
Directors Alessandro Gallenzi, Elisabetta Minervini

Contemporary literary fiction, non-fiction, European
classics, poetry, drama, art, literary, music and social
criticism, biography and autobiography, essays,
humanities and social sciences. No unsolicited MSS.
Inquiry letters must include a sae. Series include:
Alma Classics, Overture Opera Guides, Calder
Publications. Around 40% English-language
originals, 60% translations. Founded 2005.

The Alpha Press – see Sussex Academic Press

Amazon Publishing
1 Principal Place, Worship Street, London EC2A 2FA
tel 0843 504 0495
email amazonpublishing-pr@amazon.com
website https://amazonpublishing.amazon.com/
UK Publisher Eoin Purcell

Amazon Publishing is the full-service publishing arm
of Amazon. Imprints: AmazonEncore,
AmazonCrossing, Little A, Montlake Romance,
Thomas & Mercer, 47North, Montlake Romance,
Grand Harbor Press, Little A, Jet City Comics, Two
Lions, Skyscrape, Lake Union Publishing, StoryFront,
Waterfall Press, Kindle Press. Also publishes ebooks
via its Kindle Direct publishing platform. Currently
not accepting unsolicited MSS. Amazon Media EU
Sarl is Amazon Publishing's EU entity. The address is:
31–33 Rives de Clausen, 2165 Luxembourg.
Founded 2009.

Amber Books Ltd
United House, North Road, London N7 9DP
tel 020-7520 7600
email enquiries@amberbooks.co.uk
website www.amberbooks.co.uk
Facebook www.facebook.com/amberbooks
Twitter @amberbooks
Chairman Stasz Gnych, *Managing Director* Sara
McKie, *Editorial Director* Charles Catton, *Head of
Production* Peter Thompson, *Design Manager* Mark
Batley, *Picture Manager* Terry Forshaw

Illustrated non-fiction publisher for adults and
children. Subjects include photography, travel, gift
books, military technology, military history, general
history, humour, music, survival, natural history and
family reference. Works include encyclopedias and
highly illustrated reference series. Children's titles
created under Tiptoe Books imprint. Opportunities
for freelancers. Founded 1989.

Amberley Publishing‡
The Hill, Stroud, Glos. GL5 4EP
tel (01453) 847800
email info@amberley-books.com
website www.amberley-books.com
Facebook www.facebook.com/amberleybooks
Twitter @amberleybooks
Ceo Nick Hayward

General history/non-fiction and local interest;
specialisations include transport (railways, road
transport, canals, maritime), industry, sport,
biography and military history. Founded 2008.

Amgueddfa Cymru – National Museum Wales‡
Cathays Park, Cardiff CF10 3NP
tel 029-2057 3235
email post@museumwales.ac.uk
website www.museumwales.ac.uk
Twitter @AmgueddfaBooks

Books

Head of Publishing Mari Gordon

Books based on the collections and research of Amgueddfa Cymru for adults, schools and children, in both Welsh and English. Founded 1907.

Andersen Press Ltd*
20 Vauxhall Bridge Road, London SW1V 2SA
tel 020-7840 8703 (editorial) / 020-7840 8701 (general)
email anderseneditorial@penguinrandomhouse.co.uk
website www.andersenpress.co.uk
Managing Director Mark Hendle, *Publisher* Klaus Flugge, *Directors* Philip Durrance, Joëlle Flugge, Libby Hamilton (editorial picture books), Sue Buswell (editorial picture books), Charlie Sheppard (editorial fiction), Liz White (rights)

Children's books: picture books, fiction for 5–8 and 9–12 years and young adult fiction. Will consider unsolicited MSS. Include sae if response required. For novels, send three sample chapters and a synopsis only. No poetry or short stories. Do not send MSS via email. Founded 1976.

The Angels' Share – see Neil Wilson Publishing Ltd

Angry Robot Books
Unit 11, Shepperton House, 89 Shepperton Road, London N1 3DF
tel 020-3813 6940
email incoming@angryrobots.com
website www.angryrobotbooks.com
Facebook www.facebook.com/angryrobotbooks
Twitter @angryrobotbooks
Director Etan Ilfeld

Publishes modern adult science fiction, fantasy and everything in between. Part of Watkins Media (page 193). Founded 2009.

Anness Publishing
email info@anness.com
website www.annesspublishing.com
Managing Director Paul Anness, *Publisher* Joanna Lorenz

Practical illustrated books on lifestyle, cookery, crafts, reference, gardening, health and children's non-fiction. Imprints include: Lorenz Books, Armadillo, Southwater, Peony Press, Hermes House and Practical Pictures (www.practicalpictures.com). Founded 1988.

Apa Publications
7 Bell Yard, London WC2A 2JR
tel 020-7403 0284
website www.insightguides.com, www.roughguides.com, www.berlitzpublishing.com
Facebook www.facebook.com/InsightGuides, www.facebook.com/RoughGuides
Twitter @InsightGuides, @RoughGuides

Instagram @InsightGuides, @RoughGuides
Directors Agnieszka Mizak (managing), Sarah Clark (publishing), Vanessa Clarke (sales)

Publishers of Rough Guides, Insight Guides and Berlitz products for travel and language, and related digital content. Founded 1970.

Appletree Press Ltd†
164 Malone Road, Belfast BT9 5LL
tel 028-9024 3074
email editorial@appletree.ie
website www.appletree.ie
Director John Murphy

Gift books, guidebooks, history, Irish interest, Scottish interest, photography, sport, travel. Founded 1974.

Arc Publications
Nanholme Mill, Shaw Wood Road, Todmorden OL14 6DA
tel (01706) 812338
email info@arcpublications.co.uk
website www.arcpublications.co.uk
Facebook www.facebook.com/arcpublications
Twitter @arc_poetry
Directors Tony Ward (founder & managing editor), Angela Jarman (publisher & editor of Arc Music);
Editors James Byrne (international), Jean Boase-Beier (translation), Tony Ward (UK & Ireland)

Specialises in contemporary poetry and neglected work from the past: poetry from the UK and Ireland; world poetry in English; bilingual translations mainly from the smaller languages (individual poets and anthologies); and occasional books on music and musicians. Imprints: Arc Publications and Arc Music. Refer to website for current publication list/catalogue and submissions policy. Founded 1969.

Architectural Press – see Elsevier Ltd

Arena Publishing
6 Southgate Green, Bury St. Edmunds IP33 2BL
tel (01284) 754123
email arenabooks@tiscali.co.uk
email arenabooks.bse@gmail.com
website www.arenabooks.co.uk
Director James Farrell

Publishers of quality fiction, travel, history and current affairs, also of specialised social science, politics, philosophy and academic dissertations suitable for transcribing into book format. Special interest in publishing books analysing the debt-fuelled financial crisis from a non-party standpoint. New authors welcome. IPG member. Founded 1890.

Ashgate Publishing Ltd – see Taylor & Francis Group

Ashmolean Museum Publications
Beaumont Street, Oxford OX1 2PH
tel (01865) 288070
email dec.mccarthy@ashmus.ox.ac.uk
website www.ashmolean.org
Contact Declan McCarthy

Publisher of exhibition catalogues, fine and applied art of Europe and Asia, archaeology, history, numismatics. Photographic archive and picture library. Museum founded 1683.

Atlantic Books*‡
Ormond House, 26–27 Boswell Street,
London WC1N 3JZ
tel 020-7269 1610
email enquiries@atlantic-books.co.uk
website https://atlantic-books.co.uk/
Managing Director & Publisher Will Atkinson

Literary fiction, thrillers, history, current affairs, politics, sport, biography and memoir. Strictly no unsolicited submissions or proposals. In 2014 the Australian publisher Allen & Unwin became the majority owner of Atlantic Books. Founded 2000.

Atrium – see Cork University Press

Attic Press – see Cork University Press

Aureus Publishing Ltd
Castle Court, Castle-upon-Alun, St Bride's Major,
Vale of Glamorgan CF32 0TN
tel (01656) 880033
email info@aureus.co.uk
website www.aureus.co.uk
Director Meuryn Hughes

Rock and pop, autobiography, biography, sport; also music. Founded 1993.

Aurora Metro‡
67 Grove Avenue, Twickenham TW1 4HX
tel 020-3261 0000
email info@aurorametro.com
website www.aurorametro.com
Facebook www.facebook.com/AuroraMetroBooks
Twitter @aurorametro
Managing Director Cheryl Robson

Adult fiction, young adult fiction, biography, drama (including plays for young people), non-fiction, theatre, cookery and translation. Submissions: send synopsis and three chapters via our website: www.aurorametro.com/contact-us/submit-your-work/. Runs a biennial competition for women novelists (odd years): Virginia Prize For Fiction. Entry fee for submission of either adult or young adult novel. See website: www.aurorametro.com/VirginiaPrize. Imprints include Aurora Metro Books and Supernova Books. Founded 1996.

Authentic Media Ltd
PO Box 6326, Bletchley, Milton Keynes MK1 9GG
tel (01908) 268500
email info@authenticmedia.co.uk
website www.authenticmedia.co.uk
Facebook www.facebook.com/authenticmedia
Twitter @authenticmedia
General Manager Donna Harris

Biblical studies, Christian theology, ethics, history, mission, commentaries. Christian biographies, devotionals, children's books and Bibles. Imprints: Paternoster, Authentic. Founded 2001.

The Authority Guides
Unit 3 Spike Island, 133 Cumberland Road,
Bristol BS1 6UX
tel (01789) 761345
email hello@authorityguides.co.uk
website https://authorityguides.co.uk
Facebook www.facebook.com/groups/theauthorityclub
Twitter @SRA_TAG
Director Sue Richardson

Pocket-sized business books for entrepreneurs and business professionals. Concise and practical, titles range across business subjects from finance to leadership, sales and marketing to personal development. Submissions welcomed, please email for guidelines. Founded 2017.

Avon – see HarperCollins Publishers

Award Publications Ltd
The Old Riding School, The Welbeck Estate,
Worksop, Notts. S80 3LR
tel (01909) 478170
email info@awardpublications.co.uk
Facebook www.facebook.com/awardpublications
Twitter @award_books
Instagram @award.books

Publishes picture story books, fiction, early learning, information and activity books from birth to 12. No unsolicited material. Please refer to social media sites for details of submission windows. Founded 1972.

Bernard Babani (publishing) Ltd
The Grampians, Shepherds Bush Road,
London W6 7NF
tel 020-7603 2581
email enquiries@babanibooks.com
website www.babanibooks.com
Director M.H. Babani

Practical handbooks on radio, electronics and computing. Founded 1942.

Bad Press Ink‡
The Studio, High Turney Shield, Hexham NE47 8AW
tel (01434) 345529
email submissions@badpress.ink
website www.badpress.ink

Books

Directors/Commissioning Editors Pat Blayney, Iain Parke, Lord Zion

Independent UK-based publisher of alternative, cult and niche lifestyle fiction. Run by authors for authors, interested in edgy fiction with a distinctive voice including crime, horror and urban subjects and are actively looking for new and unpublished talent. Submissions test available at: https://badpress.ink/submissions/. Founded 2018.

Bailliere Tindall – see Elsevier Ltd

Banshee Press Ltd[†]
email bansheelit@gmail.com
website www.bansheelit.com
Facebook www.facebook.com/bansheelit
Twitter @bansheelit
Instagram @banshee.lit
Directors Laura Cassidy, Claire Hennessy, Eimear Ryan

Small independent Irish publisher of a print literary journal, *Banshee*, as well as a select list of books. Publishes exciting, accessible, contemporary writing in all forms. The press is open to enquiries and proposals from contributors to the journal, particularly those who have not yet published a book-length work. Occasionally opens for unsolicited submissions, check website for details. Founded 2014.

Barbican Press Ltd[‡]
tel (07507) 554731
email martin@barbicanpress.com
website https://barbicanpress.com
Twitter @barbicanpress1
Instagram @barbicanpress
Directors Martin Goodman (managing); James Thornton

An independent micro-publisher. The list includes poetry, drama, writing for children, translations and compelling non-fiction, including issues-driven memoir and vivid tales of maritime communities. LGBTQI+ friendly. Founded 2009.

Barrington Stoke*
18 Walker Street, Edinburgh EH3 7LP
tel 0131 225 4113
email info@barringtonstoke.co.uk
website www.barringtonstoke.co.uk
Chairperson Lucy Juckes

Short fiction for children, specially adapted and presented for reluctant, struggling and dyslexic readers, including picture books up to young adult fiction. No unsolicited submissions. Founded 1998.

BBC Books – see Ebury Publishing

Bearded Badger Publishing Ltd
33 High Street, Belper, Derbyshire DE56 1GF
tel 07470 458761

email paulh@beardedbadgerpublishing.com
website www.beardedbadgerpublishing.com
Facebook www.facebook.com/beardedbadgerpublishing
Twitter @beardedbadgerpc
Instagram @bearded_badger_publishing
Managing Director Paul Handley

Bearded Badger Publishing is a new, independent publishing company based in Derbyshire, with a mission to publish high-quality literature across all genres, with an initial focus on publishing writers with a link to the oft-overlooked East Midlands region. Founded 2020.

Bennion Kearny Ltd[‡]
6 Woodside, Churnet View Road, Oakamoor, Staffs. ST10 3AE
tel (01538) 703591
email info@BennionKearny.com
website www.BennionKearny.com
Publisher James Lumsden-Cook, *Marketing* Adam Walters

Non-fiction: academic, professional, popular, niche, and practical titles; all subjects considered. See website for submission details. Publishes titles both nationally and internationally. Imprints include: Bennion Kearny, Dark River, Hawksmoor Publishing, and Oakamoor Publishing. Founded 2008.

Berlitz Publishing – see Apa Publications

BFI Publishing
Bloomsbury Publishing Plc, 50 Bedford Square, London WC1B 3DP
tel 020-7631 5600
email academic@bloomsbury.com
website www.bloomsbury.com/BFI
Publisher Rebecca Barden

Film, TV and media studies; general, academic and educational resources on moving image culture. BFI books and resources are published in partnership with Bloomsbury Publishing Plc (page 136). Founded 1982.

Birlinn Ltd[‡]
West Newington House, 10 Newington Road, Edinburgh EH9 1QS
tel 0131 668 4371
email info@birlinn.co.uk
website www.birlinn.co.uk
Directors Hugh Andrew, Jan Rutherford, Andrew Simmons, Laura Poynton, Joanne Macleod

Publisher of the reissue of Neil Munro's *Para Handy* which has been in print since 1992. Publishes both in the UK and internationally. Genres include Scottish history, local interest/history, Scottish humour, guides, military, adventure, history, archaeology, sport, general non-fiction. Publishes five imprints. Founded 1992.

Arena Sport

Subjects include football, rugby, golf, running and cycling.

BC Books

Children's imprint providing quality illustrated books for young readers. Founded 2015.

Birlinn eBooks

Publishes ebooks across all imprints.

John Donald

Academic books.

Polygon

Imprint of classic and modern literary fiction and poetry. Authors include: Robin Jenkins, George Mackay Brown and Alexander McCall Smith. Publishes music and film titles including Stuart Cosgrove's *Young Soul Rebels*. International authors include Jan-Philipp Sendker.

Bitter Lemon Press‡

47 Wilmington Square, London WC1X 0ET
email books@bitterlemonpress.com
website www.bitterlemonpress.com
Facebook www.facebook.com/bitterlemonpress
Twitter @bitterlemonpub

Publishes crime fiction that exposeS the darker side of countries such as Argentina, Cuba, Mexico, Belgium, France, Germany, Italy, Netherlands, Poland, Spain, Switzerland, Turkey, India, Iraq, New Zealand, Australia, and the USA. Imprint: Wilmington Square Books publishes books about culture and society. Founded 2015.

Black & White Publishing Ltd*‡

Nautical House, 104 Commercial Street,
Edinburgh EH6 6NF
tel 0131 625 4500
email mail@blackandwhitepublishing.com
website www.blackandwhitepublishing.com
Directors Campbell Brown (managing), Alison McBride (publishing)

Non-fiction: general, sport, cookery, lifestyle, biography, humour, crime. Fiction: women's fiction, contemporary, historical, psychological thrillers, crime, young adult (Ink Road imprint). Also publisher of *Itchy Coo*, *The Broons* and *Oor Wullie* books. Please see website for latest submission guidelines: httpS://blackandwhitepublishing.com/submissions. Founded 1999.

Black Dog Press

111 Highgate Studios, 53–79 Highgate Road,
London NW5 1TL
tel 020-8371 4047
email anna@blackdogonline.com
website www.blackdogonline.com

Contemporary art, design, photography, music. Founded 1995.

Blackstaff Press Ltd†

Colourpoint House, Jubilee Business Park,
21 Jubilee Road, Newtownards, Co. Down BT23 4YH
tel 028-9182 6339 (within the UK) /
+353 (0)48 91826339 (Republic of Ireland)
email info@blackstaffpress.com
website www.blackstaffpress.com
Facebook www.facebook.com/Blackstaffpressni
Twitter @BlackstaffNI
Managing Editor Patsy Horton

Local interest titles, particularly memoir, history and humour. See website for submission guidelines before sending material. Acquired by Colourpoint Creative Ltd (page 141) in 2017. Founded 1971.

John Blake Publishing

Victoria House, Bloomsbury Squre,
London WC1B 4DA
tel 020-7490 3875
email hello@blake.co.uk
website www.bonnierbooks.co.uk
Twitter @jblakebooks
Instagram @johnblakebooks
Publisher Matthew Phillips

Aims to publish new commercial trends in non-fiction, specialising in mass-market autobiographies and real life stories, as well as history, art, humour and gift books. John Blake Publishing is an imprint of Bonnier Books UK (page 137). Founded 1991.

Blink Publishing

Victoria House, Bloomsbury Squre,
London WC1B 4DA
tel 020-7490 3875
email hello@blinkpublishing.co.uk
website www.blinkpublishing.co.uk,
www.bonnierbooks.co.uk
Twitter @blinkpublishing
Instagram @blinkpublishing
Publisher Matthew Phillips, *Editorial Director* Susannah Otter, *Senior Editor* Beth Eynon

Blink Publishing is focused on the world of commercial adult non-fiction. With an emphasis on the official and authorised, titles seek to explore the vibrant world of popular culture. Genres include memoirs, humour, cookery and sport. Blink Publishing is an imprint of Bonnier Books UK (page 137). Bonnier Group founded 1804.

Bloodaxe Books Ltd

Eastburn, South Park, Hexham,
Northumberland NE46 1BS
tel (01434) 611581
email editor@bloodaxebooks.com
website www.bloodaxebooks.com
Editor Neil Astley

Poetry. Check submissions guide on website and send sample of up to a dozen poems with sae only if the

Books

submission fits the publisher's guidelines. No email submissions or correspondence. Founded 1978.

Bloodhound Books Ltd‡

Wellington House, East Road, Cambridge CB1 1BH
email info@bloodhoundbooks.com
website www.bloodhoundbooks.com
Facebook www.facebook.com/BloodhoundBooks
Twitter @BloodhoundBook

Bloodhound Books is a digital-focused publisher that publishes commercial fiction and specialises in crime, thrillers and women's fiction. Accepts unsolicited MS. Founded 2014.

Bloomsbury Publishing Plc*‡

50 Bedford Square, London WC1B 3DP
tel 020-7631 5600
website www.bloomsbury.com
Chief Executive & Founder Nigel Newton

Bloomsbury Publishing is a leading independent publishing house with authors who have won the Nobel, Pulitzer and Booker Prizes, and is the originating publisher and custodian of the Harry Potter series. Bloomsbury has offices in London, New York (page 208), New Delhi, Oxford and Sydney (page 198). MSS must normally be channelled through literary agents, with the exception of academic and professional titles. Founded 1986.

BLOOMSBURY CONSUMER DIVISION
Managing Director Ian Hudson

Imprints include: Absolute Press, Bloomsbury Activity Books, Bloomsbury Children's Books, Bloomsbury Circus, Bloomsbury India, Bloomsbury Press, Bloomsbury Publishing, Bloomsbury USA, Bloomsbury USA Children's Books, Raven Books.

Bloomsbury Adult Trade Publishing
Adult Editor-in-Chief Paul Baggaley, *Associate Publisher* Alexis Kirschbaum, *Publishing Directors* Emma Herdman, Michael Fishwick, Alison Hennessey (Raven Books), Rowan Yapp (illustrated & cookery), *Executive Publisher* Alexandra Pringle

Part of Bloomsbury Consumer Division, publishes fiction and non-fiction. Known for literary fiction it publishes, including Elizabeth Gilbert, Khaled Hosseini, Madeleine Miller, Ann Patchett and George Saunders. In non-fiction, it publishes contemporary and history, including Reni Eddo-Lodge, William Dalrymple, Peter Francopan and Rutger Bregman. The cookery list features chefs such as Hugh Fearnley-Whittingstall, Paul Hollywood and Tom Kerridge.

Bloomsbury Children's Books
Publishing Director & International Editor-in-Chief Rebecca McNally, *Publishing Director* Sharon Hutton (non-fiction), *Head of Fiction* Ellen Holgate, *Editorial Directors* Zoe Griffiths (fiction), Saskia Gwinn (non-fiction)

Authors include J.K. Rowling, Louis Sachar, Neil Gaiman, Sarah J. Maas, Sarah Crossan and Brian Conaghan. No complete MSS; send a synopsis with three chapters.

Bloomsbury Education
Head of Education Helen Diamond, *Editorial Director* Hannah Rolls (educational fiction, poetry & digital resources), *Senior Commissioning Editor* Hannah Marston (education – CPD)

Publishes around 75 print titles per year: educational fiction, children's poetry, teacher's books, apps and digital platforms. Imprints include Bloomsbury Education, Andrew Brodie and Featherstone Education.

BLOOMSBURY ACADEMIC AND PROFESSIONAL DIVISION
website www.bloomsburyprofessional.com,
www.bloomsburyacademic.com
Managing Director Jenny Ridout

Imprints include: The Arden Shakespeare, Bloomsbury Academic, Fairchild Books, Hart Publishing (page 156), I.B. Tauris (page 189), Zed Books (page 195), Methuen Drama, T&T Clark and British Film Institute (as publishing partner).

Bloomsbury Special Interest
Global Head of Special Interest, Sarah Broadway

Publishes a wide variety of non-fiction including politics, history, business, sports and wellbeing, popular science, philosophy and religion, as well as reference books such as *Who's Who, Wisden Cricketers' Almanack, Writers' & Artists' Yearbook* and *Reeds Nautical Almanac.* Market leaders in natural history, nautical and illustrated military history.

Bloomsbury Digital Resources
Managing Director Kathryn Earle

Digital content services to expand Bloomsbury's portfolio across the humanities and social sciences, including Drama Online, Bloomsbury Collections, the Churchill Archive, Bloomsbury Fashion Central, and many others.

Blue Guides Ltd

Old Brewery Road, Wiveliscombe TA4 2PW
tel 020-8144 3509
email editorial@blueguides.com
website www.blueguides.com
Facebook www.facebook.com/blueguides
Twitter @blueguides

Blue Guides and *Blue Guide Travel Companions.* Detailed guide books with a focus on history, art and architecture for the independent traveller. Founded 1918.

Bluemoose Books*

25 Sackville Street, Hebden Bridge HX7 7DJ
email kevin@bluemoosebooks.com
website www.bluemoosebooks.com
Twitter @ofmooseandmen

Publisher Kevin Duffy

Publisher of literary fiction. No children's, young adult or poetry. Founded 2006.

Bodleian Library Publishing‡
Broad Street, Oxford OX1 3BG
tel (01865) 283850
email publishing@bodleian.ox.ac.uk
website www.bodleianshop.co.uk
Facebook www.facebook.com/bodleianlibraries
Twitter @BodPublishing
Head of Publishing Samuel Fanous

The Bodleian Library is the main library of the University of Oxford. The publishing programme creates gift, trade and scholarly books on a wide range of subjects drawn from or related to the library's rich collection of rare books, manuscripts, maps, postcards and other ephemera. Bodleian Library Founded 1602.

The Bodley Head – see Vintage

Bonnier Books UK*
Victoria House, Bloomsbury Square,
London WC1B 4DA
tel 020-377 0888
email hello@bonnierbooks.co.uk
website www.bonnierbooks.co.uk
Ceo Perminder Mann, *Managing Director* Kate Parkin (adult trade), *Managing Director* Jane Harris (children trade)

Bonnier Books UK is owned by Bonnier Books, a family-owned company headquartered in Sweden. Bonnier Books is a top-15 world publisher. Publishes across a wide variety of genres for different ages. From crime to reading group fiction; memoir to self-help; activity to reference. Publishers of twelve imprints: adult trade (Zaffre (page 195), Manilla Press (page 167), Blink (page 135), John Blake (page 135)); Embla Books; Bonnier Business; children's trade (Piccadilly Press page 177), Templar (page 189) Big Picture Press, Studio Press (page 187)). Founded 2015.

The Book Guild Ltd
14 Priory Business Park, Wistow Road, Kibworth, Leics. LE8 0RX
tel 0800 999 2982
email info@bookguild.co.uk
website www.bookguild.co.uk
Facebook www.facebook.com/thebookguild
Twitter @BookGuild
Directors Jeremy Thompson (managing), Jane Rowland (operations)

Offers traditional and partnership publishing arrangements, with all titles published being funded or co-funded by The Book Guild Ltd (does not offer self-publishing). MSS accepted in fiction, children's and non-fiction genres, please see the website for details. The Book Guild is part of parent company Troubador Publishing Ltd (page 191). Founded 1996.

Bookouture
Carmelite House, 50 Victoria Embankment,
London EC4Y 0DZ
email pitch@bookouture.com
website www.bookouture.com
Facebook www.facebook.com/bookouture
Twitter @bookouture
Managing Director Jenny Geras, *Publisher* Claire Bord, *Contracts, Rights & Author Development Director* Peta Nightingale, *Publishing Directors* Laura Deacon, Kathryn Taussig, Ruth Tross, *Associate Publishers* Natasha Harding, Lydia Vassar-Smith, Jessic Botterill, Isobel Akenhead, Christina Demosthenous, Helen Jenner, Lucy Dauman, *Commissioning Editors* Jennifer Hunt, Maisie Lawrence, Cara Chimirri, Ellen Gleeson, Emily Gowers, Therese Keating

Alternative emails: rights@bookouture.com, royalties@bookouture.com, admin@bookouture.com, pitch@bookouture.com. Bookouture is a digital imprint publishing commercial fiction. Welcomes submissions via the website. Part of Hachette UK (page 154). Founded 2012.

Thread
Publishes books by leading experts across a range of non-fiction topics including self-development, personal finance, parenting, nutrition and fitness, popular psychology and inspirational memoir.

Marion Boyars Publishers Ltd/Prospect Books
26 Parke Road, London SW13 9NG
email catheryn@marionboyars.com
email catheryn@prospectbooks.co.uk
website www.marionboyars.co.uk, www.prospectbooks.co.uk
Directors Catheryn Kilgarriff, Ella Kilgarriff, Tessa Kilgarriff *Editor (Petits Propos Culinaires)* Tom Jain

Prospect Books accepts submissions in food history. Marion Boyars Publishers has an active backlist including literary fiction, film, cultural studies, and modern music; it is however not accepting submissions. Founded 1975.

Boydell & Brewer Ltd
Bridge Farm Business Park, Top Street,
Martlesham IP12 4RB
tel (01394) 610600
email editorial@boydell.co.uk
website www.boydellandbrewer.com
Ceo James Powell

Medieval studies, early modern and modern history, maritime history, literature, archaeology, art history, music, Hispanic studies. No unsolicited MSS. See website for submission guidelines. Founded 1969.

Books

James Currey
website www.jamescurrey.com
Academic studies of Africa and developing economies.

Bradt Travel Guides Ltd‡

31A High Street, Chesham, Bucks. HP5 1BW
tel (01753) 893444
email info@bradtguides.com
website www.bradtguides.com
Twitter @BradtGuides
Managing Director Adrian Phillips, *Commissioning Editor* Claire Strange

Travel and wildlife guides with emphasis on unusual destinations and ethical/positive travel. Travel narratives and anthologies of travel writing. Submission guidelines: bradtguides.com/write-for-us. Contract publishing imprint: Journey Books. Founded 1974.

Nicholas Brealey – see John Murray Press

The Bright Press

18 Circus Street, Brighton BN2 9QF
tel (01273) 727268
website www.quartoknows.com

Illustrated books on science, lifestyle, culture, craft and adult activity. Part of The Quarto Group (page 179). Founded 2018.

Brilliant Publications Ltd*‡

Unit 10, Sparrow Hall Farm, Edlesborough, Dunstable LU6 2ES
tel (01525) 222292
email info@brilliantpublications.co.uk
website www.brilliantpublications.co.uk
Facebook www.facebook.com/Brilliant-Publications-340005555138
Twitter @Brilliantpub, @BrillCreative
Managing Director Priscilla Hannaford

Creates easy-to-use educational resources, featuring engaging approaches to learning, across a wide range of curriculum areas, including English, foreign languages, maths, art and design, thinking skills and PSHE. No children's picture books, non-fiction books or one-off fiction books. See Guidelines for Authors on website before sending proposal. Founded 1993.

Bristol University Press/Policy Press*‡

University of Bristol, 1–9 Old Park Hill, Clifton, Bristol BS2 8BB
tel 0117 954 5940
email bup-info@bristol.ac.uk
website www.policypress.co.uk, www.bristoluniversitypress.co.uk
Facebook www.facebook.com/PolicyPress
Twitter @policypress, @BrisUniPress

Ceo Alison Shaw, *Journals Director* Julia Mortimer, *Sales & Marketing Director* Jo Greig, *Head of Commissioning* Victoria Pittman

Bristol University Press specialises in politics and international relations, sociology, human geography, business and management, economics and law. Policy Press specialises in social and public policy, criminology, social work and social welfare. Bristol University Press founded 2016, Policy Press founded 1996.

British Library Publishing*

Publishing Office, The British Library, 96 Euston Road, London NW1 2DB
tel 020-7412 7294
email publishing_editorial@bl.uk
website www.bl.uk/aboutus/publishing

Publishes around 50 books a year: classic crime, science fiction, weird fiction and women's fiction, art, maps, manuscripts, history, literature and facsimiles. Founded 1979.

The British Museum Press

Great Russell Street, London WC1B 3DG
tel 020-3073 4946
email publicity@britishmuseum.org
website www.britishmuseum.org/commercial/british-museum-press
Head of Publishing Claudia Bloch

Publishes illustrated books for general readers, families, academics and students, inspired by the collections of the British Museum. Titles range across the fine and decorative arts, history, archaeology and world cultures. Division of The British Museum Company Ltd. Founded 1973.

Brown, Son & Ferguson Ltd*

Unit 1, 426 Drumoyne Road, Glasgow G51 4DA
tel 0141 883 0141 (24 hours)
email info@skipper.co.uk
website www.skipper.co.uk
Editorial Directors Richard Brown, Wendy Brown

Nautical books, plays. Founded 1860.

Bryntirion Press

Waterton Cross Business Park, South Road, Bridgend CF31 3UL
tel (01656) 655886
email office@emw.org.uk
website www.emw.org.uk/bryntirion
Publications Officer Stefan Job

Formerly Evangelical Press of Wales. Theology and religion (in English and Welsh). Founded 1955.

Burning Chair Publishing*

61 Bridge Street, Kington HR5 3DJ
email info@burningchairpublishing.com
website www.burningchairpublishing.com
Facebook www.facebook.com/BurningChairPublishing

Twitter @Burning_Chair
Directors Simon Finnie, Peter Oxley

Burning Chair is an independent publishing company based in the UK but covering readers and authors across the globe. Welcomes unsolicited fiction submissions (from authors direct as well as through agents) in the following genres: mystery, thriller, suspense, crime, action and adventure, science fiction, fantasy (including urban fantasy and young adult), paranormal, horror, historical fiction. Completed MSS of novel-length only (at least 60,000 words). A synopsis is required (no more than two pages) plus the completed MS. Email and postal submissions not accepted. Submissions only accepted through the online portal at: www.burningchairpublishing.com/submissions. Founded 2018.

Buster Books – see Michael O'Mara Books Ltd

Butterworth-Heinemann – see Elsevier Ltd

Butterworths – see LexisNexis

Cambridge University Press*‡
University Printing House, Shaftesbury Road, Cambridge CB2 8BS
tel (01223) 358331
email information@cambridge.org
website www.cambridge.org
Facebook www.facebook.com/CambridgeUniversityPress
Twitter @CambridgeUP
Chief Executive Peter Phillips; *Managing Directors* Mandy Hill (academic), Paul Colbert (ELT), Rod Smith (Cambridge Education)

Anthropology and archaeology, art history, astronomy, biological sciences, classical studies, computer science, dictionaries, earth sciences, economics, engineering, history, language and literature, law, mathematics, medical sciences, music, philosophy, physical sciences, politics, psychology, reference, technology, social sciences, theology, religion. ELT, educational (primary, secondary, tertiary), e-learning products, journals (humanitics, social sciences, science, technical and medical). The Bible and Prayer Book. In August 2021 Cambridge University Press and Cambridge Assessment joined to form a single organisation. Founded 1534.

Campbell – see Pan Macmillan

Canbury Press Ltd‡
14 Beresford Road, Kingston upon Thames, Surrey KT2 6LR
email info@canburypress.com
website www.canburypress.com
Facebook www.facebook.com/canburypress
Twitter @canburypress
Instagram @canburypress
Directors Martin Hickman (editorial), Katharine Nelson (sales & marketing)

Modern non-fiction books. Politics, philosophy, health, environment, biography, and technology. Non-fiction submissions (synopsis and two chapters) welcome by email. No fiction. Founded in 2013.

Candy Jar Books
Mackintosh House, 136 Newport Road, Cardiff CF24 1DJ
tel 029-2115 7202
email submissions@candyjarbooks.co.uk
website www.candy-jar.co.uk/books
Facebook www.facebook.com/CandyJarLimited
Twitter @Candy_Jar
Head of Publishing Shaun Russell

Publishes children's, young adult, cult media, biography, general non-fiction, military history and fantasy. Publishes about 30 titles per year. Unsolicited material welcome; submissions form on website. No children's picture books. Partner imprint of Jelly Bean Self-Publishing. Founded 2010.

Canelo Digital Publishing Ltd
C/o Rouse Partners LLP, 55 Station Road, Beaconsfield HP9 1QL
email hello@canelo.co
website www.canelo.co
Facebook www.facebook.com/canelobooks
Twitter @canelo_co
Directors Iain Millar (managing), Michael Bhaskar (publishing), Nick Barreto (technology), Louise Cullen (editorial)

Finds the best commercial storytelling and brings it to the widest possible audience with a new and fairer deal for authors. Please see canelo.co/vision for publishing and submission guidelines.

Canongate Books Ltd*
14 High Street, Edinburgh EH1 1TE
tel 0131 557 5111
email info@canongate.co.uk
Alternative address Eardley House, 4 Uxbridge Street, London W8 7SY
website www.canongate.co.uk
Ceo Jamie Byng, *Publishing Director* Francis Bickmore, *Rights & Contracts Director* Jessica Neale, *Editorial Director* Simon Thorogood, *Editorial Director* Hannah Knowles, *Commissioning Editor* Jo Dingley

Adult general non-fiction and fiction: literary fiction, translated fiction, memoir, politics, popular science, humour, travel, popular culture, history and biography. Founded 1973.

Canopus Publishing Ltd
8 Foxcombe Road, Bath BA1 3ED
tel 07970 153217
email robin@canopusbooks.com
website www.canopusbooks.com
Twitter @robin_rees

Directors Robin Rees, Sarah Tremlett

Packager of books on astronomy, aerospace, photography and rock music; publisher for the London Stereoscopic Company and Starmus. Founded 1999.

Canterbury Press – see Hymns Ancient and Modern Ltd

Jonathan Cape – see Vintage

Capuchin Classics – see Stacey Publishing Ltd

Carcanet Press Ltd*‡

4th Floor, Alliance House, 30 Cross Street, Manchester M2 7AQ
tel 0161 834 8730
email info@carcanet.co.uk
website www.carcanet.co.uk
Managing Director Michael Schmidt

Poetry, translations. Imprints include Carcanet Poetry, Carcanet Classics, Lives and Letters, Anvil Press Poetry, Northern House. Founded 1969.

Cassava Republic Press‡

9 Eri Studio C11, Mainyard Studios, 94 Wallis Road, London E9 5LN
email info@cassavarepublic.biz
website https://cassavarepublic.biz/
Facebook www.facebook.com/CassavaRepublic
Twitter @cassavarepublic
Instagram @cassavarepublicpress

Publishes contemporary Black and African writing. Founded in Abuja, Nigeria, 2006 by Bibi Bakare-Yusuf and Jeremy Weate, with the aim of bringing high-quality fiction and non-fiction for adults and children to a global audience. Has offices in Abuja and London. Founded 2006.

Caterpillar Books – see Little Tiger Group

Catholic Truth Society

42–46 Harleyford Road, London SE11 5AY
tel 020-7640 0042
email p.finaldi@ctsbooks.org
website www.ctsbooks.org
Ceo & Publisher Pierpaolo Finaldi

General books of Roman Catholic and Christian interest, liturgical books, missals, bibles, prayer books, children's books and booklets of doctrinal, historical, devotional or social interest. MSS of 10,000–20,000 words with up to six illustrations considered for publication as booklets. Founded 1868.

Cengage*

Cheriton House, Andover SP10 5BE
tel (01264) 332424
email emeahepublishing@cengage.com
website www.cengage.co.uk

Actively commissioning print and digital content for further education and higher education courses in the following disciplines: IT, computer science and computer applications; accounting, finance and economics; marketing; international business; human resource management; operations management; strategic management; organisational behaviour; business information systems; quantitative methods; psychology; hairdressing and beauty therapy. Submit content writing interest either by email or post. Founded 2007.

Century & Arrow – see Cornerstone

Chapman Publishing

4 Broughton Place, Edinburgh EH1 3RX
tel 0131 557 2207
email chapman-pub@blueyonder.co.uk
website www.chapman-pub.co.uk
Editor Dr Joy Hendry

Chapman New Writing and the Chapman Wild Women series, poetry and drama. No unsolicited MS. Founded 1986.

Chatto & Windus – see Vintage

Chicken House

2 Palmer Street, Frome, Somerset BA11 1DS
tel (01373) 454488
email hello@chickenhousebooks.com
website www.chickenhousebooks.com
Twitter @chickenhsebooks
Managing Director & Publisher Barry Cunningham,
Deputy Managing Director Rachel Hickman

Fiction for ages 7+ and young adult. No unsolicited MSS. Successes include James Dashner (the *Maze Runner* series), Cornelia Funke (*Inkheart* and the *Dragon Rider* series) and Kiran Millwood Hargrave (*The Girl of Ink & Stars*). See website for details of *Times*/Chicken House Children's Fiction Competition for unpublished writers. Part of Scholastic Ltd (page 183). Founded 2000.

Child's Play (International) Ltd

Ashworth Road, Bridgemead, Swindon, Wilts. SN5 7YD
tel (01793) 616286
email office@childs-play.com
website www.childs-play.com
Facebook www.facebook.com/ChildsPlayBooks
Twitter @ChildsPlayBooks
Chairman Adriana Twinn, *Publisher* Neil Burden

Children's educational books: board, picture, activity and play books; fiction and non-fiction. Founded 1972.

Christian Education

5/6 Imperial Court, 12 Sovereign Road, Birmingham B30 3FH

tel 0121 472 4242
email anstice.hughes@christianeducation.org.uk
website https://shop.christianeducation.org.uk/,
www.retoday.org.uk
Facebook www.facebook.com/RETodayServices
Twitter @IBRAbibleread

Incorporating RE Today Services and International Bible Reading Association. Publications and services for teachers and other professionals in religious education including *REtoday* magazine, curriculum booklets and classroom resources. Also publishes bible reading materials. Founded 2001.

Churchill Livingstone – see Elsevier Ltd

Churchwarden Publications Ltd
PO Box 420, Warminster, Wilts. BA12 9XB
tel (01985) 840189
email enquiries@churchwardenbooks.co.uk
website www.churchwardenbooks.co.uk
Directors J.N.G. Stidolph, S.A. Stidolph

Publisher of *The Churchwarden's Yearbook*. Care and administration of churches and parishes. Founded 1986.

Cicada Books*
Unit 9, 6 Cliff Road, Cliff Road Studios,
London NW1 9AN
email info@cicadabooks.co.uk
website www.cicadabooks.co.uk
Twitter @cicadabooks
Instagram @cicadabooks

Publishes a few titles a year. Specialises in highly-illustrated books for adults and children. Founded 2009.

Cicerone Press‡
Juniper House, Murley Moss Business Village,
Oxenholme Road, Kendal, Cumbria LA9 7RL
tel (01539) 562069
email info@cicerone.co.uk
website www.cicerone.co.uk
Managing Director Jonathan Williams

Guidebooks: walking, trekking, mountaineering, climbing, cycling in Britain, Europe and worldwide. Founded 1969.

Cico Books – see Ryland Peters & Small

Cisco Press – see Pearson UK

Claret Press‡
51 Iveley Road, London SW4 0EN
tel 020-622 0436
email contact@claretpress.com
website www.claretpress.com
Facebook www.facebook.com/ClaretPublisher
Twitter @Claret_Press
Founder & Editor-in-Chief Katic Isbester

Publishing stories that matter. Selecting fiction and creative non-fiction which explores the human spirit and our shared world. Flexible about genre, favouring deeply interesting and engaging narratives, often with a political edge. Founded 2015.

James Clarke & Co. Ltd‡
PO Box 60, Cambridge CB1 2NT
tel (01223) 350865
email publishing@jamesclarke.co.uk
website www.jamesclarke.co
Facebook www.facebook.com/JamesClarkeandCo
Twitter @JamesClarkeLtd
Managing Director Adrian Brink

Founded in the mid-19th century, the company originally published the religious magazine *Christian World*. Now publishes books and ebooks on: academic theology, philosophy, history and biography, biblical studies and reference books. Sister imprint The Lutterworth Press is one of the oldest independent publishing houses in the UK, see page 166. Founded 1859.

Cló Iar-Chonnachta Teo†
Indreabhán, Co. Galway H91 CHO1,
Republic of Ireland
tel +353 (0)91 593307
email eolas@cic.ie
website www.cic.ie
Director & Chairman Micheál Ó Conghaile, *Director & Secretary* Tadhg Ó Conghaile

Irish-language: novels, short stories, plays, poetry, songs, history; CDs (writers reading from their works in Irish and English). Promotes the translation of contemporary Irish fiction and poetry into other languages. Founded 1985.

Cloud Lodge Books Ltd
Niddry Lodge, 51 Holland Street, London W8 7JB
tel 020-7225 1623
email info@cloudlodgebooks.co.uk
website www.cloudlodgebooks.com
Facebook www.facebook.com/cloudlodgebooks
Twitter @CLBPressUK
Managing Director William Campos, *Fiction Editor* Oliver Walton, *Science Fiction Editor* Alexander Hernandez, *Sales & Marketing* David Wightman

Publisher of daring literary fiction, crime fiction and science fiction. Publishes up to four original titles per year, in print, digital and audio formats. Features writers (and characters) of every race, religion, nationality, gender and sexual orientation. Founded 2016.

Colourpoint Creative Ltd†
Colourpoint House, Jubilee Business Park,
21 Jubilee Road, Newtownards, Co. Down BT23 4YH
tel 028-9182 6339 (within UK) / +353 (0)48
91826339 (Republic of Ireland)

email sales@colourpoint.co.uk
website www.colourpoint.co.uk
Twitter @colourpoint
Publisher Malcolm Johnston, *Head of Educational Publishing* Wesley Johnston, *Marketing* Jacky Hawkes

Irish, Ulster-Scots and general interest including local history; transport (covering the whole of the British Isles), railways, buses, road, aviation; educational textbooks and resources. Short queries by email. Full submission in writing including details of proposal, sample chapter/section, qualification/experience in the topic, full contact details and return postage. Imprints: Colourpoint Educational, Blackstaff Press Ltd (page 135). Founded 1993.

Columba Books[†]

Unit 3B, Block 3, Bracken Business Park, Bracken Road, Sandyford, Dublin 18 D18 K277, Republic of Ireland
tel +353 (0)16 874096
email info@columba.ie
website www.columbabooks.com
Facebook www.facebook.com/columbabooks/
Twitter @columbabooks
Publisher & Managing Director Garry O'Sullivan, *Marketing & Sales Executive* Mahak Verma

Religion (Roman Catholic and Anglican) including pastoral handbooks, spirituality, theology, liturgy and prayer; counselling and self-help. Founded 1984.

Currach Books
website www.currachbooks.com
Facebook www.facebook.com/currachbooks
Irish interest including photography, poetry, history, biography and fiction.

Concord Theatricals

Head Office Concord Theatricals Ltd, Aldwych House, 71–91 Aldwych, London WC2B 4HN
tel 020-7054 7200
email customerservices@concordtheatricals.co.uk
website www.concordtheatricals.co.uk
Facebook www.facebook.com/concordukshows
Twitter @concordukshows

Concord Theatricals Ltd is a licensing, publishing, recording & producing company comprising R&H Theatricals, Samuel French and Tams-Witmark. They sell an extensive range of scripts and theatre books both online and at the Samuel French Bookshop at the Royal Court Theatre, Sloane Square, London SW1W 8AS. Email the bookshop at bookshop@royalcourttheatre.com or call on 020-7565 5024. More information on play and musical submissions can be found at concordtheatricals.co.uk. Founded 1830.

Conran Octopus – see Octopus Publishing Group

Constable & Robinson Ltd – see Little, Brown Book Group

Cork University Press[†]

Boole Library, University College Cork, College Road, Cork T12 ND89, Republic of Ireland
tel +353 (0)21 490 2980
website www.corkuniversitypress.com
Publications Director Mike Collins

Irish literature, history, cultural studies, landscape studies, medieval studies, English literature, musicology, poetry, translations. Founded 1925.

Atrium and Attic Press
email corkuniversitypress@ucc.ie
Books by and about women in the areas of social and political comment, women's studies. Cookery, psychology, biography and Irish cultural studies (trade).

Cornerstone

20 Vauxhall Bridge Road, London SW1V 2SA
tel 020-7840 8400
website www.penguin.co.uk
Managing Director Venetia Butterfield, *Director of Publicity & Media Relations* Charlotte Bush, *Associate Publisher* Nigel Wilcockson (non-fiction)

Part of Penguin Random House UK (page 176). No unsolicited MSS accepted.

Century & Arrow
tel 020-7840 8394
Publisher Selina Walker, *Publishing Director* Ben Brusey (non-fiction) *Publishing Director* Emily Griffin (fiction)
Commercial hardcover and paperback fiction and non-fiction.

Del Rey
tel 020-7139 3690
Publishing Director Ben Brusey, *Senior Editor* Sam Bradbury
Adult and young adult crossover science fiction, fantasy and horror.

Hutchinson Heinemann
tel 020-7139 8384
Publisher Helen Conford, *Publishing Director* Ailah Ahmed, *Publishing Director* Charlotte Cray (fiction)
Literary and book-club fiction, as well as a broader range of non-fiction encompassing, history, politics, popular science, polemic, memoir, and biography.

#Merky Books
tel 020-840 8454
Publisher Helen Conford, *Commissioning Editor* Lemara Lindsay-Prince
Fiction: literary fiction, commercial fiction, genre fiction, poetry. Non-fiction: current affairs, narrative non-fiction, politics, memoir.

Random House Business Books
tel 020-7840 8793
Publisher Helen Conford

Non-fiction: business, economics, smart thinking, psychology and self-development.

Windmill Books
tel 020-7840 8265
website www.windmillbooks.co.uk
Publishing Director Charlotte Cray

Literary hardcover and paperback fiction and narrative non-fiction.

Council for British Archaeology

92 Micklegate, York YO1 6JX
tel (01904) 671417
email info@archaeologyuk.org
website www.archaeologyuk.org
Facebook www.facebook.com/Archaeologyuk
Twitter @archaeologyuk
Director Mike Heyworth

British archaeology – academic; practical handbooks; general interest archaeology. *British Archaeology* magazine. Founded 1944.

Country Books

Courtyard Cottage, Little Longstone, Bakewell, Derbyshire DE45 1NN
tel (01629) 640670
email dickrichardson@countrybooks.biz
website www.countrybooks.biz,
www.sussexbooks.co.uk

Incorporating Ashridge Press. Local history (new and facsimile reprints), family history, autobiography, general non-fiction, novels, customs and folklore. Books for the National Trust, Chatsworth House, Peak District NPA, Derbyshire County Council. Founded 1995.

Countryside Books‡

35A Kingfisher Court, Hambridge Road, Newbury, Berks. RG14 5SJ
tel (01635) 43816
website www.countrysidebooks.co.uk
Partners Nicholas Battle, Suzanne Battle, Alex Batho

Publishes books of local or regional interest, usually on a county basis: walking, outdoor activities, also heritage, aviation, railways and architecture. Founded 1976.

Cranachan Publishing*

Blacksheep Croft, 52 North Galson, Isle of Lewis HS2 0SJ
tel (01851) 850700
email hello@cranachanpublishing.co.uk
website www.cranachanpublishing.co.uk
Twitter @cranachanbooks
Instagram @cranachanbooks
Publisher & Founder Anne Glennie

A small independent publisher based on the Isle of Lewis, focusing exclusively on high-quality children's fiction for 9 to 12 years (Pokey Hat imprint) and young adult fiction for teens and 12 years+ (Gob Stopper imprint) with a Scottish flavour. Also publishes educational resources for teachers. Founded 2015.

Cranthorpe Millner Publishers

Nine Hills Road, Cambridge CB2 1GE
tel 020-3441 9212
email kirsty.jackson@cranthorpemillner.com
website www.cranthorpemillner.com
Facebook facebook.com/CranthorpeMillner
Twitter @CranthorpeBooks
Instagram @CranthorpeMillner
Directors Kirsty Jackson (managing), David Hahn (chairman)

Titles include fiction and non-fiction: memoir, celeb autobiographies, history, science fiction, young adult, historical fiction, crime/thriller, literary fiction. Founded 2018.

CRC Press – see Taylor & Francis Group

Crescent Moon Publishing

PO Box 393, Maidstone, Kent ME14 5XU
tel (01622) 729593
email cresmopub@yahoo.co.uk
website www.crmoon.com
Director Jeremy Robinson *Editors* C. Hughes, B.D. Barnacle

Literature, poetry, arts, cultural studies, media, cinema, feminism. Submit sample chapters or six poems plus sae, not complete MSS. Founded 1988.

Cressrelles Publishing Co. Ltd

10 Station Road Industrial Estate, Colwall, Malvern, Herefordshire WR13 6RN
tel (01684) 540154
email simon@cressrelles.co.uk
website www.cressrelles.co.uk
Directors Leslie Smith, Simon Smith

General publishing. Founded 1973.

J. Garnet Miller

Plays and theatre textbooks.

Kenyon-Deane

Plays and drama textbooks for amateur dramatic societies. Plays for women.

New Playwrights' Network

Plays for amateur dramatic societies (page 169).

Crown House Publishing Ltd‡

Crown Buildings, Bancyfelin, Carmarthen SA33 5ND
tel (01267) 211345
email books@crownhouse.co.uk
website www.crownhouse.co.uk
Facebook www.facebook.com/CrownHousePub

Books

Twitter @CrownHousePub
Instagram @crownhousepub
Directors David Bowman (managing), Karen Bowman

Award-winning independent publisher specialising in the areas of education, coaching, business training and development, leadership, NLP, hypnotherapy, psychotherapy, self-help and personal growth. The list includes the Independent Thinking Press imprint, which brings into print the words of some of the UK's most inspiring and entertaining educational speakers and practitioners. Founded 1998.

Independent Thinking Press

email books@independentthinkingpress.com
website www.independentthinkingpress.com
Publishes CPD books and resources for teachers and school leaders. The list includes books on business, training and development, coaching, health and wellbeing, NLP, hypnosis, counselling and psychotherapy and a range of children's books.

The Crowood Press

The Stable Block, Ramsbury, Marlborough, Wilts. SN8 2HR
tel (01672) 520320
email enquiries@crowood.com
website www.crowood.com
Director Mollie Broadhead

Art, architecture, craft, general interest and hobbies, home and garden, military history, sport, performing arts, motoring and transport. Imprints include: Airlife Publishing (aviation, technical and general, military, military history), Robert Hale (general non-fiction), J.A. Allen (equestrian), N.A.G. Press (horology and gemmology) and Black Horse Westerns. Founded 1982.

Crux Publishing

34 Holford Road, Guildford, Surrey GU1 2QF
tel 020-8871 0594
email hello@cruxpublishing.co.uk
website www.cruxpublishing.co.uk
Publisher Christopher Lascelles

Boutique publisher offering to produce, distribute and market selected high-quality, non-fiction titles. Operates an open submissions policy for new authors and digitally republishes backlist titles for existing authors. Works with individual authors to create and execute a unique marketing plan that drives sales. Founded 2011.

Benjamin Cummings – see Pearson UK

James Currey – see Boydell & Brewer Ltd

Dahlia Publishing

6 Samphire Close, Hamilton, Leicester LE5 1RW
email f.shaikh@dahliapublishing.co.uk
website www.dahliapublishing.co.uk
Twitter @dahliabooks

Independent publisher of original, contemporary fiction. Short story collections welcome. Particularly keen to work with regional and diverse voices. Founded 2010.

Darf Publishers Ltd

277 West End Lane, London NW6 1QS
tel 020-7431 7009
email enquiry@darfpublishers.co.uk
website www.darfpublishers.co.uk
Facebook www.facebook.com/DarfPublishers
Twitter @DarfPublishers
Contacts Ghassan Fergiani (director), Ghazi Gheblawi (editorial)

An independent publisher based in London with diversity and inclusion at the heart of the company's work since 1980. The focus is on publishing and reprinting historical, geographic and classical works in English about the Middle East, North Africa and the UK. Also focuses on contemporary works of fiction, non-fiction and children's books from other languages into English, introducing new authors to the British market and the wider English speaking world. Recent published works from Arabic (Libya, Yemen, Sudan, Eritrea), Italian, German with plans to widen to include writers from other European countries, South America, Asia and Africa. Founded 1981.

Darton, Longman and Todd Ltd

1 Spencer Court, 140–142 Wandsworth High Street, London SW18 4JJ
tel 020-8875 0155
email editorial@darton-longman-todd.co.uk
website www.darton-longman-todd.co.uk
Editorial Director David Moloney

Spirituality, prayer and meditation; books for the heart, mind and soul; self-help and personal growth; biography; political, environmental and social issues. Founded 1959.

Daunt Books

207–209, Kentish Town Road, London NW5 2JU
email publishing@dauntbooks.co.uk
website www.dauntbooks.co.uk
Twitter @dauntbookspub
Publisher Sophie Missing

Daunt Books Publishing is an independent publisher based in London. Publishes new writing in English and in translation, whether that's literary fiction – novels and short stories – or narrative non-fiction including essays and memoir. Also publishes modern classics, reviving authors who have been overlooked. Not currently accepting unsolicited submissions, please check website for details. Founded 2010.

David & Charles Ltd‡

Tourism House, Pynes Hill, Exeter EX2 5WS
tel (01392) 790650

website www.davidandcharles.com
Managing Director James Woollam

Special interest publisher of books for hobbyists with a focus on craft and creative categories. UK and International distributor of Dover Publications. Founded 1960.

DB Publishing

29 Clarence Road, Nottingham NG9 5HY
tel (07914) 647382
email steve.caron@dbpublishing.co.uk
website www.dbpublishing.co.uk
Directors Steve Caron (managing), Jane Caron (finance)

An imprint of JMD Media Ltd. Primarily: football, sport, local history, heritage. Currently considering all topics including fiction. Unsolicited MSS welcome. Preliminary letter essential. Founded 2009.

Giles de la Mare Publishers Ltd

Bloomsbury House, 74–77 Great Russell Street, London WC1B 3DA
tel 020-7927 3800
website www.gilesdelamare.co.uk

Part of Faber & Faber Ltd (see page 148). Non-fiction: art, architecture, biography, history, music, travel. Telephone before submitting MS. Founded 1995.

Dedalus Ltd*

24 St Judith's Lane, Sawtry, Cambs. PE28 5XE
tel (01487) 832382
email info@dedalusbooks.com
website www.dedalusbooks.com
Chairman Margaret Jull Costa, *Publisher* Eric Lane, *Editorial* Timothy Lane

Original fiction in English and in translation; 12–14 titles a year. Imprints include: Original English Language Fiction in Paperback, Dedalus European Classics, Dedalus Euro Shorts, Dedalus Europe Contemporary Fiction, Dedalus Africa, Dedalus Concept books, Young Dedalus, City Noir, Dark Masters Literary Biography. Founded 1983.

Richard Dennis Publications

The New Chapel, Shepton Beauchamp, Ilminster, Somerset TA19 0JT
tel (01460) 240044
email books@richarddennispublications.com
website www.richarddennispublications.com

Books for collectors specialising in ceramics, glass, illustration, sculpture and facsimile editions of early catalogues. Founded 2008.

André Deutsch – see Welbeck Publishing Group

Digital Press – see Elsevier Ltd

Discovery Walking Guides Ltd

10 Tennyson Close, Northampton NN15 7HJ
tel (01604) 244869
email ask.discovery@ntlworld.com
website www.dwgwalking.co.uk
Chairman Rosamund C. Brawn

Publishes 'Walk!' walking guidebooks to UK and European destinations; 'Tour & Trail Super-Durable' large-scale maps for outdoor adventures; 'Bus & Touring' maps; and 'Drive' touring maps. Premium content provider to 3G phone/tablet gps apps for Digital Mapping and Hiking Adventures. Publishing in conventional book/map format along with digital platforms. Welcomes project proposals from technologically (gps) proficient walking writers. Founded 1994.

DK*

One Embassy Gardens, 8 Viaduct Gardens, London SW11 7BW
tel 020-7139 2000
website www.dk.com
Ceo Carston Coefeld

A member of the Penguin Random House (page 176) division of Bertelsmann, publishing highly visual books for adults and children: travel, licensing, children's, reference, education, gardening, food and drink. Founded 1974.

Dodo Ink

email sam@dodoink.com
website www.dodoink.com
Facebook www.facebook.com/Dodo-Ink-775175252560383
Twitter @DodoInk
Directors Sam Mills (managing), Thom Cuell (editorial)

An independent press dedicated to publishing daring and difficult literary fiction. Publishes two to three novels a year. Authors include Seraphina Madsen, Monique Roffey and James Miller. No unsolicited MSS by post; see the website for submission guidelines. Founded 2015.

Dogberry Ltd

13 The Rafters, Nottingham NG7 7FG
email contact@memoirist.org
website www.dogberrybooks.com
Publsiher Auriel Roe

English language publisher of humorous literary fiction, young adult fiction and memoir. Founded 2020.

John Donald – see Birlinn Ltd

Dorling Kindersley – see DK

The Dovecote Press Ltd

Stanbridge, Wimborne Minster, Dorset BH21 4JD
tel (01258) 840549

Books

email online@dovecotepress.com
website www.dovecotepress.com
Editorial Director David Burnett, *Office* Lynn Orchard

Books of local interest: natural history, architecture, history. Founded 1974.

Dref Wen

28 Church Road, Whitchurch, Cardiff CF14 2EA
tel 029-2061 7860
website www.drefwen.com
Directors Roger Boore, Anne Boore, Gwilym Boore, Alun Boore, Rhys Boore

Welsh language publisher. Original Welsh language novels for children and adult learners. Original, adaptations and translations of foreign and English language full-colour picture story books for children. Educational material for primary/secondary school children in Wales and England. Founded 1970.

University College Dublin Press[†]

Room H103, Humanities Institute, Belfield, Dublin 4, Republic of Ireland
tel +353 (0)17 164680
email ucdpress@ucd.ie
website www.ucdpress.ie
Twitter @UCDPress
Executive Editor Noelle Moran

North American representation: University of Chicago Press. Academic trade: humanities, Irish studies, history and politics, literary studies, social sciences, sociology, music and food science. More recently expanded to include architecture, ecology and environmental studies. Founded 1995.

Duckworth Books Ltd[‡]

1 Golden Court, Richmond TW9 1EU
tel 0777 845 2441
email info@duckworthbooks.com
website www.duckworthbooks.co.uk
Twitter @Duckbooks
Managing Director Peter Duncan

Publishers of non-fiction: biography and memoir, popular science, popular history, popular psychology, nature and travel writing. Fiction: (Duckworth) historical fiction, (Farrago) ebook first, series led humorous fiction, humorous mystery and cosy crime, social comedy and satire, science fiction and fantasy. Also represents The School of Life Press to the trade for sales. Imprints: Duckworth, Farrago. Founded 1898.

Dunedin Academic Press*

Hudson House, 8 Albany Street, Edinburgh EH1 3QB
tel 0131 473 2397
email mail@dunedinacademicpress.co.uk
website www.dunedinacademicpress.co.uk
Director Anthony Kinahan

Earth and environmental sciences. See website for submission guidelines. Founded 2000.

Dynasty Press

79 Nightingale Lane, London SW12 8LY
tel 020-8675 3435
email david@dynastypresslondon.co.uk
website www.dynastypress.co.uk
Contact David Hornsby

A boutique publishing house specialising in works connected to royalty, dynasties and people of influence. Committed to the freedom of the press to allow authentic voices and important stories to be made available to the public. Usually publishes titles which reveal and analyse the lives of those placed in the upper echelons of society. Founded 2008.

Earthscan

8–12 Camden High Street, London NW1 0JH
tel 020-7387 8558
email earthinfo@earthscan.co.uk
website www.routledge.com/sustainability

Publishes under the Routledge imprint for Taylor & Francis Group (page 189). Academic and professional: sustainable development, climate and energy, natural resource management, cities and built environment, business and economics, design and technology. Founded 1989.

Ebury Press – see Ebury Publishing

Ebury Publishing

20 Vauxhall Bridge Road, London SW1V 2SA
tel 020-7840 8400
website www.penguin.co.uk,
www.penguinrandomhouse.co.uk
Directors Joel Rickett (managing), Andrew Goodfellow (publisher), Louise Jones (communications), Loulou Clark (art)

Non-fiction publisher. Part of Penguin Random House UK (page 176). Founded 1961.

BBC Books

Publishing Director Albert DePetrillo

Non-fiction with a BBC connection from history, natural history, science to cookery, lifestyle and pop culture.

Ebury Entertainment

Publishing Director Sara Cywinski, *Senior Editorial Director* Lorna Russell

Imprint: Ebury Spotlight. Publishes autobiography, memoir, TV, sport and popular culture books.

Ebury Lifestyle

Publishing Director Lizzy Gray, *Editorial Director* Laura Higginson

Imprints: Ebury Press, Happy Place Books, Pop PressBusiness and performance publishing. Mission to make everyday life better through cookbooks, wellbeing and lifestyle guides.

Books

Ebury Partnerships
Publishing Director Elizabeth Bond

Gift books, branded and bespoke books across food/drink, health/lifestyle, museums/galleries, and entrepreneurs/business pioneers.

Ebury Self
tel 020-7840 8400
Rider Publishing Director Olivia Morris, *Vermilion Publishing Director* Susanna Abbott

Imprints: Rider, Vermilion. Rider publishes 'books with soul' across popular psychology, philosophy, inspirational memoir, spirituality and wellbeing. Vermilion publishes personal development, popular psychology, health, diet, relationships and parenting titles written by experts with influence.

Ebury Smart
Deputy Publisher Drummond Moir, *Editorial Director & Head of WH Allen* Jamie Joseph

Imprints: WH Allen, Ebury Press, Witness Books, Ebury Edge. Memoir, history, politics, current affairs, science, technology and business.

Edinburgh University Press*‡
The Tun – Holyrood Road, 12 Jackson's Entry, Edinburgh EH8 8PJ
tel 0131 650 4218
email editorial@eup.ac.uk
website www.edinburghuniversitypress.com, www.euppublishing.com
Facebook www.facebook.com/EdinburghUP
Twitter @EdinburghUP
Chair Margaret Hewinson, *Chief Executive* Timothy Wright, *Head of Editorial* Nicola Ramsey, *Head of Journals* Sarah Edwards, *Head of Sales* Charlotte Mason, *Head of Marketing* Anna Glazier

Academic publishers of scholarly books and journals: classics and ancient history, film, media and cultural studies, history, Islamic and Middle Eastern studies, history, languages and linguistics, law, linguistics, literary studies, philosophy, politics, Scottish studies, American studies, religious studies, classical and ancient history. Trade: literature and culture, Scottish history and politics. Founded 1949.

The Educational Company of Ireland
Ballymount Road, Walkinstown, Dublin D12 R25C, Republic of Ireland
tel +353 (0)14 500611
email info@edco.ie
website www.edco.ie
Ceo Martina Harford

Educational MSS on all subjects in English or Irish language. A member of the Smurfit Kappa Group plc. Founded 1910.

Educational Explorers (Publishers)
Unit 5, Feidr Castell Business Park, Fishguard SA65 9BB

tel (01348) 874890
website www.cuisenaire.co.uk
Directors J. Hollyfield

Educational. Recent successes include: mathematics: *Numbers in Colour with Cuisenaire Rods*; languages: *The Silent Way*; literacy, reading: *Words in Colour*; educational films. No longer accepting MSS. Founded 1962.

Eland Publishing Ltd‡
61 Exmouth Market, London EC1R 4QL
tel 020-7833 0762
email info@travelbooks.co.uk
website www.travelbooks.co.uk
Directors Rose Baring, John Hatt, Barnaby Rogerson

Classic travel literature. No unsolicited MSS. Email in first instance. Founded 1982.

Electric Monkey – see HarperCollins Publishers

11:9 – see Neil Wilson Publishing Ltd

Edward Elgar Publishing Ltd‡
The Lypiatts, 15 Lansdown Road, Cheltenham, Glos. GL50 2JA
tel (01242) 226934
email info@e-elgar.co.uk
website www.e-elgar.com
Managing Director Tim Williams

Economics, business, law, public and social policy. Founded 1986.

Elliott & Thompson‡
2 John Street, London WC1N 2ES
tel 020-3405 0310
email pippa@eandtbooks.com
website www.eandtbooks.com
Twitter @eandtbooks
Chairman Lorne Forsyth, *Director* Olivia Bays, *Publisher* Jennie Condell, *Senior Editor* Pippa Crane

History, biography, music, popular science, gift, sport, business, economics and adult fiction. Founded 2009.

Elsevier Ltd*
The Boulevard, Langford Lane, Kidlington, Oxford OX5 1GB
tel (01865) 843000
website www.elsevier.com
Twitter @ElsevierConnect
Ceo Kumsal Bayazit

Academic and professional reference books; scientific, technical and medical products and services (books, journals, electronic information). No unsolicited MSS, but synopses and project proposals welcome. Imprints: Academic Press, Architectural Press, Bailliere Tindall, Butterworth-Heinemann, Churchill Livingstone, Digital Press, Elsevier, Elsevier Advanced

Books

Technology, Focal Press, Gulf Professional Press, JAI, Made Simple Books, Morgan Kauffman, Mosby, Newnes, North-Holland, Pergamon, Saunders, Woodhead Publishing. Division of RELX Corp., Amsterdam. Founded 1986.

The Emma Press Ltd‡

Jewellery Quarter, Birmingham B18 6HQ
email hello@theemmapress.com
website https://theemmapress.com
Facebook www.facebook.com/TheEmmaPress
Twitter @TheEmmaPress
Director Emma Wright

Winner of the Michael Marks Award for Poetry Pamphlet Publishers in 2016, publishes single-author poetry pamphlets, prose pamphlets – including short stories and essays, and children's chapter books. Does not consider unsolicited MSS but runs occasional calls for poetry and prose pamphlets. Check website for details. Founded 2012.

Encyclopaedia Britannica (UK) Ltd

2nd Floor, Unity Wharf, 13 Mill Street, London SE1 2BH
tel 020-7500 7800
email enquiries@britannica.co.uk
website www.britannica.co.uk

Global digital educational publisher of instructional products used in schools, universities, homes, libraries and in the workplace. Founded 1999.

Enitharmon Editions

tel 020-7430 0844
email info@enitharmon.co.uk
website www.enitharmon.co.uk
Directors Stephen Stuart-Smith, Isabel Brittain

Artists' books and prints, poetry, including fine editions. Some literary criticism, fiction, translations. No unsolicited MSS. No freelance editors or proofreaders required. Founded 1967.

Everyman's Library

50 Albemarle Street, London W1S 4BD
tel 020-7493 4361
email books@everyman.uk.com
email guides@everyman.uk.com
website www.everymanslibrary.co.uk
Facebook www.facebook.com/everymanslibrary
Twitter @EverymansLib
Publisher David Campbell

Everyman's Library (clothbound reprints of the classics); *Everyman Pocket Classics*; *Everyman's Library Children's Classics*; *Everyman's Library Pocket Poets*; *Everyman Guides*; P.G. Wodehouse. No unsolicited submissions. Imprint of Knopf Doubleday Publishing Group. Founded 1905.

Everything With Words Ltd

16 Limekiln Place, London SE19 2RE
tel 020-8771 2974
email info@everythingwithwords.com
website www.everythingwithwords.com
Managing Director & Publisher Mikka Bott

Children's fiction for ages 5 to young adult and adult fiction. Publishes innovative, quality fiction. Accepts unsolicited MSS. Founded 2016.

University of Exeter Press

Reed Hall, Streatham Drive, Exeter EX4 4QR
tel 0845 468 0415
email info@exeterpress.co.uk
website www.exeterpress.co.uk
Facebook www.facebook.com/UniversityofExeterPress
Twitter @UExeterPress
Publisher Nigel Massen

Academic and scholarly books on international relations, film history, performance studies, linguistics, folklore and local history (Exeter and the South West). Founded 1958.

Helen Exley

16 Chalk Hill, Watford, Herts. WD19 4BG
tel (01923) 474480
website www.helenexleygiftbooks.com
Facebook www.facebook.com/helenexleylondon
Twitter @helen_exley
Ceo Helen Exley

Popular colour gift books for an international market. No unsolicited MSS. Founded 1976.

Eye Books

29A Barrow Street, Much Wenlock, Shropshire TF13 6EN
tel 020-3239 3027
email dan@eye-books.com
website www.eye-books.com
Twitter @EyeAndLightning
Publisher Dan Hiscocks

Publishes non-fiction with an original emphasis on travel and 'ordinary people doing extraordinary things', but with an increasingly wider remit. Founded 1996.

F100 Group

34–42 Cleveland Street, London W1T 4LB
tel 020-7323 0323
email info@f1000.com
website https://f1000.com
Chairman Vitek Tracz

Life science publishing, electronic publishing and internet communities. Founded 2012.

Faber and Faber Ltd*‡

Bloomsbury House, 74–77 Great Russell Street, London WC1B 3DA
tel 020-7927 3800
website www.faber.co.uk
Facebook www.facebook.com/FaberBooks
Twitter @FaberBooks

Managing Director Mary Cannam, *Publisher* Leah Thaxton (children's)

High-quality general fiction and non-fiction, children's fiction and non-fiction, drama, film, music, poetry. Unsolicited submissions accepted for poetry only. For information on poetry submission procedures, ring 020-7927 3800, or consult the website. No unsolicited MSS. Founded 1929.

Fabian Society
61 Petty France, London SW1H 9EU
tel 020-7227 4900
email info@fabians.org.uk
website www.fabians.org.uk
Facebook www.facebook.com/fabiansociety
Twitter @thefabians
General Secretary Andrew Harrop

Current affairs, political thought, economics, education, environment, foreign affairs, social policy. Founded 1884.

Fairchild Books – see Bloomsbury Publishing Plc

CJ Fallon
Ground Floor, Block B, Liffey Valley Office Campus, Dublin D22 X0Y3, Republic of Ireland
tel +353 (0)16 166400
email editorial@cjfallon.ie
website www.cjfallon.ie
Executive Directors Brian Gilsenan (managing), John Bodley (financial)

Educational textbooks. Founded 1927.

Farshore Books – see HarperCollins Publishers

David Fickling Books
31 Beaumont Street, Oxford OX1 2NP
tel (01865) 339000
website www.davidficklingbooks.com
Publisher David Fickling, *Publishing Director* Liz Cross

Independent publisher of picture books, novels and non-fiction for all ages, as well as graphic novels, with a focus on brilliant storytelling and world-class illustration. Currently not accepting unsolicited MSS submissions. Founded 1999.

Fig Tree – see Penguin General

Findhorn Press Ltd
tel (01309) 690582 (UK) / +1 800-246-8648 (US)
email info@findhornpress.com
website www.findhornpress.com

Mind, body & spirit and healing. Founded 1971.

Fircone Books Ltd‡
The Holme, Church Road, Eardisley, Herefordshire HR3 6NJ

tel (01544) 327182
email info@firconebooks.com
website www.firconebooks.com
Facebook www.facebook.com/firconebooks
Twitter @firconebooks
Directors Richard Wheeler, Su Wheeler

Illustrated books on church art and architecture. Welcomes submission of ideas: send synopsis first. Founded 2009.

Firefly Press Ltd*
25 Gabalfa Road, Llandaff North, Cardiff CF14 2JJ
email hello@fireflypress.co.uk
website www.fireflypress.co.uk
Facebook www.facebook.com/FireflyPress
Twitter @fireflypress
Publisher Penny Thomas, *Editor* Janet Thomas, *Marketing & Publicity Manager* Megan Farr, *Commercial Director* Robin Bennett, *Sales & Marketing Manager* Simone Greenwood

Award-winning publisher of quality fiction for ages 5 to 19. Founded 2013.

Fisherton Press
email general@fishertonpress.co.uk
website www.fishertonpress.co.uk
Facebook www.facebook.com/FishertonPress
Twitter @fishertonpress
Director Ellie Levenson

A small independent publisher producing picture books for children under 7. Not currently accepting proposals but illustrators are welcome to send links to a portfolio. Founded 2013.

Fitzrovia Press Ltd
42 Monington Road, Glastonbury BA6 8HF
tel (01458) 831926
email rprime@fitzroviapress.co.uk
website www.fitzroviapress.co.uk
Publisher Ranchor Prime

Creative writing grounded in Eastern philosophy that explores spirituality in the West. Submit outline plus sample chapter; no complete MSS. Founded 2008.

Flame Tree Publishing‡
6 Melbray Mews, Fulham, London SW6 3NS
tel 020-7751 9650
email info@flametreepublishing.com
website www.flametreepublishing.com, www.flametreepress.com
Publisher & Founder Nick Wells

Art, music, lifestyle and fiction. Accepts unsolicited MSS for fiction imprint Flame Tree Press, horror and suspense, science fiction, fantasy and crime/mystery. No young adult titles. Look out for the short story submission windows for our thematic anthologies. Founded 1992.

Books

Fleming Publications

9/2 Fleming House, 134 Renfrew Street,
Glasgow G3 6ST
tel 0141 328 1935
email info@ettadunn.com
website www.flemingpublications.com
Managing Editor Etta Dunn

Fiction, non-fiction, poetry, history, biography,
photography and self-help. Founded 2012.

Flipped Eye Publishing

Free Word Centre, 60 Farringdon Road,
London EC1R 3GA
email books@flippedeye.net
website https://flippedeye.net/
Facebook www.facebook.com/flipped.eye.publishing
Twitter @flippedeye
Instagram @flippedeye
Directors Nii Ayikwei Parkes (director & senior
editor), Mitchell Albert (editorial director – fiction &
non-fiction), Jacob Sam-La Rose (senior editor –
poetry), Niall O'Sullivan (senior editor – poetry),
Maame Aba Daisie (communications), Shamin
Kisakye (general manager), Kimberley Nyamhondera
(press & editorial officer)

Flipped eye publishing publishes an eclectic catalogue
of fiction and poetry. Founded 2001.

Floris Books*

2A Robertson Avenue, Edinburgh EH11 1PZ
tel 0131 337 2372
email floris@florisbooks.co.uk
website www.florisbooks.co.uk
Facebook www.facebook.com/FlorisBooks
Twitter @FlorisBooks
Commissioning Editors Sally Polson, Eleanor Collins

Religion; philosophy; holistic health; organics; mind,
body & spirit; crafts; parenting. Children's books:
board, picture books, activity books. See website for
submission details. Founded 1976.

Kelpies

website www.discoverkelpies.co.uk

Contemporary Scottish fiction – board books (for
1–3 years), picture books (for 3–6 years), young
readers series (for 6–8 years) and novels (for 8–15
years). Annual Kelpies Prize, see website.

Flyleaf Press

4 Spencer Villas, Glenageary, Co. Dublin A96 P2E9,
Republic of Ireland
tel +353 (0)4 429014
email books@flyleaf.ie
website www.ancestornetwork.ie
Managing Editor James Ryan

Imprint of Ancestor Network. Irish family history.
Founded 1988.

Folens Publishers

Hibernian Industrial Estate, Greenhills Road,
Tallaght, Dublin D24 DH05, Republic of Ireland
tel +353 (0)14 137200
website www.folens.ie
Facebook www.facebook.com/FolensIreland
Twitter @FolensIreland
Chairman David Moffitt

Educational (primary, secondary). Founded 1958.

Fonthill Media Ltd

Millview House, Toadsmoor Road, Stroud,
Glos. GL5 2TB
tel (01453) 886959
email office@fonthillmedia.com
website www.fonthillmedia.com
Facebook www.facebook.com/fonthillmedia
Twitter @fonthillmedia
Publisher & Ceo Alan Sutton

General history. Specialisations include biography,
military history, aviation history, naval and maritime
history, regional and local history, transport (railway,
canal, road) history, social history, sports history,
ancient history and archaeology. Also publishes
widely in the USA with American regional, local,
military and transport history under the imprints of
Fonthill, America Through Time and American
History House. Founded 2011.

W. Foulsham & Co. Ltd

The Old Barrel Store, Brewery Courtyard,
Draymans Lane, Marlow, Bucks. SL7 2FF
tel (01628) 400631
website www.foulsham.com

Publishes in print: life issues; mind, body & spirit;
health; therapies; lifestyle; popular philosophy;
practical psychology; food and drink; parenting.
Publishings in digital: content management systems
and data; iGuides travel; nutrition; self-help;
gardening; cookery. Editorial submissions to
Annemarie Howe: annemarie.howe@foulsham.com.
Founded c.1800.

Quantum

Mind, body & spirit; popular philosophy and
practical psychology.

Four Courts Press

7 Malpas Street, Dublin D08 YD81,
Republic of Ireland
tel +353 (0)14 534668
email info@fourcourtspress.ie
website www.fourcourtspress.ie
Senior Editor Martin Fanning, *Marketing & Sales
Manager* Anthony Tierney

Academic books in the humanities, especially history,
Celtic and medieval studies, art, theology.
Founded 1970.

404 Ink*

8 Albany Lane, Edinburgh EH1 3QP
email hello@404ink.com
website www.404ink.com
Facebook www.facebook.com/404Ink
Twitter @404Ink
Directors Heather McDaid, Laura Jones

Award-winning alternative, independent publisher specialising in edgy, non-conformist fiction and social issue-based non-fiction and poetry. Publications have included feminist anthology *Nasty Women*, Chris McQueer's short story collections, award-winning literary fiction from Helen McClory, poetry from Nadine Aisha Jassat, a striking novella by Elle Nash and more. Founded 2016.

4th Estate – see HarperCollins Publishers

Free Association Books

1 Angel Cottages, Milespit Hill, London NW7 1RD
email contact@freeassociationpublishing.com
website www.freeassociationpublishing.com
Twitter @Fab_Publishing
Director Trevor E. Brown, *Publishing Director* Alice Solomons, *Marketing & Editorial Consultant* Lisa Findley

Social sciences, psychoanalysis, psychotherapy, counselling, cultural studies, social welfare, addiction studies, child and adolescent studies, mental health, parenting, health studies, counselling. No poetry or fiction. Founded 1984.

Frontline – see Pen & Sword Books Ltd

FT Prentice Hall – see Pearson UK

Gaia Books – see Octopus Publishing Group

The Gallery Press

Loughcrew, Oldcastle, Co. Meath A82 N225, Republic of Ireland
tel +353 (0)49 8541779
email gallery@indigo.ie
website www.gallerypress.com
Editor/Publisher Peter Fallon

Poetry and drama – by Irish authors only at this time. Founded 1970.

Galley Beggar Press

email info@galleybeggar.co.uk
website www.galleybeggar.co.uk
Twitter @GalleyBeggars
Co-directors Eloise Millar, Sam Jordison

Independent publisher based in Norwich. Looks for authors whose writing shows great ambition and literary merit in their chosen genre. Original publishers of Eimear McBride's *A Girl is a Half-formed Thing* – winner of the Baileys Women's Prize for Fiction 2014. When submitting a MS authors must provide proof that they have read another book that Galley Beggar Press has published. Prefers completed MS; email as pdf or Word document. One submission per author. Considers a wide range of genres including fiction, non-fiction, quality science fiction, novels and short stories. No poetry or children's. See website for detailed submission guidelines. Founded 2011.

Gallic Books‡

59 Ebury Street, London SW1W 0NZ
tel 020-7259 9336
email info@gallicbooks.com
website www.gallicbooks.com
Facebook www.facebook.com/gallicbooks
Twitter @BelgraviaB
Managing Director Jane Aitken

Independent publisher with focus on French writing in translation. Publishes fiction, fiction in translation, historical fiction, crime and noir, biography and memoir. Accepts submissions from agents and foreign publishers. Part of the Belgravia Books Collective. Founded 2007.

Garland Science – see Taylor & Francis Group

J. Garnet Miller – see Cressrelles Publishing Co. Ltd

Garnet Publishing Ltd*‡

8 Southern Court, South Street, Reading RG1 4QS
tel (0118) 9597847
email info@garnetpublishing.co.uk
website www.garnetpublishing.co.uk
Publisher & Commissioning Editor Mitchell Albert

Comprises three imprints. Founded 1991.

Garnet Publishing

website www.garnetpublishing.co.uk
Trade non-fiction pertaining to the Middle East (art and architecture, cookery, culture, current affairs, history, photography, political and social issues, religion, travel and general). Accepts unsolicited material.

Ithaca Press

website www.ithacapress.co.uk
Leading publisher of academic books with a focus on Middle Eastern studies. Accepts unsolicited material.

Periscope

website www.periscopebooks.co.uk
Literary fiction and trade non-fiction from around the world (biography, crime fiction, current affairs, historical fiction, literary translations, memoir, political and social issues, popular history, popular science, reportage, general literary fiction and general trade non-fiction). Accepts unsolicited material.

Geddes & Grosset

31 Six Harmony Row, Glasgow G51 3BA
tel 0141 375 1998

Books

email info@geddesandgrosset.co.uk
website www.geddesandgrosset.com
Publishers Ron Grosset, Liz Small

An imprint of The Gresham Publishing Company Ltd. Mass market reference *Word Power* – English language learning and health and wellbeing. Associated imprint: Waverley Books. Founded 1988.

Gibson Square‡

tel 020-7096 1100
email info@gibsonsquare.com
website www.gibsonsquare.com
Facebook www.facebook.com/gibson.square
Publisher Martin Rynja

Non-fiction: general non-fiction, biography, current affairs, philosophy, politics, cultural criticism, psychology, history, travel, art history. Some fiction. See website for guidelines or email to receive an automated response. Authors include Helena Frith Powell, Alexander Litvinenko, Melanie Phillips, Bernard-Henri Lévy, Diana Mitford, Anthony Grayling, John McCain. Founded 2001.

Gill†

Hume Avenue, Park West, Dublin D12 YV96, Republic of Ireland
tel +353 (0)15 009500
email sales@gill.ie
website www.gill.ie
Founder & Chairman Michael Gill, *Managing Director* Ruth Gill

An independent publisher and distributor in Dublin. Its origins date back to 1856 when M. H. Gill & Son, whose portfolio included printing and bookselling, was founded. In partnership with the Macmillan Group in London, Gill & Macmillan was founded 1968. Now fully owned by the Gill family following the buyout of the Macmillan interest in 2013.

Gill Books

website www.gillbooks.ie
Facebook www.facebook.com/gillbooks
Twitter @gillbooks

Trade publishing. Irish interest: biography, cookery, children's, wellness, history, politics, current affairs, reference, lifestyle and fiction. Publisher of established authors and champion of new voices.

Gill Education

website www.gilleducation.ie, www.gillexplore.ie

Primary and post-primary publisher. Working with the best educators in the country to create books and resources, tailored to the Irish market. Also supplies Irish schools with a carefully selected range of the best literacy and numeracy resources available worldwide.

Gingko

4 Molasses Row, London SW11 3UX
tel 020-3637 9730
email gingko@gingkolibrary.com
website www.gingko.org.uk
Publisher Barbara Schwepcke

Gingko works with scholars of diverse backgrounds and research interests to increase understanding of the Middle East, West Asia and North Africa through conferences, public events and cultural programmes as well as publications. Founded 2014.

GL Assessment

1st Floor Vantage London, Great West Road, Brentford TW8 9AG
tel 020-8996 3333
email infon@gl-assessment.co.uk
website www.gl-assessment.co.uk
Chairman Philip Walters

Testing and assessment services for education and health care, including literacy, numeracy, thinking skills, ability, learning support and online testing. Founded 1981.

Godsfield Press – see Octopus Publishing Group

Goldsmiths Press

Room 2, 33 Laurie Grove, New Cross, London SE14 6NW
tel 020-7919 7258
email goldsmithspress@gold.ac.uk
website www.gold.ac.uk/goldsmiths-press
Twitter @goldsmithspress
Director Sarah Kember

Aims to revive and regenerate the traditions of university press publishing through print and digital media. Publishing across disciplinary boundaries and between theory, practice and fiction, aims to create a culture around inventive academic knowledge practices. Goldsmiths Press is the UK's first green Open Access monograph publisher, combining Open Access with a fair pricing model for print books. Founded 2015.

Gower Books – see Taylor & Francis Group

Granta Books‡

12 Addison Avenue, London W11 4QR
tel 020-7605 1360
website www.granta.com
Twitter @GrantaBooks
Publishing Director Bella Lacey, *Deputy Publishing Director* Laura Barber, *Editorial Director* Anne Meadows, *Commissioning Editor* Ka Bradley

Literary fiction, memoir, nature writing, cultural criticism and travel. No submissions except via a reputable literary agent. An imprint of Granta Publications. Founded 1982.

Green Print – see Merlin Press Ltd

Gresham Books Ltd

The Carriage House, Ningwood Manor, Ningwood,
Isle of Wight PO30 4NJ
tel (01983) 761389
email info@gresham-books.co.uk
website www.gresham-books.co.uk
Managing Director Nicholas Oulton

Hymn books, prayer books, service books, school
histories and other bespoke publications.
Founded 1979.

The Gresham Publishing Company Ltd

31 Six Harmony Row, Glasgow G51 3BA
tel 0141 375 1996
email info@waverley-books.co.uk
website www.waverley-books.co.uk,
www.geddesandgrosset.com
Facebook www.facebook.com/WaverleyBooks
Twitter @WaverleyBooks
Publishers Ron Grosset, Liz Small

Books for the general trade and Scottish interest
books. Founded 2013.

Grub Street Publishing‡

4 Rainham Close, London SW11 6SS
tel 020-7924 3966 / 020-7738 1008
email post@grubstreet.co.uk
website www.grubstreet.co.uk
Principals John B. Davies, Anne Dolamore

Adult non-fiction: military, aviation history, cookery.
Founded 1992.

Guild of Master Craftsman Publications Ltd*

166 High Street, Lewes, East Sussex BN7 1XU
tel (01273) 477374
email jonathanb@thegmcgroup.com
website www.gmcbooks.com
Twitter @GMCbooks
Instagram @gmcpublications
Managing Director Jonathan Phillips, *Publisher*
Jonathan Bailey

A diverse publisher of leisure and hobby project
books, with a focus on all types of woodworking;
from carving and turning to routing. Craft subjects
include needlecraft, paper crafts and jewellery-
making. The books are aimed at craftspeople of all
skill levels. Founded 1979.

Ammonite Press

email jonathanb@thegmcgroup.com
website www.ammonitepress.com
Twitter @AmmonitePress
Instagram @gmcpublications
Publisher Jonathan Bailey

Publishes highly illustrated non-fiction for the
international market. Gift books featuring
illustration, infographics and photography on pop
culture, pop reference, biography and history.

Practical photography titles written by professional
photographers provide authoritative guides to
technique and equipment.

Button Books

email jonathanb@thegmcgroup.com
website www.buttonbooks.co.uk
Twitter @GMCbooks
Instagram @GMCpublications

An imprint of GMC Publications publishing design-
led children's books, which includes award-winning
non-fiction, round-cornered board books, wipeclean
flash cards, hardbacks with poster jackets, activity
books with stickers and picture books with pop-out
animals to make. Combining beautiful illustration,
from retro to modern, with high production values
and innovative ideas.

Guinness World Records

3rd Floor, 184–192 Drummond Street,
London NW1 3HP
tel 020-7891 4567
website www.guinnessworldrecords.com

Guinness World Records, GWR Gamer's Edition, TV
and brand licensing, records processing. No
unsolicited MSS. A Jim Pattison Group company.
Founded 1954.

Gulf Professional Press – see Elsevier Ltd

Guppy Publishing Ltd‡

Bracken Hill, Cotswold Road, Oxford OX2 9JG
tel 07884 068983
email bella@guppybooks.co.uk
website www.guppybooks.co.uk
Facebook www.facebook.com/guppybooks
Twitter @guppybooks
Instagram @guppypublishing
Director Bella Pearson

Publishing children's and young adult fiction for ages
5 to 18. Illustrated books for newly emerging readers,
fiction for middle-grade readers and novels for
adults. Poetry, prose, graphic novels. Original,
thought-provoking, literary, publishing 8 to 10 titles
each year that inspire and entertain young readers.
Founded 2019.

Hachette Children's Group*

Carmelite House, 50 Victoria Embankment,
London EC4Y 0DZ
email hcg.editorial@hachettechildrens.co.uk
website www.hachettechildrens.co.uk
Facebook www.facebook.com/hachettekids

Hachette Children's Group is one of the largest
children's publishers in the UK. Publishes baby and
pre-school books, picture books, gift, fiction, non-
fiction, series fiction, books for the school and library
market and licensed publishing and comprises the
imprints Hodder Children's Books, Orchard Books,
Orion Children's Books, Little, Brown Books for

Young Readers, Quercus Children's Books, Pat-a-Cake, Wren & Rook, Franklin Watts and Wayland Books, and the owner of Enid Blyton Entertainment. Generally only accepts submissions sent via an agent. Occasionally holds periods of open submissions for a limited time period or a specific genre. See social media channels for details. Founded 1986.

Hachette UK*

Carmelite House, 50 Victoria Embankment, London EC4Y 0DZ
tel 020-3122 6000
website www.hachette.co.uk
Ceo David Shelley

Part of Hachette Livre SA since 2004. Hachette UK group companies: Bookouture (page 137), Hachette Children's Group (page 153), Hachette Ireland, Hachette Australia (page 199), Hachette New Zealand (page 204), Hachette Book Publishing India Private Ltd, Headline Publishing Group (page 157), Hodder Education Group (page 158), Hodder & Stoughton (page 158), Little, Brown Book Group (page 164), John Murray Press (page 168), Octopus Publishing Group (page 171), Orion Publishing Group (page 173), Quercus Publishing Plc (page 179). Founded 1986.

Halban Publishers

176 Goldhurst Terrace, London NW6 3HN
tel 020-7692 5541
email books@halbanpublishers.com
website www.halbanpublishers.com
Twitter @Halban_publishers
Instagram @Halban_Publishers
Directors Martine Halban, Peter Halban

General fiction and non-fiction; history and biography; Jewish subjects and Middle East. No unsolicited MSS considered; preliminary letter or email essential. Founded 1986.

Robert Hale Ltd

The Crowood Press Ltd, The Stable Block, Crowood Lane, Ramsbury, Wilts. SN8 2HR
tel (01672) 520320
email enquiries@crowood.com
website www.crowood.com

Adult general non-fiction. Imprint of The Crowood Press (page 144). Founded 1936.

Halsgrove Publishing

Halsgrove House, Ryelands Business Park, Bagley Road, Wellington, Somerset TA21 9PZ
tel (01823) 653777
email sales@halsgrove.com
website www.halsgrove.com
Facebook www.facebook.com/Halsgrove-Publishing-120746011275852
Twitter @Halsgrove
Directors Julian Davidson & Steven Pugsley, *Associate Publisher* Simon Butler

Regional books for local-interest readers in the UK. Also illustrated books on individual artists. Founded 1986.

Hamish Hamilton – see Penguin General

Hamlyn – see Octopus Publishing Group

Happy Yak

The Old Brewery, 6 Blundell Street, London N7 9BH
tel 020-7000 8084
website www.quartoknows.com/words-pictures
Associate Publisher Rhiannon Findlay

A children's imprint of the Quarto Group, Inc. (page 179). Happy Yak publishes pre-school, picture books and illustrated non-fiction for children aged 0–7 years, with a focus on fun, accessible content and contemporary illustration. Founded 2021.

Hardie Grant UK‡

5th and 6th Floors, Pentagon House, 52–54 Southwark Street, London SE1 1UN
tel 020-7601 7500
email info@hardiegrant.co.uk
website www.hardiegrant.com/uk
Managing Director Stephen King, *Publisher* Kajal Mistry

Non-fiction, categories include: food and drink, gift and humour, craft, gardening; wellness, interiors and pop culture. Founded 1994.

Patrick Hardy Books – see The Lutterworth Press

Harlequin (UK) Ltd*

HarperCollins Publishers Ltd,
1 London Bridge Street, London SE1 9EF
tel 0844 844 1351
website www.millsandboon.co.uk
Facebook www.facebook.com/millsandboon
Twitter @MillsandBoon
Executive Publisher of Mills & Boon UK Lisa Milton, *Executive Editor of Harlequin/Mills & Boon Series* Bryony Green

In 2014 Harlequin (UK) Ltd was acquired by HarperCollins Publishers (page 155). Founded 1908.

Mills & Boon Historical
Executive Editor Bryony Green
Historical romance fiction.

Mills & Boon Medical
Senior Editor Sheila Hodgson
Contemporary romance fiction in a medical setting.

Mills & Boon Modern Romance
Senior Editor Flo Nicoll
Contemporary romances – luxury and passion.

Mills & Boon True Love
Senior Editor Sheila Hodgson
Contemporary romances – emotion and escapism.

HarperCollins Publishers*

The News Building, 1 London Bridge Street,
London SE1 9GF
tel 020-8741 7070
Alternative address Westerhill Road, Bishopbriggs,
Glasgow G64 2QT
tel 0141 772 3200
website www.harpercollins.co.uk
Ceo Charlie Redmayne, *Executive Publishers* Oliver
Malcolm, Kimberly Young, *Managing Director* Kate
Elton

All fiction and trade non-fiction must be submitted
through an agent. Owned by News Corporation.
Imprints include: HarperFiction, NonFiction, Avon,
One More Chapter, HarperNorth and HarperCollins
Ireland. Founded 1817.

Avon
Executive Publisher Oliver Malcolm, *Publishing
Director* Helen Huthwaite

General fiction, crime and thrillers, women's fiction.

The Borough Press
Executive Publisher Kimberly Young, *Publishing
Director* Suzie Dooré

Literary fiction.

William Collins
Executive Publisher David Roth-Ey, *Publishing
Director* Arabella Pike, *Associate Publisher* Myles
Archibald (natural history)

Science, history, art, politics and current affairs,
biography, religion and natural history.

Collins
Managing Director Alex Beecroft

Reference publishing, including dictionaries, atlases
and bibles. Also focuses on education, publishes for
UK and international school curriculums, as well as
extensive revision and home learning support for
parents and children.

Farshore Books
website www.farshore.com
Executive Publisher Cally Poplak

Children's fiction, young adult (Electric Monkey),
picture books, non-fiction (Red Shed), novelty and
gift, and licenced books. Fiction authors include:
Michael Morpurgo, Laura Ellen Anderson, Andy
Stanton, Lemony Snicket, Holly Jackson, Michael
Grant and David Levithan. Picture Book authors
include: Matt Lucas, Julia Donaldson and Chris
Packham. Books published under licence include
Winnie-the-Pooh, Thomas the Tank Engine, Mr.
Men and Minecraft. Visit website to see current
policy on manuscript submissions. Previously known
as Egmont UK, acquired by HarperCollins Publishers
2021.

4th Estate
Executive Publisher David Roth-Ey

Fiction, literary fiction, current affairs, popular
science, biography, humour, travel.

Harper Collins Audio
Group Digital Director Joanna Surman, *Editorial
Director* Fionnuala Barrett

Publishes various audio formats. Leading publisher of
trade fiction and non-fiction audiobooks for children
and adults, as well as standalone audio projects.
Publishes in excess of 700 audiobooks each year.

HarperCollins Children's Books
Executive Publisher Ann-Janine Murtagh

Activity books, novelty books, preschool brands,
picture books, pop-up books and book and CD sets.
Fiction for 5–8 and 9–12 years, young adult fiction
and series fiction; film/TV tie-ins. Publishes approx.
265 titles each year. Picture book authors include
Oliver Jeffers, Judith Kerr and Emma Chichester
Clark, and fiction by David Walliams, Michael
Morpurgo, David Baddiel and Lauren Child. Books
published under licence include *Dr Seuss*, *Bing*,
Twirlywoos and *Paddington Bear*.

HarperCollins Ireland
Managing Director Kate Elton, *Publishing Director*
Conor Nagle

Promotes authors who are either Irish by birth or
living and working in Ireland. Fiction, non-fiction
and children's books.

HarperFiction
Executive Publisher Kimberley Young, *Publishers*
David Brawn, Lynne Drew, Julia Wisdom

General, historical fiction, crime and thrillers,
women's fiction.

HarperNorth
Executive Publisher Oliver Malcolm, *Publishing
Director* Genevieve Pegg

Fiction: general, historical, crime and thrillers,
women's fiction. Non-fiction: autobiographies,
memoir, politics, history, sport, nature writing,
smart-thinking.

One More Chapter
Executive Publisher Kimberley Young, *Editorial
Director* Charlotte Ledger

Digital first fiction.

Harper NonFiction
Executive Publisher Oliver Malcolm, *Publisher* Adam
Humphrey, *Publishing Directors* Kelly Ellis, Jack Fogg,
Katya Shipster

Autobiographies, entertainment, sport, cookery,
lifestyle and culture. Includes the imprints Element,
Mudlark and Thorsons.

Books

Harper360

This imprint aims to have all books for which the company has rights, in all markets around the world, in all formats, available for sale in the UK.

Harper Voyager

Executive Publisher Kimberley Young, *Publishing Director* Natasha Bardon

Publishes fantasy and science fiction. Authors include George R.R. Martin, Raymond E. Feist, David Eddings, Robin Hobb, Joe Abercrombie, Guy Gavriel Kay, Peter V. Brett, Isaac Asimov, Arthur C. Clarke, Philip K. Dick and Ray Bradbury. Also aims to develop new talents such as Mark Lawrence, Emmi Itäranta and Josh Malerman.

HQ

Executive Publisher Lisa Milton, *Fiction Publisher* Kate Mills, *Non-fiction Publisher* Rose Sandy

Crime and thrillers, women's fiction, historical, book club and young adult.

HQ Digital

Editorial Director Abigail Fenton

Digital-first commercial fiction list, general, crime and thrillers, women's fiction, psychological thrillers, saga.

Mills & Boon

Executive Editor Bryony Green

Times Books

Publishes a range of atlases, books and maps.

Harriman House

3 Viceroy Court, Bedford Road, Petersfield, Hants GU32 3LJ
tel (01730) 233870
email contact@harriman-house.com
email commissioning@harriman-house.com
website www.harriman-house.com

Finance, trading and investment books, ranging from personal finance, small business and lifestyle, to stock market investing, trading and professional guides. For submission guidelines see website. Founded 1992.

Hart Publishing*

Kemp House, Chawley Park, Cumnor Hill, Oxford OX2 9PH
tel (01865) 598648
email mail@hartpub.co.uk
website www.hartpublishing.co.uk
Facebook www.facebook.com/HartPublishing2
Twitter @hartpublishing
Editorial Director Sinéad Moloney

Legal academic texts for law students, scholars and practitioners. Covers all aspects of law (UK domestic, European and International). An imprint of Bloomsbury Publishing Plc (page 136). Founded in 1996.

Harvill Secker – see Vintage

Hashtag Press‡

10 Bankfields, Headcorn, Kent TN27 9RA
email submissions@hashtagpress.co.uk
website www.hashtagpress.co.uk

Hashtag Press is a female-led independent publishing house specialising in diverse and inclusive stories and writers, led by author Abiola Bello and book publicist Helen Lewis. Publishes fiction and non-fiction. Titles include *Baller Boys* by Venessa Taylor, *Hijab & Red Lipstick* by Yousra Imran and *Silver Linings* by Jess Impiazzi, their titles are spread across fiction and non-fiction genres. Founded 2018.

Hashtag BLAK

Supported by Arts Council England, Hashtag BLAK launched its first three titles – *Being Amani* by Annabelle Steele, *A Dance for the Dead* by Nuzo Onoh and *Ten Steps To Us* by Attiya Khan. Hashtag BLAK is passionate about supporting and raising up under-represented writers and own voices stories.

Haus Publishing Ltd

4 Cinnamon Row, Plantation Wharf, London SW11 3TW
tel 020-3637 9729
email haus@hauspublishing.com
website https://hauspublishing.com/
Twitter @HausPublishing
Publisher Harry Hall

Publishes history, literary fiction in translation, biography, memoir and current affairs. Founded 2003.

Hawthorn Press*‡

1 Lansdown Lane, Stroud, Glos. GL5 1BJ
tel (01453) 757040
email info@hawthornpress.com
website www.hawthornpress.com
Director Martin Large

Publishes books and ebooks for a more creative, peaceful and sustainable world. Series include *Early Years*, *Steiner/Waldorf Education*, *Crafts*, *Personal Development*, *Art and Science*, *Storytelling*. Founded 1981.

Hay House Publishers‡

The Sixth Floor, Watson House, 54 Baker Street, London W1U 7BU
tel 020-3927 7290
email info@hayhouse.co.uk
website www.hayhouse.co.uk
Facebook www.facebook.com/HayHouse
Twitter @HayHouseUK
Managing Director & Publisher Michelle Pilley

Publishers of mind, body & spirit; self-help; personal development; health; spirituality and wellness. Head office in San Diego, California. Founded 1984; in UK

2003. For submissions please use website only: www.hayhouse.co.uk/guides/.

Haynes Publishing
Sparkford, Yeovil, Somerset BA22 7JJ
tel (01963) 440635
email lmcintyre@haynes.co.uk
email jaustin@haynes.co.uk
website www.haynes.co.uk
Chairman Eddie Bell, *Chief Executive* J. Haynes,
Managing Director, consumer Jeremy Yates-Round,
Export & Rights Director Graham Cook, *Global Digital Director* Andrew Golby

Practical lifestyle manuals for the home, motorsport, space, military, aviation, entertainment and leisure activities. Founded 1960.

Head of Zeus‡
Clerkenwell House, 5–8 Hardwick Street,
London EC1R 4RG
tel 020-7253 5557
email hello@headofzeus.com
website www.headofzeus.com
Facebook www.facebook.com/headofzeus/
Twitter @HoZ_Books
Chairman Anthony Cheetham, *Publishing Director* Laura Palmer, *Editorial Director* Richard Milbank, *Publishing Director* Neil Belton

General and literary fiction, genre fiction and non-fiction. Independent Publisher of the Year 2017. Founded 2012.

Zephyr
Publisher Fiona Kennedy
Children's imprint.

Headline Publishing Group
Carmelite House, 50 Victoria Embankment,
London EC4Y 0DZ
tel 020-3122 7222
email enquiries@hachette.co.uk
website www.headline.co.uk
Twitter @headlinepg
Managing Director Mari Evans

Commercial and literary fiction (hardback, paperback and ebook) and popular non-fiction including autobiography, biography, food and wine, gardening, history, popular science, sport, TV tie-ins. Publishes under Headline, Headline Review, Tinder Press, Headline Eternal, Wildfire, Headline Home, Headline Accent. Founded 1993.

Henley Hall Press
Woofferton Grange, Brimfield, Ludlow,
Shropshire SY8 4NP
tel 07984 585861
email susanne@henleyhallpress.co.uk
website www.henleyhallpress.co.uk
Twitter @HenleyHallPress
Contact Susanne Lumsden

Henley Hall Press is an independent publisher of thought-provoking non-fiction, including topical affairs, politics, history, biography, farming, ecology and gardening. Founded 2013.

Hera Books
email submissions@herabooks.com
website www.herabooks.com
Co-founder & Publishing Director Keshini Naidoo,
Co-founder & Managing Director Lindsey Mooney

Female-led, independent digital-first publisher. Publishes crime and thriller, romance, saga and general fiction. Please note no non-fiction, young adult or children's fiction, poetry, or science fiction and fantasy. Please send a one-page synopsis and the whole MS in Word format to submissions email. Founded 2018.

Hermes House – see Anness Publishing

Nick Hern Books Ltd‡
The Glasshouse, 49A Goldhawk Road,
London W12 8QP
tel 020-8749 4953
email info@nickhernbooks.co.uk
website www.nickhernbooks.co.uk
Facebook www.facebook.com/NickHernBooks
Twitter @NickHernBooks
Publisher Nick Hern, *Managing Director* Matt Applewhite

Theatre and performing arts books, professionally produced plays, performing rights. Initial letter required. Founded 1988.

Hesperus Press Ltd
28 Mortimer Street, London W1W 7RD
tel 020-7436 0943
email publishing@hesperuspress.com
website https://hesperus.press/
Facebook www.facebook.com/hesperuspress
Twitter @HesperusPress

Under three imprints, publishes over 300 books. Hesperus Classics introduces older works of literature, Hesperus Nova showcases contemporary literature and Hesperus Minor publishes well-loved children's books from the past. Founded 2001.

Hippopotamus Press
22 Whitewell Road, Frome, Somerset BA11 4EL
tel (01373) 466653
email rjhippopress@aol.com
email mphippopress@aol.com
Editors Roland John, Mansell Pargitter, *Foreign Editor* (translations) Anna Martin

Poetry, essays, criticism. Submissions from new writers welcome. Founded 1974.

The History Press Ltd‡
97 St Georges Place, Cheltenham, Glos. GL50 3QB
tel (01242) 895310

website www.thehistorypress.co.uk
Managing Director Gareth Swain, *Publishing Director*
Laura Perehinec, *Sales Director* Jamie Kinnear, *Rights
Manager* Anette Fuhrmeister
Founded 2008.

The History Press
History and biography, general non-fiction.

Flint Books
Non-fiction books.

Hobeck Books‡
Unit 14, Sugnall Business Centre, Sugnall,
Stafford ST21 6NF
email hobeckbooks@gmail.com
website www.hobeck.net
Facebook www.facebook.com/Hobeckbooks10
Twitter @hobeckbooks
Instagram @hobeckbooks
Directors Rebecca Collins, Adrian Hobart

Family-run independent publisher in the following
genres: crime, thrillers, mystery and suspense. For
submission guidelines please see website. Also hosts a
weekly podcast called the Hobcast Bookshow for
writers and lovers of the crime fiction genre.
Founded 2019.

Hodder & Stoughton
Carmelite House, 50 Victoria Embankment,
London EC4Y 0DZ
tel 020-3122 6777
website www.hodder.co.uk
Ceo Jamie Hodder-Williams, *Managing Director*
Carolyn Mays, *Deputy Managing Director* Lisa
Highton, *Publishing Director* Carole Welch, *Non-
fiction Publisher* Drummond Moir, *Non-fiction
Publisher* Rupert Lancaster, *Hodder Lifestyle & Yellow
Kite Publisher* Liz Gough

Commercial and literary fiction; biography,
autobiography, history, humour, mind, body & spirit,
travel, lifestyle and cookery and other general interest
non-fiction; audio. No unsolicited MSS or synopses.
Publishes under Hodder & Stoughton, Sceptre,
Mobius. Part of Hachette UK (see page 154).
Founded 1960.

Hodder Children's Books – see Hachette
Children's Group

Hodder Education
Carmelite House, 50 Victoria Embankment,
London EC4Y 0DZ
tel 0123-582 7720
website www.hoddereducation.co.uk,
www.galorepark.co.uk, www.risingstars-uk.com
Managing Director Lis Tribe

School and college publishing. Includes Rising Stars,
RS Assessment, Hodder Education and Galore Park.
Part of Hachette UK (page 154). Founded 1960.

Hodder Faith – see John Murray Press

Hodder Gibson*
211 St Vincent Street, Glasgow G2 5QY
tel 0141 222 1440
email hoddergibson@hodder.co.uk
website www.hoddergibson.co.uk
Managing Director Paul Cherry

Educational books specifically for Scotland. Part of
Hachette UK (see page 154). Founded 1960.

Holland House Books
47 Greenham Road, Newbury, Berks. RG14 7HY
email contact@hhousebooks.com
website www.hhousebooks.com
Senior Editor Robert Peett

Literary fiction and non-fiction, crime, historical and
speculative fiction welcome. Happy to read
traditional and experimental work. Also runs The
Novella Project for new authors and interns, and the
literary journal *The Open Page*. Submissions welcome
from agents and authors, but please check website
first. Founded 2012.

HopeRoad‡
PO Box 55544, Exhibition Road, London SW7 2DB
email rosemarie@hoperoadpublishing.com
website www.hoperoadpublishing.com
Facebook www.facebook.com/HopeRoadPublishing
Twitter @hoperoadpublish
Instagram @hoperoadpublishing
Director/Publisher Rosemarie Hudson

HopeRoad publishes a wide range of fiction for adults
and young adults from and about Africa, Asia and the
Caribbean. Founded 2010.

Small Axes
Small Axes focuses on re-publishing out-of-print
post-colonial classics. Founded 2019.

Hopscotch
St Jude's Church, Dulwich Road, London SE24 0PB
tel 020-7501 6736
email orders@hopscotchbooks.com
website www.hopscotchbooks.com
Associate Publisher Angela Morano Shaw

A division of MA Education. Teaching resources for
primary school teachers. Founded 1997.

Practical Pre-School Books
Early years teacher resources.

Hot Key Books
Victoria House, Bloomsbury Squre,
London WC1B 4DA
tel 020-3770 8888
email hello@hotkeybooks.com
website www.hotkeybooks.com,
www.bonnierbooks.co.uk

Twitter @HotKeyBooksYA
Executive Publisher Emma Matthewson

Hot Key Books publishes books targeted at teen and older readers, some of which appeal to an adult audience. Hot Key Books is an imprint of Bonnier Books UK (page 137). Founded 2012.

House of Lochar
Isle of Colonsay, Argyll PA61 7YR
tel (01951) 200320
email sales@houseoflochar.com
website www.houseoflochar.com

Scottish history, transport, Scottish literature. Founded 1995.

John Hunt Publishing Ltd*‡
No. 3 East St, Alresford, Hants. SO24 9EE
email office@jhpbooks.com
website www.johnhuntpublishing.com
Director John Hunt

Publishes culture, politics, spirituality, Christianity, history and fiction titles for adults and children. See website for submission procedure. Imprints include: Zero Books; Iff Books; Chronos Books; Circle Books; Christian Alternative Books; Changemakers Books; Mantra Books; Moon Books; O-Books; 6th Books; Axis Mundi Books; Business Books; Dodona Books; Earth Books; Soul Rocks Books; Psyche Books; Roundfire Books; Cosmic Egg Books; Top Hat Books; Our Street Books; Lodestone Books; Liberalis Books; and Compass Press. Founded 2001.

Hutchinson Heinemann – see Cornerstone

Hymns Ancient and Modern Ltd*‡
Third Floor, Invicta House, 108–114 Golden Lane, London EC1Y 0TG
tel 020-7776 7551
website www.hymnsam.co.uk
Publishing Director Christine Smith

Theological books with special emphasis on text and reference books and contemporary theology for both students and clergy. Founded 1929.

Canterbury Press
Norwich Books and Music, 13A Hellesdon Park Road, Norwich NR6 5DR
tel (01603) 785925
website www.canterburypress.co.uk
Twitter @canterburypress

Hymnals, popular religious writing, spirituality and liturgy.

Church House Publishing
website www.chpublishing.co.uk
Twitter @CHPublishingUK

Publisher of the Church of England – church resources, stationery and Common Worship.

Saint Andrew Press
website www.standrewpress.hymns.co.uk
Twitter @standrewpress
Publisher of the Church of Scotland.

SCM Press
website www.scmpress.co.uk
Twitter @SCM_Press
Academic theology.

Icon Books Ltd‡
The Omnibus Business Centre, 39–41 North Road, London N7 9DP
tel 020-7697 9695
email info@iconbooks.com
website www.iconbooks.com
Directors: Philip Cotterell (managing), Duncan Heath (editorial), Andrew Furlow (sales, marketing, publicity, rights)

Popular, upmarket non-fiction: literature, history, philosophy, politics, psychology, sociology, sport, humour, science, current affairs, music, economics. Will consider unsolicited MSS (adult non-fiction only). Acquired by Jonathan Ball Publishers 2020. Founded 1991.

ICSA Publishing Ltd‡
Saffron House, 6–10 Kirby Street, London EC1N 8EQ
tel 020-7612 7020
email publishing@icsa.org.uk
website www.icsa.org.uk/bookshop
Publisher Saqib Lal Saleem

Publishing company of ICSA: The Charted Governance Institute, specialising in professional books, study texts for qualifications and online technical content for the governance and compliance market. Founded 1981.

Igloo Books Ltd
Cottage Farm, Mears Ashby Road, Sywell, Northants NN6 0BJ
tel (01604) 741116
email customerservices@igloobooks.com
website www.igloobooks.com
Twitter @igloo_books

Children's books: licensed books, novelty, board, picture, activity, education. Adult books: cookery, lifestyle, gift, trivia and non-fiction. Not currently accepting submissions. Founded 2005.

Imagine That Publishing Ltd
Marine House, Tide Mill Way, Woodbridge, Suffolk IP12 1AP
tel (01394) 386651
email customerservice@imaginethat.com
website www.imaginethat.com
Facebook www.facebook.com/ImagineThatPublishing
Twitter @imaginethatbook

Books

Instagram @imaginethatbook
Chairman Barrie Henderson, *Managing Director* David Henderson

Children's activity books, novelty books, picture books, reference, character, gift books and early learning books. Founded 1999.

Imprint Academic Ltd

PO Box 200, Exeter, Devon EX5 5YX
tel (01392) 851550
email graham@imprint.co.uk
website www.imprint.co.uk
Publisher Keith Sutherland, *Managing Editor* Graham Horswell

Books and journals in politics, society, philosophy and psychology for both academic and general readers. Book series include *St Andrews Studies in Philosophy and Public Affairs*, *British Idealist Studies*, *Societas* (essays in political and cultural criticism) and the *Library of Scottish Philosophy*. Also publishes under Amphora Press (biography and general historical interest titles). Unsolicited MSS, synopses and ideas welcome by email to the Managing Editor or with sae only. Founded 1980.

In Pinn – see Neil Wilson Publishing Ltd

Indigo Dreams Publishing Ltd‡

24 Forest Houses, Cookworthy Moor, Halwill, Beaworthy, Devon EX21 5UU
email publishing@indigodreams.co.uk
website www.indigodreams.co.uk
Twitter @IndigoDreamsPub
Editors Ronnie Goodyer, Dawn Bauling

Winners of Ted Slade Award for Services to Poetry. Main subject areas: (poetry) anthologies, collections, pamphlets, competitions, one monthly poetry magazine, two quarterly poetry and prose magazines. New and experienced writers welcome. Founded 2010.

Infinite Ideas

20 Stratfield Road, Oxford OX2 7BQ
tel 07802 443957
email info@infideas.com
website www.infideas.com
Managing Director Richard Burton

Publishes titles in wine (Classic Wine Library) and business. Founded 2003.

Influx Press

The Greenhouse, 49 Green Lanes, London N16 9BU
email hello@influxpress.com
website www.influxpress.com
Twitter @InfluxPress
Instagram @influxpress
Directors Gary Budden, Kit Caless

Award-winning and boundary pushing literary and experimental fiction. Imprints include New Ruins. Established 2012.

Institute of Public Administration†

57–61 Lansdowne Road, Ballsbridge, Dublin D04 TC62, Republic of Ireland
tel +353 (0)12 403600
email information@ipa.ie
website www.ipa.ie
Managing Editor John Paul Owens

Government, economics, politics, law, public management, health, education, social policy and administrative history. Founded 1957.

IOP Publishing*‡

Temple Circus, Temple Way, Bristol BS1 6HG
tel 0117 929 7481
email customerservices@ioppublishing.org
website https://ioppublishing.org/
Twitter @IOPPublishing

The company is a subsidiary of the Institute of Physics. Its portfolio includes more than 85 journals, a books programme, conference proceedings, magazines and science news websites. It focuses on physics, materials science, biosciences, astronomy and astrophysics, environmental sciences, mathematics and education. Also publishes on behalf of other scientific organisations, and represents their needs and those of their members. Founded 1874.

Irish Academic Press Ltd†

Tuckmill House, 10 George's Street, Newbridge, Co. Kildare W12 PX39, Republic of Ireland
tel +353 (0)45 432497
email info@iap.ie
website www.iap.ie
Publisher Conor Graham

General and academic publishing with a focus on Irish history, politics, biography, memoir, current affairs, literature, culture, arts and heritage. Imprints: Irish Academic Press, founded 1974: Merrion Press, founded 2012.

ISF Publishing

8 Belmont, Lansdown Road, Bath BA1 5DZ
email info@idriesshahfoundation.org
website www.idriesshahfoundation.org
Facebook www.facebook.com/idriesshah
Twitter @idriesshah

Dedicated to releasing new editions of the work of Idries Shah, who devoted his life to collecting, selecting and translating key works of Eastern Sufi classical literature, adapting them to the needs of the West and disseminating them in the Occident. Founded 2014.

Ithaca Press – see Garnet Publishing Ltd

IWM (Imperial War Museums) Publishing

Lambeth Road, London SE1 6HZ
tel 020-7416 5000

email publishing@iwm.org.uk
website www.iwm.org.uk
Facebook www.facebook.com/iwm.london
Twitter @I_W_M

IWM tells the stories of people who have lived, fought and died in conflicts involving Britain and the Commonwealth since 1914. IWM Publishing produces a range of books drawing on the expertise and archives of the museum. Books are produced both in-house and in partnership with other publishers. Founded 1917.

Jacaranda Books Art Music Ltd*‡

27 Old Gloucester Street, London WC1N 3AX
tel 020-8133 4841
email office@jacarandabooksartmusic.co.uk
website www.jacarandabooksartmusic.co.uk
Facebook www.facebook.com/jacarandabooks
Twitter @jacarandabooks
Founder & Publisher Valerie Brandes, *Publicity & Marketing Manager* Jazzmine Breary

Diversity-led independent publisher of literary and genre fiction and non-fiction. The company aims to directly address the ongoing lack of diversity in the industry, and has an interest in Caribbean, African and diaspora writing. Titles include *Tram 83* by Fiston Mwanza Mujila, *From Pasta to Pigfoot* and *Second Helpings* by Frances Mensah Williams, *Butterfly Fish* and *Speak Gigantular* by Irenosen Okojie, *Beyond the Pale* by Emily Urquhart and *The Elephant and the Bee* by Jess de Boer. Founded 2012.

JAI – see Elsevier Ltd

Jane's

163 Brighton Road, Coulsdon, Surrey CR5 2YH
tel 020-3159 3255
email communications@janes.com
website www.janes.com

Jane's delivers defence and security insight using open-source intelligence and powerful analytical tools. Jane's solutions and their publications cover key areas including: military platforms, systems and weapons; threat intelligence; defence markets, forecasts and budgets; sustainment and procurement. Founded 1898.

Joffe Books‡

111 Shoreditch High St, Hackney, London E1 6JN
email office@joffebooks.com
website www.joffebooks.com
Facebook www.facebook.com/joffebooks
Twitter @joffebooks
Publisher Jasper Joffe

A leading independent publisher of digital and print fiction, specializing in top-quality crime thrillers, mysteries, historical and psychological fiction. Accepts submissions from authors and agents, please see website for guidelines. Encourages submissions from underrepresented backgrounds. Bestselling authors include Joy Ellis, Faith Martin and Helen H. Durrant. Shortlisted for Independent Publisher of the Year 2020 at the British Book Awards. Founded 2014.

Jordan Publishing Ltd

21 St Thomas Street, Bristol BS1 6JS
tel 0117 918 1492
website www.lexisnexis.co.uk/products/jordan-publishing.html

Founded as an independent legal publisher in the UK. Produces practical information, online and in print, for practising lawyers and other professionals. Publishes textbooks, looseleafs, journals, court reference works and news services and also supplies software to law firms in the form of digital service PracticePlus, which combines step-by-step workflows, practice notes, automated court forms and links to core reference works. The company works with partners in key areas, such as the APIL series of guides, and also publishes around 40 new books and editions annually across a wide range of practice areas. Now owned by LexisNexis (page 163). Founded 1863.

Michael Joseph

One Embassy Gardens, 8 Viaduct Gardens, London SW11 7AY
tel 020-7139 3376
website www.penguin.co.uk/company/publishers/michael-joseph.html
Managing Director Louise Moore; *Editors* Louise Moore (general fiction for women, celebrity non-fiction), Maxine Hitchcock (general fiction for women, crime & thriller, general fiction), Jessica Leeke (general & literary fiction), Rowland White (crime, thriller & adventure fiction, commercial non-fiction, popular culture & military), Joel Richardson (crime & thriller, general fiction), Jillian Taylor (general fiction, historical fiction & non-fiction) Clio Cornish (commercial & literary fiction), Rebecca Hilsdon (women's fiction, saga, crime & thriller), Daniel Bunyard (commercial non-fiction, popular science & culture), Fenella Bates (commercial non-fiction, popular culture & wellbeing), Ione Walder (cookery, lifestyle & wellbeing), Charlotte Hardman (commercial non-fiction, self-help, health & memoir), Ariel Pakier (commercial narrative non-fiction, memoir, popular culture & current affairs)

Part of Penguin Random House UK (page 176). Founded 1935.

Kelpies – see Floris Books

Kenilworth Press – see Quiller Publishing Ltd

Kenyon-Deane – see Cressrelles Publishing Co. Ltd

Laurence King Publishing Ltd*

Carmelite House, 50 Victoria Embankment,
London EC4Y 0DZ
tel 020-7841 6900
email commissioning@laurenceking.com
website www.laurenceking.com
Directors Laurence King, Maria Treacy-Lord, Adrian
Greenwood, Marc Valli

Award-winning, independent publishing house based
in London. Publishes over 120 titles each year in the
illustrated mainstream, children's and gifting
markets, on topics including architecture, art, design,
fashion, film, photography and popular culture.
Founded 1976.

Kings Road Publishing

Victoria House, Bloomsbury Squre,
London WC1B 4DA
tel 020-770 3888
email hello@bonnierbooks.co.uk
website www.bonnierbooks.co.uk
Facebook www.facebook.com/KingsRoadPublishing
Ceo Perminder Mann, *Managing Director* Ben Dunn,
Head of Children's Publishing Lisa Edwards

Part of Bonnier Books UK. The children's imprints of
Kings Road Publishing are Studio Press, Weldon
Owen, which includes it's new sub-imprint 20 Watt,
and Templar Publishing (page 189), which contains
Big Picture Press. They focus on illustrated non-
fiction, picture books, novelty titles, activity books,
fiction and family reference. Blink (page 135),
including 535, Lagom and John Blake Publishing
(page 135) are the adult non-fiction imprints. Totally
Entwined Group is a leading ebook publisher, which
includes Bound Publishing, Pride Publishing and
Finch Books. Submissions to be sent to the address
above indicating which imprint they are addressed to.
Founded 2015.

Jessica Kingsley Publishers – see John Murray Press

Kitchen Press*

1 Windsor Place, Dundee DD2 1BG
tel 07951 451571
website www.kitchenpress.co.uk
Facebook www.facebook.com/kitchenpress
Twitter @Kitchen_Press
Instagram @kitchenpress

Independent publisher specialising in food writing,
particularly restaurant cookbooks. Established 2011.

Charles Knight – see LexisNexis

Kogan Page Ltd*‡

2nd Floor, 45 Gee Street, London EC1V 3RS
tel 020-7278 0433
website www.koganpage.com
Chairman Phillip Kogan, *Directors* Helen Kogan

(managing), Martin Klopstock (digital & operations),
Mark Briars (finance), Rex Elston (sales), Alison
Middle (marketing), Chris Cudmore (editorial)

Leading independent global publisher of business
books, digital solutions and content with over 1,000
titles in print. Key subject areas: accounting, finance
and banking; business and management; digital and
technology; human resources, learning and
development; marketing and communications; risk
and compliance; skills, careers and employability; and
logistics, supply chain and operations. Founded 1967.

Kube Publishing Ltd

Markfield Conference Centre, Ratby Lane,
Markfield, Leics. LE67 9SY
tel (01530) 249230
email info@kubepublishing.com
website www.kubepublishing.com
Managing Director Haris Ahmad

Formerly the Islamic Foundation. Books on Islam
and the Muslim world for adults and children.
Founded 2006.

Kyle Books

Carmelite House, 50 Victoria Embankment,
London EC4Y 0DZ
tel 020-3122 6000
email general.enquiries@kylebooks.co.uk
website www.kylebooks.co.uk
Twitter @Kyle_Books
Publisher Joanna Copestick

Food and drink; health; beauty; gardening; reference;
style; design; mind, body & spirit. Acquired by
Octopus Publishing Group in 2017 (page 171).
Founded 1990.

Peter Lang Ltd

52 St Giles, Oxford OX1 3LU
tel (01865) 502124
email oxford@peterlang.com
website www.peterlang.com
Facebook www.facebook.com/PeterLangPublishers
Twitter @PeterLangOxford
Ceo, Peter Lang Publishing Group Arnaud Béglé,
Global Publishing Director Lucy Melville, *Senior
Commissioning Editors* Tony Mason, Laurel Plapp

Part of the international Peter Lang Publishing
Group, the company publishes across the humanities
and social sciences, producing texts in print and
digital formats, as well as Open Access publications.
All forms of scholarly research as well as textbooks,
readers, student guides. Welcomes submissions from
prospective authors. Blog:
peterlangoxford.wordpress.com. Founded 2006.

Lawrence & Wishart Ltd

Central Books Building, Freshwater Road,
Chadwell Heath RM8 1RX
tel 020-8597 0090

email lw@lwbooks.co.uk
website www.lwbooks.co.uk
Book Editor Jumanah Younis

Cultural studies, current affairs, history, socialism and Marxism, political philosophy, politics, popular culture. Founded 1936.

Legend Press Ltd‡
51 Gower Street, London WC1E 6HJ
tel 020-8127 0793
email info@legendtimesgroup.co.uk
website www.legendpress.co.uk
Twitter @legend_times
Managing Director Tom Chalmers, *Commissioning Editor* Lauren Parsons

Focused predominantly on publishing mainstream literary and commercial fiction. Publishes Legend Originals, Legend Thrillers and Legend Classics. Submissions can be sent to submissions@legendtimesgroup.co.uk. Founded 2005.

Lewis Mason – see Ian Allan Publishing Ltd

LexisNexis
Lexis House, 30 Farringdon Street, London EC4A 4HH
tel 0330 1611234
email customer.services@lexisnexis.co.uk
website www.lexisnexis.co.uk

Formerly LexisNexis Butterworths. Division of Reed Elsevier (UK) Ltd. Founded 1974.

Butterworths
Legal and tax and accountancy books, journals, looseleaf and electronic services.

Charles Knight
Looseleaf legal works and periodicals on local government law, construction law and technical subjects.

Tolley
Law, taxation, accountancy, business.

Lightning Books
312 Uxbridge Road, Rickmansworth, Herts. WD3 8YL
tel 020-3239 3027
email dan@eye-books.com
website www.eye-books.com
Twitter @EyeAndLightning
Publisher Dan Hiscocks

The sister imprint for fiction of Eye Books (page 148). Literary and commercial fiction, including UK editions of award-winning work from Australia and New Zealand. Founded 2015.

The Lilliput Press Ltd†
62–63 Sitric Road, Arbour Hill, Dublin D07 AE27, Republic of Ireland

tel +353 (0)16 711647
email publicity@lilliputpress.ie
website www.lilliputpress.ie
Facebook www.facebook.com/Lilliput-Press
Twitter @LilliputPress
Managing Director Antony T. Farrell

General and Irish literature: essays, memoir, biography/autobiography, fiction, criticism; Irish history; philosophy; Joycean contemporary culture; nature and environment. Founded 1984.

Frances Lincoln
74–77 White Lion Street, London N1 9PF
tel 020-7284 9300
email reception@frances-lincoln.com
website www.quartoknows.com/Frances-Lincoln
Publisher Andrew Dunn

Imprint of The Quarto Group (page 179). Illustrated, international co-editions: gardening, architecture, environment, interiors, photography, art, walking and climbing, design and landscape, gift, children's books. Founded 1977.

Lion Hudson Ltd‡
Box 202, 266 Banbury Road, Summertown, Oxford OX2 7DL
tel (01865) 302750
email info@lionhudson.com
website www.lionhudson.com
Managing Director Suzanne Wilson-Higgins

Books for children and adults. Christian spirituality, reference, biography, history, contemporary issues, inspiration and fiction from authors with a Christian world-view. Also specialises in children's bibles and prayer collections, as well as picture storybooks and illustrated non-fiction. Adult submissions: via website, by email or hardcopy with sae if return required. Children's submissions: hardcopy only with sae if return required. Founded 1971.

Candle Books
For young children: bible story retellings, confessional prayer books, bible related activity and novelty books, and other Christian resources licensed from or created in partnership with other publishers and packagers.

Lion Books
Christian books accessible to all readers: bible related information and reference, history, spirituality and prayer, issues, self-help.

Lion Children's Books
For children of all ages: bible story retellings, prayer books, picture storybooks, illustrated non-fiction and information books on the Christian faith and world religions. Also specialises in gift books, occasion books and seasonal books for Christmas and Easter.

Lion Fiction

Historical fiction, mystery, fantasy and heart-warming tales with meaning, from authors with a Christian world-view.

Lion Scholar

Bible related reference works for the serious reader or first year undergraduate.

Monarch Books

Confessional Christian biography, issues concerning Christian faith and society, bible commentary, church resources and co-publishing with Christian events and organisations.

Little, Brown Book Group

50 Victoria Embankment, London EC4Y 0DZ
tel 020-3122 7000
email info@littlebrown.co.uk
website www.littlebrown.co.uk
Twitter @LittleBrownUK
Managing Director Charlie King, *Deputy Managing Director* Cath Burke

Hardback and paperback fiction and general non-fiction. No unsolicited MSS. Part of Hachette UK (page 154). Founded 1988.

Abacus

Publishers Richard Beswick (Abacus Non-Fiction), Clare Smith (Abacus Fiction)

Trade paperbacks.

Atom

website www.atombooks.co.uk
Editorial Director Sarah Castleton

Teen fiction with a fantastical edge.

Blackfriars

website www.blackfriarsbooks.com
Executive Publisher Clare Smith (literary fiction)

Digital imprint.

The Bridge Street Press

Executive Publisher Tim Whiting

A boutique literary non-fiction imprint.

Constable & Robinson

Publishing Directors Duncan Proudfoot (Robinson), Andreas Campomar (Constable Non-Fiction), Krystyna Green (Constable Fiction)

Fiction, non-fiction, psychology, humour, brief histories and how-to books.

Corsair

Twitter @CorsairBooks
Publisher James Gurbutt

Pioneers of literary fiction from groundbreaking debuts to established authors.

Dialogue Books

Publisher Sharmaine Lovegrove

Publishes BAME, LGBTQI+, disability and working class communities across fiction, non-fiction, literary and commercial.

Fleet

Publisher Ursula Doyle

Literary imprint, which publishes six to eight titles a year, both literary fiction and narrative non-fiction.

Hachette Digital

Publisher Sarah Shrubb (Hachette Audio)

CDs, downloads and ebooks. See page 224.

Little, Brown

Publisher Richard Beswick, *Executive Publisher* Clare Smith (literary fiction)

General books: politics, biography, crime fiction, general fiction.

Orbit

website www.orbitbooks.com
Publisher Anna Jackson

Science fiction and fantasy.

Piatkus Constable & Robinson

website www.piatkus.co.uk
Executive Publisher Tim Whiting (non-fiction), *Publishers* Zoe Bohm (non-fiction), Anna Boatman (fiction)

Fiction and general non-fiction.

Sphere

Publisher Lucy Malagoni (Sphere Fiction)

Hardbacks and paperbacks: original fiction and non-fiction.

Virago

website www.virago.co.uk
Publisher Sarah Savitt

Women's literary fiction and non-fiction.

Little Tiger Group

1 Coda Studios, 189 Munster Road, London SW6 6AW
tel 020-7385 6333
email contact@littletiger.co.uk
website www.littletiger.co.uk
Group Publishing Director Thomas Truong, *Publisher* Jude Evans, *Commissioning Editors* Sally Polson, Eleanor Collins

Religion; philosophy; holistic health; organics; mind, body & spirit; crafts; parenting. Children's books: board, picture books, activity books. See website for submission details. Acquired by Penguin Random House (page 217) in 2019. Founded 1987.

Caterpillar Books

email contact@littletiger.co.uk
website www.littletiger.co.uk/imprint/caterpillar-books

Editorial Director Pat Hegarty

Books for children, including novelty board and picture books.

Little Tiger Press

email contact@littletiger.co.uk
website www.littletiger.co.uk
Publisher Jude Evans, *Editorial Director* Eleanor Farmer

Children's picture books, board books and novelty books for preschool–7 years. See website for submissions guidelines. Founded 1987.

Stripes

email contact@littletiger.co.uk
website www.littletiger.co.uk/imprint/stripes-publishing
Editorial Director Ruth Bennett

Fiction for children aged 6–12 years and young adult. Quality standalone titles and series publishing in all age groups. Will consider new material from authors and illustrators; see website for guidelines. Founded 2005.

360 Degrees

email contact@littletiger.co.uk
website www.littletiger.co.uk/special/360degrees
Editorial Director Pat Hegarty

Non-fiction novelty for children aged 5–12 years. Founded 2015.

Little Toller Books

2 Church Street, Beaminster, Dorset DT8 3AZ
email adrian@littletollerbooks.co.uk
website www.littletollerbooks.co.uk
Facebook www.facebook.com/littletoller
Twitter @littletoller

Little Toller Books is a family-run publishing company that specialises in books about rural life and local history. Founded 2008.

Liverpool University Press*

4 Cambridge Street, Liverpool L69 7ZU
tel 0151 794 2233
email lup@liv.ac.uk
website www.liverpooluniversitypress.co.uk
Twitter @LivUniPress
Managing Director Anthony Cond

LUP is the UK's third oldest university press, with a distinguished history of publishing exceptional research since its foundation, including the work of Nobel prize winners. Rapidly expanded in recent years and now publishes approximately 150 books a year and 34 journals, specialising in literature, modern languages, history and visual culture. Founded 1899.

Logaston Press

The Holme, Church Road, Eardisley,
Herefordshire HR3 6NJ

tel (01544) 327182
email info@logastonpress.co.uk
website www.logastonpress.co.uk
Twitter @LogastonPress
Proprietors Richard Wheeler, Su Wheeler

History, social history, archaeology and guides to Herefordshire, Worcestershire, Shropshire, rural West Midlands and Mid-Wales. Welcomes submission of ideas relevant to this geographical area: send synopsis first. Founded 1985.

LOM ART

16 Lion Yard, Tremadoc Road, London SW4 7NQ
tel 020-7720 8643
email enquiries@mombooks.com
website www.mombooks.com/lom
Facebook www.facebook.com/MichaelOMaraBooks
Twitter @OMaraBooks
Managing Director Lesley O'Mara, *Publisher* Philippa Wingate

Illustrated non-fiction for children and adults. Publishes approx. 10 titles a year. Titles include *Fantomorphia, Maybe the Moon, The Van Gogh Activity Book* and *Life Lessons From My Cat*, plus a range of artist-led drawing, colouring and picture book titles. Unable to guarantee a reply to every submission received, but the inclusion of a sae is necessary for submission to be returned. Imprint of Michael O'Mara Books Ltd (page 172). Founded 2015.

Lonely Planet Publications Ltd

240 Blackfriars Road, London SE1 8NW
tel 020-3771 5100
email recruiting_contributors@lonelyplanet.com
website www.lonelyplanet.com
Ceo Luis Cabrera

A travel media company, Lonely Planet is the world's number one travel guidebook brand with 900 titles, content published in 14 different languages and products in over 150 countries. The company's ecosystem also includes mobile apps, magazines, ebooks, a website and a dedicated traveller community. Offices in USA, UK, Australia, Ireland, India and China. Founded 1973.

Longman – see Pearson UK

Lorenz Books – see Anness Publishing

Luath Press Ltd*‡

543/2 Castlehill, The Royal Mile,
Edinburgh EH1 2ND
tel 0131 225 4326
email gavin.macdougall@luath.co.uk
website www.luath.co.uk
Facebook www.facebook.com/LuathPress
Twitter @LuathPress
Director Gavin MacDougall

Books

Publishes modern fiction, history, travel guides, art, poetry, politics and more. Over 500 titles in print including recent *Sunday Times* Top 10 Bestseller and Orwell Prize Winner *Poverty Safari: Understanding the Anger of Britain's Underclass* by Darren McGarvey. Other award-winning and shortlisted titles include Angus Peter Campbell's *Memory and Straw*, Ann Kelley's *The Bower Bird*, Anne Pia's *Language of My Choosing* and Robert Alan Jamieson's *Da Happie Laand*. UK distributor BookSource. Founded 1981.

Luna Press Publishing*

149/4 Morrison Street, Edinburgh EH3 8AG
email lunapress@outlook.com
website www.lunapresspublishing.com
Founder & Owner Francesca T. Barbini (managing & editorial)

Fantasy, dark fantasy and science fiction (adult, young adult, teen) in fiction and academia. Fiction: publishes novels, novellas, graphic novels, parodies, collections, anthologies. Academia Lunare is the non-fiction, academic branch, dealing with science fiction and fantasy and non-genre: academic papers, proceedings, Calls for Papers, PhDs. Now running regular open submission days – check website for details. Submissions email: submissionsluna@outlook.com. Founded 2015.

Lund Humphries‡

Office 3, Book House, 261A City Road, London EC1V 1JX
email info@lundhumphries.com
website www.lundhumphries.com
Facebook www.facebook.com/LHArtBooks
Twitter @LHArtBooks
Instagram @lhartbooks
Managing Director Lucy Myers

Independent publishing imprint of quality art and architecture books. Lund Humphries published their first book in 1939. Founded 1895.

The Lutterworth Press

PO Box 60, Cambridge CB1 2NT
tel (01223) 350865
email publishing@lutterworth.com
website www.lutterworth.com,
www.lutterworthpress.wordpress.com
Facebook www.facebook.com/JamesClarkeandCo
Twitter @LuttPress
Managing Director Adrian Brink

A long-established independent publishing house. Originally founded as the Religious Tract Society and publisher of *The Boy's Own Paper* and *The Girl's Own Paper*. Now a publisher of educational and adult non-fiction including books and ebooks on: history, biography, literature and criticism, science, philosophy, art and art history, biblical studies, theology, mission, religious studies and collecting.

Recent titles include *Sex, Power, Control: Responding to Abuse in the Institutional Church* by Fiona Gardner, *Britain's Greatest Prime Minister: Lord Liverpool* by Martin Hutchinson and *W. H. Crossland: An Architectural Biography*. Imprints: James Clarke & Co, Acorn Editions, Patrick Hardy Books. Founded 1995.

Mabecron Books Ltd

3 Briston Orchard, St Mellion, Saltash, Cornwall PL12 6RQ
tel (01579) 350885
email ronjohns@mabecronbooks.co.uk
website www.mabecronbooks.co.uk
Twitter @mabecronbooks

Award-winning publisher. Produces beautiful children's picture books and books with a Cornish or west country subject. Linked to bookshops in Falmouth, St Ives and Padstow. Founded 1998.

McGraw-Hill Education*

8th Floor, 338 Euston Road, London NW1 3BH
tel 020-3429 3400
email emea_schools_intl@mheducation.com
website www.mheducation.co.uk
Facebook www.facebook.com/mheducationemea
Twitter @mhe_emea
Primary Contacts Emma Chambers (sales) and Parveen Bhambra (marketing)

McGraw Hill is an educational publisher and digital solution provider for primary and secondary education in English language arts, maths, science, and other subject areas, including intervention and learning support. Founded 1988.

Macmillan Education – see Springer Nature Group Ltd

Made Simple Books – see Elsevier Ltd

Management Books 2000 Ltd

36 Western Road, Oxford OX1 4LG
tel (01865) 600738
website www.mb2000.com
Directors N. Dale-Harris, R. Hartman

Practical books for working managers and business professionals: management, business and lifeskills, and sponsored titles. Unsolicited MSS, synopses and ideas for books welcome. Founded 1993.

Manchester University Press*

Floor J, Renold Building, University of Manchester, Altrincham Street, Manchester M1 7JA
tel 0161 275 2310
email mup@manchester.ac.uk
website www.manchesteruniversitypress.co.uk
Chief Executive Simon Ross

Works of academic scholarship: anthropology, archaeology and heritage, art, architecture and visual culture, economics and business, film, media and music, history, human geography, international relations, law, literature and theatre, methods and guides, philosophy and critical theory, politics, religion and sociology. Textbooks and monographs. Subscription and Open Access journals. Founded 1904.

Mandrake of Oxford
PO Box 250, Oxford OX1 1AP
tel (01865) 243671
email mandrake@mandrake.uk.net
website www.mandrake.uk.net
Director Mogg Morgan

Art, biography, classic crime studies, fiction, Indology, magic, witchcraft, philosophy, religion. Query letters only. Founded 1986.

Mango Books
18 Soho Square, London W1D 3QL
tel 020-7060 4142
email adam@mangobooks.com
website www.mangobooks.co.uk

Publishers of non-fiction books for lovers of crime, detection and mystery. Founded 2017.

Manilla Press
Victoria House, Bloomsbury Squre, London WC1B 4DA
tel 020-7490 3875
email hello@zaffrebooks.co.uk
email hello@bonnierbooks.co.uk
website www.bonnierbooks.co.uk
Publisher Margaret Stead

Manilla Press publishes 8 books a year, with an international appeal, spanning polemical writing, memoirs, popular science, social history and novels. Manilla Press is an imprint of Bonnier Books UK (page 137).

Mantra Lingua Ltd
Global House, 303 Ballards Lane, London N12 8NP
tel 020-8445 5123
email info@mantralingua.com
website https://uk.mantralingua.com/
Facebook www.facebook.com/Mantralingua
Twitter @mantralingua
Managing Director R. Dutta

Publishes bilingual picture books and educational resources for UK, US, Swedish and German audiences. Looking for illustrators with ability to draw diverse racial faces, authors and story-tellers with ability to interpret or imagine modern city lives. Commission and royalty based relationships with print runs covering between 10 and 15 language editions. Translators and audio narrators, tel: 0845 600 1361. Founded 2002.

Kevin Mayhew Ltd
Fengate Farm, Rattlesden, Suffolk IP30 0SZ
tel (01449) 737978
email info@kevinmayhew.com
website www.kevinmayhew.com
Director Barbara Mayhcw

Christianity: prayer and spirituality, pastoral care, preaching, liturgy worship, children's, youth work, drama, instant art, educational. Music: hymns, organ and choral, contemporary worship, piano and instrumental, tutors. Greetings cards: images, spiritual texts, birthdays, Christian events, musicians, general occasions. Read submissions section on website before sending MSS/synopses. Founded 1976.

Mentor Books
43 Furze Road, Sandyford Industrial Estate, Dublin D18 PN30, Republic of Ireland
tel +353 (0)12 952112
email admin@mentorbooks.ie
website www.mentorbooks.ie

General: non-fiction, humour, biographies, politics, crime, history, guidebooks. Educational (secondary): languages, history, geography, business, maths, sciences. No unsolicited MSS. Founded 1979.

The Mercier Press[†]
email info@mercierpress.ie
website www.mercierpress.ie
General Manager Deirdre Roberts

Irish literature; folklore; history; politics; humour; academic; current affairs; health; mind, body & spirit; general non-fiction; children's. Founded 1944.

Merlin Press Ltd[‡]
Central Books Building, Freshwater Road, London RM8 1RX
tel 020-8590 9700 / 020-8590 9700
email info@merlinpress.co.uk
website www.merlinpress.co.uk
Managing Director Anthony Zurbrugg

Radical history and social studies. Letters/synopses only. Founded 1957.

Green Print
Green politics and the environment.

Merrell Publishers Ltd
70 Cowcross Street, London EC1M 6EJ
email hm@merrellpublishers.com
website www.merrellpublishers.com
Publisher Hugh Merrell

High-quality illustrated books on all aspects of visual culture, including art, architecture, photography, garden design, interior design, product design and books specially developed for institutions, foundations, corporations and private collectors. Unsolicited carefully prepared proposals welcomed via email. All titles published by Merrell are sold and distributed worldwide through USA and UK distributors and international stockholding agents. Founded 1989.

Books

Methuen & Co Ltd

Orchard House, Railway Street, Slingsby,
York YO62 4AN
tel (01653) 628152 / 628195
email editorial@methuen.co.uk
email academic@methuen.co.uk
website www.methuen.co.uk
Managing Director Peter Tummons, *Editorial Director*
Naomi Tummons, *Sales* Peter Newsom, *Editor-at-Large* Dr Jonathan Tummons, *Accounts* Frank Warn

Literary fiction and non-fiction: biography,
autobiography, travel, history, sport, humour, film,
children's, performing arts. No unsolicited MSS.
Founded 1998.

Politico's Publishing

Politics, current affairs, political biography and
autobiography.

Metro Publications Ltd

tel 020-8533 7777
email info@metropublications.com
website www.metropublications.com
Twitter @metrolondon

Produces well-researched and beautifully designed
guide books on many aspects of London life.
Founded 2007.

Michelin Travel Partners UK Ltd

The Dairy, Munden Estate, Watford,
Herts. WD25 8PZ
tel (01923) 205240
email travelpubsales@michelin.com
website https://travel.michelin.co.uk

Tourist guides, maps and atlases, hotel and restaurant
guides. Founded 2001.

Miller's – see Octopus Publishing Group

Mills & Boon – see Harlequin (UK) Ltd

Milo Books Ltd

14 Ash Grove, Wrea Green, Preston, Lancs. PR4 2NY
tel (01772) 672900
email info@milobooks.com
website www.milobooks.com
Publisher Peter Walsh

True crime, sport, current affairs. Founded 1997.

Mirror Books‡

Reach plc, 10 Lower Thames Street,
London EC3R 6EN
tel 20-7293 3740
email mirrorbooks@reachplc.com
website www.mirrorbooks.co.uk
Twitter @themirrorbooks
Managing Director Steve Hanrahan, *Executive Editor*
Paul Dove

Part of Reach plc, one of the UK's leading media
companies. The imprint focus is non-fiction real-life

(memoir, crime, nostalgia, personalities and
celebrities). Accepts submissions online:
mirrorbooks.co.uk/pages/submissions.
Founded 2016.

Mitchell Beazley – see Octopus Publishing Group

Mobius – see Hodder & Stoughton

Morgan Kauffman – see Elsevier Ltd

Morrigan Book Company

Killala, Co. Mayo, Republic of Ireland
tel +353 (0)96 32555
email morriganbooks@gmail.com
website http://conankennedy.com/About.html
Publishers Gerry Kennedy, Hilary Kennedy

Non-fiction: general Irish interest, biography, history,
local history, folklore and mythology. Founded 1979.

Mud Pie

Leckford Road, Oxford OX2 6HY
tel 07985 935320
email info@mudpiebooks.com
website www.mudpiebooks.com
Facebook www.facebook.com/Mud-Pie-Books-665982096919314
Twitter @mudpiebooks
Founder & Director Tony Morris

Buddhist books and books for Buddhists. An
independent specialist online publisher, dedicated to
showcasing the best in Buddhist writing. The
company's lead title, *The Buddha, Geoff and Me*, has
sold over 100,000 copies worldwide. Founded 2016.

Murdoch Books‡

Ormond House, 26–27 Boswell Street,
London WC1N 3JZ
tel 020-8785 5995
email info@murdochbooks.co.uk
website www.murdochbooks.co.uk

Non-fiction: cookery, homes and interiors,
gardening, self-help, environment, physical and
mental well-being. Owned by Australian publisher
Allen & Unwin Pty Ltd. Founded 1991.

John Murray Press

Carmelite House, 50 Victoria Embankment,
London EC4Y 0DZ
tel 020-3122 6777
website www.johnmurraypress.co.uk
Facebook www.facebook.com/johnmurraybooks
Twitter @johnmurraypress
Managing Editor Nick Davies

No unsolicited MSS without preliminary letter. Part
of Hachette UK (page 154). Founded 1768.

Basic Books
Editor Publishing Director Sarah Caro
History, biography, science, philosophy and economics.

Nicholas Brealey Publishing
Publishing Director Iain Campbell
Coaching and leadership, personal development and popular psychology, smart thinking, business, finance and economics.

Hodder Faith
Publishing Director Andy Lyon
New International Version (NIV) bibles, Christian books, biography/memoir, gift.

Jessica Kingsley Publishers
Managing Director JKP and Director of Professional Publishing JMP Sanphy Thomas
Autism and special needs, gender, education, therapies, diversity and related issues. The Singing Dragon imprint includes books on alternative health, Chinese medicine and wellbeing.

John Murray
Publisher Jocasta Hamilton
Quality literary fiction and non-fiction: science, business, travel, history, reference, biography and memoir. The J M Originals imprint publishes distinctive new voices.

John Murray Learning
Publishing Directors Sarah Cole (languages), Iain Campbell (learning)
Professional and personal development. Home to learning brands including Teach Yourself, Michel Thomas language courses, and Brewers and Chambers reference.

Sheldon Press
Imprint of John Murray Learning. Popular medicine, health, self-help, psychology.

Two Roads
Publisher Lisa Highton
Commercial and reading-group fiction and non-fiction: biography and memoir, social history, personal development, popular culture, gift and humour.

Muswell Press‡

72 Cromwell Avenue, London N6 5HQ
email team@muswell-press.co.uk
website www.muswell-press.co.uk
Facebook www.facebook.com/MuswellPress/
Twitter @MuswellPress
Directors Kate Beal, Sarah Beal, *Editor-at-Large* Matt Bates

An independent publisher publishing an eclectic mix with the emphasis on contemporary fiction, crime, biography and travel. The queer list republishes forgotten gay classics, and a new imprint of queer writing. Founded 2008.

Myriad Editions‡

New Internationalist Publications,
The Old Music Hall, 106–108 Cowley Rd,
Oxford OX4 1JE
tel (01865) 403345
email info@myriadeditions.com
website www.myriadeditions.com
Twitter @MyriadEditions
Directors Candida Lacey (publishing), Corinne Pearlman (creative)

Independent publisher of literary fiction, crime written by women, graphic novels and feminist non-fiction. Merged with New Internationalist in 2017 as part of a joint plan to expand and embrace diversity. Founded 1993.

Natural History Museum Publishing

Cromwell Road, London SW7 5BD
tel 020-7942 5336
email publishing@nhm.ac.uk
website www.nhm.ac.uk/publishing
Head of Publishing Colin Ziegler

Natural history, life sciences, earth sciences, wildlife photography, art of natural history, books for children. Founded 1881.

New Island Books†

10 Richview Office Park, Clonskeagh,
Dublin 14 D14 V8C4, Republic of Ireland
tel +353 (0)12 784225
email info@newisland.ie
email editor@newisland.ie
website www.newisland.ie
Facebook www.facebook.com/NewIslandBooks
Twitter @NewIslandBooks
Director Edwin Higel, *Editor* Aoife K. Walsh (commissioning)

Fiction, poetry, drama, humour, biography, current affairs, history, memoir/personal essay. Unsolicited submissions during open call only via publisher's website, www.newisland.ie/submissions. See publisher's social media platforms for notice of open submission call. Founded 1992.

New Playwrights' Network

10 Station Road Industrial Estate, Colwall, Malvern,
Herefordshire WR13 6RN
tel (01684) 540154
email simon@cressrelles.co.uk
website www.cressrelles.co.uk
Publishing Director Leslie Smith

General plays for the amateur, one-act and full length.

New Riders – see Pearson UK

Newnes – see Elsevier Ltd

Books

New Welsh Rarebyte

PO Box 170, Aberystwyth, Ceredigion SY23 1WZ
tel (01970) 628410
website www.newwelshreview.com
Facebook www.facebook.com/NewWelshReview
Twitter @newwelshreview
Instagram @newwelshreview
Editor Gwen Davies

Publish prize-winners from the annual New Welsh
Writing Awards, the writer development initiative
run by New Welsh Review since 2015, which seeks
prose works of 5,000–30,000 words on a different
theme each year. See New Welsh Reader (page 74) or
website for more information.

Nexus – see Ebury Publishing

Nobrow Books

27 Westgate Street, London E8 3RL
tel 020-7033 4430
email info@nobrow.net
website https://nobrow.net/
Twitter @NobrowPress

Publishes picture books, illustrated fiction and non-
fiction and graphic novels. Nobrow Books aims to
combine good design and storytelling, quality
production value and environmental consciousness.
Founded 2008.

Flying Eye Books

email info@nobrow.net
website www.flyingeyebooks.com
Twitter @FlyingEyeBooks
Children's imprint. Focuses on the craft of children's
storytelling and non-fiction. Founded 2013.

Nordisk Books Ltd

81 Harbour Street, Whitstable CT5 1AE
tel 07437 202582
email info@nordiskbooks.com
website www.nordiskbooks.com
Facebook www.facebook.com/nordiskbooks
Twitter @nordiskbooks
Instagram @nordisk_books
Director Duncan J. Lewis

Modern and contemporary fiction from the Nordic
countries. Publishing a wide range of exciting literary
titles from across the Scandinavian peninsular and
beyond. No crime. Founded 2016.

North-Holland – see Elsevier Ltd

Northcote House Publishers Ltd

The Paddocks, Brentor Road, Mary Tavy,
Devon PL19 9PY
tel (01822) 810066
email northcotepublishers@gmail.com
website www.liverpooluniversitypress.co.uk
Directors B.R.W. Hulme, A.V. Hulme (secretary)

Imprint of Liverpool University Press (page 165).
Education and education management, educational
dance and drama, literary criticism (*Writers and their
Work*). Since April 2018 the *Writers and their Work*
series has been managed and distributed by Liverpool
University Press to whom all related enquiries should
be directed: www.liverpooluniversitypress.co.uk or
0151 794 2233. Founded 1985.

Northodox Press

email submissions@northodox.co.uk
website www.northodox.co.uk
Facebook www.facebook.com/northodoxpress
Twitter @northodoxpress
Contacts Tom Ashton, Ted O'Connor, James Gaskell

Aims to represent authentic Northern voices and
cater to readers of quality crime fiction.
Founded 2020.

W.W. Norton & Company

15 Carlisle Street, London W1D 3BS
tel 020-7323 1579
email crusselli@wwnorton.co.uk
website www.wwnorton.co.uk
Facebook www.facebook.com/WW-Norton-UK/
Twitter @wwnortonuk
Managing Director John Donovan

English and American literature, economics, music,
psychology, science. Founded 1980.

Nosy Crow*‡

14 Baden Place, Crosby Row, London SE1 1YW
tel 020-7089 7575
email hello@nosycrow.com
website www.nosycrow.com
Managing Director Kate Wilson, *Editorial Director*
Camilla Reid, *Head of Fiction* Kirsty Stansfield, *Head
of Picture Books* Louise Bolongaro, *Head of Non-
Fiction* Rachel Kellehar, *Head of Sales & Marketing*
Catherine Stokes, *Commercial Director* Adrian Soar

Award-winning children's books and apps, children's
publisher for The National Trust and The British
Museum. IPG Children's Publisher of the Year 2012,
2013, 2016, 2017 and 2020; IPG Independent
Publisher of the Year 2016; BIA Children's Publisher
of the Year 2017 and 2019; BIA Independent
Publisher of the Year 2020 and Queen's Award for
International Trade 2019. Founded 2010.

Nourish Books

Unit 11, Shepperton House, 89 Shepperton Road,
London N1 3DF
tel 020-3813 6940
email enquiries@watkinspublishing.com
website https://nourishbooks.com/
Facebook www.facebook.com/nourishbooks
Twitter @nourishbooks

Cookery, wellbeing and health. Part of Watkins
Media (page 193).

NWP – see Neil Wilson Publishing Ltd

Oak Tree Press[†]
33 Rochestown Rise, Rochestown, Cork T12 EVT0,
Republic of Ireland
tel +353 (0)86 244 1633, +353 (0)86 330 7694
email info@oaktreepress.com
website www.SuccessStore.com
Directors Brian O'Kane, Rita O'Kane

Business management, enterprise, accountancy and
finance, law. Special emphasis on titles for small
business owner/managers. Founded 1991.

Nubooks
Ebooks.

Oberon Books – see Bloomsbury Publishing Plc

The O'Brien Press Ltd[†]
12 Terenure Road East, Rathgar, Dublin D06 HD27,
Republic of Ireland
tel +353 (0)1 4923333
email books@obrien.ie
website www.obrien.ie
Directors Michael O'Brien, Ivan O'Brien, Kunak
McGann

Adult non-fiction: biography, politics, history, travel,
food & drink, sport, humour, reference. Adult fiction,
crime (Brandon). No poetry or academic. Children:
picture books; fiction for all ages; illustrated fiction
for ages 3+, 5+, 6+, 8+ years, novels (10+ and young
adult): contemporary, historical, fantasy. Non-fiction.
Unsolicited MSS (sample chapters only), synopses
and ideas for books welcome, submissions will not be
returned. Founded 1974.

Octopus Publishing Group*
Carmelite House, 50 Victoria Embankment,
London EC4Y 0DZ
tel 020-3122 6000
email info@octopusbooks.co.uk
email publisher@octopusbooks.co.uk (submissions)
website www.octopusbooks.co.uk
Publishing Director Anna Bond

Part of Hachette UK (page 154). Founded 1998.

Aster
Publisher Kate Adams
Health and wellbeing.

Brazen
Editorial Director Romily Morgan
Non-fiction.

Cassell
Popular culture, music, reference.

Conran Octopus
Quality illustrated books, particularly lifestyle,
cookery, gardening.

Gaia Books
The environment, natural living and health.

Godsfield Press
email publisher@godsfieldpress.com
Mind, body & spirit with an emphasis on practical
application.

Hamlyn
Practical non-fiction, particularly cookery, health and
diet, home and garden, sport, puzzles and reference.

Ilex Press
email info@octopusbooks.co.uk
Illustrated books on art, design and photography.

Kyle Books
Quality cookery, lifestyle and craft books (page 162).

Miller's
Antiques and collectables.

Mitchell Beazley
Quality illustrated books, particularly cookery, wine
and gardening.

Philip's
email publisher@philips-maps.co.uk
Atlases, maps and astronomy.

Pyramid
email bountybooksinfo-bp@bountybooks.co.uk
Publisher Lucy Pessell
Promotional/custom publishing.

Short Books
Popular non-fiction.

Spruce
Gift and humour.

Summersdale
Gift, humour, travel and health (page 188).

Old Barn Books[‡]
Warren Barn, Bedham Lane, Fittleworth,
West Sussex RH20 1JW
tel (01798) 865010
email ruth@oldbarnbooks.com
website www.oldbarnbooks.com
Facebook www.facebook.com/oldbarnbooks
Twitter @oldbarnbooks
Instagram @Soldbarnbooks

Independent publisher of picture books and fiction
for children up to 14 years old and the occasional gift
book for adults. Interested in the natural world and
promoting empathy. Strong line in Aussie MG
fiction. No unsolicited submissions at present.
Founded 2015.

Old Pond Publishing
3 The Bridleway, Selsey, Chichester,
West Sussex PO20 9RS

Books

email info@foxchapelpublishing.co.uk
website www.foxchapelpublishing.co.uk
Facebook www.facebook.com/OldPondPublishingLtd
Twitter @oldpondltd
Publisher Richard Dodman

A leading specialist publisher of agriculture, trucking, machinery and practical farming books. Acquired by Fox Chapel Publishers International in 2018. Founded 1997.

The Oleander Press

16 Orchard Street, Cambridge CB1 1JT
tel (01638) 500784
website www.oleanderpress.com
Managing Director Dr Jane Doyle

Travel, language, Libya, Arabia and Middle East, Cambridgeshire, history, reference, classics. MSS welcome with sae for reply. Founded 1960.

Michael O'Mara Books Ltd*

9 Lion Yard, Tremadoc Road, London SW4 7NQ
tel 020-7720 8643
email enquiries@mombooks.com
email publicity@mombooks.com
website www.mombooks.com
Facebook www.facebook.com/MichaelOMaraBooks/
Twitter @OMaraBooks
Chairman Michael O'Mara, *Managing Director* Lesley O'Mara, *Senior Editorial Director* Louise Dixon, *Deputy Managing Director & Publisher (Buster Books)* Philippa Wingate

General non-fiction: biography, autobiography, history, lifestyle, humour. See website for submission guidelines. Founded 1985.

Buster Books

website www.mombooks.com/buster
Facebook www.facebook.com/BusterBooks
Twitter @BusterBooks
Instagram @Buster_Books

Activity, novelty, picture books, fiction and non-fiction for children.

LOM ART

website www.mombooks.com/lom/

Activity, arts & crafts, reference, picture books for children (page 165).

Omnibus Press/Wise Music Group

14–15 Berners Street, London W1T 3LJ
tel 020-7612 7400
email omniinfo@musicsales.co.uk
website www.omnibuspress.com
Chief Editor David Barraclough

Music biographies, autobiographies, illustrated books, books about music. Founded 1976.

On Stream Publications

Currabaha, Cloghroe, Blarney, Cork T23 EW08, Republic of Ireland

tel +353 (0)21 4385798
email info@onstream.ie
website www.onstream.ie
Owner Rosalind Crowley

Cookery, wine, travel, human interest non-fiction, local history, academic and practical books. Contract publishing. Founded 1986.

Oneworld Publications*‡

10 Bloomsbury Street, London WC1B 3SR
tel 020-7307 8900
email info@oneworld-publications.com
website www.oneworld-publications.com
Facebook www.facebook.com/oneworldpublications
Twitter @OneworldNews
Directors & Publishers Juliet Mabey, Novin Dootscar

Fiction and general non-fiction: current affairs, politics, history, Middle East, business, popular science, philosophy, psychology, green issues, world religions and Islamic studies; literary fiction, plus fiction that sits at the intersection of the literary and commercial, with a focus on diverse voices and great stories; children and young adult fiction and upmarket crime/suspense novels, as well as fiction in translation. No unsolicited MSS; email or send non-fiction proposals via website. Founded 1986.

Open Gate Press*

51 Achilles Road, London NW6 1DZ
tel 020-7431 4391
email books@opengatepress.co.uk

Incorporating Centaur Press, founded 1954. Psychoanalysis, philosophy, social sciences, religion, animal welfare, the environment. Founded 1988.

Open University Press – see McGraw-Hill Education

Orbit – see Little, Brown Book Group

Orchard Books – see Hachette Children's Group

Orenda Books

16 Carson Road, West Dulwich, London SE21 8HU
tel 020-8355 4643
email info@orendabooks.co.uk
website www.orendabooks.co.uk
Facebook www.facebook.com/orendabooks
Twitter @OrendaBooks
Instagram @orendabooks
Publisher Karen Sullivan, *Editor* West Camel, *Digital & Publishing Assistant* Cole Sullivan

An independent publisher specialising in literary fiction, with a heavy emphasis on crime thrillers, about half in translation. Shortlisted for IPG Best Newcomer Award 2015 and 2016. Winner of the CWA Dagger for Best Crime & Mystery Publisher of 2020. Authors include Ragnar Jonasson, Eva Bjorg

Aegisdottir, Matt Wesolowski, Lilja Sigurdardottir, Gunnar Staalesen, Agnes Ravatn, Johana Gustawsson, Will Carver, Antti Tuomainen, Doug Johnstone, Thomas Enger, Louise Beech, Michael J. Malone and Helen FitzGerald. Founded 2014.

The Orion Publishing Group Ltd*
Carmelite House, 50 Victoria Embankment,
London EC4Y 0DZ
tel 020-3122 6444
website www.orionbooks.co.uk
Directors Arnaud Nourry (chairman), David Shelley (chief executive), Katie Espiner (managing director)

No unsolicited MSS; approach in writing in first instance. Part of Hachette UK (page 154). Founded 1992.

Gollancz
Contact Gillian Redfearn
Science fiction, fantasy and horror.

Orion Fiction
Contact Harriet Bourton
Trade and mass market fiction.

Orion Spring
Contact Pippa Wright
Wellbeing, health and lifestyle non-fiction.

Seven Dials
Contact Vicky Eribo
Trade and mass market: cookery, memoir and autobiography, gift and humour, personal development and parenting, lifestyle, diet and fitness.

Trapeze
Contact Anna Valentine
Trade and mass market fiction: reading group, crime and thriller, women's fiction; trade and mass market non-fiction: memoir and autobiography, lifestyle, gift and humour, popular psychology and entertainment.

W&N
Contact Ellie Freedman
Literary fiction, translated fiction; non-fiction: history, memoir, ideas-driven books, popular science, biography, sport, business, diaries and narrative non-fiction

White Rabbit
Contact Ellie Freedman
Music: memoir, history, fiction, limited editions.

Osprey Publishing Ltd
Kemp House, Chawley Park, Cumnor Hill,
Oxford OX2 9PH
tel (01865) 727022
email info@ospreypublishing.com
website www.ospreypublishing.com

Publishes illustrated military history. Over 1,600 titles in print on a wide range of military history subjects

from ancient times to the modern day. Owned by Bloomsbury Publishing Plc (page 136). Founded 1968.

Oversteps Books Ltd
6 Halwell House, South Pool, Nr Kingsbridge,
Devon TQ7 2RX
tel (01548) 531969
email alwynmarriage@overstepsbooks.com
website www.overstepsbooks.com
Director/Managing Editor Dr Alwyn Marriage

Poetry. Please check the submissions information on our website to ascertain whether we are accepting submissions at present. If the submissions window is open, you may email six poems that have either won major competitions, or been published, giving details of the competitions or magazines in which they appeared, the dates or issue numbers and the email addresses of the editors. Founded 1992.

Peter Owen Publishers
Conway Hall, 25 Red Lion Square,
London WC1R 4RL
tel 020-8350 1775
email crispin@peterowen.com
website www.peterowen.com
Facebook www.facebook.com/peter.owen.publishers
Twitter @PeterOwenPubs
Directors Nick Kent (managing), Antonia Owen (editorial)

Backlist includes ten Nobel Prize winners. Arts, belles lettres, biography and memoir, literary fiction, general non-fiction, history, theatre, philosophy and entertainment. Do not send typescripts or samples without first emailing the Editorial Department with your proposal even if an established novelist. No mass-market genre fiction, short stories or poetry; first novels rarely published. Founded 1951.

Oxford University Press*
Great Clarendon Street, Oxford OX2 6DP
tel (01865) 556767
email enquiry@oup.com
website www.oup.com
Ceo Nigel Portwood, *Global Academic Business Managing Director* David Clark, *Managing Director, Oxford Education* Fathima Dada, *Managing Director, ELT Division* Peter Marshall

Archaeology, architecture, art, belles lettres, bibles, bibliography, children's books (fiction, non-fiction, picture), commerce, current affairs, dictionaries, drama, economics, educational (foundation, primary, secondary, technical, university), encyclopedias, ELT, electronic publishing, essays, foreign language learning, general history, hymn and service books, journals, law, medical, music, oriental, philosophy, political economy, prayer books, reference, science, sociology, theology and religion; educational software; *Grove Dictionaries of Music & Art*. Trade paperbacks published under the imprint of Oxford Paperbacks. Founded 1478.

P8tech

6 Woodside, Churnet View Road, Oakamoor, Staffs. ST10 3AE
tel (01538) 703591
email info@P8tech.com
website www.P8tech.com
Publisher James Lumsden-Cook

IT and computer-related titles, including books on video games and artificial intelligence. Specialises in Oracle and Java-related titles. Founded 2012.

Palgrave Macmillan – see Springer Nature Group Ltd

Pan Macmillan

6 Briset St, Farringdon, London EC1M 5NR
tel 020-7014 6000
email publicity@macmillan.com
website www.panmacmillan.com
Managing Director Anthony Forbes Watson

Novels, literary, crime, thrillers, romance, science fiction, fantasy and horror. Autobiography, biography, business, gift books, health and beauty, history, humour, natural history, travel, philosophy, politics, world affairs, theatre, film, gardening, cookery, popular reference. No unsolicited MSS except through Macmillan New Writing. Founded 1843.

Bello

Imprint devoted to reviving classic and out-of-print titles as ebooks and print-on-demand.

Bluebird

Pan Macmillan's wellness and lifestyle imprint, publishing the very latest in diet, popular psychology, self-help as well as career and business, parenting and inspirational memoir.

Campbell

Early learning, pop-up, novelty, board books for the preschool market.

Macmillan

Hardback imprint of fiction and non-fiction.

Macmillan Children's Books

Imprint for Macmillan's children's books composed of two divisions: Macmillan Under 6s and Macmillan Over 6s.

Macmillan Collector's Library

Publishes classics in high-quality binding, from Jane Austen to Charles Dickens, from Sir Arthur Conan Doyle to F. Scott Fitzgerald. Also non-fiction, poetry, short stories and children's books.

Mantle

Focuses on publishing high-quality writing and storytelling with a broad appeal. It features the best in a vast range of genres, from crime, thriller, general and literary fiction to narrative non-fiction and memoir.

Pan

Commercial fiction.

Picador

Literary international fiction, non-fiction and poetry published in hardback and paperback. Founded 1972.

Two Hoots

Illustrated children's books.

Tor

Science fiction and fantasy published in hardback and paperback.

Parthian Books

The Old Surgery, Napier St, Cardigan SA43 1ED
tel 07890 968246
email info@parthianbooks.com
website www.parthianbooks.com
Facebook www.facebook.com/parthianbooks/
Twitter @parthianbooks
Publishing Editor Susie Wildsmith

Independent publisher of poetry, literary fiction, creative non-fiction and translations that reflect a diverse and contemporary Wales and wider world. Prizes won by authors include the Dylan Thomas Prize, the Betty Trask, the Wales Book of the Year, the Orange Futures Award, the Rhys Davies Prize, the Journey Prize, the Edge Hill Readers' Award and the Stonewall Award. Please see website for submission opportunities and guidelines on how to submit MSS. Founded 1993.

Patrician Press

12 Lushington Road, Manningtree CO11 1EF
tel 07968 288651
email patricia@patricianpress.com
website www.patricianpress.com
Facebook www.facebook.com/patricianpress,
www.facebook.com/puddingpress
Twitter @PatricianCom
Publisher Patricia Borlenghi

Paperback and digital publisher of fiction and poetry. Publisher of children's books under the imprint Pudding Press. Founded 2012.

Pavilion Children's Books‡

43 Great Ormond Street, London WC1N 3HZ
tel 020-7462 1500
website www.pavilionbooks.com
Publisher Neil Dunnicliffe

Children's books: from picture books to illustrated fiction, non-fiction and classics. Part of Pavilion

Books Company Ltd. Submissions via an agent only. Successes include *The Story of the Little Mole* by Werner Holzwarth, *The King Who Banned the Dark* by Emily Haworth-Booth, *The Journey Home* by Fran Preston-Gannon and *War Game* by Michael Foreman. Founded 2005.

Peachpit Press – see Pearson UK

Pearson UK*
Edinburgh Gate, Harlow, Essex CM20 2JE
tel 0845 313 6666
email schools@longman.co.uk
website www.pearsoned.co.uk
Ceo Andy Bird

Consists of five divisions: Virtual Learning, Higher Education, English Language Learning, Workforce Skills and Asessment and Qualifications. Founded 1998.

Allyn & Bacon
Higher education, humanities, social sciences.

BBC Active
Learning resources for children and adults.

Cisco Press
Cisco-systems authorised publisher. Material for networking students and professionals.

Benjamin Cummings
Higher education, science.

FT Prentice Hall
Business for higher education and professional.

Harcourt
Educational resources for teachers and learners at primary, secondary and vocational level. Provides a range of published resources, teachers' support and pupil and student material in all core subjects for all ages. Imprints: Ginn, Heinemann, Payne-Gallway, Raintree, Rigby.

Longman
Education for higher education, schools, ELT.

New Riders
Graphics and design.

Peachpit Press
Internet and general computing.

Penguin Longman
ELT.

Prentice Hall
Academic and reference textbooks.

QUE Publishing
Computing.

SAMS Publishing
Professional computing.

Wharton
Business.

York Notes
Literature guides for students.

Peepal Tree Press*
17 King's Ave, Burley, Leeds LS6 1QS
tel 0113 245 1703
email contact@peepaltreepress.com
website www.peepaltreepress.com
Facebook www.facebook.com/peepaltreepress
Twitter @peepaltreepress

Leading independent publisher of BAME, in particular Caribbean and Black British writing, publishing around 20 books a year. Has published over 300 titles, and are committed to keeping most of them in print. The list features new writers and established voices. In 2009 the Caribbean Modern Classics Series was launched, which restores to print essential books from the past with new introductions. Founded 1985.

Pelagic Publishing‡
PO Box 874, Exeter EX3 9BR
tel 0845 468 0415
email info@pelagicpublishing.com
website www.pelagicpublishing.com
Facebook www.facebook.com/pelagicpublishing
Twitter @pelagicpublish
Publisher Nigel Massen

Academic and trade books on natural history, ecology, conservation, data analysis and environmental science. Founded 2010.

Pen & Sword Books Ltd
47 Church Street, Barnsley, South Yorkshire S70 2AS
tel (01226) 734555 / (01226) 734222
email editorialoffice@pen-and-sword.co.uk
website www.pen-and-sword.co.uk
Managing Director Charles Hewitt, *Publisher* Jonathan Wright, *Commissioning Editors* Henry Wilson, Phil Sidnell, Rupert Harding, Claire Hopkins, Michael Leventhal, Julian Mannering, Rob Gardiner, Martin Mace

Military history, aviation history, naval and maritime, general history, local history, family history, transport, social history, archaeology, health and lifestyle, natural history, gardening, space, science, sports. Imprints: Leo Cooper, Frontline Books, White Owl, Pen & Sword Aviation, Pen & Sword Naval & Maritime, Remember When, Frontline, Seaforth, Pen & Sword Digital, Pen & Sword Transport, Pen & Sword Discovery, Pen & Sword Social History, Pen & Sword Archaeology. Founded 1990.

Penguin General*
20 Vauxhall Bridge Road, London SW1V 2SA
tel 020-7010 3000

Books

Managing Director Joanna Prior

No unsolicited MSS or synopses. Part of Penguin Random House UK (below). Penguin Books founded 1855.

Penguin Business
Publishing Director Martina O'Sullivan

Fig Tree
Publishing Director Helen Garnons-Williams
Fiction and general non-fiction.

Hamish Hamilton
Publishing Director Simon Prosser
Fiction, biography and memoirs, current affairs, history, literature, politics, travel.

Penguin Life
Publishing Director Emily Robertson
Health, lifestyle, wellbeing, trends.

Viking
Publishing Directors Mary Mount & Daniel Crewe, *Publisher,* Katy Loftus, *Editorial Director* Tom Killingbeck
Fiction, biography and memoirs, current affairs, popular culture, sport, history, literature, politics, travel.

Penguin Longman – see Pearson UK

Penguin Press*
20 Vauxhall Bridge Road, London SW1V 2SA
tel 020-7010 3000
Managing Director Stefan McGrath

Comprises the flagship non-fiction imprint Allen Lane, the innovative Particular Books, the newly revitalised Pelican imprint, new poetry and the world of Penguin Classics. Numerous international and UK bestsellers, 28 Nobel Prize winners and seven Pulitzer Prize winners. No unsolicited MSS. Founded in 1997.

Allen Lane
Non-fiction: history, science, politics, economics, philosophy, psychology, language and current affairs.

Particular Books
Non-fiction: history, science, politics, travel, biography and memoirs, current affairs and photograph.

Pelican
Non-fiction: history, science, politics, economics and finance, philosophy, psychology, language and current affairs.

Penguin Classics
Classic literature, poetry, drama, biography and memoir.

Penguin Random House Children's UK*
One Embassy Gardens, 8 Viaduct Gardens, London SW11 7AY
tel 020-7139 3000
website www.penguin.co.uk
Managing Director Francesca Dow, *Publishing Director* Amanda Punter (Puffin Fiction, non-fiction, licensing & picture books), *Publishers* Ruth Knowles (Puffin Fiction, non-fiction & licensing), Ben Horslen (Puffin Fiction), Lara Hancock (Puffin, picture books, partnerships & illustrated non-fiction), *Publishing Director* Shannon Cullen (Ladybird trade, licensing & education), *Publisher* Kate Heald (Ladybird education & international), *Licensing & Consumer Products Director* Susan Bolsover (Penguin Ventures), *Art Director* Anna Billson

Part of Penguin Random House UK (see below). Children's paperback and hardback books: wide range of picture books, board books, gift books and novelties; fiction; non-fiction, popular culture, digital and audio. Preschool illustrated developmental books for 0–6 years; licensed brands; children's classic publishing and merchandising properties. No unsolicited MSS or original artwork or text. Imprints: Ladybird, Puffin, Penguin. Founded 2013.

Penguin Random House UK*
One Embassy Gardens, 8 Viaduct Gardens, London SW11 7AY
tel 020-7840 8400
website www.penguin.co.uk
Directors Markus Dohle (Ceo Penguin Random House), Tom Weldon (Ceo Penguin Random House UK)

Penguin Random House UK publishing divisions: Penguin General (page 175), Cornerstone (page 142), Ebury Press (page 146), Michael Joseph (page 161), Penguin Random House Children's UK (above), Penguin Press (above), Penguin Random House UK Audio (page 225), Transworld (page 190) and Vintage (page 192). Founded 1927.

Pergamon – see Elsevier (Clinical Solutions)

Persephone Books
59 Lamb's Conduit Street, London WC1N 3NB
tel 020-7242 9292
email info@persephonebooks.co.uk
website www.persephonebooks.co.uk
Managing Director Nicola Beauman

Reprints of forgotten classics by 20th-century women writers with prefaces by contemporary writers. Founded 1999.

Phaidon Press Ltd
Regent's Wharf, All Saints Street, London N1 9PA
tel 020-7843 1000
email enquiries@phaidon.com
website www.phaidon.com
Editorial Director Tracey Smith

Visual arts, lifestyle, culture and food. Founded 1923.

Philip's – see Octopus Publishing Group

Piatkus – see Little, Brown Book Group

Piccadilly Press
Victoria House, Bloomsbury Squre,
London WC1B 4DA
tel 020-3770 8888
email hello@piccadillypress.co.uk
website www.piccadillypress.co.uk,
www.bonnierbooks.co.uk
Twitter @PiccadillyPress
Executive Publisher Emma Matthewson *Senior Commissioning Editor* Felicity Alexander

Publishes fun, family-orientated stories in any genre. Titles can be standalone stories or part of a series and use design and illustration that is integral to the content when appropriate. Publishes in hardback, paperback, ebook and audio formats. Publishes books primarily for readers aged 5–12 years. Piccadilly Press is an imprint of Bonnier Books UK (page 137). Founded 1983.

Pimlico – see Vintage

Pimpernel Press Ltd
22 Marylands Road, London W9 2DY
tel 07775 917202 / 07976 047767
email jo@pimpernelpress.com
website www.pimpernelpress.com
Facebook www.facebook.com/Pimpernel-Press-Ltd-456736654504879
Twitter @PimpernelPress
Instagram @Pimpernel_Press
Publisher Jo Christian, *Managing Director* Gail Lynch, *Commissioning Editor* Anna Sanderson, *Publicity* Emma O'Bryen

Independent publisher of books on gardens and gardening; art; design; architecture and places; practical books on arts and crafts; gift books and stationery. Founded 2015.

The Playwrights Publishing Company
70 Nottingham Road, Burton Joyce,
Notts. NG14 5AL
email playwrightspublishingco@yahoo.com
website www.playwrightspublishing.com
Proprietors Liz Breeze, Tony Breeze

Looking for previously performed one-act and full-length dramas to be published on the net; serious pieces or comedies, mixed cast or single sex (no musicals). Reading fee charged; email for submission guidelines. Founded 1990.

Plexus Publishing Ltd
26 Dafforne Road, London SW17 8TZ
tel 020-767 7126
email plexus@plexusuk.demon.co.uk
website www.plexusbooks.com
Editorial Director Sandra Wake

Film, music, biography, popular culture, fashion, gift. Imprint: Eel Pie. Founded 1973.

Pluto Press‡
345 Archway Road, London N6 5AA
tel 020-8348 2724
email pluto@plutobooks.com
website www.plutobooks.com
Twitter @plutopress
Editorial Director David Castle, *Commissioning Editor* David Shulman, *Editor* Neda Tehrani

An independent, political publisher of radical non-fiction. Politics, economics, history, Black studies, gender and sexuality, international relations. Founded 1969.

Policy Press – see Bristol University Press/ Policy Press

Policy Studies Institute (PSI)
35 Marylebone Road, London NW1 5LS
tel 020-7911 7500
email psi-admin@psi.org.uk
website www.psi.org.uk
Twitter @PSI_London

Economic, cultural, social and environmental policy, political institutions, social sciences. Founded 1931.

Politico's Publishing – see Methuen & Co Ltd

Polity Press‡
65 Bridge Street, Cambridge CB2 1UR
tel (01223) 324315
website www.politybooks.com

Social and political theory, politics, sociology, history, media and cultural studies, philosophy, literary theory, feminism, human geography, anthropology. Founded 1983.

Polygon – see Birlinn Ltd

Poolbeg Press Ltd
123 Grange Hill, Baldoyle, Dublin D13 N529,
Republic of Ireland
tel +353 (0)18 063825
email info@poolbeg.com
website www.poolbeg.com
Directors Kieran Devlin, Barbara Devlin

Popular fiction, non-fiction, current affairs. Imprint: Poolbeg. Founded 1976.

Portland Press Ltd*
email editorial@portlandpress.com
website www.portlandpress.com
Twitter @PPPublishing
Director of Publishing Malavika Legge

Owned by the Biochemical Society, Portland Press is embedded in the global scientific community and dedicated to promoting and sharing research for the advancement of science. Founded 1990.

Books

Prestel Publishing Ltd
16–18 Berners Street, London W1T 3LN
tel 020-7323 5004
email ahansen@prestel-uk.co.uk
website www.prestel.com
Facebook www.facebook.com/PrestelPublishing
Twitter @Prestel_pub
Instagram @prestel_publishing
Vice-President Andrew Hansen

Including pop culture, major exhibition catalogues and artist retrospectives. Publishes in the following genres: art, architecture, photography, fashion, lifestyle, design and children's books. Book submissions: submissions@prestel-uk.co.uk. Press enquiries: publicity@prestel-uk.co.uk. Founded 1924.

Princeton University Press – Europe*‡
6 Oxford Street, Woodstock, Oxon OX20 1TR
tel (01993) 814500
email claire_williams@press.princeton.edu
website www.press.princeton.edu
Facebook www.facebook.com/
PrincetonUniversityPress
Twitter @PrincetonUPress
Editor for Humanities Ben Tate, *Publisher for Sciences* Ingrid Gnerlich

Academic publishing for the social sciences, humanities and sciences. The European office of Princeton University Press. Founded 1999.

Profile Books Ltd*
29 Cloth Fair, London EC1A 7JQ
tel 020-7841 6300
email info@profilebooks.com
website www.profilebooks.com
Managing Director Helen Conford, *Associate Publisher* Rebecca Gray, *Editorial Deputy* Hannah Westland, *Publishing Directors* Cecily Gayford, Ed Lake

General non-fiction: history, biography, current affairs, popular science, politics, business, management, humour. Also publishers of *The Economist* books. No unsolicited MSS. Founded 1996.

Profile Editions
Publisher Peter Jones

Custom arts, heritage and company histories. No unsolicited MSS.

Serpent's Tail
email info@serpentstail.com
website www.serpentstail.com
Publisher Hannah Westland, *Associate Publisher* Rebecca Gray

Fiction and non-fiction; literary and non-mainstream work and work in translation. No unsolicited MSS. Founded 1986.

Souvenir Press
email info@profilebooks.com
Associate Publisher Rebecca Gray

Fiction and non-fiction; literary and non-mainstream work and work in translation. No unsolicited MSS.

Tuskar Rock
email info@profilebooks.com
Publisher Hannah Westland, *Associate Publisher* Rebecca Gray

Fiction and non-fiction; literary and non-mainstream work and work in translation. No unsolicited MSS.

Psychology Press
27 Church Road, Hove, East Sussex BN3 2FA
tel 020-7017 6000
website www.routledge.com/psychology

Psychology textbooks and monographs. Imprint of Taylor and Francis Group (page 189).

Psychology Press
website www.routledge.com/psychology

Routledge
website www.routledgementalhealth.com

Puffin – see Penguin Random House Children's UK

Pure Indigo Ltd
Publishing Department, 17 The Herons, Cottenham, Cambridge CB24 8XX
tel 07981 395258
email ashley.martin@pureindigo.co.uk
website www.pureindigo.co.uk/publishing
Commissioning Editor Ashley Martin

Adult books: submissions currently open for romance novels only. Children's books: Pure Indigo Publishing develops innovative junior series fiction. All titles are available in both print and digital formats and are distributed internationally with select partners. The company also develops software products that complement the product range. The junior series fiction titles are developed in-house and on occasion authors and illustrators are commissioned to complete project-based work. For consideration for commissions visit the website. Founded 2005.

Pushkin Press*
71–75 Shelton Street, London WC2H 9JQ
email books@pushkinpress.com
website www.pushkinpress.com
Facebook www.facebook.com/PushkinPress
Twitter @pushkinpress
Publisher Adam Freudenheim, *Deputy Publisher* Laura Macaulay, *Commissioning Editor* Daniel Seton

Having first rediscovered European classics of the 20th century, Pushkin now publishes novels, essays, memoirs, children's books (Pushkin's Children's) and everything from timeless classics to the urgent and contemporary. Imprints: Pushkin Press, Pushkin Children's Books, Pushkin Vertigo, ONE. Founded 1997.

Pyramid – see Octopus Publishing Group

Quadrille
5th and 6th Floors, Pentagon House,
52–54 Southwark Street, London SE1 1UN
tel 020-7601 7500
email enquiries@quadrille.co.uk
website www.hardiegrant.com/quadrille
Publishing Director Sarah Lavelle

Imprint of Hardie Grant UK (page 154). Non-fiction, categories include: food and drink, gift and humour, craft, wellness, lifestyle and pop culture. Founded 1994.

Quantum – see W. Foulsham & Co. Ltd

Quartet Books (The Women's Press)
27 Goodge Street, London W1T 2LD
tel 020-7636 3992
email info@quartetbooks.co.uk
website www.quartetbooks.co.uk

Independent publisher with a tradition of pursuing an alternative to mainstream. Books by women in the areas of literary and crime fiction, biography and autobiography, health, culture, politics, handbooks, literary criticism, psychology and self-help, the arts. Accepting submissions; see website for guidelines. Founded 1978.

The Quarto Group, Inc.
The Old Brewery, 6 Blundell Street, London N7 9BH
tel 020-7700 9000 / 020-7700 8066
email dan.rosenberg@quarto.com
website www.quarto.com
Chairman Peter Read

A global illustrated book publisher and distribution group. It is composed of three publishing divisions: Quarto International Co-editions Group; Quarto Publishing Group USA; and Quarto Publishing Group UK (below); plus Books & Gifts Direct (a direct seller of books and gifts in Australia and New Zealand) and Regent Publishing Services, a specialist print services company based in Hong Kong. Quarto International Co-editions Group creates illustrated books that are licensed and printed for third-party publishers for publication under their own imprints in over 30 languages around the world. The division includes: Quarto Publishing, Quarto Children's Books, Happy Yak (page 154), Qu:id, Quintessence, Quintet Publishing, QED, RotoVision, Marshall Editions, Marshall Editions Children's Books, Harvard Common Press, Small World Creations, Fine Wine Editions, Apple Press, Global Book Publishing, Iqon Editions Ltd, Ivy Press and Quantum Publishing. Book categories: practical art and crafts, graphic arts, lifestyle, reference, food and drink, gardening, popular culture. Founded 1976.

Quarto Group Publishing UK‡
6 Blundell Street, London N7 9BH
tel 020-7700 9000
website www.QuartoKnows.com
Ceo David Graham

General adult non-fiction, illustrated and non-illustrated: history, sport, entertainment, biography, autobiography, military, gardening, architecture, environment, interiors, photography, art, walking and climbing, design and landscape, gift, interiors, food and drink, lifestyle and craft. Founded 1976.

QUE Publishing – see Pearson UK

Quercus Publishing Plc
Carmelite House, 50 Victoria Embankment, London EC4Y 0DZ
website www.quercusbooks.co.uk
Managing Director Jon Butler

Fiction and non-fiction. Imprints include Quercus, Riverrun, Maclehose Press and Jo Fletcher Books. Founded 2005.

Quiller Publishing Ltd
Wykey House, Wykey, Shrewsbury SY4 1JA
tel (01939) 261616
email info@quillerbooks.com
website www.quillerpublishing.com
Managing Director Andrew Johnston

Founded 2001.

Chameleon Publishing
Custom and bespoke books for corporate clients and individuals on all subjects.

Kenilworth Press
Equestrian (riding, training, dressage, eventing, show jumping, driving, polo). Publisher of BHS official publications and exclusive distributor for *The Pony Club*.

Quiller
High-quality hardback and paperback biographies, history, food and drink, sport, art and photography, humour and gift books and specialist practical books on country pursuits including dog training, fishing, shooting, stalking, gamekeeping, deer, falconry, natural history and gardening.

Ransom Publishing Ltd*
Unit 7, Brocklands Farm, West Meon GU32 1JN
tel (01730) 829091
email ransom@ransom.co.uk
website www.ransom.co.uk
Directors Jenny Ertle (managing), Steve Rickard (creative)

Children's fiction and non-fiction, phonics and school reading programmes, and books for children and adults who are reluctant or struggling readers.

Books

Range covers high interest age/low reading age titles, quick reads and reading schemes. Series include *Alpha Stars, Reading Stars Phonics and Book Bands, Reading Stars Plus, Neutron Stars, Pick Your Path, Tales from the Pitch, Boffin Boy, PIG* and *Dark Man.* Not accepting any unsolicited submissions at this time. Founded 1995.

Raven Books
Publishes fiction for children aged 8–14 years.

Rat's Tales Ltd
Burnt House Farm, Old Fosse Road, Bath BA2 2SS
tel (07838) 460905
email enquiries@ratstales.co.uk
website www.ratstales.co.uk
Facebook www.facebook.com/ratstalespublishing
Twitter @rats_tales
Director Tatiana Polivoda

Publishes illustrated crime and thrillers that don't conform to genre standards. Founded 2016.

Reaktion Books
Unit 32 Waterside, 44–48 Wharf Road,
London N1 7UX
tel 020-7253 4965
email info@reaktionbooks.co.uk
website www.reaktionbooks.co.uk
Facebook www.facebook.com/ReaktionBooks
Twitter @reaktionbooks
Instagram @reaktionbooks
Publisher Michael R. Leaman

An independent publisher of stimulating and beautifully designed non-fiction books. Publishes around 100 new titles each year in fields including art, architecture, design and photography, popular science, food, history, nature, film, music, philosophy, economics and politics. Founded 1985.

Red Rattle Books
23 Thornfield Road, Thornton, Liverpool L23 9XY
tel 07505 700515
email editor@redrattlebooks.co.uk
website www.redrattlebooks.co.uk
Editor Howard Jackson

An independent, family-run publishing company. Produces and promotes four to six books each year. Specialises in crime and horror. Accepts submissions from young writers and unpublished authors. Full MS or samples can be submitted at editor@redrattlebooks.co.uk. Titles accepted for publication are published in paperback and Kindle editions. Fees for MS are negotiated with authors or their agents. If MS not accepted, explanation given as to why not suitable and future advice offered. Founded 2012.

Red Dog Press‡
email hello@reddogpress.co.uk
website www.reddogpress.co.uk
Facebook www.facebook.com/reddogpressuk

Twitter @reddogtweets
Director Sean Coleman

Independent publishers based in Oxfordshire. Publishes crime and thrillers. Founded 2018.

Renard Press Ltd‡
Kemp House, 152–160 City Road,
London EC1V 2NX
tel 020-8050 2928
email info@renardpress.com
website www.renardpress.com
Facebook www.facebook.com/therenardpress
Twitter @renardpress
Instagram @renardpress
Publisher Will Dady

Renard Press is a small independent press that predominantly publishes classics, supplemented by a small handful of contemporary literary fiction, non-fiction, poetry and theatre titles. Founded 2020.

Repeater Books
email enquiries@watkinsmedia.org
website https://repeaterbooks.com/
Facebook www.facebook.com/repeaterbooks
Twitter @RepeaterBooks
Publisher Tariq Goddard

Publishes books expressing new and radical ideas: counter-culture fiction and non-fiction, politics and current affairs. Part of Watkins Media (page 193). Founded 2014.

Revenge Ink
6D Lowick Close, Hazel Grove, Stockport SK7 5ED
email amita@revengeink.com
website www.revengeink.com
Editor Gopal Mukerjee (with Amita Mukerjee),
Director Amita Mukerjee

Founded by siblings Gopal and Amita Mukerjee, the company publishes adult fiction (all kinds) and prefers unsolicited, first-time novelists or established writers seeking a new outlet for edgier material. Considers poetry if presented in an original, creative manner. Currently publishes approx. seven titles a year. Does not publish children's fiction or non-fiction titles such as cookbooks, gardens and how-to books. The company is aiming to create a non-fiction imprint for new research in philosophy, history, critical theory and political analysis. Submission guidelines can be found on the website. By email, preferably, send short sample and query first. Founded 2007.

Rider – see Ebury Publishing

George Ronald
3 Rosecroft Lane, Oaklands, Welwyn,
Herts. AL6 0UB
tel (01438) 716062

email sales@grbooks.com
website www.grbooks.com
Managers E. Leith, M. Hofman

Religion, specialising in the Bahá'í Faith.
Founded 1939.

Roundhouse Group‡

Unit B, 18 Marine Gardens, Brighton BN2 1AH
tel (01273) 603717
email info@roundhousegroup.co.uk
website www.roundhousegroup.co.uk

Non-fiction adult and children's books. No
unsolicited MSS. Founded 1991.

Route

PO Box 167, Pontefract, West Yorkshire WF8 4WW
tel (01977) 793442
email info@route-online.com
website www.route-online.com
Twitter @Route_News
Contact Ian Daley, Isabel Galán

Memoir, cultural non-fiction and biography, with a
strong interest in music books. Occasional fiction.
Unsolicited MSS discouraged, book proposals in first
instance. Founded 2000.

Routledge – see Taylor & Francis Group

Rowman & Littlefield*‡

6 Tinworth Street, London SE11 5AL
tel 020-3111 1080
email info@rowmaninternational.com
website www.rowmaninternational.com
Facebook www.facebook.com/
RowmanLittlefieldInternational
Twitter @rowmaninternat
Sales & Marketing Director Ben Glover, *Directors*
James Lyons, Oliver Gadsby

One of the largest independent publishers in North
America, with a London team publishing in
philosophy, politics and international relations,
cultural studies, anthropology and geography, with a
particular focus on the interdisciplinary nature of
these academic subject areas. Founded 2013.

Royal Collection Trust

Stable Yard House, St James's Palace,
London SW1A 1JR
tel 020-7839 1377
website www.rct.uk/collection/themes/search/
publication
Head of Publishing Kate Owen, *Publishing Editor* Polly
Atkinson

Creates books, exhibition catalogues, guides and
children's books to celebrate the royal residences and
works of art found within them. Also produces
scholarly catalogues raisonnés, which demonstrate
the highest standards of academic research.
Worldwide distribution by University of Chicago

Press in the USA and Canada, and by Thames &
Hudson Ltd throughout the rest of the world.
Contact details on website. Founded 1993.

Royal National Institute of Blind People (RNIB)*

Midgate House, Midgate, Peterborough,
Cambs. PE1 1TN
tel 0303 123 9999
email helpline@rnib.org.uk
website www.rnib.org.uk

Magazines, catalogues and books for blind and
partially sighted people, to support daily living,
leisure, learning and employment reading needs.
Includes the charity's flagship Talking Books service,
providing more than 30,000 fiction and non-fiction
titles to borrow free of charge for adults and children
with sight loss and commercial audio production
services. Produced in braille, audio, large/clear print
and email. Founded 1868.

Ruby Tuesday Books Ltd‡

6 Newlands Road, Tunbridge Wells, Kent TN4 9AT
tel (01892) 557767
email shan@rubytuesdaybooks.com
website www.rubytuesdaybooks.com
Twitter @RubyTuesdaybk
Publisher & Author Ruth Owen, *All Sales & Rights*
Shan White

Publisher of children's books. Founded 2008.

Ryland Peters & Small‡

20–21 Jockey's Fields, London WC1R 4BW
tel 020-7025 2200
website https://rylandpeters.com/pages/makeetc
Managing Director David Peters

Illustrated books: food, drink, home and garden,
babies and children, gift. Founded 1995.

Cico Books

tel 020-7025 2280
email mail@cicobooks.co.uk
website www.cicobooks.co.uk

Lifestyle and interiors; crafts; and mind, body &
spirit; health. Founded 1999.

Saffron Books

PO Box 13666, London SW14 8WF
tel 020-8392 1122
email saffronbooks@eapgroup.com
website www.saffronbooks.com, www.sajidrizvi.net,
www.eapgroup.com
Twitter @saffronbooks, @Safnetoffers, @sajidrizvi,
@eapgroupnews
Founding Publisher & Editor-in-Chief Sajid Rizvi

Art criticism and art history, history, African and
Asian architecture, African and Asian art and
archaeology, Central Asian studies, East Asia journal
monographs, African and Asian linguistics including

the *Saffron Korean Linguistics* Series, general non-fiction and fiction including the *Absolute Fiction* series. European Crossroads Monographs. Founded 1989.

SAGE Publishing*‡

1 Oliver's Yard, 55 City Road, London EC1Y 1SP
tel 020-7324 8500
email info@sagepub.co.uk
website www.sagepublishing.com
Facebook www.facebook.com/SAGEPublishing
Twitter @SAGE_Publishing
Instagram @sage_publishing

Independent company that disseminates journals, books and library products for the educational, scholarly and professional markets. Founded 1965.

St. David's Press

PO Box 733, Cardiff CF14 7ZY
tel 029-2021 8187
email post@st-davids-press.wales
website www.st-davids-press.wales
Facebook www.facebook.com/StDavidsPress
Twitter @StDavidsPress
Instagram @StDavidsPress

Trade imprint of the Welsh Academic Press (page 194). Sport and popular culture including: rugby, football, cricket, boxing, horse racing, cycling, walking, music. Also general Welsh and Celtic interest. Distributed by Welsh Books Council (Wales), Ingram Publishing Services (UK & Europe), IPG (North America & Rest of World). Founded 2002.

St Pauls Publishing

St Pauls, Westminster Cathedral, Morpeth Terrace, Victoria, London SW1P 1EP
tel 020-828 5582
email editor@stpauls.org.uk
website www.stpauls.org.uk

Theology, ethics, spirituality, biography, education, general books of Roman Catholic and Christian interest. Founded 1948.

Salariya Book Company Ltd*‡

Book House, 25 Marlborough Place,
Brighton BN1 1UB
tel (01273) 603306
email salariya@salariya.com
website www.salariya.com,
www.youwouldntwantto.be
Facebook www.facebook.com/theSalariya
Twitter @theSalariya
Instagram @salariyabooks
Managing Director David Salariya

Children's art, picture books, fiction and non-fiction. Imprints: Book House, Scribblers, Scribo. No unsolicited MSS. Founded 1989.

Salt Publishing‡

12 Norwich Road, Cromer, Norfolk NR27 0AX
tel (01263) 511011
email sales@saltpublishing.com
website www.saltpublishing.com
Twitter @saltpublishing
Publishing Director Christopher Hamilton-Emery, Jennifer Hamilton-Emery

Award-winning independent publisher of fiction. Home of the annual Best British Short Story anthology. Founded 1999.

SAMS Publishing – see Pearson UK

Sandstone Press Ltd*‡

PO Box 41, Muir of Ord, Highland IV6 7YX
tel (01463) 567 080
email info@sandstonepress.com
website www.sandstonepress.com
Facebook www.facebook.com/SandstonePress
Twitter @sandstonepress
Directors Robert Davidson, Moira Forsyth, Eric Macleod, *Advisor to the Board* Jenny Todd

Publishers of quality fiction and non-fiction for adults. Literary fiction, speculative fiction, crime novels and thrillers. Literary biography, memoir, sport, natural world, outdoor and Scottish interest, other general narrative non-fiction. Submissions of non-fiction are accepted year-round, unsolicited fiction only during designated windows. Full submission guidelines are available at https://sandstonepress.com/contact/submissions. Founded 2002.

Sapere Books‡

20 Windermere Drive, Leeds LS17 7UZ
website www.saperebooks.com
Facebook www.facebook.com/saperebooks
Twitter @SapereBooks
Instagram @SapereBooks
Editorial Director & Co-Founder Amy Durant,
Marketing Director & Co-Founder Caoimhe O'Brien,
Operations Director & Co-Founder Richard Simpson

Sapere Books is a digital-first publisher, specialising in historical fiction, crime fiction, romantic fiction, thrillers, women's fiction and history. As well as signing new books and authors, we also reissue a lot of previously out-of-print titles. Founded 2015.

Saqi Books*

26 Westbourne Grove, London W2 5RH
tel 020-7221 9347
email lynn@saqibooks.com
website www.saqibooks.com
Facebook www.facebook.com/SaqiBooks
Twitter @SaqiBooks
Instagram @SaqiBooks
Publisher Lynn Gaspard, *Senior Editor & Rights Manager* Elizabeth Briggs, *Editorial & Marketing Assistant* Hassan Ali, *Sales Manager* Ashley Biles

Independent publisher of global trade and academic books on the Middle East and North Africa. Successes include *The Crusades through Arab Eyes* by Amin Maalouf, *Beyond the Veil* by Fatema Mernissi, *Black Britain: A Photographic History* by Paul Gilroy and *The White Family* by Maggie Gee. Also translates new and classic Arabic literature, including works by Naguib Mahfouz, Mahmoud Darwish, Adonis and Nawal El Saadawi. Awards: IPG Diversity Award 2013, British Book Industry Award for Diversity in Literature 2009 and the Arab British Culture and Society award 2008. Founded 1983.

Westbourne Press

Publishes alternative and progressive non-fiction works.

Telegram

Publishes new and classic international writing.

Saraband*

Digital World Centre, 1 Lowry Plaza, The Quays, Salford M50 3UB
email hermes@saraband.net
website www.saraband.net
Facebook www.facebook.com/sarabandbks
Twitter @sarabandbooks
Instagram @sarabandbooks

Publishes nature and environmental writing, memoir, history and local interest non-fiction (especially on Scotland and the North of England), as well as literary and historical fiction, occasionally in translation. Under the Contraband imprint, literary noir and dark fiction. Founded 1994.

Saunders – see Elsevier (Clinical Solutions)

Sawday's

Merchants House, Wapping Road, Bristol BS1 4RW
tel 0117 204 7810
email hello@sawdays.co.uk
website www.sawdays.co.uk
Facebook www.facebook.com/sawdays
Twitter @sawdays
Founder Alastair Sawday, *Managing Director* Mike Bevens

Independent travel. Founded 1994.

Sceptre – see Hodder & Stoughton

Schofield & Sims Ltd*

Unit 11, The Piano Works,
113–117 Farringdon Road, London EC1R 3BX
tel (01484) 607080
email editorial@schofieldandsims.co.uk
website www.schofieldandsims.co.uk

Educational: nursery, infants, primary; posters. Founded 1901.

Scholastic Ltd*

Euston House, 24 Eversholt Street,
London NW1 1DB
tel 020-7756 7756
website www.scholastic.co.uk
Chairman M.R. Robinson, *Co-Group Managing Directors* Catherine Bell, Steve Thompson

Children's fiction, non-fiction and picture books, education resources for primary schools. Owned by Scholastic Inc. Founded 1964.

Chicken House
See page 140.

Scholastic Children's Books
tel 020-7756 7761
email submissions@scholastic.co.uk
website www.scholastic.co.uk
Twitter @scholasticuk
Fiction Publisher Lauren Fortune, *Non-Fiction Publisher & Licensing* Elizabeth Scoggins, *Editorial Director, Illustrated Books* Felicity Osborne

Activity books, novelty books, picture books, fiction for 5–12 years, teenage fiction, series fiction and film/TV tie-ins. Imprints: Scholastic, Alison Green Books, Klutz. No unsolicited MSS. Unsolicited illustrations are accepted, but do not send any original artwork as it will not be returned.

Scholastic Educational Resources
Book End, Range Road, Witney, Oxon OX29 0YD
tel (01993) 893456
Publishing Director Robin Hunt

Professional books, classroom materials, home learning books and online resources for primary teachers, and GCSE support material.

Science Museum Group

Publishing Department, Enterprises, Exhibition Road, London SW7 2DD
tel 0870 870 4771
website www.sciencemuseum.org.uk

Science, technology, engineering, medicine and mathematics. Adult science non-fiction and children's science non-fiction (licensed). Museum guides.

SCM Press – see Hymns Ancient and Modern Ltd

Scotland Street Press*

email info@scotlandstreetpress.com
website www.scotlandstreetpress.com
Facebook www.facebook.com/ScotStreetPress
Twitter @ScotlandStreetPress
Instagram @scotlandstreetpress
Founder & Ceo Jean Findlay

Committed to developing a publishing house that helps promote Scotland as a distinctive creative voice in the world. For submissions please see submissions

page: https://scotlandstreetpress.com/work-with-us/.
Only accepts postal submissions. Allow three to six
months for a response. Founded 2014.

Scribe*

2 John Street, London WC1N 2ES
tel 020-3405-4218
email info@scribepub.co.uk
website https://scribepublications.co.uk/
Facebook www.facebook.com/ScribePublicationsUk
Twitter @scribeukbooks
Instagram @scribe_uk

Scribe Publications is an award-winning independent
publisher, with offices in Australia, the UK and the
USA. It publishes a range of fiction and non-fiction
for the general reader, and has a picture books
imprint called Scribble. In the UK, it is a member of
the Independent Alliance. Does not accept
submissions. Founded 1976.

Scripture Union

Trinity House, Opal Court, Fox Milne,
Milton Keynes MK15 0DF
tel (01908) 856000
email hello@scriptureunion.org.uk
website www.scriptureunion.org.uk
Director of Ministry Development (Publishing) Terry
Clutterham

Christian books and bible reading materials for
people of all ages; educational and worship resources
for churches; children's fiction and non-fiction; adult
non-fiction. Founded 1867.

Search Press Ltd‡

Wellwood, North Farm Road, Tunbridge Wells,
Kent TN2 3DR
tel (01892) 510850
email searchpress@searchpress.com
website www.searchpress.com
Directors Martin de la Bédoyère (managing), Caroline
de la Bédoyère (rights), David Grant (sales &
marketing), Katie French (editorial)

Arts, crafts, leisure. Founded 1970.

SelfMadeHero‡

139 Pancras Road, London NW1 1UN
tel 020-7383 5157
email info@selfmadehero.com
website www.selfmadehero.com
Twitter @selfmadehero
Instagram @selfmadehero
Managing Director & Publisher Emma Hayley

The UK's leading independent publisher of graphic
novels and visual narratives. The list of award-
winning fiction and non-fiction graphic novels spans
literary fiction, biography, classic adaptation, science
fiction, horror, crime and humour. Founded 2007.

September Publishing

tel 020-3637 0116
email info@septemberpublishing.org
website www.septemberpublishing.org
Facebook www.facebook.com/SeptemberPublishing
Twitter @septemberbooks
Instagram @septemberpublishing
Publisher Hannah MacDonald

Non-fiction publishers of illustrated and narrative
adult books, including memoir and biography, travel,
humour, art, politics. Founded 2013.

Seren‡

Suite 6, 4 Derwen Road, Bridgend CF31 1LH
tel (01656) 663018
email seren@serenbooks.com
website www.serenbooks.com
Publisher Mick Felton

Poetry, fiction, literary criticism, biography, art –
mostly with relevance to Wales. Founded 1981.

Severn House Publishers

Eardley House, 4 Uxbridge Street, London W8 7SY
tel 020-3011-0525
email sales@severnhouse.com
website www.severnhouse.com
Facebook www.facebook.com/severnhouse
Twitter @severnhouse

Hardback, paperback, ebook and large print adult
fiction for the library market: mysteries, thrillers,
detective, horror, romance. No unsolicited MSS;
submissions via literary agents. Imprints: Crème de la
Crime. Founded 1974.

Shearsman Books‡

PO Box 4239, Swindon SN3 9FN
tel 0330 1136514
email editor@shearsman.com
website www.shearsman.com
Facebook www.facebook.com/Shearsman-Books-
272720625528/
Twitter @ShearsmanBooks
Contact Tony Frazer

Contemporary poetry in English and in translation.

Sheldon Press – see John Murray Press

Sheldrake Press

PO Box 74852, London SW12 2DX
tel 020-8675 1767
email enquiries@sheldrakepress.co.uk
website www.sheldrakepress.co.uk
Twitter @SheldrakePress
Publisher J.S. Rigge

History and art, travel, architecture, cookery, music;
humour; stationery. Founded 1979.

Shepheard-Walwyn (Publishers) Ltd

107 Parkway House, Sheen Lane, London SW14 8LS
tel 020-8241 5927

email books@shepheard-walwyn.co.uk
website www.shepheard-walwyn.co.uk,
www.ethicaleconomics.org.uk
Director M. Lombardo, *Marketing Manager* T. Kerrigan

Independent publishing company. History, biography, political economy, perennial philosophy; illustrated gift books; Scottish interest. Founded 1971.

Shire Books
Kemp House, Chawley Park, Cumnor Hill, Oxford OX2 9PH
tel (01865) 727022
email shire@bloomsbury.com
website www.bloomsbury.com/uk/non-fiction/history/heritage
website www.bloomsbury.com/bloomsburybespoke/

Non-fiction publisher of history, heritage and nostalgia. Also provides publishing services to organisations such as museums, schools, universities and charities. Acquired by Bloomsbury Publishing Plc in 2014 (page 136).

Short Books Ltd
Unit 316, ScreenWorks, 22 Highbury Grove, London N5 2ER
tel 020-7833 9429
email info@shortbooks.co.uk
website www.shortbooks.co.uk
Facebook www.facebook.com/Short-Books/
Twitter @shortbooksuk
Editorial Directors Rebecca Nicolson, Aurea Carpenter

Non-fiction. No unsolicited MSS. Founded 2000.

Sigma Press
Stobart House, Pontyclerc, Penybanc Road, Ammanford, Carmarthenshire SA18 3HP
tel (01269) 593100
email info@sigmapress.co.uk
website www.sigmapress.co.uk
Directors Nigel Evans, Jane Evans

Leisure: country walking, cycling, regional heritage, ecology, folklore; biographies. Founded 1979.

Silvertail Books
email editor@silvertailbooks.com
website www.silvertailbooks.com
Twitter @silvertailbooks
Publisher Humfrey Hunter

Independent publisher which specialises in commercial fiction and non-fiction. Especially likes publishing newsworthy non-fiction and fiction which tells captivating stories well. Pays high royalties on both ebook and print editions. No children's books. Founded 2012.

Simon & Schuster UK Ltd*
222 Gray's Inn Road, London WC1X 8HB
tel 020-7316 1900

email enquiries@simonandschuster.co.uk
website www.simonandschuster.co.uk
Facebook www.facebook.com/simonschusterUK
Twitter @simonschusteruk
Directors Ian Chapman (Ceo), Suzanne Baboneau (managing, adult), Rachel Denwood (publishing, children's), Clare Hey (publishing, fiction), Ian Marshall (deputy publishing, non-fiction), Ali Dougal (publishing, children's), Dominic Brendon (publishing, audio)

Adult non-fiction (history, biography, current affairs, science, self-help, political, popular culture, sports books, memoirs and illustrated titles). Adult fiction (mass-market, literary fiction, historical fiction, commercial women's fiction, general fiction). Children's and young adult fiction, picture books, novelty, pop-up and licensed character. Simon & Schuster Audioworks Fiction, non-fiction and business. Founded 1986.

Siri Scientific Press
Arrow Mill, Queensway, Castleton, Rochdale OL11 2YW
tel 07770 796913
email books@siriscientificpress.co.uk
website www.siriscientificpress.co.uk
Facebook www.facebook.com/Siri-Scientific-Press-134567006626977
Publishing Consultant David Penney

Publisher of specialist natural history books including academic monographs, compiled edited volumes, photographic atlases, field guides and more general works. Specialise in works on entomology, arachnology and palaeontology, but will also consider other topics. Happy to hear directly from potential new authors. Founded 2008.

Colin Smythe Ltd
38 Mill Lane, Gerrards Cross, Bucks. SL9 8BA
tel (01753) 886000
email info@colinsmythe.co.uk
website www.colinsmythe.co.uk
Directors Colin Smythe (managing & editorial), Leslie Hayward, Ann Saddlemyer

Irish biography, phaleristics, heraldry, Irish literature and literary criticism, Irish history. Other imprints: Dolmen Press, Van Duren Publishers. Founded 1966.

Snowbooks Ltd
55 North Street, Thame, Oxon OX9 3BH
email emma@snowbooks.com
website www.snowbooks.com
Directors Emma Barnes (managing), Rob Jones

Genre fiction: steampunk, fantasy, science fiction and horror. General non-fiction. See website for submission guidelines. No postal submissions or calls please. Founded 2003.

Books

Society for Promoting Christian Knowledge

36 Causton Street, London SW1P 4ST
tel 020-7592 3900
email spck@spck.org.uk
website www.spckpublishing.co.uk
Director of Publishing Sam Richardson

Founded 1698.

IVP

Theology and academic, commentaries, biblical studies, contemporary culture.

Marylebone House

Commercial and literary fiction.

SPCK

Theology, bibles, history, contemporary culture, children's picture books and fiction, biography, liturgy, prayer, spirituality, biblical studies, educational resources, social and ethical issues, mission, gospel and culture. Imprint: Form.

Society of Genealogists Enterprises Ltd

14 Charterhouse Buildings, Goswell Road, London EC1M 7BA
tel 020-7251 8799
email sales@sog.org.uk
website www.sog.org.uk
Contact Else Churchill

Local and family history books, software and magazines plus extensive library facilities. Founded 1999.

Somerville Press Ltd

Dromore, Bantry, Co. Cork P75 NY22, Republic of Ireland
tel +353 (0)28 32873
email somervillepress@gmail.com
website www.somervillepress.com
Directors Andrew Russell, Jane Russell

Irish interest: fiction and non-fiction. Founded 2008.

Southwater – see Anness Publishing

Sparsile Books*

PO Box 2861, Glasgow G61 9ED
tel 07938 864485
email enquiries@sparsilebooks.com
website www.sparsilebooks.com
Facebook www.facebook.com/sparsilebooks
Twitter @sparsileb
Publisher James Campbell

Small independent publisher based in Scotland. Publishes books that stand out from the crowd rather than genre-specific. Contemporary fiction and non-fiction, literary fiction, biography, history, general science, memoir. Open periodically for submissions, check website for details. Founded 2018.

SPCK – see Society for Promoting Christian Knowledge

Speechmark Publishing Ltd

2nd Floor, 5 Thomas More Square, London E1W 1WY
tel 0845 450 6414
email info@speechmark.net
website www.routledge.com/collections/11164

Education, health, social care. An imprint of the Taylor and Francis Group. Founded 1990.

Sphere – see Little, Brown Book Group

Spon – see Taylor & Francis Group

SportBooks Ltd

9 St Aubyns Place, York YO24 1EQ
tel (01904) 613475
email info@sportsbooks.ltd.uk
website www.sportsbooks.ltd.uk
Directors Randall Northam, Veronica Northam

Sport. Imprints: SportsBooks, BMM. Not currently accepting submissions. Founded 1995.

Springer Nature Group Ltd*

4 Crinan Street, London N1 9XW
tel 020-7833 4000
website www.springernature.com
Chief Executive Frank Vrancken Peeters

Global and progressive research, educational and professional publisher, home to a number of trusted and respected brands, including Springer, Nature Portfolio, BMC, Palgrave Macmillan, Scientific American and Palgrave Macmillan. Committed to advancing discovery through innovative products and service. Founded 1842. Springer Nature is a leading academic book publisher, the largest Open Access publisher of primary research, and publisher of approx 3,000 journals.

BMC

website www.springer.com
Springer is a leading global scientific, technical and medical portfolio, providing researchers in academia, scientific institutions and corporate R&D departments with quality content through innovative information, products and services. Springer has one of the strongest STM and HSS ebook collections and archives, as well as a comprehensive range of hybrid and Open Access journals and books under the SpringerOpen imprint.

Macmillan Education

email info@macmillaneducation.com
website www.macmillaneducation.com
Language Learning division focuses mainly on ELT content but also produces resources in Spanish and Chinese for certain regions. The Schools Curriculum

Division creates materials to fit with the curricula of countries around the world and the Higher Education division publishes content at university level across a wide range of subject areas.

Palgrave Macmillan
website www.palgrave.com

Palgrave Macmillan is a world-class publisher of books and journals with more than 175 years' experience in the Humanities and Social Sciences. Publishes award-winning research – monographs and journals – which changes the world across the humanities, social sciences and business for academics, professionals and librarians.

Spruce – see Octopus Publishing Group

SRL Publishing Ltd
email admin@srlpublishing.co.uk
website www.srlpublishing.co.uk
Facebook www.facebook.com/srlpublishing
Twitter @srlpublishing
Instagram @srlpublishing

Award-winning, climate-positive publisher. Titles range from young adult, new adult, contemporary fiction and crime/thriller to non-fiction including autobiographies and cooking books. Founded 2014.

Stacey Publishing Ltd
14 Great College Street, London SW1P 3RX
tel 020-7221 7166
email info@stacey-international.co.uk
website www.stacey-international.co.uk
Founder Tom Stacey

Topical issues for *Independent Minds* series, encyclopaedic books on regions and countries, Islamic and Arab subjects, world affairs, children's books, art, travel, belles lettres, biography. Imprints: Capuchin Classics, Gorilla Guides. Founded 1974.

Capuchin Classics
email info@capuchin-classics.co.uk
website www.capuchin-classics.co.uk
Enduring literary fiction, mostly 19th and 20th century. Founded 2008.

Stainer & Bell Ltd
PO Box 110, Victoria House, 23 Gruneisen Road, London N3 1DZ
tel 020-8343 3303
email post@stainer.co.uk
website www.stainer.co.uk
Directors Antony Kearns (managing), Nicholas Williams (publishing), Mandy Aknai (production & secretary)

Books on music, religious communication. Founded 1907.

Stenlake Publishing Ltd
54–58 Mill Square, Catrine, Ayrshire KA5 6RD
tel (01290) 552233
email sales@stenlake.co.uk
website www.stenlake.co.uk
Managing Director Richard Stenlake

Local history, Scottish language and literature especially Robert Burns, studio pottery, bee keeping, railways, transport, aviation, canals and mining covering Wales, Scotland, England, Northern Ireland, Isle of Man, Republic of Ireland and Zambia. Founded 1987.

Alloway Publishing
website www.allowaypublishing.co.uk

Oakwood Press
Specialising in railway and transport books. Founded 1931.

Stewed Rhubarb Press
email charlie@stewedrhubarb.org
website https://stewedrhubarb.org
Facebook www.facebook.com/stewedrhubarb
Twitter @stewedbooks
Publishing Director Duncan Lockerbie, *Head of Publicity & Marketing* Charlie Roy, *Editor* Beth Cochrane

Publisher of poetry anthologies and pamphlets. Founded 2018.

Stonewood Press
email stonewoodpress@gmail.com
website www.stonewoodpress.co.uk
Facebook www.facebook.com/stonewoodpress
Twitter @stonewoodpress
Publisher & Production Editor Martin Parker

Stonewood Press is a small independent publisher dedicated to promoting new writing with an emphasis on contemporary short stories and poetry. Stonewood aims to publish challenging and high-quality writing in English without the pressures associated with mainstream publishing. Please see website for up-to-date submission guidelines and submission window. Founded 2011.

Stripes – see Little Tiger Group

Studio Press
Victoria House, Bloomsbury Squre, London WC1B 4DA
tel 020-3770 8888
email hello@studiopressbooks.co.uk
website www.studiopressbooks.co.uk, www.bonnierbooks.co.uk
Twitter @StudioPress
Executive Director Helen Wicks

Studio Press presents trend, brand and celebrity-led publishing to both the children's and adult market in the UK and seeks to capture current trends in social media, gaming, film, art and design. With a diverse range of formats, including fiction, non-fiction, picture books, gift, humour and activity, Studio Press

Books

showcases a range of books with key licensing partners including Disney, The Beano and high-profile authors including Rochelle Humes and Professor Steve Peters. Studio Press is an imprint of Bonnier Books UK (page 137). Founded 2015.

Summersdale Publishers Ltd

46 West Street, Chichester, West Sussex PO19 1RP
tel (01243) 771107
email submissions@summersdale.com
website www.summersdale.com
Editorial Director Claire Plimmer

Popular non-fiction, humour and gift books, travel writing and health and wellbeing. See website for guidelines. Imprints include Summersdale, Vie and Huck & Pucker. Acquired by Octopus in 2017 (page 171). Founded 1990.

Sunflower Books

PO Box 36160, London SW7 3WS
tel 020-7589 2377
email info@sunflowerbooks.co.uk
website www.sunflowerbooks.co.uk
Director P.A. Underwood

Travel guidebooks. Founded 1973.

Sussex Academic Press

PO Box 139, Eastbourne, East Sussex BN24 9BP
tel (01323) 479220
email edit@sussex-academic.com
website www.sussex-academic.com
Editorial Director Anthony Grahame

Founded 1994.

The Alpha Press

International relations, Middle Eastern studies, cultural studies, theatre, philosophy, literary criticism, biography, history (special emphasis on Spanish and Portuguese history, Huguenot history), First Nations studies, Latin American studies, theology and religion, Jewish and Israel studies (history, Holocaust, culture, biography), Asian studies, Art history. The Alpha Press imprint offers a wide range of popular books covering art history, religion, biography, history, sport, conservation, sociology and astrology.

Sweet & Maxwell

Thomson Reuters, PO Box 123,
Hebden Bridge HX7 9BF
tel 020-7393 7000
website www.sweetandmaxwell.co.uk

Law. Part of Thomson Reuters Ltd. Founded 1799; incorporated 1889.

Sweet Cherry Publishing*‡

Unit 36, Vulcan Business Complex, Vulcan Road, Leicester LE5 3EF
tel 0116 253 6796
email info@sweetcherrypublishing.com
website www.sweetcherrypublishing.com
Facebook www.facebook.com/sweetcherrypublishing
Twitter @sweetcherrypub
Director A. Thadha

Children's series fiction specialist. Children's picture books, novelty books, gift books, board books, educational books and fiction series for all ages. Also welcomes young adult novels, trilogies or longer series. Likes to publish a set of books as a box set or in a slipcase. See website for submission guidelines. Founded 2011.

Tango Books Ltd

PO Box 32595, London W4 5YD
tel 020-8996 9970
email sales@tangobooks.co.uk
website www.tangobooks.co.uk
Directors Sheri Safran, David Fielder

Children's fiction and non-fiction novelty books, including pop-up, touch-and-feel and cloth books. No unsolicited MSS. Founded 2004.

Tarquin Publications

Suite 74, 17 Holywell Hill, St Albans AL1 1DT
tel (01727) 833866
email info@tarquinbooks.com
website www.tarquinbooks.com

Mathematics and mathematical models, puzzles, codes and logic; paper cutting, paper engineering and pop-up books for intelligent children. No unsolicited MSS; send suggestion or synopsis in first instance. Founded 1970.

Taschen UK Ltd

5th Floor, 1 Heathcock Court, 415 Strand, London WC2R 0NS
tel 020-7845 8585
email contact-uk@taschen.com
website www.taschen.com
Ceo Hans-Peter Kübler

Publishers of art, anthropology and aphrodisia. Founded 1980.

Tate Enterprises Ltd

The Lodge, Millbank, London SW1P 4RG
tel 020-7887 8869
email submissions@tate.org.uk
website www.tate.org.uk/publishing
Publishing Director Tom Avery, *Merchandise Director* Rosey Blackmore, *Sales & Marketing Manager* Maxx Lundie, *Marketing & Publicity Coordinator* Tom Cornelius

Publishers for Tate in London, Liverpool and St Ives. Exhibition catalogues, art books, children's books and merchandise. Also product development, picture library and licensing. Founded 1911.

I.B. Tauris*

50 Bedford Square, London WC1B 3DP
tel 020-7631 5600
website www.ibtauris.com
Facebook www.facebook.com/ibtauris
Twitter @ibtauris
Editorial Director David Avital

An imprint of Bloomsbury Publishing Plc (page 136). Middle East studies. Founded 1983.

Taylor & Francis Group*

2 and 4 Park Square, Milton Park, Abingdon, Oxon OX14 4RN
tel 020-7017 6000
email enquiries@taylorandfrancis.com
website https://taylorandfrancis.com/
Ceo Annie Callanan, *Managing Director (Taylor & Francis Books)* Jeremy North

Academic and reference books. Founded 1988.

Ashgate Publishing

Art history, music, history, social work, politics and literary studies.

CRC Press

website www.crcpress.com
Science: physics, mathematics, chemistry, electronics, natural history, pharmacology and drug metabolism, toxicology, technology, history of science, ergonomics, production engineering, remote sensing, geographic information systems, engineering.

Focal Press

Animation, audio, film, gaming, music technology, photography and theatre.

Garland Science

website www.garlandscience.com
Bioscience textbooks and scholarly works.

Gower Books

Specialist business and management books and resources.

Psychology Press

See page 178.

Routledge

website www.routledge.com
Addiction, anthropology, archaeology, Asian studies, business, classical studies, counselling, criminology, development and environment, dictionaries, economics, education, geography, health, history, Japanese studies, law, library science, language, linguistics, literary criticism, media and culture, nursing, performance studies, philosophy, politics, psychiatry, psychology, reference, social administration, social studies/sociology and women's studies. Also directories, international relations, reference and yearbooks.

Spon Press

website www.sponpress.com
Architecture, civil engineering, construction, leisure and recreation management, sports science.

Templar Books

Victoria House, Bloomsbury Square, London WC1B 4DA
tel 020-3770 8888
email hello@templarco.co.uk
website www.templarco.co.uk, www.bonnierbooks.co.uk
Twitter @templarbooks
Editorial Director Katie Haworth

Publishes illustrated children's non-fiction, picture books, fiction, gift and novelty books for all ages. Templar is an imprint of Bonnier Books UK (page 137). Founded 1978.

Thames & Hudson Ltd*‡

181A High Holborn, London WC1V 7QX
tel 020-7845 5000
email sales@thameshudson.co.uk
website www.thamesandhudson.com
Facebook www.facebook.com/thamesandhudson
Twitter @thamesandhudson
Ceo & Publisher Sophy Thompson

Illustrated non-fiction for an international audience (adults and children), specialising in art and art history, photography, design, travel, history, archaeology, architecture, fashion and contemporary media. Founded 1949.

Think Books

50 Kings Lane, Northampton NN2 6QL
tel 020-3771 7200
email info@thinkpublishing.co.uk
website www.thinkpublishing.co.uk
Founder & Chairman Ian McAuliffe, *Director* Tilly McAuliffe

Specialises in books on the outdoors, gardening and wildlife. Publishes with the Wildlife Trusts, the Royal Horticultural Society and the Campaign to Protect Rural England and others. Founded 2005.

Thinkwell Books

7 Winsford Crescent, Little Bispham, Thornton-Cleveleys, Lancashire, FY5 1PS
tel 07940 933159
email thinkwellbooksuk@gmail.com
website https://thinkwellbooks.org
Managing Editors Jeff Weston & Patricia Khan

Literary fiction, academic works, sports journalism and commercial fiction. New authors and unsolicited MS welcome. See website for details regarding submissions. Founded 2019.

Thistle Publishing

36 Great Smith Street, London SW1P 3BU
tel 020-7222 7574

email david@thistlepublishing.co.uk
website www.thistlepublishing.co.uk
Facebook www.facebook.com/ThistlePublishing
Twitter @ThistleBooks
Publishers David Haviland, Andrew Lownie

Winner of The People's Book Prize 2017. Shortlisted for the Somerset Maugham Award 2018. Longlisted for the Not the Booker Prize 2018. Trade publisher of quality fiction and non-fiction. Accepts unsolicited submissions, please send three chapters and a synopsis by email. Founded 1996.

Thomson Reuters – Round Hall*

Third Floor, 12/13 Exchange Place, International Financial Services Centre, Dublin 1, Republic of Ireland
tel +353 (0)16 024808
website www.roundhall.ie
Directors M. Keen, M. McCann, M. Bolton

Law. Part of Thomson Reuters.

Three Hares Publishing

2 Dukes Avenue, London N10 2PT
tel 020-8245 8989
email submissions@threeharespublishing.com
website www.threeharespublishing.com
Facebook www.facebook.com/threeharespublishing
Twitter @threeharesbooks
Publisher Yasmin Standen

Submissions are open and will consider fiction/non-fiction, novels, children's books, young adult and short stories. No picture books. Publishes a number of established authors and first-time authors. Interested in discovering new talent. Visit website for submission guidelines – email submissions only. Founded 2014.

Tiny Owl Publishing Ltd

6 Hatfield road, London W4 1AF
email info@tinyowl.co.uk
website www.tinyowl.co.uk
Facebook www.facebook.com/tinyowlpublishing
Twitter @TinyOwl_Books
Publisher Delaram Ghanimifard

An independent publisher of global children's literature. Publishes high-quality picture books for children 3–11 years. Aims to promote diversity and human rights values. Founded 2015.

Titan Books

144 Southwark Street, London SE1 0UP
tel 020-7620 0200
website www.titanbooks.com
Divisional Head Laura Price

Publisher of original fiction under the genres science fiction, fantasy, horror, crime and young adult crossover. Licensed fiction and non-fiction covering TV, film and gaming, including licensed works for *Mass Effect, Star Trek, Alien, Planet of the Apes,*

Assassin's Creed and *DC Universe*. Graphic novel collections include The Simpsons and Modesty Blaise. No children's proposals. All fiction submissions must come from an agent. Division of Titan Publishing Group Ltd. Founded 1981.

Tolley – see LexisNexis

Tramp Press DAC

email info@tramppress.com
email submissions@tramppress.com
website www.tramppress.com
Facebook www.facebook.com/tramppress
Twitter @TrampPress
Founding Publishers Lisa Coen, Sarah Davis-Goff, *UK Head of Publishing* Laura Waddell

Publishes award-winning fiction and narrative non-fiction including authors Sara Baume, Mike McCormack and Emilie Pine. Tramp Press is a feminist press.

Transworld Publishers

One Embassy Gardens, 8 Viaduct Gardens, London SW11 7BW
tel 020-7840-8400
website www.penguin.co.uk/company/publishers/transworld.html
Publisher Bill Scott-Kerr, *Publishing Directors* Susanna Wadeson (non-fiction), Sarah Adams (fiction)

Imprints include: Bantam Press, Doubleday (UK), Black Swan, Corgi, Transworld Ireland. Part of Penguin Random House UK (page 176). No unsolicited MSS accepted. Non-fiction: autobiography, biography, business, current affairs, crime, health and diet, history, humour, memoir, military, music, natural history, personal development and self-help, science, travel and adventure. Fiction: commercial: crime, thrillers, contemporary, historical and saga fiction. Science fiction, horror and fantasy. Literary and book club fiction. Founded 1950.

Doubleday (UK)
Publishing Director Kirsty Dunseath
Literary fiction and non-fiction.

Transworld Commercial Fiction
Publishing Director Frankie Gray

Transworld Ireland
Editorial Director Fiona Murphy

Trigger Publishing

The Foundation Centre, Navigation House, 48 Millgate, Notts. NG24 4TS
tel (01636) 600825
email enquiries@triggerpublishing.com
website www.triggerpublishing.com
Facebook www.facebook.com/triggerpub
Twitter @triggerpub
Instagram @triggerpub

Publisher Jo Lal, *Managing Editor* Rachel Gregory

Independent publisher dedicated to mental health welfare, publishes for both adults and children. Founded 2016.

The Inspirational Series

Publishes titles related to mental illness by new and established authors.

Pulling the Trigger

User-friendly recovery and support books to help sufferers recover from mental health and wellbeing issues. Promotes an innovative style of cognitive behaviour therapy (CBT) with a compassion-focused approach.

Upside Down Books

Trade-focused children's imprint of fiction and non-fiction picture books, activity and middle grade that focus on mental health issues while also promoting positivity, emotional intelligence and wellness for children.

Troika*

Troika Books Ltd, Well House, Green Lane, Ardleigh, Colchester, Essex CO7 7PD
tel (01206) 233333
email info@troikabooks.com
website www.troikabooks.com
Publisher Martin West, Rights Petula Chaplin, *Publicity, Marketing & Editorial* Roy Johnson, *Sales* Saltway Global

Publishes picture books, poetry and fiction for all ages, with an emphasis on quality, accessibility and diversity. Recent fiction authors include Savita Kalhan, John Harvey and Miriam Halahmy. Poetry list includes Zaro Weil, Jay Hulme, Sue Hardy-Dawson, Shauna Darling Robertson, Hilda Offen, Coral Rumble, Neal Zetter, Roger Stevens, Dom Conlon, Ed Boxall and Brian Moses. Founded 2012.

Troubador Publishing Ltd‡

9 Priory Business Park, Wistow Road, Kibworth, Leics. LE8 0RX
tel 0116 279 2299
email books@troubador.co.uk
website www.troubador.co.uk
Facebook www.facebook.com/matadorbooks
Twitter @matadorbooks
Directors Jeremy Thompson (managing), Jane Rowland (operations)

Troubador runs several subsidiaries in the author services sector, and is organiser of the annual Self Publishing Conference. Subsidiaries include the Matador self-publishing imprint; The Book Guild Ltd partnership/mainstream imprint; and Indie-Go services for independent authors. Founded 1996.

TSO (The Stationery Office)

St Crispins, Duke Street, Norwich NR3 1PD
tel (01603) 696876

email customer.services@tso.co.uk
website www.tsoshop.co.uk

Publishing and information management services: business, directories, pharmaceutical, professional, reference, *Learning to Drive*.

Two Rivers Press Ltd‡

7 Denmark Road, Reading, Berks. RG1 5PA
tel 0118 987 1452
email tworiverspress@gmail.com
website www.tworiverspress.com
Facebook www.facebook.com/tworiverspress
Twitter @TwoRiversPress
Publisher Anne Nolan, *Editorial Director* Sally Mortimore, *Poetry Editor* Peter Robinson, *Creative Director* Nadja Guggi, *Design & Illustration* Sally Castle, Martin Andrews, *Marketing* Karen Mosman

Champions Reading and surrounding area's heritage and culture through contemporary and classic poetry, biography, art and local interest books. Publishes an international Botanical Art Portfolios series. Founded 1994.

Ulric Publishing

PO Box 55, Church Stretton, Shrops. SY6 6WR
tel (01694) 781354
email info@ulricpublishing.com
website www.ulricpublishing.com
Directors Ulric Woodhams, Elizabeth Oakes

Non-fiction military and motoring history. Licensing, bespoke bindings and publishing services. No unsolicited MSS. Visitors by appointment. Founded 1992.

Ulverscroft Ltd

The Green, Bradgate Road, Anstey, Leicester LE7 7FU
tel 0116 236 4325
email m.merrill@ulverscroft.co.uk
website www.ulverscroft.co.uk
Facebook www.facebook.com/ulverscroft
Twitter @UlverscroftUK

Offers a wide variety of large print titles in hardback and paperback format as well as unabridged audiobooks, many of which are written by the world's favourite authors and includes award-winning titles. Acquired Oakhill Publishing and its range of unabridged audiobooks April 2018. Founded 1964.

Unicorn Publishing Group LLP‡

Corporate HQ 5 Newburgh Street, London W1F 7RG
tel 01273 812066
email ian@unicornpublishing.org
Studio Charleston Studio, Meadow Business Centre, Lewes, BN8 5RW
website www.unicornpublishing.org
Twitter @UnicornPubGroup
Directors Lord Strathcarron, Lucy Duckworth, Simon Perks, Ryan Gearing

Leading independent publisher with three distinct imprints: Unicorn, specialising in the visual arts and cultural history; Uniform, specialising in military history; and Universe, specialising in historical fiction. Unicorn Sales & Distribution is UPG's and its client publishers' marketing arm, with worldwide sales and distribution operations. Submissions welcomed, see website for guidance. Founded 1985.

Merlin Unwin Books Ltd‡

Palmers House, 7 Corve Street, Ludlow, Shrops. SY8 1DB
tel (01584) 877456
email books@merlinunwin.co.uk
website www.merlinunwin.co.uk
Chairman Merlin Unwin, *Managing Director* Karen McCall

Countryside books. Founded 1990.

Usborne Publishing Ltd‡

Usborne House, 83–85 Saffron Hill, London EC1N 8RT
tel 020-7430 2800
email mail@usborne.co.uk
website www.usborne.com
Directors Peter Usborne, Jenny Tyler (editorial), Andrea Parsons, Nicola Usborne

An independent, family business which creates engaging, innovative books for curious children of all ages. Including baby, preschool, novelty, activity, non-fiction and fiction. Looking for high-quality imaginative children's fiction. No unsolicited MSS. Founded 1973.

Vallentine Mitchell‡

Catalyst House, 720 Centennial Court, Centennial Park, Elstree WD6 3SY
tel 020-8292 5637
email info@vmbooks.com (general)
email editor@vmbooks.com (submissions)
website www.vmbooks.com
Directors Stewart Cass, A.E. Cass, H.J. Cass

International publisher of books of Jewish interest, both for the scholar and general reader. Subjects published include Jewish history, culture and heritage, modern Jewish thought, Holocaust studies, Middle East studies, biography and reference. Founded 1949.

Valley Press

Woodend, The Crescent, Scarborough YO11 2PW
email hello@valleypressuk.com
website www.valleypressuk.com
Facebook www.facebook.com/valleypress
Twitter @valleypress
Publisher Jamie McGarry

Publishes poetry (collections, pamphlets and anthologies); fiction (novels and short stories); graphic novels; and non-fiction (memoirs, travel writing, journalism, music, art and more). Founded 2008.

Velocity Press

8 Holt Close, Chislehurst BR7 5FH
tel 07595 823298
email info@velocitypress.uk
website https://velocitypress.uk
Facebook www.facebook.com/velocitypressbooks
Twitter @PressVelocity
Pinterest @knowledgemag
Director Colin Steven

Velocity Press publishes electronic music and club culture non-fiction and fiction. It aims to create a catalogue that feels like a trusted record label in its integrity and vision and deliver exciting stories to serious electronic music fans who enjoy good literature. Founded 2019.

Veritas Publications†

Veritas House, 7–8 Lower Abbey Street, Dublin D01 W2C2, Republic of Ireland
tel +353 (0)18 788177
email publications@veritas.ie
website www.veritas.ie

Liturgical and church resources, religious school books for primary and post-primary levels, biographies, academic studies, and general books on religious, moral and social issues. Founded 1983.

Vermilion – see Ebury Publishing

Verso Ltd‡

6 Meard Street, London W1F 0EG
tel 020-7437 3546
email enquiries@verso.co.uk
website www.versobooks.com
Directors Jacob Stevens (managing), Rowan Wilson (sales & marketing), Robin Blackburn, Tariq Ali

Current affairs, politics, sociology, economics, history, philosophy, cultural studies. Founded 1970.

Viking – see Penguin General

Vintage

One Embassy Gardens, 8 Viaduct Gardens, London SW11 7AY
tel 020-7840 8400
website www.penguin.co.uk/vintage
Managing Director Hannah Telfer, *Deputy Managing Director* Faye Brewster, *Communications Director* Christian Lewis, *Head of Publicity* Bethan Jones, *Marketing Director* Chloe Healy, *Publisher* Rachel Cugnoni, *Publishing Director* Beth Coates (paperbacks)

Part of Penguin Random House UK (page 176). Quality fiction and non-fiction. No unsolicited MSS. Founded 1954.

The Bodley Head
tel 020-7840 8707
Publishing Director Stuart Williams, *Editorial Director* Will Hammond, *Editorial Director* Jorg Hensgen, *Editorial Assistant* Lauren Howard

Non-fiction: history, current affairs, politics, science, biography, economics.

Jonathan Cape
tel 020-7840 8608
Publishing Director Michal Shavit, *Associate Publisher* Dan Franklin, *Associate Publisher* Robin Robertson (poetry), *Deputy Publishing Director* Bea Hemming, *Editorial Director* Željka Marošević, *Senior Editor* Ana Fletcher, *Assistant Editor* Daisy Watts

Biography and memoirs, current affairs, drama, fiction, history, poetry, travel, politics, graphic novels, photography.

Chatto & Windus/Hogarth
tel 020-7840 8745
Publishing Director Clara Farmer, *Deputy Publishing Director* Becky Hardie, *Editorial Director* Poppy Hampson, *Editor* Charlotte Humphery, *Assistant Editor* Greg Clowes

Belles lettres, biography and memoirs, current affairs, fiction, history, poetry, politics, philosophy, translations, travel. No unsolicited MSS.

Classics and Paperbacks
Publishing Director Beth Coates, *Director* Hattie Adam-Smith, *Senior Editors* Victoria Murray-Browne, Charlotte Knight, Nicholas Skidmore, Alex Russell, *Editor* Lily Lindon, *Assistant Editors* Dredheza Maloku, Tom Atkins

Harvill Secker
tel 020-7840 8893
Publishing Director Liz Foley, *Deputy Publishing Director* Kate Harvey, *Editorial Director* Jade Chandler (crime), *Senior Editor* Ellie Steel, *Assistant Editor* Mikaela Pedlow

English literature, crime fiction and world literature in translation. Non-fiction (history, current affairs, literary essays, music). No unsolicited MSS.

Pimlico
tel 020-7840 8836
Publishing Director Rachel Cugnoni

History, biography, literature. Exclusively in paperback. No unsolicited MSS.

Square Peg
tel 020-7840 8541
Editor Mireille Harper, *Editorial Assistant* Maxine Sibihwana

Eclectic, idiosyncratic and commercial non-fiction including humour, illustrated and gift books, food, nature, memoir, travel, parenting. Unsolicited MSS with sae.

Yellow Jersey Press
tel 020-7840 8407
Editorial Director Joe Pickering
Sport and leisure activities. No unsolicited MSS.

Virtue Books Ltd
Edward House, Tenter Street, Rotherham S60 1LB
tel (01709) 365005
email info@virtue.co.uk
Directors Peter E. Russum, Margaret H. Russum

Books for the professional chef: catering and drink. Founded 1949.

The Vital Spark – see Neil Wilson Publishing Ltd

University of Wales Press
University Registry, King Edward VII Avenue, Cardiff CF10 3NS
tel 029-2037 6999
email press@press.wales.ac.uk
website www.uwp.co.uk, www.gwasgprifysgolcymru.org
Director Natalie Williams

Academic, educational and professional publisher (Welsh and English). Specialises in the humanities and social sciences across a broad range of subjects: Wales Studies, European studies, literary criticism, history, Celtic and Medieval studies, political philosophy. Founded 1922.

Walker Books Ltd*‡
87 Vauxhall Walk, London SE11 5HJ
tel 020-7793 0909
website www.walker.co.uk
Facebook www.facebook.com/walkerbooks
Twitter @walkerbooksuk
Directors Karen Lotz, Ian Mablin (non-executive), Roger Alexander (non-executive), Angela Van Den Belt, Jane Winterbotham, Alan Lee, Mike McGrath, John Mendelson, Hilary Berkman

Children's: activity books, novelty books, picture books, fiction for 5–8 and 9–12 years, young adult fiction, series fiction, film/TV tie-ins, plays, poetry, digital and audio. Imprints: Walker Books, Walker Studio and Walker Entertainment. Founded 1980.

Watkins Media*
Unit 11, Shepperton House, 89 Shepperton Road, London N1 3DF
tel 020-813 6940
email enquiries@watkinsmedia.org
website www.watkinsmedia.org
Owner Etan Ilfeld

Media company that incorporates magazine publishing and retail activities, as well as book publishing. Imprints: Watkins Publishing (personal development – page 194), Angry Robot (science fiction and fantasy – page 132), Nourish Books

(personal development – page 194), Angry Robot (science fiction and fantasy – page 132)

Books

(health and wellbeing, food and drink – page 170), Repeater (counter-culture fiction and non-fiction, including politics and current affairs – page 180) and Watkins Publishing (self-help, personal development; mind, body & spirit – below). Founded 1893.

Watkins Publishing‡
Unit 11, Shepperton House, 89 Shepperton Road, London N1 3DF
tel 020-3813-6940
email enquiries@watkinspublishing.com
website www.watkinspublishing.com
Facebook www.facebook.com/WatkinsPublishing
Twitter @WatkinsWisdom

Publishes personal development and mind, body & spirit books. Works in partnership with outstanding authors and aims to produce authoritative, innovative titles, both illustrated and non-illustrated. Part of Watkins Media (above). Founded 1893.

Franklin Watts – see Hachette Children's Group

Wayland – see Hachette Children's Group

Josef Weinberger Plays Ltd
12–14 Mortimer Street, London W1T 3JJ
tel 020-7580 2827
email general.info@jwmail.co.uk
website www.josef-weinberger.com

Stage plays only, in both acting and trade editions. Preliminary letter essential. Founded 1936.

Welbeck Publishing Group
20 Mortimer Street, London W1T 3JW
tel 020-7612 0400
email enquiries@welbeckpublishing.com
website www.welbeckpublishing.com
Executive Directors Marcus Leaver, Mark Smith

No unsolicited MSS; synopses and ideas welcome, but no fiction or poetry. Founded 1992.

André Deutsch
Science fiction, fantasy, crime and classic reissues.

Mortimer
Children's entertainment, licensing and gaming.

Mountain Leopard Press
Editor Christopher MacLehose
Literary and books-in-translation.

OH! Orange Hippo
Humour, nostalgia, gift.

Welbeck
General children's non-fiction, narrative and illustrated, all ages excluding preschool.

Welbeck Editions
Illustrated non-fiction.

Welbeck Fiction
Women's, thriller, crime, historical, saga, romance, reading group.

Welbeck Flame
Associate Publisher *Felicity Alexander*
Children's fiction.

Welbeck Non-Fiction
Narrative and illustrated non-fiction: smart thinking, history, memoir and biography, popular science and psychology, soft business, true crime, sport, music and film, military, puzzles and games, lifestyle.

Welsh Academic Press
PO Box 733, Cardiff CF14 7ZY
tel 029-2021 8187
email post@welsh-academic-press.wales
website www.welsh-academic-press.wales
Facebook www.facebook.com/WelshAcademicPress
Twitter @WelshAcadPress
Instagram @WelshAcademicPress

History, political studies, education, Medieval Welsh and Celtic studies, Scandinavian and Baltic studies. Distributed by Welsh Books Council (Wales), Ingram Publishing Services (UK & Europe), IPG (North America & Rest of World). Founded 1994.

Whittet Books Ltd
1 St John's Lane, Stansted, Essex CM24 8JU
tel (01279) 815871
email mail@whittetbooks.com
website www.whittetbooks.com
Director George J. Papa, *Publisher* Shirley Greenall

Natural history, wildlife, countryside, poultry, livestock, horses, donkeys. Publishing proposals considered for the above lists. Please send outline, preferably by email. Founded 1976.

Wide Eyed Editions
The Old Brewery, 6 Blundell Street, London N7 9BH
tel 020-7700 6700
website www.quartoknows.com/Wide-Eyed-Editions

Imprint of the Quarto Group, Inc. (page 179). Creates original non-fiction for children and families and believes that books should encourage curiosity about the world, inspiring readers to set out on their own journey of discovery. Founded 2014.

John Wiley & Sons Ltd
The Atrium, Southern Gate, Chichester, West Sussex PO19 8SQ
tel (01243) 779777
email customer@wiley.co.uk
Alternative address 9600 Garsington Road, Oxford OX4 2DQ
tel (01865) 776868
website www.wiley.com
Ceo Brian A. Napack

Wiley's core businesses publish scientific, technical, medical and scholarly journals, encyclopedias, books and online products and services; professional/trade books, subscription products, training materials and online applications and websites; and educational materials for undergraduate and graduate students and lifelong learners. Global headquarters in Hoboken, New Jersey, with operations in the USA, Europe, Asia, Canada and Australia.

Neil Wilson Publishing Ltd
226 King Street, Castle Douglas DG7 1DS
tel (01556) 504119
email info@nwp.co.uk
website www.nwp.co.uk
Facebook www.facebook.com/Neil-Wilson-Publishing-170187613028330
Twitter @NWPbooks
Managing Director Neil Wilson

Independent publisher of print and ebooks covering a broad range of mostly Scottish interests. Submissions by email only. Include covering letter, author CV, synopsis and sample chapter. Genres published include whisky, food, the great outdoors, history and culture, true crime and humour. Imprints: 11:9, Angels' Share, In Pinn, NWP and Vital Spark. Founded 1992.

Philip Wilson Publishers
50 Bedford Square, London WC1B 3DP
website www.philip-wilson.co.uk
Publisher Jayne Parsons

An imprint of Bloomsbury Publishing Plc (page 136). Fine and applied art, architecture, photography, collecting, museums. Founded 1975.

Windmill Books – see Cornerstone

Wooden Books
The Lawn, Walsham-le-Willows, Bury St Edmunds, Suffolk IP31 3AW
email woodenbooksoffice@gmail.com
Alternative address Red Brick Building, Glastonbury BA6 9FT
website www.woodenbooks.com
Ceo John Martineau

Liberal arts, modern and ancient arts and sciences. Quality B&W and pencil illustrators may submit samples. Founded 1996.

Y Lolfa Cyf
Talybont, Ceredigion SY24 5HE
tel (01970) 832304
email ylolfa@ylolfa.com
website www.ylolfa.com
Director Garmon Gruffudd, *Editor* Lefi Gruffudd

Welsh language and English books of Welsh/Celtic interest, biographies and sport. Founded 1967.

Yale University Press London
47 Bedford Square, London WC1B 3DP
tel 020-7079 4900
website www.yalebooks.co.uk
Managing Director Heather McCallum, *Sales & Marketing Director* David Brand, *Editorial Directors* Mark Eastment (art & architecture), Julian Loose (trade & academic)

Art, architecture, history, economics, political science, religion, history of science, biography, current affairs and music. Founded 1961.

Yellow Jersey Press – see Vintage

Zaffre
Victoria House, Bloomsbury Squre, London WC1B 4DA
tel 020-7490 3875
email hello@zaffrebooks.co.uk
website www.zaffrebooks.co.uk, www.bonnierbooks.co.uk
Twitter @zaffrebooks
Publisher Margaret Stead, *Publishing Director* Ben Willis, *Editorial Director* Sophie Orme, *Editorial Director* Katherine Armstrong

Zaffre is the flagship adult fiction imprint of Bonnier Books UK (page 137). Zaffre publishes established authors focusing on a wide range of crime, thrillers, women's and reading-group fiction.

Zambezi Publishing Ltd
22 Second Avenue, Camels Head, Plymouth PL2 2EQ
tel (01752) 367300
email info@zampub.com
website www.zampub.com
Contacts Sasha Fenton, Jan Budkowski

Mind, body & spirit. Founded 1998.

Zed Books Ltd
50 Bedford Square, London WC1B 3DP
website https://www.zedbooks.net/contact/
Twitter @ZedBooks
Editor Commissioning Editor Max Vickers

African studies. Acquired by Bloomsbury Publishing Plc 2020 (page 136). Founded 1976.

ZigZag Education
Unit 3, Greenway Business Centre, Doncaster Road, Bristol BS10 5PY
tel 0117 950 3199
email submissions@publishmenow.co.uk
website www.zigzageducation.co.uk, www.publishmenow.co.uk
Development Director John-Lloyd Hagger, *Strategy Director* Mike Stephens

Secondary school teaching resources: English, maths, ICT, geography, history, science, business, politics, P.E., media studies. Founded 1998.

Books

CROWDFUNDED PUBLISHING

Crowdfunding, the raising of small investments from a wide pool of individuals to fund a project, can be a viable option for writers wishing to publish their work.

And Other Stories*

Central Library, Surrey St, Sheffield S1 1XZ
email info@andotherstories.org
website www.andotherstories.org
Facebook www.facebook.com/AndOtherStoriesBooks
Twitter @andothertweets
Publisher Stefan Tobler

Contemporary literary fiction and non-fiction from around the world. Has an open submissions policy, but has strict submissions guidelines. Please read carefully before submitting: www.andotherstories.org/submissions. Submissions not complying with these guidelines will be disregarded. Founded 2011.

Indiegogo

website www.indiegogo.com

Acts as a 'launchpad' for creative ideas.

Inkshares

see page 213

Kickstarter

website www.kickstarter.com

Helps artists, musicians, film-makers and designers find resources and support needed for a project.

Publishizer

website https://publishizer.com/

Books only. Authors submit a proposal and launch a pre-orders campaign. Publishers receive proposals based on targets. If a publisher signals interest, an exchange is initiated between author and publisher. Alternatively approach a crowdfunding publisher to help raise finances with you. The publisher will critically assess your work before presenting it for funding opportunities and will publish and distribute the book. Some publishers seek investment from readers across their operation and not for a specific title.

Unbound‡

Unit 18, Waterside, 44–48 Wharf Road, London N1 7UX
tel 020-7253 4230
email hello@unbound.co.uk
website https://unbound.com
Facebook www.facebook.com/unbound
Twitter @unbounders

The world's first crowdfunding publisher and winner of *The Bookseller* Book of the Year Award 2015,
Unbound is home to the *Sunday Times* bestselling *Letters of Note* and the Man Booker prize longlisted *The Wake*. Considers submissions from literary agents and direct from writers. Includes an audio and podcasting arm Unbound Audio. Writers should submit projects using the website submission page: unbound.co.uk/authors. Founded 2011.

SOCIAL ENTERPRISE PUBLISHING

Organisations with social enterprise at their heart offer publishing support – expertise and funding – to those who might not otherwise be published. These initiatives, many not-for-profit charitable operations, are motivated by social, community and environmental objectives rather than by money.

Arkbound

Rogart Street Campus, 4 Rogart Street, Glasgow G40 2AA
tel (0117) 290 0386 / 0871 268 9869
email hello@arkbound.com
website httpS://arkbound.com

Social enterprise set up through the Princes' Trust in 2015. Publishes a range of fiction and non-fiction, principally focused on works that cover important social or environmental issues. Aims to support authors from disadvantaged and diverse backgrounds, giving a platform for voices who would otherwise go unheard. Based in England and Scotland, operating on behalf of the Arkbound Foundation charity.

Comma Press*

Studio 510A, 5th Floor, Hope Mill, 113 Pollard Street, Manchester M4 7JA
email info@commapress.co.uk
website https://commapress.co.uk
Facebook www.facebook.com/CommaPressMcr/
Twitter @commapress
Founder & Ceo Ra Page, *Editor-at-Large* Orsola Casagrande

A not-for-profit publishing initiative dedicated to promoting new writing with an emphasis on the short story and translated fiction. One of the Art's Council's new National Portfolio Organisations (NPOs) since 2012. For submissions please see 'resources' section of the website: https://commapress.co.uk/resources/submissions/. Founded 2002.

Dead Ink Books

Northern Lights, 5 Mann Street, Liverpool L8 5AF
email nathan@deadinkbooks.com
website https://deadinkbooks.com/
Director Nathan Connolly, *Operations Manager* Amelia Collingwood

Literary publisher based in Liverpool, supported by Arts Council England. Published books have three times made the shortlist for The Saboteur Awards, the longlists for both The Guardian's First Book Award and Not the Booker Prize, and the longlist for the Edge Hill Short Story Award. Founded 2017.

Eyewear Publishing Ltd*

Suite 333, 19–21 Crawford Street, London W1H 1PJ
tel 020-7289 0627
email info@eyewearpublishing.com
website www.eyewearpublishing.com
Facebook www.facebook.com/EyewearPublishing
Twitter @EyewearBooks
Acting Director M. John Perry, *Senior Editor* Cate Myddleton-Evans, *Senior Editor* Alex Wylie

Celebrates prose and poetry writing in English from the UK and overseas. Through the annual Melita Hume Poetry Prize, Beverly Prize and Sexton Prize, new poets are discovered, supported and developed. Founded 2012.

Fly on the Wall Press

56 High Lea Road, New Mills, Derbyshire SK22 3DP
email flyonthewallpress@hotmail.com
website www.flyonthewallpress.co.uk
Facebook www.facebook.com/flyonthewallpress
Twitter @fly_press
Instagram @flyonthewall_poetry
Managing Director Isabelle Kenyon

Small Press of the Year Finalist (British Book Awards 2021 and 2020) of socially-conscious poetry, short stories and anthologies. Titles range across poetry, both page and stage, politically-engaged short stories and cross-genre anthologies, often with a charity angle. Founded 2018.

Honno Ltd (Welsh Women's Press)‡

D41 Hugh Owen Building, Penglais Campus, Aberystwyth University, Aberystwyth SY23 3DY
tel (01970) 623150
email post@honno.co.uk
website www.honno.co.uk
Facebook www.facebook.com/honnopress
Twitter @honno
Editor Caroline Oakley

Literature written by women born or living in Wales or women with a significant Welsh connection. All subjects considered – fiction, non-fiction, autobiographies. No poetry or works for children. Honno is a community cooperative. Founded 1986.

Impress Books Ltd*‡

Innovation Centre, Rennes Drive, University of Exeter, Devon EX4 4RN
tel (01392) 950910
email enquiries@impress-books.co.uk
website www.impress-books.co.uk
Commissioning Editor Richard Willis

Founded as an independent publishing house focusing on previously unpublished writers of non-fiction and fiction, and specialising in biography, memoir, history and historical fiction. Runs the Impress Prize for New Writers. Founded 2004.

Lantana Publishing

The Oxford Foundry, 3–5 Hythe Bridge Street, Oxford OX1 2EW
email info@lantanapublishing.com
website https://lantanapublishing.com
Facebook www.facebook.com/lantanapublishing
Twitter @lantanapub
Instagram lantana_publishing
Ceo Alice Curry, *Commissioning Editor* Holly Tonks

An award-winning children's book publisher and social enterprise with a mission to publish inclusive books by under-represented voices celebrating every kind of child and family. Looking for inclusive fiction and non-fiction for babies and toddlers, 5–8 year olds and 9–12 year olds. Authors should send full MS, illustrators their portfolio and link to their website and author-illustrators a complete book dummy. See submissions page on website for how to submit. Founded 2014.

Books

Book publishers overseas

Listings are given for book publishers in Australia (below), Canada (page 201), New Zealand (page 203), South Africa (page 205) and the USA (page 207).

AUSTRALIA

Member of the Australian Publishers Association

ACER Press*
19 Prospect Hill Road, Private Bag 55, Camberwell, VIC 3124
tel +61 (0)3 9277 5555
email proposals@acer.org
website www.acer.org/au

Publisher of the Australian Council for Educational Research. Produces a range of books and assessments including professional resources for teachers, psychologists and special needs professionals. Founded 1930.

Allen & Unwin Pty Ltd*
83 Alexander Street, Crows Nest, NSW 2065
Postal address PO Box 8500, St Leonards, NSW 1590
tel +61 (0)2 8425 0100
website www.allenandunwin.com
Chairman Patrick Gallagher, *Ceo* Robert Gorman, *Publishing Director* Tom Gilliatt, *Publishing Director* Lou Johnson (Murdoch Books), *Publishing Director* Eva Mills (books for children and young adult)

General trade, including fiction and children's books, and broad-ranging non-fiction. Imprints include: Allen & Unwin, Albert Street Books, Inspired Living, Crows Nest, House of Books, Murdoch Books. Submission guidelines: will consider unsolicited MSS. Will only accept MSS through electronic Friday Pitch system. Founded 1990.

Bloomsbury Publishing Pty Ltd*
Level 6, 387 George Street, Sydney, NSW 2000
tel +61 (0)2 8820 4900
email au@bloomsbury.com
website www.bloomsbury.com/au
Facebook www.facebook.com/bloomsburypublishingaustralia
Twitter @BloomsburySyd
Managing Director Liz Bray

Supports the worldwide publishing activities of Bloomsbury Publishing: caters for the Australia and New Zealand territories. See Bloomsbury Publishing Plc (page 136). Bloomsbury Publishing Plc founded 1986.

Bonnier Publishing Australia*
Level 6, 534 Church Street, Richmond, VIC 3121
tel +61 (0)3 9421 3800
email info@bonnierpublishing.com.au
Twitter @bonnierpubau

Bonnier Publishing Australia is based in Melbourne. The company represents UK sister-company imprints across the ANZ markets, as well as creating local publishing under Five Mile, a 25-year old children's imprint, and Echo, a fresh voice in Australian adult publishing. Bonnier Publishing Australia is a division of international publishing group, Bonnier Publishing. Imprint: Echo Publishing. Founded 1979.

Cambridge University Press*
477 Williamstown Road, Private Bag 31, Port Melbourne, VIC 3207
tel +61 (0)3 8671 1400
email educationmarketing@cambridge.edu.au
website www.cambridge.edu.au/education
Executive Director Mark O'Neill

Academic, educational, reference, ESL. Founded 1534.

Cengage Learning Australia*
Level 7, 80 Dorcas Street, South Melbourne, VIC 3205
tel +61 (0)3 9685 4111
website www.cengage.com.au
Ceo Michael Hansen

Educational books. Founded 2007.

ELK Publishing
PO Box 2828, Toowoomba, QLD 4350
tel +61 (0)4 0030 1675 / +61 (0)4 7592 3670
email contactus@elk-publishing.com
website www.elk-publishing.com
Facebook www.facebook.com/elkpublishing
Twitter @elkpublish
Instagram @elkpublishing
Founder & Ceo Selina Kucks

An Australian grown, independent publishing house of children's and educational literature. Established in Korea, the company is now based in Queensland, Australia. ELK Publishing creates children's and educational books; provides opportunities for unknown artists and illustrators to collaborate with in-house authors and offers internships to university students who are presently engaged in literary scholarship. Founded in Seoul, Korea 2009.

Elsevier Australia*
Tower 1, Level 12, 475 Victoria Avenue, Chatswood, NSW 2067
tel +61 (0)2 9422 8500
email customerserviceau@elsevier.com
website www.elsevierhealth.com.au
Managing Director Rob Kolkman

Science, medical and technical books. Imprints: Academic Press, Butterworth-Heinemann, Churchill Livingstone, Endeavour, Excerpta Medica, Focal Press, The Lancet, MacLennan and Petty, MD Consult, Morgan Kauffman, Mosby, Saunders, Science Direct, Syngress. Founded 1972.

Hachette Australia Pty Ltd*
Level 17, 207 Kent Street, Sydney, NSW 2000
tel +61 (0)2 8248 0800
email auspub@hachette.com.au
website www.hachette.com.au
Ceo Louise Sherwin-Stark

General, children's. Accepts MSS via website. Founded 1971.

HarperCollins Publishers (Australia) Pty Ltd Group*
Postal address PO Box A565, Sydney South, NSW 1235
tel +61 (0)2 9952 5000
website www.harpercollins.com.au
Children's Publishing Director Cristina Cappelluto, *Head of Australian Children's Publishing* Chren Byng, *Head of HarperCollins Fiction* Catherine Milne, *Head of HarperCollins Non-fiction* Helen Littleton

Literary fiction and non-fiction, popular fiction, children's, reference, biography, autobiography, current affairs, sport, lifestyle, health/self-help, humour, true crime, travel, Australiana, history, business, gift, religion. Founded 1989.

Lawbook Co.
Level 5, 16 Harris Street, Pyrmont, NSW 2009
tel +61 (0)2 8587 7980
website www.thomsonreuters.com.au
Ceo Tony Kinnear

Law. Part of Thomson Reuters.

LexisNexis Butterworths Australia*
Tower 2, 475–495 Victoria Avenue, Chatswood, NSW 2067
tel +61 (0)2 9422 2174
Postal address Level 9, Locked Bag 2222, Chatswood Delivery Centre, Chatswood, NSW 2067
website www.lexisnexis.com.au

Accounting, business, legal, tax and commercial. Founded 1970.

McGraw-Hill Australia Pty Ltd*
Level 2, 82 Waterloo Road, North Ryde, NSW 2113
Postal address Private Bag 2233, Business Centre, North Ryde, NSW 1670
tel +61 (0)2 9900 1800
email cservice_sydney@mcgraw-hill.com
website www.mcgraw-hill.com.au

Educational publisher: higher education, primary education and professional (including medical,

general and reference). Division of the McGraw-Hill Companies. Founded 1964.

Melbourne University Press*
Level 1, 715 Swanston Street, Carlton, VIC 3053
tel +61 (0)3 9035 3333
email mup-contact@unimelb.edu.au
website www.mup.com.au
Ceo & Publisher Nathan Hollier

Trade, academic, current affairs and politics; non-fiction. Imprints: Miegunyah Press, Melbourne University Press, MUP Academic, *Meanjin* journal. Founded 1922.

New Holland Publishers (UK) Ltd
Level 1, 178 Fox Valley Road, Wahroonga 2076
tel +61 28986 4700
email orders@newholland.com.au
website www.newholland.com.au

Illustrated non-fiction books on natural history, sports and hobbies, animals and pets, travel pictorial, reference, gardening, health and fitness, practical art, DIY, food and drink, outdoor pursuits, craft, humour, gift books. New proposals accepted, send CV and synopsis and sample chapters in first instance; sae essential. Founded 1955.

Pan Macmillan Australia Pty Ltd*
Level 25, 1 Market Street, Sydney, NSW 2000
tel +61 (0)2 9285 9100
email pan.reception@macmillan.com.au
website www.panmacmillan.com.au
Directors Cate Paterson (publishing), Katie Crawford (sales), Tracey Cheetham (publicity & marketing)

Commercial and literary fiction; children's fiction, non-fiction and character products; general non-fiction; sport. Founded 1843.

Penguin Random House Australia Pty Ltd*
Sydney office Level 3, 100 Pacific Highway, North Sydney, NSW 2060
tel +61 (0)2 9954 9966
email information@penguinrandomhouse.com.au
Melbourne office 707 Collins Street, Melbourne, VIC 3008
website www.penguinrandomhouse.com.au
Ceo Julie Burland, *Publishing Director* Justin Ratcliffe, *Group Publishing Director* Nikki Christer, *Publishing Director, Penguin Young Readers* Laura Harris, *Publicity Director* Karen Reid

General fiction and non-fiction; children's, illustrated. MS submissions for non-fiction accepted, unbound in hard copy addressed to Submissions Editor. Fiction submissions are only accepted from previously published authors, or authors represented by an agent or accompanied by a report from an accredited assessment service. Imprints: Arrow, Bantam, Ebury, Hamish Hamilton, Knopf, Michael

Books

Joseph, Penguin, Viking, Vintage and William Heinemann. Subsidiary of Bertelsmann AG. Founded 2013.

University of Queensland Press*
PO Box 6042, St Lucia, QLD 4067
tel +61 (0)7 3365 7244
email reception@uqp.com.au
website www.uqp.com.au

Publishes books of high quality and cultural significance. It has launched the careers of Australian writers such as David Malouf, Peter Carey, Kate Grenville, Doris Pilkington and Nick Earls. Originally founded as a traditional university press, the company has since branched into publishing books for general readers in the areas of fiction, non-fiction, poetry, Indigenous writing and youth literature. Books and authors have received national and international recognition through literary prizes, rights sales and writers' festivals. Founded 1948.

Rhiza Edge
PO Box 302, Chinchilla, QLD 4413
tel +61 (0)7 3245 1938
email editor@rhizaedge.com.au
website www.rhizaedge.com.au
Facebook www.facebook.com/rhizaedge
Commissioning Editor Emily Lighezzolo

Aims to publish relatable, issue-based stories for today's young adult readers, ranging from books with a light, humorous touch through to deeper, more challenging tales. Imprint of Wombat Books (page 201). Founded 2018.

Scholastic Australia Pty Ltd*
76–80 Railway Crescent, Lisarow, Gosford, NSW 2250
tel +61 (0)2 4328 3555
website www.scholastic.com.au
Chairman David Peagram

Children's fiction and non-fiction. Founded 1968.

Simon & Schuster (Australia) Pty Ltd*
Office address Suite 19A, Level 1, Building C, 450 Miller Street, Cammeray, NSW 2062
Postal address PO Box 448, Cammeray, NSW 2062
tel +61 (0)2 9983 6600
email cservice@simonandschuster.com.au
website www.simonandschuster.com.au
Facebook www.facebook.com/SimonSchusterAU
Twitter @simonschusterAU
Instagram @simonschusterau
Managing Director Dan Ruffino

Part of the ViacomCBS Corporation, the company publishes and distributes in Australia and New Zealand the following: fiction, non-fiction and children's books. Imprints include: Adams Media, Atria, Avid Reader Press, Free Press, Gallery, Howard, One Signal, Pocket, Scout Press, Scribner, Simon & Schuster, Tiller Press and Touchstone. Also acts as the local sales and distribution partner for 4 Ingredients, Berbay Publishing, Black Library, Cider Mill Press, Elliott & Thompson, Fox Chapel Publishing, Gallup Press, Hazelden Publishing, Hunter Publishing, Inner Traditions, Insight Editions, Manuscript Publishing, Printer's Row Publishing, Regan Arts, Restless Books, Rockpool Publishing, Smith Street Books, Ventura Press, Viz Media, Waterhouse Press, Weldon Owen and Wild Dog Books. Founded 1987.

Spinifex Press*
PO Box 105, Mission Beach Qld 4852
email women@spinifexpress.com.au
Postal address PO Box 5270, North Geelong, VIC 3215
website www.spinifexpress.com.au
Managing Directors Susan Hawthorne, Renate Klein

Fiction, poetry, biography, autobiography, feminism, women's studies, art, astronomy, ecology, literary criticism, violence against women, education, lesbian, health and nutrition, technology, travel, ebooks. Spinifex publishes writers from every continent. No unsolicited MSS. Founded 1991.

UNSW Press*
University of New South Wales, Sydney, NSW 2052
tel +61 (0)2 8936 1400
email enquiries@newsouthpublishing.com
website www.unswpress.com
Ceo Kathy Bail

Academic and general non-fiction. Politics, history, society and culture, popular science, environmental studies, Aboriginal studies. Includes imprints UNSW Press and NewSouth. Founded 1962.

UWA Publishing*
University of Western Australia, M419, 35 Stirling Highway, Crawley, WA 6009
tel +61 (0)8 6488 3670
email admin-uwap@uwa.edu.au
website www.uwap.uwa.edu.au
Director Terri-ann White

Fiction, general non-fiction, natural history, contemporary issues. Founded 1935.

John Wiley & Sons Australia Ltd*
42 McDougall Street, Milton, QLD 4064
tel +61 (0)7 3859 9755
email custservice@wiley.com
website www.wiley.com

Educational, technical, atlases, professional, reference, trade journals. Imprints: John Wiley & Sons, Jacaranda, Wiley-Blackwell, For Dummies, Jossey-Bass, Capstone, Polity. Distribution Rights: WW Norton & Company, Yale University Press, Harvard University Press, Columbia University Press, The University of Chicago Press, University of California Press. Founded 1807.

Wombat Books*

PO Box 302, Chinchilla, QLD 4413
tel +61 (0)7 3245 1938
email wombat@wombatbooks.com.au
website www.wombatbooks.com.au
Facebook www.facebook.com/wombatbooks
Publisher Rochelle Manners, *Editor & Publicity Coordinator* Emily Lighezzolo

An independent publisher of children's picture books and books for early readers. Always on the lookout for the next story to be shared. Young adult and adult imprint: Rhiza Edge (page 200). Founded 2009.

CANADA

**Member of the Canadian Publishers' Council*
†Member of the Association of Canadian Publishers

Annick Press Ltd†

388 Carlaw Avenue, Suite 200 Toronto,
ON M4M 2T4
tel +1 416-221-4802
email annickpress@annickpress.com
website www.annickpress.com
Owner/Director Rick Wilks, *Office Manager* Asiya Awale

Preschool to young adult fiction and non-fiction. Publishes approx. 24 titles each year. Recent successes include: (picture book) *I Love My Purse*; (non-fiction) *#NotYourPrincess*; (fiction, young adult) *Fire Song*; (non-fiction) *Stormy Seas*. To send MS or illustration submission, please visit website and view submission guidelines. Founded 1975.

The Charlton Press

645 Avenue, Lepine, Dorval, Quebec H9P 2R2
tel +1 416-962-2665
email chpress@charltonpress.com
website www.charltonpress.com

Collectables, Numismatics, Sportscard price catalogues. Founded 1952.

Douglas & McIntyre (2013) Ltd†

4437 Rondeview Road, PO Box 219, Madeira Park, BC V0N 2H0
tel +1 604-883-2730
email info@douglas-mcintyre.com
website www.douglas-mcintyre.com
Publisher Anna Comfort O'Keeffe

General list: Canadian biography, art and architecture, natural history, history, native studies, Canadian fiction. Unsolicited MSS accepted. Founded 1971.

Dundurn Press†

1382 Queen St E, Toronto, ON M4L 1C9
tel +1 416-214-5544
email submissions@dundurn.com
Publisher Kirk Howard

Canadian history, fiction, non-fiction and young adult fiction, mystery fiction, popular non-fiction, translations. Founded 1972.

ECW Press Ltd†

665 Gerrard Street E, Toronto, ON M4M 1Y2
tel +1 416-694-3348
email info@ecwpress.com
website www.ecwpress.com
Facebook www.facebook.com/ecwpress
Twitter @ecwpress
Co-Publishers David Caron, Jack David. *Acquisitions Editors* Jen Knoch, Susan Renouf, Michael Holmes, Jennifer Smith

Popular culture, TV and film, sports, humour, general trade books, biographies, memoir, popular science, guidebooks. Founded 1979.

Fitzhenry & Whiteside Ltd

195 Allstate Parkway, Markham, ON L3R 4T8
tel +1 800-387-9776
email bookinfo@fitzhenry.ca
website www.fitzhenry.ca
Ceo Sharon Fitzhenry

Trade, educational, children's books. Founded 1966.

Harlequin Enterprises Ltd*

PO Box 603, Fort Erie, ON L2A 5X3
tel +1 888-432-4879
email customer_ecare@harlequin.ca
website www.harlequin.com/shop/index.html
Publisher Craig Swinwood

Fiction for women, romance, inspirational fiction, African–American fiction, action adventure, mystery. Visit SoYouThinkYouCanWrite.com for the latest writing submissions and contests. Imprints include: Harlequin Blaze, Harlequin Desire, Harlequin Heartwarming, Harlequin Historical, Harlequin Intrigue, Harlequin Kimani Romance, Harlequin Medical Romance, Harlequin Nocturne, Harlequin Presents, Harlequin Romance, Harlequin Romantic Suspense, Harlequin Special Edition, Harlequin Special Releases, Harlequin Superromance, Harlequin Western Romance, Love Inspired, Love Inspired Special Releases, Love Inspired Historical, Love Inspired Suspense. Founded 1949.

HarperCollins Publishers Ltd*

22 Adelaide Street West, 41st Floor, Toronto, ON M5H 4E3
tel +1 416-975-9334
email hcOrder@harpercollins.com
website www.harpercollins.ca
President & Publisher Jonathan Burnham

Literary fiction and non-fiction, history, politics, biography, spiritual and children's books. Founded 1989.

Books

Kids Can Press Ltd[†]

25 Dockside Drive, Toronto, ON M5A 0B5
tel +1 416-479-7000
email customerservice@kidscan.com
website www.kidscanpress.com
Editorial Director Yvette Ghione

Middle grade/young adult books. Founded 1973.

Knopf Canada – see Penguin Random House Canada Ltd

LexisNexis Canada, Inc.*

111 Gordon Baker Road, Suite 900, Toronto,
ON M2H 3R1
tel +1 800-668-6481
email info@lexisnexis.ca
website www.lexisnexis.ca

Law and accountancy. Division of Reed Elsevier plc.
Founded 1979.

Lone Pine Publishing

Suite 251, 1231 Pacific Blvd, Vancouver BC V6Z 0E2
tel +1 780-433-9333
email info@lonepinepublishing.com
website www.lonepinepublishing.com
President Shane Kennedy

Natural history, outdoor recreation and wildlife
guidebooks, self-help, gardening, popular history.
Founded 1980.

McGill-Queen's University Press[†]

1010 Sherbrooke Street West, Suite 1720, Montreal,
QC H3A 2R7
tel +1 514-398-3750
email info.mqup@mcgill.ca
Alternative address Queen's University, Douglas
Library Building, 93 University Avenue, Kingston,
ON K7L 5C4
tel +1 613-533-2155
email kingstonmqup@queensu.ca
website www.mqup.mcgill.ca
Editor-in-Chief Jonathan Crago, *Senior Editor* Kyla
Madden, *Editor* Richard Baggaley, *Editor* Richard
Ratzlaff

Academic, non-fiction, poetry. Founded 1969.

McGraw-Hill Ryerson Ltd*

145 Kings Street West, Suite 1501,
Toronto ON M5H 1J8
tel +1 800-565-5758
website www.mheducation.ca

Educational and trade books. Founded 1972.

Nelson Education*

1120 Birchmount Road, Toronto, ON M1K 5G4
tel +1 416-752-9448
website www.nelson.com
President & Ceo Steve Brown

Educational publishing: school (K–12), college and
university, career education, measurement and
guidance, professional and reference, ESL titles.
Division of Thomson Canada Ltd. Founded 1914.

NeWest Press[†]

8540, 109 Street, Edmonton, AB T6G 1E6
tel +1 780-432-9427
email info@newestpress.com
website www.newestpress.com
President Doug Barbour

Fiction, drama, poetry and non-fiction.
Founded 1977.

Oberon Press

145 Spruce Street, Ottawa, ON K1R 6P1
tel +1 613-238-3275
email oberon@sympatico.ca
website www.oberonpress.ca

General fiction, short stories, poetry, some
biographies, art and children's. Only publishes
Canadian writers. Founded 1985.

Oxford University Press, Canada*

8 Sampson Mews, Suite 204, Don Mills,
ON M3C 0H5
tel +1 416-441-2941
website www.oup.com
General Manager Geoff Forguson

Educational and academic. Founded 1586.

Pearson Canada*

26 Prince Andrew Place, North York, ON M3C 2T8
tel +1 800-361-6128
website www.pearson.com/ca/en.html
Ceo Dan Lee

Academic, technical, educational, children's and
adult, trade. Founded 1998.

Penguin Random House Canada Ltd*

320 Front Street West, Suite 1400, Toronto,
ON M5V 3B6
tel +1 416-364-4449
website www.penguinrandomhouse.ca
Ceo Kristin Cochrane

Literary fiction, commercial fiction, memoir, non-
fiction (history, business, current events, sports),
adult, teen and young readers. No unsolicited MSS;
submissions via an agent only. Imprints: Allen Lane
Canada, Anchor Canada, Appetite by Random
House, Bond Street Books, Doubleday Canada,
Emblem, Hamish Hamilton Canada, Knopf Canada,
McClelland & Stewart, Penguin Canada, Penguin
Teen, Portfolio Canada, Puffin Canada, Random
House Canada, Seal Books, Signal, Strange Light,
Tundra Books, Viking Canada, Vintage Canada.
Subsidiary of Penguin Random House.
Founded 2013.

Pippin Publishing Corporation

PO Box 242, Don Mills, ON M3C 2S2
tel +1 416-510-2918
email arayner@utphighereducation.com
website www.utppublishing.com

ESL/EFL, teacher reference, adult basic education, school texts (all subjects), general trade (non-fiction) – acquired by University of Toronto Press in 2014 (see below). Founded 1995.

Ronsdale Press†

3350 West 21st Avenue, Vancouver, BC V6S 1G7
tel +1 604-738-4688
email ronsdale@shaw.ca
website www.ronsdalepress.com
Facebook www.facebook.com/ronsdalepress
Twitter @ronsdalepress
Director Ronald B. Hatch

Ronsdale is a Canadian publisher based in Vancouver with some 290 books in print. Founded 1988.

Thompson Educational Publishing†

20 Ripley Avenue, Toronto, ON M6S 3N9
tel +1 416-766-2763
email info@thompsonbooks.com
website www.thompsonbooks.com

Social sciences. Founded 1989.

University of Toronto Press

800 Bay Street, Mezzanine, Toronto,
Ontario M5S 3A9
tel +1 416-978-2239
email publishing@utpress.utoronto.ca
website www.utorontopress.com
Vice President, Book Publishing Lynn Fisher, *Editor* Natalie Fingerhut

Imprints include: Aevo UTP; New Jewish Press; Rotman-UTP Publishing. Publishers of non-fiction, monographs, textbooks and academic books, ESL/EFL, teacher reference, adult basic education and school texts. Founded 1901.

Tundra Books

320 Front Street West, Suite 1400, Toronto,
ON M5V 3B6
tel +1 416-364-4449
email submissions@tundrabooks.com
email art@tundrabooks.com
website www.penguinrandomhouse.ca/imprints/TU/tundra-books
Facebook www.facebook.com/tundrabooks
Twitter @TundraBooks
Publisher Tara Walker

Publisher of high-quality children's picture books and novels, renowned for its innovations. Publishes books for children to teens. Imprints: Penguin Teen Canada, Puffin Canada, Tundra Books. A division of Penguin Random House Canada Ltd. Founded 1967.

NEW ZEALAND

*Member of the Publishers Association of New Zealand (PANZ)

Auckland University Press*

University of Auckland, Private Bag 92019,
Auckland 1142
tel +64 (0)9 373 7528
email press@auckland.ac.nz
website aucklanduniversitypress.co.nz
Director Sam Elworthy

Archaeology, architecture, art, biography, business, health, New Zealand history, Māori and Pacific studies, poetry, politics and law, science and natural history, social sciences. Founded 1966.

David Bateman Ltd

Unit 2/5 Workspace Drive, Auckland 0618
tel +64 (0)9 415 7664
email info@bateman.co.nz
website www.batemanbooks.co.nz
Facebook www.facebook.com/batemanbooks

General trade publisher focusing on fiction, children's, craft, natural history, gardening, health, sport, cookery, history, travel, motoring, maritime history, business, art, humour, lifestyle for the international market. Founded 1979.

The Caxton Press

32 Lodestar Ave, Wigram, PO Box 36 411,
Christchurch 8042
tel +64 (0)3 366 8516
email bridget@caxton.co.nz
website www.caxton.co.nz
Managing Director Bridget Batchelor

Local history, tourist pictorial, Celtic spirituality, parent guides, book designers and printers. Founded 1935.

Cengage Learning New Zealand*

Unit 4B, Rosedale Office Park, 331 Rosedale Road,
Albany, North Shore 0632
Postal address PO Box 33376, Takapuna,
North Shore 0740
tel +64 (0)9 415 6850
Vice President, Higher Education Paul Petrulis, *Vice President, Schools* Nicole McCarten

Educational books. Founded 2007.

Dunmore Publishing Ltd

PO Box 28387, Auckland 1541
tel +64 (0)9 521 3121
email books@dunmore.co.nz
website www.dunmore.co.nz

Education secondary/tertiary texts and other, New Zealand society, history, health, economics, politics, general non-fiction. Founded 1970.

Books

Edify Ltd*

Level 1, 39 Woodside Avenue, Northcote,
Auckland 0627
tel +64 (0)9 972 9428
email mark@edify.co.nz
website www.edify.co.nz
Ceo Adrian Keane

Edify is a publishing, sales and marketing business
providing its partners with opportunities for their
products and solutions in the New Zealand
educational market. Exclusive representatives of
Pearson and the New Zealand based educational
publisher, Sunshine Books. Founded 2013.

Hachette New Zealand Ltd*

PO Box 3255, Shortland Street, Auckland 1140
tel +64 (0)9 379 1480
email contact@hachette.co.nz
website www.hachette.co.nz
Facebook www.facebook.com/HachetteNZ
ceo Louise Sherwin Stark, *Managing Director* Melanee
Winder

International fiction and non-fiction. Local
publishing includes children's and fiction titles.
Founded 1970.

Halcyon Publishing Ltd

PO Box 1064, Cambridge 3450
tel +64 (0)9 489 5337
email info@halcyonpublishing.co.nz
website www.halcyonpublishing.co.nz
Managing Director/Publisher Graham Gurr

Hunting, shooting, fishing, outdoor interests.
Founded 1982.

HarperCollins Publishers (New Zealand) Ltd*

Unit D, 63 Apollo Drive, Rosedale, Auckland 0632
tel +64 (0)9 443 9400
email publicity@harpercollins.co.nz
Postal address PO Box 1, Shortland Street, Auckland
1140
website www.harpercollins.co.nz

General literature, non-fiction, reference, children's.
HarperCollins New Zealand does not accept
proposals or MSS for consideration, except via the
Wednesday Post portal on its website. Founded 1989.

LexisNexis NZ Ltd

Level 1, 138 The Terrace, Wellington 6011
tel 0800 800 986
email customersupport@lexisnexis.co.nz
Postal address PO Box 472, Wellington 6140
website www.lexisnexis.co.nz
Publisher Christopher Murray

Law, business, academic. Founded 1914.

McGraw-Hill Book Company New Zealand Ltd

Level 8, 56–60 Cawley Street, Ellerslie, Auckland 1005
Postal address Private Bag 11904, Ellerslie,
Auckland 1005
tel +64 (0)9 526 6200
website www.mcgraw-hill.com.au

Educational publisher: higher education, primary and
secondary education (grades K–12) and professional
(including medical, general and reference). Division
of the McGraw-Hill Companies. Always looking for
potential authors. Has a rapidly expanding publishing
programme. See website for author's guide.
Founded 1974.

New Zealand Council for Educational Research

Box 3237, Education House, 178–182 Willis Street,
Wellington 6140
tel +64 (0)4 384 7939
email david.ellis@nzcer.org.nz
website www.nzcer.org.nz
Publishing Manager David Ellis

Education, including educational policy and practice,
early childhood education, educational achievement
tests, Māori education, schooling for the future,
curriculum and assessment. Founded 1934.

Otago University Press*

533 Castle Street, Dunedin 9010
tel +64 (0)3 479 8807
email university.press@otago.ac.nz
website www.otago.ac.nz/press
Publisher Sue Wootton

Non-fiction books on New Zealand and the Pacific,
particularly history, natural history, Māori and
Pacific; also biography/memoir, poetry, literature and
the arts. Also publishes New Zealand's longest-
running literary journal, *Landfall*. Founded 1958.

Penguin Random House New Zealand Ltd*

Private Bag 102 902, North Shore, Auckland 0745
tel +64 (0)9 442 7400
email publishing@penguinrandomhouse.co.nz
website www.penguinrandomhouse.co.nz
Facebook www.facebook.com/
PenguinBooksNewZealand
Publishing Director Debra Millar, *Head of Publishing*
Claire Murdoch

Adult and children's fiction and non-fiction.
Imprints: Penguin, Vintage, Black Swan, Godwit,
Viking, Puffin Books. Part of Penguin Random
House. Founded 2013.

Victoria University Press*

Victoria University of Wellington, PO Box 600,
Wellington 6140

tel +64 (0)4 463 6580
email victoria-press@vuw.ac.nz
website https://vup.victoria.ac.nz/
Publisher Fergus Barrowman, *Publicity Manager*
Kirsten McDougall, *Publishing Manager* Craig
Gamble, *Editors* Ashleigh Young, Kyleigh Hodgson,
Editorial Assistant Jasmine Sargent

Literary fiction and poetry; scholarly works on New
Zealand history, sociology, law; Māori language;
biography, memoir and essays. Founded 1974.

Viking Sevenseas NZ Ltd
PO Box 152, Paraparaumu, Wellington 5254
tel +64 (0)4 902 8240
email vikingsevenseas@gmail.com
website www.vikingsevenseas.co.nz

Natural history books on New Zealand only.

SOUTH AFRICA

*Member of the Publishers' Association of South Africa

Ad Donker – see Jonathan Ball Publishers

Jonathan Ball Publishers*
PO Box 33977, Jeppestown 2043
tel +27 (0)11 601 8000
email services@jonathanball.co.za
Postal address PO Box 33977, Jeppestown 2043
website www.jonathanball.co.za
Ceo Eugene Ashton

Specialises in South African history, politics and
current affairs. Also acts as agents for British and
American publishers, marketing and distributing
books on their behalf in southern Africa. A division
of Media24 (Pty) Ltd. Owners of Icon Books, a UK
based publishing company, since 2020.
Founded 1977.

Ad Donker
Africana, literature, history, academic.

Jonathan Ball
General publications, current affairs, politics, business
history, business, reference.

Delta Books
Military history.

Sunbird Publishers
Illustrated wildlife, tourism, maps, travel.

Burnet Media
PO Box 53557, Kenilworth, Cape Town 7745
email info@burnetmedia.co.za
website www.burnetmedia.co.za
Twitter @BurnetMedia
Publishing Manager Tim Richman

Independent publisher of the Two Dogs and Mercury
imprints, specialising in close author–publisher
relationships. Founded 2006.

Mercury
Interesting, accessible and engaging non-fiction with
broad subject matter for the South African and
international markets. Publishes a growing number
of international titles, with a particular focus on
authors with their own platforms.

Two Dogs
Innovative and irreverent non-fiction focusing on
contemporary and lifestyle subject matter for the
South African market.

Cambridge University Press, Africa*
Lower Ground Floor, Nautica Building,
The Water Club, Beach Road, Granger Bay,
Cape Town 8005
tel +27 (0)21 773 0147
email capetown@cambridge.org
website www.cambridge.org
Publishing Director Johan Traut

Textbooks and literature for sub-Sahara African
countries, as well as primary reading materials in 28
African languages. Founded 1534.

Delta Books – see Jonathan Ball Publishers

Galago Publishing (Pty) Ltd
PO Box 1645, Alberton, 1450
tel +27 (0)11 827 9418
email lemur@mweb.co.za
website www.galago.co.za
Managing Director Fran Stiff

Southern African interest: military, political, hunting.
Founded 1980.

Juta and Company (Pty) Ltd*
1st Floor, Sunclare Building, 21 Dreyer Street,
Claremont 7708
tel +27 (0)21 659 2300
email orders@juta.co.za
website www.juta.co.za
Ceo Kamal Patel

Academic, education, agencies, learning, law and
health. Publishers of print and digital print solutions.
Founded 1853.

University of KwaZulu-Natal Press*
Private Bag X01, Scottsville, Pietermaritzburg,
KwaZulu-Natal 3209
tel +27 (0)33 260 5226
email books@ukzn.ac.za
website www.ukznpress.co.za
Facebook www.facebook.com/UKZNPress
Twitter @UKZNPress
Publisher Debra Primo

Southern African social, political and economic
history, sociology, politics and political science,
current affairs, literary criticism, gender studies,
education, biography. Founded 1948.

Macmillan Education South Africa

4th Floor, Building G, Hertford Office Park,
90 Bekker Road, Vorna Valley, Midrand 1685
tel +27 (0)11 731 3300
Postal address Private Bag X19, Northlands 2116
website www.macmillan.co.za
Managing Director Preggy Naidoo

Educational titles for the RSA market. Founded 1843.

NB Publishers (Pty) Ltd*

PO Box 879, Cape Town 8000
tel +27 (0)21 406 3033
email nb@nb.co.za
website www.nb.co.za

General: Afrikaans fiction, politics, children's and
youth literature in all the country's languages, non-
fiction. Imprints: Tafelberg, Human & Rousseau,
Queillerie, Pharos, Kwela, Best Books and Lux Verbi.
Founded 1950.

New Africa Books (Pty) Ltd

Unit 13A, Athlone Industrial Park,
10 Mymoena Crescent, Cape Town 7764
tel +27 (0)21 467 5860
email info@newafricabooks.co.za
Postal address PostNet, Suite 144, Private Bag X9190,
Cape Town 8000

New Africa Books, incorporating David Philip
Publishers, is an independent publishing house.
Currently publishes fiction and non-fiction for
adults, picture books for children and comics for
young adults in all South African languages.
Founded 1971.

Spearhead

Current affairs, also business, self-improvement,
health, natural history, travel.

Oxford University Press Southern Africa*

Vasco Boulevard, N1 City, Goodwood,
Cape Town 7460
tel +27 (0)21 596 2300
email oxford.za@oup.com
Postal address PO Box 12119, N1 City,
Cape Town 7463
website www.oxford.co.za
Managing Director Hanri Pieterse

Oxford University Press is one of the leading
educational publishers in South Africa, producing a
wide range of quality educational material in print
and digital format. The range includes books from
Grade R to Grade 12, as well as TVET textbooks,
textbooks, school literature, dictionaries and atlases.
Committed to transforming lives through education
by providing superior quality learning material and
support. Founded 1586.

Pan Macmillan SA (Pty) Ltd*

2nd Floor, 1 Jameson Avenue, Melrose Estate,
Johannesburg 2196
tel +27 (0)11 684 0400
email roshni@panmacmillan.co.za
Postal address Private Bag X19, Northlands,
Johannesburg 2116
website www.panmacmillan.co.za
Managing Director Terry Morris

Imprints: Pan Macmillan UK, Macmillan US, Pan
Macmillan Australia, Walker Books, Priddy Books,
Hachette Children's Books, Hinkler Books, Pan
Macmillan South Africa, Pan KinderBoeke/Pan
Children's Books, Guinness. Publishes titles in
autobiography, biography, business, children's books,
cookery and wine, crafts and hobbies, crime,
environment, fiction (popular and literary), humour,
inspiration, literature, business, reference, sport and
stationery. Founded 1943.

Pearson South Africa*

4th Floor, Auto Atlantic,
Corner Hertzog Boulevard and Herengracht,
Cape Town 8001
tel +27 (0)21 532 6000
email pearsonza.enquiries@pearson.com
website https://za.pearson.com/

Pearson South Africa provides learning materials,
technologies and services for use in schools, TVET
colleges, higher education institutions and in home
and professional environments. Founded 2010.

Penguin Random House (Pty) Ltd*

The Estuaries, No 4, Oxbow Crescent,
Century Avenue, Century City 7441
email info@penguinrandomhouse.co.za
Postal address PO Box 1144, Cape Town 8000
tel +27 (0)21 460 5400
website www.penguinrandomhouse.co.za
Directors Steve Connolly (managing), Fourie Bortha
(fiction), Marlene Fryer (non-fiction)

Imprints: Penguin Random House, Struik Lifestyle,
Struik Nature, Struik Travel & Heritage, Zebra Press,
Penguin Non-Fiction, Penguin Fiction, Umuzi.
Genres include general illustrated non-fiction;
lifestyle; natural history; South African politics; sport;
business; memoirs; contemporary fiction; literary
fiction; local fiction; Afrikaans; children's books. Part
of Penguin Random House. Founded 2013.

Shuter and Shooter Publishers (Pty) Ltd*

110 CB Downes Road, Pietermaritzburg,
KwaZulu-Natal 3201
tel +27 (0)33 846 8700
email sales@shuters.com
Postal address PO Box 61, Mkondeni, KwaZulu-Natal
3212

website www.shuters.co.za
Ceo Primi Chetty

Core curriculum-based textbooks for use at foundation, intermediate, senior and FET phases. Supplementary readers in various languages; dictionaries; reading development kits, charts. Literature titles in English, isiXhosa, Sesotho, Sepedi, Setswana, Tshivenda, Xitsonga, Ndebele, isiZulu and Siswati. Founded 1925.

Sunbird Publishers – see Jonathan Ball Publishers

Unisa Press*

University of South Africa, PO Box 392, Unisa, Mackleneuk, Pretoria 0003
tel +27 (0)12 429 3182
email pietehc@unisa.ac.za
website www.unisa.ac.za/press
Commissioning Editor Hetta Pieterse

All academic disciplines, African history, sustainable development, economics, the arts and the humanities generally. Imprint: UNISA. Email for MS submissions: boshosm@unisa.ac.za. Founded 1957.

Van Schaik Publishers*

PO Box 12681, Hatfield, Pretoria 0028
tel +27 (0)12 342 2765
email vanschaik@vanschaiknet.com
website www.vanschaiknet.com
General Manager Leanne Martini

Textbooks for the higher education market in southern Africa. Founded 1915.

Wits University Press*

Private Bag 3, Wits 2050
tel +27 (0)11 717 8700/1
email veronica.klipp@wits.ac.za
Postal address PO Wits, Johannesburg 2050
website www.witspress.co.za
Contact Corina Van der Spoel

Publishes well-researched, innovative books for both academic and general readers in the following areas: art and heritage, popular science, history and politics, biography, literary studies, women's writing and select textbooks. Founded 1922.

USA

Member of the Association of American Publishers Inc.

ABC-CLIO

147 Castilian Drive, Santa Barbara, CA 93117
tel +1 805-968-1911
website www.abc-clio.com
Facebook www.facebook.com/ABCCLIO
Twitter @ABC_CLIO

Academic resources for secondary and middle schools, colleges and universities, libraries and professionals (librarians, media specialists, teachers). Founded 1955.

Abingdon Press

2222 Rosa L. Parks Boulevard, Nashville, TN 37228
tel +1 800-251-3320
website www.abingdonpress.com
Facebook www.facebook.com/AbingdonPress
Twitter @AbingdonPress
President & Publisher Neil Alexander

General interest, professional, academic and reference, non-fiction and fiction, youth and children's non-fiction and Vatican Bible School; primarily directed to the religious market. Imprint of United Methodist Publishing House with tradition of crossing denominational boundaries. United Methodist Publishing founded 1789.

Harry N. Abrams, Inc.

195 Broadway, 9th Floor, New York, NY 10007
tel +1 212-206-7715
email abrams@abramsbooks.com
website www.abramsbooks.com

Art and architecture, photography, natural sciences, performing arts, children's books. Imprints include: Abrams, Abrams Appleseed, Abrams Books for Young Readers, Abrams ComicArts, Abrams Images, Abrams Noterie, Abrams Press, Amulet Books, Amulet Paperbacks, The Overlook Press, Cameron Books. Founded 1949.

Akashic Books Ltd

232 Third Street, Suite A115, Brooklyn, NY 11215
tel +1 718-643-9193
email info@akashicbooks.com
website www.akashicbooks.com
Facebook www.facebook.com/AkashicBooks
Twitter @AkashicBooks
Contacts Johnny Temple (publisher/editor-in-chief), Johanna Ingalls (managing editor/director of foreign rights), and Aaron Petrovich (production manager)

A Brooklyn-based independent company dedicated to publishing urban literary fiction and political non-fiction by authors who are either ignored by the mainstream, or who have no interest in working within the ever-consolidating ranks of the major corporate publishers. Founded 1997.

The University of Alabama Press

Box 870380, Tuscaloosa, AL 35487-0380
tel +1 205-348-5180
website www.uapress.ua.edu
Editor in Chief Daniel Waterman

American and Southern history, African–American studies, religion, rhetoric and communication, Judaic studies, literary criticism, anthropology and archaeology. Founded 1945.

Books

Applause Theatre and Cinema Book Publishers

200 Park Avenue South, Suite 1109, New York, NY 10003
tel +1 212-529-3888
email info@halleonardbooks.com
website www.applausepub.com
Facebook www.facebook.com/ApplauseBooks/
Twitter @ApplauseBooks
Publisher Michael Messina

Performing arts. Part of Rowman and Littlefield. Founded 1980.

Arcade Publishing

11th Floor, 307 West 36th Street, New York, NY 10018
tel +1 212-643-6816
website www.arcadepub.com
Executive Editor Cal Barksdale

General trade, including adult hardback and paperbacks. No unsolicited MSS. Founded 1988. Imprint of Skyhorse Publishing (page 220) since 2010.

The University of Arkansas Press

McIlroy House, 105 N. McIlroy Avenue, Fayetteville, AR 72701
tel +1 479 575-7544
email info@uapress.com
website www.uapress.com
Facebook www.facebook.com/uarkpress
Twitter @uarkpress
Instagram @urkpress
Editor-in-Chief David Scott Cunningham

Publishing Arkansas and regional history, poetry and literature, African American studies, food studies, sports studies, art and architecture. Home of the Miller Williams Poetry Prize (edited by Billy Collins), awarding publication and a cash prize for a new collections of poetry, and the Etel Adnan Poetry Prize (edited by Hayan Charara and Fady Joudah) for collections of poetry by writers of Arab heritage. Founded 1980.

Atlantic Monthly Press – see Grove Atlantic, Inc.

Avery – see Penguin Publishing Group

Avon – see HarperCollins Publishers

Barefoot Books

23 Bradford Street, Concord, MA 01742
tel +1 617-576-0660
email help@barefootbooks.com
website www.barefootbooks.com
Facebook www.facebook.com/barefootbooks
Twitter @BarefootBooks
Editorial Director Emma Parkin

Children's picture books, activity decks and board books: diverse, inclusive and global stories that build social-emotional and literacy skills. See website for submission guidelines. Founded 1993.

Basic Books

1290 Avenue of the Americas, 5th Floor, New York, NY 10104
tel +1 212 346-1100
email Basic.Books@hbgusa.com
website www.basicbooks.com
Facebook www.facebook.com/BasicBooks
Twitter @BasicBooks
Publisher Lara Heimert, *Vice-President & Associate Publisher* Thomas Kelleher

Publishes books in history, science, natural history, sociology, psychology, biography, politics, African–American studies. Basic Books is an imprint of Perseus Books, a Hachette Book Group company (page 212). Founded 1952.

Beacon Press*

24 Farnsworth, Boston, MA 02110
tel +1 617-742-2110
website www.beacon.org
Director Helene Atwan

General non-fiction in fields of religion, ethics, philosophy, current affairs, gender studies, environmental concerns, African–American studies, anthropology and women's studies, nature. Founded 1854.

Bella Books

PO Box 10543, Tallahassee, FL 32302
tel +1 800-729-4992
email info@bellabooks.com
website www.bellabooks.com

Lesbian fiction: mystery, romance, science fiction. Founded 1973.

Berkley Books – see Penguin Publishing Group

Bloomsbury Publishing USA*

1385 Broadway, New York, NY 10018
tel +1 212-419-5300
email Contact-USA@bloomsbury.com
website www.bloomsbury.com/us
Executive Director Adrienne Vaughan

Supports the worldwide publishing activities of Bloomsbury Publishing Plc: caters for the US market. For submission guidelines see: www.bloomsbury.com/us/authors/submissions/. Established in 1998 as an American subsidiary of Bloomsbury Publishing Plc. Founded 1986.

Bold Strokes Books, Inc.

648 South Cambridge Road, Building A, Johnsonville, NY 12094

email service@boldstrokesbooks.com
website www.boldstrokesbooks.com
Facebook www.facebook.com/BoldStrokesBooks/
Twitter @boldstrokebooks
Publisher Len Barot

Offers a diverse collection of LGBTQI+ general and genre fiction. Fiction includes romance, mystery/intrigue, crime, erotica, speculative fiction (science fiction/fantasy/horror), general fiction, and, through the Soliloquy imprint, young adult fiction. Since its inception in 2004, the company's mission has remained unchanged to bring quality queer fiction to readers worldwide and to support an international group of authors in developing their craft and reaching an ever-growing community of readers via print, digital and audio formats. Over 1,300 titles in print. For submission instructions see www.boldstrokesbooks.com/submissions. Founded 2004.

R.R. Bowker

630 Central Avenue, New Providence, NJ 07974
tel +1 908-286-1090
website www.bowker.com

Bibliographies and reference tools for the book trade and literary and library worlds, available in hardcopy, on microfiche, online and CD-Rom. Reference books for music, art, business, the computer industry, cable industry and information industry. Division of Cambridge Information Group. Founded 1868.

Boyds Mills & Kane

19 West 21st Street, #1201, New York NY10010
email info@bmkbooks.com
website www.boydsmillsandkane.com
Facebook www.facebook.com/BMKbooks
Twitter @kanepress

Fiction, non-fiction and poetry trade books for children and young adults. Founded 1991.

Boyds Mills Press

Publishes a wide range of high-quality fiction and non-fiction titles for young readers.

Kane Press

Publisher of illustrated titles for children ages 3 to 11.

Burford Books, Inc.

757 Warren Rd, #4137, Ithaca, NY 14852
tel +1 607-319-4373
email pburford@burfordbooks.com
website www.burfordbooks.com
President Peter Burford

Outdoor activities: golf, sports, fitness, nature, travel. Founded 1997.

Cambridge University Press*

1 Liberty Plaza, Floor 20, New York, NY 10006
tel +1 212-337-5000

email customer_service@cambridge.org
website www.cambridge.org/us

Academic and professional; Cambridge Learning (ELT, primary and secondary education). Founded 1534.

Candlewick Press

99 Dover Street, Somerville, MA 02144
tel +1 617-661-3330
email bigbear@candlewick.com
website www.candlewick.com
President & Publisher Karen Lotz, *Creative Director & Associate Publisher* Chris Paul, *Executive Editorial Director & Associate Publisher* Liz Bicknell, *Editorial Director & Director of Editorial Operations* Mary Lee Donovan

Books for babies through teens: board books, picture books, novels, non-fiction, novelty books. Submit material through a literary agent. Subsidiary of Walker Books Ltd, UK. Founded 1991.

Candlewick Entertainment

Group Editorial Director Joan Powers

Media-related children's books, including film/TV tie-ins.

Candlewick Studio

Group Editorial Director Karen Lotz, *Group Art Director* Chris Paul

Books for book-lovers of all ages.

Center Street

Hachette Book Group USA, 6100 Tower Cir #210, Franklin, TN 37067
email centerstreetpub@hbgusa.com
website www.centerstreet.com

Books with traditional values for readers in the US heartland. Imprint of Hachette Book Group (page 212). Founded 2005.

University of Chicago Press*

1427 East 60th Street, Chicago, IL 60637
tel +1 773-702-7700
website www.press.uchicago.edu

Scholarly books and monographs (humanities, social sciences and sciences); general trade books; reference books; and 70 scholarly journals. Founded 1891.

Chronicle Books*

680 Second Street, San Francisco, CA 94107
tel +1 415-537-4200
email hello@chroniclebooks.com
website www.chroniclebooks.com,
www.chroniclebooks.com/titles/kids-teens
Facebook www.facebook.com/ChronicleBooks
Twitter @ChronicleBooks
Instagram @chroniclekidsbooks
Chairman & Ceo Nion McEvoy, *Publisher* Christine Carswell

Books

Publishes award-winning, innovative books. Recognized as one of the 50 best small companies to work for in the USA. Publishing list includes illustrated books and gift products in design, art, architecture, photography, food, lifestyle, pop culture and children's titles. Founded 1967.

Coffee House Press

79 13th Avenue NE, Suite 110, Minneapolis, MN 55413
tel +1 612-338-0125
email info@coffeehousepress.org
website www.coffeehousepress.org
Interim Publisher Carla Valadez

Literary fiction, essays and poetry; collectors' editions. Founded 1984.

Columbia University Press*

61 West 62nd Street, New York, NY 10023
tel +1 212-459-0600
email jc373@columbia.edu
email es3387@columbia.edu
website https://cup.columbia.edu/
Twitter @ColumbiaUP
Associate Provost & Director Jennifer Crewe, *Editorial Director* Eric Schwartz

General interest, scholarly and textbooks in the humanities, social sciences, sciences and professions; reference works in print and electronic formats. Subjects include Asian studies, business, earth science and sustainability, economics, English and comparative literature, film and media studies, global and American history, international relations, journalism, life science, Middle Eastern studies, neuroscience, palaeontology, philosophy, political science and international relations, religion, sociology and social work. Publishes Asian and Russian literature in translation. For MSS submission information see https://cup.columbia.edu/manuscript-submissions. Founded 1893.

Concordia Publishing House

3558 South Jefferson Avenue, St Louis, MO 63118
tel +1 314-268-1000
website www.cph.org
Facebook www.facebook.com/concordiapublishing
Twitter @concordiapub
President & Ceo Bruce G. Kintz

Religious books, Lutheran perspective. Few freelance MSS accepted; query first. Founded 1869.

Contemporary Books

130 East Randolph Street, Suite 400, Chicago, IL 60601
tel +1 800-621-1918
website www.mheducation.com/prek-12/segment/adulted.html

Non-fiction. Imprints: Contemporary Books, Lowell House, Passport Books, VGM Career Books. Division of the McGraw-Hill companies.

Cooper Square Publishing

4501 Forbes Boulevard, Suite 200, Lanham, MD 20706
tel +1 301-459-3366

Part of the Rowman & Littlefield Publishing Group (page 219). Founded 1949.

Cornell University Press

Sage House, 512 East State Street, Ithaca, NY 14850
tel +1 607-253-2338
email cupressinfo@cornell.edu
website www.cornellpress.cornell.edu
Director Jane Bunker

Comstock Publishing Associates, Cornell East Asia Series, ILR Press, NIU Press, SEAP Publications and Three Hills. Scholarly books. Founded 1869.

The Countryman Press

500 Fifth Avenue, New York, NY 10110
tel +1 212-354-5500
email countrymanpress@wwnorton.com
website www.countrymanpress.com
Editorial Director Ann Treistman

Cooking and lifestyle, outdoor recreation guides for anglers, hikers, cyclists, canoeists and kayakers, US travel guides, New England non-fiction, how-to books, country living books, books on nature and the environment, classic reprints and general non-fiction. No unsolicited MSS. Division of W.W. Norton & Co., Inc. Founded 1973.

Crown Publishing Group – see Penguin Random House.

DAW Books, Inc.

1745 Broadway, New York, NY 10019
tel +1 212-366-2096
email daw@penguinrandomhouse.com
website www.dawbooks.com
Publishers Elizabeth R. Wollheim, Sheila E. Gilbert

Science fiction, fantasy, horror and paranormal: originals and reprints. Founded 1971.

Tom Doherty Associates, LLC

120 Broadway, 22nd Floor, New York, NY 10271
tel +1 212-388-0100
email enquiries@tor.com
website www.torforgeblog.com
Facebook www.facebook.com/tordotcom
Twitter @tordotcom

Fiction: general, historical, western, suspense, mystery, horror, science fiction, fantasy, humour, juvenile, classics (English language); non-fiction: adult and juvenile. Imprints: Tor, Forge, Orb, Starscope, Tor Teen. Founded 1980.

Forge

Publishes general fiction, both contemporary and historical; thrillers, mysteries and suspense novels;

westerns and Americana; military fiction and non-fiction.

Tor

Science fiction and fantasy published in hardback and paperback.

Dover Publications, Inc.

31 East 2nd Street, Mineola, NY 11501
tel +1 516-294-7000
website https://store.doverpublications.com/
Facebook www.facebook.com/doverpublications
Twitter @doverpublications

Art, architecture, antiques, crafts, juvenile, food, history, folklore, literary classics, mystery, language, music, mathematics and science, nature, design and ready-to-use art. Founded 1941.

Dutton – see Penguin Publishing Group

Elsevier (Clinical Solutions)

1600 John F. Kennedy Boulevard, Philadelphia, PA 19103-2398
tel +1 215-239-3900
website www.elsevierhealth.co.uk
website www.elsevier.com/clinical-solutions
President Dr. John Danaher

Medical books, journals and electrical healthcare solutions. No unsolicited MSS but synopses and project proposals welcome. Imprints: Bailliere Tindall, Churchill Livingstone, Elsevier, Mosby, Pergamon, Saunders. Founded 1880.

Farrar, Straus and Giroux, LLC

175 Varick Street, 9th Floor, New York, NY 10014
tel +1 212-741-6900
website https://us.macmillan.com/fsg
Facebook www.facebook.com/fsgoriginals
Twitter @FSOriginals
President & Publisher Jonathan Galassi

Founded 1946.

Sarah Crichton Books

Publishes a wide variety of literary and commercial fiction and non-fiction.

FSG Originals

website www.fsgoriginals.com
Original fiction that does not fit into any obvious category.

Hill and Wang

General non-fiction, history, public affairs, graphic novels. Founded 1956.

North Point Press

Literary non-fiction, with an emphasis on natural history, ecology, yoga, food writing and cultural criticism.

Scientific American

website https://books.scientificamerican.com/fsg/
Publishes non-fiction science books for the general reader.

Flyaway Books

100 Witherspoon Street, Louisville, KY 40202–1396
tel +1 502-569-5000
website www.flyawaybooks.com
President & Publisher David Dobson

Children's picture books with a social justice and spiritual angle. Division of Presbyterian Publishing Corp. Founded 1938.

Fonthill Media LLC

12 Sires Street, Charleston, SC 29403
tel +1 843-203-3432
email info@fonthillmedia.com
website www.fonthillmedia.com
Publisher & President (Charleston SC Office) Alan Sutton

General history. Specialisations include biography, military history, aviation history, naval and maritime history, regional and local history, transport history, social history, sports history, ancient history and archaeology. US imprints: Fonthill, America Through Time and American History House. Founded 2012.

Fulcrum Publishing

4690 Table Mountain Drive, Suite 100, Golden, CO 80403
tel +1 303-277-1623
website www.fulcrum-books.com

Publishes a wide variety of educational non-fiction texts and children's books, also books and support materials for teachers, librarians, parents and elementary through middle school children. Subjects include: science and nature, literature and storytelling, history, multicultural studies and Native American and Hispanic cultures. Founded 1965.

Getty Publications*

1200 Getty Center Drive, Suite 500, Los Angeles, CA 90049
tel +1 310-440-6536
email booknews@getty.edu
website www.getty.edu

Art, art history, architecture, classical art and archaeology, conservation. Founded 1983.

Gibbs Smith

tel 801-544-9800
email info@gibbs-smith.com
website www.gibbs-smith.com

A Utah-based publisher. Its trade and special interest division publishes home reference, cookbook and children's titles. The Gibbs Smith Education division is the nation's leading publisher of state history programs. All unsolicited queries, submissions and correspondence should be via email. Due to the number of submissions received, the policy is to respond only to projects the company wishes to explore. Founded 1969.

David R. Godine, Publisher, Inc.
15 Court Square, Suite 320, Boston, MA 02108
tel +1 617-451-9600
website www.godine.com
Publisher David Alexander

Fiction, non-fiction, poetry, biography, children's, essays, history, photography, art, typography, architecture, nature and gardening, music, cooking, words and writing and mysteries. No unsolicited MSS. Founded 1970.

Grand Central Publishing
1290 6th Avenue, New York, NY 10104
tel +1 212-364-1100
email grandcentralpublishing@hbgusa.com
website www.grandcentralpublishing.com
Facebook www.facebook.com/grandcentralpub
Twitter @grandcentralpub

Previously Warner Books, Inc. Fiction and non-fiction. Imprints: Twelve (publishes authors with unique perspectives), Forever (romance), Forever Yours (romance) and Twelve. Division of Hachette Book Group (see below). Founded 1970.

Grove Atlantic, Inc.*
154 West 14th Street, 12 Floor, New York, NY 10011
tel +1 212-614-7850
email info@groveatlantic.com
website www.groveatlantic.com
Facebook www.facebook.com/groveatlantic
Twitter @groveatlantic
Associate Publisher Judy Hottensen, *Vice-President & Editorial Director* Elisabeth Schmitz, *Senior Editor & Rights Director* Amy Hundley

Fiction, biography, autobiography, history, current affairs, social science, belles lettres, natural history. No unsolicited MSS. Imprints: Atlantic Monthly Press, Black Cat, Mysterious Press, Grove Press. Founded 1952.

Hachette Book Group*
1290 Avenue of the Americas, New York, NY 10104
tel +1 212-364-1100
website www.hachettebookgroup.com

Divisions: Grand Central Publishing (above); Hachette Audio; Hachette Nashville; Little, Brown and Company (page 214); Little, Brown Books for Young Readers; Orbit; Perseus Books; Yen Press. Imprints: Grand Central: Forever; Forever Yours; Goop Press; Twelve; Vision. Hachette Nashville: Center Street; FaithWords; Worthy Books. Little, Brown and Company: Back Bay Books; Jimmy Patterson; Little, Brown Spark; Mulholland Books; Voracious. Little, Brown Books for Young Readers:

LB Kids; Poppy. Orbit: Redhook. Perseus Books: Avalon Travel, Basic Books; Black Dog & Leventhal; Bold Type Books; Hachette Books; Hachette Go; Moon Travel; Rick Steves; Running Press; PublicAffairs; Seal Press. Founded 1996.

Orbit
website www.orbitbooks.net
Science fiction and fantasy.

HarperCollins Publishers*
195 Broadway, New York, NY 10007
tel +1 212-207-700
website https://corporate.harpercollins.com/us
President & Ceo Brian Murray

Fiction, history, biography, poetry, science, travel, cookbooks, juvenile, educational, business, technical and religious. Founded 1817.

Harpeth Road Press
PO Box 158184, Nashville, TN 37215
website www.harpethroad.com
Facebook www.facebook.com/harpethroad
Twitter @harpethroad
Instagram @harpethroad
Founder Jenny Hale

Romantic fiction publishers. Currently accepting mainstream commercial romantic fiction in all categories (no erotica please). Founded 2020.

Harvard University Press*
79 Garden Street, Cambridge, MA 02138
tel +1 617-495-2600
email contact_hup@harvard.edu
website www.hup.harvard.edu
Director George Andreou, *Editorial Director* Sharmila Sen

History, philosophy, literary criticism, politics, economics, sociology, music, science, classics, social sciences, behavioural sciences, law. Founded 1913.

Hill and Wang – see Farrar, Straus and Giroux, LLC

Hippocrene Books, Inc.
171 Madison Avenue, New York, NY 10016
tel +1 718-454-2366
email info@hippocrenebooks.com
website www.hippocrenebooks.com

International cookbooks, foreign language dictionaries, travel, military history, Polonia, general trade. Founded 1971.

Holiday House, Inc.*
120 Broadway, New York NY10271
tel +1 212-646 5025
email submissions@holidayhouse.com
website www.holidayhouse.com

General children's books. Send entire MS. Only responds to projects of interest. Founded 1935.

Henry Holt and Company LLC
175 Fifth Avenue, New York, NY 10010
tel +1 646-307-5238
website https://us.macmillan.com/henryholt

History, sports, politics, biography, memoir, novels.
Imprints: Henry Holt, Metropolitan Books, Times
Books, Holt Paperbacks. Founded 1866.

Johns Hopkins University Press*
2715 North Charles Street, Baltimore,
MD 21218–4319
tel +1 410-516-6900
email tcl@press.jhu.edu
website www.press.jhu.edu
Director Barbara Kline Pope, *Associate Director* Erik
A. Smist, *Editorial Director* Gregory M. Britton

History, literary studies, classics, environmental
studies, biology, history of STEM, bioethics, public
health and health policy, health and wellness, physics,
astronomy, mathematics, education. Founded 1878.

Houghton Mifflin Harcourt*
3 Park Avenue, Floor 19, New York, NY 10016
tel +1 212-598-5730
website www.hmhco.com

Educational content and solutions for K-12 teachers
and students of all ages; also reference, and fiction
and non-fiction for adults and young readers.
Founded 1832.

University of Illinois Press*
1325 South Oak Street, Champaign, IL 61820
tel +1 217-333-0950
email uipress@uillinois.edu
website www.press.illinois.edu
Director Laurie Matheson

American studies (history, music, literature, religion),
working-class and ethnic studies, communications,
regional studies, architecture, philosophy, women's
studies, film, sports history, folklore, food studies.
Founded 1918.

Indiana University Press
Office of Scholarly Publishing,
Herman B Wells Library 350, 1320 East 10th Street,
Bloomington, IN 47405–3907
tel +1 812-855-8817
email iupress@indiana.edu
website www.iupress.indiana.edu
Director Gary Dunham

Specialises in the humanities and social sciences:
African, African–American, Asian, cultural, Jewish
and Holocaust, Middle East, Russian and East
European, and women's and gender studies;
anthropology, film, history, bioethics, music,
palaeontology, philanthropy, philosophy and religion.
Imprint: Quarry Books (regional publishing).
Founded 1950.

Infobase Publishing
132 West 31st Street, New York, NY 10001
tel +1 800 322-8755
website www.infobase.com/about
Editorial Director Laurie E. Likoff

General reference books and services for colleges,
libraries, schools and general public. Founded 1940.

Inkshares
95 Linden Street, Suite 6, Oakland, CA 94607
email hello@inkshares.com
website www.inkshares.com
Facebook www.facebook.com/inkshares
Twitter @Inkshares
Co-founder & Ceo Adam Gomolin, *Co-founder & Cpo*
Thad Woodman, *Co-founder* Larry Levitsky

A book publisher that has readers, not agents or
editors, decide what is published. Publishes books
that successfully hit a pre-order threshold on the
company's platform, or win a contest run in
partnership with an imprint on the platform. The
process is as follows: authors pitch, readers pre-order,
and the company publishes. Any author can submit a
proposal for a book. Once the project goes live,
readers support the project by pre-ordering copies of
the book. Once the 750 pre-order goal is hit, the
work is published: authors are assigned an editor, a
designer and the company deals with printing,
distribution, marketing and publicity once the MS is
finished. Founded 2013.

Inner Traditions Bear & Company
1 Park Street, Rochester, Vermont 05767-0388
tel +1 800-246-8648
email comcustomerservice@InnerTraditions.com
website www.innertraditions.com
Founder/Publisher Ehud C. Sperling

Subjects included spirituality, the occult, ancient
mysteries, new science, holistic health and natural
medicine. Founded 1975.

Jolly Fish Press
2297 Waters Drive, Mendota Heights, MN 55120
tel +1 888-417-0195
email publicity@jollyfishpress.com
email submit@jollyfishpress.com
website www.jollyfishpress.com
Facebook www.facebook.com/JollyFishPress
Twitter @JollyFishPress
Managing Editor Mari Kesselring

Jolly Fish Press is dedicated to promoting
exceptional, unique new voices in middle grade
fiction and jumpstarting writing careers. See website
above for submission guidelines. Accepts electronic
submissions only. Jolly Fish Press is an imprint of
North Star Editions, Inc. Founded 2011.

University Press of Kansas
2502 Westbrooke Circle, Lawrence, KS 66045–4444
tel +1 785-864-4154

email upress@ku.edu
website www.kansaspress.ku.edu
Interim Director Kevin Smith, *Editor-in-Chief* Joyce Harrison, *Acquisitions Editors* David Congdon, Bethany Mowr

American history (political, social, cultural, environmental), military history, American political thought, American presidency studies, law and constitutional history, political science. Founded 1946.

Knopf Doubleday Publishing Group
1745 Broadway, New York, NY 10019
tel +1 212-782-9000
website https://knopfdoubleday.com/
President & Publisher Maya Mavjee, *Executive Vice-President (Knopf, Pantheon & Schocken)* Reagan Arthur

Alfred A. Knopf was founded in 1915 and has long been known as a publisher of distinguished hardback fiction and non-fiction. Imprints: Alfred A. Knopf, Vintage Books, Anchor Books, Doubleday, Everyman's Library, Nan A. Talese, Pantheon Books, Schocken Books, Black Lizard and Vintage Español. Founded 2008.

Krause Publications
700 East State Street, Iola, WI 54990–0001
tel +1 800-258-0929
website www.krausebooks.com

Antiques and collectables: coins, stamps, automobiles, toys, trains, firearms, comics, records; sewing, ceramics, outdoors, hunting. Imprint of F&W Publications, Inc. Founded 1952.

Little, Brown & Company
1290 Ave of the Americas, New York, NY 10104
tel +1 212-364-1100
email lbpublicity.Generic@hbgusa.com
website www.littlebrown.com
Facebook www.facebook.com/littlebrownandcompany
Twitter @littlebrown

General literature, fiction, non-fiction, biography, history, trade paperbacks, children's. Founded 1837.

Back Bay Books
Fiction and non-fiction. Founded 1993.

Jimmy Patterson
website www.littlebrown.com/imprint/little-brown-and-company/jimmy-patterson
Publishes James Patterson's *Middle School Years* series and other books by the same author and other popular writers of middle grade fiction.

Little, Brown Spark
Publishes books for young people and adults that spark ideas, feelings and change. Looking for authors who are experts and thought leaders in the fields of health, lifestyle, psychology and science.

Mulholland Books
Suspense and crime.

Voracious
Non-fiction: cookery, self-help, current issues and interest.

Llewellyn Worldwide
2143 Wooddale Drive, Woodbury, MN 55125
tel +1 651-291-1970
email publicity@llewellyn.com
website www.llewellyn.com
Facebook www.facebook.com/LlewellynBooks
Twitter @llewellynbooks
Publisher Bill Krause

For over a century Llewellyn Worldwide Ltd has been a publisher of new age and mind, body & spirit books, including self-help, holistic health, astrology, tarot, paranormal and alternative spirituality titles. Imprints: Llewellyn, Midnight Ink, Flux. Founded 1901.

Lonely Planet
230 Franklin Road, Building 2B, Franklin, TN 37064
email pressusa@lonelyplanet.com
website www.lonelyplanet.com
Facebook www.facebook.com/lonelyplanet
Twitter @lonelyplanet
Ceo Luis Cabrera

Lonely Planet is an international travel publisher, printing over 120 million books in 11 different languages, along with guidebooks and ebooks to almost every destination on the planet. Also produces a range of gift and reference titles, a website, a magazine and a range of digital travel products and apps. Founded 1973.

The Lyons Press
246 Goose Lane, Guilford, CT 06437
tel +1 203-458-4500
website www.lyonspress.com, www.globepequot.com
Contact Stephanie Scott

Fishing, hunting, sports, outdoor skills, history, military history, reference, true crime, entertainment and non-fiction. An imprint of Globe Pequot Press. Founded 1978.

McGraw-Hill Professional*
2 Penn Plaza, 12th Floor, New York, NY 10121
tel +1 212-904-2000
website www.mhprofessional.com

McGraw-Hill Business
Management, investing, leadership, personal finance.

McGraw-Hill Consumer
Non-fiction: from health, self-help and parenting, to sports, outdoor and boating books. Publishing partnerships include Harvard Medical School and Standard & Poor's.

McGraw-Hill Education
Test-prep, study guides, language instruction, dictionaries.

McGraw-Hill Medical
Harrison's and reference for practitioners and medical students.

McGraw-Hill Technical
Science, engineering, computing, construction references.

Macmillan Publishers, Inc.
120 Broadway, New York, NY 10271
tel +1 646-307-5151
email press.inquiries@macmillanusa.com
website https://us.macmillan.com

Publishers: Celadon Books; Farrar, Straus and Giroux (page 211); Flatiron Books; Henry Holt and Co. (page 213); Macmillan Children's Publishing Group; Macmillan Audio; St. Martin's Publishing Group (page 219); and Tor/Forge. Macmillan Publishers is based in New York City. Founded 1843

McPherson & Company
PO Box 1126, Kingston, NY 12402
tel +1 845-331-5807
email bmcphersonco@gmail.com
website www.mcphersonco.com
Facebook www.facebook.com/McPherson-and-Company
Twitter @bookmaverick
Publisher Bruce R. McPherson

Literary fiction; non-fiction: art criticism, writings by artists, film-making; occasional general titles (e.g. anthropology). No poetry. No unsolicited MSS; query first. Distributed in UK by Central Books, London. Imprints: Documentext, Treacle Press, Saroff Books. Founded 1974.

The University of Massachusetts Press*
New Africa House, 180 Infirmary Way, 4th Floor, Amherst, MA 01003-9289
email info@umpress.umass.edu
website www.umass.edu/umpress
Director Mary Dougherty, *Executive Editor* Matt Becker

Scholarly books and works of general interest: American studies and history, Black and ethnic studies, women's studies, cultural criticism, architecture and environmental design, literary criticism, poetry, fiction, philosophy, political science, sociology, books of regional interest. Founded 1964.

The University of Michigan Press*
839 Greene Street, Ann Arbor, MI 48104-3209
tel +1 734-764-4388
email um.press@umich.edu
website www.press.umich.edu
Director Charles Watkinson

Scholarly and general interest works in literary and cultural theory, classics, history, theatre, women's studies, political science, law, American history, American studies, anthropology, economics, jazz; textbooks in English as a second language; regional trade titles. Founded 1930.

Microsoft Press
One Microsoft Way, Redmond, WA 98052–6399
tel +1 425-882-8080
email 4bkideas@microsoft.com
website www.microsoft.com/en-gb/learning/microsoft-press-books.aspx

Computer books. Division of Microsoft Corp. Founded 1983.

Milkweed Editions
1011 Washington Avenue South, Suite 300, Minneapolis, MN 55415
tel +1 612-332-3192
website www.milkweed.org
Editors Daniel Slager, Joey McGarvey

Fiction, poetry, essays, the natural world. Founded 1979.

University of Missouri Press
113 Heinkel Building, 201 South 7th Street, Columbia, MO 65211
tel +1 573-882-7641
email upress@missouri.edu
website https://upress.missouri.edu
Facebook www.facebook.com/umissouripress
Twitter @umissouripress
Editor-in-Chief Andrew Davidson

American History (esp. US military, African American, political), journalism, political science, Missouri history and regional studies, and literary criticism. Founded 1958.

The MIT Press
One Rogers Street, Cambridge, MA 02142–1209
tel +1 617-253-5646
website https://mitpress.mit.edu
Director Amy Brand

Art and architecture; cognitive sciences, philosophy, and bioethics; computer science; culture and technology; design and visual culture; education and learning; economics, finance and business, environmental studies, urbanism, and food studies; information science and communication; life sciences, neuroscience, and trade science; linguistics, new media, game studies, and digital humanities; physical sciences, mathematics, and engineering; science, technology, and society, and MIT and regional interest. Founded 1962.

Thomas Nelson Publisher
PO Box 141000, Nashville, TN 37214
tel +1 800-251-4000

Books

email publicity@thomasnelson.com
website www.thomasnelson.com

Bibles, religious, non-fiction and fiction general trade books for adults and children. Acquired by HarperCollins in 2012. Founded 1798.

New Harbinger Publications
5674 Shattuck Avenue, Oakland, CA 94609
tel +1 800 748 6273
email customerservice@newharbinger.com
website www.newharbinger.com
Facebook www.facebook.com/NewHarbinger
Twitter @NewHarbinger

An independent, employee-owned publisher of books on psychology, health, spirituality and personal growth. Their evidence-based self-help books and pioneering workbooks aim to help readers make positive changes to improve mental health and well-being. Their professional books serve as resources for mental health clinicians to build their practice and better serve clients. And their spirituality books offer timeless wisdom for living consciously in the modern world. Imprints include: New Harbinger, Instant Help, Impact Publishers, Context Press, Non-duality Press, Reveal Press. For submission guidelines see: www.newharbinger.com/publishing-new-harbinger. Founded 1973.

University of New Mexico Press
1717 Roma NE, MSC05 3185, Albuquerque, NM 87131-0001
tel +1 505-277-3495
email custserv@unm.edu
website www.unmpress.com
Director Stephen Hull, *Managing Editor* James Ayers

Western history, anthropology and archaeology, Latin American studies, photography, multicultural literature, fiction, poetry. Founded 1929.

The University of North Carolina Press*
116 South Boundary Street, Chapel Hill, NC 27514
tel +1 919-966-3561
website https://uncpress.org/
Facebook www.facebook.com/newmexicopress
Twitter @UMPress
Editorial Director James Ayers

American history, American studies, Southern studies, European history, women's studies, Latin American studies, political science, anthropology and folklore, classics, regional trade. Founded 1922.

North Point Press – see Farrar, Straus and Giroux, LLC

W.W. Norton & Company, Inc.*
500 Fifth Avenue, New York, NY 10110
tel +1 212-354-5500
website www.wwnorton.com
Vice President & Editor-in-Chief John Glusman

Literary fiction and narrative non-fiction, history, politics, science, biography, music and memoir. Founded 1923.

University of Oklahoma Press
2800 Venture Drive, Norman, OK 73069–8216
tel +1 405-325-2000
website www.oupress.com
Interim Director Dale Bennie, *Managing Editor* Stephen Baker

American West, American Indians, classics, political science. Founded 1928.

OR Books
137 West 14th Street, New York, NY 10011
tel +1 212 514 6485
email info@orbooks.com
website www.orbooks.com
Facebook www.facebook.com/orbooks/
Twitter @orbooks
Co-founders John Oakes & Colin Robinson

OR Books publishes by printing on demand, selling directly to the customer, and focusing on creative promotion through traditional media and the Internet. Publishes non-fiction: literature, history and politics, activism, society, the Internet and the Middle East. Founded 2009.

Orbit – see Hachette Book Group

The Overlook Press
141 Wooster Street Suite 4B, New York, NY 10012
tel +1 212-673-2210
website www.overlookpress.com
Facebook www.facebook.com/overlookpress
Twitter @overlookpress

Non-fiction, fiction, children's books (*Freddy the Pig* series). Imprints: Ardis Publishing, Duckworth. Imprint of Abrams. Founded 1971.

Oxford University Press*
198 Madison Avenue, New York, NY 10016
tel +1 212-726-6000
website https://global.oup.com/academic
Ceo Nigel Portwood

Academic and trade, bibles; ELT and ESL; dictionaries; higher education and science, technology, medicine and scholarly; law, medicine and music; journals; online; reference. Publishes globally for a range of audiences, across a multitude of cultures, education systems and languages. Currently publishes more than 6,000 titles a year worldwide, in a variety of formats. Many of these titles are created specifically for local markets and are published by regional publishing branches. Founded 1586.

Paragon House Publishers
3600 Labore Road, Suite 1, St. Paul, Minnesota, MN 55110–4144

tel +1 651-644-3087
email paragon@ParagonHouse.com
website www.ParagonHouse.com
President Gordon L. Anderson

Academic and general interest books in philosophy, religion, social sciences and non-fiction.

Pelican Publishing

400 Poydras Street, Suite 900, Gretna, LA 70130
tel +1 504-684-8976
email editorial@pelicanpub.com
website www.pelicanpub.com
Publisher & President Christen Thompson

Art and architecture, cookbooks, biography, history, business, children's, motivational, political science, social commentary, holiday. Founded 1926.

Penguin Publishing Group*

1745 Broadway, New York, NY 10019
tel +1 212-366-2000
website www.penguin.com
President Allison Dobson

The Penguin Publishing Group is a leading adult trade book division with a wide range of imprints. Imprints include: Avery, Berkley, Dutton, G. P. Putnam's Sons, Optimism Press, Pamela Dorman Books, Penguin Books, Penguin Classics, Penguin Press, Plume, Portfolio, TarcherPerigee, Riverhead, Sentinel, Viking and Writer's Digest Books. Founded 1935.

Penguin Random House*

1745 Broadway, New York, NY 10019
tel +1 212-782-9000
website www.penguinrandomhouse.com
Ceo Madeline McIntosh

With 300 independent imprints and brands, more than 15,000 new print titles and close to 800 million print, audio and ebooks sold annually, Penguin Random House is the world's leading trade book publisher. The company was formed in 2013, and is owned by Bertelsmann. Like its predecessor companies, Penguin Random House is committed to publishing adult and children's fiction and non-fiction print editions, and is a pioneer in digital publishing. Its book brands include storied imprints such as Doubleday, Viking and Alfred A. Knopf (US); Ebury, Hamish Hamilton and Jonathan Cape (UK); Plaza & Janés and Alfaguara (Spain); and Sudamericana (Argentina); as well as the international imprint DK. See Crown Publishing Group (page 210), Knopf Doubleday Publishing Group (page 214), Penguin Publishing Group (above), Random House Publishing Group (page 218), Penguin Young Readers (below) and Random House Children's Books (page 218). Founded 2013.

Penguin Young Readers*

1745 Broadway, New York, NY 10019
tel +1 212-366-2000
website www.penguin.com/children
President Jen Loja

Penguin Young Readers is one of the leading children's book publishers in the USA. The company owns a wide range of imprints and trademarks including Dial Books, Dutton, Grosset & Dunlap, Kathy Dawson Books, Kokila, Nancy Paulsen Books, Penguin Workshop, Philomel, Puffin, G.P. Putnam's Sons, Razorbill, Speak, Viking and Frederick Warne. Penguin Young Readers is also the proud publisher of perennial brand franchises such as the *Nancy Drew* and *Hardy Boys* series, *Peter Rabbit, Corduroy, The Very Hungry Caterpillar, Llama Llama, Mud Libs, Last Kids On Earth, Who Was?*, Roald Dahl, Jacqueline Woodson, S.E. Hinton and John Green among many others. Penguin Young Readers is a division of Penguin Group LLC, a Penguin Random House company. Founded 1935.

University of Pennsylvania Press

3905 Spruce Street, Philadelphia, PA 19104–4112
tel +1 215-898-6261
email custserv@pobox.upenn.edu
website www.pennpress.org
Director Mary Francis

American and European history, African-American studies, anthropology, Atlantic studies, architecture, cultural studies, ancient studies, human rights, literature, medieval and early modern studies, Jewish studies, religious studies, current affairs, politics and public policy, urban studies and Pennsylvania regional studies. Founded 1890.

Pennsylvania State University Press*

820 North University Drive, USB1, Suite C,
University Park, PA 16802
tel +1 814-865-1327
email info@psupress.org
website www.psupress.org
Director Patrick Alexander, *Assistant Director & Editor-in-Chief* Kendra Boileau, *Executive Editor* Eleanor Goodman, *Acquisitions Editors* Kathryn B. Yahner, Ryan Peterson

Art history, literary criticism, religious studies, philosophy, political science, sociology, history, Latin American studies and medieval studies. Founded 1956.

The Permanent Press

4170 Noyac Road, Sag Harbor, NY 11963
tel +1 631-725-1101
website www.thepermanentpress.com
Facebook www.facebook.com/ThePermanentPress
Twitter @TPermanentPress
Publisher Judith Shepard

Books

Literary fiction. Imprint: Second Chance Press. Founded 1978.

Plume – see Penguin Publishing Group

Potomac Books, Inc.
c/o Longleaf Services, Inc, 116 S Boundary St, Chapel Hill, NC 27514
tel +1 800-848-6224
email customerservice@longleafservices.org
website www.nebraskapress.unl.edu/potomac

National and international affairs, history (military and diplomatic); reference, biography. Purchased by the University of Nebraska Press in 2013. Founded 1984.

powerHouse Books
32 Adams St, Brooklyn, NY 11201
tel +1 718-666-3049
email madison@powerhousebooks.com
website www.powerhousebooks.com
Facebook www.facebook.com/pages/powerHouseBooksNY
Twitter @powerhousebooks
Instagram @powerhousebooks
Ceo/Publisher Daniel Power

World-renowned and critically acclaimed publisher, best known for a diverse publishing program which specialises in fine art, documentary, pop culture, fashion, and celebrity books. Check submissions page on website for submissions procedure. Founded 1995.

Princeton University Press*
Princeton, NJ 08540
tel +1 609-258-4900
Postal address 41 William Street, Princeton, NJ 08540
website www.press.princeton.edu
Director Christie Henry

Scholarly and scientific books on all subjects. Founded 1905.

Puffin – see Penguin Young Readers

Quarto Publishing Group USA
142 West 36th Street, Fourth Floor, New York, NY 10018
website www.quarto.com

Creates and publishes illustrated books in North America and sells co-editions of them internationally. Subject categories include home improvement, gardening, practical arts and crafts, licensed children's books, transport, graphic arts, food and drink, sports, military history, Americana, health and body, lifestyle, pets and music. The division comprises 15 imprints; Book Sales, Cool Springs Press, Creative Publishing International, Fair Winds Press, Motorbooks, Quarry Books, QDS, Quiver, Race Point Publishing, Rock Point, Rockport Publishers,

Voyageur Press, Walter Foster Publishing, Walter Foster, Jr. and Zenith Press. Details of the imprints can be found on the website. Founded 2004.

Rand McNally
PO Box 7600, Chicago, IL 60680
tel +1 847-329-8100
website www.randmcnally.com

Maps, guides, atlases, educational publications, globes and children's geographical titles and atlases in print and electronic formats. Founded 1856.

Random House Children's Books*
1745 Broadway, New York, NY 10019
tel +1 212-782-9000
website www.rhcbooks.com, www.randomhouse.com/teachers
President & Publisher Barbara Marcus

Random House Children's Books is the world's largest English-language children's trade book publisher. Creates books for preschool children through young adult readers, in all formats from board books to activity books to picture books, graphic novels, novels and non-fiction. Imprints: Dragonfly, Ember, Laurel-Leaf, Little Golden Books, Make Me A World, Princeton Review, Random House Books for Young Readers, Random House Graphic, Rodale Kids, Schwartz & Wade Books, Sylvan Learning, Wendy Lamb Books, Yearling Books. Part of Penguin Random House (page 217). Founded 1925.

Random House Publishing Group*
1745 Broadway, New York, NY 10019
tel +1 212-782-9000
website www.randomhousebooks.com
President & Publisher Gina Centrello

Random House publishes literary and commercial fiction; narrative non-fiction across genres such as history, science, politics, current affairs, biography, memoir, religion and business; as well as in the preeminent culinary and lifestyle illustrated published program in the USA. Imprints: Ballantine Books, Bantam Books, Broadway Books, Clarkson Potter, Convergent Books, Crown, Crown Archetype, Crown Forum, Currency, Delacorte Press, Dell, Del Rey, The Dial Press, Harmony Books, Hogarth, Hogarth Shakespeare, Ink & Willow, Lorena Jones Books, Modern Library, One World, Random House, RocLit 101, Rodale Books, SJP for Hogarth, Ten Speed Press, Three Rivers Press, Tim Duggan Books, WaterBrook Multnomah and Watson-Guptill. Part of Penguin Random House (page 217). Founded 1927.

Razorbill – see Penguin Young Readers

Rizzoli International Publications, Inc.
300 Park Avenue South, New York, NY 10010
tel +1 212-387-3400

email publicity@rizzoliusa.com
website www.rizzoliusa.com
Publisher Charles Miers

Art, architecture, photography, fashion, gardening, design, gift books, cookbooks. Founded 1976.

Rodale Book Group
733 Third Avenue, New York, NY 10017
tel +1 212-573-0300
website https://crownpublishing.com/archives/imprint/rodale-books
Ceo Maria Rodale

General health, women's health, men's health, senior health, alternative health, fitness, healthy cooking, gardening, pets, spirituality/inspiration, trade health, biography, memoir, current affairs, science, parenting, organics, lifestyle, self-help, how-to, home arts. Imprint of the Crown Publishing Group. Founded 1932.

Routledge
711 Third Avenue, New York, NY 10017
tel +1 212-216-7800
website www.routledge.com

Music, history, psychology and psychiatry, politics, business studies, philosophy, education, sociology, urban studies, religion, film, media, literary and cultural studies, reference, English language, linguistics, communication studies, journalism. Editorial office in the UK. Subsidiary of Taylor & Francis, LLC. Imprint: Routledge. Founded 1834.

Rowman & Littlefield
4501 Forbes Boulevard, Suite 200, Lanham, MD 20706
tel +1 301-459-3366
email customercare@rowman.com
website www.rowman.com
Facebook www.facebook.com/rowmanuk
Twitter @rowmanuk
President & Ceo James E. Lyons

Rowman & Littlefield is an independent publisher specialising in academic publishing in the humanities and social sciences, government and official data and educational publishing. Founded 1925.

Running Press Book Publishers
2300 Chestnut Street, Suite 200, Philadelphia, PA 19103
tel +1 215-567-5080
email perseus.promos@perseusbooks.com
website www.runningpress.com

General non-fiction, TV, film, humour, history, children's fiction and non-fiction, food and wine, pop culture, lifestyle, illustrated gift books. Imprints: Running Press, Running Press Miniature Editions, Running Press Kids, Running Press Adults. Member of the Perseus Books Group. Founded 1972.

Rutgers University Press
106 Somerset Street, Third Floor, New Brunswick, NJ 08901
tel +1 800-848-6224
website www.rutgersuniversitypress.org
Director Micah Kleit, *Editorial Director* Kimberly Guinta

Women's studies, LGBTQI+ studies, anthropology, childhood studies, Latin American and Caribbean studies, higher education, human rights, television, film and media studies, communication, sociology, public health, history of medicine, Asian American studies, African American studies, American studies, Latinx studies, Jewish studies, religious studies, regional titles. Founded 1936.

St Martin's Press, Inc.
175 Fifth Avenue, New York, NY 10010
tel +1 212-677-7456
website https://us.macmillan.com/smp

Trade, reference, college. No unsolicited MSS. Imprint of Macmillan. Founded 1952.

Santa Monica Press
PO Box 850, Solana Beach, CA 92075
tel +1 858-793-1890
email acquisitions@santamonicapress.com
website www.santamonicapress.com
Facebook www.facebook.com/santa-monica-press
Publisher Jeffrey Goldman

Titles are sold in chain, independent, online and university bookstores around the world, as well as in retail outlets in North America and the UK. Publishes modern non-fiction titles: pop culture, film, music, humor, biography, travel and sports, as well as regional titles focused on California. Young adult historical fiction and young adult narrative non-fiction recently added to the list. Please visit website to view author guidelines. Founded 1994.

Sasquatch Books
1904 Third Ave, Suite 710 Seattle, WA 98101
tel +1 206-467-4300
email custserv@sasquatchbooks.com
website www.sasquatchbooks.com

Independent press, located in downtown Seattle. The mission is to seek out and work with gifted writers, chefs, naturalists, artists and thought leaders in the Pacific Northwest and bring their talents to a national audience. Publishes a variety of non-fiction books, as well as children's books under the Little Bigfoot imprint. Are happy to consider queries and proposals from authors and agents for new projects that fit into the company's West Coast regional publishing programme. Founded 1986.

Scholastic, Inc.*
557 Broadway, New York, NY 10012
tel +1 212-343-6100

email news@scholastic.com
website www.scholastic.com
Facebook www.facebook.com/scholastic
Twitter @scholastic

Scholastic is the world's largest publisher and distributor of children's books and a leader in education technology and children's media. Divisions: Scholastic Trade Publishing, Scholastic Book Clubs, Scholastic Book Fairs, Scholastic Education, Scholastic International, Media, Licensing and Advertising. Imprints include: Arthur A. Levine Books, Cartwheel Books, Chicken House, David Fickling Books, Graphix, Orchard Books, Point, PUSH, Scholastic en español, Scholastic Focus, Scholastic Licensed Publishing, Scholastic Nonfiction, Scholastic Paperbacks, Scholastic Press, Scholastic Reference and The Blue Sky Press. In addition, Scholastic Trade Books includes Klutz, a highly innovative publisher and creator of 'books plus' for children. Founded 1920.

Seal Press

1290 Avenue of the Americas, 5th Floor, New York, NY 10104
tel +1 212 364-1100
email Basic.Books@hbgusa.com
website www.sealpress.com
Facebook www.facebook.com/sealpress
Twitter @SealPress
Instagram @sealpress
Publisher Lara Heimert

Publishes radical feminist, antiracist and LGBTQIA+ non-fiction books. Seal Press is an imprint of Basic Books, an imprint of Perseus Books, a Hachette Book Group company. Founded 1976.

Sentinel – see Penguin Publishing Group

Simon & Schuster Children's Publishing Division*

1230 Avenue of the Americas, New York, NY 10020
tel +1 212-698-7200
website www.simonandschuster.com/kids
President & Publisher Jon Anderson

Preschool to young adult, fiction and non-fiction, trade, library and mass market. Imprints: Aladdin Paperbacks, Atheneum Books for Young Readers, Beach Lane Books, Little Simon, Margaret K. McElderry Books, Salaam Reads, Simon & Schuster Books for Young Readers, Simon Pulse, Simon Spotlight, Paula Wiseman Books. More details on some of the imprints are given below. Division of Simon & Schuster, Inc. Founded 1924.

Simon & Schuster, Inc.*

1230 Avenue of the Americas, New York, NY 10020
tel +1 212-698-7000
website www.simonandschuster.com
President & Publisher Jonathan Karp, *VP & Deputy Publisher* Richard Rhorer

General fiction and non-fiction. No unsolicited MSS. Imprints: 37 Ink, Adams Media, Aladdin, Atria Books, Atheneum Books for Young Readers, Avid Reader Press, Beach Lane Books, Beyond Words, Caitlyn Dlouhy Books, Denene Millner Books, Emily Bestler Books, Folger Shakespeare Library, Free Press, Gallery Books, Gallery 13, Howard Books, Jeter Publishing, Little Simon, Marble Arch Press, Margaret K. McElderry, Paula Wiseman Books, Pocket Books, Pocket Star, Saga Press, Salaam Reads, Scout Press, Scribner, Signal Press, Simon & Schuster, Simon & Schuster Books for Young Readers, Simon Pulse, Simon Spotlight, Skybound Books, Star Trek®, Strebor Books, Threshold Editions, Tiller Press, Washington Square Press. Founded 1924.

Skyhorse Publishing

307 West 36th Street, 11th Floor, New York, NY 10018
tel +1 212-643-6816
website www.skyhorsepublishing.com
Facebook www.facebook.com/SkyhorsePublishing
Twitter @skyhorsepub
Instagram @skyhorsepub

Publishes outdoor sports, adventure, team sports, nature and country living, with a good dose of politics, true crime, history and military history, reference and humor (practical, literary and general trade). Imprints include: Sky Pony Press, Sports Publishing, Allworth Press and Arcade Publishing (page 208). Founded 2006.

Soho Press, Inc.

853 Broadway, New York, NY 10003
tel +1 212-260-1900
email soho@sohopress.com
website www.sohopress.com
Facebook www.facebook.com/SohoPress
Twitter @soho_press
Publisher Bronwen Hruska

Literary fiction, commercial fiction, mystery, memoir. Founded 1986.

Sourcebooks, Inc.

P.O. Box, 4410, Naperville, IL 60567-4410
website www.sourcebooks.com
Editorial Director Todd Stocke, *Editorial Director, Sourcebooks & Sourcebooks Landmark* Shana Drehs, *Editorial Director, Sourcebooks & Poisoned Pen Press* Anna Michels, *Editorial Director, Sourcebooks Fire & Sourcebooks Kids* Steve Geck, *Editorial Director, Sourcebooks eXplore (non-fiction)*, Kelly Barrales-Saylor, *Editorial Director, Sourcebooks Casablanca* Deb Werksman

A leading independent publisher with a wide variety of genres including fiction, romance, children's, young adult, gift/calendars and college-bound. E-commerce businesses include *Put Me In the Story*, the number one personalised books platform. Imprints include: Cumberland House, Dawn Publications, Little Pickle Press, Poison Pen Press, Simple Truths, Sourcebooks, Sourcebooks Casablanca, Sourcebooks Fire, Sourcebooks Kids, Sourcebooks Landmarks. Founded 1987.

Sourcebooks

Publishes narrative history, science, memoirs, study aids, self-help and personal development, and topics of particular interest to women, as well as practical and prescriptive books that help readers improve their lives under our trade imprint.

Sourcebooks Casablanca

Publishes six to eight romance novels per month: contemporary, paranormal, romantic suspense and historical romance.

Sourcebooks Fire

Aims to publish books with authentic teen voices that create and validate the teen experience in all of its diversity. Bridging both the commercial and literary, publishes across genres, and is known for books that teens want to recommend to their friends.

Sourcebooks Kids

Publishes notable fiction and non-fiction projects including board books, picture books, chapter books and middle-grade works with the hope of engaging children in the pure fun of books and the wonder of learning new things.

Sourcebooks Landmarks

Publishes contemporary women's and feel-good fiction, historical fiction, speculative crossover and mysteries, thrillers and suspense – all perfect for the book club audience.

Stanford University Press*

485 Broadway, First Floor, Redwood City, CA 94063-8460
tel +1 650-723-9434
email information@www.sup.org
website www.sup.org

Scholarly (humanities and social sciences), professional (business, law, economics and management science), high-level textbooks. Founded 1893.

Ten Speed Press

1745 Broadway, 10th Floor, New York, NY 10019
tel +1 510-559-1600
website https://crownpublishing.com/archives/imprint/ten-speed-press

Career/business, cooking, practical non-fiction, health, women's interest, self-help, children's. Imprints: Celestial Arts, Crossing Press, Tricycle Press. Founded 1971.

University of Tennessee Press

110 Conference Center Building, Knoxville, TN 37996

tel +1 865-974-3321
website www.utpress.org
Director Scot Danforth

American studies: African–American studies, Appalachian studies, history, religion, literature, historical archaeology, folklore, vernacular architecture, material culture. New series, *Legacies of War and America's Baptists*. Founded 1940.

University of Texas Press*

3001 Lake Austin Blvd, 2,200 Stop E4800, Austin, TX 78703–4206
tel +1 800-252-3206
email info@utpress.utexas.edu
website https://utpress.utexas.edu/
Facebook www.facebook.com/utexaspress
Editorial Assistant Jon Boggs

A book and journal publisher – a focal point where the life experiences, insights and specialised knowledge of writers converge to be disseminated in both print and digital format. Founded 1950.

Tuttle Publishing/Periplus Editions

Airport Business Park, 364 Innovation Drive, North Clarendon, VT 05759
tel +1 802-773-8930
email info@tuttlepublishing.com
website www.tuttlepublishing.com
Ceo Eric Oey, *Publishing Director* Ed Walters

Asian art, culture, cooking, gardening, Eastern philosophy, martial arts, health. Founded 1948.

Viking Press – see Penguin Publishing Group

Walker Books US

99 Dover Street, Somerville, MA 02144
tel +1 617-661-3330
website www.walkerbooksus.com, www.candlewick.com
Facebook www.facebook.com/CandlewickPressBooks
Directors Susan Van Metre (editorial), Maria Middleton (art)

Walker Books US is a division of Candlewick Press. Founded 2017.

University of Washington Press

4333 Brooklyn Avenue NE, Seattle, WA 98105
Postal address Box 359570, Seattle, WA 98195-9570
tel +1 206-543-4050
website https://uwapress.uw.edu/
Director Nicole Mitchell

American studies; anthropology; art history and visual culture; Asian American studies; Asian studies; critical ethnic studies; environmental history; Native American and Indigenous studies; nature and environment; women's, gender, and sexuality studies; and Western and Pacific Northwest history. The press also publishes a broad range of books about the Pacific Northwest for general readers, often in

Books

partnership with regional museums, cultural organizations, and local tribes. Founded 1920.

WaterBrook Multnomah Publishing Group

10807 New Allegiance Drive, Suite 500, Colorado Springs, CO 80921
tel +1 719-590-4999
email info@waterbrookmultnomah.com
website www.waterbrookmultnomah.com

Fiction and non-fiction with a Christian perspective. No unsolicited MSS. Subsidiary of Penguin Random House (page 217). Founded 1996.

Watson-Guptill Publications

c/o Penguin Random House, 1745 Broadway, New York, NY 10019
tel +1 212-782-9000 / +1 212-572-6066
website https://crownpublishing.com/imprint/watson-guptill/

Art, crafts, how-to, comic/cartooning, photography, performing arts, architecture and interior design, graphic design, music, writing, reference. Imprints: Amphoto Books, Watson-Guptill. Founded 1937.

John Wiley & Sons, Inc.*

111 River Street, Hoboken, NJ 07030
tel +1 201-748-6000
email info@wiley.com
website www.wiley.com
President & Ceo Brian A. Napack

Specialises in scientific, technical, medical and scholarly journals; encyclopedias, books and online products and services; professional/trade books, subscription products, training materials and online applications and websites; and educational materials for undergraduate and graduate students and lifelong learners. Founded 1807.

Workman Publishing Company*

225 Varick Street, New York, NY 10014
tel +1 212-254-5900
email info@workman.com
website www.workman.com
Publisher & Editorial Director Susan Bolotin

General non-fiction for adults and children. Calendars. Founded 1968.

Writer's Digest Books

1745 Broadway New York, NY 10019
tel +1 212-782-9000
email writersdigest@fwmedia.com
website www.penguinrandomhouse.com

Market directories, books and magazine for writers, photographers and songwriters. Imprint of Penguin Random House. An imprint of Penguin Random House LLC, see page (217). Founded 1920.

Yale University Press*

PO Box 209040, New Haven, CT 06520-9040
tel +1 203-432-0960
UK office 47 Bedford Square, London WC1B 3DP
website www.yale.edu/yup

Scholarly, trade books and art books. Founded 1908.

Yen Press

Hachette Book Group, 1290 Avenue of the Americas, New York, NY 10104
email yenpress@hbgusa.com
website www.yenpress.com
Facebook www.facebook.com/yenpress
Twitter @yenpress

Graphic novels and manga in all formats for all ages. Currently not seeking original project pitches from writers who are not already working with an illustrator. For submission guidelines see under Contact on website. Division of Hachette Book Group (page 212). Founded 2006.

Audio publishers

Many of the audio publishers listed below are also publishers of print books. As the audio market grows and evolves in line with listeners' preferences, new entrants are offering a range of digital streaming solutions, often on a monthly subscription basis.

Audible
email bizdev_uk@audible.co.uk
website www.audible.co.uk
Twitter @audibleuk

Producer and seller of digital audio entertainment, including fiction and non-fiction audiobooks for adults and children. Publishers keen to enquire about business opportunities with Audible may email the address above, or find out more about turning print books into audiobooks at www.acx.com. Founded 1995; acquired by Amazon 2008.

Audio Factory
Unit 8, High Jarmany Rural Workshops, Barton Saint David, Somerset TA11 6DA
email contact@audiofactory.co.uk
website www.audiofactory.co.uk
Facebook www.facebook.com/audiofactoryuk
Co-founders Dave Perry, Arran Dutton

Audiobook production company. Recommends narrators based on an author's brief, followed by an audition process at the end of which the author makes the final decision. Studio recording takes place over multiple sessions and is guided by a detailed plan created by producers with guidance and feedback from the author. The audiobook goes through editing, mixing, mastering and proofing before being delivered to the author or their chosen distributor.

Audiobook Creation Exchange (ACX)
email support-uk@acx.com
website www.acx.com
Facebook www.facebook.com/goacx
Twitter @acx_com

Authors are invited to create a profile for their book, including a synopsis and a brief sample. If authors choose not to narrate for themselves, interested narrators will submit an audition tape reading from the sample; authors can then make an offer to their preferred narrator. Once the full audiobook is completed, ACX will distribute on the author's behalf to Audible, Amazon and iTunes and return monthly payments and sales reports. ACX take a percentage of earnings and narrators can be compensated either through a one-off payment or through a share of royalties.

Audiobooks.com
email acquisitions@audiobooks.com
website www.audiobooks.com
Facebook www.facebook.com/audiobookscom
Twitter @audiobooks_com

Subscription audio book service, offering a wide range of fiction and non-fiction genres, as well as some children's titles. Publishers interested in having their titles included in the company's library may get in touch via the email address above.

Author's Republic
email info@authorsrepublic.com
website https://authorsrepublic.com/
website https://authorsrepublic.com/creation
Facebook www.facebook.com/authorsrepublic
Twitter @AuthorsRepublic

Global operation. Accepts completed audiobooks which are then submitted on the author's behalf to over 30 audiobook retailers, including Audible and iTunes. Does not assist with the production process, but offers hints and tips about how to create an audiobook (see above) and the quality of all submissions is tested before they are shared. All income from these retailers is combined into one monthly payment which is delivered alongside a sales report showing how many audiobooks an author is selling and where. Services cost a percentage of all audiobook profits.

BookBeat
email info@bookbeat.com
website www.bookbeat.com/uk
Twitter @BookBeatUK

Digital streaming service for adult and children's audiobooks across a variety of fiction and non-fiction genres. Monthly subscription model. Owned by Bonnier. Founded 2017.

Canongate Audio Books
14 High Street, Edinburgh EH1 1TE
tel 0131 557 5111
email support@canongate.co.uk
website www.canongate.co.uk
Twitter @canongatebooks
Audio and Online Manager Joanna Lord

Classic literature including the works of Jane Austen, Charles Dickens, D.H. Lawrence and P.G. Wodehouse; also current literary authors, such as Yann Martel and Nick Cave. Founded 1991 as CSA Word; acquired by Canongate 2010.

Cló Iar-Chonnacht Teo
Cheardlann, Spiddal, Co. Galway, Republic of Ireland
tel +353 (0)91 593307

email eolas@cic.ie
website www.cic.ie
Twitter @CloIarChonnacht
Ceo Micheál Ó Conghaile, *General Manager* Deirdre Ní Thuathail

Irish-language novels, short stories, plays, poetry, songs; CDs (writers reading from their works), downloads and bilingual books. Promotes the translation of contemporary Irish poetry and fiction into other languages. Founded 1985.

Creative Content Ltd
Roxburghe House, 273–287 Regent Street, London W1B 2HA
tel 07771 766838
email ali@creativecontentdigital.com
website www.creativecontentdigital.com
Twitter @CCTheLowdown
Publisher Ali Muirden, *Editorial Director* Lorelei King

Publishes audio digital downloads, ebooks and print-on-demand books in the business, language improvement, self-improvement, lifestyle, crime fiction, classic fiction, sci-fi, short stories and young adult genres. Founded 2008.

Findaway Voices
31999 Aurora Rd, Solon, OH 44139, USA
email support@findawayvoices.com
website https://findawayvoices.com/creating-audiobooks/
Facebook www.facebook.com/FindawayWorld
Twitter @wearefindaway
Instagram @wearefindaway

US-based audio technology company. Offers a range of services for authors and distributors. For audiobooks, authors do not have to commit to recording their audiobook until they have chosen a narrator from a supplied shortlist based on their manuscript. Production will then begin, followed by editing and quality control. Findaway distributes to over 40 audiobook retailers and supports authors with marketing, promotion and real time and monthly sales reports showing how many and where audiobooks are being sold. Production prices range between $1,000 and $2,000 for up to 50,000 words plus 20% of royalties for distribution.

Hachette Audio
Carmelite House, 50 Victoria Embankment, London EC4Y 0DZ
email sarah.shrubb@littlebrown.co.uk
website www.littlebrown.co.uk
Twitter @HachetteAudioUK
Audio Publisher Sarah Shrubb

Audiobook list that focuses on unabridged titles from Little, Brown's bestselling authors such as Iain Banks, J.K. Rowling, Sarah Waters, Donna Tartt and Mark Billingham, as well as classics including Joseph Heller's *Catch-22*, John Steinbeck's *Of Mice and Men*

and Hans Fallada's *Alone in Berlin*. Publishes approx. 300 audiobooks per year. Founded 2003.

HarperCollins Publishers
The News Building, 1 London Bridge Street, London, SE1 9GF
tel 020-8285 4016
website www.harpercollins.co.uk
Twitter @HarperCollinsUK
Senior Audio Editors Jessica Barnfield, Rebecca Fortuin, Tanya Hougham

Publishers of award-winning fiction and non-fiction audiobooks for adults and children. An imprint of HarperCollins. Founded 1990.

Hodder & Stoughton Audiobooks
Carmelite House, 50 Victoria Embankment, London EC4Y 0DZ
tel 020-7873 6000
email dominic.gribben@hodder.co.uk
website www.hodder.co.uk
Twitter @HodderPod
Audio Publisher Dominic Gribben

Specialist audiobook team publishing fiction and non-fiction audiobooks from within the Hodder group by authors including Stephen King, John Grisham, Jodi Picoult, Graham Norton, John Connolly and David Mitchell. The team also commissions and publishes original audiobook content and podcasts.

W. F. Howes Ltd
Unit 5, St George's House, Rearsby Business Park, Gaddesby Lane, Rearsby, Leicester LE7 4YH
tel (01664) 423000
email info@wfhowes.co.uk
website www.wfhowes.co.uk

Independent audiobook publisher. Also large-print publisher and digital-services provider to libraries. Releases c. 80 new and unabridged audiobooks monthly. Works with authors/agents directly and a range of large UK publishers, including Penguin Random House and HarperCollins. Founded 1999; UK subsidiary of RBMedia.

Isis/Soundings
Isis Publishing Ltd, 7 Centremead, Osney Mead, Oxford OX2 0ES
tel (01865) 250333
Facebook www.facebook.com/Isis.Soundings/
Twitter @Isisaudio
Chief Executive Michele Petty

Complete and unabridged audiobooks: fiction, non-fiction, autobiography, biography, crime, thrillers, family sagas, mysteries, romances.

Kobo
website www.kobo.com/gb/en
Twitter @kobo

Audiobook streaming service, for a monthly fee. Offers fiction, non-fiction, adult, children's and YA titles.

Macmillan Digital Audio
20 New Wharf Road, London N1 9RR
tel 020-7014 6000
email audiobooks@macmillan.co.uk
website www.panmacmillan.com
Publishing Director, Audio Rebecca Lloyd

Adult fiction, non-fiction and autobiography, and children's. Founded 1995.

Media Music Now
email support@mediamusicnow.com
website www.mediamusicnow.co.uk/voice-overs/audio-book-narration.aspx
Facebook www.facebook.com/mediamusicnow
Twitter @MusicMediaNow
Co-founders Lee Pritchard, Adam Barber

Audio production company. Supplies royalty-free music and sound effects as well as voice-overs and narration. For the latter, authors submit a brief indicating their preferred choice of narrator from a catalogue. Once a narrator has accepted, production will begin, with the author being given the opportunity to review and make edits to a completed proof copy. If authors have already recorded an audiobook, Media Music Now can edit and/or polish it as required. Completed audiobooks are returned to authors who are responsible for organising distribution. Founded 2005.

Naxos AudioBooks
5 Wyllyotts Place, Potters Bar, Herts. EN6 2JD
tel (01707) 653326
email info@naxosaudiobooks.com
website www.naxosaudiobooks.com
Twitter @NaxosAudioBooks
Managing Director Anthony Anderson

Recordings of classic literature, modern fiction, non-fiction, drama and poetry. Founded 1994.

The Orion Publishing Group Ltd
Carmelite House, 50 Victoria Embankment, London EC4Y 0DZ
tel 020-3122 6876
website www.orionbooks.co.uk
Twitter @OrionBooksAudio
Senior Audio Manager Paul Stark

Adult fiction and non-fiction. Founded 1998.

Penguin Random House UK Audio
Penguin Studios, One Embassy Gardens, Nine Elms Lane, London SW8 5BL
website www.penguinrandomhouse.co.uk
Executive Producer Roy McMillan, *Senior Producer* Chris Thompson, *Studio Manager* Kate MacDonald

Includes classic and contemporary fiction and non-fiction, autobiography, poetry and drama. Authors include Jo Nesbø, Lee Child, Kathy Reichs, Claire Tomalin, Zadie Smith and Paula Hawkins.

Simon & Schuster Audio
Simon & Schuster UK, 1st Floor, 222 Gray's Inn Road, London WC1X 8HB
tel 020-7316 1900
email enquiries@simonandschuster.co.uk
website www.simonandschuster.co.uk/audio
Publisher Dominic Brendon

Fiction, children's, young adult and non-fiction audiobooks. Fiction authors include Graham Swift, Philippa Gregory, Milly Johnson and Caroline Kepnes. Non-fiction authors include Bruce Springsteen, Walter Isaacson and Anita Anand. Founded 1997.

Ulverscroft Ltd
The Green, Bradgate Road, Anstey, Leicester LE7 7FU
tel 0116 236 4325
email m.merrill@ulverscroft.co.uk
website www.ulverscroft.co.uk
Facebook www.facebook.com/ulverscroft
Twitter @UlverscroftUK

Offers a wide variety of large print titles in hardback and paperback format as well as unabridged audiobooks, many of which are written by the world's favourite authors and includes award-winning titles. Acquired Oakhill Publishing and its range of unabridged audiobooks April 2018. Founded 1964.

Books

Book packagers

Many illustrated books are created by book packagers, whose particular skills are in the areas of book design and graphic content. In-house desk editors and art editors match up the expertise of specialist writers, artists and photographers who usually work on a freelance basis.

Aladdin Books Ltd
PO Box 53987, London SW15 2SF
tel 020-3174 3090
email sales@aladdinbooks.co.uk
website www.aladdinbooks.co.uk

Full design and book packaging facility specialising in children's non-fiction and reference. Founded 1980.

Nicola Baxter
16 Cathedral Street, Norwich NR1 1LX
tel (01603) 766585 / 07778 285555
email nb@nicolabaxter.co.uk
website www.nicolabaxter.co.uk
Director Nicola Baxter

Full packaging service for children's books in both traditional and digital formats. Happy to take projects from concept to finished work or supply bespoke authorial, editorial, design, project management or commissioning services. Produces both fiction and non-fiction titles in a wide range of formats, for babies to young adults, and experienced in novelty books and licensed publishing. Founded 1990.

Bender Richardson White
PO Box 266, Uxbridge, Middlesex UB9 5NX
tel (01895) 832444
email brw@brw.co.uk
website www.brw.co.uk
Directors Lionel Bender (editorial), Kim Richardson (sales & production), Ben White (design)

Specialises in children's and young people's natural history, science and family information. Opportunities for freelancers. Founded 1990.

Brown Bear Books Ltd
Unit 1/D, Leroy House, 436 Essex Road, London N1 3QP
tel 020-3176 8603
website www.windmillbooks.co.uk
Children's Publisher Anne O'Daly

Specialises in high-quality illustrated reference books and multi-volume sets for trade and educational markets. Opportunities for freelancers. Imprint of Windmill Books (page 228). Founded 1967.

John Brown Group – Children's Division
10 Triton Street, Regents Place, London NW1 3BF
tel 020-7565 3000
email andrew.hirsch@johnbrownmedia.com
website www.johnbrownmedia.com
Director Chris Dicey (business development)

Creative development and packaging of children's products including books, magazines, teachers' resource packs, partworks, CDs and websites. Founded 2000.

Chase My Snail
19 Darnell House, Royal Hill, London SE10 8SU
tel 0785 267 5689 / +27 (0)82 822 8221 (South Africa)
email headsnail@chasemysnail.com
Publishing Director Daniel Ford

Produces top-quality books, especially non-fiction sports, fitness and travel publications, for the co-edition market. Handles writing, editing, proofing and design to take the book through from concept to final files. Has a wide range of book ideas already developed for publishers looking to extend their lists. Operates in London and Johannesburg. Founded 2008.

Diagram Visual Information Ltd
34 Elaine Grove, London NW5 4QH
tel 020-7485 5941
email info@diagramgroup.com
website www.diagramgroup.com
Directors Jane Johnson, Patricia Robertson

Research, writing, design and illustration of reference books, supplied as disks. Founded 1967.

Elwin Street Productions Ltd
10 Elwin Street, London E2 7BU
tel 020-7033 6706
email silvia@elwinstreet.com
website www.elwinstreet.com
website www.modern-books.com
Director Silvia Langford, *Art Director* Moira Clinch, *Editor* Florence Ward, *Operations Manager* Claire Anouchian

Trade imprint: Modern Books. Upmarket illustrated co-edition publisher of adult non-fiction: reference, visual arts, popular culture and science, lifestyle, food, health and nutrition, parenting, gift. Founded 2001.

Global Blended Learning Ltd
Singleton Court, Wonastow Road, Monmouth NP25 5JA
tel (01993) 706273
email info@hlstudios.eu.com
website www.globalblendedlearning.com

Primary, secondary academic education (geography, science, modern languages) and co-editions (travel guides, gardening, cookery). Multimedia (CD-Rom programming and animations). Opportunities for freelancers. Founded 1985.

Graham-Cameron Publishing & Illustration

59 Hertford Road, Brighton BN1 7GG
tel (01273) 385890
email enquiry@gciforillustration.com
Alternative address The Art House, Uplands Park, Sheringham, Norfolk NR26 8NE
tel (01263) 821333
website www.gciforillustration.com
Partners Helen Graham-Cameron, Duncan Graham-Cameron

Educational and children's books; information publications; sponsored publications. Illustration agency with 37 artists. Do not send unsolicited MSS. Founded 1985.

Hart McLeod Ltd

14A Greenside, Waterbeach, Cambridge CB25 9HP
tel (01223) 861495
email jo@hartmcleod.co.uk
website www.hartmcleod.co.uk
Director Joanne Barker

Primarily educational and general non-fiction with particular expertise in illustrated books, school texts, ELT and electronic and audio content. Opportunities for freelancers and work experience. Founded 1985.

Heart of Albion

2 Cross Hill Close, Wymeswold, Loughborough LE12 6UJ
tel (01509) 881342
email albion@indigogroup.co.uk
website www.hoap.co.uk
Director Bob Trubshaw

Not currently seeking submissions. Founded 1989.

Ivy Press Ltd

Ovest House, 58 West Street, Brighton, East Sussex BN1 2RA
tel (01273) 487440
email ivypress@quarto.com
website www.ivypress.co.uk
Twitter @QuartoExplores

Publishers of illustrated trade books on art, science, popular culture, design, children's non-fiction, natural history and conscious living. Opportunities for authors and freelancers. Part of the Quarto Group (page 179). Founded 1996.

Lexus Ltd

47 Broad Street, Glasgow G40 2QW
tel 0141 556 0440
email peterterrell@lexusforlanguages.co.uk
website www.lexusforlanguages.co.uk
Director P.M. Terrell

Publisher of language books. Lexus Travelmate series (15 titles; French and Spanish also as ebooks) and Chinese Classroom series (two textbooks and CD-Rom with speech recognition); Insider China; UK4U (written in Chinese). Also dual language books: Cross Over into Gaelic series (Maggie Midge, Scottish Folk Tales); Scottish Folk Tales in English and French; ScotlandSpeak, a wordbook for Scotland. For children: dual language books for young children, Mess on the Floor, with audio app (French, German, Spanish and Scottish Gaelic); Gaelic Gold, a learner's dictionary/phrasebook; Placename books: What's in a Scottish Placename?; Edingow and Glasburgh. Learning French: Me and My Mobile; Colourful Languages, a new series of colouring books: Round the Glasgow Underground (with Gaelic), Colour My Zoo (with French). Founded 1980.

Little People Books

The Home of BookBod, Knighton, Radnorshire LD7 1UP
tel (01547) 520925
email littlepeoplebooks@thehobb.tv
website www.littlepeoplebooks.co.uk
Directors Grant Jessé (production & managing), Helen Wallis (rights & finance)

Packager of audio, children's educational and textbooks, digital publications. Parent company: Grant Jessé UK.

Market House Books Ltd

Suite B, Elsinore House, 43 Buckingham Street, Aylesbury, Bucks. HP20 2NQ
tel (01296) 484911
email books@mhbref.com
website www.markethousebooks.com
Twitter @markethousebook
Directors Jonathan Law (editorial), Anne Kerr (production)

Book packagers with experience in producing reference books from small pocket dictionaries to large multi-volume colour encyclopedias and from specialist academic reference books to popular books for crossword enthusiasts. Deals with publishers worldwide. Services offered include: start-to-finish project management; commissioning of writers and editors; writing and rewriting; editing and copy-editing; proofreading; checking of final pages; keyboarding; typesetting; page design and make-up; text conversion; data manipulation; database management. Founded 1970.

Orpheus Books Ltd

6 Church Green, Witney, Oxon OX28 4AW
tel (01993) 774949
email info@orpheusbooks.com
website www.orpheusbooks.com, www.Q-files.com
Executive Directors Nicholas Harris, Sarah Hartley

Children's illustrated non-fiction/reference books and ebooks. Orpheus Books are the creators of Q-files.com, the online educational resource for schools and libraries. Founded 1993.

Toucan Books Ltd

The Old Fire Station, 140 Tabernacle Street, London EC2A 4SD
tel 020-7250 3388
website www.toucanbooks.co.uk

International co-editions; editorial, design and production services. Founded 1985.

Windmill Books Ltd

Unit 1/D, Leroy House, 436 Essex Road, London N1 3QP
tel 020-3176 8603
website www.windmillbooks.co.uk
Children's Publisher Anne O'Daly

Publisher and packager of books and partworks for trade, promotional and international publishers. Opportunities for freelancers. Imprint: Brown Bear Books Ltd (page 226). Founded 2009.

Working Partners Ltd

9 Kingsway, 4th Floor, London WC2B 6XF
tel 020-7841 3939
email enquiries@workingpartnersltd.co.uk
website www.workingpartnersltd.co.uk
Managing Director (Working Partners & Director of IP Creation, Coolabi Group) Chris Snowdon

Genres include: animal fiction, fantasy, horror, historical, detective, magical, adventure. No unsolicited MSS or illustrations. Pays advance and royalty; retains copyright on all works. Selects writers from unpaid writing samples based on specific brief. Looking to add writers to database: to register visit website. Founded 1995.

Inspiring Writers

Becoming a bestselling author: my writing story

Peter James shares his first-hand experience of the ups and downs, false starts and challenges a writer may face along the route to success, and the value of passion and persistence – and chance moments of opportunity.

I am so pleased to have been invited to write this piece for the *Writers' & Artists' Yearbook*, not only because it was the first place I turned to when I finished my first novel in 1967, but also because I want to share with all of you all to know that a successful writing career does not come overnight. Mine had many detours but I always kept my destination in mind.

I often get asked why I became a writer. I always wanted to be one, right from the age of seven, but I had very little self-confidence and never believed I would ever actually succeed. I kept a notebook by my bed and used to write my thoughts and ideas into it. I remember the very first entry, a great pearl of wisdom: 'Life is a bowl of custard – it's all right until you fall in.' When I went to my boarding school, Charterhouse, I had one English teacher, David Summerscale, who believed in me and encouraged me. He went on to become headmaster of Westminster School and we are still in touch today. At 15 I won a school poetry prize and then at 17 I won a BBC short story competition, and these both gave my confidence a boost – but I was still a troubled, uncertain kid. My housemaster, Ted Hartwell, turned out to be absolutely bang on prophetic in his leaving report for me: 'Enigmatic and unpredictable, a literary career seems inevitable, but there may be some false starts.'

I guess it really started when my dad bought me a portable electric typewriter for my 17th birthday, along with a real battle-axe of a typing tutor, who would put sticky tabs on the keys to make them unreadable and then rap my fingers with a ruler if I looked down! I learned to touch-type within days and it has stood me in good stead ever since. Eighteen months later I set to work writing my first novel, *Ride Down A Rollercoaster*, in a garage converted into a bedsit on the Fulham Road, and when I finished I went straight out and bought *Writers' & Artists' Yearbook* so that I could send my manuscript off to literary agents. The replies I received said it was 'too American' and, instead of letting that deter me, I referred to the American section of the *Yearbook* and started sending copies to the States. After mailing countless letters, I finally received a reply from Kurt Helmer, a New York literary agent who said I showed 'real promise' and encouraged me to re-work the book and send him another draft. However, in the arrogance of youth, I insisted the second novel that I had written in the meantime, a zany sci-fi comedy, was much better. He didn't agree and asked me to return to the first book. Instead, now 21, I wrote a third. Again, he told me to go back to the first book, and again I ignored him.

During this time, I had been attending Ravensbourne Film School, after trying to get into Oxford. Although I got in on my second attempt, I turned down Oxford's offer as the idea of telling stories through film had got under my skin. However, after graduation from Ravensbourne I realised how hard it is to get your first job in film without having a contact on the inside. Nor had I managed to publish a novel yet. On the advice of my Canadian uncle, I moved to Canada and got my first job in television as a gofer on a children's show called *Polka Dot Door*. Through a twist of fate, I had the chance to write an episode and, following the success of that first episode, was asked to take on the writing three days a week. I sent a letter to Kurt Helmer, my literary agent, sharing my excitement. He replied, 'You a**hole, never do both. Don't have a job writing in the day and expect to write a novel in the night.' He told me the only way I'd ever write a good novel was if I got a job in a factory and wrote after work. This proved to have been very good advice, after I went on to work on a 'movie-gone-wrong' in Spain called *Spanish Fly* (that I had had to help finance on my own credit card during production) starring Terry-Thomas and Lesley Philips. It was described by the eminent critic Barry Norman as 'the worst British film since the Second World War and the least funny British funny film ever made'. So I joined the family business and started working in the factory of Cornelia James Glovemakers by day and writing at night. I decided to write a spy novel and wrote my first published book, *Dead Letter Drop* (W.H. Allen 1981). I would love to say this was a shining start to my career as a published author, but it was, as my teacher had predicted, a false start. *Dead Letter Drop* sold around 1,800 copies and 1,500 of those were to libraries. I remember a particularly bad press interview where the journalist asked me how I had found Namibia, a location in my second published novel, and I couldn't answer … because I had never been. I vowed then to never write about something I had not fully researched and experienced. This was reinforced by a chance meeting with the author Elizabeth Buchan who told me, 'You'll never be successful writing something you're not passionate about and can't research.' This was a real turning point for me in terms of how I approached my writing.

An unexpected lucky break came when my former wife and I were burgled after moving into a house in Brighton. Sussex Police arrived to take my statement and eagle-eyed detective, Mike Harris, noticed my books. He said that if I ever needed help with research I should let him know. This was the beginning of my long-term relationship with Sussex Police. Ever since, after years of earning their trust, I have been privileged to join officers on shifts, to go out in response and traffic patrol cars, attend raids, and some crime scenes, as well as social events and I have been able to talk to officers about their experiences. I am regularly reminded of the breadth of life a police officer sees over their career, and the extraordinary situations they experience. I have been told many times over the years that I have 'become part of the furniture' in the station! So, at this point, I knew I needed to write a crime novel, but my protagonist still eluded me. It would be a few more years before I would meet the man who would inspire Roy Grace.

Writing from what I knew and what I was passionate about took a surprisingly supernatural turn after the death of the son of good friends in a car accident, soon after the death my own father. My friends consulted a medium to try and make contact with their son, and this gave me an idea: how the intense love between a mother and her son might continue, but with dangerous consequences, from beyond the grave. The result was my supernatural thriller, *Possession* (Gollancz 1988), and for the first time I experienced a bidding war, with every major publisher in the UK vying for it. I had started to be called 'Britain's answer to Stephen King' in the press and I was encouraged by my publisher to write further horror books. But this would once again prove to be a false start, as the sales of horror books started a sharp decline in the 1990s.

Knowing I was keen to meet police officers with an interesting story to tell, my friends at Sussex Police invited me down to the station to chat with a young Detective Inspector called Dave Gaylor. I walked into his office and was surprised to see there were plastic crates all over the floor, piled with documents. When I asked if he was moving Dave explained that, in addition to being an active homicide investigator, he was also in charge of reviewing all the county's unsolved murders where there was still a perpetrator at large or someone alive who could benefit from a successful conclusion: 'I'm the last chance the victims have for justice, and I'm the last chance the families have for closure.' In talking to Dave I realised that he had the rare qualities that make a truly great homicide detective – that is to be calm, to have a high degree of emotional intelligence and empathy, and to be highly methodical yet, at the same time, open to creative, blue-sky thinking. Over the next few years, I switched from supernatural to psychological thrillers, putting policing more and more into my novels.

In 2002 Dave was promoted to Detective Chief Superintendent, and effectively became head of major crime for Sussex Police. My publishers, Pan Macmillan, approached me just and asked if I'd ever thought of creating a fictional detective as my central character. I went straight to Dave and asked him, 'Would you like to be a fictional cop?'. He loved the idea! Dave, my notebook and I spent many nights in Brighton pubs talking in detail about his life and police procedure. From this, we then worked out the plot of *Dead Simple* (Pan Macmillan 2005) together, with Dave ensuring that I was absolutely correct in my research. We've worked closely on every Roy Grace novel since and we've become great friends, with Dave being best man when my wife Lara and I married. Dave reads all my manuscripts to make sure they are entirely accurate in how I portray the way the police would approach a case. This was when I finally, and thankfully, got my writing career on the trajectory I had been hoping for. My first Roy Grace novel was published in 2005, my 17th Roy Grace novel came out in May 2021, as well as an ITV series, *Grace*, with John Simm playing Detective Superintendent Roy Grace.

The most important lesson I can offer – and I hope that this has come across – is never to give up. If you believe you have a story to tell, keep going. Even when I was published for the first time, it was not the end of my struggles; in fact, it was still the beginning. Another lesson that I learned the hard way is that research is paramount and frequently bizarre. For example, when a character in *Dead Simple* got buried alive, I asked a funeral parlour to nail me into a coffin so that I could understand the experience and write about it in a convincing way. Too often an author who has spent years working on their writing is called an 'overnight success', and this is hardly ever accurate. Writers are craftspeople and we need to spend time making mistakes and honing our skills. I often liken writing to being a mechanic; the best way to learn is to take things apart and put them back together in your own way. Read and reread the bestselling novels in the genre you want to write, pick apart what makes them great novels, and apply that in your own work.

Good luck, and never let a false start send you off course.

Peter James is an international bestselling author and film producer. His crime thriller series featuring Detective Superintendent Roy Grace has included 17 consecutive *Sunday Times* Number 1 bestsellers and he has won over 40 awards, including WHSmith Best Crime Author of All Time Award and the Crime Writers' Association Diamond Dagger. Born in Brighton, he graduated from Ravensbourne Film School, and worked as a film producer and screenwriter for some years before starting to write novels. His first book, *Dead Simple* (W.H. Allen) was published in 1981. His latest book, *Left You Dead*, was published by Macmillan in May 2021. Peter's Roy Grace novels are now a major ITV series, *Grace*, starring John Simm and Richie Campbell. His website is www.peterjamesuk.com; follow him on Twitter @peterjamesuk.

See also...

• *Turning to crime: writing thrillers,* page 265

First chapters: how to grab your reader's attention

Emma Flint lists the important considerations for a writer embarking on a new book and pinpoints some key elements that make for success when composing that all-important first chapter.

The first chapter of your book is your one chance to hook your reader. If you don't draw your reader in and make them want to continue, it doesn't matter how thrilling the climax in chapter eight is or how thought-provoking the ending is. If your first chapter doesn't work, your reader won't make it past chapter one.

On the plus side, no other part of your book can provide you with the kind of pay-off that a good first chapter can. A good first chapter can get the attention of a reader. Or an agent. Or a publisher.

Viewpoint

There are a number of decisions that you need to make in your first chapter. Firstly, from whose point of view are you telling the story? What kind of voice will work best for the story you're telling?

One of the most common mistakes novelists make is to have too many viewpoints and too many narrators. Keep it as simple as you can and never include more than one narrator if it's not absolutely essential to the plot.

You should never write your opening from a particular viewpoint and then abandon that voice. Don't allow your readers to invest emotionally in a character, and then neglect that character or kill them off early in the story – it will annoy and alienate your audience.

Setting

Your novel will almost certainly have more than one setting. However, in your first chapter you need only set up the rough location and the rough period for the opening of your main character's narrative.

Avoid trying to set up an opening scene in too much depth. Two pages of description about landscape or weather before you've begun the actual story is unlikely to draw a reader in. Conversely, if you can relate the setting of your novel to your characters, you give your reader a reason to care about the history of a building or the colours of a landscape before you start describing it in detail. Sarah Waters does this beautifully: look at how she introduces setting through character.

Character

In your opening chapter, your main character has one job and one job only: *to make your reader care about their story*.

Your readers don't need to like your main character. In the first chapter, they don't need to know everything about her, or understand her childhood. You need to give the reader just enough so that they care about her, about the situation she's in, and about what she wants.

And in order to show these things, you need to work out what you want your reader to learn about that character. If you're writing a murder mystery in which your main character poisons his wife, your reader probably needs to know in the first chapter that the character is having an affair, or that he's desperate for his wife's money.

The easiest way to bore your reader is to *tell* them about your main character, while the most effective way to *show* your readers something about your characters is through dialogue. Dialogue tells you about a person's background – where they're from, sometimes what kind of education they've had, often how old they are. It tells you their beliefs, their prejudices, and how they see the world.

What's the starting point of your story?

Broadly speaking, there are four ways in which you can open a novel:

• **Start with a prologue** – an episode that is not part of chapter one, but that relates somehow to your main story. It might not include the main character, or it might include the main character at a time outside of the central narrative – for example, when she's a child, or when he's looking back on the events of the novel from years later.
• **Put your main character in a scene**, doing something interesting related to the main story. It's almost always more effective to start your story with action rather than description. That action doesn't have to be dramatic – it can be as gentle as someone taking a bath or buying coffee. But what it must *not* be is a description of a character doing nothing – staring out of the window, reflecting on their broken marriage, fantasising. If it wouldn't be interesting to watch a character doing it at the beginning of a film, don't put it in the opening of your novel.
• **Begin in the middle**. Start at a point deep in the story and show a dramatic event; then, at the end of the scene, jump back to an earlier, quieter part of the narrative. To create this effect, you need to bring the reader into the scene late. Bring them in moments before the flight takes off, seconds before the gun is fired.

If you choose to use this method, you need to be aware of two things: firstly, this type of opening is used so often in mysteries and thrillers that it's in danger of becoming a bit of a cliché. Yours must be both original and surprising. Secondly, it can sacrifice suspense for that whole portion of the story until the narrative catches up with the first moment. If you open with your main character fleeing from a guy with a gun, how nervous will the reader be in chapter four when that same character is at risk of drowning? They already know that she survives, at least until she encounters the gunman. The risk is that this kind of opening can deflate any later tension you want to set up.
• **Use a framing device**, where your story is bookended at the front and back (and sometimes in a few instances in the middle) by a story that is outside the main story.

Think of *Alice in Wonderland*, where the main narrative is bookended by dreams. Or Mary Shelley's *Frankenstein*, which uses multiple framed narratives.

If you're writing a story that's very removed from the real life of your reader – perhaps set in a fantasy world – a framing device can be used to show someone like your reader coming in to hear the main story. Show the reader a character like them getting involved, and that way you make it easier for *them* to follow you as well.

In deciding how to open your novel, you need to work out what information is relevant to your story. Your characters have pasts and futures (unless you plan to kill them off).

The setting of your novel also has a past and a future. So, in a sense, every writer jumps into their story midway through.

Create immediacy

One way to plunge your reader into the story is to add detail that makes your writing realistic and credible. If you're writing an historical novel, do your research. If you're writing about a location that you're familiar with, show the reader that you know it well. But be careful to use that detail sparingly, rather than piling it on to show off your knowledge.

Another way is to create tension – and the easiest way to do this – is to set up conflict in the first chapter. Conflict feeds readers. It creates drama.

To generate conflict, you need a mini-plot. A fight scene is an example of conflict. But a fight scene alone isn't enough if the reader doesn't know who the characters are. They're not yet invested in them. A fight scene between two brothers is better. It ups the stakes a little. But a fight scene between two brothers, one of whom suspects the other of killing their mother, is better still. *Now* you have a story.

It's no accident that many great novels have first chapters that could stand as short stories. Every chapter should have its own mini-plot and its own mini-narrative arc, and this element is most important in chapter one.

Move the reader on

As you will know from your own reading, the more of a book you read and enjoy, the more you'll want to read; if you read the first page and liked it, you will read the second. If you read ten pages, you're likely to read twenty.

One of the functions of your first chapter is to get your reader on to the second. As a writer, you're like the witch in Hansel and Gretel … you're giving the reader breadcrumbs to follow. If they pick up one – in the form of a well-crafted line, or a believable character, or a moment of suspense – they'll be looking for the next one.

At the opening of your novel, those breadcrumbs need to be close together – because your reader isn't yet engaged. Following the fairy tale metaphor, they're still looking back at the edge of the forest. You need to *entice* them in.

And your first breadcrumb comes in the form of your first line.

First lines

A great first line is like a welcome marriage proposal: it makes the reader commit.

A first line needs to do one or more of several things:

1. It needs to be well-written, and memorable, and confident. There's no room in a first line for flabby language or clumsy wording.
– Take *Love in the Time of Cholera* by Gabriel Garcia Marquez: 'It was inevitable: the scent of bitter almonds always reminded him of the fate of unrequited love.'
2. The first line needs to give an indication of the story to come. It is a promise, or a question, or an unproven idea, which will be explored in the novel itself.
– Think of Jane Austen's *Pride and Prejudice*: 'It is a truth universally acknowledged, that a single man in possession of a good fortune must be in want of a wife.'
– or Dickens' *A Tale of Two Cities*: 'It was the best of times, it was the worst of times'.
3. A first line needs to say something interesting; it can show the reader a shattered status quo or subvert their expectations.

– Perhaps the best-known example of this is the opening line of George Orwell's *1984*: 'It was a bright cold day in April, and the clocks were striking thirteen.'
– The most effective examples of this type of opening line are often the shortest. Take Iain Banks' opening of *The Crow Road*: 'It was the day my grandmother exploded.'
– or the opening line of *Peter Pan* by J.M. Barrie: 'All children, except one, grow up.'

Ask yourself what questions you are raising in your opening sentence and paragraph, and whether they are interesting or memorable enough to draw readers in.

And two final and key points about opening chapters:

Firstly, your reader needs to understand from the first chapter what your book is about, and why you've written it. They need to feel the interest or the motivation or the passion that made you want to write it.

Secondly, *your first chapter must be interesting*. The absolute worst thing you can do is bore your reader. So be brave. Be bold. Open your book in a way that commands attention and engages curiosity.

Emma Flint graduated from the University of St Andrews with an MA in English Language and Literature and completed a novel-writing course at the Faber Academy. Her debut *Little Deaths*, a crime novel set in 1960s New York and based on a real-life murder, was published to wide acclaim in January 2017 and was longlisted for the Bailey's Women's Prize for Fiction, for the Desmond Elliott Prize and for the Crime Writers' Association Gold Dagger Award. Emma's second novel, *Other Women*, set in 1920s London and Sussex, will publish in 2022. Find her online at https://emmaflint.com.

Keeping the writing dream alive

S.J. Watson proves why no writer should give up on their dream of being published one day.

I'm writing this in late March 2020, sitting not in my office but at a table I've set up in the bay window of my sitting room. From here I have a view of the garden – I can watch the birds as they flit from branch to branch and eventually settle at the feeder outside the window; I can chart the day's progress by the changing light. But the world has changed – suddenly I can move no further than I can see, other than in an emergency or to collect provisions and, even then, I must stay a minimum of two metres from anyone I may meet. A virus is tearing through the population, threatening to overwhelm us, and it must be slowed. Collectively, we're in lockdown.

And so, unable to travel, we temporarily escape our surroundings in other ways. We reach out to our friends on social media and through meet-up apps, checking in, lifting each other up. And we turn to stories – to our books and films, our TV shows and, yes, even our plays, as theatres stream recorded performances direct to our living rooms. Through words we bond, we are entertained and amused, offered ways to escape and expand. Never before has the importance of a shared story been more apparent.

Yet it has always been so. I grew up in the Black Country, an only child, gay. My childhood was far from unhappy, but it felt … limited, confusing. I turned to books at a very early age, visited the local library weekly, taking out and reading my allotted five books without fail. They were my escape, my life raft, and it wasn't long before I began to write stories of my own. Encouraged by teachers, I dreamt of one day seeing a book of mine on a shelf in a library or bookshop, of having the power to transport people as I had been transported. When asked what I wanted to be when I grew up, I replied, 'A writer!' – without hesitation, every time.

It took me a long time (or a long time to be a *published* writer, at least; I've been a writer my whole life, and the distinction is important). Seduced by the idea that I needed a sensible career alongside my writing, I studied physics and eventually worked in the NHS. But the writing was always there. I filled notebooks, I wrote stories and poems and started novels, I pushed forward. I vowed I wouldn't stop as long as my output was improving. My dream never left me.

The publishing side of things, though? That remained a mystery. I hoovered up as much advice as I could, yet much of it was conflicting, and the path to publication remained impossibly opaque. I read somewhere that one needed an agent to be published, then read somewhere else that to get an agent one needed to have been published. 'Win a prize!', they said, 'or no one will even look at your work. Get some short stories into magazines!', though no one told me how, or which magazines.

But then, one day, in a now-vanished bookshop in North London, I lifted down from the shelf an earlier version of the book you're holding now. And my eyes were opened. Here was a guide, a clear way through what had previously been misty and unclear – not only a reference guide that listed agents, publishers and other helpful organisations along with their contact details and preferences, but also a treasure trove of invaluable and inspirational articles and guides covering every stage of the writer's journey. Here, at last, was a beacon that could guide me through the choppy waters ahead. I kept it on hand the whole time and referred to it frequently for information, inspiration or support. And when, in my late thirties and ground down by working in an overstretched health service, I decided it was time my career took a back seat to my writing ambitions, it was *this* book that gave me the courage to drop to part-time at work and really go for it.

A definitive guide, in here you'll find everything you need. It won't write your book for you, quite, but it'll demystify the whole process of getting your book into the hands of readers, however you choose to do that, as well as illuminating the 'business' side of being a writer. There can be few published writers who haven't turned to the *Writers' & Artists' Yearbook* at some stage in their development, and many use it still. All writing is an act of optimism, including this foreword – I hope that, by the time you're reading it, the world will be in a different, better place. But we'll still need stories, perhaps more than ever. We'll always need stories. They make us human. They connect us – across space, across time. The only way to learn to write is by doing it, by practising, over and over … but for every other aspect of the world of publishing, we have this book.

Foreword from *Writers' & Arists' Yearbook 2021*

S.J. Watson is the award-winning author of the international bestsellers *Before I Go to Sleep* (Doubleday 2011), winner of the Crime Writers' Association Award for Best Debut Novel and the Galaxy National Book Award for Crime Thriller of the Year, and *Second Life* (Doubleday 2015). He was born in the Midlands and studied physics at Birmingham University, later working as an audiologist in the NHS, before enrolling on the first Faber Academy 'Writing a Novel' course in 2009. He now lives in London. The film adaption of *Before I Go to Sleep*, directed by Rowan Joffe, starring Nicole Kidman and Colin Firth, was released in 2014. S.J. Watson's latest book, *Final Cut*, was published by Transworld in August 2020. Follow him on Twitter @SJ_Watson.

Advice to a new writer

Rachel Joyce advocates that you take yourself seriously as a writer, so that others will too. It's important to 'know your stuff' and allow your writing to find its place in the world.

When I was 14, I finished my first novel. *Sisters* was short, I admit – possibly no more than 500 words. It was written in couplet form and was autobiographical. During the course of this tale, the older sister (*me*) did everything to save her two younger sisters (*mine*) from unhappiness, general uncleanliness and also TB (we had just made a family visit to Haworth). For lots of reasons, it was important for me to tell that story. But here is the thing – as soon as I finished my book, I wanted more. Even then. I wanted it *published*. I tell you this in a light-hearted way but you have to understand that, when I wrote it, it was not light-hearted. That story was a part of me. It marked who I was – and I wanted people to know that.

I find it hard to explain why it isn't enough for me to write a story and keep it to myself; why I must take it into the world; why I need … *what*? What is it I need? The approval of others? The affirmation? The challenge? The sharing? More and more, I feel that writing is about saying, 'This is how the world seems to me' – followed by a question mark. Writing is a deeply solitary process but it is also, I think, the most generous piece of reaching out. I write in order to understand.

But back to *Sisters*. I didn't mention to anyone I had written a book. I didn't dare. I was a quiet child. I wanted people to know who I was, but I didn't seem to be very good at showing it, at least not in a day-to-day way. I decided to give myself a pseudonym as a writer: Mary Thorntons. *Mary* because I thought it sounded intellectual and *Thorntons* because I made a mistake (I misremembered Thornfield from *Jane Eyre*). I had a hunch Mary Thorntons sounded altogether more writerly than Rachel Joyce.

So I had my BOOK. I had my WRITER'S NAME. What next? I went to my local library in West Norwood because that was where we always went for information. I headed for the reference section (I knew it well) and, with a beating heart, I found a heavy manual called the *Writers' & Artists' Yearbook*. We are talking 1976. I sat alone, where no one could see me, and I opened it.

All I can tell you is that it was like discovering a friend – someone who took my writing seriously and who had practical knowledge in spadefuls. It provided a bridge between my story and the professional world of publishing. I couldn't believe that everything I needed to know was in one book. I wrote down the names and addresses of publishers who were interested in rhyming books (there weren't many). I noted the word count they expected (short) and the kind of accompanying letter. I also discovered that it was important to include my name and address (Mary Thorntons, West Norwood).

Now, over 40 years later, I have done at last what I wasn't able or ready to achieve when I was 14. Over the years, I have written in different media: short stories and novels, for radio and television. And here too is a new edition of the *Writers' & Artists' Yearbook* – the 114th to be exact. The book you are holding will give you all the up-to-date information it offered me when I was 14, but it also offers far more. Along with clear detailing of all the contacts you can possibly need, it now provides advice from many well-respected voices in the publishing industry about editing, how to pitch your book, writing for the theatre, copyright law, finance, how to attract the attention of an agent, self-publishing (to name just a few of the topics). If you take your writing at all seriously, and that part of you that wants your writing not only to be finished but to find its place in the world, then … well done, you have come to the right place. There may be a lot of information to be found if you trawl the internet, but here it is all under one roof. Think of yourself as being in the best writers' Christmas market. It is all here.

People ask me sometimes for my advice to a new writer. I say the obvious things: 'Keep going' and 'Don't let go until you really believe you have scraped right down to the bare bones of the truth'. But it might be better to say, 'Take yourself seriously'. If you don't take yourself seriously as a writer then how can you expect anyone else to? Nurture the part of yourself that needs to write. Listen to how it works, what it needs, its ups and downs. Don't think of it as short term. It is a part of you, in the same way that your thoughts are part of you and so is your blood. And when your writing is done, be practical. Know your stuff about the world you are entering. Know where to place what you have done.

Read this book very carefully. Treasure it. Keep it beside you. It is your friend.

Rachel Joyce is the author of the *Sunday Times* and international bestsellers *The Unlikely Pilgrimage of Harold Fry* (2012), *Perfect* (2013), *The Love Song of Miss Queenie Hennessy* (2014), *The Music Shop* (2018) and *Miss Benson's Beetle*, all published by Doubleday. *The Unlikely Pilgrimage of Harold Fry* was shortlisted for the Commonwealth Book Prize and longlisted for the Man Booker Prize and has been translated into 34 languages. Rachel was awarded the Specsavers National Book Awards 'New Writer of the Year' in December 2012 and shortlisted for the 'Writer of the Year' 2014. She has written over 20 original afternoon plays for BBC Radio 4 and major adaptations for the *Classic Series* and *Woman's Hour*, including all of the Brontë novels. See more at www.penguin.co.uk/authors/1069732/rachel-joyce.html.

Reading as a writer

Cathy Rentzenbrink shares her life-long passion for reading. She shows how it can open up new worlds and possibilities, providing an invaluable learning resource for aspiring writers as well as pleasure for the reader, and how studying the lives, work and technique of other authors can drive, inform and enhance your own individual practice.

I have always loved reading more than pretty much anything else. It enables exploration and escape, gives consolation and pleasure, and fuels my desire to know the world. I don't remember learning how to do it, so it doesn't feel like a skill I had to acquire, more like a gift bestowed by a benevolent fairy godmother. 'I will make this one a reader,' she said, as she waved her wand over my crib. Perhaps it was this way for you, too, or maybe you came to reading later in life. My dad only learnt to read as an adult, and it strengthens my gratitude for books and reading to know that what is a comfort and joy for me, is not always easy for everyone. So welcome, dear reader, no matter what your journey to this page has been. My mission today is to share with you that, as well as everything else it offers, reading is probably the single best thing you can do in the service of your writing.

If reading was my first love, then writing was hard on its heels. When asked what I wanted to do when I grew up, I would announce that I wanted to be a writer or a detective (the influence of all those Enid Blytons, I'm sure) and would be told not to be silly by my teachers. Luckily my parents were encouraging and I had books where children were always striking out on adventures, solving crimes, and ruling magical kingdoms.

This, perhaps, is the first thing reading can do for us as well as offering entertainment – it opens up alternative realities. If you are struggling to find your tribe, if you are surrounded by people who care less about words and stories than you do, then look for friends in books. As a child I loved Anne Shirley as much as if she existed in my real life and I could visit her at Green Gables. I've never really stopped imagining myself into books in this way and it is a great cure for loneliness. In addition to fiction, I have always loved books about writers – both memoir and biography – and I see now that I was looking for clues as to how writing could be done. I was looking for the granular details: what time someone got up; where they wrote; how they earned money; and how they transitioned between the states of aspiration and arrival. When I had a child, I wanted to read about how authors managed their childcare, and when my first book, *The Last Act of Love* (Picador 2015), came out I wanted to read about how they dealt with attention. This is all available to you, dear reader, this mentoring via what writers say about themselves. Consider it all as you forge your own path.

And engage with the process: read a novel and then seek out what the writer says about how they made it. Go to events in bookshops, libraries and festivals (see *Festivals and conferences for writers, artists and readers* on page 596). If you can see authors in the flesh – our scruffy shoes, our bitten nails – the prospect of joining the ranks becomes less intimidating. There is a vast amount of stuff, often free, that you can access online. I have taken huge inspiration over the years from Hilary Mantel; from her books, yes, but also from her Reith Lectures and her interviews with the *Paris Review* and the *Guardian*. This is about chemistry. Maya Angelou, Maggie O'Farrell and Kit de Waal all float my boat, but your search might lead you to a different writer. Experiment. Read around. Find your soulmates. They don't have to know you for a relationship to have a significant impact and influence on your work.

Some writers send me directly to the page. And this doesn't seem to have anything to do with the subject. When I read Maggie Nelson or Elena Ferrante then I yearn to wield my own pen. One of the things that makes me happiest is when people tell me that reading my books has encouraged them in their own practice. I go forth into my day with great joy that someone out there is opening a notebook and sharpening their pencil because of me.

The most useful way to learn about technique, the nuts-and-bolts stuff, is to look at what other writers do. What point of view they have chosen? How do they handle any time shifts? How have they selected the start and end point of their story? When I get stuck on a point like this, I will look for the answer on my bookshelves. If I'm struggling with handling the dialogue when there are lots of characters present, then I'll search out dinner party scenes. At the moment I'm considering writing a novel that happens largely in flashback, but when I tried this before I found it too hard. This time I am going to reread *The Secret History* by Donna Tartt, *Rebecca* by Daphne du Maurier and *The Confessions of Frannie Langton* by Sara Collins and carefully study exactly how it is done.

And I'm always on the lookout. I read a book for pleasure first, racing through, and then, if it fits the bill, I go back and read it again with forensic attention. How did they do it? How did they capture and then hold my attention? How did they make me care so much about that really quite unpleasant character? As well as doing this with a brilliant book, it can be useful to do it when a book has fallen short. Where did the author lose your interest? Where did the pace drop? What didn't quite ring true? If you were this book's editor, what would you suggest to make it better? Would it be less confusing if there were fewer characters? Does that relentless present tense get on your nerves? Is there too much back story? If so, how could you fix this?

A word of caution, though. Don't compare your work in progress with a finished book – that's like watching the Oscars from the sofa in your pyjamas and berating yourself for not being red-carpet-ready. If a book is good, and the author has done their job; it will read as though they sat down one day and it just flowed out in the time it takes you to read it. That is the magic trick of literature; we all sign up to suspend disbelief and allow the wizard to wave their wand – but, if you are going to write as well as read, you need to know just how much work is involved in that sleight of hand. A finished book has almost always involved gargantuan effort, sometimes years of wailing and gnashing of teeth and pulling out of hair and endless drafts, and then finally – finally – the writer got an agent who made suggestions, and an editor who worked on several drafts, and then a copy-editor and a proofreader made the manuscript the best version of itself it could be. I didn't always know this – I would allow myself to be swamped with despair and I'd down tools because I didn't see how I could ever measure up. Eventually I realised how futile it is to brood on the knowledge that I will never be as good as Julian Barnes or Bernardine Evaristo. How pointless! I don't want to be trying to sound like them, I want to be putting all my time and energy into trying to sound like *myself*.

When you get deep into your work-in-progress you might want to be careful about exposing yourself to new ideas. I do press pause on certain things every so often. When I was finishing my novel *Everyone is Still Alive* (Phoenix 2021) I stopped reading new fiction and confined myself to memoirs or rereading Agatha Christie and Georgette Heyer. Then, when the novel was safely dispatched to my editor, I went on a fiction binge to make up for lost time. Another tip is an occasional week or two of complete deprivation. If you can make your manuscript the most interesting thing in your life, if you have no other sources of distraction – no email, no Netflix, no books – then you'll have to get all your entertainment from your own words. This isn't terribly compatible with living a 21st-century life, but I find it pays great dividends every so often, especially at the start of a project when the green shoots are tender and need a bit of protection, and when I'm coming towards the end of a draft; at that stage I feel like a juggler with all the colourful balls of my own story up in the air and I'm ready to commit to dedicated concentration as I bring the novel to an end with a flourish. But most of the time I am reading and think you should be too. These days, I have to carve out and protect both writing and reading time so that I am not seduced by the easy, empty pleasure of the internet. I write in the mornings, before I have looked at my email, and then, unless I have an event, I firmly shut down my computer and phone in the evening and give myself up to someone else's book.

So, read. Because it's useful. Because it's pleasurable. Because books are the best that humanity has to offer. Because your life will be enlarged when you spend as much of it as you can engaged in long-form narrative. Because you will feel better than if you toss away your time on the internet. And because you can take it all back to your own work; then one day you will know the joy of having readers of your own, as well as being a reader, and maybe someone will tell you that your book has inspired them to start writing their own and you will fill up with a sense of meaning and purpose that makes it all worthwhile.

Cathy Rentzenbrink is the author of the memoir *The Last Act of Love* (2015), *A Manual for Heartache* (2017) and *Dear Reader: The Comfort and Joy of Books* (2020), all published by Picador. *Everyone is Still Alive* (Phoenix 2021) is her first novel. Cathy has worked for the Reading Agency and Waterstones and regularly contributes to the media on all aspects of books and reading. For more information see https://cathyreadsbooks.com. Follow her on Twitter @catrentzenbrink.

See also...
• *Festival fun: your guide to how, why and what,* page 501

Books

Real people write books

Samantha Shannon reflects on the unknowable and untraceable mystery of the published author from the perspective of the fledgling writer. She sheds light on what finally allowed her to 'illuminate every dark corner of publishing' and become a bestselling author herself.

Some years ago, I wrote my first story. I believe I was seven or eight years old. From what little I remember of it, it was about a princess who inherited the moon. The reason I know nothing else about this piece of my juvenilia is that I only printed one copy, and I sent that copy to a publishing house (don't do this). I used spotless paper and double-checked that the ink had dried. I stapled the pages together, sealed them in an envelope, and penned the address in my very best handwriting. My grandmother walked me down the street to the postbox and, together, we sent my little story to the only publisher I could recall off the top of my head.

For a long time, I forgot about that story. I have no proof that it existed; it survives as a cobweb in the corner of my memory. Still – for a short time – it was out in the world. I imagine someone heaved a sigh when it arrived as it did, bereft of an agent to represent it or a synopsis to describe it. Perhaps a kind-hearted editor would have sent me a reply, had they known I was a child with a vivid imagination and no idea how publishing worked – but they would have hit a dead end if they'd tried. I had sent no letter to introduce myself, nor included a self-addressed envelope. I'm not confident I even thought to include my name on the cover.

Perhaps it was because I never got an answer that in my young mind a silence grew around publishing. My impression of it was all shadow and clockwork. Perhaps machines created books. Perhaps they grew on trees. Either way, it was clear that little girls like me had no place in the process. I continued to write stories, but I set aside the notion that anyone would ever find them in a bookshop. The author became an abstract concept. I glossed over the names on my favourite books, for they belonged to ethereal beings whose lives were worlds away from mine.

Then a media storm around a certain author brought her name to my attention. People weren't just talking about a book but about its creator – about her life, her dreams, and how she had conjured a universe in a café and on trains. There was fierce interest in her personal story. She was telling marvellous tales, but she was not a clockwork toy, not a shadow. Reading about her reminded me of what I must have always known – that people wrote books. Real people. From then on, I plunged back in to writing ferociously, with a luminous dream: I was going to be an author.

When I was 15, I started a full-length novel. Once it was finished, I decided to try to get it published but found myself with as little knowledge of publishing as I'd possessed when I was a child. All I had gained was a suspicion that there were many more pieces in the jigsaw than one author and one story, and I had no sense of how to fit those pieces together. I turned to the internet, where I found a local freelance editor and paid her all of my saved-up pocket money to look at a few chapters. Countless websites sang to me, promising me they could publish my book if I paid them far more money than I had ever had. I had only a tenuous understanding of what an agent was. In short, I was overwhelmed.

When I found the *Writers' & Artists' Yearbook* it was like striking a match in the dark. After someone mentioned it to me in passing, I got my hands on a copy straight away. With every page I turned, I understood more about the trade that had flummoxed me since I was a child. Soon I was armed with the knowledge I needed to begin my journey.

Writers' & Artists' Yearbook does not come with a guarantee of publication. There is no formula to publishing, no code to crack, no single 'right answer' that will launch your book onto the shelves. I don't think I've ever heard exactly the same publication story twice. All writers are wayfarers, and there are many paths we travel on ... some longer than others. That novel I wrote when I was 15 never saw the light of day. Even though I followed agency guidelines, even though I used the right font and the right line spacing – it was not to be.

You might have a book like that. You might have several. Trying to get someone to see them can sometimes feel like knocking on a door that never opens. But, if there's one thing I can tell you from the other side, it's that each minute you spend writing is worthwhile. Every story whets your craft. Every story hones your ability to see a tale through to its end. I would not have written my debut novel, *The Bone Season* (Bloomsbury 2013), without having first written the one I had to put away.

I got my book deal when I was 20. I've now been in the industry for seven years and have three bestsellers under my belt – yet there are still things I'm only just learning, things that take me by surprise. As with any vocation, getting to grips with being a writer is a lifelong process. But, by opening *Writers' & Artists' Yearbook*, you've taken your first step. This is your toolbox, your skeleton key, and the torch that will illuminate every dark corner of publishing. I wish you all the luck in the world.

Samantha Shannon is the *New York Times* and *Sunday Times* bestselling author of *The Bone Season* series: *The Bone Season* (2013), *The Mime Order* (2015), *The Song Rising* (2017) and *The Mask Falling* (2021), all published by Bloomsbury. Her other works, also published by Bloomsbury, include the novellas *On the Merits of Unnaturalness* (2016) and *The Pale Dreamer* (2016). Her fourth and most recent novel is *The Priory of the Orange Tree* (2019). Samantha's work has been translated into 26 languages.

Books

Shelf space: a debut writer's journey to claim his place

Femi Kayode looks back at how, mid-career, he turned a creative compulsion into an award-winning reality with his debut novel; he describes the specific sense of purpose that drove him to take that leap, building on previous experience and working through challenges, and explains why crime fiction was his chosen genre.

As I considered how to approach this article, Burna Boy, a Nigerian musician, won the Grammy for his album, *African Giant*. In his acceptance speech, he said something along the lines of: 'Here's to every African. You must know that no matter where you are, you can make it.' For some reason, this well-meaning but erroneous advice (placing a whole continent in the category of marginalised minorities) struck a chord. My debut novel, *Lightseekers* (Bloomsbury 2021), had just been published in a pandemic that prevented the traditional publicity circuit. At home in Windhoek, toasting with my publishers on Zoom, I felt like I was looking in on someone else's life. Even as reviews poured in from all over the English-speaking world and I received my first reader mail from New Zealand, it all seemed to be happening to someone else. Not Femi Kayode, father of two, husband, writer of soaps by night and advertising copywriter by day. 'But you said all this will happen,' my wife reminds me whenever the imposter syndrome takes over. Indeed, I remember ...

After writing across mediums for almost three decades, I suffered something I had assumed was beneath me: a crisis of purpose. A lot of my works were the products of workshops, a complex and convoluted production-value chain with outcomes that bear little or no resemblance to my initial creative vision. At 45, I looked back on my life and desired something uniquely mine that I could brandish as a testament to a life of story-telling. I can admit now that I was assailed by a crushing sense of my mortality. I realised that this wish for something wholly my own was in fact worry about my legacy, and this realisation came with a yearning to write a novel, a compulsive need that overtook every waking moment, spurring me into action.

I catalogued all the reasons why I couldn't write a novel (there were a lot) and all the reasons why I should do it anyway. I made friends with published writers, attended writers' festivals in the region where I lived, and applied for every writing workshop I could find on the internet. I had prepared a 500-word short story that I deemed pretty good, but no one on the selection panels of those workshops agreed. I made the decision not to write for the screen or theatre during this time, convinced that my experience in scriptwriting was impeding my ability to write The Novel. I knew I could tell a compelling story in script form, so if these competitions/workshops were rejecting my story, it had to be because I had not mastered the art of prose. Despite amassing books on writing and endless YouTube tutorials, the words did not tumble out of me with the urgency I expected. Deep inside, I knew I was scared, insecure and in need of a community of peers. So ... I went back to school. This was a decision few understood. I was relatively successful in advertising, I had teenage sons whose education was more a priority and, well, I was old. The guilt I felt about this rather selfish decision was only outweighed by my conviction: I was going to write a novel and it was now or never.

The response to my application to the inaugural MA in Crime fiction at University of East Anglia went to spam and I missed my interview. I contacted the university and was told my application could only be considered in the next year. 'I will be 46, practically close to my grave!', I nearly screamed at the poor Admissions Officer over the phone. Still, I had to wait and, in that time, desperate to occupy my mind with something other than my writing ambition, I enrolled for a postgraduate programme in Futures Studies where I learned to use Systems Thinking as a storytelling tool. Perhaps afraid for my sanity based on our initial interaction, UEA did offer me a place in the Crime Writing programme the next year. I was now at the end of one postgraduate programme while starting another one. The pressure was immense, but from the first day of class at UEA, sitting with a dozen other writers – some already published – I felt a sense of purpose, as though everything I did in the past had led to this place.

'I want to debunk this myth of "African literature",' I said when asked why I was taking the course. While waiting to be accepted into a creative writing programme, I had scoured enough bookshops and attended enough festivals to notice that novels written by writers of African origin (including African Americans!), no matter the genre, were placed in the African Literature category – even the ones marked with little stickers as long/shortlisted for one prize or another. On the shelves that housed the authors who had entertained me in my youth – Stephen King, Sidney Sheldon, David Baldacci, – I would search for an indication that the publishing world treated all narratives as equally important, but found none.

Apart from the popularity of the genre, crime fiction is one of the most expansive forms of novel. Perhaps because no one, no class or race, is immune from the cause and effect of crime, the genre lends itself to lateral thinking and allows for the synthesis of a modern world. I wanted to write grand, complex stories with tropes reminiscent of the movies I watched and the books I read while growing up. I wanted to present a world that defied classification, stories that genre-hopped and characters that inhabited an exciting and evolving world, not one 'developing' by the standards of an amorphous rating system. Certainly not one consigned by a reductionist model to 'African literature'. As I sat in class at UEA, the only black student, struggling to make out the accents of my equally ardent classmates, I knew it was important to create a character they could relate to in the same way they did with me. I set about creating a hero with a deliberateness that employed all my experience as a psychologist-turned-advertising-practitioner. I understood the concept of branding, the importance of a consistent narrative that brands need to appeal to their target audience, and I was learning the tropes of crime fiction at one of the best creative writing programmes in the world. I was ready.

From the get-go, I planned a series. Before attending UEA, I had created several TV shows. To pitch a TV series required a sound knowledge of the target audience, the characters' back stories, the main plot arc, the world of the show, and more. I was adept at creating what the industry called 'show bibles', not least because, as an advertising practitioner, I was well versed in the elements of a document like this, and I applied the same principles to the book series I planned to write. Now I needed a story befitting of the pilot episode of a series.

The story was always there ... an event which left me horrified at the scale of its inhumanity: the 'necklace killing' of four undergraduates in a university town in southern Nigeria. The many questions this incident raised in my mind made it the perfect case for my protagonist, an investigative psychologist who, despite being Nigerian, had lived most of his life in the States. Then self-doubt appeared abruptly. I started asking myself: who am I writing for? The more I developed the character(s), the more I became concerned that I was becoming alienated from the story. I realized that I may have taken my desire to appeal to a predominantly western audience a bit too far. I was writing through what Toni Morrison referred to as the 'white gaze'. For months, I could not write. Indeed, I *was* ready ... but now was stuck. 'Write a love letter to Nigeria,' my tutor advised when I shared my challenge, and snap, everything fell into place. I realised I was apportioning blame, delivering judgment, and meting out my version of justice to victim and perpetrator from the pedestal I placed my protagonist on; my story was rebelling. To move forward, I needed to go beyond empathy to demonstrating love: love for the characters – victim, accused, witness. I had to appreciate that, as soon as the characters became living and breathing beings in *my* story, they came with *their* stories to tell. I had to give them space.

To complement the feedback from my mostly British classmates, I did what any self-respecting advertising practitioner would do – I created a focus group. I reached out to a diverse group of people in different parts of the world with two critical things in common: they were avid readers and they were all Nigerian. Their brief was simple – to tell me how my protagonist made them feel. Are there red flags of disdain and judgment in his tone? Did he come across as standoffish, patronising, warm or caring? Was he sufficiently invested in the case and in the people that the tragedy had affected? Most of all, did he exhibit an ambivalence towards Nigeria that almost every national, both in the country and the diaspora, could relate to?

The completion of the manuscript, graduation and subsequently winning the Little, Brown/UEA Award for Crime Fiction gave me the perfect subject line for my emails to agents: 'Award-winning writer seeks representation'. I got referrals from the university and from the judging panel at Little, Brown. While the award may have inspired prompt feedback from agents, I quickly realised that the genre I was writing in was not consistent with their expectation of what an African should be writing. I used this as a benchmark in my search for an agent, never failing to ask that critical question: 'Where do you see my book on the shelves?'

On 1 February 2020 my UK publishers sent me a congratulatory note. *Lightseekers* was reviewed as the Standout Thriller of the Month by the *Independent*. By the end of the first week of publication, *Lightseekers* had made nine Best of the Month Crime Fiction lists in the UK, including *The Times*, *Sunday Times*, *Guardian*, *Observer*, *Independent*, *Literary Review*, *Financial Times*, *Irish Times* and the *Herald*.

When they spot the novel at bookshops I cannot visit because of the pandemic, friends take pictures of the shelf labels and send them to me. In nearly all cases, it resides in the 'new releases' section, not in New African Writing or World Literature (we need to talk about this category, but not today). My book is placed next to the works of other writers from around the world, both known and unknown, but all storytellers. Just like me.

Burna boy was right. No matter where you are, you can make it. First, believe. Then, do.

Femi Kayode has worked as an advertising copywriter and as a screenwriter and developer of several award-winning TV shows. He was a Packard Fellow in Film and Media at the University of Southern California. While studying for an MA in Creative Writing – Crime Fiction at the University of East Anglia, he wrote his first novel, *Lightseekers* (Bloomsbury 2021), which won the Little, Brown/UEA Award for Crime Fiction in 2018. Femi lives in Windhoek, Namibia. Follow him on Twitter @FemiKay_Author.

Books

The winning touch: the impact of winning an award

Ingrid Persaud traces the zigzag route, via law, art and parenting, that led to the discovery of her writing voice. She describes the powerful life-changing effect award-winning success had on her fledgling writing career, and encourages others to pursue their own writing passion at whatever stage of life.

Books

Writing is one of the few careers that you can start at any time – and the later in life the better. But I am bound to say that, given that I took the scenic route myself. Writing is my third (and final) act. If you were born into a lower-middle-class Trinidadian family like mine, particularly one with East Indian roots, there were only three career options: a young person with academic leanings could become a doctor, a lawyer or a failure. Keen to please, I read law at the LSE with every intention of returning home to practise as a barrister, have children and die. But it didn't take long to discover that practising law wasn't for me. I was horrified, but I couldn't lie; I just preferred hanging out at university. So I stayed on at LSE, only leaving when I got a job teaching law across the Aldwych at King's College. I was living my dream.

And yet ... deep within myself I knew something was missing. I was desperate for some form of self-expression which aligned my head, heart and hands. But I couldn't articulate the unease – I took time off to reflect. That's when I stumbled across the Slade Art Foundation Course. I had no background in art, and arrived at the entrance interview with my two hands swinging. They politely asked for my portfolio. Unfazed, I said I didn't have one; I was enthusiastic though, and would that be enough? I don't know why, but they decided to take a chance on me. At the end of a few intense months of immersion in art and art history, I had decided that I wanted to be an artist. That crazy decision took me back to university – this time to Goldsmiths College as an art undergraduate, and then to Central Saint Martins for a Masters in Fine Art. Oh, and along the way I gave birth to gorgeous identical twin boys. As is my wont, I stuck around institutions of higher education, picking up bits of teaching at Saint Martins and occasionally exhibiting work.

I might have made this mix of teaching, art practice and parenting work, but my then partner decided the twin babies deserved a childhood away from the confines of city life. We had ties to Barbados, and with reluctance I packed us in boxes and shipped us there, all the while grieving for the London art scene I would no longer inhabit. Writing a weekly essay became my way of interrogating this new life on a small rock. I discovered classified ads for Boss Fix, Uncrossing and Come to Me magical oils and went to the fish market with a bar full of ballroom dancers. Somewhere during the writing of that blog, I fell in love with the act of writing. When I tried to express myself on the page, I found the logic of law meeting the play of art, and melding. What I was discovering was the beginnings of a writing voice.

When I am introduced now, people often mention that I won both the Commonwealth Short Story Prize and the BBC National Short Story Award (NSSA) for my first short story, 'The Sweet Sop'. But I'm not a genius who opened her laptop and immediately wrote an award-worthy text. 'The Sweet Sop' flowed out of years spent grappling with language, with meaning, and with finding a way to express my *self*. I felt immensely lucky and honoured to win those two awards. But in the wake of the ceremonies and celebrations, I quickly found out just how much of an impact winning awards could have on a fledgling writing career. Agents are the first gatekeepers in the publishing world and I, of course, didn't have one; but on the night I won the BBC NSSA I let slip that I wasn't yet represented. Agents who a day before would not have read my emails, much less the unfinished novel manuscript I was working on, queued up to offer their services. Add serendipity to the mix and I signed with Zoë Waldie of RCW Literary Agency, and three years on I know I've chosen well. She is a fierce critic and my loyal champion. Her integrity and expertise means I can entrust the management of my writing life to her hands.

Right this minute, if industry surveys are correct, about one million people are writing a novel. A goodly proportion will not finish what they started. But that still leaves a lot of competition. As Zoë helped me realise, the awards I had won meant that – for a moment at least – I had name recognition. If ever there was an opportunity to sell my novel manuscript, it was then. But Zoë was hampered by one slight problem – although I could hand over 20,000 words, the other 80,000 were as-yet unwritten. So I sat down at my desk and for the next three months wrote with back-breaking intensity, leaving off only for the most essential bodily needs: eating, sleeping and going to the bathroom. The work paid off. With Zoë's light editing, the MS was sent off to all the major UK-based publishing houses.

Love After Love was bought by Faber after a seven-way auction. And what a great publisher: I worked with a super-bright editor, Louisa Joyner, who took a decent manuscript and transformed it into an excellent novel. But then something happened that none of us could have predicted … Almost overnight, the world shut down. Borders closed and nations retreated as Covid-19 raged. It was in this scary, precarious atmosphere that *Love After Love* was published in April 2020. And here is where I understood the value of a small, nimble publisher like Faber: marketing and sales changed tack and pushed all their resources online; they lined up Zoom events to promote the book; and somehow, the book managed to gain visibility.

No spin can change the fact that 2020 was a ghastly year – on top of the pandemic, my long marriage was ending. Bookstores shuttered their doors just as my novel came out. I would have continued crying into my breakfast cereal except for the amazing good fortune of winning another life-changing award: the Costa First Novel Award. And let's be clear that prizes are simply what a particular panel of judges on a particular day decide about a particular book. Chance is a huge component. When I was told I'd won, it took me a good 20 minutes to speak. All the anxiety, hard work and sacrifice were vindicated. Positive reviews from publications such as the *Economist*, the *Guardian* and the *New York Times* were now independently justified. Zoë's faith as my agent and the Faber publishing team's trust had paid off. I exhaled.

My writing life post-Costa has shifted. The prize is now my calling card. Invitations to bookish events, never in short supply, now overwhelm and threaten my productivity. Commissions to write articles, short stories and essays arrive with increasing regularity. Foreign rights to *Love After Love* are being sold. The Italian iteration of the novel is being published earlier than planned to catch the wave of publicity that has accompanied the prize. Sales have increased. I can let go – because *Love After Love* has found its way in the world. But the real shifts have been internal. More than anything else, my long bouts of self-doubt have shortened. I sit a little straighter at my desk, and I am relishing this third act of my life. Not only am I doing what I love, but I'm making a modest living. Every morning I wake up ready to work. It doesn't mean I don't have unproductive, uninspired days; but I know now that I can get past these dips because I am doing what I love and I've been lucky enough to have some recognition.

In a crowded field, prizes and awards help to give our work a platform – a fighting chance of finding the readership it deserves. I hope my zigzag path and inability to qualify as a best young thing to hit the writing scene give you hope and courage. Now, get back to your desk, open that blank page and write. The muse will come, but she's often stuck in traffic. Meanwhile your passion awaits you.

Ingrid Persaud was born in Trinidad. Her debut novel, *Love After Love*, won the Costa First Novel Award 2020. She also won the BBC National Short Story Award in 2018 and the Commonwealth Short Story Prize in 2017. She read law at the LSE and was an academic before studying fine art at Goldsmiths and Central Saint Martins. Her writing has appeared in several newspapers and magazines including *Granta, Prospect, Five Dials*, the *Guardian* and *National Geographic*. Follow her on Twitter @IngridPersaud.

The 'how to' of writing how-to books

Author Kate Harrison had published 12 novels when she made the unexpected move of writing a diet book. Here she talks through the six things you need to know to write a how-to book.

Becoming a how-to author was not part of my plan – and as for being a diet guru, my lifelong battle with the scales meant I was surely never going to be in a position to tell others how to eat. Yet here I am, the author of four books on the intermittent fasting approach to weight loss: the first, *The 5:2 Diet Book*, was turned down by my own publisher, but I published it myself and it became a bestseller, shifted more copies than my (still successful) novels and, at the last count, has been translated into 16 languages. And I'm two stone lighter than I was before this whole new world opened up ....

Maybe dieting isn't your area of expertise, but all of us have some specialist knowledge. Whether you're the go-to person for assembling flat-pack furniture, organising kids' birthday parties or training wilful puppies, there are readers out there who'd love to know how.

But how can you turn your skills into book sales? Here's the 'how to' of how-to books:

1. Know your stuff

What do you know more about than the average Joe or Joanna? Do your friends regularly ask you for help with something? Do you have a job or a hobby that gives you expertise?

Understanding a subject inside out is the key to a great how-to book. But that doesn't mean you need academic qualifications. Decades of experience in a practical skill will give you the understanding – and the short cuts and tips – that readers may prefer.

My experience: I'd spent years of my life losing and regaining weight on different regimes, yet when I tried intermittent fasting after watching the BBC's 'Horizon', I immediately sensed this could be different for me. There wasn't much practical information around, so I tried different approaches, and set up a Facebook group to share tips with friends. I was both an expert in dieting – including emotional factors and the reasons for failure – and a natural sceptic because, as a journalist, I was trained to question everything.

2. Know your readership

Often, the readership of a how-to book will be people like you, but the you *before* you went on the journey that equips you to write the book. Or they might be people you already teach in your day job or as a volunteer.

Whether you're a craftsperson with tricks that have taken you decades to learn, or a therapist who wants to help people in print as well as face to face, you need to understand the readers who might buy your book, so you can get the tone right.

My experience: I knew my ideal reader was me, six months earlier. But I did understand that, while I was fascinated by the science of fasting, not all readers would share my interest. So when I planned the book I aimed for the middle ground, interspersing real-life experiences, with more complex biology. I included a glossary, and lots of hyperlinks – particularly useful in an ebook – so that readers could easily read the research for themselves.

3. Know the question your book will answer

All how-to books answer a question or solve a problem. It's worth spending time thinking through what that question or need is, to help refine what your book will offer. One

Books

practical way to do this is to use Google or Amazon search functions. When you type in the beginning of a phrase, search engines predict what the rest of your phrase might be, based on millions of previous searches. It can be hilarious, but useful too.

For example, type 'DIY' into the Amazon books search bar, and you'll see: projects, for women, complete manual … Or type 'vegan eating' on Google and you'll see other people have searched for 'meal plan' or 'breakfast'. Do this around lots of possible combinations and write down key words.

Once you understand what people want to know, you can structure your book around telling them, dealing with one key point or area per chapter. Use the key words in the title of the book itself: it makes it easier for readers to find your book!

Some questions or needs are very niche, which is not a problem if you're writing an ebook. Because the costs of producing the book are low, you can create shorter books – at lower prices – that address single issues and work well at the shorter length. Or bring different questions on one topic together in a 'complete' guide.

One important point: if you're writing about health, or potentially risky activities, include clear and appropriate warnings to ensure you're not putting readers in danger. If you have any doubt at all, look at the warnings in books on similar topics, or take professional advice. The last thing you want is to be sued!

My experience: 'How can I lose weight and keep it off?' is a need shared by millions of people worldwide. Discovering what worked for me was a life-changer, and I focused on explaining why the approach was different, and on practical ways to fit it into your life.

4. Know your unique story/point of view

Stories aren't just for children. We learn the three-act structure of stories – beginning, middle, end – from movies, books and even jokes. Structuring your non-fiction book around a story makes it more enjoyable. For example, a book about money or changing your job could easily follow the 'rags to riches' Cinderella storyline.

Your book doesn't have to be a fairy tale, but readers will enjoy reading your own story and/or case studies or people you've helped. Explaining your own struggles or problems, and then how you found the solution, establishes you as credible. Your story also makes your book unique. Even if you're a high-powered expert – a brain surgeon or a leading detective – talking as one person to another will make your book accessible, and help you stand out, even if there are many other books already on your topic.

My experience: as a consumer of previous 'diet books' written by scientific experts, I knew they could be patronising. I decided to be 100% honest about my struggles, interspersing research and advice with my own weight-loss diary. After the book was published, I had countless emails from other dieters saying 'it was like reading my own story' and my success, after years of failure, helped inspire them to try the plan.

5. Know how to publish your book

Writing may be a solitary activity, but publishing your book will almost certainly be a team effort!

You have two main options: look for an agent and publishing deal, or self-publish your work as an ebook and a print-on-demand title. The decision is worthy of an article in itself, but how-to books are very well suited to self-publishing. If your subject is quite niche, then it may not be worthwhile for a mainstream publisher, but if you get your title and cover right, readers can find you easily online, and will you will receive the lion's share of the profits. Agents and publishers are more likely to be interested if you're well-known in your field and already have thousands of followers on social media, and they may offer you an advance based on a proposal.

Self-publishing doesn't mean going it alone: you will need an editor/proofreader, and a cover designer who can make your cover as appealing as possible. The investment will help make your book stand out. Formatting an ebook is straightforward, but you may also want to hire someone for that, especially if it contains illustrations or photographs.

My experience: I thought my book had potential, but my publishers didn't agree. So I worked with my agent to self-publish on Amazon Kindle. It went to Number 1 in the diet charts within a few days – and later my publisher did republish an expanded version, plus we worked together on three recipe books and a self-help title, *5:2 Your Life*.

In 2020, I decided to expand the approach I outline in this article in *Pitch Power: Discover what makes your book irresistible & how to sell it*. I knew the market for this was smaller than a diet book so a mainstream publisher wouldn't be interested – so decided to publish it myself and love the fact I could pick the perfect cover and publish instantly and I can revise it whenever I wish, adding in new examples.

6. Know how to sell your book

Hooray – your book is ready! But the hard work is not over. You need to let potential readers know it exists.

If you already have a blog or a website, post there, and on Twitter or Facebook. Be generous with your knowledge and content; offering free samples of your work is far more convincing than just screaming BUY MY BOOK! Ebooks can be given away for free or at a reduced price, which can help get you early reviews, or increase your visibility by helping the book rise in the charts. But use with caution; don't undersell yourself.

Good reviews on Amazon and other sites are very important, but never post them under fake names or via family members' accounts. You will be found out. A better idea is to put a note to readers at the end of your ebook asking them to review it if they've enjoyed it.

Articles in newspapers or magazines can really boost your sales. Press releases are simple to write but do research the right format online. Offer yourself, or people you've taught, as case studies. Local media often like to feature authors, so approach your local radio station or newspaper.

My experience: I had already shared tips in a private Facebook group I'd set up with a few friends who were also fasting. The group grew massively and when I decided to write the book, I included members' experiences. This meant that, when it went on sale, they were keen to read and discuss it. The group is now 70,000 members strong, and I still use their comments to influence my books.

7. Finally, know what to do next

Whether you find a handful of readers, or many thousands, writing a how-to book can be rewarding and fun. And it can be a platform to so much more: a new book, a podcast or YouTube channel, an e-course, or offering yourself as a public speaker.

The possibilities are endless, but whatever you do, there's nothing like that first email from a reader thanking you for making something easy … or even for changing their lives.

My experience: I've hosted my own podcast, and still enjoy chatting to people about diet and health. But after eight years of fasting – and writing about it – I decided to return to my fiction writing roots, and have separate pen names for thrillers and love stories. Plus I offer tips for new writers on social media. I'm living proof we can find an audience for anything we are passionate about. Whatever your ambitions, remember that writing is a labour of love, and we can and should follow our hearts.

Kate Harrison worked at the BBC as a TV correspondent and news producer before becoming a full-time writer. Kate wrote nine adult novels, including the *Secret Shopper* series, and a young adult thriller trilogy, *Soul Beach* (Orion 2011), before starting her non-fiction journey. She first self-published *The 5:2 Diet Book* as an ebook in 2012, followed by a print version with Orion, and six more recipe/self-help titles. Her books have been translated into more than 20 languages. She still writes fiction as Kate Helm (*The Secrets You Hide* and *The House Share*), and in 2021 her epic love story *How to Save a Life* will be published under the name Eva Carter. Read more about Kate's 7-step method for planning and writing books in *Pitch Power: discover what makes your book irresistible & how to sell it* and visit her website at https://kate-harrison.com/for-writers or follow her on Twitter, Instagram and YouTube, @KateWritesBooks.

Finding my agent

Martina Cole describes how her writing career started.

The *Writers' & Artists' Yearbook* holds a very dear place in my heart. Without it, I would never have been published as quickly, or as well, of that much I am sure.

I had written my first novel, *Dangerous Lady*, when I was 21 and it had been a dream of mine to become an author. I wasn't expecting fortune, or fame; all I had ever wanted was to see my name on the cover of a book. Books are probably the most important things in my life, apart from the family of course! I have loved books since I was a small child, when my father, a merchant seaman, brought home from his travels a cardboard theatre. When I opened the crimson faux velvet curtains, hidden behind them were the smallest books I had ever seen. The stories they contained were all old Aesop fables, and fairy tales, and I was absolutely entranced.

After that, a book was second nature to me. I even played truant from school so I could lie all day long in the park reading books from the local library – books I had taken out in my parents' names as well as my own. Books I would never otherwise have been allowed to read at such a young age. My parents died never knowing they had library memberships!

So, when I wrote *Dangerous Lady* all those years ago, it was the start of my writing career, though I didn't know it at the time.

Over the next nine years I wrote three more novels, film scripts, television scripts, and even a play for the theatre. But I had no confidence in myself as a writer, and I wrote for the sheer pleasure of it. I'm sure many of the people reading this are doing exactly the same thing!

Coming up to 30 was my personal watershed. I was running a nursing agency and had been offered a partnership. I was also moving house, so there were big upheavals all round. I was going to throw out all my writing efforts, and put away the dream of being an author. Then I glanced through *Dangerous Lady* – and I knew instinctively that it was much better than I had ever realised and that I had to at least try and fulfil my ambition, whatever the outcome might be.

I purchased then read the *Writers' & Artists' Yearbook* from cover to cover, and was fascinated by this world I craved but knew absolutely nothing about. It told me the correct way to set out a manuscript, both for a novel and for television, who published what, and more importantly, where I could find them! It was a mine of information, and it gave me the push I needed to pursue my dream.

I found my agent, Darley Anderson, tucked away among the pages, and taking a deep breath I rang him up – I nearly passed out when he answered the phone himself. I explained that I had written a book, what it was about, and he said, 'Send it to me, I'm intrigued'.

I posted it to him on the Thursday night, and he phoned me on the Monday at teatime: Darley's first words were, 'You are going to be a star!' It was the start of a long and happy friendship. It was also the beginning of my career in publishing.

When I am at a writers' conference, or a library event, I always tell the audience they must purchase the *Writers' & Artists' Yearbook*. On signings, if I am approached by someone who is writing a novel and I think they are serious about it, I purchase the book for them, and tell them that if they get published I want the first signed copy!

Books

When I was asked to write this article, I was thrilled because all those years ago when I bought my first copy of the *Yearbook* I never dreamt that one day I would be lucky enough to actually be a small part of it. It's a truly wonderful introduction to the world of literature, and it also contains everything you need to know about writing for television, film *et al*. If it's relevant to what you are writing about, be it a novel or a newspaper article, you can find it in this *Yearbook*.

There's so much of interest, and so much that the budding writer needs explained. By the time I finally had a meeting with Darley in person, the *Writers' & Artists' Yearbook* had helped me understand exactly what I needed to ask about, and more importantly, what to expect from the meeting itself.

I wish you all the very best of luck. Publishing is a great business to be a part of.

I wrote for years in my spare time, for free – I loved it. It was a part of me and who I was. I still love writing, every second of it. I was asked once by a journalist if I ever got lonely – writing is such a solitary occupation, as we all know. But I said no. I spend all day with people that I've created. I put the wallpaper on the walls, and I give them families, lives to live, cars to drive, and in some cases I have even killed them! Not many people can that say about their jobs.

The *Writers' & Artists' Yearbook* is a wonderful tool for any budding writer, so use it and enjoy it. Good luck.

Martina Cole's first novel *Dangerous Lady* caused a sensation when it was published in 1992. 29 years later, Martina is the bestselling author of 25 highly successful novels, published ny Headline, 17 of which reached No. 1 and her books have collectively spent over four years in the bestseller charts. Total sales stand at over 17 million copies, making her Britain's bestselling female crime writer. *The Take*, which won the British Book Award for Crime Thriller of the Year in 2006, was adapted for Sky One, as was *The Runaway*. Three of her novels have been adapted for the stage: *Two Women*, *The Graft* and *Dangerous Lady* were all highly acclaimed when performed at the Theatre Royal Stratford East. In 2021, Martina was awarded the highest honour in British crime writing, the Crime Writers' Association Diamond Dagger.

See also...
• *Literary agents* section, page 405

Notes from a successful children's author

J.K. Rowling shares her experiences of writing success.

I can remember writing *Harry Potter and the Philosopher's Stone* in a cafe in Oporto. I was employed as a teacher at the language institute three doors along the road at the time, and this café was a kind of unofficial staffroom. My friend and colleague joined me at my table. When I realised I was no longer alone I hastily shuffled worksheets over my notebook, but not before Paul had seen exactly what I was doing. 'Writing a novel, eh?' he asked wearily, as though he had seen this sort of behaviour in foolish young teachers only too often before. *'Writers' & Artists' Yearbook*, that's what you need,' he said. 'Lists all the publishers and … stuff,' he advised, before ordering a lager and starting to talk about the previous night's episode of *The Simpsons*.

I had almost no knowledge of the practical aspects of getting published; I knew nobody in the publishing world, I didn't even know anybody who knew anybody. It had never occurred to me that assistance might be available in book form.

Nearly three years later and a long way from Oporto, I had almost finished *Harry Potter and the Philosopher's Stone*. I felt oddly as though I was setting out on a blind date as I took a copy of the *Writers' & Artists' Yearbook* from the shelf in Edinburgh's Central Library. Paul had been right and the *Yearbook* answered my every question, and after I had read and reread the invaluable advice on preparing a manuscript, and noted the time-lapse between sending said manuscript and trying to get information back from the publisher, I made two lists: one of publishers, the other of agents.

The first agent on my list sent my sample three chapters and synopsis back by return of post. The first two publishers took slightly longer to return them, but the 'no' was just as firm. Oddly, these rejections didn't upset me much. I was braced to be turned down by the entire list, and in any case, these were real rejection letters – even real writers had got them. And then the second agent, who was high on the list purely because I liked his name, wrote back with the most magical words I have ever read: 'We would be pleased to read the balance of your manuscript on an exclusive basis …'.

This piece was written for the very first edition of the *Children's & Writers' Yearbook*, published in 2004.

J.K. Rowling OBE CH is best known as the author of the seven *Harry Potter* novels (Bloomsbury), published between 1997 and 2007. The series has sold over 500 million copies worldwide, been translated into over 80 languages and made into eight blockbuster films. She also wrote three short companion volumes to the series for the charities Comic Relief and Lumos. In 2016 J.K. Rowling collaborated with playwright Jack Thorne and director John Tiffany to continue Harry's story in a stage play, *Harry Potter and the Cursed Child*, which is now playing in London, the USA and Australia. In the same year, she made her screenwriting debut with the film *Fantastic Beasts and Where to Find Them*. The second, *Fantastic Beasts: The Crimes of Grindelwald*, was released in 2018. J.K. Rowling also writes novels for adults. *The Casual Vacancy* (Little, Brown) was published in 2012 and adapted for television in 2015. Under the pseudonym Robert Galbraith, she is the author of the acclaimed *Strike* crime series. There are five books in the series so far: *The Cuckoo's Calling* (2013), *The Silkworm* (2014), *Career of Evil* (2015), *Lethal White* (2018) and *Troubled Blood* (2020). The first four books have been adapted for television. In 2020, J.K. Rowling released, *The Ickabog* (Little, Brown Books for Young Readers), an original fairy tale, first in free online instalments and then as a book illustrated by children, with her royalties donated to assist vulnerable groups impacted by the Covid-19 pandemic.

Books

Writing advice

Changing lanes: writing across genres and forms

Mark Illis describes the shifting path, form and shape his writing career has taken – from adult novels and short stories, through TV and radio drama to Young Adult novels – and shows how the unexpected challenges and changes writers may encounter serve to develop and refresh their work.

I started early. My first short story was published in 1984, when I was 21, and my first novel when I was 25 (it was a short novel with a young male protagonist whose experiences weren't a million miles from my own). I had another two books published by Bloomsbury before I was 30, and at that point I thought that the road ahead was clear: I wrote literary novels for adults. If the process of writing the novel got a bit stodgy around the middle, I'd pause to write a couple of short stories, send them off to magazines or competitions and return to the novel refreshed. Novels and short stories. I was pretty sure that I knew what I was going to write for the rest of my life.

I was wrong. A writer's career is seldom that straightforward. Writing novels is what I love, it's what I always return to, it's the thread that runs through my writing life, but I've stepped – or sometimes lurched, and occasionally been shoved – in other directions many times over the years.

The first time this happened was when Bloomsbury turned down my fourth novel. This was a blow after the relatively smooth road I'd travelled up to that point. I'd only ever wanted to be a writer and, amazingly, up till then I'd succeeded in being a writer. Now I had to stop and think. What could I do if no one wanted to publish me? I wrote a couple of calling card scripts for TV – one-off, one-hour dramas that gave a sense of what my writing was like. I sent them to *EastEnders* and *The Bill*. These days you might try *Doctors*, the BBC Writers' Room, its Channel 4 equivalent, or the Northern Writers' Awards. *EastEnders* and *The Bill* replied, and then I was writing for TV.

For a while I felt like I was having an affair. I was married to novels but I'd run away with this glamorous stranger. But after two or three years the first excitement of the affair began to wear off, and I started thinking about going back to my first love – to novels. However, TV is where the money is, and it sort of sidled up to me and whispered in my ear: 'Stay with me, and I'll buy you a house.' So I stayed with TV. My screen agent was happy, my book agent dropped me, and the years slipped by.

I enjoyed working in TV because it didn't just buy me a house, it introduced me to a new way of writing. This is one of the great advantages of writing across different genres and forms – your technique, your assumptions, your approach to your craft will all be challenged, shaken up and enriched. My TV journey took me on to *Peak Practice* and then to *Emmerdale*, where I stayed for over a decade. It was all new to me. Soap writing is collaborative, it loves big characters and big stories, it trades in jeopardy, high stakes and cliffhangers, and it explores the art of finding surprise in the context of the familiar. I found some of this strange at first, even alienating, but as I discovered the rhythm of soap, and got accustomed to how it worked, it became increasingly satisfying. Writing for soap deepened my understanding and appreciation of story. How do you keep people coming back for more, night after night, week after week, year after year? A soap writer is like a modern Scheherazade, spinning story to stop the fickle audience from changing channels.

I enjoyed the collaborative aspect of writing for TV. At *Emmerdale* we had a story conference every month, with about 20 writers, along with storyliners, script editors and the producer, all sitting round a table and talking story for two days – and then going out for a meal together in the evening. It was a major change in my life. Until then, writing had involved me sitting alone with my laptop. I would unpeel myself from the screen occasionally and find some pretext to leave the house, to get some fresh air and meet some humans. Writing for TV came with fellow humans included.

Diving into story was fascinating, and collaborating at story conferences was usually creative, productive and fun. Having your script edited was often like that too ... but sometimes it wasn't. When you're writing a novel, you're the god of your own world for a year or so, as you write it and polish it and get it into its best possible form. Then an agent and an editor will almost certainly have suggestions and your manuscript will develop, but it's unlikely that you'll need to make radical changes. Script editing on a soap is different. It's your episode, but it's not your story. They can decide at a late stage to strip out your 'A' story and replace it with something else. They can – and probably will – tell you that your favourite scene, where you've used humour and nuance to really delve into character, has to be cut to make way for another story beat. So writing for soap was sometimes frustrating, but it's a distinct way of working; it's skilled and involving, and it produces six episodes a week watched by millions.

Still, I couldn't write exclusively for soap. It was my enjoyable, intellectually stimulating, income-generating day job, but I needed to do other writing as well. I got on to a course that the BBC was running, on writing radio plays, and over the next few years I had two and a half plays on Radio 4 (one of them was co-written). It was fascinating to explore a new medium, with new difficulties and opportunities, while in terms of collaboration it was an interesting halfway house, in that I had to get an idea accepted, and then a producer would have notes on my script, but still it was *my* script, my story. In fact, it felt a bit like writing a short story. I also wrote a screenplay, which won a prize, but it was based closely on someone else's storyline, so it wasn't fully satisfying.

The truth is, I wanted to be writing novels again. That thread I mentioned, running through my writing life, was still there, even if it was currently a bit buried under TV scripts. I'd never stopped writing short stories, because they fit nicely in between TV deadlines, and I began to notice that there were thematic and character-based links between some of these stories. I'd been reading the wonderful *Olive Kitteridge* (Random House 2008) by Elizabeth Strout around this time, which is a book of linked short stories, and I realised that I could use the same approach. So I took six months off *Emmerdale* to work on the project. I sent the collection to Salt Publishing, and *Tender* appeared in 2009. I was delighted to finally be a novelist again. My novel *The Last Word* (Salt Publishing 2011) followed, and I was starting to think that I had achieved an ideal situation, in which I could write both TV and fiction.

Then, in 2013, *Emmerdale* sacked me. As when that fourth novel was rejected back in the 1990s, it was a bit of a shock. Around that time, my children were becoming teenagers and I was reading some of the books they were reading: *The Knife of Never Letting Go* (Walker Books 2008) by Patrick Ness, *The Hunger Games* (Scholastic 2008) by Suzanne

Collins, *Maggot Moon* (Hot Key Books 2012) by Sally Gardner, *Noughts and Crosses* (Random House 2001) by Malorie Blackman. My geeky, angsty, inner teenager who loved reading and writing – and who is never very far beneath the surface – sat up. I thought, 'I'd like to write something like that; I'd like to use what I've learnt from TV, along with what I've learnt from writing novels for adults, in order to produce stories for teenagers.' So that's what I did. My novel *The Impossible* (Quercus Children's 2017) is about four teenagers navigating the tricky world of relationships and family – but there are also aliens and mutants in the mix, and there's a metaphorical (and autobiographical) layer involving the alarming changes that occur in teenagers' lives. It's influenced by John Wyndham, whom I read as a teenager, and the US science fiction series *Stranger Things*, which I watched on Netflix, and yet in some ways it's just as personal as my first novel.

So … I got a new book agent, *The Impossible* was published, a sequel came out in 2018, and I recently finished a new YA book. I love writing for teenagers, and it feels exciting at my age to set out into a new field. I think it's probably very good for a writer to experience the occasional upheaval. Change refreshes your work and refreshes your brain as well. Writing novels for teens has spilled over into my TV work, as I wrote a couple of episodes of *Jamie Johnson* for CBBC, and I spent some time developing my own children's drama with Lime Pictures..

Some days I'll work on the novel in the morning and on TV in the afternoon. Some weeks it'll be all about a TV project. Pre-Covid I'd be off to a school to do a reading, a talk or a workshop, and I'd still squeeze in the odd short story now and then. I think the variety is helpful, but novels, I'm happy to say, are still the essential thread running down the centre of my writing life.

I hope it's clear from all the above that – like a lot of writers – I've been demoralised in the past and tempted to give up. For the most part I've been very lucky, but writing isn't easy, and rejection, compromise and outright failure are occasional or regular visitors for most of us. New genres and forms have been a lifeline for me; they've kept me writing, kept me working, kept me earning, and kept me excited about my craft. When change comes, I think we should try to welcome it, and when it doesn't come … perhaps we should seek it.

Mark Illis is a novelist, short story writer, and writer for TV, radio and film. He took an MA in Creative Writing at UEA, and his first three novels, *A Chinese Summer* (1988), *The Alchemist* (1990) and *The Feather Report* (1992) were published by Bloomsbury. In 1992 Mark moved to West Yorkshire to be a Centre Director for the Arvon Foundation. He went on to write for TV serials *EastEnders*, *The Bill* and *Peak Practice*, and then for *Emmerdale*, and has written three radio plays. Mark's other books are *Tender* (2009) and *The Last Word* (2011), published by Salt Publishing, and his YA novels *The Impossible* (2017) and *The Impossible: On the Run* (2018), published by Quercus. *The Impossible* has been optioned for TV. Visit his website http://markillis.co.uk.

Turning to crime: writing thrillers

Crime writer Kimberley Chambers describes how her life took a new direction when she began writing, and recalls the help and advice that have brought her success. She provides her own top tips for other aspiring authors.

I grew up in Dagenham and left school at 16, with hardly any qualifications. I then spent years working on East End markets such as Roman Road, Petticoat Lane and Whitechapel. When the markets took a turn for the worse, I began DJ-ing and then, in my thirties, I took up minicab driving.

At the age of 38, I was wondering what to do next. I hadn't written anything since school, but always thought that one day I'd have a crack at writing a book. That was the start of my career. Before I started writing my first book, *Billie Jo* (Preface 2008), I made a list of all the main characters. I recall slightly struggling with the first three chapters, but I stuck with it and, from chapter four onwards, it started to get easier. By chapter seven I was flying, and was positive that I'd found my vocation in life.

Because I was still minicabbing, it took me a whole year to write that first book. My friend Pat, who had a bookstall on Romford market at the time, told me about the *Writers' & Artists' Yearbook*. I wasn't particularly great at technical stuff – I'm still not – and if it hadn't been for Pat's advice I wouldn't have had a clue about getting an agent or getting published. She ordered me a copy and I remember reading through it from cover to cover. For someone uneducated like myself, I found it was written in a way that I could understand. I took all the advice on board, including the need to create a strong covering letter and to polish up the first few chapters; they, as the *Yearbook* explains, could be the only chance you have to catch someone's interest.

The day after I sent those chapters off to about 25 agents, an agent rang me up asking to see the rest. Another four agents contacted me the following week. I went to meet a few of them and ended up choosing Tim Bates (then of Pollinger Limited, now at PFD), who is still my agent to this day. And, since then, it really has been a rollercoaster of a journey for both of us.

I recall the initial wait was horrid – waiting to find out if I'd got that first book deal. Every day seemed like a week. I think a few of the publishers were worried because I was so uneducated and because I wrote by hand (which I still do). Penguin Random House had just launched a new imprint called Preface and they decided to take a chance on me. My first book deal was very small but, by the time *Billie Jo* came out in July 2008, I had finished my second novel, *Born Evil* (Preface 2009) and already signed another deal, which enabled me to give up the minicabbing for good. Obviously, there's always a chance, as a new author, that your book will flop or that you won't be able to get your name out there; but my sales still grew, by word of mouth, and I always believed in myself and that one day I would make it to the top.

My fortunes changed when I moved to HarperCollins. They decided to bring out the third book they published for me in hardback, because they knew I had a loyal following. *Payback* (HarperCollins 2013) shot straight to Number One on the *Sunday Times* bestseller list, where it stayed for a couple of weeks. Since that day, I've never looked back.

I'm not the biggest planner when it comes to plotting my books. I tend to mostly go with the flow, and let the storyline come to me as I get into the book. For instance, my novel *The Feud* (Preface 2010) was meant to be a standalone but, when I got five chapters from the end, I decided to change the ending in order to carry on with the story. A similar thing happened with *The Trap* (Harper 2013). That was also meant to be a standalone, but yet again I loved the characters and thought there was so much more to come from them, so I ended up with five books.

I often get asked by others wanting to write a book how to go about it, and I always tell them to get the *Writers' & Artists' Yearbook* and go through it with a fine-tooth comb like I did. I also advise them to write to as many agents as possible. As the old saying goes, one man's trash is another man's treasure. I sometimes wonder what I would be doing now if I hadn't been given the advice that I was.

As far as advising others on their writing, I personally find that I bring more colour to a book when I set it in an era that I'm interested in. I much prefer writing stories set in the '60s, '70s or '80s. I love to recreate the music and fashion of those days and the way life was back then. For example, my parents used to have a caravan on King's Holiday Park in Eastbourne, which back in the day had the biggest nightclub in the Southeast. So I set part of the *Butler* series at King's – my main characters bought a bungalow there – and I went back and recreated those days and how I remembered it. The markets usually pop up in my books too. Queenie Butler, one of my characters, loves shopping with her sister Vivvy up the Roman Road. That was recalling the time I worked there myself and it was like a competition between the women back then, about who was the most glamorous on a Saturday afternoon! As I was writing those scenes, it felt like stepping back in time.

I'm not the biggest reader myself but, as a child, I was addicted to Enid Blyton and I remember reading the *Famous Five* books repeatedly. I didn't pick up a book again until I went on a girls' holiday in my late teens. I found a Jackie Collins novel at the airport, and that's what got me back into reading, although, since becoming an author myself, I don't tend to read a great amount. I still enjoy a good holiday book, but I relax by watching a drama or film on TV. I have no set pattern to the hours I work, but I tend to write more in the evening than earlier in the day. In summer I like to sit at the kitchen table because it looks out onto my garden and it's quite tranquil; in winter I prefer sitting in the front room opposite the open fire.

My top tips for anybody who aspires to be a published author are:

1. Think about your **characters** carefully. I tend to visualize what mine would look like, give them strong names that suit them, and focus on their separate personalities.

2. Pick a **genre** you like to read or a world you are familiar with. I chose the genre I write in as it's the one I enjoy reading the most. I had led a reasonably colourful life, so choosing to write crime from the other side of the fence, rather than from the usual police perspective, was much easier for me. I don't like doing hours and hours of research.

3. Think of a strong **beginning, middle and ending**. This might change as your book develops, as it has in a few of mine, but it's always best to know in which direction you are heading.

4. Believe in yourself. If you are having a bad day when you are writing, **don't give up**. Just take a break, then return to the story with a fresh mind and eye.

5. Try to go down the route of getting properly published before considering self-publishing. To do that, you need **an agent**. You will find literary agents listed in this

Yearbook, along with tips about how to approach them (listings for agents start on page 430).

That is exactly how I got published, and I wish all of you doing the same the very best of luck.

Kimberley Chambers worked as a market trader, DJ and minicab driver before becoming a full-time author after the success of her first two books, *Billie Jo* and *Born Evil*. The second book in her *Butler* series, *Payback* (HarperCollins 2013), was No. 1 in the *Sunday Times* bestseller list, as were *Tainted Love* (HarperCollins 2016), *Life of Crime* (HarperCollins 2018) and *Queenie* (HarperCollins 2020), the last two of which were also *Sunday Times* Top 10 bestsellers in paperback. Her latest book, *The Family Man* (HarperCollins), will be published in Autumn 2021. Kimberley's other books include the Mitchell & O'Haras trilogy: *The Feud*, *The Traitor* and *The Victim*. For more information visit http://kimberleychambers.com and follow her on Twitter @kimbochambers or www.facebook.com/kimberleychambersofficial.

Writing character-led novels

Kerry Hudson knows that fully-rounded, engaging and nuanced characters, developed through detailed observation and thought, are fundamental to character-led novels. She shares her experience and tested techniques that help build up a character thoroughly before writing their story.

The frequent question 'Where do you get your ideas from?' is given a bad rap, but I understand why it's often the first question people ask authors about their writing. After all, there are so many things that might be explored in a novel: our own lives; the lives of others; our world; and what lies beyond our understanding of our own world and lives. For me, my books and stories, fiction and non-fiction, have always begun with a character. The genesis of each narrative has been a single figure who I've then built a world around – a character I'll get to know so well that I can understand how they'll interact with the people, setting and situations they encounter.

In writing this article, in trying to work out and break down my writing process so it might be of help to someone else, I realised that I build my characters in exactly the same way that I've developed my *process* for building characters. The thoughts and exercises described below have developed over many years of reading, conversation, teaching and listening. I have worked out what feels important to me in my work, what 'speaks' to me and feels authentic.

When I begin to create a character, I find myself looking for them in the people I meet, in the people I watch on the bus or on TV, in films or read about in newspapers and magazines. I look out for characteristics; it might be the unusual way someone holds their phone, how they order their coffee, the way they hold their body as they walk through the rain, the music that slips from their headphones, the rhythm of their language, the way they eat spaghetti. Any small gesture or behaviour can spark recognition: this is something my character would do in the event of a certain situation, interaction or emotion. *My character would hold their phone that way because they are a germaphobe/they saw someone on Instagram doing it that way/they suffer from chronic pain.*

So, my first writing tip is to watch and observe. Really look and notice, not the sweeping and obvious, but the grit – the tiny specks of uniqueness that we all carry. This is about evoking a 'real' character and making them not just what, as a writer, you want them to be, but turning them into rounded individuals, flesh and blood with flaws and hopes. It's about capturing and using these tiny details, which relate to the readers' own lives and experiences, to fill in the gaps, making your character come 'alive' and making your writing more universal. When writing character-driven work, you think first of all the things – all the layers and factors, social, emotional, genetic and environmental – that make up who your character is.

Exercise 1: What makes a person?

• Make a list of all the factors you can think of that describe the character you have in mind. If it's easier, you can draw up a list about yourself. This would be my list: woman, queer, working class, Caucasian, Scottish, 41, anxious but often seems confident, writer, former NGO worker, world traveller, home body, married, friendly, warm, socially avoidant, organised, occasionally lazy, careful about clothes only when necessary, tough, vulnerable, intelligent but not educated. The list is long and will never be exhaustive because, of course, it changes from day to day, context to context, setting to setting. You might also see that many of the characteristics I've listed are contradictory – and this is often the case with people. Part of developing a nuanced character is not simply conveying the surface details but the more in-depth complexity.

• Now do the same for your fictional character. Consider everything – absolutely *everything* – that impacts on who they are, why they behave the way they do, and why they interact with others and the world as they do. Keep this list close by as you write, as you think, as you magpie-steal from real-life people and add to it. Soon you will know your character as well as your closest friend or your partner. And then they are ready to guide the story and move through the world you are creating.

So what makes a 'good character' ('good' here meaning believable, compelling, evocative, alive and dynamic)? Here's a list of the elements I strive for when creating my characters:

• **Uniqueness** – I believe each of us are wondrously unique and therefore the characters we write should be too. When you're writing, the first thing you might think of is a 'type' – a curmudgeonly academic, a wild, free-spirited woman, a classic hard man. That's OK as a starting point, but then go deeper. Consider the aspects that make that person, that archetype, into a human with flaws – the individual grit and grains of reality.

• **Investment** – We need to actually care about our protagonist. This does not mean we have to like them. I am very over the idea that female protagonists in particular must be likeable but, even when their behaviours are questionable, we *must* root for them on some level – this is what keeps readers reading and the stakes and consequences of the action in your novel high. Perhaps it would be best to call this quality 'relatability': it doesn't mean the character is like you or like the reader, it means you can follow their actions and say, 'I can see how they might behave that way ...'.

• **Ambiguity** – No one person is all good or all bad, and characters are much more interesting with a good dose of light and dark and shades of grey. It is helpful, however, to decide who your character is 'at core' and then show the reader that they are also flawed and can make mistakes. After all, with mistakes comes conflict and that's where narrative tension is found.

• **Consistency** – It's important to maintain consistency of actions, reactions, thought and character traits, even though these may evolve and gradually change throughout the narrative. This can be difficult – because ultimately you are in control of your characters – but you must get to know them intimately, so that you know exactly how they would behave, why and when.

Exercise 2: How would your character react?

I use this exercise to see how well I understand the way my character thinks and acts (or not). Understanding their response to unusual situations helps me gauge the credibility of their actions, reactions and behaviours:

Bring to mind a character you've written about in the past. Your character is at a petrol station buying something. They come out and see a car driving away quickly and a near dying cat lying in the forecourt ...

How to they respond? What do they feel? What were they buying and why were they at that particular garage? How would their response change depending on when this scene occurred within the novel?

When you can send your characters to Tesco or Brazil, or to a figure-skating championship and know how they would behave, what they'd say and what might happen to them there, *then* you have a good sense of who your character is; from that comes the ease of guiding them through your setting and plot as if by second nature.

Revealing character through setting

The reader learns about the context of the story through the setting, and at the same time, through the setting, the author is able to show things about the character, as well as some character development.

When you're creating a setting, consider what the environment – and the objects it is filled with – says about your character, particularly if it is the character's own space. If it is a space that isn't the character's, or is one entirely alien to them, then consider how they would interact with it – what they (not you) would notice and how it would make them feel. There are two things to consider here:

• **Specificity** – It's not just a glass, a hairbrush, a chair, a sweater; are they drinking coffee from a Dunkin' Doughnuts mega-mug or a bone china teacup? Do they wear holey cashmere or a sequin-embellished slouch sweater? If they encounter a beanbag, do they view it with excitement or suspicion?

• **Precision** – Know why you're including the detail. Each little detail should have a purpose; why is it valuable to your intention for the narrative and the character? Use these details wisely and sparingly – and try to avoid falling in love with your detail 'darlings'. Less is usually more in this case.

The essential goal is to understand who your character is and what has made them as they are. Consider who they were before and who they will be long after you have written about a period of their life. Ask yourself if they feel like a person you could really meet one day, with all the chaos, creativity, strength, vulnerability and complexity that real people encompass. Consider where their barriers are and what they hope for; and understand *why* those things are that way.

Ultimately, if you listen to your character's wants and needs and deepest fears, they will take you by the hand and lead you through the writing of their story.

Kerry Hudson is a Scottish writer whose first novel, *Tony Hogan Bought Me An Ice-Cream Float Before He Stole My Ma* (Vintage 2012), won the Scottish First Book Award. Her second novel, *Thirst* (Vintage 2014), was translated into French and won Le prix Femina étranger 2015. Kerry's most recent book, *Lowborn* (Chatto & Windus 2019), is a work of non-fiction about poverty and homelessness. For more information visit https://kerryhudson.co.uk. Follow her on Twitter @ThatKerryHudson.

Writing romantic fiction

Raffaella Barker describes the lure of romantic fiction for reader and writer alike, the pleasure and challenge of creating characters real enough for the reader to fall in love with, and the importance of providing structure and the promise of a satisfying resolution as the story unfolds.

The first time I fell in love it was in a book. I was 11 and I fell in love with a boy called Dion in *Fire in the Punchbowl* (Collins 1969), a novel by Monica Edwards. I knew Dion quite well by the time I fell in love with him; he was one of the family in Edwards' series of novels set on Punchbowl Farm in Sussex, where the topography and detail of daily life, the weather, animals, journey to school, and the granular experience of their day-to-day existence made a believable world I wanted to be part of – indeed, one I really felt I *was* part of. By the time I read this penultimate novel in the series, the family I myself had grown up with was doing just that, and I, on the cusp of adolescence, stepped forward with these characters. As Dion grappled with a terrifying fire on the farm, taking a characteristically brave and tenacious part in putting out the flames, I fell for his unassuming strength, his gentle thoughtfulness and his noble motives. I could love him safely, within the confines of my imagination, rehearsing something I was not at all ready, or likely, to experience in real life at that point (11 years old, I attended a girls' school and spent the holidays riding my pony in the wild countryside of '70s rural North Norfolk, with no one my age for miles around).

From that moment, though, I never stopped falling in love in literature. After Dion came many more infatuations: older, less suitable, engaging, dashing, silent, injured, brooding, married, blind … the possibilities were endless. I read romantic fiction hungrily, always with an eye for humour and fallibility in the object of my affections. From novelists Georgette Heyer, Jilly Cooper, Elizabeth Jane Howard, Olivia Manning and Daphne du Maurier I learnt several things: writing a romance can be funny (as in Jilly Cooper's joyful early novels); it can be part of a much bigger picture (as in Olivia Manning's wonderful Balkan Trilogy); it can be epic (as in Elizabeth Jane Howard's series on the Cazelet family); and it can be an engine of fear and of what is left unsaid (as in Daphne du Maurier's *Rebecca*). Later Maggie O'Farrell and Audrey Niffenegger showed me that it can be tragic. My take on what defines romantic fiction remains broad; for me, there just needs to be someone I can fall in love with.

Romance, and the love affair in fiction, hit the spot like nothing else – unlike real-life romance which can be awkward, fleeting, and too frequently riddled with clichés and the uneasy awareness that things are not going to plan. Things may not always turn out right for the characters in romantic fiction, but the reader can take pleasure in the journey – packaged as it is within the trajectory of a novel, and with the promise of resolution.

In fiction, the reader gets to inhabit the world of the characters as an observer, no matter how close to the story. Even if the piece is written in the first person, the act of reading provides a flexible distance that keeps us outside the experience of the protagonists. Yet we have the intimacy of moving inside the characters' lives, which sometimes brings us closer to them than to anyone we live with or love. It is this, I think, that makes romantic fiction a most useful insight into human beings and the way we behave. In fiction, the reader is there with the characters, living in their altered temporal universe, as they misunderstand and make up, separate then come together, kiss, experience loss, joy, yearning and confusion – all on their way to the kingdom of happy-ever-after. Romance is wonderful to read, and it is also wonderful to write.

It can be a daunting challenge to create believable characters and set up a world in which it is impossible yet inevitable that two people (or maybe more) will fall in love. We tend to think that so many good writers have done this already, that too many instances depict the rules of love and attachment being broken just to be mended with an intoxicating embrace. The idea of romantic love as the core of a novel is wide open to the hazards of cliché and overfamiliarity. But there is nothing more interesting than the way human beings relate to one another, and romantic love manifests this in myriad forms. This is what is exciting for the writer embarking on the romantic novel. Who is it about, why is it about these people, and what will be revealed to bring something different to the genre?

In *Poppyland* (Headline 2008) I took up the challenge of how a novelist creates two people who could believably fall in love with one another, and how to make real the magnetic, hypnotic, unstoppable collision that occurs when they do. This was a volte-face from my previous novel, *A Perfect Life* (Headline 2006), which depicts a divorce. In another novel, *Hens Dancing* (Headline 1999), I had played with the romantic idea differently; my central character was unaware of the attraction and the 'rightness' of the love interest, even though the reader could see their chemistry in the scenes they appeared in together. Long before Venetia, the central character, knew she was in love with David, *we* knew it, and we were on the complex journey of discovery with our heroine, cheering her on to the finish line. Well, everyone loves a happy ending.

There are many ways of approaching the job of writing romantic fiction but, to me, it always makes sense to start with character. After all, there can be no hope of romance without two people between whom the chemistry will ignite. And here lies the first and most important decision for the author. For the purposes of satisfactory storytelling, the characters need to be very different from one another, to present apparently insurmountable clashes of temperament or timing, and to exist with a vivid and believable autonomy bringing veracity to the paradoxical notion that, while they are completely capable of having full and vivid lives without one another, they can only thrive and be the best version of themselves when they find their way together. The path of true love is never smooth, but it leads to an end at some point; the writer must lay this out clearly for the reader, if obscurely for the characters.

Given that the engine of the narrative is driven by these characters, now it's important to decide on perspective. Will the story be told from one character's perspective or both? Or will it be told by someone else observing them? Will we only ever see one of the two characters through the eyes of the other, or will we know both through an omniscient overarching voice from outside? These questions determine the structure of the novel. If they are both telling the story, for example, the urgency might be contained in two parallel narratives, one for each central character, with the energetic heart of the novel being exploited when they finally meet and spend time together. In this way the ending is lit with the possibility of a potential get-together, a state of 'happily ever after', and creates a trajectory with a pleasing arc. On the other hand, the author might opt for a third party telling the story, so that the lovers are seen from the outside, their motivation opaque, the journey of their romance filtered through the perspective of this third party, and our relationship to it similarly distanced.

Perspective is one issue; the unfolding of the action is another. Misunderstandings are a vital element of romance – plenty of them. Think of *Pride and Prejudice*. The title alone suggests a constant seesawing of confusion and wrong-footedness. The author is managing both the expectations of the characters and those of the readers, so the placing of these devices must be strategic. If the difficulties the characters face are too profound, the pulse that keeps the story moving forward will cease to beat, both on the page and off. Readers are sophisticated – their interest needs to be stoked, and the way love and romance is built is crucial. The writer is best to avoid recourse to stereotypes, as in fairy tales, instead applying focus and depth to the individual characteristics of the protagonists. The more human these characteristics are, the more relatable, the more satisfying the romance.

'Satisfying' is a word I use advisedly here. It describes the task that romantic fiction is meant to fulfil. By the end of the narrative, romantic fiction is meant to deliver a fully believable love story, one that suggests a beginning of something else for the characters – they deserve it, the reader deserves it. In romantic fiction, perhaps more than any other genre, the potential of the future needs to be lit, like a touch paper, by the bright joy of the ending. It is not that the characters' future needs to be implied or discussed, more that it is plausible; its foundations have been laid. In *Pride and Prejudice* we know, when Mr Darcy and Elizabeth walk down the aisle, that their marriage will be filled with discussion, energy, amusement, and deep respect for the intelligence each has finally seen in the other. In romantic fiction, the characters focus the beam of their attention on one another, not on their circumstances. This is the intensity the reader seeks.

The love affairs we create in our writing are like the music we hear in our dreams – they exist in a dimension beyond those in which we inhabit our lives. They are, by definition, unreal yet also hyper-real. Any writer who knows the pleasure of living alongside their characters as they develop will enjoy the experience of writing a love life for them – even one that will never work out. We agree with the Romantic poet Alfred Lord Tennyson that ''Tis better to have loved and lost than to have never loved at all.' To write about people finding love, and make it real enough for a reader to follow that experience with them, is a joy – worth any amount of hard work.

Raffaella Barker is an author and journalist who published her first novel *Come and Tell Me Some Lies* (Hamish Hamilton) in 1994. Her later books include *The Hook* (Bloomsbury 1996), *Hens Dancing* (1999), *Summertime* (2001), *Green Grass* (2002), *A Perfect Life* (2006) and *Poppyland* (2008), all first published by Headline Review, *From A Distance* (Bloomsbury 2014), and the children's book *Phosphorescence* (Macmillan Children's 2005). Raffaella has written short stories for radio, worked at *Harpers & Queen* magazine, as a columnist for *Country Life* and has been a regular contributor to the *Sunday Times*, the *Sunday Telegraph*, *Harper's Bazaar* and the *Spectator*. She teaches Creative Writing at the University of East Anglia and the *Guardian* Novel Writing Masterclass. Her website is www.raffaellabarker.co.uk.

Books

Ever wanted to write a saga?

Bestselling author Di Redmond (aka Daisy Styles) outlines the key elements required for a successful saga, and shares her insights into the market, character and demands of this popular genre.

Be prepared for the long haul!

A saga, by definition, is a genre of literature which chronicles the life of a family, interconnecting dramatic events over a long period of time – think *Game of Thrones*, *The Crown*, *The Archers* and *Coronation Street*. The saga as an art form is as old as the Norse myths, but more recently writers like Jeffrey Archer, Maeve Binchy, Danielle Steele, Anne Tyler and Catherine Cookson (to name but a few) have put them firmly at the top of the bestseller list. The key ingredients of any successful saga are: background content (e.g. the Napoleonic Wars, the Victorians, WW2); the pace of the writing; the accuracy to historical detail; and the strength of the core characters who hold the entire structure tightly together.

A series can run from two to six books, with each book usually having a word count of 100,000 words, roughly 40 chapters, and with a swift turnaround from the end of one book to the start of the next. The public appetite for sagas is surprisingly voracious … I know this for certain from my 'Daisy Styles' Facebook page (I had to take Daisy Styles as a nom de plume, since my real name – I'm proud to say – is often associated with writing *Bob the Builder*!). People who buy sagas (mostly women) regularly treat themselves to a new paperback whilst doing their weekly shop in any of the big supermarkets – Tesco, Asda, Sainsburys, Morrisons. They sell cheaply – usually on offer at two for £7 – thereby undercutting regular bookshop prices. With a short shelf life of about 12 weeks, the books have their popularity ratings flagged up beside the titles; these are based on the success of their sales figures and run from No. 1 Bestseller to No. 20. Believe me, these books virtually fly off the shelf! As they sell, their numbers are regularly topped up until a batch of newly published sagas arrive, immediately replacing the previous batch; it's a case of 'out with the old and in with the new' – a never-ending cycle.

Sagas follow a seasonal pattern; mine covered *Bomb Girl Brides* (Penguin 2018) and *Christmas with the Bomb Girls* (Penguin 2017), but for other seasons the sagas might have covered springtime and rationing, or summertime and evacuees. Saga readers are a dedicated fan base – hence the ever-hungry market – and their loyalty and dedication is such that they each build up their own personal library of favourite authors, and (touchingly) they're hot on ordering the next saga – the very one the author is in the process of writing – well in advance on Amazon. They also like to keep in touch with their saga author on Facebook, relishing details of work in progress, deadlines, edits, research and travel related to the forthcoming book. It's almost as if you were having a baby!

A fan base can also be very exacting; get a fact wrong, such as confusing Prime Minister Chamberlain's WW2 timeline with Prime Minister Churchill's, and you'll know about it. As they respect you, they in turn expect you to respect the territory – which is where research comes in …

The research

When I launched into my saga-writing career, I spent more time researching the period than I did writing the book. I had to back up almost every paragraph I wrote with hard facts and it nearly drove me crazy. Was I writing a history text or a novel? With the plotline rapidly unfolding in my head, and my fabulous characters champing at the bit, I was as eager to get cracking as they were, but I felt thwarted at every turn. I was constantly checking and re-checking references in my mounting pile of history books and endlessly on a search engine. When it came to googling 'how to build a bomb' for a spy plotline, a good friend advised me to always insert a date – 1941 or 1944 for example – otherwise I would have a Special Branch officer knocking on my front door!

After decorating my study walls with a printout of WW2's timeline, I decided I was going to go for it – otherwise I would never meet my deadline. Though I was nervous, I told myself that wherever I felt uncertain about a date I would leave a blank and address the problem at the end of the working day, rather than spend the entire working day thumbing through history books. I'm happy to say, it worked. As the story unrolled and my fabulous *Bomb Girls* stepped out of the woodwork, I became more and more familiar with the dreaded timeline. At the drop of a hat I could have told you when the Canadians joined the war ('God love 'em', as the nation chorused), when the Yanks bombed Pearl Harbor, how to slaughter a pig, build an air-raid shelter, read Morse code, and the price of nylons on the black market. The moral of the story is not to get bogged down by facts, which I know are very important and must be respected, but there has to come a point when you have to let the writing flow, secure in the knowledge that if you make a mistake you can go back and rectify it later.

The setting

Once you've got your timeframe, you have to establish exactly where your saga will be played out. When I was asked by my agent if I might be interested in writing a saga series, my mind immediately flew to Lancashire where I was brought up and where, as a child, I rambled for miles across the moors – sometimes coming across a crumbling ruin of a mill which locals told me had been a munitions factory. During wartime the locations of these sites were kept top secret, for fear of spies reporting their whereabouts to the Luftwaffe who would unquestionably bomb both the site and the workers to kingdom come. I'd considered writing about land girls, nurses on the front line, WRNS, Special Ops, Women's Auxiliary Air Force (WAAF) and the Auxiliary Territorial Services (ATS), but memories of that dark ruin defined my choice – I'd write about conscripted women building bombs in a former cotton mill on Pendle Moor.

The core characters

It's vital that your core group of characters can pack a punch! My *Bomb Girls* were all very different characters; the lead girl was savvy and a brilliant cook, the second shy and bookish, the third poor and bullied and the fourth sexy and a bit of a comedian, whilst the fifth girl was posh. Though vastly different in every respect, they complemented each other in rather surprising and unexpected ways, stirring up plots and complications because of their intrinsic differences. Conscription was a great leveller, bringing together the rich and the poor, forcing them to live under the same roof whether they liked it or not. Poor girls, used to an outside privy and an old water pump, couldn't believe the luxury of having hot and cold running water in their domestic lodgings and a flush toilet too, whilst the rich girls were appalled at the thought of sharing a bathroom and queuing for the toilet.

In my enthusiasm I went for five women and thereby created a problem for myself; not that the women were a problem – all of them were fantastic to write for – but five characters going off in different directions is just too many to juggle. My advice is to keep your core group down to three or four; it's a more manageable number, especially as the characters develop and become stronger than you originally anticipated (a little mouse of a girl can grow into a lion when she's building bombs to fight Hitler!). The environment in which these women worked round-the-clock shifts fed them propaganda that didn't just strengthen their muscles to do the gruelling hard work, but strengthened their mindset too. The women who entered the factory at the start of the war had changed into very different women by the time they left at the end.

Location, location ...

The setting for saga-based novels is important for both the reader and the writer. Big old industrial towns like Glasgow, Manchester, Liverpool, Leeds, Sheffield, Bristol and Birmingham bring their own history – cotton and woollen mills, docks, steelworks, shipyards and harbours. Added to which, there's a war raging, bombs are falling, men dying, telegrams arriving, sweethearts grieving, and innocent children being evacuated. It's drama upon drama; at the heart of any saga there are irrefutable facts. In every reader's family there will be someone who lived through the war and has a story to tell – a true and cherished story which they are proud to pass on to the next generation.

When it came to writing my latest book, *The Wartime Midwives* (Penguin 2019), my love of the Lake District lured me further north; on visiting Grange-over-Sands, Cartmel, Kendal and the whole breathtaking sweep of Morecambe Bay and the Irish Sea, I knew with a certainty that made my spine tingle that this was the perfect setting for the secluded mother-and-baby home where my story would unfold. On top of that, the location was within walking distance of the Southern Fells, which were essential to the denouement of my story (which I knew before even starting the first chapter).

A word of warning

Although Catherine Cookson – queen of the saga – made a fortune from her books, it would be insincere of me to suggest you're going to get rich from this genre. You will get royalties when you've paid off your publisher's advance, but the royalty payment depends on how big your sales are and if the book goes to a reprint. The plus side is that sagas don't stop with one publication; the demand will grow, and so will your fan base, as your books become a regular feature on the supermarket shelves.

If you have an agent, approach them with an outline of your characters, location and an exact timeframe (be warned – taking on the entire six years of the war is huge, so focus on a section of the WW2 you want to work around, such as after Dunkirk, before Pearl Harbor, or during the Blitz). Your agent may ask you to write three sample chapters and then present to a number of publishers known to be on the lookout for a new saga series. If you haven't got an agent, you should do extensive research on the publishers that have a particular interest in the genre (there are a lot), then submit your outline and three sample chapters to the editor of that department.

If you love writing on a broad canvas, about a pivotal point in history with a possible cast of thousands, and you can keep a convoluted plot line running over 100,000 words, this is the one for you!

Di Redmond, under the pen name Daisy Styles, is the author of the bestselling *Bomb Girls* and *Wartime Midwives* series published by Penguin. Di is also a prolific writer for children's television, writes for stage and radio and is an established celebrity ghostwriter. She has published over 120 books and is the Audio-Visual Director on ALCS's Board of Directors.

Writing speculative fiction

Author Claire North considers the nature of 'speculative fiction', and the blurry nature of genres more broadly, and provides advice for writers on the boundless world-building possibilities that writers of fantastical fiction can develop to grab a reader's imagination.

You could spend as much time arguing about what 'speculative fiction' is as writing it. Magic realism? Literature with a twist? Science fiction? Hi-tech social commentary? It's worth asking this question as – although hopefully you are writing out of love for words on the page – your experience of being a published author will vary hugely, depending on where (rather arbitrarily) the world decides your speculative fiction falls.

The question of genre

Revolutions in film, TV and games now mean that science fiction and fantasy have never been more popular and accepted in the mainstream. Yet the world of literary criticism and review frequently still treats genre as if it were less worthy of note than literature, despite its potent selling power. Without making 'literature' a term of exclusions (NOT crime, NOT thriller, NOT romance) it can be hard to say what 'literary' actually means, and the inclusion of writers such as Margaret Atwood, David Mitchell, Kazuo Ishiguro and George Orwell on mainstream shelves only adds to the justified arch of your raised eyebrow.

Partly in response to this, 'speculative fiction' has grown in recent years as a term that tweaks the definition of genre into something mainstream – and therefore perhaps more acceptable. Not quite 'hard' science fiction or pure fantasy, but laced through with an element of something strange, fantastical or other, it is the land of Emily St. John Mandel, Nick Harkaway, Naomi Alderman, and – in film/TV terms – of *Black Mirror* or *Stranger Things*. Speculative fiction is, in short, an excellent corner to claim for marketing purposes, encompassing the best of so many worlds: if only you can work out what it means.

The simplest truth may be the truth of all genres, namely that the key difference between, say, hard science fiction and speculative fiction is a publisher's marketing choice. In the case of M.R. Carey's *Girl with all the Gifts* (Orbit 2014) this meant removing any reference to 'zombies' from both book and blurb, transforming an excellent apocalypse story into something sold as nuanced character-study in a difficult world. Both aspects are of course true – it is both a character study and a straight-up zombie book – but most books are more than one thing, and it could have been positioned a dozen other ways. Genre is an increasingly blurry line – a comforting tool for helping us find books that we love, as well as an imprisoning categorisation used to define what we don't read as much as what we do. What we read defines us; there is still a social pressure to be seen to read the 'right' thing. Men do not read books about shopping with Comic Sans lettering on pink covers; adults do not read Harry Potter unless they have silver embossed jackets – and so on. The world is changing, perhaps, but social pressures remain.

Does genre even matter?

Of course, appreciating the nuances of how genre is positioned in the changing world of bookshop categories and predictive algorithms may not affect what you write. Indeed, I would argue that at the early stages of writing, it shouldn't. Writing is a business, but it is also a joy, a gift. Forget market positioning, forget reviewer bias; the best book you can possibly write is the one you loved writing the most. And if you have chosen to write speculative fiction – embrace it, enjoy it! In the future you might find yourself making artistic choices based on where a publisher seeks to sell you, but this makes *now* the moment to choose a path that you'll always love walking. That said, there are a few things to bear in mind in those earliest stages, that may help you on your quest:

1. Have confidence

Easier said than done, but this is key, especially in speculative fiction, to bringing a reader into a place where their imagination has never been before. You do not need to explain your choices; you do not need to info-dump your world. If you know every detail of it already, it will manifest in the actions of your text, in the story that you *show* rather than the information that you tell. In doing so, you have already won half the battle.

'Show, don't tell' is one of the classic rules. It is the art of revealing information through story, rather than through exposition.

- 'The witches are coming!'
- *'No – not the witches of the west!'*
- 'Yes, the very ones, who drink the blood of infants!'
- *'Oh my God – and who wear blue robes while chanting to their pagan gods?'*
- 'That's them!'

Nah, mate. Think of the tools you have available to you as a writer to help us **live** a story – third person, first person, extracted texts, second person, biased narrator, past tense, present tense, future tense, flashback. There is a tool out there that is waiting for you to **show** us your world, and to transform information into experience. It is the secret of every great medical drama. Very few people know why the CT scan matters or what the spleen does, but we all hear the truth of **feeling** beneath this language and are caught up by the emotional urgency beneath the technobabble.

Where information must be given, be succinct:

- 'The western witches in robes of blue, who drank the blood of babies and worshipped their pagan gods, came upon the town as it was sleeping.'

Job done. You have imparted data. Now move on; there's a story to tell.

2. Use story for world-building

The same 'show, don't tell' applies to speculative fiction world-building. Show us what we need to know. It is the difference between:

- 'She was one of the sisters, an ancient order of healers, who look after dying men on the battlefield.'

and

- 'The sister's robe was still caked in the blood of the men she had tended on the battlefield ...'

The immediacy of one brings us into the moment; the other is just information. Resist putting every detail of your world on the page; the story must come first, and the world will unfold as it does. A focus on story allows you to start harder, faster, and let the reader invest more in building the world for themselves.

3. Obey your own rules

It is the classic *Dr Who/Buffy the Vampire Slayer* trope: around 40 minutes into a 45-minute episode (or 250 pages into an average book), when things have got just about as bad as they can possibly get, someone finds a giant button/a mystic spell that fixes everything. In crime, this is the unexpected witness who busts the case wide open; thrillers have the dramatic helicopter rescue. But in speculative fiction, if you try to write yourself out of that plot-hole with an unexpected *deus ex machina*, there is a danger that you will undermine a reader's immersion in what that world is. Don't be afraid of deleting your way to freedom and take time to structure your story. Especially in speculative fiction, death need not be the thing that *matters*. In thrillers in the Chris Ryan vein, soldiers live and soldiers die, but *betrayal* hurts more than actual bullets. Gout doesn't kill Falstaff; the betrayal of Prince Hal does. What matters to the story is not life or death, but what these things mean to our characters. Mount Doom erupting in Middle-Earth has nothing on Frodo succumbing to the dark side. Find what matters to your world and characters; obey your own rules.

4. Humanity is your gift

Speculative fiction is a genre that offers you so many possibilities, from the pure joy of space cowboy adventure through to tales of horror and deceit. But, more than anything, it lets you ask what humanity *is*. What is it to be human, in a world where apps and algorithms run our lives? Are we still ourselves with 30% of our brain grown from something else? 40%? 50%? Are we still ourselves, unique and true, when our clone sits opposite us? Is it human nature to build or to destroy? If we know the thoughts of others, does that elevate us or destroy the very essence of humanity? Is Kafka's twisted human cockroach still a man? Does humankind need gender? Can humans be grown in a lab?

We ask these questions, and in doing so we can tear down the barriers that are used to stratify humanity into exclusionary ideas of 'not I', such as class, race, ethnicity and sex. Fiction tells stories that catch the heart and then bring the head along after. We can do all of this, and we can have fun doing it, poking at the world while having badass, awesome adventures.

This being so, embrace the scope of humanity that is offered to you. Forget normative, oppressive ideas of women, men or culture. Speculative fiction opens up realms of boundless imagination to you; be awesome, and imagine humanity – lots and lots of it.

Claire North is the pen name of Catherine Webb, who also writes under the name Kate Griffin. Her novel, *The First Fifteen Lives of Harry August* (Orbit 2014) was shortlisted for the Arthur C. Clarke Award and was selected for the Richard and Judy Book Club, the Waterstones Book Club and the Radio 2 Book Club. Also published by Orbit, her novel *The Sudden Appearance of Hope* (2017) won the 2017 World Fantasy Award for Best Novel and *The End of the Day* (2017) was shortlisted for the *Sunday Times*/PFD Young Writer of the Year Award. Recent books under the Claire North pseudonym are: *84K* (2018), which won a special citation at the 2019 Philip K. Dick Award, *The Pursuit of William Abbey* (2019) and the novella *Sweet Harmony* (2020), all published by Orbit. Follow her on Twitter @ClaireNorth42.

Breaking into comics

Antony Johnston has advice for any writer keen to build a career in comics and graphic novels on how to showcase and pitch their work in a challenging field where networking, quality and enthusiasm are essential.

Writing comics and graphic novels is challenging and fun. The medium of sequential narrative art is unique in its applications and possibilities, one that can produce a similar level of immersion and engagement to books yet is as visually striking as movies or TV. It's also littered with the bodies of writers who've taken on the form without truly understanding it.

I won't belabour the point but, suffice it to say, if you have little experience of comics, I strongly urge you to immerse yourself in them before you try to write one. Must you have been reading comics since you were a child? Not at all. There are some great writers who came to comics later in life, but those people did their homework: they fell in love with the medium and set about analysing how it works, how to achieve wondrous immersion through the combination of words and still images. If you're new to comics, you must do the same.

It also won't hurt to read up on the industry itself. Monthly comics is a strange business, punching far above its weight in cultural influence, yet conducted with almost shocking informality. Seminal works are lionised and commemorated for decades; yet, to make a living, writers must constantly generate new work, new ideas, and (with only very rare exceptions) write several different titles per month. In some ways the job is closer to being a magazine writer than a novelist. Instead of submitting a single manuscript to many publishers, you will submit many pitches to a few publishers. And 99% of the time you will be pitching, rather than submitting a finished manuscript.

'But wait!', you say, 'I don't want to write monthly comics. I want to write graphic novels.' To which I say, 'Godspeed, and don't give up the day job.' I am (to the best of my knowledge) the most prolific Anglophone graphic novelist, with 20 published 'Original Graphic Novels', aka OGNs[1]. I believe graphic novels are the future of the comics medium, and for two decades I've backed up that belief with my output. But I've also supplemented my income by writing monthly comics, videogames, film, books and more, because English-language graphic novels do not yet pay a living wage for 99% of their practitioners.

To break into monthly comics is to join a small club that, to the novice, can feel impenetrable. The old joke goes that it's like breaking out of prison; whenever someone discovers a new route, it's sealed up behind them to prevent others using it. This is partly because there's no formal path to becoming a professional comics writer – no union, no industry programs, no official mentors. Some further education institutions now teach graphic novel writing modules (see box on page 281), but there is no route from there to getting hired that doesn't require the same shoe leather as it does for everyone else. Comics only cares about the quality of your work.

---

1. The majority of books in a store's Graphic Novel section are actually collections of previously-published monthly comics. A 'true' graphic novel is one that has never been serialised and is published as a single volume, like a prose novel. OGNs are increasingly common, but still in the minority.

Despite changing technology, then, the problem for aspiring writers will always be the same: how do you showcase that work to the people who can buy it from you or commission you to write other work? The good news is that the answer is also unchanged: write comics in your own time, find aspiring artists to draw them, and show them to editors. By necessity, such scripts should be short. Nobody will draw your 800-page epic for free. Frankly, it's unfair to expect any artist to draw more than half a dozen pages gratis, no matter how good you think it may look in their portfolio. And from your perspective, there's no need; an experienced editor can judge your work within five or six pages.

Graphic novel writing courses

University of Dundee
MLitt/MDes Comics & Graphic Novels
www.dundee.ac.uk/postgraduate/comics-graphic-novels-mdes

Edinburgh Napier University
MA Creative Writing

University Centre Grimsby
BA (Hons) Professional and Creative Writing
https://grimsby.ac.uk/higher-education-course/ba-hons-professional-creative-writing

University of Worcester
Creative Writing and Illustration BA (Hons)
www.worcester.ac.uk/courses/creative-writing-and-illustration-ba-hons

So get used to writing short comic stories and finding artistic collaborators to draw them (unless you can also draw your own stories, but even in that case much of what follows will still apply).

How you show this work to editors depends on many factors, including your comfort with technology, your geographical location, your financial means, and your ease in social interactions. There's no 'One True Way' and comics is not an agent-driven industry[2], so it really is up to you to determine the best path. The simplest method nowadays is to put your work online. Facebook, Tumblr, even Twitter and Instagram – along with gallery sites such as DeviantArt – have made it essentially free to post your comic samples where anyone with a link can see them. The real hurdle is getting editors to click that link in the first place, and this is where the importance of *networking* rears its head.

Let's clear something up: despite its bad reputation, networking does not mean getting work by charm alone. It's about building a relationship with people – editors, yes, but also other writers, artists, and publishers – so that when they see your name on a piece of work, they'll be inclined to look at it. An inclination is all it will get you; there are no guarantees. But the alternative is to build online buzz about your talent and wait for editors to come knocking on your door. That's not impossible, but it takes a rare talent, and it subjects your destiny to the whims of others. The best way to build those relationships, meanwhile, is at the whim of changing times. Some editors still prefer to meet new creators, especially writers, at conventions. The time and effort it takes to attend a comic-con shows them you're serious; this is especially true for UK creators travelling to the US, still where the biggest are held (it's a truism that some of us fly 6,000 miles every year to spend time with people who live in the next town over). But, increasingly, relationships with editors and other creators are reinforced, and sometimes entirely built, online – which is good news for anyone unable to make it to a convention.

2. Very few comic creators have agents. There's rarely enough money in it, and in any case not many agents are familiar with the industry's idiosyncrasies. Comics publishers know this, however; they won't object if you have an agent, but not having one is entirely normal and won't count against you.

Conventions themselves are the second way to get your work in front of editors, by giving them photocopied samples. Make sure you have many copies, and that you can afford to give them all away; editors will expect to keep them for reference. What hasn't changed, whether online or in person, are the ground rules about behaviour: be polite, be professional, and take criticism or feedback on board with decorum. Under no circumstances argue with an editor who criticises your portfolio – you may think that warning unnecessary, but I've seen it happen, and such people do not get hired.

Let's progress to pitching. You've cultivated a relationship, made some impressive sample comics, and an editor wants to read/hear your new pitch. This is a true achievement, and merely reaching this stage puts you well ahead of the pack. But now you're competing for a publisher's budget against other creators, many of whom will be seasoned pros. So focus on quality and on a compelling tale, well-told.

There are scant resources on writing pitches, because everyone approaches them differently. If possible, ask the editor what they prefer to see, or if they can give you a sample to use as a template; but equally, remember that they don't know exactly what you're pitching. Ultimately, it's your decision what's relevant to the pitch in question. (The Marvel/DC superhero market is an exception; new writers are expected to pitch very short takes on existing characters in just a few sentences.)

The golden rule of pitches is, paraphrasing Einstein, to make them 'as short as possible, but no shorter'. Plot and main characters, yes, of course. Tone and format, if they're important. And finally, if the editor doesn't know you, any *relevant* credentials. But no more. The only other thing required is your name and email address on the title page.

If you're pitching at a convention, you'll be expected to do so verbally. Don't panic! Nobody expects you to be a slick salesman, and the same principle applies to pitching by email. Editors understand that writers are not always the best advocates of our own work. But whether in person or in writing, they will expect to see enthusiasm. So stick to the story, to your idea, and don't be afraid of getting excited – I might even say *get over yourself*, because writers are often humble, self-effacing and modest to a literal fault. Remember, when an editor asks you to pitch, they've already decided they might want to work with you. It's up to you to convince them they're right. I'm not suggesting you become an egotist, but if your pitch is filled with hedging caveats (… 'I'm not sure about that', 'I haven't figured this part out yet', 'I don't know how many people will be interested' …) who could blame an editor for passing on it? Believe in your ideas without apology. Nobody else will do it for you.

So, finally, your pitch has been accepted. You've negotiated a contract and been commissioned to write something. What happens now? What should you expect, when you reach the promised land of being paid to write comics? Well, that's when the real work starts. From this point on your destiny is firmly in your own hands, and to give specific advice about comics scriptwriting would require a whole book. The most important things to remember are not about your script, but about your conduct. Be professional; be clear upfront about what your editor expects from you; maintain good communication with your collaborators; and always, *always* hit your deadlines, because an artist, colourist, letterer, and even printer, are all waiting on you.

Follow those principles, create good work, and one day you'll look up from your keyboard to remind yourself you're being paid to write comics. Have fun.

Antony Johnston is a *New York Times* bestselling graphic novelist, author and screenwriter, and the creator of *Atomic Blonde*, which was adapted from his graphic novel *The Coldest City* (Oni Press 2012). His other comics work includes its sequel *The Coldest Winter* (Oni 2016), the epic series *Wasteland* (Oni 2006-14), adaptations of Antony Horowitz's *Alex Rider* novels (Walker Books 2006-), Marvel's *Daredevil* series (2010-12), *The Fuse* (Image Comics 2014-17) and many more. Antony also writes the Brigitte Sharp spy novels *The Exphoria Code* (2017) and *The Tempus Project* (2020), both published by Lightning Books. His work for writers includes the productivity guide *The Organised Writer* (Bloomsbury 2020) and his podcast *Writing and Breathing*. Find him online at www.antonyjohnston.com and @antonyjohnston.

Books

Writing a romcom

Rachel Winters defines the essential constituents of a successful romcom, offering her experience as both editor and writer.

The first short story I ever wrote was when I was eight, and it was about a serial killer. So when I say my journey to being a romcom writer hasn't exactly been straightforward, I don't exaggerate. In my defence, I was reading a lot of Point Horror at the time.

In time I moved on to writing more wholesome fantasy. My undergrad degree was in creative writing, as I'd harboured dreams of becoming the next Robin Hobb (creator of the *Assassin's Apprentice* series). Sadly, though I loved being a student (classes were four hours a week and the campus was so small most people turned up in their slippers), at the end of the course I was told I wasn't very good. I'd never had much confidence and this was the deal-breaker for me – I pretty much stopped writing altogether.

I still loved books and decided to go into publishing – which, it turned out, was fiercely competitive. Cue several years of being a personal assistant (a very bad one), a part-time Publishing MA student, an academic editor, and then, finally, landing my dream job – working at HarperVoyager. During this time, while I barely typed a sentence of fiction, I was writing. I had my own column for a cat newspaper (though I didn't own a cat) and spent five years writing entertainment reviews for an online magazine. By the time I became a commissioning editor at Gollancz, the UK's oldest and biggest science fiction and fantasy imprint, I thought that my writing days were well and truly behind me. Thankfully, I was wrong.

My job is a creative one – we get to work with incredible writers; some are debut authors, some are well established, all of them have spent years honing their craft. As editors we learn to pick apart the building blocks of narrative and examine how it all works. A key aspect of my job is to develop ideas. This involves building a book from the ground up – coming up with a concept, thinking about the readership, creating an overarching plot, characters, a grand finale. Doing this for my day job gave me the confidence I needed to start writing fiction again. I've always loved the romantic comedy genre, and I had an idea that would utilise my healthy appreciation of 90s Hugh Grant. My idea was that of a self-referential romcom, because readers are savvy and well aware of the tropes, while still being a love letter to the genre. Maybe, this time, I could silence the person's voice who'd told me I wasn't good enough – and write.

So I did (assisted by my good friends: chocolate and coffee). With the help of brilliant editors, it became *Would Like to Meet* (Trapeze 2020), which to date has sold in 15 territories and has been optioned for a major film deal. There's no set formula to writing a book, but as a debut author I found it useful to consider the following elements. It's no coincidence that these are also what I focus on as an editor:

1. Concept

The concept helps you find your audience by hooking them in and revealing the genre. It is, to use a familiar term, the 'elevator pitch' – your book's USP. It is what makes it stand out from the market, while at the same time appealing to a certain readership. Simple, eh? (Laughs forever …)

The concept of *Would Like to Meet* is this: Assistant Evie Summers has to prove romcoms are realistic, in order to convince an arrogant screenwriter to write one and save the film agency she works for. It's tricky trying to narrow a whole book down to its core idea, but it's worth it. It will help you establish your book's goal. I raised a question at the beginning of *WLTM* – one that interested me: can real love ever be like the movies? And by the end of the book I had to answer it. The concept is what you can keep coming back to when you wander from the story path that leads to your conclusion. Ask yourself: am I still honouring that initial premise? Is it working? If not, why not?

2. Plot development

Next, you can unpack the plot. I'd established the goal in *WLTM* – to save the agency, and how my main character would achieve this goal – by proving it was possible to fall in love via a romcom 'meet-cute' (the moment the two love interests meet for the first time). And, of course, she had to unexpectedly, for her at least, find love along the way. Now, every step of the plot – from the settings to the best friend characters – had to serve that story.

I'd advise outlining the plot first to give your book its best possible start. You have to lay out the playing field before you can begin the game (which is the only sports analogy I'll ever use). You might prefer to write a particular type of romcom: love-to-hate, friends-to-lovers, enemies-to-lovers, etc. There are tropes associated with these categories, which can help when plotting (whether you follow or subvert them).

Know your ending – not just who the main character ends up with, but how. With a romantic comedy, the end is likely to be at least partially predictable, and yet it must still be satisfying. It's often not so much about the ending but the journey. What are all your key plot points to get you there? What obstacles will the love interests face? Will you weave in some red herrings? What are the emotional conflicts? When planning, I used the meet-cute re-enactments as focal points which served as my plot skeleton. In practice, I had to revise most of these scenes for myriad reasons – characters will often surprise you; you'll come up with multiple new ideas as you write; you accidentally overwrite the first draft by 40,000 words, etc. It's totally ok for your book to veer from your initial outline – it was just your playing field, after all. Having laid the groundwork, now you can start moving your pieces around.

3. Characters

You might choose to have two main characters who share the narrative, as in Beth O'Leary's *The Flatshare* (Quercus 2019). *Would Like to Meet* was a first-person narrative with one main character, Evie. I have a confession: in the first draft she was (whisper it) sort of based on me. She had my sense of humour and a good dose of my social anxiety. The more I wrote, however, I realised that how I would act within the story wasn't how Evie could act (big surprise). Yes, she had to have flaws, and I wanted her to go on a journey of self-discovery as much as finding love, but she also had to be far bolder than I would be. I wouldn't spill a drink on a stranger – she would.

Ask yourself, who does your main character have to be in order to achieve what they need to within the story? Evie needed to be incredibly passionate about her job, if she was to go to such extremes for it. And she had to start out with a lack of self-belief in order to grow, eventually, to a place of self-confidence. As you plot out your story, also consider how each step along the way will grow and shape your character on their own journey.

They can be likeable, but their flaws and emotional conflicts still need to get in their way occasionally, to create tension.

As for the rest – every character should fulfil a function that the other characters don't. Parents. Friends. Bosses. Enemies. What role are they playing that's crucial to the story? How do their personalities and goals affect your main characters?

4. Love interest

As in Helen Fielding's *Bridget Jones's Diary* (Picador 1996), with Mark Darcy and Daniel Cleaver, you might choose to have more than one prospective partner for your character. What makes yours swoon-worthy? Looks help of course, but in that story it's Mark Darcy's uptight stoicism and Daniel Cleaver's rakish arrogance and wit that readers thirst for – two opposing personalities, each bringing their own emotional conflict for Bridget.

Does your love interest enter the stage fully formed, or do they have some growing to do? What is their own journey through the plot, and how does that intersect with your main character's? Do their characters complement or oppose each other? If there are two love interests, does one fit with your main character at the start, and the other the person they become by the end? Ben, the widower dad in *WLTM*, is a closed book at the start, whereas the arrogant screenwriter, Ezra, is seemingly an open one. As I progressed the plot, and Ben's and Ezra's characters, I wanted to convince readers to change their allegiances as to who they wanted Evie to choose, right up until the end.

Conflict can create sparks or drama; so can competition. What creates those essential sparks between your characters?

5. Conflict

Ah, sweet, sexy conflict. It's what drives romcoms and keeps them so ridiculously compelling. In the plot itself there will be setbacks for your character, as when other characters have goals that conflict with theirs, and conflict between the love interests.

In romcoms people expect obstacles; they want to see emotional (i.e. 'internal') conflict – something that creates enough tension that makes it all the more satisfying when the two love interests eventually do get together. External conflict – a missed plane, a dead phone battery – doesn't really have the zing romcom readers crave. Internal conflict, however, that's the good stuff – loyalty to family, or ambition to succeed in your career, whatever it takes (here's looking at you, Tom Hanks in *You've Got Mail*).

Of course, external conflict can (and should) lead to internal conflict: what if your character missed that plane when they were trying to prove they could be reliable? Or the battery dies on their phone midway through an important sentence ('I absolutely hate you[niversity]')? By the end, your love interests have to survive the conflict. It can't be insurmountable, but it does have to be satisfying, effective and believable. A classic example is Nora Ephron's script for the film *When Harry Met Sally*. The initial conflict is that Harry believes men and women can't be friends. Sally believes they can. Eventually, that conflict manifests in their friendship, until it finally resolves itself through emotional growth.

6. Pace

Romcoms tend to be fairly short, pacey books (75,000-95,000 words), with attention-keeping chapters. Write what you need to get the story out, then trim. Be brutal with yourself. Do you need that scene? Does that indulgently lengthy Christmas chapter move the story along, or can it (as in *WLTM*) be reduced to a single email? Can you halve that dialogue? Is every single sentence serving your story?

7. Comedy

Ah, the essential 'com' part of the romcom. There are all kinds of comedy you can include: slapstick, situational, observational, wordplay. Whatever works for you. Trimming will help keep it snappy. What makes other people laugh is often indefinable. My rule is, it's a romance first. After that, if it makes me laugh, it goes in (though always listen to your editors, no matter how funny you might find toilet humour).

Finally, write because you love it – it always shows – and don't let someone else's thoughtless words prevent you doing so.

Rachel Winters is the author of *Would Like to Meet* (Trapeze 2020). She has a degree in Creative Writing and an MA in Publishing. After writing freelance for local papers and online magazines, she later worked as an editor for Orion and is currently a commissioning editor with Gollancz. Follow her on Twitter @Frostycheeks.

See also...
• *Writing romantic fiction*, page 271

Books

Writing historical fiction: lessons learned

Award-winning novelist Tim Pears shares the seven valuable lessons he learned as – prompted by snippets of family memoir and narrative – his writing shifted from contemporary into historical fiction.

A kindly poet once advised me: 'Never give advice; someone might take it'. But what I can perhaps do is to share the lessons I've learned while writing historical fiction ... a genre which, incidentally, I never planned to write.

I was a chronicler of contemporary life, having written seven novels describing the times we'd lived through; but I'd been given a sign and should have taken note. My second novel, *In a Land of Plenty* (Doubleday 1997), was made into a ten-part BBC TV series, broadcast in 2001. I visited the set when they were filming the reconstruction of a concert featuring The Clash, attended by the main characters. For me it seemed as though the concert, from 1978, had happened yesterday. I was chatting to a makeup girl, and asked if she was enjoying the job. 'Oh yes,' she said, 'I do like working on period drama.'

It was my father's fault, really. As a young man he'd had short stories published in *The Strand* and other magazines. But he became a Church of England priest and, with the demands of his ministry and then a growing family, he found no time to continue writing. Upon retirement he looked forward to resuming, only to be afflicted by cancer. Before he died, in 1986, he managed to scribble a rough draft of memoir, the most interesting part of which covered his experiences in Yugoslavia during the Second World War. He was a young intelligence officer sent in 1943 to encourage resistance to the German occupiers; he found a fully organised Communist partisan army and liaised with them.

I'd been interested in Yugoslavia from childhood, through the stories Dad told my sisters and me, and I became captivated by it during the autumn of 1991 when a film-maker friend and I travelled through a country on the chaotic brink of civil war.

My friend later returned to Yugoslavia to make a brilliant documentary, *Serbian Epics*. I wrote a film script that didn't get anywhere, then watched in fascination and horror as events unfolded in the Balkans. The poison of the 20th century funnelled towards the century's end, gathering in the sump of Srebrenica.

The seeds of the Balkan Wars of the 1990s had been planted in WW2. I found myself re-reading my father's memoir and then some books retained from his library: Deakin, Maclean, Djilas. And that was it. I was hooked, mind whirring, researching material for a novel about a young British officer in Yugoslavia from 1943 to 1945.

I soon learned **Writing Historical Fiction lesson 1**: serious background research. My father witnessed extraordinary events, but he was sent here and there almost at random. His actions were haphazard, they did not cohere into a satisfying narrative. I had to ditch his actual experiences and began to write a novel not about my father, but about a different young Englishman and his physical and spiritual journey through the furnace of war. I've always been a realist writer, seeking the authentic detail that convinces and illuminates, but doing research for a historical novel is of a quite different order to covering the events of one's own lifetime.

I travelled to Slovenia, met elderly men and women who'd been teenage peasant partisans, visited museums, and hiked in the forests and mountains my hero and his comrades would have walked in. Back home, I took up residence in the Bodleian Library; I found the research enthralling and buried myself in it. Was there anyone who knew more about British involvement in Yugoslavia in WW2 than I did? About events in a particular valley in northern, occupied Slovenia? I gained an insight into the crepuscular joy of academics, tunnelling deep down into a limited subject.

Then I woke up. What was I thinking? I was not an academic, but a novelist. I had to wrench my miserable body out of the library and back to the study, having learned **Writing Historical Fiction lesson 2**: you need to do the research, but you also need to know when to stop. You can't amass ingredients forever – you have to start cooking.

In all my novels there has been an engine – a deep theme – that drives the story. Perhaps all authors need this. It's usually implicit, and sometimes there are more than one of these themes. I wrote *In the Light of Morning* (Heinemann 2014), set in Yugoslavia in the Second World War, while British troops were in Helmand Province, Afghanistan, and the engine was the nature of occupation. Natives respond to occupiers with resentment, however benign those occupiers may wish to be. I was struck by the assertion that a small number of people resist, a small number collaborate, while most keep their heads down, try to get on with daily life, survive. But if the tide turns – through successful resistance or through outside forces – then the quiescent masses will rise up against an occupier.

Writing Historical Fiction lesson 3 was the discovery that an engine linking the past to the present adds an entire extra gear to one's writing process. After I finished *In the Light of Morning*, I realised there was another family myth to explore: our paternal grandfather's experience as a young gunnery officer aboard a light cruiser at the heart of the maelstrom that was – and remains – the greatest naval battle in history, the Battle of Jutland, in 1916.

Like his son, Pop also wrote a memoir, when he was young, in a series of exercise books. I tracked these down, to a cousin in Northumberland. He assured me that Pop's handwriting was both archaic and atrocious; there was no chance of me deciphering it, but he knew an expert who would type it up for him, and he'd send me a copy.

While waiting for this precious document, I started musing – walking the dog more often than she wanted, probably. I neglected my housework duties to read, take notes. Gradually a story took shape ... a boy, Leo, born in 1899, a horseman in the making, his father works as a ploughman on an estate on the Devon-Somerset border; a girl, Lottie, born the same year, only child of the aristocrat widower who owns the estate; their friendship, forged in a shared love of horses. *The Horseman* (Bloomsbury 2017), about their childhood, became the first book in a trilogy. Periodically I asked my cousin how the deciphering was coming along: 'Fine', he said, 'Be with you shortly.'

The Horseman was set in 1911/12, during the long Edwardian summer before the war, and threw into stark relief one of the common problems of writing anything set in the past. Cue **Writing Historical Fiction lesson 4**: the reader knows what is coming; the characters do not. Certainly, the inhabitants of a remote valley in the West Country had no idea of the conflagration ahead of them and I had to stop myself putting anything into their speech that was suggestive of foreknowledge.

I did not establish an actual location for *The Horseman*, nor even visit the general area. The estate was a kind of Garden of Eden, a dream place somehow (... so much for the details of realism). I'd learned **Writing Historical Fiction lesson 5**: be prepared to change your customary writing habits.

The second book in the trilogy, *The Wanderers* (Bloomsbury 2018), depicts my heroes' youth up to the eve of war, 1914. It follows Leo's odyssey from the estate across the south-west peninsular to Penzance, and I walked his route, gleaning those authenticating details I've always considered necessary. Leo reaches Penzance and walks along the seafront. Research showed that this was called the Esplanade, but when I visited Penzance every local I met referred to the seafront as the Prom. What had happened? Had 'the Esplanade' gradually mutated into 'the Promenade'? Or, although the Victorian architects and town worthies named and recorded it as the Esplanade, had locals always called it the Prom?

India Vaughan-Wilson at the Morrab Library and Katie Herbert at Penlee House in Penzance kindly attempted to clarify what the seafront was known as in 1914. Katie wrote to me: 'I have looked at several postcards and reference books in our collections/archive and have come to the conclusion that there is no definitive answer! I think you would be safe to call it either Promenade or Esplanade ....' It was inevitable, however, that if I called it the Promenade then a historically knowledgeable reader would decide 'He's got his facts wrong', while if I called it the Esplanade a local reader would think 'He doesn't know what he's talking about'! **Writing Historical Fiction lesson 6**: don't expect written records to authenticate every detail.

Just as I began writing the third book, *The Redeemed* (Bloomsbury 2019), our grand-father's memoir arrived, deciphered and typed. To my stupefaction, the family myth turned out to be erroneous. In those exercise books, Pop recorded his time as a midshipman before the First World War. So I had to plunge into the kind of research I love, and write the relevant chapter with no trace of my grandfather. Between them, four historical novels inspired by my father's and grandfather's experiences in war only feature one single tiny incident from those two men's lives.

The greatest and most enjoyable challenge of writing a novel set in an earlier epoch brings with it **Writing Historical Fiction lesson 7**: people were different from us; and people were the same as us. For example, a hundred years ago most people in a Somerset village went to church; today few do, though I don't believe people have any less appetite for the transcendent, the numinous, a meaning beyond evolution's random beauty.

John Tyndale, translator of the Bible, famously told a fellow priest who had denounced him, 'If God spare my life, 'ere many years, I will cause the boy that driveth the plow to know more of the Scriptures than thou dost.' My main character, Leo, is an unwilling schoolboy – he would rather be out in the fields, with animals. But he is extraordinarily attentive and, just as he notices nature, so he goes to church every week and hears the King James Bible. I tried to see the world through Leo's eyes and to let the challenge posed by Writing Historical Fiction lesson 7 take care of itself, i.e. he saw things differently from me; he saw things the same as me.

And a single engine for the whole trilogy emerged. At the end of the first book, Leo is expelled from his Eden, from the life he should have led. This is his tragedy. Yet as a result he has adventures that enlarge his existence far beyond what it could have been. I thought of the courage it takes to migrate, to move to a different culture and language, to lose all that is familiar, and of how many in the world today undergo that journey. The trilogy is for them.

Tim Pears' first novel, *In the Place of Fallen Leaves* (Hamish Hamilton 1993), was awarded the Hawthornden Prize and the Ruth Hadden Memorial Award. His second, *In a Land of Plenty* (Doubleday 1997), was made into a ten-part drama series for the BBC. His other novels include *A Revolution of the Sun* (Doubleday 2000), *Landed* (Heinemann 2010; MJA Open Book Award winner) and his West Country trilogy set before, during and in the aftermath of the First World War: *The Horseman* (2017), *The Wanderers* (2018) and Walter Scott Historical Fiction Prize shortlisted *The Redeemed* (2019), all published by Bloomsbury. Tim is a Fellow of the Royal Society of Literature. His website is https://timpears.com.

See also...
● *Writing popular history books*, page 292

Books

Writing popular history books

On turning from fiction to non-fiction, author Tom Holland was able to re-connect fully with his childhood love of history and find a fulfilling place as a writer. He reflects on the importance of historical accuracy in popular history, and on the literary and scholarly giants whose work has combined to influence and inspire him.

When I began writing, I wanted to be Proust. No novel had ever inspired me quite as much as his *À la recherche du temps perdu* (1913-27) – and so, with the lunatic hubris of youth, I decided that I would devote my career to emulating it. Naturally, it did not turn out well. My laborious attempt to write a 'Great Novel' proved abortive. My first published work of fiction, *The Vampyre* (Little, Brown 1995), instead featured Lord Byron as a vampire. Two more in the series followed, set respectively in 1880s London and the Restoration. My final vampire novel featured Howard Carter, a deranged Fatimid caliph, and blood-sucking pharaohs. It was all a long way from madeleines dipped in tea.

Or was it? Proust's great theme was memory – the hold that it has on us, and the tricks that it can play on our minds. My mistake had been to imagine that my formative experiences, my formative passions, were best served by fiction. In truth, the emotions that lived most vividly in my memory, I came to realise, were those bred of my childhood love of history. That all my novels were set in the past was, perhaps, a desperate cry for recognition to my ego from my id. In writing historical fiction, I could now see that what really stirred me was less the fiction than the history. To invent things that had happened in the reign of Akhenaten, the heretic pharaoh who served as the central protagonist in my last vampire novel, was to gild the lily. He was quite extraordinary enough as he was, without me giving him a taste for human blood.

So I decided to turn to non-fiction. Pointedly, though, I chose as my subject the period that had given me my first ever rush of fascination with vanished empires. It was a book on the Roman army (complete with a gory cover showing one of Caesar's officers getting spitted by a Gaul) that had first persuaded me, at the age of eight, to abandon an obsession with palaeontology for one with humanity's past. Rome was the apex predator of the ancient world: like a tyrannosaur, it was lethal, glamorous, and extinct. Yet it was also a civilisation of astonishing brilliance, possessed of poets and historians who, over the course of my studies, and then into my adult life, had allowed my fascination with it to mature as I myself grew older. Rome, as a theme, was unavoidably steeped in my memories. In researching the age of Caesar and the collapse of the Roman Republic, I was exploring an aspect of my own past, as surely as if I been writing an autobiography.

Which is not to say that *Rubicon* (Little, Brown 2003), my first work of non-fiction, did not aspire to stringent accuracy and objectivity. History has always had pretensions to rank as a science. Thucydides, writing back in the 5th century BC, scorned the exaggerations of poets and the meretricious taste for fantasy of chroniclers; presenting his account of the great war between Athens and Sparta, he assured his readers that 'the conclusions I have drawn from the proofs quoted may, I believe, safely be relied upon.'

History today, as an academic discipline, is recognisably the descendant of such a methodology. Scholarship, in university history departments, ranks as a vocation. The books that result tend to be written by experts for experts, and in a style that is distinctively academic. Historians who write for the general reader cannot afford to indulge in jargon; but neither can they afford to jettison the exacting standards that serve to qualify a book published by a university press. With large readerships come large responsibilities. No less than academics, writers of popular history are dependent for their career upon a reputation for not making mistakes.

An evident aspect of history's enduring appeal beyond the groves of academe, though, is precisely the fact that it is *not* a science. Herodotus, Thucydides' great predecessor and rival, declared – in the first sentence of the first work of history ever written – that it was his ambition to ensure that 'human achievement may be spared the ravages of time'. Literally, he spoke of not allowing them to become *exitẹla*, a word that could be used in a technical sense to signify the fading of paint from inscriptions or works of art. To Thucydides, the colours applied by Herodotus to his history were too bright, too distracting, to qualify him as a true historian – a criticism that would see him, in due course, named the 'Father of Lies' as well as the 'Father of History'. Herodotus himself, though, might have retorted that Thucydides was too dry, too narrow, too lacking in colour. His own history was rich with the plenitude that is the mark of great literature. If his concern with the means of gathering evidence was something revolutionary, then so too was the sheer scope and range of his interests. No one before him had ever thought to write on such a heroically panoramic scale. Unlike the austere narrative of Thucydides, with its focus on politics and war, that of Herodotus might lead in an often bewildering variety of directions: to a laugh-out-loud story of a drunk man dancing on a table, perhaps, or to the chilling account of a eunuch's revenge on the man who had him castrated as a child. 'Clio,' as Isaiah Berlin once put it, 'is, after all, a muse.'

It is the mark of the direction that my career took, I now recognise, that the great literary influence on my life has turned out to be, not Proust, but Herodotus. He too, like Caesar's legions, was a part of my childhood; and ever since I first read him at the age of 12, he has been a constant companion. I translated him for Penguin Classics, and *Persian Fire* (Little, Brown 2005), the book I wrote after *Rubicon,* was in large part a refraction of his work. Much of what we know about the early 5th century BC – the Persian Empire, the Greek world, and the wars that were fought between them – is dependent upon Herodotus; and it was as a quarry full of data that I gleefully mined him for my own history of the Persian wars. Yet Herodotus – in his love of wonders, in his complex relationship to evidence, and in his style, which today can appear closer to *Tristram Shandy* than to any conventional work of history – was a great literary artist as well as a historian. To write in his shadow is, of necessity, to acknowledge that. Which is why, in academia, the study of Herodotus is as much the prerogative of literary critics as it is of historians; and it is why, to the writer of popular history, he affords quite as many opportunities to meditate upon the nature of memory and narrative as any novelist would.

'*Stat rosa pristina nomine, nomina nuda tenemus.*' So Umberto Eco ended his bestselling novel, *The Name of the Rose* (Secker & Warburg 1983). 'The rose that once was now exists just in name – for bare names are all we have.' It is given to few writers to combine scholarship with fiction to the remarkable degree that Eco did; but to write about the distant past is, perforce, to wrestle with the implications of Eco's Latin tag. Even when the sources are at their most plentiful, uncertainties and discrepancies crop up everywhere. This is the fascination of ancient history, as well as its frustration. Although to write about it is, indeed, to impose upon the past an artificial pattern, that need be no drawback. The ancients, after all, when they wrote their own histories, did the same. Rare, for instance, in the era of Caesar, was the citizen who did not fancy himself the hero of his own history. This was an attitude which did much to bring Rome to disaster, but it also gave the epic of the Republic's fall its peculiarly lurid and heroic hue. Barely a generation after it had occurred, men were already shaking their heads in wonderment, astonished that such a time, and such giants, could ever have been.

A half-century later, the panegyrist of the Emperor Tiberius, Velleius Paterculus, could exclaim that 'It seems an almost superfluous task, to draw attention to an age when men of such extraordinary character lived,' – and then promptly write it up. He knew, as all Romans knew, that it was in action, in great deeds and remarkable accomplishments, that the genius of his people had been most gloriously displayed. Accordingly, it was through narrative that this genius could best be understood.

This intersection between the reliability of ancient sources and their unreliability, between their value as a record of facts and their often incorrigibly literary character, is the furrow which, as a writer, I find I most enjoy ploughing. It has led me to various dimensions in which reality and fantasy can easily seem intermingled: to the court of Nero; to the origins of Islam; to Viking England; to the First Crusade. The pleasure I have taken in writing about all of them is the pleasure of someone who, after years of restless wandering, has finally found somewhere that feels like home. I am not Proust, nor was I meant to be. The relief of this discovery is what enabled me at last, after many false starts, to become fulfilled as a writer.

Tom Holland is the author of the prize-winning history titles *Rubicon: The Triumph and Tragedy of the Roman Republic* (2003) and *Persian Fire* (2005), as well as *Millennium: The End of the World and the Forging of Christendom* (2008), *In the Shadow of the Sword* (2012) and *Dynasty* (2015), all published by Little, Brown. Tom's translation of *Herodotus: The Histories* was published in 2013 by Penguin Classics, and his translation of Suetonius will be published by Penguin Classics in 2022. His novels include *The Vampyre* (1995), *Deliver Us From Evil* (1997) and *The Bonehunter* (Abacus 2001). His latest book is *Dominion: The Making of the Western Mind* (Little, Brown 2019). Tom has adapted Herodotus, Homer, Thucydides and Virgil for BBC Radio 4 and is the presenter of BBC Radio 4's *Making History*, and co-host of the podcast *The Rest Is History*. He has written and presented TV documentaries on subjects ranging from religion to dinosaurs. Tom is currently Chair of the PLR Advisory Committee. Visit www.tom-holland.org or follow him on Twitter @holland_tom.

Blurring facts with fiction: memoir and biography

Nell Stevens explores the murky literary territory that lies somewhere between truth and fiction, full of creative possibilities, risks and responsibilities, where memoir and imagination mingle.

'But what is it, exactly?' When I was working on my first book, *Bleaker House* (Picador 2017), this question was posed repeatedly, by friends who were the first to read it, then by agents, then publishers and then, even later, by readers. The book was about my attempts to write a novel by sequestering myself in the Falkland Islands. It was a story that included descriptions of earlier experiences – when I had pushed myself to extremes in order to find material for fiction – as well as the fiction those experiences produced. The final product seemed resistant to categorisation, and nobody was quite sure what to do with it. Was *Bleaker House*, a book about trying to write a novel, itself a novel? Or was it a memoir?

I should have seen these questions coming. *Bleaker House* began its life as fiction, then morphed into something resembling my own life; in its final form, it incorporated both – in obvious and less obvious ways. It did not feel accurate to say it was a novel; much of the text explores my real experiences, after all, and involves real people. And yet, the term 'memoir' implied a weighty responsibility to tell the truth, which was not a burden I was particularly keen to shoulder. I was a storyteller and had used all the tools of the novelist to tell my story. In doing so, I had changed chronologies, timelines and dialogue, created composite characters, omitted information and allowed my imagination to kick in when my memory failed (I have a bad memory, so that was an awful lot of imagination). In the end, my publisher and I reached a compromise. The book was published as a memoir with a very prominent disclaimer: 'This is a work of memory and invention by someone who set out to be a novelist.'

I love the playfulness inherent in that compromise. There's a mischievous joy in saying, 'This is true, but maybe it isn't, but maybe it is, but I never meant it to be, but just maybe …'. There's something generative and exciting in the idea of all those 'maybes'. It opens up a space in which real life, in all its complicated strangeness, can be used as raw material with which the writer is free to do what she wants. It allows me to use my own experiences in roughly the same way I imagine a sculptor uses a block of marble: they are mine to chip away at, to shape, to transform as I see fit. The statue the sculptor creates is made of marble, but it isn't *just* marble. It's also a portrait, a depiction, a piece of art.

The murky middle

Since writing *Bleaker House*, I've become increasingly aware that the idea of a story being either one thing or the other, fact or fiction, truth or lies, is an illusion. If we imagine a spectrum, with absolute truth at one end and absolute fiction at the other, the temptation would be to place novels on the 'fiction' side and non-fiction (an unwieldy, amorphous category that includes investigative journalism, recipe books and celebrity memoir) under 'truth'. But the reality of most writing is, of course, much murkier.

The middle ground of the truth-fiction spectrum is heavily populated by works of every genre. There are plenty of overlaps: novels that cleave closely to real life, for example;

Books

cookbooks whose authors haven't tried every recipe; biographies that incorporate imaginative work about their subjects. Most memoirs are works of immense artifice. Humans are unreliable narrators of our own experiences; memories are fallible and often entirely false; the very act of translating life into language transforms it.

There is a plethora of terms designed to make sense of this no-man's-land between fact and fiction. 'Autobiographical fiction' takes the author's life as a starting point for storytelling, though without making any demands for accuracy. French writers have been producing 'autofiction', in which the protagonist and the author tend to share a name and the story plays with the biographical details of the author's life, for over 40 years; it has reached the mainstream of literature in English more recently, practised by writers such as Ben Lerner and Sheila Heti. Then there's the idea of the 'non-fiction novel', associated with Truman Capote's *In Cold Blood* (Random House 1965); this was defined by Capote as 'a narrative form that employed all the techniques of fictional art but was nevertheless immaculately factual'. Perhaps the most forgiving, capacious term we have for in-between writing is simply 'creative non-fiction', which marries the imaginative labour of creativity with a sense that the form is nonetheless invested in the possibilities of evoking real life.

Risk and responsibility

Despite an increasing interest in and appetite for genre-bending literature, both from readers and publishers, there remains a risk inherent in writing that sits between or beyond easily identifiable truths or fictions. In one sense, that risk is very real: blurring fact and fiction has legal consequences that are difficult to parse. In libel cases, the legal defences for the fiction writer and the non-fiction writer are contradictory: the novelist asserts everything is made up and that any resemblance to real life is purely coincidental; the memoirist states that everything is absolutely true. Navigating the legal consequences of writing that blurs these lines is perilous, especially in writing that involves the lives of people other than author. There have been high-profile complaints made against novelists for too accurately portraying real people, and against memoirists for mischaracterising their own or others' experiences. The media attorney who read my work prior to publication, checking for legal issues, described the genre as 'a doozy'.

There is another kind of risk associated with these kinds of projects, too: a sense that its purpose is to disturb, to make uneasy, to complicate. A strange thing that happened when *Bleaker House* came out was that readers almost invariably interpreted the fact and fiction sections the 'wrong' way round; they assumed the fictional elements were real and the sections I considered more straightforwardly autobiographical to be made up. I can only explain this by the overused truism that truth is stranger than fiction, but it highlighted something innately slippery and disruptive in the genre – an unknowability, or rather an acknowledgement that 'truth' in all kinds of writing is unknowable.

Geoff Dyer, whose works of non-fiction revel in the generative possibilities of unreliability, puts it this way: 'All that matters is that the reader can't see the joins, that there is no textural change between reliable fabric and fabrication.' In other words, the story is what matters to Dyer, the creative whole rather than its constituent parts.

I think about this question in terms of responsibility. Writers have a responsibility to readers not to waste their time. There are more specific responsibilities, some more relevant to specific genres than others, but all important and valid: the responsibility to delight, to amaze, to entertain; the responsibility not to mislead; the responsibility to respect people's privacy; the responsibility to protect our *own* privacy; the responsibility to tell a great story no matter what. These obligations often compete with and contradict each other. Writers of in-between narratives must make our own, very personal decisions about which of them we feel most bound to honour.

Other creative forms, notably poetry and stand-up comedy, occupy this in-between space more comfortably than narrative prose does. A discerning reader of poetry comprehends that the truth of a poem is independent of its literal accuracy; poets mine their own lives and experiences in their work, but the speaker of a poem is not the poet personally. Similarly, an audience member at a stand-up gig intuitively understands that the comedian's persona is a *version* of the comedian, that the stories the performer is telling on stage are truths in the loosest sense – exaggerated, warped, fabricated, but nonetheless showing us something real about the world. The demands of form, both poetic and comedic, are transformative; once reality is moulded into its new shape, it is both entirely new and wholly recognisable.

Finding your place

When *Bleaker House* came out I went, giddily, to a bookshop to visit it. I was excited to admire it in situ and needed reassurance that it was real, so on publication day I hurtled into my local Waterstones to see it on a shelf with my own eyes. Except, I couldn't find it. I searched the 'New Non-fiction' table, scanning the covers for mine; then I went to the non-fiction shelves, speed-reading spines looking for my own name. My book was nowhere to be seen. I tried 'Memoir and biography'. Nothing. 'Travel writing'? No. I felt too shy to ask a bookseller and was about to retreat, forlornly, when I passed the 'New Fiction' table and saw *Bleaker House* stacked between a historical novel and a thriller. After all those fraught conversations at the beginning of the publication process about whether the book was a novel or a memoir, and after coming to the decision to publish it as non-fiction, *Bleaker House* had found its way onto a table where, ostensibly, it did not belong.

But being out of place felt fitting for a book that didn't really fit anywhere. Having begun its life as a novel and morphed into something that was published as a memoir, it had somehow wound up back where it started. And until we – writers, publishers and readers – reach a point of collectively abandoning categories altogether, putting poetry and drama in amongst the cookbooks and popular history under the banner of 'words about life', I will wander through bookshops never knowing where my work will pop up next. That uncertainty and surprise is part of the joy of breaking the rules: you never know where you'll end up.

Nell Stevens is a writer of memoir and fiction and the author of *Bleaker House* (Picador 2017). Her second book, *Mrs Gaskell & Me* (Picador 2018), which is also published by Doubleday in the US and Knopf in Canada as *The Victorian & the Romantic* (2018), won the 2019 Somerset Maugham Award. She currently lectures in Creative Writing at Goldsmiths, University of London. For more information visit www.nellstevens.com.

Books

Ghostwriting

Gillian Stern sheds light on the invisible role of the ghostwriter, describing the often intense process involved in the art of writing another person's story in their own voice.

Everyone has a story. I learned this as a Saturday dental nurse at my father's NHS practice in Tottenham. Even the smallest details of people's lives are important, he would tell me. Listen carefully and you will hear.

His tiny surgery vibrated with life. Even before I had a chance to show a patient to the chair, they took up whatever they had been telling him during their last visit, which may have been six months or a year previously. They talked about their children, their families; they pre-emptively repeated their vow to quit eating sugary things; they gave their opinions on what Thatcher was or wasn't doing; told him how they brushed their teeth, what dental problems they were having. And as he filled their mouth with cotton wool rolls and started probing, he would take up the thread of their conversation, to which the patient would nod their head or roll their eyes, trying to make themselves understood.

As I mixed the mercury and amalgam for fillings, or held the hand of a nervous patient, I would listen. Everyone who sat in that chair had a distinctive voice; they were mostly living hard, complex lives. And I learned to hear, I learned to ask questions, and eventually I learned that sometimes what a patient *wasn't* saying was as interesting as what they were saying. My father made each and every one of his patients feel as if they mattered and how I wish now that I had written down the words that filled his surgery, in the rich and varied voices of his patients.

Maybe, then, it is no surprise that I am a ghostwriter – a writer who gives voice to other people's stories. I am paid to listen, to hear, to become someone else, to tell their story in their voice. In this, I am completely invisible, a siphon for their words, their story, their life, their soul. I do not interpret or pass judgement and though I might steer my questions in a direction I think their story should head, ultimately the book I am ghosting is entirely theirs, made up of their words.

While there are a range of ghostwriters – from those who ghost speeches to others ghosting novels – I ghost memoirs. I am a more reactive type of ghost in that I take commissions; many ghosts are more proactive, coming up with the idea of who they are going to ghost, taking responsibility for the outline, and involving themselves in all aspects of the publishing deal to writing the book itself. Ghostwriters are proper writers, often excellent writers, and in a world where we suspend our egos almost entirely, swapping recognition for invisibility, ghostwriters deserve all the accolades the industry and public are so keen not to throw our way. Going into a large, unnamed publishing house, where they were painting beautiful swirls of their author's names up and down the walls, I was completely unsurprised to see my own and other ghostly colleagues' names *not* included.

There is a peculiar snobbery and fuss out there about ghostwritten books and I can't quite work out why. There are plenty of people with book-worthy stories, from the already famous to the completely unknown, who have been busy living their lives – noisily or quietly – but who have never written a book before and are honest enough to know that writing is not one of their talents. While everyone has a story, not everyone has the ability to write that story. So, in order for their *commissioned* book to be the best possible read, they, their agent and publisher decide that it is better to employ the services of a professional writer rather than have them inflict underdeveloped, clumsy prose on their readers. I can see nothing wrong with this. The art is in how that story is told.

I came to ghosting through being a structural editor. A publisher handed me a manuscript by someone pretty famous (signing Non-Disclosure Agreements means I am not allowed to disclose who I am ghosting, before, during and after) and asked me to edit it. It was so tortuously written – so oblique and wooden – that I simply couldn't, and I requested time with the author, persuading them to let me have a go at re-working what they had written. The book went on to do extremely well and so the same publisher commissioned me to ghost another memoir. Publishing is a small world and publishers get used to reading between the lines in acknowledgements. 'A special thank you to Gillian Stern, without whom none of this would have hit the page' is a bit of a giveaway in the industry (and to my family), and so the acknowledgement, on many levels, is everything.

Often I am asked to attend what is, quaintly and oddly, still known as a 'beauty parade', where the person who needs a ghost – the author – with their agent and the publisher interview a number of potential ghosts, offering the job to the person whom the author feels best fits the profile of whatever it is they are looking for. I have walked into some such events and it is obvious immediately, or as the interview proceeds, that there is no way I fit, either because of a massive difference in outlook or voice or a complete lack of connection; I have walked into others and the connection and fit have been instant – not that that means I always then got the job. Mostly, though, because I've been around a bit, I am asked directly by a publisher to meet the author, with a view that I am the right person for the job. I am careful about what I accept; I am likely to be spending a great deal of time with the author, investing emotionally in them and their story, even 'becoming' them as I get into and develop the writing. I can only write someone's story if I can *imagine* myself in their voice. I will not accept a job if I think I will bring judgment and bias to the page.

Once I accept a commission, I either involve my agent or negotiate the contract myself. I read as much as I can about the author that already exists. Sometimes that can be just the outline on which the publisher has bought the book; in general, though, there is a body of material online, in existing books or articles and often they have diaries or letters or papers. I listen to, or watch, whatever programmes or clips I can and then spend time with the author, chatting, walking, eating (– for one author even frenetically working out with them at their gym while they talked!). I tape as much as I can and in the early stages, as I go about my day, I stick in my headphones and listen to their voice, allowing their way of talking, the patterns in their speech, to become mine too. I try it out as I shop or talk to friends. I try to understand the way they look at the world, the way they see the everyday, what it is they want to convey. I love that aspect of the job, the beginning of becoming part of someone else's life so intimately. It's a strange internal intimacy; *becoming* them – as I write and *am* them – can be overwhelming, although when I'm actually with that person, I can feel oddly detached.

Typically, the author and I have a couple of sessions where we decide how we are going to work and then we get going. I generally spend as much time as I can with them; some like me to tape everything over a number of days or weeks and get writing; others prefer to get together once a week or so, with me writing and them going over what I have written in between times. Most authors I have worked with like to pore over every word, checking that I am expressing them as they believe they express themselves, hearing the flow of the narrative, the timbre of the tone, the sound of their words. I have the world's best transcriber and I download tapes to her as soon as I get home and write from the transcripts. One thing I would strongly advise aspiring ghosts to do is to insist that your publisher or author pay for all transcribing expenses.

Once we settle on style and rhythm, I like my editor or the author's agent to see a few initial draft chapters so that there are no great surprises near to the delivery deadline. I didn't do this on the first book I ghosted, and a couple of days before delivery received 18 pages of vicious criticism from the author's agent, none of which I disagreed with.

I get emotionally attached to my authors, of course I do. I have fallen in (appropriate) love; I have wanted to be the person I am ghosting; I have been a part of the lives of people I would never have otherwise had access to and I have seen things that would fill a book I can never write. And I have learned, painfully at first, that once the script is delivered and the book goes into production, I need to get out of there. I don't own the book; I don't own the story and I have no part in the publishing process once the script is delivered. Quite often the author and I stay in touch; quite often they tell me I am the most important person in their lives, the person who 'knows them the best', but that is moonshine and after the launch, after the razzmatazz, after the sales (and even prizes), life moves on. I did ghost two memoirs for one author and she told me shocking things she had genuinely never told anyone before, which was a burden for me but one I was prepared to carry and not include in the book. But I am not in this business to make friends. Ghosting, like editing, is a job and, once a book is written, I need to write the next.

The questions I am most frequently asked are: Why don't you write your own book? and How can you write a book without your name on the front? Here are my answers: I do not have a novel in me; I do not have a story about my life or an aspect of my life that I believe would interest readers; I have no desire to see my name on the front of a book when the story belongs to someone else. I get a great deal of satisfaction bringing interesting stories to life, in capturing someone else's voice so convincingly that they hear themselves come off the page. Ghostwriting is challenging and complex and a great privilege.

These days, well into his eighties, my father is still collecting stories – be it on the streets of his neighbourhood as he goes for his daily 'ball of chalk', in the stands at White Hart Lane, or around the table with his grandchildren. And, if I had time, I would tell you his story. Or maybe, one day, I will ghost it.

United Ghostwriters

United Ghostwriters is a leading collective of bestselling UK ghostwriters. Their work covers all genres including memoirs, business books, celebrity, self-help, social history and fiction. Other services include structural edits, copywriting, blogs, and columns. Their writers include *Sunday Times* bestselling ghostwriters and award-winning writers, who work internationally and consider projects on a case-by-case basis. As industry experts in the field, they have links with agents and major publishers and can advise on all stages of the publishing process. United Ghostwriters have produced over 350 books to date. www.unitedghostwriters.co.uk.

Gillian Stern is a former non-fiction commissioning editor, who happily discovered a novel that went on to win prizes and become a bestseller. She then crossed over into the world of commercial and literary fiction and has since been a freelance fiction and non-fiction editor for literary agents and publishers including Bloomsbury, Hodder, Penguin Random House and Orion as well as a judge for the Lucy Cavendish Fiction Prize for the past six years. She combines this with her work as a ghostwriter. A memoir she ghosted was named as WHSmith's Non-Fiction Book of the Year and she has since ghosted a sequel for the same author, as well as other memoirs that have been *Sunday Times* and Amazon bestsellers. Contact her at gillybethstern@hotmail.com or follow her on Twitter @gillybethstern.

Becoming a successful copywriter

Freelance strategic copywriter Carina Martin explains the multitude of roles that fall under the banner of copywriting and offers pointers for breaking into the industry.

Copywriting is a job you can start straight out of college or something you can switch to later in life. So what do copywriters do? (clue – it has nothing to do with trademarking). Copywriters use words to attract attention and to persuade readers to behave in a certain way.

For a role that relies on clarity and simplicity, the term 'copywriter' is something of an archaic misnomer, harking back to the invention of the printing press. In those early days, newspapers would differentiate between news writers and advertising copywriters, with the latter producing factual, rational sales messages. The 1950s were a turning point. US advertising pioneer Bill Bernbach was the first to place art directors (responsible for the visual elements of an ad) and copywriters in teams of two, believing that the dynamic between those disciplines would result in more creative, emotional advertising. And it did. Bernbach's humorous writing for Volkswagen and David Ogilvy's long copy for Rolls-Royce have stood the test of time and have earned their places in advertising's Hall of Fame. The team model worked then, and it still exists in agencies to this day.

Fast forward to the 2020s and copywriting has exploded in a million different directions. Sadly, the popularity of long advertising copy has, to some extent, succumbed to today's shorter attention spans, but what the copy lacks in volume is more than made up for in variety.

The many faces of copywriting

Advertising copywriting is probably the area that has experienced the least change over the years, although digital channels such as YouTube, Facebook and Instagram have brought new challenges. It remains the domain of *creative teams*, also known as *concept teams*, under the watchful eye of the creative director. The focus here is on idea generation, while the roles of art director and copywriter are sometimes blurred. These creative duos often begin agency life as paid interns, plucked from Creative Advertising degree courses at reputable universities like Bucks New or Falmouth. This is done either formally – through graduate schemes – or informally through direct approaches.

Teams may be given a single execution to work on or they may be responsible for overarching campaign ideas that are then optimised for different media. Given how much creatives are expected to learn about the client, teams are generally employed full-time by an agency, with freelancers being brought in when fresh ideas and perspectives are needed.

Beyond creative teams, it's common for copywriters to work on their own as *long-form copywriters* (persuading potential customers to choose your product or service over a competitors') and *content writers* (less hard-sell, more subtle ways of engaging prospective audiences). These solo operators might choose to work for an agency, a business (known as working 'in-house'), or for one or both as a freelancer. There are many different types of agency that hire copywriters, including branding, design, advertising and PR agencies, and there are many different job titles within each. If you are strongly drawn to write about a particular subject, you may prefer to take the in-house route.

Books

In-house or freelance?

My own decision to freelance was a lifestyle choice as much as anything. I was tired of commuting and wanted to get a dog. It suits me. I enjoy working on my own, away from distractions, and I like the variety of work I get – from agencies and businesses in equal measure. I can write a website about a medical breakthrough one day and be naming an ice lolly the next. As such, I can turn my hand to pretty much any brief.

That's not for everyone, though. Freelance life can be lonely, and the cliché about feast and famine couldn't be more true. My friends working in agencies get a buzz from being in a creative environment while enjoying the range of work coming from the agency's clients. Those who work in-house love getting to know one business thoroughly, rather than being a jack-of-all-trades. It's a personal choice, and there are highs and lows which-ever route you choose.

Squiggly career paths

I discovered copywriting by accident. I was working in-house as a marketing manager and my budget had been slashed; I needed to reduce my external expenses and one way to do this was for me to write all our copy rather than outsource it. I already had experience of writing from working in PR and advertising, so it was a logical step. And it soon became clear that copywriting was my true love. I moved into full-time writing, at a content agency, and subsequently became Head of Copy at a digital agency. To broaden my skill set, I also did a Masters in Screenwriting for Film and TV. I've now been freelancing as a copywriter and screenwriter for around 12 years.

Whenever I've recruited copywriters, I've always been interested in candidates' previous lives and what those experiences can bring. For example, an account manager wanting to make the switch to copywriting might bring discipline and diplomacy. Someone with an acting background might find it easy to get into character, becoming the 'voice' of different clients. If you're thinking of a career change, just think about the transferable skills you can offer. My own experience in marketing has proved invaluable, as I understand the pressures my clients are under and am good at mediating if creative differences arise. A good command of the English language is, of course, a must – but a natural ability to write interesting, informative copy triumphs over any number of qualifications.

Day-to-day life

An entry-level copywriter may be tasked with writing product descriptions or SEO (search engine optimised) articles, which are designed to improve rankings on search engines. You'll be given a brief, with the key messages to convey, and your job is to produce copy that grabs attention and persuades the reader to buy/find out more/make an appointment, etc. You might work in the social media team, writing tweets and posts on behalf of different brands, or help the human resources team to generate attractive job ads. In a nutshell, copy requests can come from virtually anywhere and they can take many different forms. If something needs to be written well, it tends to fall to the copywriter.

A senior copywriter might help the board of a company to draft the non-financial section of its annual report or write white papers and thought-leadership articles. They may help develop businesses' manifestos, shape their brand tone of voice, or name their product ranges. The higher up the chain, the more strategic the job becomes.

Getting started

My advice to new copywriters is to create a portfolio website. You can do this even if you have yet to find your first role. I created mine by following YouTube videos; you don't need to throw money at it, just time. If you are interested in becoming one half of a creative team, start writing ads now. Maybe pick a campaign and deconstruct it until you've figured out what the client's original brief was. You'll notice there are some variables between different ads, and some mandatory elements. Stick to those rules and write a better ad.

Pick up a product in a supermarket and find a great hook for it that grabs attention. It's important to make it clear on your website that your idea is independently created and not linked in any way to the agency or client. That said, if you're proud of it, it's worth sharing. Think, too, about how you might stretch that idea into other media. The more life an idea has, the more likely it is to be bought.

You can do the same as a solo copywriter. Write speculative press releases, articles, social media posts and website pages. Show an understanding of pace, prioritisation of messaging and subbing. Get into the habit of writing succinct copy – less is nearly always more. And think about your audiences; you have to wear many hats as a copywriter, and you need to be able to flex your language to appeal to the intended reader.

Try writing for business-to-business (B2B) clients as well as business-to-consumer (B2C). Target social posts at influencers and a press release to a broadsheet newspaper. The more variety you can show, the more flexible you will appear to potential employers.

Building your personal brand

It's a good idea, right from Day One, to think of yourself as a brand. As Jeff Bezos once said, 'A brand is what other people say about you when you're not in the room.' Consider how you want to be perceived and make sure you permeate that message consistently – from the way you dress in your profile picture on LinkedIn to the colours you use on your website. It is about playing to your strengths and not trying to be someone you're not.

As well as your website, which will act as your calling card, you will need a well-crafted CV and some business cards. I use shocking pink consistently on everything from my email signature to my laptop cover. It acts as an aide memoire when I leave my (shocking pink) business card behind. Another way to reinforce 'brand you' is to write opinion pieces that you can post on your social media. Write blogs, articles in local magazines, even thank-you letters. Take any excuse you can to practise writing. The more you do it, and the more you're known for it, the higher your chances of getting spotted.

Getting yourself out there

Once you've got a website (or a PDF portfolio) that you're proud of, you need to drive traffic to it. I recommend you look at other copywriters' profiles on LinkedIn and make yours as powerful as possible. Then make it work for you. Connect with potential employers, comment on creative directors' posts and be an active contributor to online debates. Set up job alerts and follow recruitment agencies that specialise in creative appointments. Join networks such as The Dots (https://the-dots.com), YunoJuno (www.yunojuno.com) and Creativepool (https://creativepool.com) where you can build a profile and apply for jobs. There's also a lot of good advice for copywriters on LinkedIn and Twitter.

It's old school, I know, but try writing some letters to clients or agencies where you believe you have a natural fit. Structure it like a compelling argument, explaining your

Books

strengths and selling your benefits. When was the last time you received a handwritten letter? I bet you opened it straight away. And remember – you'll write better copy if you're interested in the product or service you're marketing, so rather than writing to the top ten agencies, or the biggest spending clients, think how you'd *feel* writing for them (I love design, art and innovation, so I'll always jump at those briefs). Get as much experience on as many subjects as you can, then find your niche and chase your dream.

Carina Martin has been a freelance copywriter and screenwriter since 2011. Her previous experience includes roles as Marketing Manager at Capital Radio and Channel 4 (FilmFour), and at digital marketing agency Dare, where she later became Head of Copy. Carina has an MA in Screenwriting for Film & TV from Royal Holloway. For more information see www.carinamartin.co.uk and her LinkedIn profile. Follow her on Twitter @copycatch.

Making facts your mission: the pleasure of writing non-fiction

Jane Robinson describes what led her to become a non-fiction writer, and gives advice on the key elements and requirements of this disciplined and enjoyable work.

I didn't mean to be an author. I've always loved books; my obsession with collecting them began when I was banned from our local library at the age of seven – for using a jam tart as a bookmark in their copy of *Squirrel Nutkin*. After university I bought and sold books for a living, but never dreamed of writing them myself. That happened by accident. One day, while I was working in an antiquarian bookshop, a customer asked me for a guide to all the travel books ever written by women. He wanted to make a complete collection. I asked him to wait a few days; if there wasn't already a published list, I was sure I could work one up. After all, there couldn't be that many female first-hand travel accounts. Didn't history's women traditionally stay at home?

Off I went to the library to begin research. I discovered a handful of volumes by women and then a handful more, and by the time my customer returned I had a catalogue of over 100. He disappeared, disappointed that his task was now probably beyond his purse. And I went back to the library to see how many more forgotten travellers' voices I could find.

I was entranced by these intrepid adventurers. Encouraged by a friend who was a published historian, I decided to attempt a reference bibliography of their work – a book about books – just so that dealers like me could appreciate how many of these surprising authors there were. By now I had unearthed getting on for 1,000, spanning 16 centuries. But when I started reading the books I was only supposed to be listing (how could I resist *On Sledge and Horseback to Outcast Siberian Lepers* or *To Lake Tanganyika in a Bath Chair*?) my life swerved onto a new course. The same friend introduced me to his editor at Oxford University Press. We had a meeting, I wrote a proposal, and a few weeks later was the stunned possessor of a contract for my first book: *Wayward Women: A Guide to Women Travellers* (OUP 1990). One book led to another; I gave up my job at the shop, became self-employed, and now here I am, twelve books later, working on the thirteenth. I fell into a career as an author specialising in social history through women's eyes – and couldn't enjoy my job more.

I'm making it sound easy, and to some extent it was – back then. I had found a **subject** virtually untouched by other historians by which I was completely enthused; I knew I could **research** it given time; I had an introduction to and subsequently a **commission** from a respectable publisher; and I have never found it hard to **discipline** myself to meet deadlines. When *Wayward Women* came out, the publishing business was not as restricted as it is now by the aggressive need to make money on every book. OUP could afford to take a chance on me. But it is still possible to start from scratch as a non-fiction writer, as I did, and **enjoy success**.

Here's some advice about those five key elements of the job, with reference to my own work as a narrative historian.

1. Subject

Everything begins with this. Fiction writers can make up reality for themselves; we non-fiction authors must stick to the facts. The trick is to root your book in a subject you find irresistibly fascinating (enthusiasm is infectious) and write about it engagingly. Easily said, I know, but you'll develop your style with practice. Read aloud everything you write – that helps you gauge what readers are hearing in their heads as they turn the pages. It's no less important to pay attention to the cadence of a sentence in a biography, for instance, than in a novel. Good writing is good writing.

On a book-by-book level, I seek out well-known historical events or social attitudes and approach them from an unexpected angle, using the testimony of 'ordinary' people rather than history's celebrities. I like challenging stereotypes. The popular assumption is that before the 20th century, for instance, women were mostly seen, not heard, and did what they were told. *Wayward Women* smashes that one. In *Bluestockings* (Penguin 2009), about the first women to fight for higher education, I highlight the drama behind something we take for granted: the right of women to attend university. Did you realise that they were not given degrees at Cambridge until 1948? Or that Victorian medics believed that if women thought too much their wombs would wither? *Hearts and Minds* (Doubleday 2018) focuses on a massed, six-week women's march though the UK which won (some) women the vote in 1918 – and they weren't suffragettes. Who knew?

Choose a common approach like this for each book, and your work will amass a recognisable USP, which helps enormously when pitching for new commissions.

2. Research

Don't choose a subject you can't research thoroughly. While writing *Wayward Women* I had access to the British Library, which is a copyright library. Every book published in the UK must be deposited there by law. Anyone can become a registered reader, provided they have a referee and a valid reason for study. Other copyright libraries are in Aberystwyth, Cambridge, Dublin, Edinburgh and Oxford. It's important, when trying to present a fresh perspective to your readers, to find as many original sources as possible; hence I spend a great deal of research time in local archives and record offices, listening to oral history collections and advertising in judiciously chosen magazines for reader contributions. For *Bluestockings* I asked for family stories through university alumni magazines. Authenticity is crucial – try to get straight to the horse's mouth.

3. Commissions

I was fortunate to have an introduction to my first editor, which helped. If it's your debut you might not have an agent yet, so do try to find a champion – perhaps a friend or mentor in the business. Editors are swamped by unsolicited manuscripts (some refuse them altogether), so they welcome anything that marks you out from the crowd.

I have never written a book, chapter or article without a commission. It's not about the advance – only a quarter of that is due on signing the contract anyway (the rest coming on delivery, hardback and then paperback publication). Very few of us get rich writing. It's more that I need the confidence of a promise to publish and the impetus of having a contractual deadline. I value the framework provided by the proposal I've had to submit to achieve the deal. A good proposal is a thorough document with a detailed chapter-plan, as well as the usual information about why me, why the subject and what's the competition.

Mine are blueprints; they are the most important element of the whole process of writing non-fiction. They express the flavour of the book and of my style to a potential editor and guide me through my work until I've finished.

4. Discipline

I happen to be temperamentally incapable of submitting work late. Always was, however hard I tried – even at university. I don't have the bravado to break deadlines, terrified that if something doesn't get done in time, it won't get done at all. I set myself a series of achievable targets. I decide when I'm realistically likely to finish the book, stating this in the proposal. Usually I allow a year for research and a year for writing. That includes a little leeway for other commitments (and life) to get in the way. Within that timeframe I'll mentally apportion periods for: research; collating my notes into a usable resource; completing each chapter; a second draft; and finally organising the notes, bibliography and illustrations.

Like most writers, I suspect, I have a routine. Once the research is done – all of it, so that I have an overview of the whole subject before I metaphorically put pen to paper – I start pretending I have a proper job, by disappearing into my study during office hours, with a break for some exercise at lunch. Because I write at home, I demarcate my working life from my domestic life by (bizarrely) putting on an apron before I sit down at my desk and removing it when I've switched off the computer. Weird, I know, but it works for me. There's probably a psychological fest of hidden agendas swirling around this ritual to do with the subversion of my role as a wife and mother … let's not go there.

5. Enjoy success

Sometimes I dream of being a fiction writer, of sitting somewhere inspirational for a while, inviting some characters into my empty head, then floating off to my study to see where they lead me and eventually lapping up the awards when my tour de force is made into a blockbuster film. Imagine! No research other than my own life and that of my friends and family (more or less disguised); no wearisome checking of the facts, compiling of the bibliography, sifting of the footnotes and fear of having misconstrued the truth.

But then I remember how much I enjoy having the outline of a plot already in place and then colouring it in to my own design. To me, non-fiction is a mission: I aim to restore a voice to people whose part in history has been forgotten. Hence my passion for women's lives. If I write well, I will paint no less involving a picture for my readers than a fiction-writer might; share some astonishing stories with them; inspire them and make them proud of those unknown ancestors who belong to us all. Never think of non-fiction as a poor relation.

Added extras

Don't think that you can't make money from it, either. The days of publishers taking a punt on young authors may have disappeared in the glare of hard-nosed commercialism, but it is possible to supplement your earnings by learning how to deliver a good talk. A significant part of my income comes from author appearances. Publish a blog about your work; interest in that could attract invitations to write opinion pieces elsewhere. Choose your subject carefully enough, and write about it in a lively, revealing way, and – who knows – the film and TV companies might come knocking at your door. It happens. Take advantage of every opportunity offered around publication day in terms of media and

Books

speaking engagements; they'll push up sales and, anyway, after all that work you deserve your day in the sun.

Every time a book of mine comes out, I thank that nameless customer who walked into the bookshop all those years ago. He changed the way I look at the world. And by writing non-fiction, I can now do the same for my readers. It's a privilege. Do try it.

Jane Robinson worked in the antiquarian book trade before becoming a full-time writer, social historian and lecturer. Her first book was *Wayward Women: A Guide to Women Travellers* (OUP 1990) and later publications include *Bluestockings: the Remarkable Story of the First Women to Fight for an Education* (Penguin 2009, currently in development as a TV series) and most recently *Ladies Can't Climb Ladders* (Doubleday 2020). Her biography of the Victorian artist and activist Barbara Leigh Smith Bodichon is due out in 2023. For more information see www.jane-robinson.com and follow her on Twitter @janerobinson00.

See also...
- *How to submit a non-fiction proposal,* page 423
- *Libraries,* page 682

How to become a travel writer

Jonathan Lorie looks at the ever-widening range and opportunity that travel writing offers, as the digital world opens up new territory and new forms of storytelling. He outlines the three main routes into this hybrid genre, each with its differing demands, focus and appeal.

'But is it travel writing?' The famous explorer leans across a table full of books and frowns ... 'I mean, it's more like a history book or a memoir. And then there's all the food.'

We're sitting in the boardroom of the world's largest map and travel bookshop, Stanfords in London, for the final judging of the Stanford Dolman Travel Book of the Year Award (2020). In front of us lies a pile of books that reveal the range and ambition of travel writing today. Some of them are classic stuff: an edgy road trip through Mexico and its mafias, or a gentle memoir of Trieste and its ghosts of Hapsburg glory. Others are experimental: a tour of Tokyo led by temple bells and written like a haiku, or a journey following Europe's ancient epics from the Greek Odyssey to the Icelandic sagas. And some are political: a wander around Putin's Russia from oligarchs' yachts to villagers' huts, or a dive into the underground places where humankind has laid its dead, mined its minerals and now is storing up its nuclear waste and other troubles for the future.

Is it travel writing? We judges all think so. What a range – and what opportunities – this genre offers any writer, combining aspects of thriller, memoir, discovery, culture,

My top travel book recommendations

These classic travel books illustrate the four key skills of this genre, which are the ability to write about places, adventures, people and yourself.

Describing places

The Lost Continent (Abacus 1998), by Bill Bryson: comical road trip through small-town America, with all its eccentricities.

Voices of the Old Sea (Hamilton 1984), by Norman Lewis: poignant evocation of life in a Spanish fishing village in the 1950s, before tourism changed everything.

Recounting adventures

Terra Incognita (Jonathan Cape 1996), by Sara Wheeler: seventh months on research stations at the South Pole, swinging between endurance and exhilaration.

A Time of Gifts (John Murray 2002), by Patrick Leigh Fermor: an epic walk across 1930s Europe, sleeping in barns one night and castles the next.

Describing people

In Patagonia (Jonathan Cape 1977), by Bruce Chatwin: perhaps the greatest travel book since 1945, glittering with vivid portraits of local people.

The Great Railway Bazaar (Hodder & Stoughton 1989), by Paul Theroux: the other contender for that title, a riot of characters and their stories.

Personal memoir

Driving Over Lemons (Sort of Books 2011), by Chris Stewart: hilarious tale of buying a run-down farm and trying to build the good life, hampered by the author's many foibles.

As I Walked Out One Midsummer Morning (Deutsch 1969), by Laurie Lee: a young man's journey to adulthood as he busks his way across Spain, poetically retold.

Books

history, reportage and anthropology. This is the ultimate crossover genre and you can make of it whatever you want.

Glancing down the judging table, it's easy to see that travel writing is enjoying a new-found confidence. For the past decade, our bookshops have been filled with a boom in 'nature writing' – journeys around the British Isles to rediscover our wild places, local cultures and varied landscapes. Now travel writers are turning their attention to changes in the wider world. What is the reality of Donald Trump's wall on the Mexican border? asks Paul Theroux in his book *On the Plain of Snakes: A Mexican Road Trip* (Hamish Hamilton 2019). Where has Russia gone wrong? inquires Rory Maclean in *Pravda Ha Ha: True Travels to the End of Europe* (Bloomsbury 2019). Will we prove good ancestors to the generations coming after us? ponders Robert Macfarlane in the masterpiece that won the prize in 2020, *Underland: A Deep Time Journey* (Hamish Hamilton 2019).

So this is an interesting time to start out as a travel writer, and full of possibilities. As well as the resurgence in travel books, there is a wild frontier of travel blogs for you to explore. Out there, bloggers are creating viable careers from personal passions – train travel, luxury hostels, cookery in Italy. Some have become digital nomads, living with just a backpack and a laptop, others are running start-up businesses with staff and subscribers. As the digital world expands, new forms of storytelling will take travel writing to new territory, alongside visual platforms like Instagram and its successors.

That might seem a little optimistic at the time of writing, when the planet has been locked down by a coronavirus pandemic, and wider environmental concerns are changing the way we will travel in future. But when actual journeys are rare, imaginative journeys have greater value, and armchair travellers will turn to books and media for ways to wander the world. My sense is that as we start to travel less often but more meaningfully, a well-told traveller's tale will be just what people want.

So if all this tickles your taste buds, where do you begin? I would start by considering where you currently are as a writer. If you're just starting out, or new to this genre, then my advice is to begin by reading well and writing simple. Try the authors I've just mentioned, or some from my recommended list (see box). Read them to see what you'd like to write, and how these authors achieved their effects. Then start to draft something simple – descriptions of places you've visited, things that happened, people you met and how you felt about these experiences. Those are the four building blocks of travel writing: places, adventures, people and you.

The personal element – 'you' – is unusual. In travel, unlike some other genres, you're almost always a character in your story. Often you're the central character, the narrator recalling experiences and emotions, whose presence and personality hold the whole thing together. Sometimes this deepens into a metaphorical journey of personal transformation, which can supply a narrative arc. You'll need to consider how to present yourself: as an expert who knows it all, or an innocent abroad who's encountering things for the first time? Think about how much of your real self and backstory you would like to include: flashbacks to your childhood, inner thoughts about the meaning of life, personal responses to the strangenesses of foreign lands ... Especially in travel blogs, the personality of the writer can add a powerful dimension.

If you're beyond the beginner stage, you'll know that building these blocks into the shape of a story is your next challenge. How you do that will depend on the form in which you're planning to write. In our genre, there are three main forms – blogs, articles and books – and they carry different expectations and conventions. Blogs are short and self-defining, articles are written to please editors in the marketplace, and books are huge personal projects with great creative satisfactions. You can explore them all to see which suits. Many travel writers build their careers on success in more than one.

1. Travel blogs

Blogging is the quickest route to seeing your writing published. In just a couple of hours you can set up a free space on Wordpress.com, choose one of their design templates, drop in your text, add photos from a free library like Pixabay, and you're done. This approach is perfect if you're aiming to write about your travels as a hobby or as a journal for friends. Travel blogs tend to be written in a direct, first-person style, as though chatting with the reader, and their length varies from perhaps 800 to 2,000 words. You can format them how you like – first person, third person, narratives, lists or whatever.

If you think your blogging might have commercial possibilities, then try setting yourself up on the sister site Wordpress.org; with this you pay a small subscription but can use your own domain name, and you receive much more functionality in terms of plug-ins that allow you to sell merchandise, for example, or gather a mailing list of followers. If you're going down this route, where you're hoping to reach the public, then have a hard think beforehand about the brand identity and purpose of your blog. Professionals call this your 'niche': what is your subject matter, what sort of readers will be attracted by it and what kind of 'persona' will you present to them? These will be the foundations of what you write, and what you will sell to your fanbase or 'tribe'.

Travel bloggers make their money from a variety of sources: advertisements and links on their site; merchandise such as books or training; and, crucially, paid relationships with travel brands. For example, a tourist board in a particular destination might hire you by the day to visit their location and write about it on your blog. This might extend to a lucrative retainer-type partnership, where you become a brand ambassador for a travel company or product. Such relationships should be declared, for ethical and legal reasons.

Travel blogs to try

- **NomadicMatt.com**

The world's most popular travel blogger, Matthew Kepnes gave up his day job to live on the road and launch this site, which offers advice on affordable travel experiences.

- **Seat61.com**

Classic blog based on a single mode of transport – railway travel – set up by railway executive Mark Smith as a hobby that became a business.

- **ALuxuryTravelBlog.com**

Winner of *Wired* magazine's Best Travel Influencer award, blogger Paul Johnson now has 1.1 million followers reading articles by his 700 guest writers.

- **BudgetTraveller.org**

Hugely successful consumer blog by Kash Battacharya, who now lives as a digital nomad and was *National Geographic Traveller*'s Blogger of the Year in 2016.

- **LiveShareTravel.com**

Successful mix of affordable luxury holidays and authentic travel experiences, developed from 20 years of traditional journalistic experience by Sarah Lee.

2. Travel articles

By contrast to the freedom and fluidity of a blog, articles for magazines or newspapers are written for the marketplace. They must obey strict journalistic formats (such as features or round-ups) and need to please your chosen commissioning editor. Each will focus on a clearly defined angle, delivered in an agreed number of words (somewhere between 900 and 1,600 words). Most are written by freelancers like yourself, and no one will mind whether you're doing it full-time or just feeling your way with a story or two.

As with any form of freelance journalism, start by looking at the range of outlets and who is publishing what. The question in any editor's mind is, 'What will interest my readers?' So, research what will – and offer it. Travel magazines differ hugely, from the stylish luxury of *Condé Nast Traveller*, to the family holidays of *Sunday Times Travel*, to the solo adventures of *Wanderlust*. That will affect what topics you can offer them. Remember, too, to pitch early: magazines work 8-12 months ahead of publication date, and newspapers 6-10 weeks ahead.

The pitch itself can be fairly simple:

Dear X

Would you consider a feature on a new river safari in Zambia during the rainy season, when travellers are rare and game is plentiful?

I have visited safari parks all over Africa and written for the *Independent* and *The Times*.

You can read my writing here [link].

With best wishes

Jonathan Lorie.

The key elements in that pitch are:
• the right name for the recipient (probably a commissioning editor, whose name you've found online)
• which slot you're pitching for (in this case, a feature)
• the angle and destination, and why this is interesting
• anything about your credentials
• a link to samples of your writing (if you don't have any cuttings yet, set up a little blogsite, as described above, to showcase pieces of unpublished work)
• it is short and to the point: editors are very busy.

It is fairly standard that, after emailing your pitch, nothing happens. So resend it with a polite nudge about two weeks later. Then let it go and try another pitch. Statistically, it must be the case that you send more pitches than are accepted, and this effect is bound to be exaggerated when you are an unknown. It is also true that the market for articles is shrinking in all sectors. A short cut for beginners is to aim for outlets that are less prestigious or are not travel publications at all: a golf magazine will probably take a piece about a golf resort somewhere gorgeous, or a food magazine might like an article on a cookery school in Goa. The beauty of a hybrid genre like travel is that it crosses into other areas of interest, where there is less competition for travel articles.

3. Travel books

Compared to the shorter forms of blogs and articles, a travel book is a mighty beast. Readers (and publishers) expect at least 90,000 words in a book, which requires a lot of material and a good strong theme. It also allows you considerable freedom in the shape and style of writing. Readers will be interested in meeting you and spending time in your company, so the writing style and range of interests can be much more personal. What will make it work as a commercial proposition is a theme that is interesting for both writer and readers – sufficient that you will be motivated to complete it well and they will be attracted to buy it.

Getting it published traditionally involved finding yourself a literary agent, who would advise on the manuscript and then sell it to a publisher. This is still the preferred route for many authors, as agents understand the industry and publishers put funds and expertise into the marketing. The way to reach them is with a 'book proposal', which typically consists of a cover letter followed by a synopsis. This describes what the book is about (i.e. the theme), whether there are other books like it already, who might read it and why you are the person to write it. You also need to include a chapter breakdown, which is a list of what happens in each chapter, plus at least one finished chapter, as good as you can make it. You can send the book proposal to several agents at once and see what happens. If they like it, they'll contact you.

Alternatively, these days you can avoid the middleman by self-publishing online. You go onto a website like Amazon or Lulu, drop your manuscript into a design template, and publish it there at once. No agent, no editor, no fuss: but, unfortunately, also no advice and no marketing. Self-publishing is a route that works if you just want to see printed copies of your story, or if you think you can do the marketing yourself. If not, then the traditional route is worth trying first.

The choice of publication route is up to you. What is not really negotiable, however, is the amount of time involved in completing a book. Travel authors often spend three to six months on the road, gathering material and experiences, then six months or more at home, writing it up. Before they take the plunge, they spend many months developing a theme that will work. Do bear this in mind.

But I hardly know a short-form travel writer who does not hanker for the space and freedom of a book-length tale. And I hardly meet a traveller who does not long to write up their trips in some form or other. So whichever of these major routes you choose, it's a wonderful adventure. If you can make a go of this, it will take you around the world. Doors will open, people will talk, experiences will begin. There's not a lot of money in it, but there is a fabulous journey.

Jonathan Lorie is the author of *The Travel Writer's Way: Turn Your Travels into Stories* (Bradt 2019) and director of Travellers' Tales (www.travellerstales.org), the training agency for travel writers. He writes freelance travel features for UK newspapers and magazines and was formerly the editor of *Traveller Magazine* for Wexas Travel. He can be contacted at www.jonathanlorie.com.

See also...
- *Life's a pitch: how to get your ideas into print*, page 7
- *How to submit a non-fiction proposal*, page 423

Writing about science for the general reader

Consultant neurologist Suzanne O'Sullivan has advice for science writers on communicating ideas clearly, without jargon and with purpose and passion, to engage and inform a general audience.

I recently happened upon a museum of barbed wire. I assure you, barbed wire is not a subject to which I had given a moment's thought before, but I have learned that it's fascinating. The museum reminded me that everything has the potential to be interesting if it is told to you in a story. The curators didn't try to draw me into the subject by giving me a dry explanation about the evolution of wire fences from single to double strand, or by describing the numerous types of twists and barbs. I know about these things now, but only because I was told them through the chronicles of cowboys, barbed wire barons and the Wild West. Yeehaa!

The principles of writing about technical subjects for a general audience are the same as those for any other sort of creative writing – it is all about telling a compelling human story, in a language to which the audience can relate. Five years ago, I started writing about my work as a neurologist. I had never written for the public before. It may have seemed to others that I had a radical change of direction in my career. That was not the case. I regard my writing as nothing more than an extension of my everyday interactions with my patients. The skills required to be a good doctor are much more closely aligned to those a writer needs than people realise. Fundamental to medicine is the ability to communicate ideas clearly to audiences of all levels – while never forgetting the person at the heart of the story.

Of course, neuroscience is more innately interesting than barbed wire – but it is also considerably more complex. I have my patients in mind in several different ways when I write about them. Ella came to my clinic in a state of high anxiety. She had had a cluster of seizures and was convinced that she was dying; another doctor had told her that her brain scan was abnormal. Ella had come to me for help. After reviewing her tests, I was able to reassure her that things weren't as bad as she thought. Her scan showed a small scar that was likely to be an anomaly present since birth. It wasn't growing or changing but it was causing epileptic seizures. There was a good chance I could treat those successfully. The scar presented no imminent threat to her life.

I could have given Ella the diagnosis in a completely different way. I could have told her she had a brain tumour – because that's technically what she has. I could have immediately labelled the 'scar' by its proper name: a *dysembryoplastic neurepithelial tumour*. I would of course give her all that information as our conversation progressed, but first I needed to translate the diagnosis into language she could understand and, in doing so, dispel the myths that were frightening her. Things were not as bad as the scientific terminology made them sound.

My first piece of advice to any science writer would be to avoid excessive jargon and to use technical terms very carefully. Think of the audience. Lots of specialist terminology have different meanings to different people. If I told you that you had a brain tumour, what would you think? To a doctor a tumour is just a swelling; not all tumours grow unabated and not all require treatment. But to many people the word 'tumour' is synonymous with cancer … a death sentence. It is a good example of how easily misunderstandings can arise.

Communicating in plain English allows a science writer to avoid the pitfalls caused by the different ways in which specialists and the general public use terminology. Plain English doesn't mean dumbing down. In fact, I would say it is the opposite; people often use complicated terminology to appear knowledgeable, but the ability to express detailed ideas without it is a much more sophisticated skill. Then there is the question of just how technical and detailed one should get. Although science is a body of facts and truth, there are few absolutes. The scientific world is fraught with controversies and disagreements. Medical conferences are hotbeds of debate and rivalry. It would be impossible for any one book to represent every single expert view without simultaneously getting bogged down in unnecessary detail. When I am writing, I have as a constant companion an imaginary panel of angry-looking colleagues sitting on my shoulder criticising my choices. So my second piece of advice is, never forget the purpose of the book you set out to write. I quieten my critics gallery by never allowing myself to lose sight of who I am writing for, and why. Science books written for non-science audiences are not supposed to be textbooks. Textbooks are available if your reader wants to take the next step.

So far so good – you write clearly and keep the audience and the purpose of the book in mind – except, of course, that translating science into an accessible language is the easy bit; it doesn't conflict with a scientist's natural repertoire of abilities. If a reader only wanted the facts, they could read a scientific paper for that; something more is required of creative non-fiction. My next piece of advice is to take a leaf out of the Barbed Wire Museum's book and learn how to be entertaining. That is the bigger challenge, particularly for career scientists who have never been required to be entertaining before – but it's far from impossible because, when you think about it, science is intrinsically full of mystery and high stakes. Science is trying to save the planet and cure cancer and find extraterrestrials. What could be more exciting than that? Show the reader the bigger picture and give them something or someone to root for. Apply the scientific fact to a circumstance from life that people can understand. In medicine that is of course easier than in other fields of science writing.

Ella had her first seizure when she was 15. She was at breakfast with her family when she reported feeling unwell. She started to behave strangely. She became convinced that she could smell something burning. She started talking rubbish, telling her sister over and over again that she could see cartoon horses romping around the room. Her anxiety level built slowly until she abruptly lost consciousness and fell to the floor. When she woke up in hospital, her only memory of the event was eating bagels one moment and battling with paramedics the next. Like so many of my patients, Ella has taught me about resilience and humanity. But the specifics in her story also offer a lesson about how the brain works. From hallucinatory smells, to confusion and illusory visions of cartoon horses, once examined, Ella's experience provides an anatomical tour through the brain. It can be used to cast a light on hallucinations and consciousness, the brain's way of processing smell and vision. The fact that Ella has kindly allowed her story to be shared means that I can do without lists and flow charts and diagrams when talking about the brain.

There is always a story, you just have to find it. Sometimes it is the scientist's own: I was a fledgling doctor once and had many of the same misconceptions about neuroscience as anybody else; I have made lots of mistakes and learned from them; I fell in love with the work I do for a reason. I took a journey to get to where I am now and, when I write, I try to bring people on that journey with me. Scientific discoveries come from hard-fought research, from wrong turns and blind alleyways, and from errors. Sometimes I tell my patients' stories and sometimes I tell my own.

All of science explains something apparently ordinary – but actually extraordinary – in the world around us. So many breakthroughs have come from a brilliant mind observing something that the rest of us took for granted. When I think of gravity, the first thing I think of is Newton sitting under a tree. I cannot picture Archimedes anywhere but in his bath. Evolution brings to mind Darwin's travel to the Galapagos. A teacher wouldn't dream of trying to engage a child in physics or chemistry by showing them an equation. Everything can be related to something that interests people, even if they never considered it as being scientific before; did you know that, by the time a batsman or batswoman sees the ball leave the bowler's hand, they are seeing something that happened a quarter of a second in the past? That was one writer's introduction to a discussion on the speed of light.

There is something incredibly invigorating about enthusing others about your work. I suppose some science writers jump on a bandwagon, exploit the zeitgeist, but I think science writing works best when the writer is genuinely passionate about their subject. If you are not entertaining yourself, how can you expect anybody else to join you? The same applies to the act of writing.

To write a book one must love to write. I started writing in 2013 – writing, apparently out of nowhere, to people who didn't know me. In truth, though, I had had a love of writing since my school days; my greatest ambition as a child was to write a book. Being a doctor distracted me from that ambition for a long time, but I never abandoned the basic building block of writing – which is reading. It may seem obvious, but to write any book (science or otherwise) you have to love reading and you have to love writing. Writing a book is hard work: it takes a long time; there's no guarantee of success; the monetary rewards are measly; sacrifice is required. When I was *just* a doctor my evenings, weekends and holidays were largely free time to do with what I wished. I no longer have time off. I have ever-present deadlines and a constant fear that if I stop writing I'll forget how. My medical career will always be there, my writing career requires maintenance. But if you are honestly driven to write, doing so will enrich your life to such a degree that sacrifices become irrelevant.

Suzanne O'Sullivan is the author of *It's All in Your Head* (Vintage 2016), which won the Wellcome Book Prize and the Royal Society of Biology General Book Prize. She has been a consultant in neurology since 2004 and currently works as a consultant in clinical neurophysiology and neurology at the National Hospital for Neurology and Neurosurgery and for a specialist unit based at the Epilepsy Society. She is the author of *Brainstorm: Detective Stories From the World of Neurology* (Chatto & Windus 2018); her latest book, *The Sleeping Beauties*, about the social life of illness, was published in 2021 (Picador).

So you want to write about nature ...

Melissa Harrison celebrates the resurgence of interest in nature writing, a genre in which honesty, authenticity and integrity are valued above all by readers. She has advice and encouragement for writers on how best to nourish and communicate their personal connection with nature.

It's often said, these days, that nature writing is enjoying something of a boom. But 'nature writing' is a broad church, and a term that's arguably more useful to bookshops and publishers than it is to authors, including travel writing, memoir, psychogeography, landscape archaeology, craft, zoology, botany and ornithology, essay collections, fiction, ecology, poetry and many other types of books. Still, shelf space devoted to writing that is in some way about the outdoors does seem to have increased in the last decade, and I can attest to the fact that the trickle of proofs crossing my desk in the hope of a 'blurb', or an endorsement, has swelled from a trickle to – well, not a flood, but certainly a steady stream.

This recent surge of interest should not obscure the fact that the UK has a long tradition of writing about the natural world, one that stretches back in an unbroken line for several hundred years (and one which will vastly enrich the imaginations of all hopeful nature writers). It could be said, with some justification, that we have never *not* been writing about nature. However, during that time there have been some distinct 'golden eras', often linked to anxiety-inducing events like war or economic depression, in which more books than usual have been produced and read. And now, in a time of great financial, political and environmental uncertainty, it seems that once again writers are turning to the outdoors as their subject. Publishers, picking up on the trend, have commissioned greater numbers of books about nature, and agents have found themselves looking favourably on manuscripts they might not have perceived a market for, if not for the current upswell in public appetite for writing about the wild.

As with every bubble, there is a risk of the moment passing and that appetite dissipating – particularly if shops become oversaturated with cynically conceived, unfelt books all with 'retro' covers, earnest quotes, a hint of personal tragedy and the same clichéd 'quest' or 'three-act' structures inside (if you're starting to suspect I may have come across a few of these already, you'd be right). But let's assume you're neither a Johnny-come-lately bandwagon-jumper nor a writer in search of a project, *any* project. Let's assume that you're someone with a way with words and a genuinely deep and heartfelt connection to nature who wants to communicate that interest and connection to others. How should you go about doing so?

The first thing (as with writing of any kind) is not to set much store by writing tips or 'how to' guides – including this one, which is why I won't be offering you detailed advice on how to actually produce your manuscript. The best work is born of deep, clear-eyed and hard-won self-knowledge, with a side-helping of trial and error, courage and mistakes; seeking to emulate the techniques or the oeuvre of others will only distract from the difficult but necessary path of getting to know and accept yourself and your creative method, with all your oddities, foibles and individual strengths.

The goal, when making art of any kind, isn't to produce something similar to what already exists; the goal is to discover what it is that you uniquely need to say to the world, and then find a way to say it. In a genre like nature writing, which prizes authenticity and integrity particularly highly, this is perhaps the most important thing to keep in mind. If you find yourself trying to come up with a subject that hasn't been done to death, thinking you might produce a new twist on an existing book, or researching which subjects are selling well, your book will lack any authenticity; worse, it may become part of an embarrassing glut of similar books by writers who are casting about (as you have) for 'the next big thing'. So don't look to the market for ideas, or to how-to guides for your working method. When it comes to creativity, the place to begin is always inside; if what comes from that place is exceptional enough, it won't have to fit in – it will create a space of its own.

When I began to write, all I knew was that nature most moved me – yet I didn't think I could write about it as others did, because I wasn't an 'expert'. That's partly why my first book, *Clay* (Bloomsbury 2013), took the form of a novel rather than descriptive non-fiction about urban ecology (which, frankly, might have been quite boring, and definitely wouldn't have reached the wide audience of ordinary people that a work of fiction did). Thankfully, times have changed in the nature writing world, and I don't think I would feel the same insecurity now.

You certainly don't have to be an expert to write about any aspect of nature as long as: 1) you are willing to bring rigour to your research (including trying to keep in mind that there will always be things you don't know you don't know!); 2) you have the humility to ask questions and allow yourself to be corrected; 3) most importantly, you're brave enough to bring the truth about your doubts and lack of expertise into your work. If you're an interested amateur with a great angle, that's fine – just don't pretend to have knowledge you don't have, for in a small world peopled with highly knowledgeable people you'll be found out sooner or later. Instead, let the reader see when you've had to look something up; allow the truth of your subjective experience into your work. If it's done well, readers – most of whom won't be experts either – will identify with your writing more, and what you produce will have the crucial ring of authenticity. Marc Hamer, in his memoir *How to Catch a Mole: And Find Yourself in Nature* (Harvill Secker 2019), sees little birds fly past and doesn't know what they are (he finds out later); in *Timesong: Searching for Doggerland* (Vintage 2019), Julia Blackburn describes repeatedly getting lost, misclassifying fossils, and identifying a seagull as a peregrine falcon and a roe deer as a hare. Both books are wonderful; neither is diminished by the author's honesty. Quite the reverse.

Many people who write about the natural world bring to it something of a crusading spirit. They want to draw the public's attention to global warming, or habitat loss or species decline. Few books – let's be honest – will by themselves create any sort of lasting change, but they may form part of a wider conversation; and anyway, there's nothing wrong with a little idealism if it helps you find a sense of meaning in your chosen path. *Clay*, in its way, was strongly evangelical; I wanted to open people's eyes to the overlooked richness of the natural world in cities, as it had been so transformative in my own life.

If creating change is your driving motivation, think carefully about how you want to effect it: do you want to wake readers up with hard facts and nudge them into action of some kind, or do you want to inspire a love of nature and a sense of emotional connection? It's possible to do both – see, for instance, Michael McCarthy's *The Moth Snowstorm* – but it's difficult. The risk with writing that campaigns explicitly is that it can end up bashing people over the head with bad news and paralysing them with guilt, while the accusation that can be levelled at purely inspiring or descriptive writing is that it is self-indulgent or – worse – falsely comforting, allowing readers to turn away from the issues we currently face.

Every nature writer must choose their own ground on this central dilemma; even David Attenborough has found himself caught on its horns. To work out your position, read widely, critically, but non-judgmentally, and don't assume that the things that inspire you or stir you into action will necessarily have the same effect on everyone else. For that is crucial. If you can constantly challenge yourself to de-centre your own experience and bear in mind how different others' lives are, the writing you produce about the natural world will reach more people and change more lives – for long gone are the days of supposed objectivity; there is no 'view from nowhere', we know now. It's so easy, as a nature-lover, to start from the assumption that our own relationship with nature is obviously, universally beneficial and desirable. But that assumption leads to an inward-looking, homogenous sector – one that leaves behind individuals and communities who may need to prioritise employment, housing, personal safety or immigration status over the far less tangible benefits of time spent outdoors, or who simply prefer other pursuits.

Above all, feed your compost heap, and feed it carefully and well. The compost is the fertile soil of your imagination, and you need to keep chucking good things on it if you want anything worthwhile to grow. Get out and explore with your sketchbook, binoculars, sound recorder or camera; go to photography exhibitions and art galleries that relate to nature, place or landscape, or find electrifying art to look at online; follow interesting, creative people on social media who make things you never could, and educators who will expand your knowledge of your subject; play beautiful, groundbreaking computer games, watch documentaries, box sets or disaster movies if they chime with your interests in writing or the natural world; and read, read, read ... Not just contemporary nature writing, or the nature writers of the past (though don't neglect them!), but whatever feeds the central spark of your imagination, no matter how obliquely – whether that's graphic novels or social history, critical theory or crime. Ideas come from all sorts of places, and the wider the range of high-quality (which doesn't mean highbrow) material you feed it, the more productive your compost heap will prove.

Then, when your pile is fully fertile, when you've discovered exactly what it is you are driven to put out into the world, when you're clear on the good you want it to do, if any, and you've found the courage to risk failing (the courage every writer needs for every book, no matter how experienced) – only then is it time to take off your muddy boots, go indoors, and begin writing.

Melissa Harrison is the author of three novels, all published by Bloomsbury: *Clay* (2013), *At Hawthorn Time* (2016), which was shortlisted for the Costa Novel Award and longlisted for the Bailey's Women's Prize, and *All Among the Barley* (2018), which won the European Union Prize for Literature. She has also published a non-fiction book, *Rain: Four Walks in English Weather* (Faber 2016) and edited four seasonal collections, *Spring/Summer/Autumn/Winter: An Anthology for the Changing Seasons* (Elliott & Thompson 2016). A collection of her *Nature Notebook* columns for *The Times*, *The Stubborn Light of Things* (Faber 2020), became a *Sunday Times* Nature Book of the Year. Her debut children's book, *By Ash, Oak and Thorn* was published in 2021 by Chicken House. Melissa is a regular contributor to the *Guardian*, the *Weekend FT* and the *New Statesman*. For more information see https://melissaharrison.co.uk or follow her on Twitter @M_Z_Harrison.

Books

Writing for the health and wellness market

Health writer Anita Bean offers advice on how to find success in the popular and fast-moving health and wellness market, using some essential ingredients – fresh ideas, careful research, trustworthy content and strong, clever marketing.

When I began writing freelance in 1990, the health and wellness market was quite niche compared to what is today. Back then, it comprised mostly slimming magazines, which were targeted exclusively at women. As a nutritionist, I was – fortunately – in high demand. My first regular commission was a column for *Slimmer* magazine, and after that folded I had a regular column in *Zest* and *She*. In those days, most publications preferred to use freelancers rather than staff writers, so there was certainly plenty of work around.

The market has changed hugely over the past 25 years, thanks largely to the internet. So many more people are interested in health and wellness, not just slimmers. You'll find regular health and wellness features in just about every print and digital medium – even the financial and business press! The other major change is the decreased use of freelancers by mainstream media, as tighter budgets mean many more health and wellness features are now written in-house.

This is both good and bad for health writers. More media channels and bigger audiences mean there's loads of potential work out there for us. Editors need to fill more column inches and digital space, so they are perpetually on the lookout for new health content. The downside is that every man and his dog now seem to be an 'expert' and there's nothing to stop them writing about health and wellness on the internet. As a result, good (that is, evidence-based) content has become diluted in a tsunami of poor content put out there by bloggers, self-styled 'experts' and social media stars with a large Instagram following and impressive six-packs. The public are often left confused and, nowadays, no longer know who to trust for health advice.

How I got into writing

As a child, I was always curious about the science of food – what's in it, what happens when you add this to that, what happens to food in the body – and I was forever experimenting in the kitchen, cooking and creating recipes. I also loved reading cookery books and built up quite a collection over the years – I would devour every morsel of information I could find about food and nutrition.

At school, I loved home economics (now food technology) but was more fascinated by food chemistry. So I went on to study for a degree in Nutrition and Food Science at the University of Surrey and – unusually for a girl back in the 80s – started lifting weights. I qualified both as a registered nutritionist and, after winning the British bodybuilding championships in 1991, as a fitness instructor.

I honed my writing skills while I worked as a nutritionist for the Dairy Council. I wrote booklets and articles about health and nutrition, and also developed an interest in the organisation's sports sponsorship activities. I realised that there was virtually no nutrition information available for athletes or regular exercisers. There was clearly a gap in the market for such a book! So, I handed in my notice and decided to enter the world of freelance health writing.

Getting your lucky break

As with many things in life, getting that lucky break in writing is often a case of being in the right place at the right time, seizing an opportunity and taking a risk. You also need to have a strong belief in your idea, and be persistent. That's essentially how I got my first book deal in 1992 (*The Complete Guide to Sports Nutrition*) when I sent my proposal to Bloomsbury (then A&C Black), as well as many other publishers. There was nothing on sports and exercise nutrition in the UK trade market but, luckily, this commissioning editor happened to be on the lookout for a sports nutrition book to add to her sports list. My proposal landed at just the right time. But it was a risk for both of us, as it was an untapped and unknown market.

Fortunately, the market turned out to be a lot bigger than anticipated; as well as publicising the book to athletes, I also looked up my contacts list and targeted fitness training providers, schools and universities. The book was soon placed on the recommended list for many higher education courses, which now account for a large proportion of its sales. There's no single secret to a book's success, but it's often a combination of fresh ideas, excellent content and savvy marketing.

Build your brand

The other aspect of writing is longevity. It's tempting to sit back on your laurels after you've published a book and let sales look after themselves. But that won't happen. You need to put sustained effort into building your reputation and marketing yourself and your work. As a new writer, I offered to provide nutrition talks for health clubs and fitness training organisations who then recommended my books to their students. I also gave talks to athletes, spoke at conferences, and provided quotes and commentary to the media. Much of this was either underpaid or unpaid but it was always done in return for a book plug. And any editorial coverage is worth so much more in terms of endorsement. Whether you're a new or an established author, it's important to get your name out there – and keep it there!

In the world of health and wellness, trends change fast, and what's hot one minute can be out of favour the next. The key to a book's longevity is to update it regularly to reflect new thinking and the demands of a fast-changing market. I've now written eight editions of my first book. Each time, I re-examine the content to ensure it is current and relevant to my readership. I add extra material and cut sections that I feel are no longer engaging my readers.

Market your work

In the highly competitive world of health and wellness, doing your own marketing is more important than ever before. I strongly recommend having your own website. This is not only a brilliant way of marketing your books and writing services but is also a platform to showcase your published work. Providing free information in the form of articles and recipes is also a great way of establishing your credibility and attracting potential book sales. You don't need to spend a fortune (you can build your own site) but the more time and effort you put into your website, the greater will be the return in terms of future commissions. It's also crucial to update your site regularly, add new content, ditch stuff

Books

that has become less relevant and learn a bit about search engine optimisation. I've re-designed my website (https://anitabean.co.uk) three times since 2004. I provide free articles and recipes, and a free downloadable ebook. To sustain a regular readership, I aim to post a new blog a minimum of once a month.

Having a social media presence is also crucial for a health writer. It's not only a great way of letting people know about your work but is also essential for keeping up to date and finding out what people are talking about. I recommend focusing your efforts on just two or three platforms, whichever are most relevant to your target market. For me, Twitter and Instagram work very well. I use Twitter for sharing new information, publicising my work (e.g. new books, blog posts and articles) and finding out what's new in health. I post photos of recipes from my latest book on Instagram to help spread the word.

Seven tips on breaking into the health and wellness market

1. Identify a gap in the market

Read, read, read – find out what's new and emerging. Research what's already out there, your competition, and then work out how you can make your product better. Keep an eye on trends and try to stay ahead of the game – be the first to write about a new topic, not the last.

2. Generate new ideas

Network with colleagues and experts at conferences; this is also useful for building up a contact list of experts for quotes. Mingle with your audience before and after presentations – what do they want to know, what are their concerns? Social media can be a great place to pick up on what's trending and on ideas for blogs, articles and books.

3. Know your readership

Do your research – actually *read* the magazine you want to write for, so you get a feel of who the readers are and what they want to read about. Get on their level and talk their language.

4. Improve your content

Accuracy is paramount; always use evidence (not just 'research says…') and cite or link to the source or study abstract. Always add a practical element ('– now here's how you can use this info...').

5. Adapt your style

Be adaptive and always write to, not at, your reader as if you were speaking to them. Aim to inspire them, and for your reader to say, 'Oh, I didn't know that!' by the end of the piece. Make your article or book unique and different from the competition, not just a companion to what's already out there.

6. Be consistent

Ensure your messages are consistent across everything you write (e.g. you can't be pro-carb one minute and low-carb the next), but be prepared to change your view if new research comes to light.

7. Don't slavishly follow trends

Just because other writers are raving about a new thing – say, coconut oil – doesn't mean you have to. Question a trend; where did it start? Often it stems from clever PR rather than science. And don't believe everything a PR sends you; look beyond the headlines – where did the story come from? Read the original research, and only write about the product if you believe it stands up to scrutiny, not just to fill a column or to generate a grabby headline.

Anita Bean is an award-winning registered nutritionist, freelance health writer and author of 30 books, including *The Complete Guide to Sports Nutrition, The Vegetarian Athlete's Cookbook, The Runner's Cookbook, Food for Fitness* and *The Complete Guide to Strength Training* and *Nutrition for Young Athletes* (all published by Bloomsbury). Her latest book is *The Vegan Athlete's Cookbook* (Bloomsbury 2021). She has written features for many national magazines, including *Good Housekeeping, Cycling Weekly, Runner's World, Waitrose Weekend, Waitrose Health* and *Women's Running*. Visit Anita's website at https://anitabean.co.uk.

Writing sports books

Frances Jessop describes how, in sports publishing, a quick-thinking and creative author can grasp an opportunity or take advantage of a new angle to find success. Here she gives clear advice on what an editor is looking for in a proposal for a sports book.

A book of his quotes, a compilation of the season's programme notes, a self-described love letter to him, multiple biographies, numerous accounts telling the story of the season, and a fictional diary of life married to him – so many books have been published about manager Jürgen Klopp following Liverpool's Premiership win of 2019/20 that he's practically a football sub-genre. Liverpool's triumph and their highly quotable and likeable manager have spawned books that perfectly illustrate both the breadth and depth of sports writing and the opportunities open to authors and publishers who can think quickly and imaginatively.

What makes a good (and successful) sports book?

There are as many types of sports books as there are types of non-fiction, however many fit into one of three varieties. Firstly, the autobiography or biography of a sporting figure – what many people imagine when they think of a sports book. Their subjects range from household names to pioneers of a sport and everything in between. What the good ones have in common are insight and access. Many autobiographies are ghostwritten and the more time the writer has had to spend with the subject, the better the book. If they have been able to interview people surrounding their subject, then a much more nuanced and layered portrait will emerge. A gold standard in autobiography (across all genres) is Andre Agassi's *Open* (HarperCollins 2010). As the title suggests, he is breathtakingly honest about his relationship with tennis and the struggles he has faced in his career. This candour and vulnerability, combined, of course, with a highly successful career and an engaging character, make for a terrific book.

Secondly, many of the books I have published could be described as narrative non-fiction that happens to be set in the sporting world. One of the best non-fiction books I've read is *Friday Night Lights* by H.G. Bissinger (Yellow Jersey Press 2005), which was subsequently adapted into a film and a long-running television drama. It's 'about' American football in Texas, but it's actually about small town life, growing up, hopes and dreams. The best sporting narratives are often described as books you'd enjoy even if you aren't a fan of the particular sport. Sport is a great leveller; there's a universality to sport that makes it an excellent prism through which to tell bigger stories, something which good books do to great effect.

Sports publishing is opportunistic, as can be seen by the flurry of books that inevitably appear following a successful Olympic Games or a triumph that captures the imagination. A third type of book is one that has a clear opportunity of this kind – perhaps due to a tournament, an anniversary or a spectacular result. These books are often a gamble – after all, as every football manager knows, the only result that counts is the most recent one – but when they work can be very successful. It is often said that you need to be the best or the first, and with this type of book being *first* is often what really counts, which makes for some hair-raising schedules! A good sports book of this kind has a clear market, an excellent hook for publicity and timeliness. In 2016 at Yellow Jersey Press, I published one of those biographies of Liverpool manager Jürgen Klopp. We knew that he was popular with fans, who tend to heavily support books about the club and its players and managers. He was doing well, which meant we hoped he'd be a long-term appointment, plus the book would be out in advance of any trophies he won with the club. And we had the perfect author, someone who had excellent access to Klopp's friends, family and colleagues and could deliver the definitive story of his career. Happily for everyone, Klopp fulfilled that promise, as did the book.

More than anything, finding a new angle or a story that hasn't been told is key. Some people are brilliant at this, with a knack for spotting sides of their sport that haven't been explored. Most great sports books start with a question, such as: 'Will anyone ever run a marathon in under two hours?' [Ed Caesar's *Two Hours* (Viking 2015)]; 'What's it really like to be a professional athlete? Could I do it?' [George Plimpton's *Paper Lion* (Yellow Jersey Press 2016)].

Pitching a sports book: the proposal

Like any other non-fiction, most sports books are sold on proposal. Whether you're submitting directly to a publisher or to an agent, a good proposal contains an introduction to the project, which includes: an overview of the story; why now is the time to tell it; why you are uniquely qualified (this is just as important as your professional experience – I've commissioned new writers who are perfectly placed to write their book just as often as experienced writers); and research to show the book's place in the market. Also needed is a detailed summary of the chapters, in order to assess the shape of the story, although, as you write it this might change, so don't be concerned about being beholden to a structure that doesn't work. Finally, a sample of your writing is essential – a chapter or two will do, and make sure it's as polished as possible.

You will need to give an idea of when you'll deliver the manuscript. With most sports books there's likely to be an obvious time to publish it – for example, ahead of the Tour de France for cycling books, before a World Cup or the start of the season for football books. Also important are gifting opportunities – many sports books are given as gifts, so Father's Day and Christmas are sales peaks. Ideally, books are delivered a year in advance of publication to allow time for editorial work, for the cover to be designed, the production process (copy-editing, typesetting, proofreading, etc), and to have the final book in plenty of time for the sales department to sell it in to retailers and for the publicity and marketing team to plan and execute their campaigns. However, in order to make the most of a window of opportunity, this process is often compressed – so being able to work quickly and deliver in a reasonable timeframe is very attractive to a publisher. But do be realistic: late delivery is intensely frustrating for publishers, resulting in either a book being rushed or it having to be moved on, possibly missing the ideal publication date. Both scenarios can severely affect its commercial potential.

Many publishers only accept submissions from agents, but in sports publishing we do see far more direct approaches from authors. In principle, publishers are happy to see a well-written and comprehensive proposal, no matter how it comes to them, and if time is a factor then it can make sense to come directly to publishers, particularly if there is an obvious home for a book. However, agents can contribute a great deal to the publishing process, not least by taking care of the contract negotiations, so it's often worth taking advantage of that extra step. See section *Literary agents*, page 405.

Most sports books will require interviews, so it's helpful to have an idea of who you intend to interview and to show if you've already got links to them. By all means include a wish list, but where you do have contacts make this clear, and where you don't, outline how you might get to those interviewees.

Some research into the market and competitor titles is useful. Publishers do this research too, but it helps to be given a view on how you see your book positioned and what the market looks like, particularly in less mainstream sports. And just because a sport isn't mainstream it doesn't mean they won't want to publish it. On the contrary, more diversity in sports writing, such as more books on women's sport and sports that are underrepresented on television, would be very much welcomed. It does mean, though, that author and editor will need to work a bit harder to build a case and to prove there's an audience out there waiting for this book. As well as comparison titles, think about providing viewing figures, attendance numbers, the sport's social media reach and ways in which the athletes reach their fans.

Finally, it's important to understand that not all books get commissioned and the vast majority are turned down by at least one publisher. Please don't get disheartened. Publishing is an extremely subjective industry: editors must fall in love with a book (or spy an unmissable publishing opportunity), enough to make colleagues fall for it too; those colleagues, in turn, will make retailers and book reviewers desperate to stock or review it, and they will persuade readers to buy it. We all have different tastes; what leaves one person cold will be perfect for another.

There are many things editors consider when evaluating a proposal, other than simply whether it's good enough to be published. Numerous questions run through their minds as they look at a proposal: Is it well written? Does the story grab them? Do they know there's a market for it? What publicity and marketing opportunities are there? Is the schedule already full (publishing schedules are usually filled at least a year ahead, barring one or two late must-haves)? What's the balance of the list like – do they have space for another football/cycling/tennis book? We've all turned down books we loved but which just weren't right for us at that particular time, for any of the above reasons and more.

What an editor wants you to know

If you've got a commission, congratulations! Your editor will be excited to publish your book and to share it with colleagues. Here are a few things that I've told almost every writer during the writing and editing process.

Firstly, you're doing a great job – writing a book is hard. Most writers have a wobble at some point and your editor is there to be a sounding board and to offer some advice or just moral support. They would always rather hear from you than for you to suffer in silence.

Don't panic if you don't already have loads of industry contacts. Most people are willing to help you or to point you in the right direction. Be clear about what you want, polite and willing to travel or be flexible. Often one interviewee will lead you to another and your network will blossom. Be persistent; PR offices are hectic places, so keep trying in a variety of ways and your patience may well be rewarded. Be creative about who you approach –

the star names would be ideal, but you might get more insight (and time) from someone recently retired or the next level down.

When writing, keep notes on your sources. Many sports book need a libel read if the subjects are still living and you will save yourself a lot of time (and money – the cost of libel reads are shared between publishers and authors) if you have this information to hand.

Finally, it's surprising how little sport you actually want in a sports book. Endless descriptions of what happened in a football match are superfluous and drain the pace from a narrative. Save the blow-by-blow detail for when it's necessary and when it adds real drama. On a similar note, the usual adage applies: *show, don't tell*. Don't tell us why something is important, show it; where possible, let us hear directly from interviewees instead of telling us what they said.

In summary: be curious, be creative, think strategically about where opportunities might be found and read widely for inspiration and instruction. There are some wonderful stories out there waiting to be turned into brilliant sports books – I look forward to reading your take on them.

Frances Jessop is a senior editor at Simon & Schuster working across sport and general non-fiction. She spent nine years at Penguin Random House commissioning literary sports books at Yellow Jersey Press, as well as working on fiction and non-fiction paperbacks for Vintage. She started her publishing career at Blackwell Publishing in Oxford and then worked in the literary agency at the William Morris Agency. Follow her on Twitter @francesjessop.

Poetry
How to become a poet

Poet Andrew McMillan knows that poetry is a state of mind and being, a full-time commitment, and has practical advice for would-be poets looking to find their own voice and a path to publication.

The most important thing is to choose exactly the right size of beret to accommodate the shape of your head; everything else will hinge on this first decision.

OK, don't worry, this article will contain much more practical help (hopefully) than that first sentence, though it strikes me that, even in the writing of it, I was doing what one of the key processes of being a poet is: paying attention to the rhythm and feel of language as it is spoken out loud. Originally, my jokey opening line read '… exactly the right shape of beret to accommodate the size of your head'. That didn't quite work, for reasons I can't quite put my finger on. There's a nicer echo between 'right' and 'size'; also, 'shape' and 'head' feel more companionable than 'size' and 'head' which – perhaps because of that 'z' sound and the 'd' – just don't sit well together.

Paying attention to language, then, but also to the world – that's really the only trick to master. Poetry is a state of mind rather than a vocation (disclaimer: it's also impossible to write about it without straying into the realms of vaguely pretentious cliché). Being a poet isn't something you can really sit down at the desk and just 'do', in the same way that you might sit down and turn out 500 more words of your novel. It's not about the fancy notebook that cost £15 that's too nice to ever write in; it's not about berets or fashion choices, or the perfect desk space; it's a mode of being in the world.

I've always thought that if a choreographer witnessed a fight in a bar, they'd probably see it as different dance moves; they'd focus on the movements and the arc of a particular uppercut swing. It's the same with poetry – it's a way of inhabiting every moment, looking at things a certain way, seeing how a certain small thing might speak to something wider. If you're a student studying on a course or at a university, you can't just be a poet for the two or three hours you're in class that day; it has to be something you endeavour to do all the time, in the background, as you go about the rest of your life.

Perhaps I'm getting ahead of myself though. The first step towards becoming a poet must be to *read poetry*. Read as much of it as you can. It's a cliché by now, but it certainly has some truth to it, that if everyone who was writing poetry was also actively *buying* it, then all poets would be millionaires. We all come to writing because we were readers first, and that's always important to remember. Every so often I encounter someone who repeats the mantra, 'I don't read other people's work because I don't want to be influenced.' That is basically the same thing as saying, 'I want to be a tennis player, but I don't think I should ever watch a tennis match. It would distract me from my own training to become Wimbledon Champion.'

Obviously, we read poetry because we love poetry and it's the thing that sustains us through our lives, but we also read to see what other people are managing to do with the page, with language, with rhythm, with rhyme, with ideas. So, the first step is to read as much as you can get your hands on. Read widely, from the so-called 'mainstream' across to the avant-garde; read things from the past and read a lot of contemporary poetry. That way you'll get a sense of the lie of the land, too; you'll see which publishers publish which type of work, which publishers are the ones who always seem to be publishing the poets you're really drawn to.

Don't be afraid of reading things you *don't* like as well ... spend some time with your discomfort and your displeasure. Why is it you don't like this book? What could it have done differently? What does it make you want to do differently in your own practice? Reading in this way is how we come to find our own 'voice' in poetry. At first you'll wear your influences heavily, but then they will start to become simply your own voice, like the finished soup that is boiling in the pot, made up of all the different ingredients that have been flung in.

Getting published

So ... you're reading lots, you're beginning to get a handle on what the world of poetry looks like out there, but it probably still feels impossibly far off. You've got your sheaf of poems, sitting on your desk or on the dining table or in your bottom drawer, and you think you're ready to start sending them off. There is no fixed trajectory for a poet in terms of how it's best to do things, but the perceived wisdom would be that a typical path might be:

Single poems in magazines/competitions → pamphlet → first full collection.

I've oversimplified that wildly, so I'll spend some time now unpacking each of those.

Poetry **magazines** are really the coalface of poetry; they're where the really new work is published, and a great way for new poets to begin to get their name out there. They might not have vast readerships, but people do read them and if your name starts turning up on the pages of different ones people will begin to recognize you, and that's how you begin to build a reputation. One of the most exciting things to witness in the last few years has been an explosion of brilliant new places to be published, both online and in print.

There's a huge variety of poetry magazines out there, all of which cater to a different sort of work: new modernism, accessible, experimental (see **Poetry magazines** on page 337). Spend some time with the magazines (libraries, particularly dedicated poetry libraries or university campus libraries, will often stock them). Try and compare your work to the work you're seeing published on their pages, not in terms of quality, but in terms of style. There's no point in sending your highly experimental language-breaking poetry to the magazine that likes accessible, anecdotal, 20-line poems, but there will be a magazine out there that suits you much more. When you've found one that does, check the submission guidelines, and send off your work. If the work's accepted, there'll be a few months' wait until it appears, but that thrill of your first poem in print is one that never goes away. If you do get published and the magazine offers you the chance to read at a launch event, or asks you to take part in an online launch, do take part if you can find any way of doing so. That experience of meeting the editors, or giving a reading, is vital.

Once you've done a few years of that kind of thing, you might have a smallish stack of poems that you think is ready for the world; this is when you'd begin to think about publishing a **pamphlet**, almost like the EP before the full album. Pamphlets are great as a testing ground for your work; they carry much less weight than a full first collection, and

I think of them almost like a business card that you can hand out (or hopefully sell) or send on to the people you're hoping to impress.

Then, far off in the distance, is that first **collection**, but we probably don't need to worry about that … yet. Except to say that it can and will happen, and it will be the most thrilling feeling in the world when you first open the box that contains the books.

I'm saying all this because it's the process I went through myself. I was lucky enough to grow up in a house of poetry, so I saw that it was a tangible living thing; I know not everyone has that kind of privilege, and that's why in writing things like this, I hope to demystify some of the process.

When I was still an undergraduate I sent off a couple of my poems to a magazine called *The North* and, by some sort of beginner's fluke, they got accepted … and I thought I'd made it! Of course, what followed were loads and loads of rejections, which if compiled would probably make a volume as thick as this *Yearbook* you're holding. But eventually, I did have enough poems for a pamphlet.

A new pamphlet prize called the Michael Marks Award had just started, and so I looked at a list of the pamphlet publishers who had submitted to it. I found one that seemed as though it would like the sort of stuff I was writing, Red Squirrel Press, and sent an email followed by lots of work to them. They accepted a first pamphlet, which came out in 2009, and then published a second in 2011, and then a third in 2013.

Finally, I felt I was ready for a first collection, and I looked around at the books on my shelves and asked myself whose list would I dream of being on. I wanted to try it; if I failed, I'd work my way down my imaginary list. I chose Jonathan Cape, and was lucky enough to get taken on.

It all started with that love of poetry, staying up too late reading poets, and repeating lines or phrases back to myself as I walked around the house. I knew I wanted, in however small a way, to be a part of that conversation, and that's why I wanted to become a poet. Hopefully that's why you do, as well.

Andrew McMillan's first collection, *physical* (Jonathan Cape 2015), was the first poetry collection to win the *Guardian* First Book Award; it also won a Somerset Maugham Award, an Eric Gregory Award, a Northern Writers' Award and the Aldeburgh First Collection Prize. In 2019 it was voted one of the top 25 poetry books of the past 25 years by the Booksellers Association. His second collection, *playtime* (Jonathan Cape 2018) won the inaugural Polari Prize. He is a senior lecturer at the Manchester Writing School at Manchester Metropolitan University and a Fellow of the Royal Society of Literature.

See also...
- *Notes from a passionate poet*, page 334
- *Getting your poetry out there*, page 336

Poetry

Poems for the page and on stage

Raymond Antrobus celebrates poetry on the page and in performance, a passion he shares with fellow poet Anthony Anaxagorou. Here he records their views on writing and reading poetry in private and in public spaces to offer comfort, particularly in times of change.

While London was in lockdown, I and my fellow poet Anthony Anaxagorou, curator of Out-Spoken and Out-Spoken Press, decided to choose four poems (by other poets) to read on Instagram live. We started this series a month ago [in March 2020] and, as of the time of writing this article, each week we have attracted between 300 and 400 viewers. We discuss the poems and why they resonated with us in these times of uncertainty.

At first, I was unsure of how this would be received. I was anxious that at times it felt more like exploiting the moment rather than living it but, after a month of these sessions, I can see how it is sharing the moment we're living in with people – giving a sort of fly-on-the-wall perspective to the kind of private discussions Anthony and I, as peers, have been having for years about the writing and reading of poetry. We found that these discussions have helped give a wider dimension to the Audenesque anxieties of our times; the crucial element to it is that it is improvised, unrehearsed sharing.

For example, Anthony and I don't know in advance which poems each of us is going to read; everything is revealed live, but there is often a natural relationship of some kind that happens between each of the poems. In the third episode we both happened to choose poems with animals and children in them, poems that ask questions rather than claim answers; in some there were tones of cynicism woven around sentimentality. Sometimes images even reoccur within the poems we chose, and Anthony and I delight in these mystic synchronicities.

Last week I asked Anthony if he missed giving readings and performances. He said no – he prefers reading poetry alone and engaging with poems on the page to reading for an audience. Watching poetry readings online, I notice that a lot of poems do sound the same in the air even though they make different sounds and shapes on the page. There is an assumed poetry voice for every poem – a kind of jolting, careful reading where, even if the content has different tones, it is still read in that same kind of stately, over-pronounced voice.

Coming from the spoken word scene, I know that part of the craft is knowing how to surprise an audience beyond just the words; the voice and body also have agency, in the same way that line-breaks and line length do on the page. In performance, monotony bores audiences – you see it – but this is craft talk for poems in performance, something rarely considered by poets who only think of the readers who come to them on the page.

Anthony's preference for engaging on his own with poems on the page is significant, because both of us started out on the London 'open mic' circuit. We both co-curate poetry nights (mine were Chill Pill and Keats House Poets Forum, and his was Out-Spoken). Anthony, as well as running a live night, also runs a publishing house (Out-Spoken Press). I miss giving readings where you feel your poems connecting with audiences in real time, but I do also love quietly reading other people's poems privately on the page. I love geeking out about enjambments and voltas and how to create volume and surprise around the white space. I read poetry collections the way most people read novels; first poem to last poem fast, then going again – first poem to last poem – marking the poems that moved me.

For years Anthony has been the one person I know who has both that kind of sustained, intense relationship with poetry on the page and also comes from the stage. Polarising stage and page has always felt like a loaded issue to me, in the sense that the open mic and spoken word scene is a lot more diverse culturally than the literary scene. The dismissal of spoken word as low art, from the *Guardian* to *PN Review*, came with racial and class undertones; it's a kind of prejudice hidden in language, but it works both ways. Poets I know who also come from the spoken word scene say literary poets are too posh, that they write poems where you don't know if they're starting or finishing. I do understand that, but this is a discussion about the expectations of audience. Those poems that end quietly without declaring some kind of resolve or punch line are often expecting their audience to meet the poem halfway. This requires a different kind of listening – a kind of listening that engages subtlety with meanings that are sometimes less immediate. Often there are no digressions or statements or opinions of the poet guiding the poem; it's more of a focusing-in on smaller moments or ideas.

Now, I don't want to privilege one style over the other. To pull off a quality spoken-word performance and a good page poem takes craft and talent. But talking to Anthony about performance has highlighted to me that, as we've grown older, our taste has developed and our expectations of poetry have changed. However, there is still a fundamental integrity in what we expect from poems, and that is a kind of widening curiosity and wonder about the world and our existence – an openness. I think an easier way to put it is: heart and imagination.

Even now, I remember the slam poems from my days in Slam. 'Gay Poem' by Keith Jarrett beat me in a national Slam championship final back in 2009. The poem is a conversation between the poem and the poet: the poem comes to life to ask the poet, 'Am I gay?' In spoken word, there is a lot of space for self-affirmation because of how active the body and voice is in the way poems are received. This poem stood out because it engages with the visibility and *invisibility* of the poet.

Other memorable poems from the London spoken word scene include Ross Sutherland's poem about how the language of customer service has changed over the centuries (Ross performs his dramatic poem in the dialect of each period of history between a customer and a shopkeeper), and Kate Tempest's poem 'Ballad of a Hero' about a soldier returning from war, which she performed at a reading commemorating the poet Christopher Logue. These live experiences are an important part of my poetry history as a reader and as a listener, so I can't privilege page over stage … or vice versa. I acknowledge them as two different species of poetry that coexist with my poetry eye and ear.

Raymond Antrobus is the author of *Shapes & Disfigurements* (Burning Eye Books 2012), *To Sweeten Bitter* (Out-Spoken Press 2017), *The Perseverance* (Penned in the Margins 2018) and *All The Names Given* (Picador 2021). His children's picture book *Can Bears Ski?* was published in 2021. In 2019 Raymond was awarded the Rathbones Folio Prize for best work of literature in any genre, the first poet to receive the prize. Other accolades include the Ted Hughes Award, *Sunday Times* Young Writer of the Year Award and *Guardian* Poetry Book of the Year 2018. He has been shortlisted for the Griffin Prize and the Forward Prize. Raymond is a founding member of Chill Pill and Keats House Poets Forum and is an Ambassador for the Poetry School. For more information see www.raymondantrobus.com.

See also ...
• *Getting your poetry out there*, page 336

Poetry

Notes from a passionate poet

Benjamin Zephaniah describes his route to being published.

'How did you first get published?' and 'Can you give me any advice on getting published?' must be the two questions I am most regularly asked as I go poeting around this planet. And what really gets me is that for most of my poetic life I have found them so hard to answer without doing a long talk on race and culture, and giving a lesson on the oral traditions of the Caribbean and Africa. I'm trying hard not to do that now but I have to acknowledge that I do come out of the oral tradition and to some extent I am still very much part of the Jamaican branch of that tradition, which has now established itself in Britain. In reality, getting published wasn't that hard for me: I came to the page from the stage. I didn't wake up one day and decide to join the oral tradition, I simply started performing in churches and community centres, on street corners and at political rallies, and I really didn't care about being published in books – I used to say I just want to be published in people's hearts. Now I don't want to sound like a royal seeking sympathy or a surgeon evaluating her or his work, I just feel there's something very special about hearing people recite a poem of yours back to you when you know that it has never been written down: it means that they must have heard me recite the poem and it had such an impact on them that it left an impression on their minds – but I say hearts because it sounds more sensitive.

Someone with a PhD once told me that the most important thing I could do was to get published, so for what seemed like an eternity (in fact it was just a couple of months) I became the most depressed kid on the block as the rejections flooded in, and I took each rejection very personally. I soon stopped punishing myself and went back to performing. Within the black and Asian communities there was a large network of venues to perform in and I was happy there, performing for 'my people'. But it wasn't long before I started to make a bit of a name for myself in what we now call the mainstream, and then the publishers came running back to me, many of them apologising and saying that the person who sent the rejection letter to me had now moved on and they weren't very good anyway. I didn't blame the publishers; I wasn't angry with them. It was a time when the British publishing industry simply didn't understand Reggae and Dub poetry, and the performance scene as we know it today had hardly taken root. It's not practical to advise all budding poets to go down the route that I chose. Some poets simply don't want to perform whilst others want something published before they take to the stage – they literally want something to cling to as they recite – but I have to say there is nothing like looking your audience in the face and delivering your work to them in person.

I used to be able to give a run-down of the poetry publishing and performance scene in Britain in about 30 minutes, but not any longer, with the internet and all that, the universe has changed. Not only are there hundreds of ways to get your poetry published, you can now publish your performance and have a worldwide hit without ever actually having a book or leaving your bedroom. You don't even have to tread the boards to become a performance poet. The choice is now yours: you can be a Dub poet, a pub poet, a cyber poet, a graffiti poet, a rap poet, a naked poet, a space poet, a Myspace poet, or a street poet. You can be a geek poet, a YouTube poet, an underground poet, a Facebook poet, a sound poet, an Instagram poet, and if you like to keep it short you can be a Twitter poet. You can go any way you want, but you must never forget to be a poet. You must never forget why you started writing (or performing) and you must love your art. The love I had for words as a baby has never left me, and when I was getting all those rejection letters and feeling so unwanted, my love for poetry never waned.

And another thing: read poetry. Many people tell me that they love poetry but after a minute or so of investigation I find that they only love their own poetry, and in many cases they only understand their own poetry. You can get a lot of help from teachers or in workshops, but reading other people's poetry is the best way of understanding poetry, it is the best way of getting into the minds of other poets. This great book that you now have in your hands and learned people who understand the industry are able to give you much better advice on getting published than I can, and if you do get published your publisher or agent should be offering you all the practical help you need. But you have to have the passion, you have to have the inspiration, you have to be a poet. Stay true.

Benjamin Zephaniah has been performing poetry since he was 11 years old. He has written 13 books of poetry, six novels, and recorded seven music CD albums. He spends much of his time encouraging young people to write and perform poetry and has received 18 honorary doctorates in recognition of his work. His publications include a martial arts travelogue *Kung Fu Trip* (Bloomsbury 2011), *To Do Wid Me*, a book and DVD of live performances (Bloodaxe Books 2013) and *Terror Kid* (Hot Key Books 2014). *The Life and Rhymes of Benjamin Zephaniah: The Autobiography* was published in 2018 by Simon & Schuster and *Windrush Child*, a novel for young adults, was published by Scholastic in 2020. He is currently Visiting Professor at De Montfort University and Professor of Poetry and Creative Writing at Brunel University. His website is www.benjaminzephaniah.com.

Poetry

Getting your poetry out there

Neil Astley knows that you need talent, passion, patience and dedication to become a published poet. He gives valuable advice on the possibilities, pitfalls and rewards that any budding poet might encounter.

Are you a poet – yet?

This article assumes that you have a potential readership or audience for your poetry, and that where you need guidance is in how to reach all those readers. But most poets just starting out believe that. There is, however, *no* readership for poets who *think* they are ready to publish but whose work isn't really *there* yet. If you've *not* immersed yourself in poetry for years – which involves intensive reading and absorbing poetry from all periods – to think of yourself as a poet is self-delusion. No one will want to read you, and your attempts to get your work out there will be met with rejection, frustration and disappointment – and self-righteous indignation if you're one of those would-be writers who think they're geniuses waiting to be discovered. People either have talent or they don't, and no amount of self-promotion and/or even education in the way of poetry workshops or MA courses will make you a poet if you don't have an insatiable passion for *reading* poetry (not just your own) and an original way of writing it. But if you've been drawn to poetry, and have *read* as much poetry as you can get hold of, I'd say you're halfway there.

A poet's reading list

One of the poets I publish, Hannah Lowe, was an English teacher who'd always loved poetry but wasn't familiar with the full range of contemporary poetry until her mother gave her a copy of the Bloodaxe anthology *Staying Alive* as a birthday present. That book made her think that *she* could write poetry. With other younger poets writing now, the process has often been the other way round; maybe they've read Simon Armitage, Carol Ann Duffy, Seamus Heaney and Philip Larkin, but they haven't read their Shakespeare, Donne, Keats, Wordsworth, Coleridge, Browning, Dickinson, Frost, Yeats, Auden and Eliot, all essential reading for anyone who wants to write poetry.

Without that groundwork reading, your own work will go nowhere. But all is not lost. If you really do have a gift for poetry, but life circumstances have been such as to make your reading patchy, stop thinking of getting your work out there now, and for the next year, just read and reread judiciously without thinking of writing. Start with the *Norton Anthology of Poetry* (W.W. Norton, 6th edn 2018) and the *Penguin Book of English Verse* (Penguin, new edn 2004), and get hold of books by the major figures they include; then *The Rattle Bag* (Faber 1982, 2005), *Emergency Kit* (Faber 2004) and the *Staying Alive* anthology series (Bloodaxe Books 2002, 2004, 2011 and 2020) and read more by the poets who most appeal to you. When you come back to writing, a year or more later, both you and your poetry will have changed. The poems you had wanted to get out there earlier will go in the bin, and you'll be writing poetry that should interest other readers.

Getting critical feedback

Next you need feedback. If you can find a good writing group or workshop in your area, that can be helpful. Even if you disagree with other people's comments on your work, their feedback should still show what aspects of your poems don't work for other readers. Later, once you've been working on your poetry for at least a year or two, it would be helpful to go on one of the writing courses (which are more week-long workshops than taught courses as such) run by the Arvon Foundation at three centres in England, or by Tŷ Newydd in Wales or Moniack Mhor in Scotland. Or contact the Poetry School in London (https://poetryschool.com) which offers online tuition, downloads, workshops and summer schools. There are also part-time MA courses run by numerous universities and colleges throughout Britain, but I don't think those are right for relative beginners; to gain full benefit from such courses (which cost thousands of pounds in fees) I think you need to have been writing seriously for at least five years. (See page 691 for a list.)

You can also start sending out poems to magazines; their websites will say whether you should submit online or if you need to send half a dozen poems with a stamped addressed envelope for their possible return. It won't be hard to get poems taken by the smallest of the magazines. The real challenge will be in sending work to the long-standing, leading poetry or literary magazines edited by significant poets or critics. These might include *Acumen, Agenda, Ambit, The Dark Horse, Granta, Iota, The London Magazine, Magma Poetry, The North, Orbis, PN Review, Poetry London, The Poetry Review, Poetry Wales* or *The Rialto*. There are also literary and cultural journals that publish poems, but these are much harder for new writers to break into, such as the *London Review of Books* and the *Times Literary Supplement*; somewhat perversely, you may find you have more luck with the political press: the *Morning Star, New Statesman* and the *Spectator* all publish newcomers as well as established poets.

Just as important as getting poems accepted is getting them rejected, especially if that includes getting a note back from an editor with a comment on your submission that makes something click. You may think that what you're writing now is great, but there will be flaws. There are always improvements that can be made that make all the difference between a half good poem and a really good one. Poets judging poetry competitions talk

Poetry magazines

Acumen	**The North**
See page 36	https://poetrybusiness.co.uk/the-north-magazine/
Agenda	**PN Review**
See page 37	See page 76
Ambit	**Poetry London**
See page 37	See page 77
The Dark Horse	**The Poetry Review**
www.thedarkhorsemagazine.com	See page 77
The London Magazine	**Poetry Wales**
See page 69	See page 77
Magma Poetry	**The Rialto**
See page 69	See page 82

For a fuller list see www.bloodaxebooks.com/links

See also *Magazines UK and Ireland* starting on page 36 and *Poetry organisations* on page 342.

about 'the wrong note', a line or phrase in a poem that sticks out as not belonging there or needing to be changed even with just one word added or a phrase taken out, and they can't give the prize to that poem because readers will see it too, but the poet is too close to the work and isn't aware of it.

To submit or not to submit?

So the first lesson in how to get your poetry out there is *not* to send it out, or not yet. Put it in a drawer for six months and come back to it; with that amount of distance from the work, you should be able to fix that 'wrong note' and also make the whole poem read more smoothly. Also – and this is absolutely essential – read the poem aloud. As you're writing it, and when you think you've finished it, and when you come back to it months later. Again, poets who haven't done this all talk about only realising what doesn't work in a poem when they were reading it aloud to an audience; trying not to let their expression show that they've just read a bum line at the live event, but rushing home afterwards to correct it. And if you do all your writing on a computer, print out your poems, and read through and edit them on paper. What may look right on a computer screen will often not *feel* right on paper, and then you'll see what needs to be edited. This is also where magazine rejections are helpful: six months later, going back to the poem you thought was your best but which kept being returned, you see the 'wrong note', fix the problem, send it out, and the poem is taken right away.

Don't submit to magazines unless you're familiar with the kind of work each one publishes. They are all different, and you will not be able to publish much unless you research the field and send to those whose output you like and respect. If you live in or can get to London or Edinburgh, spend a day in the National Poetry Library (formerly the Saison Poetry Library) at the Southbank Centre or the Scottish Poetry Library (there's also the Northern Poetry Library in Morpeth, Northumberland) and read the latest issues of the current magazines, and afterwards take out subscriptions to those you like most. Familiarity with the work of other poets is an important part of that process: if you're expecting others to read your work, you should read theirs too and learn from it; and support the magazines which support you. Join the Poetry Society and you'll receive *The Poetry Review* and *Poetry News* every quarter; join the Poetry Book Society and you'll receive their four Choices over the course of the year with the PBS *Bulletin* (including highly illuminating pieces by the poets about their books). The National Poetry Library also has two websites: www.nationalpoetrylibrary.org.uk, which includes listings of all the current print and online magazines, and http://poetrymagazines.org.uk, which has an archive covering many of the leading journals where you can read their back issues.

You can familiarise yourself with the editorial taste of online magazines much more easily. Some magazines publish both print and online editions, while others that started out as print have gone over completely to online publication. But so much poetry is published online now – and online imprints come and go – that readers and writers alike find it hard to see the wood for the trees, an appropriate metaphor to use here given that the cost and labour involved in printing and distributing magazines used to discourage poorly edited publications from flourishing. For a list of significant webzines which currently publish poetry, see the box below. These are the webzines (some quite new, not all exclusively poetry) picked out by poets I've consulted as the places where they'd most like to see their work, and where the younger poets in particular go to read their peers. It's worth adding that they also want their work to be featured or discussed in several webzines which don't take submissions, notably *The Quietus* (http://thequietus.com), *Sabotage Reviews* (http://sabotagereviews.com) and *Wild Court* (http://wildcourt.co.uk). And the ultimate accolade is getting your poems into America's *Poetry* magazine, with all the work it publishes being added to an historic online archive that goes back to 1912. The recently established reciprocal publication by *Poetry* and *The Poetry Review* of selections by US and UK poets has helped make this less of a pipe dream for British poets.

Get noticed through competitions and performance

Building up a coherent body of work can take years. As your work matures, so your confidence grows, and you start getting more and more poems taken by magazines and perhaps win prizes in poetry competitions. And some of the poetry competitions are worth trying, but as with the magazines, don't submit blindly, do your research. Just as you can almost predict which poets will win each year's poetry prizes from who the judges are, or what kind of work the combination of judges on each prize's judging panel is likely to favour, so it is with the poetry competitions. And the timing of their deadlines is such that you can't usually submit the same poems to more than one of the main poetry competitions in any one year. So check out the main competitions and submit to those judged by the poets you admire. As well as the Poetry Society's National Poetry Competition, these might include the Basil Bunting, Bridport, Bristol, Cardiff, Cheltenham, Ledbury, Manchester, *Mslexia* (women only) and *Poetry London* competitions. (See *Competitions* on page 348 under *Poetry organisations*.)

Popular webzines

And Other Poems
http://andotherpoems.com

Atrium
https://atriumpoetry.com

The Fortnightly Review
http://fortnightlyreview.co.uk

Ink Sweat and Tears
www.inksweatandtears.co.uk

The Lake
www.thelakepoetry.co.uk

London Grip
http://londongrip.co.uk

The Manchester Review
www.themanchesterreview.co.uk

Molly Bloom
https://mollybloompoetry.weebly.com

The Poetry Shed
https://abegailmorley.wordpress.com

Pulsar Poetry
www.pulsarpoetry.com

Riggwelter Press
https://riggwelterpress.wordpress.com

Three Drops from a Cauldron
https://threedropspoetry.co.uk

The White Review
www.thewhitereview.org

The recent growth of festivals and venues with open mic slots has given new writers opportunities to read their work in public; and you don't have to be a performance poet for your work to go down well with audiences, you just have to read strong work and read it well. Don't overrun your time slot and give a straightforward presentation of your work, which means a short introduction only, use your 'natural' voice and don't adopt the highly mannered whining delivery style favoured by poets who should know better.

Once you've published widely in magazines and are starting to do readings, you'll be at the stage of seeking out a small press willing to publish a pamphlet or chapbook (15 to

Poetry

20 poems). Most pamphlets are sold at readings, and having a pamphlet to give to organisers and to sell at events can lead to more opportunities to read your work. And finally – we're talking about years now – you might have a book-length manuscript (= typescript) of around 50 poems which you think worthy of publication. But the chances of having this taken up by one of the 'big eight' leading poetry imprints (Bloodaxe, Cape, Carcanet,

Poetry publishers

THE BIG EIGHT
Bloodaxe Books
See page 135

Jonathan Cape
See page 193

Carcanet
See page 140

Chatto & Windus
See page 193

Faber and Faber
See page 148

Granta Books
See page 60

Penguin
See page 176

Picador
See page 174

SMALLER PRESSES
Arc Publications
See page 132

Blue Diode
www.bluediode.co.uk

Burning Eye Books
https://burningeyebooks.wordpress.com

Cinnamon Press
www.cinnamonpress.com

Dedalus Press
(Ireland)
www.dedaluspress.com

The Emma Press
https://theemmapress.com

Eyewear Publishing/The Black Spring Press Group
https://blackspringpressgroup.com

The Gallery Press
(Ireland) See page 151

Happenstance
www.happenstancepress.com

Nine Arches Press
www.ninearchespress.com

Offord Road Books
www.offordroadbooks.co.uk

Pavilion Poetry
https://liverpooluniversitypress.co.uk/series/series-12328/

Peepal Tree Press
(Black British & Caribbean)
www.peepaltreepress.com

Penned in the Margins
www.pennedinthemargins.co.uk

Salmon Poetry
(Ireland)
www.salmonpoetry.com

Seren
See page 184

Shearsman Books
See page 184

Smith/Doorstop Books
www.poetrybusiness.co.uk/smith-doorstop

Smokestack Books
https://smokestack-books.co.uk

Templar Poetry
http://templarpoetry.com

Valley Press
www.valleypressuk.com

Verve Poetry Press
https://vervepoetrypress.com

The Waywiser Press
https://waywiser-press.com

For a fuller list of poetry publishers visit www.bloodaxebooks.com/links.

Poetry

Chatto, Faber, Granta, Penguin and Picador) are exceedingly slim. Apart from Granta, Penguin and Picador, which don't consider unsolicited submissions except from literary agents, we all receive *thousands* of submissions every year, but the annual output of first collections from *all* six imprints is rarely more than a dozen books *in total*. Much wiser to try the smaller poetry presses you'll find listed in this *Yearbook*, and you won't need an agent to do this. The only poets with agents are writers who are also novelists, journalists or playwrights. Don't think of ebooks as any kind of solution. Ebooks don't give poets the massive readership reached by writers of thrillers or romance, amounting to just 4% of total poetry sales.

Poets, beware!

Finally, a word of warning. There are certain firms which charge poets to publish their work or which require payment for copies of anthologies in which your work appears as a condition of publication. Poets starting out are particularly susceptible to what is known as vanity publishing. Reputable publishers or magazines of any size will pay authors for their work, usually with royalties in the case of books. If you are asked to pay for the production of your book by a publisher who sends you a flattering 'reader's report' on your work, try asking a local printer to give you an estimate for printing a few hundred copies of your book. The likelihood is that the cost will be considerably lower, and if you want your work to be read by friends, colleagues and people in your local community, the circulation you can achieve by this DIY method will be more effective. The normal arrangements for publishing also involve the author receiving complimentary copies of a book or a free contributor's copy of a magazine or anthology. If you're asked to pay to see your own work in print, you are paying to have it published. For more information see the website Vanity Publishing (www.vanitypublishing.info) and also the advice offered by the Society of Authors (www.societyofauthors.org/SOA/MediaLibrary/SOAWebsite/Guides/Vanity-Publishing.pdf).

If you're unable to get your book published but are confident of selling enough copies at readings, there are effective ways of self-publication covered by other articles in this *Yearbook*. As an alternative to local printers, a number of poets use the self-publishing website www.lulu.com, which offers a distribution channel in addition to well-produced books and ebooks.

Neil Astley is the editor of Bloodaxe Books, which he founded in 1978. His books include novels, poetry collections and anthologies, most notably the Bloodaxe *Staying Alive* series: *Staying Alive* (2002), *Being Alive* (2004), *Being Human* (2011) and *Staying Human* (2020). He has edited three collaborations with Pamela Robertson-Pearce, *Soul Food: nourishing poems for starved minds* (2008), and the DVD-books *In Person: 30 Poets* (2008) and *In Person: World Poets* (2017). He has published two novels, *The End of My Tether* (Scribner 2002), which was shortlisted for the Whitbread First Novel Award and *The Sheep Who Changed the World* (Flambard Press 2005).

Poetry

Poetry organisations

Below are some organisations which provide budding poets with opportunities to explore, extend and share their work. However, readers should note that some poetry events will not go ahead in their usual way due to coronavirus-related restrictions. Please check websites for details.

WHERE TO GET INVOLVED

A range of organisations – from local groups to larger professional bodies – exists at which emerging and established poets can access support or learn more about others' work. A concise selection appears below.

The British Haiku Society
36–38 Station Parade, PC Mail Box 25, Barking, Essex IG11 8DR
email cblundell2929@gmail.com
website www.britishhaikusociety.org.uk
Facebook www.facebook.com/thebritishhaikusociety

Pioneers the appreciation and writing of haiku in the UK, publishes books concerning haiku and related matters, and is active in promoting the teaching of haiku in schools and colleges. Publishes a quarterly journal, *Blithe Spirit*, an annual members' anthology and a newsletter. Also runs the prestigious annual British Haiku Society Awards in three categories: haiku, tanka and haibun. Registered charity. Founded 1990.

Literature Wales
Glyn Jones Centre, Wales Millennium Centre, Bute Place, Cardiff CF10 5AL
tel 029-2047 2266
email post@literaturewales.org
website www.literaturewales.org

National company for the development of literature in Wales. Working to inspire communities, develop writers and celebrate Wales' literary culture. Activities include the Wales Book of the Year Award, the Children's Laureate Wales and Bardd Plant Cymru schemes, creative writing courses at Tŷ Newydd Writing Centre, writer's bursaries and mentoring, and the National Poet of Wales initiative. The organisation is a member of the Arts Council of Wales' Arts Portfolio Wales.

The Poetry Book Society
Milburn House, Dean Street, Newcastle Upon Tyne NE1 1LF
tel 0191 230 8100
email enquiries@poetrybooksociety.co.uk
website www.poetrybooks.co.uk
Facebook www.facebook.com/poetrybooksoc
Twitter @poetrybooksoc

Book club for readers of poetry founded in 1953 by T.S. Eliot. Every quarter, expert poet selectors choose one outstanding publication (the PBS Choice), and recommend four other titles to deliver to PBS Members. The PBS also produces the quarterly membership magazine, the *Bulletin*, which contains in-depth reviews, interviews with international poets and extensive listings. PBS Members also enjoy 25% off all book orders and access to a lively poetry community with nationwide events.

The Poetry Business
Campo House, 54 Campo Lane, Sheffield S1 2EG
tel 0114 438 4074
email office@poetrybusiness.co.uk
website www.poetrybusiness.co.uk

Publishes books, pamphlets and audio under its Smith|Doorstop imprint; runs the literary magazine, *The North*. Also organises an international book & pamphlet competition, Writing Days, residential courses and runs an advanced writing school for published poets.

Poetry Ireland
11 Parnell Square East, Dublin D01 ND60, Republic of Ireland
tel +353 (0)1 6789815
email info@poetryireland.ie
website www.poetryireland.ie

Organisation committed to achieving excellence in the reading, writing and performance of poetry throughout the island of Ireland. Poetry Ireland receives support from The Arts Council / An Chomhairle Ealaíon and The Arts Council of Northern Ireland and enjoys partnerships with arts centres, festivals, schools, colleges and bookshops at home and abroad. Its commitment to creating performance and publication opportunities for poets at all stages of their careers helps ensure that the best work is made available to the widest possible audience. Poetry Ireland publishes the well-regarded journal, *Poetry Ireland Review*.

The Poetry Society
22 Betterton Street, London WC2H 9BX
tel 020-7420 9880
email info@poetrysociety.org.uk
website www.poetrysociety.org.uk

A leading voice for poets and poetry in Britain. Founded in 1909 to promote a more general recognition and appreciation of poetry, the Society has more than 3,000 members. With education initiatives, commissioning and publishing programmes, and a calendar of performances, readings and competitions, the Society champions poetry in its many forms.

The Society offers advice and information to all, with exclusive offers and discounts available to members. Every quarter, members receive copies of *The Poetry Review* and the Society's newsletter, *Poetry News*. The Society also publishes education resources; organises events including an Annual Lecture and National Poetry Day celebrations; runs Poetry Prescription, a critical appraisal service available to members for £40 and non-members for £50; and provides an education advisory and training service, as well as school and youth memberships.

Competitions run by the Society include the annual National Poetry Competition, with a first prize of £5,000, and the Foyle Young Poets of the Year Award.

The Seamus Heaney Centre at Queen's

c/o School of Arts, English and Languages, Queen's University Belfast, Belfast BT7 1NN
tel 028-9097 1077
email shc@qub.ac.uk
website www.seamusheaneycentre.com
Director Professor Glenn Patterson

The Centre runs a prestigious Poetry Summer School, and awards an annual First Collection Poetry Prize. It hosts an array of visiting Fellows, and a programme of talks, readings and performances throughout the year. The current Seamus Heaney Chair in Poetry is Nick Laird. The Centre's founding director was Ciaran Carson. Founded 2003.

Shortlands Poetry Circle

Ripley Arts Centre, 24 Sundridge Avenue, Bromley BR1 2PX
tel 020-8464 9810
email shortlands@poetrypf.co.uk
website www.poetrypf.co.uk/shortlands.html
President Anne Stewart

Founded in 1911, the Circle continues to meet twice a month during term time (meetings may be online). Visitors welcome.

Survivors' Poetry

95 Wick Hall, Furze Hill, Hove BN3 1NG
tel (01273) 202876
email info@survivorspoetry.org.uk
email drsimonjenner@gmail.com
Director Simon Jenner

National charity and survivor-led arts group which coordinates artistic activities using poetry to make connections between creativity and mental health. The quarterly newsletter, *Poetry Express*, is free to download from the website. Also monthly readings and open mic at Poetry Cafe, Covent Garden.

Tower Poetry

Christ Church, Oxford OX1 1DP
tel (01865) 286591
email tower.poetry@chch.ox.ac.uk
website www.chch.ox.ac.uk/towerpoetry
Facebook www.facebook.com/towerpoetry/
Twitter @towerpoetry

Exists to encourage and challenge everyone who reads or writes poetry. Funded by a generous bequest to Christ Church, Oxford, by the late Christopher Tower, the aims of Tower Poetry are to stimulate an enjoyment and critical appreciation of poetry, particularly among young people in education, and to challenge people to write their own poetry.

Ver Poets

tel (01582) 715817
email gregsmith480@gmail.com
website www.verpoets.co.uk
Secretary Gregory Smith
Membership £18 p.a. UK; £24 p.a. overseas; £12 p.a. students

Encourages the writing and study of poetry. Holds evening meetings and daytime workshops in the St Albans area. Holds members' competitions and the annual Open Competition. Founded 1966.

WHERE TO GET INFORMATION

Your local library is a good first port of call, and should have information about the poetry scene in the area. Many libraries are actively involved in spreading the word about poetry as well as having modern poetry available for loan.

Alliance of Literary Societies (ALS)

email allianceoflitsocs@gmail.com
website www.allianceofliterarysocieties.org.uk
Acting Hon Treasurer and Membership Secretary Linda J. Curry

Umbrella organisation for literary societies and groups in the UK. It provides support and advice on a variety of literary subjects, as well as promoting cooperation between member societies. Its publications include a twice-yearly members' newsletter, *Not Only But…*, and an annual journal, *ALSo*. ALS holds an AGM weekend which is hosted by a different member society each year, moving around the UK, or online. Founded 1973.

Arts Council England

tel 0161 934 4317
email enquiries@artscouncil.org.uk
website www.artscouncil.org.uk

National development agency for the arts in England, providing funding for a range of arts and cultural activities. It supports creative writing including poetry, fiction, storytelling, spoken word, digital work, writing for children and literary translation. It funds a range of publishers and magazines as well as providing grants to individual writers. Contact the enquiries team for more information on funding support and advice.

Arts Council of Wales

Bute Place, Cardiff CF10 5AL
tel 0845 8734 900

email information@arts.wales
website www.arts.wales

Independent charity, established by Royal Charter in 1994. It has three regional offices and its principal sponsor is the Welsh Government. It is the country's funding and development agency for the arts, supporting and developing high-quality arts activities. Its funding schemes offer opportunities for arts organisations and individuals in Wales to apply, through a competitive process, for funding towards a clearly defined arts-related project.

Manchester Poetry Library

Manchester Metropolitan University, Oxford Road, Manchester M15 6BR
email poetrylibrary@mmu.ac.uk
website www.mmu.ac.uk/poetrylibrary
Twitter @McrPoetryLib
Director Becky Swain

New public poetry library, due to open in 2021. Sets out to expand access to poetry and to encourage the writing of it at all levels, from primary school to professional standard. Its core collection will include 19th- to 21st-century poetry in English from around the world, as well as poetry in translation. Audio and print versions will be available. Will run events for children and adults, celebrating the role of local communities and languages in the process.

National Association of Writers' Groups

Old Vicarage, Scammonden, Huddersfield HD3 3FT
email info@nawg.co.uk
website www.nawg.co.uk

Aims to bring cohesion and fellowship to isolated writers' groups and individuals, promoting the study and art of writing in all its aspects. There are many affiliated groups and associate (individual) members across the UK.

National Poetry Library

Level 5, Royal Festival Hall, Southbank Centre, London SE1 8XX
tel 020-7921 0943
email info@poetrylibrary.org.uk
website www.nationalpoetrylibrary.org.uk
Facebook www.facebook.com/NationalPoetryLibrary
Twitter @natpoetrylib
Instagram @nationalpoetrylibrary
Membership Free with two forms of ID, one photographic and the other showing a UK address

The largest public collection of modern poetry in the world. It is open to everyone and free to join (see above stipulations and please check website for opening times). Members can borrow from the extensive loan collections, including audio items and take advantage of the library's e-loan service through which ebooks can be loaned at distance. The extensive collection of current poetry magazines gives a window into the breadth of poetry in the UK and beyond. The library runs regular live readings, a programme of exhibitions which run throughout the year and a book club. The library's website features publishers' information, poetry news and a list of UK-wide events.

Northern Poetry Library

The Chantry, Bridge Street, Morpeth, Northumberland NE61 1PD
tel (01670) 620391
email mylibrary@northumberland.gov.uk
website www.northernpoetrylibrary.org.uk
Twitter @nplpoetry

Largest collection of contemporary poetry outside London, housing over 15,000 titles and magazines covering poetry published since 1945. Founded 1968.

Scottish Poetry Library

5 Crichton's Close, Canongate, Edinburgh EH8 8DT
tel 0131 557 2876
email reception@spl.org.uk
website www.scottishpoetrylibrary.org.uk

Houses over 45,000 items: books, magazines, pamphlets, recordings and the Edwin Morgan Archive (featuring rare works by Morgan). The core of the collection is contemporary and classic poetry written in Scotland, in Scots, Gaelic and English, but classic Scottish poetry as well as contemporary works from almost every part of the world are also available. All resources, advice and information are readily accessible, free of charge. The SPL holds regular poetry events, including reading and writing groups, details of which are available on the library website. Closed Saturday and Sunday. Founded 1984.

ONLINE RESOURCES

There is a wealth of information available for poets at the click of a mouse: the suggestions below are a good starting point.

The Poetry Archive

website www.poetryarchive.org
Facebook www.facebook.com/PoetryArchive
Twitter @PoetryArchive
Instagram @thepoetryarchive

World's premier online collection of recordings of poets reading their work. Over 500 authors featured. Features the voices of contemporary English-language poets as well as those from the past, including C. Day Lewis, Paul Farley and Dorothea Smartt. The Archive is added to regularly. Some content can be accessed free of charge, but paid-for membership is available for frequent users.

The Poetry Kit

email info@poetrykit.org
website www.poetrykit.org

Collates a wide variety of poetry-related information, including events, competitions, courses and more for an international readership.

Poetry Space
email susan@poetryspace.co.uk
website www.poetryspacc.co.uk

Specialist publisher of poetry and short stories, as well as news and features, edited by Susan Jane Sims. Operatcs as a social enterprise with all profits being used to publish online and in print, and to hold events to widen participation in poetry. Submissions of poems, stories, novel extracts, photographs and artwork accepted all year for Young Writers' and Artists' Space (18s and under; work by under 16s particularly welcomed).

Poets and Writers
website www.pw.org
Twitter @poetswritersinc

US-based online magazine and e-newsletter on the craft and business of writing.

Sabotage Reviews
email director@sabotagereviews.com
email poetry@sabotagereviews.com
website www.sabotagereviews.com
Contacts Charley Barnes (general enquiries), Karen Goodwin (poetry), Phil Olsen (fiction)

Small press review site. Welcomes articles and reviews of 500–1000 words on poetry, fiction and the spoken word but check website guidelines carefully prior to submitting any work – full poetry collections or novels are rarely covered on the site.

Write Out Loud
email info@writeoutloud.net
website www.writeoutloud.net

Poetry news, features and reviews, with comprehensive listings of poetry events, publications, festivals and competitions. Members may post poems, join discussions, add their profile, etc. 50,000+ monthly users.

WHERE TO CELEBRATE POETRY

Festival information should be available from Arts Council England offices (see page 520). See also *Festivals and conferences for writers, artists and readers* on page 596. As well as the list below, major poetry festivals each year include Ledbury, Aldeburgh and Cheltenham. Poetry also often features prominently at the Glastonbury and Latitude Festivals when they are staged.

The British Council
British Council Customer Service UK, Bridgewater House, 58 Whitworth Street, Manchester M1 6BB
tel 0161 957 7755
email uk-literature@britishcouncil.org
website https://literature.britishcouncil.org
Twitter @litbritish

Visit the website for information on events, authors and projects.

Canterbury Festival
Festival House, 8 Orange Street, Canterbury, Kent CT1 2JA
tel (01227) 452853
email info@canterburyfestival.co.uk
website https://canterburyfestival.co.uk
Takes place 16–30 October 2021

Kent's international arts festival, one of the most important cultural events in the South East. The Festival showcases performing arts from around the world and runs year-round projects to inspire creativity in people of all ages. It commissions new work, champions emerging talent and supports those seeking careers in the cultural industries.

Ledbury Poetry Festival
The Master's House, St Katherine's, Bye Street, Ledbury HR8 1EA
tel (01531) 636232
email manager@poetry-festival.co.uk
website www.poetry-festival.co.uk
Festival Director Chloe Garner, *Festival Manager* Phillippa Slinger
Takes place July and throughout the year

The UK's biggest celebration of poetry and spoken word, attended by poets from all over the world. Established and upcoming talents take part in a wide variety of events, from masterclasses, walks, talks and films through to breakfasts, music, exhibitions and bike rides. International Poetry Competition launches every February.

WHERE TO PERFORM

Poetry evenings are held all over the UK and the suggestions listed below are worth checking out. Others can be found by visiting your local library or your Arts Council office, or by visiting the What's on section of the Poetry Society website (https://poetrysociety.org.uk/events/). The Poetry Library (www.nationalpoetrylibrary.org.uk/events-exhibitions) is also an excellent source for upcoming poetry events. Also look out for local groups at which members can share their work.

As we go to press, many established poetry events are on hold (or online) due to the coronavirus pandemic. Please check their website or social media contacts for any status updates.

Allographic
tel 07904 488009
email info@allographic.co.uk
website https://sites.google.com/site/allographica
Twitter @allographica
Instagram @allographica
Contact Fay Roberts

Cambridge-based live or Zoom events with new and upcoming names from the spoken word scene and a set of workshops for aspirant poets, storytellers and other writers and performers. Also produces a range of publications, from anthologies to books and pamphlets, that can be purchased online.

Apples and Snakes

The Albany, Douglas Way, London SE8 4AG
tel 020-8465 6140
email info@applesandsnakes.org
website www.applesandsnakes.org

Organisation for performance poetry and spoken word, whose goal is to produce engaging and transformative work in performance and participation. Founded 1982.

Bang Said the Gun

email info@bangsaidthegun.com
website www.bangsaidthegun.com
Twitter @bangsaidthegun
Contact Daniel Cockrill

High-energy monthly spoken word night with a limited open mic section. See website for up-to-date gig listings and venues.

Book Slam

email info@bookslam.com
website www.bookslam.com
Contact Elliott Jack

Founded with the aim of returning literature to the heart of popular culture, Book Slam invites authors, poets, singer-songwriters and comedians to a thinking person's cabaret. Various venues; see website for details.

Café Writers Norwich

Louis Marchesi, Tombland,
Norwich NR3 1HF (also on Zoom)
email info@cafewriters.co.uk
website www.cafewriters.co.uk
Twitter @cafewriters
Contacts Ramona Herdman, Julia Webb

Readings of poetry and prose in a relaxed and welcoming atmosphere, on the second Monday of every month. Open mic slots available.

CB1 Poetry

The Blue Moon, Norfolk Street, Cambridge CB1 2LF
email info@cb1poetry.org.uk
website www.cb1poetry.org.uk

Regular readings featuring new and well-known artists. Previous participants include Owen Sheers, George Szirtes, Don Paterson and Emily Berry. Check website for dates and times of meetings; some may be online.

Coffee House Poetry at The Troubadour

PO Box 16210, London W4 1ZP
email coffpoetry@aol.com
website www.coffeehousepoetry.org

Readings & classes take place at The Troubadour, 263–267 Old Brompton Road, London SW5 9JA.

Find the Right Words

Upstairs at the Western, 70 Western Road,
Leicester LE3 0GA
email jess_green@hotmail.co.uk
website www.jessgreenpoet.com
Twitter @ftrwpoetry
Contact Jess Green

Monthly poetry event. Two headliners every month, ten open mic spots (five in advance, five on the door).

Flint & Pitch Productions

email flintandpitch@gmail.com
website www.flintandpitch.com
Twitter @flintandpitch
Contact Jenny Lindsay

Scotland-based literature, poetry, theatre and music organisation specialising in multi-act revue shows, touring spoken word theatre shows and live literature events.

Hammer and Tongue

The Old Fire Station, George Street,
Oxford OX1 2AQ
email oxford@hammerandtongue.com
website www.hammerandtongue.com
Twitter @htoxford
Regional Coordinator Steve Larkin

Poetry slam and touring guest artist events in London, Bristol, Brighton, Cambridge, Southampton and Oxford. See website for timings and contact details.

Jawdance

Rich Mix, 35–47 Bethnal Green Road,
London E1 6LA
email info@applesandsnakes.org
website www.applesandsnakes.org
Host Yomi Sode

Poetry, film and music night, currently every third Wednesday of the month. Check website for details.

Kent & Sussex Poetry Society

The Vittle & Swig, Camden Road, Tunbridge Wells,
Kent TN1 2PT
email kentandsussexpoetry@gmail.com
website www.kentandsussexpoetry.com

Local group with national reputation. Organises monthly poetry readings (third Tuesday of each month at 8pm), workshops and an annual poetry competition.

Out-Spoken

100 Club, 100 Oxford Street, London W1D 1LL
email info@outspokenldn.com
website www.outspokenldn.com
Facebook www.facebook.com/outspokenLDN

Twitter @OutSpokenLDN

Monthly poetry and live/online music event. See website or social media accounts for forthcoming dates and start times.

Out-Spoken also runs an annual poetry prize awarded in three categories: Performance; Page; and Film. Submissions open in January, with winners in each category and a cash prize for the overall winner. Submissions can be made via the website (see above); a fee may be applicable. Previous winners include Momtaza Mehri, who was appointed the Young People's Laureate for London in April 2018.

Poetry Unplugged at the Poetry Café
22 Betterton Street, London WC2H 9BX
tel 020 7420 9888
email poetryunplugged@gmail.com
website http://poetrysociety.org.uk/poetry-cafe/
Twitter @poetniall
Host Niall O'Sullivan

Open mic session, welcoming to new poets. Every Tuesday, sign-up between 6.45pm and 7.15pm; spaces are limited.

Poets' Café
South Street Arts Centre, 21 South Street, Reading RG1 4QU
email info@poetscafereading.co.uk
website www.poetscafereading.co.uk
Twitter @Poets_Cafe
Hosts Vic Pickup, Zannah Kearns, Damon Young

Reading's longest-running poetry platform is organised and hosted by The Poetry Society's Reading Stanza. Held on the second Friday of each month, it consists of an open mic section and a full reading by an established poet.

Polari
Royal Festival Hall, Southbank Centre, Belvedere Road, London SE1 8XX
email paulburston@btinternet.com
website www.polarisalon.com
Contact Paul Burston

Multi-award-winning LGBTQ+ literary salon, held once a month at the Southbank Centre (see website for details). Focuses on established authors but has some pre-arranged spots per event for up-and-coming LGBT writers.

Rainbow Poetry Recitals
2 Old Farm Court, Shoreham BN43 5FE
tel (01273) 465423
email rainbow.poetry@hotmail.co.uk
Administrator Hugh Hellicar

Poetry meetings and recitals at two branches in London and four in Sussex. Membership £5 p.a. Poetry appreciation and members' poems. Magazine available on request. Founded 1994.

SoapBox
tel 07879 353396
email amy@getonthesoapbox.co.uk
website www.getonthesoapbox.co.uk
Facebook www.facebook.com/getonthesoapbox
Twitter @getonthesoapbox
Contact Amy Wragg

Based in Norfolk and Suffolk, SoapBox promotes and organises live music, poetry and comedy events in a variety of settings, from pubs to arts centres, festivals and street performances.

WHERE TO WRITE POETRY

Arvon
Lumb Bank – The Ted Hughes Arvon Centre, Heptonstall, Hebden Bridge, West Yorkshire HX7 6DF
tel (01422) 843714
email lumbbank@arvon.org
Totleigh Barton, Sheepwash, Beaworthy, Devon EX21 5NS
tel (01409) 231338
email totleighbarton@arvon.org
The Hurst – The John Osborne Arvon Centre, Clunton, Craven Arms, Shrops. SY7 0JA
tel (01588) 640658
email thehurst@arvon.org
website www.arvon.org

Arvon's three centres run five-day residential courses throughout the year for anyone over the age of 16, providing the opportunity to live and work with professional writers. Writing genres explored include poetry, narrative, drama, writing for children, song-writing and the performing arts. Bursaries are available to those receiving benefits. Arvon also runs online courses and events throughout the year. Founded 1968.

Cannon Poets
22 Margaret Grove, Harborne, Birmingham B17 9JH
email martin@cannonpoets.co.uk
Meets at The Moseley Exchange, The Post Office Building, 149–153 Alcester Road, Moseley, Birmingham B13 8JP usually on the first Sunday of each month (except August) at 2pm
website www.cannonpoets.org.uk

Cannon Poets have met monthly since 1983. The group encourages poetry writing through:

• workshops run by members or visitors
• break-out groups where poems are subjected to scrutiny by supportive peer groups
• ten-minute slots where members read a selection of their poems to the whole group
• publication of its journal, *The Cannon's Mouth* (email submissions to greg@cannonpoets.org.uk).

Members are encouraged to participate in poetry events and competitions. Cannon Poets' annual poetry competition, Sonnet or Not, invites poems of just fourteen lines in length. Entrants may choose any one of the traditional sonnet forms, or experiment with alternative fourteen-line forms, perhaps using half rhyme, metarhyme or blank verse. The first prize is £500 and the deadline for entries is 31 December of each year. See website for details.

City Lit
1–10 Keeley Street, London WC2B 4BA
tel 020-7831 7831
email advice@citylit.ac.uk
website www.citylit.ac.uk
Twitter @citylit

Offers classes and courses (currently online only, but check website for updates) on poetry appreciation, as well as a wide range of other topics.

The Poetry School
1 Dock Offices, Surrey Quays Road, Canada Water, London SE16 2XU
tel 020-7582 1679
website www.poetryschool.com

Teaches the art and craft of writing poetry, with courses in London and around the UK, ranging from evening classes, small seminars and individual tutorials, to one-day workshops, year-long courses and an accredited MA. Activities for beginners to advanced writers, with classes happening face-to-face and online. Three termly programmes a year, plus professional skills development projects and CAMPUS, a social network for poets.

Tŷ Newydd Writing Centre
Llanystumdwy, Criccieth, Gwynedd LL52 0LW
tel (01766) 522811
email tynewydd@literaturewales.org
website www.tynewydd.wales

Runs residential writing courses encompassing a wide variety of genres and caters for all levels, from beginners to published poets. All the courses are tutored by published writers. Writing retreats are also available.

Wey Poets (Surrey Poetry Centre)
Friends Meeting House, 3 Ward Street, Guildford GU1 4LH
tel (01252) 702450 (admin)
email bb_singleton@hotmail.com
website www.weyfarers.com
Contact Belinda Singleton

Small, long-standing group with quality input. New members/visitors and enquiries very welcome. Group meets 2–4.30 for each event: third Wednesday of the month for workshops, September to June (first Wednesday in December). Additional speaker events on first Wednesday in November, March, April and May. (Please see website for any changes.) Supportive workshops for original poetry. Some events may run on Zoom or by email exchange.

COMPETITIONS

There are now hundreds of competitions to enter. As a rule, as the value of the prize increases, so does the prestige associated with winning. To decide which ones are most appropriate for your work, make sure you know who the judges are and think twice before paying large sums for an anthology of 'winning' poems which will be read only by entrants wanting to see their own work in print. The Poetry Library publishes a list online (www.nationalpoetrylibrary.org.uk/write-publish/competitions). See also *Prizes and awards* on page 556.

Literary prizes are given annually to published poets and as such are non-competitive. Information on some high-profile awards can be found on the Booktrust website (www.booktrust.org.uk/what-we-do/awards-and-prizes/).

HELP FOR YOUNG POETS AND TEACHERS

National Association of Writers in Education (NAWE)
Tower House, Mill Lane, off Askham Fields Lane, Askham Bryan, York YO23 3FS
tel 0330 3335 909
email admin@nawe.co.uk
website www.nawe.co.uk

National membership organisation which aims to further knowledge, understanding and enjoyment of creative writing and to support good practice in its teaching and learning at all levels. NAWE promotes creative writing as both a distinct discipline and an essential element in education generally. Its membership includes those working in Higher Education, the many freelance writers working in schools and community contexts, and the teachers and other professionals who work with them. It runs a national database of writers, produces a weekly opportunities bulletin, publishes two journals – *Writing in Education* and *Writing in Practice* – and holds a national conference. Professional membership includes public liability insurance cover.

Poetry Society Education
The Poetry Society, 22 Betterton Street, London WC2H 9BX
tel 020-7420 9880
email educationadmin@poetrysociety.org.uk
website www.poetrysociety.org.uk

An arm of The Poetry Society aiming to facilitate exciting and innovative education work. For over 30 years it has been introducing poets into classrooms, providing comprehensive teachers' resources and producing accessible publications for pupils. It develops projects and schemes to keep poetry flourishing in schools, libraries and workplaces, giving work to hundreds of poets and allowing thousands of children and adults to experience poetry for themselves.

Through projects such as the Foyle Young Poets of the Year Award and Young Poets Network, The Poetry Society gives valuable encouragement and exposure to young writers and performers.

Schools membership offers a range of benefits, including quarterly Poetry Society publications, books and posters, and free access to the Poets in Schools placement service. Youth membership is also available (for ages 11–18; from £20 p.a.) and offers discounts, publications, poetry books and posters.

Young Poets Network

email educationadmin@poetrysociety.org.uk
website https://ypn.poetrysociety.org.uk
Facebook www.facebook.com/YoungPoetsNetwork
Twitter @youngpoetsnet

Online resource from The Poetry Society comprising features about reading, writing and performing poetry, plus new work by young poets and regular writing challenges. Open to anyone under the age of 25.

YOUNG POETRY COMPETITIONS

Children's competitions are included in the competition list provided by the Poetry Library: this is free online at www.nationalpoetrylibrary.org.uk/write-publish/competitions. Further information on literary prizes can be found on the BookTrust website (www.booktrust.org.uk/what-we-do/awards-and-prizes/).

Foyle Young Poets of the Year Award

The Poetry Society, 22 Betterton Street,
London WC2H 9BX
tel 020-7420 9880
email fyp@poetrysociety.org.uk
website www.foyleyoungpoets.org
Facebook www.facebook.com/thepoetrysociety
Twitter @PoetrySociety

Annual competition for writers aged 11–17. Prizes include publication, mentoring and a residential writing course. Deadline 31 July. Free to enter. Founded 2001.

Christopher Tower Poetry Prize

Christ Church, Oxford OX1 1DP
tel (01865) 286591
email tower.poetry@chch.ox.ac.uk
website www.chch.ox.ac.uk/towerpoetry
Twitter @TowerPoetry

Annual poetry competition (open from November to March) from Christ Church, Oxford, aimed at students aged between 16 and 18 in UK schools and colleges. The poems should be no longer than 48 lines, on a different chosen theme each year. Prizes: £3,000 (1st), £1,000 (2nd), £500 (3rd). Every winner also receives a prize for his or her school.

See also...

• *Publishers of poetry*, page 770

Further reading

Addonizio, Kim, *Ordinary Genius: A Guide for the Poet Within* (W.W. Norton and Co. 2012)

Bell, Jo, and Jane Commane, *How to Be a Poet: A 21st Century Guide to Writing Well* (Nine Arches Press 2017)

Bell, Jo, and guests: *52: Write a Poem a Week – Start Now, Keep Going* (Nine Arches Press 2015)

Chisholm, Alison, *A Practical Guide to Poetry Forms* (Compass Books 2014)

Fairfax, John, and John Moat, *The Way to Write* (Penguin Books, 2nd edn revised 1998)

Greene, Roland, *et al.*, *Princeton Encyclopedia of Poetry and Poetics* (Princeton University Press, 4th edn 2012)

Hamilton, Ian, and Jeremy Noel-Tod, *The Oxford Companion to Modern Poetry in English* (Oxford University Press, 2nd edn 2014)

Kowit, Steve, *In the Palm of Your Hand: A Poet's Portable Workshop* (Tilbury House, 2nd edn 2017)

Maxwell, Glyn, *On Poetry* (Oberon Books 2017)

Oliver, Mary, *Rules for the Dance: Handbook for Writing and Reading Metrical Verse* (Houghton Mifflin 1998)

Padel, Ruth, *52 Ways of Looking at a Poem: A Poem for Every Week of the Year* (Vintage 2004)

Padel, Ruth, *The Poem and the Journey: 60 Poems for the Journey of Life* (Vintage 2008)

Roberts, Philip Davies, *How Poetry Works* (Penguin Books, 2nd edn 2000)

Sampson, Fiona, *Poetry Writing: The Expert Guide* (Robert Hale 2009)

Sansom, Peter, *Writing Poems* (Bloodaxe 1993, repr. 1997)

Whitworth, John, *Writing Poetry* (A&C Black, 2nd edn 2006)

Poetry

Screen and audio
Successful screenwriting

Anna Symon suggests what it takes to forge a career as a screenwriter. She gives practical advice on how to develop the skills and traits needed to succeed in this creative, collaborative and competitive field.

In 2018 I had my first series on television, *Mrs Wilson*, on BBC One and, in 2019, my second, *Deep Water*, for ITV. As a result of this, there's plenty more work for me on the horizon – both here and in the US. It doesn't feel that long since I was sitting at home in my proverbial pyjamas, desperately wanting to make it, and I'm still puzzling out how I got here.

How do you become a screenwriter? The straight answer is there is no answer: every writer I know has taken a different route. However, I do think that all of us screenwriters have one key thing in common. It's not something people talk about very often and it's hard to pin it down in a word or two, but it's a certain curiosity about life, an interest in scratching below the surface, a compulsion to express a point of view. I think it makes us writers a fun bunch of people to hang out with, because we like to question what we see around us, try to make sense of the world or simply enjoy observing its complexity and absurdity. If you're that kind of person – and I don't mean necessarily having something deep and meaningful to say, but an original 'take' or 'insight' – and you want to get your thoughts out there, the next step is sitting down and writing.

… And writing. And more writing. Practise as hard as you would a piano if you wanted to be a concert pianist. Because I truly believe that, with enough time and effort, the majority of screenwriting skills can be learnt. If you think in an interesting way, and have something interesting to say, you can surely learn how to put a screenplay together. That said, they say it takes ten years to become an overnight success and I think, in screenwriting, that's true. It was certainly true for me. The good news is that the ten years honing your craft are extremely rewarding. They are certainly some of the most fun times I've had in my life. It's the time when you are reading books, watching films, reading scripts, avidly trying to absorb what everyone else is doing, while all the time writing your own stuff. Perhaps thinking about whether you have a voice and, if you do, what the hell it is? Personally, I wouldn't worry too much about that. Write from the heart, lay down the story as you see it, and leave it to others to discover your voice.

For some lucky new screenwriters, they'll get off to a flying start and get paid while they are still learning their craft – although they will then make their mistakes in public (which can be a significant downside for the ego). For others at the start of their writing journey, they are penning spec scripts, unpaid and largely unnoticed, each one hopefully better than the last until, one day, they find that people ask to read their work and then pay for it. (It should be said that these writers will also continue to make mistakes – so the ego will get battered at some point, whichever way your career progresses.)

If 'a career' means getting paid for your writing, then in the world of books that means getting something published. In television and film it means getting a project into so-called 'development'. You may well make a healthy living as a full-time, paid screenwriter (particularly in film) for quite a long time before you get a project green lit and on screen. There's a reason it's known as 'development hell', as scripts go back and forth from broadcaster to producer to writer, with a pile of notes and tweaks along the way. There's also a reason for the much-quoted saying: 'Writing is re-writing.' Be prepared for the long haul – and don't become a screenwriter unless you genuinely enjoy collaboration with other creatives. Professional input from script editors, directors and producers can, and should, massively improve your work. However, at times it can feel like your insides are being scraped with a rusty blade. Get used to it.

If, given all this, you still want to write screenplays I believe there are a few steps you can take along the way to give yourself the best chance. Firstly, I would sign up for as much good quality training as you can afford. I did an MA in Screenwriting and it went a long way towards demystifying both the craft and the business. The course had links with the industry, so it was a first shot at meeting producers and agents and learning how I could turn what I had written into a commercial proposition that a broadcaster would want to finance and an audience would want to watch. More importantly, it was the first time I had met a whole cohort of others on the same journey as me. It was a lot of fun. I found my tribe. It was also an opportunity for us all to get people to read and critique our work, to develop that thick skin for what was coming down the road. There were a few people on the course who genuinely couldn't take criticism of their work, however positively it was offered, and for those people it was useful to discover that screenwriting was not right for them.

The second step comes out of the first, really, and it is to find a clever, sensitive first reader of your work. This person doesn't have to be a writer, but it should be someone who will be honest with you and whose opinion you value. It does feel extremely exposing to have someone question work that took you so long to think about and then express, but having those fresh eyes on it is an incredibly valuable process. It means that when you sit down to write another draft, as you must if you're serious about it, you'll have a sense of where its strengths and weaknesses are – which parts are intriguing, which bits a little slow. Quite often the most useful feedback is to learn which scenes or sequences don't really make sense yet – even if they do to you. 'It's not on the page yet' is a common note given. This means that, despite the fact you feel you have expressed a particular storyline or character point, it is not 'landing' for the reader.

In that sense your first reader is your best friend, who will protect you from less helpful criticism from the outside world. Listen to them … carefully. Try not to be too defensive or write off their notes as them just not 'getting' you. You don't have to alter anything. But you may find that what they pick up on is an area of the script that you weren't quite sure about yourself, a problem you thought you had solved but in your heart of hearts knew wasn't working. Let the criticism settle and then buoy yourself up to tackle the problem head on in your next pass. On the other hand, the reader's thoughts may be inexplicable to you – a real surprise. In that case, I'd suggest finding another reader if you can. Listen carefully to them too. If they come up with a similar point, then I'd suggest you try and do some work on that area of the script.

Try out a few readers if you can. See who you are in tune with – but by that I don't mean the person who simply says: 'Amazing, I loved every bit of it'. Whatever stage a script is at, there should always be something to talk about. Sometimes the most useful thing is simply to discuss the script with someone who has read it. It forces you to articulate what you are trying to express, as your work develops. If you feel really stuck, with lots of contradictory thoughts on your work, and are not sure if something's there yet, I'd suggest sending it to a professional script editor. Make sure you have done everything you possibly can to get the script to this stage, so you don't waste your money getting notes you could have given yourself.

Finally, I think the most important piece of advice is not to send your work out into the world too soon. If you are looking for an agent, or you have met a producer, and you have that precious email address and their invitation to send in a script, pause a moment. Think carefully. This person would not have suggested you send something in unless they intend to read it. Contrary to popular opinion, everyone is looking for new talent, new voices. There is no reason that new voice won't be yours, but the field is very competitive. You are new and therefore a risk. There are lots of talented writers out there already, with long track records. Your work has to have the potential to be as good as theirs … or better. So you need to seriously impress at this point. You almost certainly won't get another chance with this particular person. So, force yourself to look at your script again; if there is a character that you think is still rather two-dimensional or a plot point that feels coincidental, your reader will pick that up too. If, on the other hand, you read through your script one final time and you genuinely feel there is nothing more you can do to improve it, then you are ready to hit 'send'. Good luck!

Anna Symon is currently adapting *The Essex Serpent* by Sarah Perry for Apple TV. Her scriptwriting credits include the BBC series *Mrs Wilson* (2018), the ITV series *Deep Water* (2019) and Channel 4's *Indian Summers* (2015-16). She is a graduate of the Channel 4 Screenwriting Programme and previously worked as a producer/director in current affairs and documentaries. Follow her on Twitter @AnnaSymon.

Adapting books for stage and screen

Ana Garanito outlines the essential elements of the adaptation process, an exciting journey of deconstruction and reconstruction, and stresses the importance of seeking out, understanding and protecting the authored voice and the crucial 'pillars' of a book.

Books provide proof of concept for any commissioner. The American TV market is producing more adaptations than ever before and some of the UK film market's biggest successes of recent years have been adaptations. Adapting a book for stage or screen allows us to use the leverage of the original and create even more around it – think *Game of Thrones*, *American Gods* or *The Handmaid's Tale*.

How you adapt a novel will prompt various outcomes. Hopefully it will get commissioned after initial development. When it's made (and if it's based on a much-loved book) it could meet with a ready-made audience's approval … or not. And if you have built a relationship with the author or the estate, your approach may receive the ultimate blessing. No pressure!

This article is not an exhaustive list of what to do, but it focuses on a few key essentials for tackling an adaptation. As Head of Scripted at Green Door Pictures, I'm currently developing a number of adaptations across TV and film, but the advice below can absolutely apply to any form of adaptation, such as optioning life rights, a stage show, a documentary, radio, literature, even music.

The 'why?'

Before beginning any adaptation, we always ask: Why this novel? Why now? Why is it relevant? Why should we (the producer) make it and why should you (the writer) adapt it? We also have to make sure it is not competing with anything else already in development or production that will hamper its chances of a commission; a similar project is an excuse to reject your one.

It's also worth considering which is the best format – stage, film, TV, digital short, audio series, etc. Then it's necessary to break it down even further; for example – if you choose TV, which broadcaster? Which slot? As you do this, you will inevitably start to consider who your audience is. If you are planning to start an adaptation without a producer alongside you just yet, ask yourself all the same questions, because the answers should certainly be part of your sales pitch as you look to option it from the author, find a production company, or pitch to a commissioner.

If adapting someone else's work, before optioning the book you should meet or speak with the author if you can. Having the two of you discuss the book and any potential approach to the adaptation is invaluable, and it's even better if you have your producer by your side.

And again, when you're ready to dive in, the most important question to ask the author is 'Why?' Why did they write this book? What do they want an audience to take away from reading the book? Knowing the author's reasoning means you can understand the beating heart of the book and in turn become a genuine custodian of it. An adaptation will inevitably carry changes from the original book, but truly embracing the 'why' can help inform the decisions you make. If you need to lose anything from the original because the film or

TV series can't accommodate it, as long as the 'why' still remains within its reimagining, you're protecting the very essence of the whole book.

I have worked on adaptations where the author has been dead for a number of years and the book is out of copyright, which means that understanding the 'why' happens through research on the internet, digging deep within books around the author or novel and doing the necessary analysis and evaluation. It's important – especially if it's a classic – to understand the motivation for the book, because any reimagining will be analysed (and potentially criticised) by a long-established fanbase.

The 'how?'

How you handle the adaptation will be a key consideration for anyone commissioning you to write. Not only must you be clear about how you would tackle the adaptation so it can be translated successfully to stage or screen, but you need to articulate this with confidence to the author, producer and/or commissioner. The one thing that everyone (myself included) is looking for is an authored voice – a truly unique and singular take on a story, theme or issue. What is it about your handling of the book that makes this a must-have and yet still retains the tone of the original?

After establishing the 'Why?', we must turn to the nuts and bolts of adapting a piece of work. This largely means breaking down the whole book and rebuilding it, from the ground up, into your desired format. Narrative arc, characters, tone, timeline – the whole lot. Get under its skin. Know it inside and out, but always keep the 'Why?' close by. If and when you decide that some elements can't make their way into the adaptation or need to be reconfigured, as long as it's in service of the 'Why?', you can justify it to all those around you.

When you have all the components laid out in front of you, you can then determine 'the pillars of the novel', as I like to call them. These are the essential elements that it's important to retain even when you make significant changes from the original. These could be tone, key characters, setting, story points, themes or issues that are unique to the book. I've worked on adaptations that have been difficult either because they were structurally complex or sometimes because of their rather dated handling of diversity or other themes. However, in both cases, the pillars of the original lay beneath. By simplifying the through-line of the emotional journey, it was then possible to create an alternative structure or commentary for the adaptation.

Film, TV, theatre and audio series are all completely different disciplines and you could take a single text and adapt it in different ways for each of those formats. Your take on that adaptation will be important and will inevitably change the original. That's fine and as it should be, but it can be a shock to an author – so be sure to warn people! You should always be as transparent as possible. I say all this knowing the author may not necessarily have right of approval, or any final decision may sit with someone else such as a producer, but a good relationship managed by you or your producer means you will build trust and also ensure that everyone involved understands the transformation that is about to take place.

Diversity and representation

Whatever story you're adapting, I assume you want it to be seen by the biggest and widest audience possible. Diversity may be considered a buzz word, but it's actually just good practice. Consider the diversity within your world and amongst your characters. Is it relevant to the audience you want to sell your story to? Do you understand the backgrounds you're writing about? Research them if you don't. The word that should be considered more often is 'representation'. This is about authenticity. Are you reinforcing stereotypes, or can you accurately depict a character through understanding their upbringing, religion, disabilities, cultural heritage, sexuality or gender?

Consider the language you use to describe those characters and the world. This means the terminology you use in your script to describe a disability or culture, for example. It will say a lot about how you see the world. Whether describing a character's cultural heritage, faith or disability, your words are the blueprint for how an entire crew will discuss those characters, how an actor approaches and reflects on a character (even how comfortable they will feel discussing it openly) and how an audience will finally consider the representation of that character. Are you promoting or dismantling stereotypes?

Your people

Whether you are adapting your own book, have been commissioned to adapt a book or are bringing it to a production company, it is important that the producer you're working with gets the novel and gets you, and that you are all aligned on how to tackle the adaptation. Life is short and development is long, so you don't want to spend that time feeling a disconnect with the people who are supposed to be steering you and selling your adaptation. How do they intellectually and emotionally respond to the book and your plans for it? Do you like them? Will they have your back? They need to help protect you from multiple voices, navigate the whole process efficiently and manage the expectations of the author if needed.

If you have optioned the book yourself and are looking for a producer, always consider their company ethos and back catalogue. I'm always surprised when projects have been pitched to me that are very similar to shows we have already produced and aired. Do your homework. Watch their shows.

Take a moment

Everyone is on the lookout for a good story, an authored voice and a new creative challenge. It is an exciting time to be a creator of content because there are so many more outlets to pitch to. As much as your adaptation may change the original, if you can retain the 'Why?' and honour the pillars of the book, you can create an adaptation from an honest place that is endorsed by all the stakeholders. Some of the criticism around the handling of the new *Star Wars* films or the final seasons of *Game of Thrones* is about how they failed to honour the essential pillars of the original and all the rules that were established previously.

There is always a time, just before I start any development, when I take a deep breath and appreciate that – regardless of whether we have a manuscript in front of us at that moment – we still have a blank page before us. It may seem overwhelming to consider how to deconstruct and reconstruct, but that's the good stuff! Rediscovering that work as a film, TV series, audio series or theatre piece is a glorious journey. Enjoy every minute of it because, if you do, your audience will also.

Ana Garanito has over 20 years' broadcast industry experience. Her work for Green Door Pictures includes *In The Long Run* (Sky One), *Turn Up Charlie* (Netflix), *Tree* (a theatre co-production with the Young Vic and Manchester International Festival) and *Concrete Cowboy*, a feature film based on the novel by Greg Neri, released on Netflix in 2021.

Writing series for television

Scriptwriter Russell Lewis has tough-talking advice about making your way into the competitive and collaborative business of writing for television, and describes how, when that break comes, you can succeed if you give it your all and never stop learning.

The first rule of Write Club is: you do not talk about Write Club.

The stock reply to the question, 'What advice would you give to someone who wanted to be a television writer?' is, of course, 'Don't.' Seriously. Develop another ambition. Become the fluffer for a tiger-mating program, or a teething ring for rattlesnakes. But you've invested in a copy of *Writers' & Artists' Yearbook*, so you must believe that it's something you want to do – you crazy, idealistic little fool! Let's see if I can put you off.

It's difficult to catch a break and find a way into the industry – but then, you know that, or you wouldn't be reading this. No short cuts or magic formulae lie within the body of this article, only some vestigial amount of fellow feeling. We have all been there. Every writer you like has been there, and every writer you detest. They have all been on the same journey. There is only graft, and patience, and frustration, and more patience, and anger, and even more patience, and very, very occasionally, a bit of luck. And that's just to get a foot in the door. So, why do it at all? Well – let's be honest, it beats working for a living … Who was it said: 'Find the thing you love, and let it kill you'? Those who answered Ethel Christie, go to the back of the class.

However, I promise you, if you have talent then somewhere, amongst all the pain and patience and frustration and anger and more patience, something will happen. You will get better at what you're doing. And 'getting better at what you're doing' is a process without end. Every day is a school day. You know that scene or line of dialogue that yesterday was a line in the sand that you scratched out with your own blood and sweat, and which you swore to defend against all comers to your last breath? Today, you will decide that you don't need it. You will find a more elegant and infinitely more economical way to make the same point, or a better one, or decide that you don't need it at all, and the piece will be improved a thousandfold by its excision. Very likely, your good colleagues will have been telling you this – or something like it – for some time. They couldn't tell you exactly what needed to be done, but they just knew they were bumping on something around that section. But – *here's the important bit* – you absolutely had to walk that lonely moonlit mile yourself to get to the moment of epiphany. That's the drug. That's what keeps us coming back for more. Like the Devil's candy – we know we shouldn't but, like the beat-up old ex-con in every heist movie, we keep coming back for one … last … job.

You will hear your peers (and others) talk self-mockingly about 'Writer Monkeys'. It's okay when we do it, but the 'others' aren't allowed to disparage. I'm proud to be a Writer Monkey, and you should be, too. Because it's a slight misnomer. What we actually are is the 'Problem-Solving Ape'. A script – any script – is, at its most basic level, a sequence of problems and solutions. In the first instance – be they physical, emotional or moral – those problems are intentional points of plot and narrative, the building blocks of story. Bring me the Broomstick of the Wicked Witch of the West. What's a saloon bar owner to do with two letters of transit? What did he mean, 'Rosebud'? What should Sophie choose, and how can she live with that choice? How could anyone? Resolving those problems, answering those questions – while maintaining the established integrity of the imagined world in which they exist, and retaining the audience's interest in the solution – is more than half the job. I suppose it's what the late, great William Goldman called 'the spine'. Find the spine of your story, and all else follows. (Seriously, if you want to do this, read Goldman; let *Adventures in the Screen Trade* (Warner Books 1983) become your Bible.) Another way of putting it is, 'What's it about?'. When you begin, you may not have that answer down pat. You may not know. You may have a vague idea, a mood you want to catch, a feeling. Some things we wish to express are so gossamer and fragile that they're nigh on impossible to nail down straight out of the traps. In part, the process of writing is an uncovering – a chipping away at the block of marble to discover the form that lies within.

But back to the advice … Outside of the 'soaps', long-form drama series with high volume and turnover where a writer can develop their chops are few. The BBC has its writing scheme – and that's a way in for some. That route leads, typically – in the first instance – to continuing drama, a.k.a. the aforementioned 'soap'. And that's terrific. There are many fantastic talents who have come through that forcing ground – some of my favourite writers. I started with drama on a variation of the same, a show called *The Bill*, which was then a bi-weekly policier. The difference between that show and the current continuous dramas is that *The Bill* wasn't storylined; the 'episodes' were essentially 22-minute playlets. You could take it pretty much anywhere you wanted to go, provided you stuck to the one Golden Rule (and we only had one rule) – everything had to be seen from a police point of view. Otherwise, you could do what you liked.

It took me about a year to get through the door on that show. I'd been turned down, repeatedly. I'd come from a performing background – and that kind of weighed against being taken seriously – but the greatest bit of good luck that ever came my way arrived in the shape of a young woman by the name of Gina Cronk (insert Hollywood Recognition Applause here). Gina had been working in Reception, but – like your faithful correspondent – had ambition and ideas above her station. She'd just been made up from assistant script editor to script editor and consequently was looking to fill her flight roster with her own writers. If that hadn't happened, I would never have been seen and may have never got started. I don't doubt that the spec half-script I put in was pretty awful, but she saw something in there and gave me a break. I owe her pretty much everything.

The other thing the BBC's Writersroom has (at least at the time of writing) is a brilliant resource of scripts that you can download and read at your leisure, by people who really know what they're doing. Read every play, script and screenplay you can get your hands on. *That's* how you learn to know your way around a script. You watch the shows, and you read the scripts. See what was dropped; see what was added. Take note of who the script editor was. If it's a recent show, odds are that the script editor is still a script editor and hasn't ascended to the purple of Producerdom. Get in touch with them. If you're local, offer to buy them a cup of tea in a brightly lit public place and throw yourself upon their mercy. Beg, weep, grovel, offer whatever inducements you both consider legal, acceptable and, moreover, physically possible to get them to clue you in to what's going on in their department and the wider industry. They will know far better than anyone which shows are crewing up, which are looking for writers, what's in development, which of the afternoon dramas have a slot. If you are not local, try to do the same thing, initially, via email. Become pen pals, but (useful tip) – *don't be weird*. And remember – TV doesn't have to be your first port of call. A well-received fringe play or radio play can open just as many doors as the spec script. Get a rehearsed reading together. Invite agents and script editors and producers – especially agents – because representation is important. It will help get you in the room; after that you're on your own.

When that break comes, be ready to throw everything you've got at it. If you're pitching for a slot on an existing show, find the gap in the internal market. Know that show inside out. If everyone else is turning left, you turn right. Nothing to frighten the horses – you're not there to reinvent the wheel – but there will be characters who have been a bit under-served, or a coming curve that you can get ahead of. Furthermore, leave your pride and ego at the door; they're surplus to requirements. No matter how much you privately disagree, you will attend to the notes you are given diligently and with utmost dispatch, as if they were the Word of God. If that means you have to go a couple of nights without sleep to make the production deadline, then that is what you will do. This is not your great oeuvre or *meisterwerk*; this is episode 5, series 3, of whatever it might be. SERVE THE SHOW. Cut the throat of your favourite lines and characters and scenes if ordered to do so, without flinching or a moment's remorse. Stay light on your feet as production issues arise which will inevitably impact your script. Don't be precious about any of it. You've just lost the most important location? Write around it. *One of the regulars has had an accident and won't be available to shoot scenes 3, 24, 55A, 57 and 103B tomorrow … however, another character is available. Oh, and the first assistant director says the schedule is still 'over' and they won't be able to make the day; the request is to amalgamate scenes 55A and 57 while losing a page from their current page-count of three. We'll also have to cut 103B – and fold in the important information into scene 24. And, by the way, we're going to need it by close of play … today.*

Here's my modern heresy: I don't believe you can teach someone how to write. I think the snake-oil salesmen who tell you they can are exactly that. You can learn how to write – and you never stop learning – but that's a different thing. We learn by *doing*. You can no more teach someone to write than you can teach them to think or feel. You can provide them with a supportive environment, a creative soft space where they can stumble and fall frequently and safely. You can be a sounding board who offers thoughts about their work – a new angle, a different approach to a narrative problem or a way to rework the plot; but these are creative and editorial conversations you can expect to have all the time with your colleagues – commissioners, executives, producers, directors, actors – and especially, above all else, your editor. The good ones are worth their weight in diamonds and will save your arse more times than you can thank them, without it becoming an embarrass-ment – and really, you *do* need to thank them. So will many of the others on that list; because … (all together now) television – or film, radio or theatre – is a collaborative medium. This places the writer (who, you will remember, 'does not play well with others') in something of a cleft stick.

To illustrate this dichotomy, I keep two messages on my wall. The first reads, 'Television is a collaborative medium.' The second reads, 'COLLABORATORS WILL BE SHOT!' As Morgan Freeman's Detective Somerset observes at the end of the film *Se7en*: 'I agree with the second part.'

In the beginning was the word. Stay limber.

Oh, and the second rule of Write Club is …?

Russell Lewis has has written for TV series including *Between the Lines* (1992), winner of the Writers' Guild of Great Britain TV Original Drama Series Award, and *Murphy's Law* (2003). He devised and wrote the TV series *Endeavour* (2012) and has recently adapted two of Peter James' books featuring DS Roy Grace for *Grace* (2021) on ITV starring John Simm. He also co-wrote three of the *Sharpe* films. Russell began his career as a child actor. His earlier TV credits include episodes of *Perfect Scoundrels*, *Taggart*, *The Bill*, *Wycliffe*, *Inspector Morse*, *Kavanagh QC*, *Spooks* and *Lewis*.

See also...

- *Successful screenwriting*, page 351
- *Becoming a bestselling author: my writing story*, page 230

Podcasting: how to get creative and make money

Sam Delaney describes the versatility, creative freedom and financial rewards of podcasting. He shares his experience and gives practical advice about making your own podcasts and the many career opportunities this accessible medium presents.

Screen and audio

You've got a bright idea and you would like to expose it to the public. But first you need the patronage and approval of the media gatekeepers. Developing your idea is only half the battle. Selling it to an agent, a publisher, a TV commissioner or movie studio is the real challenge. Often, creative people are neither keen nor particularly competitive salespeople. Why should they be?

The good news is that, if you have an idea – whether it's for a science fiction novel, a history of the shovel or a slim volume of poetry about recycling – you no longer have to ask for permission from bigwigs to make it public. An idea you had in the bath before breakfast can plausibly be a bona fide piece of intellectual property being consumed by the great unwashed by teatime. All you need to do is pivot to podcasting.

Podcasting is a versatile medium that can be used as an initial testing ground for ideas eventually intended to be books, films, plays, TV shows – or anything really. There are few barriers to getting a podcast published and distributed: all you really need is a cheap microphone, a laptop and an internet connection. Rather than keep toiling to flog your idea to an agent, publisher or commissioner, you can get it out there via social media, build an audience, test and adapt the content and establish a brand. Eventually – if your idea is as good as you hope it is – you may well have the agents, publishers and commissioners coming to you.

In 2008 Ricky Gervais and Stephen Merchant first made the term 'podcast' famous by releasing highlights of their popular XFM radio show as a downloadable iTunes file you could listen to whenever you liked. It got so big that they started making bespoke shows exclusively as podcasts and charging people a pound a time to download them. It seemed like the birth of a brand-new lucrative industry. But it didn't really work out that way: lots of people were inspired to start podcasts, then quickly dropped them when they realized that, without millions of devoted listeners (which Merchant and Gervais had migrated across from their TV careers), there was no way they could make any money out of the medium.

I was one of those disappointed podcasters. I was a freelance journalist at the time and launched a TV review pod called *Stupid Telly* with a couple of mates. We worked with a production company who provided us with a studio and engineer. I would plan the show, write a skeleton script and book celebrity guests. We were proud of the content, got a couple of nice reviews in the press, but attracted about 500 listeners per show. We did it because we enjoyed it, but in the end we just couldn't devote all that time and energy to something that we weren't making any money out of. So, we all got full-time jobs and went our separate ways.

Fast forward 12 years and I am still a journalist, but I also have a podcast called *Top Flight Time Machine*. It has been downloaded over 4.5 million times since it started in

2018. It has been sponsored by a series of major brands, has a lucrative online merchandise shop and has completed two nationwide sell-out tours. We release two free-to-air episodes per week, plus another two via a subscription service which costs £3 per month. My co-host and I earn a few grand a month from *TFTM* and have created a brand: the idea – if you can call it that – is just two middle-aged dads chatting to each other about football nostalgia and any other ephemera that happens to cross our minds. We have managed to extend that to a live show, merchandise range, video content and, perhaps soon, a book too.

What's interesting is that you have probably never heard of us. I think we've proved that you don't need to be Ricky Gervais and Stephen Merchant to turn your podcast into something that is both creatively fulfilling and commercially lucrative. The size of your audience is one thing, but their engagement is just as important. You might build a weekly listenership of just 10,000 people but, if they are sufficiently passionate about you and your content, they will help you build a viable enterprise. Getting the balance right, so that you don't exploit or alienate your fans by harassing them for money, is all you need to focus on beyond creating great output.

Podcasting is not a very new medium, but it has only recently found its moment. In 2020, over seven million British adults (one in eight of the population) currently listen to a podcast at least once a week, according to Ofcom figures. That figure has more than doubled in the last five years. There are currently 850,000 active podcasts in the world, leading some people to deride the format as whimsical or ten-a-penny, and there is some truth in this; but if you're someone with a story to tell, the ability to turn it into a compelling piece of audio and the commitment to do it consistently, then a podcast could change your life and your career.

You might have heard of the big success stories. *My Dad Wrote A Porno*, a podcast where three mates talk about the porno one of their dads wrote, is so huge that its live show has sold out the Albert Hall, the Sydney Opera House and numerous other huge venues across the globe. Fern Cotton's *Happy Place*, a podcast in which the BBC broadcaster chats to friends, writers, celebrities and experts about mental health and wellbeing, is so enormously popular that it morphed into a sell-out, outdoor festival that stretched across two weekends in the summer of 2019. Dramatic fiction has found similar success via podcasts: psychological thriller *Homecoming* started life as a pod written by Eli Horowitz and Micah Bloomberg. It became so popular that Amazon commissioned a TV adaptation starring Julia Roberts.

Of course, not all podcasts prove so successful. Of those 850,000 pods, a huge number (I'm guessing 75% at least) are ill-thought-out, self-indulgent ramblings that only ever get listened to by the host, the host's mother, and the poor dope at iTunes who has to listen to Episode One in order to clear the content as suitable for broadcast. Even worse, there are numerous excellent podcasts, full of fresh ideas beautifully delivered, that never make it past Episode Five because the talent behind them can't make a living (or even a half-decent side-hustle) out of them. Taking the time to write, produce, record and edit something worth listening to will soak up a chunk of your schedule. Eventually, the need to do something that might actually help pay your gas bill is likely to get in the way.

The big difference between the success of my current podcast and the failure of *Stupid Telly* back in 2008 was that my *Top Flight* co-host and I started out with a commercial plan. That's not because we are cynical money-grubbers who create stuff only for profit. Okay, we do like money, but we genuinely love the content we create and the relationship we share with our band of listeners. We did it because we knew that unless we could see some sort of monetary return we'd be unlikely to stick with it as a project. We have bills to pay … which is a great focus for the mind. I am 45 with a mortgage and two kids. I need to know that anything which takes more than a couple of hours out of my working week has got at least a chance of paying dividends – both financially and in terms of career development.

So instead of just making a podcast, chucking it out there into the ether, and sitting at home waiting for some ad revenue to arrive one day, we looked at all the commercial angles. Once we started to build an audience, we thought about different revenue streams beyond plain old ad sales (which we do get, via a distribution platform we use called Acast, though to begin with this was way too sporadic to rely on). So we started to sell T-shirts, then to book live shows and then started offering the subscription service. Sponsors came on board to supplement the revenue from normal ads that played at the start and end of each episode. The sponsors pay you more than ordinary advertisers, in return for you taking a minute or two to weave promotion of their brand into the editorial content of the show. We manage to do it pretty unobtrusively and the audience don't seem to mind.

Top Flight Time Machine started as a TV idea: we tried to convince ITV to let us watch old episodes of the Big Match and talk about it as we went along. It was basically a nostalgic football version of Gogglebox. For whatever reasons, ITV didn't bite. So we did it as a podcast and stuck at it for the first six months when the audience was relatively small, until the 2018 World Cup seemed to boost our appeal and, by the end of that year, we had enough listeners for us to start making a bit of money and producing more episodes.

In the past year we've had approaches from TV companies, live promoters and publishers about 'extending the brand' – which is flattering – but on the whole we have rejected their offers because we have found it possible to build our audience and make money ourselves without having to pay a percentage to any middlemen. And, best of all, we have no one overseeing our creative output; we are 100% uncensored and unproduced. I have spent my whole career working in the media and have never enjoyed such creative freedom – at least, not for something I was actually getting paid for. I know a household-name TV star who has a podcast that started out as an outlet for ideas he could never get past commissioners. Now, he says, he makes more money out of the podcast than he does any of his high-profile TV gigs – and not a penny of it goes to anyone other than him.

I have had three books published and still have aspirations to write a fourth. If I do, I will build the idea as a podcast first – testing the creative limits, seeing what works and what doesn't, cultivating an audience and collecting loads of lovely data with which to impress publishers when I eventually take out my written proposal. Any literary agent is going to find their life a great deal easier if they can pitch a book idea with a pre-existing audience already attached (even if that audience is only in the thousands, not millions).

At this stage you might be frustrated that you have read this far without being told how to actually *make* the podcast. Well, that is the easiest bit to explain. Plug a microphone into your laptop. Record yourself using GarageBand, Quicktime or any other free audio tool (there are loads). Upload your file (for free) to Soundcloud. Generate an RSS code (google it if you don't know how – it is extremely easy) and then post that code to wherever you want people to listen. Get a logo designed using Canva. Start telling people about it on social media, and keep doing it – every episode will be better than the last. And anyway, even if the first ones are rubbish, it is a disposable medium. No one expects this to be a piece of gorgeously produced, meticulous audio journalism. This is podcasting – half the appeal is that it feels lo-fi, authentic and a bit rough round the edges. Just make it unique and sincere.

Right now your idea is living inside your head. The quickest way to extract it is saying it into a microphone and releasing it as a podcast. You might just be launching it into a bright new future.

Sam Delaney is a journalist, author and broadcaster. He has published three books: *Get Smashed!* (Sceptre 2007), *Night of the Living Dad* (John Murray 2010) and *Mad Men And Bad Men* (Faber 2015). His writing appears regularly in the *Guardian* and *The Big Issue*, among others, and is the former editor-in-chief of *Heat* magazine. Sam has hosted radio shows on BBC 5 Live, BBC Radio London and talkSPORT; from 2016-18 he hosted Drivetime on national network Talk Radio. He now runs 11-29 Media (www.11-29media.com), a podcast company that helps creators monetise their content.

Audio dramatist or novelist?

Writer Jonathan Myerson describes what has drawn him towards audio drama, how closely this form of storytelling relates to the art of a novelist, and where it differs. He explains the freedom offered by audio drama, as well as its dangers and demands, and outlines some crucial elements for success.

I cannot leave home without a book. The thought of being stuck with spare minutes and nothing to read … it's agony. So there is always a book – usually a novel – in my coat pocket. Even the dog complains.

As a chain-reader of fiction since my teenage years, I am not quite sure how I became a dramatist. But then again, I'm not surprised that audio drama has become my chosen form – I've dabbled in TV drama (too melodramatic), film (too much second-guessing) and even animation (still can't even draw stick men), but it is audio drama that I keep coming back to. I have also written novels, which is probably the one *un*surprising element in that spectrum: there's a clear affinity between a story told on the page and a story conveyed purely in sound.

To begin with, both the novel and the audio drama take shape only in the reader's or listener's mind. The well-worn maxim that 'the pictures are better on radio' rings equally true for the novel, whose scenes exist in that netherworld between the actual and the imagined, forcing the reader-audience to add the missing elements. And audio dramas, like novels, must tread the thin line between what the character might observe and what the story demands. A novelist – any good novelist, anyway – includes only the elements which are crucial for the given scene. Anything else – as we all discover when editing our own prose – is just typing.

This is also the stricture which a good audio dramatist must obey. Back when the BBC believed that younger audiences craved an alternative soap to *The Archers*, I wrote for a drama called *Citizens*. And it taught me one glorious lesson: very sporadically would you be reminded that one character (it was the landlord of the pub, I think) was in a wheelchair. For most scenes it was wholly irrelevant and therefore not mentioned (not even as a sound effect). A novelist would do the same. But in any other storytelling form, it would be inescapable in every frame, and would inevitably misdirect the audience's attention constantly.

Perhaps this is why so many of our great novelists have turned simultaneously to audio drama – William Trevor, Rose Tremain and Hilary Mantel, for instance – and so many audio dramatists have tried their hand at novels – recently and most notably Rachel Joyce. In fact, the latter's breakout bestseller, *The Unlikely Pilgrimage of Harold Fry*, started life as a (somewhat shorter) play for BBC Radio 4. Apart from the budget-busting range of eras and locations available to audio dramas and novels, both forms crucially enable the writer to tell you only what they want you to focus on – leaving you to pour your own imaginative fuel onto the rest.

I'll admit that, when I started writing my first novel after more than a decade as a dramatist, I went through a period of shock. I was accustomed to simply typing terse scene-settings (maybe 'deck of freighter during force 8 storm' or 'the characters stroll through an autumnal forest glade') and leaving it to the crew to execute my demands. Suddenly, with no production staff, I was going to have to bring all of this to life myself, to find the precise and most convincing sequence of words to make it real. And then my second realisation: this wouldn't be simply 'Sound Effects Disc 37B' or a studio manager waltzing across crisp packets. No, here my words were free to evoke exactly what it feels like for the characters to endure that storm or breathe the leafy mist coming in on that October air. It would all be about the characters' response to these surroundings. Their perspective would be my liberation.

And perspective brings us back to that crucial element of audio drama storytelling: just as many novels are written either in the first person or in close third person, audio dramas thrive on that same intense bond between listener and central character. If asked to define the role of the modern novel, I would say it's a 300-page exploration of What It's Like To Be X (whether X is a woman of 60 who has just discovered her husband's secret love child or X is a mixed-race teen on a West London estate where it's all about to kick off). At their most successful, audio dramas perform the same function. Sure, you can choose to bounce around between different characters in different places, but any audio drama gains hugely from a central pivot - the sort of viewpoint you'd take for granted in a novel. Emile Zola defined art as 'a corner of creation seen through a temperament' and that ticks the audio drama boxes just as neatly.

As always in the writing game, though, there's no such thing as a free lunch. That central temperament will also do its best to pull you down the fatal primrose path for audio drama writers: the internal monologue. Many novels thrive on this kind of commentary, but at this point drama and prose must part ways. For me, the internal monologue is the enemy of live drama, and any play must feel *live*, must hum with the danger of *now*, with the unknowingness of its characters. And that's why the internal monologue is the dramatist's sworn enemy. For so many seemingly good reasons, voice-over will feel like the solution to all your problems: anything which you cannot convey in sound can instantly get itself described. What's more, it's your chance to speak directly and unimpeded to the audience. But characters in drama, unlike prose fiction, must always be up against a ticking clock and, as soon as a character has unlimited and unopposed time to unleash her thoughts and reflections, that clock stops ticking.

So my advice on the 'narratorly voice-over' is: Handle With Extreme Caution. That direct channel into the mind and feelings of the protagonist, that self-dissecting honesty, will erode any genuine suspense. If the central character understands himself, why does the audience need to even try? Imagine if the curtain went up on the latest production of *Hamlet* and the title character strode to the front of the stage and announced he has an issue with getting things done, is probably a bit confused about his sexuality, and let's not even talk about his mother issues. Would you bother to watch the ensuing four hours? No, you watch the five acts in order to work all this out for yourself.

Worse than self-knowledge, a voice-over becomes a safety net underlying your plot, because however bad things turn out, this character is still able to tell us about what happened, and how they have come to terms with those events. Often, when I fulminate about voice-overs, people throw something like *Sunset Boulevard* back at me (non-spoiler alert: Scene 1 reveals William Holden's corpse floating in the swimming pool and the rest of the film unravels his journey to that point), but even that trades on a Zen-like resignation in Holden's narration. In other words, he survived, he's down with it, and you don't need to worry.

So how then to ensure that the audio drama remains your protagonist's story? How to generate that solidity of POV? It's not easy, but now we come full circle back to the novelist's skill set. Any novelist writing in first or close third person takes for granted that their protagonist appears in every scene. Yes, in a shorter drama that can make the plotting tricky, but you can always contrive the setting and 'agenda' of your scenes so that everything is revealed (though beware those faux voice-overs: the Therapist's Couch, the Endlessly Patient Best Friend!). Once you have finagled your plotting to tell it all through action involving your protagonist, the coherence and focus of your play is assured. The listener is now freed to walk a single, ribbon-like journey – and we're back to Harold Fry.

Of course, in this sense, a protagonist is not always a single person. In 1998 Bruce Springsteen agreed to play a concert in East Germany, behind the Berlin Wall. My play, *Born in the GDR*, dramatises how three young people first had the crazy idea of asking him, and how they squeezed the whole scheme past the Stasi and then staged a concert in front of what is still the largest audience ever in Europe. Those three people, as a joint enterprise, are the protagonist – one or more of them is in every scene. They are the ribbon; they are the temperament through whom we view this particular corner of creation.

In fact, many of my plays – because they dramatise actual events – have demanded this approach. In my trilogy of plays about *The Clintons*, Bill and/or Hillary is in every scene; it was their show, their unfolding. We never jump to the other side's POV. What happens is happening to them. Or think sideways: Anthony Minghella's *Cigarettes and Chocolate* explores the mystery of why the pivotal character has stopped speaking. The result is a brilliant set of agonised, one-sided conversations with a woman who won't reply. The other characters can say what they want, but they are still talking to someone – it's not just narration into a convenient theatrical void. And the clock remains ticking ... until, at the last, she reveals the reason for her silence.

And why stop there? We now all carry a device engineered for self-advertisement and this hands the audio dramatist a sledgehammer with which to demolish the fourth wall entirely. My podcast serial *That Was Then* has the central character secretly recording everything – for her own safety, as much as anything – into her phone, both the events and her follow-up diary. In fact, we even recorded it on location on an iPhone in order to generate that kind of scratchy, amateurish recording (but Apple outwitted us, and the quality was barely distinguishable from the BBC's best in-house microphones). But the protagonist's need to hide the recordings from everyone, including her own family, kept that clock ticking loudly; the drama remains set firmly in the now.

So I am often asked, how do you know if your next idea is a novel or an audio drama? And the truthful answer is, I don't know. In so many respects, they're the same thing and ask the same from their audiences – but don't forget that they make slightly different demands on the writer.

A word on words: throughout this piece I have used the term 'audio drama'. Now that the world of podcasts has reinvented this particular wheel, the words 'radio drama' seem needlessly old-fashioned. Nowadays audio dramas are sometimes known as 'scripted podcasts', but I find that dull and unwieldy. Certainly, someday soon, podcast providers will be creating more hours of audio drama than the BBC – and the Corporation is the only reason still to call it 'radio' drama.

Jonathan Myerson is the author of over 50 individual dramas for the BBC (Radio 4, Radio 3 and World Service), as well as episodes of radio drama series *Westway* and *Citizens*. His audio drama series include *The Republicans*, *Doctor Zhivago*, *The Way We Live Right Now*, and *Number 10* (winner of the Writers' Guild Award for Best Radio Drama). His most recent podcasts are *Mueller: Trump Tower Moscow* and *That Was Then*. Jonathan has been nominated for an Oscar and won a BAFTA in 1999 for his animated film of *The Canterbury Tales*. After ten years running the prestigious Novel Writing MA at City University London, he now consults for finishyournovel.org.

See also...

● *Advice to a new writer*, page 239

Should I make an audiobook?

James Peak looks at the rapid growth, popularity and profitability of the audiobook market that has been made possible by new technology, and lays out a clear route and valuable tips for anyone considering producing their own audiobook.

It was 1999. I was lost and disoriented at the London Book Fair. I staggered into a lopsided little tent right at the back, where a wizened old lady whose palm I crossed with silver peered into her misty orb. 'What does the future of book publishing hold?', I asked her. Then, more stridently (thinking of the small Caribbean island I so richly deserve), 'And how can it make me some money?' Focusing deep inside the glass, she muttered something about young wizards, colouring-in for adults and rebooted ladybirds. Staring deeper, she whispered a mysterious incantation: 'Buy Amazon' and rushed outside to phone her stock-broker. I seized her crystal ball. The mist inside cleared to reveal a strange vision: some books would become peculiar electronic files, beamed straight to the pockets and handbags of readers via their tiny, shiny, computery-phoney things; some books would be read on scrolling screens; some would even be listened to with stylish white headphones. I ran from the tent. I'd seen the future. I was going to be rich.

Twenty years later that future is here – and 70,000 of my colouring books about wizarding ladybirds have been pulped. Authors today must expect to be heard as well as read. It's a change that begs several questions: should I write differently if my words are destined for the ear as well as the eye? Whose voice will my readers be hearing? What will this all cost me? Should I bother to make an audiobook at all?

The market is growing

Over the last few years, the UK's big four publishers have been racing to hire teams of audio editors, build in-house studios and forge links with independent audio producers, in order that they may deep-fill their back catalogues with spoken versions, not only of their bestsellers but their midsellers too. Why is this land-grab for audio making good business sense? One reason might be that audiobook distribution has vastly simplified. Publishers no longer need to cough up to burn CDs, expensively design and package boxed sets and lobby for shelf space in high-street bookshops. Instead, the ubiquity of the smartphone has enabled a streamlined distribution network from printed page to listener's ear.

The economics look great. In common with ebooks, the endless replicability of the mp3 file negates all physical costs of production. An eight-hour book can retail at well over £20. Once produced, it's re-deliverable, pretty much free, forever (or at least until the tech changes again). As a result, the entire audiobook market has digitised and found millions of new listeners ready to put their hands into their pockets. According to the 2020 Audio Publishers Association survey, unit sales of audiobooks in 2019 increased with 16% growth in revenue, taking the total earned to US$1.2b, the eighth consecutive year of double-digit growth. US adults each listened to, on average, 8.1 audiobooks in 2020, up from 6.8 in 2019 (Edison Research and Triton Digital's *The Infinite Dial 2020*). Voice-enabled home smart speakers, like Amazon Echo and Google Home, support digital audiobooks; 60% of listeners over 18 in the USA own a smart speaker, with 46% using them to listen to audiobooks.

Excitingly, the same report found that, with audiobooks, people are finding new time in their day to listen. This is big: that's 50% of people choosing to consume more book content through audiobooks. They are also multi-tasking as they do so. Print books demand a reader's full attention. If you exercise or bake with a printed book on the go, you'll sustain terrible injuries and your muffins will be dreadful.

Who is behind all this?

So who is behind this sensational reboot? Amazon – through its subsidiary Audible, the early-to-market US audiobook producer that was snapped up back in 2008 for a mere bagatelle ($300m) and which now presides over an estimated 90% of the global audiobook market. There are other players on the audiobook market (Scribed, Kobo, Storytel) but competition-wise, the dominance has raised hackles. In 2015 anti-trust regulators began investigating, as simply too much, an exclusivity agreement that made Audible the only provider of audiobooks to Apple's massive, global iStore. The Amazon-Apple arrangement came to an end in 2017, which the European Commission said was 'likely to improve competition' in the future. For now, though, the Amazon-Audible platform is overwhelmingly the biggest game in town, and it is most probably the main place where your audiobook will live.

Audiobooks are not just for big publishers. Amazon has extended its jaw-droppingly efficient infrastructure to the self-publishing sector, through Audible's Audiobook Creation Exchange (ACX). It is aimed at book rights-holders and self-publishing authors in the USA, UK and Canada. Although the quality of the most cheaply produced audiobooks can vary, it has lowered the barriers to entry. An audiobook can now cost just a few hundred pounds to produce if you are prepared to narrate and edit it yourself, and a couple of thousand if working with a professional voice actor and studio. Amazon then advertises the audiobook on the same page as the printed book on Amazon.com. Royalties of up to 40% of the cover price can quickly add up to significant sums, if it sells. After an initial production outlay, writers are finding it's possible to turn a profit. How much of a profit is difficult to establish, as Amazon are cagey about releasing their sales data.

How to do it

If you are going to make an audiobook, there are pitfalls into which you should not stumble. Here is an overview of a linear route to market:

Writing → voice casting → recording → editing → releasing → marketing

Writing

Your book is a strong candidate to become an audiobook if it's literary, historical, thrilling, romantic, fantastical or erotic, or if it's a memoir, diary or self-help book. Sci-fi can also be enormously popular, and a few specialist UK audio companies (including Big Finish Ltd) found success with audio products before the current land grab, working within classic sci-fi like *Dr Who* and *Blake's 7*. Graphic novels, art books and cookbooks may struggle with audio, as they depend so heavily on a visual element. However, some big publishers are experimenting with recording children's picture books, using familiar voices, high-end sound design and music to create adaptations. Imelda Staunton's version of *The Gruffalo* (Macmillan 1999) is a lovely example of this. If you have a children's picture book that you can adapt to work without pictures, its brevity can be its saving grace, as the finished audiobook might be only five or ten minutes long, and costs or recording and editing correspondingly low.

Voice casting

Deciding whose voice to use may be easy if cost is an issue: your own will be cheapest, and nobody knows the nuances of your book like you do. However, if time is a factor, or you are not sure if your own voice is strong enough, you could book a test session at a local recording studio (£50-£100) or find a quiet space and read into your smartphone for a full 30 minutes, taking feedback from sample listeners. At the end of a test session you'll know if narrating is something you have an appetite for and if your voice will do your book justice.

Alternatively, hiring a professional narrator can be a really effective way to draw out the drama, romance, thrills and mystery in your book, particularly if there is lots of multi-character dialogue or if it needs careful pacing or tone. The best narrators are absolutely spellbinding, bringing emotion and passion to your words.

A typical 100,000-word novel might be 8-10 hours long and will take a professional 'voice' 20-25 hours to record properly. Their services do not have to be horrifically expensive if you have your negotiating hat on. Often, voices combine audiobook work with lucrative commercial work and acting careers. Many are represented by agents keen to monetise time, and recording audiobooks can soak up spare hours. Reasonable charges for audiobook voices are around £200-£400 per day, and for this you can expect adequate preparation and reading time thrown in.

If only a particular (high-profile, celebrity) narrator will do, or you really need transparency on costs at the outset, try passing your book on via that person's agent, with a letter explaining why they simply must do it! If you can enthuse them, you might be able to 'buy them out' to record the whole thing for a fixed price.

Recording

If you decide to voice your own book in your own home, you'll need a very quiet and small space, and ideally it should be soundproofed and acoustically deadened. Bare, flat walls reverberate sound, but hanging heavy fabrics at angles can minimize this.

You'll need a decent condenser microphone, a 'pop shield' to stop plosive sounds like 'P' and 'B' distorting your recording and a computer with a solid-state drive or the fan turned off so that it is near silent.

You'll need decent audio recording software, like ProTools or the open-source programme Audacity, with GarageBand being a simple entry-level programme that is already pre-installed on many Apple computers.

Make sure you read your book from a tablet, as rustling noises from paper scripts will be picked up by your microphone. Regular hydration will stop horrid clicky mouth noises being picked up by the microphone. You will quickly get into the habit of re-doing sentences that you've fluffed, and these mistakes can be edited out afterwards.

Recording in a studio with an engineer can be expensive (£75-£150 per hour) but many will consider buy-outs for a project, particularly if they can schedule sessions around other work. As the author, you should be welcome at all recording sessions, to review production and comment on pace and narration style. Beware of studios that don't welcome you to sit in, as it might indicate quality isn't key. Many studios provide a producer to sit alongside the engineer, to listen to performances, ask for retakes and rewrite sentences that read better on the page than they sound. Having several pairs of ears in these recording sessions can eliminate the need to re-record later.

Editing

If you are producing your own audiobook at home, you'll have to review and edit every page into chapter-sized chunks for ACX. This can be fiddly, but it is immensely satisfying if you are a tech-savvy multitasker. Editing consists of: removing extraneous noises from the recording; joining different takes together without losing the sense of drama and pace; adding music and effects; and delivering sound files to exact technical specifications.

To pass ACX's quality control for release for sale on Audible and Amazon, you'll need to deliver audio files 'at 44.1khz … measuring between -23dB and -18dB RMS … with a maximum -60dB noise floor.' This sounds more difficult than it is.

If you recorded in a professional studio, then you'd be well advised to keep the editing with the same team, because they know your book very well by this stage.

Releasing

Once edited, your audiobook's individual chapters are uploaded onto ACX, where it enters a quality-control queue. Audible learned quickly that consumers won't pay £20-odd for distorted or echoing audio recordings. Their quality control is stringent but, equally, their feedback about problems with files is helpful and precise.

If all is well, a couple of weeks after submission your book will appear for sale. Because of the quality-control filter, and a greater volume of audiobooks being submitted than even a year ago, you'd be well advised to pause advance marketing activity until your new audiobook is confirmed as available.

Marketing

Increasingly, reviewers are listening to audiobooks and plumbing them into their blogs and channels. There are many audiobook specialists, e.g. at www.rtbookreviews.com, https://audiobookreviewer.com, www.hotlistens.com and http://briansbookblog.com.

Just as for books, marketing audiobooks is effort-based. If you're prepared to run a campaign of social media ads, serenade bloggers, lobby to appear on podcasts, organise online book tours and engage in all those dark arts, then your sales will benefit. Upon request, ACX provides free download codes to send out to reviewers, so you may push your audiobook as much or as little as you please.

Making an audiobook is a fascinating, exacting, collaborative process that can give your book another dimension, and, hopefully, your bank balance a boost. There are many brilliant audio engineers and narrators out there who can help your words reach ears as well as eyes. If you decide to start production, good luck, and don't forget your pop shield.

James Peak runs Essential Music Ltd (http://essentialmusic.co.uk), which has been producing BBC comedies, dramas and documentaries since 1996, and audiobook and podcasts since they were invented. He is co-author, with Duncan Crowe, of the series of comic novels, *Scoundrels*, published by Farrago Books (http://farragobooks.com) and Black Door Press (www.blackdoorpress.com). James welcomes questions about your audiobook projects at james@essentialmusic.co.uk.

Writing for videogames: a guide for the curious

Chris Bateman shines a light on videogame writing, its nature and challenges, and has essential advice for anyone hoping to build a career in the rewarding and creative world of game narrative and design.

So you've played a few videogames, and marvelled at the production values and the intensity of the experience, but were perhaps a little underwhelmed by the stories you've encountered. Like any writer, you can't resist a creative challenge and you know that with the right tools you could do a better job. The question is: what do you need to create videogame narrative? How do you begin? Where do you go to make it happen?

Let's start with the bucket of cold water – you will not end up writing for videogames if it's just an idle fancy; it takes a real commitment to work in games writing and – make no mistake – this is the toughest medium to work in. But at the same time, working on a game story, helping a team bring characters into beautifully animated life and working with voice actors to give a soul to those animations, can be hugely rewarding. Working on an animated movie or TV show carries the same emotional payoff, is substantially easier, and gives more creative control to the writing team, but if you're dedicated to your dream of writing for games, or don't think anything else would quite satisfy your creative needs, videogame writing is a path you can take.

Getting started

So how do you get the opportunity? As with most jobs, you frustratingly need to have prior experience to get hired. If you've already written novels, short stories, radio plays, screenplays, stage plays or anything of the kind, you can try fishing for work with that experience but you're likely to come up against a certain resistance from game developers. One way around this, especially if you're a writer with time to invest in career-building, is to lend your support to indie games (i.e. low-budget projects) that are advertising on sites like Gamasutra (www.gamasutra.com) or via social media asking for help. They may be willing to take on a writer (typically unpaid) and in return you can get experience working in games. It's not a glamorous way to start, but gaining experience seldom is.

If you have a little money to invest in your career, consider attending one of the major industry events like Develop in Brighton or GDC in San Francisco (see box for details), where you can hear from experienced game writers and get networking. This was more or less how my company, International Hobo, built up clients in the early years, although admittedly I'd already worked on several critically acclaimed games at that point. You can also go to these events and set up meetings with developers to talk about what you can offer. There's usually a meeting app provided with the ticket, and there are also third-party options, like MeetToMatch (www.meettomatch.com), which are often worth the extra cost.

How game projects begin

Let's say you've found a developer willing to work with you. Now is the time to pitch that screenplay you wrote as a dynamite basis for a videogame, right? Sorry, no. Videogames are never made from screenplays (we don't even have a standard format for one!) and very few start as story concepts either. If you want to make your own glossy digital masterpiece for games consoles, you'd better have a few million in your back pocket to fund production. Otherwise, accept that your job as game writer is to assist a development team to get the most out of the game they're making, by helping them discover opportunities to get more out of characters or settings or theme (a subtlety many game developers tend to overlook).

Typically, a game begins as either a prototype, showing off what the game is like, or as a concept document – a short pitch for a game. Concept documents are quite similar to the proposals that a book publisher or agent expects to be submitted (and often written after the manuscript is completed). Laying out the story in broad strokes is part of the concept and so can be an element of the documentation from the very beginning – although, in practice, writers seldom get attached to projects this early. This, however, is short-sightedness on the part of developers, who actually could use your input at this stage. You can pitch your services to companies in this way – but expect scepticism if you can't show evidence that you have a handle on how stories in games work.

Networking opportunities

Develop Conference

www.developconference.com

Europe's leading convention and expo for those working in game development. Held annually in Brighton for three days in July.

Game Development Conference (GDC)

www.gdconf.com

The world's largest professional gaming industry event, incorporating The Independent Games Festival and The Game Developers Choice Awards. Takes place over five days every March in San Francisco.

Gamescom

www.gamescom.global

Europe's largest expo, and a good networking opportunity. Held in August each year in Cologne.

International Game Developers Association (IGDA)

https://igda.org

US-based with a global network of over 150 Chapters and Special Interest Groups (SIGs) with individual members from all fields of game development: programmers and producers, designers and artists, writers and other experts.

WGA – Writers Guild of America

www.wga.org

Union that represents writers for film, TV and games, combining WGA West and WGA East. Like the WGGB, its UK equivalent, the WGA honours writers for games in its annual awards. See page 520.

WGGB – Writers' Guild of Great Britain

https://writersguild.org.uk

Union that supports UK-based writers, including games writers, with a useful guide *Writing for videogames* on its site. See page 512.

How do you build up your understanding of the workings of videogame? The easiest way is to play games. You can learn a lot from playing videogames, but don't just play the latest releases or you'll end up playing solely what are called AAA games (i.e. multi-million-dollar blockbusters) and, as a writer trying to break into games, you won't be working on these. Play older games, play new games made on a low budget, and play games from wildly different genres. While you're networking, you can even ask game developers which games they rate for clever use of story materials ... you'll get plenty of suggestions! Another option is to watch online videos of other people playing games. Some game writers will cluck their tongues at this suggestion, but you don't need to be able to play a certain kind of game to work on its story, you just have to be able to appreciate how it works; other people's player experiences can be just as useful for this (in some cases, more useful) because games are not played in the same ways by all players.

Narrative design

In the early 2000s, when I was setting up International Hobo, my colleagues and I conceived of our job as 'narrative design'. It's a term that has now crept out into the industry thanks to the International Game Developers Association, for which I set up the Game Writing Special Interest Group (you might want to check this out as a helpful community for game writers at all stages of their careers; see box). Narrative design is the intersection of game design and writing: it's about putting a player into the centre of your story or, perhaps more accurately, about turning a story inside-out so that it can work when the central character is (nearly) beyond your control. A player isn't an actor, so you'll need to provide reasons for them to take on the role provided – or alternatively give them opportunities to mess around with the world.

There are several key aspects of narrative design you'll need to consider:

1. Dialogue

You'll need to decide if your focus will just be on dialogue – in which case, expect the scenarios to be almost entirely dictated to you, and prepare to work with a low level of creative influence – or if you're going to get involved with narrative design. This means having a hand in the structuring of the game materials, which in turn means understanding game design as well as writing. Woe betide the conventional screenwriter who thinks they will 'fix' videogames by making them more like movies!

2. Cut scenes and voice actors

Almost everything you want to do to make a conventional narrative work is too expensive. You will struggle to get much budget for animated sequences (called *cut scenes*, or *FMV* – full motion videos) and if you're having to tell your story in this way you're working in the wrong medium. Talking heads (i.e. voice actors providing dialogue to animated characters in the game) is a powerful and relatively cost-effective tool, but the moment you need one of the characters to be animated in a specific way (say, banging their fist on a table for emphasis) you're draining money from the budget. As a writer, words are your greatest tool so use them to great effect. If the game has voice recording (most mid-budget or higher games do) the voice actors will be able to 'sell' your dialogue to the player without you having to specify animations for emphasis. If it doesn't, well then you get an even greater opportunity to make every word count, because it's your text being read directly by the players. Either way, don't use more lines than you need to advance the narrative.

3. Narrative spaces

The other key element of narrative design is location: games typically flow through environments and, as a writer, you can use your grasp of locations to great effect in discussions with the developer. As always, though, every location costs money to make and, unlike for film or TV, you can't just nip out with a location crew if you need footage; everything has to be painstakingly built by the team. That means nothing should go into the game that isn't absolutely necessary, and ideally you shouldn't be creating more locations than are needed.

Theatre is a much better guide than film in this regard. The playwright has to think about how it works on stage; you don't have an entire set put up just for an actor to say two lines and walk off. In a game, every location has to earn its time. Unlike theatre sets, however, videogame environments are typically vast open spaces; that gives you the opportunity to paint in stories, without text or dialogue, by using environmental storytelling. You won't get the budget to show, say, a werewolf tearing apart a village, but you can show the aftermath and let the player piece together the back story from what they can find.

4. World-building

Some games, particularly computer role-playing games, also rely on a depth of lore – and the need for the associated texts can be a way for a writer to get added to a project. World-building is part of the writer's toolkit, and while few game developers will let you put together the world for their game single-handed, they may well be delighted for you to write short texts that fill in the substance of their setting. I won't lie to you – this may involve a great deal of writing descriptions for weaponry, but I have to say I found it very rewarding to paint a picture of a fantasy world solely from the swords, shields, jewellery and clothing players will encounter. There's a challenge here that no other medium will give you.

Part of the team

Ultimately, writing for games is about working in a team in which different professionals have a hand in making everything happen. The most important thing you can do, as a writer, when you join a developer is to acknowledge that the programmers and artists are the ones who are actually making the game – your job is to help bring out the best in what they're doing. If you can place yourself in the service of a developer, your writing can take videogames to another level. That's what keeps me going. There are always new ways to tell stories in games, and it's my pleasure and honour to work with developers to help them discover the right one for their project.

Chris Bateman is a game designer, philosopher, author and founder of the game design, narrative design and scriptwriting consultancy International Hobo. He is best known for the games *Discworld Noir* and *Ghost Master* and his books *Game Writing: Narrative Skills for Videogames* (Cengage Learning 2007, 2nd edition Bloomsbury 2021). His other books include *Imaginary Games* (2011) and *Chaos Ethics* (2014), both published by Zero Books, and *The Virtuous Cyborg* (Eyewear Publishing 2018). Chris has an MSc in Artificial Intelligence/Cognitive Science and a PhD in game aesthetics, and has worked on over 70 published games. He teaches at the University of Bolton and Laguna College of Art and Design in California. Find out more by visiting his blog *Only a Game* (http://onlyagame.typepad.com) or his company's blog (http://blog.ihobo.com).

Television and radio

The information in this section has been compiled as a general guide for writers, artists, agents and publishers to the major companies and key contacts within the broadcasting industry. As personnel, corporate structures and commissioning guidelines can change frequently, readers are encouraged to check the websites of companies for the most up-to-date information.

REGULATION

Advertising Standards Authority

Castle House, 37–45 Paul Street, London EC2A 4LS
tel 020-7492 2222
website www.asa.org.uk
Facebook www.facebook.com/adauthority
Twitter @ASA_UK
Chief Executive Guy Parker

The UK's independent regulator of advertising across all media. Its work includes acting on complaints and taking action against misleading, harmful or offensive advertisements.

Ofcom

Riverside House, 2A Southwark Bridge Road, London SE1 9HA
tel 020-7981 3000, 0300 123 3000
website www.ofcom.org.uk
Facebook www.facebook.com/ofcom
Twitter @Ofcom
Chief Executive Melanie Dawes

Accountable to parliament and exists to further the interests of consumers by balancing choice and competition with the duty to encourage plurality, protect viewers and listeners, promote diversity in the media and ensure full and fair competition between communications providers.

TELEVISION

There are five major TV broadcasters operating in the UK: the BBC, ITV, Channel 4 (S4C in Wales), Channel 5 and Sky. In Ireland, RTÉ is the country's public service broadcaster.

The BBC

BBC Broadcasting House, Portland Place, London W1A 1AA
website www.bbc.co.uk

The BBC is the world's largest broadcasting organisation, with a remit to provide programmes that inform, educate and entertain. Established by a Royal Charter, the BBC is a public service broadcaster funded by a licence fee. Income from the licence fee is used to provide services including:

• eight national TV channels plus regional programming

• ten national radio stations
• 39 local radio stations
• two national radio services each in Scotland, Wales and Northern Ireland
• BBC Online Services
• BBC World Service

Anyone in the UK who watches or records TV programmes (whether via TV, online, mobile phone, games console, digital box, etc) or watches or downloads any BBC programmes from BBC iPlayer needs a TV licence. The Government sets the level of the licence fee; it was announced in 2016 that the licence would rise in line with inflation for five years from 1 April 2017. The annual cost from 1 April 2021 is £159. For full details of which services require a TV licence, visit: www.tvlicensing.co.uk.

Governance

BBC Board

Since January 2021, the BBC has been governed by a board chaired by Richard Sharp. Tim Davie, Director-General, sits on the board alongside four other BBC executive members. There are ten non-executive members. More information is available at: www.bbc.co.uk/aboutthebbc.

Ofcom

External regulation of the BBC is carried out by Ofcom.

What does the BBC do?

The following provides a selective overview of the BBC's main services and key contact information we consider most relevant to our readership.

Television

The BBC's eight national TV channels, provide entertainment, news, current affairs and arts programming for the whole of the UK: BBC One, BBC Two, BBC Three, BBC Four, CBBC, CBeebies, BBC News and BBC Parliament. BBC Three is an online-only service.

Chief Content Officer Charlotte Moore
Controller, BBC Two Patrick Holland
Controller, BBC Three Fiona Campbell
Channel Editor, BBC Four Cassian Harrison
Controller, Programming & iPlayer Dan McGolpin
Director, Children's Alice Webb
Director, Sport Barbara Slater

BBC Radio and Education

Network radio, arts, music, learning, and children's form one division.

BBC Strategy and Digital

BBC's online services include news, sport, weather, CBBC, CBeebies, BBC iPlayer and the school learning and revision site, BBC Bitesize. Sites are developed to provide audiences with access to content on a variety of devices including tablets, smartphones, computers and internet-connected TVs. Also provides access to the BBC's radio and TV programme archives, through BBC iPlayer.

News Group

This is the largest of the BBC's departments in terms of staff. BBC News incorporates network news (the newsroom, news programmes such as Newsnight, political programmes such as Daily Politics, and the weather team), English Regions and Global News.

Director, News and Current Affairs Fran Unsworth

Nations and Regions

The Nations and Regions division is one of the largest divisions in the BBC with staff working for the BBC in England, Scotland, Wales and Northern Ireland. The division produces a range of content across TV, radio and online for audiences locally, across all of the UK and globally.

Director, Nations Rhodri Talfan Davies

BBC Studios

BBC Studios works with British writers, directors and programme-makers to create over 2,500 hours of content every year through seven production bases in the UK and in partnership with countries around the world.

Interim Ceo Tom Fussell

BBC Studioworks

A wholly owned subsidiary of the BBC, works with media companies to create and manage content across all genres for a diverse range of broadcasters and platforms, including ITV, Channel 4 and Sky, as well as the BBC.

Ceo Andrew Moultrie

BBC World Service Group

Incorporates BBC World Service and BBC Global News and includes the BBC World News Television Channel, the BBC's international-facing online news services in English, BBC Monitoring Service and BBC Media Action (the BBC's international development charity).

Director, World Service Group Jamie Angus

Britbox

website www.britbox.com

A digital video subscription service created by the BBC and ITV Plc, serving the UK, the USA and Canada. It is focused on British television series and films, mainly featuring current and past series and films supplied from the main UK public service broadcasters.

Commissioning

For full details of editorial guidelines, commissioning, production and delivery guidelines, and how to submit a proposal, see www.bbc.co.uk/commissioning.

Developing and producing programmes is complex and requires substantial knowledge of production and broadcasting. **BBC Pitch** (www.bbc.co.uk/commissioning/pitch) is the BBC's commissioning tool designed for UK-based production companies and BBC in-house production teams to submit content proposals for BBC Network Television. Individuals and members of the public cannot use BBC Pitch. If you are a member of the public with an idea, see www.bbc.co.uk/commissioning/talent.

Who's who in commissioning?

Television (genre commissioning) *Chief Content Officer* Charlotte Moore

Children's *Head of Content BBC Children's* Cheryl Taylor

Comedy *Controller* Shane Allen, *Commissioning Editors* Gregor Sharp, Ben Caudell, Tanya Qureshi

Daytime and Early Peak *Head of Daytime and Early-Peek Commissioning* Carla-Maria Lawson, *Commissioning Editors* Lindsay Bradbury, Alex McLeod, Neil McCallum, Rachel Platt, Julie Shaw, Muslim Alim

Drama *Controller* Piers Wenger, *Commissioning Editors* Lucy Richer, Jo McClellan, Gaynor Holmes, Mona Qureshi, Tommy Bulfin, Ben Irving

Entertainment *Interim Controller* Jo Wallace, *Commissioning Editors* Neil McCallum, Rachel Ashdown, Ruby Kuraishe, Pinki Chambers, Sarah Clay, Kalpna Patel-Knight

Factual (covers arts, current affairs, documentaries, features and formats, history, business, learning, music, religion and ethics, science, natural history, Open University, acquisitions and BBC iPlayer) *Controller* Alison Kirkham

BBC Nations and Regions *Director Northern Ireland* Peter Johnston, *Director BBC Scotland* Stephen Carson, *Director Cymru Wales* Rhodri Talfan Davies, *Head of BBC Midlands* Stuart Thomas, *Director South West* Pat Connor

BBC Writersroom

email writersroom@bbc.co.uk
website www.bbc.co.uk/writersroom
Facebook www.facebook.com/BBCWriters
Twitter @bbcwritersroom

BBC Writersroom is the first port of call at the BBC for unsolicited scripts and new writers. It champions writing talent across a range of genres and is always on the lookout for writers of any age and experience who can show real potential for the BBC. Unsolicited scripts are accepted twice a year as part of Script Room (comedy and drama scripts only) and those shortlisted get offered a development group placement. The BBC Writersroom blog provides a wealth of behind-the-scenes commentary from writers and producers who have worked on BBC TV and radio programmes: www.bbc.co.uk/blogs/writersroom.

Education and training

The BBC has adopted a recruitment system called the BBC Careers Hub. It allows candidates to apply for jobs, source interview tips, learn about the BBC's recruitment processes and get advice about CVs, applications and assessments: www.bbc.co.uk/careers/

Trainee Schemes and Apprenticeships

website www.bbc.co.uk/careers/trainee-schemes-and-apprenticeships

For full details of the BBC's trainee and apprenticeship schemes, see website.

Work Experience

website www.bbc.co.uk/careers/work-experience

For full details of the BBC's work experience placements, see website.

BBC Academy

website www.bbc.co.uk/academy

A free, online learning resource providing practical advice and information on all aspects of working in TV, radio and online.

Channel 4

124–126 Horseferry Road, London SW1P 2TX
tel 020-7396 4444
website www.channel4.com
Facebook www.facebook.com/Channel4/
Twitter @Channel4

A publicly owned, commercially funded, not-for-profit public service broadcaster with a remit to be innovative, experimental and distinctive. Its public ownership and not-for-profit status ensure all profit generated by its commercial activity is directly reinvested back into the delivery of its public service remit. As a publisher-broadcaster, Channel 4 is also required to commission UK content from the independent production sector and currently works with over 400 creative companies across the UK every year. In addition to the main Channel 4 service, its portfolio includes: E4, More4, Film4, 4Music, 4seven, channel4.com and a digital service, All 4, which presents all of C4's on-demand content, digital innovations and live linear channel streams in one place online for the first time.

Management team

Chief Executive Alex Mahon
Director of Programmes Ian Katz

Chief Marketing and Communications Officer Zaid Al-Qassab
Director of People Kirstin Furber

Commissioning

Information about commissioning and related processes and guidelines can be found at www.channel4.com/info/commissioning. Email addresses for most individuals named below can be found on the relevant parts of the website under 4Producers.

Arts

Commissioning Editor Sharminder Nahal

Comedy

Head of Comedy Fiona McDermott, *Commissioning* Jack Bayles, Jon Petrie, Laura Riseam

Daytime and Features

Head of Daytime Jo Street, *Programme Coordinator and Assistant* Barry Agnew, *Commissioning Editors* Kate Thomas, Jayne Stranger, Jonny Rothery, Tim Hancock, Christian Kehoe

Documentaries

Heads of Factual Danny Horan, *Commissioning Editors* Will Rowson, Sacha Mirzoeff, Harjeet Chhokar, Alisa Pomeroy, Shaminder Nahal, Jonah Weston, Fozia Khan, Rita Daniels, *Commissioning Executive* Madonna Benjamin

Drama

Head of Drama Caroline Hollick, *Head of Development* Gemma Boswell, *Commissioning Executive* Rebecca Holdsworth, *Commissioning Editors* Lee Mason, Gwawr Lloyd, Gwen Gorst

Entertainment, TV Events and Sport

Head of Entertainment Phil Harris, *Head of Live Events and Commissioning Editor, Entertainment* Tom Beck, *Commissioning Editors, Entertainment* Steven Handley, *Head of Sport* Pete Andrews, *Commissioning Executive, TV Events and Sport* Antonia Howard Taylor, *Commissioning Editor, Sport* Joe Blake-Turner

Factual Entertainment

Head of Factual Entertainment Alf Lawrie, *Commissioning Editors* Ian Dunkley, Gilly Greenslade, Becky Cadman, Lee McMurray, Deborah Dunnett, Daniel Fromm, Tim Hancock, Vivienne Molokwu

Nations and Regions

Nations and Regions Executives Karen Kelly

News and Current Affairs

Head of News and Current Affairs Louisa Compton, *Commissioing Executive* Sarah Hey, *Commissioning Editors* Siobhan Sinnerton, Louisa Compton, Adam Vandermark

All 4

Commissioning Editors Shaminder Nahal (Arts and Topical), Jonah Weston (Science and Adventure)

4Skills

website http://careers.channel4.com/4skills

Through 4Skills, Channel 4 aims to help people wanting to work in the broadcasting industry gain experience, qualifications and career development. There are a range of options including apprenticeship, graduate and scholarship programmes, work experience, training, events and workshops. For full details see website.

Channel 5

17–29 Hawley Crescent, Camden Town, London NW1 8TT
tel 020-3580 3600
website www.channel5.com
Facebook www.facebook.com/channel5uk/
Twitter @channel5_tv
Director of Programming Ben Frow

Brands include Channel 5, 5Star, 5Select and 5USA, and an on-demand service, My5. Channel 5 works with independent production companies to provide its programmes.

Commissioning

Information about commissioning and related processes and guidelines can be found at: www.channel5.com/commissions.

Factual, News and Current Affairs
Commissioning Emma Westcott, Adrian Padmore, Guy Davies, Lucy Willis

Factual Entertainment, Features and Entertainment
Commissioning Greg Barnett

Acquisitions
Acquisitions Manager Cherry Yeandle

Children's Programming: Milkshake!
Head of Children's Louise Bucknole

ITV Plc

2 Waterhouse Square, 138–142 Holborn, London EC1N 2AE
website www.itv.com
website www.itvplc.com
Facebook www.facebook.com/itv/
Twitter @ITV
Chief Executive Carolyn McCall
Director of Television Kevin Lygo
Managing Director of Commercial Kelly Williams
Managing Director Julian Bellamy
Director of Group Strategy Julian Ashworth
Group Communications and Corporate Affairs Director Paul Moore
General Counsel and Company Secretary Kyla Mullins
Human Resources Director David Osborn

The ITV network is responsible for the commissioning, scheduling and marketing of network programmes on ITV1 and its digital channel portfolio including ITV2, ITV3, ITV4, CiTV and ITVBe. It is the UK's largest commercial TV network. In addition to TV broadcasting services, ITV also delivers programming via a number of platforms, including ITV Hub. Britbox is a digital video subscription service created by the BBC and ITV plc, serving the UK, the USA and Canada. It is focused on British television series and films, mainly featuring current and past series and films supplied from the main UK public service broadcasters.

ITV Studios is the UK's largest production company and produces over 8,500 hours of original content annually. ITV Studios (UK) produces programming for the ITV network's own channels as well as other UK broadcasters including the BBC, Channel 4, Channel 5 and Sky. ITV also has an international production business which produces for local broadcasters in the USA, Australia, France, Germany and Scandinavia.

Commissioning

ITV's commissioning areas include entertainment and comedy, factual, daytime, drama, sport, current affairs, digital and online. Information, FAQs and guidelines for commissioning can be found at www.itv.com/commissioning.

Entertainment and Comedy
email comedy.commissioning@itv.com
email entertainment.commissioning@itv.com
Head of Entertainment Katie Rawcliffe, *Development Coordinator* Emma Barnard

Factual
email factual.commissioning@itv.com
Controller, Popular Factual Jo Clinton-Davis, *Head of Factual Entertainment* Sue Murphy, *Commissioning* Priya Singh, Satmohan Panesar, Nicola Lloyd, Kate Teckman, Amanda Stavri

Daytime
Commissioning Editor Lara Akeju

Drama
Commissioning Huw Kennair-Jones, Chloe Tucker, *Head of Drama* Polly Hill

Sport
Director of Sport Niall Sloane
Current Affairs
Controller of Current Affairs Tom Giles

Digital
Controller, Digital Channels Paul Mortimer

Recruitment, training and work experience

Information about training schemes, work experience and recruitment at ITV can be found at www.itvjobs.com, including details of ITV Insight, a volunteering scheme which enables people seeking experience in the TV industry to gain hands-on knowledge.

ITV Network regions

The ITV Network is made up of the following regions:

ITV Anglia www.itv.com/news/anglia

ITV Border www.itv.com/news/border

ITV Calendar www.itv.com/calendar

ITV Central www.itv.com/news/central

ITV Granada www.itv.com/news/granada

ITV London www.itv.com/news/london

ITV Meridian www.itv.com/news/meridian

ITV TyneTees www.itv.com/news/tyne-tees

ITV Wales www.itv.com/news/wales

ITV West Country www.itv.com/news/westcountry

STV Group www.stv.tv (Scotland)

UTV www.itv.com/news/utv (Northern Ireland)

Channel TV www.itv.com/news/channel

RTÉ

Donnybrook, Dublin 4, Republic of Ireland
email info@rte.ie
website www.rte.ie
Facebook www.facebook.com/ExploreRTE
Twitter @rte
Director General Dee Forbes

RTÉ (Raidio Teilifís Éireann) is Ireland's national public service broadcaster. A leader in Irish media, it provides comprehensive, free-to-air multimedia services.

Commissioning

RTÉ works in partnership with independent producers to create many of Ireland's favourite TV programmes. It commissions content in seven groups: drama and comedy; entertainment and music; factual; arts and culture; Cláracha Gaeilge; sport; and young people's programmes. Full details of commissioning guidelines, specifications and submissions can be found at www.rte.ie/commissioning.

S4C

Canolfan S4C Yr Egin, Carmarthen, SA31 3EQ
tel 0370 600 4141
website www.s4c.cymru/en
Facebook www.facebook.com/S4C
Twitter @S4C
Ceo Owen Evans
Chief Operating Officer Elin Morris
Director of Content Amanda Rees
Director of Communications Gwyn Williams

S4C is a Welsh language television channel which transmits live between 6 a.m. and late at night, and features news, drama, documentaries, music, entertainment and children's programmes. Shows are available to stream 24 hours a day on the S4C app. An online service called Hansh is aimed mainly at the 16–34 audience. Independent production companies produce most of the programmes; the BBC also produces around 520 hours a year for the channel. See website for full details of commissioning and production guidelines and personnel.

DIGITAL TV PROVIDERS

Amazon Prime/Amazon Studios

website https://studios.amazon.com/
Facebook www.facebook.com/amazonstudios
Twitter @AmazonUK
Head of Amazon Studios Jennifer Salke, *Head of Amazon UK* John Boumphrey

Amazon Prime streams to over 200 territories. Its original content includes film, television shows and live coverage of events and sport. All Amazon Prime original content is acquired and created by Amazon Studios. Amazon Studios does not accept submissions but their IMDbPro service gives subscribers access to industry contacts, in-development projects looking for creatives, casting notices, and box office trends and insights. More information can be found at: https://pro.imdb.com.

Apple TV+

website www.apple.com/uk/apple-tv-plus/
Facebook www.facebook.com/appletv/
Twitter @AppleTV
Creative Director, Europe Worldwide Video Jay Hunt

Apple TV+ is one of the newest additions to Apple's services. Original content is added monthly and focuses primarily on scripted content across a range of genres, including children's, as well as documentaries and talk shows.

BT

81 Newgate Street, London EC1A 7AJ
tel 020-7356 5000 (switchboard) or 0800 800 152 (customers)
Customer postal address BT Correspondence Centre, Providence Row, Durham DH98 1BT
website www.player.bt.com/#/home
Chief Executive Philip Jansen

BT offers subscription television services in the UK, through BT TV, which provides on-demand content, over 30 extra entertainment channels and live sports channels including BT Sport and Sky Sports.

Disney+

website www.disneyplus.com/en-gb/
Facebook www.facebook.com/DisneyPlus
Twitter @DisneyPlusUK
President of Content and Marketing Jo Early

Disney's digital streaming service brings together over 80 years of Disney and Pixar television and film including the entire Disney-owned Star Wars and Marvel catalogues, and new original and exclusive content from the four brands plus National Geographic. Through their Star channel they also stream films and television shows produced by FOX and 20th Century Studios.

Facebook Watch

website www.facebook.com/watch/
Twitter @FacebookWatch
Head of Global Creative Strategy Ricky van Veen,
Head of Product Mike Bidgoli

Facebook's digital streaming service is available to its two billion users and focuses on scripted, reality and talk shows which are available live and on demand. Aims to share content which will spark discussion and engagement across the social media site.

Freesat

23–24 Newman Street, London W1T 1PJ
tel 0345 313 0051
website www.freesat.co.uk
Facebook www.facebook.com/freesat/
Ceo Alistair Thom

Freesat is a British free-to-air satellite television service provided by joint venture between the BBC and ITV.

Hulu

website https://press.hulu.com/corporate/
Facebook https://en-gb.facebook.com/hulu/
Twitter @hulu
Senior Vice President, Originals Craig Erwich

An American-only streaming service that incorporates both live channels and on-demand television and film and has over 30.7 million subscribers. Original content is streamed first on Hulu and then screened around the world through partnerships with national companies such as the BBC and Channel 4.

Netflix

website https://media.netflix.com/en/
Facebook www.facebook.com/NetflixUK/
Twitter @NetflixUK
Co-Ceos Reed Hastings, Ted Sarandos

Netflix was the world's first digital streaming service and now has over 167 million members from over 190 countries. Netflix's original film and television shows cover all genres, including children's and young adult, and is available in a range of languages.

Sky

Grant Way, Isleworth TW7 5QD
tel 020-7032 2000
website www.skygroup.sky/corporate/home
Facebook www.facebook.com/sky/

Twitter @skytv
Chief Executive Jeremy Darroch

Sky is a British telecommunications company which provides a range of television and internet services in the UK, including entertainments, news and sport. It owns a number of subsidiaries including NOW and Freesat from Sky. Through Sky Studios they produce original films and television shows throughout Europe. Full details of commissioning guidelines and contacts can be found at www.skygroup.sky/skystudios/commissioning.

Virgin Media

Griffin House, 161 Hammersmith Road, London W6 8BS
website www.virginmedia.com
Facebook www.facebook.com/virginmedia
Twitter @virginmedia
Ceo Lutz Schuler

Virgin Media provides a range of television and internet services throughout the UK. Virgin TV is the largest cable television provider in the country.

YouTube Originals

website www.youtube.com/channel/
UCqVDpXKLmKeBU_yyt_QkItQ
Facebook www.facebook.com/youtube/
Twitter @YouTube
Global Head of Original Content Susanne Daniels,
Head of UK and Ireland Partnerships Richard Lewis

YouTube has almost two billion users worldwide. Its Originals service offers a range of content including interviews, documentaries, celebrity-hosted shows and scripted television.

YouView

3rd Floor, 10 Lower Thames Street, London EC3R 6YT
email info@youview.com
website www.youview.com
Ceo Susie Buckridge

YouView is a hybrid television platform in the UK, developed by a partnership of telecommunications operators including BT, TalkTalk and Arqiva, and broadcasters including the BBC, ITV, Channel 4 and Channel 5.

ORGANISATIONS CONNECTED TO TELEVISION BROADCASTING

BARB

20 Orange Street, London WC2H 7EF
tel 020-7024 8100
email enquiries@barb.co.uk
website www.barb.co.uk
Twitter @BARBtelevision
Chief Executive Justin Sampson

The Broadcasters Audience Research Board is the official source of viewing figures in the UK.

Ipsos MORI

3 Thomas More Square, London E1W 1YW
tel 020-3059 5000
website www.ipsos.com
Twitter @IpsosMORI
Ceo Ben Page

One of the UK's leading research companies and conducts surveys for a wide range of major organisations (such as BARB and RAJAR) as well as for other market research agencies.

Pact (Producers Alliance for Cinema and Television)

3rd Floor, Fitzrovia House,
153–157 Cleveland Street, London W1T 6QW
tel 020-7380 8230
website www.pact.co.uk
Twitter @PactUK
Ceo John McVay

The trade association representing the commercial interests of UK independent TV, film, digital, children's and animation media companies. For details of children's independent TV and film production companies, see the website.

Public Media Alliance

Arts 1.80, DEV, University of East Anglia,
Norwich NR4 7TJ
tel (01603) 592335
email info@publicmediaalliance.org
website www.publicmediaalliance.org
Twitter @PublicMediaPMA

World's largest association of public broadcasters. Provides advocacy, support, knowledge exchange, research and training opportunities for public media worldwide.

Royal Television Society

3 Dorset Rise, London EC4Y 8EN
tel 020-7822 2810
email info@rts.org.uk
website www.rts.org.uk
Facebook www.facebook.com/RoyalTelevisionSociety
Twitter @RTS_media

An educational charity promoting the art and science of television and is the leading forum for discussion and debate on all aspects of the TV community.

RADIO

UK domestic radio services are broadcast across three wavebands: FM, medium wave and long wave. A number of radio stations are broadcast in both analogue and digital and there are growing numbers of stations broadcasting in digital alone. Digital radio (DAB – digital audio broadcasting) is available through digital radio sets, car radios, online, and on games consoles and mobile devices such as smartphones and tablets. Radio provision in the UK comprises of public service radio programming provided by the BBC and programming provided by independent, commercial stations.

BBC Radio

The BBC operates 10 national radio stations offering music and speech programming for the whole of the UK: Radio 1, Radio 1 Xtra, Radio 2, Radio 3, Radio 4, Radio 4 Extra, Radio 5 Live, Radio 5 Live Sports Extra, Radio 6 Music and Asian Network. In addition, there are 39 regional/local radio stations. The BBC Sounds website and app host all of the BBC's live radio stations alongside a catalogue of 80,000 hours of BBC programmes, interviews, podcasts and playlists available to stream.

Commissioning

For full details of commissioning and delivery guidelines, see www.bbc.co.uk/commissioning/radio/. For details of how to pitch programme ideas to BBC Radio, see www.bbc.co.uk/programmes/articles/4fC4NcVXqkZntJv8ZHpClD8/pitching-ideas.
  Radio 1/1Xtra/Asian Network *Head of Radio 1* Aled Haydn Jones, *Head of Radio 1 Xtra* Faron McKenzie, *Head of Asian Network* Ahmed Hussai
  Radio 2 *Head* Helen Thomas, *Commissioning Editor* Robert Gallacher, *Commissions and Schedules Manager* Julian Grundy
  Radio 3 *Controller* Alan Davey, *Head of Speech* Matthew Dodd, *Head of Music* Edward Blakeman, *Commissioning Manager* David Ireland
  Radio 4/4 Extra *Controller* Mohit Bakaya, *Commissioning Editors* Rhian Roberts (Digital), Alison Hindell (Drama), Sioned William (Comedy), Richard Knight (Factual), Daniel Clarke (Factual)
  Radio 5 Live/5 Live Sports Extra *Controller* Heidi Dawson, *Commissioning Editor* Richard Maddock
  Radio 6 Music *Head* Samantha Moy, *Commissioning Editor* Robert Gallacher
  World Service *Controller (English)* Mary Hockaday, *Senior Commissioning Editor* Steve Titherington

Commercial radio

There are around 300 commercial radio stations operating in the UK, most of which serve a local area or region. A number of commercial radio stations operate nationally, including Classic FM, Absolute Radio, talkSport and LBC. The majority of commercial radio stations are owned by one of three groups:

Bauer Media

website www.bauermedia.co.uk

Global Radio

website https://global.com/radio

Wireless Group

website www.wirelessgroup.co.uk

ORGANISATIONS CONNECTED TO RADIO BROADCASTING

Media.info
website https://media.info/uk

This website provides detailed listings of UK radio stations plus information about TV, newspapers, magazines and media ownership in the UK.

The Radio Academy
GO8 The Pillbox, 115 Coventry Road, London E2 6GG
email info@radioacademy.org
website www.radioacademy.org
Facebook www.facebook.com/radioacademy/
Twitter @radioacademy

The Radio Academy is a registered charity dedicated to the promotion of excellence in UK radio broadcasting and production. For over 30 years the Radio Academy has run the annual Audio and Radio Industry Awards (ARIAS), which celebrate content and creativity in the industry.

Radiocentre
6th Floor, 55 New Oxford Street, London WC1A 1BS
tel 020-7010 0600
website www.radiocentre.org
Facebook www.facebook.com/RadiocentreUK
Twitter @Radiocentre
Chief Executive Ian Moss

Radiocentre is the voice of UK commercial radio and works with government, policy makers and regulators, and provides a forum for industry-wide debate and discussion.

RAJAR
6th Floor, 55 New Oxford Street, London WC1A 1BS
tel 020-7395 0630
website www.rajar.co.uk
Twitter @RAJARLtd
Chief Executive Jerry Hill

RAJAR – Radio Joint Audience Research – is the official body in charge of measuring radio audiences in the UK. It is jointly owned by the BBC and the RadioCentre on behalf of the commercial sector.

Theatre
How to get your play published and performed

Playwright Temi Wilkey offers her experience and practical steps for the writer who is ready to discover, share and develop their own dramatic voice, to fulfil the dream of seeing their work performed on stage.

Getting your play published and performed is a long road – and people have taken many different routes. I don't think there's any one way to achieve it, and I'm by no means an expert (especially given the uncertain times ahead) but I was fortunate enough to have my first play, *The High Table*, programmed in a co-production with Birmingham Rep and the Bush Theatre last year [2019] and staged earlier this year.

How on earth did a first-time writer get her debut play programmed at these two prestigious theatres? you may ask. Reader, that's a question I've asked myself every day for the past twelve months. I'm not entirely sure I have all the answers but, if you keep reading, we'll explore the process in detail.

First things first …

Write a play

Okay, so this seems an obvious first step – but it's crucial and is the only bit you have any real control over. Putting pen to paper is sometimes the hardest thing to do. How do you wrestle with all the ideas in your head and get them down into one comprehensible narrative? How do you structure it? What if … it is really bad?

I can't answer those questions for you, but I'm sure you can resolve them yourself if you sit down and write. Some would-be playwrights seek help in getting creative answers to these questions through creative writing courses where they are taught how to write for the theatre. Others are brave enough to get started on their own, without external support. I knew that I couldn't afford another course or degree after my undergraduate study, but I didn't feel confident enough to try writing a play on my own, so I applied to be in a writers' group.

Writers' groups are brilliant if you need some guidance or encouragement to write your play. I applied for the Royal Court's 'Introduction to Playwriting' group, as I only needed to send in ten pages for my application. I'd highly recommend doing this if you think a writers' group could be helpful for you (see https://royalcourttheatre.com/playwriting/writers-groups for more information). Even if you can't write a full-length play, you can definitely have a go at writing ten pages; if you're accepted into the group, you get much closer to answering the questions we're all asking at the start. For those who live outside London, this is also a brilliant group to apply to because the Royal Court covers your travel to attend sessions.

I was accepted into the group and each week, over a ten-week period, I met with a teacher and ten other aspiring playwrights. We read plays and talked about character, plot and structure. The guidance from our group leader was incredible, but the most helpful thing for me was having a group of peers who were also trying to write a play. I learnt so much from them about how other people write; sometimes it confirmed that the way I was doing things was okay, but far more often it challenged me to try and approach things in different ways.

One of the greatest things that a writers' group can give you is a deadline. Usually at the end of a group's duration you're expected to hand in a draft of an original play. External deadlines can be a really motivating force to get you to finish your play. If you're not in a writers' group, I'd recommend finding other external deadlines, whether they're play-writing awards or theatre submissions windows. Whatever it is, find a deadline (with a realistic timeframe) so that there is somewhere you *have* to send a finished play to (no matter what state it's in).

Apart from seeking out the external impetus provided by award deadlines and writers' groups run by theatres, the biggest advice I'd give to any writer is to write the play that *you* need to write. Remember, those external forces are helpful on a purely pragmatic basis; use them for the time pressure they exert, but not as an artistic goalpost. When I was in the Royal Court writers' group, they made it very clear that we should not try to write whatever it is we thought a 'Royal Court play' was. Of course, there's always a part of you that hopes they'll read the first draft of the play you've written after the group finishes and say, 'Wow. This is perfect! We have to stage this immediately.' And that may just happen! Being a writer is about developing your own voice and creating work that speaks to what *you* care about.

So write the play that you need to write, the play that you've always wanted to see – whether you do it on your own, by taking a course, or by attending a writers' group. And when it's ready, the right theatre will find it.

Which brings us neatly onto our next step …

Share the play

Once you've written your play, it's time to share it. Send it in for submissions windows, to literary departments, to 'scratch nights'. Send it far and wide. We writers – especially women – can be notoriously shy about sharing our work. Lisa Spirling (Artistic Director of Theatre 503) said, when I was on a panel with her, that men are much more likely to share their work with her, even when it's not very good. Whereas women and non-binary writers are more likely to wait until they think their play is as close to perfect as possible before they do. News flash: your work is never going to be perfect, even in performance. The point of a new writing theatre is to find new writers – that's literally their job! And

Scratch

Scratch is about sharing an idea with the public at an early stage of its development. When you scratch an idea, you can ask people questions and consider their feedback. This helps you work out how to take your idea on to the next stage. It's an iterative process that can be used again and again. Over time, ideas become stronger because they are informed by a wide-range of responses.

The feedback is an important part of the process but scratch is not about doing everything that people's feedback suggests; it is about using the responses to help you understand how people currently receive it and to help you shape your idea. The feedback doesn't have to be a Q&A, you can simply share your idea 'live' and, by doing this, you can often tell what works and what doesn't. Scratch recognises that when an idea does not fully succeed, or even when it crashes and burns, that there is great learning to be gathered.

© Battersea Arts Centre

lots of them are very good at it. They might see some potential in your work, even if the draft you send in isn't perfect. So don't get in your own way, and do share your work.

That being said, I didn't send my play, *The High Table*, straight out to all the new writing theatres immediately on completion of my first draft. I sent it to lots of friends first. I sent it to people I trusted in the industry, whom I knew would give me their honest opinion. I also sent it into theatre companies with windows of submission that were just for feedback and got some thoughts back from them. However, nothing can compare to the drama-turgical support you get from someone who is interested in staging your text. I'd really recommend sharing your work with any directors you know, or can get an introduction to through your other contacts, and trying to organise a rehearsed reading.

A friend shared a call-out for LGBTQ+ plays and I sent my play to established playwright Tom Wright, who was organising some rehearsed readings alongside the opening of his play *My Dad's Gap Year* at the Park Theatre. When I met him, his approach to giving notes was so different from everyone else's. His feedback was bold, honest and practical. I often use the image of 'getting under the hood' when I talk about writing; well, Tom got under the hood of my play with me. And this was because he had a stake in it. Because it was a rehearsed reading, he was directly considering how the play would work in front of an audience. It gave the writing a new lease of life.

You learn so much about what needs to change in your play when you're collaborating and when you hear it read by actors. The redrafting carried out on *The High Table* during the rehearsed reading process was an instrumental step towards it eventually being staged. It was important not only for its creative development, but also because Tom championed the play to the Bush Theatre before I met their directorial team.

If you're planning to invite theatres to a rehearsed reading, make sure you give them lots of notice (at least a month) and then remind them again a week beforehand. A re-hearsed reading is a great way of sharing your work because it's something to invite people to that brings your work off the page. Literary departments in theatres read a lot of plays, but they're in this industry because they love live theatre, and a rehearsed reading comes as close to that experience as possible.

On my podcast, *Making it with Temi Wilkey* (www.bushtheatre.co.uk/artists/podcast-making-it-with-temi-wilkey), I interview emerging playwrights about how they write and make a living. Ella Road's experience was very similar to mine. When we discussed the process of programming her play, *The Phlebotomist*, Ella told me that, although many theatre managers she invited to her rehearsed reading didn't end up coming, the literary manager of The Hampstead did – and that's how it came to be programmed and performed there in 2018.

The important thing about sharing your work is it increases your chances of it getting staged. Someone *might* bite. Here's what to do if they do.

Work with a theatre

If you're lucky enough to have a theatre interested in staging your work, my advice is: be open to their notes and work fast. When you meet them they're trying to suss out what it would be like to work with you. So be nice . . . but not too nice! If they're the right theatre for your play, they'll understand your work and their suggestions will illuminate the in-consistencies within your play and, hopefully, make you feel inspired and excited to write the next draft. But you know your text better than anyone. If their notes are wrong,

Theatre

disregard them; but listen with an open heart and, if their notes feel right, take them on board.

After the Bush Theatre read *The High Table*, I went in to speak to them and they gave me some great notes, most of which I agreed with, and then they said they'd be really interested in reading the next draft. They didn't give me any timelines, but Lynette Linton, the artistic director, said she was 'interested in it being quite quick'. Assuming they couldn't give me any firm deadlines without giving me a fee, I took the hint. Who knows what their actual programming timelines were?! This was my shot so, I turned the next draft around in a matter of days. Not everyone needs to do this, but it felt important for me to seem reliable. It was my first play and I knew that it might need more work in the run-up to it being staged, so I wanted to show them that I could take notes and come back on things if necessary, but ultimately be easy to work with and reliable in submitting drafts.

They liked the next draft and organised an internal reading of the play. After that, there was a lot of waiting around, a lot of anxiety, doubt. But eventually they said they wanted to programme it. Elation, happy screams and tears of joy ensued ... and the rest is history. Ultimately, I think *The High Table* was staged because it found a home at the right theatre at the right time. They were interested in it because it fitted the artistic vision of the theatre and they were willing to invest their creative energy into making it happen.

It feels like it had a lot to do with luck. But, looking back, I realise that you can certainly help to create your luck by: 1) writing a play that's true to your artistic voice; 2) sharing it far and wide and getting feedback to develop it; and if a theatre shows interest in it, 3) doing your very best to prove that you can deliver.

Temi Wilkey is an actor and playwright. Her theatre credits include the National, RSC and Manchester Royal Exchange. She was a member of the Royal Court's Young Writers' Group in 2017. Her debut play, *The High Table*, was produced at the Bush Theatre, London, in Lynette Linton's debut season in early 2020 and won the Stage Debut Award for Best Writer. She is a writer on Season 3 of *Sex Education* for Netflix.

Writing about theatre: reviews, interviews and more

Mark Fisher compares popular perceptions of the theatre critic with the realities, and outlines what it takes to succeed in the business.

The critic

In the award-winning movie *Birdman*, Michael Keaton plays Riggan Thomson, a main-stream Hollywood actor trying to earn some late-career credibility. He's banking on people seeing him in a different light if he has a Broadway hit with his adaptation of a Raymond Carver story. As opening night approaches, the stakes are high. He loses his lead actor, his last-minute replacement is an unpredictable maverick and his budget is at breaking point.

As the tensions mount, he comes across Tabitha Dickinson in a bar. Played by Lindsay Duncan, she is the lead theatre critic of the *New York Times* and seems to exist less as a character in her own right than as a projection of his actorly neuroses.

In the short time she is in the film, this is what we learn about her:
• She is always alone. We first see her perched at the end of a counter having a drink and writing longhand in a notepad. In the theatre, she sits at the end of a row and leaves before the rest of the audience.
• She is prepared to wield the power of the *New York Times* to shut down a show that she hasn't even seen – at least, she says she is. Having decided Thomson is indulging in a vanity project, she regards him as a threat to Broadway's artistic standards. She tells him she will give him a bad review on principle.
• She gets it all wrong. When, finally, she does file a rave review, she appears not to have realised that the onstage violence was a genuine suicide attempt.

Watching the movie as a theatre critic, I naturally tried to weigh this portrayal against my own experience. If I were the sensitive type, I'd be worried. This is especially the case because the majority of fictional critics share the same characteristics. In films, novels and television programmes, my profession is dominated by misanthropic loners, arrogant opinion-mongers, writers who love the sound of their own voice and destructive zealots who detest the theatre – unless, of course, they happen to be having an affair with someone on stage. Variations on this theme include Addison DeWitt in *All About Eve*, Sheridan Whiteside in *The Man Who Came to Dinner* and Moon and Birdboot in Tom Stoppard's *The Real Inspector Hound*.

Critical characteristics

For anyone considering a career as a theatre critic, it's reasonable to wonder not so much whether the characteristics described above pertain to you, but whether you're prepared for other people to see you in this light. To the theatre profession, you can seem like the only sober guest at the party, the spoilsport who is all head and no heart, the one who's prepared to break the magic spell that keeps the whole enterprise alive. They may not want to be your friend any more.

In reality, the quality common to nearly all the critics I have known is their love of theatre. The job involves long journeys to out-of-the-way venues, spending evenings at work when you could be with friends and family and sitting through mediocre shows that were not made for someone like you in the first place. Only someone with blind optimism and a passionate belief in the artform would sign up to such working conditions. I've seen cynical critics write entertainingly, but they invariably burn out in a matter of months. In real life, the negativity of a fictional critic is not sustainable.

There is a kind of truth, though, in the solitariness of *Birdman*'s Tabitha. Theatre criticism suits lone wolves. You may be friendly and sociable in the right circumstances, but when it comes to the job, it's just you, your opinion and a blank computer screen. It's not something you can do collectively. You can't get a friend to help. Everything is down to you. This takes a certain resourcefulness. You need to be self-motivated or, at least, motivated by the pressure of a deadline (and not freaked by it) and happy in your own company. You have to be content to work antisocial hours in sociable circumstances. When those around you are on their feet applauding or wiping the tears from their eyes, you have to be thinking of a catchy first sentence.

Becoming a critic

When I told people I was writing a book called *How to Write About Theatre* (Bloomsbury Methuen Drama 2015), some questioned my timing. After all, if you read anything about criticism these days, it tends to be about newspapers cutting back on their arts coverage and laying critics off. Shouldn't I have called it *How Not to Write About Theatre*? Certainly, it seems unlikely that a journalist starting today would have quite the career trajectory I have enjoyed. I was employed in the late 1980s by the *List* magazine, then a fortnightly arts and entertainment guide, and now, since 2015, a predominantly online publication. My first job there was as a production assistant, but with my drama degree and previous interest in writing, it was perhaps inevitable that I would start contributing to the theatre section. Eventually I became the theatre editor and then took up a freelance career in which I founded and edited a quarterly theatre magazine, became theatre critic for the *Herald* in Glasgow and, latterly, Scottish theatre critic for the *Guardian*.

Even if I add that most of the money I have earned has come from feature writing rather than reviewing, there's no question that today's critics have fewer paid opportunities open to them. There are, however, more opportunities than ever for unpaid criticism – and more people than ever writing about theatre. No need for contacts or job interviews, you can just set up a blog right now and start writing. This is having two beneficial effects. One is that a wider range of voices are being heard and the old cultural hegemony – what Nicholas Hytner called the 'dead white men' of the critical establishment – is breaking down. The other is that the idea of what constitutes a 'proper' review is being upturned: the interactive and responsive nature of the internet is well suited to a discursive form of criticism, one that needn't be the final word, just an addition to the debate.

The good news for writers is that it's now possible to make an impression from a standing start. If you have something to say and an arresting way of saying it, you can build up a reputation on the internet without the endorsement of a traditional media publication. The bad news – until somebody comes up with a better idea – is that you're likely to have to treat your writing as a kind of loss leader, an investment in your future career that may (or may not) pay dividends at some later date. The industrious Matt Trueman (http://matttrueman.co.uk) is a case in point. From being a predominantly on-line critic, he went on to pick up paid work from publications including the *Guardian*, the

Matador® Serious Self-Publishing

Reliable and realistic advice on self-publishing from the UK's most widely recommended author services company

Whether it be writers' services like Jericho Writers, high street or online retailers, literary agents, other publishers – not to mention the *Writers' & Artists' Yearbook*... time and again Matador is recommended to authors wishing to self-publish a book, ebook or audiobook for pleasure or profit.

> "A new breed of self-publishing companies offer authors a kind of halfway house between conventional self-publishing and the commercial kind. Of these, the company that has gone the furthest is Matador..." *Writers' & Artists' Yearbook Guide to Getting Published*

We produce books for authors to their specifications at a realistic price, as print on demand, or as a short or longer print run book. As well as a high quality of production, we insist on a high quality of content, and place great emphasis on the marketing and distribution of our books to high street retailers. We also offer great customer service.

Matador is ranked as the best self-publishing services supplier in the world by *The Independent Publishing Magazine* (Nov 2018 & Nov 2019)

But publishing a book is the easy part... getting it into the shops is harder. We offer a full sales representation and distribution service through our distributor and dedicated sales team. We also offer a full ebook and/or audiobook creation and distribution option to our authors, distributing ebooks and audiobooks worldwide.

> "We've always liked Matador because they have the best values in their industry. Apart from anything else, they actually try to sell books. It sounds crazy, but most of their rivals don't. They print 'em, but don't care about selling 'em. Matador do." *Jericho Writers*

Ask for a free copy of our guide to self-publishing, or download a copy from our website. Or call us if you want to speak to a human being!

www.troubador.co.uk/matador

Matador, Troubador Publishing Ltd,
9 Priory Business Park, Kibworth, Leics LE8 0RX

Tel: 0116 279 2299
Email: matador@troubador.co.uk

Matador
exhibiting at
the 2019
London
Book Fair

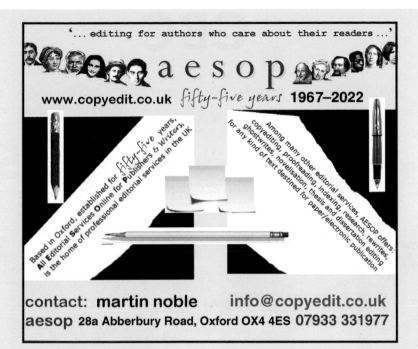

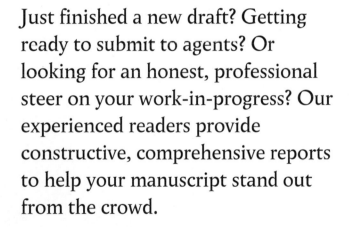

Writers &Artists

A FREE WRITING PLATFORM TO CALL YOUR OWN

- Share your writing
- Build reward points
- Free writing advice articles
- Publishing guidance
- Save margin notes
- Exclusive discounts

REGISTER NOW

WWW.WRITERSANDARTISTS.CO.UK

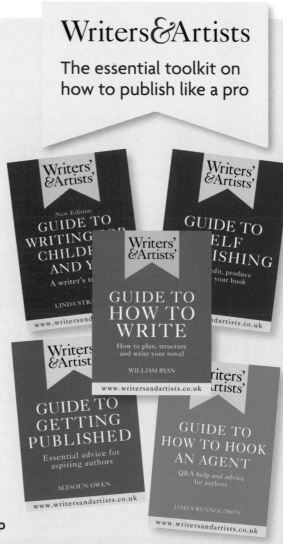

THE BOOK GUILD PUBLISHING

Mainstream & Partnership Publishing

The Book Guild Ltd has a solid reputation in publishing quality books for over 35 years. Authors are invited to submit manuscripts with commercial sales potential in all genres for consideration, particularly in non-fiction. All submissions are first considered for traditional publishing; if we do not feel a manuscript is suitable for traditional publishing, we then consider it for our partnership (co-funded) publishing option. We only make any sort of publishing offer on around 10% of submissions.

Traditional Publishing

Under our traditional publishing model, we bear all the expense of publishing a book, and we usually pay an 'advance' on royalties to the author. Around 70% of our non-fiction and 30% of our fiction is published under our traditional publishing route.

Partnership (co-funded) Publishing

If we can't offer a traditional publishing arrangement for a new manuscript, we may offer a partnership publishing arrangement, but only if we believe the manuscript has commercial potential. Our partnership (co-funded) option enables us to publish the more risky commercial titles in partnership with the author, sharing the risk and rewards.

The Book Guild will always fund some of the costs of publishing under our Partnership Publishing arrangement, ranging from 25% to 75% of the cost. We do *not* offer a wholly author-financed option for publishing (i.e. self-publishing).

For further details and submission information, visit our website; or give us a call!

the novelry

The online creative writing course that takes you to the literary agent's desk

BESTSELLING TUTORS

A team of supportive, and energetic tutors at your side while you write to keep you on track. From children's fiction and YA to romance, historical murder, mystery, and psychological thrillers...

INSPIRING COURSES

Voted 'The best course to write your novel' by The Bookfox. With five star reviews. Original and exciting daily guidance to complete your novel step-by-step in style.

WHERE WRITERS BECOME AUTHORS

Guest tutors: Val McDermid, Adele Parks, Kathy Lette, Meg Rosoff. Guest sessions with our literary agency partners.

A warm welcome to writers at all stages of their writing.

Stage, *What's On Stage* and *Variety*. In 2019, he left criticism to become a creative ass
at Sonia Friedman Productions.

How typical this route will be in the future remains to be seen, although, as a form
editor, I would expect anyone with a serious interest in becoming a professional theat
critic to be doing the job without waiting to be asked. Whether you get published in a
student newspaper, a zine, your own website or someone else's, you'll never get a foothold
on the critical ladder unless you first do it of your own volition. Without that, you will
have no opportunity to develop your writing skills, learn how to translate a live experience
into words and extend your knowledge of contemporary theatre. It's also a way to advertise
yourself. If you can't show an editor examples of your work, he or she will have nothing
to go on and no reason to employ you.

For the first-time critic, the question of authority comes into play. 'Who do you think
you are, passing comment on other people's work – what makes you so special?' Your self-
confidence is the only adequate answer to this question, especially as there is no expected
qualification for the job. Yes, you can study drama, yes, you can take a course in journalism
-- and there's a strong case to say you should – but nobody will ask to see your certificates.
Criticism is a practical occupation and the evidence of whether you can do it or not is in
your writing. Taking a course will widen your knowledge, develop your skills and give you
confidence, but it will be your passion for communication and passion for theatre, as well
as an insatiable desire to get better at both, that will make you a good critic.

Features, interviews and other writing

If you have such a passion, there's no reason you should confine your writing to criticism.
On the contrary, there are many more opportunities for writing about theatre – and at
greater length – than in reviewing it. For the keen-eyed journalist, the theatre is a rich
source of material. The people who work in it, the relationship it has with the wider
community, the ideas it deals with and the pragmatics of putting it on all offer potential
stories.

Feature writing can range from interviews with the theatremakers to research-based
pieces inspired by the themes of a production. If one of the creative team has a fascinating
story to tell, you may be able to write a human-interest piece that is only tangentially
connected to the show. You may find outlets for think-pieces and blogs about theatrical
issues or news stories about artistic fall-outs and funding problems. Think too about
publications aimed at special-interest groups such as lighting designers, educationalists
and marketing managers. You may also find other ways to exploit your specialist knowledge
– I have given seminars to theatre students and led cultural tours for foreign visitors, for
example.

Staff or freelance?

My assumption underlying all this is that you will be working freelance. That's not entirely
fair because, of course, there are many full-time staff with some responsibility for theatre,
whether it be a BBC arts reporter, a theatre editor on a national newspaper or an in-house
critic. I worked as an editor back at the *List* magazine from 2000 to 2003, but have been
freelance for the majority of my career. Staff jobs have the advantage of relative security,
a team of colleagues, pension schemes, wage rises and some kind of career structure.
Unsurprisingly, there is tough competition to get one.

...kes a particular temperament to cope with the freelance life. You have to be resilient, -skinned and comfortable with unpredictability. If you can't stomach the thought of knowing where next week's money is going to come from, it probably isn't for you. ...t in uncertain economic times, when increasing numbers are shifting into portfolio ...areers, your adaptability can be an asset. It's also a little more likely that you'll be able to spread your knowledge of theatre around a number of publications than to find one publication that can sustain a single theatre-related job.

If that's a life you're happy to lead, then be prepared for a few knocks, keep on generating the ideas and say yes to anything that comes your way (worry about practicalities later). As with any journalistic writing, you need to be accurate, reliable and punctual. If you have a dazzling turn of phrase, your editors will like you even more, but most important is being easy to work with. And as far as the theatre community is concerned, the more you can let your passion and erudition show through, the better they will appreciate you and the more you will enjoy yourself.

Mark Fisher is one of Scotland's foremost commentators on the arts. With over 30 years' experience, he is a critic for the *Guardian*, a former editor of the *List* and a freelance journalist. He is the author of *The Edinburgh Fringe Survival Guide* (Bloomsbury Methuen Drama 2012) and *How to Write About Theatre* (Bloomsbury Methuen Drama 2015), and editor of *The XTC Bumper Book of Fun for Boys and Girls* (Mark Fisher Ltd 2017) and *What Do You Call That Noise? An XTC Discovery Book* (Mark Fisher Ltd 2019).

See also...
- *Managing your finances: a guide for writers*, page 721
- *National Insurance contributions*, page 732

Theatre

Theatre producers

This list is divided into metropolitan theatres (below), regional theatres (page 396) and touring companies (page 401). See also *Literary agents for television, film, radio and theatre* on page 772.

⚠ Readers should note that theatrical performances may not go ahead in their usual way due to coronavirus-related restrictions. Please check websites for details.

There are various types of theatre companies and it is helpful to know their respective remits. Many of those that specialise in new writing are based in London (for example, Hampstead Theatre, Royal Court, Bush Theatre, Soho Theatre), but also include the Royal Exchange Manchester, Everyman Theatre Liverpool, Leeds Playhouse, etc. Regional repertory theatre companies are based in towns and cities across the country and may produce new plays as part of their repertoire. Commercial production companies and independent producers typically are unsubsidised profit-making theatre producers who may occasionally be interested in new plays to take on tour or to present in the West End. Small- and/ or middle-scale touring companies are companies (mostly touring) which may exist to explore or promote specific themes or are geared towards specific kinds of audiences.

You may also be able to find independent theatre producers who could be keen to collaborate, especially at the start of their careers, or consider drama schools or amateur companies, both of whom sometimes develop and produce new work. See the *Actors' and Performers' Yearbook* (Bloomsbury, annual) for further information.

LONDON

The Bridge Theatre
3 Potters Fields Park, London SE1 2SG
tel 0333 320 0052
email info@bridgetheatre.co.uk
website www.bridgetheatre.co.uk
Twitter @bridgetheatre
Founders Nicholas Hytner, Nick Starr

The home of the London Theatre Company. Commissions and produces new shows, as well as staging occasional classics. Can seat up to 900 in its adaptable auditorium.

Bush Theatre
7 Uxbridge Road, London W12 8LJ
tel (admin) 020-8743 3584
email info@bushtheatre.co.uk
website www.bushtheatre.co.uk/artists/get-involved/ submissions
Twitter @bushtheatre
Artistic Director Lynette Linton

The Bush has produced hundreds of groundbreaking premieres since its inception in 1972 – many of them Bush commissions – and has hosted guest productions by leading companies and artists from around the world. Check the website for the unsolicited submissions policy and guidelines on when and how to submit.

Chiswick Playhouse
2 Bath Road, London W4 1LW
tel 020-8995 6035
email info@chiswickplayhouse.co.uk
website www.chiswickplayhouse.co.uk
Twitter @ChiswickPlay
Executive Director Mark Perry

Hosts a variety of live entertainment, from classical adaptations to revivals and new musical works. Also produces in-house shows. Formerly the Tabard Theatre.

Michael Codron Plays Ltd
Aldwych Theatre Offices, Aldwych, London WC2B 4DF
tel 020-7836 5537

Finborough Theatre
118 Finborough Road, London SW10 9ED
tel 020-7244 7439
email admin@finboroughtheatre.co.uk
website www.finboroughtheatre.co.uk
Facebook www.facebook.com/FinboroughTheatre
Twitter @finborough
Artistic Director Neil McPherson

Presents new writing, revivals of neglected plays from 1800 onwards, music theatre and UK premieres of foreign work, particularly from Ireland, Scotland, the USA and Canada. Unsolicited scripts are accepted, but see literary policy on website before sending. Founded 1980.

Robert Fox Ltd

29 Wingate Road, London W6 0UR
email info@robertfoxltd.com
website www.robertfoxlimited.com
Twitter @RobertFoxLtd

Independent theatre and film production company. Stages productions mainly in the West End and on Broadway. Not currently accepting submissions. Founded 1980.

Hampstead Theatre

Eton Avenue, London NW3 3EU
tel 020-7449 4200
email info@hampsteadtheatre.com
website www.hampsteadtheatre.com
Twitter @Hamps_Theatre
Artistic Director Roxana Silbert

The company's theatre, built in 2003, was designed with writers in mind, allowing for flexible staging within an intimate main house auditorium and a second studio space. The theatre accepts full-length plays from unagented UK-based writers throughout the year; writers with agents may submit directly to the Literary Manager. See website for full details of the submission process and new writing initiatives.

Bill Kenwright Ltd

BKL House, 1 Venice Walk, London W2 1RR
tel 020 7446 6200
email info@kenwright.com
website www.kenwright.com
Twitter @BKL_Productions
Managing Director Bill Kenwright

Award-winning prolific commercial theatre and film production company, presenting revivals and new works for the West End, international and regional theatres. Productions include: *Blood Brothers, Heathers, Joseph and the Amazing Technicolor Dreamcoat, Evita, Cabaret* and *The Sound of Music.* Films include: *My Pure Land, Another Mother's Son, Broken, Cheri* and *Don't Go Breaking My Heart.*

Kiln Theatre

269 Kilburn High Road, London NW6 7JR
tel 020-7372 6611
email info@kilntheatre.com
website https://kilntheatre.com
Twitter @KilnTheatre
Artistic Director Indhu Rubasingham, *New Work Associate* Tom Wright

Presents at least six productions per year, aiming to provoke debate and engage the audience. Many of these are commissioned and written specifically for the theatre, or are programmed in collaboration with national or international companies. Unable to accept unsolicited submissions. Formerly the Tricycle Theatre.

King's Head Theatre

115 Upper Street, London N1 1QN
tel 020-7226 8561
email info@kingsheadtheatre.com
website www.kingsheadtheatre.com
Twitter @KingsHeadThtr

Off-West End theatre producing opera, LGBTQI+ plays and revivals.

Lyric Hammersmith

Lyric Square, King Street, London W6 0QL
tel 020-8741 6850
email enquiries@lyric.co.uk
website www.lyric.co.uk
Twitter @LyricHammer
Artistic Director Rachel O'Riordan

West London's largest producing and receiving theatre. Unsolicited scripts for in-house productions not accepted.

Neal Street Productions Ltd

1st Floor, 26–28 Neal Street, London WC2H 9QQ
tel 020-7240 8890
email post@nealstreetproductions.com
website www.nealstreetproductions.com
Twitter @NealStProds
Founders Sam Mendes, Pippa Harris, Caro Newling

Film, TV and theatre producer of new work and revivals. No unsolicited scripts. Founded 2003.

The Old Red Lion Theatre

418 St John Street, London EC1V 4NJ
tel 020-7837 7816
email info@oldredliontheatre.co.uk
website www.oldredliontheatre.co.uk
Twitter @ORLTheatre
Executive Director Damien Devine

Interested in contemporary pieces, especially from unproduced writers. No funding: incoming production company pays to rent the theatre. All submissions should be sent via email. Founded 1977.

Orange Tree Theatre

1 Clarence Street, Richmond, Surrey TW9 2SA
tel 020-8940 0141
email literary@orangetreetheatre.co.uk
website www.orangetreetheatre.co.uk
Facebook www.facebook.com/OrangeTreeTheatre
Twitter @OrangeTreeThtr
Artistic Director Paul Miller, *Literary Associate* Guy Jones

Producing theatre presenting a mixture of new work, contemporary revivals and rediscoveries in an intimate in-the-round space. Unsolicited work is not accepted but writers should visit the website for up-to-date information about opportunities.

Enquiries can be addressed to the Literary Associate at the email address above.

The Questors Theatre

12 Mattock Lane, London W5 5BQ
email enquiries@questors.org.uk
website www.questors.org.uk
Twitter @questorstheatre
Executive Director Andrea Bath

Largest independent community theatre in Europe.
Produces 15–20 shows a year, specialising in modern
and classical world drama. Also hosts visiting
productions. No unsolicited scripts. Also runs a
youth theatre for young people aged between 6–18, as
well as summer workshops.

Royal Court Theatre

(English Stage Company Ltd)
Sloane Square, London SW1W 8AS
tel 020-7565 5050
email literary@royalcourttheatre.com
website https://royalcourttheatre.com/script-submissions/
Twitter @royalcourt

Programmes original, exciting new plays that ask
bold questions about the way we live now. Looks for
outstanding plays which are original in form or
theme and unlikely to be produced elsewhere.
  Submissions accepted all year round using online
submissions portal on website, which also outlines
full submission criteria.

Royal National Theatre

South Bank, London SE1 9PX
tel 020-7452 3333
email scripts@nationaltheatre.org.uk
website www.nationaltheatre.org.uk
Twitter @NationalTheatre
Artistic Director Rufus Norris

New Work Department considers submissions from
the UK and Ireland. No synopses, treatments or hard
copy submissions; full scripts can be sent in as pdfs or
Word documents to the email address above.

Soho Theatre

21 Dean Street, London W1D 3NE
tel 020-7478 0117
email submissions@sohotheatre.com
website www.sohotheatre.com
Twitter @sohotheatre
Executive Director Mark Godfrey, *Creative Director*
David Luff

Aims to discover and develop new playwrights,
produce a year-round programme of new plays and
attract new audiences. Producing venue of new plays,
cabaret and comedy. The Writers' Centre offers an
extensive unsolicited script-reading service and
provides a range of development schemes such as
writers' attachment programmes, commissions, seed
bursaries and more. Three venues: the main Soho
Theatre has 150 seats; Soho Upstairs is self-contained
and seats 90; and Soho Downstairs is a 150-seat

capacity cabaret space. Also theatre bar, restaurant,
offices, rehearsal, writing and meeting rooms.
Founded 1972.

Theatre Royal, Stratford East

Gerry Raffles Square, London E15 1BN
tel 020-8534 7374
website www.stratfordeast.com
Twitter @stratfordeast
Artistic Director Nadia Fall, *Executive Director* Eleanor
Lang

Middle-scale producing theatre. Specialises in new
writing, including developing contemporary British
musicals. Welcomes new plays that are unproduced,
full in length, and which relate to its diverse
multicultural, Black and Asian audience.

Unicorn Theatre

147 Tooley Street, London SE1 2HZ
tel 020-7645 0560
email hello@unicorntheatre.com
website www.unicorntheatre.com
Facebook www.facebook.com/unicorntheatre
Twitter @unicorn_theatre
Artistic Director Justin Audibert, *Executive Director*
Bailey Lock

Produces a year-round programme of theatre for
children and young people under 21. In-house
productions of full-length plays with professional
casts are staged across two auditoria, alongside
visiting companies and education work. Unicorn
rarely commissions plays from writers who are new
to it, but it is keen to hear from writers who are
interested in working with the theatre in the future.
Do not send unsolicited MSS, but rather a short
statement describing why you would like to write for
the Unicorn along with a CV or a summary of your
relevant experience.

White Bear Theatre Club

138 Kennington Park Road, London SE11 4DJ
tel 07496 442747
email info@whitebeartheatre.co.uk
website https://whitebeartheatre.co.uk/
Twitter @WhiteBearTheatr
Artistic Director Michael Kingsbury

Metropolitan new writing theatre company.
Welcomes scripts from new writers: send queries to
whitebearliterary@gmail.com. Founded 1988.

Young Vic Theatre Company

66 The Cut, London SE1 8LZ
tel 020-7922 2922
email boxoffice@youngvic.org
website www.youngvic.org
Facebook www.facebook.com/youngvictheatre
Twitter @youngvictheatre
Artistic Director Kwame Kwei-Armah, *Executive
Director* Despina Tsatsas

Leading London producing theatre. Founded 1969.

A Younger Theatre

website www.ayoungertheatre.com
Facebook www.facebook.com/AYoungerTheatre
Twitter @ayoungertheatre
Instagram @ayoungertheatre_
Managing Director Samuel Sims

Online theatre publication reviewing theatre both in London and across the UK, with features on high-profile industry names and discussions on issues facing young and marginalised people. Writers do so for free in return for seeing a show or in order to build a portfolio of work or promote their own performance work. Content is generally aimed at those aged 35 and under.

REGIONAL

Abbey Theatre Amharclann na Mainistreach

26 Lower Abbey Street, Dublin D01 K0F1, Republic of Ireland
tel +353 (0)1 8872200
email info@abbeytheatre.ie
website www.abbeytheatre.ie
Twitter @AbbeyTheatre
Artistic Directors Graham McLaren, Neil Murray, *Dramaturg* Louise Stephens

Ireland's national theatre. The Abbey Theatre commissions and produces new Irish writing and contemporary productions from the canon, alongside hosting and presenting work by other Irish and international artists and companies

Yvonne Arnaud Theatre Management Ltd

Millbrook, Guildford, Surrey GU1 3UX
tel (01483) 440077
email yat@yvonne-arnaud.co.uk
website www.yvonne-arnaud.co.uk
Twitter @YvonneArnaud
Director and Chief Executive Joanna Reid

Producing theatre which also receives productions.

The Belgrade Theatre

Belgrade Square, Coventry CV1 1GS
tel 024-7625 6431
email admin@belgrade.co.uk
website www.belgrade.co.uk
Twitter @BelgradeTheatre
Artistic Director and Chief Executive Hamish Glen

Repertory theatre producing drama, comedy and musicals. Does not accept unsolicited scripts; email short synopses first to the address above. Runs a series of training development opportunities, including its Springboard initiative.

Birmingham Repertory Theatre Ltd

Broad Street, Birmingham B1 2EP
tel 0121 245 2000
email stage.door@birmingham-rep.co.uk
website www.birmingham-rep.co.uk
Twitter @BirminghamRep
Artistic Director Sean Foley

Producing theatre company and pioneer of new plays whose programme includes new versions of the classics as well as contemporary writing. Recently refurbished alongside the Library of Birmingham, the theatre now includes a 300-seat studio theatre. Founded 1913.

The Bootleg Theatre Company

23 Burgess Green, Bishopdown, Salisbury, Wilts. SP1 3EL
tel (01722) 421476
email colinburden281@gmail.com
website www.bootlegtheatre.com/tearawayfilms
Contact Colin Burden

New writing theatre company whose recent productions include *Girls Allowed* by Trevor Suthers, *A Rainy Night in Soho* by Stephen Giles, and *The Squeaky Clean* by Roger Goldsmith. Also produces compilation productions of monologues/duologues: these have included *15 Minutes of Fame*, *Tales from The Street* and *Parting Shots*. Founded 1985.

The company has a sister company, Tearaway Films (founded 2018), that produces music videos and short films.

Bristol Old Vic

King Street, Bristol BS1 4ED
tel 0117 949 3993
email admin@bristololdvic.org.uk
website www.bristololdvic.org.uk
Twitter @BristolOldVic
Artistic Director Tom Morris, *Executive Director* Charlotte Geeves

Oldest theatre auditorium in UK (opened in 1766). See website for more details. Founded 1946.

Chichester Festival Theatre

Oaklands Park, Chichester, West Sussex PO19 6AP
tel (01243) 784437
website www.cft.org.uk
Twitter @chichesterFT
Artistic Director Daniel Evans

Stages annual Summer Festival Season April–Oct in Festival and Minerva Theatres together with a year-round education programme, winter touring programme and youth theatre Christmas show. See website for unsolicited scripts policy.

Contact Theatre Company

Oxford Road, Manchester M15 6JA
tel 0161 274 0600
website https://contactmcr.com/
Twitter @ContactMcr

Artistic Director Matt Fenton, *Head of Creative Development* Suzie Henderson

Multidisciplinary arts organisation focused on working with and for young people aged 13 and above.

Creation Theatre Company

tel (01865) 766266
email boxoffice@creationtheatre.co.uk
website www.creationtheatre.co.uk
Facebook https://en-gb.facebook.com/CreationTheatre/
Twitter @creationtheatre
Instagram creationtheatre
Chief Executive Lucy Askew, *General Manager* Charlie Morley

Stages classic stories in special locations. Commended as leaders in innovative digital theatre and for award-winning digital interactive productions. Creators of a range of holiday and term-time online theatre workshops for ages 5 to 19. No unsolicited manuscripts.

Curve

Rutland Street, Leicester LE1 1SB
tel 0116 242 3560
email contactus@curvetheatre.co.uk
website www.curveonline.co.uk
Twitter @CurveLeicester
Chief Executive Chris Stafford, *Artistic Director* Nikolai Foster

Regional producing theatre company.

Derby Theatre

15 Theatre Walk, St Peter's Quarter, Derby DE1 2NF
email creatives@derbyplayhouse.co.uk
website www.derbytheatre.co.uk
Twitter @DerbyTheatre
Artistic Director and Chief Executive Sarah Brigham, *Creative Learning Director* Caroline Barth

Regional producing and receiving theatre.

Druid

The Druid Building, Flood Street, Galway H91 PWX5, Republic of Ireland
tel +353 (0)91 568660
email info@druid.ie
website www.druid.ie
Twitter @DruidTheatre
Artistic Director Garry Hynes

Producing theatre company presenting a wide range of plays, with an emphasis on new Irish writing. New submission window for scripts: May–September (see website for details). Tours nationally and internationally.

The Dukes

Moor Lane, Lancaster LA1 1QE
tel (01524) 598505

email info@dukes-lancaster.org
website https://dukes-lancaster.org/
Twitter @TheDukesTheatre
Chief Executive Karen O'Neill

Producing theatre and cultural centre. Its Young Writers scheme was launched in January 2017. See website for up-to-date information about the theatre's productions and programming approach.

Dundee Rep and Scottish Dance Theatre Limited

Tay Square, Dundee DD1 1PB
tel (01382) 227684
email info@dundeereptheatre.co.uk
website www.dundeereptheatre.co.uk
Twitter @DundeeRep
Artistic Director (Dundee Rep)/Joint Chief Executive Andrew Panton, *Executive Director/Joint Chief Executive* Liam Sinclair

Regional repertory theatre company with resident ensemble. Mix of classics, musicals and new commissions.

Everyman Theatre Cheltenham

7 Regent Street, Cheltenham, Glos. GL50 1HQ
tel (01242) 512515
email admin@everymantheatre.org.uk
website www.everymantheatre.org.uk
Twitter @Everymanchelt
Creative Director Paul Milton

Regional presenting and producing theatre promoting a wide range of plays. Small-scale experimental, youth and educational work encouraged in The Studio Theatre. Contact the Creative Director before submitting material.

Exeter Northcott Theatre

Stocker Road, Exeter, Devon EX4 4QB
tel (01392) 722417
email info@exeternorthcott.co.uk
website www.exeternorthcott.co.uk
Twitter @ExeterNorthcott
Artistic Director and Chief Executive Daniel Buckroyd

460-seat producing and receiving venue offering a varied programme of shows and touring productions.

Harrogate Theatre

Oxford Street, Harrogate, North Yorkshire HG1 1QF
tel (01423) 502710
email info@harrogatetheatre.co.uk
website www.harrogatetheatre.co.uk
Twitter @HGtheatre
Chief Executive David Bown, *Associate Director* Phil Lowe

Predominantly a receiving house, Harrogate Theatre rarely produces productions in-house. Unsolicited scripts not accepted.

HOME: Theatre

2 Tony Wilson Place, First Street,
Manchester M15 4FN
tel 0161 200 1500
email info@homemcr.org
website www.homemcr.org
Twitter @HOME_mcr
Director & Ceo Dave Moutrey

Purpose-built centre for international contemporary art, theatre and film. Hosts drama, dance, film and contemporary visual art with a strong focus on international work, new commissions and talent development. Founded 2015.

Leeds Playhouse

Playhouse Square, Quarry Hill, Leeds LS2 7UP
tel 0113 213 7700
website https://leedsplayhouse.org.uk
Twitter @LeedsPlayhouse
Artistic Director James Brining, *Executive Director* Robin Hawkes

Leeds Playhouse has been welcoming audiences for 50 years. As a registered charity (No. 255460), the theatre seeks out the best companies and artists to create inspirational theatre in the heart of Yorkshire. A dedicated collaborator, Leeds Playhouse works with distinctive, original voices from across the UK.

Its Artistic Development programme, Furnace, discovers, nurtures and supports new voices, while developing work with established practitioners. It provides a creative space for writers, directors, companies and individual theatre-makers to refine their practice at all stages of their career. The sector-leading Creative Engagement team works with more than 12,000 people aged 0–95 every year reaching out to refugee communities, young people, students, older people and people with learning disabilities. The Playhouse pioneered Relaxed Performances ten years ago.

Live Theatre

Broad Chare, Quayside,
Newcastle upon Tyne NE1 3DQ
tel 0191 232 1232
email info@live.org.uk
website www.live.org.uk
Twitter @LiveTheatre
Chief Executive Jim Beirne

New writing theatre company and venue. Stages three to six productions per year of new writing, plus touring plays from other new writing companies.

Liverpool Everyman and Playhouse

Liverpool and Merseyside Theatres Trust Ltd,
5–11 Hope Street, Liverpool L1 9BH
tel 0151 708 3700
email scripts@everymanplayhouse.com
website www.everymanplayhouse.com/script-submissions

Facebook www.facebook.com/everymanplayhouse
Twitter @LivEveryPlay
Chief Executive Mark Da Vanzo

Produces and presents theatre. Looks for original work from writers based within the Liverpool city region: email pdfs or Word documents along with a completed submission form (see website for this and further details of submission specifications).

Mercury Theatre Colchester

Balkerne Gate, Colchester, Essex CO1 1PT
tel (01206) 577006
email info@mercurytheatre.co.uk
website www.mercurytheatre.co.uk
Twitter @mercurytheatre
Executive Producer Tracey Childs, *Executive Director* Steve Mannix, *Creative Director* Ryan McBryde

Active producing theatre in East Anglia, aiming to put theatre at the heart of the community it serves and to make work in Colchester that reaches audiences regionally and nationally. Runs a comprehensive Creative Learning & Talent programme to support artists and theatre-makers at all stages of their development.

The New Theatre: Dublin

The New Theatre, Temple Bar, 43 East Essex Street, Dublin D02 XH92, Republic of Ireland
tel +353 (0)1 6703361
email info@thenewtheatre.com
website www.thenewtheatre.com
Artistic Director Anthony Fox, *New Writing Coordinator* Nora Kelly Lester

Innovative theatre supporting plays by new Irish writers and others whose work deals with issues pertaining to contemporary Irish society. Welcomes scripts from new writers. Seats 66 people. Founded 1997.

New Vic Theatre

Etruria Road, Newcastle under Lyme ST5 0JG
tel (01782) 717954
email admin@newvictheatre.org.uk
website www.newvictheatre.org.uk
Twitter @NewVicTheatre
Artistic Director Theresa Heskins, *Managing Director* Fiona Wallace

Europe's first purpose-built theatre-in-the-round, presenting drama, contemporary and new plays, comedy and a range of one-night concerts. Also runs the award-winning *Borderlines* community programme and creative learning opportunities for ages four to adults.

The New Wolsey Theatre

Civic Drive, Ipswich, Suffolk IP1 2AS
tel (01473) 295900
email info@wolseytheatre.co.uk
website www.wolseytheatre.co.uk
Facebook www.facebook.com/NewWolsey

Twitter @NewWolsey
Chief Executive Sarah Holmes, *Artistic Director* Peter Rowe

Mix of producing and presenting in 400-seater main house and studio. Founded 2000.

Northern Stage (Theatrical Productions) Ltd

Barras Bridge, Newcastle upon Tyne NE1 7RH
tel 0191 242 7210
email info@northernstage.co.uk
website www.northernstage.co.uk
Twitter @northernstage
Artistic Director Natalie Ibu, *Executive Director* Kate Denby

The largest producing theatre company in the north east of England. Presents local, national and international theatre across three stages and runs an extensive participation programme.

Nottingham Playhouse

Nottingham Playhouse Trust Ltd, Wellington Circus, Nottingham NG1 5AF
tel 0115 941 9419
website www.nottinghamplayhouse.co.uk
Twitter @NottmPlayhouse
Artistic Director Adam Penford, *Chief Executive* Stephanie Sirr

Seeks to nurture new writers from the East Midlands primarily through its Artist Development programme, Amplify. There are two official Ideas Submission windows per year, one in the Spring and one in the Autumn. The Playhouse will select the best material and look at bespoke ways of developing these projects. See the website for full information and dates.

Octagon Theatre

Howell Croft South, Bolton BL1 1SB
tel (01204) 520661
email literary@octagonbolton.co.uk
website www.octagonbolton.co.uk
Twitter @octagontheatre
Chief Executive Roddy Gauld, *Artistic Director* Lotte Wakeham

Fully flexible professional theatre. Year-round programme of own productions and visiting companies, including a Studio Theatre for creative engagement, family theatre, new work and emerging artists. The theatre is due to reopen later in 2021 following extensive remodelling.

Oldham Coliseum Theatre

Fairbottom Street, Oldham OL1 3SW
tel 0161 624 1731
email mail@coliseum.org.uk
website www.coliseum.org.uk
Twitter @OldhamColiseum
Artistic Director Chris Lawson

Interested in new work, particularly plays set in the North. Alongside the programme in its Main Auditorium, the Studio programme aims to support and showcase the best in new writing and emerging talent to explore issues that affect the local community. The theatre's learning and engagement department runs a variety of outreach programmes and courses for young people, adults and schools.

Queen's Theatre, Hornchurch

(Havering Theatre Trust Ltd)
Billet Lane, Hornchurch, Essex RM11 1QT
tel (01708) 443333
email info@queens-theatre.co.uk
website www.queens-theatre.co.uk
Twitter @QueensTheatreH
Artistic Director Douglas Rintoul, *Executive Director* Mathew Russell

Regional theatre with a rich heritage, working in Outer East London, Essex and beyond, which celebrated its 65th birthday in 2018. Each annual programme includes home-grown theatre, visiting live entertainment and inspiring learning and participation projects.

Royal Exchange Theatre Company Ltd

St Ann's Square, Manchester M2 7DH
tel 0161 833 9833
email suzanne.bell@royalexchange.co.uk
website www.royalexchange.co.uk
website www.writeaplay.co.uk
Facebook www.facebook.com/rx
Twitter @rxtheatre
Executive Director Steve Freeman, *Artistic Directors* Bryony Shanahan and Roy Alexander Weise, *Dramaturg* Suzanne Bell

Varied programme of major classics, new plays, musicals, contemporary British and European drama. Focus on new writing, writer development, creative collaborations and community participation. Facilitates and delivers the Bruntwood Prize for Playwriting biennially.

Royal Lyceum Theatre Company

Royal Lyceum Theatre, 30B Grindlay Street, Edinburgh EH3 9AX
tel 0131 248 4800
email info@lyceum.org.uk
website www.lyceum.org.uk
Twitter @lyceumtheatre
Artistic Director David Greig

Scotland's busiest producing theatre, creating a diverse year-round programme of classic, contemporary and new drama in Edinburgh. Interested in work of Scottish writers.

Royal Shakespeare Company

The Royal Shakespeare Theatre, Waterside, Stratford-upon-Avon, Warks. CV37 6BB

Theatre

tel (01789) 296655
email literary@rsc.org.uk
website www.rsc.org.uk
Facebook www.facebook.com/thersc
Twitter @TheRSC
Artistic Director Gregory Doran, *Deputy Artistic Director* Erica Whyman, *Head of Literary* Pippa Hill

On its two main stages in Stratford-upon-Avon, the RST and the Swan Theatre, the Company produces a core repertoire of Shakespeare alongside new plays and the work of Shakespeare's contemporaries. In addition, its studio theatre, The Other Place, produces festivals of cutting-edge new work. For all its stages, the Company commissions new plays, new translations and new adaptations that illuminate the themes and concerns of Shakespeare and his contemporaries for a modern audience. The Literary department does not accept unsolicited work but rather seeks out writers it wishes to work with or commission, and monitors the work of writers in production in the UK and internationally. Writers are welcome to invite the Literary department to readings, showcases or productions by emailing the address above.

Salisbury Playhouse

Wiltshire Creative, Salisbury Playhouse,
Malthouse Lane, Salisbury, Wilts. SP2 7RA
tel (01722) 320117; box office (01722) 320333
email info@wiltshirecreative.co.uk
website www.wiltshirecreative.co.uk
Facebook www.facebook.com/salisburyplayhouseofficial/
Twitter @salisburyplay
Artistic Director Gareth Machin, *Executive Director* Sebastian Warrack

Regional producing and presenting theatre with a broad programme of classical and contemporary plays in two auditoria. Does not accept unsolicited scripts. The Playhouse is committed to a programme of original drama with a particular focus on South-West writers. Please check website for current information on script submission.

Sheffield Theatres

(Crucible, Crucible Studio & Lyceum)
55 Norfolk Street, Sheffield S1 1DA
tel 0114 249 5999
website www.sheffieldtheatres.co.uk
Chief Executive Dan Bates

Large-scale producing house with distinctive thrust stage; studio; Victorian proscenium arch theatre used mainly for touring productions.

Sherman Theatre

Senghennydd Road, Cardiff CF24 4YE
tel 029-2064 6900
website www.shermantheatre.co.uk
Twitter @shermantheatre

Executive Director Julia Barry, *Artistic Director* Joe Murphy

Produces new work and revivals. Seeks to stage high-quality and innovative drama with a local, national or international perspective. Develops work by Welsh and Welsh-based writers, both in English and Welsh. Supports writers through the New Welsh Playwrights' Programme. Participatory work with youth theatres (age 5 to 25), community engagement, and mentorship of new artists. Currently unable to read and respond to unsolicited scripts. Founded 2007.

Show of Strength Theatre Company Ltd

74 Chessel Street, Bedminster, Bristol BS3 3DN
tel 0117 953 5976
email info@showofstrength.org.uk
website www.showofstrength.org.uk
Facebook www.facebook.com/showofstrength
Twitter @Showofstrength
Creative Producer Sheila Hannon

Small-scale company committed to producing new and unperformed work. Unsolicited scripts not accepted. Founded 1986.

Stephen Joseph Theatre

Stephen Joseph Theatre, Westborough, Scarborough, North Yorkshire YO11 1JW
tel (01723) 370540
email scripts@sjt.uk.com
website www.sjt.uk.com/aboutus/new_writing
Twitter @thesjt
Assistant Producer & Literary Coordinator Fleur Hebditch

Regional repertory theatre company presenting approx. eight productions a year, many of which are premieres. Unsolicited scripts accepted from represented and unrepresented writers; see website for details.

Swansea Grand Theatre

Singleton Street, Swansea SA1 3QJ
tel (01792) 475715
email swansea.grandmarketing@swansea.gov.uk
email paul.hopkins2@swansea.gov.uk
website www.swanseagrand.co.uk
Facebook www.facebook.com/swanseagrandtheatre
Twitter @swanseagrand
Theatre Manager Paul Hopkins

Regional receiving theatre.

Theatr Clwyd

Mold, Flintshire CH7 1YA
tel (01352) 344101
email newplays@theatrclwyd.com
website www.theatrclwyd.com
Twitter @ClwydTweets

Largest producing theatre in Wales, creating up to fourteen productions each year in English, Welsh and bilingually. Productions are a mix of classic plays, contemporary revivals, musicals and new writing. Will consider plays by writers, particularly Welsh, Wales-based or with Welsh themes, and has six resident writers a year. No literary department, so authors will need to be patient when waiting for a response to an unsolicited script.

Theatre Royal Bath
Sawclose, Bath BA1 1ET
tel 01225 448815
website www.theatreroyal.org.uk
Twitter @TheatreRBath
Director Danny Moar

One of the oldest theatres in Britain. Comprising three auditoria – the Main House, the Ustinov Studio Theatre and the Egg theatre for children and young people – the Theatre Royal offers a varied programme of entertainment all year round.

Theatre Royal Plymouth
Royal Parade, Plymouth PL1 2TR
tel 01752 668282
email literary@theatreroyal.com
website www.theatreroyal.com
Twitter @TRPlymouth

Specialises in the production of new plays. Its engagement and learning work engages young people and communities in Plymouth and beyond. The award-winning waterfront production and learning centre, TR2, offers set, costume, prop-making and rehearsal facilities.

Theatre Royal Windsor
32 Thames Street, Windsor, Berks. SL4 1PS
tel (01753) 863444
email info@theatreroyalwindsor.co.uk
website www.theatreroyalwindsor.co.uk
Facebook www.facebook.com/TheatreWindsor/
Twitter @TheatreWindsor
Executive Producer Bill Kenwright, *Co-Directors* Anne-Marie Woodley, Jon Woodley

Regional producing theatre presenting a wide range of productions, from classics to new plays.

Traverse Theatre
10 Cambridge Street, Edinburgh EH1 2ED
tel 0131 228 3223
website www.traverse.co.uk
Twitter @traversetheatre
Co-Artistic Directors Gareth Nicholls, Debbie Hannan

Produces and presents new theatre work from Scotland and internationally. Scripts submissions are accepted at certain points throughout the year; see the website for submission guidelines and further information.

Visible Fictions
Suite 325/327, 4th Floor, 11 Bothwell Street, Glasgow G2 6LY

email office@visiblefictions.co.uk
website https://visiblefictions.co.uk
Twitter @visiblefictions
Artistic Director Dougie Irvine, *Producer* Laura Penny

Accessible theatre for young people and adults. Also works in creative learning settings – community, educational, institutional and professional – to create bespoke and immersive projects.

Watford Palace Theatre
20 Clarendon Road, Watford, Herts. WD17 1JZ
tel (01923) 235455
website www.watfordpalacetheatre.co.uk
Twitter @watfordpalace
Artistic Director Brigid Larmour

Regional theatre. Produces and co-produces seasonally, both classic and contemporary drama and new writing. Accepts unsolicited scripts from writers in Hertfordshire.

York Theatre Royal
St Leonard's Place, York YO1 7HD
tel (01904) 658162
website www.yorktheatreroyal.co.uk
Facebook www.facebook.com/yorktheatreroyal
Twitter @yorktheatre
Instagram yorktheatreroyal
Chief Executive Tom Bird

Repertory productions, tours.

TOURING COMPANIES

Actors Touring Company
ICA, 12 Carlton Terrace, London SW1Y 5AH
tel 020-7930 6014
email atc@atctheatre.com
website www.atctheatre.com
Facebook www.facebook.com/actorstouringcompany
Twitter @ATCLondon
Artistic Director Matthew Xia

Small- to medium-scale company producing international new writing.

Boundless Theatre
B2–B4 Galleywall Road, Bermondsey, London SE16 3PB
tel 020-7928 2811
email hello@boundlesstheatre.org.uk
website www.boundlesstheatre.org.uk
Instagram boundlessabound
Artistic Director and CEO Rob Drummer

Creates new plays with and for audiences aged 15 to 25. Tours the UK and internationally. Also runs a variety of projects to help young people develop their creativity; these focus on performance, writing and digital innovation. Founded 2001 (as Company of Angels).

Theatre

Theatre

Eastern Angles

Sir John Mills Theatre, Gatacre Road,
Ipswich IP1 2LQ
tel (01473) 218202
email admin@easternangles.co.uk
website www.easternangles.co.uk
Twitter @easternangles
Artistic Director Ivan Cutting

Touring company producing new work with a
regional theme. Stages three to four productions per
year. Welcomes scripts from new writers in the East
of England region. Founded 1982.

Graeae Theatre Company

Bradbury Studios, 138 Kingsland Road,
London E2 8DY
tel 020-7613 6900
email info@graeae.org
website www.graeae.org
Facebook www.facebook.com/graeae
Twitter @graeae
Instagram graeaetheatrecompany
Artistic Director Jenny Sealey MBE, *Executive Director*
Kevin Walsh, *Finance Director* Charles Mills, *Head of
Marketing and Development* Richard Matthews, *Access
Manager* Lizzy Leggat, *Producer* Kate Baiden, *Creative
Learning Director* Jodi-Alissa Bickerton

Small- to mid-scale touring company boldly placing
D/deaf and disabled artists centre stage. Welcomes
scripts from D/deaf and disabled writers.
Founded 1980.

Headlong Theatre

17 Risborough Street, London SE1 0HG
tel 020-7633 2090
email info@headlong.co.uk
website https://headlong.co.uk
Twitter @HeadlongTheatre

Mid-/large-scale touring company presenting a
provocative mix of new writing, reimagined classics
and influential twentieth-century plays.

Hull Truck Theatre Co. Ltd

50 Ferensway, Hull HU2 8LB
tel (01482) 224800
email admin@hulltruck.co.uk
website www.hulltruck.co.uk
Twitter @HullTruck
Artistic Director Mark Babych, *Executive Director*
Janthi Mills-Ward

Producing and receiving theatre with a national
reputation for new writing. Premieres of new plays,
including own commissions, have included works by
Tanika Gupta, Amanda Whittington, Bryony Lavery,
James Graham and Richard Bean.

The London Bubble

(Bubble Theatre Company)
5 Elephant Lane, London SE16 4JD
tel 020-7237 4434
email admin@londonbubble.org.uk
website www.londonbubble.org.uk
Twitter @LBubble

Aims to provide the artistic direction, skills,
environment and resources to create inspirational,
inclusive and involving theatre for the local
community and beyond. Also runs a number of
groups for children and young people as well as an
adult drama group, a Creative Elders group and the
Rotherhithe Shed initiative.

M6 Theatre Company

Studio Theatre, Hamer C.P. School,
Albert Royds Street, Rochdale, Lancs. OL16 2SU
tel (01706) 355898
email admin@m6theatre.co.uk
website www.m6theatre.co.uk
Twitter @M6Theatre
Artistic Director Gilly Baskeyfield

Touring theatre company specialising in creating and
delivering innovative theatre for young audiences.

New Perspectives Theatre Company

Park Lane Business Centre, Park Lane, Basford,
Nottingham NG6 0DW
tel 0115 927 2334
email info@newperspectives.co.uk
website www.newperspectives.co.uk
Facebook www.facebook.com/
newperspectivestheatrecompany
Twitter @NPtheatre
Artistic Director Jack McNamara

Touring theatre company, staging up to four
productions a year, many of which are new
commissions. The company tours new writing and
adaptations of existing works to theatres, arts centres,
festivals and rural village halls around the country.
Founded 1973.

Out of Joint

49 South Molton Street, London W1K 5LH
email ojo@outofjoint.co.uk
website www.outofjoint.co.uk
Twitter @Out_of_Joint
Executive Producer Martin Derbyshire, *Artistic
Director* Kate Wasserberg

Touring company producing 'plays for the nation' for
audiences across the UK. Founded 1993.

Paines Plough

2nd Floor, 10 Leake Street, London SE1 7NN
tel 020-7240 4533
email office@painesplough.com
website www.painesplough.com
Facebook www.facebook.com/painesploughHQ
Twitter @painesplough
Joint Artistic Directors Katie Posner, Charlotte Bennett

Commissions and produces new plays by British and
Irish playwrights. Tours at least six plays per year

nationally for small- and mid-scale theatres. Also runs The Big Room, a concierge-style development strand for professional playwrights: see website for further details. Welcomes unsolicited scripts and responds to all submissions. Seeks original plays that engage with the contemporary world and are written in a distinctive voice.

Proteus Theatre Company

Proteus Creation Space, Council Road, Basingstoke, Hants RG21 3DH
tel (01256) 354541
email info@proteustheatre.com
website www.proteustheatre.com
Twitter @proteustheatre
Artistic Director and Chief Executive Mary Swan

Small-scale touring company particularly committed to new writing and new work, education and community collaborations. Produces up to three touring shows per year plus community projects. Founded 1981.

Red Ladder Theatre Company

3 St Peter's Buildings, York Street, Leeds LS9 8AJ
tel 0113 245 5311
email rod@redladder.co.uk
website www.redladder.co.uk
Twitter @RedLadderTheatr
Artistic Director Rod Dixon

Theatre performances with a radical and dissenting voice. National touring of theatre venues and community spaces. Commissions one or two new plays each year. Runs the Red Grit Project, a free theatre training programme for over-18s.

Sphinx Theatre Company

email info@sphinxtheatre.co.uk
website www.sphinxtheatre.co.uk
Twitter @Sphinxtheatre
Artistic Director Sue Parrish

Specialises in writing, directing and developing roles for women.

Talawa Theatre Company

Fairfield Halls, Park Lane, Croydon CR9 1DG
020-7251 6644

email contact@talawa.com
website www.talawa.com
Facebook www.facebook.com/TalawaTheatreCompany
Twitter @TalawaTheatreCo
Artistic Director Michael Buffong

Script-reading service available twice a year. Visit the website for further details of submission windows.

Theatre Absolute

Shop Front Theatre, 38 City Arcade, Coventry CV1 3HW
tel 07799 292957
email info@theatreabsolute.co.uk
website www.theatreabsolute.co.uk
Facebook www.facebook.com/TheatreAbsolute
Twitter @theatreabsolute
Contact Julia Negus

Independent theatre producer of contemporary work. Opened the Shop Front Theatre, a 50-seat flexible professional theatre space for new writing, performances, script development, theatre lab and other live art events, in 2009. The company is funded project to project and unfortunately not able to receive unsolicited scripts. Founded 1992 by Chris O'Connell and Julia Negus.

Theatre Centre

The Albany, Douglas Way, Deptford, London SE8 4AG
tel 020-7729 3066
email admin@theatre-centre.co.uk
website www.theatre-centre.co.uk
Facebook www.facebook.com/TheatreCentreUK
Twitter @TClive
Artistic Director (Interim) Rob Watt

Young people's theatre company producing plays and workshops which tour nationally across the UK. Productions are staged in schools, arts centres and other venues. Keen to nurture new and established talent, encouraging all writers to consider writing for young audiences. Also runs creative projects and manages writing awards: see website for details. Founded 1953.

Theatre

Literary agents
What a debut novelist should expect from an agent

Sallyanne Sweeney explains what a literary agent's job entails, and the range of roles that may include as they work closely with and for an author to ensure the best possible outcome for a debut novel.

Congratulations! You've beaten the slush pile. You have a literary agent. Dream realised, job done, right?

Signing to an agency is an exciting time both for authors and agents. One of the best parts of my job is taking on a new client – that fizz of anticipation mixed with a slight trepidation, as now the work really begins. You may well be wondering what happens next, and it's okay not to know what to expect at this stage; your agent is there to guide you through everything that lies ahead. You may have been in the position of choosing between multiple offers of representation or you may have found 'the one' on your first try. Either way, it's a good idea to meet your new agent or at least have a phone conversation before accepting their offer. This is your chance to ask about their process and discuss expectations – and if you don't feel comfortable asking these questions, are they the right agent for you?

The debut

When I started working in publishing, the submissions pile tended to tower precariously in the office corner, gathering dust. Since then, the attitude towards debuts has completely shifted (and, thankfully for everyone, electronic submissions have become the norm). Publishers have proven they can launch debuts into the world as major brands, with marketing campaigns to match. The competition between agents to sign talented new authors is fierce, and for good reason: Nielsen BookScan records more debut novels in the top 150 fiction titles published in 2020 than in 2019, with sales of the top 10 debutants up 151%.

No two paths to publication are the same and my relationship with clients differs according to their individual needs and styles. Last year, I sold five debut novelists across children's and adult fiction. With one of these authors, the period from their joining the agency to agreeing a publication deal was a matter of weeks, after a contracted round of edits and a swift auction. With another, we had been working together for five years by the time I sold her manuscript, so her 'debut' was actually the second novel I'd 'gone on submission' with. Many debut novels are anything but. Sometimes that first book will be published later; more often than not, it remains in a drawer.

Below are the key elements the agent will bring to your new partnership.

1. The edit

By the time of securing an agent, you will have already revised and honed your manuscript, sometimes over multiple drafts. The bad news: you need to be prepared for several more. The good news: this time, you're not working alone.

An agent will work with you to get the manuscript into as polished a state as possible for submission. This creative back-and-forth is one of the most rewarding (and time-consuming) aspects of my job. It's a vital investment from your agent and one that will hopefully pay off – remember, you have one chance to make a winning first impression on publishers. I start with the 'big picture' or structural edits, homing in on how to get the best out of the story and characters, and identifying what might not be working as well as it could be. The final stage focuses on a line edit and looking for anything that might have been missed in previous drafts. How many rounds come in between completely depends on the individual manuscript.

Your agent should share your vision and ambition for your book and want to work with you to make it the best it can be. You don't have to agree with, or implement, all these edits, but they should serve as a useful guide through your revisions. I'm always happy for an author to find their own solutions to my editorial concerns; the magic is often in the unexpected and I love when an author thinks around the issue and elevates their work in a way I could never have anticipated.

2. The sale

While my client is working on their edits, I'll be progressing things behind the scenes, discussing the manuscript with editors, and finessing both the pitch and the submission list.

Passion sells and, in the same way you might rush to tell all your friends and family about a wonderful book you've just read, I want to be 'going on submission' feeling excited about pressing a manuscript into the hands of editors I think will love it. This entails knowing editors' tastes, keeping in constant touch about what publishers are buying and looking for, researching the market, looking at trends, and reading recently published titles. You won't necessarily be aware of all of this going on as you're working on edits, but it's a good idea to keep your agent informed of your progress so that they can plan their timing for submission. Once you've both signed off on the final manuscript, you're ready to go.

Most authors find being on submission tough. You've now done everything you can, and your manuscript is out of your hands. I'd advise trying to keep yourself occupied while waiting on news, whether that's throwing yourself into your next book or scrubbing your skirting boards, as is one client's habit – whatever it takes! It can be a nerve-wracking time for agents, too. At Mulcahy Sweeney Associates we are extremely selective about new authors we take on because we want to maintain our high success rate in sales. An agent's reputation is on the line with each submission and we want editors to respond quickly and positively to every manuscript from our agency, ideally to immediately call and tell us they love it as much as we do (and make us a compelling offer at the same time).

3. The deal

Hopefully, you'll have one or multiple publishers wishing to acquire your debut novel and your agent will guide you through this process. My job is to get the best deal for my author, thinking strategically beyond this first book to look ahead at the author's career as a whole. This means not only orchestrating a competitive auction to secure the optimal advance, royalties and rights, but also matchmaking the author with the right editor and ensuring the commitment of the full publishing team for the book.

When you have accepted a publisher offer, your agent will cast a forensic eye over the finer detail of the contract. This is the less glamorous side of agenting, but no less important, examining the small print (for example, negotiating favourable high discount, reversion and option clauses) and worrying about the minutiae of the deal – so that the author doesn't have to.

4. Rights

All along the way, an agent will be thinking about subsidiary rights – in particular, US, translation and dramatic rights – ensuring that they build momentum after that primary deal. This initial energy surrounding a title can create ripples around the world that lead to a wave of international offers, which in turn maintains that buzz at home. To try to achieve this, I'll regularly discuss forthcoming projects with literary scouts (employed by international publishers to flag up the 'hot' titles in the English language markets) and our co-agents, and pitch to international publishers or production companies myself at the London, Bologna and Frankfurt Book Fairs.

5. Advocacy

An agent's job doesn't end once you have a publisher on board (or indeed, many publishers around the world). As my client's foremost champion, I stay involved throughout the whole publication process and beyond, bringing my own ideas and experience and making sure things flow as smoothly as possible. As a debut author, you may not know which concerns are worth raising and which are standard practice. What do you do if you hate your cover or the publisher's proposed title, if no copies have shown up at a scheduled event, or if your signature advance is nowhere to be seen? Your agent can tell you what's acceptable – or not – and advocate on your behalf so that your relationship with the publisher stays purely creative.

6. The long game

What happens when (… whisper it …) things go wrong? If your debut novel doesn't sell, or it does but isn't the success you'd hoped for? Your agent should be there in bad times as well as good, as your creative and business partner throughout your whole career and not just your debut. As great as it is to get immediate offers on a book, I find immense satisfaction in securing a harder-fought deal for an author. Agents get rejected too (and it hurts!), but when I believe in a book I will persist in fighting for it. Sometimes, if I think we just haven't found the right match yet and there hasn't been a common editorial concern flagged in the responses, I'll start a second submission round; one such novel on my list ended up selling at auction and winning awards, after being rejected across the board in its first publisher outing. In some instances, this might first entail a further round of edits with the author, after going through the publisher feedback together. Or, in what's a tougher call, you and your agent might decide that it's time to move on to your next novel … which might be the one that sets the world alight.

What can an author can do throughout this whole journey? Keep the faith and keep writing. Most authors with long careers will work with different publishers and editors along the way but usually with the same agent. Your debut should be only the very beginning of this long and successful partnership.

Sallyanne Sweeney started her career at Watson, Little Ltd, where she became a Director in 2011. In 2013 she joined Mulcahy Associates, part of the MMBcreative group, and since 2021 has been a Director of the renamed Mulcahy Sweeney Associates. Sallyanne was Chair of the Children's Agents' Circle 2014–18. See https://mmbcreative.com/agents/sallyanne-sweeney for more information and follow her on Twitter @sallyanne_s.

Literary agents

What does a literary agent do?

An agent has three main roles. James Rennoldson briefly encapsulates what these are.

The job of a literary agent is to sell your manuscript to publishers and secure terms beneficial in both the short- and long-term life of your book. They understand you creatively and look to support and develop your career as a writer. Agents act on your behalf by championing your book, brokering the best deal possible for it and acting as a buffer between you and your publisher. They do the worrying so you can do the writing.

Broadly speaking, an agent's job can be broken down into three areas: **creative**, **business** and **people-related**.

In a **creative** sense, an agent has to be in sync with what their writers are working towards and hone manuscripts so that they reach their potential. In being offered representation, you will have gained a passionate, influential supporter of your book and creative outlook in general. Agents may work through several versions of your manuscript with you ahead of sending it out to commissioning editors they have identified as potentially interested in bidding for the rights. If the process of rewriting means tightening up character arcs, concentrating on giving your book more 'heart' or restructuring to create a pacier plot, then your agent will support you in that. This means you need to trust them and be willing to let go of your book enough to be guided by someone with your best interests at heart and an eye on what they know editors are looking for. Before approaching an agent, you should have a reasonable idea where your book would sit within a bookstore; an agent will be an expert on the market, with knowledge as to how books are categorised and in which genre they are likely to sit.

This overarching appreciation of publishing as a commercial enterprise is where an agent's creative support meets their eye for **business**. Agents constantly have their ear to the ground for deals being done; the sorts of books editors are buying and where rights are being sold for particular titles. This informs their strategy when it comes to approaching potential buyers of a manuscript, and also how much to push for during financial negotiations. All of which, of course, needs to be tied up contractually, and an agent's keen eye for small print is something that benefits their authors. It's the meat and potatoes of an agent's job to look into any sort of contractual query (financial or otherwise) and find solutions so that their authors are rewarded for their writing.

The third attribute of a literary agent complements both the creative and commercial elements of their role. Like most jobs in the Arts (and beyond!) being able to **relate to people** counts for a great deal. The business side of their job, for example, comes down to having good contacts. This requires acquiring an understanding of what commissioning editors have on their wish-lists and is built up over time through chance conversations or more formal meetings. These are the moments when they can put forward manuscripts, either by planting a seed and mentioning how excited they are by a book one of their unpublished clients is putting finishing touches to, or by proclaiming a book to be ready and one an editor must read. As a yet-to-be published writer, this, as far as you're concerned, is the primary role of the agent – to champion your book and pitch it with such passion that an editor feels compelled to put everything else aside and read it. Whether it be in-person over a coffee or by email, an agent's ability to transfer their enthusiasm for your project is integral to their job.

Being able to relate to people is more than an agent being a good salesperson for their authors, though. There's a huge difference in approach between chasing royalty payments or interrogating the terms of a publishing agreement, for example, to that needed to support overwhelmed debut author suddenly stifled by 'imposter' syndrome. Perhaps the greatest test of an agent's emotional dexterity is how they handle their authors in order to bring out the best in them and their work. Do they need 'tough love' and hard deadlines, or will they respond more to a sympathetic ear that coaxes them through a crisis of confidence?

Extracted from the *Writers' & Artists' Guide to How to Hook an Agent* (Bloomsbury 2020) by **James Rennoldson**, Senior Digital Product Manager for Writers & Artists.

Putting together your submission

Hellie Ogden spells out what the time-pressed agent is looking for in a book submission, and provides advice and examples of what *is*, and what *is not*, likely to help a new author secure an agent.

Any agent will tell you they get huge numbers of submissions sent to them daily – perhaps up to 100 or so each week. And it's true, we do, but that fact shouldn't be unduly intimidating. It always amazes me, despite the amount of information available on agents' sites and from resources such as this *Yearbook* and the Writers' & Artists' website (www.writersandartists.co.uk), how many of these submission emails are hastily and sloppily written – full of spelling, punctuation and, in some cases, factual errors. These I will reject straightaway. The number of smart, professional cover letters that I receive is much smaller (approximately 25% of all those I see) and these will be bumped up my submission pile.

The cover letter

There are some key points to remember when putting your submission together: personalise your covering letter/email, addressing it to a specific, correctly named agent, and send it in line with each agent's guidelines on their site. Include a brief introduction about yourself and your book and what material you are attaching as specified by each agency. This would typically include three sample chapters and a synopsis, which should be in documents attached to your cover letter email, and not added to the body of the email itself.

Knowing the market

What will elevate your submission package, comes down to two things. Firstly, knowing where your book sits in the market or which genre it falls within. It may sound obvious, but having market awareness is really smart. It shows that you have done your research and, because of that, that you have an idea of what other published titles it might sit alongside on the booksellers' shelves or in online stores. On top of falling in love with your writing, agents themselves will be strategising and formulating a pitch around how your book will be positioned. Is your book YA, upmarket commercial, narrative non-fiction, literary, psychological suspense? Your agent will have a good idea of what 'type' of book you have written, but it's encouraging to see an author considering these questions too, showing an awareness of the commercial side of publishing and some understanding of the market.

The elevator pitch

The second crucial element of your submission is the 'elevator pitch'. This need only be a paragraph long, around 100-150 words, but contains the most important lines you will write in your cover email. This is your opportunity to be creative and to stand out positively. The elevator pitch is your chance to sell your hook – an agent's eyes will flip to that part of the letter first. Take inspiration from blurbs on the back of published books in your genre; don't rush it and don't overcomplicate; focus on one key plot point and one unique angle.

A good and a not-so-good example

Opposite is an example of a submission letter I received a few years ago. I subsequently took on the author. I was instantly drawn to her letter: in her opening lines, she provides a clear sense of the book's genre and highlights her relevant writing experience. She has an understanding of my client list and her elevator pitch is really strong and compelling. The book's title isn't perfect, but it does feel relevant to the genre. She finishes by including a brief biography and (what I always appreciate) her telephone number, so I can be in touch quickly! It's always useful, too, to mention when you have submitted to other agents and to remain honest and transparent throughout the submission process.

As an extreme example of a bad cover letter(!), overleaf is one that I've cobbled together to highlight the errors a surprising number of authors make:

• It's not directed at an individual agent, it's arrogant in tone, and it's packed full of spelling mistakes.

• The writer has sent in a random selection of chapters – the ones that she thinks are the best. *All* your chapters should be the best examples of your writing and equally strong; send the first three chapters, not a random selection.

• Although I'm a big fan of comparison titles to highlight where your book might sit, the ones included here are contradictory and confusing.

Synopsis

The synopsis can challenge even the most confident of writers, and it shouldn't take precious time away from perfecting the manuscript itself. I would never turn down a manuscript if I loved the book but the synopsis didn't stylistically blow me away. In fact, I won't even open it until I've had a look at the manuscript itself. It's a simple map of the book, ideally a page long, detailing the beginning, middle and end of your story. Concentrate on the key points and don't overload it with detail.

It's an extremely exciting stage getting your manuscript ready to go out to agents, but I can't stress enough the importance of spending a good chunk of time on your approach. Do your research; read widely so you are aware of the market; spend time in bookshops looking at the backs of books and at titles too. Write, rewrite and write that pitch again! Keep it tight and compelling. Spend time on your synopsis but don't fret over it and, more importantly, try to make those opening three chapters of your work as wonderful as possible.

I often recommend to new writers that they read *The Bookseller* online – the publishing trade magazine (www.thebookseller.com). It's a great resource not only for researching an agent, but also for understanding a little about the market. Remember that agents are reading constantly, so don't nag if you don't hear back from them immediately; do check individual agency guidelines for response times. It's worth noting, too, that around the time of the three major book fairs each year – Bologna (usually March/April, children's and YA only, www.bolognachildrensbookfair.com), London (usually March, www.londonbookfair.co.uk) and Frankfurt (usually October, www.buchmesse.de/en) – agents are extremely busy, so I would suggest not submitting during the weeks running up to, during and just after the fairs.

From: Heidi Hopeful   14/02/2018

Subject: Submission of Bones by Heidi Hopeful

To: agent@literaryagency.com

Dear Hellie,

I hope you don't mind me contacting you directly. You have been highly recommended to me by an editor at Faber, who I worked with on the Faber Writing-a-Novel course a few years ago.

I would love you to be one of the first people to look at my upmarket thriller. I have thought long and hard about agents and I would absolutely love to work with you if you felt *Bones* was right for you. You have a wonderful, eclectic list and I hope that I might fit in well alongside your existing clients. I particularly love M.J. Arlidge's *Eeny Meeny*, which is just unputdownable, and the character of Helen Grace is fascinating - a detective who struggles with her demons so differently from other crime novel detectives.

My novel, *Bones*, tells the story of how Beth Chase's life is shattered when her 17-year-old son goes missing. When a body is pulled from the Thames outside her riverside home, Beth is convinced it is her missing son. Although it is soon evident the bones have been in the water far longer, she becomes fixated on them, her search for Louis becoming ever more frantic. As strange things begin to happen in the river house, the life of a former inhabitant emerges and Beth grows obsessed by events that unfolded there centuries ago.
But are these things really happening, or are they all in Beth's mind? Can the house on the river and its secrets lead Beth to her son, or is it spinning her away from him?

In my day job I write for a number of national parenting magazines and websites, on everything from how to travel across a continent with a potty-training toddler, to persuading your monsters that Haribo Sours are not one of the major food groups. Recent titles include *Families Magazine* and *Families Online*. I also write the blog *21stCenturyMum*.

I hope you don't mind but I have taken the liberty of attaching my novel, as well as a brief synopsis.

Thank you so much, and apologies for the excruciating length of this email! I look forward to hearing from you. My telephone number is *XXX* and I have submitted to a small number of agents.

Best wishes,

Heidi Hopeful

An example of a good submission email

From: Neil Chance
Subject: HEY, LOOK AT THIS!!!!
To: agent@literaryagency.com

01/04/2018

Dear Sir/Madam/Miss/Mz (that should cover you all),

I am writing to give you an exclusive first look at the future of publishing. A book that will literally change our society.

'The Face of God is an ugly one my son' is a fast-paced but literary thriller that follows the adventures of an innocent postie who gets sucked into the world of forensic archaeology and the dark underbelly of the Christian church, and must race across the world to stop a terrifying prophecy from coming true.

Dan Brown sold buckets of 'The DaVinci Code' and I plan to do the same. But where his book was based on cheap and easy hearsay, the myths and truths exposed in my book are the result of years of my own painstaking research into Christian conspiracies which I undertook during my twenty-five year career as a post office manager. I thin the book will hopefully steal away some of Mr Brown's fans but also appeal to readers of the likes of Graham Greene and John Updike.

If you're interested then read on – I've included the opening, closing and middle chapter to give you a flavour of the novel at its best places! I've already mapped out four possible sequels to this book – each more death defyingly thrilling than the last. I also have a backlist of more historical adventures – very Indiana Jones-esque, when men were men and women were in distress – which I'm sure you'll love as much as 'The Face of God is an ugly one my son.'

I look forward to a long and fruitful career with you,

Best,

N.O. Chance

An example of a poor submission email

Good luck! It's the best feeling in the world discovering new talent and nurturing debut writers.

Hellie Ogden is a literary agent at Janklow & Nesbit UK Literary Agency. She featured in *The Bookseller* Rising Stars list 2013 and was shortlisted for the Kim Scott Walwyn Prize 2014. She is looking for series crime, psychological thrillers, commercial and upmarket fiction, YA and children's debuts and accessible, charming literary fiction. In non-fiction Hellie is looking for unique personal stories and work that has a large social following with cross-media potential. As an editorially focused agent, she has a keen interest in helping to develop and nurture debut writers. Follow her on Twitter @HellieOgden.

Advice from an 'accidental' agent

Clare Grist Taylor, experienced publisher turned literary agent, highlights the importance of building trust between agent and author. She believes that a big part of her role is to provide editorial and emotional support for her authors; here she considers what a budding non-fiction author should take into account when preparing to publish.

I founded The Accidental Agency after a long career on the other side of the publishing fence and with a deep and enduring love of being a non-fiction editor and publisher. The words 'poacher' and 'gamekeeper' have been used. But I'm sure that my experience of working with all types of authors writing so many different types of books for all sorts of readers could have provided no better starting point for my work as an agent.

For me, the best editors have always combined market and commercial nous and judgement with the interpersonal skills needed to encourage and enable their authors. It is a relationship based on trust and respect, requiring the editor to act variously as counsellor, challenger, confidante and sounding board. As an agent, while market knowledge and judgement remain essential, I find that these 'soft' communication skills loom even larger. Writing is inherently exposing, and it's important that I provide a safe haven for my authors to explore and test new ideas, suffer crises of confidence, moan and rage, exult and despair. It's about being a true critical friend who is, usefully, at one remove from their publishers.

It is not a relationship to be taken lightly either, which is why it's so important that authors understand what an agent can (and can't) do for them, and that both parties are prepared for the journey ahead. Writing is hard, even for the most natural and accomplished of writers. Convincing a publisher that your book should be published can be even harder. All of this takes hard work, resilience, persistence and often (whisper it) a healthy dose of being in the right place at the right time. It also means being realistic – taking a good, hard look at what you want to achieve and why.

Does a non-fiction author really need an agent?

Be honest with yourself. You need to understand your motivations for writing, and the true size and scope of the audiences you're writing for; both of these will have implications on how your book might be published.

Many non-fiction authors will not be giving up the day job any time soon. There's nothing wrong with writing a book to reflect, reinforce or support your professional or personal credentials, or for a more defined market – which is the basis, after all, of much academic, professional and, increasingly, self-publishing. But, given that the immediate monetary rewards are likely to be minimal, you're unlikely to secure the services of an agent to help you ... and you might not need to. Many academic or professional publishers actively invite submissions and provide lists of their editors on their websites. So, find an in-house editor sympathetic to your work or, if self-publishing, a freelance editor to coach and inspire you, and to help you marshal and communicate your ideas. Partnership publishing – where you make an up-front investment to support publication – can be a good halfway house; do check any contracts carefully though, and be aware of potential vanity publishing scams (see *What do self-publishing providers offer?* on page 618).

If you have different ambitions for your book, aiming for a more general audience or a more traditional publishing deal, then the world becomes trickier, the rewards potentially greater but often more elusive. That's when an agent can really add value, and not simply in terms of helping you to find the right editor and publisher, negotiating the best deals and maximising what you'll earn as a result, crucial though that is. Because, before that, there's plenty of editorial work and thinking to do. The right agent will help you to marshal your ideas into book form, whether that's creating a book proposal that will also act as a blueprint and guide when it comes to writing or reviewing, or helping to craft draft chapters. It's a competitive world out there, so you need to think carefully about what your book offers and why it should be published, and how to anticipate and meet the objections you'll face. A properly persuasive book proposal, accompanied by well-constructed and compellingly written sample chapters, can make all the difference.

Before I wrote this piece, I talked to some of my authors about this process, what they'd learnt and what they wanted to pass on to others embarking on their own journeys. Below are some of the points they wanted to share.

1. Have a vision for what you want to achieve

Although most authors won't have in-depth knowledge of the world of publishing or the latest publishing trends, you can start to create a vision for yourself of the book you want to write. What will it look like? Where will it sit in a bookshop? Who can you imagine reading it? What other books will it be like? Visit the largest bookshop you can and spend time with comparable books. Think about things you might not have considered before, such as the relationship between the type of content and the book format and price. Consider titles and subtitles. Look at which publisher is publishing which types of books. Read author acknowledgements to identify likely agents and editors.

2. Stop and think before you write

Bear in mind Abraham Lincoln's famous advice that, if he were given six hours to cut down a tree, he would spend the first four sharpening the axe. Starting to write non-fiction without a very clear idea about what you want to say, and how, is a very bad idea indeed. I have lost track of the number of manuscripts that have crossed my desk with an appeal for help to sort them out; this is never, I can assure you, a task to be taken on lightly. In my experience, there are two main culprits:

• **Blog as would-be book**

This is my shorthand for a book that may start with a convincing argument or story but can't sustain the narrative in book-length form. If it's meant to be a blog, let it be a blog.

• **If I were to start again, I wouldn't start from here …**

Diving straight into writing without a proper sense of structure, focus, key messages or narrative arc will only make the (already difficult) task of writing a book even harder. Don't be tempted to make it up as you go along. Although plans will inevitably morph and change as the writing progresses, doing the serious thinking up front is essential.

Creating a convincing and compelling case for your book is not just about making it attractive for publishers. It's also about challenging yourself to hone your argument, sharpen your structure and write the best book you can. This is harder to do in retrospect than at the outset.

3. Non-fiction is about telling stories

Telling stories is about creating a connection with the reader. This is as true for even the most hard-nosed, 'how to' non-fiction as it is for the latest Booker Prize winner. Think about the narrative arc for your book: how can you communicate your story/information to create maximum resonance with readers? What's going to grab and hold their attention? Look at books you admire and ask yourself why. The chances are that they created a powerful connection that has stayed with you. This is also true when creating book proposals. A proposal is a mini book in its own right; it needs the right elements in a logical order, in order to be compelling and to engage the reader's attention. You need to tell your story.

4. Trust, collaboration and iteration

Whether you're working with an agent or an editor, that relationship must be based on trust. Publishing is a collaborative business, and, for me, that starts with the content. We all like to think that the best books emerge fully formed, with little intervention along the way. Some do – but, in my experience, that's rare. Even the most talented authors benefit from well-delivered and insightful feedback and input from someone whose opinion they value.

Being open to this collaboration and a healthy dose of iteration (write; review; edit; repeat) will undoubtedly result in a better book – but make sure the trust is there. You need a sounding board that works for you.

What goes in a good non-fiction book proposal?

- A compelling title, often with a more descriptive subtitle.
- An overview of the book's purpose and vision, showing clearly what the book will do and why it should be published; its key themes; what's special or unique about it; what does it offer?
- The markets/audiences for the book: who will buy it and why; how will you reach them?
- Positioning statement: how your book compares with similar and competing titles.
- Proposed overall length and schedule for writing.
- An outline of chapters, with clear synopses and notes on sources, as relevant.
- (Where relevant) thoughts on illustrations and where they can be sourced.
- Author profile and credentials.
- Publicity contacts and links; access to marketing channels; how you can help to support publication.
- Ideas for potential endorsers and reviewers.
- Sample chapters.

5. Content is king – but positioning matters too

No publisher is going to take on a book with uninteresting, flawed or badly written content, but even the best content in the world often needs a helping hand to get noticed. That's why you need to consider and identify how your book can be positioned in its markets. Some authors find this difficult or distasteful but, if you want to be published, it's simply part of the deal.

Positioning involves everything from the right attention-grabbing title and subtitle through to a strong sense of how you, as author, can help to publicise and promote the book. It's strongly related to that vision of your work I mentioned earlier, and it requires you to think carefully about how your book will compare and contrast with other, similar titles in the market. There may be a tricky balancing act between taking a sensible decision to look and feel a bit like the other fish in the sea – for familiarity's sake – and offering something genuinely new or different. Comparisons with other writers and titles can work – but be careful not to over-use shorthand descriptions of the 'Malcolm Gladwell meets Daniel Pink' type, unless they're spot on. And don't try to shoehorn your work into a genre or type that is currently in vogue just to make it sound more marketable.

That's because you need to …

Literary agents

6. Write the book *you* want to write

Way back in my career, a wise colleague warned me off pairing a recalcitrant author with a more reliable co-author with the phrase: 'Publisher marriages don't work'. In some areas of non-fiction, using an author's expertise to write to a brief can work but, in general, I firmly believe that authors should write the books they want to write. That doesn't mean you should not accept guidance and support along the way, or that you should write books that have no potential or market. But the best books come from an author's passion, and passion is hard to manufacture.

Good luck! Non-fiction is a buoyant, stimulating and deeply satisfying area of publishing. It'll be good to have you on board.

Clare Grist Taylor is founder of The Accidental Agency, specialising in intelligent and inspiring non-fiction. She has worked in publishing for over 35 years, with experience across trade, professional and academic sectors. She still gets a buzz when talking to potential authors, from matching authors with publishers and from seeing books well published. Clare is a Trustee of the Montgomeryshire Literary Festival and an advisory board member at the University of Wales Press. See www.claregristtaylor.com for more information. Follow her on Twitter @claregt.

Cross-format representation: what a literary agent can do for you

Literary agent Sarah Such explains her role and the reasons why it's worth engaging an agent to represent you as an author in our multimedia world.

I founded Sarah Such Literary Agency in 2007. My list of authors is wide-ranging and varied, and includes award-winners and bestsellers, such as Jeffrey Boakye, Anne Charnock, Antony Johnston and Vina Jackson. As well as debut writers like Sabrina Pace-Humphreys. They are representative of my own broad reading tastes and publishing experience (I was previously editorial director at Duckworth and publicity director at Penguin Books) in both literary and commercial publishing.

I look for distinct and original voices and/or writers who are outstanding in their field. And I help shape the long-term careers of authors who are often writing across genre and format. Some writers prefer to represent themselves; others may not see the need for a literary agent, since some publishers now offer authors the chance of submitting their work un-agented. The offer of a publishing deal direct from an enthusiastic editor following a publisher's open submission can look enticing to a new author excited to be published for the first time, while the prospect of paying a literary agent commission for the whole lifetime of a work can be daunting.

How a literary agent earns their commission

The reality is that a good literary agent should always earn their commission by adding value to every publishing deal they negotiate; as often as not, that means not only increasing an author's financial terms through bettering advances, nuanced negotiation and deals in numerous territories, but also by ceding far fewer rights.

1. Finding the right publisher for your work

Because reputable literary agents work solely by commission, to justify their time they can only take on authors when they feel strongly enough about a work, and when they think there is a good chance of placing a work with a publisher. It's quite possible that I will spend several months working editorially with an author prior to submission, and if the author's book is not placed, there is no payment due to me as agent.

So, from the outset, a literary agent will give serious thought not only to the traditional publishing potential for the work (what revisions are necessary, how to pitch the work, where it lies in the market place and submission to the right editor and publisher) but also to the work's potential in some, if not all, of the following areas: newspaper serial extract, foreign rights, film, TV, theatre and radio (dramatic, documentary or serialisation), audiobook (one of the fastest growing areas of publishing, served by specialist audiobook publishers, such as W.F. Howes, as well as by traditional publishers), picturisation or graphic novel rights, as well as electronic versions rights and merchandising rights. Whereas ebook rights, i.e. the verbatim text of the work (mirroring the print title) for the sole purpose of reading, are usually part of a traditional publishing contract, electronic version rights – or multimedia rights, as they are sometimes known – allow adaptations that include images, sounds and graphics.

I'll give some examples of what this means in practice. Over and above traditional publishing agreements, I am currently in discussions about licensing the electronic adaptation rights to a graphic novel, which will allow for an interactive experience with both text and pictures. These are separate from ebook rights or film and television rights. Even in manuscript, some books are clearly filmic or have potential to tell a story in a different format. The film rights to Matthew De Abaitua's seminal artificial intelligence novel *The Red Men* (Snowbooks 2007; shortlisted for the Arthur C. Clarke Award) were acquired by Shynola Films before it was even published, as were virtual reality rights to another author's work before it was submitted. By contrast, the tv rights to cyber-thriller *The Exphoria Code* by Antony Johnston, the first in the Brigitte Sharp series, were acquired in 2020 by Red Planet Pictures three years after publication. The popularity of podcasts and the listening experience, in addition to the increased global market for audiobooks, has led to publishers such as Audible commissioning Audible Originals (books commissioned specifically for audiobook listeners, that will only appear in print at a later date). One of my authors has a radio idea under consideration with a major broadcaster, as well as a submission under way for both a children's book and a serious adult non-fiction work. Others are writing original film scripts and video games. The writing life of an author can be a varied one over the course of a career.

The starting point for any writer, therefore, should be to ensure that they value and take their own work seriously, either by finding a literary agent to advise them or, if unagented, by understanding exactly what they are signing up to, as well as the long-term implications of any publishing contract they enter into. Publishing contracts (in all their many varied forms) have become more complicated in a global market place, and choosing the right publisher for your work – crucially which rights are granted to a publisher – is one of the fundamental reasons why a writer needs an experienced literary agent to navigate increasingly complex waters. A poor publishing deal is frequently a lost opportunity, because it results in valuable rights that could be exploited separately (i.e. earn an author greater remuneration) being tied up as part of the publishing agreement.

An un-agented author should think carefully before signing a publishing contract without either seeking advice from the Society of Authors (SoA; see page 509), who have an excellent contract vetting service for members where an author has a publishing contract in-hand, or from publishing industry contract experts such as Contracts People (www.contractspeople.co.uk) who are not literary agents but rather offer a contract service to review, advise and negotiate publishing contracts on a professional fee basis.

2. Negotiating deals

Most successful writers appoint a literary agent because a strong author/literary agent relationship plays a pivotal role for any writer serious about their work and long-term future in an ever-fluctuating industry where there are few guarantees. It is also done because a writer does not have time – nor often the inclination – to negotiate their own publishing deals, never mind numerous publishing deals in foreign languages throughout the world (when a book has a global market).

The impact that the covid-19 global pandemic has had on the global print publishing industry cannot be underestimated, with rapid growth in online book sales and an increase in ebook and audiobook sales, particularly now VAT has been removed from the price of ebooks. This may well lead to literary agents pushing to negotiate stronger royalty positions for their authors in these areas where sales are increasing dramatically. It is now not unusual to receive high advance offers from specialist audiobook publishers for the audiobook rights alone. An author needs to be aware of the value of their work in different formats. Once the publishing industry readjusts, it may be more necessary than ever to find a good literary agent to place work in a very competitive new publishing landscape. Literary agents spend time working editorially with writers honing their work and submission. And they have close relationships with editors and publishers, know their lists and what they are looking for.

3. Championing you as an author

The literary agent plays a key role in the publishing process by working to give voice to an author's work, initially through the submission process, but then primarily with the author's publisher and to the outside world, including media and readers. A writer can go from having a six-figure publishing deal at the dizzying heights of the publishing experience, with sizeable marketing budgets, to finding their next book is not acquired if sales figures are less than expected. Or, at a more mundane level, an author can find the simplest things – such as their editor leaving before their book is published – can impact their publication and longer-term relationship with a publisher. In the long trajectory of a writer's publishing life, having a literary agent who is able to champion a writer, voice their concerns with the publisher on their behalf, retrench in times of difficulty and help plan and shape their publishing career is vital for professional longevity.

What an agent provides

Authors say they value Sarah's:

'... passion and commitment .... I am thrilled by the opportunities and feel protected and supported going forward.'

Jeffrey Boakye, author of *Hold Tight* (Influx Press 2017), *Black, Listed* (Dialogue Books 2019), *Musical Truth* (Faber Children's 2021) and *I Heard What You Said* (Picador 2022)

'... experience, tenacity, tranquillity, charm and professionalism. She conducts her business with the utmost integrity.'

Kit Caless, author of *Spoon's Carpets: An Appreciation* (Square Peg 2016, Vintage Digital 2016), and *Secrets: An Investigation* (Audible Original 2021), co-publisher of Influx Press and a *Bookseller* Rising Star 2019

' ... help in shaping and developing my career. Thanks to her input I'm now in a situation where I can be a full-time writer, doing what I love, with deals in the UK, around Europe and also in the US. Over the years she has helped me make decisions that are business-smart but that also feel "right" for me.'

Louisa Leaman, debut author of *The Perfect Dress* (Transworld Digital 2019, Corgi 2020)

' ... rare combination of skills. Whenever I seek her opinion on my work, I know that she will always take time to give me the honest and thorough answer I need. She also applies the excellent market knowledge and broader cultural savviness, which is so essential to any writer working today.'

Caroline Sanderson, author of *Someone Like Adele* (Omnibus 2012) and *A Rambling Fancy: in the footsteps of Jane Austen* (Cadogan Guides 2006)

'... [her role as] guide, philosopher, and friend. Her editorial input has been absolutely invaluable. She has managed always to tread that delicate line between being endlessly supportive and encouraging without giving false expectations, which from the perspective of the author (and authors are a needy bunch) is so vital.'

Heather Cooper, debut author of *Stealing Roses* (Allison & Busby 2019)

Literary agents

4. Long-term support

As a minimum, working with a literary agent should result in considerably more favourable and industry-competitive contracts, and therefore substantially more earnings over the lifetime of a work. It ensures greater accountability from UK and/or US publishers, as agents work closely with their authors and their publishers throughout the publication process, and also a direct relationship with foreign publishers, for example, where foreign rights are retained – since literary agents broker separate publishing deals with publishers in each separate territory. Some eight years after the original UK publication, I've recently agreed a repeat deal for the Danish rights to Vina Jackson's *Eighty Days Trilogy* (Orion 2012). Books can have long lives in many territories. Ensuring that new deals are being brokered, new opportunities are explored and that an author is issued payment promptly is all part of a literary agent's role.

More broadly, a literary agent works with their author to advise, shape and help plan their career. I first started working with Antony Johnston because at one time I was one of the few literary agents who represented graphic novelists. I negotiated mainstream publishing deals for his graphic novel adaptations of Anthony Horowitz's *Alex Rider* novels with Walker Books. Since then his graphic novel *The Coldest City* (Oni Press 2012) was adapted into the film *Atomic Blonde*, and he has written the highly praised *Brigitte Sharp* thriller series (Lightning Books 2017-) as well as *The Organised Writer* for Bloomsbury (2020) – a non-fiction book about the writing process.

Confidential conversations and trust between author and literary agent are crucial to steer major decisions – such as moving from one publisher to another, or advising on shaping a career that traverses different genres and formats including fiction, non-fiction and children's books. It is also telling that publishing industry insiders who are also published writers nearly always appoint literary agents, even though they are wholly familiar with industry practice and publishing contracts. At times in any writer's career there can be concerns about how their work is being promoted or published by their publisher, or whether the publication date is optimum, or when an author needs more input or information; perhaps the author needs to go in a different writing direction altogether. Quite often an author may be successful in one area of publishing but yearns to write in another genre. The ability to navigate such decisions and aspects of the publishing process astutely is something that an author needs to be able to sustain in the longer term; at these times authors can benefit immensely from having a literary agent.

In all writers' careers there will be difficulties as well as celebrations. It is the literary agent's role to champion, represent and lobby for the author, to get to the bottom of issues and to help even the most successful author navigate the many troughs and peaks of their publishing career.

Sarah Such founded Sarah Such Literary Agency in 2007. Her previous roles have included publicity and marketing manager at Chatto & Windus, publicity director at Penguin Books UK, senior editor at Hodder & Stoughton and editorial director at Duckworth. She was shortlisted for Literary Agent of the Year at the British Book Awards 2017, 2014 and 2013. Sarah was a judge for Mslexia's 2017 first novel competition and the London Short Story competition 2018. Follow her at https://sarahsuchliteraryagency.tumblr.com and on Twitter at @sarahsuch.

See also...

- *Breaking into comics*, page 280
- *Defining genre fiction*, page 124

How to submit a non-fiction proposal

Literary agent and author Andrew Lownie provides a tried-and-tested format for your book proposal, and valuable advice on how to get the attention of an agent or publisher.

Good proposals are essential. The proposal is usually the first – and only – thing publishers will read before making their offer. It will usually determine whether or not you are published, the offer that is made and how your book is published.

The principles of a good non-fiction proposal are the same whether you are submitting to an agent or to a publisher. It needs to give them a good sense of the book, your qualifications to write it, how the book fits into the market and how the book can reach that market. It should also be layered, so that the agent and/or publisher can assess the proposal quickly but obtain more detailed information as they read more of it. Remember – some 30 people in an editorial meeting may be considering your submission, one of dozens they consider each week, so it needs to be concise and it needs to be structured so that even if they only read the first page they will know what it's about.

The format that has served me well over the last 30+ years in publishing is as follows:

1. Introductory page

A first page introducing the *subject* in a paragraph, followed by *bullet-point revelations* and a note on proposed *word count* and *delivery date*. Word counts vary but are generally around 90,000 words for a commercial book, up to no more than 140,000 words including footnotes for a serious academic book.

Publishers tend to commission for lists about 12–18 months ahead and to take about 12 months to publish from delivery of manuscript. They don't like to put their money down for too long and they worry about competing books sneaking in, so they don't give long delivery periods. Try to hook your publication to an anniversary and be aware that publishers tend to put fiction for heavyweight prizes, as well as their Christmas books, bestselling and gift titles, in the autumn list – which runs from July to end of the year.

The spring list, from January to July, tends to be for books which would be lost in autumn lists with the plethora of titles jostling for Christmas sales. Here are books which need room to breathe while there is less competition in bookshops and in the media. January, as a quiet month of good resolutions, tends to be for diet books and first novelists, along with travel books and commercial fiction for holiday-reading promotions.

The key in this section is to show what makes your book different and commercial. What is its Unique Selling Point (USP) or Proposition? Perhaps it's a new hook, interpretation or information. If you can extrapolate this to one exciting strap line which the editor can use to pitch in a meeting or the salesman can push to a bookshop, then all the better.

A *strong title* always helps. I sold a biography of a Tudor poet as *Henry VIII's Last Victim*.

2. Personal profile

A page on you and your qualifications to write the book, together with a photo. Have you an academic background, published widely in the field? Are you respected as an authority on the subject? Have you written lots of successful books before or won awards? Give details of your social media following (Facebook, LinkedIn, Instagram, Twitter) as this shows you are focused on marketing. No need to give your shoe size or GCSE results (as one author proffered) but provide details which might be helpful for publicity, such as links to media appearances, contacts who might endorse the book, and book review extracts.

3. Comparable/competing books

Give the title, author, publisher and date of publication of between five and ten reasonably successful books published in the last 20 years by trade publishers, with a few lines on how they compare to your book. You are trying to plant subliminally in the reader's mind that there is interest in the subject but that you have a slightly different take. This will help the publisher place the book in the market.

Be careful not to make meaningless comparisons, such as 'J.K. Rowling meets John Le Carré' or resort to clichés, such as 'Another *Eat, Pray, Love*'. It may seem fresh to you but will not impress jaded editors and agents. Amazon's search engine is a good place to research not just published titles but also forthcoming ones. Remember that publishers, often run by former sales directors, want 'the same but different'.

4. Sources

The fourth page lists primary sources – whether it's archives or interviews – and demonstrates that there is something new and original in the book rather than simply a synthesis of the existing information.

5. Market

Finally include a note on the market and how it might be reached; who is going to buy the book, why and how can they be reached. Perhaps there are specialist organisations, websites, magazines, television or radio programmes or bloggers with a particular interest in the subject? Give details, if possible, of numbers of members, subscribers, followers, etc.

The purpose is to show you are thinking about the market, but also to give information to the publisher about publicity or marketing outlets of which they might not be aware. If you have particular publicity ideas or contacts, then mention them. Is there potential for extracts in newspapers, for audio or film or for selling the book in other languages?

When I initially pitch to editors often that's all I send. It's short and should be sufficient for the editor to know if they want to see more.

6. Chapter synopses and samples

The next stage of the layered approach are the chapter *synopses*. I would suggest about 20-25 of these, each about half a page long and written in continuous prose, numbered and with chapter titles – as if you were paraphrasing the book. This should give a clear sense of content and structure of the book without being overwhelming.

Now come the *sample chapters*, perhaps on a separate Word attachment. The more you supply the better – a finished script means the publisher knows exactly what they are buying so they will be less cautious – but certainly include the first chapter. Authors sometimes choose the chapter they feel is best or most exciting, but you have to have confidence that all your chapters are good. Selecting a chapter from the middle of the book can be confusing and suggests that you don't rate your first chapter. Indeed, the first has to be particularly good because that tends to be the chapter the purchaser will dip into first. Chapters should be between 3,000 and 5,000 words – short enough for the reader to feel they are making progress but not so short as to appear superficial.

7. Covering note

The covering note with the proposal doesn't need to be long, but tailor it to the agent or publisher, explaining why you are approaching them by naming specific other books they have handled in the same genre. This is flattering and shows you have done your research and focused your submission.

Don't say you are approaching lots of other agents or publishers, even if you have. No one likes to feel they are in a beauty parade and may be wasting their time assessing the book. I tend to submit in waves of about five, so I can adjust the proposal in the light of the response. Ask if you can have a response within a month and then do a gentle chase. If you don't get a response – I'm afraid a lot of agents and publishers are rude – then move on.

Make sure you address the person properly. I have received supposedly exclusive submissions addressed to other agents and sometimes cc'd to numerous agencies, letters beginning Mr Loonie, Mrs Downie and with the firm described as a litter agency! The covering note may help to explain why you choose that particular agency or publisher. One explanation I received began: 'Warm greetings from Australia. I am very pleased to have found you via a psychic's recommendation to my mother a few weeks ago.'

Make sure the agent you are approaching actually handles what you are offering. Well over half my submissions are for genres which, in all the reference books and on my website, I categorically say I don't represent. It is easy enough, now that agencies have websites, to find out the authors they handle. Look at the acknowledgements pages of books which are comparable to yours and try approaching the agent who handled these.

Important dos and don'ts

• Pitch by email rather than phone as it's the writing which will sell you. If leaving a phone message, explain why you phoned. You are unlikely to receive a return call to Australia if you simply say, 'Steve called.' Agents and editors tend to communicate by email as the easiest method and I suggest you do the same. The days of manuscripts by post are over; just think of the logistical problems and expense of sharing material which isn't in email attachments.

• Don't submit too early. You only have one chance to impress an agent or publisher so make sure the proposal is absolutely right. It shouldn't have grammatical or spelling mistakes, and it should be polished – consistently formatted, fully justified and ideally double-spaced in 12 point – and lucid.

• Don't assume too much knowledge, but equally don't become bogged down in detail.

• Don't underline, use bold or lots of exclamation marks, or write in pencil or green ink.

• Don't boast. Your mother may – indeed should – think the book is wonderful, but her opinion doesn't count in the publishing world.

• Make it easy for an agent to respond. An email address is preferred to an address or phone number. If you are going to submit by post, ensure there is sufficient postage on the envelope, so the receiver isn't surcharged. Including return postage is a courtesy, preferably in UK stamps, and the envelope should be large enough to take the returned material.

• Follow instructions. If agencies have a preferred format, then follow it and customise your proposal. That said, I still think my format is best!

• Don't worry about being rejected. There may be lots of reasons behind it – maybe the book isn't suitable for the list, they already handle authors in the genre and don't want more, they got out of bed the wrong side that morning, they are incompetent, etc – it doesn't have to mean the book is rubbish. Not every idea makes a book. Perhaps it's better as an article, short-form ebook or would suit being self-published. Don't get upset, even, or write back to point out the error of their ways, but move on to the next person on your list.

Remember that editors and agents are busy people and will be making quick decisions. Anything that jars with them or makes them lose interest means they will move on to the next script. You don't want that to happen – which is why the proposal is so important.

Andrew Lownie has been a Cambridge history fellow, bookseller, publisher, journalist and director of Curtis Brown. He has run his own literary agency (www.andrewlownie.co.uk) since 1988 and according to publishersmarketplace.com is the top-selling non-fiction agent in the world. He is President of the Biographers Club and an award-winning biographer in his own right. He is the author of the *Sunday Times* bestseller *The Mountbattens: Their Lives & Loves* (Blink Publishing 2019) and *Stalin's Englishman: Guy Burgess, the Cold War, and the Cambridge Spy Ring* (St Martin's Press 2016). Follow him on Twitter @andrewlownie.

A day in the life of a literary agent

Charlotte Seymour reveals the many different strands of an agent's day-to-day work. She explains how fulfilling the role of literary matchmaker and author's champion requires endless perseverance – and makes for a full and often unpredictable day.

One of the best things about working as a literary agent is the variety that fills each and every day and night (I often wake up in the morning surrounded by pages from manuscripts I'm looking at, a published novel I'm reading for pleasure and probably a cookbook too – always good for browsing if you can't get to sleep …). It's a common misconception that people who work in publishing spend all day reading; in fact, most of us do all our reading at home in the evenings and at weekends – otherwise, books would simply never make it onto readers' shelves or Kindles.

So exactly what do agents do in their daily work? Agents come in all shapes and sizes, and have varying interests and ways of working, but an agent is by necessity protean, acting as an author's reader, editor and mentor, their greatest champion and staunchest defender. Here are some of the key elements of my day-to-day work:

1. Discovering authors

Discovering and supporting writing is at the essence of what we do, and as with everything else about the job, we do it in a variety of ways. I always keep an eye on the unsolicited submissions coming in, for although the vast majority are blanket submissions, rather than being targeted to my personal interests, there are gems to be found from time to time. Existing clients and contacts will also often recommend writers to us.

There are an ever-growing number of creative writing courses and writers' festivals which agents are invited to attend, and while it's by no means a requirement of getting published to undertake a costly MA or similar qualification, such courses do offer writers access to industry professionals and vice versa. I make sure also to visit local writers' groups and other book-related events, from launches to readings – you just never know who you might meet.

Finally, when it comes to non-fiction, I will regularly approach someone who is an expert in their field – whether a chef or a scientist – with a view to developing a proposal. So the process of finding new authors to work with is a very proactive one; occasionally, something special will land in your inbox but, more often than not, you have to go out and find it for yourself!

2. Developing an author's work

Once I've signed up a new author, I will do whatever it takes to get the manuscript or proposal to the stage where I feel it is ready to show to editors. Sometimes it's a case of going through multiple drafts until the work feels as polished as I know how to make it. At other times, and with non-fiction in particular, you can take an idea and working proposal to editors and offer them more input on how they would shape and publish a project.

3. Submitting to editors

When the material is ready, I make an initial round of submissions to those publishing houses I think would be the best fit for the author. In some cases, a book will sell very quickly at auction; in others, it's a question of persisting for many months, or even longer, until you find the one editor who falls for the book. If that book doesn't work, rather than giving up, you think about why it didn't sell and then get working on something new with the author.

A year ago, at Strand Bookstore in New York, I saw a tote bag (every publishing girl and boy's best friend) for sale bearing the well-known feminist slogan 'Nevertheless she persisted', and I always think this sums up my job. As an agent, you need endless perseverance – and often a bit of luck …

4. Negotiating a publishing deal

When a publisher or several publishers offer for a book, I will negotiate the best possible publishing deal for the author, not just in terms of the money being offered but also the publisher's plans for how to edit, position and promote the book and the author. Sometimes, in an auction, an agent will choose a publisher who offers slightly less money than another but who is a better overall fit for the author.

5. The run-up to publication, and beyond …

Getting a publishing deal for an author is a hugely exciting moment, but it's by no means the end of an agent's job. From the moment we have a signed contract, in the run-up to and following publication, I will be regularly checking in with the publisher to ensure that everything is on track, finding out how many copies are being printed, what coverage the publicist has lined up, how the book is performing, and so on. I will also be working with my colleagues and partner agents who sell foreign rights, and film and TV rights, to bring the work to as many other territories and platforms as possible.

6. Keeping up with editors and the book market

An agent is essentially a literary matchmaker, so we dedicate a lot of time to getting to know the individual editors who acquire in the genres we represent, and to understanding their tastes and interests. For those of us based in London and the UK, we can meet fairly easily at any time of year, and a week will rarely go by when I don't see an editor for coffee or visit their office to find out what they've been buying recently and tell them about the projects I have coming up.

I work with English-language publishers across the world as well, so the London Book Fair every spring is a good opportunity to meet with visiting editors; I will also spend a week in New York each year if I can. From time to time I meet with film and TV scouts and producers who are looking for content to adapt. Whoever I'm seeing and wherever we are, I am constantly championing my authors, even if the book in question won't be ready for another year.

Finally, in addition to keeping in touch with editors, I try to stay on top of the book market by reading reviews every week, making sure to read newly published books as well as those I'm working on and just spending hours in bookshops, familiarising myself with what's new on the shelves. I go into a bookshop at least once a week, ostensibly for 'research purposes', though I often leave with something to add to the ever-growing pile!

Highs and lows

One of the best moments as an agent is when you can call an author to let them know you've found them a publisher – and the right publisher for them. After that, the point when it starts to feel more real is when you see the final cover, and of course when you get to hold a print copy for the first time. There are low moments too: brilliant books that you just can't sell, ideas that never quite come to fruition, disappointing sales and dashed expectations. For every peak there's usually a trough, and as an agent you have to weather the storms with and for your authors, as well as celebrating the successes.

The very unpredictability of the job is also one of the greatest joys: some books are instant hits and others are slow burners; reviews can be amazing and sales minuscule; 30 publishers might turn down a book and it goes on to win prizes. You never know quite what's around the corner – and it's thrilling.

A typical day ...

Sometimes I'm out all day to meet with editors, and if I'm reading or editing a new manuscript, I usually work from home, but when I'm in the office, a typical day might go something like this:

Morning

– I get to work and answer any emails that have come in overnight. Two publishers have sent draft contracts for books they have acquired from me, so I will check that the contracts accurately reflect what we've agreed and mark any amendments I want to make before sending back to the publisher.

– I send a new book out on submission, calling editors first to pitch it to them if we haven't already spoken about it, or not recently.

– Then I check in with any editors who are considering other projects I have out on submission and set a deadline for offers on a book for which I've received a first offer.

Afternoon

– After lunch, I have a phone call with an author to discuss progress on his or her latest book, and then another call with one of our US co-agents to catch up on the authors we are representing for one another.

– Towards the end of the day, I usually look at any unsolicited submissions that have come in by email. It's very rare that I will call in a full manuscript, but I have taken on several wonderful authors from the so-called 'slush pile', one of whose work sold in my biggest deal to date.

Evening

– As I spend so much of the day looking at a computer screen, I'll often print off anything I want to read and take it home with me.

Charlotte Seymour is a literary agent at Andrew Nurnberg Associates and has previously worked as a literary scout at Eccles Fisher Associates. She was Secretary of the Association of Authors' Agents (2019–21).

This article first appeared on the author Sarah Pearse's website https://sarahpearse.co.uk. Sarah's debut novel, *The Sanatorium*, was published by Transworld in February 2021 and Charlotte is her agent.

Literary agents

Literary agents UK and Ireland

The *Writers' & Artists' Yearbook,* along with the Association of Authors' Agents and the Society of Authors, takes a dim view of any literary agent who asks potential clients for a fee prior to a manuscript. We advise you to treat any such request with caution and to let us know if that agent appears in the listings below. It is assumed that all agents listed do *not* charge a 'reading fee'. However, agents may charge additional costs later in the process but these should only arise once a book has been accepted by a publisher and the author is earning an income. We urge authors to make the distinction between upfront and additional charges. Authors should also check agents' websites before making an enquiry and should familiarise themselves with submission guidelines.

*Member of the Association of Authors' Agents   sae = self-addressed envelope

The Accidental Agency

email clare.gristtaylor@accidentalagency.co.uk
website www.accidentalagency.co.uk
Contact Clare Grist Taylor

Agency specialising in non-fiction for adults. Represents memoir, nature writing, history, current affairs, popular science and psychology, lifestyle and wellbeing, smart thinking, business/personal-professional development and humour/gift. *Commission* Home 15%, overseas 20%, film/TV 20%. Submissions should be made via the website. No fiction, academic texts, poetry or children's books. *Founded* 2019.

Aevitas Creative Management UK Limited

49 Greek Street, London W1D 4EG
email UKenquiries@aevitascreative.com
website https://aevitascreative.com
Twitter @aevitascreative
Ceo ACM UK Toby Mundy *Agents* Trevor Dolby, Max Edwards, Natalie Jerome, Toby Mundy, Sara O'Keeffe, Simon Targe

A management company that represents writers, speakers and brands. Wide range of genres represented including history, science, biography, autobiography, politics and current affairs, literary fiction, crime, thrillers. *Commission* Fiction and non-fiction: home 15%, USA/translation 20%. Submissions via website. No plays or poetry.
  Clients include Rachel Botsman, Stephen Bush, James Crabtree, Armand D'Angour, Daniel Finkelstein, David Goodhart, Charles Handy, Ivan Leslie, Clive Myrie, Jonathan Rowson, Geoffrey Wheatcroft. *Founded* 2014.

The Agency (London) Ltd*

24 Pottery Lane, London W11 4LZ
tel 020-7727 1346
email childrensbooksubmissions@theagency.co.uk
website https://theagency.co.uk/childrens-books/childrens-home/
Twitter @TALLChildrens

Works in conjunction with overseas agents. The Agency also represents screenwriters, directors, playwrights and composers; for more information check the agency's website. Represents picture books, including novelty books, fiction for all ages including teenage fiction and series fiction. *Commission* Home 15%, overseas 20%. Submission guidelines on website. *Founded* 1995.

Aitken Alexander Associates Ltd*

291 Gray's Inn Road, London WC1X 8QJ
tel 020-7373 8672
email reception@aitkenalexander.co.uk
website www.aitkenalexander.co.uk
Twitter @AitkenAlexander
Instagram AitkenAlexander
Agents Clare Alexander, Lesley Thorne, Lisa Baker, Chris Wellbelove, Emma Paterson (Directors), Monica MacSwan, Amy St Johnston; *Film/TV/stage rights* Lesley Thorne, Steph Adam, Jazz Adamson

Fiction and non-fiction. *Commission* Home 15%, USA 20%, translation 20%, film/TV 15%. Email preliminary letter with half-page synopsis and first 30 pages to submissions@aitkenalexander.co.uk. No plays.
  For a full list of clients, see the website. *Founded* 1977.

AMP Literary

76 Nowell Road, London SW13 9BS
email anna@ampliterary.co.uk
email submissions@ampliterary.co.uk
website www.ampliterary.co.uk
Founder Anna Pallai

The agency is searching for a fresh generation of unique non-fiction writers. With strong connections across various media platforms, from digital to TV, AMP develops ideas beyond print to maximise exposure. Specialises in commercial non-fiction with a particular interest in bold female voices. *Commission* UK 15%, USA 20%. Submissions to be sent via email, to include synopsis and at least three chapters.

Authors include Natasha Devon, Terri White, Anita Mangan, Annalisa Barbieri, Eleanor Ross, Nadine White, Nichi Hodgson, Maddy Anholt. *Founded* 2016.

The Ampersand Agency Ltd*

Ryman's Cottages, Little Tew, Oxon OX7 4JJ
tel (01608) 683677/683898
email info@theampersandagency.co.uk
website www.theampersandagency.co.uk
Contacts Peter Buckman, Jamie Cowen, Anne-Marie Doulton

Literary and commercial fiction and non-fiction. *Commission* Home 15%, USA 15–20%, translation 20%. Writers should consult the website for information on agents' preferences and submission guidelines. No poetry, books for young children or scripts.

Clients include Tariq Ashkanani, Quentin Bates, Helen Black, Sharon Bolton, Ben Crane, Cora Harrison, Mark Hill, Tendai Huchu, Adrian Selby, Vikas Swarup, and the estates of Georgette Heyer, Jin Yong, Angela Thirkell, Winifred Foley and John James. *Founded* 2003.

Darley Anderson Literary, TV and Film Agency*

Estelle House, 11 Eustace Road, London SW6 1JB
tel 020-7386 2674
website www.darleyanderson.com
website www.darleyandersonchildrens.com
Twitter @DA_Agency
Instagram darleyanderson_agency
Agents Adult fiction: Darley Anderson (international thrillers and crime featuring a memorable central character, tear-jerking love stories and commercial non-fiction), Camilla Bolton (crime, thrillers, suspense, general fiction), Sheila David (TV and film rights), Tanera Simons (women's fiction, accessible literary/reading group fiction). Children's fiction: Clare Wallace (middle grade, YA, picture books and illustrators), Lydia Silver (middle grade), Darley Anderson (animal books), Chloe Davis (Junior Agent/Assistant to Clare Wallace). *Contacts* Rosanna Bellingham (Financial Controller), Mary Darby (Head of Rights), Kristina Egan (Rights Agent), Georgia Fuller (Rights Agent), Rebeka Finch (Assistant to Darley Anderson), Jade Kavanagh (Junior Agent/Assistant to Camilla Bolton).

Overseas associates APA Talent & Literary Agency (LA/Hollywood) and leading foreign agents in selected territories. All commercial fiction and non-fiction. Special interests (fiction): all types of thrillers, crime and mystery. All types of American and Irish novels. Comic fiction. All types of popular women's fiction and accessible literary/reading group fiction. Special interests (non-fiction): autobiographies, biographies, sports books, 'true-life' women in jeopardy, revelatory history and science, popular

psychology, self improvement, diet, beauty, health, fashion, animals, humour/cartoon, cookery, gardening, inspirational, religious. *Commission* Home 15%, USA/translation 20%, film/TV/radio 20%. Send covering letter, short synopsis and first three chapters. Return postage/sae essential for reply. No poetry, academic books, scripts or screenplays.

Clients include Chris Carter, Lee Child, Martina Cole, John Connolly, Margaret Dickinson, Tana French, T.M. Logan, Stephen Spotswood, Annie Murray, Beth O'Leary, B.A. Paris, Phaedra Patrick, K.L. Slater, Catherine Steadman, Tim Weaver. *Founded* 1988.

ANDLYN

tel 020-3290 5638
email submissions@andlyn.co.uk
website www.andlyn.co.uk
Twitter @andlynlit
Founder and Agent Davinia Andrew-Lynch

Fiction interests: intersectional/inclusive – women's commercial fiction, cosy crime, rom-coms, humour, high-octane action/thrillers, accessible speculative fiction. Non-Fiction interests: intersectional/inclusive/accessible – lifestyle (particularly interiors and horticulture), gift and business. Also represents children's authors (picture book to YA – all genres). *Commission* Home and audio 15%, USA, foreign/translation, film/TV, multi-platform and online media rights 20%. See website for submission guidelines. *Founded* 2015.

Anubis Literary Agency

7 Birdhaven Close, Lighthorne, Warwick CV35 0BE
tel (01926) 642588
Contact Steve Calcutt

No telephone calls. Works with The Marsh Agency Ltd on translation rights. Genre fiction: science fiction, fantasy and horror. No other material considered. *Commission* Home 15%, USA/translation 20%. Send 50 pages with a one-page synopsis (sae essential). *Founded* 1994.

Artellus Ltd*

30 Dorset House, Gloucester Place,
London NW1 5AD
tel 020-7935 6972
email artellussubmissions@gmail.com
website www.artellusltd.co.uk
Twitter @Artellus
Contacts Leslie Gardner (Agent and Director), Gabriele Pantucci (Agent and Chairman), Darryl Samaraweera (Agent and Company Secretary), Jon Curzon (Associate Agent), Angus MacDonald (Social Media), Raffaello Pantucci (Consultant)

International literary agency representing writers in all fields and genres. Handles a wide range of fiction (from literary to crime, fantasy and sci-fi) and non-fiction, in areas including history, current affairs, science, economics, investigative journalism, culture and food. Also interested in fine writers in translation. *Commission* 15% UK, 20% direct sales to USA, 15% rest of world. Submissions in the form of a covering note attaching the first three chapters and synopsis. Submissions also accepted by post.

See the website for a full client list. *Founded* 1986.

Tassy Barham Associates

23 Elgin Crescent, London W11 2JD
tel 020-7229 8667
email tassy@tassybarham.com
Proprietor Tassy Barham

Specialises in representing European and American authors, agents and publishers in Brazil and Portugal, as well as the worldwide representation of Brazilian authors. *Founded* 1999.

Kate Barker Literary Agency*

tel 020-7688 1638
email kate@katebarker.net
website www.katebarker.net

Commercial and literary fiction for adults including crime, thriller, suspense, women's fiction, historical and reading group fiction. Non-fiction including narrative non-fiction, popular psychology and science, smart thinking, business, history, memoir, biography, lifestyle and wellbeing. *Commission* Home 15%, overseas 20%, TV/film 20%. Submissions via the website. Does not represent science fiction, fantasy or children's picture books. *Founded* 2016.

Bath Literary Agency*

5 Gloucester Road, Bath BA1 7BH
tel (01225) 317894
email submissions@bathliteraryagency.com
website www.bathliteraryagency.com
Twitter @BathLitAgency
Instagram bathlitagency
Contact Gill McLay

Specialist in fiction for children and young adults. Also accepts submissions in picture books, non-fiction and author illustrators. *Commission* UK 15%, overseas 20%, film/TV 20%. For full submission details, refer to the website.

Clients include Lou Abercrombie, Fox Benwell, Conor Busuttil, Philippa Forrester, Dr Jess French, Tweedy, Joe Haddow, Demelsa Haughton, Harry Heape, Laura James, Pippa Pixley, Dr Shini Somara, Tessa Strickland, Anna Terreros Martin, Chris Wakling. *Founded* 2011.

The Bell Lomax Moreton Agency*

Suite C, Victory House, 131 Queensway, Petts Wood, Kent BR5 1DG
tel 020-7930 4447
email agency@bell-lomax.co.uk
website www.belllomaxmoreton.co.uk
Twitter @BLM_Agency

Executives Paul Moreton, Lauren Gardner, Jo Bell, Katie Fulford, Justine Smith, John Baker, Lorna Hemingway, Rory Jeffers, Sarah McDonnell

Will consider most fiction, non-fiction and children's (including picture books, middle grade and young adult) book proposals. Submission guidelines on website. Physical submissions should be accompanied by an sae for return and an email address for correspondence. Does not represent poetry, short stories or novellas, education textbooks, film scripts or stage plays. *Founded* 2000.

Lorella Belli Literary Agency Ltd (LBLA)*

54 Hartford House, 35 Tavistock Crescent, Notting Hill, London W11 1AY
tel 020-7727 8547
email info@lorellabelliagency.com
website www.lorellabelliagency.com
Facebook www.facebook.com/LorellaBelliLiteraryAgency
Twitter @lblaUK
Proprietor Lorella Belli

Full service literary and management agency. Works with film/TV and overseas associates; represents American literary agencies in the UK. Sells translation rights on behalf of British publishers, literary agents and independent authors. Fiction and general non-fiction. Particularly interested in first-time writers, books which have international appeal, multicultural writing, books on Italy, successful self-published authors, crime, mysteries, thrillers, psychological suspense, reading group fiction, women's fiction, historicals, memoirs, personal development, popular history, popular science, current affairs, soft business, investigative journalism. *Commission* Home 15%, overseas/dramatic 20%. Send a query email about your work before submitting it. Only online submissions considered. May suggest revision. No children's, science fiction, fantasy, academic, poetry, original scripts and short stories.

Clients include Ingrid Alexandra, Crux Publishing, Renita D'Silva, Karen Dionne, Ruth Dugdall, Joy Ellis, Joffe Books, Ana Johns, Angela Marsons, Carol Mason, Nicola May, Rick Mofina, Kirsty Molesley, Lara Prescott, Silvertail Books. *Founded* 2002.

The Bent Agency*

17 Kelsall Mews, Richmond TW9 4BP
email info@thebentagency.com
website www.thebentagency.com
Agents Molly Ker Hawn, Nicola Barr, Gemma Cooper, Sarah Hornsley, Zoe Plant (UK); Jenny Bent, Claire Draper, Louise Fury, James Mustelier, John Silbersack, Laurel Symonds, Desiree Wilson (USA)

Full-service literary agency with offices in the UK and USA. Represents authors of fiction and non-fiction for adults, children and teenagers. Unsolicited submissions welcome by email only: query and first ten pages pasted into body of email. See complete guidelines on the website.

Clients include Faridah Abike-Iyimide, Gary John Bishop, Dhonielle Clayton, Stephanie Garber, Alwyn Hamilton, Anstey Harris, Mariam Khan, Matt Killeen, Hilary McKay, Jo Spain, Robin Stevens, Jessica Townsend. *Founded* 2009.

Berlin Associates Ltd

7 Tyers Gate, London SE1 3HX
tel 020-7836 1112
email submissions@berlinassociates.com
website www.berlinassociates.com
Twitter @berlinassocs
Agents Marc Berlin, Stacy Browne, Matt Connell, Alexandra Cory, Rachel Daniels, Yas Lewis, Julia Mills, Maddie O'Dwyer, Laura Reeve, Fiona Williams, Emily Wraith, Julia Wyatt

A boutique agency representing writers, directors, producers, designers, composers and below-the-line talent across theatre, film, TV, radio and new media. All genres represented. The majority of new clients are taken on through recommendation or invitation, however, if you would like your work to be considered for representation, email a CV along with a brief outline of your experience and the work you would like to submit for consideration. No prose/fiction. *Founded* 2003.

The bks Agency

website www.thebksagency.com
Contacts Jason Bartholomew, Jessica Killingley, James Spackman

A literary management agency specialising in non-fiction. A division of Midas. Genres represented include history, politics, current affairs, biography, memoir, narrative non-fiction, business, personal development, general lifestyle and wellbeing, sport, music, culture and smart thinking. Pitch ideas via the online form. See website for full guidelines.

Authors include Noor Hibbert, Alexa Shoen, Eleanor Tweddell, Jo Wimble-Groves, Ellie Wallace, Timi Merriman Johnson, Melanie Blake, Roberto Sendoya Escobar, Eva Mozes Kor, Tim Sullivan, Mark Pallis, Paul Jones, Paul Maunder, Dan Bigham, Katie Archibald, Orla Chennaoui, Dani Garavelli, Stephen McGinty, Dr Marlon Moncrieffe, Kate Rawles, Alasdair Fotheringham, Steve Cummings.

The Blair Partnership*

PO Box 7828, London W1A 4GE
tel 020-7504 2520
email info@theblairpartnership.com
email submissions@theblairpartnership.com
website www.theblairpartnership.com
Twitter @TBP_agency
Founding Partner and Agent Neil Blair, *Agency Director* Rory Scarfe, *Associate agent* Jordan Lees
Agents Josephine Hayes, Hattie Grünewald

Represents a range of people internationally from debut and established writers to broader talent across business, politics, sport and lifestyle. Range of work spans fiction, non-fiction, digital, TV and film production. Considers all genres of fiction and non-fiction for adults, young readers and children. Will consider unsolicited MSS. Fiction: email a covering letter, a one-page synopsis and the first three chapters. Non-fiction: email a proposal document and writing sample. Not currently accepting screenplays, short stories or poetry.

Clients include Ronen Bergman, Michael Calvin, Emma Farrarons, Henry Fraser, Robert Galbraith, Dr Pippa Grange, Sir Chris Hoy, Louise Jensen, Frank Lampard, Kieran Larwood, Maajid Nawaz, Jon Sopel, J.K. Rowling, Pete Townshend and Brian Wood. *Founded* 2011.

Blake Friedmann Literary, TV & Film Agency Ltd*

Ground Floor, 15 Highbury Place, London N5 1QP
tel 020-7387 0842
email info@blakefriedmann.co.uk
website www.blakefriedmann.co.uk
Agents Books: Isobel Dixon, Kate Burke, Juliet Pickering, Samuel Hodder; Film/TV: Julian Friedmann, Conrad Williams, Louisa Minghella

Full-length MSS. Fiction: crime, thrillers, women's fiction, historical fiction, speculative fiction and literary fiction; a broad range of non-fiction. Media Department handles film and TV rights, and represents scriptwriters, playwrights and directors. *Commission* Home 15%, overseas 20%. Preliminary letter, synopsis and first three chapters via email. See website for full submission guidelines.

Authors include Bolu Babalola, Graeme Macrae Burnet, Edward Carey, Will Dean, Barbara Erskine, David Gilman, Kerry Hudson, Peter James, Lucy Mangan, Deon Meyer, Joseph O'Connor, Sheila O'Flanagan. *Scriptwriters* include Andy Briggs, Marteinn Thorisson, Stuart Urban. *Founded* 1977.

The Book Bureau Literary Agency

7 Duncairn Avenue, Bray, Co. Wicklow A98 R293, Republic of Ireland
tel +353 (0)12 764996
email thebookbureau123@gmail.com
Managing Director Ger Nichol

Works with agents overseas. Sub-agents: The Rights People. Full-length MSS. Fiction only – thrillers, crime, Irish novels, literary fiction, women's commercial novels and general fiction. *Commission* Home 15%, USA/translation 20%. Send preliminary letter, synopsis and three sample chapters (single line spacing); return postage required. Email preferred. No horror, science fiction, children's or poetry.

Clients include Ciara Geraghty, Patricia Gibney, Caitriona Lally, Claire Allan, Amanda Robson, Clodagh Murphy, Sian O'Gorman, Paula McGrath,

Dan Brotzel, Cormac O'Keeffe, Aidan Conway Gillian Harvey and others. *Founded* 1998.

BookBlast® Ltd

PO Box 20184, London W10 5AU
tel 020-8968 3089
email gen@bookblast.com
website www.bookblast.com
Facebook www.facebook.com/bookblastofficial
Twitter @bookblast
Instagram bookblastoffical

Promotes cultural diversity. Supports the independent publishing sector and translation via The BookBlast® Diary & Podcast. Also offers editorial and translation services. Literary and general adult fiction and non-fiction (memoir, travel, popular culture, multicultural writing). *Commission* Full-length MSS (home 15%, overseas 20%). Not currently accepting new clients.

Represents Onyekachi Wambu and Philip Mann; and the literary estates of Prof. Elton Mayo, Gael Elton Mayo. Literary executor(s) of Lesley Blanch. *Founded* 1997.

The Bravo Blue Agency*

email charlotte@bravoblue.co.uk
website www.bravoblue.co.uk
Contact Charlotte Colwill

Boutique literary agency. Literary fiction and narrative non-fiction, category fiction, lifestyle, health, history, children's fiction and non-fiction, picture books. Send first five pages, synopsis and covering letter via email.

Authors include Bill Swiggs, Megan Vickers, Cecily Blench, Brian Schofield, Gianni Washington, Jacob Avila. *Founded* 2018.

Alan Brodie Representation

Paddock Suite, The Courtyard,
55 Charterhouse Street, London EC1M 6HA
tel 020-7253 6226
email abr@alanbrodie.com
website www.alanbrodie.com
Twitter @abragency
Instagram abragency
Managing Director Alan Brodie, *Agent* Victoria Williams

Specialises in stage plays, literary estates, radio, TV and film. Represented in all major countries. *Commission* Home 10%, overseas 15%. No unsolicited scripts; recommendation from known professional required. No prose, fiction or general MSS. *Founded* 1996.

Brotherstone Creative Management*

Mortimer House, 37–41 Mortimer Street,
London W1T 3JH
tel 07908 542886
email info@bcm-agency.com
email submissions@bcm-agency.com

website www.bcm-agency.com
Contact Charlie Brotherstone

Represents an eclectic list of authors, from academics, musicians and cookery writers through to novelists of commercial and literary fiction. The agency guides each client through every part of the publishing process and draws upon a wide contact network to develop their careers across all media. *Commission* UK 15%, USA direct 20%, dramatic 20% direct (20% if sub-agented), translation 20%, TV 15%. Submissions by email: for fiction, include the first three chapters or 30 pages, a one- to two-page synopsis and a short covering letter; for non-fiction, send a detailed outline with a sample chapter and a covering note. Does not handle scripts for theatre, film or television.

Clients include Brett Anderson, Raymond Blanc, A.A. Gill, Kirstin Innes, George The Poet, Anna Stothard, Jessie Ware, Giles Yeo. *Founded* 2017.

Jenny Brown Associates*

31 Marchmont Road, Edinburgh EH9 1HU
tel 0131 229 5334
email info@jennybrownassociates.com
website www.jennybrownassociates.com
Contact Jenny Brown, Lucy Juckes

Literary fiction, crime writing and writing for children; narrative non-fiction including literary memoir and nature writing. Has a strong preference for working with writers or illustrators based in Scotland. *Commission* Home 15%, overseas/translation 20%. A small agency which only reads submissions at certain points in the year; always check website before sending work. No poetry, science fiction, fantasy or academic.

Clients include Lin Anderson, Shaun Bythell, Christopher Edge, Gavin Francis, Alex Gray, Joanna Hickson, Kathleen Jamie, Helen Kellock, Sarah Maine, Sally Magnusson, Sara Maitland, Jonathan Meres, Ann O'Loughlin, Chitra Ramaswamy. *Founded* 2002.

Felicity Bryan Associates*

2A North Parade, Banbury Road, Oxford OX2 6LX
tel (01865) 513816
email agency@felicitybryan.com
website www.felicitybryan.com

Translation rights handled by Andrew Nurnberg Associates; works in conjunction with US agents. Literary and commercial upmarket fiction and general non-fiction, with emphasis on history, biography, science and nature. *Commission* Home 15%, overseas 20%. All submissions and queries through website. No science fiction, fantasy, horror, erotica, romance, self-help, graphic novels, scripts or poetry.

Clients include Karen Armstrong, Louis de Bernières, Jonathan Coe, Edmund de Waal, Reni Eddo-Lodge, Peter Frankopan, Damon Galgut, A.C.

Grayling, Tim Harford, Lindsey Hilsum, Anna Hope, Gill Hornby, Diarmaid MacCulloch, Jon Savage, Lucy Worsley. *Founded* 1988.

Juliet Burton Literary Agency*
2 Clifton Avenue, London W12 9DR
tel 020-8762 0148
email juliet@julietburton.com
Contact Juliet Burton

Handles fiction and some non-fiction. Special interests include crime and women's fiction. *Commission* Home 15%, USA/translation 20%. Approach either via email or in writing with synopsis and the opening three chapters and sae. No science fiction/fantasy, children's, short stories, plays, film scripts, articles, poetry or academic material.
   Clients include Rosie Archer, Kay Brellend, Barbara Cleverly, Marjorie Eccles, Edward Enfield, Anthea Fraser, Veronica Heley, Mick Herron, Maureen Lee, Priscilla Masters, Gwen Moffat, Barbara Nadel, Sheila Norton and Pam Weaver. *Founded* 1999.

C&W Agency*
(previously Conville & Walsh)
Haymarket House, 28–29 Haymarket, London SW1Y 4SP
tel 020-7393 4200
website www.cwagency.co.uk
Twitter @CWAgencyUK
Directors Clare Conville, Jake Smith-Bosanquet, Sue Armstrong, Sophie Lambert

Handles all genres of fiction, non-fiction and children's worldwide. *Commission* Home 15%, overseas 20%. Submissions welcome: first three chapters, cover letter, synopsis by email. Part of the Curtis Brown Group of Companies; simultaneous submission accepted.
   Fiction clients include notable prize winners and bestsellers such as Matt Haig, M.L. Stedman, Rachel Joyce, Kevin Barry, Andrew Michael Hurley, Joanna Cannon, Nathan Filer, S.J. Watson, D.B.C. Pierre and Jess Kidd.
   Non-fiction clients include Dolly Alderton, Misha Glenny, Dr. Megan Rossi, Tim Spector, Christie Watson and Ben Wilson. *Founded* 2000.

Charlie Campbell Literary Agents*
49 Greek Street, London W1D 4EG
email info@cclagents.com
website www.cclagents.com
Twitter @CCLAgents
Directors Charlie Campbell, Hitesh Shah *Agents* Charlotte Atyeo, Natalie Galustian, Julia Silk

Fiction and non-fiction. *Commission* Home 15%, USA, film/tv and translation 20%. Submissions via website. No plays, poetry or scripts.
   Clients include SJ Bennett, Ruqsana Begum, Edward Brooke-Hitching, Jen Campbell, Rebecca Front, Julian Gough, Sofie Hagen, Ed Hawkins, Maisie Hill,

Will Hill, Michael Holding, Bella Mackie, Anthony McGowan, Charlotte Philby, the Estate of Alan Rickman. *Founded* 2020.

Georgina Capel Associates Ltd*
29 Wardour Street, London W1D 6PS
tel 020-7734 2414
email firstname@georginacapel.com
website www.georginacapel.com
Agents Georgina Capel, Rachel Conway

Literary and commercial fiction, history, biography; film and TV; also writers for children and young adults. *Commission* Home/overseas 15%. Postal submissions preferred, but do accept email. Include a covering letter, synopsis of work and first three chapters of your work. Film & TV scripts for established clients only.
   Clients include Julia Copus, Adrian Goldsworthy, Philip Hoare, Dan Jones, Tobias Jones, Adam Nicolson, Ben Okri, Chibundu Onuzo, Olivette Otele, Andrew Roberts, Ian Sansom, Simon Sebag Montefiore, Jo Shapcott, Lesley Thomson, Fay Weldon. *Founded* 1999.

Casarotto Ramsay & Associates Ltd
7 Savoy Court, Strand, London WC2R 0EX
tel 020-7287 4450
email info@casarotto.co.uk
website www.casarotto.co.uk
Directors Jenne Casarotto, Giorgio Casarotto, Mel Kenyon, Jodi Shields, Rachel Holroyd, Ian Devlin, Elinor Burns

Works in conjunction with agents in USA and other foreign countries. Preliminary letter essential. MSS – theatre, films, TV, sound broadcasting only. *Commission* 10%. Preliminary letter essential. *Founded* 1989.

Robert Caskie Ltd
tel 07900 431005
email robert@robertcaskie.com
website www.robertcaskie.com
Twitter @rcaskie1

Represents a broad range of writers of fiction and non-fiction. *Commission* Home 15%, overseas 20%. Fiction submissions: send an introductory email, a brief synopsis and the first three chapters. Non-fiction submissions: send an introductory email, a detailed outline and a sample chapter. All submissions need to be sent to submissions@robertcaskie.com. Does not represent children's, crime and thriller, YA, horror, or science fiction.
   Authors include Louis Theroux, Sarah Winman, Libby Page, Emma Barnett, Sir Trevor McDonald, Lord Michael Cashman, Ilana Fox, Manda Scott, Ece Temelkuran, Kate Spicer, Lorraine Candy. *Founded* 2020.

The Catchpole Agency

53 Cranham Street, Oxford OX2 6DD
tel 07789 588070
email james@thecatchpoleagency.co.uk
website www.thecatchpoleagency.co.uk
Proprietor James Catchpole

Agents for authors and illustrators of children's books
from picture books through to young adult novels,
with a specialism in editorial work. See website for
contact and submissions details.
   Authors include Polly Dunbar, SF Said, Michelle
Robinson, Emer Stamp, Sean Taylor. *Founded* 1996.

Chapman & Vincent*

21 Ellis Street, London SW1X 9AL
email chapmanvincent@hotmail.co.uk
Directors Jennifer Chapman, Gilly Vincent

A specialist agency acting mainly as a packager.
Works with Elaine Markson in the USA. Non-fiction
agent packagers for texts suitable for major
illustration in heritage, interiors, gardening and
cookery. *Commission* Home 15%, overseas 20%. Not
currently seeking new clients but will reply to all
sensible approaches by email without attachments in
this limited area. No postal submissions.
   Clients include George Carter, Leslie Geddes-Brown,
Lucinda Lambton and Eve Pollard.

Teresa Chris Literary Agency Ltd*

43 Musard Road, London W6 8NR
tel 020-7386 0633
email teresachris@litagency.co.uk
website www.teresachrisliteraryagency.co.uk
Director Teresa Chris

All fiction, especially crime, women's commercial,
general and literary fiction. Representation in all
overseas territories. *Commission* Home 10%, overseas
20%. Send introductory letter describing work, first
three chapters and sae. No science fiction, horror,
fantasy, short stories, poetry or academic books.
   Clients include Dilly Court, Stephen Booth, Rory
Clements, Julie Cohen, Kate Rhodes, M.A. Bennett.
Founded 1988.

Anne Clark Literary Agency*

email submissions@anneclarkliteraryagency.co.uk
website www.anneclarkliteraryagency.co.uk
Facebook www.facebook.com/anneclarkliterary
Twitter @AnneClarkLit
Contact Anne Clark

Specialist in fiction, picture books and non-fiction for
children and young adults. *Commission* Home 15%,
overseas 20%. Submissions by email only. See website
for submission guidelines.
   Clients include Mike Barfield, Anne Booth, Moira
Butterfield, Lou Carter, Patricia Forde, Pippa
Goodhart, Miriam Halahmy, Cath Howe, Penny
Joelson, Rebecca Patterson, Lucy Rowland.
Founded 2012.

Mary Clemmey Literary Agency*

6 Dunollie Road, London NW5 2XP
tel 020-7267 1290
email mcwords@googlemail.com

High-quality fiction and non-fiction with an
international market. TV, film, radio and theatre
scripts from existing clients only. Works in
conjunction with US agent. *Commission* Home 15%,
overseas 20%, performance rights 15%. No
unsolicited MSS. Approach first by letter (including
sae). No children's books or science fiction.
Founded 1992.

Jonathan Clowes Ltd*

10 Iron Bridge House, Bridge Approach,
London NW1 8BD
tel 020-7722 7674
email admin@jonathanclowes.co.uk
website www.jonathanclowes.co.uk
Directors Ann Evans, Nemonie Craven, Cara Lee
Simpson

Literary and commercial fiction and non-fiction, film,
TV, theatre (for existing clients) and radio. Email for
general enquiries. Works in association with agents
overseas. *Commission* Home 15%, overseas 20%. See
website for submission guidelines.
   Clients include Dr David Bellamy, Angela Chadwick,
Arthur Conan Doyle Characters Ltd, Bethany Clift,
Simon Critchley, Brian Freemantle, Ben Halls,
Francesca Hornak, Carla Lane, David Nobbs,
Okechukwu Nzelu, Gruff Rhys, Jacqueline Bublitz
and the literary estates of Doris Lessing, Elizabeth
Jane Howard, Michael Baigent and Richard Leigh.
Founded 1960.

Rosica Colin Ltd

1 Clareville Grove Mews, London SW7 5AH
tel 020-7370 1080
Director Joanna Marston

All full-length MSS (excluding science fiction and
poetry); also theatre, film and sound broadcasting.
Commission Home 10%, overseas 10–20%. May take
three to four months to consider full MSS. Send
synopsis only in first instance, with letter outlining
writing credits and whether MS has been previously
submitted, plus return postage.
   Authors include Richard Aldington, Samuel Becket
(publication rights), Steven Berkoff, Alan Brownjohn,
Sandy Brownjohn, Donald Campbell, Nick Dear, Neil
Donnelly, J.T. Edson, Bernard Farrell, Jean Genet,
Franz Xaver Kroetz, Don McCamphill, Graham Reid,
Alan Sillitoe, Anthony Vivis. *Founded* 1949.

Jane Conway-Gordon Ltd*

38 Cromwell Grove, London W6 7RG
tel 020-7603 7504
email jane@conway-gordon.co.uk
website www.janeconwaygordon.uk

Full length MSS. Represented in all foreign countries. *Commission* Home 15%, overseas 20%. Preliminary letter and return postage essential. No poetry, science fiction or children's. *Founded* 1982.

Coombs Moylett Maclean Literary Agency

120 New Kings Road, London SW6 4LZ
tel 020-8740 0454
website www.cmm.agency
Contacts Lisa Moylett, Jamie Maclean, Zoe Apostolides

Interested in well-written commercial fiction, particularly historical, crime/mystery/suspense and thrillers, women's fiction from chick-lit sagas to contemporary and literary fiction. Also looking to build YA fiction list. Considers most non-fiction particularly history, biography, current affairs, politics, how-to, true crime and popular science. *Commission* Home 15%, overseas 20%, film/TV 20%. Works with foreign agents. Please note that whole books and manuscript submissions via post and/or email will not be accepted. Check the website for details on how to submit. Does not handle poetry, plays or scripts for film and TV.

   Authors include Leye Adenle, Helen Batten, Simon Brett, Ian Dunt, Jonathan Gash, John Gardner, Jonathon Green, Lisa Hall, Chris Hart, Mark McCrum, Frankie McGowan, Catriona McPherson, Malachi O'Doherty. *Founded* 1997.

Creative Authors Ltd

11A Woodlawn Street, Whitstable, Kent CT5 1HQ
email write@creativeauthors.co.uk
website www.creativeauthors.co.uk
Twitter @creativeauthors
Instagram creativeauthors
Director Isabel Atherton

Fiction, women's fiction, literary fiction, non-fiction, humour, history, science, autobiography, biography, business, memoir, health, cookery, arts and crafts, crime, children's fiction, picture books, young adult, graphic novels and illustrators. *Commission* Home 15%, overseas 20%. Only accepts email submissions.

   Authors and illustrators include Guojing, Ged Adamson, Zuza Zak, Tristan Donovan, Nick Soulsby, Mark Beaumont, Lucy Scott, Coll Muir, Kenneth Womack, Colleen Kosinski, Anthony Galvin, Dr Keith Souter, E.A. Hanks, Cassie Liversidge, Caroline Young, Megan Tadden. *Founded* 2008.

Rupert Crew Ltd*

Southgate, 7 Linden Avenue, Dorchester DT1 1EJ
tel (01305) 260335
email info@rupertcrew.co.uk
website www.rupertcrew.co.uk
Managing Director Caroline Montgomery

International representation, handling accessible literary and commercial fiction and non-fiction for adult and children's (8+) markets. *Commission* Home 15%, overseas, TV/film and radio 20%. No unsolicited MSS: see website for current submission guidelines. No picture books, plays, screenplays, poetry, journalism, science fiction, fantasy or short stories. *Founded* 1927.

Curtis Brown*

Haymarket House, 28–29 Haymarket, London SW1Y 4SP
tel 020-7393 4400
email cb@curtisbrown.co.uk
website www.curtisbrown.co.uk
website www.curtisbrowncreative.co.uk
Twitter @CBGBooks
Twitter @cbcreative
Contacts Jonny Geller (Chair), Sheila Crowley, Gordon Wise (Managing Directors), Felicity Blunt, Jonathan Lloyd, Alice Lutyens (inc Audio and Podcast), Lucy Morris, Cathryn Summerhayes, Karolina Sutton, Stephanie Thwaites (Agents and Senior Agents), Becky Brown, Norah Perkins (Heritage), Lisa Babalis, Isobel Gahan, Viola Hayden, Jess Molloy (Associates), Luke Speed (Media)

Represents prominent writers of fiction and non-fiction, from winners of all major awards to international bestsellers and from debuts to literary estates, and formats ranging from print and audio to digital and merchandise. Also manages the international careers of authors, with strong relationships in translation and US markets as well as a growing European-language business. The Book Department works closely with the wider team of Curtis Brown agents and Curtis Brown Group companies, offering full-service representation in film, TV and theatre, audio, events and other performance. Activities include the creative writing school, Curtis Brown Creative, established with the aim of finding and fostering new talent. In fiction, works across many genres, both literary and those aimed at a popular audience, and looks for strong voices and outstanding storytellers in general fiction, crime, thrillers, psychological suspense, speculative and historical fiction, young adult and children's books. Non-fiction list includes leading commentators and thinkers, historians, biographers, social media influencers, lifestyle brands, scientists and writers of quality narrative non-fiction. See website and individual agent webpages. Simultaneous submissions with C&W.

   Clients include fiction and non-fiction debuts and established brands, and a number of well-known thinkers and personalities, from world-renowned politicians to business leaders and performers. *Founded* 1899.

Judy Daish Associates Ltd

2 St. Charles Place, London W10 6EG
tel 020-8964 8811

email judy@judydaish.com
website www.judydaish.com
Agents Judy Daish, Howard Gooding, Tracey Elliston

Theatre, film, TV, radio, opera. Commission Rates by negotiation. No unsolicited MSS. Founded 1978.

Dalzell & Beresford Ltd

Paddock Suite, The Courtyard,
55 Charterhouse Street, London EC1M 6HA
tel 020-7336 0351
email mail@dbltd.co.uk
website www.dalzellandberesford.com

A long-established and well-respected leading UK theatrical agency representing outstanding British and international actors, writers and directors. Maintains a selective client list providing focused and sustained career management for its creative talent. Accepts postal and electronic submissions, including links to showreels. Send an sae for the return of materials. All submissions are reviewed and where there is interest in a meeting or attending a show, applicants will be contacted.

Caroline Davidson Literary Agency*

5 Queen Anne's Gardens, London W4 1TU
tel 020-8995 5768
email enquiries@cdla.co.uk
website www.cdla.co.uk

Handles exceptional novels, memoirs and non-fiction of originality and high quality. Commission 12.5%. All submissions must be in hard copy. Email submissions are not considered. For non-fiction send letter with CV and detailed, well thought-out book proposal, including chapter synopsis. With fiction, send letter, CV, three-line pitch, synopsis and the first 50 pages and last ten pages of text. No reply without large sae with correct return postage. CDLA dislikes fantasy, horror, crime and science fiction.

Authors (frontlist) include Peter Barham, Andrew Beatty, Andrew Dalby, Emma Donoghue, Chris Greenhalgh, Richard Hobday, John Phibbs, Helena Whitbread. Founded 1988.

Felix de Wolfe

20 Old Compton Street, London W1D 4TW
tel 020-7242 5066
email info@felixdewolfe.com
website https://felixdewolfe.com
Twitter @felixdewolfe
Instagram felixdewolfe
Agents Caroline de Wolfe, Wendy Scozzaro

Theatre, films, TV, sound broadcasting and fiction. Works in conjunction with many foreign agencies. Commission Home 10–15%, overseas 20%. For fiction, send a CV/biography with a synopsis and the first 15 pages of your work. Founded 1947.

DGA Ltd

2nd Floor, 40 Rosebery Avenue, Clerkenwell,
London EC1R 4RX
tel 020-7240 9992

email amandine@davidgodwinassociates.co.uk
email sebastiangodwin@davidgodwinassociates.co.uk
website www.davidgodwinassociates.com
Twitter @DGALitAgents
Instagram DGALiterary
Directors David Godwin, Heather Godwin

Broad range of fiction and non-fiction with a strong focus on literary. Send MS with synopsis and cover letter to Sebastian Godwin at the above email address.

Clients include Simon Armitage, Christina Lamb, Richard Holmes, Claire Tomalin, Jeremy Paxman, Norman Davies, Vikram Seth, Arundhati Roy, William Dalrymple. Founded 1995.

DHH Literary Agency*

23–27 Cecil Court, London WC2N 4EZ
tel 020-7836 7376
email enquiries@dhhliteraryagency.com
website www.dhhliteraryagency.com
Facebook www.facebook.com/dhhliteraryagency
Twitter @dhhlitagency
Agents David H. Headley, Broo Doherty, Hannah Sheppard, Harry Illingworth, Emily Glenister

Fiction, women's commercial fiction, crime, thriller, literary fiction, speculative fiction, science fiction and fantasy. Non-fiction special interests include narrative non-fiction, memoir, history, cookery and humour. Also children's and YA fiction. Commission UK 15%, overseas 20%. Send informative preliminary email with first three chapters and synopsis. New authors welcome. No plays or scripts, poetry or short stories.

Authors include Stuart Turton, Anna Stephens, Ada Palmer, Adam Simcox, Anna Jacobs, Jules Wake, Phillipa Ashley, Amanda Jennings, Jo Thomas, Ragnar Jonasson, M.W. Craven, Anita Frank, Adam Hamdy, Chris McGeorge, Abi Elphinstone. Founded 2008.

Diamond Kahn & Woods Literary Agency*

Top Floor, 66 Onslow Gardens, London N10 3JX
tel 020-3514 6544
email info@dkwlitagency.co.uk
email submissions.ella@dkwlitagency.co.uk
email submissions.bryony@dkwlitagency.co.uk
website www.dkwlitagency.co.uk
Twitter @DKWLitAgency
Agents Ella Diamond Kahn, Bryony Woods

Literary and commercial fiction (including all major genres) and non-fiction for adults; and children's, young adult and crossover fiction. Interested in new writers. Commission Home 15%, USA/translation 20%. Email submissions only. Send three chapters and synopsis to one agent only. See website for further details on agents, their areas of interest and submission guidelines.

Clients include Virginia Macgregor, S.E. Lister, Chris Lloyd, Nicole Burstein, David Owen, Caroline O'Donoghue, Sharon Gosling, Sylvia Bishop,

Katherine Orton, Calum McSwiggan, Laura Jane Williams, Catriona Silvey, Jayne Cowie, Natalie Hart, Daisy May Johnson. *Founded* 2012.

Elise Dillsworth Agency

9 Grosvenor Road, Muswell Hill, London N10 2DR
email elise@elisedillsworthagency.com
website www.elisedillsworthagency.com
Twitter @EliseDillsworth
Owner/Literary Agent Elise Dillsworth

Represents literary and commercial fiction and non-fiction in the area of memoir, biography, travel and cookery, with a keen aim to reflect writing that is international. *Commission* Home 15%, overseas 20%. Send preliminary letter, synopsis and first three chapters (or approximately 50 pages). No postal submissions accepted. See website for full submission guidelines. Does not represent science fiction, fantasy, plays, film/TV scripts or children's books.

Authors include Yvonne Battle-Felton, Maria Bradford, Anthony Joseph, Charlotte Morgan-Nwokenna, Irenosen Okojie, Yewande Omotoso, Hanna Randall, Noo Saro-Wiwa, Stephanie Victoire, Aisling Watters and the estate of Roy Heath. *Founded* 2012.

Robert Dudley Agency

135A Bridge Street, Ashford, Kent TN25 5DP
tel 07879 426574
email info@robertdudleyagency.co.uk
website www.robertdudleyagency.co.uk
Proprietor Robert Dudley

Non-fiction only. Specialises in history, biography, sport, management, politics, military history, current affairs. *Commission* Home 15%, overseas 20%, film/TV/radio 20%. Will suggest revision. Email submissions preferred. All material sent at owner's risk. No MSS returned without sae.

Authors include Edoardo Albert, Nigel Barlow, Ben Barry, Tim Bentinck, Rachel Bridge, Michael Broers, Prit Buttar, Ambrogio Caiani, Halik Kochanski, Mungo Melvin, Adrian Phillips, Tim Phillips, Brian Holden Reid, Mary Colwell, Chris Sidwells, Martyn Whittock. *Founded* 2000.

Eddison Pearson Ltd*

West Hill House, 6 Swains Lane, London N6 6QS
tel 020-7700 7763
email enquiries@eddisonpearson.com
website www.eddisonpearson.com
Contact Clare Pearson

Small, personally run agency. Children's and young adult books, fiction and non-fiction, poetry. *Commission* Home 10–15%, overseas 15–20%. Enquiries and submissions by email only; email for up-to-date submission guidelines by return. May suggest revision where appropriate.

Authors include Valerie Bloom, Sue Heap, Caroline Lawrence, Robert Muchamore, Mary Murphy, Megan Rix. *Founded* 1997.

Edwards Fuglewicz Literary Agency*

49 Great Ormond Street, London WC1N 3HZ
tel 020-7405 6725
Contacts Ros Edwards, Jill McCluskey

Literary and commercial fiction; non-fiction: biography and narrative non-fiction (including animal stories). *Commission* Home 15%, USA/translation 20%. No email submissions. No children's fiction, science fiction or horror. *Founded* 1996.

Faith Evans Associates

27 Park Avenue North, London N8 7RU
tel 020-8340 9920
email faith@faith-evans.co.uk

Small agency. Co-agents in most countries. *Commission* Home 15%, overseas 20%. List currently full. No phone calls or submissions.

Authors include Melissa Benn, Eleanor Bron, Helena Kennedy, Tom Paulin, Sheila Rowbotham, Harriet Walter, and the estates of Madeleine Bourdouxhe and Lorna Sage. *Founded* 1987.

Fillingham Weston Associates

20 Mortlake, 20 Mortlake High Street, London SW14 8JN
tel 020-8748 5594
website www.fillinghamweston.com
Agents Janet Fillingham, Kate Weston

Film, TV and theatre only. *Commission* Home 15%, overseas 15–20%. Strictly no unsolicited MSS; professional recommendation required. No books. *Founded* 1992.

Film Rights Ltd

11 Pandora Road, London NW6 1TS
tel 020-8001 3040
email information@filmrights.ltd.uk
website www.filmrights.ltd.uk
Directors Brendan Davis, Joan Potts

Represented in USA and abroad. Theatre, films, TV and sound broadcasting. *Commission* Home 10%, overseas 15%.

Clients include Carlo Ardito, John Chapman, Peter Coke, Ray Cooney OBE, Dave Freeman, John Graham, Robin Hawdon, Jeremy Lloyd (plays), Dawn Lowe-Watson, Glyn Robbins, Edward Taylor, the estate of Dodie Smith, the literary estate of N.C. Hunter, the estate of Frank Baker and the literary estate of Michael Pertwee. *Founded* 1935.

Laurence Fitch Ltd

(incorporating The London Play Company 1922)
11 Pandora Road, London NW6 1TS
tel 020-8001 3040
email information@laurencefitch.com
website www.laurencefitch.com
Directors F.H.L. Fitch, Joan Potts, Brendan Davis

Agents representing film and TV. *Commission* Home 10%, overseas 15%.

Authors include Carlo Ardito, John Chapman, Peter Coke, Ray Cooney OBE, Dave Freeman, John Graham, Robin Hawdon, Jeremy Lloyd (plays), Dawn Lowe-Watson, Glyn Robbins, Edward Taylor, the estate of Dodie Smith, the literary estate of N.C. Hunter, the estate of Frank Baker and the literary estate of Michael Pertwee. *Founded* 1935.

Fox & Howard Literary Agency*
Denbighshire LL16 4LE
tel (01824) 790817
email enquiries@foxandhoward.co.uk
email fandhagency@googlemail.com
website www.foxandhoward.co.uk
Contact Charlotte Howard

General non-fiction: biography and memoirs, history and current affairs, mind, body & spirit, health and personal development, popular science and maths. *Commission* Home 15%, overseas 20%. The client list is currently closed. *Founded* 1992.

FRA*
(formerly Futerman, Rose & Associates)
91 St Leonards Road, London SW14 7BL
tel 020-8255 7755
email enquiries@futermanrose.co.uk
website www.futermanrose.co.uk
Contacts Guy Rose, Alexandra Groom

Non-fiction, biography (especially sport, music and politics), show business, current affairs, teen fiction and scripts for TV and film. No unsolicited MSS. Send brief résumé, synopsis, first 20 pages and sae. No children's, science fiction or fantasy.
Clients include Jill Anderson, Larry Barker, Rt Hon. Sir Iain Duncan Smith MP, Paul Ferris, Keith Gillespie, Mike Gooley CBE, Sara Khan, Keith R. Lindsay, Tony McMahon, Max Morgan-Witts, His Hon. Judge Peter Murphy, Paul Nicholas, His Hon. Judge Chris Nicholson, Liz Rettig, Paul Stinchcombe QC, Simon Woodham. *Founded* 1984.

Fraser Ross Associates
6 Wellington Place, Edinburgh EH6 7EQ
tel 0131 553 2759, 0131 657 4412
email agentlmfraser@gmail.com
email kjross@tiscali.co.uk
website www.fraserross.co.uk
Facebook www.facebook.com/fraserrossassociates
Twitter @FraserRossLA
Instagram fraserrossassociates
Partners Lindsey Fraser, Kathryn Ross

Writing and illustration for children's books, fiction and non-fiction for adults. See website for submission guidelines.
See website for a complete list of writers and artists represented. *Founded* 2002.

Jüri Gabriel
35 Camberwell Grove, London SE5 8JA
tel 020-7703 6186
email juri@jurigabriel.com

Jüri Gabriel was the chairman of Dedalus (publishers) for nearly 30 years. Quality fiction and non-fiction (i.e. anything that shows wit and intelligence); radio, TV and film, but selling these rights only in existing works by existing clients. *Commission* Home 10%, overseas 20%, performance rights 10%. Submit three sample chapters plus a one-to two-page synopsis and sae (if using snail mail) in the first instance. Will suggest revision where appropriate. No short stories, articles, verse or books for children.
Authors include Jack Allen, Gbontwi Anyetei, Nick Bradbury, Prof. Christopher Day, Paul Genney, Pat Gray, Mikka Haugaard, Robert Irwin, Pat Johnson, David Madsen, Richard Mankiewicz, David Miller, John Outram, Philip Roberts, Roger Storey. *Founded* 1983.

Gleam Titles
3rd Floor, 20 Triton Street, Regent's Place, London NW1 3BF
email gleamtitles@gleamfutures.com
website www.gleamfutures.com/gleamtitles

Looking for original, brave and exciting new voices. Particularly interested in writers who are using social media and the online space to share their content in a creative and effective way. Works with clients to help them nurture a direct connection with their audience across their channels with the aim of developing a strategy to grow long-term value in their books across multiple media platforms. Email submissions only. See website for details. Part of Gleam Futures talent management company. Represents a wide range of fiction and non-fiction. The agency works with all sorts of writers and experts, including journalists, comedians, scientists, illustrators and podcasters.
Authors include Dr Becky, Dr Soph, Emma Gannon, Gina Martin, Katherine Ormerod, Laura Bates, Liv Little, Mrs Hinch, Munroe Bergdorf, Olivia Purvis, Paula Sutton, Penny Wincer, Sam Baker, Scarlett Curtis, Zoe Sugg.

The Good Literary Agency*
email info@thegoodliteraryagency.org
website www.thegoodliteraryagency.org
Twitter @thegoodagencyuk
Instagram thegoodagencyuk

Represents authors from backgrounds underrepresented in UK publishing including writers of colour, working class, disability, LGBTQ+ and anyone who feels that they or their stories are under-represented. Non-fiction (including history, science, economics, politics, self-help, lifestyle, pop culture and memoir); fiction (all genres, in particular crime and thriller, contemporary love stories, family sagas, science fiction and fantasy and historical); children's and YA. For detailed submission guidelines, visit the website.
Authors include Saima Mir, Hafsa Zayyan, Musa Okwonga, Irfan Master, Lizzie Huxley-Jones, Paula

Akpan, Elijah Lawal, Eva Verde, Jon Ransom, Nicole Crentsil, Sharan Dhaliwal, Nicola Garrard, Penny Pepper and Clare Weze. *Founded* 2018.

Bill Goodall Literary Agency
26 Lower Road, Malvern, Worcs. WR14 4BX
email bill@billgoodall.co.uk
website www.billgoodall.co.uk
Twitter @BGLitAgency
Owner/Director Bill Goodall

Adult fiction, including (but not exclusively) commercial/literary crime and thriller, and general fiction. *Commission* Home 15%, overseas/translation 20%, film/TV 15% (home)/20% (overseas). Send synopsis plus first three chapters or 50 pages, whichever is shorter, by email as Word attachments. No postal submissions. No sci-fi/horror, short stories, poetry or children's books.
  Clients include Tom Benjamin, C J Farrington, Mandy Byatt, Leigh Russell, Diana Finley, Kevin Sullivan, James Brydon, Mark Dowd.

Graham Maw Christie*
37 Highbury Place, London N5 1QP
email enquiries@grahammawchristie.com
website www.grahammawchristie.com
Twitter @litagencyGMC
Instagram @litagencyGMC
Contacts Jane Graham Maw, Jennifer Christie, Maddy Belton

General non-fiction: autobiography/memoir, business/smart thinking, humour and gift, food and drink, craft, health and wellness, lifestyle, parenting, self-help/how to, popular science/history/culture/reference. Email submissions only. Will suggest revisions. See website for submission guidelines. Also represents ghostwriters. No fiction, children's or poetry.
  Authors include Seyi Akiwowo, Sarah Akwisombe, Shaun Deeney, Natalie Fée, Milli Hill, Tim James, Vex King, Freya Lewis, Prof. Tom Oliver, Kajal Odedra, Suzy Reading, Clemmie Telford, Graeme Tomlinson, Raynor Winn. *Founded* 2005.

Annette Green Authors' Agency
5 Henwoods Mount, Pembury,
Tunbridge Wells TN2 4BH
tel (01892) 263252
email annette@annettegreenagency.com
website www.annettegreenagency.co.uk
Partners Annette Green, David Smith

Fiction: Literary, general and teenage fiction. Non-fiction: popular culture, history and science. *Commission* Full-length MSS: home 15%, overseas 20–25%. Preliminary letter, synopsis, sample chapter and sae essential. No picture books, dramatic scripts, poetry, science fiction or fantasy.
  Authors include Andrew Baker, Louis Barfe, Tim Bradford, Bill Broady, Katherine Clements, Terry

Darlington, Elizabeth Haynes, Jane Kerr, Maria McCann, Adam Macqueen, Ian Marchant, Audrey Reimann, Kirsty Scott, Elizabeth Woodcraft. *Founded* 1998.

Christine Green Authors' Agent*
PO Box 70078, London SE15 5AU
email info@christinegreen.co.uk
website www.christinegreen.co.uk
Twitter @whitehorsemews
Contact Christine Green

Literary and commercial fiction, narrative (novelistic) non-fiction. General, young adult, women's, crime and historical fiction welcome. *Commission* Home 15%, overseas 20%. Preliminary queries by email welcome. Email submissions only. No genre science fiction or fantasy, travelogues, self-help, picture books, scripts or poetry.
  Clients include Maeve Binchy, Mary Beckett, Ita Daly, Sairish Hussain, Ali Lewis, Gaile Parkin, Alice Redmond. *Founded* 1984.

Louise Greenberg Books Ltd*
The End House, Church Crescent, London N3 1BG
tel 020-8349 1179
email louisegreenberg@btinternet.com
website https://louisegreenbergbooks.co.uk

Literary fiction and non-fiction. *Commission* Full-length MSS: home 15%, overseas 20%. New writers by recommendation. No telephone enquiries. *Founded* 1997.

Greene & Heaton Ltd*
37 Goldhawk Road, London W12 8QQ
tel 020-8749 0315
email submissions@greeneheaton.co.uk
email info@greeneheaton.co.uk
website www.greeneheaton.co.uk
Twitter @GreeneandHeaton
Contacts Carol Heaton, Judith Murray, Antony Topping, Claudia Young, Laura Williams, Holly Faulks, Imogen Morrell, Kate Rizzo (Translation Rights Director)

Handles translation rights directly in all major territories. Fiction and non-fiction. *Commission* Home 15%, USA/translation 20%. Email submissions accepted, but no reply guaranteed. Postal submissions not accepted. No poetry or original scripts for theatre, film or TV.
  Clients include Laura Barnett, Lucy Clarke, Sabine Durrant, Marcus du Sautoy, Hugh Fearnley-Whittingstall, Michael Frayn, Joseph Knox, Ian McGuire, Thomasina Miers, Barney Norris, Temi Oh, C.J. Sansom, Andrew Taylor, Sarah Waters and the estate of P.D. James. *Founded* 1963.

The Greenhouse Literary Agency
tel 020-7841 3958
email info@greenhouseliterary.com
website www.greenhouseliterary.com
Twitter @sarahgreenhouse

Twitter @chelseberly
Director Sarah Davies, *Agent* Chelsea Eberly

Specialist children's book agency with a reputation for impressive transatlantic deals. Represents picture book author-illustrators through to writers for teens/young adults. Select children's/teen non-fiction and women's fiction by referral. Represents UK, Irish and North American authors. *Commission* USA/UK 15%, elsewhere 25%. No postal submissions. All submissions by e-query via Query Manager. Strict submission criteria (see website for details). No poetry, short stories, educational or religious/inspirational work, erotic, pre-school/novelty material or screenplays. No picture book texts unless also illustrated by author.
   Authors include Julie Bertagna, Sarwat Chadda/Joshua Khan, Tae Keller, Dawn Kurtagich, Cori McCarthy, Megan Miranda, Ali Standish, Brenna Yovanoff. *Founded* 2008.

Gregory & Company Authors' Agents*

(Now part of David Higham Associates)
6th Floor, Waverley House, 7–12 Noel Street, London W1F 8GQ
tel 020-7434 5900
email maryjones@davidhigham.co.uk (submissions)
website www.davidhigham.co.uk
Twitter @DHABooks
Contacts Jane Gregory (UK, USA), Stephanie Glencross and Mary Jones (editorial), Camille Burns (assistant)

Editorial advice given to own authors. Translation and film/TV rights handled by DHA team. Special interests (fiction): crime, suspense, thrillers, commercial women's fiction and literary. Particularly interested in books which will also sell to publishers abroad. *Commission* Home 15%, USA/translation/radio/film/TV 20%. No unsolicited submissions. Submissions by email: first 50 pages of typescript, but due to volume will only respond if interested in reading more. Submissions by post: send preliminary letter with CV, synopsis (three pages maximum), first ten pages of typescript and future writing plans plus return postage. No science fiction, fantasy, poetry, academic or children's books, original plays, film or TV scripts.
   Authors include Val McDermid, Minette Walters, Belinda Bauer, Tan Twang Eng, Paula Daly, Sarah Hilary, Martyn Waites. *Founded* 1987.

David Grossman Literary Agency Ltd

9 Lamington Street, London W6 0HU
tel 020-8741 2860
email submissions@dglal.co.uk

Works in conjunction with agents in New York, Los Angeles, Europe, Japan, China. Preliminary letter required. *Commission* Full-length MSS: home 10–15%, overseas 20% including foreign agent's commission, performance rights 15%. Preliminary

letter required. No submissions by email without a preceding preliminary letter or message briefly describing the work and justifying its publication. *Founded* 1976.

Marianne Gunn O'Connor Literary, Film/TV Agency

Morrison Chambers, Suites 52 & 53, 32 Nassau Street, Dublin D02 RX59, Republic of Ireland
email submissions@mariannegunnoconnor.com
Contact Marianne Gunn O'Connor

Literary fiction, upmarket fiction including book club and psychological suspense. Also handles children's books, middle grade, young adult, new adult and crossover fiction, as well as exciting new non-fiction authors with a focus on narrative non-fiction, health, some memoir and biography. No screenplays.
   Clients include Liz Nugent, Louise Nealon, Christy Lefteri, Mike McCormack, Patrick McCabe, Nana Oforiata Ayim, Shane Hegarty, Orlagh Collins, Susie Lau aka Stylebubble, Claudia Carroll, Caitriona Perry, Kevin Power, Kate Kerrigan, Sinead Moriarty, Kathleen McMahon. *Founded* 1996.

Gwyn Palmer Associates (Literary Agents) Ltd

email robertgwynpalmer@gmail.com
Contact Robert Gwyn Palmer

Non-fiction only including, but not limited to, self-help, memoir and autobiography, history, cookery, economics, popular science, graphic design, architecture and design. *Commission* Home 15%. Make initial contact via email with an outline of the proposal. No fiction, poetry, children's.
   Authors include Bobby Seagull, Daniel Fryer, Ben Aldridge, Tom Goodwin, Sarah Stamford, Paul Farrell, Tiffany Wood, Anne Atkins, Dr Elizabeth English and Marcus Bawdon. *Founded* 2005.

The Hamilton Agency

12A Portland Road, London W11 4LA
email matthew@thehamiltonagency.co.uk
website https://thehamiltonagency.co.uk/
Twitter @MWHamilton
Founder and agent Matthew Hamilton

Represents writers of literary fiction and non-fiction, with a particular interest in politics, music and entertainment. Submissions via the website using the form provided. No queries by post or phone. Submissions must include a covering letter, short author bio and a brief synopsis. An excerpt or the full MS can be included at submission.
   See website for client list. *Founded* 2019.

The Hanbury Agency Ltd, Literary Agents*

Suite 103, Lower Marsh, London SE1 7AB
email enquiries@hanburyagency.com
website www.hanburyagency.com
Twitter @HanburyAgency

Represents general fiction and non-fiction. See website for submission guidelines.

Authors include George Alagiah, Tom Bergin, Simon Callow, Jane Glover, Oscar de Muriel, Luke Dormehl, Nick Frost, Paul Gorman, Roman Krznaric, Margarette Lincoln, Judith Lennox, Kate Raworth, Simon Sharpe, Charles Saumarez Smith, Jerry White. The agency has a strong stable of ghostwriters. *Founded* 1983.

Hardman & Swainson*
S86 Somerset House, London WC2R 1LA
tel 020-3701 7449
email submissions@hardmanswainson.com
website www.hardmanswainson.com
Twitter @hardmanswainson
Directors Caroline Hardman, Joanna Swainson

Literary and commercial fiction, crime and thriller, women's, accessible literary, YA and middle-grade children's fiction. Non-fiction, including memoir, biography, popular science, history, philosophy. *Commission* Home 15%, USA/translation/film/TV 20%. Submissions by email only; check the website for details. Will work editorially with the author where appropriate. No poetry, screenplays or picture books.

Clients include Dinah Jefferies, Liz Trenow, Cathy Bramley, Ali McNamara, Giovanna Fletcher, Helen Fields, Isabelle Broom, The Unmumsy Mum, Daniel M. Davies, Alex Bell, Beth Kempton, Tracy Buchanan, Rachel Edwards. *Founded* 2012.

Antony Harwood Ltd
103 Walton Street, Oxford OX2 6EB
tel (01865) 559615
email mail@antonyharwood.com
website www.antonyharwood.com
Contacts Antony Harwood, James Macdonald Lockhart, Jo Williamson (children's)

General and genre fiction; general non-fiction. *Commission* Home 15%, overseas 20%. Will suggest revision.

Clients include Louise Doughty, Peter F. Hamilton, Alan Hollinghurst, A.L. Kennedy, Douglas Kennedy, Dorothy Koomson, Amy Liptrot, George Monbiot. *Founded* 2000.

A.M. Heath & Co. Ltd*
6 Warwick Court, London WC1R 5DJ
tel 020-7242 2811
email enquiries@amheath.com
website www.amheath.com
Twitter @amheathltd
Contacts Bill Hamilton, Victoria Hobbs, Euan Thorneycroft, Alexandra McNicoll (translation rights), Oliver Munson, Julia Churchill (children's), Rebecca Ritchie, Zoe King, Florence Rees

Literary and commercial fiction and non-fiction, children's and film/TV. *Commission* Full-length MSS:

home 15%, USA/translation 20%. Film/TV 15–20% by agreement. Digital submission via website. No screenplays, poetry or short stories except for collections.

Clients include Christopher Andrew, Lauren Beukes, Sarah Crossan, Lindsey Davis, Katie Fforde, Michelle Harrison, Salma El-Wardany, Lady Hale, Conn Iggulden, Cynan Jones, Sophia Money-Coutts, Hilary Mantel, Maggie O'Farrell, Kamila Shamsie and the estate of George Orwell. *Founded* 1919.

Sinead Heneghan Literary Agency
website https://sineadheneghan.com/
Twitter @sinead_heneghan

A Manchester based agency actively looking for submissions. Represents fiction: well-written crime, thrillers, psychological suspense, high-concept novels, romance, women's fiction, historical fiction and reading group fiction. Submissions via form on website. Include a short synopsis, first three chapters and author bio. Does not represent Children's, YA, fantasy, poetry or non-fiction.

hhb agency ltd*
62 Grafton Way, London W1T 5DW
tel 020-7405 5525
email heather@hhbagency.com
email elly@hhbagency.com
website https://hhbagency.com/
Twitter @hhbagencyltd
Contacts Heather Holden-Brown, Elly James

Non-fiction: journalism, history and politics, contemporary autobiography and biography, ideas, entertainment and TV, business, memoir, food and cookery a speciality. Fiction: women's commercial, book club, historical and thrillers. *Commission* 15%.

Authors include Darina Allen, Anjum Anand, Dr Nick Barratt, Charlotte Betts, Emma Burstall, Rory Cellan-Jones, Ben Chu, Suzanne Goldring, Molly Green, Nick Hewer, Mishal Husain, Dr Max Pemberton, Saliha Mahmood Ahmed, Louise Parker, Rosemary Shrager, Rachel Trethewey. *Founded* 2005.

Sophie Hicks Agency*
email info@sophiehicksagency.com
website www.sophiehicksagency.com
Twitter @SophieHicksAg
Agents Sophie Hicks, Sarah Williams

Adult fiction and non-fiction. Also handles children's books for 9+. Represented in all foreign markets. *Commission* UK/USA 15%, translation 20%. Email submissions only, see website for guidelines. No poetry or scripts.

Authors include: Tamsin Calidas, Anne Cassidy, Lucy Coats, Eoin Colfer, Ruth Fitzmaurice, Tristan Gooley, Shahroo Izadi, Benedict Jacka, Signe Johansen, Kathryn Evans, Emerald Fennell, Padraig Kenny, Andrew Meehan, Amanda Reynolds, Tom Whipple. *Founded* 2014.

David Higham Associates Ltd*

6th Floor, Waverley House, 7–12 Noel Street,
London W1F 8GQ
tel 020-7434 5900
email dha@davidhigham.co.uk
website www.davidhigham.co.uk
Managing Director Anthony Goff, *Books* Veronique
Baxter, Nicola Chang, Jemima Forrester, Georgia
Glover, Anthony Goff, Andrew Gordon, Jane
Gregory, Lizzy Kremer, Harriet Moore, Caroline
Walsh, Jessica Woollard, *Foreign Rights* Alice Howe,
Emma Jamison, Lucy Talbot, Margaux Vialleron,
Imogen Bovill, Johanna Clarke, *Film/TV/Theatre*
Nicky Lund, Georgina Ruffhead, Clare Israel,
Penelope Killick

Agents for the negotiation of all rights in literary and
commercial fiction, general non-fiction. Represented
in all foreign markets either directly or through sub-
agents. All genres, children's fiction and picture
books, plays, film and TV scripts, offering a full
service across all media. *Commission* Home 15%,
USA/translation 20%, scripts 10%. See website for
submissions policy.

Clients include Naomi Alderman, Belinda Bauer,
J.M. Coetzee, Bernard Cornwell, Stephen Fry, Paula
Hawkins, Owen Jones, Robert Macfarlane, Carole
Matthews, Val McDermid, Alexander McCall Smith.
The children's list features Roald Dahl, Michael
Morpurgo, Liz Pichon, Cressida Cowell and
Jacqueline Wilson. *Founded* 1935.

Holroyde Cartey Ltd*

website www.holroydecartey.com
Contacts Claire Cartey, Penny Holroyde

A literary and artistic agency representing a list of
award-winning and bestselling authors and
illustrators. Welcomes submissions from debut and
established authors. *Commission* 15% headline. See
website for submission guidelines. *Founded* 2015.

Vanessa Holt Ltd*

59 Crescent Road, Leigh-on-Sea, Essex SS9 2PF
tel (01702) 473787
email v.holt791@btinternet.com

General fiction and non-fiction. Works in
conjunction with foreign agencies and publishers in
all markets. *Commission* Home 15%, overseas 20%,
TV/film/radio 15%. No unsolicited MSS and
submissions preferred by arrangement. No overseas
submissions. *Founded* 1989.

Kate Hordern Literary Agency Ltd*

KHLA Ltd, 18 Mortimer Road, Clifton,
Bristol BS8 4EY
tel (01179) 239368
email kate@khla.co.uk
email anne@khla.co.uk
website https://khla.co.uk
Agents Kate Hordern, Anne Williams

A small agency with an international reach
representing a wide range of fiction, some non-fiction
and some children's. See website for further details of
what the agency is looking for and for submission
guidelines. *Founded* 1999.

Valerie Hoskins Associates Ltd

20 Charlotte Street, London W1T 2NA
tel 020-7637 4490
email vha@vhassociates.co.uk
website www.vhassociates.co.uk
Proprietor Valerie Hoskins, *Agent* Rebecca Watson

Film, TV and radio; specialises in animation. Works
in conjunction with US agents. *Commission* Home
12.5%, overseas max. 20%. No unsolicited MSS;
preliminary letter and sae essential.

Authors include Joe Alexander, Andy Amfo, Bill
Armstrong, Paul Boateng, Tom Bradby, Guy Burt,
Laurence Davey, Michelle Gayle, Matthew Graham,
Sarah Gordon, Henrietta Hardy, Sarah Louise
Hawkins, Paul Mari, Jeff Povey, E.L. James.
Founded 1983.

Clare Hulton Literary Agency*

email info@clarehulton.co.uk
website www.clarehulton.com
Director Clare Hulton

Represents numerous bestselling and award-winning
authors. Specialises in non-fiction especially cookery
and lifestyle, health and fitness, music, humour,
television tie-ins, self-help, commercial non-fiction,
history, business and memoir. The agency also has a
small but growing fiction list. Submissions consisting
of a synopsis and sample chapter should be sent by
email. No fantasy, poetry, screenplays, YA or
children's proposals.

Authors include Kay Featherstone and Kate
Allinson, Yasmin Khan, Jackie Kabler, Dale Pinnock,
Dan Toombs, James Haskell, Chloe Madeley, John
Partridge, Matt Roberts, Emma Rowley, Craig and
Shaun McAnuff, Catherine Phipps, Kwoklyn Wan,
Willow Crossley, and Becca Maberley. *Founded* 2012.

IMG UK Ltd

Building Six, Chiswick Park,
566 Chiswick High Road, London W4 5HR
tel 020-8233 5000
email sarah.wooldridge@img.com
website www.img.com
Literary Agent Sarah Wooldridge

Celebrity books, sports-related books, non-fiction
and how-to business books. *Commission* Home 15%,
USA 20%, elsewhere 25%. No emails. No theatre,
fiction, children's, academic or poetry.

Authors include Michael Johnson, Colin
Montgomerie, John McEnroe, Katherine Grainger,
Ken Brown, Nicole Cooke, Dave Alred, Judy Murray,
Thomas Bjorn, Padraig Harrington. *Founded* 1960.

Independent Talent Group Ltd
40 Whitfield Street, London W1T 2RH
tel 020-7636 6565
website www.independenttalent.com
Twitter @ITG_Ltd

Specialises in scripts for film, theatre, TV, radio. Client base encompasses actors, directors, writers, producers and their production companies, below-the-line talent, casting directors, presenters, comedians and voice-over artists.

Intercontinental Literary Agency Ltd*
5 New Concordia Wharf, Mill Street,
London SE1 2BB
tel 020-7379 6611
email ila@ila-agency.co.uk
website www.ila-agency.co.uk
Contacts Nicki Kennedy, Sam Edenborough, Jenny Robson, Katherine West, Clementine Gaisman, Alice Natali

Represents translation rights only. *Founded* 1965.

Janklow & Nesbit (UK) Ltd*
13A Hillgate Street, London W8 7SP
tel 020-7243 2975
email submissions@janklow.co.uk
website www.janklowandnesbit.co.uk
Twitter @JanklowUK
Instagram janklownesbituk
Agents Will Francis, Rebecca Carter, Claire Paterson Conrad, Hellie Ogden, *Translation rights* Zoe Nelson

Represents a bestselling, global and award-winning range of commercial and literary fiction and non-fiction, children's and YA. Handles translation rights directly or through sub-agents in all territories. US rights handled by Janklow & Nesbit Associates in New York. Send informative covering letter with full outline (non-fiction), synopsis and first three sample chapters (fiction) by email only. See website for full submission guidelines. No plays or film/TV scripts.

Clients include Dr Rangan Chatterjee, Ed Yong, Rutger Bregman, Adam Rutherford, Mya-Rose Craig, Hannah Fry, Matt Parker, Michel Faber, Olivia Laing, Sunjeev Sahota, Kiran Millwood Hargrave, MJ Arlidge, Elly Griffiths, Xiaolu Guo, Sharna Jackson. *Founded* 2000.

JFL Agency Ltd
48 Charlotte Street, London W1T 2NS
tel 020-3137 8182
email agents@jflagency.com
website www.jflagency.com
Agents Alison Finch, Dominic Lord, Gary Wild

TV, radio, film. *Commission* 10%. Initial contact by preliminary email; do not send scripts in the first instance. See website for further information. No novels, short stories or poetry.

Clients include Humphrey Barclay, Adam Bostock-Smith, Bill Dare, Ed Dyson, Phil Ford, Rob Gittins,

Gabby Hutchinson Crouch, Anji Loman Field, Lisa McMullin, Julie Parsons, David Semple, James Serafinowicz, Pete Sinclair, Paul Smith, Fraser Steele. *Founded* 2011.

Johnson & Alcock Ltd*
Bloomsbury House, 74–77 Great Russell Street,
London WC1B 3DA
tel 020-7251 0125
website www.johnsonandalcock.co.uk
Contacts Michael Alcock, Anna Power, Ed Wilson

All types of commercial and literary fiction, and general non-fiction. Young adult and children's fiction (ages 9+). *Commission* Home 15%, USA/translation/film 20%. For fiction and non-fiction, send first three chapters, full synopsis and brief covering letter with details of writing experience. For email submission guidelines see website. Return postage essential. No short stories, poetry or board/picture books. *Founded* 1956.

Tibor Jones & Associates
PO Box 74604, London SW2 9NH
email enquiries@tiborjones.com
website www.tiborjones.com
Contact Kevin Conroy Scott

Literary fiction and non-fiction, category fiction, music autobiographies and biographies. Send first five pages, synopsis and covering letter via email.

Authors include Wilbur Smith, Guillermo Arriaga, Deborah Curtis, Olafur Eliasson, Hala Jaber, Paul Lake, Hans Ulrich Obrist, Bernard Sumner, Christopher Winn. *Founded* 2007.

Robin Jones Literary Agency (RJLA)
66 High Street, Dorchester on Thames OX10 7HN
tel (07916) 293681
email robijones@gmail.com
Twitter @AgentRobinJones
Director Robin Jones

Adult fiction and non-fiction: literary and commercial. Script consultancy, structural and editorial development, indexing, proofreading, self-publishing consultancy and copy editing services. High-concept non-fiction. Russian and Slavonic themed fiction and non-fiction. Literary, experimental, translated and international fiction. *Commission* Home 15%, overseas 20%. In first instance, send synopsis, 50-page sample, and cover letter detailing writing experience. No theatre/plays, YA or Childrens

Clients include Sir David Madden, Ben Rowland, Alex Flynn, Waqas Ahmed, Chrissie Hynde, Philip Lymbery, Isabel Oakeshott, Paul Jackson. Co-founder of Unthank Books, Unthology, Unthank School and UnLit Festival. *Founded* 2007.

Jane Judd Literary Agency*
18 Belitha Villas, London N1 1PD
tel 020-7607 0273

website www.janejudd.com
Twitter @janelitagent

General non-fiction and fiction. Works with agents in the USA and most foreign countries. *Commission* Home 10%, overseas 20%. No longer accepting new clients.

Authors include Jill Mansell, Anne O'Brien, John Brunner, David Winner, S.W. Perry, Michelle Birkby, Andy Dougan, Quentin Falk, Margaret Rooke, Margret Geraghty. *Founded* 1986.

Kane Literary Agency*

2 Dukes Avenue, London N10 2PT
tel 020-8351 9680
website www.kaneliteraryagency.com
Twitter @YasminKane3
Director Yasmin Kane

Interested in discovering new writers and launching the careers of first-time writers. Literary and commercial fiction, YA and children's fiction – middle grade upwards. Non-fiction: memoirs, metaphysics. *Commission* Home 15%, overseas 20%. Send submissions by email only; no submissions by post. Send first three chapters, a synopsis (one side of A4) and a covering letter, all double-line spaced. See website for further information.

Authors include Mark Stibbe, Richard Butchins, Sarah Harris, Sebastian Siegel, Min Day, Reena Kumarasingham. *Founded* 2004.

Michelle Kass Associates Ltd*

85 Charing Cross Road, London WC2H 0AA
tel 020-7439 1624
website www.michellekass.co.uk
Agents Michelle Kass, Russell Franklin

Literary and commercial fiction. Scripts for film and TV. Works with agents around the world. *Commission* Home 10%, overseas 15–20%. Submit first three chapters. No unsolicited material, phone in first instance. *Founded* 1991.

Keane Kataria Literary Agency

email info@keanekataria.co.uk
website www.keanekataria.co.uk
Partners Sara Keane, Kiran Kataria

Boutique agency representing quality commercial fiction and non-fiction. Women's fiction (including historical and saga), crime, narrative non-fiction/ memoir. *Commission* Home 15%, USA/translation 20%. See website for current submission guidelines. No children's, YA, science fiction/fantasy, academic, short stories, poetry, plays, film/TV scripts.

Clients include Tommy Barnes, Jan Casey, Lucy Coleman, Sareeta Domingo, Lynne Francis, Helen Fripp, Claire Heywood, Jenny Kane, Fay Keenan, Judy Leigh, Rosie Meddon, Beth Moran, Amy Myers, Fiona Veitch Smith, Alexandra Walsh. *Founded* 2014.

Ki Agency Ltd*

Studio 315, ScreenWorks, 22 Highbury Grove,
London N5 2ER
tel 020-3214 8287
email meg@ki-agency.co.uk
email roz@ki-agency.co.uk
email anne@ki-agency.co.uk
website www.ki-agency.co.uk
Twitter @kiagency
Director Meg Davis, *Agents* Roz Kidd, Anne C. Perry

Represents writers of fiction, non-fiction and screenplays for film or TV. Email synopsis and three chapters or full screenplay. No unsolicited MSS. No children's or poetry.

Clients include Anne Perry, M.R. Carey, Claire North, Angela Slatter, Helena Coggan, John Allison, the estate of Fred Hoyle. *Founded* 2011.

Knight Features Ltd

Trident Business Centre, 89 Bickerseth Road,
London SW17 9SH
tel 020-3051 5650
website www.knightfeatures.com
Contacts Gaby Martin, Sam Ferris, Andrew Knight

Business and communication, history and military history, puzzles, general interest and literary estates management. Send letter accompanied by synopsis, three sample chapters and sae, or via website submission page. No fiction, poetry, cookery, memoirs or books for children.

Authors include David J. Bodycombe, Frank Dickens, Barbara Minto, Ralph Barker, Frederic Mullally, David Kerr Cameron, W. H. Canaway, Patrick MacGill. *Founded* 1985.

Knight Hall Agency Ltd

Lower Ground Floor, 7 Mallow Street,
London EC1Y 8RQ
tel 020-3397 2901
email office@knighthallagency.com
website www.knighthallagency.com
Contacts Charlotte Knight, Katie Langridge, Carolin Wolfsdorf

Specialises in writers for stage, screen and radio but also deals in TV and film rights in novels and non-fiction. *Commission* Home 10%, overseas 15%.

Clients include Simon Beaufoy, Jeremy Brock, Sally Gardner, Francis Lee, Liz Lochhead, Martin McDonagh, Simon Nye, Ol Parker, Lucy Prebble, Philip Ridley, Robert Thorogood, Laura Wade, the estate of Siegfried Sassoon. *Founded* 1997.

Laxfield Literary Associates*

email submissions@laxfieldliterary.com
website https://laxfieldliterary.com/
Founder Emma Shercliff

Represents authors from Norfolk and Suffolk plus writers from under-represented backgrounds.

Translation rights, screen rights and permissions are handled by Blake Friedmann Literary Agency. Looking for literary and commercial fiction and non-fiction, particularly creative non-fiction, travel writing, memoir and nature writing. See website for submission guidelines. Does not represent poetry, plays, children's books or YA. *Founded* 2020.

LBA Books*
91 Great Russell Street, London WC1B 3PS
tel 020-7637 1234
email info@lbabooks.com
website www.lbabooks.com
Twitter @LBA_Agency
Agents Luigi Bonomi, Amanda Preston, Louise Lamont, Hannah Schofield

Fiction and non-fiction. Keen to find new authors and help them develop their careers. Works with foreign agencies and has links with film and TV production companies. Fiction: commercial and literary fiction, thrillers, crime, psychological suspense, young adult, children's, women's fiction, fantasy. Non-fiction: history, science, memoir, parenting, lifestyle, cookery, TV tie-in. *Commission* Home 15%, overseas 20%. Send preliminary letter, synopsis and first three chapters. No postal submissions. No poetry, short stories or screenplays.
  Authors include Sarah Alderson, Fern Britton, Emma Cooper, Lesley Kara, Simon Kernick, Susan Lewis, Amy Lloyd, Fiona Lucas, Rachael Lucas, Tom Marcus, Alice Roberts, Simon Scarrow, Heidi Swain, Karen Swan, Alan Titchmarsh. *Founded* 2005.

Susanna Lea Associates Ltd*
South Wing, Somerset House, Strand, London WC2R 1LA
tel 020-7287 7757
email london@susannalea.com
website www.susannalea.com
Twitter @SLALondon
Directors Susanna Lea, Kerry Glencorse

General fiction and non-fiction. Send query letter, brief synopsis, the first three chapters and/or proposal to london@susannalea.com. No plays, screenplays or poetry.
  Authors include Carole Cadwalladr, Tom Service, Ramla Ali, Susan Spindler, Tom Mustill, Marie Phillips, Alice O'Keeffe, Alice Adams, Ingrid Betancourt, Dr Mukwege, Marc Levy, Sabri Louatah, Violaine Huisman, Adélaïde de Clermont-Tonerre. *Founded* in Paris 2000, New York 2004 and London 2008.

Barbara Levy Literary Agency*
64 Greenhill, Hampstead High Street, London NW3 5TZ
tel 020-7435 9046
email submissions@barbaralevyagency.com
website www.barbaralevyagency.com
Director Barbara Levy, *Associate* John Selby (solicitor)

Translation rights handled by the Buckman Agency; works in conjunction with US agents. Adult fiction and general non-fiction. Film and TV rights for existing clients only. *Commission* Full-length MSS: home 15%, overseas by arrangement. Preliminary letter with synopsis and sae essential, or by email. *Founded* 1986.

Limelight Celebrity Management Ltd*
10 Filmer Mews, 75 Filmer Road, London SW6 7JF
tel 020-7384 9950
email mail@limelightmanagement.com
website www.limelightmanagement.com
Facebook www.facebook.com/LimelightCelebrityManagement/
Twitter @Fionalimelight
Contacts Fiona Lindsay, Maclean Lindsay

General fiction, crime, thrillers, historical, suspense, mystery, women's commercial fiction. Also non-fiction in the areas of arts and crafts, cookery, biography, autobiography, popular science, business, natural history, sport, travel and health. *Commission* Full-length and short MSS: home 15%, overseas 20%, TV and radio rights 10–20%. Will suggest revision where appropriate.
  Clients include James Martin, Oz Clarke, Theo Randall, Paul Gayler, Antony Worrall Thompson, Nigel Colborn, Tim Wonnacott, Pierre Koffman, Salvatore Calabrese, Lesley Waters. *Founded* 1991.

Lindsay Literary Agency*
East Worldham House, Alton, Hants GU34 3AT
tel (01420) 831430
email info@lindsayliteraryagency.co.uk
website www.lindsayliteraryagency.co.uk
Twitter @LindsayLit
Director Becky Bagnell

Specialists in children's fiction and non-fiction, teen/YA, middle grade, picture books. *Commission* Home 15%, translation 20%. Send first three chapters, synopsis and covering letter by email. No submissions by post. Will suggest revision.
  Authors include Pamela Butchart, Christina Collins, Donna David, Sam Gayton, Ruth Hatfield, Larry Hayes, J. M. Joseph, Giles Paley-Phillips, Sharon Tregenza, Rachel Valentine, Sue Wallman, Joe Wilson. *Founded* 2008.

The Liverpool Literary Agency
tel 07742 603459, 07917 788964
email contact@liverpoolediting.co.uk
website www.liverpool-literary.agency
Twitter @LiverpoolLit
Agents Clare Coombes, Matthew McKeown, Laura Bennett

Looking for fiction novels across all genres. Submissions should include a synopsis and the first three chapters by email, with an author bio included in the covering email. See website for further submission guidelines. Do not accept children's, scripts, non-fiction, poetry, short stories or YA. *Founded* 2020.

Andrew Lownie Literary Agency

36 Great Smith Street, London SW1P 3BU
tel 020-7222 7574
email andrew@andrewlownie.co.uk
website www.andrewlownie.co.uk
Twitter @andrewlownie
Director Andrew Lownie

Handles non-fiction, working in association with a range of sub-agents around the world. The list includes biography, history, reference, current affairs and packaging journalists and celebrities for the book market. Represents inspirational memoirs (Cathy Glass, Casey Watson) and ghostwriters. *Commission* Home and USA 15%, translation and film 20%. Non-fiction submissions should include synopsis, author profile, chapter summaries and sample material. Will suggest revision.
   Authors include Jeremy Dronfield, Juliet Barker, the Joyce Cary estate, Roger Crowley, Tom Devine, Robert Hutchinson, Lawrence James, the Julian Maclaren-Ross estate, Sean McMeekin, Daniel Tammet, *The Oxford Classical Dictionary*, *The Cambridge Guide to Literature in English*. *Founded* 1988.

Luithlen Agency

88 Holmfield Road, Leicester LE2 1SB
tel 0116 273 8863
email penny@luithlenagency.com
website www.luithlenagency.com
Agents Jennifer Luithlen, Penny Luithlen

Children's fiction, all ages to YA. *Commission* Home 15%, overseas 20%, performance rights 15%. See website for submission information. *Founded* 1986.

Lutyens & Rubinstein*

21 Kensington Park Road, London W11 2EU
tel 020-7792 4855
email submissions@lutyensrubinstein.co.uk
website www.lutyensrubinstein.co.uk
Agents Sarah Lutyens, Felicity Rubinstein, Jane Finigan, Daisy Parente, Jenny Hewson, Francesca Davies *Contact* Susannah Godman

Fiction and non-fiction, commercial and literary. *Commission* Home 15%, overseas 20%. Send material by email with a covering letter and short synopsis. Submissions not accepted by hand or by post. *Founded* 1993.

David Luxton Associates Ltd*

23 Hillcourt Avenue, London N12 8EY
website www.davidluxtonassociates.co.uk
Twitter @DLuxAssociates
Instagram davidluxtonassociates
Agents David Luxton, Rebecca Winfield, Nick Walters

Agency specialising in non-fiction, especially sport, memoir, history, politics and nature writing. Also handles foreign rights for September Publishing, Judith Murdoch, Eve White, Kate Nash and Graham Maw Christie Literary Agency. Consult website for submission guidelines. Sports and general non-fiction submissions should be directed to Stella Dodwell (admin@davidluxtonassociates.co.uk). For Memoir, history, travel and popular reference email Rebecca Winfield (rebecca@rebeccawinfield.com). *Founded* 2011.

Duncan McAra

3 Viewfield Avenue, Bishopbriggs, Glasgow G64 2AG
tel 0141 772 1067
email duncanmcara@mac.com

Literary fiction; non-fiction. Art, architecture, archaeology, biography, military, Scottish, travel. *Commission* Home 15%, USA/translation 20%. Preliminary email or letter with sae essential.
   Clients include Lorna Almonds-Windmill, Devon Cox, Rosemary Hannah, Brian Izzard, James Miller, Jules Stewart and Helen Crisp. *Founded* 1988.

Eunice McMullen Ltd

Low Ibbotsholme Cottage, Off Bridge Lane, Troutbeck Bridge, Windermere, Cumbria LA23 1HU
tel (01539) 448551
email eunice@eunicemcmullen.co.uk
website www.eunicemcmullen.co.uk
Director Eunice McMullen

All types of children's fiction, particularly picture books and older fiction. *Commission* Home 15%, overseas 15%. No unsolicited scripts. Telephone or email enquiries only.
   Authors include Ross Collins, Emma Dodd, Alison Friend, Charles Fuge, Cally Johnson Isaacs, Sarah Massini, James Mayhew, David Melling, Angela McAllister, Angie Sage. *Founded* 1992.

Andrew Mann Ltd*

6 Quernmore Road, London N4 4QU
tel 020-7609 6218
email tina@andrewmann.co.uk
website www.andrewmann.co.uk
Twitter @AML_Literary
Contacts Tina Betts

Currently closed to new submissions. *Founded* 1975.

Marjacq Scripts Ltd*

The Space, 235 High Holborn, London WC1V 7LE
tel 020-7935 9499
email firstname@marjacq.com
website www.marjacq.com
Twitter @MarjacqScripts
Contacts Diana Beaumont (commercial fiction and non-fiction), Leah Middleton (commercial fiction and non-fiction, Film & TV rights, screenwriters), Philip Patterson (commercial and literary fiction, and

non-fiction), Imogen Pelham (literary and upmarket fiction and non-fiction), Catherine Pellegrino (children's, YA, and romance), Sandra Sawicka (genre and speculative fiction)

Full-service agency. Handles all rights. In-house legal, foreign rights, book-to-film and interactive media support. Commercial and literary fiction and non-fiction, crime, thrillers, horror, science fiction, commercial women's fiction, graphic novels, children's, history, lifestyle, contemporary issues, screenwriting. *Commission* Home 15%, overseas/film 20%. Send first 50 pages with synopsis by email to appropriate agent. See website for further submission guidelines. No poetry. No theatre.

Clients include Daisy Buchanan, Angela Clarke, Roopa Farooki, Helen FitzGerald, Finbar Hawkins, Paul Herron, David Keenan, Marie Le Conte, Stuart MacBride, Claire McGowan, Alex North, Bryony Pearce, Kassia St Clair, Luca Veste, Matt Wesolowski. *Founded* 1973.

The Marsh Agency Ltd*

50 Albemarle Street, London W1S 4BD
tel 020-7493 4361
email hello@marsh-agency.co.uk
website www.marsh-agency.co.uk

The Marsh Agency offers international representation to a wide range of writers, literary agents and publishing companies. No unsolicited submissions. *Founded* 1994.

MBA Literary and Script Agents Ltd*

62 Grafton Way, London W1T 5DW
tel 020-7387 2076
website www.mbalit.co.uk
Twitter @mbaagents
Book agents Diana Tyler, Laura Longrigg, David Riding, Susan Smith, Sophie Gorell Barnes, *Film/TV/Radio/Theatre agent* Diana Tyler

Fiction and non-fiction, children's books. Foreign rights handled by Louisa Pritchard Associates. *Commission* Home 15%, overseas 20%, TV/theatre/radio 10%, films 15%. See website for submission guidelines.

Clients include Amanda Brown, Jeffrey Caine, Alex Dahl, Jean Fullerton, Jay Jayamohan, Julian Jones, Rosanna Ley, estate of Anne McCaffrey, Alice Nutter, Ollie Ollerton, Stef Penney, Iain Sinclair. *Founded* 1971.

Madeleine Milburn Literary, TV & Film Agency*

The Factory, 1 Park Hill, Clapham, London SW4 9NS
tel 020-7499 7550
email submissions@madeleinemilburn.com
website www.madeleinemilburn.co.uk
Facebook www.facebook.com/MadeleineMilburnLiteraryAgency
Twitter @MMLitAgency

Contacts Madeleine Milburn (Director & Agent), Giles Milburn (Managing Director & Agent), Liane-Louise Smith (Rights Director), Georgina Simmonds (Rights Agent), Hannah Ladds (Dramatic Rights Agent), Emma Dawson (Operations), Hayley Steed (Agent), Olivia Maidment (Associate Agent), Emma Bal (Non-Fiction Agent), Chloe Seager (Children's & YA Agent), Rachel Yeoh (Assistant), Georgia McVeigh (Editorial)

Special interest in launching the careers of debut authors. Represents a dynamic and prize-winning range of bestselling adult fiction and non-fiction, young adult and children's fiction.

Represents British, American, Canadian and international authors. Builds the international careers of authors. Handles all rights in the UK, USA and foreign markets including film/TV/radio and digital. Literary fiction, upmarket commercial fiction, book club, women's, crime, thrillers, psychological suspense, historical, romance, mystery, horror, comedy, fantasy and science fiction, true crime, self-help, wellbeing, cookery, food writing, narrative non-fiction, history, biography, memoir, lifestyle, science, popular psychology, nature, travel, politics, illustrated non-fiction, film/TV tie-ins. Children's fiction for all ages including picture books, 6–8 years, 9–12 years, teen, YA, new adult and crossover. *Commission* Home 15%, USA/translation/film 20%. No longer accepts submissions by post. See submission guidelines and agency news on website. Works editorially with all clients.

Authors include Gail Honeyman, Ashley Audrain, C.J. Tudor, C.L. Taylor, Fiona Barton, Clare Pooley, Elizabeth Kay, Abbie Greaves, Beth Morrey, Holly Bourne, Elizabeth Macneal, Stephanie Wrobel, Nita Prose, Emma Stonex, Mark Edwards, Katherine May, Leah Hazard, Alexandra Wilson. *Founded* 2012.

Rachel Mills Literary Ltd*

email submissions@rmliterary.co.uk
website www.rachelmillsliterary.co.uk
Twitter @rmliterary
Instagram rachelmillsliterary

Focused on fiction and non-fiction which can effect positive change, aimed at an upmarket, mainstream audience. Non-fiction: big ideas books, popular science, popular economics, popular psychology, narrative non-fiction, literary memoir, memoir plus, health, wellbeing, lifestyle, food, the environment, feminism, nature writing. Fiction: literary, commercial, clever and upmarket female fiction, historical, suspense, thrillers, crime, high concept. *Commission* Home 15%, overseas 20%, film/TV 20%. Send synopsis and first three chapters for fiction. For non-fiction send proposal and full biography. Does not represent erotica, children's science fiction, fantasy, business, educational or academic books.

Authors include Elizabeth Day, Bryony Gordon, Sara Collins, Heidi Perks, Catherine Gray, Alice Vincent, Hassan Akkad, David Nutt, Peter Walker, Uju Asika,

Claire Ratinon, Max La Manna and Twisted. *Founded* 2019.

MMB Creative (Mulcahy Sweeney Associates Ltd)*
The Old Truman Brewery, 91 Brick Lane, London E1 6QL
tel 020-3582 9379
website https://mmbcreative.com/
Twitter @MulcahyLitAgent
Contacts Ivan Mulcahy, Sallyanne Sweeney

Fiction, non-fiction. Biography, crime, finance, historical, lifestyle, sport, thrillers, women's interests, adult, children's, youth, commercial, literary. Send query with synopsis, author bio and sample writing via website only. See website for full guidelines.

Clients include Benet Brandreth, Ha-Joon Chang, Sarah Davis-Goff, Juno Dawson, Felicity Everett, Ian Kelly, Steven Lenton, Lisa McInerney, Alan McMonagle, Roisin Meaney, David Mitchell, Sarah Painter, Simon Philip, E.M. Reapy, Robert Webb.

Morgan Green Creatives Ltd
157 Ribblesdale Road, London SW16 6SP
email kirsty@morgangreencreatives.com
website www.morgangreencreatives.com
Founder Kirsty McLachlan

Actively looking for fresh talent and want to be challenged with new ideas, inspired and moved by great writing, and to find unique and distinct voices with compelling stories to tell. Represents fiction and non-fiction, children's book writers, poets, scriptwriters, and illustrators. Submission by email which includes a covering letter within the body of the email, plus 30 pages of your work attached.
See website for full client list. *Founded* 2020.

Judith Murdoch Literary Agency*
19 Chalcot Square, London NW1 8YA
tel 020-7722 4197
website www.judithmurdoch.co.uk
Contact Judith Murdoch

Full-length fiction only. Translation rights handled by Rebecca Winfield (rebecca@rebeccawinfield.com). Especially interested in commercial women's fiction and crime. *Commission* Home 15%, overseas 20%. Approach by post, sending the first two chapters and synopsis. Send email address or return postage; no email submissions. Editorial advice given. No science fiction/fantasy, poetry, short stories or children's.

Clients include Diane Allen, Trisha Ashley, Frances Brody, Rosie Clarke, Diney Costeloe, Kate Eastham, Leah Fleming, Faith Hogan, Emma Hornby, Lola Jaye, Sheila Jeffries, Jill McGivering, Kitty Neale, Mary Wood. *Founded* 1993.

Mushens Entertainment*
email jmsubmissions@mushens-entertainment.com
email ldbsubmissions@mushens-entertainment.com
email sesubmissions@mushens-entertainment.com
website www.mushens-entertainment.com
Twitter @mushenska, @lizadeblock, @sileloquies
Twitter @MushensEnt
Contact Juliet Mushens, Liza DeBlock, Silé Edwards

Represents all genres except picture books, non-fiction, novellas, poetry, erotica or children's books. *Commission* Home 15%, overseas 20%. For fiction: email with the subject line QUERY, the cover letter in the body of the email, and a synopsis and the first three chapters or approximately first 50 pages as attachments. Juliet responds to every submission within four weeks of receipt of email. For non-fiction: email with the subject line QUERY, the cover letter in the body of the email and a proposal attached. Please submit to only one agent. Please check website for specific genres they each represent, and to check whether they are currently open to submissions.

Authors include Jessie Burton, Claire Douglas, Stacey Halls, Ali Land, Laura Jane Clark, Taran Matharu, Kuchenga, Della Hicks-Wilson, James Oswald, and Richard Osman. *Founded* 2020.

Kate Nash Literary Agency*
email submissions@katenashlit.co.uk
website www.katenashlit.co.uk
Facebook www.facebook.com/KateNashLiteraryAgency
Twitter @katenashagent
Twitter @robbieguillory
Twitter @justinnashlit
Contacts Kate Nash, Justin Nash, Robbie Guillory

Represents general, genre fiction and popular non-fiction. Open to approaches from both new and established authors. General fiction, literary fiction, crime and thriller, historical fiction, romantic fiction, SFF, popular non-fiction. *Commission* UK and Ireland 15%, USA 15% (direct) and 20% (sub-agented), overseas 20%, book to screen 20%. See website for full submission guidelines. No poetry, drama or children's picture books.

Clients include Amanda Brittany, PR Black, Sylvia Broady, Lesley Cookman, Lucy Cruickshanks, Helena Dixon, Neil Lancaster, Naomi Joy, Jane Lovering, Faith Martin, Andie Newton, Bella Osborne, Alex Shaw, Maggie Sullivan, Joma West. *Founded* 2009.

The North Literary Agency
The Chapel, Market Place, Corbridge, Northumberland NE45 5AW
email hello@thenorthlitagency.com
website www.thenorthlitagency.com
Agents Julie Fergusson, Allan Guthrie, Lina Langlee, Kevin Pocklington, Mark Stanton

Agency based across the north of England and Scotland, doing business globally. Looking for all types of fiction and narrative non-fiction. Email synopsis and 15,000-word sample. Check website for full submission guidelines. No academic writing, poetry, self-help, picture books or screenplays.

Clients include Ned Boulting, Simon Conway, Gavin Extence, Simon Goddard, Cass Green, Sophie Hardach, Roger Hutchinson, John Ironmonger, Ed James, Andy Jones, Sheena Kalayil, Guy Kennaway, Craig Robertson, Adam Southward, the estate of Paul Torday. *Founded* 2017.

Northbank Talent Management*
email info@northbanktalent.com
email fiction@northbanktalent.com
email nonfiction@northbanktalent.com
website www.northbanktalent.com
Twitter @northbanktalent

Commercial fiction, non-fiction and children's books. Fiction: women's fiction, reading group fiction, crime, thrillers, literary fiction with a strong storyline, high-concept fantasy, young adult, middle grade, children's. Non-fiction: politics, current affairs, memoir, real-life stories, celebrity, autobiography, biography, business, popular history, popular science, self-help, popular psychology, children's. *Commission* Home 15%, overseas and rights in other media 20%. Send cover letter, synopsis and first three chapters as Word or Open Document attachments. Aims to give initial response within two weeks. No poetry, academic books, plays, scripts or short stories.

Authors include Brian Cox, Iain Dale, Anthony Seldon, Camilla Cavendish, Damian Collins, Carla Valentine, Christopher Harding, Jonathan Rugman, Katerina Diamond, Rachel Wells, Marion Todd, Catherine Mangan. *Founded* 2006.

Andrew Nurnberg Associates Ltd*
3–11 Eyre Street Hill, London EC1R 5ET
tel 020-3327 0400
email info@nurnberg.co.uk
website www.andrewnurnberg.com
Twitter @nurnberg_agency

Represents adult and children's authors, agent and publisher clients in the fields of literary and commercial fiction and general non-fiction for the sale of rights throughout the world via offices in the UK and overseas. *Founded* 1977.

Deborah Owen
78 Narrow Street, Limehouse, London E14 8BP
tel 020-7987 5119/5441
Contact Deborah Owen

Small agency specialising in only two authors: Delia Smith and David Owen. No new authors. *Founded* 1971.

Paper Lion Ltd
13 Grayham Road, New Malden, Surrey KT3 5HR
tel 07748 786199, (01276) 61322
email katyloffman@paperlionltd.com
email lesleypollinger@paperlionltd.com

website www.paperlionltd.com
Agents Katy Loffman, Lesley Pollinger

A cross-media literary agency which brings together the digital publishing expertise of Katy Loffman and Lesley Pollinger's extensive experience as a literary agent. The client list includes award-winning authors, literary estates and publishers. The agency has a strong focus on the exploration of digital opportunities and expertise in solving complex copyright, dramatic rights and literary issues from the present and past.

Clients include Max Allen, Diane Barker, Cordelia Feldman, Stewart Ferris, Catherine Fisher, Bruce Hobson, Nick Drake-Knight, Bruce Montague, Saviour Pirotta, HopeRoad, and the estates of authors including Grantley Dick-Read, D.H. Lawrence, Ada Lovelace and John Wyndham. *Founded* 2017.

PBJ & KBJ Management
22 Rathbone Street, London W1T 1LG
tel 020-7287 1112
email general@pbjmanagement.co.uk
website www.pbjmanagement.co.uk
Contacts Peter Bennett-Jones, Caroline Chignell

Represents writers, performers, presenters, podcasters, composers, directors, producers and DJs. Specialises in comedy. *Commission* Theatre 15%, film/TV/radio 12.5%.

Clients include Rowan Atkinson, Armando Iannucci, Eddie Izzard, Lenny Henry, Hannah Gadsby, Simon Blackwell, Adam Buxton, Richard Ayoade, Tim Minchin, Tim Key, Vic & Bob, Nina Conti, Dylan Moran, Sally Phillips, James Acaster. *Founded* 1987.

Maggie Pearlstine Associates*
31 Ashley Gardens, Ambrosden Avenue, London SW1P 1QE
tel 020-7828 4212
email maggie@pearlstine.co.uk
Contact Maggie Hattersley

Small agency representing a select few authors. No new authors.

Authors include Matthew Baylis, Lord (Menzies) Campbell, Jamie Crawford, Mark Douglas-Home, Roy Hattersley, Prof. Lesley Regan, Winifred Robinson and Christopher Ward. *Founded* 1989.

Kay Peddle Literary*
email kay@kaypeddleliterary.co.uk
website https://kaypeddleliterary.co.uk/
Twitter @KayPeddle
Instagram kaypeddlebooks

Specialist non-fiction agency focusing on narrative non-fiction, literary memoir, cookery & food writing, travel writing, nature writing, journalism with a social justice angle, politics, current affairs, history and popular science. Submission by email only. Include a brief pitch about your book/idea in the body of the email and attach a word document that includes the cover letter and proposal. See website for what should be included in the letter and proposal. Does not represent fiction, including children's.

Authors include Helen Graves, Kimberly McIntosh, Jess Morgan, Dr Joe Mulhall, Rebecca Omonira-Oyekanmi, Tom Rowley.

Jonathan Pegg Literary Agency*
67 Wingate Square, London SW4 0AF
tel 020-7603 6830
email submissions@jonathanpegg.com
email info@jonathanpegg.com
website www.jonathanpegg.com
Founder and Agent Jonathan Pegg

Specialises in full-length quality fiction and non-fiction. See website for genre categories represented. *Commission* Direct 15%, co-agented 20%. Email submissions accepted. See website for submission guidelines. Does not represent children's fiction, YA, pure fantasy.

Authors include Dr Nafeez Ahmed, Michael Blastland, Steve Bloomfield, Alex Brummer, Alex Christofi, Nick Davies, Dr Stuart Farrimond, Kaffe Fassett OBE, Zac Goldsmith, Robert Lacey, Tom McCarthy, General Sir Michael Rose, Jonathan and Angela Scott, Carolyn Steel and Professor Sir David Spiegelhalter OBE. *Founded* 2008.

PEW Literary*
46 Lexington Street, London W1F 0LP
tel 020-7734 4464
email info@pewliterary.com
website www.pewliterary.com
Agents Patrick Walsh, Margaret Halton, John Ash, Eleanor Birne, Doug Young

Boutique agency with a strong list of prize-winning authors. Non-fiction, fiction, graphic novels. *Commission* Home 15%, overseas 20%, film and TV 20%. See website for submission guidelines. No poetry, children's picture books, plays or academic titles.

Clients include: novelists Nick Harkaway, H.M. Naqvi, Luke Jennings and Keggie Carew; non-fiction writers Laura Cumming, Jim al-Khalili, Tom Holland, Helen Castor, Andrea Wulf, Anita Anand, Gaia Vince, Simon Singh, Bill Browder and Mark Cocker; and artists including David Shrigley. *Founded* 2016.

Peters Fraser & Dunlop Ltd*
55 New Oxford Street, London WC1A 1BS
tel 020-7344 1000
email info@pfd.co.uk
website www.petersfraserdunlop.com
Facebook www.facebook.com/pfdagents
Twitter @PFDAgents
Ceo Caroline Michel, *Book agents* Caroline Michel, Annabel Merullo, Elizabeth Sheinkman, Tim Bates, Adam Gauntlett, Silvia Molteni, Fiona Petheram,

Tessa David, Lucy Irvine, Laurie Robertson, *Theatrical Rights* Adam Gauntlett, *Children's agent and Audio Rights* Silvia Molteni, Lucy Irvine, *Theatrical Rights* Adam Gauntlett, *Foreign Rights* Rebecca Wearmouth, Lisette Verhagan, Lucy Barry, Antonia Kasoulidou, Silvia Molteni, Lucy Irvine, *Estates* Dan Fenton, Giulia Bernabe, *Broadcast and Live Events* Tris Payne, Riman Salim, *TV and Film Rights* Jonathan Sissons, Rosie Gurtovoy, *Journalism* Laurie Robertson

Represents authors of fiction and non-fiction, presenters and public speakers throughout the world. PFD runs its own digital publishing imprint called Agora Books Ltd (www.agorabooks.co). Covering letter, synopsis or outline and first three chapters as well as author biographies should be addressed to individual agents. Return postage necessary. See website for submission guidelines. Does not represent scriptwriters.

Authors include Jeanette Winterson, Simon Schama, Edna O'Brien, Bear Grylls, Michael Caine, Onjali Q. Rauf, Lisa Thompson, Jamie Bartlett, Lesley Pearce, Chi-chi Nwanoku, Rose Tremain, Niall Williams, Jamie Susskind, Kenya Hunt, Ruby Wax. *Founded* 1924.

Shelley Power Literary Agency Ltd*
33 Dumbrells Court, North End, Ditchling, East Sussex BN6 8TG
tel (01273) 844467
email sp@shelleypower.co.uk
Contact Shelley Power

General fiction and non-fiction. Works in conjunction with agents abroad. No longer accepting submissions. *Commission* Full-length MSS: home 12.5%, USA/translation 20%. Preliminary letter essential – may be sent by email. No children's books, YA, science fiction, fantasy, short stories, poetry, screenplays or plays. *Founded* 1976.

Joey Quincey Literary Agency
17 Carlton House Terrace, St James's, London, SW1Y 5AH
tel 07396 344505
email joey@jq-agency.co.uk
website www.jq-agency.co.uk
Director Joey Quincey

Actively looking for authors from BAME backgrounds who explore identity, cultural duality and diaspora, particularly in urban, inner-city areas. The Agency represents Children's middle grade, YA and fantasy fiction; commercial literary fiction and lifestyle non-fiction. Email in first instance with a summary of the book plus an author bio. *Founded* 2019.

Redhammer Management Ltd
website www.redhammer.info
Vice President Peter Cox

A boutique literary agency providing in-depth management for a restricted number of clients. Specialises in works with international book, film and television potential. Submissions must follow the guidelines given on the website. Do not send unsolicited MSS by post. No radio or theatre scripts.

The Lisa Richards Agency

108 Upper Leeson Street, Dublin D04 E3E7, Republic of Ireland
tel +353 (0)1 637 5000
email info@lisarichards.ie
website www.lisarichards.ie
Contact Faith O'Grady

Handles fiction and general non-fiction. Overseas associate: The Marsh Agency for translation rights. *Commission* Ireland 10%, UK 15%, USA/translation 20%, film/TV 15%. Approach with proposal and sample chapter for non-fiction and three to four chapters and synopsis for fiction (sae essential).
   Clients include Prof. Marie Cassidy, Dr Alan Desmond, Aoife Dooley, Austin Duffy, Christine Dwyer Hickey, Paul Howard (aka Ross O'Carroll-Kelly), Gerry Hussey, Ann Ingle, Trish Kearney, Laura McKenna, Daniella Moyles, David O'Doherty, The Happy Pear, Gillian Perdue, Deborah Somorin. *Founded* 1998.

Richford Becklow Agency

2 Church Street, Peasenhall, Suffolk IP17 2HL
tel (01728) 660879
email enquiries@richfordbecklow.co.uk
website www.richfordbecklow.com
Twitter @richfordbecklow
Contact Lisa Eveleigh

Literary and commercial fiction and non-fiction. Historical fiction, saga, crime, romantic comedy, biography and memoir. *Commission* Home 15%, overseas 20%. No postal submissions; will only respond to email submissions. Ensure you visit the website regarding submissions before approaching the agency. Does not represent books for children or young adults.
   Authors include Amanda Austen, Mary Alexander, Caroline Ashton, Hugo Barnacle, Stephen Buck, Anne Corlett, Jane Gordon-Cumming, A.D. Lynn, R.P. Marshall, Madalyn Morgan, Tony Slattery, Jonathan Socrates, Grace Wynne-Jones, Sophie Parkin, Adrienne Vaughan. *Founded* 2011.

Robertson Murray Literary Agency

3rd Floor, 37 Great Portland Street, London, W1W 8QH
tel 020-7580 0702
email info@robertsonmurray.com
website https://robertsonmurray.com/
Facebook www.facebook.com/
RobertsonMurrayLiteraryAgency
Twitter @RMLitAgency

Co-founders Charlotte Robertson, Hilary Murray, *Agent* Jenny Heller

Fiction: commercial and literary fiction in any genre except science fiction. Non-fiction: welcomes all non-fiction, including memoir and biography, personal development, lifestyle, cookery, history, current affairs, popular science, sport and humour. Submission via the website which includes full submission guidelines. Does not represent academic texts, poetry, or scripts for film, TV or stage. Currently closed for new children's submissions.
   Full client list on website. *Founded* 2019.

Rocking Chair Books Literary Agency*

2 Rudgwick Terrace, St Stephens Close, London NW8 6BR
email representme@rockingchairbooks.com
website www.rockingchairbooks.com
Twitter @rockingbooks
Contact Samar Hammam

Dedicated to original and page-turning books and looking for stories that are both inspired and inspiring. Focuses on adult commercial fiction, literary fiction, graphic novels and non-fiction for publication around the world. Also works with other agencies to represent their translation or English language rights, including Mulcahy Sweeney Associates and the Raya Agency. *Commission* Home 15%, translation/adaptation rights 20%. Submission by email only. No children's, YA or science fiction (unless they are crossover).
   Authors include Warsan Shire, Brian Turner, Mike Medaglia, Amita Murray, Nydia Hetherington, Laura Coleman. As co-agent alongside The Raya Agency for Arabic Literature in Translation: Dima Wannous, Khaled Khalifa, Samar Yazbek, Hoda Barakat. *Founded* 2013.

Rogers, Coleridge & White Ltd*

20 Powis Mews, London W11 1JN
tel 020-7221 3717
email info@rcwlitagency.com
website www.rcwlitagency.com
Twitter @RCWLitAgency
Instagram rcwliteraryagency
Managing Director Peter Straus, *Finance Director* Nelka Bell, *Directors* Sam Copeland, Stephen Edwards, Natasha Fairweather, Georgia Garrett, Laurence Laluyaux, Zoe Waldie, Claire Wilson, *Agents* Cara Jones, Jon Wood

International representation for all genres of fiction, non-fiction, children's and YA. *Commission* Home 15%, USA 20%, translation 20%. Note that due to the volume of unsolicited queries, it is policy to respond (usually within six weeks) only if interested in the material. See website for submissions information.
   Clients include household names, bestsellers and winners of Nobel, Booker, Pulitzer, Waterstones,

Blue Peter, Costa and Carnegie prizes. *Founded* 1967 as Deborah Rogers Ltd, 1989 as Rogers, Coleridge and White Ltd.

Elizabeth Roy Literary Agency
White Cottage, Greatford, Nr Stamford,
Lincolnshire PE9 4PR
tel (01778) 560672
website www.elizabethroy.co.uk

Children's fiction, picture books and non-fiction – writers and illustrators. *Commission* Home 15%, overseas 20%. Send preliminary letter, synopsis and sample chapters with names of publishers and agents previously contacted. Return postage essential. *Founded* 1990.

The Ruppin Agency
website www.ruppinagency.com
Twitter @ruppinagency
Directors Jonathan Ruppin, Emma Claire Sweeney

Represents both commercial and literary fiction, and serious non-fiction. Looking for writing with ambition, originality and relevance. Particularly interested in submissions from writers from under-represented communities: working class, LGBTQ+, people of colour, those with disabilities, those outside London catchment area. Also operates Writers' Studio, a nationwide mentoring scheme for writers of fiction, YA and non-fiction, directed by author Emma Claire Sweeney. *Commission* Home 15%, translation 20% (rights handled by The Marsh Agency). Full details of areas of interest and submission requirements on website. No science fiction, fantasy, horror, poetry, plays, graphic novels, children's/YA, professional or academic.

   Clients include Selma Carvalho, Aoife Mannix, Rebecca Monks, Sally J. Morgan, Jude Piesse, Devika Ponnambalam, Mark Thwaite, Nicola Williams, Richard Zimler. *Founded* 2017.

The Sayle Literary Agency*
1 Petersfield, Cambridge CB1 1BB
tel (01223) 303035
email info@sayleliteraryagency.com
website www.sayleliteraryagency.com
Proprietor and Agent Rachel Calder

Uses specialist co-agents to sell books in foreign language markets, in the USA and for film/TV. Translation rights handled by The Marsh Agency Ltd. Film and TV rights handled by Sayle Screen Ltd. US rights handled by Dunow, Carlson and Lerner. Fiction: general, literary and crime. Non-fiction: current affairs, social issues, travel, biographies, history. *Commission* Home 15%, USA/translation 20%. List is currently closed. No plays, poetry, textbooks, children's, technical, legal or medical books. *Founded* 1896.

Sayle Screen Ltd
11 Jubilee Place, London SW3 3TD
tel 020-7823 3883

email info@saylescreen.com
website www.saylescreen.com
Agents Jane Villiers, Matthew Bates, Kelly Knatchbull, Eva Robinson

Specialises in scripts for film, TV, theatre and radio. Represents film, TV and theatre rights in fiction and non-fiction for The Sayle Literary Agency, JULA Ltd, Greene & Heaton Ltd and Rogers, Coleridge and White Ltd. Works in conjunction with agents in New York and Los Angeles. Unable to consider unsolicited material unless recommended by producer, development executive or course tutor. If this is the case, email a CV, covering letter and details of your referee or course tutor to submissions@saylescreen.com. Every submission carefully considered, but responds only to submissions it wishes to take further; not able to return material sent in.

The Science Factory Ltd
Scheideweg 34C, 20253 Hamburg, Germany
tel +49 (0)40 4327 2959 (Germany), 020-7193 7296 (Skype)
email info@sciencefactory.co.uk
website www.sciencefactory.co.uk
Twitter @sciencefactory
Director/Agent Peter Tallack (Germany), *Agents* Jeff Shreve, Tisse Takagi (New York)

With experience in both scholarly and commercial publishing, the agency specialises in stimulating non-fiction written by public intellectuals, academics and journalists, and offers an enthusiastic, personal and dedicated service in all markets, media and languages across the world. Represents all areas of non-fiction including history, biography, memoir, politics, current affairs and travel, as well as science. *Commission* Home 15%, overseas 20%. In first instance send proposal with chapter summaries and sample chapter (not the first). Email submissions only (material sent by post not returned). May suggest revision. No fiction.

   Clients include Adam Becker, Jesse Bering, Matthew Cobb, Trevor Cox, Lone Frank, Kate Greene, David Hand, Simon Ings, Mark Miondownick, Michael Nielsen, Abby Norman, Massimo Pigliucci, Quanta magazine, Angela Saini and Ramesh Srinivasan. *Founded* 2008. UK-registered limited company.

Linda Seifert Management Ltd
29-30 Fitzroy Square, London W1T 6LQ
tel 020-3327 1180
email contact@lindaseifert.com
website https://lindaseifert.com
Twitter @lindaseifert
Agent Edward Hughes

Represents writers, directors and producers for film, TV and radio only. *Commission* Home 10%, overseas 20%. No book authors.
   Client list ranges from the highly established to the emerging talent of tomorrow – see website for details.

Not currently accepting unsolicited submissions. *Founded* 2002.

The Sharland Organisation Ltd

The Manor House, Manor Street, Raunds, Northants NN9 6JW
tel (01933) 626600
email tso@btconnect.com
website www.sharlandorganisation.co.uk
Directors Mike Sharland, Alice Sharland

Specialises in film, TV and stage rights throughout the world. Preliminary letter and return postage is essential. *Founded* 1988.

Sheil Land Associates Ltd

52 Doughty Street, London WC1N 2LS
tel 020-7405 9351
email info@sheilland.co.uk
website www.sheilland.co.uk
Twitter @sheilland
Agents UK and USA Sonia Land, Vivien Green, Piers Blofeld, Ian Drury, Gaia Banks *Film/theatre/TV* Lucy Fawcett, *Foreign Rights* Gaia Banks, Alba Arnau

Quality literary and commercial fiction and non-fiction, fantasy, military history and saga. Also film, TV, radio and theatre representation, adult and children's. Overseas associates Georges Borchardt, Inc. US film and TV representation: CAA, APA and others. Genres include politics, history, military history, gardening, thrillers, crime, romance, drama, science fiction, fantasy, young adult, biography, travel, cookery, humour, popular fiction and non-fiction, literary and commercial. *Commission* Home 15%, USA/translation 20%. Welcomes approaches from new clients to start or to develop their careers. See website for submission instructions.

Clients include Sally Abbott, Peter Ackroyd, Pam Ayres, Steven Carroll, Nadine Dorries, Robert Fabbri, Graham Hancock, Susan Hill, Mark Lawrence, The Brothers McLeod, Gill Paul, Diane Setterfield, Neil White, and the estates of Catherine Cookson and Patrick O'Brian. *Founded* 1962.

Caroline Sheldon Literary Agency Ltd*

71 Hillgate Place, London W8 7SS
tel 020-7727 9102
email info@carolinesheldon.co.uk
website www.carolinesheldon.co.uk
Twitter @CarolineAgent
Twitter @FelicityTrew
Contacts Caroline Sheldon, Felicity Trew

Represents fiction, non-fiction, children's books and illustration. Interested in all the major fiction genres – historical, romance, contemporary, humour, fantasy, crime and thriller. In non-fiction, interested in personal stories and anything involving animals. Represents children's books in every genre and age range from picture books through middle grade to YA. In illustration, the agency is looking for high-quality work in every style. *Commission* Home 15%, USA/translation 20%, film/TV 20%. Authors – send an introductory email addressed to either Caroline or Felicity with the first three chapters or equivalent length attached. In the subject line write 'Proposal' and title of the work. At head of the email include a three-line synopsis of the work and give further full information in the email about the work and about yourself. Illustrators – send an introductory email addressed to either Caroline or Felicity with work attached or a link to your work. In the subject line write 'Proposal from Illustrator', and include information about yourself and your work in the email.

Represents prominent, award-winning and bestselling clients in all fields including books, audio, digital and theatre. Works closely with a media agent on film, TV and other opportunities. *Founded* 1985.

Sinclair-Stevenson

3 South Terrace, London SW7 2TB
tel 020-7581 2550
Directors Christopher Sinclair-Stevenson, Deborah Sinclair-Stevenson

General – no children's books. *Commission* Full-length MSS, home 15%, USA/translation 20%. Will suggest revision. *Founded* 1995.

Skylark Literary Limited

19 Parkway, Weybridge, Surrey KT13 9HD
tel 020-8144 7440
email info@skylark-literary.com
email submissions@skylark-literary.com
website www.skylark-literary.com
Facebook www.facebook.com/SkylarkLiteraryLtd
Twitter @skylarklit
Directors Joanna Moult, Amber Caraveo

Specialists in children's and young adult fiction. All genres considered. *Commission* Home 15%, overseas 20%. Keen to support new and established authors. Will consider unsolicited submissions. Agents have editorial backgrounds and will work closely with clients on their manuscripts to increase chances of publication. Submissions by email only. Will suggest revision where appropriate. No adult fiction/non-fiction.

Clients include Amy Wilson, Simon James Green, Alyssa Hollingsworth, Rachel Burge, Nizrana Farook. *Founded* 2014.

Robert Smith Literary Agency Ltd*

12 Bridge Wharf, 156 Caledonian Road, London N1 9UU
tel 020-7278 2444
email robert@robertsmithliteraryagency.com
website www.robertsmithliteraryagency.com
Directors Robert Smith, Anne Smith

Predominantly non-fiction. Autobiography and biography, topical subjects, history, lifestyle, popular culture, entertainment, sport, true crime, cookery, health and nutrition, illustrated books. *Commission* Home 15%, overseas 20%. No unsolicited MSS. Will suggest revision.

Authors include Victoria Aitken, Sarbjit Athwal, Peta Bee, Clive Driscoll, Mike Dunn, Penny Farmer, Stephen Fulcher, Roberta Kray, Mo Lea, Carol Ann Lee, Marie McCourt, Ann Ming, Theo Paphitis, Derek and Pauline Tremain, James Reed. *Founded* 1997.

The Soho Agency Ltd*

(previously LAW/Lucas Alexander Whitley Ltd)
16–17 Wardour Mews, 2nd Floor, London W1F 8AT
tel 020-7471 7900
email admin@thesohoagency.co.uk
website www.thesohoagency.co.uk
Twitter @TheSohoAgencyUK
Agents Mark Lucas, Julian Alexander, Araminta Whitley, Rowan Lawton, Alice Saunders, Ben Clark, Sophie Laurimore, Helen Mumby, Carina Rizvi, Philippa Milnes-Smith (Children's and YA), *Associate Agents* Marina de Pass, Niamh O'Grady

Full-length commercial and literary fiction, non-fiction, fantasy, young adult and children's books. Special interests (fiction): accessible literary fiction, character-led narrative, contemporary romance, crime, domestic dramas, historical, psychological suspense and thrillers, reading group fiction, romantic comedy, women's fiction. Special interests (non-fiction): big ideas, business, history, inspirational stories and people, leadership, memoir, philosophy, science. *Commission* Home 15%, USA/translation 20%. Representation in all markets. Unsolicited MSS considered. See website for further information about the clients and genres represented and essential information on submissions. No postal submissions. No plays, poetry or textbooks. Film, TV and stage handled for established clients only.

Clients include Tom Bradby, Kate Eberlen, Frank Gardner, Bettany Hughes, Lindsey Kelk, Sophie Kinsella, Andy McNab, Kate Mosse, Henry Marsh, Chris Riddell, Michael Robotham, Jasvinder Sanghera, Nigel Slater, Tabitha Webb, Alison Weir. *Founded* 1996.

SP Literary Agency

email info@sp-agency.co.uk
website https://sp-agency.co.uk/
Facebook www.facebook.com/sp.literary.agency
Agents Philippa Perry, Abigail Sparrow

Represents authors and illustrators across children's, YA and adult fiction and non-fiction. Email submissions are preferred; attach a synopsis and the first three chapters to a covering email. Children's or YA submissions should also be clearly marked in the subject line.

See website for client list.

Elaine Steel Writers' Agent*

49 Greek Street, London W1D 4EG
tel (01273) 739022
email info@elainesteel.com
website www.elainesteel.com
Contact Elaine Steel

Represents screen, radio, theatre and book writers. Does not read unsolicited material. Any consideration for representation must be by email and accompanied by a CV together with a short outline of the work to be submitted.

Authors include Gwyneth Hughes, Penny Woolcock, James Lovelock, Michael Eaton, Ian Kennedy Martin, Pearse Elliott, Neil Brand, Brian Keenan. *Founded* 1986.

Abner Stein*

Southbank House, Suite 137, Black Prince Road, London SE1 7SJ
tel 020-7373 0456
email info@abnerstein.co.uk
website www.abnerstein.co.uk
Contacts Caspian Dennis, Sandy Violette

Fiction, general non-fiction and children's. *Commission* Home 15%, overseas 20%. Not taking on any new clients at present.

Micheline Steinberg Associates

Studio 315, ScreenWorks, 22 Highbury Grove, London N5 2ER
email info@steinplays.com
website www.steinplays.com
Twitter @SteinbergAssocs
Agent Micheline Steinberg, *Literary Associate* Helen MacAuley

Represents writers/directors for theatre, opera, musicals, television, film, radio and animation, as well as writer-directors, translators and librettists. Media rights in fiction and non-fiction on behalf of book agents, including Juliet Burton Literary Agency and Watson Little Ltd. Also works in association with agents overseas. *Commission* Home 10%, with associates 15–20%. No unsolicited submissions. Industry recommendation preferred. No poetry or prose (except for existing clients).

Authors include David K. Barnes, Hilary Brooks and Clive King, Julie Jones, Rob Kinsman, Jonathan Larkin, Susie McKenna, Glyn Maxwell, Robin Norton-Hale, Debbie Owen, Lisa Parry, Mark Robertson, Danny Spring, Jane Upton, Steve Waters, Sarah Woods. *Founded* 1987.

Rochelle Stevens & Co

2 Terretts Place, Upper Street, London N1 1QZ
tel 020-7359 3900
email info@rochellestevens.com
website www.rochellestevens.com
Twitter @TerrettsPlace
Directors Rochelle Stevens, Frances Arnold

Scripts for TV, theatre and radio. *Commission* 10%. Send preliminary letter, CV, short synopsis and opening ten pages of a drama script by post (sae essential for return of material). See website for full submission guidelines. *Founded* 1984.

Sarah Such Literary Agency
81 Arabella Drive, London SW15 5LL
tel 020-8876 4228
email info@sarah-such.com
website https://sarahsuchliteraryagency.tumblr.com
Twitter @sarahsuch
Director Sarah Such

High-quality literary and commercial non-fiction and fiction for adults, young adults and children. Always looking for exciting new writers with originality and verve. Translation representation: The Buckman Agency. Film/TV representation: Lesley Thorne, Aitken Alexander Associates Ltd. Particular focus on literary and commercial debut novels, thrillers, topical fiction and quality women's fiction, biography, narrative non-fiction, memoir, history, popular culture and humour. *Commission* Home 15%, TV/film 20%, overseas 20%. Will suggest revision. Submit synopsis and three sample chapters (as a Word attachment by email) plus author biography. No postal submissions unless requested. No unsolicited MSS or telephone enquiries. TV/film scripts for established clients only. No radio or theatre scripts, poetry, fantasy, self-help or short stories (unless full collections).

Authors include Matthew De Abaitua, Jeffrey Boakye, Kit Caless, Rob Chapman, Anne Charnock, Heather Cooper, Vina Jackson, Maxim Jakubowski, Antony Johnston, Amy Lankester-Owen, Louisa Leaman, Vesna Maric, Caroline Sanderson, Nikhil Singh, Mike Wendling. *Founded* 2007.

The Susijn Agency Ltd
820 Harrow Road, London NW10 5JU
tel 020-8968 7435
email info@thesusijnagency.com
website www.thesusijnagency.com
Agents Laura Susijn

Specialises in world rights in English- and non-English-language literature: literary fiction and general non-fiction. *Commission* Home 15%, overseas 20%, theatre/film/TV/radio 15%. Send synopsis and three sample chapters.

Authors include Peter Ackroyd, Saud Alsanousi, Robin Baker, Gwynne Dyer, Hwang Sok-yong, Radhika Jha, Uzma Aslam Khan, Christine Leunens, Mazen Maarouf, Jeffrey Moore, Parinoush Sainee, Sunny Singh, Paul Sussman, Alex Wheatle, Yan Lianke. *Founded* 1998.

Emily Sweet Associates
35 Barnfield Road, London W5 1QU
tel 020-8997 6696, 07980 026298
website www.emilysweetassociates.com
Director Emily Sweet

Primarily represents non-fiction genres including history, biography, memoir, topical non-fiction with a particular focus on cookery and lifestyle. *Commission* Home 15%, overseas and translation 20%. No children's or YA.

Clients include Anja Dunk, Joe Trivelli, Anna Koska, Alex Jackson, Joseph Massie, Sumayya Usmani, Shu Han Lee, Heidi Sze, Fliss Chester, N.J. Crosskey. *Founded* 2014.

The Tennyson Agency
109 Tennyson Avenue, New Malden,
Surrey KT3 6NA
tel 020-8942 1039
email agency@tenagy.co.uk
website www.tenagy.co.uk
Agent Adam Sheldon

Scripts and related material for theatre, film, radio and TV only. *Commission* Home 15%, overseas 20%. See website for full submission guidelines. *Founded* 2002.

Simon Trewin Literary and Media Rights Agency
Adam House, 7 Adam Street, London WC1N 6AA
email simon@simontrewin.co.uk
website www.simontrewin.co.uk
Twitter @simontrewin
Instagram simontrewin

Represents fiction and non-fiction. Email in first instance to introduce yourself and the book you are working on.

See website for client list. *Founded* 2019.

Jane Turnbull Agency*
Postal address Barn Cottage, Veryan Churchtown, Truro TR2 5QA
tel (01872) 501317
email jane@janeturnbull.co.uk
website www.janeturnbull.co.uk

Specialises in high quality non-fiction. Works in conjunction with Aitken Alexander Associates Ltd for sale of translation rights. Genres: biography, history, natural history, lifestyle, memoir, humour, TV tie-ins, cookery, some literary and YA fiction. *Commission* Home 15%, USA/translation 20%, performance rights 15%. See website for submission guidelines.

Authors include Kevin McCloud, Prue Leith, Penny Junor, David Lindo, Kate Bradbury, Kate Watson-Smyth, Lucy O'Brien, Andy Mulligan, Frederick Taylor, Lynne Murphy, Richard Van Emden. *Founded* 1986.

Nick Turner Management Ltd
tel 020-7450 3355
email nick@nickturnermanagement.com
website www.nickturnermanagement.com
Twitter @nickturnermgmt
Agents Nick Turner, Phil Adie

Represents writers and directors for film, TV and radio worldwide. Specialises in TV drama, comedy, continuing drama and children's. *Commission* Home 10%, overseas 15–20%. See website for submission guidelines.

See website for client list. *Founded* 2016.

Two Piers Literary Agency
email hello@twopiersagency.com
website https://twopiersagency.com/
Facebook www.facebook.com/TwoPiersAgency
Twitter @TwoPiersAgency
Instagram twopiersagency
Agent Rufus Purdy

Represents fiction and non-fiction including children's (from 7+) and memoir. Submissions through form on website. For fiction, submit the first three chapter and synopsis, while for non-fiction send three chapters and proposal. Submissions must include a covering letter. *Founded* 2021.

United Agents LLP*
12–26 Lexington Street, London W1F 0LE
tel 020-3214 0800
email info@unitedagents.co.uk
website www.unitedagents.co.uk
Agents Seren Adams, Sarah Ballard, Caroline Dawnay, Ariella Feiner, James Gill, Jodie Hodges (children's/young adult writers and illustrators), Millie Hoskins, Caradoc King, Robert Kirby, Laura Macdougall, Yasmin McDonald, Amy Mitchell, Zoe Ross, Sophie Scard, Rosemary Scoular, Emily Talbot (children's/young adult writers and illustrators), Charles Walker, Anna Webber, Jane Willis

Fiction and non-fiction. *Commission* Home 15%, USA/translation 20%. See website for submission details. *Founded* 2008.

Jo Unwin Literary Agency*
West Wing, Somerset House, London WC2R 1LA
email submissions@jounwin.co.uk
website www.jounwin.co.uk
Twitter @jounwin
Twitter @rachelphilippa
Twitter @MillyReilly
Agents Jo Unwin, Rachel Mann, Milly Reilly

Represents authors of literary fiction, commercial women's fiction, non-fiction, cookery, YA fiction and fiction for children aged 5+ (picture books only accepted if written by established clients).

Authors include Richard Ayoade, Charlie Brooker, Candice Carty-Williams, Jenny Colgan, Kit de Waal, A.J. Pearce, Cathy Rentzenbrink, Nina Stibbe, Eliza Clarke, Caleb Femi. *Founded* 2016.

Wade and Co. Literary Agency Ltd
33 Cormorant Lodge, Thomas More Street, London E1W 1AU
tel 020-7488 4171

email rw@rwla.com
website www.rwla.com
Director Robin Wade

General fiction and non-fiction. Most genres represented. *Commission* Home 10%, overseas 20%. See website for submission guidelines. Email submissions preferred. New authors welcome. No poetry, plays, screenplays, science fiction and fantasy, children's books, picture books or short stories.

For details of clients, see the website. *Founded* 2001.

Watson, Little Ltd*
Suite 315, ScreenWorks, 22 Highbury Grove, London N5 2ER
tel 020-7388 7529
email office@watsonlittle.com
email submissions@watsonlittle.com
website www.watsonlittle.com
Twitter @watsonlittle
Contacts James Wills (Managing Director), Laetitia Rutherford (Agent), Donald Winchester (Agent), Megan Carroll (Agent), Rachel Richardson (Rights Director)

Film and TV Associates: Ki Agency and The Sharland Agency; US Associates: Howard Morhaim Literary Agency and The Gersh Agency. Adult Fiction: literary, commercial women's, historical, reading group, crime and thriller. Non-fiction: history, science, popular psychology, memoir, humour, cookery, self-help. Children's: YA and middle grade fiction, picture books and children's non-fiction in all genres. *Commission* Home 15%, USA/translation 20%. Send informative preliminary letter, synopsis and sample chapters by email only. No poetry, TV, play or filmscripts.

Authors include Jenny Blackhurst, Susan Blackmore, Martin Edwards, Christopher Fowler, Tim Hall, Greg Jenner, Holan Liang, Alex Marwood, Margaret Mahy, Colin Wilson. *Founded* 1970.

Josef Weinberger Plays Ltd
(formerly Warner/Chappell Plays Ltd)
12–14 Mortimer Street, London W1T 3JJ
tel 020-7580 2827
email general.info@jwmail.co.uk
website www.josef-weinberger.com

Specialises in stage plays. Works in conjunction with overseas agents. All genres considered. No unsolicited MSS; preliminary letter essential. No radio plays, screenplays, fiction or non-fiction.

Clients include Arthur Miller, Ingmar Bergman, Sam Shepard, Eugene O'Neill, John Steinbeck, Debbie Isitt, Vanessa Brooks, Peter Gordon, Ron Aldridge, Eric Chappell. *Founded* 1938.

WGM Atlantic Talent and Literary Group
5 Chancery Lane, London WC2A 1LG
tel 020-3637 2064

email hello@wgmatlanticgroup.com
website www.wgmtalent.com
Facebook www.facebook.com/wgmtalent
Twitter @WGMAtlantic

Represents international and UK-based screenwriters, playwrights and authors and is recognised for developing northern talent and close relationships with industry partners. Builds long-lasting careers for clients, offers guidance and support in project development and guides authors through the publication process by encouraging, mentoring and advising on all aspects of editorial where necessary. For detailed submission guidelines, see www.wgmtalent.com/representation/.

Whispering Buffalo Literary Agency Ltd
97 Chesson Road, London W14 9QS
tel 020-7565 4737
email info@whisperingbuffalo.com
website www.whisperingbuffalo.com
Director Mariam Keen

Commercial/literary fiction and non-fiction, children's and young adult fiction. Special interest in book-to-screen adaptations; TV and film rights in novels and non-fiction handled in-house. *Commission* Home 15%, overseas 20%. Only accepts submissions by email. Will suggest revision. *Founded* 2008.

Eve White Literary Agency Limited*
15 Alderney Street, London SW1V 4ES
tel 020-7630 1155
email eve@evewhite.co.uk
email ludo@evewhite.co.uk
website www.evewhite.co.uk
Twitter @EveWhiteAgency
Contact Eve White, Ludo Cinelli

Boutique agency representing commercial and literary fiction and non-fiction, children's fiction and film/TV tie-ins. *Commission* Home 15%, overseas 20%. Will suggest revision where appropriate. See website for up-to-date submission requirements. No submissions by post.
  Clients include Ruth Ware, Jane Shemilt, Andy Stanton, Rae Earl, Sarah J Naughton, Saskia Sarginson, Rebecca Reid, Damian Le Bas, Luan Goldie, Sarah Ockwell-Smith, Tracey Corderoy, Abie Longstaff, Darran Anderson, James Clarke, James Norbury. *Founded* 2003.

Dinah Wiener Ltd*
12 Cornwall Grove, London W4 2LB
tel 020-8994 6011
email dinah@dwla.co.uk
Director Dinah Wiener

Fiction and general non-fiction, film and TV in association. *Commission* Home 15%, overseas 20%, film and TV in association 15%. Taking on no new clients. No plays, scripts, poetry, short stories or children's books. *Founded* 1985.

Alice Williams Literary*
tel 020-7385 2118
email submissions@alicewilliamsliterary.co.uk
website www.alicewilliamsliterary.co.uk
Twitter @alicelovesbooks
Contact Alice Williams

Specialist literary agency representing writers and illustrators of picture books, children's fiction and teen/young adult fiction. Also children's non-fiction. *Commission* Home 15%, USA/translation/film/TV 20%. Open to submissions, by email only. Attach full typescript and synopsis, two or three picture book texts, or illustration portfolio. See website for further guidelines.
  Clients include Zoe Armstrong, Lauren Beard, Jo Clarke, Rachel Delahaye, Lucy Freegard, Rebecca Harry, Lara Hawthorne, Natelle Quek, Rose Robbins, Fabi Santiago, Suzy Senior, Ciara Smyth, Cat Weldon, Clare Helen Welsh, Pete Williamson. *Founded* 2018.

WME*
(William Morris Endeavour, UK)
100 New Oxford Street, London WC1A 1HB
tel 020-7534 6800
email ldnsubmissions@wmeagency.com
website www.wmeentertainment.com
Books Matilda Forbes Watson, Fiona Baird, Anna Dixon *Foreign Rights* James Munro, *TV* Antonia Melville

Worldwide talent and literary agency with offices in London, New York, Beverly Hills, Nashville and Miami. Literary and commercial fiction, crime, thrillers, young adult fiction, middle-grade fiction, memoir, self-help, lifestyle, sci-fi, fantasy, women's fiction, serious non-fiction and popular culture. *Commission* Film/TV 10%, UK books 15%, USA books/translation 20%. Please submit via email to the address above with the first three chapters, a synopsis and a covering email.

The Writers' Practice
mobile 07940 533243
email jemima@thewriterspractice.com
website www.thewriterspractice.com
Twitter @writerspractice
Literary Agent and Editorial Consultant Jemima Hunt, *Editorial Consultant, manuscripts and scripts* Jeremy Page

The Writers' Practice is a boutique literary agency and editorial consultancy that specialises in launching debut authors. Jemima Hunt is interested in commercial and literary fiction and specialises in memoir and narrative non-fiction. She works closely with writers on all aspects of book development.
  Clients include H.B. Lyle, Mikey Cuddihy, Emma Baxter-Wright, Turning Earth. *Founded* 2011.

The Wylie Agency (UK) Ltd

17 Bedford Square, London WC1B 3JA
tel 020-7908 5900
email mail@wylieagency.co.uk
website www.wylieagency.co.uk

Literary fiction and non-fiction. No unsolicited MSS. *Founded* 1996.

Susan Yearwood Agency*

2 Knebworth House, Londesborough Road, London N16 8RL
tel 020-7503 0954
email submissions@susanyearwoodagency.com
website www.susanyearwoodagency.com
Twitter @sya_susan
Contact Susan Yearwood

Book club fiction, commercial fiction and non-fiction; children's fiction 9+ and YA. *Commission* Home 15%, overseas 20%. Send submission with covering letter and brief synopsis via email. Submissions not accepted by hand or post. Tends not to read science fiction/fantasy in adult fiction, short stories or poetry. *Founded* 2007.

Zeno Agency Ltd*

Primrose Hill Business Centre,
110 Gloucester Avenue, London NW1 8HX
tel 020-7096 0927
email info@zenoagency.com
website www.zenoagency.com
Twitter @zenoagency
Director John Berlyne

Represents most fiction genres (crime, thrillers, YA, historical, etc), with particular specialism in science fiction, fantasy and horror. Also some non-fiction. *Commission* Home and direct overseas 15%, overseas via sub-agents 20%. See website for client list and submission guidelines. *Founded* 2008.

Literary agents overseas

This list includes only a selection of agents across the English-speaking world. Additional agency listings can be found at www.writersandartists.co.uk/listings. Before submitting material, writers are advised to visit agents' websites for detailed submission guidelines and to ascertain terms.

AUSTRALIA

ALM: Australian Literary Management
tel +61 (02) 9818 8557
email alphaalm8@gmail.com
website www.austlit.com

For full details of genres represented and submission guidelines, see website. Does not consider TV or Film scripts of any kind, poetry, science fiction, self help, fantasy or books for children by unpublished authors. Does not accept self-published work or previously published works including ebooks or writing by non-Australian authors.

The Authors' Agent
PO Box 577, Terrigal, NSW 2260
email briancook@theauthorsagent.com.au
website www.theauthorsagent.com.au

Specialises in adult fiction, narrative non-fiction and children's books. Accepts submissions by email. For detailed guidelines, see website.

The Cameron Creswell Agency/ Cameron's Management
Level 7, 61 Marlborough Street, Surry Hills, NSW 2010
tel +61 (0)2 9319 7199
email info@cameronsmanagement.com.au
website www.cameronsmanagement.com.au

Cameron's Management is an agency representing writers, directors, actors, presenters, designers, cinematographers, editors, composers and book authors across the full range of the film, television, live performance and publishing industries. Only accepts submissions in accordance with guidelines on website.

Curtis Brown (Australia) Pty Ltd
PO Box 19, Paddington, NSW 2021
tel +61 (0)2 9361 6161
email submissions@curtisbrown.com.au
website www.curtisbrown.com.au
Twitter @curtisbrownaus

Australia's oldest and largest literary agency representing a diverse range of Australian and New Zealand authors. Submissions open for a month at a time in February, June and October. See website for more details. *Founded* 1967.

Jenny Darling & Associates
PO Box 5328, South Melbourne, VIC 3205
email office@jennydarling.com.au
website www.jennydarling.com.au
Contact Jenny Darling

Adult fiction and non-fiction (home 15%, international/translation 20%, film/TV 20%). Currently closed for submissions. *Founded* 1998.

Drummond Agency
PO Box 572, Woodend, VIC 3442
tel +61 (0)3 5427 3644
email info@drummondagency.com.au
website www.drummondagency.com.au/index.htm

Considers both fiction and non-fiction for adults and YA fiction, but no fantasy or science fiction. Query by telephone, email or letter. Do not send attachments unless requested. See website for full submission guidelines and author listing.

Authors include Randa Abdel-Fattah, Vikki Wakefield, Claire Zorn, Deborah Burrows, Margareta Osborn, Yvette Walker. *Founded* 1997.

Golvan Arts Management
website www.golvanarts.com.au
Facebook www.facebook.com/Golvan-Arts-Management-153871021304383/

Represents a wide range of writers including writers of both adult and children's fiction and non-fiction, poetry, screenwriters and writers of plays. Also represents visual artists and composers. See the General Information section on the website before making contact via online form.

Margaret Kennedy Agency
PO Box 1433, Toowong, Brisbane, QLD 4066
tel +61 (0)7 3870 9996
email hannah@margaretkennedyagency.com
website www.margaretkennedyagency.com
Twitter @mkliterary
Agent Hannah Douglas, *Consultant* Margaret Kennedy

A full-service literary agency representing general non-fiction, a limited range of fiction and high-quality children's literature. Areas of special interest in non-fiction include biography, current affairs and social issues, language, philosophy, religion, science, history, food and wine and Australia and the Pacific. Does not accept fantasy, science fiction, chick lit, chook lit, horror and erotica. Children's picture books, chapter books and teen and YA literature, including non-fiction, are welcomed from established writers. For fiction, send a brief query letter with the first 50 pages by email. For non-fiction, send a brief query letter with a proposal by email. *Founded* 1996.

Left Bank Literary

website www.leftbankliterary.com
Instagram @leftbankliteraryagency
Agents Gaby Naher, Grace Heifetz, *Rights Manager* Rebecca Slater

A Sydney-based literary agency specialising in quality fiction and non-fiction. Works closely with clients to develop their manuscripts to their greatest potential before representing them to publishers and other media organisations. To submit your work for consideration, send a preliminary 'pitch' through the website form including book title, genre, brief synopsis and author bio. Agents will be in contact should they wish to read your manuscript. Does not represent self-help, fantasy, romance, early reader, middle grade and picture books, stage/screenplays, comics or poetry.

Sarah McKenzie Literary Management

email submissions@smlm.com.au
website www.smlm.com.au

Provides advice, advocacy and representation for Australian authors, helping them to shape and polish their writing projects, negotiate the best possible terms in their contracts and identify and create opportunities to build a writing career. Actively seeks established and emerging authors of fiction, non-fiction and children's fiction. Does not represent works that have been previously self-published in any form. For detailed submission guidelines and for a full list of genres accepted, see the website.

Jane Novak Literary Agency

PO Box 774, Five Dock NSW 2046
tel +61 (0)2 9281 8648
email jane@janenovak.com
website www.janenovak.com

Represents writers across all genres as well as a number of literary estates. Submissions are currently closed for fiction and children's/YA. Non-fiction submissions will be considered in digital form only. You must inform the agency if you have submitted your work to a publisher or another agency.

Zeitgeist Agency

Sydney office: Level 1, 142 Smith Street, Summer Hill, NSW 2130

tel +61 (0)4 1035 5790
email query_@zeitgeistagency.com
Brussels office: 75 Rue E. Van Driessche, 1050 Brussels
website www.zeitgeistagency.com
Twitter @literaryagent1

International literary, screen, theatre and talent management agency representing writers (fiction, non-fiction, memoir, screen and stage) and illustrators. Submit query or submission to either the Sydney or Brussels office with 'Query' in the subject line. Specific submission guidelines for each genre can be found on the website. *Founded* 2006.

CANADA

Acacia House Publishing Services Ltd

51 Chestnut Avenue, Brantford, Ontario N3T 4C3
tel +1 519-752-0978
email bhanna.acacia@rogers.com
Managing Director Bill Hanna

Literary fiction/non-fiction, quality commercial fiction, most non-fiction (English worldwide 15%, translation 25%, performance 20%). No horror or occult. Works with overseas agents. Query first by email with sample of 50 pages max. *Founded* 1985.

Rick Broadhead & Associates

47 St. Clair Avenue West, Suite 501, Toronto M4V 3A5
tel +1 416-929-0516
email info@rbaliterary.com
email submissions@rbliterary.com
website https://rbaliterary.com

Interested in non-fiction, especially in the following categories: history, politics, business, true crime, investigative journalism, natural history/environment, national security/intelligence, current affairs, biography, science, pop culture, self-help, health, medicine, humour. Not currently accepting fiction novels, screenplays, poetry or children's books. Email/electronic (via website) queries preferred.

The Bukowski Agency Ltd

20 Prince Arthur Avenue, Suite 12-I, Toronto M5R 1B
email info@bukowskiagency.com
website www.bukowskiagency.com
Agent Denise Bukowski

Specialises in international literary fiction and up-market non-fiction for adults. Does not represent genre fiction, children's literature, plays, poetry or screenplays. See website for submission guidelines. *Founded* 1986.

CookeMcDermid

email admin@cookemcdermid.com
website https://www.cookemcdermid.com

Agents Dean Cooke, Sally Harding, Martha Webb, Suzanne Brandreth, Ron Eckel, Rachel Letofsky, Stephanie Sinclair, Paige Sisley

CookeMcDermid was formed when two pre-eminent literary agencies, The Cooke Agency and The McDermid Agency, amalgamated, combining over 47 years of experience. CMD represents authors of literary, commercial and sci-fi/fantasy fiction; a broad range of narrative non-fiction; health and wellness resources; and middle grade and young adult books. See https://cookemcdermid.com/submissions for submissions guidelines and form. Sells Canadian and American rights directly. Cooke International represents UK and translation rights, in conjunction with a network of co-agents around the world. CMD also sells film and TV rights directly, in addition to working with associates in New York and LA. *Founded* 2017.

Donaghy Literary Group

website www.donaghyliterary.com
Facebook www.facebook.com/DonaghyLiteraryGroup
Twitter @DonaghyLiterary

Provides full-service literary representation to clients at all stages of their publishing career. Specialises in commercial fiction and seeking young adult and adult novels. Genres represented include romance, women's fiction, thriller, mystery, suspense, science fiction, fantasy, historical fantasy and historical fiction. Visit agent pages on the website for information on each agent and what they are currently looking for. Only accepts query submissions via the website. Welcomes both established and new writers.

P.S. Literary Agency

2nd Floor, 2010 Winston Park Drive, Oakville, Ontario L6H 5R7
email info@psliterary.com
website www.psliterary.com
Twitter @PSLiterary
President and Principal Agent Curtis Russell, *Senior Literary Agent and Senior Advisor* Carly Watters, *Senior Literary Agents* Maria Vicente, Eric Smith, Claire Harris, *Associate Agents* Stephanie Winter, Cecilia Lyra

Represents both fiction and non-fiction works to publishers in North America, Europe and throughout the world. Categories include commercial, upmarket, literary, women's fiction, mystery, thriller, romance, science fiction, fantasy, historical, LGBTQ+, young adult, middle grade, picture books, graphic novels, memoir, history, politics, current affairs, business, wellness, cookbooks, sports, humour, pop science, pop psychology, pop culture, design and lifestyle. Does not accept submissions via mail or telephone. Send queries to query@psliterary.com. Do not send email attachments unless specifically requested.

Seventh Avenue Literary Management

16708 20th Avenue, South Surrey, BC V3Z 9R4
email info@seventhavenuelit.com
website www.seventhavenuelit.com

One of Canada's largest non-fiction and personal management agencies. With more than 35 years in business, it has a substantial client list of recognised non-fiction authors and public figures. Helps authors develop proposals and manuscripts for submission and negotiates on their behalf with publishing houses in Canada, the USA and worldwide. Authors' books are published by a range of publishers including international houses, independents and specialist presses. Send short query via email including a short description of your project and a brief bio. Submissions are also accepted via post: see the website for specific guidelines.

Beverley Slopen

131 Bloor Street West, Suite 711, Toronto M5S 1S3
tel +1 416-964-9598
email beverley@slopenagency.ca
website www.slopenagency.com/sa/
Agent Beverley Slopen

Represents a diverse list of authors in fields ranging from literary and commercial fiction to history, non-fiction, anthropology, biography and selected true crime and self-help. Does not handle poetry, horror, romance or illustrated books, and publishes very few children's titles. Does not take on many new authors and tends to concentrate on Canadian-based writers. See website for details of authors, titles and submission guidelines.

Carolyn Swayze Literary Agency Ltd

7360-137th Street, Suite 319, Surrey, BC V3W 1A3
email reception@swayzeagency.com
website www.swayzeagency.com
Proprietor Carolyn Swayze

Literary fiction and non-fiction. Some romance and mystery. No science fiction, poetry, self-help, spiritual, screenplays. Eager to discover strong voices writing narrative non-fiction in history, science, nature, popular culture, food and drink. Some memoir. Primarily Canadian authors. No telephone calls; make contact by email. Provide CV, publication credits, writing awards, education and experience relevant to the book project. Allow six weeks for a reply. *Founded* 1994.

Westwood Creative Artists

386 Huron Street, Toronto M5S 2G6
email wca_office@wcaltd.com
website www.wcaltd.com

Represents literary fiction, quality commercial fiction including mysteries and thrillers and non-fiction in the areas of memoir, history, biography, science, journalism and current affairs. See website for submission guidelines.

NEW ZEALAND

High Spot Literary
email nadine@highspotlit.com
email vicki@highspotlit.com
website www.highspotlit.com
Facebook www.facebook.com/highspotlit
Twitter @HighSpotLit
Agents Vicki Marsdon, Nadine Rubin Nathan

A full-service agency dedicated to guiding authors to success through working with the best publishing partners and providing guidance and support to manage their author profile. Prefers to work with authors who have had their manuscripts professionally assessed before making an approach. Does not represent science fiction, fantasy, horror, erotica, poetry or children's picture books. Email only the agent that best suits your project. See website for submissions guidelines.

Playmarket
PO Box 9767, Wellington 6141
email info@playmarket.org.nz
website www.playmarket.org.nz
Director Murray Lynch

Playwrights' agent, adviser and bookshop. Representation, licensing and script development of New Zealand plays and playwrights. Licenses productions of New Zealand plays nationally and around the world. *Founded* 1973.

Frances Plumpton Literary Agency
PO Box 15061, New Lynn, Auckland 0640
tel +64 (0)9 827 6785
email submissions@francesplumpton.com
website www.francesplumpton.com
Facebook www.facebook.com/Frances-Plumpton-Literary-Agency-685680644791804/

Represents picture books, junior and young adult fiction and children's non-fiction by New Zealand writers and/or illustrators. No poetry or short stories. Submissions should be sent as an attachment (Word or PDF) with the manuscript title in the subject line. See website for submission guidelines. *Founded* 2012.

TFS Literary Agency
PO Box 6292 Dunedin North, Dunedin 9059
email tfs@elseware.co.nz
website www.elseware.co.nz

General fiction, non-fiction, children's books. No poetry, individual short stories or articles. Enquiries from New Zealand authors only. Email queries but no attachments. Hard copy preferred. Also offers assessment reports, mentoring and courses. *Founded* 1988.

USA

Member of the Association of American Literary Agents

3 Seas Literary Agency*
PO Box 444, Sun Prairie, WI 53590
tel +1 (608) 834-9317
website www.threeseasagency.com
Twitter @threeseaslit
Agents Michelle Grajkowski, Cori Deyoe, Stacey Graham

A full-service literary agency representing authors who write romance, women's fiction, science fiction/fantasy, thrillers, young adult and middle-grade fiction as well as select non-fiction titles. Accepts email submissions only to the 'queries' address above, and should include QUERY: in the subject line. Submissions must appear in the body of the email and not as an attachment. Genre-specific submission guidelines can be found on the website. Will only reply if interested in your work.

Aevitas Creative Management*
website https://aevitascreative.com
Facebook www.facebook.com/AevitasCreative/
Twitter @AevitasCreative

A full-service literary agency with offices in New York, Boston, Washington DC, Los Angeles and London, representing scores of award winning authors, thinkers and public figures. See website for full submission and agent details.

The Axelrod Agency*
55 Main Street, PO Box 357, Chatham, NY 12037
tel +1 518-392-2100
email steve@axelrodagency.com
email lori@axelrodagency.com
President Steven Axelrod, *Foreign Rights Director* Lori Antonson

Full-length MSS. Fiction (home 15%, overseas 20%), film and TV rights (15%); will suggest revision where appropriate. Works with overseas agents. *Founded* 1983.

The Bent Agency*
529 W 42nd St, New York, NY 10036
email info@thebentagency.com
website www.thebentagency.com
Instagram thebentagency
Agents Nicola Barr, Jenny Bent, Victoria Cappello, Gemma Cooper, Nissa Cullen, Claire Draper, Louise Fury, Molly Ker Hawn, Amelia Hodgson, Sarah Hornsley, James Musterlier, Martha Perotto-Wills, Zöe Plant, John Silbersack, Laurel Symonds, Desiree Wilson

Represents a diverse range of genres including history, humour, lifestyle, inspiration, memoir, literary fiction, children's and commercial fiction.

Only accepts email queries. See website for detailed query and submission guidelines.

The Bindery Agency
email info@thebinderyagency.com
website www.thebinderyagency.com
Founder Alexander Field, *Managing Director* Ingrid Beck, *Agents* Trinity McFadden, John Blase, Estee Zandee

Currently represents authors of general non-fiction, religion, literary fiction, science fiction and fantasy, biography and memoir, pop culture, leadership, spiritual growth, Christian spirituality and more. To query about literary representation, email your book proposal along with a cover letter. Include a summary of your book concept, table of contents, author biography, at least one sample chapter, relevant contact information and your publishing story. Will respond within ten to 12 weeks if interested in pursuing further. In addition to literary representation, the agency also consults with businesses and organisations on publishing strategy and develops highly specialised book projects offering a variety of boutique publishing options.

Blue Heron Literary*
email submissions@blueheronliterary.com
website www.blueheronliterary.com

A Seattle-based boutique agency that places fiction and non-fiction with publishers throughout the USA and internationally. Accepts non-fiction manuscripts and proposals from both first-time and established authors. Submissions currently closed.

Georges Borchardt Inc.*
136 East 57th Street, New York, NY 10022
tel +1 212-753-5785
website www.gbagency.com
Directors Georges Borchardt, Anne Borchardt, Valerie Borchardt

Full-length and short MSS (home/performance 15%, British and translations 20%). Agents in most foreign countries. No unsolicited MSS. *Founded* 1967.

Bradford Literary Agency*
5694 Mission Center Road, Suite 347, San Diego, CA 92108
email queries@bradfordlit.com
website www.bradfordlit.com

Currently looking for fiction (romance, speculative fiction, women's, science fiction/fantasy, mystery, thrillers, historical, horror, magical realism, children's and YA) and non-fiction (relationships, biography, memoir, self-help, lifestyle, business, parenting, narrative humour, pop culture, illustrated/graphic design, parenting, food and cooking, mind/body/spirit, history and social issues). Not currently looking for poetry, screenplays, short stories, westerns, inspirational/spiritual, horror, New Age,

religion, crafts or gift books. Query by email only. For detailed submission guidelines, see website.

Brandt & Hochman Literary Agents Inc.*
1501 Broadway, Suite 2310, New York, NY 10036
tel +1 212-840-5760
website www.brandthochman.com
Contact Gail Hochman

Fiction and non-fiction for the general trade market (home 15%, overseas 20%), performance rights (15%). See website for full list of genres represented. No screenplays or textbooks. Queies by email or letter.

The Brattle Agency
PO Box 380537, Cambridge, MA 02238
tel +1 617-721-5375
email submissions@thebrattleagency.com
website https://thebrattleagency.com

A full-service agency providing assistance to clients in all areas related to their work including editorial guidance, submission and sale of works to both large and small publishers, contract negotiations, foreign language sales, film and television licences and marketing and publicity strategies. Semi-annual reading period for open submissions; see website for details. Queries should include a formal cover letter, brief synopsis and a CV (if submitting an academic manuscript). *Founded* 2008.

Barbara Braun Associates Inc.*
7 East 14th Street, 19F, New York, NY 10003
email bbasubmissions@gmail.com
email barbara@barbarabraunagency.com
website www.barbarabraunagency.com
Twitter @212bard
President Barbara Braun

Represents literary and commercial fiction and serious non-fiction (home 15%, overseas 20%). Does not represent poetry, science fiction, fantasy, horror or screenplays. Send queries by email, doesn't accept postal submissions. See website for full submission guidelines.

Browne & Miller Literary Associates*
52 Village Place, Hinsdale, IL 60521
tel +1 312-922-3063
email mail@browneandmiller.com
website www.browneandmiller.com
Twitter @BrowneandMiller
Contact Danielle Egan-Miller

General adult fiction and non-fiction (home 15%, overseas 20%). Works in conjunction with foreign agents. Will suggest revision. No children's (inc. YA), science fiction, fantasy, horror, short stories, poetry, screenplays or academic work. Query by email in first instance. *Founded* 1971.

Maria Carvainis Agency Inc.*

Rockefeller Center, 1270 Avenue of the Americas, Suite 2915, New York, NY 10020
tel +1 212-245-6365
email mca@mariacarvainisagency.com
website www.mariacarvainisagency.com
President and Literary Agent Maria Carvainis

Represents a wide range of fiction and non-fiction with special interest in literary and mainstream fiction, mystery and suspense, thrillers, historicals, contemporary women's fiction, young adult and middle grade, memoir, biography, history, business, psychology, pop culture and popular science (home 15%, overseas 20%). Send a query letter, a synopsis of the work, first 5–10 pages and a note of any writing credentials. See website for full submission guidelines. *Founded* 1977.

The Chudney Agency

72 North State Road, Suite 501, Briarcliff Manor, NY 10510
tel +1 914-465-5560
email steven@thechudneyagency.com
website https://thechudneyagency.com
Contact Steven Chudney

Represents authors of children's books and adult fiction. Does not accept science fiction, non-fiction, plays, screenplays or film scripts. See website for full guidelines for queries and submissions, and for details of genres represented. *Founded* 2002.

Frances Collin Literary Agency*

PO Box 33, Wayne, PA 19087-0033
email queries@francescollin.com
website www.publishersmarketplace.com/members/slyyake
website www.francescollin.com
Owner Frances Collin, *Agent* Sarah Yake

Home 15%, overseas 20%, performance rights 20%. Specialisations of interest to UK writers: literary fiction, mysteries, women's fiction, history, biography, science fiction, fantasy. No screenplays. No unsolicited MSS. Query via email only. Query letter in the body of the email with the first five pages of the manuscript pasted in the message, no attachments. Works in conjunction with agents worldwide. *Founded* 1948.

Concord Theatricals

250 W. 57th Street, 6th Floor, New York, NY 10107-0102
tel +1 866-979-0447
email info@concordtheatricals.com
website www.concordtheatricals.com
Twitter @ConcordShows

Concord Theatricals is the new home of Samuel French. Provides comprehensive services to the creators and producers of plays and musicals, including theatrical licensing, music publishing, script publishing, cast recording, artists protection and first-class production. Passionate about cultivating theatre and making it accessible for all.

Don Congdon Associates Inc.*

110 William Street, Suite 2202, New York, NY 10038
tel +1 212-645-1229
email dca@doncongdon.com
website www.doncongdon.com
Agents Cristina Concepcion, Michael Congdon, Katie Grimm, Katie Kotchman, Maura Kye Casella, Susan Ramer

Full-length and short MSS. General fiction and non-fiction (home 15%, overseas 20%, performance rights 15%). Works with co-agents overseas. No unsolicited MSS. Query/submissions by email only; see website for full guidelines. *Founded* 1983.

The Doe Coover Agency*

PO Box 668, Winchester, MA 01890
tel +1 781-721-6000
email info@doecooveragency.com
website www.doecooveragency.com
Agents Doe Coover, Colleen Moyyde

Specialises in non-fiction: business, history, popular science, biography, social issues, cooking, food writing, gardening; also literary and commercial fiction (home 15%, overseas 10%). No poetry or screenplays. Email queries only; see website for submission guidelines. *Founded* 1986.

Cullen Stanley International*

745 Fifth Avenue, Suite 500, New York, NY 10151
tel +1 917-677-4074
email submissions@cullenstanleyinternational.com
website www.cullenstanleyinternational.com
Contacts Cullen Stanley, Jaclyn Gilbert

Specialises in international rights representation on behalf of authors, agencies and publishers. Represents books with international appeal that will find readers in many languages around the world. Authors seeking representation are encouraged to send a query via email. Query letters should contain your publication history, biographical information and a brief synopsis of your work; attach the first ten pages of your manuscript. Does not accept hard copy submissions. Query letters should be addressed to one agent only – see the website for details of agents' requirements. *Founded* 2017.

Richard Curtis Associates Inc.*

200 East 72nd Street, Suite 28J, New York, NY 10021
tel +1 212-772-7363
website www.curtisagency.com
President Richard Curtis

All types of commercial fiction and non-fiction (home 15%, overseas 25%, film/TV 15%). Foreign rights handled by Baror International. *Founded* 1970.

Curtis Brown Ltd*
228 East 45th Street, New York, NY 10017
tel +1 212-473-5400
email info@cbltd.com
website www.curtisbrown.com
Twitter @CurtisBrownLtd
Instagram curtisbrown.ltd
Ceo Timothy Knowlton, *President* Peter Ginsberg (at
CA branch office), *Contacts* Ginger Clark (*Vice
President*), Katherine Fausset, Jonathan Lyons (*Vice
President*), Laura Blake Peterson (*Vice President*),
Kerry D'Agostino, Steven Salpeter, *Film and TV rights*
Holly Frederick, *Translation rights* Sarah Perillo

Fiction and non-fiction, juvenile (see Agent page on
website as not all agents handle juvenile), film and
TV rights. No unsolicited MSS. See individual agent's
entry on the Agents page of the website for specific
query and submission information. *Founded* 1914.

Liza Dawson Associates*
121 West 27th Street, Suite 1201, New York,
NY 10001
email lwu@lizadawson.com
website www.lizadawsonassociates.com
Twitter @LizaDawsonAssoc
Ceo Liza Dawson

A full-service agency which draws on expertise as
former publishers. Commercial and literary fiction
and non-fiction. See website for full details of genres
represented by individual agents, submission
guidelines and email contacts. *Founded* 1996.

Sandra Dijkstra & Associates*
PMB 515, 1155 Camino Del Mar, Del Mar, CA 92014
tel +1 858-755-3115
website www.dijkstraagency.com
Contacts Sandra Dijkstra, Elise Capron, Jill Marr,
Thao Le, Andrea Cavallaro, Jessica Watterson, Suzy
Evans, Jennifer Kim

Fiction: literary, contemporary, women's, romance,
suspense, thrillers and science fiction. Non-fiction:
narrative, history, journalism, business, psychology,
self-help, science and memoir/biography (home 15%,
overseas 20%). Works in conjunction with foreign
and film agents. Email submissions only. Please see
website for the most up-to-date guidelines.
Founded 1981.

Dunham Literary Inc.*
email dunhamlit@gmail.com
website www.dunhamlit.com
Contact Jennie Dunham, Leslie Zampetti

Literary fiction and non-fiction, children's books
(home 15%, overseas 20%). Send query by email to
query@dunhamlit.com. Submission guidelines on
website. *Founded* 2000.

Dunow, Carlson & Lerner*
27 West 20th Street, Suite 1107, New York, NY 10011
email mail@dclagency.com
website www.dclagency.com

Represents literary and commercial fiction, a wide
range of non-fiction and children's literature for all
ages. Query letters with first ten pages of your work
preferred by email (no attachments). For query letters
by post, include sase. *Founded* 2005.

Dystel, Goderich & Bourret LLC*
1 Union Square West, New York, NY 10003
tel +1 212-627-9100
website www.dystel.com
Facebook www.facebook.com/DGandB/
Twitter @DGandBTweets
Contacts Jane Dystel, Miriam Goderich, Michael
Bourret, Jim McCarthy, Lauren Abramo, Stacey
Glick, Ann Leslie Tuttle, Jessica Papin, John Rudolph,
Sharon Pelletier, Amy Bishop, Michaela Whatnall

General fiction and non-fiction (home 15%, overseas
19%, film/TV/radio 15%): literary and commercial
fiction, narrative non-fiction, self-help, cookbooks,
parenting, science fiction/fantasy, children's and
young adults. See website for submission guidelines.
Founded 1994.

The Ethan Ellenberg Literary Agency*
155 Suffolk Street, Suite 2R, New York, NY 10002
tel +1 212-431-4554
email agent@ethanellenberg.com
website www.ethanellenberg.com
President and Agent Ethan Ellenberg, *Senior Agent*
Evan Gregory, *Associate Agent* Bibi Lewis

Fiction and non-fiction (home 15%, overseas 20%).
Commercial fiction: science fiction, fantasy, romance,
thrillers, suspense, mysteries, children's and general
fiction; also literary fiction with a strong narrative.
Non-fiction: history, adventure, true crime, science,
biography. Children's fiction: interested in young
adult, middle grade and younger, of all types. Will
consider picture books and other illustrated works.
No scholarly works, poetry, short stories or
screenplays.

Accepts unsolicited MSS and seriously considers all
submissions, including first-time writers. For fiction,
submit synopsis and first three chapters. For non-
fiction, send a proposal (outline, sample material,
author CV, etc). For children's works, send complete
MS. Illustrators should send a representative selection
of colour copies (no original artwork). Unable to
return any material from overseas. See website for full
submission guidelines. *Founded* 1983.

Diana Finch Literary Agency*
116 West 23rd Street, Suite 500, New York, NY 10011
tel +1 646-375-2081
email diana.finch@verizon.net
website https://dianafinchliteraryagency.submittable.
com
Facebook www.facebook.com/DianaFinchLitAg
Twitter @DianaFinch
Owner and Agent Diana Finch

Memoirs, narrative non-fiction, science, history, environment, business, literary fiction, current affairs, health and how-to, science fiction and fantasy, YA and middle grade fiction (domestic 15%, foreign 20%). Queries through website (preferred). No queries by telephone.

Clients include Noliwe Rooks, Azadeh Moaveni, Antonia Juhasz, Loretta Napoleoni, Owen Matthews, Greg Palast, Thaisa Frank, Eric Simons, Thomas Goltz, Mark Schapiro, Joanna Russ (estate), Christopher Leonard, Robert Marion MD. Recent sales to W.W. Norton, Farrar, Straus & Giroux, Beacon Press, The New Press, Island Press. Previously agent with Ellen Levine Literary Agency. *Founded* 2003.

FinePrint Literary Management*
207 West 106th Street, Suite 1D, New York, NY 10025
email firstname@fineprintlit.com
website www.fineprintlit.com
Ceo Peter Rubie, *Agents* Laura Wood, Lauren Bieker, June Clark, Bobby O'Neil

Represents fiction and non-fiction. Also handles book-to-film and TV dramatic rights, and worldwide subsidiary rights for US-based authors. Each agent has specific interests; these are detailed on the website. Query by email to the appropriate agent, including a query letter, synopsis and first two chapters, but do not send any attachments without an invitation to do so.

Folio Literary Management*
The Film Center Building, 630 9th Avenue, Suite 1101, New York, NY 10036
website www.foliolit.com
Twitter @FolioLiterary

Represents both first-time and established authors. Seeks upmarket adult fiction, literary fiction, commercial fiction that features fresh voices and/or memorable characters, and narrative non-fiction. Folio Jr is devoted exclusively to representing children's book authors and artists. Consult agents' submission guidelines on the website before making contact.

Jeanne Fredericks Literary Agency Inc.*
221 Benedict Hill Road, New Canaan, CT 06840
tel +1 203-972-3011
email jeanne.fredericks@gmail.com
website www.jeannefredericks.com

Quality non-fiction, especially health, science, women's issues, gardening, antiques and decorative arts, biography, cookbooks, popular reference, business, natural history (home 15%, overseas 20%). Query first by email or mail, enclosing sase. Member of Authors Guild and AALA. *Founded* 1997.

Sarah Jane Freymann Literary Agency
tel +1 212-362-9277
email submissions@sarahjanefreymann.com
website www.sarahjanefreymann.com
Contacts Sarah Jane Freymann, Steven Schwartz, Katharine Sands, Jessica Sinsheimer

Book-length fiction and general non-fiction. Fiction interests include sophisticated mainstream and literary fiction with a distinctive voice, crime, thrillers and historical novels. Also looking for edgy YA fiction. Non-fiction interests include spiritual, psychology, self-help, women/men's issues, books by health experts (conventional and alternative), cookbooks, narrative non-fiction, natural science, nature, memoirs, cutting-edge journalism, travel, multicultural issues, parenting, lifestyle. See website for detailed submission guidelines. *Founded* 1974.

The Friedrich Agency*
email mfriedrich@friedrichagency.com
email lcarson@friedrichagency.com
email hcarr@friedrichagency.com
email hbrattesani@friedrichagency.com
website www.friedrichagency.com
Agents Molly Friedrich, Lucy Carson, Heather Carr, Hannah Brattesani

Represents literary and commercial fiction for adults and YA, plus narrative non-fiction and memoir. Accepts queries by email only. Query only one agent. No unsolicited MSS. No attachments to query emails unless invited. See website for detailed submission guidelines.

Gelfman Schneider ICM Partners*
850 Seventh Avenue, Suite 903, New York, NY 10019
email mail@gelfmanschneider.com
website www.gelfmanschneider.com
Agents Jane Gelfman, Deborah Schneider, Heather Mitchell, Penelope Burns

General adult fiction and non-fiction (home 15%, overseas 20%). See website for detailed submission guidelines and information on which agents are accepting queries/submissions. Works in conjunction with ICM Partners and Curtis Brown, London. *Founded* 1992.

Global Lion Intellectual Property Management Inc.
PO Box 669238, Pompano Beach, FL 33066
tel +1 754-222-6948
email peter@globallionmgt.com
website www.globallionmanageiment.com
Facebook www.facebook.com/GlobalLionManagement/
Twitter @AbundantLion
President/Ceo Peter Miller

Peter Miller has been a literary and film manager for several decades and is President and Ceo of Global

Lion Intellectual Property Management Inc. (previously PMA Literary & Film Management Inc. of New York). He has represented more than 1,500 books, including over 25 *New York Times* bestsellers.

Global Lion specialises in non-fiction and commercial fiction including thrillers and true crime, as well as books with film, TV or global publishing potential as Global Lion works in conjunction with agents worldwide. Authors and clients include Sir Ken Robinson, Jean Pierre Isbouts, Rabbi Mordecai Schreiber, Anthony DeStefano and Ann Pearlman. Initial submissions should include a synopsis, author biography, manuscript sample and details of personal social media and self-promotion.

Barry Goldblatt Literary LLC*
594 Dean Street, Brooklyn, NY 11238
website https://bgliterary.com
Contact Barry Goldblatt

Represents young adult and middle-grade fiction, as well as adult science fiction and fantasy. No non-fiction. Has a preference for quirky, offbeat work. Query only. See website for full submission guidelines. *Founded* 2000.

Frances Goldin Literary Agency*
214 West 29th Street, Suite 1006, New York, NY 10001
tel +1 212-777-0047
email agency@goldinlit.com
website www.goldinlit.com
Agents Ellen Geiger, Matt McGowan, Sam Stoloff, Ria Julien, Caroline Eisenmann, Roz Foster, Jade Wong-Baxter

Fiction (literary and high-quality commercial) and non-fiction. See website for submission guidelines. *Founded* 1977.

Sanford J. Greenburger Associates Inc.*
55 Fifth Avenue, New York, NY 10003
tel +1 212-206-5600
website www.greenburger.com
Facebook www.facebook.com/GreenburgerAssociates/
Twitter @GreenburgerLit
Agents Heide Lange, Faith Hamlin, Daniel Mandel, Matt Bialer, Rachel Dillon Fried, Stephanie Delman, Ed Maxwell, Wendy Gu, Sarah Phair, Abigail Frank

Fiction and non-fiction, film and TV rights. Only accepts queries by email. See website for submission guidelines. *Founded* 1932.

The Joy Harris Literary Agency Inc.*
1501 Broadway, Suite 2310, New York, NY 10036
tel +1 212-924-6269
email contact@joyharrisliterary.com
website www.joyharrisliterary.com
Twitter @JoyHarrisAgency
Agents Joy Harris, Adam Reed, Alice Fugate

Represents works of literary fiction and non-fiction. Does not currently accept poetry, screenplays, genre

fiction or self-help submissions. Submissions should be emailed, comprising a query letter and an outline or sample letter. See website for detailed submission guidelines. No unsolicited manuscripts. *Founded* 1990.

Hartline Agency
123 Queenton Drive, Pittsburgh, PA 15235
tel +1 412-829-2483
email firstname@hartlineliterary.com
website https://hartlineagency.com
Agents Joyce Hart, Jim Hart, Diana Flegal, Linda Glaz, Cyle Young, Patricia Riddle-Gaddis

Actively seeking new and established authors in a variety of genres and categories of both fiction and non-fiction. Does not represent short fiction, screenplays, scripts, poetry or magazine articles. Detailed submission guidelines are available on the website and on individual agent pages. Works primarily with authors living in the USA or Canada but international authors are considered on an individual basis by each agent.

John Hawkins & Associates Inc.*
80 Maiden Lane, Suite 1503, New York, NY 10038
tel +1 212-807-7040
email jha@jhalit.com
website www.jhalit.com
Agents Moses Cardona (President), Warren Frazier, Anne Hawkins

Fiction, non-fiction, young adult. *Founded* 1893.

The Jeff Herman Agency LLC
PO Box 1522, Stockbridge, MA 01262
tel +1 413-298-0077
email jeff@jeffherman.com
website www.jeffherman.com

Business, reference, popular psychology, technology, health, spirituality, general non-fiction (home/ overseas 15%); will suggest revision where appropriate. Works with overseas agents. *Founded* 1986.

Hill Nadell Literary Agency
6442 Santa Monica Blvd., Suite 201, Los Angeles, CA 90038
tel +1 310-860-9605
email queries@hillnadell.com
website www.hillnadell.com
Twitter @HillNadell
Agents Bonnie Nadell, Dara Hyde, Kari Erickson

Literary and commercial fiction, narrative non-fiction, current affairs, memoirs and popular culture (home 15%, overseas 20%). Send query electronically via the form on the website. No scripts or screenplays. Due to the high volume of submissions the agency receives, a response to all emailed queries cannot be guaranteed. Works in conjunction with agents in Scandinavia, France, Germany, Holland, Japan, Spain and more. *Founded* 1979.

ICM Partners*

65 East 55th Street, New York, NY 10022
tel +1 212-556-5600
website www.icmpartners.com

One of the world's leading talent agencies dedicated to the representation of authors, artists, content creators, broadcasters and journalists. No unsolicited MSS.

InkWell Management

521 Fifth Avenue, 26th Floor, New York, NY 10175
tel +1 212-922-3500
email info@inkwellmanagement.com
email submissions@inkwellmanagement.com
website https://inkwellmanagement.com
Twitter @inkwellmgmt

Fiction and non-fiction (home/overseas 15%). See website for submission guidelines. *Founded* 2004.

JABberwocky Literary Agency Inc.

49 West 45th Street, Suite 12N, New York, NY 10036-4603
website www.awfulagent.com
Twitter @awfulagent
President Joshua Bilmes, *Vice President* Eddie Schneider, *Coo* Brady McReynolds, *Agents* Lisa Rodgers, Bridget Smith, *Subsidiary Rights Director* Susan Velazquez

Agency specialising in science fiction and fantasy. There are six acquiring agents; for their individual submission and query guidelines, visit the website. *Founded* 1994.

Heather Jackson Literary Agent*

email query@hjlit.com
website www.hjlit.com

Specialises in practical and narrative commercial non-fiction and 'can't put it down, must-read now' fiction. Represents novelists and authors in personal health and wellbeing, history, popular science and psychology, politics and current affairs, business, memoir and self-help. Does not accept unsolicited proposals or manuscripts. Send a query email with a brief description of your book, its uniqueness in the marketplace and why you, and only you, can write it. Do not send attachments. Can only respond to projects of interest.

Janklow & Nesbit Associates

285 Madison, 21st Floor, New York, NY 10017
tel +1 212-421-1700
email info@janklow.com
email submissions@janklow.com
website www.janklowandnesbit.com
Twitter @JanklowNesbit
Chairmen Morton L. Janklow, Lynn Nesbit

Commercial and literary fiction and non-fiction. Submissions: send an informative cover letter, synopsis/outline and the first ten pages. For picture book submissions, include a dummy and at least one full-colour sample. Address submissions to an individual agent, including your email address or a return envelope with sufficient postage for material to be returned. Works in conjunction with Janklow & Nesbit (UK) Ltd. *Founded* 1989.

Keller Media Inc.

578 Washington Boulevard, No. 745, Marina Del Rey, CA 90292
website www.kellermedia.com
Facebook www.facebook.com/KellerMediaInc
Twitter @KellerMediaInc
Ceo/Senior Agent Wendy Keller, *Agent* Megan Close Zavala

Non-fiction for adults: business, science, self-improvement, psychology, relationships, wellness, health and non-traditional health, career, personal finance, nature, history, and ecology/green movement. Autobiographies and memoirs considered only by well-known people. No children's books, young adult, fiction, poetry, memoirs, screenplays or illustrated books. To inquire, please refer to www.kellermedia.com/submission-guidelines/. *Founded* 1989.

Harvey Klinger Inc.*

email queries@harveyklinger.com
website www.harveyklinger.com
Twitter @HKLiterary
Agents Harvey Klinger, David Dunton, Andrea Somberg, Wendy Levinson, Rachel Ridout, Cate Hart, Jennifer Herrington, Analieze Cervantes

Commercial and literary adult and children's fiction and non-fiction – serious narrative through to self-help psychology books by authors who have already established strong credentials in their respective field. (Home 15%, overseas 25%). See website for submission guidelines and submission form. *Founded* 1977.

The Knight Agency*

email admin@knightagency.net
website www.knightagency.net
Facebook www.facebook.com/knightagency/
Twitter @KnightAgency
Instagram the.knight.agency

Represents both first-time and established authors across a wide range of genres. For the genre interests of individual agents and detailed submission guidelines, see website. All queries should be sent via QueryManager. *Founded* 1996.

kt literary*

9249 S. Broadway 200–543, Highlands Ranch, CO 80129
tel +1 720-344-4728

email contact@ktliterary.com
website https://ktliterary.com
Twitter @ktliterary
Agents Kate Testerman, Sara Megibow, Hannah Fergesen, Renee Nyen, Hilary Harwell, Kelly Van Sant, Jas Perry, Chelsea Hensley, Aida Z. Lilly

Primarily middle-grade and young adult fiction. No picture books. In adult, also seeking romance, science fiction, fantasy and erotica (Sara Megibow and Hannah Fergesen). Email a query letter and the first three pages of manuscript in the body of the email (no attachments) as per website instructions. No snail mail.

Clients include Maureen Johnson, Stephanie Perkins, Matthew Cody, Ellen Booraem, Trish Doller, Amy Spalding, Roni Loren, Tiffany Reisz, Stefan Bachmann, Jason Hough. *Founded* 2008.

Susanna Lea Associates
331 West 20th Street, New York, NY 10011
tel +1 646-638-1435
email ny@susannalea.com
website www.susannalea.com
Twitter @SLANYC

General fiction and non-fiction with international appeal. No plays, screenplays or poetry. Send query letter, brief synopsis, the first three chapters and/or proposal via website. *Founded* in Paris 2000, New York 2004, London 2008.

Levine Greenberg Rostan Literary Agency*
307 Seventh Avenue, Suite 2407, New York, NY 10001
tel +1 212-337-0934
email submit@lgrliterary.com
website www.lgrliterary.com
Twitter @LGRLiterary

Represents literary and commercial fiction, non-fiction and books for young readers across a diverse range of genres. Refer to the How to Submit section of the website before querying or submitting work.

Julia Lord Literary Management*
38 West Ninth Street, New York, NY 10011
email query@julialordliterarymgt.com
website www.julialordliterarymgt.com
Contacts Julia Lord, Ginger Curwen

Currently looking for submissions in the following genres: narrative non-fiction, reference, biography, history, lifestyle, sports, humour, science, adventure, general fiction, historical fiction, thrillers, mysteries, graphic fiction and non-fiction. Email and postal queries accepted. See website for details about the agency, its authors and submission guidelines.

Donald Maass Literary Agency*
Suite 252, 1000 Dean Street, Brooklyn, NY 11238
tel +1 212-727-8383

email info@maassagency.com
website www.maassagency.com
Agents Donald Maass, Jennifer Jackson, Cameron McClure, Katie Shea Boutillier, Michael Curry, Caitlin McDonald, Paul Stevens, Jennifer Goloboy, Kiana Nguyen, Kat Kerr, Anne Tibbets

Specialises in fiction, all genres (home 15%, overseas 20%). See website for submission guidelines. *Founded* 1980.

Margret McBride Literary Agency*
PO Box 9128, La Jolla, CA 92038
tel +1 858-454-1550
email mmla@mcbridelit.com
website www.mcbrideliterary.com
President Margret McBride

Business, mainstream fiction and non-fiction (home 15%, overseas 25%). No poetry or children's books. See website for submission guidelines. *Founded* 1981.

McIntosh & Otis Inc.*
207 E. 37th Street, Suite BG, New York, NY 10016
tel +1 212-687-7400
email info@mcintoshandotis.com
website www.mcintoshandotis.com
Agents Elizabeth Winick Rubinstein, Adam Muhlig, Christa Heschke

Adult and children's literary fiction and non-fiction. No unsolicited MSS; query first via email, see website for instructions. *Founded* 1928.

MacKenzie Wolf*
Suite 1602, 115 Broadway, New York, NY 10006
email queries@mwlit.com
website www.mwlit.com
Twitter @MWLiterary

As of April 2021, the Agency is now functioning as two separate but affiliated agencies: Gillian MacKenzie Agency and Wolf Literary. Whilst the transition takes place, the existing website and contact information should be used for both new agencies. To submit a project email a query letter along with a 50-page writing sample (for fiction) or a detailed proposal (for non-fiction). Samples may be submitted as an attachment or embedded in the body of an email. Does not accept mailed queries. Does not represent screenplays.

Carol Mann Agency*
55 Fifth Avenue, New York, NY 10003
tel +1 212-206-5635
email submissions@carolmannagency.com
website www.carolmannagency.com
Twitter @carolmannagency
Contacts Carol Mann, Laura Yorke, Gareth Esersky, Myrsini Stephanides, Joanne Wyckoff, Iris Blasi, Maile Beal, Agnes Carlowicz

Interested in books on animals, business, food, fiction, health, history and politics, humour and popular culture, memoir, relationships and parenting, science and technology, spirituality and religion (home 15%, overseas 20%). Works in conjunction with foreign and film agents. See website for submission guidelines. *Founded* 1977.

The Evan Marshall Agency*
1 Pacio Court, Roseland, NJ 07068-1121
tel +1 973-287-6216
email evan@evanmarshallagency.com
website www.evanmarshallagency.com
President Evan Marshall

General fiction (home 15%, overseas 20%). Works in conjunction with overseas agents. Will suggest revision. Considers new clients by referral only. *Founded* 1987.

Jean V. Naggar Literary Agency Inc.*
216 East 75th Street, Suite 1E, New York, NY 10021
tel +1 212-794-1082
email jvnla@jvnla.com
website www.jvnla.com
President and Agent Jennifer Weltz, *Agents* Alice Tasman, Ariana Philips, Alicia Brooks

Mainstream commercial and literary fiction, non-fiction (narrative, memoir, journalism, psychology, history, pop culture, humour and cookbooks), young readers (picture, middle grade, young adult). Works in conjunction with foreign agents. Submit queries via form on website. *Founded* 1978.

Alison Picard, Literary Agent
PO Box 2000, Cotuit, MA 02635
tel +1 508-477-7192
email ajpicard@aol.com

Adult fiction and non-fiction, children's and young adult (15%). No short stories, poetry, plays, screenplays or sci-fi/fantasy. Please send query via email (no attachments). *Founded* 1985.

Pippin Properties Inc.
110 West 40th Street, Suite 1704, New York, NY 10018
tel +1 212-338-9310
email info@pippinproperties.com
website www.pippinproperties.com
Facebook www.facebook.com/pippinproperties
Twitter @LovethePippins
Contact Holly McGhee, Elena Giovinazzo, Sara Crowe, Cameron Chase, Ashley Valentine, Rakeem Nelson

Focuses on children's book authors and artists (home 15%, overseas 25%), from picture books to middle grade, graphic novels and young adult novels, and adult trade books on occasion. Query by email. *Founded* 1998.

Rees Literary Agency*
One Westinghouse Plaza, Suite A203, Boston, MA 02136
email lorin@reesagency.com
website www.reesagency.com
Agents Ann Collette, Lorin Rees, Rebecca Podos, Kelly Peterson, Ashley Herring Blake

Business books, self-help, biography, autobiography, political, literary fiction, memoirs, history, current affairs, YA, middle grade, romance, women's fiction, mystery (home 15%). Check agency bios for submission guidelines on the website. *Founded* 1982.

The Angela Rinaldi Literary Agency*
email info@rinaldiliterary.com
website www.rinaldiliterary.com
President Angela Rinaldi

Mainstream and literary adult fiction; non-fiction (home 15%, overseas 25%). *Founded* 1994.

Root Literary*
email submissions@rootliterary.com
email illustrators@rootliterary.com
website www.rootliterary.com
Twitter @RootLiterary

Identifies talent, negotiates deals and advocates for books all the way from submission to publication. Represents authors, author-illustrators, graphic novelists and illustrators. See website for specific submission guidelines. No postal, telephone or in-person pitches. No screenplays or poetry, no authors of picture book texts only.

Jane Rotrosen Agency*
318 East 51st Street, New York, NY 10022
tel +1 212-593-4330
email info@janerotrosen.com
website www.janerotrosen.com
Twitter @Jane_Rotrosen

Represents authors of fiction and non-fiction. Client list includes over 1,000 international and domestic bestsellers in all formats. Genres represented include women's fiction, suspense, thrillers, mysteries, crime fiction, historical novels, YA, fantasy, psychological suspense and romantic comedy. Visit individual agent pages on the website for their specific interests and to contact them by email. *Founded* 1974.

Susan Schulman Literary Agency LLC*
454 West 44th Street, New York, NY 10036
tel +1 212-713-1633
email susan@schulmanagency.com
website www.schulmanagency.com

Agents for negotiation in all markets (with co-agents) of fiction and general non-fiction, children's books, academic and professional works, and associated subsidiary rights including plays, television and film (home 15%, UK 7.5%, overseas 20%). Return postage required. Email enquiries to queries@schulmanagency.com.

Scott Meredith Literary Agency

PO Box 3090, Grand Central Post Office, New York, NY 10163-3090
email info@scottmeredith.com
website www.scottmeredith.com
President Arthur Klebanoff

General fiction and non-fiction. *Founded* 1946.

Scovil Galen Ghosh Literary Agency, Inc.*

276 Fifth Avenue, Suite 708, New York, NY 10001
tel +1 212-679-8686
email info@sgglit.com
website www.sgglit.com
Contacts Russell Gallen (russellgalen@sgglit.com), Jack Scovil (jackscovil@sgglit.com), Anna Ghosh (annaghosh@sgglit.com), Ann Behar (annbehar@sgglit.com)

Represents a wide range of commercial and literary fiction, with an emphasis on novels with strong characters and distinct, new voices. Non-fiction tastes generally lean towards the literary scale and favours works that have something new to teach their reader. Areas of interest include biography and memoir, business and politics, contemporary culture, journalism, nature, history, science and sport. Picture books, children's, middle-grade and young adult fiction also of interest. Foreign rights handled by co-agency Baror International, Inc. Query by post or email to one agent or to info@sgglit.com. Email queries preferred. For full submission guidelines and agent preferences see website. *Founded* 1992.

Philip G. Spitzer Literary Agency Inc.*

50 Talmage Farm Lane, East Hampton, NY 11937
tel +1 631-329-3650
email annelise.spitzer@spitzeragency.com
website www.spitzeragency.com
Facebook www.facebook.com/SpitzerLit/
Twitter @SpitzerLit
Agents Philip Spitzer, Anne-Lise Spitzer, Lukas Ortiz, *Office* Kim Lombardini

General fiction and non-fiction; specialises in mystery/suspense/thriller, true crime, biography and memoir.

The Strothman Agency*

63 East 9th Street, Suite 10X, New York, NY 10003
email info@strothmanagency.com
website www.strothmanagency.com
Twitter @strothmanagency

Specialises in history, science, narrative journalism, nature and the environment, current affairs, narrative non fiction, business and economics, YA fiction and non-fiction, middle-grade fiction and non-fiction. Only accepts electronic submissions. Query by email to strothmanagency@gmail.com but first see website for detailed submission guidelines. *Founded* 2003.

Trident Media Group

355 Lexington Avenue, New York, NY 10017
tel +1 212-333-1511
email info@tridentmediagroup.com
website www.tridentmediagroup.com
Facebook www.facebook.com/TridentMediaGroup
Twitter @Trident_Media

Full-length MSS: see website for genres represented (home 15%, overseas 20%); in conjunction with co-agents, theatre, films, TV (15%). Will suggest revision. See website for submission guidelines. *Founded* 2000.

Watkins/Loomis Agency Inc.

PO Box 20925, Park West Finance Station, New York, NY 10025
email assistant@watkinsloomis.com
website www.watkinsloomis.com

Specialises in literary fiction, biography, memoir and political journalism. No unsolicited MSS. Representatives Abner Stein (UK), The Marsh Agency Ltd (foreign).

WME

11 Madison Avenue, 18th Floor, New York, NY 10010
tel +1 212-586-5100
website www.wmeentertainment.com

Represents bestselling authors, critically acclaimed literary writers, award-winning thought leaders and up-and-coming talent.

WordLink Incorporated

PO Box 395, Enola, Pennsylvania 17025
tel +1 631-882-3462
website www.wordlink.us
Facebook www.facebook.com/wordlink.us/

Founded as a cooperative of writers, editors and agents in the USA and New Zealand. Represents works of fiction and non-fiction as well as television and film internationally. Send a query letter or use online form. See website for detailed submission guidelines. *Founded* 1998.

Writers House LLC*

21 West 26th Street, New York, NY 10010
tel +1 212-685-2400
website www.writershouse.com

Fiction and non-fiction, including all rights; film and TV rights. See website for submission guidelines and contact details for agents. *Founded* 1973.

The Wylie Agency Inc.

250 West 57th Street, Suite 2114, New York, NY 10107
tel +1 212-246-0069
email mail@wylieagency.com
website www.wylieagency.com

Literary fiction/non-fiction. Offices in New York and London. No unsolicited MSS accepted.

Art and illustration
Freelancing for beginners

Fig Taylor describes the opportunities open to freelance illustrators and discusses types of fee and how to negotiate one to your best advantage.

Full-time posts for illustrators are extremely rare. Because commissioners' needs tend to change on a regular basis, most artists have little choice but to freelance – offering their skills to a variety of clients in order to make a living.

Illustration is highly competitive and a professional attitude towards unearthing and targeting potential commissioners, and presenting, promoting and delivering your work will be vital to your success. Likewise, a realistic understanding of how the industry works and of your place within it will be key. Without adequate research into your chosen field(s) of interest, you may find yourself approaching inappropriate clients – a frustrating and disheartening experience for both parties and a waste of your time and resources.

Who commissions illustration?
Magazines and newspapers

Whatever your illustrative ambitions, you are most likely to receive your first commissions from editorial clients. The comparatively modest fees involved allow art editors the freedom to take risks, so many are keen to commission newcomers. Briefs are generally fairly loose though deadlines can be short, particularly where daily and weekly publications are concerned. However, fast turnover means you will establish yourself sooner rather than later, thus reassuring clients in other, more lucrative, spheres of your professional status. Given then that it is possible to use magazines as a springboard, it is essential to research them thoroughly when seeking to identify your own individual market. See the directories starting on page 36. Collectively, editorial clients accommodate an infinite variety of illustrative styles and techniques. Don't limit your horizons by approaching only the most obvious titles and/or those you would read yourself. Consider also trade and professional journals, customer magazines (such as in-flight magazines or those produced for supermarkets, insurance companies, etc.) and those available on subscription from membership organisations or charities. You will often find obscure titles in the reference section of public or university libraries, where the periodicals they subscribe to will reflect the subjects taught. Seeking out as many potential clients as possible will benefit you in the long term. In addition to the titles listed in this *Yearbook*, the Association of Illustrators (AOI) publishes an *Editorial Directory* which gives specific client contact details and is updated annually. Don't just confine yourself to the world of print; online publications commission illustration – and gifs – too. There are a number of useful online resources to further aid your research such as www.magforum.com, https://magpile.com, www.express.yudu.com, and https://issuu.com.

Book publishing

With the exception of children's picture books, where illustration is unlikely to fall out of fashion, some publishers are using significantly less illustration than they once did on print or ebook covers. Certain publishers of traditional mass market fiction genres, such as horror, science fiction and fantasy, still favour strong, representational work on their covers, however it no longer predominates and a wider variety of styles are now used. While photography still predominates in other genres, such as the family saga and historical romance, quirky, humorous and fashion-influenced styles continue to be synonymous with the packaging of women's contemporary romance. A very diverse range of styles can be accommodated within literary fiction, including classics, though a smaller, independent publisher specialising in this area might opt to use stock imagery in order to operate within a limited budget. While specialist, scientific and technical illustrators still have a vital part to play in non-fiction publishing, decorative work is proving popular with lifestyle publishers covering subjects such as cookery, gardening and mind, body & spirit. Overall, however, photography continues to predominate in non-fiction, much of which is celebrity led.

Children's publishers use a wide variety of styles, covering the gamut from baby books, activity and early learning, through to full-colour picture books, transitional readers, national curriculum-related educational books, covers for YA fiction and black-and-white spot illustrations for the 8–11 age group. Author/illustrators are particularly welcomed by picture book publishers – though some have a policy of working only with those represented by a literary agent. Whatever your style, being able to develop believable characters and sustain them throughout a narrative is paramount. Some children's book illustrators initially find their feet in educational publishing. However, all ages are catered for within this area, including adults with learning difficulties, those learning a second language and teachers working right across the educational spectrum. Consequently, a wide variety of illustrators can be accommodated, even those working in comic book, graphic novel or manga styles. With the exception of educational publishing, which tends to have a faster turnaround, most publishing deadlines are civilised and mass market covers particularly well paid. There are numerous publishing clients listed elsewhere in this *Yearbook* (see the directories starting on page 130 and page 198) and visiting individual websites is a good way to get a flavour of the kind of illustration they may favour. In addition, the AOI publishes a *Publishing Directory*, which is updated yearly and gives specific client contact details.

Greeting cards

Many illustrators are interested in providing designs for cards and giftwrap. Illustrative styles favoured include decorative, graphic, humorous, fine art, children's, quirky and cute. For specific information on the gift industry which, unlike the areas covered here, works on a speculative basis, see *Card and stationery publishers that accept illustrations and photographs* on page 497. The UK Greeting Card Association also has some excellent resources for those who are new to the industry on their website, www.greetingcardassociation.org.uk/resources.

Design and branding agencies

Both design commissioners and their clients (who are largely uncreative and will, ultimately, be footing the bill) will be impressed and reassured by relevant, published work so wait until you're established before approaching them or illustrators' agents who cater to this market. Although fees are significantly higher than those in newspapers, magazines and book publishing, this third-party involvement generally results in a more restrictive brief. Deadlines may vary and styles range from conceptual through to realistic, decorative, humorous, stylised, and informational – with those involved in multimedia and web design favouring illustrators with character development and basic animation skills.

Magazines such as *Creative Review* and the online *Design Week* (both published by Centaur Media Plc) will keep you abreast of developments in the design world and help you identify clients' individual areas of expertise. Free online directories, such as www.designdirectory.co.uk and www.dexigner.com, carry listings; and you can scour Instagram and any number of well-curated graphic design blogs for leads. Individual contact names are also available at a price from database specialists Agency Access, who can provide creative suppliers with up-to-date information on commissioners in all areas. A similar service is provided by Bikinilists, an online annual subscription-based resource that specialises in providing categorised contact data. The AOI's annually updated *Advertising Directory* incorporates a number of design consultancies, reflecting the fact that lines between advertising, marketing and branding are becoming increasingly blurred.

Useful addresses

Association of Illustrators (AOI)
Somerset House, Strand, London WC2R 1LA
tel 020-7759 1010
email info@theaoi.com
website https://theaoi.com

The UK's professional trade organisation. Organisers of the World Illustration Awards and publishers of *Varoom* magazine, *The Illustrator's Guide to Law and Business Practice* and various client directories.

Agency Access
360 Motor Parkway, Suite 700, Hauppauge, NY 11788
tel (+1) 631-951-9500
email via contact form on website
website www.agencyaccess.com

Offers practitioners a variety of creative services, including access to up-to-date information on commissioning clients in a wide variety of spheres.

Bikinilists: Creative Buyers Database
Unit 18, Govanhill Workspace, 69 Dixon Road, Glasgow G42 8AT
tel 020-7112 1105
website www.bikinilists.com

Maintains an up-to-date database of creative commissioners and practitioners. Provides a boutique platform and support to those wishing to create and send promotional email marketing campaigns.

Centaur Media Plc
Floor M, 10 York Road, Lambeth, London SE1 7ND
tel 020-7970 4000
website www.creativereview.co.uk, www.designweek.co.uk

Publishes *Creative Review* magazine and free online resource, *Design Week*.

Haymarket Business Media
Bridge House, 69 London Road, Twickenham TW1 3SP
tel 020-8267 5000
email campaign@haymarket.com
website www.campaignlive.co.uk

Publishes *Campaign* magazine monthly, plus an additional quarterly publication.

Serbin Creative Inc.
813 Reddick Street, Santa Barbara, CA 93103
email hello@serbincreative.com
website www.serbincreative.com, www.directoryofillustration.com

Publishes the *Directory of Illustration* and hosts portfolios online. Also publishes the accompanying catalogue of The World Illustration Awards in conjunction with the Association of Illustrators.

Workbook
email support@workbook.com
website www.workbook.com

Publishes printed sourcebooks and showcases portfolios online.

Advertising agencies

You should ideally be established before seeking advertising commissions. Fees can be high, deadlines short and clients extremely demanding. A wide range of styles are used and commissions might be incorporated into direct mail or press advertising, featured on websites or elsewhere in cyberspace, billboards, hoardings, themed installations or animated for television. Fees will depend on whether a campaign is local, national or global and how many forms of media are used to attract the target demographic's attention.

Most agencies employ at least one art buyer to look at portfolios, increasingly online. A good one will know what campaigns each creative team is currently working on and alert creatives to work that meets their criteria. While some art buyers are open to being approached by freelance illustrators, the chances of them being able to use a total newbie on a big-budget job remain slim. Monthly periodicals, *Creative Review* and the monthly *Campaign* (see page 46) carry agency news, while the AOI also publishes an *Advertising Directory*, updated annually. The online directory www.adforum.com is another invaluable resource.

The 21st-century portfolio

These days it's hard to define a portfolio as any one thing. Put simply, it's a curated, ever-evolving body of your best work geared towards getting you the type of commissions you want, whether showcased on a website, slideshow, pdf, Instagram feed, or displayed in a ring-bound folder. Given the wide variety of self-promotional tools and formats available, most illustrators' portfolios will take multiple concurrent forms. Traditionally UK commissioners have shown a marked preference for illustrators with a strong, consistent, recognisable style to a generic jack-of-all-trades. Widespread use of the internet has gradually rendered this requirement universal as the world contracts and the talent pool widens. Thus, when assembling a selection of work for professional purposes, try to exclude samples which are, in your own eyes, weak, irrelevant, outdated, derivative, uncharacteristic or simply unenjoyable to do, and focus on your strengths instead. Should you be one of those rare, multi-talented individuals who finds it hard to limit themselves stylistically, or someone with more than one creative career, you will probably find it helpful to split conflicting work up to minimise the risk of confusion. You may, for instance, choose to create separate sections on a website aimed at the needs of different types of commissioner, or opt to have more than one website and/or trading name.

A lack of formal training or published work need not be a handicap providing your portfolio accurately reflects the needs of the clients you're targeting. Some illustrators find it useful to assemble 'mock-ups' using existing magazine layouts. By responding to the copy and replacing the original images with your own, it is easier to see how your work will look in context. If you'd rather not reproduce the layout, a concise caption or title can suffice unless the work clearly speaks for itself, such as a food still life or political caricature. This advice is particularly relevant to conceptual illustrators, as commissioners are paying for the way you think in addition to your style/technique. Eventually, as you become more established, you'll be able to replace these with published pieces.

Face-to-face meetings with clients are a rarity unless there's a job on the go and you're based in the same location. If you are fortunate enough to get one, strive to keep a laptop or tablet presentation as focused and streamlined as you would a print one, i.e. have a finite number of images and a set running order. Either bring your own device or borrow one with which you are familiar. Make sure it is fully charged and that you have emergency back-up. If your presentation involves talking a client through your website or blog rather than a pdf or slideshow, check you will have wireless internet access and, if not, take screen captures. Don't attempt to deliver a professional presentation on your phone – and if you are opting for a print presentation bear in mind that most commissioners have limited desk space and never exceed A3. Regardless of method of delivery, complexity of style and diversity of subject matter will dictate how many samples to include. Since it will be taken for granted that you know how to draw from observation, don't show academic life drawings and remember that sketch books are optional extras unless specifically requested.

Austerity and technology have contrived to shrink the size of the average art department while increasing individual workload. Consequently even illustrators' agents can struggle to make appointments with commissioners for speculative purposes. But reaching out to potential clients is still very much part of your remit. In other words, quietly sitting on social media and trusting they'll somehow magically find you is not going to cut it. Having established the correct contact name (either from a written source, asking the company directly, or consulting your good friends, Google, Instagram, and LinkedIn), and checking that your work is relevant to their needs, your chosen target clients are best initially approached by letter or telephone call. Emails can be overlooked, ignored or simply end up in the company spam filter. Avoid generic 'Dear Sir or Madam' communications of any kind as well as indiscriminate blanket bombing. Take your time, always do your homework, and make sure it shows in what you write and the samples and/or links you send. This alone will separate you from the herd. Commissioners are divided on the use of gimmicky promotional material so keep it simple and affordable. A couple of hi-res printouts should see you right as an introduction; politely followed up by a phonecall or email within a week or two.

If you are summoned for a personal briefing (again this isn't a given in the age of Skype and clients in different geographical locations), cleanliness, punctuality and enthusiasm are more important to clients than how you dress – as is a professional attitude to taking and fulfilling a brief. A thorough understanding of each commission is paramount from the outset. You will need to know your client's requirements regarding roughs; content and format; preferred medium if you work in more than one; resolution and size of the finished artwork when reproduced; and preferred file type and resolution for delivery of final image(s). You will also need to know when the deadline is. Never, under any circumstances agree to undertake a commission unless you are certain you can deliver on time and always work within your limitations. Talent is nothing without reliability.

Self-promotion

There are many ways an illustrator can ensure their work stays uppermost in the industry's consciousness, some more expensive than others. On the affordable front, images can be emailed in a variety of formats, stored on disc, posted in a blog, or showcased on a website/ online portfolio. Social networking platforms, such as Twitter, Dribbble, Tumblr, Pinterest, Facebook and Instagram, can also be invaluable when raising your professional profile. You might also consider advertising in a professional directory such as the US-based *Workbook* or *Directory of Illustration*, which tend to have a long shelf life and are well respected by industry professionals. While sourcebooks like these are generally available free to commissioners in print and digital format, exposure doesn't come cheap to advertisers. However, those represented by illustration agencies who advertise in them can promote themselves at a cheaper rate. Unlike freelancers, agents purchase multiple pages which can be divided up and shared by their artists.

Competitions are another effective means of self promotion. The annual World Illustration Awards, run by the Association of Illustrators, is open to students and new graduates as well as professional illustrators over the age of 18. There are ten categories and a 500 project longlist is published online by the AOI. 200 shortlisted projects, in addition to those of the award winners, are included in an annual competition showcase and awards catalogue. Keep your eyes open for other competitions too. Even comparatively low-key online challenges such as *Illustration Friday* and *InkTober* can result in commissions.

As commissioners routinely use internet resources, websites have become an essential method of self-promotion. Make sure yours loads quickly, is simple and straightforward to navigate and displays decent-sized images. Many illustrators make poor use of their 'About Me' section, which is effectively your shop window. Use your bio page to discuss the way you work and the type of commissions you've had or hope to work on. Likewise incorporate links to where else your work can be found on the web. The more you keep them clicking, the more likely they are to remember you. Currently, both AOI members and non-members can promote their work online at https://theaoi.com/folios, though members can do so at a reduced rate.

Be organised

Once you are up and running, it is imperative to keep organised records of all your commissions. Contracts can be verbal as well as written, though details – both financial and otherwise – should always be confirmed in writing (an email fulfils this purpose) and duplicated for your files. Likewise, keep corresponding client letters, emails and order forms. The AOI publication *The Illustrator's Guide to Law and Business Practice* offers a wealth of practical, legal and ethical information. Subjects covered include contracts, fee negotiation, agents, licences, royalties and copyright issues.

Money matters

The type of client, the purpose for which you are being commissioned and the usage of your work can all affect the fee you can expect to receive, as can your own professional attitude. Given that it is *extremely* inadvisable to undertake a commission without first agreeing on a fee, you will have to learn to be upfront about funds.

Licence v copyright

Put simply, according to current legislation, copyright is the right to reproduce a piece of work anywhere, *ad infinitum*, for any purpose, for a period ending 70 years after the death of the person who created it. This makes it an extremely valuable commodity.

By law, copyright automatically belongs to you, the creator of your artwork, unless you agree to sell it to another party. In most cases, clients have no need to purchase it, and the recommended alternative is for you to grant them a licence instead, governing the precise usage of the artwork. This is far cheaper from the client's perspective and, should they subsequently decide to use your work for some purpose other than those outlined in your initial agreement, will benefit you too as a separate fee will have to be negotiated. It's also worth noting that even if you were ill-advised enough to sell the copyright, the artwork would still belong to you unless you had also agreed to sell it.

Rejection and cancellation fees

Most commissioners will not expect you to work for nothing unless you are involved in a speculative pitch, in which case it will be up to you to weigh up the pros and cons of your possible involvement. Assuming you have given a job your best shot, i.e. carried out the client's instructions to the letter, it's customary to receive a rejection fee even if the client doesn't care for the outcome: 25% is typical at developmental/rough stage and 50% at finished artwork stage. (Clear this with the client before you start, as there are exceptions to the rule.) Cancellation fees are paid when a job is terminated through no fault of the artist; rates in this instance are around 25% before rough stage, 33% on delivery of roughs and 100% on delivery of artwork.

Fixed *v* negotiable fees

Editorial and publishing fees are almost always fixed with little, if any, room for haggling and are generally considerably lower than advertising and design fees, which tend to be negotiable. A national full-colour 48-sheet poster advertising Marks & Spencer is likely to pay more than a black-and-white ad in the local freebie newspaper plugging a poodle parlour. If, having paid your editorial dues, you find yourself hankering after commissions from the big boys, fee negotiation – confusing and complicated as it can sometimes be – will become a fact of life. However you choose to go about the business of cutting a deal, it will help if you disabuse yourself of the notion that the client is doing you a whopping favour by considering you for the job. Believe it or not, the client *needs* your skills to bring his/her ideas to life. In short, you are worth the money and the client knows it.

Pricing a commission

Before you can quote on a job, you'll need to know exactly what it entails. For what purpose(s) is the work to be used? Will it be used several times? Will its use be local, national or international? For how long is the client intending to use it? Who is the client and how soon do they want the work? Are you up against anyone else (who could possibly undercut you)? Ask the client what the budget is. There's a fair chance they might tell you. Whether they are forthcoming or not, don't feel you have to pluck a figure out of thin air or agree to their offer immediately. Play for time. Tell them you need to review your current workload and that you'll get back to them within a brief, specified period of time. If nothing else, haggling over the phone is less daunting than doing it face to face. If you've had no comparable commissions to date and are an AOI member, you can contact the membership desk for advice on fee negotiation and use their online calculator and resources. Pricing is at the heart of being a successful illustrator and it's important you are confident.

   When you begin negotiating, have in mind a bottom-line price you're prepared to do the job for and always ask for slightly more than your ideal fee as the client will invariably try to beat you down. You may find it useful to break down your asking price in order to explain exactly what it is the client is paying for. How you do this is up to you. Some people find it helpful to work out a daily rate incorporating overheads such as rent, heating, materials, travel and telephone charges, while others prefer to negotiate on a flat fee basis. There are also illustrators who charge extra for something needed yesterday, time spent researching, model hire if applicable and so on. It pays to be flexible, so if your initial quote exceeds the client's budget and you really want the job, tell them you are open to negotiation. If, on the other hand, the job looks suspiciously thankless, stick to your guns. If the client agrees to your exorbitant demands, the job might start to look more appetising.

Getting paid

Once you've traded terms and conditions, done the job and invoiced the client, you'll then have the unenviable task of getting your hands on your fee. It is customary to send your invoice to the accounts department stating payment within 30 days. It is also customary for them to ignore this entreaty and pay you when it suits them. Magazines pay promptly, usually within 4–6 weeks; everyone else takes 60–90 days.

Be methodical when chasing up your invoice. Get on the accounts department's case the moment the 30 days has elapsed and keep on chasing until payment is made. Don't worry about your incessant nagging scuppering plans of further commissions as these decisions are solely down to the art department, and they think you're a gem. If payment is still not forthcoming three months down the line, ask your commissioner to follow things up on your behalf. Chances are they'll be horrified you haven't been paid and things will be speedily resolved. In the meantime, you'll have had a good deal of practice talking money, which can only make things easier next time around.

And finally ...

Basic book-keeping – making a simple, legible record of all your financial transactions, both incoming and outgoing – will be crucial to your sanity once the tax inspector starts to loom. It will also make your accountant's job easier, thereby saving you money. If your annual turnover is less than £85,000 (over a twelve-month period), HM Revenue & Customs do not insist on you giving them a detailed breakdown of your business income and allowable expenses. Instead, they allow you to provide three summary figures in your tax return: turnover, one figure for the total

> ### Further reading
>
> • Fig Taylor, *How To Create A Portfolio and Get Hired* (Laurence King Publishing, 2nd edn 2013)
> • Derek Brazell and Jo Davies, *Understanding Illustration* (Bloomsbury 2014)
> • Derek Brazell and Jo Davies, *Becoming a Successful Illustrator* (Bloomsbury, *Creative Careers* series, 2nd edn 2017)
> • Alison Branagan, *The Essential Guide to Business for Artists and Designers* (Bloomsbury, 2nd edn 2017)
> • Darrel Rees, *How To Be An Illustrator* (Laurence King Publishing, 2nd edn 2014)
> • Lawrence Zeegen, *The Fundamentals of Illustration* (Bloomsbury, 3rd edn 2020)

of allowable expenses, and net profit or loss. Although an accountant is not necessary to this process, many find it advantageous to employ one. The tax system is complicated and dealing with HM Revenue & Customs can be stressful, intimidating and time consuming. Accountants offer invaluable advice on tax allowances, National Insurance and tax assessments, as well as dealing expertly with HM Revenue & Customs on your behalf – thereby enabling you to attend to the business of illustrating.

Fig Taylor began her career as an illustrators' agent in 1983. She has been the resident 'portfolio surgeon' at the Association of Illustrators since 1986 and also operates as a private consultant to non-AOI member artists. She lectures extensively in Professional Practice to illustration students throughout the UK and is the author of *How to Create a Portfolio and Get Hired* (Laurence King Publishing, 2nd edn 2013).

Illustrating non-fiction books

Freelance illustrator Frances Moffatt describes her route into professional non-fiction illustration and gives practical advice for aspiring illustrators on finding that first commission, and the process from contract through to publication and beyond.

The world of non-fiction books provides a wealth of illustration opportunities for the freelance illustrator, but is often overlooked by illustration graduates in favour of children's middle-grade fiction and picture books. It is an exciting, diverse sector of publishing to work in, and can range from commissions for cookery books and instructional guides on exercise and fashion to adult colouring books.

My own journey to illustrating non-fiction began after I graduated from my MA in Illustration and, fittingly, consulted the *Writers' & Artists' Yearbook* to identify potential clients. I had come to the conclusion that my portfolio was suited to the 'lifestyle' market, with a predominantly female focus, and subjects such as fashion, health and beauty. I duly combed the *Yearbook* to find appropriate publishers and then sent off small promotional packs containing a bundle of postcards, a business card and a covering letter to my chosen publishers. I put all this information in a spreadsheet so I could keep track of whom I had contacted and when, and whether I had followed that up with a phone call.

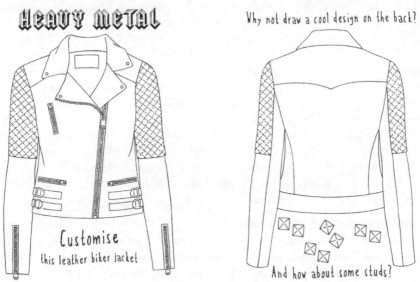

Illustrations by Frances Moffatt from *Fashion Exercise Book* (Batsford)

Around 18 months later, I received an exciting email from Pavilion Books asking me if I would like to illustrate a fashion-themed colouring and doodle book aimed at the young adult and adult markets, to which I swiftly replied a resounding 'Yes!'. It turned out that one of the designers in their art department had liked the promo package I had sent, and had pinned up one of my postcards on her desk to keep me in mind if any suitable projects came up. *Fashion Exercise Book* was published in 2014 by Batsford (a Pavilion imprint), and I went on to illustrate a further book, *Pick up a Pen*, in 2018, for their Portico list.

It's a commonly held belief that if you want to work in any aspect of the creative industries it is important to have 'contacts', but I can honestly say that, in my own experience and that of many other illustrators I know, this has not been the case. If your work is good, and you have a solid online portfolio, and knowledge of where your work sits in the publishing market, then you have every chance of seeing your work in print. Also keep in mind that building a sustainable career as an illustrator is a marathon not a sprint, and not getting an immediate response from potential clients is not a failure. In my case, I had some positive and encouraging feedback from art directors at various publishing houses, but it took nearly two years to receive an actual commission.

Commission, ideas and initial meeting

So … you have been commissioned to illustrate a book, either following an approach by a publisher or your own pitch. The next step is to sign your contract. Publishing contracts are long and have many clauses, so it is essential to read them carefully and to seek advice if there are any sections you don't understand. If you are a member of the Association of Illustrators (AOI), the professional body for illustration within the UK (https://theaoi.com/ see page 539), you can access free legal and contracts advice.

In a publishing contract for illustrating a book, you will generally get an advance and a percentage of royalties from any sales. Your advance will then be paid in three parts: the first instalment on signing the contract, the second on submitting the final illustrations, and the third on publication. Therefore your full payment will be spread out over a long period of time, which means it's important to manage your time and budget accordingly, and to understand that your book project will inevitably run alongside other shorter projects.

After agreeing the contract, the next step is a meeting with your commissioning editor and the team working on the book. This can be done over Skype or Zoom or in person, which I prefer. The team can vary in size depending on the nature of the project. It's a great opportunity to visit your publisher's headquarters, have a face-to-face meeting with the people you will be working with, and to discuss potential directions and possibilities. For the initial meeting, it's a good idea to prepare some rough sketches and ideas, any visual inspiration, and some examples of similar successful titles on the market. This doesn't have to be anything elaborate or polished; for this stage I usually use a PowerPoint for images and a sketchbook for ideas and roughs.

Synopsis, layouts and pencil roughs

Your book concept may be taken to a book fair, such as London or Frankfurt, which is an opportunity for co-editions to be sold to foreign publishers. For this, your publisher will need a written synopsis of the book and around three finished spreads. This is a really helpful step for you as an illustrator, because it means you get a clear idea of the publisher's vision for the book and the feel and the tone that they, and you, are looking for.

Once the synopsis has been pinned down, it's time to do the roughs for each spread and this can take different forms, depending on the book. For example, when I was working on *Fashion Exercise Book*, a colouring book with brief slogans on each page rather than proper 'text', it was quite an organic process. We started off with a list of ideas for page content, and then I worked closely with the designer, sending work back and forth until we arrived at a consistent look and feel for the illustrations. As a result, after a couple of spreads we had established a routine of sending through the rough pencil spreads for any adjustment and approval, and then sending the inked-up finals as I completed them, until the book was finished.

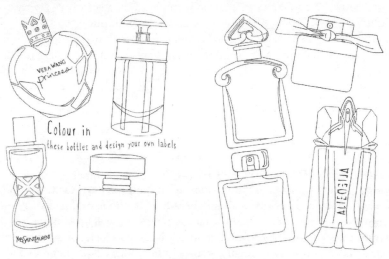

Illustrations by Frances Moffatt from *Fashion Exercise Book* (Batsford)

However, for *Pick up a Pen*, because there was copy involved it required a bigger team, so the process was slightly different and more formalised. I had input into the synopsis of the book, which was written up by a ghostwriter; I then submitted a pdf of pencil roughs of the whole book for approval, outlining what was going to be on each spread. Clearly at this point the text had not been written, but from the initial three spreads sent to book fairs I had an idea of the amount of text that would be on each page, which meant I could plan out the size and number of illustrations. As a result, my images for this book were a whole series of black-and-white 'spot' illustrations, which I submitted to the publisher in one batch at the end of the development stage; these were then sent to the book designer for page layout and the addition of limited accent colour.

So you will find that, when working on illustration for non-fiction books, there is commonality in the different stages of the project, but there is not just one set process or way of working. The main thing to remember is that clear and professional communication with the client and team at all times is paramount. It's likely that most of this communication will be conducted by email if you don't live near the publisher's offices (and they may well even be in a different time zone), so it's important to respond to all emails in a timely manner, and to just ask if you have questions or queries about any aspect of the brief or process. It's also really important to manage expectations; if you feel you are struggling with your deadline, it's best to speak up straightaway. It is much better to bring up any timing issues with as much notice as possible, and to negotiate an extension, than to struggle on and miss your deadline, as there is generally a little space in the schedule to allow for delays. And remember to *enjoy* the process! Freelance illustration can be a solitary profession at times, so illustrating a book allows you to be part of a creative team of experts in their field, which is an inspiring and rewarding experience.

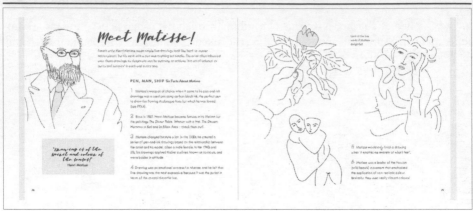

Illustrations by Frances Moffatt from *Pick up a Pen* (Portico)

Proofs, publication, marketing and beyond

After you've submitted your final illustrations, what happens next? First, you will receive proofs to check. Proofs are prints of all the spreads of the book on loose sheets of paper; they will give you a pretty clear idea of what the final book will look like. After that you will receive a sample copy of the book, which for me is always a high point – the culmination of many months of hard work brought together in final form, ready to be sold.

The process of creating a book, from commission to publication, is a long one, usually around 12 months. Therefore you will have a long break between completing your illustrations and promoting the publication of your book, which involves a very different mindset and skills. You will need to work with your publisher on a marketing strategy, and you will also need to take responsibility for promoting the book yourself through social media, traditional media and in-person events.

In the weeks leading up to publication, you need to start building excitement and anticipation for your product across social media. You can start dropping 'teaser' images (small excerpts) from your book, along with a link to where people can pre-order; you can give your audience an insight into your development process, showing images of your pencil roughs or filming a short 'behind the scenes' video. In addition, you can work with your publisher to organise a book launch event – which is a great opportunity to both promote your book and to celebrate too! Venues for these can range from bookshops to restaurants to galleries.

At this stage you may also see your book published in co-editions across various countries with different publishers. In these cases, the front cover design may be amended or changed, and the book may be given a new title. For example, *Fashion Exercise Book* was published in France as *My Fashion Book – Coloriages Creatifs* (Éditions Marie Claire 2015) with a red and purple rather than an orange cover.

Once the process is over it's a great idea to keep in touch with your publishers, sending them updates on your new work, through further promotional packs or email links to your updated website, so they can keep you in mind for any future projects. When you have one book illustration project in your portfolio, you'll be in a strong position as you go back to your trusty *Writers' & Artists' Yearbook* for your next round of marketing. Potential clients will be more likely to commission you, as they have evidence you have already successfully handled illustrating a book from start to finish.

The good news is, if you're reading this, you are already on Step One of your journey towards being a published illustrator for non-fiction. If you have the passion and drive to continue to refine your illustrative practice, and have a considered and consistent marketing plan, you can move forward with confidence knowing that you are equipped with the knowledge and skills to make your publishing dreams a career reality. Good luck!

Frances Moffatt is a freelance illustrator, writer, speaker and educator. She has worked on a range of commissions for clients across editorial, publishing, fashion, beauty, product and live event illustration and is the author/illustrator of *Fashion Exercise Book*, *Pick up a Pen* and *Fashion Colouring and Doodling*, all published by Pavilion Books. She has many years' experience of lecturing in Illustration at degree level and has spoken at design events and festivals, including TEDx Bloomsbury. She is a co-founder of The School of Illustration (www.theschoolofillustration.com), an online learning space for both aspiring and professional illustrators. For more information see www.francesmoffatt.com.

See also...
● *Freelancing for beginners,* page 475

How to make a living:
money matters

Alison Branagan explores the ways in which the self-employed artist, illustrator or writer can make their creative work pay in the current financial environment.

As professional writers, illustrators or artists we are all vulnerable to periods of economic uncertainty, often temporary in nature, but which might be anything from a sudden shortage of ready cash to suffering longer-term hardship and poverty.

During 2020 and 2021, creative people were forced to learn much more about online communication: making use of Zoom, setting up online shops or promoting their services via social media. More emergency funding became available as did new ways to support yourself and others, such as the #artistsupportpledge movement on Facebook and Instagram. Unexpectedly the world had more time for hobbies and leisure with the upshot that book sales and magazine subscriptions flourished.

In recent years there have been various organisations and professional bodies that have dissuaded artists, illustrators and writers from taking on unpaid commissions, for example, #NoFreeWork, #NotAHobby, and #payingartists. I still think it is worth writing or illustrating a one-off piece of work if your association with the business, brand, publication or organisation is of longer-term benefit to you. If the project is promoted properly, it can raise your profile and introduce you to new contacts. But in most cases, creative work needs to be paid for, or politely turned down if a suitable fee can't be negotiated. Taking the opportunity to recommend a competitor who regularly charges the most eye-watering sums (with a wry smile to yourself, of course) might be an even more fitting response to would-be clients seeking your services at low or no cost.

Free royalties

Unclaimed royalties from the ALCS (Authors' Licensing and Collecting Society; see page 715), PLR (Public Lending Right; see page 665) and DACS (Design and Artists' Copyright Society; see page 717) do add up. If you are a member or associate of the SoA (Society of Authors), which is highly recommended, you gain free membership of the ALCS which usually costs £36. The annual 'payback' royalty claimed by an illustrator from images printed in books, newspapers, magazines or even captured on television via DACS can amount to anywhere from a small sum to several thousand pounds.

If you are currently a member of ALCS you can now also submit claims for illustrations, photographs and diagrams you have submitted to publications. However, you can't claim twice, meaning if you are already claiming through DACS Payback, you can't also apply through ALCS Visual Claims.

Though some of these annual royalty payments are often quite small, over time they can mount up; they are well worth the tiny amount of effort involved in signing up and submitting your claim online at: www.alcs.co.uk, www.bl.uk/plr, and www.dacs.org.uk.

Trusts, grants and charities

Grants are difficult to come by, but I recommend contacting charitable organisations who have funds for artists or writers experiencing financial difficulty. Turn2Us can be used to find trusts and foundations for which you might be eligible, simply by entering your postcode into their 'Search for a Grant' section.

The SoA (Society of Authors) has a number of trusts that members can apply to, such as those set up to allay general financial difficulty or to assist with a specific publishing project by way of a research or writing grant.

If illustration is not your main focus and you are a visual artist, then subscribing to 'a-n' The Artists Information Company, is recommended. Other useful resources for funding information are the Arts Council (DYCP fund and 'Grants for the Arts and How to Apply' guide), Artquest, and Funding For Artists (see box for websites). The Elephant Trust (http://elephanttrust.org.uk) is a charity for fine artists. Creative England is also worth exploring for competitions and support projects especially for scriptwriters.

In-work and out-of-work benefits

The benefit system in the UK has changed dramatically, with six benefits now merged into one: this benefit is called Universal Credit (UC). You might be able to claim Employment Support Allowance (ESA) if you are self-employed and unwell. There are other benefits if you are very ill or disabled. (See *National Insurance contributions*, on page 732). I would strongly urge you to apply for any you are eligible for if you have been without any paid commissions for some time, especially if you have dependents, rent or a mortgage to pay. It is worth bearing in mind that if you have substantial savings this can limit your eligibility for assistance.

UC is an 'in-work' and also 'out-of-work' payment, which may support you in the first year of self-employment. However, if claiming UC you may have to look for a job if trading income continues to be at subsistence levels and you still require financial support beyond your first year of trading. It's a complicated benefit and is unsuited to the fluctuations of *ad hoc* freelance work, erratic sales and commissions. Visit Turn2Us or the UK Government portal (www.gov.uk/browse/benefits) and look at eligibility guidelines, try out the online calculators or contact Citizens Advice (www.citizensadvice.org.uk) if you are bewildered by the complexity of it all.

Understanding how taxation works

Many creative people fail to fully understand what they can count as expenses as part of their self-employment, and thereby reduce their net profits, and in turn their income tax or Class 4 National Insurance liability. Visit www.gov.uk/income-tax-rates/ for more in-

---

Trusts, grants and charities: useful websites

a-n The Artists Information Company
www.a-n.co.uk

Artquest
www.artquest.org.uk

The Arts Council
www.artscouncil.org.uk

Creative England
www.creativeengland.co.uk

Developing Your Creative Practice (DYCP)
www.artscouncil.org.uk/DYCP

Funding For Artists
www.fundingforartists.org.uk

Society of Authors (SoA)
www.societyofauthors.org

Society of Children's Book Writers and Illustrators
www.scbwi.org/awards/grants/for-illustrators/

Turn2Us
www.turn2us.org.uk

Art and illustration

formation. You can offset any trading losses against tax paid on a salary, or possibly become eligible for Tax Credits or UC if you record a reduced level of income on your tax return. If you are a member of the AOI, SoA or other professional body, you may have access to advice from an accountant as part of your membership. Tax Aid (https://taxaid.org.uk) is a very useful organisation if your annual income is under £20,000. They offer free advice and are used to working with artists, illustrators and writers.

Saving small sums

Credit Unions (www.findyourcreditunion.co.uk) are like local community banks you can join and save regular small amounts of money. In return there are a number of benefits, including access to personal and business loans. Equally, if you only save a small amount each week there will always be a small sum of money held in reserve to pay for the odd unexpected bill or tax demand.

What is crowdfunding?

Crowdfunding works by attracting pledges from a number of sources to help fund or pay for a new (creative) project and is well worth exploring. The best way to see how this can work successfully is by visiting some of the websites listed in the box. It can be helpful to have some form of social media presence to make the opportunity work best for you, but it is also now the case that these platforms are garnering their own brand of enthusiastic supporters.

Kickstarter and Indiegogo are two of the leading platforms, but there are more specialist publishing platforms aimed at authors and illustrators such as Unbound. If Unbound supports your proposed campaign, once the advance, print and distribution costs are raised they will print your book and make it available to buy through their online bookshop.

Crowdfunding platforms
Crowdfunder   www.crowdfunder.co.uk
GoFundMe   https://uk.gofundme.com
Indiegogo   www.indiegogo.com
JustGiving   www.justgiving.com
Kickstarter   www.kickstarter.com
Patreon   www.patreon.com
Spacehive   www.spacehive.com
Unbound   https://unbound.com

Patreon is a popular crowdfunding portal which is for all creatives not only for vloggers on YouTube; artists, illustrators and writers can also create projects to attract paid monthly support from subscribers known as patrons. GoFundMe and JustGiving are crowdfunding platforms closer in nature to traditional sponsorship or philanthropic support. Spacehive supports projects that benefit the wider community both socially and culturally.

Sponsorship

Major art festivals and book competitions are often sponsored by large businesses, but sponsorship can also work at a more localised and personal level. Attracting sponsorship often isn't just about money; it can take other forms such as the loan of a vehicle, assistance with travel costs, access to accommodation, resources, materials, hospitality, technology or a space to work. Often businesses like to become involved with interesting projects that not only work in a commercial sense, e.g. by attracting new consumers, but also provide a positive association with an emerging or established writer, illustrator, artist or collective.

Negotiation

Developing the skills of negotiation and persuasion are vital if you want to gain a better financial deal for your work. Negotiation is not just about money.

It is helpful, as a starting point, to obtain some guidance about what to charge, and the SoA provides fact sheets on rates and a useful guide to publishing contracts to its members. The AOI also provides access to brilliant resources and an extensive Pricing Calculator which helps you work out what fees to charge.

These days, many people are using email and texts to negotiate fees. I usually wouldn't advise this as you don't know what frame of mind the other party is going to be in when they see your communication. It is possible to negotiate on the phone, but face to face is always best when possible. Suitable non-verbal cues, facial expressions and tone of voice are important factors in any discussion.

Building relationships which withstand the test of time is essential and nurturing trust and goodwill with your clients will improve the likelihood of gaining a successful outcome when it comes to agreeing commissions, rates, licensing, and securing further opportunities.

Persuasion is something that needs to be cultivated as a personal attribute; you should never let a little thing like a potential client being utterly disinterested in your ideas or work put you off from pitching another idea! If you experience difficulties with a client, try to remain professional, upbeat and confident. A shiny disposition and outlook will always be attractive to those who commission, buy and hire creative freelancers.

Alison Branagan is an author and visual arts consultant. She is an associate lecturer at Central Saint Martins and a tutor at The Art Academy, London. She has written several business start-up and enterprise books, including *The Essential Guide to Business for Artists and Designers* (Bloomsbury, 2nd edn 2017, updated reprint 2019). For more information, go to www.alisonbranagan.com. Her Twitter and Instagram handle is @alisonbranagan.

See also...
- *Managing your finances: a guide for writers*, page 721
- *National Insurance contributions*, page 732
- *Authors' Licensing and Collecting Society*, page 715
- *DACS (Design and Artists Copyright Society)*, page 717
- *Public Lending Right*, page 665

Art agents and commercial art studios

Before submitting work, artists are advised to make preliminary enquiries and to ascertain terms of work. Commission varies but averages 25–30%. The Association of Illustrators (see page 539) provides a valuable service for illustrators, agents and clients.

*Member of the Society of Artists Agents
†Member of the Association of Illustrators

Advocate Art Ltd

Suite 7, The Sanctuary, 23 Oakhill Grove, Surbiton, Surrey KT6 6DU
tel 020-8390 6293
email mail@advocate-art.com
website www.advocate-art.com
Director Edward Burns

Has seven agents representing 300 artists and illustrators. Bespoke illustration for children's books, greeting cards and fine art publishers, gift and ceramic manufacturers. For illustrators' submission guidelines see website. New: animation, design and original content represented through LaB – Writers and Artists colLaBorate. Also original art gallery, stock library and website in German, Spanish and French. Founded 1996.

Allied Artists/Artistic License

tel 07971 111256
email info@allied-artists.net
website www.alliedartists-illustration.com
Contact Gary Mills

Represents over 90 illustrators ranging in styles from realistic through stylised to cute for all types of publishing but particularly children's illustration. Commission: 35%. Founded 1983.

Arena Illustration Ltd*†

Arena Illustration Ltd, 31 Eleanor Road, London E15 4AB
tel 020-8555 9827
website www.arenaillustration.com
Contact Tamlyn Francis

Represents 27 artists illustrating mostly book covers, children's books and design groups. Average commission: 25%. Founded 1970.

The Art Agency

21 Morris Street, Sheringham, Norfolk NR26 8JY
tel (01263) 823424
email artagency@me.com
website www.the-art-agency.co.uk
Facebook www.facebook.com/illustrationagency

Provides non-fiction, reference and children's book illustration. Specialises in non-fiction illustrations across a wide variety of subjects and age groups. Submit by email up to six samples along with a link to your website. Founded 1990.

The Art Market

51 Oxford Drive, London SE1 2FB
tel 020-7407 8111
email info@artmarketillustration.com
website www.artmarketillustration.com
Director Philip Reed

Represents 40 artists creating illustrations for publishing, design and advertising. Founded 1989.

Artist Partners Ltd*†

22 Albion Hill, Ramsgate, Kent CT11 8HG
tel 020-7401 7904
email christine@artistpartners.com
website www.artistpartners.com
Managing Director Christine Isteed

Represents artists, including specialists, producing artwork in every genre for advertising campaigns, storyboards, children's and adult book covers, newspaper and magazine features and album covers. New artists are considered if their work is of high standard. Submission should be by post and include a sae. Commission: 30%. Founded 1951.

Artistique International

Suite 7, The Sanctuary, 23 Oakhill Grove, Surbiton KT6 6DU
tel 07532 712002
email mail@artistique-int.com
website www.artistique-int.com
Contact Alison Berson

Specialises in editorial and advertising. The mission is to bring the highest quality illustrations to their clients. Offices in London, Marbella, New York and Singapore. Founded 2016.

The Artworks†

14 Cranbourne Avenue, London E11 2BQ
email submissions@theartworksinc.com
website www.theartworksinc.com
Contacts Stephanie Alexander-Jinks, Alex Hadlow, Lucy Scherer

Represents 35 illustrators for design and advertising work as well as for non-fiction children's books, book jackets, illustrated gift books and children's picture books. Commission: 25% advances, 15% royalties, 25% book jackets. Founded 1983.

Beehive Illustration

42A Cricklade Street, Cirencester, Glos. GL7 1JH
tel (01285) 644001
email enquiries@beehiveillustration.co.uk
website www.beehiveillustration.co.uk
Contact Paul Beebee

Represents 200 artists specialising in ELT, education and general children's publishing illustration. Commission: 25%. Founded 1989.

The Big Red Illustration Agency

tel 0808 120 0996
email enquiries@bigredillustrationagency.com
website www.bigredillustrationagency.com
Director Adam Rushton

Offers a high standard of talented, professional and dedicated illustrators. Over the years has developed strong relationships with a wide range of clients including children's book publishers, design agencies, greeting card companies and toy manufacturers. Founded 2012.

Central Illustration Agency

17B Perseverance Works, 38 Kingsland Road, London E2 8DD
tel 020-3222 0007
email info@centralillustration.com
website www.centralillustration.com
Contact Benjamin Cox

An international resource for commercial art and motion graphics for the advertising, design and publishing industries. Commission: 30%. Founded 1983.

Collaborate Agency

Unit 7, Hove Business Centre, Fonthill Road, Hove, Brighton BN3 6HA
tel (01273) 251700
email hello@collaborate.agency
website https://collaborate.agency/
Facebook www.facebook.com/collaborate
Twitter @c0llab0rate
Instagram @collaborateagency

Works on books for all ages and in all genres. Artists are skilled across all creative disciplines. Illustrators, editors, photographers, designers, web developers and animators are based in Brighton, London, New York, Gibraltar, Singapore and Seville studios.

Column Arts Agency

33 Kelmscott Road, Harborne, Birmingham B17 8QW
tel 07803 244202
email hi@columnartsagency.co.uk
website www.columnartsagency.co.uk
Facebook www.facebook.com/ColumnArtsAgency
Twitter @columnartagency
Artists' Agent & Project Manager William Ashbury

An illustration, design and animation agency that represents a range of author-cum-illustrators, artists and commercial creatives. Represents portfolios of individuals in the UK and USA. Founded 2012.

Creative Coverage

49 Church Close, Locks Heath, Southampton, Hants. SO31 6LR
tel (01489) 564536
email info@creativecoverage.co.uk
website www.creativecoverage.co.uk
Facebook www.facebook.com/CreativeCoverage
Twitter @CreativeCov
Instagram @creativecov
Co-founders Tim Saunders, Caroline Saunders

Fine art book publisher and artists' agent. Marketing for selected professional artists. Founded 2013.

Darley Anderson Illustration Agency

Suite LG4, New Kings House, 136–144 New Kings Road, London SW6 4LZ
tel 020-7385 6652
email clare@darleyanderson.com
website www.darleyandersonillustration.com
Twitter @Illustration_da
Managing Director Clare Wallace, *Directors* Darley Anderson, Rosanna Bellingham, *Agent* Lydia Silver, *Agent's Assistant* Chloe Davis

Represents bestselling and award-winning illustrators. Works across all areas of publishing, from picture books to gift titles to graphic novels, across fiction and non-fiction, collaborating with both adult and children's publishers worldwide. Actively looking for new talent, especially illustrators from under-represented backgrounds. Commission: 20%. Submission guidelines: send an email with portfolio attached as a pdf or in the body of the email, along with information about yourself and links to social media channels used to display your work. Author-illustrators should send texts as pdf or Word attachments, along with a brief synopsis and illustration samples. Submissions should be made directly to the agent of choice. Founded 1988.

David Lewis Agency

3 Somali Road, London NW2 3RN
tel 020-7435 7762 / 07931 824674
email david@davidlewisillustration.com
Director David Lewis

Considers all types of illustration for a variety of applications but mostly suitable for book and magazine publishers, design groups, recording companies and corporate institutions. Also offers a comprehensive selection of images suitable for subsidiary rights purposes. Send return postage with samples. Commission: 30%. Founded 1974.

Début Art & The Coningsby Gallery*†
30 Tottenham Street, London W1T 4RJ
tel 020-7636 7478
email info@coningsbygallery.com
website www.coningsbygallery.com
Directors Andrew Coningsby, Jonathan Hedley, Laura Lee

Offices in London and New York and a gallery in Bloomsbury, central London, which is available for exhibitions by fine artists and graphic artists on a hire or fully represented basis. Since it was founded, the gallery has helped many leading and up-and-coming artists mount successful exhibitions. The gallery offers artists many highly specialist marketing support services. Email submissions from artists are welcome. Founded 1985.

Dutch Uncle
5th Floor, 22 Upper Ground, London SE1 9PD
tel 020-7336 7696
email info@dutchuncle.co.uk
website www.dutchuncle.co.uk
Facebook www.facebook.com/dutchuncle
Twitter @AgencyDU
Instagram @agencydu

Represents and seeks out creative talent for clients looking to commission content such as animation, illustration, book design and data visualisations. Offices in New York and Tokyo. Founded 2006.

Eastwing†
99 Chase Side, Enfield EN2 6NL
tel 020-8367 6760
email art@eastwing.co.uk
website www.eastwing.co.uk
Contacts Andrea Plummer, Abby Glassfield

Represents artists who work across advertising, design, publishing and editorial. Commission: 25–30%. Founded 1985.

Eye Candy Illustration
Field Cottage, Saintbury WR12 7PX
tel 020-8291 0729
email info@eyecandyillustration.com
website www.eyecandyillustration.com
Managing Director Mark Wilson

Represents 50+ artists producing work for advertising campaigns, packaging, publishing, editorials, greeting cards, merchandising and a variety of design projects. Submit printed samples with sae or email low-res jpg files via website. Founded 2002.

Ian Fleming Associates – see Phosphor Art Ltd

Folio Illustration Agency†
tel 020-7242 9562
email info@folioart.co.uk
website www.folioart.co.uk

All areas of illustration. Founded 1976.

Good Illustration Ltd
71–75 Shelton Street, Covent Garden, London WC2H 9JQ
tel 020-8123 0243 (UK) / +1 347-627-0243 (US)
email draw@goodillustration.com
website www.goodillustration.com
Directors Doreen Thorogood, Kate Webber, Tom Thorogood

Represents 50+ artists for advertising, design, publishing and animation. Send return postage and samples. Commission: 25% publishing, 30% advertising. Founded 1977.

Graham-Cameron Illustration
59 Hertford Road, Brighton BN1 7GG
tel (01273) 385890
email enquiry@gciforillustration.com
Alternative address The Art House, Uplands Park, Sheringham, Norfolk NR26 8NE
tel (01263) 821333
website www.gciforillustration.com
Partners Helen Graham-Cameron, Duncan Graham-Cameron

Represents 37+ artists and undertakes illustration for publishing and communications. Specialises in educational, children's and information books. Phone before sending A4 samples with sae or email samples or link to a website. No MSS. Founded 1985.

Holroyde Cartey
email claire@holroydecartey.com
website www.holroydecartey.com

Represents high-quality illustrators. Welcomes submissions from debut and established illustrators. Only accepts submissions via email. Aims to respond to every submission within about six weeks. Please send a portfolio of a dozen or so images in either jpg or pdf format of up to 5MB in size. Founded 2015.

IllustrationX*†
2 Salamanca Place, Albert Embankment, London SE1 7HB
tel 020-7720 5202
email hello@illustrationx.com
website www.illustrationx.com
Facebook www.facebook.com/weareillustrationx
Twitter @_illustrationx

Welcomes submissions from illustrators and animators whose work is distinctive and innovative. Only accepts applications from artists through submissions page: www.illustrationx.com/applications. Founded 1929.

Image by Design Art Licensing

Suite 3, 107 Bancroft, Hitchin, Herts. SG5 1NB
tel (01462) 451190
email hugh@ibd-licensing.co.uk
website www.ibd-licensing.co.uk
Contact Hugh Brenham

Art licensing agency representing talented creatives. Artwork for greeting cards, stationery, home decor, wall art, tableware, textiles, puzzles, giftware and more. Represents an extensive portfolio of designs or commissions bespoke artwork. Founded 1987.

Inky Illustration

Kemp House, 152–160 City Road,
London EC1V 2NX
tel (0121) 330 1312
email info@inkyillustration.com
website https://inkyillustration.com/
Facebook www.facebook.com/inkyillustration
Twitter @inkyillo

Showcases the work of talented artists from across the globe. The range of illustrators have experience working with clients, on international advertising campaigns, publications and editorials, as well as commissions for smaller companies. Always happy to receive new work. New artists should fill out the application form on the website or email to: submissions@inkyillustration.com. Hard copies of work are accepted with a sae if the work is to be returned.

JSR

Unit 4, 3 Lever Street, London EC1V 3QU
tel 020-7228 6667
email illustration@jsragency.com
website www.jsragency.com
Facebook www.facebook.com/jsragency
Twitter @jsragency
Founder & Director Jamie Stephen

Represents some of the most highly skilled artists in the industry. Before submitting work for consideration artists should take a look at roster and make sure their work does not overlap with the artists currently represented. Please provide a pdf of your best work and website details in your submission: submissions@jsragency.com. Founded 2005.

B.L. Kearley Art & Antiques

Glebe House, Bakers Wood, Denham,
Bucks. UB9 4LG
tel (01875) 832145
email christine.kearley@kearley.co.uk
website www.kearley.co.uk
Agent C.R. Kearley

Represents over 30 artists and has been supplying top-quality illustrations for over 70 years. Mainly specialises in children's book and educational illustration for the domestic market and overseas. Known for realistic figurative work. Specialises in the sale of original book illustration artwork. Commission: 25%. Founded 1948.

Kids Corner

The Old Candlemakers, West Street, Lewes BN7 2NZ
tel 020-7593 0506
email claire@meiklejohn.co.uk
website www.kidscornerillustration.co.uk
Managing Director Claire Meiklejohn

Represents illustrators, from award-winning to emerging artists for children's publishing. Styles include fun, cute, stylised, picture book, young fiction, reference, graphic, traditional, painterly and digital. See also Meiklejohn Illustration (page 496). Founded 2015.

Lemonade Illustration Agency

Hill House, Suite 231, 210 Upper Richmond Road, London SW15 6NP
tel 07891 390750
email gary@lemonadeillustration.com
US office 347 Fifth Ave, Suite 1402, New York, NY 10016
website www.lemonadeillustration.com

Represents 150+ illustrators and character designers for all kinds of media from TV to children's books. Offices in London, New York, Austin, Sydney and Wakefield. Works with leading children's book, kidslit, ELT and educational publishers in the industry. Any submissions from illustrators by email must contain a website link (no attachments) or hard copies of samples can be sent by post with a sae to the London office. The company cannot reply to all emails because so many artist submissions are received.

Lipstick of London*

78 Clarendon Drive, London SW15 1AH
tel 07966 176989
email mc@lipstickillustration.com
website www.lipstickillustration.com
Twitter @LipstickAgency

Agency with artists who have experience spanning advertising, design, fashion, packaging, publishing, editorial, digital and motion and live events. Founded 2012.

Frances McKay Illustration

17 Church Road, West Mersea, Essex CO5 8QH
tel (01206) 383286
email frances@francesmckay.com
website www.francesmckay.com
Proprietor Frances McKay

Represents 15–20 artists for illustration mainly for children's books. For information on submissions please look at the website. Submit email with low-res scans or colour copies of recent work; sae essential for return of all unsolicited samples sent by post. Commission: 25%. Founded 1999.

Meiklejohn Illustration*†
The Old Candlemakers, West Street, Lewes BN7 2NZ
tel 020-7593 0506
email claire@meiklejohn.co.uk
website www.meiklejohn.co.uk
Managing Director Claire Meiklejohn

Represents illustrators, covering a wide range of styles, from traditional, children's publishing, photorealistic, cartoon to contemporary. See also Kids Corner (page 495). Founded 1973.

The Monkey Feet Illustration Agency
email enquiries@monkeyfeetillustration.com
website www.monkeyfeetillustration.com

Presents portfolios for artists creating work for children's book publishers, design agencies, greeting cards and toy companies. Founded 2012.

NB Illustration*
Home Farm, East Horrington, Somerset BA5 3EA
tel 07720 827328
email info@nbillustration.co.uk
website www.nbillustration.co.uk
Directors Joe Najman, Charlotte Dowson

Represents over 50 artists and will consider all material for the commercial illustration market. For submission details see website. Submissions by email only. Commission: 30%. Founded 2000.

Outline Artists
90 The Avenue, London NW6 7NN
tel 020-8451 3400
email ellie@outlineartists.com
website www.outlineartists.com
Contacts Camilla Parsons, Ellie Phillips

Represents a diverse roster of international image-making and animation talent.

Phosphor Art Ltd*†
19 Acacia Way, The Hollies, Sidcup, Kent DA15 8WW
tel 020-7064 4666
email info@phosphorart.com
website www.phosphorart.com
Directors Jon Rogers, Catriona Wydmanski

Represents 46 artists and specialises in innovative graphic digital illustration with artists working in watercolour, oil and gouache as well as pen and ink, scraper, charcoal and engraving styles. Also animation. Incorporates Ian Fleming Associates and The Black and White Line. Commission: 33.3%. Founded 1988.

Plum Pudding Illustration
Chapel House, St. Lawrences Way, Reigate, Surrey RH2 7AF
tel (01737) 244095
email letterbox@plumpuddingillustration.com
website www.plumpuddingillustration.com
Director Hannah Whitty

Represents 100+ artists, producing illustrations for children's publishing, advertising, editorial, greeting cards and packaging. See website for submission procedure. Commission: 30%. Founded 2006.

Sylvie Poggio Artists Agency
36 Haslemere Road, London N8 9RB
tel 020-8341 2722
email sylviepoggio@blueyonder.co.uk
website www.sylviepoggio.com
Directors Sylvie Poggio, Bruno Caurat

Represents 40 artists producing illustrations for publishing and advertising. Founded 1996.

Tallbean
tel (01728) 454921
email heather@tallbean.co.uk
website www.tallbean.co.uk
Founder Heather Richards

Provides a single source of specialist illustrators offering a range of styles. The team of well-established and creative illustrators is kept relatively small to ensure a close working relationship. Founded 1996.

Vicki Thomas Associates
195 Tollgate Road, London E6 5JY
tel 020-7511 5767
email vickithomasassociates@yahoo.co.uk
website www.vickithomasassociates.com
Twitter @VickiThomasA
Instagram @VickiThomasA
Consultant Vicki Thomas

Considers the work of illustrators and designers working in greetings/gift industries, and promotes work to gift, toy, publishing, licensing and related industries. Email sample images, covering letter and CV. Commission: 30%. Founded 1985.

Card and stationery publishers that accept illustrations and photographs

Before submitting work, artists and photographers are advised to ascertain requirements of the company they are approaching, including terms and conditions. Only high-quality material should be submitted.

*Member of the Greeting Card Association

The Almanac Gallery*
Waterwells Drive, Gloucester GL2 2PH
tel (01452) 888999
email submissions@greatbritishcards.co.uk
website www.greatbritishcards.co.uk

Specialises in contemporary art and beautiful charity Christmas cards. Acquired by The Great British Card Company (page 498) in 2015.

Card Connection Ltd*
Park House, South Street, Farnham,
Surrey GU9 7QQ
tel (01252) 892300
email enquiries@cardconnection.co.uk
website www.card-connection.co.uk
Managing Director Michael Johnson

Everyday and seasonal designs. Styles include cute, fun, traditional, contemporary, humour and photographic. Humorous copy and jokes plus sentimental verse. Founded 1992.

CardsWorld Ltd t/a 4C For Charity
114 High Street, Stevenage, Herts. SG1 3DW
tel 0845 230 0046
email design@charitycards.org
website www.charitycards.org

Contemporary and traditional Christmas cards for the corporate and charity market (London, international and festive themes). Submit low-res artwork by email no larger than 5MB. No verses or cute styles. Works with over 70 charities. Founded 1966.

Caspari Ltd
Linden House, John Dane Player Court, East Street, Saffron Walden, Essex CB10 1LR
tel 01799 513010
email info@caspari.co.uk
website https://international.casparionline.com/uk
Facebook www.facebook.com/casparionline

Traditional fine art/classic images; 5 x 4in transparencies. No verses. Founded 1990.

Colneis Marketing Ltd
3 Manning Road, Felixstowe IP11 2AS
tel (01394) 271668
email colneiscards@btconnect.com
website www.colneisgreetingcards.com
Proprietor John Botting

Photographs (preferably medium format) and colour artwork of nature and cute images. Founded 1994.

Dry Red Press*
Metway Studios, 55 Canning Street,
Brighton BN2 0EF
tel (01273) 241210
email info@dryredpress.com
website www.dryredpress.com
Facebook www.facebook.com/dryredpress
Twitter @dryredpress
Contacts Laura McDonald, Kicki Ringqvist

Publishes the work of contemporary British artists to produce high-quality greeting cards. See website for details. Founded 2009.

Simon Elvin Ltd*
Wooburn Industrial Park, Wooburn Green,
Bucks. HP10 0PE
tel (01628) 526711
email studioadmin@simonelvin.com
website www.simonelvin.com
Art Director Fiona Buszard, *Studio Manager* Rachel Green

Female/male traditional and contemporary designs, female/male cute, wedding/anniversary, birth congratulations, fine art, photographic animals, flowers, traditional sympathy, juvenile ages, special occasions and giftwrap. Looking for submissions that show flair, imagination and an understanding of greeting card design. Artists should familiarise themselves with the ranges, style and content. Submit a small collection of either colour copies or prints (no original artwork) and include a sae for return of work. Alternatively email jpg files. Founded 1977.

Graphic Humour Ltd
PO Box 717, North Shields, Tyne & Wear NE30 4WR
tel 0191 280 5019
email enquiries@graphichumour.com
website www.graphichumour.com

Risqué and everyday artwork ideas for greeting cards; short, humorous copy. Founded 1984.

The Great British Card Company

Unit 3, St Modwen Park, Haresfield, Stonehouse,
Gloucester GL10 3EZ
tel (01452) 888999
email submissions@paperhouse.co.uk
website www.greatbritishcards.co.uk
Facebook www.facebook.com/
GreatBritishCardCompany
Twitter @GreatBritCards

Incorporating Paper House (below), Medici Cards
(below) and The Almanac Gallery (page 497).
Publishers of everyday, Christmas and spring greeting
cards, notecards, gift wrap and gift bags. Particularly
welcomes new humorous submissions. For a full
listing of brands published visit website.
Founded 1980.

Green Pebble*

The Studio, Hall Farm (Behind Urban Jungle),
London Road, Weston, Beccles NR34 8TT
tel (01502) 710427
email ruby@greenpebble.co.uk
website www.greenpebble.co.uk
Publisher Michael Charles

Publisher of fine art greeting cards and associated
products by artists. See website for style before
submitting. Send a minimum of six design
thumbnails via email. Founded 2010.

Hallmark Cards Plc*

Dawson Lane, Dudley Hill, Bradford BD4 6HN
tel (01274) 252000
email creativesubmissions@hallmark-uk.com
website www.hallmark.co.uk
Facebook www.facebook.com/hallmarkukandireland
Twitter @HallmarkUK

See website for freelance opportunities and
submission details. Founded 1997.

Leeds Postcards

4 Granby Road, Leeds LS6 3AS
email xtine@leedspostcards.com
website www.leedspostcards.com
Contact Christine Hankinson

Publisher and distributor of postcards; feminism,
animal rights and socialism. Send only suitable and
relevant jpg files to email above. If published, paid by
advance royalty on print run.

Ling Design Ltd*

Westmoreland House, Westmoreland Street,
Bath BA2 3HE
tel (01225) 838574
email enquiries@lingdesign.co.uk
website www.lingdesign.co.uk
Twitter @GreetingsByLing
Head of Design Claire Twigger

Publishers of exceptional greetings cards and
premium gift packaging with a heritage that stretches
back to the 1950s. Founded 1998.

Medici Cards

Unit 3, St Modwen Park, Haresfield, Stonehouse,
Gloucester GL10 3EZ
tel (01452) 888999
email submissions@greatbritishcards.co.uk
website www.greatbritishcards.co.uk

Specialises in market-leading art and photographic
cards. Brands include National Geographic, English
Heritage, Royal Horticultural Society and Medici
Cards Blue Label. Founded 1997.

Miko Greetings

85 Landcroft Road, East Dulwich, London SE22 9JS
tel 020-8693 1011 / 07957 395739
email info@miko-greetings.com
website www.miko-greetings.com
Head Creative & Illustrator, Mik Brown aka Miko,
Creative Photographer Toby Brown, *Consultant* Annie
Horwood

Produces high-end, quality, humorous illustrated and
photographic greetings cards. Cards are mainly blank
for any occasion. Currently introducing some
occasions cards. Also produces 'Wall Art' of all the
company's designs. Founded 2014.

Moonpig

Herbal House, 10 Back Hill, London EC1R 5EN
email hellodesign@moonpig.com
Facebook www.facebook.com/Moonpig
Twitter @moonpiguk
Ceo Nickyl Raithatha

Offers designs from many of the leading card
publishers in the UK, such as Paperlink, The Great
British Card Company, Carte Blanche Greetings,
Disney, Ling Design, Last Lemon and Quitting
Hollywood, as well as many smaller publishers and
designers. The company is always on the lookout for
new design, humour and inspirational talent. If you
have created a range of cards that you think would be
suitable, please send them to the email above with a
short covering letter. Founded 2000.

Paper House

Unit 3, St Modwen Park, Haresfield, Stonehouse,
Gloucester GL10 3EZ
tel (01452) 888999
email art@paperhouse.co.uk
website www.greatbritishcards.co.uk

Producers of everyday birthday, special occasions and
family relations greeting cards; plus spring seasons
and Christmas. Specialising in the following: funny/
humorous cards and always looking for new copy/
ideas; photographic ranges; and contemporary and
trend-driven imagery.

Paperlink Ltd*

356 Kennington Road, London SE11 4LD
tel 020-7582 8244
email info@paperlink.co.uk
website www.paperlink.co.uk

Publishes a range of humorous and contemporary art greeting cards. Produce products under licence for charities. Always keen to hear from new artists, cartoonists and copywriters. Please check submission guidelines. Founded 1986.

Pineapple Park*

Unit A & B High Road, Deadmans Cross, Haynes, Shefford, Beds. SG17 5QQ
tel (01234) 381214
email info@pineapplepark.co.uk
website www.pineapplepark.co.uk
Director Sally Kelly

Illustrations and photographs for publication as greeting cards. Contemporary, cute, humour: submit artwork or laser copies with sae. Photographic florals always needed. Humour copy/jokes accepted without artwork. Founded 1993.

Nigel Quiney Publications Ltd*

Cloudesley House, Shire Hill, Saffron Walden, Essex CB11 3FB
tel 01799 520200
email carl.pledger@nigelquiney.com
website www.nigelquiney.com
Contact Carl Pledger

Everyday and seasonal greeting cards including traditional, photographic, humour, contemporary and cute. Submit by email or colour copies and photographs by post, no original artwork. Founded 1987.

Felix Rosenstiels Widow & Son Ltd

Fine Art Publishers, 33–35 Markham Street, London SW3 3NR
tel 020-7352 3551
email artists@rosenstiels.com
website www.rosenstiels.com

Invites offers of artwork of a professional standard for reproduction as picture prints for the picture framing trade. Any type of subject considered. See website for submission details. Founded 1880.

Santoro London*

Rotunda Point, 11 Hartfield Crescent, London SW19 3RL
tel 020-8781 1100
email submissions@santoro-london.com
website www.santoro-london.com
Directors Lucio Santoro, Meera Santoro

Publishers of innovative and International award-winning designs for three-dimensional pop-up cards, greeting cards, giftwrap and gift stationery. Bold, contemporary images with an international appeal. Subjects covered: contemporary, humour, photography, pop-up, cute, kawaii, quirky, fashion, retro. Submit samples in digital format (jpg or pdf files). Founded 1985.

Second Nature Ltd*

10 Malton Road, London W10 5UP
tel (01983) 209590
email design@secondnature.co.uk
website www.secondnature.co.uk
Facebook www.facebook.com/SecondNatureLtd

Contemporary artwork for greeting cards and handmade cards; jokes for humorous range; short modern sentiment; verses. Founded 1981.

Noel Tatt Group/Impress Publishing*

Appledown House, Barton Business Park, Appledown Way, New Dover Road, Canterbury, Kent CT1 3TE
tel (01227) 811600
email mail@noeltatt.co.uk
website www.noeltatt.co.uk

General everyday cards including Christmas. Will consider verses. Founded 1964.

UK Greetings Ltd*

Mill Street East, Dewsbury, West Yorks. WF12 9AW
tel (01924) 465200
website www.ukgreetings.co.uk
Ceo James Conn, *Creative & Product Development Director* Sandi Parisi

For submissions, please visit website. Founded 1997.

Wishing Well Studios*

Chichester Business Park, City Fields Way, Tangmere PO20 2FT
tel (01243) 792600
email creative.recruitment@cbg.co.uk
website www.carteblanchegreetings.com
Studio Manager Jude Williams

Part of Carte Blanche Group. Rhyming and prose verse 4–24 lines; also jokes. All styles considered. Don't send originals. Email attachments less than 3MB. Founded 1996.

Woodmansterne Publications Ltd*

1 The Boulevard, Blackmoor Lane, Watford, Herts. WD18 8UW
tel (01923) 200600
website www.woodmansterne.co.uk

Publisher of greeting cards and social stationery featuring fine and contemporary art and photography (colour and b&w). Submit colour copies, photographs or jpg files by email. Founded 1968.

Societies, prizes and festivals

Festival fun: your guide to why, how and what

Author and screenwriter Adam Hamdy, co-founder of crime and thriller festival Capital Crime, sings the praises of literary festivals. He has tips on how to find, prepare for, enjoy, and reap rewards from the festival experience and all it has to offer both authors and readers.

Why go to a literary festival?

Whether you're an aspiring or established author, or reader, if you've never been to a literary festival I'd highly recommend going. I went to my first literary festival in 2016, shortly before my debut novel, *Pendulum* (Headline 2016), hit the shelves. My publisher sent me to the Theakston Old Peculier Crime Writing Festival (see page 604) to promote the book and build relationships with bloggers, journalists and other authors. Unsure of what to expect, I was nervous on the drive up, but within an hour of arriving my only regret was that I hadn't been to a festival sooner.

I've been to the Cannes Film Festival, but I can't imagine walking up to Martin Scorsese or Steven Spielberg and managing to say anything more than, 'It's lovely to meet …' before suited bouncers whisked me away. Literary festivals are nothing like that. I soon found myself chatting to new, established and downright legendary authors. Perhaps it's because we spend so much time alone, with nothing but our imaginations and the tyranny of a daily word count, but most writers are a gregarious bunch, always up for a chat and a laugh. And, because every writer you ever meet has their own horror story of rejections and knockbacks, you will find that, as a group, we're very accessible and happy to share our thoughts and experiences of the industry. If you want to learn about publishing a book, finding an agent, or the craft of writing, hang out at a festival bar.

In addition to informal opportunities to forge new relationships and learn from the pro's, most festivals offer a structured programme of events designed to interest everyone from the general reader to the most established author. In our first year at Capital Crime, we had Ian Rankin and Don Winslow in conversation, an industry panel on how to become published, a creative masterclass with Anthony Horowitz, an interview with Kate Atkinson and so much more. There were heavyweight discussions about true-life crime and fun sessions; the role-play and banter of the Capital Crime debut novelists quiz – 'Whose Crime Is It Anyway?' - had the audience in stitches.

While they're fun and entertaining experiences for readers, I would advise aspiring authors to go to festivals as soon as they can. Most festivals feature discussion about the craft and business of writing, so authors can learn a lot. I wish I'd gone to festivals when I was starting out as a writer because I think I could have saved myself a lot of heartache. They're great places to meet agents, hear what the industry is looking for and learn what life as an author is really like. A number of aspiring authors who attended Capital Crime went on to be signed with agents; it really can be a springboard for your career.

How to prepare for your first festival

If the idea of going to a festival has piqued your interest, you might want to start with a local event. Most UK towns and cities host a literary event, and if it's local it's likely to be a less costly experience than a distant, travel-and-hotel festival. If you belong to a writers' group, book club or have bookish friends, you might be able to convince others to attend with you, reducing potential angst. You might also want to check your local bookshops, as many run regular events that are good warm-ups for the full-blown festival experience. Even in deepest, darkest Shropshire, I have been to some amazing events run by independent bookshops – Booka in Oswestry is brilliant at attracting big-name authors as well as showcasing debut writers – which can give you a taste of the live experience.

When you're ready for one of the big festivals – Cheltenham, Hay, Harrogate, Capital Crime – make sure you plan ahead to get the most from the experience. Research the travel and accommodation available and ask around on social media for hints and tips on where to stay and how to reduce costs. Most festivals offer an 'early bird' discount for people who buy their tickets well in advance so, if you're sure you're going, save money by booking early.

Some festivals offer tickets to individual events, others sell 'rover' passes. Check the programme and make sure your ticket allows you to get into the events you're keen to attend. Capital Crime and a few other festivals offer concession prices for people on low incomes or specific groups, such as librarians. Make sure you check to see what discounts might be available before booking.

Once you've booked and sorted out travel and accommodation, take time to plan your schedule. When you're there, it's all too easy to get drawn into conversation at the bar, lose track of time and miss events. Allow yourself enough time to rest and grab tea, coffee or a bite to eat. If you're planning to go to author signings, make sure you know when they are and don't dawdle! Some big-name authors limit how many books they'll sign and will rarely be seen in the bar, so their signing appearance is the only time you'll be able to grab them.

Dress code is whatever you feel comfortable in. It helps to know a bit about the festival you're attending. At the Theakston Old Peculier Crime Writing Festival in Harrogate, for example, a lot of time is spent outside socialising in the beer tent and on the lawns of the famous Old Swan Hotel – so take clothes that reflect the vagaries of the British summer! Many festival sessions are held in large conference venues, and some can be chilly if the air-conditioning is too high or overwarm if there's no AC at all, which means layers are a good idea – so you can cool down or wrap up, depending on your internal climate control.

Most festivals provide tote bags and goodies. These are much sought-after and hugely helpful to stow all the books you may end up buying at the festival bookshop. You may not go *intending* to add to your reading pile but, believe me, you will. We had to buy another bookcase to accommodate all the books purchased at Capital Crime last year!

Every festival is different

Do your research. Find out which festivals fit your personality and interests. Bloggers and journalists review festivals and talk about their experiences, which means you can get a good sense of a festival's ethos and atmosphere by reading what's been written about them online.

Some festivals run competitions or host special events. Capital Crime runs its New Voices Award, which is designed to give unsigned authors the opportunity to win a cash prize and garner some industry attention. Harrogate hosts an author dinner, where guests are able to spend a couple of hours with published authors over a meal. ThrillerFest in New York runs a best first-line competition in addition to its more widely publicised awards. Scour the festival's website and check on social media to ensure you know exactly what your chosen festival offers.

Attending as a panellist

As an author, you might be eligible to appear at the festival as a panellist. The right time to introduce yourself to a festival organiser is when you have a debut novel heading towards publication. If your book is going to be traditionally published, your publisher will usually make the festival organiser aware of the debut, but it doesn't hurt to connect with them directly as well. Check the festival website for information on being a panellist and how to get in touch.

If you are fortunate enough to be invited to appear at a festival, have a think about the panel topic the organisers give you and prepare some thoughts on interesting angles or subjects for discussion. Festivals are a live event, and you're there to entertain and engage the audience, not to sell your book. Selling your book is a happy by-product of an appreciative audience. If the audience feels you're an interesting or entertaining person, they will expect those qualities to be found in your work.

Perhaps you're nervous about speaking in public – I think most people are – but remember the audience is there because they're interested in what you have to say. Booklovers tend to be a friendly crowd and will be sympathetic to the fact that you're out of your comfort zone. Take some deep breaths (it really does help) and speak a little slower and a little louder than normal, so your audience can hear you.

Although this may not sound very 'artist-in-a-garret', do think about your author brand. Hopefully, you've taken time to find your author voice and to discover who you are as a storyteller. Do the same with your public persona. What makes you stand out as a person? What do you bring to an event that no one else can? Once you've understood who you are, practise – take the opportunity to appear at as many events as possible, large or small.

Societies, prizes and festivals

Festival dos and don'ts

- Do network with authors and other readers. Festival-goers are a friendly bunch and are generally happy to chat and provide advice.
- Dress code is whatever you feel comfortable in.
- Do have fun. Festivals are supposed to engage and entertain. Make the most of your time.
- Do read as many books by attending authors as possible. This will help you get more out of their events and to ask informed questions. Which brings us to the next point...
- Do ask questions. Authors love to be challenged and engaged. But...
- Don't hog the microphone. Keep your question short and to the point. If you have something you'd like to discuss with an author in more detail, save it for the signing.
- Don't be rude. Publishing is a polite world and rudeness doesn't generally get results.
- Don't be afraid to ask for help. Festivals employ staff and volunteers who are there to help you. Don't be afraid to approach them with any issue, no matter how big or small.

Hone your public speaking. It's like anything else in life – practice makes perfect, and the more preparation you do, the better the experience should be for you and your audience.

Also, given the times we live in, be sure to promote your appearance on social media. Sometimes, amid the buzz and busyness of the festival, it can be easy to forget to take photos and the obligatory selfie. Do try to record these moments – it's not only a useful tool for connecting with other authors and promoting your book, but it's also a lovely way to remember the experience. Writing brings plenty of lows, so it's always important to celebrate the highs; I certainly count all my festival experiences as among the highs. In fact, it was while I was in New York, buzzing with the excitement of ThrillerFest (https:// thrillerfest.com), that I joined forces with bookseller and agent extraordinaire David Headley to set up Capital Crime.

Adam Hamdy is an author and screenwriter, and co-founder of the crime and thriller festival Capital Crime (www.capitalcrime.org). Adam has a law degree from Oxford University and worked as a strategy consultant before taking up his writing career. He is the author of the *Pendulum* trilogy (Headline) – *Pendulum* (2016), *Freefall* (2017) and *Aftershock* (2018), and *Black 13* (Pan Macmillan 2020). He has co-written *Private Moscow* (Arrow 2020) and *Private Rogue* (Arrow 2021) with James Patterson. His latest novel, *Black 13*, is a top 20 bestseller. For more information see www.adamhamdy.com.

See also...
● *Developing talent: support and opportunities for writers*, page 505
● *Festivals and conferences for writers, artists and readers*, page 596

Developing talent: support and opportunities for writers

Helen Chaloner shares her knowledge of the many agencies, networks, awards and opportunities available to writers, to provide funding, inspiration and encouragement as they develop their talents.

Prizes, bursaries, awards and other opportunities for developing your writing are widespread and can really support your efforts. The process of putting yourself forward for one of these provides focus in the form of a deadline. It can lift your horizons and help you view your writing ambitions in a wider context. However, there is a balance to be sought, as always; the hard graft of seeking and applying for opportunities will eat into precious writing time.

Writer development agencies

A good place to start is your regional literature development agency. These agencies are Arts Council England-funded, not-for-profit organisations that exist to support writers and generate opportunities. I am writing this article in my role as Chief Executive Officer of Literature Works (https://literatureworks.org.uk), the literature development agency for South West England. The other agencies are: New Writing South (https://newwriting-south.com), New Writing North (https://newwritingnorth.com), Spread the Word, London (www.spreadtheword.org.uk), National Centre for Writing, covering the East of England (https://nationalcentreforwriting.org.uk), Writing East Midlands (www.writingeastmidlands.co.uk) and Writing West Midlands (https://writingwestmid-lands.org). There are non-regional agencies, too, such as Speaking Volumes (www.speakingvolumes.org) which produces *Breaking Ground: Celebrating British Writers of Colour*, a resource aimed at improving representation and diversity in live literature events.

Signing up for your regional agency's online newsletter will instantly connect you to networks and opportunities. Amongst other things, we run writing courses, offer mentoring and bursaries, administer prizes, oversee festivals and tour live literature. Some of us have membership schemes, through which you can access advance information and connect with other writers. Creative Scotland supports an equivalent in the Scottish Book Trust (www.scottishbooktrust.com), and the Arts Council of Wales supports Literature Wales (www.literaturewales.org). We all survey writers on a regular basis about their priorities and needs, so that you can have your say and feed into what we offer as well.

See also *Arts councils, Royal Societies and funding* on page 520.

Prizes

In a constantly changing landscape, there are hundreds of writing prizes. They sometimes charge a small fee per entry and often offer publication in an anthology as part of the prize package. A significant number recognise new talent or previously unpublished work.
• The Bridport Prize (see page 560) is one of the biggest and aims specifically to encourage emerging writers, with categories for short stories, poems, flash fiction and first novels.

Societies, prizes and festivals

• The Royal Society of Literature's annual V.S. Pritchett Memorial Prize (see page 579) is for the best unpublished short story of the year, which is then published in *Prospect Magazine* and the *RSL Review*.

• The Betty Trask Prize (see page 586) distributes substantial prize money every year to the best published or unpublished first novels by writers under the age of 35.

• The Creative Future Writers' Awards (see page 564) showcase the work of talented writers from under-represented groups, with prizes and mentoring offered for writers of poems and flash fiction.

There are many others and the smaller prizes should not be overlooked. They offer better odds of winning, with closely defined areas of interest that may just dovetail nicely with your interests. See full listings in the *Prizes and awards* section, page 556. To give just one example, Literature Works runs an annual poetry prize to accompany a project about the positive impact of poetry on people living with memory loss. In order to focus attention on the meaning of our project, we have a prize category for poems by a primary carer who is looking after a loved one with dementia.

Awards

Awards and bursaries are another prospect. They can provide crucial cash support that reduces financial pressure and frees up time for writing and research.

• The Deborah Rogers Foundation Writers' Award supports an unpublished prose writer to complete their first book.

• The Royal Society of Literature's Giles St Aubyn Awards help writers complete their first commissioned work of non-fiction.

• The Royal Society of Literature (RSL) and the Society of Authors (SoA) both offer a range of support and awards.

• For more experienced writers, the Royal Literary Fund (www.rlf.org.uk) runs year-long writers' fellowships at universities and colleges to help students with their academic writing.

Be aware, though, that demand outstrips supply for all high-profile awards; your regional literature development agency may well be running similar schemes on a smaller, more attainable scale.

Do also sign up for information about Arts Council England's funding streams (see www.artscouncil.org.uk/funding). These are generally grants for activities over a set period that engage people in arts activities and help artists and arts organisations to carry out their work. Individual writers can apply to the 'Developing Your Creative Practice Fund' for a grant of between £2,000 and £10,000 to support periods of research, developing new ideas, international work and training, networking or mentoring.

Feedback, writing courses and residencies

If you are looking for objective external feedback on your writing, there are a number of services on offer. The Literary Consultancy's 'Free Reads' scheme (https://literaryconsultancy.co.uk/editorial/ace-free-reads-scheme) produces detailed assessments from professional readers for promising writers on low incomes or from under-represented groups. The regional literature development agencies select and submit work to the scheme each year and the same service is also available from The Literary Consultancy (on a paid basis).

Perhaps you crave time and space to write, away from day-to-day responsibilities and in the company of other writers? Arvon (see page 691) has been making this possible for

50 years at residential writers' centres in secluded locations in Devon, Shropshire and West Yorkshire. Course members make the house their home for five days and immerse themselves in writing. They are tutored and guided by two established authors, who encourage them to take themselves seriously as writers. Courses run all year round, in many genres and for different writing stages. The list of tutors, past and present, is an impressive roll call of contemporary writing talent. Arvon offers substantial bursaries to people who cannot afford the full course fee and works in partnership with other organisations to provide bespoke courses for particular interest groups. Moniack Mhor runs a similarly impressive programme in the Scottish Highlands and Tŷ Newydd, on the Llŷn Peninsula in North Wales, is the National Writing Centre of Wales. (See *Writers' retreats and creative writing courses* on page 691.)

If you enjoy time away from the desk, bringing writing to other people, opportunities for paid writer-in-residence work come in many other forms and settings. A writers' residency can be a one-off event, or it may actually involve a writer living at a property. Usually it entails some combination of activities for the writer, between running workshops and developing their own work.

Writers can be paid to work in prisons, in commercial firms and, in the south west, at National Trust properties with a literary heritage. Literature Works also places poets in community dementia care settings, remembering and creating poetry with people living with memory loss and their loved ones.

Schools will often engage a local writer to work with children and there is good guidance on this from the National Association of Writers in Education (NAWE; see page 348). It is well worth looking out for opportunities to train as a facilitator or writing workshop leader. This can not only provide you with essential guidance on things like safeguarding and insurance, but will sometimes feed directly into projects as well.

Festivals and promotions

Literary festivals are springing up everywhere and there will be at least one near you. Get to know the organisers; volunteer if you can spare the time. The big ones are well established and attract high-profile media sponsorship. Smaller ones are thriving, too, and they are often keen to promote local writers. (See *Festivals and conferences for writers, artists and readers* on page 596.)

There are now a range of themed literary days or weeks throughout the year:

• **World Book Day**, in early spring, is a celebration of books and reading marked by many schools and a great opportunity for author events.

• The most prominent of the longstanding generic promotions must be **National Poetry Day**, celebrated in the autumn and firmly on the agenda of publishers, booksellers, schools and poets.

• A relatively new and welcome addition is **National Writing Day**, which takes place in the summer and provides a focus for all sorts of writing courses and opportunities. Check the dates for these and others, and put them in your calendar. Opportunities may well arise for events, volunteering and connecting.

Libraries

In the south west of England, we have a long track record of working closely with libraries, based on the absolute knowledge that writers need readers and vice versa. Libraries often host or run writing groups and these, for many people, are a great place to start and sustain your writing. Libraries run regular author events and themed or local promotions. Though operating in a harsh climate and often under-resourced, they can be fantastic early champions of local writers and it's worth letting them know that you're around.

For an up-to-date overview of library sector innovations and latest news, the Libraries Taskforce blog (https://dcmslibraries.blog.gov.uk/) is well worth a read.

In summary, there is a vibrant culture of development opportunities for writers, whether just starting out or more established. It is worth doing your research and it's very easy these days to keep informed by signing up for newsletters. If you can meet face to face, pop into your local library or get involved with writers' group that will pay dividends, too. None of this replaces precious hours spent writing, but writing is a craft that can be improved over time and there are many people and organisations out there, ready to share their expertise with you.

Helen Chaloner is Ceo of Literature Works, the literature development agency for South West England. After studying French and Comparative Literature at UEA, Helen worked in publishing PR at Penguin Books and at Faber and Faber, before taking up leadership positions with the Arvon Foundation and with the educational charity, Farms for City Children. Before joining Literature Works, Helen ran her own consultancy offering charities support with developing, funding and growing their organisations. Follow her on Twitter @litworksceo.

See also...

- *Festivals and conferences for writers, artists and readers*, page 596
- *Prizes and awards*, page 556
- *Writers' organisations*, page 547
- *Arts councils, Royal Societies and funding*, page 520

Society of Authors

The SoA is the UK trade union for all types of writers, illustrators and literary translators at every stage of their careers.

Founded in 1884, the Society of Authors now has over 10,000 members. Members receive unlimited free advice on all aspects of the profession, including confidential clause-by-clause contract vetting, and a wide range of exclusive offers. It campaigns and lobbies on the issues that affect authors, and holds a wide range of events across the UK, offering opportunities for authors to network and learn from each other. It manages more than 50 literary estates, the income from which helps to fund their work. It also administers a range of literary grants and prizes, awarding more than £400,000 to authors annually.

Members

SoA members include household names, such as J.K. Rowling, Philip Pullman and Joanne Harris, but they also include authors right at the start of their careers. Amongst the SoA membership are academic writers, biographers, broadcasters, children's writers, crime writers, dramatists, educational writers, ELT writers, health writers, ghostwriters, graphic novelists, historians, illustrators, journalists, medical writers, non-fiction writers, novelists, poets, playwrights, radio writers, scriptwriters, short story writers, translators, spoken word artists, YA writers and more.

The benefits available to all SoA members include:

• assistance with contracts, from negotiation and assessment of terms to clause-by-clause, confidential vetting;

• unlimited advice on queries, covering any aspect of the business of authorship;

Membership

The Society of Authors
24 Bedford Row, London WC1R 4EH
tel 020-7373 6642
email info@societyofauthors.org
website www.societyofauthors.org
Chief Executive Nicola Solomon
President Philip Pullman

There are two membership bands: Full and Associate membership.

Full membership is available to professional writers, poets, translators and illustrators working in any genre or medium. This includes those who have: had a full-length work traditionally published, broadcast or performed commercially; self-published or been published on a print-on-demand or ebook-only basis and who meet sales criteria; published or had broadcast or performed an equivalent body of professional work; or administrators of a deceased author's estate.

Authors at the start of their careers are invited to join as Associates.

Associate membership is available to anyone actively working to launch a career as an author. This includes: authors who are starting out in self-publishing but who are not yet making a profit; authors who have been offered a contract for publication or agent representation but who are not yet published; students engaged on a course of at least one academic year's duration that will help them develop a career as an author, as well as other activities that mark the early stages of an author's career. Associate members enjoy all the same services and benefits as Full members.

Membership is subject to election and payment of subscription fees.

The subscription fee (tax deductible) starts at £27 per quarter, or £19 for those aged 35 or under. From the second year of subscription there are concessionary rates for over 65s who are no longer earning a significant amount of income from writing.

• taking up complaints on behalf of members on any issue concerned with the business of authorship;

• pursuing legal actions for breach of contract, copyright infringement and the non-payment of royalties and fees, when the risk and cost preclude individual action by a member and issues of general concern to the profession are at stake;

• conferences, seminars, meetings and other opportunities to network and learn from other authors;

• regular communications and a comprehensive range of publications, including the SoA's quarterly journal, the Author;

• discounts on books, exclusive rates on specialist insurance, special offers on products and services and free membership of the Authors' Licensing and Collecting Society (ALCS; see page 715);

• Academic and Medical Writers Groups – investigating and highlighting the issues faced by these authors, including confusion and concern around Open Access requirements and Creative Commons licensing.

• Broadcasting Group – representing members working in radio, TV and film;

• Children's Writers and Illustrators Group – a professional community of writers and illustrators who create content for the children's publishing market;

• Educational Writers Group – protecting the interests of educational authors in professional matters, especially contracts, rates of pay, digitalisation and copyright;

• Poetry and Spoken Word Group – a new, increasingly active group to which all new member poets are subscribed on joining SoA;

• Society of Authors in Scotland – organises a varied and busy calendar of activities in Scotland through a committee of volunteers;

• Translators Association – a source of expert advice for individual literary translators and a collective voice representing the profession (see page 546);

• Writers as Carers Group – a new group designed to help keep writers writing when they take on caring responsibilities for someone with an illness or disability.

The SoA also facilitates many local groups across the UK.

Campaigning and lobbying

The SoA is a voice for authors and works at a national and international level to improve terms and treatment of authors, negotiating with all parties including publishers, broadcasters, agents and governments. Current areas of campaigning include contract terms, copyright, freedom of expression, tax and benefits arrangements and Public Lending Right (PLR; see page 665) – which the SoA played a key role in establishing. It also campaigns on wider matters which affect authors, such as libraries, literacy and a fair playing field for publishing.

In the UK the SoA lobbies parliament, ministers and departments and makes submissions on relevant issues, working closely with the Department for Culture, Media and Sport and the All Party Parliamentary Writers Group. The SoA is a member of the British Copyright Council and was instrumental in setting up ALCS. It is recognised by the BBC in the negotiation of rates for authors' contributions to radio drama, as well as for the broadcasting of published material.

The SoA is highly active and influential at a European level and is a member of the European Writers' Council and applies pressure globally, working with sister organisations as part of the international Authors' Foundation.

The SoA also works closely with other professional bodies, including the Association of Authors' Agents, the Booksellers Association, the Publishers Association, the Independent Publishers Guild, the British Council, the National Union of Journalists and the Writers' Guild of Great Britain. (See the societies listings that start on page 516.)

Awards and grants

The SoA supports authors through a wide range of awards and grants. Over £100,000 is given in prizes each year and more than £230,000 is distributed in grants.
The SoA administers:
• the Authors' Foundation and K Blundell Trust, which give grants to assist authors working on their next book;
• the Francis Head Bequest and the Authors' Contingency Fund, which assist authors who, through physical mishap, are temporarily unable to maintain themselves or their families;
• the Women's Prize for Fiction;
• the *Sunday Times*/University of Warwick Young Writer of the Year Award;
• the *Sunday Times* EFG Short Story Award;
• Travelling Scholarships, which give honorary awards;
• three prizes for first novels: the Betty Trask Awards, the McKitterick Prize and inaugural Paul Torday Memorial Prize;
• the Somerset Maugham Awards for a full-length published work;
• two poetry awards: the Eric Gregory Awards and the Cholmondeley Awards;
• the ALCS Tom-Gallon Award for short story writers;
• two audio drama prizes: the Imison Award for a writer new to radio drama and the Tinniswood Award;
• awards for translations from Arabic, Dutch/Flemish, French, German, Greek, Italian, Spanish and Swedish into English;
• the ALCS Educational Writers' Awards.

WGGB (Writers' Guild of Great Britain)

The WGGB is the TUC-affiliated trade union for writers.

WGGB represents writers working in film, television, radio, theatre, books, poetry, animation, comedy and videogames. Formed in 1959 as the Screenwriters' Guild, the union gradually extended into all areas of freelance writing activity and copyright protection. It comprises professional writers in all media, united in common concern for one another and regulating the conditions under which they work.

Apart from necessary dealings with Government and policies on legislative matters affecting writers, the WGGB is, by constitution, non-political, has no involvement with any political party and members pay no political levy.

WGGB employs a permanent general secretary and other permanent staff and is administered by an Executive Council of around 20 members.

WGGB agreements

WGGB's core function is to negotiate minimum terms in those areas in which its members work. Those agreements form the basis of the individual contracts signed by members. It also gives individual advice to its members on contracts and other matters and maintains a benevolent fund to help writers in financial trouble.

Membership

The Writers' Guild of Great Britain
First Floor, 134 Tooley Street, London SE1 2TU
tel 020-7833 0777
email admin@writersguild.org.uk
website www.writersguild.org.uk
Facebook www.facebook.com/thewritersguild
Twitter @The WritersGuild
General Secretary Ellie Peers
Full membership: Members pay approximately 1.2% of earnings from professional writing using a banding system (min. £198, max. £2,000 p.a.).

Candidate membership: £108 p.a. restricted to writers who have not had work published or produced at WGGB-approved rates.

Student membership: £30 p.a. for student writers aged 18 or over, studying at BA level or below.

Affiliate membership: £300 p.a. for people who work professionally with writers, e.g. agents, technical advisers.

Members receive a weekly email newsletter. The WGGB website contains full details of collective agreements and WGGB activities, plus a 'Find a Writer' service and a dedicated Members' area; information is also made available on Twitter and Facebook. Other benefits include: legal advice and contract vetting; free training; member events, discounts and special offers (subject to membership tier).

Television

WGGB negotiates minimum terms agreements with the BBC, ITV, Pact (Producers' Alliance for Cinema and Television; see page 545) and TAC (representing Welsh-language television producers).

WGGB TV agreements regulate minimum fees, residuals and royalties, copyright, credits and general conditions for television plays, series and serials, dramatisations and adaptations, soaps, sitcoms and sketch shows. One of the WGGB's most important achievements has been the establishment of pension rights for members. The BBC, ITV and independent producers pay a pension contribution on top of the standard writer's fee on the understanding that the WGGB member also pays a contribution.

The switch to digital television, video-on-demand and download-to-own services, mobile phone technology and the expansion of the BBC's commercial arm have seen WGGB in constant negotiation over the past decade. WGGB now has agreements for all of the BBC's digital channels and for its joint venture channels. In May 2012 it signed new agreements with the BBC extending minimum terms over online services such as iPlayer. From April 2015 the first payments under the Writers Digital Payments scheme (a not-for-profit company) were paid out to writers whose work had been broadcast on BBC iPlayer and ITV Player. In 2016 WGGB negotiated a 75% fee increase for writers working under its 2003 Pact agreement, and also started work on rewriting the agreement. In 2017 it negotiated a new script agreement for television and online with the BBC.

Film

In 1985 an agreement was signed with the two producer organisations: the British Film and Television Producers' Association and the Independent Programme Producers' Association (now known as Pact). Since then there has been an industrial agreement covering UK film productions and pension fund contributions have been negotiated for WGGB members. The Agreement was renegotiated in February 1992 and consultations on an updated arrangement are in progress.

Radio

WGGB has a standard agreement for Radio Drama with the BBC, establishing a fee structure that is reviewed annually. It was comprehensively renegotiated in 2005 resulting in an agreement covering digital radio. In 1985 the BBC agreed to extend the pension scheme already established for television writers to include radio writers. WGGB has special agreements for Radio 4's *The Archers* and for BBC iPlayer. A separate agreement covers the reuse of old comedy and drama material on digital BBC Radio 4 Extra. It has also negotiated rates for podcasts.

Books

WGGB fought for the loans-based Public Lending Right (PLR, see page 665) to reimburse authors for books lent in libraries. The scheme is now administered by the British Library; WGGB is represented on its advisory committee. WGGB has a Books Committee, which works on behalf of book writers and poets. Issues affecting members include authors' earnings, self-publishing, print-on-demand services and ebooks.

Theatre

In 1979 WGGB, together with the Theatre Writers' Union, negotiated the first industrial agreement for theatre writers. The Theatres National Committee Agreement (TNC) covers the Royal Shakespeare Company, the Royal National Theatre Company and the English Stage Company at the Royal Court. When their agreement was renegotiated in 2007, WGGB achieved a long-standing ambition of a minimum fee of £10,000 for a new play; this has since risen to £12,997.

In June 1986, a new agreement was signed with the Theatrical Management Association (now UK Theatre), which covers 95 provincial theatres. In 1993, this agreement was comprehensively revised and included a provision for a year-on-year increase in fees in line with the Retail Price Index. The agreement was renegotiated in 2015.

After many years of negotiation, an agreement was concluded in 1991 between WGGB and the Independent Theatre Council (ITC), which represents 200 of the smaller and fringe theatres as well as educational and touring companies. This agreement was revised in 2002 and the minimum fees are reviewed annually. WGGB is currently talking to the ITC about updating the agreement. The WGGB Theatre Committee holds an annual forum for Literary Managers and runs the Olwen Wymark Theatre Encouragement Award scheme.

Videogames

WGGB counts games writers amongst its members and holds regular networking events for them, as well as celebrating their achievements at the annual Writers' Guild Awards. The union publishes guidelines for games writers and those who work with them, outlining best practice in this growing area.

Other activities

WGGB is in touch with Government and national institutions wherever and whenever the interests of writers are in question or are being discussed, for example, submitting evidence to a Parliamentary Inquiry on the lack of working-class writers. It holds cross-party Parliamentary lobbies with Equity and the Musicians' Union to ensure that the various artforms they represent are properly cared for, and writers' voices are heard during, for example, the Brexit transition and the Covid-19 pandemic. Working with the Federation of Entertainment Unions, WGGB makes its views known to bodies, such as Arts Council England, the BBC Trust and Ofcom on a broader basis.

WGGB is an active affiliate of the British Copyright Council, Creators' Rights Alliance and other organisations whose activities are relevant to professional writers. An Anti-Censorship Committee has intervened strongly to protect freedom of speech.

Internationally, WGGB plays a leading role in the International Affiliation of Writers Guilds, which includes the American Guilds East and West, the Canadian Guilds (French and English) and the Irish, Mexican, French, Israeli, South African and New Zealand Guilds. When it is possible to make common cause, the Guilds act accordingly. WGGB takes a leading role in the European Writers' Council and the Fédération des Scénaristes d'Europe.

On a day-to-day basis, WGGB gives advice on contracts, and takes up issues that affect the lives of its members as professional writers. Other benefits include access to free and discounted training, exclusive events and discounts and a dedicated online members' area. Full members are entitled to submit a profile for inclusion in the WGGB online *Find A Writer* directory; pay no joining fee for membership to Writers Guild of America East or West; and are eligible for Cannes accreditation. Regular committee meetings are held by specialist WGGB Craft Committees and its active branches across the UK organise panel discussions, talks and social events.

Recent campaigns include Equality Writes, following an independent report commissioned by WGGB and launched in 2018, which revealed the shocking lack of gender equality in the UK screen industries. The union has also campaigned on bullying and harassment in the creative industries.

Each year WGGB presents the Writers' Guild Awards, covering all the areas in which its members work. These are the only cross-media awards in which writers are honoured by their peers.

Alliance of Independent Authors

The ALLi is a professional association of self-publishing writers and advisors.

The Alliance of Independent Authors (ALLi) is a global organisation with a mission of fostering ethics and excellence in self-publishing and advocation for author-publishers globally.

Founded in 2012 at the London Book Fair by author, poet and creative entrepreneur, Orna Ross, ALLi is headquartered in London but with members all over the world. In addition to its member services, the organisation offers outreach education to the self-publishing community through its popular online Self-Publishing Advice Center, which features a blog, podcast, bi-annual online conference and series of guidebooks.

ALLi has an Advisory Board of successful author-publishers, educators and service providers, and an active Watchdog desk which runs a publicly available ratings board of the best and worst self-publishing services. It also publishes an annual Directory of its Partner Members (https://selfpublishingadvice.org/best-self-publishing-services/): vetted self-publishing services, from large global players like Amazon KDP and Ingram Spark to local freelance editors and designers. Many of these offer discounted services to ALLi author members.

Membership

The Alliance of Independent Authors
email info@allianceindependentauthors.org
website www.allianceindependentauthors.org,
https://selfpublishingadvice.org

ALLi offers three grades of membership:

Author membership (£89 p.a.) is open to writers or translators of books for adults who have self-published a full-length title (55,000+ words) or series of shorter books; writers of children's/young adult books who have self-published one or more titles.

Authorpreneur membership (£119 p.a.) is open to full-time self-publishing authors who earn their living from their author business and can show evidence of 50,000 book sales in the last two years; applications are assessed.

Associate membership (£69 p.a.) is open to writing/publishing students with an interest in self-publishing and non-published writers (or translators) preparing a book for self-publication.

Benefits include self-publishing advice, guidance and community; vetted services, service ratings and watchdog desk; legal and contract appraisal; discounts and deals; professional and business development; campaigns and advocacy.

ALLi advocates for the interests of independent, self-publishing authors within and outside the literary, publishing and bookselling industries. 2021 saw the launch of the 'Self-Publishing for All' campaign, where ALLi works with ambassadors, other authors associations, and grassroots organizations to bring self-publishing skills to marginalised voices, those currently denied involvement in mainstream cultural, education or social activity. Other campaigns include 'Open Up To Indie Authors', which urges booksellers, festivals, prize-giving committees, libraries, book clubs and corporate media to include author–publishers in their programmes; and 'Self-Publishing 3.0', which calls on government and creative industry bodies to support authors' digital business development.

Societies, prizes and festivals

Societies, associations and clubs

This list is divided into the following sections: Representation and publishing; Arts councils, Royal Societies and funding; Copyright and licensing; Editorial, journalism and broadcasting; Literacy; Libraries and information; Literary; Art, illustration and photography; Film, theatre and television; Translation; Bibliographical and academic; Members' Clubs; Writers' organisations; and Music. Some also offer prizes and awards (see page 556).

REPRESENTATION AND PUBLISHING

American Booksellers Association
333 Westchester Avenue, Suite S202, White Plains, NY 10604
tel +1 800-637-0037
email info@bookweb.org
website www.bookweb.org
Twitter @ABAbook

A national non-profit trade organisation that works with booksellers and industry partners to ensure the success and profitability of independently owned book retailers and to assist in expanding the community of the book. Provides education, information dissemination, business products and services, creates relevant awareness programmes and engages in public policy. Founded 1900.

Association of American Literary Agents
302A West 12th Street, Suite 122, New York, NY 10014
email assistant@aalitagents.org
website aalitagents.org

A professional organisation of over 400 agents who work with book authors and playwrights. Founded 1991.

Association of American Publishers
455 Massachusetts Avenue, NW Suite 700, Washington DC 20001
tel +1 202-347-3375
email info@publishers.org
website https://publishers.org
Twitter @AmericanPublish

AAP is the largest trade association for US books and journal publishers, providing advocacy and communications on behalf of the industry and its priorities nationally and worldwide. Founded 1970.

The Association of Authors' Agents
c/o Andrew Nurnberg Associates,
3–11 Eyre Street Hill, London EC1R 5ET
tel 020-3327 0400
website www.agentsassoc.co.uk
President Isobel Dixon, *Secretary* Johanna Clarke

The AAA exists to provide a forum which allows member agencies to discuss issues arising in the profession; a collective voice for UK literary agencies in public affairs and the media; and a code of conduct to which all members commit themselves. Founded 1974.

Association of Canadian Publishers
174 Spadina Avenue, Suite 306, Toronto, Ontario M5T 2C2
tel +1 416-487-6116
email admin@canbook.org
website https://publishers.ca
Executive Director Kate Edwards

Represents approximately 115 Canadian-owned and controlled book publishers from across the country. Founded 1976.

Australian Publishers Association
60/89 Jones Street, Ultimo, NSW 2007
tel +61 (0)2 9281 9788
email office@publishers.asn.au
website www.publishers.asn.au
Twitter @AusPublish

The APA is the peak industry body for Australian book, journal and electronic publishers. Founded 1948.

The Australian Society of Authors
Suite C1.06, 22–36 Mountain Street, Ultimo, NSW 2007
tel +61 (0)2 9211 1004
email asa@asauthors.org
website www.asauthors.org

The ASA is the professional association for Australia's authors and illustrators. Provides advocacy, support and advice for authors and illustrators in matters relating to their professional practice. Founded 1963.

Australian Writers' Guild
Level 4, 70 Pitt Street, Sydney, NSW 2000
tel +61 (0)2 9319 0339
email admin@awg.com.au
website www.awg.com.au

The professional association representing writers for stage, screen, radio and online and has protected and promoted their creative and professional interests for more than 50 years. Founded 1962.

The Booksellers Association of the United Kingdom & Ireland Ltd
6 Bell Yard, London WC2A 2JR
tel 020-7421 4640
email mail@booksellers.org.uk
website www.booksellers.org.uk
Twitter @BAbooksellers
Managing Director Meryl Halls

A membership organisation for all booksellers in the UK and Ireland, representing over 95% of bookshops. Key services include National Book Tokens and Batch Payment Services. Founded 1895.

Canadian Authors Association
192 Spadina Avenue, Suite 107, Toronto, Ontario M5T 2C2
tel +1 705-955-0716
website www.canadianauthors.org
Facebook www.facebook.com/canadianauthorsassociation
Twitter @canauthors
Executive Director Anita Purcell

Provides writers with a wide variety of programmes, services and resources to help them develop their skills in the craft and business of writing. A membership-based organisation for writers in all areas of the profession. Branches across Canada. Founded 1921.

Canadian Publishers' Council
3080 Yonge Street, Toronto, Ontario M4N 3N1
tel +1 647-255-8880
email dswail@pubcouncil.ca
website https://pubcouncil.ca
Twitter @pubcouncil_ca
President David Swail

Represents the interests of Canadian publishing companies that publish books and other media for schools, colleges and universities, professional and reference markets, the retail and library sectors. Founded 1910.

Canadian Society of Children's Authors, Illustrators & Performers (CANSCAIP)
720 Bathurst Street, Suite 503, Toronto, Ontario M5S 2R4
tel +1 416-515-1559
email office@canscaip.org
website www.canscaip.org
Twitter @CANSCAIP
Administrative Director Helena Aalto
Membership $85 p.a. member; $45 p.a. friend

A membership-based non-profit organisation that supports the professional development of Canada's community of authors, illustrators and performers for children and teens. Founded 1977.

Creative Access
3rd Floor, 2 Waterhouse Square, 140 Holborn, London EC1N 2AE
email info@creativeaccess.org.uk
website www.creativeaccess.org.uk
Facebook www.facebook.com/CreativeAccessUK
Twitter @_CreativeAccess
Instagram @_CreativeAccess

A social enterprise and one of the UK's leading diversity organisations which helps those from under-represented communities to secure paid training opportunities and full-time jobs in the creative industries and support them to progress into leadership roles. Working with leading creative organisations across the UK, Creative Access provides a range of services to help support employer partners create inclusive workplaces; including recruitment of trainees and permanent staff, mentoring programmes and employer training. Founded 2012.

Creative Industries Federation
22 Endell Street, London WC2H 9AD
tel 020-3771 0350
website www.creativeindustriesfederation.com
Twitter @Creative_Fed

The national organisation for the UK's creative industries, cultural education and arts. Through a unique network of member organisations, influential policy and advocacy work and a UK-wide events programme it brings together the many sectors that comprise the UK's world-leading creative industries. Its membership network includes more than 10,000 individuals from creative organisations, businesses and educational institutions across the UK. Founded 2014.

Cwlwm Cyhoeddwyr Cymru
Elwyn Williams, Bryntirion Villa, Ffordd Penglais, Aberystwyth SY23 2EU
tel 07866 834109
email elwyn_williams@btinternet.com

Represents and promotes Welsh-language publishers. Founded 2002.

Federation of European Publishers
Chaussee d'Ixelles, 29 box 4-1050, Brussels, Belgium
tel +32 2770 1110
email info@fep-fee.eu
website www.fep-fee.eu
Twitter @FEP_EU

Represents the interests of European publishers on EU affairs; informs members on the development of EU policies which could affect the publishing industry. Founded 1967.

Independent Publishers Guild
PO Box 12, Llain, Login SA34 0WU
tel (01437) 563335

email info@independentpublishersguild.com
website www.independentpublishersguild.com
Chief Executive Bridget Shine
Membership open to new and established publishers from all sectors and of all sizes, plus suppliers and service providers.

The IPG is the UK's largest network of publishers and has served, supported and represented independents for nearly 60 years. It delivers two popular annual conferences, a range of other events and numerous resources to help members do better business. Coordinates the Independent Publishing Awards, a mentoring scheme, collective stands at book fairs and training via the IPG Skills Hub, and provides members with weekly ebulletins, a business support helpline and special deals on publishing products and services. Due to the impact of the coronavirus outbreak, its 2020 Autumn and 2021 Spring Conferences took place virtually, featuring a wide range of speakers from across publishing and beyond. Founded 1962.

International Authors Forum
5th Floor, Shackleton House, 4 Battle Bridge Lane, London SE1 2HX
tel 020-7264 5707
email luke.alcott@internationalauthors.org
website www.internationalauthors.org
Twitter @IntAuthors
Executive Administrator Luke Alcott

Represents authors around the world and has a membership made up of over 70 authors' organisations from every continent. Campaigns for authors' rights at the UN and national levels. Organises events, publications and collaborates with other organisations representing authors to promote the importance of creative work financially, socially and culturally. Keeps members up to date with international developments in copyright law.

International Publishers Association
23 Avenue de France, 1202 Geneva, Switzerland
tel +41 22-704 1820
email info@internationalpublishers.org
website www.internationalpublishers.org
Facebook www.facebook.com/
InternationalPublishersAssociation
Twitter @IntPublishers
President Bodour Al Qasimi, *Secretary-General* José Borghino

The IPA is a federation of national, regional and international publishers associations. It promotes and protects publishing worldwide, with a focus on copyright and freedom to publish. Its membership comprises 86 organisations from 71 countries worldwide. Founded 1896.

Irish Writers Centre
19 Parnell Square, Dublin D01 E102,
Republic of Ireland

tel +353 (0)1 872 1302
email info@writerscentre.ie
website https://irishwriterscentre.ie
Facebook www.facebook.com/irishwritersctr
Twitter @IrishWritersCtr
Director Valerie Bistany

The national resource centre for Irish writers, the Irish Writers Centre supports and promotes writers at all stages of their development. It runs workshops, seminars and events related to the art of writing which are run by established writers across a range of genres. It hosts professional development seminars for writers, and provides space for writers, writing groups and other literary organisations. Founded 1991.

Irish Writers' Union/Comhar na Scríbhneoirí
Irish Writers Centre, 19 Parnell Square, Dublin D01 E102, Republic of Ireland
email info@irishwritersunion.org
website https://irishwritersunion.org
Facebook www.facebook.com/IrishWritersUnion
Twitter @WritersUnion_ie
Chairman and Secretary Lissa Oliver, *Treasurer* Roy Hunt

The Union aims to advance the cause of writing as a profession, to achieve better remuneration and more favourable conditions for writers and to provide a means for the expression of the collective opinion of writers on matters affecting their profession. Offers free contract advice and negotiation for members. Founded 1986.

New Zealand Association of Literary Agents
PO Box 6292, Dunedin North 9059
email tfs@elseware.co.nz
website www.elseware.co.nz/NZALA/Index.htm

Set up to establish standards and guidelines for literary agents operating in New Zealand. All members subscribe to a code of ethics which includes working on commission and not charging upfront fees for promotion or manuscript reading.

New Zealand Writers Guild
145 Carrington Road, Auckland 1026
tel +64 (0)9 360 1408
email guildhq@nzwg.org.nz
website www.nzwg.org.nz

Represents the interests of New Zealand writers (TV, film, radio and theatre); to establish and improve minimum conditions of work and rates of compensation for writers; to provide professional services for members. Founded 1975.

The Personal Managers' Association Ltd
tel 0845 602 7191
email info@thepma.com
website www.thepma.com

Membership organisation for agents representing talent in film, television, theatre and radio. Has over 180 member agencies which comprise more than 800 individual agents.

Professional Publishers Association

White Collar Factory, 1 Old Street Yard,
London EC1Y 8AF
tel 020-7404 4166
email info@ppa.co.uk
website www.ppa.co.uk
Twitter @PPA_Live

The association for publishers and providers of consumer, customer and business media in the UK. PPA's role is to promote and protect the interests of the industry in general, and member companies in particular. The association's membership consists of around 250 publishing companies.

The Publishers Association

First Floor, 50 Southwark Street, London SE1 1UN
tel 020-7378 0504
email mail@publishers.org.uk
website www.publishers.org.uk
Twitter @PublishersAssoc
President David Shelley, *Ceo* Stephen Lotinga

A member organisation for UK publishing, representing companies of all sizes and specialisms. Their members produce digital and print books, research journals and educational resources across genres and subjects. The Publishers Association exists to champion publishing to the wider world and to provide their members with everything they need to thrive. They have helped change laws, improved business conditions and inspired people to become publishers. Founded 1896.

Publishers Association of New Zealand

Level 6, 19 Como Street, Takapuna, Auckland 0622, New Zealand
tel +64 (0)9 280 3213
email admin@publishers.org.nz
website www.publishers.org.nz
Twitter @Publishers_NZ

PANZ represents book, educational and digital publishers in New Zealand. Members include both the largest international publishers and companies in the independent publishing community.

Publishers' Association of South Africa

House Vincent, Wynberg Mews, 1st Floor, Unit 104, Brodie Road, Wynberg 7800
tel +27 (0)21 762 9083
email pasa@publishsa.co.za
website www.publishsa.co.za

PASA is the largest publishing industry body in South Africa and is committed to creativity, literacy, the free flow of ideas and encouraging a culture of reading. It aims to promote and protect the rights and responsibilities of the publishing sector in South Africa.

Publishers' Publicity Circle

email publisherspublicitycircle@gmail.com
website www.publisherspublicitycircle.co.uk
Secretary/Treasurer Madeline Toy

Enables all book publicists to meet and share information regularly. Monthly meetings provide a forum for press journalists, TV and radio researchers and producers to meet publicists collectively. Awards are presented for the best PR campaigns. Monthly newsletter includes recruitment advertising. Founded 1955.

Publishing Ireland/Foilsiú Éireann

63 Patrick Street, Dun Laoghaire,
Co Dublin A96 WF25, Republic of Ireland
tel +353 (0)1 639 4868
email info@publishingireland.com
website www.publishingireland.com
Facebook www.facebook.com/PublishingIreland
Twitter @PublishingIRL
General Manager Orla McLoughlin

Publishing Ireland enables publishers to share expertise and resources in order to benefit from opportunities and solve problems that are of common concern to all. It comprises most of the major publishing houses in Ireland with a mixture of trade, general and academic publishers as members. Founded 1970.

Publishing Scotland

Scott House, 10 South St Andrew Street,
Edinburgh EH2 2AZ
tel 0131 228 6866
email enquiries@publishingscotland.org
website www.publishingscotland.org
Chief Executive Marion Sinclair

A network for trade, training and development in the Scottish publishing industry. Founded 1973.

Society of Artists Agents

website https://saahub.com
Twitter @SaaAgents

Formed to promote professionalism in the illustration industry and to forge closer links between clients and artists through an agreed set of guidelines. The Society believes in an ethical approach through proper terms and conditions, thereby protecting the interests of the artists and clients. Founded 1992.

The Society of Authors

– see page 509

Society of Young Publishers

c/o The Publishers Association, First Floor,
50 Southwark Street, London SE1 1UN

email sypchair@thesyp.org.uk
website www.thesyp.org.uk
Twitter @SYP_UK
Twitter @SYPIreland, @SYP_LDN, @SYPNorth,
@Oxford_SYP, @SYPScotland, @SYP_SouthWest
Membership £30 p.a. employed standard;
£24 p.a. student/unemployed;
£18 p.a. digital membership

Supports those of any age looking to get into publishing, or those within the first ten years of their career who are looking to get ahead. The SYP is made up of six regional committees (Ireland, London, North, Oxford, Scotland and South West), and a UK team responsible for the organisation's oversight. These committees organise mentorship schemes for current and aspiring publishers based in the UK and Ireland. Two annual conferences are held, as well as numerous in-person and digital events each month – including socials, career panels, and more. The website is routinely updated with articles and guides on how to progress in the publishing industry. Founded 1949.

Theatre Writers' Union – see page 513

Writers Guild of America, East Inc.
250 Hudson Street, Suite 700, New York, NY 10013
tel +1 212-767-7800
website www.wgaeast.org
Facebook www.facebook.com/WGAEast
Twitter @WGAEast

WGAE represents writers in screen, TV and new media for collective bargaining. It provides member services including pension and health, as well as educational and professional activities. Founded 1954.

Writers Guild of America, West Inc.
7000 West 3rd Street, Los Angeles, CA 90048
tel +1 323-951-4000
website www.wga.org

WGAW represents and services writers in film, broadcast, cable and multimedia industries for purposes of collective bargaining, contract administration and other services, and functions to protect and advance the economic, professional and creative interests of writers. Founded 1933.

Writers Guild of Canada
366 Adelaide Street West, Suite 401, Toronto, Ontario M5V 1R9
tel +1 416-979-7907; toll free +1-800-567-9974
email info@wgc.ca
website www.writersguildofcanada.com

Represents professional screenwriters. Negotiates and administers collective agreements with independent producers and broadcasters. The Guild also publishes *Canadian Screenwriter* magazine.

WGGB (Writers' Guild of Great Britain) – see page 512

Writers Guild of Ireland
Art House, Curved Street, Temple Bar, Dublin 2, Republic of Ireland
tel +353 (0)1 670 9970
email info@script.ie
website http://script.ie/
Ceo Hugh Farley, *Chairperson* Jennifer Davidson

Represents writers' interests in theatre, radio and screen. Founded 1969.

The Writers' Union of Canada
600–460 Richmond Street West, Suite 600, Toronto, Ontario M5V 1Y1
tel +1 416-703-8982
email info@writersunion.ca
website www.writersunion.ca

National arts service organisation for professionally published book authors. Founded 1973.

ARTS COUNCILS, ROYAL SOCIETIES AND FUNDING

Arts Council/An Chomhairle Ealaíon
70 Merrion Square, Dublin D02 NY52, Republic of Ireland
tel +353 (0)1 618 0200
website www.artscouncil.ie/home

The national development agency for the arts in Ireland. Founded 1951.

Arts Council England
tel 0161 934 4317
website www.artscouncil.org.uk
Facebook www.facebook.com/artscouncilofengland
Twitter @ace_national

The national development agency for arts and culture in England, distributing public money from the government and the National Lottery. Between 2018 and 2022, Arts Council England will invest £1.45 billion of public money from government and an estimated £860 million from the National Lottery to deliver its objectives. Through its funding schemes organisations, artists, events and initiatives can receive funding and help achieve the Council's mission of providing art and culture for everyone. There are nine regional offices: Newcastle, Leeds, Manchester, Nottingham, Birmingham, Cambridge, Brighton, Bristol and London. Visit the website for information on funding support and advice, an online funding finder and funding FAQs. Founded 1946.

Arts Council of Northern Ireland
Linen Hill House, 23 Linenhall Street, Lisburn BR29 1FJ
tel 028-9262 3555

email info@artscouncil-ni.org
website www.artscouncil-ni.org
Chief Executive Roisín McDonough

Promotes and encourages the arts throughout Northern Ireland. Artists in drama, dance, music and jazz, literature, the visual arts, traditional arts and community arts can apply for support for specific schemes and projects. The value of the grant will be set according to the aims of the programme. Artists of all disciplines and in all types of working practice, who have made a contribution to artistic activities in Northern Ireland for a minimum period of one year within the last five years, are eligible.

Australia Council

PO Box 576, Pyrmont, NSW 2009
tel +61 (0)2 9215 9000
website www.australiacouncil.gov.au
Ceo Adrian Collette

Provides a broad range of support for the arts in Australia, embracing music, theatre, literature, visual arts and crafts, dance, indigenous arts, community and experimental arts.

Books Council of Wales/Cyngor Llyfrau Cymru

Castell Brychan, Aberystwyth, Ceredigion SY23 2JB
tel (01970) 624151
email castellbrychan@books.wales
website https://Illyfrau.cymru/en/
website www.gwales.com
Ceo Helgard Krause

A national charity which supports and develops the publishing industry in Wales. It promotes literacy and reading for pleasure through a range of public campaigns, activities and events across Wales, often working in partnership with schools, libraries and other literary organisations. The Council works with publishers to nurture new talent and content in Welsh and English as well as offering specialist editing, design, marketing and distribution services. It administers grants to publishers and independent booksellers. Partly funded by the Welsh Government through Creative Wales and from the commercial operations of its wholesale book distribution centre. Founded 1961.

British Academy

10–11 Carlton House Terrace, London SW1Y 5AH
tel 020-7969 5200
website www.britishacademy.ac.uk
Facebook www.facebook.com/TheBritishAcademy
Twitter @BritishAcademy_
Ceo Hetan Shah

The British Academy is the voice of humanities and social sciences. The Academy is an independent fellowship of world-leading scholars and researchers; a funding body for research, nationally and internationally; and a forum for debate and engagement. It produces a wide range of publications, for academic and more general readerships.

The British Council

British Council Customer Service UK,
Bridgewater House, 58 Whitworth Street,
Manchester M1 6BB
tel 0161 957 7755
website www.britishcouncil.org
Twitter @BritishCouncil
Interim Chief Executive Kate Ewart-Biggs, *Director of Arts* Skinder Hundal

The UK's international organisation for cultural relations and educational opportunities. It builds connections, understanding and trust between people in the UK and other countries through arts and culture, education and the English language. It finds new ways of connecting with and understanding each other through the arts, to develop stronger creative sectors around the world that are better connected with the UK. Working in close collaboration with book trade associations, the Literature team participates in major international book fairs.

It works with hundreds of writers and literature partners in the UK and collaborates with offices overseas to broker relationships and create activities which link artists and cultural institutions around the world. It works with writers, publishers, producers, translators and other sector professionals across literature, publishing and education. The Visual Arts team shares UK visual arts around the world, connecting professionals internationally through collaborative exhibition programmes, digital networking, training and development and delegations. It manages and develops the British Council Collection and the British Pavilion at the Venice Biennale.

Creative Scotland

Waverley Gate, 2–4 Waterloo Place,
Edinburgh EH1 3EG
tel 0330 333 2000 (switchboard); 0345 603 6000 (enquiries line)
email enquiries@creativescotland.com
website www.creativescotland.com

The public body that supports the arts, screen and creative industries across all parts of Scotland on behalf of everyone who lives, works or visits there. Through distributing funding from the Scottish Government and the National Lottery, Creative Scotland enables people and organisations to work in and experience the arts, screen and creative industries in Scotland by helping others to develop great ideas and bring them to life. Creative Scotland supports writers and publishers based in Scotland through a range of funds and initiatives.

The Gaelic Books Council/Comhairle nan Leabhraichean

32 Mansfield Street, Glasgow G11 5QP
tel 0141 337 6211

email alison@gaelicbooks.org
website www.gaelicbooks.org
Director Alison Lang

Stimulates Scottish Gaelic publishing by awarding publication grants for new books, commissions new works from established and emerging authors and provides editorial advice and guidance to Gaelic writers and publishers. Has a bookshop in Glasgow that stocks all Gaelic and Gaelic-related books in print. All stock is listed on the website. Founded 1968.

Guernsey Arts Commission

Candie Museum, Candie Road, St Peter Port, Guernsey GY1 2UG
tel (01481) 709747
email info@arts.gg

The Commission's aim is to help promote, develop and support the arts in Guernsey through exhibitions, a community arts programme and public events.

Literature Wales

Glyn Jones Centre, Wales Millennium Centre, Bute Place, Cardiff CF10 5AL
tel 029-2047 2266
email post@literaturewales.org
website www.literaturewales.org
Facebook www.facebook.com/LlenCymruLitWales
Twitter @LitWales
Chief Executive Lleucu Siencyn

Literature Wales is the national company for the development of literature in Wales. Working to inspire communities, develop writers and celebrate Wales' literary culture, its vision is a Wales where literature empowers, improves and brightens lives. Activities include the Wales Book of the Year Award, the Children's Laureate Wales and Bardd Plant Cymru schemes, creative writing courses at Tŷ Newydd Writing Centre, writer's bursaries and mentoring, the National Poet of Wales initiative, and more. The organisation is a member of the Arts Council of Wales' Arts Portfolio Wales.

Literature Works

c/o The Arts Institute Office, Roland Levinsky Building, Plymouth University, Drake Circus, Plymouth PL4 8AA
tel (01752) 585073
email info@literatureworks.org.uk
website www.literatureworks.org.uk
Twitter @LitWorks

Literature Works is the regional literature development agency for South West England, a registered charity and an Arts Council England National Portfolio organisation. Its aim is to open up the flexible literature artform of poetry and story, creative writing and reading as widely as they can to the benefit of all in the South West of England. They host a thriving online community of emerging and established writers, nurture talent and provide resources for writers in the region.

Royal Academy of Arts

Burlington House, Piccadilly, London W1J 0BD
tel 020-7300 8090
website www.royalacademy.org.uk
President Rebecca Salter

Royal Academicians are elected from the most distinguished artists in the UK. Holds major loan exhibitions throughout the year including the annual Summer Exhibition. Also runs Royal Academy Schools, a free fine art postgraduate programme, for 51 early career artists.

Royal Birmingham Society of Artists

RBSA Gallery, 4 Brook Street, St Paul's, Birmingham B3 1SA
tel 0121 236 4353
email rbsagallery@rbsa.org.uk
website www.rbsa.org.uk
Facebook www.facebook.com/rbsagallery
Twitter @rbsagallery
Instagram rbsagallery
Membership Friends £40 p.a.

The Royal Birmingham Society of Artists (RBSA) is an artist-led charity, which supports artists and promotes engagement with the visual arts through a range of exhibitions, events and workshops. It runs its own exhibition venue, the RBSA Gallery, in Birmingham's historic Jewellery Quarter, a short walk from the city centre. The gallery is open seven days a week and admission to all exhibitions is free.

Royal Institute of Oil Painters

17 Carlton House Terrace, London SW1Y 5BD
tel 020-7930 6844
website https://theroi.org.uk
Twitter @InstituteRoi

Promotes and encourages the art of painting in oils. Open Annual Exhibition at the Mall Galleries, The Mall, London SW1.

Royal Institute of Painters in Water Colours

17 Carlton House Terrace, London SW1Y 5BD
tel 020-7930 6844
email info@mallgalleries.com
website www.royalinstituteofpaintersinwater colours.org
Facebook www.facebook.com/RIwatercolours
Twitter @RIwatercolours
Instagram royal_institute_watercolours
President Rosa Sepple
Membership Elected from approved candidates' list

Promotes the appreciation of watercolour painting in its traditional and contemporary forms, primarily by means of an annual exhibition at the Mall Galleries,

The Mall, London SW1 of members' and non-members' work and also by members' exhibitions at selected venues in Britain and abroad. The Royal Institute of Painters in Water Colours is one of the oldest watercolour societies in the world. Founded 1831.

The Royal Musical Association
Dr Jeffrey Dean, 4 Chandos Road,
Chorlton-cum-Hardy, Manchester M21 0ST
tel 0161 861 7542
email exec@rma.ac.uk
website www.rma.ac.uk
Twitter @RoyalMusical
President Prof. Barbara Kelly

Promotes the investigation and discussion of subjects connected with the art and science of music. Sponsors conferences, study days and research/training events. Publishes the *Journal of the Royal Musical Association*, *Royal Musical Association Research Chronicle*, and the RMA Monographs series. Founded 1874.

The Royal Photographic Society
RPS House, 337 Paintworks, Arnos Vale,
Bristol BS4 3AR
tel 0117 316 4450
email frontofhouse@rps.org
website www.rps.org
Facebook www.facebook.com/
royalphotographicsociety
Twitter @The_RPS
Instagram royalphotographicsociety
Membership £122 p.a. UK; £110 p.a. overseas; £92 p.a. over-65s; £56 p.a. under-25s, students and concessions.

The Society promotes the public appreciation of photography in all its forms and supports and encourages individuals to develop their skills, which it does through exhibitions, public events, film screenings, workshops and a qualifications programme. It acts as an advocate for photography and photographers and speaks to the media on relevant matters. Membership is open to anyone with an interest in photography. Founded 1853.

The Royal Scottish Academy of Art and Architecture
The Mound, Edinburgh EH2 2EL
tel 0131 624 6110
website www.royalscottishacademy.org
Director Colin Greenslade

Led by eminent artists and architects, the Royal Scottish Academy (RSA) is an independent voice for cultural advocacy and one of the largest supporters of artists in Scotland. It administers a number of scholarships, awards and residencies and has a historic collection of Scottish artworks and an archive, recognised by the Scottish Government as

being of national significance. The Academy cherishes its independence from local or national government funding, relying instead on bequests, legacies, sponsorship and earned income. For information on open submission exhibitions, artist scholarships and residencies, or to discuss making a bequest to the Academy, visit the website. Founded 1826.

The Royal Society
6–9 Carlton House Terrace, London SW1Y 5AG
tel 020-7451 2500
email library@royalsociety.org
website https://royalsociety.org
Facebook www.facebook.com/theroyalsociety
Twitter @royalsociety
President Sir Adrian Smith PRS, *Treasurer* Prof. Andrew Hopper FRS, *Biological Secretary* Dame Linda Partridge FRS, *Physical Secretary* Prof. Peter Bruce FRS, *Foreign Secretary* Sir Richard Catlow FRS, *Executive Director* Dr Julie Maxton

The independent scientific academy of the UK and the Commonwealth, dedicated to promoting excellence in science.

RSA (Royal Society for the Encouragement of Arts, Manufactures and Commerce)
8 John Adam Street, London WC2N 6EZ
tel 020-7930 5115
email general@rsa.org.uk
website www.thersa.org
Twitter @theRSAorg

The RSA works to remove barriers to social progress, driving ideas, innovation and social change through an ambitious programme of projects, events and lectures. Supported by 30,000 Fellows, an international network of influencers and innovators from every field and background across the UK and overseas. Welcomes people of any nationality and background who will support the organisation's aims. Founded 1754.

Royal Society of British Artists
email info@royalsocietyofbritishartists.org.uk
website www.royalsocietyofbritishartists.org.uk
Facebook www.facebook.com/
RoyalSocietyBritishArtists
Twitter @RoyalSocBritArt
Instagram royal_society_british_artists
Honorary Secretary Brenda Davies

Incorporated by Royal Charter for the purpose of encouraging the study and practice of the arts of painting, sculpture, drawing and printmaking. The RBA Annual Exhibition at the Mall Galleries, The Mall, London SW1 is open to non-member artists, with many awards offered to both members and non-members alike. Work from younger artists is also encouraged and a month-long Rome Scholarship offered, as well as other awards and the possibility of exhibiting work in the RBA RISING STARS exhibition in central London for artists aged 35 or under.

Royal Society of Literature

Somerset House, Strand, London WC2R 1LA
tel 020-7845 4679
email info@rsliterature.org
website www.rsliterature.org
Facebook www.facebook.com/RoyalSocietyLiterature
Twitter @RSLiterature
Membership £60 p.a.; £40 for those aged 18–30.

The RSL is the UK's charity for the advancement of literature. It acts as a voice for the value of literature, engages people in appreciating literature, and encourages and honours writers through its events programme, awards and prizes and outreach programme. Founded 1820.

Royal Society of Marine Artists

17 Carlton House Terrace, London SW1Y 5BD
tel 020-7930 6844
email rsma.contact@gmail.com
website www.rsma.org

The aim of the society is to promote and encourage the highest standards of marine art and welcomes submissions for their Annual Open Exhibition at The Mall Galleries in London, which is usually held in October (more information at www.mallgalleries.org.uk). Membership is achieved by a consistent record of success in having work selected and hung at this event and ultimately by election by the members.

The Royal Society of Miniature Painters, Sculptors and Gravers

email info@royal-miniature-society.org.uk
website www.royal-miniature-society.org.uk
Facebook www.facebook.com/RoyalMiniatureSociety
Twitter @royalminiature
Instagram royalminiature
Executive Secretary Claire Hucker
Membership By selection and standard of work over a period of years (ARMS associate, RMS full member)

An open Exhibition is held annually at the Mall Galleries, The Mall, London SW1. Entry forms for the next exhibition will be available from the website in July. Applications and enquiries to the Executive Secretary. Patron HRH The Prince of Wales. Founded 1895.

Royal Society of Painter-Printmakers

Bankside Gallery, 48 Hopton Street, London SE1 9JH
tel 020-7928 7521
email info@banksidegallery.com
website www.re-printmakers.com
President Prof. David Ferry

Open to British and overseas artists. An election of Associates is held annually; for details check the

website. New members are elected by the Council of the Society based on the quality of their work alone, in a tradition reaching back over one hundred years. Holds three members' exhibitions per year. Founded 1880.

Royal Society of Portrait Painters

17 Carlton House Terrace, London SW1Y 5BD
tel 020-7930 6844
email enquiries@therp.co.uk
website www.therp.co.uk
website www.mallgalleries.org.uk
President Richard Foster

Annual Exhibition at Mall Galleries, The Mall, London SW1, of members' work and work drawn from an open selection. Awards are made including: the Ondaatje Prize for Portraiture (£10,000), the De Laszlo Award (£3,000), the Prince of Wales's Award for Portrait Drawing (£2,000), the Changing Faces Prize (£2,000), the Burke's Peerage Foundation Award (£2,000), Smallwood Architects' Contextual Portraiture Prize (£1,000). A commissions consultancy service to help those wishing to commission portraits runs throughout the year. Founded 1891.

Royal Society of Sculptors

Dora House, 108 Old Brompton Road, London SW7 3RA
tel 020-7373 8615
email info@sculptors.org.uk
website www.sculptors.org.uk

An artist-led membership organisation which supports and connects sculptors throughout their careers and offers exhibitions, artists' talks, creative workshops and events for all.

Royal Watercolour Society

Bankside Gallery, 48 Hopton Street, London SE1 9JH
tel 020-7928 7521
email info@royalwatercoloursociety.com
website www.royalwatercoloursociety.co.uk
Twitter @RWS_Art
Membership Open to British and overseas artists; election of Associates held annually. Friends membership is open to all those interested in watercolour painting.

An artist-led society whose members work in a variety of media including gouache, acrylic, pen and ink, pigment, collage and mixed media as well as traditional watercolour. Promotes, by example and education, the understanding, appreciation and enjoyment of these media. Founded 1804.

Royal West of England Academy

Queens Road, Clifton, Bristol BS8 1PX
tel 0117 973 5129
email info@rwa.org.uk
website www.rwa.org.uk
Director Alison Bevan

The RWA, Bristol's first art gallery, brings world-class visual art from around the world to the South West. Its vision is to be the South West's leading centre for the exhibition, exploration and practice of the visual arts, recognised as a place that enriches the lives of people from all communities and backgrounds. Founded 1844.

COPYRIGHT AND LICENSING

Australian Copyright Council

PO Box 1986, Strawberry Hills, NSW 2012
tel +61 (0)2 9101 2377
email info@copyright.org.au
website www.copyright.org.au
Facebook www.facebook.com/
AustralianCopyrightCouncil
Twitter @AusCopyright
Chief Executive Officer Eileen Camilleri

Provides easily accessible and affordable practical information, legal advice, education and forums on Australian copyright law for content creators and consumers. It represents the peak bodies for professional artists and content creators working in Australia's creative industries and Australia's major copyright collecting societies, including the Australian Society of Authors, the Australian Writers' Guild and the Australian Publishers Association.

    The Council advocates for the contribution of creators to Australia's culture and economy; the importance of copyright for the common good. It works to promote understanding of copyright law and its application, lobby for appropriate law reform and foster collaboration between content creators and consumers. Founded 1968.

Authors' Licensing and Collecting Society Ltd – see page 715

British Copyright Council

2 Pancras Square, London N1C 4AG
email info@britishcopyright.org
website www.britishcopyright.org
Vice-President Geoffrey Adams, *President of Honour* Maureen Duffy, *Chairman* Trevor Cook

Aims to defend and foster the true principles of copyright and its acceptance throughout the world, to bring together bodies representing all who are interested in the protection of such copyright, and to keep watch on any legal or other changes which may require an amendment of the law.

Copyright Clearance Center Inc.

222 Rosewood Drive, Danvers, MA 01923, USA
tel +1 978-750-8400
email info@copyright.com
website www.copyright.com

Aims to remove the complexity from copyright issues and make it easy for businesses and academic institutions to use copyright-protected materials while compensating publishers and content creators for their work.

The Copyright Licensing Agency Ltd – see page 713

Design and Artists Copyright Society (DACS) – see page 717

FACT

Regal House, 70 London Road, Twickenham, Middlesex TW1 3QS
tel 020-8891 1217
email contact@fact-uk.org.uk
website www.fact-uk.org.uk
Twitter @factuk

Protects the content, product and interests of the film and television broadcasting industries and is regarded as the leader in intellectual property protection. Founded 1983.

The Irish Copyright Licensing Agency

63 Patrick Street, Dun Laoghaire, Co Dublin A96 WF25, Republic of Ireland
tel +353 (0)1 662 4211
email info@icla.ie
website www.icla.ie
Executive Director Samantha Holman

Licenses schools and other users of copyright material to photocopy or scan extracts of such material, and distributes the monies collected to the authors and publishers whose works have been copied. Founded 1992.

PICSEL (Picture Industry Collecting Society for Effective Licensing)

112 Western Road, Brighton, East Sussex BN1 2AB
tel (01273) 746564
email info@picsel.org.uk
website www.picsel.org.uk

PICSEL is a not-for-profit collecting society that ensures that all visual artists, creators and representative rights holders of images receive fair payment for various secondary uses of their works. It works to ensure that all licence fees collected are distributed equitably, efficiently and in a transparent manner. Founded 2016.

EDITORIAL, JOURNALISM AND BROADCASTING

American Society for Indexing

1628 E. Southern Ave. 9–223, Tempe, AZ 85282, USA
tel +1 480-245-6750
email info@asindexing.org
website www.asindexing.org
Facebook www.facebook.com/theaac/
Executive Director Gwen Henson

Increases awareness of the value of high-quality indexes and indexing; offers members access to educational resources that enable them to strengthen their indexing performance; keeps members up to date on indexing technology; advocates for the professional interests of indexers.

Association of Freelance Editors, Proofreaders and Indexers of Ireland

email info@afepi-ireland.com
website www.afepi-ireland.com
Twitter @AFEPI_Ireland

AFEPI Ireland protects the interests of members and serves as a point of contact between publishers/ independent authors and members. Membership is available to experienced professional editors, proofreaders and indexers. For services for publishers and authors, see our online directory of freelance professional editors, proofreaders and indexers based in Ireland and Northern Ireland. Founded 1985.

Association of Freelance Writers

8–10 Dutton Street, Manchester M3 1LE
tel 0161 819 9922
email studentservices@writersbureau.com
website www.writersbureau.com/writing/association-of-freelance-writers.htm
Membership £24.99 p.a.

Members of the association receive resources to help with their writing career including: a membership card identifying them as a freelance writer, free online course, free appraisal of up to 2000 words, free writing guide plus discounts on writing resources, competitions, courses, self-publishing and more.

British Association of Journalists

PO Box 742, Winchester SO23 3QB
email office@bajunion.org.uk
website www.bajunion.org.uk
General Secretary Matthew Myatt

Non-political trade union for professional journalists. Aims to protect and promote the industrial and professional interests of journalists. Founded 1992.

British Guild of Agricultural Journalists

444 Westwood Heath Road, Coventry CV4 8AA
tel 07584 022909
email secretary@gaj.org.uk
website www.gaj.org.uk
Twitter @gajinfo
President Baroness Boycott, *Chairman* Catherine Linch, *General Secretary* Nikki Robertson
Membership £78 p.a. (full membership); £39 (retired/ student membership)

Promotes high standards among journalists, photographers and communicators who specialise in agriculture, horticulture, food production and other rural affairs, and contributes towards a better understanding of agriculture. Founded 1944.

British Society of Magazine Editors

4 Conway Road, London N14 7BA
tel 020-8906 4664
email admin@bsme.com
website www.bsme.com
Twitter @bsmeinfo
Instagram bsme_insta

The only society in the UK exclusively for magazine and digital editors. Represents the needs and views of editors and acts as a voice for the industry.

Chartered Institute of Editing and Proofreading

Apsley House, 176 Upper Richmond Road, London SW15 2SH
tel 020-8785 6155
email office@ciep.uk
website www.ciep.uk
Facebook www.facebook.com/EditProof
Twitter @The_CIEP

The CIEP is a non-profit body promoting excellence in English language editing. It sets and demonstrates editorial standards, and is a community, training hub and support network for editorial professionals – the people who work to make text accurate, clear and fit for purpose. The CIEP publishes an online directory of experienced editorial professionals and also runs online courses and workshops in copyediting, proofreading and related skills, for people starting an editorial career and those wishing to broaden their competence.

As well as professional practice, training covers business skills for the self-employed. It also offers in-house training to businesses and organisations on various writing-related skills. The Institute will be instrumental in developing recognised standards of training and accreditation for editors and proofreaders. The CIEP was known as the Society for Editors and Proofreaders before being awarded its Royal Charter in 2019. It has close links with and works alongside other bodies in the publishing sector.

The Chartered Institute of Journalists

PO Box 765, Waltham Abbey EN8 1NT
tel 020-7252 1187
email memberservices@cioj.org
website https://cioj.org
Twitter @CIoJournalist

The senior organisation of the profession, the Chartered Institute is an independent organisation that promotes standards and ethics throughout the profession. There are three parts to the work carried out on behalf of members: professional, charitable and trade union. Founded 1884.

Editors' and Proofreaders' Alliance of Northern Ireland

email info@epani.org.uk
website www.epani.org.uk
Twitter @epa_ni
Coordinator Averill Buchanan

Aims to establish and maintain high professional standards in editorial skills in Northern Ireland. For services for authors, see our directory of freelance professional editors, proofreaders and indexers based in Northern Ireland.

European Broadcasting Union

L'Ancienne Route 17A, Postal Box 45,
CH–1218 Grand-Saconnex, Geneva, Switzerland
tel +41 (0)22-717 2111
email info@ebu.ch
website www.ebu.ch
Twitter @EBU_HQ
Director General Noel Curran

The European Broadcasting Union (EBU) is the world's foremost alliance of public service media (PSM). Its mission is to make PSM indispensable. It has 115 members in 56 countries, and an additional 33 associates in Asia, Africa, Australasia and the Americas. Members operate nearly 2,000 television, radio and online channels and services, broadcasting in more than 160 different languages. Together they reach audiences of more than one billion people around the world. EBU's television and radio services operate under the trademarks of Eurovision and Euroradio.

Foreign Press Association in London

8 St James's Square, London SW1Y 4JU
tel 020-7792 4565
email briefings@fpalondon.org
website www.fpalondon.org
Facebook www.facebook.com/foreignpressassociation
Twitter @FPALondon
Director Deborah Bonetti

The oldest and largest association of foreign journalists in the world. All major international news outlets are represented. Provides access and accreditation to a wide variety of events in the UK, chairs Foreign Lobby briefings with N10 and the FCDO and provides access to the House of Commons and to annual Buckingham Palace Garden Parties. Organises press trips and briefings with ministers and leading figures in all departments. The FPA is one of the gatekeepers of the UKPCA and provides UK Press Cards to bona fide international journalists. Founded 1888.

Independent Press Standards Organisation

Gate House, 1 Farringdon Street, London EC4M 7LG
tel 0300 123 2220
email inquiries@ipso.co.uk
website www.ipso.co.uk
Twitter @ipsoneus

IPSO is the independent regulator of the newspaper and magazine industry. It exists to promote and uphold the highest professional standards of journalism in the UK and to support members of the public in seeking redress where they believe that the Editors' Code of Practice has been breached.

Journalists' Charity

Dickens House, 35 Wathen Road, Dorking,
Surrey RH4 1JY
tel (01306) 887511
email enquiries@journalistscharity.org.uk
website https://journalistscharity.org.uk
Twitter @JournoCharity
Ceo James Brindle

For the relief of hardship amongst journalists, their widows/widowers and dependants. Financial assistance and retirement housing are provided. Founded 1864.

Magazines Canada

Mailbox 201, 555 Richmond Street West, Suite 604,
Toronto, Ontario M5V 3B1
tel +1 416-994-6471
email info@magazinescanada.ca
website www.magazinescanada.ca
Twitter @magscanada
Executive Director Melanie Rutledge

The national trade association representing Canadian consumer, cultural, speciality, professional and business media magazines.

The Media Society

Broadgate Tower, 3rd Floor, 20 Primrose Street,
London EC2A 2RS
email admin@themediasociety.com
website www.themediasociety.com/index.php
Honorary President Peter York
Membership £45 p.a., £10 p.a. students

Exists to promote and encourage collective and independent research into the standards, performance, organisation and economics of the media and to hold regular discussions and debates on subjects of topical or special interest and concern to print and broadcast journalists and others working in or with the media. Up to 22 evening debates and events organised throughout the year, currently all online using Zoom but once venues re-open, these will continue with a mixture of physical and online events. Founded 1973.

National Council for the Training of Journalists

The New Granary, Station Road, Newport,
Essex CB11 3PL
tel (01799) 544014
email info@nctj.com
website www.nctj.com
Facebook www.facebook.com/nctjpage
Twitter @NCTJ_news

The NCTJ is a registered charity and awarding body which provides multimedia journalism training. Full-time accredited courses run at various colleges/

independent providers/universities in the UK. Distance learning programmes and short courses are also available. Founded 1951.

National Union of Journalists

Headland House, 72 Acton Street,
London WC1X 9NB
tel 020-7843 3700
email info@nuj.org.uk
website www.nuj.org.uk
Facebook www.facebook.com/groups/nujournalists
Twitter @NUJofficial

Trade union for journalists and photographers, including freelances, with over 30,000 members and branches in the UK, Republic of Ireland, Paris, Brussels and the Netherlands. It covers the newspaper press, news agencies, magazines, broadcasting, periodical and book publishing, public relations departments and consultancies, information services and new media. The NUJ mediates disputes, organises campaigns, provides training and general and legal advice. Official publications: *The Journalist* (bi-monthly), e-newsletters *NUJ Active* and *NUJ Informed*, the online *Freelance Directory* and *Freelance Fees Guide*, the *NUJ Ethical Code of Conduct* and policy pamphlets and submissions.

News Media Association

2nd Floor, 16–18 New Bridge Street,
London EC4V 6AG
tel 020-3848 9620
email nma@newsmediauk.org
website www.newsmediauk.org
Twitter @newsmediaorg

Promotes the interests of news media publishers to government, regulatory authorities, industry bodies and other organisations whose work affects the industry.

Reporters Without Borders

CS 90247, 75083 Paris Cedex 02, France
tel +33 (0)1 4483 8484
email secretariat@rsf.org
website https://rsf.org
Facebook www.facebook.com/Reporterssansfrontieres
Twitter @RSF_en

Provides information on the media freedom situation worldwide and issues regular press releases about abuses against journalists and about different kinds of censorship. It also protects journalists and bloggers in danger, acts as a pressure group and publishes the World Press Freedom Index. Its main activities are advocacy, awareness campaigns, assistance and legal aid and cyber-security. Founded 2014.

Scottish Newspaper Society

17 Polwarth Grove, Edinburgh EH11 1LY
email info@scotns.org.uk
website www.scotns.org.uk

Represents and safeguards the interests of the Scottish newspaper industry, to maintain press freedom and improve the industry's profile. Founded 2009.

Society of Editors

University Centre, Granta Place, Mill Lane,
Cambridge CB2 1RU
tel (01223) 304080
email office@societyofeditors.org
website www.societyofeditors.org
President Alison Gow
Membership up to £230 p.a. depending on category

Formed from the merger of the Guild of Editors and the Association of British Editors, the Society of Editors has members in national, regional and local newspapers, magazines, broadcasting and digital media, journalism education and media law. It campaigns for media freedom, self regulation, the public's right to know and the maintenance of standards in journalism.

Society of Indexers – see page 660

Society of Women Writers & Journalists

email enquiries@swwj.co.uk
website www.swwj.co.uk
Facebook www.facebook.com/societyofwomenwriters
Twitter @SWWJ

The SWWJ aims to encourage literary achievement, to uphold professional standards, to promote social contact with fellow writers and to defend the dignity and prestige of the writing profession in all its aspects. Full and Associate members can now use the appropriate post-nominals (e.g., MSWWJ and FSWWJ) after their name and receive a Press Card. See website for a full list of benefits and information. Founded 1894.

Sports Journalists' Association

tel 020-8916 2234
email info@sportjournalists.co.uk
website www.sportsjournalists.co.uk
Twitter @SportsSJA

The SJA represents sports journalists across the country and is Britain's voice in international sporting affairs. Offers advice to members covering major events and acts as a consultant to organisers of major sporting events on media requirements. Member of the BOA Press Advisory Committee. Founded 1948.

Voice of the Listener & Viewer

The Old Rectory Business Centre, Springhead Road,
Northfleet DA11 8HN
tel (01474) 338716
email info@vlv.org.uk
website www.vlv.org.uk
Facebook www.facebook.com/VLVUK

Twitter @vlvuk
Administrator Sarah Stapylton-Smith
Membership From £30 p.a. Academic, corporate and student rates available

VLV's mission is to campaign for accountability, diversity and excellence in UK broadcasting, seeking to sustain and strengthen public service broadcasting to the benefit of civil society and democracy in the UK. It holds regular conferences and seminars and publishes a bulletin and an e-newsletter. Founded 1983.

Yachting Journalists' Association

website www.yja.world
Honorary Secretary Chris English, *Honorary Treasurer* Cliff Webb
Membership £50 p.a. (£45 p.a. if paid by Standing Order)

Aims to further the interests of yachting and yachting journalism. Members vote annually for the Yachtsman of the Year and the Young Sailor of the Year Award and host several important functions annually on both the British and international maritime calendar. Founded 1969.

LITERACY

BookTrust

G8 Battersea Studios, 80 Silverthorne Road, London SW8 3HE
tel 020-7801 8800
email query@booktrust.org.uk
website www.booktrust.org.uk
Twitter @Booktrust
Ceo Diana Gerald, *Chair of Trustees* John Coughlan

The UK's largest children's reading charity, dedicated to getting children reading because children who read are happier, healthier, more empathetic and more creative; they also do better at school. BookTrust gets children reading in lots of different ways, but its priority is to get children excited about books and stories.

  BookTrust reviews at least one children's book each day and runs the Blue Peter Book Awards, Waterstones Children's Laureate, BookTrust Storytime Prize and BookTrust Lifetime Achievement Award. In 2019, it launched BookTrust Represents, a project to promote authors and illustrators of colour. See website to learn more about BookTrust's work.

The Children's Book Circle

website www.childrensbookcircle.org.uk
Twitter @ChildBookCircle
Membership £25 p.a.

Provides a discussion forum for anybody involved with children's books. Monthly meetings are addressed by a panel of invited speakers and topics focus on current and controversial issues. Holds the annual Patrick Hardy lecture and administers the Eleanor Farjeon Award. Founded 1962.

Children's Books Ireland

17 North Great George's Street, Dublin D01 R2F1, Republic of Ireland
tel +353 (0)1 872 7475
email info@childrensbooksireland.com
website www.childrensbooksireland.ie
Ceo Elaina Ryan, *Deputy Ceo* Jenny Murray, *Programme and Events Manager* Aoife Murray

The national children's books resource organisation of Ireland. Its mission is to make books part of every child's life. It champions and celebrates the importance of authors and illustrators and works in partnership with the people and organisations who enhance children's lives through books. Core projects include: the Children's Books Ireland International Annual Conference; the KPMG Children's Books Ireland Awards and its Junior Juries programme for school groups and book clubs; the annual Children's Books Ireland Recommended Reads, a guide to the best books of the year; nationwide Book Clinics; various book gifting initiatives including the Robert Dunbar Memorial Libraries; Bookseed and *Inis* magazine in print and online – a forum for discussion, debate and critique of Irish and international books. CBI administers the Laureate na nÓg project on behalf of the Arts Council and runs live literature events throughout the year. Founded 1996.

Free Word

tel 020-7324 2570
email info@freeword.org
website https://freeword.org
Artistic Director Roma Backhouse

An arts organisation focused on the power and politics of words. Also a home for organisations interested in who gets to speak and be heard in society. Produces two seasons a year in collaboration with artists and activists, with an emphasis on fresh voices and on influencing the range of perspectives heard in our society. Free Word associates include: Apples & Snakes, Article 19, Arvon, BookTrust, English PEN, Index on Censorship, The Literary Consultancy, The Reading Agency and Reporters Without Borders. Founded 2009.

LoveReading4Kids

PTC International Ltd, Turnbridge Mills, Quay Street, Huddersfield HD1 6QT
tel 020-3004 7204
website www.lovereading4kids.co.uk
Facebook www.facebook.com/lovereading4kids
Twitter @lovereadingkids

A book recommendation site for children's books ranging from toddlers to teens and ensures that whatever their age or interest, there is a steady stream of book recommendations available. Offers a variety of free services for parents and anyone who is interested in buying the best books for boys and girls of all ages. Supports parents, teachers and school librarians in helping engender a lifelong love of reading in children. The website features Kids' Zone, an area designed specifically for children, with competitions, quizzes and book-related material. Founded 2005.

LoveReading4Schools

PTC International Ltd, Turnbridge Mills, Quay Street, Huddersfield HD1 6QT
tel 020-3004 7204
website www.lovereading4schools.co.uk
Facebook www.facebook.com/lovereading4schools
Twitter @lr4schools

A book recommendation website which promotes a love of books and reading to all by offering the tools, advice and information needed to help members and browsers to find their next book, including time-strapped teachers and librarians in schools to help engender a lifelong love of reading in their students. Publishes book lists of relevance to schools including lists of inspirational books, cultural books, reluctant readers recommendations and books related to mental health and wellbeing.

National Literacy Trust

68 South Lambeth Road, London SW8 1RL
tel 020-7587 1842
email contact@literacytrust.org.uk
website https://literacytrust.org.uk
Facebook www.facebook.com/nationalliteracytrust
Twitter @Literacy_Trust

An independent charity that aims to help change lives through literacy. It campaigns to improve public understanding of the importance of literacy, as well as delivering projects and working in partnership to reach those most in need of support.

Read for Good

26 Nailsworth Mills, Avening Road, Nailsworth, Glos. GL6 0BS
tel (01453) 839005
email reading@readforgood.org
website www.readforgood.org
Facebook www.facebook.com/readforgood
Twitter @ReadforGoodUK

Read for Good aims for all children in the UK to be given the opportunity, space and motivation to develop their own love of reading, benefiting them throughout their lives. Many studies show that reading changes lives: from educational outcomes and social mobility to emotional wellbeing. Runs a readathon programme in 3,000 schools and a hospital programme, which focuses on the supply of books and storyteller visits to brighten up the days of 150,000 children in the UK's main children's hospitals.

The Reading Agency

email info@readingagency.org.uk
website www.readingagency.org.uk
Twitter @readingagency

A charity whose mission is to tackle life's big challenges through the proven power of reading. Works closely with public libraries, publishers, health partners and volunteers to bring reading programmes to adults and young people across the UK. Funded by Arts Council England, The Reading Agency supports a wide range of reading initiatives for adults and young people including Reading Ahead, designed to build people's reading confidence and motivation; and World Book Night, an annual celebration of books and reading which takes place on 23 April. In 2018, supported by the Big Lottery Fund, The Reading Agency launched Reading Friends – a programme that tackles loneliness and isolation among older people by starting conversations through reading.

Scottish Book Trust

Sandeman House, Trunk's Close, 55 High Street, Edinburgh EH1 1SR
tel 0131 524 0160
email info@scottishbooktrust.com
website www.scottishbooktrust.com
Facebook www.facebook.com/scottishbktrust
Twitter @ScottishBkTrust

Scotland's national agency for the promotion of reading, writing and literature. Programmes include: Bookbug, a free universal book-gifting programme which encourages families to read with their children from birth; an ambitious schools programme including national tours, the virtual events programme Authors Live and the Bookbug Picture Book Prize; the Scottish Teenage Book Prize; the Live Literature funding programme, a national initiative enabling Scottish citizens to engage with authors, playwrights, poets, storytellers and illustrators; a writer development programme, offering mentoring and professional development for emerging and established writers; and a readership development programme featuring a national writing campaign, as well as Book Week Scotland, during the last week in November. Founded 1998.

Seven Stories – The National Centre for Children's Books

30 Lime Street, Ouseburn Valley, Newcastle upon Tyne NE1 2PQ
tel 0300 330 1095
email info@sevenstories.org.uk
website www.sevenstories.org.uk
Facebook www.facebook.com/7stories
Twitter @7stories

Seven Stories champions the art of children's books to ensure its place as an integral part of childhood and national cultural life. The world of children's books is celebrated through unique exhibitions, events for all ages and a national archive. The work of over 200 British authors and illustrators, including Judith Kerr, Enid Blyton, Michael Morpurgo and David Almond is cared for in the archive collection – and it is still growing. Seven Stories is a charity – all the money earned and raised is used to save, celebrate and share children's books so that future generations can enjoy Britain's rich literary heritage. Arts Council England and Newcastle Culture Investment Fund regularly fund Seven Stories' work, giving children's literature status and establishing new ways of engaging young audiences. Founded 1996.

Story Therapy CIC

1 Sugworth Lane, Radley, Abingdon-on-Thames, Oxon OX14 2HZ
email admin@storytherapyresources.co.uk
website www.storytherapyresources.co.uk
Facebook www.facebook.com/storytherapy
Twitter @StoryTherapy
Contact Hilary Hawkes

A non-profit social enterprise creating resources, especially story-themed, that support children's emotional health and mental wellbeing. Founded 2016.

LIBRARIES AND INFORMATION

Campaign for Freedom of Information

tel 020-7324 2519
email admin@cfoi.org.uk
website www.cfoi.org.uk
Twitter @CampaignFOI

A non-profit organisation working to defend and improve public access to official information and to ensure that the Freedom of Information Act is implemented effectively. Advises members of the public about their rights to information under FOI and related laws, helps people challenge unreasonable refusals to disclose information, encourages good practice by public authorities and provides FOI training.

CILIP (The Library and Information Association)

7 Ridgmount Street, London WC1E 7AE
tel 020-8159 4925
website www.cilip.org.uk
Facebook www.facebook.com/CILIPinfo
Twitter @CILIPinfo
Membership varies according to level and income

The leading professional body for librarians, information specialists and knowledge managers, with members in the UK and internationally. CILIP's objective is to put library and information skills at the heart of a democratic, equal and prosperous information society.

English Association

University of Leicester, University Road, Leicester LE1 7RH
tel 0116 229 7622
email engassoc@leicester.ac.uk
website www2.le.ac.uk/offices/english-association
Chair Rob Penman

A membership body for individuals and organisations passionate about the English language and its literatures. Membership includes teachers, students, authors, writers and readers, and is made up of people and institutions from around the world. Its aim is to further the knowledge, understanding and enjoyment of English studies, and to foster good practice in their teaching and learning at all levels by:

• encouraging the study of English language, literature and creative writing;
• working towards fuller recognition of English as core to education;
• fostering discussion about methods of teaching English at all levels;
• offering timely conferences and lectures alongside a uniquely diverse and extensive portfolio of publications; and
• responding to national consultations and policy decisions about the subject.

English Speaking Board (International)

9 Hattersley Court, Burscough Road, Ormskirk L39 2AY
tel (01695) 573439
email customer@esbuk.org
website www.esbuk.org

An internationally accredited awarding organisation with a mission to promote clear, effective communication at all levels by providing high-quality speech and language qualifications. ESB International's range of assessments support learners to possess the oracy and English language skills they need in order to achieve their aspirations.

Offers an extensive portfolio of speech qualifications including a new speech pathways qualification which gives greater flexibility to learners. These qualifications are designed for schools who wish to use spoken language to raise pupil achievement and develop enrichment programmes. ESOL Skills for Life and ESOL international qualifications are also accessible for individuals for whom English is not a first language.

The English-Speaking Union

Dartmouth House, 37 Charles Street, London W1J 5ED
tel 020-7529 1550
email esu@esu.org
website www.esu.org

Societies, prizes and festivals

Promotes international understanding and tolerance through the widening use of the English language throughout the world. The English-Speaking Union is an educational charity which runs programmes, competitions and exchanges promoting oracy (speaking and listening) skills and cross-cultural understanding. Members contribute to its work across the world. Founded 1918.

Institute of Internal Communication

Scorpio House, Rockingham Drive, Linford Wood, Milton Keynes MK14 6LY
tel (01908) 232168
email enquiries@ioic.org.uk
website www.ioic.org.uk

As the only professional body dedicated to internal communication in the UK, it exists to help organisations and people succeed through promoting internal communication of the highest standard. Founded 1949.

Private Libraries Association

29 Eden Drive, Hull HU8 8JQ
email maslen@maslen.karoo.co.uk
website www.plabooks.org
President Matthew Haley, *Honorary Secretary* Jim Maslen, *Honorary Journal Editors* David Chambers, David Butcher, James Freemantle
Membership £30 p.a.

International society of book collectors and lovers of books. Publications include *The Private Library* (quarterly), annual *Private Press Books*, and other books on book collecting. Founded 1956.

LITERARY

Alliance of Literary Societies

email allianceoflitsocs@gmail.com
website www.allianceofliterarysocieties.wordpress.com
President Claire Harman

An umbrella organisation of about 130 literary societies which aims to act as a valuable liaison body between member societies to share knowledge, skills and expertise, and also acts as a pressure group when necessary. The Alliance can assist in the preservation of buildings, places and objects which have literary associations. Its publications include a twice-yearly newsletter and an annual journal, *ALSo*. The ALS holds an annual literary weekend hosted by a different member society each year.

Association for Scottish Literary Studies

c/o Dept of Scottish Literature,
University of Glasgow, 7 University Gardens,
Glasgow G12 8QH
tel 0141 330 5309
email office@asls.org.uk
website www.asls.org.uk

President David Goldie, *Secretary* Craig Lamont, *Director* Duncan Jones
Membership £60 p.a. individuals; £15 p.a. UK students; £90 p.a. corporate

ASLS promotes the study, teaching and writing of Scottish literature and furthers the study of the languages of Scotland. Publishes annually *New Writing Scotland*, an anthology of new Scottish writing; an edited text of Scottish literature; a series of academic journals; and the eZine *The Bottle Imp*. Also publishes *Scotnotes* (comprehensive study guides to major Scottish writers), literary texts and commentaries designed to assist the classroom teacher, and a series of occasional papers. Organises two conferences a year. Founded 1970.

The Jane Austen Society

20 Parsonage Road, Henfield, West Sussex BN5 9JG
email hq@jasoc.org.uk
website www.janeaustensoci.freeuk.com
Membership £28 p.a.; £33 p.a. joint membership for two people living at the same address; £12 p.a. student membership (UK); £38 p.a. overseas; £43 p.a joint overseas rate; £50 p.a. corporate

The Society fosters the appreciation and study of the work, life and times of Jane Austen (1775–1817), and the Austen family. Regular publications, meetings and conferences. Ten branches and groups in UK. Founded 1940.

The Beckford Society

The Timber Cottage, Crockerton,
Warminster BA12 8AX
tel (01985) 213195
email sidney.blackmore@btinternet.com
website www.beckfordsociety.org
Membership from £20 p.a.

Promotes an interest in the life and works of William Beckford of Fonthill (1760–1844) and his circle. Encourages Beckford studies and scholarship through exhibitions, lectures and publications, including *The Beckford Journal* (annual) and occasional newsletters. Founded 1995.

Arnold Bennett Society

4 Field End Close,
Trentham, Stoke on Trent ST4 8DA
email arnoldbennettscty@btinternet.com
website www.arnoldbennettsociety.org.uk
Facebook www.facebook.com/arnoldbennettsociety
Twitter @BennettSoc
Chairman Professor Ray Johnson MB
Membership £17.50 p.a. individuals; £20 p.a. family

Promotes the study and appreciation of the life, works and times not only of Arnold Bennett (1867–1931), but also of other provincial writers with a particular relationship to north Staffordshire.

The E.F. Benson Society

The Old Coach House, High Street, Rye,
East Sussex TN31 7JF
tel (01797) 223114
email info@efbensonsociety.org
website www.efbensonsociety.org
Secretary Allan Downend
Membership £12 p.a. single; £15 p.a. for two people at
same address; £20 p.a. overseas

Promotes interest in the author E.F. Benson
(1867–1940) and the Benson family. Arranges an
annual literary evening, annual outing to Rye (July)
and other places of Benson interest, talks on the
Bensons and exhibitions. Archive includes the Austin
Seckersen Collection, transcriptions of the Benson
diaries and letters. Publishes postcards, anthologies of
Benson's works, a Mary Benson biography, books on
Benson and an annual journal, *The Dodo*. Also sells
out-of-print Bensons to members. Founded 1984.

The George Borrow Society

60 Upper Marsh Road, Warminster, Wilts. BA12 9PN
email mkskillman@blueyonder.co.uk
website http://georgeborrow.org/home.html
Membership Secretary Michael Skillman

Promotes knowledge of the life and works of George
Borrow (1803–81), traveller and author. The Society
has waived its subscription fee until further notice.
Founded 1991.

The Brontë Society

Brontë Parsonage Museum, Church Street, Haworth,
Keighley, West Yorkshire BD22 8DR
tel (01535) 642323
email bronte@bronte.org.uk
website www.bronte.org.uk
Twitter @bronteparsonage

The Society cares for and promotes the accredited
collections and literary legacy of the Brontë family. It
is an Arts Council National Portfolio Organisation
and presents an exciting contemporary arts
programme, alongside changing exhibitions and
learning and engagement programmes. *Brontë Studies*
and the *Brontë Gazette* are published three times a
year. The museum is open Wednesday to Sunday all
year round. Please visit our website for the latest
information.

The Browning Society

64 Blythe Vale, London SE6 4NW
email browningsociety@hotmail.co.uk
website www.browningsociety.org
Honorary Secretary Jim Smith
Membership £20 p.a.

Aims to widen the appreciation and understanding of
the lives and poetry of Robert Browning (1812–89)
and Elizabeth Barrett Browning (1806–61), as well as
other Victorian writers and poets. Founded 1881;
refounded 1969.

The John Buchan Society

72 Ravensdowne, Berwick-upon-Tweed,
Northumberland TD15 1DQ
tel (01289) 302913
website www.johnbuchansociety.co.uk
Membership Secretary Alison Gallico
Membership £20 p.a. full; overseas and other rates on
application

Promotes a wider understanding of the life and works
of John Buchan (1875–1940). Encourages publication
of Buchan's works and supports the John Buchan
Story Museum in Peebles. Also holds regular
meetings and social gatherings; produces a newsletter
and a journal. Founded 1979.

Byron Society (Newstead Abbey)

Acushla, Halam Road, Southwell NG25 0AD
website www.newsteadabbeybyronsociety.org
Chairman P.K. Purslow
Membership £30 p.a.

Promotes research into the life and works of Lord
Byron (1788–1824) through seminars, discussions,
lectures and readings. Publishes *The Newstead Review*
(annual). Founded 1988.

The Lewis Carroll Society

email secretary@lewiscarrollsociety.org.uk
website https://lewiscarrollsociety.org.uk
Facebook www.facebook.com/groups/68678994062
Twitter @LewisCarrollSoc
Membership £25 p.a. UK; £30 p.a. Europe; £35 p.a.
elsewhere. Special rates for students and institutions

Promotes interest in the life and works of Lewis
Carroll (Revd Charles Lutwidge Dodgson, 1832–98)
and to encourage research. Activities include regular
meetings, exhibitions and a publishing programme
that includes the first annotated, unexpurgated
edition of his diaries in nine volumes, the Society's
journal *The Carrollian* (two p.a.), a newsletter,
Bandersnatch (quarterly) and the *Lewis Carroll Review*
(occasional). Founded 1969.

The John Clare Society

tel (01353) 668438
email sueholgate@hotmail.co.uk
website https://johnclaresociety.wordpress.com/
Membership £15 p.a. UK individual; other rates on
application

Promotes a wider appreciation of the life and works
of the poet John Clare (1793–1864). Founded 1981.

The Wilkie Collins Society

email paul@paullewis.co.uk
website https://wilkiecollinssociety.org
Secretary Paul Lewis
Membership £16 p.a. EU; £28 p.a. international

Aims to promote interest in the life and works of
Wilkie Collins (1824–89). Publishes a newsletter, an

annual scholarly journal and reprints of Collins's lesser known works. Founded 1981.

The Joseph Conrad Society (UK)

c/o The Polish Social and Cultural Association, 238–246 King Street, London W6 0RF
email theconradian@aol.com
email hughepstein@hotmail.co.uk
website www.josephconradsociety.org
Chairman Robert Hampson, *Honorary Secretary* Hugh Epstein, *Editors of The Conradian* Alex Fachard, Robert Hampson, Laurence Davies

Activities include an annual international conference; publication of *The Conradian* and a series of pamphlets; and maintenance of a substantial reference library as part of the Polish Library at the Polish Social and Cultural Association. Administers the Juliet McLauchlan Prize, a £200 annual award for the winner of an essay competition, and travel grants for scholars wishing to attend Conrad conferences. Founded 1973.

Walter de la Mare Society

email info@walterdelamare.co.uk
website www.walterdelamare.co.uk
Membership £10 p.a.

Established to promote the study and deepen the appreciation of the works of Walter de la Mare (1873–1956) through a magazine, talks, discussions and other activities. Founded 1997.

Dickens Fellowship

The Charles Dickens Museum, 48 Doughty Street, London WC1N 2LX
tel 020-7405 2127
email postbox@dickensfellowship.org
website www.dickensfellowship.org
Honorary Secretary Paul Graham
Membership £17 p.a.

Based in the house occupied by Charles Dickens (1812–70) during the period 1837–9. Publishes *The Dickensian* (3 p.a.). Founded 1902.

The George Eliot Fellowship

website www.georgeeliot.org
Facebook www.facebook.com/TheGeorgeEliotFellowship
Twitter @GeorgeEliotLove
Chairman John Burton
Membership £18 p.a. (£15 p.a. concessions) individuals; £23 p.a. (£20 p.a. concessions) couples; £15 p.a. students (under 25)

Promotes an interest in the life and work of George Eliot (1819–80) and helps to extend her influence; arranges meetings, study days and conferences; produces an annual journal (*The George Eliot Review*), newsletters and other publications. Back numbers of all editions of the *George Eliot Review* are now online, via the website. Works closely with educational establishments in the Nuneaton area. The Fellowship is hoping to open a George Eliot Visitor Centre in the future. Awards the annual George Eliot Fellowship Prize (£500) for an essay on Eliot's life or work, which must be previously unpublished and not exceed 4,000 words. Founded 1930.

The Folklore Society

50 Fitzroy Street, London W1T 5BT
tel 020-3915 3034
email thefolkloresociety@gmail.com
website www.folklore-society.com

Collection, recording and study of folklore. Founded 1878.

The Gaskell Society

37 Buckingham Drive, Knutsford, Cheshire WA16 8LH
tel (01565) 651761
email pamgriff54@gmail.com
website www.gaskellsociety.co.uk
Facebook www.facebook.com/TheGaskellSociety
Twitter @GaskellSociety
Membership Secretary Jackie Tucker
Membership £23 p.a.; £28 p.a. joint annual member/European member/institutions; £15 p.a. student in full-time education; £30 p.a. non-European member

Promotes and encourages the study and appreciation of the work and life of Elizabeth Cleghorn Gaskell (1810–65). Holds regular meetings in Knutsford, London, Manchester and Bath; visits and residential conferences; produces an annual journal and bi-annual newsletters. Founded 1985.

Graham Greene Birthplace Trust

email secretary@grahamgreenebt.org
website https://grahamgreenebt.org
Facebook www.facebook.com/Graham-Greene-International-Festival-55327438605
Twitter @FestivalGreene
Membership £14, £19 and £22 p.a. for the UK, Europe and rest of world respectively; £38, £52 and £60 respectively for three years, all including the quarterly newsletter

Exists to study the life and the wide-ranging works (novels, stories, plays, films, non-fiction and journalism) of Graham Greene (1904–91). For over 20 years, the Trust has presented the popular and engaging Graham Greene International Festival, which is held annually in or around the third week of September at Berkhamsted School. It publishes a quarterly newsletter, *A Sort of Newsletter*, available to Friends of the Trust, and organises the Graham Greene audio trails in Berkhamsted. The Trust also runs an annual Graham Greene Film Review Competition, organised in partnership with the Centre for New Writing at the University of Manchester. It has a very active website and a presence on social media.

The Thomas Hardy Society

c/o Dorset County Museum, High West Street,
Dorchester, Dorset DT1 1XA
tel (01305) 251501; 07867 666737
email info@hardysociety.org
website www.hardysociety.org
Membership £24 p.a. UK or £35 p.a. overseas for print
and online journals; £18 p.a. UK or £22.50 p.a.
overseas for online only; £10 p.a. students for print
and online journals; £7.50 p.a students for online
only.

Promotes and celebrates the life and work of Thomas
Hardy (1840–1928). Publishes *The Thomas Hardy
Journal* (annual) and *The Hardy Society Journal*
(two p.a.). Biennial conference and festival held in
Dorchester in July. Annual Study Day conference
held in Dorchester in April. Annual THS invited
lecture held in London in November. Regular events
throughout the year. Over 1000 members
internationally, we also have a large and interactive
online presence. Founded 1967.

The James Hilton Society

22 Well House, Woodmansterne Lane, Banstead,
Surrey SM7 3AA
email info@jameshiltonsociety.co.uk
website www.jameshiltonsociety.co.uk
Chairman Richard Hughes
Membership £13 p.a.; £10 p.a. concessions; £18 p.a.
overseas

Promotes interest in the life and work of novelist and
scriptwriter James Hilton (1900–54). Publishes a
newsletter three times a year and a bi-annual
scholarly journal, and organises conferences.
Founded 2000.

The Sherlock Holmes Society of London

email shjournal@btinternet.com
website www.sherlock-holmes.org.uk
Press and Publicity Officer Roger Johnson

The Society is open to anyone with an interest in
Sherlock Holmes, Dr John H. Watson and their
world. A literary and social society, publishing a bi-
annual scholarly journal and occasional papers, and
holding meetings, dinners and excursions.
Founded 1951.

Housman Society

Abberley Cottage, 7 Dowles Road, Bewdley DY12 2EJ
email info@housman-society.co.uk
website www.housman-society.co.uk
Twitter @housmansoc
Membership £15 p.a. UK; £20 p.a. overseas

Aims to foster interest in and promote knowledge of
A.E. Housman (1859–1936) and his family. Sponsors
a lecture at the Hay Festival. Publishes an annual
journal and bi-annual newsletter. Founded 1973.

The Johnson Society

Johnson Birthplace Museum, Breadmarket Street,
Lichfield, Staffs. WS13 6LG
tel (01543) 264972
email info@thejohnsonsociety.org.uk
website www.johnsonnew.wordpress.com
General Secretary Marilyn Davies

Aims to encourage interest in, and study of, the
writings, life and times of Dr Samuel Johnson
(1709–84); support the Samuel Johnson Birthplace
Museum, by helping to maintain and enhance its
contents, and by working with the Johnson
Birthplace Advisory Committee; assist in preserving
other physical memorials of Johnson and his
contemporaries, including books, manuscripts,
artefacts, buildings, statues, plaques and Johnson's
Willow; participate in the annual commemorations
of Johnson's birthday, and promote knowledge of
eighteenth-century history in general.

Johnson Society of London

email memsec@johnsonsocietyoflondon.org
website www.johnsonsocietyoflondon.org
Membership £25 p.a. individual; £30 p.a. joint; £20
p.a. student

Promotes the study of the life and works of Dr
Johnson (1709–84) and perpetuates his memory in
the city of his adoption. Founded 1928.

Keats-Shelley Memorial Association

KSMA Registered Office, 11 Staple Inn,
London WC1V 7QH
email hello@keats-shelley.org
website www.keats-shelley.org
Facebook www.facebook.com/keatsshelleyhouse
Twitter @Keats_Shelley

Owns and supports the house in Rome where John
Keats died in 1821. Since 1909, a museum open to
the public; celebrates the poets Keats (1795–1821),
Shelley (1792–1822), Lord Byron (1788–1824) and
the novelist Mary Shelley (1797–1851). Regular
events; bursaries for young scholars, bi-annual Keats-
Shelley Review; two literary awards; and online
resources, including the Keats-Shelley Blog and
Keats-Shelley Podcast. The Keats-Shelley Memorial
Association runs the annual Keats-Shelley Prize and
the Young Romantics Prize, open to young writers
aged 16–18. Founded 1903.

The Kipling Society

Bay Tree House, Doomsday Garden, Horsham,
West Sussex RH13 6LB
tel (07801) 680516
email michaelrkipling@gmail.com
website www.kiplingsociety.co.uk
Chairman Prof. Jan Montefiore
Membership £29 p.a. UK; £31 p.a Europe; £35 p.a rest
of world; £10 p.a student (worldwide)

Encourages discussion and study of the work and life
of Rudyard Kipling (1865–1936) by assisting in the

study of his writings, holding discussion meetings, publishing a quarterly journal and website (with a Readers' Guide to Kipling's work), maintaining a Kipling Library at Haileybury School in Hertfordshire and running an annual story-writing competition for primary schools.

The Charles Lamb Society
BM-ELIA, London WC1N 3XX
email h.goodman@bathspa.ac.uk
website www.charleslambsociety.com
Chairs Felicity James, John Strachan, *Membership Secretary* Helen Goodman
Membership Personal: £24/$45 p.a. individual;
£32 p.a. couple; £32/$60 p.a. corporate

Publishes the academic journal *The Charles Lamb Bulletin* (twice a year). The Society's extensive library of books and MSS by and about Charles Lamb (1775–1834) is housed at the Guildhall Library, Aldermanbury, London EC2P 2EJ. Founded 1935.

The D.H. Lawrence Society
email brenda.sumner@gmail.com
website www.dhlawrencesociety.com
Facebook www.facebook.com/dhlawrencesociety/
Twitter @DHLawrenceSoc
Chairman Alan Wilson, *Treasurer* Sheila Bamford,
Secretary Brenda Sumner
Membership £20 p.a. ordinary; £22 p.a. overseas; £18 p.a. concessions/students

Aims to bring together people interested in D.H. Lawrence (1885–1930), to encourage study of his work, and to provide information and guides for people visiting Eastwood. Founded 1974.

The T.E. Lawrence Society
PO Box 728, Oxford OX2 9ZJ
email chairman@telsociety.org.uk
website www.telsociety.org.uk
Membership £24 p.a. UK; £32 p.a. overseas

Promotes the memory of T.E. Lawrence (1888–1935) and furthers education and knowledge by research into his life; publishes a journal (bi-annual) and newsletter (three p.a.). Founded 1985.

The Marlowe Society
email secretary@marlowe-society.org
website www.marlowe-society.org
Facebook www.facebook.com/marlowesociety/
Twitter @MarloweSociety_

Aims to extend appreciation and widen recognition of Christopher Marlowe (1564–93) as the foremost poet and dramatist preceding Shakespeare, whose development he influenced. Founded 1955.

The John Masefield Society
40 Mill Way, Bushey, Herts. WD23 2AG
tel (01923) 246047
email robert.vaughan110@gmail.com
website www.ies.sas.ac.uk/node/496
Chairman Bob Vaughan

Membership £5 p.a.; £10 p.a. overseas; £8 p.a. family/institution

Promotes the life and works of the poet John Masefield (1878–1967). Holds an annual lecture and other, less formal, readings and gatherings; publishes an annual journal and frequent newsletters. Founded 1992.

William Morris Society
Kelmscott House, 26 Upper Mall, London W6 9TA
tel 020-8741 3735
website www.williammorrissociety.org
Twitter @WmMorrisSocUK
Honorary Secretary Natalia Martynenko-Hunt

Spreads knowledge of the life, work and ideas of William Morris (1834–96); publishes a magazine (three times p.a.) and an academic journal (two p.a.). Visit the website for details of how to access the library, archive and collections. Founded 1955.

The Edith Nesbit Society
21 Churchfields, West Malling, Kent ME19 6RJ
email edithnesbit@gmail.com
website www.edithnesbit.co.uk
Membership £10 p.a. individual; £12 p.a. joint; £15 p.a. organisations

Promotes an interest in the life and works of Edith Nesbit (1858–1924) by means of talks, a regular newsletter and other publications, and visits to places associated with her. Founded 1996.

Wilfred Owen Association
email woa@1914-18.co.uk
website www.wilfredowen.org.uk
Membership £15 p.a. UK; £25 p.a. overseas; £12 p.a. concession

Commemorates the life and work of Wilfred Owen (1893–1918); encourages and enhances appreciation of his work through visits, public events and a bi-annual journal. Founded 1989.

The Beatrix Potter Society
email info@beatrixpottersociety.org.uk
website www.beatrixpottersociety.org.uk

Promotes the study and appreciation of the life and works of Beatrix Potter (1866–1943) as author, artist, diarist, farmer and conservationist. Regular lecture meetings, conferences and events in the UK and USA. Quarterly newsletter. Small publishing programme. Founded 1980.

The Powys Society
Flat D, 87 Ledbury Road, London W11 2AG
tel 020-7243 0168
email chris.d.thomas@hotmail.co.uk
website www.powys-society.org
Honorary Secretary Chris Thomas
Membership £22 p.a. UK; £26 p.a. overseas

Promotes the greater public recognition and enjoyment of the writings, thought and contribution to the arts of the Powys family, particularly John Cowper (1872–1963), Theodore Powys (1875–1953) and Llewelyn Powys (1884–1939), and the many other family members and their close friends. Publishes an annual scholarly journal (*The Powys Journal*) and three newsletters per year, as well as books by and about the Powys family, and holds an annual weekend conference in August, as well as organising other activities throughout the year. Founded 1967.

The J.B. Priestley Society
Eldwick Crag Farm, High Eldwick, Bingley, West Yorkshire BD16 3BB
email reavill@globalnet.co.uk
website www.jbpriestleysociety.com
General Secretary Rod Slater (rodslater7@gmail.com), *Information Officer* Michael Nelson (m.nelson928@btinternet.com), *Membership Secretary* Tony Reavill
Membership £15 p.a. single; £20 p.a. family; £10 p.a. concessions

Promotes the knowledge, understanding and appreciation of the published works of J.B. Priestley (1894–1984) and the study of his life and career. Holds lectures and discussions and shows films. Publishes a newsletter and journal. Organises walks to areas with Priestley connections, Annual Priestley Luncheon and other social events. Founded 1997.

The Ruskin Society
email info@theruskinsociety.com
website www.theruskinsociety.com
Twitter @ruskinsociety
Membership £15 p.a.

Celebrates the life, work and legacy of John Ruskin (1819–1900). Organises lectures and events exploring Ruskin's ideas and placing them in a modern context. Organises a regular programme of events including talks, visits and study days in the UK. Founded 1997.

The Malcolm Saville Society
11 Minster Court, Windsor Close, Taunton TA1 4LW
email mystery@witchend.com
website www.witchend.com
Facebook www.facebook.com/MalcolmSaville
Twitter @MSavilleSociety
Membership £15 p.a. UK; £17.50 p.a. Europe; £21 p.a. elsewhere

Promotes interest in the work of children's author Malcolm Saville (1901–82). Regular social activities, library, contact directory and magazine (four p.a.). Founded 1994.

The Dorothy L. Sayers Society
Gimsons, Kings Chase, Witham, Essex CM8 1AX
tel (01376) 515626

email info@sayers.org.uk
website www.sayers.org.uk
Chair Seona Ford, *Bulletin Secretary* Jasmine Simeone
Membership e-version of *Bulletin*: £20 p.a. UK and worldwide; £10 p.a. under-25s; Printed version (mailed): £27 p.a. UK; £33 p.a. Europe; £36.50 p.a rest of world

Aims to promote and encourage the study of the works of Dorothy L. Sayers (1893–1957); to collect archive materials and reminiscences about her and make them available to students and biographers; to hold an annual conference and other meetings; to publish *Proceedings*, pamphlets and a bi-monthly *Bulletin*; to make grants and awards. Founded 1976.

The Shaw Society
tel 020-7435 6497
email contact@shawsociety.org.uk
website www.shawsociety.org.uk
Twitter @ShawSoc
Chair Dr Anne Wright CBE
Membership £25 p.a., £30 p.a. family membership

Works towards the improvement and diffusion of knowledge of the life and works of Bernard Shaw (1856–1950) and his circle. Publishes *The Shavian*. Meets regularly for script-in-hand performances and discussion. SHAW2020, the theatre company affiliated to The Shaw Society, is dedicated to promoting Shaw's plays and writing, bringing them to wider, diverse audiences, especially now that Shaw's works are out of copyright.

The Robert Louis Stevenson Club
website http://robert-louis-stevenson.org/rls-club/

Aims to foster interest in Robert Louis Stevenson's life (1850–94) and works through various events and its newsletter. Founded 1920.

The Tennyson Society
Lincolnshire Archives, St Rumbold Street, Lincoln LN2 5AB
tel (01522) 687837
email tennysonsociety@gmail.com
website www.tennysonsociety.org.uk
Twitter @TennysonSociety
Membership £14 p.a.; £16 p.a family; £25 p.a. institutions

Promotes the study and understanding of the life and work of the poet Alfred, Lord Tennyson (1809–92) and supports the Tennyson Research Centre in Lincoln. Holds lectures, visits and seminars; publishes the *Tennyson Research Bulletin* (annual), Monographs and Occasional Papers; tapes/recordings available. Founded 1960.

The Edward Thomas Fellowship
Fairlands, Finchmead Lane, Stroud, Petersfield, Hampshire GU32 3PF

email mitchjd.etf@outlook.com
website www.edward-thomas-fellowship.org.uk
Chairman Jeremy Mitchell
Membership £15 p.a.

Celebrates the life and work of Edward Thomas (1878–1917), poet and writer, and assists in the preservation of places associated with him and arranges events which extend fellowship amongst his admirers. In partnership with Petersfield Museum, the Fellowship has established the Edward Thomas Study Centre at the museum based around the Tim Wilton-Steer collection of books by and about Edward Thomas. There are over 2,000 books and artefacts in the collection, which are available to researchers and readers. Contact Jeremy Mitchell for access arrangements. Founded 1980.

Dylan Thomas Society
email info@dylanthomassociety.com
website www.dylanthomassociety.com
website www.dylanthomasbirthplace.com
Chairman Geoff Haden
Membership £15 p.a. single; £20 p.a. couple; £10 p.a. student

Based at the Dylan Thomas Birthplace and Family Home. The society promotes an interest in the works of Dylan Thomas (1914–53) and other writers. Founded 1977.

The Tolkien Society
website www.tolkiensociety.org
Facebook www.facebook.com/TolkienSociety
Twitter @TolkienSociety
YouTube The Tolkien Society
Membership £30 p.a. online or £10 p.a. students; Postal: £30 p.a. UK; £35 p.a. EU; £45 p.a. rest of the world; add £15 p.a. for family membership

An educational charity and literary society devoted to the study and promotion of the life and works of J.R.R. Tolkien.

The Trollope Society
PO Box 505, Tunbridge Wells, Kent TN2 9RW
tel (01747) 839799
email info@trollopesociety.org
website www.trollopesociety.org
Chairman Dominic Edwardes
Membership £26 p.a. UK; £36 p.a. international

Has produced the first ever complete edition of the novels of Anthony Trollope (1815–82). Founded 1987.

The Walmsley Society
18 Pinfold Close, Barkisland, Halifax, West Yorkshire HX4 0EY
website www.walmsleysoc.org
Secretary Margaret Higson
Membership £13 p.a. UK; £20 p.a. overseas; £12 p.a. concession

Promotes and encourages an appreciation of the literary and artistic heritage left to us by Leo Walmsley (1892–1966) and J. Ulric Walmsley (1860–1954). Founded 1985.

Mary Webb Society
c/o Anne Williams, Concord College, Acton Burnell, Shrewsbury SY5 7PF
tel (01694) 731631
website www.marywebbsociety.co.uk
Secretary Anne Williams

For devotees of the literature and works of Mary Webb (1881–1927) and of the Shropshire countryside of her novels. Publishes two newsletters p.a., organises four events p.a. including a two-day Summer School in various locations related to Webb's life and works. Lectures and tours arranged for individuals and groups. The Society archive is continually being added to. Founded 1972.

The H.G. Wells Society
153 Kenilworth Crescent, Enfield, Middlesex EN1 3RG
email secretaryhgwellssociety@hotmail.com
website https://hgwellssociety.com
Chairman Dr Emelyne Godfrey, *Secretary* Brian Jukes
Membership £22 p.a. UK (£15 retired/student/unwaged); £27 p.a. EU (£17); £30 rest of world (£20); Institutions: £30 p.a. UK, £35 p.a. EU, £40 p.a. rest of world

Promotes an active interest in and an appreciation of the life, work and thought of H.G. Wells (1866–1946). Publishes *The Wellsian* (annual) and *The Newsletter* (bi-annual). Founded 1960.

The Oscar Wilde Society
email vanessaheron1@outlook.com
website https://oscarwildesociety.co.uk
Membership Secretary Veronika Binoeder, *Honorary Secretary* Vanessa Heron

Promotes knowledge, appreciation and study of the life, personality and works of the writer and wit Oscar Wilde (1854–1900). Activities include meetings, lectures, readings and exhibitions, and visits to associated locations. Members receive a journal, *The Wildean* (two p.a.), a newsletter/journal, *Intentions* (four p.a.) and regular e-newsletters. Founded 1990.

The Henry Williamson Society
email paulmcglonegoshawk@gmail.com
email margaretmurphy567@gmail.com
website www.henrywilliamson.co.uk
General Secretary Paul McGlone, *Membership Secretary* Margaret Murphy

Encourages a wider readership and greater understanding of the literary heritage left by Henry Williamson (1895–1977). Founded 1980.

The P.G. Wodehouse Society (UK)

email info@pgwodehousesociety.org.uk
website www.pgwodehousesociety.org.uk
Membership £22 p.a.

Promotes the enjoyment of P.G. Wodehouse
(1881–1975). Publishes *Wooster Sauce* (quarterly) and
By The Way papers (four p.a.) which cover diverse
subjects of Wodehousean interest. Holds events,
entertainments and meetings throughout Britain.
Founded 1997.

Virginia Woolf Society of Great Britain

Fairhaven, Charnleys Lane, Banks,
Southport PR9 8HJ
tel (01704) 225232
email stuart.n.clarke@btinternet.com
website www.virginiawoolfsociety.org.uk
Facebook www.facebook.com/VWSGB
Membership Secretary Stuart N. Clarke
Membership £20 p.a.; £26 p.a. Europe; £30 p.a.
outside Europe (2021 fees)

Acts as a forum for British admirers of Virginia
Woolf (1882–1941) to meet, correspond and share
their enjoyment of her work. Publishes the *Virginia
Woolf Bulletin*. Founded 1998.

Francis Brett Young Society

92 Gower Road, Halesowen, West Midlands B62 9BT
tel 0121 422 8969
email michael.hall10@gmail.com
website www.fbysociety.co.uk
Chairman Dr Michael Hall, *Secretary* Mrs J. Hadley
Membership £7 p.a., £70 life for individual; £10 p.a.,
£100 life joint; £5 p.a. full-time students; £7 p.a.
societies and institutions

Provides opportunities for members to meet,
correspond, and to share the enjoyment of the works
of Francis Brett Young (1884–1954). Publishes a
journal (two p.a.). Founded 1979.

ART, ILLUSTRATION AND PHOTOGRAPHY

The Association of Illustrators

Somerset House, Strand, London WC2R 1LA
tel 020-7759 1010
email info@theaoi.com
website www.theaoi.com
Facebook www.facebook.com/theaoi
Twitter @theaoi

Trade association which supports illustrators,
promotes illustration and encourages professional
standards in the industry. Publishes *Varoom*
magazine. Presents an annual programme of events
and holds an annual competition, exhibition and
tour of the World Illustration Awards in partnership
with the *Directory of Illustration* (www.theaoi.com/
awards). Founded 1973.

The Association of Photographers

2nd Floor, 201 Haverstock Hill, London NW3 4QG
tel 020-7739 6669
website www.the-aop.org
Facebook www.facebook.com/
AssociationOfPhotographers
Twitter @AssocPhoto
Instagram assocphoto

Exists to protect and promote the worth and standing
of its members, to vigorously defend, educate and
lobby for the interests and rights of all photographers,
especially in the commercial photographic industry.
Founded 1968.

Axisweb

The Art House, Drury Lane, Wakefield WF1 2TE
tel (01924) 200502
email hello@axisweb.org
website www.axisweb.org
Facebook www.facebook.com/axisweb.org
Twitter @axisweb
Instagram axisweb

Axisweb is an independent charity providing a
platform to support artists and profile what they do.
Axisweb's programme reflects the artists' voice,
presenting new aspects and forms of expression to
local, national and international audiences. Through
membership, Axisweb supports artists and art
professionals with insurance, networking, space,
opportunities, awards, profiling, advice and
mentoring.

BAPLA (British Association of Picture Libraries and Agencies)

52 High Street, Pinner, Middlesex HA5 5PW
tel 020-8297 1198
email enquiries@bapla.org.uk
website https://bapla.org.uk
Twitter @baplaUK

The British Association of Picture Libraries and
Agencies (BAPLA) is the trade association for picture
libraries in the UK. Members include the major news,
stock and production agencies as well as sole traders
and cultural heritage institutions. Founded 1975.

The Blackpool Art Society

The Studio, Wilkinson Avenue,
Off Woodland Grove, Blackpool FY3 9HB
tel (01253) 768297
email sec@blackpoolartsociety.co.uk
website www.blackpoolartsociety.co.uk/index.htm

Various exhibitions (members' work only). Studio
meetings, demonstrations, workshops, lectures, out-
of-door sketching. New members always welcome.
Founded 1884.

British Institute of Professional Photography

The Artistry House, 16 Winckley Square,
Preston PR1 3JJ

Societies, prizes and festivals

tel (01772) 367968
email admin@bipp.com
website www.bipp.com
Facebook www.facebook.com/theBIPP
Twitter @thebipp

An internationally recognised qualifying organisation with over 100 years' experience in supporting and networking photographers. Delivers education, qualifications and professional development to photographers through a challenging qualifications structure alongside a full programme of training courses and events. Founded 1901.

British Interactive Media Association

49 Greek Street, London W1D 4EG
tel 020-3538 6607
email web@bima.co.uk
website https://bima.co.uk
Membership open to any organisation or individual with an interest in multimedia

BIMA is Britain's digital community which connects, develops and champions the industry. Membership of BIMA can lead to the extension of professional networks, attracting and developing talent, business growth and raising professional profiles. It also gives members a voice on issues affecting the industry. Founded 1985.

Cartoonists Club of Great Britain

website www.ccgb.org.uk
Facebook www.facebook.com/TheCartoonistsClub
Twitter @CartoonistsGB
Instagram Cartoonistsclub

The UK's largest cartoonists' organisation, started by Fleet Street cartoonists in the 1960s and providing a social base for cartoonists wherever they may live/work. It has grown to include many different types of cartoonist. Social gatherings are held several times a year at different places around the country, and occasionally members also attend events abroad. It has a thriving online presence with its own website with several forums, including one for non-members that helps interested budding cartoonists to raise their game. Members have their own private forum and a members' portfolio so that they can promote their work. The club's Facebook page is another lively cartoon-related news source, as is the monthly magazine *The Jester*.

The Chartered Society of Designers

1 Cedar Court, Royal Oak Yard, Bermondsey Street, London SE1 3GA
tel 020-7357 8088
email info@csd.org.uk
website www.csd.org.uk
Facebook www.facebook.com/charteredsocietyofdesigners
Twitter @csdminerva

The internationally recognised body for the design profession, providing support and guidance for designers at every stage of their career. Works to promote and regulate standards of competence, professional conduct and integrity, including representation on government and official bodies, design education and awards. The services to members include general information, publications and guidance on copyright and other professional issues.

Event & Visual Communication Association

23 Golden Square, London W1F 9JP
tel 020-3771 5642
email info@evcom.org.uk
website www.evcom.org.uk
Twitter @EVCOMUK

Created from two highly successful organisations, eventia and IVCA, EVCOM is comprised of a wide variety of leading professionals, agencies, freelancers, destinations, production companies and suppliers; all working throughout the events and visual communications sector.

Federation of British Artists

17 Carlton House Terrace, London SW1Y 5BD
tel 020-7930 6844
email info@mallgalleries.com
website www.mallgalleries.org.uk
Facebook www.facebook.com/mallgalleries
Twitter @mallgalleries

Administers nine major National Art Societies at Mall Galleries, The Mall, London SW1.

Fine Art Trade Guild

2 Wye House, 6 Enterprise Way, London SW18 1FZ
tel 020-7381 6616
email info@fineart.co.uk
website www.fineart.co.uk
Managing Director Louise Hay

Promotes the sale of fine art prints and picture framing in the UK and overseas markets; establishes and raises standards amongst members and communicates these to the buying public. The Guild publishes *Art + Framing Today*, the trade's longest established magazine, and various specialist books. Founded 1910.

FOCAL International Ltd (Federation of Commercial AudioVisual Libraries International Ltd)

27 Mortimer Street, London W1T 3BL
tel 020-3948 1999
email info@focalint.org
website www.focalint.org
Twitter @FOCALint

A not-for-profit trade association for the commercial audio-visual library industry, with over 300 members. Founded 1985.

Free Painters & Sculptors London

59A Charlton Road, Harlesden, London NW10 4BB
email info@freepaintersandsculptors.co.uk
website www.freepaintersandsculptors.co.uk
Facebook www.facebook.com/fpsartistgroup/
Twitter @fpsartistgroup

FPS is an established, artist-led organisation that promotes and exhibits a talented membership of painters, sculptors, printmakers and photographers at renowned central London galleries twice a year. With over 65 years of experience, FPS helps artists build long-term networks that develop artistic sustainability, exposure and sales, while also encouraging artists to create work on their own terms and therefore be 'free'. FPS was originally associated with the ICA (Institute of Contemporary Arts) and founding members included Roy Rasmussen, Lyall Watson and Maurice Jadot, who all feature in the permanent Tate Collection. FPS welcomes applications from talented artists at all stages of their career. Founded 1952.

The Greeting Card Association

United House, North Road, London N7 9DP
tel 020-7619 9266
email hello@gca.cards
website www.gca.cards
Facebook www.facebook.com/
GreetingCardAssociation
Twitter @GCAUK
Instagram GCA_UK
Chief Executive Amanda Fergusson

The trade association for greeting card publishers. See website for information and contacts for freelance designing and writing for greeting cards. Official magazine: *Progressive Greetings Worldwide.* Founded 1919.

The Guild of Aviation Artists

(incorporating the Society of Aviation Artists)
Studio 100, 161 High Street, Ruislip HA4 8JY
tel (03331) 302223
email admin@gava.org.uk
website www.gava.org.uk
President Michael Turner PFGAVA
Membership £70 p.a. Full; £55 p.a. Associates; £35 p.a. Friends; £15 p.a. Young Friends (aged under 25 years and in continuing education)

Formed to promote aviation art through the organisation of exhibitions and meetings. Holds annual open exhibition in July in London; £1,000 prize for 'Aviation Painting of the Year'. Quarterly members' newsletter. Founded 1971.

Guild of Railway Artists

website www.railart.co.uk
Facebook www.facebook.com/The-Guild-of-Railway-Artists-520306528057416

Aims to forge a link between artists depicting railway subjects and to give members a corporate identity; also stages railway art exhibitions and members' meetings and produces books of members' works. Founded 1979.

Hesketh Hubbard Art Society

17 Carlton House Terrace, London SW1Y 5BD
tel 020-7930 6844
email info@mallgalleries.com
website www.mallgalleries.org.uk
President Simon Whittle
Membership £225 p.a.

Offers both amateur and professional artists the opportunity to work from life models in untutored sessions. Membership includes 48 drawing sessions and no cover charge. Prospective members are invited to attend one session free before deciding if they wish to apply for membership.

The Hilliard Society of Miniaturists

tel 07582 019359
email hilliardsociety@aol.com
website www.hilliardsociety.org
President Maggy Pickard
Membership £60 p.a.; £25 p.a. friend member

Aims to increase knowledge and promote the art of miniature painting. Annual exhibition held in June at Wells; produces a newsletter. Founded 1982.

Imaginative Book Illustration Society

email ibissec@martinsteenson.co.uk
website www.bookillustration.org
Membership enquiries Martin Steenson

IBIS was established to encourage research into, and to facilitate, the exchange of information on book and periodical illustrations, the artists and their publishers. The Society has a worldwide membership including artists, collectors, bibliographers, writers and general enthusiasts. Whilst IBIS embraces all aspects of illustrative art, the main emphasis is on the illustration of texts in English since the 1830s. Founded 1995.

Institute of Designers in Ireland

WeWork, Charlemont Exchange, Charlemont Street, Dublin DO2 UN88, Republic of Ireland
email info@idi-design.ie
website www.idi-design.ie
Facebook www.facebook.com/idiireland
Twitter @IDIIreland

Irish design profession's representative body, covering every field of design. Founded 1972.

International Society of Typographic Designers

email info@istd.org.uk
website www.istd.org.uk

Working closely with graphic design educationalists and the professional community, the International Society of Typographic Designers establishes, maintains and promotes typographic standards through the forum of debate and design practice.

Membership is awarded to practising designers, educators and students who demonstrate, through the quality of their work, their commitment to achieving the highest possible quality of visual communication. It publishes a journal, *Typographic*. Students of typography and graphic design are encouraged to gain membership of the Society by entering the annual student assessment scheme. Founded 1928.

Master Photographers Association

Jubilee House, 1 Chancery Lane, Darlington, Co. Durham DL1 5QP
tel (01325) 356555
email membership@thempa.com
website www.thempa.com

Promotes and protects professional photographers. With over 60 years in the professional photography industry, the MPA prides itself in developing some of the industry's leading photographers.

National Acrylic Painters' Association

28 Polmennor Drive, Carbis Bay, Cornwall TR26 2SQ
email contact@napauk.com
website www.napauk.com

Promotes interest in, and encourages excellence and innovation in, the work of painters in acrylic. Holds an annual exhibition and regional shows; awards are made. Worldwide membership. Publishes a newsletter known as the *International NAPA Newspages*. Founded 1985.

National Society for Education in Art and Design

3 Masons Wharf, Potley Lane, Corsham, Wilts. SN13 9FY
tel (01225) 810134
email info@nsead.org
website www.nsead.org
Twitter @NSEAD1
General Secretary Michele Gregson

The leading national authority concerned with art, craft and design across all phases of education in the UK. Offers the benefits of membership of a professional association, a learned society and a trade union. Has representatives on national and regional committees concerned with art and design education. Publishes *International Journal of Art and Design Education* online (three p.a.; Wiley Blackwell) and *AD* magazine for teachers. Founded 1888.

The Pastel Society

email info@mallgalleries.com
website www.thepastelsociety.org.uk
Facebook www.facebook.com/thepastelsociety
Twitter @PastelSociety

Pastel and drawings in all dry media. Annual Exhibition open to all artists working in dry media held at Mall Galleries, The Mall, London SW1. Members elected from a list of approved candidates. Founded 1898.

The Picture Research Association

website www.picture-research.org.uk
Twitter @PRA_Association

The PRA is a professional organisation of picture researchers and picture editors specifically involved in the research, management and supply of visual material to the media industry. Registered members are listed on the website and can be located through the Find Researchers page, along with lots of useful information about the picture industry. Founded 1977.

Printmakers Council

Ground Floor Unit, 23 Blue Anchor Lane, London SE16 3UL
tel 07531 883250
email admin@printmakerscouncil.com
website www.printmakerscouncil.com
Facebook www.facebook.com/PrintmakersCouncil
Twitter @PMCouncil
Instagram printmakerscouncil
Membership £75 p.a.; £30 students, join online

Artist-led group which aims to promote the use of both traditional and innovative printmaking techniques by holding exhibitions of prints, providing information on prints and printmaking to both its membership and the public, and encouraging cooperation and exchanges between members, other associations and interested individuals. Archives held by the V&A and Scarborough Museums Trust. Founded 1965.

Professional Cartoonists' Organisation

email info@procartoonists.org
website www.procartoonists.org
Facebook www.facebook.com/UKProfessionalCartoonists
Twitter @procartoonists
Instagram procartoonists
Membership £80 p.a.

The organisation showcases UK cartoonists through its portfolio pages, a cartoon news blog and public events such as The Shrewsbury International Cartoon Festival and the Herne Bay Cartoon Festival. Founded 2006.

SAA

PO Box 50, Newark, Notts. NG23 5GY
tel 0800 980 1123
email info@saa.co.uk
website www.saa.co.uk
Facebook www.facebook.com/SupportingAllArtists
Instagram supportingallartists
Membership from £45 p.a.

Supporting all artists, from complete beginners and enthusiasts to professionals. SAA is the largest art community with 37,000 members, and welcomes new members. Membership includes access to hundreds of member-only inspirational videos, Paint magazine (delivered bi-monthly), exclusive discounts and offers on materials, paintings insurance for exhibitions and third-party public liability. Founded 1992.

The Society of Botanical Artists

1 Knapp Cottages, Wyke, Gillingham,
Dorset SP8 4NQ
tel (01747) 825718
email info@soc-botanical-artists.org
website www.soc-botanical-artists.org
Co-Presidents Billy Showell and Gael Sellwood,
Executive Secretary Mrs Pam Henderson
Membership by election, £130–£145 p.a.

Aims to encourage the art of botanical painting. Entry details for the open exhibitions are available on the website. Founded 1985.

Society of Graphic Fine Art

email enquiries@sgfa.org.uk
website www.sgfa.org.uk
Facebook www.facebook.com/
SocietyofGraphicFineArt
Twitter @SGFADrawing
President Les Williams

With over 130 elected members across the UK, the Society of Graphic Fine Art (The Drawing Society) exists to promote and exhibit works of high quality in colour or black and white, with the emphasis on good drawing and draughtsmanship, in pencil, pen, brush, charcoal or any of the forms of original printmaking. The Society holds an annual Open Exhibition with prizes and awards in many categories. Founded 1919.

Society of Heraldic Arts

Chairman of the Appointments Board,
8 Abbot Close, Ottery St Mary, Devon EX11 1FH
email k.arkinstall@tiscali.co.uk
website www.heraldic-arts.com
President Anthony Wood, *Chairman of the Appointments Board* Kevin Arkinstall

Serves the interests of heraldic artists, craftsmen, designers and writers, to provide a 'shop window' for their work, to obtain commissions on their behalf and to act as a forum for the exchange of information and ideas. Also offers an information service to the public. Candidates for admission as craft members should be artists or craftsmen whose work comprises a substantial element of heraldry and is of a sufficiently high standard to satisfy the requirements of the Society's advisory council. Founded 1987.

Society of Scribes and Illuminators

6 Queen Square, London WC1N 3AT
email honsec@calligraphyonline.org
website www.calligraphyonline.org

Membership £46 Fellows; £37 Lay members; £30 Friends

Aims to promote and preserve the art of calligraphy, bringing the beauty of handwritten letters to the modern world, moving with the times to embrace contemporary lettering whilst upholding the traditions of the craft. Education programme includes a correspondence course, an advanced training scheme, mentorship towards fellowship, a programme of study days, a series of masterclasses and recommendations for local learning opportunities. A specialist sales shop and an archive/library are available to members. Founded 1921.

Society of Wildlife Artists

17 Carlton House Terrace, London SW1Y 5BD
tel 020-7930 6844
website www.swla.co.uk
President Harriet Mead

Aims to promote and encourage the art of wildlife painting and sculpture. Open Annual Exhibition at Mall Galleries, The Mall, London SW1, for any artist whose work depicts wildlife subjects (botanical and domestic animals are not admissible).

The Society of Women Artists

Foxcote Cottage, Foxcote, Cheltenham,
Glos. GL54 4LP
email rebeccacottonswa@gmail.com
website www.society-women-artists.org.uk
President Dr Linda Smith, *Executive Secretary* Rebecca Cotton
Membership election by invitation, based on six works submitted to the exhibition. Digital submissions open March to June

Receiving day to be confirmed for annual open exhibition usually held in September at Mall Galleries, The Mall, London SW1. Continues to promote art by women. Founded 1855.

The Turner Society

BCM Box Turner, London WC1N 3XX
website www.turnersociety.com
Membership £30 p.a. individuals; £30 p.a. overseas surface mail; £45 p.a. overseas airmail; £600 life member

Promotes the study and appreciation of the life and works of J.M.W. Turner (1775–1851). Publishes *Turner Society News* (two p.a.). Founded 1975.

Women Who Draw

email hello@womenwhodraw.com
website www.womenwhodraw.com
Facebook www.facebook.com/womenwhodraw/
Twitter @thewomenwhodraw

Women Who Draw is an open directory of female professional illustrators, artists and cartoonists. It was created by two women to increase the visibility of female illustrators, emphasising female illustrators of colour, LBTQ+ and other minority groups of female illustrators. Women Who Draw is trans-inclusive and includes women, trans and gender non-conforming illustrators. Since its launch, it has become the place to go to discover talented illustrators from all over the world and features over 2,700 professional artists, interviews with industry professionals, monthly member collaborations and a resources page for artists and the people who hire them. Founded 2017.

FILM, THEATRE AND TELEVISION

AITA/IATA asbl International Amateur Theatre Association

email secretariat@aitaiata.net
website www.aitaiata.net
Facebook www.facebook.com/aitaiata
Twitter @aita_iata
President Béatrice Cellario, *Vice Presidents and Councillors* Rob Van Genechten, Aled Rhys-Jones, *Treasurer and Councillor* Villy Dall

Encourages, fosters and promotes the exchanges of non-professional theatre organisations and individuals and of student, educational and adult theatre activities at international level. Organises international seminars, workshops, courses and conferences, and collates information of all types for national and international dissemination. Holds an annual General Assembly and International Amateur Theatre Festival and a biennial World Festival of Children's Theatre. Every fourth General Assembly is held in Monaco and every other Festival of Children's Theatre is held in Lingen, Germany.

BAFTA (British Academy of Film and Television Arts)

195 Piccadilly, London W1J 9LN
tel 020-7734 0022
email reception@bafta.org
website www.bafta.org
Facebook www.facebook.com/bafta
Twitter @BAFTA
Chief Executive Amanda Berry OBE

The UK's pre-eminent, independent charity supporting, developing and promoting the art forms of the moving image (film, games and television) by identifying and rewarding excellence, inspiring practitioners and benefiting the public. BAFTA's awards are presented annually by its members to their peers in recognition of their skills and expertise. BAFTA's year-round learning programme offers unique access to some of the world's most inspiring talent through workshops, masterclasses, lectures and mentoring schemes, connecting with audiences of all ages and backgrounds across the UK, Los Angeles and New York. Founded 1947.

BECTU (Broadcasting Entertainment Communications and Theatre Union)

373–377 Clapham Road, London SW9 9BT
tel 020-7346 0900
email info@bectu.org.uk
website htpps://bectu.org.uk
Head of BECTU Philippa Childs

BECTU (a sector of the trade union Prospect) aims to defend the interests of writers in film, TV and radio. By virtue of its industrial strength, the union is able to help its writer members to secure favourable terms and conditions. In cases of disputes with employers, the union can intervene in order to ensure an equitable settlement. Its production agreement with Pact lays down minimum terms for writers working in the documentary area. Founded 1991.

BFI (British Film Institute)

21 Stephen Street, London W1T 1LN
tel 020-7255 1444
website www.bfi.org.uk
Facebook www.facebook.com/BritishFilmInstitute
Twitter @BFI

The BFI supports, nurtures and promotes the art of film, television and the moving image. A registered charity, funded by government and earned income, and a distributor of National Lottery funds, the BFI is at the heart of the UK's fast-growing screen industries, protecting the past and shaping their future across the UK. It works in partnership with cultural organisations, government and industry to make this happen. Founded 1933.

Independent Theatre Council

The Albany, Douglas Way, London SE8 4AG
tel 020-7403 1727
email admin@itc-arts.org
website www.itc-arts.org
Twitter @itc_arts

Enables the creation of high-quality professional performing arts by supporting, representing and developing the people who manage and produce it. It has around 500 members from a wide range of companies, venues and individuals in the fields of drama, dance, opera, musical theatre, puppetry, mixed media, mime, physical theatre and circus. Founded 1974.

Little Theatre Guild of Great Britain

tel (01207) 545280
email caroline.chapman1816@gmail.com
website www.littletheatreguild.org
Secretary Caroline Chapman

Promotes closer cooperation amongst the little theatres constituting its membership, acts as a coordinating and representative body on behalf of the little theatres, maintains and advances the highest standards in the art of theatre, and assists in encouraging the establishment of other little theatres.

Pact (Producers Alliance for Cinema and Television)

3rd Floor, Fitzrovia House,
153–157 Cleveland Street, London W1T 6QW
tel 020 7380 8230
email info@pact.co.uk
website www.pact.co.uk
Twitter @PactUK
Chief Executive John McVay

The UK trade association that represents and promotes the commercial interests of independent feature film, television, animation and interactive media companies. Headquartered in London, it has regional representation throughout the UK, in order to support its members, including an office in Leeds. An effective lobbying organisation, it has regular and constructive dialogues with government, regulators, public agencies and opinion-formers on all issues affecting its members, and contributes to key public policy debates on the media industry, both in the UK and in Europe. It negotiates terms of trade with all public service broadcasters in the UK and supports members in their business dealings with cable and satellite channels and streaming services. It also lobbies for a properly structured and funded UK film industry and maintains close contact with other relevant film organisations and government departments.

Player–Playwrights

email lynneplay@gmail.com
website www.playerplaywrights.co.uk
Facebook www.facebook.com/groups/playerplaywrights
Secretary Lynne O'Sullivan
Membership £12 in first year and £8 thereafter (plus £2.50 per attendance). Guests and audience welcome (non-members £4 entrance).

The society reads, performs and discusses plays and scripts submitted by members, with a view to assisting the writers in improving and marketing their work and enabling actors to showcase their talents. New writers and new acting members are always welcome. Check website for details of group meets. Founded 1948.

The Society for Theatre Research

c/o Department of Theatre and Performance,
V & A Blythe House, 23 Blythe Road,
London W14 0QX
email contact@str.org.uk
website www.str.org.uk
Twitter @TheSTR
Honorary Secretary Diana Fraser

Supports and promotes theatre research. Publishes the journal *Theatre Notebook* along with at least one major book per year, holds public lectures, and makes annual research grants. Also awards an annual prize for best book published in English on British Theatre. Founded 1948.

TRANSLATION

American Literary Translators Association

email elisabeth@literarytranslators.org
website www.literarytranslators.org
Executive Director Elisabeth Jaquette

ALTA is a broad-based professional association dedicated to the promotion of literary translation through services to literary translators, forums on the theory and practice of translation and collaboration with the international literary community. Hosts an annual conference, offers fellowships and mentorship for emerging translators and bestows four translation awards. Founded 1978.

British Centre for Literary Translation

School of Literature, Drama and Creative Writing,
University of East Anglia, Norwich Research Park,
Norwich NR4 7TJ
tel (01603) 592785
email bclt@uea.ac.uk
website www.bclt.org.uk
Facebook www.facebook.com/bcltuea
Twitter @bcltuea

A research centre within the School of Literature at the University of East Anglia in Norwich. It supports an MA in Literary Translation at the University of East Anglia, an increasing variety of undergraduate modules in the subject, and an extensive programme of PhD research. BCLT works in close partnership with the National Centre for Writing and a wide range of other national and international organisations to deliver a programme of activities which support the professional development of literary translators and promote the recognition of literary translation as a profession. These include the annual Sebald Lecture, held in the spring at the British Library in London, and the International Literary Translation and Creative Writing Summer School, held in July at UEA in Norwich. Founded 1989.

Chartered Institute of Linguists

7th Floor, 167 Fleet Street, London EC4A 2ES
tel 020-7940 3100
website www.ciol.org.uk
Facebook www.facebook.com/charteredinstituteoflinguists
Twitter @CIOLinguists

The Chartered Institute of Linguists (CIOL) is the foremost international membership organisation for all language professionals and is the only one offering a pathway to Chartership. Its diverse membership includes translators and interpreters, language teachers, university lecturers and linguists who use their foreign language skills in business, the professions and government.

CIOL's associated charity, CIOL Qualifications, is an Ofqual-accredited awarding body offering professional qualifications in translation and public service interpreting. CIOL publishes a bi-monthly magazine, *The Linguist*, free to members and available to non-members by subscription. *The Linguist* offers its readers a wide range of articles that are of interest to anyone working with languages. Founded 1910.

The Institute of Translation and Interpreting

Milton Keynes Business Centre, Foxhunter Drive, Linford Wood, Milton Keynes MK14 6GD
website www.iti.org.uk
Facebook www.facebook.com/ITofficial
Twitter @ITIUK

The ITI is the independent professional association of practising translators and interpreters. With the aim of promoting the highest standards in the profession, ITI serves as a focal point for all those who understand the importance of translation and interpreting to the economy and community. It offers guidance to those entering the profession and advice to both people offering their language services and their potential customers. Founded 1986.

Translators Association

24 Bedford Row, London WC1R 4EH
tel 020-7373 6642
email info@societyofauthors.org
website www.societyofauthors.org/Groups/Translators

Specialist group within the membership of the Society of Authors (see page 509), exclusively concerned with the interests of literary translators. Offers contract vetting and industry advice to members, runs literary translation events and provides specialist resources.

BIBLIOGRAPHICAL AND ACADEMIC

The Association of Learned and Professional Society Publishers

Egale 1, 80 St Albans Road, Watford,
Herts. WD17 1DL
email admin@alpsp.org
website www.alpsp.org
Twitter @alpsp

ALPSP is the international membership trade body which supports and represents not-for-profit organisations that publish scholarly and professional content and those that partner with and provide services to not-for-profit publishers. ALPSP has nearly 300 members in 30 countries. Its mission is to connect, inform, develop and represent the international scholarly and professional publishing community.

Bibliographical Society

c/o Institute of English Studies,
University of London, Senate House, Malet Street,
London WC1E 7HU
tel 020-7782 3279
email admin@bibsoc.org.uk
website www.bibsoc.org.uk
Facebook www.facebook.com/BibSoc
Twitter @BibSoc

The senior learned society dealing with the study of books and their history. Promotes and encourages study and research in the fields of historical, analytical, descriptive and textual bibliography as well as the history of printing, publishing, bookselling, bookbinding and collecting. Publishes the journal *The Library*. Founded 1892.

Cambridge Bibliographical Society

University Library, West Road, Cambridge CB3 9DR
email cbs@lib.cam.ac.uk
website www.lib.cam.ac.uk/collections/cambridge-bibliographical-society

Aims to encourage the study of bibliography, including book and MS production, book collecting and the history of libraries. It publishes *Transactions* (annual) and a series of monographs, and arranges a programme of lectures and visits. Founded 1949.

Classical Association

email office@classicalassociation.org
website www.classicalassociation.org
Honorary Secretary Prof. J. Robson

Exists to support the study, and teaching, of the Greek and Roman world in all its inspiring forms. This includes its history, civilisations and languages plus its interaction with other cultures, both ancient and modern. The Association sponsors the UK's largest annual classics conference, working to promote access to the classical world in schools, universities and beyond.

Early English Text Society

Faculty of English, St Cross Building, Manor Road,
Oxford OX1 3UL
website www.eets.org.uk
Twitter @EEngTextSoc
Honorary Director Prof. V. Gillespie, *Executive Secretary* Prof. D. Wakelin
Membership £30 p.a.

Aims to bring unprinted early English literature within the reach of students in sound texts. Founded 1864.

Edinburgh Bibliographical Society

c/o 102A Findhorn Place, Edinburgh EH9 2NZ
email secretary@edbibsoc.org
website www.edbibsoc.org
Secretary D. Taylor
Membership £18 p.a.; £25 p.a. corporate; £12 p.a. full-time students

Encourages bibliographical activity through organising talks for members, particularly on bibliographical topics relating to Scotland, and visits to libraries. See website for submission guidelines and prizes. Publishes a journal (annual, free to members) and other occasional publications. Founded 1890.

Oxford Bibliographical Society

Bodleian Library, Broad Street, Oxford OX1 3BG
email secretary@oxbibsoc.org.uk
website www.oxbibsoc.org.uk
Membership £35 p.a. UK; £45 rest of world

Exists to encourage bibliographical research. Publishes monographs. Founded 1922.

MEMBERS' CLUBS

The Arts Club

40 Dover Street, London W1S 4NP
tel 020-7499 8581
email membership@theartsclub.co.uk
website www.theartsclub.co.uk

A private members' club for all those connected with or interested in the arts, literature and science. Founded 1863.

Authors' Club

Authors' Club, Whitehall Place, London SW1A 2HE
email info@authorsclub.co.uk
website www.authorsclub.co.uk
Facebook www.facebook.com/authorsclub1891
Twitter @AuthorsClub
President John Walsh, *Chairperson* Lucy Popescu

A club for all those professionally engaged with literature, the Authors' Club welcomes as members writers, publishers, critics, journalists and academics. Administers the Authors' Club Best First Novel Award, the Art Book Prize and the Stanford Dolman Travel Book of the Year Award. Founded 1891.

New English Art Club

email info@neac.co.uk
website www.newenglishartclub.co.uk

The New English Art Club is an elected society of contemporary painters whose ethos resides in art informed by the visual world and personal interpretation. Its Annual Exhibition held at London's Mall Galleries showcases work by its members and aspiring artists selected from an open submission.

Scottish Arts Club

24 Rutland Square, Edinburgh EH1 2BW
tel 0131 229 8157
email administrator@scottishartsclub.com
website www.scottishartsclub.com
Facebook www.facebook.com/scottishartsclub
Twitter @ScottishArtsCL
Instagram thescottishartsclub

The Scottish Arts Club is a social hub for Artists and those interested in the Arts. Professional members include painters, sculptors, filmmakers, actors, musicians, playwrights, poets, novelists, journalists, architects, designers, dancers and diplomats. The Club also welcomes Lay members and anyone who is interested in the Arts. Founded 1873.

WRITERS' ORGANISATIONS

All Party Parliamentary Writers Group

tel 020-7264 5700
email barbara.hayes@alcs.co.uk
website www.allpartywritersgroup.co.uk
Chair Giles Watling MP, *Administrator* Barbara Hayes

The Group has some 60 Members from both Houses and seeks to represent the interests of all writers; to safeguard their intellectual property rights and ensure they receive a fair level of recognition and reward for their contribution to the economy and society as a whole. Founded 2007.

Alliance of Independent Authors – see page 515

Association of British Science Writers

email info@absw.org.uk
website www.absw.org.uk
Facebook www.facebook.com/BritishScienceWriters
Twitter @absw
Chair Andy Extanle, *Honorary President* Pallab Ghosh

An association for media professionals who cover science, medicine, environment, mathematics, engineering and technology. Champions independence and excellence in the reporting of science, medicine, engineering and technology. Trains and supports journalists and writers at all stages of their careers through conferences, summer schools and awards, in addition to a range of networking, training and debating events. Membership details/application through website only.

Association of Christian Writers

email admin@christianwriters.org.uk
website www.christianwriters.org.uk
Facebook www.facebook.com/groups/24831838019
Twitter @ACW1971
Membership from £26 p.a. Membership year runs from 1 April to 31 March and includes quarterly issues of *Christian Writer* magazine sent by post.

ACW aims to inspire excellence in writing from a Christian world view. Equips Christian writers through writers' days around the UK, workshops and writing competitions. Members encourage each other online and in affiliated local groups. Publishes a daily blog, *More Than Writers*. Please note that ACW is not a publisher.

Authors Aloud UK

72 Castle Road, St Albans, Herts. AL1 5DG
tel (01727) 893992
email info@authorsalouduk.co.uk
website www.authorsalouduk.co.uk
Facebook www.facebook.com/Authors-Aloud-UK-497942623573822
Twitter @AuthorsAloudUK
Instagram AuthorsAloudUK
Directors Naomi Cooper, Annie Everall

An author booking agency which brings together authors, illustrators, poets, storytellers and trainers with schools, libraries and festivals in the UK and Internationally, to promote enthusiasm for reading, both for enjoyment and information. Works with children's authors who wish to visit schools and libraries, in person and virtually and who are published by mainstream children's publishers. Also arranges author tours and book related events for publishers and other organisations.

Book Aid International

39–41 Coldharbour Lane, London SE5 9NR
tel 020-7733 3577
email info@bookaid.org
website www.bookaid.org
Twitter @Book_Aid

Book Aid International is the UK's leading international book donation and library development charity. The charity works for a world where everyone has access to books that will enrich, improve and change their lives.

Book Marketing Society

email admin@bookmarketingsociety.co.uk
website www.bookmarketingsociety.co.uk
Twitter @BMSoc

Launched with the objective of becoming the representative body of marketing within the book industry. It provides a forum for sharing best practice, inspiration and creativity across the sector through regular awards and a lively programme of member meetings, development workshops, masterclasses and social events. Anyone who works for a book publisher, book retailer or book wholesaler is eligible for membership, including those working in associated areas of the publishing and book retailing industry.

BookTrust Represents

BookTrust, G8 Battersea Studios,
80 Silverthorne Road, London SW8 3HE
tel 020-7801 8826

email booktrust.represents@booktrust.org.uk
website www.booktrust.org.uk/booktrustrepresents
Twitter @Booktrust

A project to support and promote authors and illustrators of colour and to reach more readers through school visits, special events and festivals. The project also supports aspiring and new authors and illustrators of colour with training, mentoring, events and an online community. Find out more about the project and the associated research into the ethnicity of authors and illustrators in the UK on the website. Aspiring and established authors and illustrators of colour are encouraged to get in touch and join the group via email at the above address.

The British Fantasy Society

email secretary@britishfantasysociety.org
website www.britishfantasysociety.org
Membership £20 p.a. for digital membership. Print editions: £35 p.a. single; £40 p.a. joint (same address); £60 p.a. rest of world

For readers, writers and publishers of fantasy, horror and related fields, in literature, art and the cinema. There is an annual convention, FantasyCon, and the British Fantasy Awards are sponsored by the Society. Publications are the *BFS Journal* and *BFS Horizons*. Founded 1971.

British Guild of Beer Writers

c/o Cask Marque, B10 Seedbed Centre, Wyncolls Road, Severalls Business Park, Colchester CO4 9HT
tel 07490 425345
email secretary@beerguild.co.uk
website www.beerguild.co.uk
Twitter @Britbeerwriters
Secretary Natalya Watson
Membership £55 p.a.

Aims to improve standards in beer writing and at the same time extend public knowledge of beer and pubs. Awards are given annually to writers, broadcasters and other communicators judged to have made the most valuable contribution to this end. Publishes a directory of members with details of their publications and their particular areas of interest, which is circulated to the media. Founded 1988.

The British Guild of Travel Writers

Larking Garden, 1 Clayton Business Park, Great Blakeham, Ipswich IP6 0NL
tel 020-8144 8713
email secretariat@bgtw.org
website www.bgtw.org
Facebook www.facebook.com/TravWriters
Twitter @TravWriters

Arranges meetings, discussions and visits for its members (who are all professional travel journalists) to promote and encourage the public's interest in travel. Publishes a monthly newsletter (for members only), website and annual Yearbook, which contains details of members and lists travel industry PRs and contacts. Annual awards for journalism (members only) and the travel trade. Founded 1960.

The British Haiku Society
36–38 Station Parade, PC Mail Box 25, Barking, Essex IG11 8DR
email cblundell2929@gmail.com
website www.britishhaikusociety.org.uk
Facebook www.facebook.com/thebritishhaikusociety

Pioneers the appreciation and writing of haiku in the UK, publishes books concerning haiku and related matters, and is active in promoting the teaching of haiku in schools and colleges. Publishes a quarterly journal, Blithe Spirit, an annual members' anthology and a newsletter. Also runs the prestigious annual British Haiku Society Awards in three categories: haiku, tanka and haibun. Registered charity. Founded 1990.

British Science Fiction Association Ltd
email info@bsfa.co.uk
website www.bsfa.co.uk
Twitter @bsfa
Membership £29 UK standard; £20 UK concession; £31 UK joint; £45 international

A membership organisation for authors, publishers, booksellers and readers of science fiction, fantasy and allied genres. Currently publishes The BSFA Review, a free digital magazine reviewing recent science fiction and fantasy releases across all media and runs regular events with authors, which are free and open to the public. Exclusively for members, BFSA publishes Focus, aimed at writers of all levels, as well as Vector, a critical journal featuring interviews, essays, reviews and other features, including peer-reviewed academic articles. Members can also participate in Orbiters, BSFA's network of online writers' workshops.

The BSFA has historically had strong ties with Eastercon, the UK's largest annual science fiction convention; Eastercon is home to the annual BSFA Awards, where awards are given in four categories: best novel, best short story, best artwork and best non-fiction. Founded 1958.

British Society of Comedy Writers
61 Parry Road, Ashmore Park, Wolverhampton, West Midlands WV11 2PS
tel (01902) 722729
email info@bscw.co.uk
website www.bscw.co.uk/index.htm

Aims to bring together writers and industry representatives in order to develop new projects and ideas. Holds an annual international comedy conference, networking days and workshops to train new writers to professional standards. Founded 1999.

Circle of Wine Writers
tel (01753) 882320
email administrator@circleofwinewriters.org
website www.circleofwinewriters.org
Membership by election

An association for those engaged in communicating about wines and spirits. Produces The Circular (monthly online newsletter), organises tasting sessions as well as a programme of meetings, talks and trips. Founded 1960.

Crime Readers' Association
email hello@thecra.co.uk
website www.thecra.co.uk
Facebook www.facebook.com/groups/CRAbookchat
Twitter @CrimeReaders
Contact Dea Parkin

Offers readers an insight into the novels and non-fiction of the largest community of crime writers in the world: the Crime Writers' Association (CWA). Subscribers to the Crime Readers' Association receive multiple benefits free of charge: Case Files, a bi-monthly eZine focusing on new books and containing fascinating features and articles from members of the CWA; a monthly newsletter containing insider news of books and their authors; crime-writing events; and crime writing opportunities such as competitions and courses as well as exclusive discounts and giveaways

Crime Writers' Association
email secretary@thecwa.co.uk
website www.thecwa.co.uk
Facebook www.facebook.com/CrimeWritersAssociation
Twitter @The_CWA
Secretary Dea Parkin

The CWA is a growing, thriving community representing writers of all kinds of crime fiction and non-fiction and at all stages of their careers. Membership is open to crime writers of both fiction and non-fiction, who at one time have had a traditional publishing contract, from anywhere in the world plus anyone whose business is closely connected with crime writers. Provisional membership is available for writers with a valid contract whose first book will be published within two years. Associate and corporate membership is open to editors, reviewers, bloggers, publishers, journalists and booksellers specialising in crime literature, and literary agents.

Membership benefits include book promotional platforms such as Case Files eZine and the Crime Readers' Association Newsletter, read by around 12,000 subscribers, active social media platforms, monthly members' magazine Red Herrings, local chapters for social events, annual conference, free tax helpline from H.W. Fisher, discounted festival passes to CrimeFest, links with organisations such as the

Society of Authors and HWA, Find an Author webpage, plus blogging opportunities on the Crime Readers' Association website. The CWA initiates National Crime Reading Month in June where members participate in library, festival and bookshop events, and runs the Debut Dagger and Margery Allingham Short Mystery competitions. The CWA has appointed Library Champions and a Booksellers' Champion. Founded 1953.

The Critics' Circle

c/o Rick Jones, 17 Rosenthal Road, Catford, London SE6 2BX
email criticscircleallsections@gmail.com
website https://criticscircle.org.uk
President Anna Smith, *Honorary Treasurer* Peter Cargin, *Honorary Secretary* Rick Jones
Membership by invitation of the Council

The Critics' Circle was established to promote the art of criticism, uphold its integrity, foster and safeguard the professional interests of its members, provide opportunities for socialising and networking, and support the advancement of the arts. Membership is by invitation only and granted only to persons engaged regularly and substantially in the writing or broadcasting of criticism of dance, drama, film, literature, music and the visual arts. Founded 1913.

TheFED – A Network of Writing and Community Publishers

email fedonline1@gmail.com
website www.thefed.btck.co.uk
Facebook www.facebook.com/groups/TheFEDfriends
Membership Secretary/Treasurer Louise Glasscoe
Membership £25 p.a. funded groups; £15 unfunded; £10 waged/higher income individuals; £5 unwaged/low income

TheFED is a not-for-profit organisation, run by volunteers, and continues the work started by the Federation of Worker Writers and Community Publishers. Details of the annual Festival of Writing and AGM at Syracuse University's London campus, as well as other activities associated with TheFED, are advertised on the website. TheFED runs a monthly writing challenge and hosts TheFED archive in collaboration with TUC Library Collections, London Metropolitan University and Syracuse University, New York; it has associations with other local and national events and encourages networking between member groups.

The Garden Media Guild

Katepwa House, Ashfield Park Avenue, Ross-on-Wye, Herefordshire HR9 5AX
tel (01989) 567393
email admin@gardenmediaguild.co.uk
website www.gardenmediaguild.co.uk
Facebook www.facebook.com/gdnmediaguild
Twitter @gdnmediaguild

Chairmen Tamsin Westhorpe
Membership £75 p.a.; associate membership £120 p.a.; probationary membership £55 p.a. Full membership is open to those who earn a significant part of their income from communicating information on the subject of gardening and horticulture.

Aims to raise the quality of garden writing, photography and broadcasting, to help members operate efficiently and profitably, to improve communication between members and to promote liaison between members and the broader horticultural industry. The Guild administers annual awards to encourage excellence in garden writing, photography, trade and consumer press journalism, TV and radio broadcasting, online media and blogging. Founded 1991.

Gay Authors Workshop

BM Box 5700, London WC1N 3XX
email eandk2@btinternet.com
website http://gayauthorsworkshop.uk/
Contact Kathryn Bell
Membership £8 p.a.; £5 p.a. unwaged

Exists to encourage writers who are lesbian, gay or bisexual. Quarterly newsletter and monthly meetings. Founded 1978.

Guild of Food Writers

255 Kent House Road, Beckenham, Kent BR3 1JQ
tel 020-8659 0422
email guild@gfw.co.uk
website www.gfw.co.uk
Twitter @GuildFoodWriter
Instagram thegfw
Administrator Jonathan Woods
Membership £85 p.a.

Aims to bring together professional food writers including journalists, broadcasters and authors, to compile a comprehensive and detailed directory of members, to extend the range of members' knowledge and experience by arranging discussions, tastings and visits, and to encourage the development of new writers by every means, including competitions, awards, bursaries and mentorship. Awards entry is not restricted to members of the Guild. Founded 1984.

Guild of Health Writers

Dale Lodge, 88 Wensleydale Road, Hampton, Middlesex TW12 2LX
tel 020-8941 2977
email admin@healthwriters.com
website www.healthwriters.com
Twitter @HealthWritersUK
Membership £50 p.a.

The Guild of Health Writers is a national, independent membership organisation representing Britain's leading health journalists and writers. It was founded to encourage the provision of readable and accurate health information to the public. Members write on every aspect of health and wellbeing, from innovative medical science to complementary therapies and lifestyle issues. They value the training and networking opportunities that the Guild provides. Founded 1994.

The Guild of Motoring Writers

General Secretary: Melissa Chadderton, Argyll House, 1 River Road, Littlehampton, West Sussex BN17 5BN
tel (01903) 386423
email generalsec@gomw.co.uk
website www.gomw.co.uk
Facebook www.facebook.com/gomwuk
Twitter @gomw_uk

The largest organisation of its kind in the world representing automotive journalists, photographers, broadcasters and artists. Based in the UK, it represents more than 500 members. It aims to raise the standard of motoring journalism, to encourage motoring, motorsport and road safety, and to promote professional training of journalists. Works closely with the motor industry and provides a link between fellow members around the world. Also aims to safeguard the interests of members in relation to the aims of the Guild. Founded 1944.

Hakluyt Society

c/o The Map Library, The British Library, 96 Euston Road, London NW1 2DB
tel (07568) 468066
email office@hakluyt.com
website www.hakluyt.com

Publication of original narratives of voyages, travels, naval expeditions and other geographical records. Founded 1846.

Harleian Society

College of Arms, 130 Queen Victoria Street, London EC4V 4BT
tel 020-7236 7728
email thsduke@gmail.com
website http://harleian.org.uk
Chairman T. Woodcock CVO, DL, FSA, *Honorary Secretary* T.H.S. Duke FSA, Clarenceux King of Arms

Instituted for transcribing, printing and publishing the heraldic visitations of Counties, Parish Registers and any manuscripts relating to genealogy, family history and heraldry. Founded 1869.

Historical Novel Society

Marine Cottage, The Strand, Starcross, Devon EX6 8NY
tel (01626) 891962
email richard@historicalnovelsociety.org
website http://historicalnovelsociety.org/
Facebook www.facebook.com/historicalnovelsociety
Twitter @histnovsoc

Contact Richard Lee
Membership £40 p.a.

Promotes the enjoyment of historical fiction. Based in the US and UK but welcomes members (who can be readers or writers) from all over the world. Publishes print magazines, organises conferences and local chapters. Founded 1997.

Historical Writers' Association

The Union Building, 51– 59 Rose Lane, Norwich NR1 1BY
email admin@historicalwriters.org
website https://historicalwriters.org
Facebook www.facebook.com/HistoriaHWA
Twitter @HistoriaHWA

Association created by authors, publishers and agents of historical writing, both fiction and non-fiction, which provides professional and social support to members and creates opportunities online and in person for members to meet with fellow writers and enthusiasts of all things historical. Organises a range of regional events.

Horror Writers Association

PO BOX 56687, Sherman Oaks, CA 91413, USA
tel +1 818-220-3965
email hwa@horror.org
website https://horror.org
Facebook www.facebook.com/groups/Horrorwritersassoc
Twitter @horrorwriters
President John Palisano

The HWA is a worldwide organisation of around 1,400 writers and publishing professionals dedicated to promoting the interests of writers of horror and dark fantasy. There are various levels of membership including new writers, established writers, professionals, academics and non-writing horror professionals. The HWA gives the iconic Bram Stoker Awards® on an annual basis, as well as hosting horror conventions, and provides a range of services to its horror writer, editor and publisher membership base. Founded 1987.

The Mythopoeic Society

website www.mythsoc.org

A non-profit international literary and educational organisation for the study, discussion and enjoyment of fantastic and mythic literature, especially the works of Tolkien, C.S. Lewis and Charles Williams. 'Mythopoeic' (myth-oh-PAY-ik or myth-oh-PEE-ik) means 'mythmaking' or 'productive of myth' and aptly describes much of the fictional work of the three authors who were also prominent members of an informal Oxford literary circle (1930s–50s) known as the Inklings. Membership is open to all scholars, writers and readers of these literatures. The Society sponsors three periodicals: *Mythprint* (a bulletin of book reviews, articles and events), *Mythlore* (scholarly articles on mythic and fantastic literature), and *Mythic Circle* (a literary annual of original poetry and short stories). Each summer the Society holds an annual conference, Mythcon. Founded 1967.

National Association of Writers' Groups

Old Vicarage, Scammonden, Huddersfield HD3 3FT
email info@nawg.co.uk
website www.nawg.co.uk
Facebook www.facebook.com/NAWGNews
Twitter @NAWGnews
Secretary Chris Huck
Membership £50 p.a. per group; £25 p.a. individuals

NAWG aims to advance the education of the general public throughout the UK, including the Channel Islands, by promoting the study and art of writing in all its aspects. Publishes *LNK*, a bi-monthly magazine. Festival of Writing held annually in August/September. New members always welcome. Founded 1995.

National Centre for Writing

Dragon Hall, 115–123 King Street,
Norwich NR1 1QE
email info@nationalcentreforwriting.org.uk
website https://nationalcentreforwriting.org.uk
Facebook www.facebook.com/
NationalCentreforWriting
Twitter @WritersCentre

Celebrates and explores the artistic and social power of creative writing and literary translation. An ongoing programme of innovative collaborations engages writers, literary translators and readers in projects that support new voices and new stories and respond to the rapidly changing world of writing. Based at the historic Dragon Hall in Norwich, where workshops and mentoring are regularly available for writers at all levels, both face-to-face and online. Projects range from major international partnerships to vibrant festivals such as the Noirwich Crime Writing Festival and the Norfolk & Norwich Festival. Founded 2018.

New Writing North

3 Ellison Terrace, Ellison Place,
Newcastle upon Tyne NE1 8ST
email office@newwritingnorth.com
website https://newwritingnorth.com
Facebook www.facebook.com/newwritingnorth
Twitter @NewWritingNorth

Supports writing and reading in the North of England. Commissions new work, creates development opportunities and nurtures talent. Founded 1996.

New Writing South

email hello@newwritingsouth.com
website www.newwritingsouth.com
Facebook www.facebook.com/newwritingsouth
Twitter @newwritingsouth

New Writing South champions all kinds of new creative writing in the South East and beyond. It develops writers' careers and helps fresh talent to flourish by providing development opportunities and commissioning new work. NWS is committed to nurturing an inclusive community of writers, regardless of background or previous experience.

Outdoor Writers and Photographers Guild

email secretary@owpg.org.uk
website www.owpg.org.uk
Twitter @owpg
Membership £80 p.a.

Association of the leading practitioners in outdoor media. Represents members' interests to representative bodies in the outdoor industry, circulates members with news of media opportunities and provides a forum for members to meet colleagues and others in the outdoor industry. Presents annual literary and photographic awards. Members include writers, journalists, broadcasters, illustrators, photographers, bloggers, editors and publishers. Founded 1980.

Owned Voices

website https://ownedvoices.com/
Facebook www.facebook.com/OwnedVoices
Twitter @OwnedVoices
Instagram ownedvoices

Creative writing workshop created specifically for writers from backgrounds traditionally underrepresented in publishing including BAME, working class, LGBTQ+ writers, or writers with disabilities.

Paper Nations

email writers@papernations.org
website https://papernations.org/
Facebook www.facebook.com/papernationsuk
Twitter @PaperNationsUK

A creative writing incubator nurturing communities and creating partnerships to build an inclusive literary ecology. They commission writers in the South West of England to create new work, with particular focus on establishing creative writing opportunities for children and young people, and have recently launched 'Writing for All' programme, for writers of all ages and backgrounds. Founded 2016.

PEN International

Unit A Koops Mill Mews, 162–164 Abbey Street,
London SE1 2AN
tel 020-7405 0338
email info@pen-international.org
website https://pen-international.org
Twitter @pen_int

A world association of writers. PEN was founded to promote friendship and understanding between writers and to defend freedom of expression within and between all nations. The initials PEN stand for Poets, Playwrights, Editors, Essayists, Novelists – but membership is open to all writers of standing (including translators), whether men or women, without distinction of creed or race, who subscribe to these fundamental principles. PEN takes no part in state or party politics. Founded 1921.

English PEN Centre
tel 020-7324 2535
email enquiries@englishpen.org
website https://englishpen.org

Scottish PEN Centre
The Writers' Museum, Lady Stair's House, Lady Stair's Close, Lawnmarket, Edinburgh EH1 2PA
tel 0131 226 5590
email info@scottishpen.org
website https://scottishpen.org

Irish PEN Centre
Irish Writer's Centre, 19 Parnell Square, Dublin 1
email vanessa@writing.ie
website https://irishpen.com

Pen to Print
tel 020-8227 2267
email pentoprint@lbbd.gov.uk
website https://pentoprint.org/
Facebook www.facebook.com/OfficialPentoPrint
Twitter @Pen_to_Print
Instagram officialpentoprint

Located in East London, Pen to Print is a free writer development programme based in libraries. As an Arts Council funded programme, Pen to Print provides a safe, collaborative environment aiming to develop writers' authentic voices. Aspiring writers are encouraged to reach communities with their stories reflecting not just their own journeys but also inspiring potential in others. Pen to Print has translated this ethos into a relevant library service for writers which creates a shared accessible storytelling experience, while supporting writers into publication. Free activities include:

- classes and workshops;
- competitions including The Book Challenge;
- author talks;
- ReadFest literary festival; and
- *Write On!* magazine

The Poetry Book Society – see page 342

The Poetry Society – see page 342

The Romantic Novelists' Association
email rnahonsec@romanticnovelistsassociation.org
website https://romanticnovelistsassociation.org
Chairwoman Alison May

Promotes romantic fiction and encourages good writing within the genre. Inclusive of all forms of romantic fiction and welcomes authors from all backgrounds. Represents around 1,000 writers, agents, editors and other publishing professionals. See also The Romantic Novel of the Year Awards page 580. Founded 1960.

Scattered Authors' Society
email scatteredauthorssociety@gmail.com
website www.scatteredauthors.org

Provides a forum for informal discussion, contact and support for professional writers in children's fiction. Founded 1998.

Scottish Association of Writers
Brackenbank, Crosshands, By Mauchline KA5 5TP
email secretary@scottishassociationofwriters.com
website www.scottishassociationofwriters.com
Facebook www.facebook.com/groups/Sawriters
Secretary Susan McVey

Promotes writing in Scotland. Organises an annual conference attended by writers who are members of affiliated clubs and runs alternating annual satellite events: Write Up North and Write Down South. Competitions organised throughout the year. Website features group and writer resources. The Council organises outreach visits to writing clubs to promote good practice, offer workshops and advise on the current writing market. This can often be coupled with competitions and specific talks. Founded 1969.

Scottish Fellowship of Christian Writers
website www.sfcw.info
Facebook www.facebook.com/Scottish-Fellowship-of-Christian-Writers-393556520670479
Membership £12 p.a.

To inspire, encourage and support Christians living in Scotland to make use of their creative writing talents. It publishes *Showcase*, a quarterly magazine which includes members' own writing, and *FUN* (Fellowship Update and News), a bi-monthly e-newsletter. The group also runs two, two-day conference in May and November each year. Over 100 members. Founded 1980.

Society of Children's Book Writers and Illustrators (SCBWI)
email ra@britishscbwi.org
website https://britishisles.scbwi.org
Facebook www.facebook.com/groups/SCBWI
Twitter @scbwi
Instagram scbwi_british_isles
Co-Regional Advisers, SCBWI-British Isles Natascha Biebow and Kathy Evans

An international network for the exchange of knowledge between professional writers, illustrators, editors, publishers, agents, librarians, educators, booksellers and others involved with literature for young people. Sponsors conferences on writing and illustrating children's books and multimedia as well as dozens of regional conferences and events throughout the world. Publishes a quarterly newsletter, *The Bulletin*, and information publications. Awards grants for: works in progress, portfolios, humour, marketing your book, excellence in non-traditional publishing and diversity in books. The SCBWI also presents the annual Golden Kite and Crystal Kite Awards for the best fiction and non-fiction books, and the Spark Award for the best book published through a non-traditional publishing route.

The SCBWI British Isles region meets regularly for speaker, networking or professional development events, including the annual two-day conference, industry insiders series, 1-to-1 opportunities with Industry professionals, PULSE events for published members, agents' party, masterclasses for writers and illustrators and annual fiction and picture book retreats. Also sponsors local and online critique groups and publishes *Words and Pictures* blog magazine (www.wordsandpics.org). Member showcase features: find a speaker, illustrator gallery and awards (www.scbwishowcase.org). Founded 1971.

The Society of Civil and Public Service Writers

website www.scpsw.org

Welcomes serving and retired members of the civil service, armed forces, police, local government, NHS and other public servants. Members can be aspiring or published writers. Holds monthly competitions for short stories, articles and poetry, mostly with a cash prize. In 2020, the Society published a major Anthology, *Dancing with Words*, with 40 contributors, 200 pieces, 490 pages of stories, anecdotes and poetry. Founded 1935.

The Society of Medical Writers

SoMW, Acre-Rise Cottage, Upper Ludstone, Claverley, Wolverhampton WV5 7DH
website https://somw.org.uk

Recruits members from all branches of the medical profession, together with all professions allied to medicine, to foster interest in literature and in writing – not solely about medicine but also about art, history, music, theatre, etc. Members are encouraged to write fiction, poetry, plays, book reviews and non-fiction articles. Prizes are awarded for short story, poetry, unpublished article or essay, best non-fiction and best written clinical paper. Publishes *The Writer* (two p.a.) and a register of members and their writing interests. Holds a bi-annual conference in which various aspects of literature and writing are explored in a relaxed and informal atmosphere. Founded 1989.

South African Writers' Circle

email southafricanwriterscircle@gmail.com
website https://sawriters.org.za

Encourages all writers, new and experienced, in the art of writing. Publishes a monthly newsletter and runs competitions with prizes for the winners. Please see the website for latest membership fees and details of payment. Founded 1960.

Southwest Scriptwriters

website https://southwestscriptwriters.uk
Facebook www.facebook.com/southwestscriptwriters
Twitter @swscriptwriters

Workshops members' drama scripts for stage, screen, radio and TV with the aim of improving their chances of professional production, meeting at Bristol Old Vic. Projects to present members' work to a wider audience have included theatre and short film productions, as well as public rehearsed readings. Monthly e-newsletter. Founded 1994.

Spread the Word

The Albany, Douglas Way, London SE8 4AG
tel 020-8692 0231 extension 249
email hello@spreadtheword.org.uk
website www.spreadtheword.org.uk
Facebook www.facebook.com/spreadthewordwriters
Twitter @STWevents
Instagram spreadthewordwriters

London's writer development agency, helping writers make their mark on the page, the screen and in the world. Kick-starts the careers of London's best new writers, and energetically campaigns to ensure mainstream publishing truly reflects the diversity of the city. Supports the creative and professional development of talent, by engaging those already interested in literature and those who will be, and by advocating on behalf of both.

The Worshipful Company of Stationers and Newspaper Makers

Stationers' Hall, Ave Maria Lane, London EC4M 7DD
tel 020-7248 2934
email admin@stationers.org
website www.stationers.org
Master Trevor Fenwick, *Clerk* William Alden MBE, DL

One of the Livery Companies of the City of London. Connected with the printing, publishing, bookselling, newspaper and allied trades. Founded 1403.

Writers Advice Centre for Children's Books

Shakespeare House, 168 Lavender Hill, London SW11 5TG
tel 020-7801 6300
email info@writersadvice.co.uk
website www.writersadvice.co.uk
Facebook www.facebook.com/writersadvice
Twitter @writersadvice
Managing Editor Louise Jordan

Dedicated to helping new and published children's writers by offering both editorial advice and tips on how to get published. The Centre also runs workshops, an online children's writing correspondence course and publishes a small list of its own under the name of Wacky Bee Books (www.wackybeebooks.com). Founded 1994.

MUSIC

American Society of Composers, Authors and Publishers

website www.ascap.com

An organisation owned and run by its members, it is the leading performance rights organisation representing more than 800,000 songwriters, composers and music publishers.

The Guild of International Songwriters & Composers

Prospect Business Park, West Wing, Leadgate, Consett DH8 7PW
tel 0330 202 0760
email gisc@songwriters-guild.co.uk
website www.songwriters-guild.co.uk
Membership £65 p.a.

Gives advice to members on contractual and copyright matters; assists with protection of members' rights; online copyright service free to all members; international collaboration register free to members; outlines requirements of record companies, publishers, artists.

Incorporated Society of Musicians

4–5 Inverness Mews, London W2 3JQ
tel 020-7221 3499
email membership@ism.org
website www.ism.org
Facebook www.facebook.com/ISMusicians
Twitter @ISM_music
Chief Executive Deborah Annetts
Membership £181 p.a.

Professional body for musicians. Aims to promote and support the art of music and protect the interests of those working as professionals within the music profession. Provides unrivalled services and expert advice for its members. Publishes a bi-monthly magazine, *Music Journal*, and an annual Handbook. Founded 1882.

The Ivors Academy of Music Creators

The Ministry, 79 Borough Road, London SE1 1DN
tel 020-7636 2929
website www.ivorsacademy.com
Membership £92 p.a. Standard membership; £50 p.a. for under-25s

The Ivors Academy of Music Creators (formerly the British Academy of Songwriters, Composers and Authors) is the trade association for songwriters and composers of all genres in the UK. As champions of music creators, it has three pillars of activity: celebrating, cultivating and campaigning. Flagship awards – The Ivors and The Ivors Composer Awards – recognise the power and brilliance of music creators. A programme of educational and inspirational events runs throughout the year, where members can share their insights and expertise, develop their craft and collaborate with one another. The Ivors Academy's most powerful and important role is as a campaigning voice: to research, consult and lobby to ensure that the rights of members are protected, now and tomorrow. To become a member, you must be a member of PRS for Music or another performance rights organisation.

Music Publishers Association

2nd Floor, Synergy House,
114–118 Southampton Row, London WC1B 5AA
tel 0333 077 2350
email info@mpagroup.com
website https://mpaonline.org.uk
Facebook www.facebook.com/MusicPublishersAssociation
Twitter @the_MPA

Trade organisation representing over 270 UK music publisher members: promotes and safeguards its members' interests in copyright, trade and related matters. Sub-committees and groups deal with particular interests. Founded 1881.

PRS for Music

41 Streatham High Road, London SW16 1ER
tel 020-7580 5544
website www.prsformusic.com
Twitter @PRSforMusic

Represents the rights of songwriters, composers and music publishers in the UK. As a membership organisation it ensures creators are paid whenever their music is played, performed or reproduced, championing the importance of copyright to protect and support the UK music industry. Founded 1914.

Prizes and awards

This section has two parts: an alphabetical listing of prizes, competitions and awards; and an alphabetical list of grants, bursaries and fellowships for writers and artists, and the organisations that award them. See page 772 for details of prizes and awards by genre.

⚠ Awards presentations and ceremonies may not go ahead in their usual way due to coronavirus restrictions.

PRIZES, COMPETITIONS AND AWARDS

Academy of British Cover Design: Annual Cover Design Competition
website https://abcoverd.co.uk
Twitter @ABCoverD

This annual competition awards covers produced for any book published between 1 January and 31 December each year, by any designer in the UK, for a UK or overseas publisher. Ebooks are eligible. Designers may enter their own work or the work of other designers. There are ten categories: children's, young adult, sci-fi/fantasy, mass market, literary fiction, crime/thriller, non-fiction, series design, classic/reissue and women's fiction. A cover can only be submitted in one category unless it is entered as an individual cover and again as part of a series design. Entry is free.

The Aeon Award
Albedo One, 8 Bachelor's Walk, Dublin 1, Republic of Ireland
email fraslaw@yahoo.co.uk
website www.albedo1.com/aeon-award

An annual contest for short fiction (up to 10,000 words) in genres of fantasy, science fiction, horror or anything in between. The Award will be on hiatus during 2021 pending consideration of a redesign and upgrade of the contest and its rules. Visit the website for updates.

ALCS Educational Writers' Award
The Society of Authors, 24 Bedford Row, London WC1R 4EH
tel 020-7373 6642
email prizes@societyofauthors.org
website www.societyofauthors.org/ALCS-award

This is an annual award alternating each year between books in the 5–11 and 11–18 age groups. It is given to an outstanding example of traditionally published non-fiction (with or without illustrations) that stimulates and enhances learning. The work must have been first published in the UK, in the English language, within the previous two calendar years.

The ALCS Tom-Gallon Trust Award
The Society of Authors, 24 Bedford Row, London WC1R 4EH
tel 020-7373 6642
email prizes@societyofauthors.org
website www.societyofauthors.org/tom-gallon
Twitter @Soc_of_Authors

An annual award of £1,000, with £500 for a runner-up, for a submitted short story, open to writers who have had at least one short story accepted for publication and are ordinarily resident in the United Kingdom, Commonwealth or the Republic of Ireland. The submission can be unpublished or published, written in English and should be traditional, not experimental, in character. Closing date: 31 October.

Dinesh Allirajah Prize for Short Fiction
email commaprizes@gmail.com
website https://commapress.co.uk/resources/prizes

Hosted by Comma Press and the University of Central Lancashire, the Dinesh Allirajah Prize for Short Fiction is open to anyone 18 years or over who is a UK resident, and the story submitted must not have been published anywhere previously in print or online. One entry per author. For full details regarding this year's theme for entries and submission guidelines, see the Comma website.

The Hans Christian Andersen Awards
International Board on Books for Young People, Nonnenweg 12, Postfach CH–4009 Basel, Switzerland
tel +41 61 272 2917
email ibby@ibby.org
website www.ibby.org
Facebook www.facebook.com/ibby.international
Twitter @IBBYINT

This Award is the highest international recognition given to an author and an illustrator of children's books. Given every other year by IBBY, the awards recognise lifelong achievement and are presented to an author and an illustrator whose complete works have made an important, lasting contribution to children's literature. The selection criteria include the aesthetic and literary qualities of writing and illustrating, as well as the ability to see things from the child's point of view and the ability to stretch the child's curiosity and imagination. The complete works of the author and of the illustrator are taken into consideration. The Author's Award has been given since 1956 and the Illustrator's Award since 1966.

ARIAS (Audio & Radio Industry Awards)

website www.radioacademy.org
Twitter @radioacademy

Run by The Radio Academy, the ARIAS recognise the best in the UK audio and radio industry and celebrate outstanding achievement. The awards offer stations, podcasters, publishers, presenters and production companies an annual opportunity to enter work in a range of categories reflecting today's UK audio and radio landscape. Founded 1982.

The Australian/Vogel's Literary Award

email vogel@allenandunwin.com
website www.allenandunwin.com/being-a-writer/the-australian-vogel-s-literary-award

An annual award of $20,000 for a chosen unpublished work of fiction, Australian history or biography. Entrants must be under 35 years of age on the closing date and must normally be residents of Australia. The MS must be between 50,000 and 80,000 words and must be an original work entirely by the entrant written in English. It cannot be under consideration by any publisher or award. Closing date: 31 May. Founded 1980.

Authors' Club Awards

Whitehall Place, London SW1A 2HE
email info@authorsclub.co.uk
website www.authorsclub.co.uk
Twitter @AuthorsClub

The Authors' Club supports the best in contemporary writing through its four annual literary awards:

• The Richard Schlagman Art Book Awards, in association with the Whitechapel Gallery, for the best book on art or architecture published in English, anywhere in the world, in the previous year. Awards are given in eight categories, including an overall Book of the Year.
• The Best First Novel Award, for the most promising debut novel first published in the UK in the previous year. Open to British, Irish or UK-based authors; there is no age limit.
• The Jhalak Prize, in association with Media Diversified, for black, Asian and minority ethnic writing across all genres in the UK. See page 571.
• The Stanford Dolman Award, in partnership with Stanfords, for the most outstanding work of literary travel writing of the past year.

For full details of each prize and links to individual submission guidelines, see the website.

The Baillie Gifford Prize for Non-Fiction

website www.thebailliegiffordprize.co.uk
Twitter @BGPrize

The Prize aims to reward the best of non-fiction and is open to authors of any nationality. It covers all non-fiction in the areas of current affairs, history, politics, science, sport, travel, biography, autobiography and the arts. Formerly known as The Samuel Johnson Prize (1999–2015), it is the most prestigious non-fiction prize in the UK, worth £50,000 to the winner.

Bardd Plant Cymru (Welsh-Language Children's Poet Laureate)

Books Council of Wales, Castell Brychan, Aberystwyth, Ceredigion SY23 2JB
tel (01970) 624151
email castellbrychan@books.wales
website https://Illyfrau.cymru/en/

Aims to raise the profile of poetry amongst children and to encourage them to compose and enjoy poetry. During his/her term of office the bard will visit schools as well as help children to create poetry through electronic workshops. The scheme's partner organisations are: S4C, the Welsh Government, the Books Council of Wales, Urdd Gobaith Cymru and Literature Wales.

Verity Bargate Award

Soho Theatre, 21 Dean Street, London W1D 3NE
email vba@sohotheatre.com
website www.sohotheatre.com/writers/verity-bargate-award

The Award was established to honour Soho Theatre's co-founder and is presented biennially to an artist resident in the UK or Ireland with fewer than three professional productions. The winner receives £7,500 in respect of an exclusive option to produce the winning play at Soho Theatre. See website for information on workshops and events associated with the award. Founded 1982.

Bath Flash Fiction Awards

6 Old Tarnwell, Stanton Drew, Bristol BS39 4EA
website https://bathflashfictionaward.com/enter/
Facebook www.facebook.com/bathflashaward
Twitter @BathFlashAward

Host to two international flash fiction writing competitions; the Bath Flash Fiction Award, and the Bath Novella-in-Flash Award. Entrants have the opportunity to appear in print and digital anthology collections, published by Ad Hoc Fiction, with overall winners receiving cash prizes.

Bath Flash Fiction Award

This award has three rounds per year: March to June, July to October, and November to February. The flash fiction has a 300 word limit and entries are made online via website and cost from £9. £1,000 prize for the winner, while 50 longlisted entrants will be offered publication in the end of year print and digital anthology.

Bath Novella-in-Flash Award

Runs once per year and has a 6000 to 18,000 word limit – each flash that makes up the novella should not be more than about 1000 words. Entries can be on any theme or subject but must be original and written in English. They must also be for adult or young adult readers, Non-fiction and fiction written for children are not permitted.

The Bath Novel Award

PO Box 5223, Bath BA1 0UR
email info@bathnovelaward.co.uk
website www.bathnovelaward.co.uk
Twitter @bathnovelaward

This annual international prize is for unpublished or independently published writers of novels for adults or young adults. Submissions: first 5,000 words plus one-page synopsis. Prize: £3,000 plus introductions to literary agents. Entries open December until May. Entry fee: £28 per novel with sponsored places available for low-income writers. See website for full entry and submission guidelines.

BBC National Short Story Award

website www.bbc.co.uk/programmes/b0079gw3

In partnership with Cambridge University, this award is one of the most prestigious awards for a single short story; it aims to expand opportunities for British writers, readers and publishers of the short story, and to honour the UK's finest exponents of the form. The winner receives £15,000 and their story will be broadcast on Radio 4. Visit the website to meet the judges and find out how to enter. Founded 2005.

BBC Young Writers' Award

website www.bbc.co.uk/ywa

With Cambridge University, this award seeks out writers between 14 and 18 who submit a story of no more than 1,000 words on any topic they choose. The winner will have their story broadcast on the BBC and published in an anthology, and will receive a personalised mentoring session with an author. Entry is by online form.

The David Berry Prize

Administrative Secretary, Royal Historical Society, University College London, Gower Street, London WC1E 6BT
tel 020-7387 7532
email adminsecretary@royalhistsoc.org
website https://royalhistsoc.org/prizes/david-berry/

Candidates may submit an essay/article on any subject dealing with Scottish history. The article/essay must have been published in a journal or edited collection during the calendar year 2020. Advanced access publisher versions are also eligible, but an item cannot be entered more than once in subsequent years. Candidates must be doctoral students in a historical subject in a UK institution, or be within two years of having a submitted a corrected thesis in a historical subject in a UK institution at the time of the closing date for entries. Value of prize: £250. Closing date: 31 December each year.

The James Berry Poetry Prize

Newcastle Centre for the Literary Arts, Percy Building, Newcastle University NE1 7RU
tel 0191 208 7787
email jamesberrypoetryprize@gmail.com
website www.ncl.ac.uk/ncla/james-berry/#theprize

Newcastle University's Centre for Literary Arts (NCLA) and Bloodaxe Books are working in partnership to award three equal winners a £1,000 cash prize, with mentoring and a debut collection published by Bloodaxe. Open to poets of colour who have not published a book-length collection, with special consideration given to LGBTQ+/disabled poets and poets from disadvantaged socio-economic backgrounds. See website for entry criteria. Founded 2021.

Besterman/McColvin Medals – see The K&IM Information Resources Awards

The Biographers' Club Slightly Foxed Best First Biography Prize

tel 07985 920341
email ariane.bankes@gmail.com
website www.biographersclub.co.uk
Prize Administrator Ariane Bankes

The prize is awarded to the best book written by a first-time biographer. The Prize, worth £2,500, is sponsored by *Slightly Foxed, The Real Reader's Quarterly*. Only entries submitted by publishers will be accepted for consideration. Literary memoirs are also eligible but celebrity autobiographies and ghostwritten books are not.

To qualify, books must have a publication date between 1 January and 31 December 2021 (proofs are acceptable). Four copies of each book should be submitted no later than 31 October (enclose a press release to confirm publication date) along with an entry form (downloadable from the website) and entry fee of £25 per title to: The Slightly Foxed Best First Biography Prize, c/o Jane Mays, 21 Marsden Street, London NW5 3HE.

The Biographers' Club Tony Lothian Prize

E6 Albany, Piccadilly, London W1J 0AR
tel 07985 920341
email ariane.bankes@gmail.com
website www.biographersclub.co.uk
Prize Administrator Ariane Bankes

The £2,000 Tony Lothian Prize (sponsored by her daughter, Elizabeth, Duchess of Buccleuch) supports uncommissioned first-time writers working on a biography. Applicants should submit a proposal of no more than 20 pages including a synopsis and ten-page sample chapter (double-spaced, numbered pages), CV and a note on the market for the book and competing literature (all unbound), to the prize administrator. Entry fee: £15. For further details and mandatory entry form, see website.

Blue Pencil Agency First Novel Award
website https://bluepencilagency.com/bpa-first-novel-award-2021/

The Award is open to unrepresented and unpublished authors for a novel in any adult fiction genre. Cash prize, manuscript review and agent introductions for winner and runners up. Entry fee: £20. See website for submission guidelines, entry deadlines, eligibility, and announcement of future awards. Founded 2017.

Blue Peter Book Awards
BookTrust, G8 Battersea Studios,
80 Silverthorne Road, London SW8 3HE
tel 020-7801 8843
email bluepeter@booktrust.org.uk
website www.booktrust.org.uk/books/awards-and-prizes

Awarded annually, winners are shortlisted by a panel of expert adult judges, then a group of young *Blue Peter* viewers judge the two categories, which are: the Best Story and the Best Book with Facts. Winning books are announced on *Blue Peter* in March. Founded 2000.

The Boardman Tasker Prize
tel (01332) 342246
website www.boardmantasker.com
Twitter @BoardmanTasker

This annual prize is given for a work of fiction, non-fiction, drama or poetry, the central theme of which is concerned with the mountain environment. The prize of £3,000 commemorates the lives of mountaineers Peter Boardman and Joe Tasker. Authors of any nationality are eligible but the work must be published or distributed in the UK. Entries from publishers only. Founded 1983.

The Bollinger Everyman Wodehouse Prize for Comic Fiction
website www.everymanslibrary.co.uk
Twitter @Everymanslib

The UK's leading prize dedicated to comic fiction for adults. Awarded to the most original comic novel of the previous 12 months. The winner receives a case of Bollinger Special Cuvée, a jeroboam of Bollinger, a complete set of the Everyman Wodehouse collection and a rare breed pig named after the winning novel. Eligible novels are published in the UK between 1 June and 31 May. The winner is announced at the Hay Festival in late May/early June. Closing date:

February; shortlist announced in late March/early April. Launched in 2000 on the 25th anniversary of the death of P.G. Wodehouse.

Bookbug Picture Book Prize
Scottish Book Trust, Sandeman House,
Trunk's Close, 55 High Street, Edinburgh EH1 1SR
tel 0131 524 0160
email info@scottishbooktrust.com
website www.scottishbooktrust.com/reading-and-stories/bookbug-picture-book-prize

Scotland's national picture book prize which recognises the favourite picture book of children in Scotland by writers and illustrators resident in Scotland. Visit the Scottish Book Trust website for more details.

The Booker Prize
Four Culture, 20 St Thomas Street, London SE1 9BF
tel 020-3697 4256
email marion.fraser@fourcommunications.com
website www.thebookerprizes.com

This annual prize for fiction of £50,000, plus £2,500 to each of six shortlisted authors, is awarded by the Booker Prize Foundation to the author of the best (in the opinion of the judges) eligible novel. Any novel in print or electronic format, written originally in English and published in the UK and Ireland by an imprint formally established in the UK or Ireland is eligible. Entries are accepted only from UK and Irish publishers who may each submit novels based on their previous longlisting with scheduled publication dates between 1 October of the previous year and 30 September of the current year. The judges may also ask for other eligible novels to be submitted to them. In addition, publishers may submit eligible titles by authors who have either won or been shortlisted in the past. Sponsored by Man Group plc for 18 years until 1 June 2019, when a new sponsor, Crankstart, took over the role.

The International Booker Prize
Four Culture, 20 St Thomas Street, London SE1 9BF
tel 020-3697 4256
email marion.fraser@fourcommunications.com
website www.thebookerprizes.com

Awarded annually for a single work of fiction, translated into English and published in the UK and Ireland. Both novels and collections of short stories are eligible. As a further acknowledgement of the importance of translation, the £50,000 prize will be divided equally between the author and the translator. Each shortlisted author and translator will receive £1,000. Entries only from UK and Irish publishers.

Books Are My Bag Readers Awards
website www.nationalbooktokens.com/vote

Curated by bookshops and chosen by readers, categories include Fiction, Non-Fiction, Poetry, YA

Fiction, Children's fiction, Breakthrough author and Readers' choice. Reader's choice is nominated exclusively by readers.

BookTrust Storytime Prize

BookTrust, G8 Battersea Studios,
80 Silverthorne Road, London SW8 3HE
tel 020-7801 8826
email StoryTimePrize@booktrust.org.uk
website www.booktrust.org.uk/prizes

An annual prize to celebrate the best books for sharing with young children aged 0–5 with a particular focus on books that have a wide appeal to parents and carers across our diverse nation, and for stories which can be read and enjoyed over and over again. The prize is run in collaboration with Youth Library Group (YLG) and the shortlisted titles are shared with families by public librarians across the UK to find the best book. Publishers are invited to enter up to five books per imprint. See website for further details and timings.

The Branford Boase Award

8 Bolderwood Close, Bishopstoke, Eastleigh,
Hants SO50 8PG
tel 023-8060 0439
email anne.marley@tiscali.co.uk
website www.branfordboaseaward.org.uk

An annual award of £1,000 is made to a first-time writer of a full-length children's novel (age 7+) published in the preceding year; the editor is also recognised. Its aim is to encourage new writers for children and to recognise the role of perceptive editors in developing new talent. The Award was set up in memory of the outstanding children's writer Henrietta Branford and the gifted editor and publisher Wendy Boase who both died in 1999. Closing date for nominations: end of December. Founded 2000.

The Bridport Prize

Bridport Arts Centre, South Street, Bridport,
Dorset DT6 3NR
email kate@bridportprize.org.uk
website www.bridportprize.org.uk

Annual prizes are awarded for poetry and short stories (1st £5,000, 2nd £1,000, 3rd £500 in both categories), £1,000 for flash fiction stories (under 250 words) and £1,500 for the Peggy Chapman-Andrews First Novel Award. Novel award open to writers based in Britain and the Republic of Ireland, British citizens living, working or studying overseas and residents of the 14 British Overseas Territories. All other categories open internationally. Entry fees: £9 flash fiction, £10 poems, £12 short stories, £20 novel. A Young Writer Award of £500 is given to the writer aged 16–25 who places highest in the competition each year.

Closing date 31 May each year. Enter by post or online. See website for rules and eligibility. Entries should be in English, original work, typed or clearly written, and never published or read on radio/TV/stage. Winners and highly commended winners are notified by email in September and results announced in October. Shortlisted winners are notified by email between mid-September and early October. Winning stories are read by a leading London literary agent, without obligation, and two anthologies of winning entries are published each autumn. Top three poems are submitted to the Forward Poetry Prizes and top 13 eligible stories are submitted to the BBC National Short Story Award and *The Sunday Times* Short Story Prize. Send sae for entry form or enter online.

British Academy Medals and Prizes

The British Academy, 10–11 Carlton House Terrace,
London SW1Y 5AH
tel 020-7969 5200
email prizes@thebritishacademy.ac.uk
website www.thebritishacademy.ac.uk/prizes-medals

A number of prizes and medals are awarded by the British Academy for outstanding work in various fields of the humanities and social sciences on the recommendation of specialist committees: Brian Barry Prize in Political Science; British Academy Medal; Burkitt Medal (Biblical studies); Derek Allen Prize (made annually in turn for Musicology, Numismatics and Celtic studies); Edward Ullendorff Medal (Semitic languages and Ethiopian studies); Grahame Clark Medal (Prehistoric Archaeology); Sir Israel Gollancz Prize (English studies); Kenyon Medal (Classical Studies and Archaeology); Nayef Al-Rodhan Prize for Global Understanding; Peter Townsend Prize (Social Policy); Rose Mary Crawshay Prize (English Literature); Serena Medal (Italian studies); Leverhulme Medal and Prize (Humanities and Social Sciences); The Landscape Archaeology Medal. Nominations open in December 2021.

The British Book Awards

The Bookseller, Stage House, 47 Bermondsey Street,
London, SE1 3XT
email events@thebookseller.com
website www.thebookseller.com/awards

Affectionately known as The Nibbies, these awards seek to showcase and honour the best books, the best publishers and the best bookshops. The year 2020 celebrates 30 years of the awards. The Nibbies are supported by all major industry associations including the Publishers Association, the Booksellers Association and the Independent Publishers Guild. For full entry criteria and details for all award categories, see the website.

British Czech and Slovak Association Writing Competition

24 Ferndale, Tunbridge Wells, Kent TN2 3NS
tel (01892) 543206

email prize@bcsa.co.uk
website www.bcsa.co.uk
Contact BCSA Prize Administrator

Annual BCSA competition (1st prize: £400; 2nd prize: £150) for fiction or non-fiction on the theme of the links between Britain and the Czech and Slovak Republics, at any time in their history, or society in those republics since the Velvet Revolution in 1989. See website for suggested (optional) theme for 2022. Winning entries published in *British Czech & Slovak Review*. Length: 2,000 words max. Entry is free. Closing date: 30 June each year. Founded 2002.

British Fantasy Awards

The Apex, 2 Sheffiels Orchards, Coventry CV1 3PP
tel 07557 389878
email bfsawards@britishfantasysociety.org
website www.britishfantasysociety.org/british-fantasy-awards
Facebook www.facebook.com/britishfantasysociety
Twitter @BritFantasySoc
Awards Administrator Katherine Fowler

Awarded in up to 14 categories including best novel, novella, short story and collection, and are presented each autumn at FantasyCon (24–26 September 2021) to works published the previous year. Past winners include Neil Gaiman, Angela Slatter, Lavie Tidhar and Tanith Lee. Publishers, writers, editors and readers are able to contribute to a list of eligible works. The shortlist is currently decided by a vote of British Fantasy Society members and FantasyCon attendees, and the winners decided by a jury. Founded 1972.

British Science Fiction Association Awards

email info@bsfa.co.uk
website https://bsfa.co.uk/
Twitter @bsfa

These awards have been presented annually by the British Science Fiction Association, based on a vote of BSFA members and – in recent years – members of the British national science fiction convention, Eastercon. They seek to honour the most worthy examples in each category, promote the genre of science fiction and get people reading, talking about and enjoying all that contemporary science fiction has to offer. Awards are made to the Best Novel, work of Short Fiction, Artwork and work of Non-Fiction. There are three rounds: longlist (September to December), shortlist (January) and final vote (opens February and closes at noon on the day of the awards ceremony). Founded 1970.

Gordon Burn Prize

email will@newwritingnorth.com
website http://gordonburnprize.com/

Run in partnership by the Gordon Burn Trust, New Writing North, Faber and Faber and Durham Book Festival, this fiction prize seeks to celebrate the writing of those whose work follows in late novelist Gordon Burn's footsteps. See website for submission details. Founded 2012.

The AKO Caine Prize for African Writing

51 Southwark Street, London SE1 1RU
email info@caineprize.com
website www.caineprize.com
Twitter @caineprize

A literature prize awarded to an African writer of a short story published in English. The prize, worth £10,000, was launched to encourage and highlight the richness and diversity of African writing by bringing it to a wider audience internationally. The focus on the short story reflects the contemporary development of the African story-telling tradition. See the website for eligibility and submission guidelines. Founded 1999, launched 2000.

Caledonia Novel Award

email enquiries@thecaledonianovelaward.com
website https://thecaledonianovelaward.com/

Award for unpublished and self-published novelists. Novels can be of any genre for adult or YA fiction. The award is open to writers of any nationality who are over 18+. Entries cost £25, with the winner receiving £1,500. The Award provides a number of sponsored places to eligible, low-income writers who are unable to afford the fee. For more information, see the competition rules on the website.

Canterbury Festival Poet of the Year

Festival House, 8 Orange Street, Canterbury, Kent CT1 2JA
tel (01227) 452853
email tina@canterburyfestival.co.uk
website https://canterburyfestival.co.uk/poet-of-the-year-competition-2021/

Managed by the Festival Friends, the competition attracts entries locally, nationally and internationally. Entries that make the longlist will be published in an anthology. The overall winner, announced on National Poetry Day, will receive a £200 cash prize. Submission costs £5; see website for full submission details. Founded 2007.

Carnegie Medal – see The CILIP Carnegie and Kate Greenaway Children's Book Awards

Peggy Chapman-Andrews First Novel Award

The Bridport Prize, Bridport Arts Centre, South Street, Bridport, Dorset DT8 3NR
email kate@bridportprize.org.uk
website www.bridportprize.org.uk/peggy-chapman-andrews-award-first-novel

Enter first chapter(s) of novel, up to 8,000 words, plus 300-word synopsis. 1st prize £1,500 plus mentoring from the Literary Consultancy, through their Chapter & Verse mentoring scheme, and possible publication. Extracts from the 20 longlisted novels are published in an annual anthology in October. Closing date 31 May each year. Enter by post or online. Entry fees £20 per novel. Open to writers based in Britain and the Republic of Ireland only, British citizens living, working, or studying overseas, and residents of the 14 British Overseas Territories. See website for rules and eligibility. Founded 2014.

Cheltenham Illustration Awards

email eevans@glos.ac.uk
website www.cheltenham-illustration-awards.com

Exhibition and Annual submissions are invited and can be freely interpreted in a narrative context. Submissions of work are free and open to all students, emerging and established illustrators and graphic novelists. A selection panel will assess entries. The selected work will be showcased in an exhibition and published in the *Cheltenham Illustration Awards Annual*, which will be distributed to education institutions and publishers. Deadline for submissions: June.

The Children's Book Award

email childrensbookaward@fcbg.org.uk
website https://childrensbookaward.org.uk/
Twitter @CBACoordinator

This award is given annually to authors and illustrators of children's fiction published in the UK. Children participate in the judging of the award. Awards are made in the following categories: Books for Younger Children, Books for Younger Readers and Books for Older Readers. Founded 1980.

The KPMG Children's Books Ireland Awards

Children's Books Ireland,
17 North Great George's Street, Dublin 1 D01 R2F1
tel +353 (0)1 872 7475
email info@childrensbooksireland.ie
website www.childrensbooksireland.ie

Formerly the CBI Book of the Year Awards/Bisto Awards, the awards are the leading annual children's book awards in Ireland. The awards are: the Book of the Year, the Eilís Dillon Award (for a first children's book), the Honour Award for Fiction, the Honour Award for Illustration, the Judges' Special Award and the Junior Juries Award. The awards are made annually by Children's Books Ireland to authors and illustrators who were born in Ireland, are permanently resident in Ireland or are citizens of Ireland, and are open to books written in Irish or English. Schools and reading groups nationwide take part in the Junior Juries programme: participating groups make their own selection of suitable titles from the books shortlisted for the awards in March, using a specially devised activity pack to guide them in their reading. Each group then votes for their favourite book, the results of which form the basis for the Junior Juries Award. Closing date: December for work published between 1 January and 31 December of an awards year. Shortlist announced in March; winners announced in May. Founded 1990.

The Children's Laureate

BookTrust, Studio G8, Battersea Studios,
80 Silverthorne Road, London SW8 3HE
tel 020-7801 8800
email childrenslaureate@booktrust.org.uk
website www.childrenslaureate.org.uk
Contact Charlotte Copping

The idea for the Children's Laureate originated from a conversation between (the then) Poet Laureate Ted Hughes and children's writer Michael Morpurgo. The post was established to celebrate exceptional children's authors and illustrators and to acknowledge their importance in creating the readers of tomorrow. Quentin Blake was the first Children's Laureate (1999–2001), followed by Anne Fine (2001–2003), Michael Morpurgo (2003–2005), Jacqueline Wilson (2005–2007), Michael Rosen (2007–2009), Anthony Browne (2009–2011), Julia Donaldson (2011–2013), Malorie Blackman (2013–2015), Chris Riddell (2015–2017), Lauren Child (2017–2019) and Cressida Cowell (2019–2022). Founded 1999.

Cholmondeley Awards

The Society of Authors, 24 Bedford Row,
London WC1R 4EH
tel 020-7373 6642
email prizes@societyofauthors.org
website www.societyofauthors.org/prizes/Society-of-Authors-Awards/Cholmondeley
Twitter @Soc_of_Authors

These honorary awards recognise the achievement and distinction of individual poets. Submissions cannot be accepted. Total value of awards is about £8,000.

The CILIP Carnegie and Kate Greenaway Children's Book Awards

CILIP, 7 Ridgmount Street, London WC1E 7AE
tel 020-7255 0650
email ckg@cilip.org.uk
website www.ckg.org.uk

Nominations for the following two awards are invited from members of CILIP (the library and information association), who are asked to submit one title per Medal, accompanied by an explanation of how the book they have selected meets the Medal criteria. The awards are selected by librarian judges from the Youth Libraries Group of CILIP. One title from each shortlist will receive a prize awarded by children who take part in the Awards shadowing scheme who vote for their favourites.

Carnegie Medal

Awarded annually for an outstanding book for children (fiction or non-fiction) written in English and first published in the UK during the preceding year or co-published elsewhere within a three-month time lapse. The Carnegie Medal winner is awarded £5,000 prize money from the Colin Mears Award annually.

Kate Greenaway Medal

Awarded annually for an outstanding illustrated book for children first published in the UK during the preceding year or co-published elsewhere within a three-month time lapse. Books intended for older as well as younger children are included, and reproduction will be taken into account. The Colin Mears Award (£5,000) is awarded annually to the winner of the Kate Greenaway Medal.

Arthur C. Clarke Award

website www.clarkeaward.com

An annual prize consisting of a number of pounds sterling equal to the current year (e.g. £2,021 in 2021) plus an engraved bookend is given for the best science fiction novel with first UK publication during the previous calendar year. Titles are submitted by publishers. Founded 1985.

The David Cohen Prize for Literature

PO Box 1277, Newcastle upon Tyne NE99 5BP
tel 0191 204 8850
email office@newwritingnorth.com
website www.newwritingnorth.com
website www.davidcohenprize.com

The David Cohen Prize for Literature is one of the UK's most distinguished literary prizes. It recognises writers who use the English language and are citizens of the UK or the Republic of Ireland, encompassing dramatists as well as novelists, poets and essayists. Former winners include Harold Pinter, William Trevor, Doris Lessing, Seamus Heaney, Hilary Mantel, Tom Stoppard and Edna O'Brien.

The biennial prize, of £40,000, is for a lifetime's achievement and is donated by the John S. Cohen Foundation. Established in 1965 by David Cohen and his family, the trust supports education, the arts, conservation and the environment. Arts Council England funds an additional prize of £10,000 (The Clarissa Luard Award) which is given by the winner to a fellow author or literary organisation. The David Cohen Prize for Literature is not open to applications but is awarded by an independent judging panel. Founded 1993.

Comedy Women in Print Awards

email hello@comedywomeninprint.co.uk
website www.comedywomeninprint.co.uk
Twitter @CWIPprize
Instagram cwipprize

The first UK and Ireland comedy literary prize to shine a light on witty women authors. Awards include Published Comedy Novel and Unpublished Comedy Novel. Every two years includes Humorous Comic Graphic Novel category in association with LDComics. Entry forms, terms and conditions and submission guidelines can be found on the website. Founded 2019.

Commonwealth Short Story Prize

Commonwealth Writers,
Commonwealth Foundation, Marlborough House, Pall Mall, London SW1Y 5HY
email writers@commonwealth.int
website www.commonwealthwriters.org/our-projects/the-short-story
Facebook www.facebook.com/cwwriters
Twitter @cwwriters

Run by the cultural programme of the Commonwealth Foundation. It is awarded for the best piece of unpublished short fiction (2,000–5,000 words) in English. Regional winners receive £2,500 and the overall winner receives £5,000. Translated entries are also eligible, as are stories written in selected languages other than English. The competition is free to enter and open to any citizen of a Commonwealth country who is aged 18 and over.

The Pol Roger Duff Cooper Prize

email info@theduffcooperprize.org
website www.theduffcooperprize.org

An annual prize for a literary work in the field of biography, history, politics or poetry published in English and submitted by a recognised publisher during the previous 12 months. The prize of £5,000 comes from a trust fund established by the friends and admirers of Duff Cooper, 1st Viscount Norwich (1890–1954) after his death, with a £1,000 contribution from Pol Roger Champagne.

Copy*right* Essay Prize

The Copyright Licensing Agency Ltd, 5th Floor, Shackleton House, 4 Battle Bridge Lane, London SE1 2HX
email LAessayprize@cla.co.uk
website https://cla.co.uk/essayprize

The annual competition is open to 16–19 year olds based in UK schools and colleges to write a 1,500 word essay around subjects concerning copyright and intellectual property. The overall winner will receive a £300 cash prize. Each year the CLA will set a specific essay question that the students must respond to. See website for more details. Founded 2020.

Costa Book Awards

The Booksellers Association, 6 Bell Yard, London WC2A 2JR
tel 020-7421 4640

email costabookawards@booksellers.org.uk
website www.costa.co.uk/costa-book-awards
Contact Naomi Gane

The awards celebrate and promote the most enjoyable contemporary British writing. There are five categories: Novel, First Novel, Biography, Poetry and Children's, plus one overall winner. Each category is judged by a panel of judges and the winner in each category receives £5,000. Judges then choose the Costa Book of the Year from the five category winners. The overall winner receives £30,000. There is also a seventh award, the Short Story Award, given for a single short story. Total prize money for the Costa Book Awards is £60,000. Submissions must be received from publishers. Shortlist announced: November. Closing date: end of June. For full eligibility and submission guidelines, see the website. Founded 1971.

The Rose Mary Crawshay Prize

The British Academy, 10–11 Carlton House Terrace, London SW1Y 5AH
tel 020-7969 5200
email prizes@thebritishacademy.ac.uk
website www.thebritishacademy.ac.uk

Worth £500, is awarded each year for an historical or critical book by a woman, on any subject connected with literature. Eligible nominations must be for books published within the last three years. Nominations for the 2022 Rose Mary Crawshay Prize opens December 2021 and are invited from Fellows of the British Academy. Founded 1888.

Creative Future Writers' Award

Community Base, 113 Queens Road, Brighton BN1 3XG
tel (01273) 234780
email info@creativefuture.org.uk
website www.creativefuture.org.uk

A national writing competition and high-profile awards ceremony for under-represented writers. The Award showcases talented writers who lack opportunities due to mental health issues, disability, identity or other social circumstance. Prizes are awarded for poetry and short fiction, including £10,000 of cash and writing development prizes. See website for information about eligibility, rules and how to apply. Founded 2013.

Cundill History Prize

840 Dr Penfield Avenue, Room 233, Montreal, Quebec H3A 1A4, Canada
tel +1 514-398-4400
email cundill.prize@mcgill.ca
website www.cundillprize.com
Facebook www.facebook.com/cundillprizemcgill
Twitter @CundillPrize

Offered each year to an individual who has published a book in English determined to have had, or likely to

have, a profound literary, social and intellectual impact. Administered by Montreal's McGill University, the Cundill Prize recognises outstanding works of non-fiction that are grounded in scholarly research while retaining wide appeal and interest to the general public. Submissions are judged on their literary merits, their scholarship, and their contribution to historical understanding. The Prize is the largest non-fiction history prize in the world and welcomes submissions on any historical period or subject, regardless of the nationality or place of residence of the author. See website for submission guidelines.

The Curtis Brown Prize for Prose Fiction (University of East Anglia)

School of Literature, Drama and Creative Writing, University of East Anglia, Norwich Research Park, Norwich NR4 7TJ
email ldc.schooloffice@uea.ac.uk
website www.uea.ac.uk/literature/scholarships-and-funding/prizes

The prize of £1,500 is awarded annually to the best writer of prose fiction on the University of East Anglia MA in Creative Writing (Prose Fiction) course. The prize is open to all students enrolled on the MA in Prose Fiction in a given year and based on the material submitted by students for their MA assessment. The winner will be chosen by a panel of Curtis Brown agents from a shortlist comprising all students in the year who achieve MA with Distinction. For further details, contact the School of Literature, Drama and Creative Writing.

CWA Dagger Awards

c/o CJAM, Peershaws, Berewyk Hall Court, White Colne, Colchester CO2 2QB
email admin@thecwa.co.uk
email secretary@thecwa.co.uk
website www.thecwa.co.uk/the-daggers
Contacts Dea Parkin (CWA Secretary), Mike Stotter (Daggers Liaison)

Every year, the Crime Writers' Association awards the world-renowned Daggers for crime writing. Winners of the Diamond Dagger and the Publishers' Dagger are nominated by CWA members. The Gold Dagger, the Ian Fleming Steel Dagger, the John Creasey Dagger, the International Dagger, the ALCS Gold Dagger for Non-Fiction, the Short Story Dagger and the Sapere Books Historical Dagger are all nominated by publishers via the CWA website (email dagger.liaison@thecwa.co.uk). The Dagger in the Library winner is nominated by library staff via the CWA website.

CWA Debut Dagger

email secretary@thecwa.co.uk
website www.thecwa.co.uk/debuts/debut-dagger
Facebook www.facebook.com/groups/thedebuts

Sponsored by ProWritingAid, the Debut Dagger is the UK's prestigious, international crime-writing competition. Entrants are eligible who have never had a traditional publishing contract for any kind of full-length novel and who don't have a literary agent at the time the competition closes for entries.

Shortlisted writers get feedback from the panel of judges – comprising of top crime agents, editors and a bestselling crime author – and have their work shown to agents and publishers who specialise in crime. Every year, shortlisted authors secure representation and/or a contract this way. The winner receives £500. Entrants should read the rules and T&Cs closely. They should submit the opening of a crime novel of no longer than 3,000 words and a synopsis of 1,500 words via the website portal. The novel does not need to be completed. Entry costs £36 and the deadline is 6pm the last working day of February. The competition opens October 1.

CWA Margery Allingham Short Mystery Prize
email secretary@thecwa.co.uk
website www.thecwa.co.uk/ma

A prestigious annual competition for a short story of up to 3,500 words that follows Margery Allingham's definition of a mystery. The international competition is open to all writers, published or unpublished. The story itself must not previously have been published in any form and it's very important it follows the definition as shown on the website. Entry costs £12 and the prize is £500 plus two tickets to CrimeFest the following year. The competition opens on 1 October and closes at 6pm on the last working day of February. Entry is via the website where the mystery definition, T&Cs and past winning stories can be found.

Derwent Art Prize
tel 020-3653 0896
email info@parkerharris.co.uk
website www.derwent-artprize.com
Facebook www.facebook.com/derwentartprize
Twitter @DerwentArt
Instagram derwentartofficial

Rewards excellence by showcasing the very best 2D and 3D artworks created in pencil or coloured pencil as well as water soluble, pastel, graphite and charcoal by British and international artists. Prizes totalling over £12,500 are awarded. Since the Derwent Art Prize began, the competition has attracted more than 7,000 entries from over 67 countries. For detailed submission guidelines and entry fees, see the website. Founded 2012.

Desperate Literature Short Fiction Prize
tel +34 911-88-80-89
email prize@desperateliterature.com
website https://desperateliterature.com/prize/
Twitter @DesperateLit

This prize celebrates the best of new short fiction. Run in partnership with 14 different literary and artistic institutions, we offer not only a cash prize and writing retreats but the opportunity to be published in multiple print and online journals, have your work put in front of literary agents and performed in multiple countries. The overall winner receives €1,500 cash prize, a week's residency at the Civitella Ranieri Foundation and consultation with a Literary Agent from Andrew Nurnberg Associates. See website for full entry criteria. Founded 2018.

Deutsche Börse Photography Foundation Prize
email foundation@deutsche-boerse.com
email info@tpg.org.uk
website www.deutscheboersephotographyfoundation. org/en/support/photography-prize.php
Facebook www.facebook.com/ DeutscheBoersePhotographyFoundation

Rewards a living photographer, of any nationality, who has made the most significant contribution to the medium of photography in Europe during the previous year (1st prize £30,000). Founded by the Photographers' Gallery and awarded together with the Deutsche Börse Photography Foundation, a non-profit organisation dedicated to the collection, exhibition and promotion of contemporary photography. Founded 1996.

The DSC Prize for South Asian Literature
Writu Bose, C-66, South Extension Part-II, New Delhi 11049, India
+91 (0)11 4132 0192
email admin@dcsprize.com
website www.dscprize.com
Facebook www.facebook.com/DSCPrize
Twitter @thedscprize

This Prize celebrates the rich and varied world of literature of the South Asian region. Authors can belong to the region through birth or be of any ethnicity, but the writing should pertain to the South Asian region in terms of content and theme. The prize aims to bring South Asian writing to a new global audience through a celebration of the achievements of South Asian writers. Prize value: $25,000. See website for submission guidelines and eligibility. Founded 2010.

East Anglian Book Awards
email competitions@nationalcentreforwriting.org.uk
website www.nationalcentreforwriting.org.uk/east-anglian-book-awards

Awarded annually, the Awards comprise six categories: fiction, general non-fiction, poetry, children's, history and tradition, and biography and memoir, with the £1,000 prize money going to the East Anglian Book of the Year. Additional categories: Book by the Cover, sponsored by East Anglian Writers, offering £100 to the best cover from the shortlisted books, and Exceptional Contribution Award given to a key figure in the world of literature, publishing, writing and editing, etc. Books must be largely set in East Anglia or be written by an author living in the region, which for the Awards' purposes is defined as the counties of Norfolk, Suffolk and Essex, and the area of Fenland District Council. Awards are staged in partnership with *Eastern Daily Press*, Jarrold, and the National Centre for Writing, sponsored by the University of East Anglia Faculty of Humanities and the PACCAR Foundation.

Closing date for entries: July. Books must have been published within the calendar year of the previous award's closing date and the one for the current year. Once entries are open (June), two copies of the book and a covering note explaining which category it is to be submitted to should be sent to: East Anglian Book Awards, National Centre for Writing, Dragan Hall, 115–123 King Street, Norwich NR1 1QE.

Edge Hill Short Story Prize

Edge Hill University, St Helens Road, Ormskirk, Lancs. L39 4QP
tel (01695) 584133
email cowanb@edgehill.ac.uk
website www.edgehill.ac.uk/shortstory
Contact Billy Cowan

This prize is awarded annually by Edge Hill University for excellence in a published single-authored short story collection. The winner will receive £10,000. There is also a Readers' Choice prize of £1,000. Publishers are entitled to submit collections published during the preceding year. Authors must be normally resident in the UK or Ireland.

The T.S. Eliot Prize

50 Penn Road, London N7 9RE
website http://tseliot.com/prize/
Director Chris Holifield

An annual prize of £25,000, with £1,500 for each of the ten shortlisted poets, is awarded by the T.S. Eliot Foundation to the best collection of new poetry published in the UK or the Republic of Ireland during the year. Submissions are invited from publishers in June with a closing date of early August. The shortlist is announced in October and the winner in January, the day after the T.S. Eliot Prize Readings in the Royal Festival Hall.

The Desmond Elliott Prize

National Centre for Writing, Dragon Hall, 115–123 King Street, Norwich NR1 1QE
tel (01603) 877177
email awards@nationalcentreforwriting.org.uk
website www.nationalcentreforwriting.org.uk

An annual prize for a first novel written in English by an author resident in the UK or Ireland and published in the UK. The winning author receives the £10,000 prize to support their writing future, alongside a year of bespoke support from National Centre for Writing. The prize is named after the literary agent and publisher, Desmond Elliott, who died in 2003. The prize seeks to award and support a debut novel of depth and breadth with a compelling narrative, original and arresting characters, vividly written and confidently realised. This award is part of the National Centre for Writing's suite of Early Career Awards. Founded 2007.

Encore Award

Royal Society of Literature, Somerset House, London WC2R 1LA
tel 020-7845 4679
email info@rsliterature.org
website https://rsliterature.org/award/encore-award/

The £10,000 Encore Award for the best second novel of the year was founded by Lucy Astor in 1990. The award fills a niche in the catalogue of literary prizes by celebrating the achievement of outstanding second novels. See the website for full submission guidelines. The RSL has administrated the award since 2016.

English Association English 4–11 Children's Book Awards

The English Association, University of Leicester, Leicester LE1 7RH
tel 0116 229 7622
email engassoc@leicester.ac.uk
website www2.le.ac.uk/offices/english-association/primary/english-4-11-book-awards

The Awards are presented by the English Association to the best children's picture books of the year. Categories are Fiction and Non-fiction in the age ranges 4–7 years and 7–11 years. The winning books are chosen by the editorial board of *English 4–11*, the journal for primary teachers published by the English Association and the United Kingdom Literacy Association from a shortlist selected by a panel of teachers and primary education specialists. Founded 1995.

European Union Prize for Literature

email info@euprizeliterature.eu
website www.euprizeliterature.eu

Supported by the Creative Europe programme of the European Union, this award is an annual initiative to recognise the best emerging fiction writers in Europe. Each year, national juries set up in a rotating third of the participating countries decide on a shortlist of two to five books before electing their winner. All laureates of the year are collectively announced and later celebrated at the occasion of an EUPL award ceremony. To encourage translation and circulation of literature, an anthology of the winning books is published, featuring excerpts both in original language and in an English or French translation. See website for full details. Founded 2008.

FAB Prize for Undiscovered Talent

email prize@fabfaber.co.uk
website www.fabprize.org
Twitter @FaberChildrens

Set up by Faber Children's and Andlyn Literary
Agency, this is an annual competition for unagented
and unpublished writers and illustrators from Black,
Asian and/or non-white minority ethnic
backgrounds. Now with the additional backing of
BookTrust and the Association of Illustrators, the
competition winners and runners up are not only
offered mentoring, but also exposure to literary
agents and editors alongside access to training and
shadowing schemes. The prize offers a unique
opportunity to kick start a writing or illustrating
career and get a foot in the door. Entries must be text
or artwork for children aged 1 to 18 years. First prize
of £500 for text and £500 for illustration. To follow
the results of the 2021 prize and for further
information about future prizes, visit the website.
Founded 2017.

The Geoffrey Faber Memorial Prize

website www.faber.co.uk/geoffrey-faber-prize
Twitter @FaberBooks

The Prize of £1,500 is awarded annually and it is
given, in alternate years, for a volume of verse and for
a volume of prose fiction. It is given to that volume
of verse or prose fiction first published originally in
the UK during the two years preceding the year in
which the award is given which is, in the opinion of
the judges, of the greatest literary merit. To be eligible
for the prize the volume of verse or prose fiction
must be by a writer who is not more than 40 years
old at the date of publication of the book and a
citizen of the UK, or any other Commonwealth state,
of the Republic of Ireland or of the Republic of South
Africa. No submissions for the prize are to be made.
Founded 1963 by Faber and Faber Ltd, as a memorial
to the founder and first Chairman of the firm.

The Alfred Fagon Award

email info@alfredfagonaward.co.uk
website www.alfredfagonaward.co.uk
Facebook www.facebook.com/alfredfagonaward
Twitter @AlfredFagonAwrd
Administrator Pauline Walker

An annual award of £6,000 for the Best New Play of
the Year (which need not have been produced) for
the theatre in English. TV and radio plays and film
scripts will not be considered. Only writers of
Caribbean and African descent resident in the UK are
eligible. Applicants should submit two copies of their
play plus sae for return of their script and a CV
which includes details of the writer's Caribbean and
African connection. Closing date: end July.
Founded 1997.

The Eleanor Farjeon Award

website www.childrensbookcircle.org.uk

An annual award which may be given to an
individual or an organisation. Librarians, authors,
publishers, teachers, reviewers and others who have
given exceptional service to the children's book
industry are eligible for nomination. It was instituted
in 1965 by the Children's Book Circle (page 529) for
distinguished services to children's books and named
after the much-loved children's writer Eleanor
Farjeon.

Financial Times and McKinsey Business Book of the Year Award

email bookaward@ft.com
website www.ft.com/bookaward

This award aims to identify the book that provides
the most compelling and enjoyable insight into
modern business issues including management,
finance and economics. Submissions should be made
via the publisher. The winner receives £30,000 and
five runners up each receive £10,000. Founded 2005.

First Novel Prize

c/o Daniel Goldsmith Associates Ltd,
Gridiron Building, One Pancras Square,
London N1C 4AG
email hello@danielgoldsmith.co.uk
website www.firstnovel.co.uk

A literary contest organised by the literary
consultancy Daniel Goldsmith Associates, open to
previously unpublished and independently published
novelists. Open to novels of more than 50,000 words
and of any adult genre. Judges include a leading
literary agent and an adult fiction commissioning
editor. First prize £1,000, second prize £250 and third
prize £100. For full entry guidelines and entry fees,
see the website. Entries are open February to May
every year.

Fish Publishing Writing Prizes

Fish Publishing, Durrus, Bantry, Co. Cork,
Republic of Ireland
email info@fishpublishing.com
website www.fishpublishing.com/writing-contests
Facebook www.facebook.com/FishPublishingIreland
Twitter @fishpublishing

International writing prizes set up to publish and
encourage new writers. There are a number of prizes
available including the Fish Short Story Prize, the
Fish Memoir Prize, the Fish Flash Fiction Prize and
the Fish Poetry Prize. Winners from each prize are
published in the annual Fish Anthology and each
competition has cash and other prizes including
residencies and other courses. Founded 1994.

FOCAL International Awards

email awards@focalint.org
website www.focalintawards.com
website www.focalint.org

The awards celebrate achievement in the use of footage in all variety of genres, across all media platforms plus its restoration. Producers, film-makers and other creative professionals who have used library footage in a documentary, feature film or any other form of production are encouraged to submit their work for consideration. See website for full submission guidelines and further information.

Rathbones Folio Prize
email info@rathbonesfolioprize.com
website www.rathbonesfolioprize.com
Twitter @RathbonesFolio
Instagram rathbones_folio
Executive Director Minna Fry

Open to all works of literature written in English and published in the UK. All genres and all forms of literature are eligible, except work written primarily for children. The format of first publication may be print or digital. The Prize will be awarded in March for books published in the previous calendar year. The prize is worth £30,000. See the website for submission details and dates.

Fool for Poetry Chapbook Competition
Frank O'Connor House, 84 Douglas Street, Cork T12 X802, Republic of Ireland
email foolforpoetry@munsterlit.ie
website www.munsterlit.ie

An annual poetry chapbook competition run by the Munster Literature Centre. The competition is open to new, emerging and established poets from any country, but at least one of the winners will be previously unpublished. First prize €1,000 and second prize €500. Both winners will receive a chapbook publication and 25 complimentary copies. The winning poets are also offered a reading and three nights' accommodation at the Cork International Poetry Festival. See website for entry fees and submission guidelines.

Forward Prizes for Poetry
Forward Arts Foundation, Somerset House, Strand, London WC2R 1LA
tel 020-7845 4655
email info@forwardartsfoundation.org
website www.forwardartsfoundation.org

Three prizes are awarded annually:

• The Forward Prize for Best Collection published in the UK and Republic of Ireland (£10,000);
• The Felix Dennis Prize for Best First Collection (£5,000); and
• The Forward Prize for Best Single Poem, published but not as part of a collection, pamphlet or anthology (£1,000).

   All poems entered are also considered for inclusion in the *Forward Book of Poetry*, an annual anthology. Entries for the Best Collection and Best First Collection must be submitted by book publishers

and, for Best Single Poem, by editors of newspapers, periodicals, magazines or online journals, or by competition organisers, in the UK and Ireland. Entries accepted online. See website for full details and submission guidelines. Entries from individual poets of their unpublished or self-published work will not be accepted. Founded 1992.

The Franco-British Society's Literary Prize
Franco–British Society, 3 Dovedale Studios, 465 Battersea Park Road, London SW11 4LR
email francobritsoc@gmail.com
website www.franco-british-society.org
Executive Secretary Isabelle Gault

This annual prize is given for a full-length work of literature which contributes most to Franco–British understanding. It must be first published in the UK between 1 January and 31 December, and written in English by a citizen of the UK, British Commonwealth or the Republic of Ireland. Closing date: 31 December.

Fresh Ink Award
email freshink@littlebrown.co.uk
website https://www.littlebrown.co.uk/uncategorized/2015/11/20/launching-the-fresh-ink-award/

Run by Little, Brown imprints Sphere and Piatkus, in association with The Tandem Collective, this prize seeks to champion underrepresented voices in crime and romance fiction. Open to unpresented or unpublished Black, Asian and minority ethnic writers, the winners (one for each imprint) will receive a publishing contract and a £250 cash prize. See website for full entry requirements. Founded 2020.

The Ginkgo Prize for Ecopoetry
email jaz@ginkgoprize.com
website https://ginkgoprize.com/
Twitter @ginkgoprize
Instagram ginkgo.prize

The Prize, in association with the Poetry School, aims to highlight the role poetry can play in raising awareness, gaining insight, and provoking concern for the ecological imperatives of our time. Awarded to a single poem, the overall winner receives £5,000. Applicants must be 18 or over and submissions cost £7 then £4 for each additional poem entered. Poems can be be of any length or form but must, in some way, explore ecology. See website for further terms and conditions. Founded 2015.

Gladstone History Book Prize
Administrative Secretary, Royal Historical Society, University College London, Gower Street, London WC1E 6BT
tel 020-7387 7532

email adminsecrctary@royalhistsoc.org
website https://royalhistsoc.org/prizes/gladstone-history-book-prize/
Administrative Secretary Imogen Evans

An annual award (value £1,000) for a history book. The book must:

• be on any historical subject which is not primarily related to British history;
• be its author's first solely written history book;
• have been published in English during the previous calendar year;
• be an original and scholarly work of historical research.

One non-returnable copy of an eligible book should be submitted by the publisher before 31 December. Should the book be shortlisted, two further copies will be required.

The Goethe-Institut Award for New Translation
The Society of Authors, 24 Bedford Row, London WC1R 4EH
tel 020-7373 6642
email prizes@societyofauthors.org
website www.societyofauthors.org/prizes/translation-prizes/Goethe-Institut

This biennial award is open to emerging British translators of literature who translate from German into the English language. The winner will be awarded prize money of €1,000 and a place at the International Translator's seminar, including a visit to the Leipzig Book Fair. The 2021 Award will open for submissions on 13 September and will close on 11 November, 5pm.

The Goldsmiths Prize
c/o Department of English & Comparative Literature, Goldsmiths University of London, New Cross, London SE14 6NW
email goldsmithsprize@gold.ac.uk
website www.gold.ac.uk/goldsmiths-prize
Twitter @GoldsmithsPrize
Literary Director Tim Parnell

Celebrates the qualities of creative daring associated with the University and rewards fiction that breaks the mould or extends the possibilities of the novel form. The annual prize of £10,000 is awarded to a book that is deemed genuinely novel and which embodies the spirit of invention that characterises the genre at its best.

Prize open for submissions late January; closing date for submission of entry forms late March; closing date for submission of books early July; shortlist announced late September/early October; winner announced November. Founded 2013.

The Gourmand World Cookbook Awards
Pintor Rosales 50, 28008, Madrid, Spain
email pilar@gourmandbooks.com
email edouard@gourmandbooks.com

website www.cookbookfair.com
President Edouard Cointreau

The annual Gourmand World Cookbook Awards were created by Edouard Cointreau. Entries are free and any book published within the year can be entered by sending three copies of the book to the Gourmand Library at the address above. The Gourmand Library was created in 2013 to house the reference collection of cookbook and wine book titles of the awards. For further details about past winners, see the website. Founded 1995.

Kate Greenaway Medal – see The CILIP Carnegie and Kate Greenaway Children's Book Awards

The Griffin Poetry Prize
The Griffin Trust for Excellence in Poetry, 363 Parkridge Crescent, Oakville, Ontario L6M 1A8, Canada
tel +1 905-618-0420
email info@griffinpoetryprize.com
website www.griffinpoetryprize.com
Facebook www.facebook.com/GriffinPoetryPrize
Twitter @griffinpoetry

Two annual prizes of Can$65,000 (and an additional Can$10,000 to each shortlisted poet) are awarded for collections of poetry published in English during the preceding year. One prize goes to a living Canadian poet, the other to a living poet from any country. Collections of poetry translated into English from other languages are also eligible and are assessed for their literary quality in English. Submissions are accepted from publishers only. Founded 2000.

Jane Grigson Trust Award
tel 07951 777407
email award@janegrigsontrust.org.uk
website https://janegrigsontrust.org.uk/the-award/

Award for first-time Food and Drink writers who have been commissioned but not yet published. The Award is open to non-fiction books on food and drink including cookbooks, memoir, travel and history so long as the primary subject is food and/or drink. Winner receives £2,000. Founded 2016.

Harvill Secker Young Translators' Prize
email youngtranslatorsprize@penguinrandomhouse.co.uk
website www.penguin.co.uk/youngtranslatorsprize

The Prize recognises the achievements of young translators at the start of their careers. The prize is open to anyone between the ages of 18 and 34, with no restriction on the country of residence. The first prize includes £1,000 and a selection of Vintage titles. Founded 2010.

The Hawthornden Prize
The Prize Administrator,
International Retreat for Writers,

Hawthornden Castle, Lasswade,
Midlothian EH18 1EG
email office@hawthornden.org

This £15,000 prize is awarded annually to the author of the book the judges consider the best work of imaginative literature published during the preceding calendar year by a British, Irish or British-based author. Books are chosen rather than received by submission.

The PEN Hessell-Tiltman Prize for History

English PEN, 49–51 East Road, London N1 6AH
tel 020-7324 2535
email enquiries@englishpen.org
website www.englishpen.org/prizes/pen-hessell-tiltman-prize

An annual prize of £2,000 awarded to a non-fiction work of high literary merit covering any historical period and published during the previous year. Biography, autobiography and books written primarily for the academic market are excluded. Submissions must come through publishers. Full details can be found on the English PEN website. Founded 2002.

William Hill Sports Book of the Year Award

website https://news.williamhill.com/sports/sports-book-of-the-year/
Twitter @BookiePrize

The world's longest-established and most valuable literary sports-writing prize. Winner receives £30,000 and a trophy. Shortlisted authors receive a leather-bound copy of their book and £3,000. See website for rules and submission guidelines. Founded 1989.

The Calvin and Rose G. Hoffman Memorial Prize for Distinguished Scholarly Essay on Christopher Marlowe

The King's School, 25 The Precincts, Canterbury, Kent CT1 2ES
email bursar@kings-bursary.co.uk
Contact The Hoffman Administrator

This annual prize is awarded to the writer of the best distinguished scholarly essay on Christopher Marlowe. Closing date: 1 September 2021. An application form and further details must be obtained from the Hoffman Administrator.

The Ted Hughes Award for New Work in Poetry

The Poetry Society, 22 Betterton Street, London WC2H 9BX
tel 020-7420 9886

email marketing@poetrysociety.org.uk
website www.poetrysociety.org.uk/competitions/ted-hughes-award/
Facebook www.facebook.com/thepoetrysociety
Twitter @PoetrySociety

An annual award of £5,000 for a living UK poet, working in any form, who has made the most exciting contribution to poetry over the year. Organised by the Poetry Society and funded by Carol Ann Duffy with the honorarium which the Poet Laureate traditionally receives from H.M. the Queen.

The Imison Award

The Broadcasting Committee,
The Society of Authors, 24 Bedford Row,
London WC1R 4EH
tel 020-7373 6642
email info@societyofauthors.org
website www.societyofauthors.org/prizes/audio-drama/imison

This annual prize of £3,000, sponsored by the Peggy Ramsay Foundation, is awarded to an audio drama script by a writer new to the medium. Submissions are accepted from any party, e.g., producer, broadcasting organisation, writer, agent. Founded 1994.

The Impress Prize for New Writers

13–14, Crook Business Centre, New Road, Crook, Co. Durham DL15 8QX
email prize@impress-books.co.uk
website www.impress-books.co.uk/impress-prize-for-new-writers/
Twitter @ImpressPrize

An annual literary prize run by Impress Books, an imprint of Untold Publishing, that allows new writers the chance to see their work published. The prize is open to all writers who have not been traditionally published before (e.g. self-published authors, or writers who have had other work published including short stories, poetry, and academic work). Both fiction and non-fiction entries are accepted across all genres, but poetry is not accepted. Submit a 6,000 word manuscript sample, a synopsis, book proposal and author biography. Winning prize: £500 and the opportunity to attend a writer's workshop in France. Founded 2006.

Indie Book Awards

6 Bell Yard, London WC2A 2JR
tel 020-7421 4656
email emma.bradshaw@booksellers.org.uk
website www.indiebookshopweek.org.uk
Twitter @booksaremybag
Instagram booksaremybag

Awards are given in four categories: fiction, non-fiction, children's fiction and picture book. For entry guidelines and shortlist details see the website.

International Dublin Literary Award

Dublin City Library and Archive,
138–144 Pearse Street, Dublin D02 HE37,
Republic of Ireland
tel +353 (0)1 6744802
website https://dublinliteraryaward.ie
Facebook www.facebook.com/DubLitAward
Twitter @DublinLitAward

This award is the largest and most international prize of its kind. Administered by Dublin City Public Libraries, nominations are made by libraries in capital and major cities throughout the world. Novels are nominated solely on the basis of 'high literary merit'. Books may be written in any language, but must be translated into English. The prize is €100,000 which is awarded to the author if the book is written in English. If the winning book is in English translation, the author receives €75,000 and the translator €25,000. Founded 1996.

The International Poetry Business Book & Pamphlet Competition

The Poetry Business, Campo House,
54 Campo Lane, Sheffield S1 2EG
tel 0114 438 4074
email office@poetrybusiness.co.uk
website www.poetrybusiness.co.uk
Directors Peter Sansom, Ann Sansom

Entrants are invited to submit a collection of 20 pages of poetry. Four winners will be selected by the judges to be published by award winning imprint, Smith|Doorstop books. There is also an opportunity to submit a full-length manuscript, which, where the judges feel it is appropriate, will be published as a book in the following year. Full-price entry is £28. Subscribers to *The North*, Friends of the Poetry Business, and members of the Poetry Society are eligible for the discounted fee of £25. A number of free entries are available for those who cannot afford the entry fee to the International Book & Pamphlet (see website for full details). Poets over the age of 18 writing in English from anywhere in the world are eligible. Founded 1986.

International Prize for Arabic Fiction

Mailbox V100, Hill House,
210 Upper Richmond Road, London SW15 6NP
email fleurmontanaro@yahoo.co.uk
website https://arabicfiction.org
Facebook www.facebook.com/
InternationalPrizeArabicFiction
Twitter @Arabic_Fiction
Prize Administrator Fleur Montanaro

The IPAF is recognised as the leading prize for literary fiction in the Arab world. Its aim is to reward excellence in contemporary Arabic creative writing and increase the international reach of Arabic fiction through the English translation of its winners. The six shortlisted finalists receive USD$10,000, with a further USD$50,000 going to the winner.

An Post Irish Book Awards

137 Hillside, Dalkey, County Dublin A96 DP86,
Republic of Ireland
tel +353 (0)85 1449574
email bert@agile-ideas.com
website www.irishbookawards.irish/
Administrator Bert Wright

The Awards are a set of industry-recognition awards set up by a coalition of Irish booksellers in 2007. The awards are owned by Irish Book Awards Ltd, a not-for-profit company, and were established to celebrate the extraordinary quality of Irish writing, to help bring the best books to a wider readership annually, and to promote an industry under severe competitive pressures. The awards include 18 categories spanning the entire spectrum of literary genres. Thousands of ordinary readers vote to select the winners every year and the awards are presented at a Gala Dinner and Awards Ceremony in late November each year.

The current headline sponsor is An Post, the state-owned provider of postal services in the Republic of Ireland. Submissions open 1 June; shortlist announced late October. Founded 2007.

Jhalak Prize

email info@jhalakprize.com
website www.jhalakprize.com
Twitter @jhalakprize

Awarded annually, this prize seeks out the best books by British/British resident BAME writers and awards one winner £1,000. Entries can be for fiction, non-fiction, short story, graphic novel, poetry, and all genres. Started by authors Sunny Singh and Nikesh Shukla and Media Diversified, with support from The Authors' Club and a prize donated by an anonymous benefactor, the prize exists to celebrate the achievements of writers of colour. For submission guidelines and details of key dates see the website. Founded 2016.

The K&IM Information Resources Awards

CILIP, 7 Ridgmount Street, London WC1E 7AE
tel 020-7255 0500
email jdburntoak@virginmedia.com
website www.cilip.org.uk

Information Resources Award

Awarded annually for outstanding information resources that are available and relevant to the library and information sector in the UK. There are two categories, one for electronic formats and one for printed works. Recommendations are invited from Members of CILIP (the Chartered Institute of Library and Information Professionals), publishers and others, who are asked to submit nominations via the website. Winners receive a certificate.

The Walford Award

Awarded annually to an individual for an outstanding contribution to the knowledge and information management services and information services in the UK. Recommendations may be made for the work of a living person or persons, or for an organisation.

Kent and Sussex Poetry Society Open Poetry Competition

email kentandsussexpoetry@gmail.com
website www.kentandsussexpoetry.com
Facebook www.facebook.com/kentandsussexpoetrysoc
Twitter @KentSusXPoetry

This competition is open to all unpublished poems, no longer than 40 lines. Prizes: 1st: £1,000, 2nd: £300, 3rd: £100, 4th: four at £50. Closing date: 31 January. Entry fee £5 per poem (£4 per poem if submitting 3+ poems). Founded 1985.

Kerry Group Irish Novel of the Year Award

Listowel Writers' Week, 24 The Square, Listowel, Co. Kerry V31 RD93, Republic of Ireland
tel +353 (0)68 21074
email info@writersweek.ie
website www.writersweek.ie/competitions/

An annual award of €17,000 for a published novel by an Irish author. Listowel Writers' Week is an acclaimed literary festival devoted to bringing together writers and audiences at unique and innovative events in the historic and intimate surroundings of Listowel, County Kerry. Events include workshops, readings, seminars, lectures, book launches, art exhibitions and a comprehensive children's and teenagers' programme. See website for submission guidelines and dates. Founded 1971.

Killing It: The Killer Reads Competition for Undiscovered Writers

HarperCollins Publishers, The News Building, 1 London Bridge St, London SE1 9GF
tel 0141 306 3100
email crimesubmissions@harpercollins.co.uk
website www.killerreads.com/killing-it/

Prize for unrepresented authors, especially those from under-represented backgrounds writing a crime, thriller or suspense novel. The winner will receive editorial reports and mentoring from HarperFiction crime editors on their full manuscripts. Submit the first 10,000 words, short synopsis and author bio by email. See website for full details. Founded 2021.

Kindle Storyteller Award

website www.amazon.co.uk/
b?ie=UTF8&node=12061299031

Open to submissions of new English-language books in any genre. Titles must be previously unpublished and be available as an ebook and in print via Kindle Direct Publishing or CreateSpace (print edition only). The winning author will receive £20,000. Competition entry period runs from 1 May to 31 August.

The Kitschies

email submissions@thekitschies.com
website www.thekitschies.com
Facebook www.facebook.com/Kitschies
Twitter @TheKitschies

Awarding the year's most progressive, intelligent and entertaining works that contain elements of the speculative or fantastic. Four awards: Red Tentacle (Novel), Golden Tentacle (Debut), Inky Tentacle (Cover art) and Black Tentacle (Special recognition). Open for submissions in late spring/early summer and closed in late autumn/early winter, with awards presented in late winter each year. Prizes total £2,000. There is no fee to enter. Founded 2009.

Kraszna-Krausz Book Awards

email info@kraszna-krausz.org.uk
website www.kraszna-krausz.org.uk
Twitter @kraszna_krausz

Awards which recognise individuals or groups of individuals who, in the opinion of the judges, have made an outstanding original or lasting contribution to the literature of, or concerning the art and practice of, photography or the moving image. Two winning titles are selected; one in the field of photography and one in the field of the moving image (including film, television and digital media). From the total submissions, a long list of ten books is selected in both categories by the judges. This is then reduced to shortlists of three, from which two final winning publications will be chosen. Each winning book receives a £5,000 cash prize. Founded 1985.

Laurel Prize for Ecopoetry

39 Mosedale, Moreton in Marsh, Glos. GL56 0HP
website https://laurelprize.com/
Twitter @laurelprize
Instagram thelaurelprize

Established by Simon Armitage and in association with the Poetry School, this prize is awarded to the best collection of nature or environmental poetry that highlights the challenges and potential solutions to the climate crisis. The overall winner receive £5000, donated by Poet Laureate's Honorarium and is open to published poetry collections of over 40 pages written in English. Founded 2020.

Laxfield Literary Launch Prize

website https://laxfieldliterary.com/new-anglia-manuscript-prize/

Debut novel prize of any genre is open to all unpublished writers. Winners receive £500 and representation from Laxfield Literary Agency. There is no fee to enter and submissions open in early October and close in early December. See website for submission guidelines. Founded 2020.

The Lindisfarne Prize for Crime Fiction

email admin@darkskiespublishing.co.uk
website www.ljrossauthor.com/philanthropy/lindisfarne-prize
Publishing Director James Ross

A literary prize which recognises outstanding writing in the genre of crime or thriller fiction, sponsored by the author L.J. Ross through her publishing imprint, Dark Skies Publishing, and in association with the Newcastle Noir Crime Writing Festival and Newcastle Libraries. It is open to all writers who are from, or whose work celebrates, the North East of England and who have not previously had their submission published in any form (though they might have had other stories published before). Entrants must submit a short story of no more than 10,000 words or the first two chapters and a synopsis of their work in progress, to be considered.

The winning entry will be awarded a prize of £2,500 to support the completion of their work and funding towards a year's membership of industry associations. Entries are open from 31 October 2021 –28 February 2022 and the winner will be announced at a ceremony forming part of the Newcastle Noir Crime Writing Festival. For full terms and conditions, see the website.

Listowel Writers' Week Poetry Competitions

Listowel Writers' Week, 24 The Square, Listowel, Co. Kerry V31 RD93, Republic of Ireland
tel +353 (0)68 21074
email info@writersweek.ie
website www.writersweek.ie/competitions

Holds three poetry competitions (poetry book: €10,000; poetry single: €700; poetry collection: €2,500). Full details and submission guidelines are on the website. No entry form required. No entry fee. Not taking place in 2021. Founded 1971.

Little, Brown Award for Crime Fiction (University of East Anglia)

School of Literature, Drama and Creative Writing, University of East Anglia, Norwich Research Park, Norwich NR4 7TJ
email ldc.schooloffice@uea.ac.uk
website www.uea.ac.uk/literature/scholarships-and-funding/prizes

This prize of £3,000 is awarded annually for the best writer of crime fiction on the University of East Anglia MA in Creative Writing (Crime Fiction). The prize is open to all students enrolled on the MA in Crime Fiction in a given year and will be based on the material submitted by students for their final assignment of a full-length crime fiction manuscript.

The winner will be chosen by a panel of Little, Brown editors. For further information, contact the School of Literature, Drama and Creative Writing.

The London Magazine Short Story, Poetry and Essay Competitions

Flat 5, 11 Queen's Gate, London SW7 5EL
tel 020-7584 5977
website www.thelondonmagazine.org/category/tlm-competition
Twitter @TheLondonMag

A chance to be published in the UK's oldest literary magazine, established in 1732. Annual competitions held for poetry, essays and short stories. Dates announced online throughout the year. First prize: £500, second prize: £300, third prize: £200, plus publication in the magazine.

The London Hellenic Prize

The Hellenic Centre, 16–18 Paddington Street, London W1U 5AS
email msm@londonhellenicprize.org
website www.londonhellenicprize.cu
Twitter @LHellenicPrize

Established by the London Hellenic Society, the Prize is worth £10,000 and runs annually with a submission deadline of 31 January for books published in the preceding calendar year. It is awarded to authors of original works written in (or translated into) English and inspired by Greece or Greek exploits, culture or history at any time from the ancient past to the present day. Although the Prize will always strive to recognise works of excellence, any winner must be accessible to a broad readership. Founded 1996.

London Press Club Awards

c/o London & Partners, 6th Floor, 2 More Riverside, London SE1 2RR
tel 020-7520 9082
email info@londonpressclub.co.uk
website https://londonpressclub.co.uk/
Twitter @londonpressclub

The London Press Club is a membership organisation for journalists and other media professionals. It organises debates, Q&As and social events at exclusive venues across the capital, as well as the annual Press Ball. The London Press Club Awards take place each year, honouring categories which include: Daily Newspaper of the Year, Sunday Newspaper of the Year, Business Journalist of the Year, Scoop of the Year, Blog of the Year, Reviewer of the Year and Broadcast Journalist of the Year.

The Elizabeth Longford Prize for Historical Biography

The Society of Authors, 24 Bedford Row, London WC1R 4EH
tel 020-7373 6642

email prizes@societyofauthors.org
website www.societyofauthors.org/prizes/non-fiction/
Elizabeth-Longford
website www.elhb.uk
Twitter @Soc_of_Authors

A prize of £5,000 is awarded annually for an historical
biography published in the year preceding the prize
in memory of acclaimed biographer Elizabeth
Longford, and sponsored by Flora Fraser and Peter
Soros. No unsolicited submissions are accepted and
works in translation are not eligible. Founded 2003.

Longman-History Today Book Prize

History Today Ltd, 2nd Floor, 9/10 Staple Inn,
London WC1V 7QH
email admin@historytoday.com
website www.historytoday.com/longman-history-
today-awards

The Book of the Year Award is open to an author's
first or second book, written in English, on any aspect
of history, published between 1 October and 30
September. The winning book, which receives an
award of £2,000, will display innovative research and
interpretation and will have made its subject
accessible to the general reader. Publishers may
submit up to three entries each. The Historical
Picture Researcher of the Year Award is given to a
researcher who has done outstanding work to
enhance a text through the selection of creative,
imaginative and wide-ranging images. Founded 1997.

The Sir William Lyons Award

Argyll House, 1 River Road, Littlehampton,
West Sussex BN17 5BN
email generalsec@gomw.co.uk
website www.gomw.co.uk
Facebook www.facebook.com/gomwuk
Twitter @gomw_uk

Sponsored by Jaguar Cars in memory of Sir William
Lyons, founder and president of Jaguar Cars, this
annual award was set up to encourage young people
to foster interest in motoring and the motor industry
through automotive journalism. Open to any person
of British nationality resident in the UK aged 17–23
years at the closing date of 1 October. Full details are
available on the website.

McIlvanney Prize for the Scottish Crime Novel of the Year and The Bloody Scotland Debut of the Year

Bloody Scotland, c/o The Mitchell Library,
North Street, Glasgow G3 7DN
website https://bloodyscotland.com/mcilvanney-
prize-entry/
Twitter @BloodyScotland

For the purposes of both prizes, a crime book is
eligible if the author was born or raised in Scotland.
If the author was not born or raised in Scotland, a
book will still be deemed eligible if the author lives in
Scotland and has done so for at least six years, and
the book submitted for the award is substantially set
in Scotland. The winner of The McIlvanney Prize will
receive a cheque for £1,000 and a prize of £500 will be
awarded for the debut prize. See website for full
submission guidelines.

The McKitterick Prize

The Society of Authors, 24 Bedford Row,
London WC1R 4EH
tel 020-7373 6642
email prizes@societyofauthors.org
website www.societyofauthors.org/prizes/fiction/
mckitterick
Twitter @Soc_of_Authors

This annual award of £4,000 is open to first published
novels (excluding works for children) and
unpublished submissions by authors over the age of
40. The runner-up receives £1,250. Closing date: 31
October.

Bryan MacMahon Short Story Award

Listowel Writers' Week, 24 The Square, Listowel,
Co. Kerry V31 RD93, Republic of Ireland
tel +353 (0)68 21074
email info@writersweek.ie
website www.writersweek.ie
Facebook www.facebook.com/writersweek

An annual award for the best short story (up to 3,000
words) on any subject. Prize: €1,000. Entry fee: €10.
No entry form required, enter online. Listowel
Writers' Week is an acclaimed literary festival
devoted to bringing together writers and audiences at
unique and innovative events in the intimate and
historic surroundings of Listowel, County Kerry.
Founded 1971.

The Macmillan Prize for Illustration

Macmillan Children's Books, The Smithson,
6 Briset Street, London EC1M 5NR
email macmillanprize@macmillan.co.uk
website www.panmacmillan.com/macmillanprize

Three prizes are awarded annually for unpublished
children's book illustrations by art students in higher
education establishments in the UK. Prizes: 1st:
£1,000, 2nd: £500 and 3rd: £250. Founded 1985.

The Sarah Maguire Prize

Poetry Translation Centre, The Albany,
Douglas Way, Deptford SE8 4AG
tel 020-8692 4446
email info@poetrytranslation.org
website www.poetrytranslation.org/sarah-maguire-
prize

Biennial prize in the memory of Sarah Maguire
(1957–2017), the founder of the Poetry Translation
Centre and champion of international poetry.
Awarded to the best book of poetry from a living

poet from Africa, Asia, Latin America or the Middle East in English translation, published anywhere in the world. Winning poets and translators will divide a prize of £3,000. See website for entry criteria. Founded 2019.

The Manchester Prizes for Fiction and Poetry

The Manchester Writing School at Manchester Metropolitan University,
Arts & Humanities Building, Cavendish Street, Manchester, M15 6BG
tel 0161 247 1787
email writingschool@mmu.ac.uk
website www.mmu.ac.uk/writingcompetition/
Twitter @McrWritingSchl
Chair of Judges Nicholas Royle (fiction), Malika Booker (Poetry)

The Manchester Writing School, the home of creative writing within the Department of English at Manchester Metropolitan University, hosts this competition which was created by UK Poet Laureate (2009–19) Carol Ann Duffy and is designed to celebrate Manchester as an international city of writers, find diverse new voices, and create opportunities for writer development.

The Manchester Fiction Prize

Entrants are asked to submit a short story of up to 2,500 words. An award of £10,000 is made to the overall winner or winners. The competition currently opens for entries in spring each year with a September deadline and winners announced the following February.

The Manchester Poetry Prize

Entrants are asked to submit a portfolio of three to five poems totalling up to 120 lines. An award of £10,000 is made to the overall winner or winners. The competition currently opens for entries in spring each year with a September deadline and winners announced the following February.

The Michael Marks Awards for Poetry Pamphlets

tel (01539) 435544
email admin@michaelmarksawards.org
website www.michaelmarksawards.org
Facebook www.facebook.com/MichaelMarksAwards
Twitter @MarksAwards
Instagram MichaelMarksAwards

Inaugurated by the British Library and supported by the Michael Marks Charitable Trust (in partnership with the Wordsworth Trust, the *TLS* and Harvard University's Center for Hellenic Studies), the awards aim to raise the profile of poetry pamphlets and reward the enormous contribution that poets and their pamphlet publishers make to the poetry world in the UK. The awards include prizes for Poetry Pamphlet, Publisher, Illustration, and writing in a Celtic Language. They range from £1,000 to £5,000, and include a writer-in-residence cultural tour of Greece with the Harvard Center for Hellenic Studies. Founded 2009.

The Somerset Maugham Awards

The Society of Authors, 24 Bedford Row, London WC1R 4EH
tel 020-7373 6642
email prizes@societyofauthors.org
website www.societyofauthors.org/somerset-maugham
Twitter @Soc_of_Authors

These annual awards are for writers under the age of 30. Candidates must be a British national, or resident in Great Britain and Northern Ireland for three years prior to the date of submission for the award. Poetry, fiction, non-fiction, *belles lettres* or philosophy, but not dramatic works, are eligible. Entries should be of full-length and submitted by the publisher. Total prize money of £16,000 which should be used for foreign travel. Closing date: 30 November.

The Mogford Prize for Food and Drink Short Story Writing

36 St Giles, Oxford OX1 3LD
email steve@mogford.co.uk
website www.mogfordprize.co.uk
Facebook www.facebook.com/TheOxfordCollection1987
Twitter @theoxcollection
Contact Steve Holmes

A £10,000 annual award for a short story based, to a greater or lesser extent, on the theme of food and/or drink. The story can be any form of fiction – a romance, a mystery, an observation on life, a comedy, or any other theme. The Prize is open to all published or unpublished writers. Each year judging is conducted by Prize founder Jeremy Mogford as well as two different acclaimed literary authors or established food/cookery writers. In addition to the winning story, there are three runners-up. The winning story is published in small booklet form and distributed throughout The Oxford Collection's venues. For the 2022 prize, submissions open in November 2021 and close in early January 2022. See the website for full details. Founded 2013.

The Moth Art Prize

email mothartprize@themothmagazine.com
website www.themothmagazine.com

Awarded annually to an artist for a body of figurative or representational work (images of which can be sent electronically). Anyone over 16 can enter, and the winner receives €1,000 plus a two-week stay at The Moth Retreat in rural Ireland. There is a fee of €20 per portfolio. Closes 31 August 2021. For full entry details and guidelines, see the website.

The Moth Poetry Prize

email enquiries@themothmagazine.com
website www.themothmagazine.com

Awarded annually to four unpublished poems, chosen by a different judge each year. Prizes: 1st €6,000, with three runner-up prizes of €1,000. Anyone over 16 can enter. There is a fee of €15 per poem. All four poems appear in *The Moth* magazine. Closes 31 December. For full entry details and guidelines, see the website.

The Moth Short Story Prize

email enquiries@themothmagazine.com
website www.themothmagazine.com

Awarded annually to three unpublished stories, chosen by a different judge each year. Prizes: 1st €3,000; 2nd, a week-long retreat at Circle of Misse in France plus €250; 3rd €1,000. Anyone over 16 can enter. The word limit is 5,000 and there is a fee of €15 per story. All three stories appear in *The Moth* magazine. Closes 30 June. For full entry details and guidelines, see the website.

Michael Murphy Memorial Poetry Prize

email engassoc@leicester.ac.uk
website http://bit.ly/MurphyPoetryPrize

This biennial prize celebrates a distinctive first book of poetry in honour of the eponymous poet. The winner receives £1,000 and a review of their collection appears in a selection of the English Association's publications. See the website for more information and to enter.

The Mythopoeic Fantasy Award for Adult Literature

email awards@mythsoc.org
website www.mythsoc.org

Given to the fantasy novel, multi-volume novel or single-author story collection for adults published during the previous year that best exemplifies the spirit of the Inklings.

The Mythopoeic Awards are chosen from books nominated by individual members of the Mythopoeic Society and selected by a committee of Society members. Authors, publishers and their representatives may not nominate their own books for any of the awards, nor are books published by the Mythopoeic Press eligible for the awards. The Mythopoeic Society does not accept or review unsolicited manuscripts.

The Mythopoeic Scholarship Award in Inklings Studies

email awards@mythsoc.org
website www.mythsoc.org

Given to books on J.R.R. Tolkien, C.S. Lewis and/or Charles Williams that make significant contributions to Inklings scholarship.

The Mythopoeic Scholarship Award in Myth and Fantasy Studies

email awards@mythsoc.org
website www.mythsoc.org

Given to scholarly books on specific authors in the Inklings tradition, or to more general works on the genres of myth and fantasy.

National Poetry Competition

The Poetry Society, 22 Betterton Street, London WC2H 9BX
tel 020-7420 9880
email info@poetrysociety.org.uk
website https://poetrysociety.org.uk/competitions/national-poetry-competition/
Facebook www.facebook.com/thepoetrysociety
Twitter @PoetrySociety

One of the UK's major annual open poetry competitions. Accepts poems up to 40 lines long on any theme (previously unpublished and written in English). Judged by a panel of three leading poets. First prize: £5,000. For entry guidelines visit the website. Entry costs £7 for the first poem submitted and £4 for each subsequent poem in the same submission. Closing date: 31 October each year. Founded 1978.

New Angle Prize for East Anglian Literature

Ipswich Institute, Reading Room and Library, 15 Tavern Street, Ipswich IP1 3AA
tel (01473) 253992
email library@ipswichinstitute.org.uk
website www.ipswichinstitute.org.uk/NAP.html
Twitter @PrizeNewAngle
Prize Coordinator Jo Rook

A biennial award for a recently published book of literary merit, associated with or influenced by the UK region of East Anglia (defined here as Norfolk, Suffolk, north Essex, Cambridgeshire and the Fens).

The 2022 award will be open to works of fiction or poetry, first published between 1 January 2019 and 31 December 2021. Past winners include Mark Cocker (*Crow Country*), Jim Kelly (*Death Watch*), Jules Pretty (*This Luminous Coast*), Kate Worsley (*She Rises*) and Julia Blackburn (*Threads, the Delicate Life of John Craske*) and Anna Mackmin (*Devoured*). Current sponsors of the £2,000 single category first prize (£500 for runner-up) are Suffolk-based Gotelee Solicitors.

New Anglia Manuscript Prize

website https://laxfieldliterary.com/new-anglia-manuscript-prize/

Sponsored by the National Centre for Writing in Norwich, this debut novel prize is open to unpublished writers from Suffolk and Norfolk. There is no fee to enter and submissions open in early

October and close in early December. See website for submission guidelines. Founded 2020.

New Media Writing Prize

website http://newmediawritingprize.co.uk
Facebook www.facebook.com/newmediawritingprize
Twitter @NMWPrize

The prize showcases exciting and inventive stories that integrate a variety of formats, platforms and digital media. Encourages and promotes the best in new media writing and seeks to lead the way toward the future of the 'written' word and storytelling. The NMWP has attracted entries from the very best and most innovative writers in the field. There are five prizes: The if:book UK New Media Writing Prize, the Unicorn Student Award, the Dot Award, and the Future Journalism Award and the Skylab Innovation Award. Founded 2010.

The New Poets Prize

The Poetry Business, Campo House, 54 Campo Lane, Sheffield S1 2EG
tel 0114 346 3037
email office@poetrybusiness.co.uk
website www.poetrybusiness.co.uk
Directors Peter Sansom, Ann Sansom

A pamphlet competition for writers between the ages of 17 and 24. Entrants are invited to submit short poetry collections of 12 pages. Four outstanding collections will be selected to receive a year of support from The Poetry Business: a publisher and writer development agency with a strong reputation for discovering, developing and publishing outstanding new poets. All four New Poets Prize winners will also have their winning collection published under The New Poets List, our imprint dedicated to discovering, mentoring, and publishing young and emerging poets. Poets, writing in English, from anywhere in the world are eligible. Entry £8. A number of free entries are available for those who cannot afford the entry fee to the New Poets Prize (see website for full details). Entries can be submitted by post (with a cheque and completed entry form) or online via the website.

New Welsh Writing Awards

PO Box/Blwch Post 170, Aberystwyth, Ceredigion SY23 1WZ
tel 01970 628410
website https://newwelshreview.com/awards

The awards include the Rheidol Prize for Prose with a Welsh Theme or Setting. This recognises the best writing in short form (5,000–30,000 words) with the winner receiving £1,000 cash as an advance against e-publication, a critique by a leading literary agent and a year-long subscription to New Welsh Review. Entries cost £12 with some free entries available for low income writers. See website for further details. Founded 2015.

New Zealand Book Awards for Children and Young Adults

c/o NZ Book Awards Trust, Te Wharepōuri Street, Wellington 6023, New Zealand
tel +64 (0)27 773 9855
email childrensawards@nzbookawards.org.nz
website www.nzbookawards.nz/new-zealand-book-awards-for-children-and-young-adults

Annual awards to celebrate excellence in, and provide recognition for, the best children's books published in New Zealand. Awards are presented in six categories: Picture Book, Junior Fiction (the Wright Family Foundation Esther Glen Award), Young Adult Fiction, Non-Fiction (the Elsie Locke Award), Illustration (the Russell Clark Award) and te reo Māori (the Wright Family Foundation Te Kura Pounamu Award). Each of these awards carries prize money of $7,500. The overall prize, the Margaret Mahy Book of the Year award, carries a further prize of $7,500. A Best First Book prize of $2,000 is also awarded to a previously unpublished author or illustrator. Eligible books must have been published in New Zealand between April and March in the period preceding the awards' August ceremony date.

Nielsen Bestseller Awards in association with Coutts

c/o Agile Ideas, Studio 10, Glove Factory Studios, Brook Lane, Holt BA14 6RL
tel (01225) 302266
email hazel.kenyon@agile-ideas.com
website https://nielsenbestsellerawards.com
Twitter @BestsellerAwards

The Awards were originally launched in September 2001, and were presented to publishers and authors of books that achieved outstanding sales through the UK retail book trade. Any one title, in all its print editions, that had sold more than 500,000 copies (Gold) or 1,000,000 copies (Platinum) over a period of five consecutive years qualified.

In 2017, the Awards were re-launched with new criteria. Both print and ebook sales are counted and all sales from publication (or from when Nielsen BookScan UK TCM records began: 1998 for print books and January 2014 for ebooks) are included. In addition, a new Award has been added: Silver, for sales of over 250,000 copies in all editions over the same time period. The former Nielsen Book Gold and Platinum Awards are now called the Nielsen Bestseller Awards in association with Coutts. This is a continual award scheme but there is an annual review ceremony held every January when multiple awards are given out to various successful authors.

The Nobel Prize in Literature

website www.nobelprize.org/prizes/literature
Twitter @NobelPrize

One of the annual awards stipulated in the will of the Swedish scientist Alfred Nobel. No direct application for a prize will be taken into consideration.

The Observer/Jonathan Cape/Comica Graphic Short Story Prize

website www.theguardian.com/books/series/observer-graphic-short-story-prize

An annual graphic short story competition offering a £1,000 cash prize and the chance to see your story printed in the *Observer New Review*. £250 runner-up prize and the author's work will appear on theguardian.co.uk. Founded 2007.

Ockham New Zealand Book Awards

c/o Auckland Writers Festival, Suite 9A, 44–52 Wellesley Street West, Auckland 1010
tel +64 (0)9 376 8074
email awards@nzbookawards.org.nz
website www.nzbookawards.nz

Annual awards to celebrate excellence in, and provide recognition for, the best books published annually in New Zealand. Awards are presented in four categories: fiction, poetry, illustrated non-fiction and general non-fiction. The winner of the fiction category, the Jann Medlicott Acorn Prize for Fiction, wins more than $55,000. Winners of the other three categories each receive $10,000. Other awards include a Best First Book Award for each of the four categories, and Te Murau o te Tuhi, a special Māori Language Award presented at the judges' discretion. Eligible books must have been published in New Zealand in the calendar year preceding the awards ceremony date.

OCM Bocas Prize for Caribbean Literature

email info@bocaslitfest.com
website www.bocaslitfest.com
Twitter @bocaslitfest

An annual prize for literary books by Caribbean writers (writers must have been born in the Caribbean or hold Caribbean citizenship). Books published in the calendar year 2021 will be eligible for the 2022 prize. There are two deadline dates for entries: books published before November 2020 (which should be received by the prize administrators by mid-November) and books published between 1 November and 31 December 2021 (which should be received by the prize administrators by the first week of January 2022). Books are judged in three categories: poetry; fiction (including novels and short stories); and literary non-fiction (including books of essays, biography, autobiography, history, current affairs, travel and other genres which demonstrate literary qualities and use literary techniques, regardless of subject matter). Textbooks, technical books, coffee-table books, specialist publications and reference works are not eligible. There is an entry fee of US$35. The overall winner will receive an award of US$10,000. Prize guidelines and entry forms available via the website.

The Orwell Prizes

The Institute of Advanced Studies, University College London, Gower Street, London WC1E 6BT
tel 020-3108 1618
email books@theorwellprize.co.uk
website www.orwellfoundation.com
Contact Jeremy Wikeley

Awarded annually for books and journalism that come closest to George Orwell's ambition to 'make political writing into art'. Four prizes are awarded annually: the Orwell Prize for Political Fiction, the Orwell Prize for Political Writing, the Orwell Prize for Journalism and the Orwell Prize for Exposing Britain's Social Evils (sponsored by the Joseph Rowntree Foundation). Each prize is worth £3,000 to the winner; shortlists and longlists published on the website and widely publicised. Deadline for entry is December for Books, and early January for Journalism and Social Evils. Work with a British or Irish connection first published in the calendar year before the date of the prize is eligible; books must be first published in the UK or Ireland. Founded 1994.

Owned Voices Novel Award

website https://ownedvoices.com/novel-award
Facebook www.facebook.com/OwnedVoices
Twitter @OwnedVoices
Instagram ownedvoices

Rewarded to two writers who receive £250 plus one-to-one mentoring and feedback with an agent or editor on their novel. Writers must be from an under-represented background, be unagented and their novel must fall into one of the following categories: crime, thriller and mystery; contemporary romance; historical fiction; contemporary women's fiction; and cook club fiction. Entries open in December, with submission through the website. Founded 2020.

The PEN Ackerley Prize for Autobiography and Memoir

English PEN, 49–51 East Road, London N1 6AH
tel 020-7324 2535
email enquiries@englishpen.org
website www.englishpen.org/prizes/pen-ackerley-prize

An annual prize of £2,000 is given for an outstanding work of literary autobiography/memoir written in English and published during the previous year by an author of British nationality. No submissions: books are nominated by the judges only. Founded 1982.

The People's Book Prize

email thepeoplesbkpr@aol.com
website www.peoplesbookprize.com

Facebook www.facebook.com/pages/The-Peoples-Book-Prize/200637717319384
Twitter @PeoplesBkPrize
Founder and Prize Administrator Tatiana Wilson,
Patron Emeritus Frederick Forsyth CBE, *Founding Patron* Dame Beryl Bainbridge DBE

Awards are given in six categories: fiction, non-fiction, children's, first-time author (the Beryl Bainbridge First Time Author Award), TPBP Best Achievement Award and TPBP Best Publisher Award. Titles must be submitted by publishers, with a limit of three titles per category, per collection. Winners are announced at an awards ceremony in May at the Worshipful Company of Stationers and Newspaper Makers, Stationers' Hall, London.

The Samuel Pepys Award
Paul Gray, Haremoor House, Faringdon, Oxon SN7 8PN
tel 07802 301297
email plgray@btinternet.com
website www.pepys-club.org.uk

A biennial prize is given to a book published in English making the greatest contribution to the understanding of Samuel Pepys, his times, or his contemporaries. The winner receives £2,000 and the Robert Latham Medal. Closing date: 30 June 2023 (for publication between 1 July 2021 and 30 June 2023). Founded by the Samuel Pepys Award Trust in 2003 on the tercentenary of the death of Pepys.

The Plough Prize
The Plough Arts Centre, 9–11 Fore Street, Great Torrington, Devon EX38 8HQ
tel (01805) 622552
website www.theploughartscentre.org.uk/poetry-prize
Twitter @PloughArts

Poetry competition; poems should contain no more than 40 lines. There are three top prizes: 1st: £1,000, 2nd: £500, 3rd: £250. Visit website for full entry criteria, submission guidelines and a downloadable entry form.

Polari Book Prize
email paulburston@btinternet.com
website www.polarisalon.com
Facebook www.facebook.com/groups/36989183143
Twitter @polarisalon

Recognises emerging and established LGBTQ+ literary talent in two categories: the Polari Book Prize and the Polari First Book Prize. Any full length novel (Book Prize), debut novel (First Book Prize), novella, short story collection, memoir, book of poetry or published play text written in English by a writer born or based in the UK or Ireland is eligible. For the First Book Prize, Writers must explore LGBTQ+ themes and characters in the work submitted. For the Book Prize, writers must identify as LGBTQ+ or explore LGBTQ+ characters in the work submitted.

The winner of the First Book Prize receives £1,000 and the winner of the Book Prize receives £2,000. Full eligibility and submission guidelines can be found on the website.

The Portico Prize
Portico Library, 57 Mosley Street, Manchester M2 3HY
tel 0161 236 6785
email prize@theportico.org.uk
website www.theportico.org.uk
Facebook www.facebook.com/ThePorticoLibrary
Twitter @ThePortico
Instagram porticolibrary

This biennial prize is awarded for a published or self-published work of fiction, non-fiction or poetry which best evokes the spirit of the North of England. The winning prize is £10,000. There is a standard £50 fee per entry, with discounted fees available to non-profit publishers and self-published entries. Founded 1985.

The Press Awards
Society of Editors, University Centre, Granta Place, Cambridge CB2 1RU
tel (01223) 304080
email office@societyofeditors.org
website www.societyofeditors.org
Twitter @PressAwardsuk

Annual awards for British journalism judged by a number of influential judges as well as representatives from all the national newspaper groups.

V.S. Pritchett Short Story Prize
Royal Society of Literature, Somerset House, Strand, London WC2R 1LA
tel 020-7845 4679
email info@rsliterature.org
website www.rsliterature.org

An annual prize of £1,000 is awarded for a previously unpublished short story of between 2,000 and 4,000 words. Entry fee: £7.50 per story. Closing date for entries: June. See website for full details and submission guidelines. Founded 1999.

Queen Mary Wasafiri New Writing Prize
email wasafirinewwritingprize@qmul.ac.uk
website www.wasafiri.org/new-writing-prize

Awarded in three categories: fiction, life writing, and poetry and is open to anyone worldwide who has not published a complete book in the category they wish to enter. The three category winners will be published by *Wasafiri* magazine and receive a cash prize of £1,000 each. They will also be offered mentoring (depending on eligibility). The prize was launched to support new writers, with no limits on age, gender, nationality or background. See website for submission guidelines, terms and conditions and entry fees (some subsidised entry fees are available).

The Queen's Knickers Award

The Society of Authors, 24 Bedford Row,
London WC1R 4EH
tel 020-7373 6642
email prizes@societyofauthors.org
website www.societyofauthors.org/Prizes/Society-of-Authors-Awards/The-Queens-Knickers-Award
Twitter @Soc_of_Authors

An annual prize, generously funded by the author of *The Queen's Knickers*, Nicholas Allan, for outstanding children's illustrated books for ages 0–7. The prize recognises books that strike a quirky, new note, in any combination of words and/or pictures and in any physical format including pop-ups, flap books and board books. Submissions must be made by the print publisher. The winner receives £5,000 as well as a golden Queen's Knickers badge, and the runner-up receives £1,000 and a silvered badge. The prize will be shared between the author and illustrator if applicable. Closing Date: 30 November.

Republic of Consciousness Prize for Small Presses

email republicofconsciousness@gmail.com
website www.republicofconsciousness.com/prize

The Republic of Consciousness supports, promotes and celebrates small presses in the UK and Ireland. The Prize for Small Presses rewards the best fiction published by publishers with fewer than five full-time employees, yearly. In four years over £45,000 has been awarded to publishers and authors. Money is split between shortlistees, rather than focussed all on the winner. Winners: CB Editions for *Murmur* by Will Eaves and Galley Beggar Press for *Lucia* by Alex Pheby (2019); Fitzcarraldo Editions for *Animalia* by Jean-Baptiste Del Amo, translated by Frank Wynne (2020). Also runs a monthly small press book subscription service and a book club. Founded 2017.

The Rialto Nature and Place Poetry Competition

The Rialto, PO Box 309, Aylsham NR11 6LN
email info@therialto.co.uk
website www.therialto.co.uk/pages/nature-poetry-competition-2021

The Rialto, working in association with the RSPB, Birdlife International and the Cambridge Conservation Initiative invites poems that deal with any aspect of nature and place. First prize £1,000, second prize £500 and third prize £250. Additional prizes include a personal tour with Nick Davies, one of Britain's most celebrated nature writers. For full submission guidelines and to enter the competition, see the website.

Deborah Rogers Foundation Writers Award and David Miller Bursary

email info@deborahrogersfoundation.org
website www.deborahrogersfoundation.org/writers-award
website www.deborahrogersfoundation.org/bursary

Set up in memory of Deborah Rogers, a literary agent, who died in 2014. The Foundation aims to seek out and support emerging talent by means of two biennial awards: the Writers Award, which gives £10,000 to an unpublished author to enable them to complete a first book; and the DRF David Miller Bursary, which offers work placements in publishing houses worldwide together with £10,000 to help a young agent or publisher gain international work experience. For full submission guidelines, see the website.

The Romantic Novel of the Year Awards

website www.romanticnovelistsassociation.org
Awards Organiser Celia Anderson

The reader-judged awards, presented in early March, are: the Contemporary Romantic Novel of the Year and the Historical Romantic Novel of the Year (both sponsored by Goldsboro Books); the Debut Romantic Novel of the Year (sponsored by Katie Fforde); the Romantic Comedy Novel of the Year (sponsored by Simon and Schuster's Books and the City community); the Fantasy Romantic Novel of the Year; the Liberta Shorter Romantic Fiction Novel of the Year; the Romantic Saga of the Year; and the Jackie Collins Romantic Thriller of the Year. In addition, the RNA awards a Popular Romantic Fiction Prize sponsored by Sapere publishing for a book nominated and selected by booksellers, book bloggers and librarians, and an Outstanding Achievement Award for an individual nominated by RNA members for their exceptional contribution to romantic fiction.

Awards are open to both members and non-members of the RNA. Novels must be first published between 1 January and 31 December of the year of entry. There is an entry fee and entrants are required to provide a PDF and cover image for their novel. With later publications, where the PDF and cover are not yet available, an entry can still be made to hold the place. Print copies are no longer accepted. The entry form can be found on the website. The Joan Hessayon Award is only open to members of the Romantic Novelists' Association's New Writers' Scheme who submit a MS from January until the end of August. All will receive a critique. Any MSS subsequently accepted for publication become eligible for the Award.

RSL Christopher Bland Prize

Royal Society of Literature, Somerset House, Strand,
London WC2R 1LA
tel 020-7845 4679
email info@rsliterature.org
website www.rsliterature.org

This £10,000 prize encourages and celebrates older writers. First awarded in 2019, the prize is given annually to a debut novelist or popular non-fiction writer, first published at the age of 50 or over.

RSL Giles St Aubyn Awards for Non-Fiction

Royal Society of Literature, Somerset House, Strand, London WC2R 1LA
tel 020-7845 4679
email info@rsliterature.org
website www.rsliterature.org

Awards offering financial assistance to authors engaged in writing their first major commissioned works of non-fiction. The awards are open to UK and Irish writers and writers who have been resident in the UK for at least three years. These awards are made possible thanks to a generous bequest from author and RSL Fellow Giles St Aubyn.

RSL Ondaatje Prize

Royal Society of Literature, Somerset House, Strand, London WC2R 1LA
tel 020-7845 4679
email info@rsliterature.org
website www.rsliterature.org

This annual £10,000 prize, administered by the Royal Society of Literature and endowed by Sir Christopher Ondaatje, is awarded to a book of literary merit: fiction, poetry or non-fiction, best evoking the spirit of a place. The writer must be a citizen of the UK, Commonwealth, Republic of Ireland or have been a resident of the UK for three years. Books may be entered only by publishers based in the UK.

The Royal Society Young People's Book Prize

The Royal Society, 6–9 Carlton House Terrace, London SW1Y 5AG
tel 020-7451 2500
email sciencebooks@royalsociety.org
website https://royalsociety.org/grants-schemes-awards/book-prizes/young-peoples-book-prize/
Facebook www.facebook.com/theroyalsociety
Twitter @royalsociety

This prize is open to books for under-14s that have science as a substantial part of their content, narrative or theme. An expert adult panel choose the shortlist, but the winner is chosen by groups of young people in judging panels across the UK. The winning entry receives £10,000 and shortlisted entries receive £2,500. Entries open in December each year. Pure reference works including encyclopedias, educational textbooks and descriptive books are not eligible. The Prize is offered thanks to the generosity of an anonymous donor. Founded 1988.

RSPCA Young Photographer Awards

Brand Marketing and Content Department, RSPCA, Wilberforce Way, Southwater, Horsham, West Sussex RH13 9RS
email ypa@rspca.org.uk
website https://young.rspca.org.uk/ypa/home

Annual awards open to anyone aged 18 or under. The aim of the competition is to encourage young people's interest in photography and to show their appreciation and understanding of the animals around them. See website for a full list of categories and submission guidelines. Founded 1990.

RTÉ Radio, Drama On One, P.J. O'Connor Awards for Radio Drama

RTÉ Radio, Drama on One, Radio Centre, Donnybrook, Dublin 4, Republic of Ireland
email dramaonone@rte.ie
website www.rte.ie/dramaonone

For over 30 years the annual P.J. O'Connor Awards for Radio Drama have celebrated the best in new Irish writing. Candidates should submit radio plays of 40 minutes in duration. First prize: €5,000.

RTÉ Radio 1 Short Story Competition in Honour of Francis MacManus

RTÉ Radio 1 Short Story Competition, RTÉ Radio Centre, Donnybrook, Dublin 4, Republic of Ireland
website www.rte.ie/writing

An annual competition for short stories, open to writers who hold an Irish passport or are resident on the island of Ireland. Entries, in Irish or English, should not have been previously published or broadcast. Winning entries are broadcast on RTÉ Radio.

Rubery Book Award

PO Box 15821, Birmingham B31 9EA
email enquiries@ruberybookaward.com
website www.ruberybookaward.com

An annual award for published books on any subject, including children's books, with prizes totalling £2,000 (Book of the Year receives £1,500 and category winners £150 each). Books published by independent presses and self-published books are eligible. See website for entry fees and submission guidelines.

Runciman Award

email info@anglehellenicleague.org
website https://runcimanaward.org/

An annual award, given by the Anglo-Hellenic League, to promote Anglo-Greek understanding and friendship. The Anglo-Hellenic League has decided to make the next Runciman Award in 2021, to coincide with the celebrations of the bicentenary of the start of the Greek War of Independence. Founded 1986.

The Saltire Society Literary Awards

The Saltire Society, 9 Fountain Close, 22 High Street, Edinburgh EH1 1TF
tel 0131 556 1836
email saltire@saltiresociety.org.uk
website www.saltiresociety.org.uk
Twitter @saltire_society

Books published between 1 September and 31 July are eligible. The Scottish Book of the Year is an annual award selected from the Saltire Society Book Award categories – see categories listed below. The Saltire Society also celebrates the wider publishing landscape of Scotland with its Scottish Publisher of the Year Award (company) and Emerging Publisher of the Year Award (individual). Both of these recognise the work of publishers in creating and nurturing readership and writing in Scotland.

Scottish Book Cover of the Year

A new annual Award for book covers for any category of book, made by a designer working with Scottish based publishers.

Scottish First Book of the Year

Annual award open to any author who has not previously published a book. Authors from or living in Scotland or any book which deals with the work or life of a Scot or with a Scottish problem, event or situation are eligible.

Scottish Fiction Book of the Year

Annual award for all fiction by an author of Scottish descent or living in Scotland, or for any book which deals with the work or life of a Scot or with a Scottish problem, event or situation.

Scottish History Book of the Year

Annual award for a work of Scottish historical research from authors of Scottish descent or living in Scotland, or for any book which deals with the work or life of a Scot or with a Scottish problem, event or situation. Editions of texts are not eligible. Nominations are invited from professors of Scottish history and editors of historical reviews.

Scottish Non-Fiction Book of the Year

Annual award for non-fiction books such as biography, travel and political writing. Authors of Scottish descent or living in Scotland, or any book which deals with the work or life of a Scot or with a Scottish problem, event or situation are eligible.

Scottish Poetry Book of the Year

Annual award for a collection of new poetry from authors of Scottish descent or living in Scotland, or for any book which deals with the work or life of a Scot or with a Scottish problem, event or situation.

Scottish Research Book of the Year

Annual award for a book representing a significant body of research by authors of Scottish descent or living in Scotland, or for any book which deals with the work or life of a Scot or with a Scottish problem, event or situation. Research books must offer insight or dimension to the subject and add to the knowledge and understanding of Scotland and the Scots.

Walter Scott Prize for Historical Fiction

c/o StonehillSalt PR,
10 Brewery Park Business Centre, Haddington,
East Lothian EH41 3HA
tel (01620) 829800
email rebecca@stonehillsalt.co.uk
website www.walterscottprize.co.uk
Facebook www.facebook.com/walterscottprize
Twitter @waltscottprize
Administration, Publicity and Marketing Rebecca Salt

Founded by the Duke and Duchess of Buccleuch. Awarded annually, the Prize rewards fiction of exceptional quality which is set in the past (according to Walter Scott's subtitle for Waverley, at least sixty years ago). The Prize is among the richest UK fiction prizes; the winner receives £25,000, and shortlisted authors receive £1,500 each. The Prize is usually awarded at the Borders Book Festival in Melrose each June, with a longlist announced in February and a shortlist announced in March or April.

The rules governing submission are on the website. Books must be written in English and have been published in the UK, Eire or the Commonwealth during the previous calendar year. Books written in English by authors of British nationality first published outside the UK, Eire or the Commonwealth are also eligible provided they are also published in the UK in that calendar year. Authors who have already won the prize twice are precluded from submitting a new work until a period of seven years has elapsed since they last won the Prize. Books must be submitted by publishers, and self-published authors are not eligible. Founded 2009.

The Kim Scott Walwyn Prize

website https://kimscottwalwyn.org
Twitter @KSWPrize

The Prize honours the life and career of Kim Scott Walwyn (who was Publishing Director at Oxford University Press and who died in 2002), and celebrates exceptional women in publishing. The Prize is open to any woman who has worked in publishing in the UK for up to seven years and recognises the professional achievements and promise of women in the industry. Founded 2003.

Scottish Book of the Year – see The Saltire Society Literary Awards

Scottish First Book of the Year – see The Saltire Society Literary Awards

Scottish Research Book Award – see The Saltire Society Literary Awards

Segora International Writing Competitions

email simms.gordon@orange.fr
website www.poetryproseandplays.com
Organisers Gordon and Jocelyn Simms

The Competitions are held annually for poetry, short story, vignette (short prose) and one-act play. Deadline for all competitions 15th June each year. Full details available on the website.

The André Simon Memorial Fund Book Awards
1 Westbourne Gardens, Glasgow G12 9XE
tel 07801 310973
email katie@andresimon.co.uk
website www.andresimon.co.uk
Twitter @AndreSimonAward

Celebrating excellent new writing in the fields of food and drink. Two awards of £2,000 are given annually, one each for the best new books on food and on drink. There is also a Special Commendation of £1,500 in either category. All works first published in the calendar year of the award are eligible (publisher entry only). See website for entry guidelines and form. Founded 1978.

Wilbur Smith Adventure Writing Prize
The Wilbur & Niso Smith Foundation, Unit 9, 5–7 Wells Terrace, London N4 3JU
email submissions@wilbur-niso-smithfoundation.org
website www.wilbur-niso-smithfoundation.org
Facebook www.facebook.com/WNSmithFoundation
Twitter @Wilbur_Niso_Fdn

An international writing prize that supports and celebrates today's best adventure writing. The Prize is open to writers of any nationality, writing in English. Awards are presented for fiction in three categories: Best Published Novel (prize: £10,000); Best Unpublished Manuscript (prize: a publishing deal with Bonnier Books UK) and Author of Tomorrow (prizes: £150–£1,000 depending on age category, plus book tokens and digital publication). The Author of Tomorrow award seeks to find the adventure writers of the future and is open to young people across the world (in age categories 16–21 years, 12–15 years and age 11 and under) who have completed a short piece of adventure writing in English. Submission guidelines, eligibility criteria, entry fees, shortlist dates and details of the previous winners for each category can be found on the website.

The Jill Smythies Award
The Linnean Society of London, Burlington House, Piccadilly, London W1J 0BF
tel 020-7434 4479
email nominations@linnean.org
website www.linnean.org

A prize of £1,000 for a botanical artist for outstanding illustrations. Established in honour of Jill Smythies whose career as a botanical artist was cut short by an accident to her right hand. The rubric states that 'the Award, to be made by Council usually annually consisting of a silver medal and a purse … is for published illustrations, such as drawings and paintings, in aid of plant identification, with the emphasis on botanical accuracy and the accurate portrayal of diagnostic characteristics. Illustrations of cultivars of garden origin are not eligible.' Closing date for nominations: 30 November. Founded 1988.

The Stephen Spender Prize
PO Box 1618, Oxford OX4 9LW
email charlotte@stephen-spender.org
website www.stephen-spender.org/spender_prize.html

Annual competition for poetry in translation, with categories for young people (14 and under, 16 and under, and 18 and under) as well as an open category for adults. Translate into English any poem from any language. Overall winner will win a £1,000 cash prize. All entrants must be UK or Irish citizens or residents, or pupils at a British School overseas. Founded 2004.

The Telegraph Sports Book Awards
c/o Agile Ideas Ltd, Studio 10, Glove Factory Studios, Brook Lane, Holt BA14 6RL
tel (01225) 302266
email danielle@sportsbookawards.com
website https://sportsbookawards.com
Twitter @sportsbookawards

The Awards is the major annual promotion for sports writing and publishing. The awards exist to highlight the most outstanding sports books of the previous calendar year, to showcase their merits and to enhance their reputation and profile. The campaign and event are sponsored by *The Telegraph* and winners are announced at an annual awards ceremony in May/June at Lord's Cricket Ground. There are over ten categories to reflect every sport and genre sub-category in sports writing, including sports health and fitness and children's sports writing. See website for full details.

Staunch Book Prize
email info@staunchbookprize.com
website www.staunchbookprize.com
Facebook www.facebook.com/StaunchBookPrize
Twitter @StaunchBkPrize

Launched to draw attention to the prevalence of violence towards women in fiction, the prize is awarded to the author of a novel in the thriller genre in which no woman is beaten, stalked, sexually exploited, raped or murdered. Any genre of thriller is welcome – crime, mystery, science fiction, cyber, comedy, psychological, spy, suspense, political, disaster, etc – but no horror or fantasy. The prize is open to published, self-published and unpublished thrillers that fulfil all the criteria. The winner receives £1,000. Entry is £20 and submission should include the first 5,000 words plus a one page synopsis. Open to entries February to July. For full details of rules and submission guidelines, see the website. The inaugural prize in 2018 was won by Jock Serong for *On The Java Ridge*. The 2020 winner was *Heaven, My Home* by Attica Locke. Founded 2018.

The Sunday Times Audible Short Story Award

c/o Books Department, *The Sunday Times*,
The News Building, 1 London Bridge Street,
London SE1 1GF
email shortstoryaward@sunday-times.co.uk
website www.shortstoryaward.co.uk

The richest prize for a single short story in the English language, worth £30,000 to the winner. The award, for a story of 6,000 words or less, is open to writers from anywhere in the world, as long as they have had at least one work of creative writing published in the UK or Ireland. A unique feature of the award since 2019 is that Audible produces an exclusive audiobook anthology of the shortlisted stories, which will dramatically broaden the audience for the short story, and allow the award's stories to be enjoyed in a brand new way. Shortlisted authors will receive an extra £1,000 fee, on top of a prize payment of £1,000, for being included in the anthology. For full details of the prize and eligibility, see the website.

Winners and shortlistees of the prize, which is international in reach and rewards stories of outstanding literary merit, have included some of the world's great writers, including Pulitzer Prize-winners Junot Díaz, Anthony Doerr and Adam Johnson, alongside a proud track record of discovering writers at the very start of their literary careers. Other alumni include Kevin Barry, Sally Rooney, Emma Donoghue, Mark Haddon, Sarah Hall, Bret Anthony Johnston, Yiyun Li, Hilary Mantel, Ali Smith, C.K. Stead, Elizabeth Strout, Jonathan Tel, David Vann and Gerard Woodward. The 2020 winner was Niamh Campbell. Founded 2010.

The Sunday Times/University of Warwick Young Writer of the Year Award

email pjohnson@societyofauthors.org
website www.youngwriteraward.com
Facebook www.facebook.com/YoungWriterAward
Twitter @YoungWriterYear

A prize of £5,000 is awarded for a full-length published or self-published (in book or ebook format) work of fiction, non-fiction or poetry, by a British or Irish author aged 18–35. Runners-up receive £500 each. The winning book will be a work of outstanding literary merit. For submission information, see the website.

Swansea University Dylan Thomas Prize

tel (01792) 606245
email DTPrize@swansea.ac.uk
website www.swansea.ac.uk/dylan-thomas-prize

The £20,000 Swansea University Dylan Thomas Prize is awarded to the best published literary work in the English language, written by an author aged 39 or under. Launched in 2006.

The James Tait Black Memorial Prizes

English Literature, School of Literatures,
Languages and Cultures,
The University of Edinburgh, c/o Room 4.12,
David Hume Tower, George Square,
Edinburgh EH8 9JX
tel 0131 650 3619
email s.strathdee@ed.ac.uk
website www.ed.ac.uk/events/james-tait-black
Contact Sheila Strathdee. For the James Tait Black Prize for Drama, contact Nicola McCartney at jtbdrama@ed.ac.uk.

The James Tait Black Fiction and Biography Prizes

English Literature, c/o Room 2.24, School of Literatures, Languages, and Cultures, The University of Edinburgh, 50 George Square, Edinburgh EH8 9LH (for submissions for the Fiction prize)
English Literature, c/o Room 3.07, School of Literatures, Languages, and Cultures, The University of Edinburgh, 50 George Square, Edinburgh EH8 9LH (for submissions for the Biography prize)
website www.ed.ac.uk/events/james-tait-black

Two prizes of £10,000 are awarded annually: one for the best biography or work of that nature, the other for the best work of fiction, published during the calendar year 1 January to 31 December. The adjudicators are lecturers in English Literature at the University of Edinburgh, with the assistance of teams of postgraduate readers. Eligible works of fiction and biographies are those written in English and first published in the year of the award. Eligible works must be available for purchase in the UK. Works in translation will be considered. Both prizes may go to the same author, but neither to the same author a second time.

Publishers should submit three copies of any appropriate biography, or work of fiction, as early as possible with a note of the date of publication, marked 'James Tait Black Prize'. Closing date for submissions: 1 December. Founded 1918.

The James Tait Black Prize for Drama: University of Edinburgh in association with Playwright Studio Scotland

A prize of £10,000 for a professionally produced play which displays an original voice in theatre and one that has made a significant and unique contribution to the art form. The prize is open to any new work originally written in English, Scots or Gaelic, by playwrights from any country at any stage in their career. The judges will be students and staff of the University's School of Literatures, Languages and Cultures and representatives from the wider European theatre industry.

Plays must be formally commissioned and have had a full professional production. Eligible plays will have been produced between 1 January and 31 December in the year preceding the year of the award, and run for a minimum of six performances. A typed copy of the script and a digital copy must be sent with details of the first production, which should include venue, company and date, and proof of production if possible. The submissions must come from the producing company or the agent of the playwright, and should be submitted with the submission form to the Department of English Literature by the date specified on the website. Applications which do not have the submission form complete will be considered ineligible. For full criteria visit the website.

Reginald Taylor and Lord Fletcher Essay Competition

British Archaeological Association, 18 Stanley Road, Oxford OX4 1QZ
email jsmcneill@btinternet.com
Honorary Secretary John McNeill

A prize of a medal and £500 is awarded biennially for the best unpublished essay of high scholarly standard, which shows original research on a subject of archaeological, art-historical or antiquarian interest within the period from the Roman era to AD1830. The successful competitor will be invited to read the essay before the Association and the essay may be published in the Association's journal. Competitors should notify the Honorary Editor in advance of the intended subject of their work. Next award: Spring 2022. The essay should be submitted not later than 1 November 2021 to the Hon. Editor, Dr Tom Nickson, Courtauld Institute of Art, Vernon Square, Penton Rise, London WC1X 9EW. Founded in memory of E. Reginald Taylor FSA and Lord Fletcher FSA.

The Royal Society Science Book Prize

The Royal Society, 6–9 Carlton House Terrace, London SW1Y 5AG
tel 020-7451 2500
email sciencebooks@royalsociety.org
website https://royalsociety.org/awards/science-books/
Facebook www.facebook.com/theroyalsociety
Twitter @royalsociety

Sponsored by Insight Investment, this prestigious prize is open to authors of science books written for a non-specialist audience. The winner will receive £25,000 and each shortlisted author will receive £2,500. Eligible books should be written in English and their first publication in the UK must have been between 1 July and 30 September the following year.

Publishers may submit any number of books for the Prize. Entries may cover any aspect of science and technology but educational textbooks published for professional or specialist audiences are not eligible. Nominations open early in the calendar year and the winner is announced in the autumn. Founded 1988.

The Times/Chicken House Children's Fiction Competition

Chicken House, 2 Palmer Street, Frome, Somerset BA11 1DS
tel (01373) 454488
email competitions@chickenhousebooks.com
website www.chickenhousebooks.com
Twitter @chickenhsebooks
Contact Kesia Lupo

This annual competition is open to unpublished writers of a full-length children's novel (age 7–18). Entrants must be over 18 and novels must not exceed 80,000 words in length. The winner will be announced in *The Times* and will receive a worldwide publishing contract with Chicken House with a royalty advance of £10,000. The winner is selected by a panel of judges which includes children's authors, journalists, publishers, librarians and other key figures from the world of children's literature. For competition opening and closing dates, please consult the Chicken House website.

The Tinniswood Award

Society of Authors, 24 Bedford Row, London WC1R 4EH
email info@societyofauthors.org
website www.societyofauthors.org/prizes/audio-drama/the-tinniswood-award

Presented annually for the best original audio drama script of the year. The Society of Authors perpetuate the memory of radio and TV comedy scriptwriter, Peter Tinniswood, through the Award, which aims to celebrate and encourage high standards in radio drama. Prize: £3,000. Submissions will be accepted from any party (producer, broadcasting organisation, writer, agent, etc). For entry guidelines and details of the application procedure, see the website.

Tir na n-Og Awards

Books Council of Wales, Castell Brychan, Aberystwyth, Ceredigion SY23 2JB
tel (01970) 624151
email wbc.children@books.wales
website https://llyfrau.cymru/en/gwobrau/tir-na-nog
Facebook www.facebook.com/LlyfrDaFabBooks
Twitter @LlyfrDaFabBooks

Established with the intention of promoting and raising the standard of children's and young people's books in Wales. Three awards are presented annually by the Welsh Books Council and are sponsored by the Chartered Institute of Library and Information Professionals Cymru/Wales:

• The best English-language book of the year with an authentic Welsh background. Fiction and factual books originally in English are eligible; translations from Welsh or any other language are not eligible. Prize: £1,000.
• The best original Welsh-language book aimed at the primary school sector. Prize: £1,000.
• The best original Welsh-language book aimed at the secondary school sector. Prize: £1,000. Founded 1976.

The Paul Torday Memorial Prize

The Society of Authors, 24 Bedford Row,
London WC1R 4EH
tel 020-7373 6642
email prizes@societyofauthors.org
website www.societyofauthors.org/prizes/authors-awards/fiction/the-paul-torday-prize
Twitter @Soc_of_Authors

A prize for debut novelists aged 60 or over, set up in honour of Paul Torday, who published his first novel *Salmon Fishing in the Yemen* aged 60. The winner receives £1,000 and a set of Paul Torday's collected works. Runners-up receive one specially selected Paul Torday novel with a commemorative book plate. Closing date: 30 November.

The Translation Prizes

The Society of Authors, 24 Bedford Row,
London WC1R 4EH
tel 020-7373 6642
email prizes@societyofauthors.org
website www.societyofauthors.org/prizes/translation-prizes
Twitter @Soc_of_Authors

The Society of Authors offers a number of prizes for published translations into English from Arabic, Dutch, French, German, Hebrew, Italian, Spanish and Swedish. The Society also administers the TA First Translation Prize, which is an annual prize of £2,000 for debut literary translation from any language published in the UK. See website for entry guidelines and deadlines.

The Betty Trask Prize and Awards

The Society of Authors, 24 Bedford Row,
London WC1R 4EH
tel 020-7373 6642
email prizes@societyofauthors.org
website www.societyofauthors.org/betty-trask
Twitter @Soc_of_Authors

An annual prize for first novels (published or unpublished), of a traditional or romantic nature, by authors who must be under the age of 35, a resident in Great Britain and Northern Ireland or the Commonwealth for three years prior to the date of submission for the award, or a British national, and writing in English. Total prize money from £25,000. Closing date: 30 November.

The V&A Illustration Awards

Victoria & Albert Museum, London SW7 2RL
email villa@vam.ac.uk
website www.vam.ac.uk/info/va-illustration-awards

These annual awards are open to illustrators living or publishing in the UK and students who have attended a course in the UK over the last two years. Awards are made in the following categories: book illustration, book cover design, illustrated journalism and student illustrator. Founded 1972.

Ver Poets Open Competition

181 Sandridge Road, St Albans, Herts. AL1 4AH
tel (01727) 762601
email gillknibbs@yahoo.co.uk
website www.verpoets.co.uk
Competition Secretary Gill Knibbs

A competition open to all for poems of up to 30 lines of any genre or subject matter, which must be an unpublished work in English. Prizes: 1st: £600, 2nd: £300, 3rd: £100. Send two copies of each poem with no name or address; either put address on separate sheet or send sae or email for entry form. Closing date: 30 April. Entry fee: £4 per poem, three poems for £10 (£3 per poem thereafter). Anthology of winning and selected poems with Adjudicator's Report usually available from mid-June, free to those included.

The Wainwright Prize

c/o Agile Ideas, Studio 10, Glove Factory Studios,
Brook Lane, Holt BA14 6RL
email alastair@agile-ideas.com
website https://wainwrightprize.com
Twitter @wainwrightprize

In association with the National Trust, this prize seeks to reward the best writing on the outdoors, nature and UK-based travel writing. The prize is awarded to the work which best reflects Wainwright's core values of Great British writing and culture and a celebration of the outdoors. See website for submission guidelines and key dates. In 2020 an additional prize, the Global Conservation Prize, was created under the Wainwright Prize umbrella to reflect the increased interest in conservation and climate change issues in nature writing. A £5,000 prize fund will be shared between the two awards.

Wales Book of the Year Award

Glyn Jones Centre, Wales Millennium Centre,
Bute Place, Cardiff CF10 5AL
tel 029-2047 2266
email post@literaturewales.org
website www.literaturewales.org/our-projects/wales-book-year
Facebook www.facebook.com/LlenCymruLitWales
Twitter @litwales
Literature Wales Chief Executive Lleucu Siencyn

Wales Book of the Year, administered by Literature Wales, is an annual award which is presented to the best Welsh and English-language works first published in the year preceding the ceremony in the fields of creative writing and literary criticism in four categories: Poetry, Fiction, Creative Non-fiction and Children and Young People. Annual highlights include the shortlist announcement in May and the awards ceremony in June. Previous winners include Robert Minhinnick, Owen Sheers, Rhian Edwards, Patrick McGuinness, Thomas Morris and Alys Conran.

The Warwick Prize for Women in Translation
email womenintranslation@warwick.ac.uk
website https://warwick.ac.uk/fac/cross_fac/
womenintranslation
Coordinators Chantal Wright and Holly Langstaff

Awarded annually to the best eligible work of fiction, poetry, literary non-fiction, work of fiction for children or young adults, graphic novel, or play text, written by a woman, translated into English by a translator (or translators) of any gender, and published by a UK or Irish publisher. The £1,000 prize is divided between the writer and her translator/s. Founded 2017.

Wellcome Book Prize
email bookprize@wellcome.ac.uk
website https://wellcomebookprize.org
Twitter @wellcomebkprize

Celebrates the best of medicine in literature by awarding £30,000 each year for the finest fiction or non-fiction book that engages with some aspect of medicine, health or fitness. This prize aims to stimulate interest, excitement and debate about medicine and literature, reaching audiences not normally engaged with medical science. At the time of going to press the prize is on pause while the team plans for its future. See the website for the latest information. Founded 2009.

The White Review Short Story Prize
email prizes@thewhitereview.org
website www.thewhitereview.org/prize/
Twitter @TheWhiteReview

An annual short story competition for emerging writers, established with support from a Jerwood Charitable Foundation Small Grant in 2013. The prize awards £2,500 to the best piece of short fiction by a writer resident in the UK or Ireland who has yet to secure a publishing deal. For submission and eligibility guidelines and entry terms and conditions, see the website.

The Whitfield Prize
Administrative Secretary, Royal Historical Society, University College London, Gower Street, London WC1E 6BT
tel 020-7387 7532
email adminsecretary@royalhistsoc.org
website https://royalhistsoc.org/prizes/whitfield-book-prize/

The Prize of £1,000 is awarded for the best work on a subject within a field of British or Irish history. It must be its author's first solely written history book, an original and scholarly work of historical research and published in English. For full information on how to enter and for eligibility guidelines, see the website.

Wildlife Photographer of the Year
The Natural History Museum, Cromwell Road, London SW7 5BD
website www.nhm.ac.uk/visit/wpy/competition.html

This annual award is given to the photographer whose individual image is judged to be the most striking and memorable. There is an adult competition for photographers aged 18 or over and a young competition for photographers aged 17 or under. See website for submission guidelines.

Winchester Poetry Prize
c/o 41 Nuns Road, Winchester, Hampshire SO23 7EF
email hello@winchesterpoetryfestival.org
website www.winchesterpoetryfestival.org/prize

An annual prize awarded for poetry of up to 40 lines (1st £1,000, 2nd £500, 3rd £250). Entries should be in English, typed and never before published. Entry fee: £5 for first poem, £4 for subsequent poems. An anthology of longlisted entries is published annually. Enter online or by post. Closing date: 31 July each year. Judge for the 2021 prize is Jacqueline Saphra. Founded 2016.

Wingate Literary Prize
email admin@wingate.org.uk
website www.wingatefoundation.org.uk/
literary_prize.php
Twitter @Wingateprize

Celebrating its 44th anniversary in 2021, an annual prize of £4,000 is awarded, in association with JW3, for a work of fiction or non-fiction which best translates the idea of Jewishness to the general reader. Founded 1977.

The Wolfson History Prize
email wolfsonhistoryprize@wolfson.org.uk
website www.wolfsonhistoryprize.org.uk
Twitter @wolfsonhistory

Awarded annually to promote and recognise outstanding history written for a general audience, the Wolfson History Prize is the most valuable non-fiction writing prize in the UK. Books are judged on the extent to which they are carefully researched, well-written and accessible to the non-specialist reader. Books must be published in the UK in the calendar year preceding the year of the award. The subject matter of the book may cover any aspect of history, including historical biography. The author must be normally resident in the UK during the year of publication and not be a previous winner of the Prize. Previously shortlisted authors are eligible. The winning author will receive a prize of £40,000. The five remaining shortlisted authors will be awarded a prize of £4,000 each. All submissions must come via the publisher. Full details on the process are available online. Founded 1972.

Women Poets' Prize at the Rebecca Swift Foundation

email info@rebeccaswiftfoundation.org
website www.rebeccaswiftfoundation.org/women-poets-prize/

Biennial award given to three women poets who write about the empowerment of women. The Prize is free to enter and the winners will each receive a bursary of £1,000 plus poetry mentorship and pastoral coaching. Founded 2018.

Women's Prize for Fiction

email submissions@womensprizeforfiction.co.uk
website www.womensprizeforfiction.co.uk

The Prize celebrates excellence, originality and accessibility in writing by women in English from throughout the world. It is the UK's most prestigious annual book award for fiction written by a woman and also provides a range of educational, literacy and research initiatives to support aspiring or emerging writers and readers.

The Women's Prize for Fiction is awarded annually for the best full novel of the year written by a woman and published in the UK. Any woman writing in English – whatever her nationality, country of residence, age or subject matter – is eligible, submitted by a publisher. The winner receives £30,000 and a limited edition bronze figurine known as a Bessie, created and donated by the artist Grizel Niven.

World Illustration Awards

Association of Illustrators, Somerset House, Strand, London WC2R 1LA
tel 020-7759 1010
email awards@theaoi.com
website www.theaoi.com/world-illustration-awards
Facebook www.facebook.com/theaoi
Twitter @theaoi
Instagram WorldIllustrationAwards

Presented in partnership with the *Directory of Illustration*, the awards programme sets out to celebrate contemporary illustration across the globe. A panel of international judges create a 500 strong longlist and shortlists 200 projects, which are celebrated in an online showcase, a printed catalogue and with an online industry events programme. For submission guidelines, categories and prizes, see the website.

Writers' & Artists' Yearbook 2022 Short Story Competition

website www.writersandartists.co.uk/competitions

See information panel on page vi of this edition or visit our website for details.

YouWriteOn.com Book Awards

tel 07948 392634
email edward@youwriteon.com
website www.youwriteon.com

Arts Council-funded site publishing awards for new fiction writers. Random House and Orion, the publishers of authors such as Dan Brown and Terry Pratchett, provide free professional critiques for the highest rated new writers' opening chapters and short stories on YouWriteOn.com each month. The highest rated writers of the year are then published, three in each of the adult and children's categories, through YouWriteOn's free paperback publishing service for writers. The novel publishing awards total £1,000. Writers can enter at any time throughout the year: closing date is 31 December each year. Join YouWriteOn.com to participate. Previous YouWriteOn.com winners have been published by mainstream publishers such as Random House, Orion, Penguin and Hodder, including Channel 4 TV Book Club winner and bestseller *The Legacy* by Katherine Webb. Founded 2005.

Zooker Award

Arkbound, Backfields House, Upper York Street, Bristol BS2 8QJ
email editorial@arkbound.com
website http://arkbound.com/zooker-award/

The Award aims to encourage first-time authors from disadvantaged backgrounds and to reward works of social value; principally those that touch upon the themes of environmental sustainability and social inclusion, encouraging positive changes in behaviour or attitude for readers. Submitted work must have been published (not self-published) in the last two years. Entry fee £4.50. The prize is £500 and in the event that there is insufficient sponsorship or entry fees, the Award will be carried over to the next year. For full details, visit the website.

GRANTS, BURSARIES AND FELLOWSHIPS

Arts Council England

tel 0161 934 4317
email enquiries@artscouncil.org.uk
website www.artscouncil.org.uk
Facebook www.facebook.com/artscouncilofengland
Twitter @ace_national

Arts Council England is the national development agency for the arts in England, providing funding for a range of arts and cultural activities. Through its funding schemes organisations, artists, events and initiatives can receive funding and help achieve the Council's mission of providing art and culture for everyone. Visit the website for information on funding support and advice, an online funding finder and funding FAQs.

The Arts Council/An Chomhairle Ealaíon

70 Merrion Square, Dublin D02 NY52, Republic of Ireland

tel +353 (0)1 618 0200
website www.artscouncil.ie/home
Facebook www.facebook.com/artscouncilireland
Twitter @artscouncil_ie

Outlines all of its funding opportunities for individuals, groups and organisations on website. Also publishes regular information on grants and awards, news and events, and arts policy.

The Authors' Contingency Fund

Grants Department, The Society of Authors, 24 Bedford Row, London WC1R 4EH
tel 020-7373 6642
email grants@societyofauthors.org
website www.societyofauthors.org

This fund makes modest grants to established, published authors who find themselves in sudden financial difficulty. Apply for guidelines and application form.

The Authors' Foundation

The Society of Authors, 24 Bedford Row, London WC1R 4EH
tel 020-7373 6642
email funding@societyofauthors.org
website www.societyofauthors.org/grants/grants-for-works-in-progress
Twitter @Soc_of_Authors

The Authors' Foundation provides grants to writers to assist them while writing books. There are two rounds of grants each year (check website for deadlines). The Authors' Foundation provides funding (in addition to a proper advance) for research, travel or other necessary expenditure.

Open to applications from authors commissioned by a commercial British publisher to write a full-length work of fiction, poetry or non-fiction, or those without a publishing contract, who have had one previous book published commercially and where there is a strong likelihood that a further book will be published in the UK. Closing dates for applications are 1 September and 1 February. Download application guidelines from the website or send an sae for an information sheet; apply by email. Founded 1984.

Carole Blake Open Doors Project

Blake Friedmann Literary Agency, Ground Floor, 15 Highbury Place, London N5 1QP
email sian@blakefriedmann.co.uk
website http://blakefriedmann.co.uk/carole-blake-open-doors-project
Twitter @BFLAgency

The Carole Blake Open Doors Project is a programme specifically aimed at encouraging candidates from a diverse range of backgrounds to enter the publishing industry. The programme offers ten days of work shadowing to a selected applicant over a two-week period, including funding for travel and up to twelve nights' accommodation in London. The programme runs twice a year, includes close mentorship with Blake Friedmann agents, the opportunity to attend meetings with editors and clients and the chance to be involved in the day-to-day life of a literary agent. For full details of candidate specifications, how to apply and terms and conditions, see the website.

The K. Blundell Trust

The Society of Authors, 24 Bedford Row, London WC1R 4EH
tel 020-7373 6642
email funding@societyofauthors.org
website www.societyofauthors.org/grants/grants-for-works-in-progress
Twitter @Soc_of_Authors

Grants are given to published writers under the age of 40 to assist them with their next book. This work must 'contribute to the greater understanding of existing social and economic organisation' and may be fiction or non-fiction. Closing dates for applications are 1 September and 1 February. Please visit the Society of Authors' website to download application guidelines or send sae for an information sheet; apply by email.

Alfred Bradley Bursary Award

website www.bbc.co.uk/writersroom/about/successes/alfred-bradley-award
Facebook www.facebook.com/BBCWriters
Twitter @bbcwritersroom

This biennial development opportunity is awarded to a writer or writers resident in the North of England. This scheme allows the winning writer to devote a period of time to writing and to develop an idea for a Radio 4 drama commission. Founded 1992.

Creative Scotland

tel 0330 333 2000
email enquiries@creativescotland.com
website www.creativescotland.com/funding
Twitter @CreativeScots

The public body that supports the arts, screen and creative industries across all parts of Scotland on behalf of everyone who lives, works or visits there. Through distributing funding from the Scottish Government and the National Lottery, Creative Scotland enables people and organisations to work in and experience the arts, screen and creative industries in Scotland by helping others to develop great ideas and bring them to life. Creative Scotland supports writers and publishers based in Scotland through a range of funds and initiatives.

The Julia Darling Travel Fellowship

email office@newwritingnorth.com
website http://newwritingnorth/projects/the-julia-darling-travel-fellowship/

website www.juliadarling.co.uk
Facebook www.facebook.com/newwritingnorth
Twitter @NewWritingNorth

New Writing North, in conjunction with the family and friends of the late writer, Julia Darling, have established a travel fellowship for creative writers in her name. Julia's work covered a variety of forms, from plays and novels to poetry and performance. The fellowship is to be used to fund travel and accommodation both in the UK and internationally. It will also support group applications from writers who would like to undertake joint residential retreats.

Open to novelists, poets and playwrights over the age of 18 who live and work in the North of England and who have at least one professionally produced or published work to their name. Entry is by online submission only. See the website for full details.

E.M. Forster Award
American Academy of Arts and Letters,
633 West 155th Street, NY 10032, USA
tel +1 212-368-5900
email academy@artsandletters.org
website www.artsandletters.org/award

The distinguished English author, E.M. Forster, bequeathed the American publication rights and royalties of his posthumous novel *Maurice* to Christopher Isherwood, who transferred them to the American Academy of Arts and Letters, for the establishment of an E.M. Forster Award, currently $20,000, to be given annually to a British or Irish writer for a stay in the USA. Applications for this award are not accepted.

The Eric Gregory Awards
The Society of Authors, 24 Bedford Row,
London WC1R 4EH
tel 020-7373 6642
email prizes@societyofauthors.org
website www.societyofauthors.org/eric-gregory
Twitter @Soc_of_Authors

These awards are for poets under the age of 30, made annually for the encouragement of young poets who can show that they are likely to benefit from an opportunity to devote more time to writing. Candidates must be a British National, resident in Great Britain and Northern Ireland or the Commonwealth for three years prior to the date of submission. Submissions must be in English. Candidates must be under the age of 30 on 31 March in the year of the Award (i.e. the year following submission). The work submitted may be a published or unpublished volume of poetry, drama-poems or *belles lettres*, and no more than 30 poems should be submitted. Closing date: 31 October.

Hawthornden Fellowships
The Administrator, International Retreat for Writers,
Hawthornden Castle, Lasswade,
Midlothian EH18 1EG

tel 0131 440 2180
email office@hawthornden.org

Applications are invited from novelists, poets, dramatists and other creative writers whose work has already been published. The Retreat provides four-week fellowships in a peaceful setting. Application forms are available from January for Fellowships awarded in the following year. Deadline for applications 30 June.

Francis Head Bequest
Grants Department, Society of Authors,
24 Bedford Row, London WC1R 4EH
tel 020-7373 6642
email grants@societyofauthors.org
website www.societyofauthors.org

This fund provides grants to published British authors over the age of 35 who need financial help during a period of illness, disablement or temporary financial crisis. Apply for guidelines and application form.

The P.D. James Memorial Fund
Society of Authors, 24 Bedford Row,
London WC1R 4EH
email funding@societyofauthors.org
website www.societyofauthors.org/grants/P-D-James-memorial-fund

This fund offers regular payments to a small number of Society of Authors members who find themselves in financial hardship. Awards are given by committee to long-term members who are either aged 60 or over or who are completely incapacitated for work. The fund currently distributes £2,200 per annum to each recipient. For more information, see the website.

Jerwood Compton Poetry Fellowships
email info@jerwoodarts.org
website www.jerwoodarts.org
Twitter @Jerwoodarts

Funded by Jerwood Arts and Arts Council England, the Jerwood Compton Poetry Fellowships offer a significant development opportunity for poets. Running between 2017 and 2022 and supporting a total of nine artists, successful artists will receive £15,000 to support their Fellowship, during which time they will be matched with a mentor and given access to a range of advisers to support their work. For further details, see the website. The opportunity is selected through a nomination process.

Leverhulme Research Fellowships
The Leverhulme Trust, 1 Pemberton Row,
London EC4A 3BG
tel 020-7042 9888
email grants@leverhulme.ac.uk
website www.leverhulme.ac.uk/research-fellowships
Twitter @LeverhulmeTrust

The Leverhulme Trust Board offer annually approximately 120 fellowships to experienced researchers in aid of original research. These awards are not available as replacement for past support from other sources. Applications in all subject areas are considered, with the exception of clinical medical or pharmaceutical research. Applications must be completed online by early November 2021 for 2022 awards. Refer to the website for further details. Founded 1933.

The John Masefield Memorial Trust

Grants Department, The Society of Authors,
24 Bedford Row, London WC1R 4EH
tel 020-7373 6642
email grants@societyofauthors.org
website www.societyofauthors.org

This trust makes occasional grants to professional poets who find themselves with sudden financial problems. Apply for guidelines and application form.

Northern Writers' Awards

email awards@newwritingnorth.com
website http://northernwritersawards.com/
Facebook www.facebook.com/newwritingnorth
Twitter @NewWritingNorth

Established by New Writing North, the Northern Writers' Awards support work-in-progress by new, emerging and established writers across the North of England. The Awards support writers creatively as they develop their work through publication, as well as helping them to progress professionally and to navigate their way through the publishing industry. Founded 2000.

The Peggy Ramsay Foundation

7 Savoy Court, London WC2R 0EX
email prf@harbottle.com
website www.peggyramsayfoundation.org

Grants are made to writers of stage plays in accordance with the criteria on the Foundation's website. Awards are made at intervals during each year. A total of approx. £200,000 is expended annually. Founded 1992.

The Royal Literary Fund

3 Johnson's Court, off Fleet Street,
London EC4A 3EA
tel 020-7353 7150
website www.rlf.org.uk
Facebook www.facebook.com/rlfwriters
Twitter @rlfwriters

The RLF is a charity for writers in financial difficulties. It does not offer grants to writers who can earn their living in other ways, nor does it provide financial support for writing projects, but it helps authors who are in financial difficulties due to personal or professional setbacks. Applicants must have published several works of approved literary merit. Applicants are requested to send copies of their books with their completed application forms. Founded 1790.

TLC/Arts Council England Free Reads Scheme

East Side, Kings Cross Station, London N1C 4AX
tel 020-7324 2563
email info@literaryconsultancy.co.uk
website www.literaryconsultancy.co.uk/editorial/ace-free-reads-scheme
Director Aki Schilz

In 2001, TLC received funding from Arts Council England to enable the provision of bursaried manuscript assessments for writers from low-income households. The scheme is known as the Free Reads Scheme and offers access to TLC's core services to writers who might not be able to afford them. Free Reads are selected by a range of literature development bodies from across the UK, and there are currently seventeen organisations benefitting from the scheme. For detailed submission guidelines and eligibility information, see the website.

The Travelling Scholarships

The Society of Authors, 24 Bedford Row,
London WC1R 4EH
tel 020-7373 6642
email prizes@societyofauthors.org
website www.societyofauthors.org/prizes/fiction/travelling-scholarships
Twitter @Soc_of_Authors

These honorary awards were established by an anonymous benefactor to enable British creative writers to keep in touch with their colleagues abroad. Founded 1944.

David T.K. Wong Fellowship

School of Literature, Drama and Creative Writing, University of East Anglia, Norwich NR4 7TJ
tel (01603) 592272
email davidtkwongfellowship@uea.ac.uk
website www.uea.ac.uk/literature/fellowships

The David T.K. Wong Fellowship is an annual award of £26,000 to enable a fiction writer who wants to write in English about the East and Southeast Asia to spend a year in the UK, at the University of East Anglia in Norwich. The Fellowship is named after its sponsor David T.K. Wong, a retired Hong Kong businessman, who has also been a teacher, journalist and senior civil servant, and is a writer of short stories. The Fellowship will be awarded to a writer planning to produce a work of prose fiction in English which deals seriously with some aspect of life in East and Southeast Asia (Brunei, Cambodia, Hong Kong, Indonesia, Japan, Korea, Laos, Macau, Malaysia, Mongolia, Myanmar, People's Republic of China, Philippines, Singapore, Taiwan, Thailand and Vietnam). The 2020/21 Fellow is Che Yeun.

Opportunities for
under-represented writers

There has been an acknowledgement across the publishing industry that many voices have not found it easy to be heard and promoted amongst the many hundreds and thousands of books published every year. Publishers, agents, authors and prize-awarding organisations have started to actively encourage and nurture a more diverse range of writers who have new stories to tell. There has been an increase in open submissions, prizes, bursaries and other schemes in 2020–21 aimed at previously less represented groups. Some of the more established awards have full entries in this *Yearbook* (as indicated below) and some of the newer ones are listed in full here.

PRIZES AND AWARDS

Comic Creators' Prize

website www.thoughtbubblefestival.com/comiccreatorprize
Twitter @ThoughtBubbleUK

Organised by Jonathan Cape, in partnership with Thought Bubble Festival and BLM Leeds. An initiative for Black creatives for long-form projects, such as a graphic novel, or a selection of unfinished projects or proposals. Winners receive editorial feedback.

Creative Future Writers' Award

See page 564

FAB Prize for Undiscovered Talent

See page 567

Fresh Ink Award

page 568

Jhalak Prize

See page 571

Joffe Books Prize for Crime Fiction Writers of Colour

email prize@joffebooks.com
website www.joffebooks.com/prize

In conjunction with writer Dorothy Koomson and literary agent Susan Yearwood, this prize, launched in 2021, is for crime fiction writers of colour. The winner will recieve a two-book deal contract with Joffe Books and submissions are open until 30 September 2021. See website for full submission details.

Killing It: The Killer Reads Competition for Undiscovered Writers

See page 572

#Merky Books New Writers' Prize

email merkybooks@penguinrandomhouse.co.uk
website www/penguin.co.uk/campaigns/merky-new-writers-prize.html
Twitter @MerkyBooks
Instagram MerkyBooks

A prize for unpublished and unagented writers of fiction, non-fiction or poetry.

The Nature Writing Prize for Working Class Writers

email workingclassnatureprize@gmail.com

For writers who self-idetify as working class, this prize includes editorial feedback from Gaia Books, a stay with National Trust Holidays worth £500 along with a nature writing commission based on it, publication in the *Countryman* magazine, and a selection of Little Toller Books. *Founded* 2020.

Owned Voices Novel Award

See page 578

Polari Book Prize

See page 579

RSL Christopher Bland Prize

See page 580

Mo Siewcharran Prize

email mosiewcharranprize@hachette.co.uk
website www.littlebrown.co.uk/landing-page/the-mosiewcharran-prize-2021
Twitter @MoPrize

The initiative aims to nuture talent from Black, Asian and Marginalised ethnic backgrounds writing in English. Run by Hachette UK's Changing the Story diversity and inclusivity initiative, the winner will receive £2,500 prize money plus the offer of a publishing deal, subject to contract, with Little, Brown and Abacus. The prize is for a full-length, unpublished novel for adults of any literary fiction genre which is compelling, unique and relatable. See website for full submission guidelines. *Founded* 2019.

Sky Arts RSL Writers Awards

The Royal Scoiety of Literature, Somerset House, Strand, London WC2R 1LA
tel 020-7845 4678
email martha.stenhouse@rsliterature.org
website https://rsliterature.org/awards/sky-arts-rsl-writers-awards/
Twitter @RSLiterature

Launched in 2021, five awards will be given to British writers of colour who are at the beginning of their careers. The categories are: non-fiction, fiction, screenwriting, poetry, and playwriting. Each winner will receive a year's worth of mentoring sessions from a RSL Fellow writing in their form, plus additional mentoring from Bernardine Evaristo.

Writers & Artists Working-Class Writers' Prize

Bloomsbury Publishing plc, 50 Bedford Square, London WC18 3DB
tel 020-7631 5985
email waybcompetitions@bloomsbury.com
website HYPERLINK www.writersandartists.co.uk/competitions

Open to unpublished writers who consider themselves to be from a working-class background. The winner will receive one year's writing mentoring, plus £200, one year's free subscription to The Society of Authors, free admission to any one-day Writers & Artists' Yearbook or Children's Writers' & Artists' Yearbook. See website for full submission guidelines and application process.

EVENTS, BURSARIES AND OTHER SCHEMES

BookTrust Represents

See page 548

Creative Access

See page 517

Carole Blake Open Doors Project

See page 589

Curtis Brown Creative

website www.curtisbrowncreative.co.uk/the-breakthrough-writers-programme
email cbccourses@curtisbrown.co.uk

CBC runs the Breakthrough Writers' programme, providing programmes, mentoring and scholarships for under-represented writers. See page 693.

Elevate Mentoring Scheme

2 Green Barton, Swyre, Dorchester, Dorest DT2 9DN
tel (01308) 897374

email helen@cornerstones.co.uk
website https://cornerstones.co.uk/elevate-mentoring-scheme/

An Arts Council funded scheme that pairs low-income and/or under-represented writers with specialist editors best suited to help them develop their craft.

Emerging Writers Programme

tel 020-7766 4765
email email emergingwriters@londonlibrary.co.uk
website www.londonlibrary.co.uk/emerging-writers

Open to all writers above the age of 16, writers, in all genres, receive one year's free membership of The London Library, plus writing development masterclasses, literary networking opportunities and peer support. The Virago Participation Bursary (funded by Virago Books) is awarded to black female and black non-binary writers to assist with any financial issues that might prevent them from accessing the full Programme.

Future Bookshelf

website www.thefuturebookshelf.co.uk
Twitter @FutureBookshelf

Part of Hachette UK's Changing the Story programme, this free creative writing resource is for under-represented writers, providing tips and exercies on writing a book and inspiring content from authors, agents and experienced editors.

Inscribe

website www.peepaltreepress.com/inscribe
Twitter @INSCRIBEwriters

Supporting writers of colour in England to professionally advance their creative work and their careers through coaching, mentoring, workshops, residentials, training, newsletters, publications and general advice.

Megaphone Writer Development Scheme

email megaphone.write@gmail.com
website https://megaphonewrite.com/
Twitter @MegaphoneWrite

An Arts Council England funded project which offers a year of one-to-one mentoring and masterclasses for writers of colour based in England who are wrtiting a novel for children or teenagers.

TLC/Arts Council England Free Reads Scheme

See page 591

Working Class Writers Festival

Twitter @ClassFestival
Instagram @classfestival
Artistic Director Natasha Carthew

Takes place *21–24 October 2021*

Run as part of Bristol's Festival of Ideas, it aims to give exposure to working-class writers and make the event physically and financially available to all audiences, regardless of income.

Writers & Artists

Bloomsbury Publishing plc, 50 Bedford Square, London WC1B 3DP
tel 020-7631 5985
email AccessWA@bloomsbury.com
website www.writersandartists.co.uk/accessible-to-all
website www.writersandartists.co.uk/bursary-opportunities

Bursary places worth a combined total £4,000 are available to help ensure that everything W&A offers – events, writing courses and editing services – is accessible to all. See the website for more details and eligibility.

WriteNow Programme

WriteNow - The Penguin Random House Group, 20 Vauxhall Bridge Road, London SW1V 2SA
email writenow@penguinrandomhouse.co.uk
website www.penguin.co.uk/company/creative-responsibility/writenow.html
Twitter @PenguinUKBooks

A programme by PRH which aims to nurture and publish new, unpublished writers from under-represeneted communities. Its workshops provide the aspiring writer with tools, contacts, information and access to getting published.

OPEN SUBMISSIONS

Hashtag BLAK

See page 156

Lantana Publishing

see page 197

One More Chapter

See page 155

Out-Spoken Press

Unit 39, Containerville, 1 Emma Street, London E2 9FP
email press@outspokenldn.com
website www.outspokenldn.com/about
Twitter @outspoken_press
Instagram @out_spoken_press
Editors Anthony Anaxagorou
Publishing Coordinator Patricia Ferguson

An independent publisher of poetry and critical writing. Established by poet and editor Anthony Anaxagorou to provide a platform for compelling writing from voices under-represented in mainstream publishing. *Founded* 2015.

Peepal Tree Press

See page 175

Prize winners

This is a selection of high-profile literary prize winners from 2020–21 presented chronologically. Some awards have been postponed due to the coronavirus lockdowns, please see individual awards websites for details. Entries for many of these prizes are included in the *Yearbook*, starting on page 556.

May 2020

International Booker Prize
The Discomfort of Evening by Marieke Lucas Rijneveld, translated by Michele Hutchison

International Dylan Thomas Prize
Lot by Bryan Washington

Jhalak Prize
Afropean by Johny Pitts

June

The CILIP Carnegie Medal
Lark by Anthony McGowan

The CILIP Kate Greenaway Medal
Tales from the Inner City by Shaun Tan

Walter Scott Prize for Historical Fiction
The Narrow Land by Christine Dwyer Hickey

Women's Prize for Fiction
Hamnet by Maggie O'Farrell

July

Commonwealth Writers' Short Story Award
The Great Indian Tee and Snakes by Kritika Pande

August

James Tait Black Memorial Prizes
Ducks, Newburyport by Lucy Ellmann (Fiction); *The Photographer at Sixteen: The Death and Life of a Fighter* by George Szirtes (Biography); *J'Ouvert* by Yasmin Joseph (Drama)

October

BBC National Short Story Award
The Grotesques by Sarah Hall

BBC Young Writers' Award
The Changeling by Lottie Mills

The Booker Prize
Shuggie Bain by Douglas Stuart

The Bridport Prize
Low Tide by Michael Lavers (Poetry); *Mum Died* by Rowena Warwick (Flash Fiction); *Oh, Hululu* by Deborah Waters (Short Story); *Helen and the Fires* by Joseph Piersen (The Peggy Chapman-Andrews Award for a First Novel)

Crime Writers' Association Gold Dagger Award
Good Girl, Bad Girl by Michael Robotham

Forward Prizes for Poetry
Vertigo & Ghost by Caroline Bird (Best Poetry Collection); *RENDANG* by Will Harris (Best First Collection); *The Little Miracles* by Malika Booker (Best Single Poem)

Nobel Prize for Literature
Louise Glück

November

The Baillie Gifford Prize for Non-fiction
One, Two, Three, Four: The Beatles in Time by Craig Brown

National Book Awards (USA)
Interior Chinatown by Charles Yu (Fiction); *The Dead are Arising: The Life of Malcolm X* by Tamara Payne and Les Payne (Non-fiction); *King and the Dragonflies* by Kacen Callender (Young People's Literature); *DMZ Colony* by Don Mee Choi (Poetry); *Tokyo Ueno Station* by Yu Miri, translated by Morgan Giles

Waterstones Book of the Year
Hamnet by Maggie O'Farrell

January 2021

T.S. Eliot Prize for Poetry
How to Wash a Heart by Bhanu Kapil

Costa Book of the Year
The Mermaid of Black Conch by Monique Roffey (Novel and Overall Winner); *Love After Love* by Ingrid Persaud (First Novel); *The Louder I Will Sing* by Lee Lawrence; *Flèche* by Mary Jean Chan (Poetry); *Voyage of the Sparrowhawk* by Natasha Farrant (Children's Book)

Bookbug Picture Book Award
This is a Dog by Ross Collins

March

Blue Peter Book Awards
A Kind of Spark by Elle McNicoll (Best Story); *A Day in the Life of a Poo, a Gnu and You* by Mike Barfield (Best Book with Facts)

Rathbones Folio Prize
The Dream House: A Memoir by Carmen Maria Machado

Festivals and conferences for writers, artists and readers

There are hundreds of arts festivals and conferences held in the UK each year – too many to mention in this *Yearbook*. We list a selection of literature, writing and general arts festivals which include literature events. Space constraints and the nature of an annual publication together determine that only brief details are given; contact festival organisers for a full programme of events.

⚠ Events may not go ahead in their usual way due to coronavirus restrictions. Please check websites for details.

Aldeburgh Poetry Festival
website www.poetryinaldeburgh.org
Facebook www.facebook.com/AldeburghPoetry
Twitter @poetryaldeburgh
Takes place November

A volunteer-led annual festival of contemporary poetry with a relaxed weekend feel. Founded 1989.

Appledore Book Festival
Festival Office, Docton Court Gallery,
2 Myrtle Street, Appledore, Bideford,
Devon EX39 1PH
email director@appledorebookfestival.co.uk
website www.appledorebookfestival.co.uk
Facebook www.facebook.com/appledorebookfestival
Twitter @AppledoreBkFest
Instagram appledorebookfestiva
Festival Director Ann Juby
Takes place 16–25 September 2021

Founded by children's author Nick Arnold, this annual festival aims to increase enjoyment of reading and encourages creative writing through providing access to inspirational events. Includes a schools programme and public events for all ages. Founded 2006.

Asia House Bagri Literature Festival
Asia House, 63 New Cavendish Street,
London W1G 7LP
tel 020-7307 5454
email arts@asiahouse.co.uk
website www.asiahousearts.co.uk
Twitter @asiahousearts
Takes place September and October

The only festival in the UK dedicated to pan-Asian literature. Content covers writing from Turkey to Tokyo as well as exploring the Asian diaspora experience. Speakers have included literary heavyweights such as Jung Chang, Hanif Kureishi and Elif Shafak, and speakers that appeal to a millennial crowd such as Insta-Poet Nikita Gill, comedian Nish Kumar and online satirist Karl reMarks. Founded 2006.

Aspects Irish Literature Festival
email arts@ardsandnorthdown.gov.uk
website www.aspectsfestival.com
Twitter @aspectsfestival

An annual celebration of contemporary Irish writing with novelists, poets and playwrights. Includes readings, children's events and exhibitions.

Aye Write! Glasgow's Book Festival
Glasgow Life, Commonwealth House,
38 Albion Street, Glasgow G1 1LH
email ayewrite@glasgowlife.org.uk
Takes place May

Brings together the best undiscovered local talent with a wealth of established writers from the city, and nationwide. A free children's festival runs in tandem with the main festival. Creative writing workshops and masterclasses are on offer at the Festival. Founded 2005.

Baillie Gifford Borders Book Festival
Harmony House, St Mary's Road, Melrose TD6 9LJ
tel (01896) 822644
email info@bordersbookfestival.org
website www.bordersbookfestival.org
Facebook www.facebook.com/bordersbookfestival
Twitter @BordersBookFest
Instagram bordersbookfest
Takes place September 2021

An annual festival with a programme of events featuring high-profile and bestselling writers, including a Family Festival programme. Winner of the Walter Scott Prize for Historical Fiction is announced during the festival. Founded 2004.

The Bath Festival
The Bath Festival, 9–10 Bath Street, Bath BA1 1SN
tel (01225) 614180 , Box Office (01225) 463362
email info@bathfestivals.org.uk
website https://bathfestivals.org.uk/the-bath-festival
Twitter @TheBathFestival
Takes place May

An annual festival with leading guest writers. Includes readings, debates, discussions, workshops and events.

Birmingham Literature Festival
Studio 130, Zellig, Gibb Street, Birmingham B9 4AT
tel 0121 246 2770
email programming@writingwestmidlands.org
website www.birminghamliteraturefestival.org
Twitter @BhamLitFest
Programmes Director Antonia Beck
Takes place October

The annual Birmingham Literature Festival is firmly established in the cultural calendar as the region's brightest literary event. It gathers household names and rising stars to celebrate the power of words. The Festival has a varied, ambitious programme that has won a loyal and growing audience over the years. A project of Writing West Midlands.

Bloody Scotland Festival
email info@bloodyscotland.com
website www.bloodyscotland.com
Twitter @BloodyScotland
Takes place September

Based in Stirling, Bloody Scotland has brought hundreds of crime writers, both new and established, to the stage. The Bloody Scotland Festival strives to put on entertaining as well as informative events during a weekend in September, covering a range of criminal subjects from fictional forensics, psychological thrillers, tartan noir, cosy crime and many more. With an international focus at the heart of Bloody Scotland, crime writing talent from outside of Scotland is always welcome. Founded 2012.

Bread and Roses
c/o Five Leaves Bookshop, 14A Long Row, Nottingham NG1 2DH
email bookshop@fiveleaves.co.uk
website www.fiveleavesbookshop.co.uk

An annual weekend of radical politics, music and literature held at various venues in Nottingham. The only book festival supported by trade unions.

Brighton Festival
Church Street, Brighton BN1 1UE
tel (01273) 700747
email info@brightonfestival.org
website www.brightonfestival.org
Facebook www.facebook.com/brightonfestival
Twitter @brightfest
Takes place May

An annual arts festival with an extensive national and international programme featuring theatre, dance, music, opera, literature, outdoor and family events.

Buxton International Festival
3 The Square, Buxton, Derbyshire SK17 6AZ
tel (01298) 70395
email info@buxtonfestival.co.uk
website https://buxtonfestival.co.uk
Takes place July

The renowned opera and music programme is complemented by a Books Series, featuring distinguished authors largely but not exclusively in the sphere of history, biography, music and politics. The festival includes 'Perspectives' – a series of debates in partnership with the British Academy.

Cambridge Literary Festival
209 Wellington House, East Road, Cambridge CB1 1BH
tel (01223) 515335
email hello@cambridgeliteraryfestival.com
website https://cambridgeliteraryfestival.com
Facebook www.facebook.com/CamLitFest
Twitter @camlitfest
Takes place April and November

From poetry to politics, fiction to finance, history to hip-hop and comedy to current affairs, Cambridge Literary Festival brings an eclectic mix of today's best writers, thinkers and speakers to Cambridge all year round. Founded 2003.

Canterbury Festival
Festival House, 8 Orange Street, Canterbury, Kent CT1 2JA
tel (01227) 452853
email info@canterburyfestival.co.uk
website https://canterburyfestival.co.uk
Takes place 16–30 October 2021

Kent's international arts festival, one of the most important cultural events in the South East. The Festival showcases performing arts from around the world and runs year-round projects to inspire creativity in people of all ages. It commissions new work, champions emerging talent and supports those seeking careers in the cultural industries.

Capital Crime Festival
61–65 Great Queen Street, Holborn, London WC2B 5DA
email info@capitalcrime.org
website www.capitalcrime.org
Twitter @CapitalCrime1
Takes place October

One of the world's largest celebrations of crime and thriller fiction featuring leading crime and thriller creatives. It welcomes some of the world's favourite authors and filmmakers to London and brings the best of everything crime and thriller-related to fans in a packed two-day schedule of entertaining and thought-provoking events. Founded 2019.

Charleston Festival
The Charleston Trust, Charleston, Firle, Lewes, East Sussex BN8 6LL
email info@charleston.org.uk
website www.charleston.org.uk/festival
Twitter @CharlestonTrust
Takes place 19–22 May 2022

Charleston, country home of Bloomsbury artists Duncan Grant and Vanessa Bell, hosts an annual literary festival involving writers, performers, politicians and thinkers – both high profile and up and coming, national and international.

The Times and The Sunday Times Cheltenham Literature Festival

109–111 Bath Road, Cheltenham, Glos. GL53 7LS
tel (01242) 511211
email boxoffice@cheltenhamfestivals.com
website www.cheltenhamfestivals.com/literature
Facebook www.facebook.com/cheltenhamfestivals
Twitter @cheltlitfest
Takes place 8–17 October 2021

The annual festival is one of the oldest literary events in the world and is one of the largest of its kind in Europe. Events include debates, talks and lectures, poetry readings, novelists in conversation, exhibitions, discussions, workshops and a Lit Crawl. The festival has both an adult and family programme, with events for toddlers to teenagers. Founded 1949.

Cliveden Literary Festival

tel 020-3488 3401
email info@clivedenliteraryfestival.org
website https://clivedenliteraryfestival.org
Facebook www.facebook.com/clivedenlitfest
Twitter @clivedenlitfest
Takes place 23–24 October 2021

Set in Cliveden, the magnificent English country house with a unique and extraordinary history of politics and intrigue, the Cliveden Literary Festival aims to evoke the spirit of the great writers and potentates who have stayed there and to continue the tradition of the house as a sanctuary for literature lovers. Since 1666 the house has been known for its literary salon, helping to inspire writers from Alexander Pope and George Bernard Shaw, Jonathan Swift and Lord Tennyson to Sir Winston Churchill. Various events, key speakers and panel discussions.

Cork International Short Story Festival and Poetry Festival

Frank O'Connor House, 84 Douglas Street, Cork T12 X802, Republic of Ireland
tel +353 (0)21 4312955
email info@munsterlit.ie
website www.munsterlit.ie
website www.corkshortstory.net
website www.corkpoetryfest.net
Twitter @MunLitCentre
Takes place September (Short Story Festival), March (Poetry Festival)

Run by the Munster Literature Centre, these festivals include readings, workshops, seminars and public interviews involving some of the world's best writers and poets. Founded 2000.

CrimeFest

email info@crimefest.com
website www.crimefest.com
Facebook www.facebook.com/crimefest.bristol
Twitter @CrimeFest
Takes place May

An annual, Bristol-based convention for people who like to read an occasional crime novel as well as for die-hard fanatics. Drawing top crime novelists, readers, editors, publishers and reviewers from around the world, it gives all delegates the opportunity to celebrate the genre in a friendly, informal and inclusive atmosphere. The CrimeFest programme consists of interviews with its featured and highlighted guest authors; over 60 events with more than 150 participating authors; and a gala awards dinner.

Cúirt International Festival of Literature

Galway Arts Centre, 47 Dominick Street, Galway H91 X0AP, Republic of Ireland
tel +353 (0)91 565886
email info@cuirt.ie
website www.cuirt.ie
Twitter @CuirtFestival
Takes place 21–25 April

One of Europe's oldest book festivals, and a leading voice for literature both internationally and across Ireland. The festival began as a celebration of poetry and has since grown to a week-long celebration of all forms of writing.

Cúirt bring readers and writers together to tell stories, share new perspectives, and to celebrate writing, books and reading in all forms. Through our festival every April and our year-round programme of engagement, we nurture a community of readers interested in the world, creating a space for conversation, debate and reflection. The name Cúirtis is Irish, drawing on Ireland's history of bardic poetry and oral storytelling. Founded 1985.

Dalkey Creates

tel +353 (0)87 2235124
email info@dalkeycreates.com
website www.dalkeycreates.com
Twitter @DalkeyCreates
Festival Director Anna Fox
Takes place November

Held annually in the picturesque seaside town of Dalkey in Dublin, Dalkey Creates aims to encourage and inspire writers with an excellent range of workshops and writer-focused events. It also features annual short story and poetry competitions.

The Daunt Books Festival

83–84 Marylebone High Street, London W1U 4QW
tel 020-7224 2295

email enquries@dauntbooks.co.uk
website https://dauntbooks.co.uk/festival
Twitter @dauntbooks
Takes place Spring

The Festival takes place in a beautiful Edwardian bookshop in Marylebone. This annual celebration of literature goes to show that a bookshop is not just a place to buy books but a space to bring readers together, to foster a literary community and to have a great deal of fun in the process. Key speakers over the years have included Michael Palin, Antonia Fraser, Colin Thubron, Claire Tomalin, Owen Jones, George Saunders, Sebastian Barry, Sarah Perry, Peter Frankopan and Michael Morpurgo.

Derby Book Festival
13 Lavender Row, Darley Abbey, Derby DE22 1DF
email hello@derbybookfestival.co.uk
website www.derbybookfestival.co.uk
Takes place over 10 days in May/June and a weekend Autumn Edition

Celebrates the joy of books and reading for all ages and interests, with a programme featuring great writers, poets, historians, politicians, illustrators, storytellers and musicians. Each year the festival welcomes internationally celebrated bestselling authors as well as a broad range of local writing talent and includes a children's, families and educational programme. Founded 2015.

Dublin Book Festival
email info@dublinbookfestival.com
website www.dublinbookfestival.com
Twitter @DublinBookFest
Takes place 12–15 November 2021

The Festival brings together the best of Irish publishing, offering a chance for the voices of both established and up-and-coming authors to be heard. Mostly held in Smock Alley Theatre, the festival's events include book launches, interviews, workshops, a children's and schools programme and lots more. Founded 2006.

Durham Book Festival
New Writing North, PO Box 1277, Newcastle upon Tyne NE99 5PB
email office@newwritingnorth.com
website https://durhambookfestival.com
Twitter @durhambookfest
Takes place October

A book festival for new and established writers, taking place in the historic city of Durham in a variety of historic venues including Durham Town Hall, Durham Cathedral and the Gala Theatre. Founded 1990.

East Riding Festival of Words
East Riding Libraries, Redcliff Road, Melton, North Ferriby, East Riding of Yorkshire HU14 3RS
email festivalofwords@eastriding.gov.uk
website www.festivalofwords.co.uk
Facebook www.facebook.com/erwordfest/
Twitter @erwordfest
Instagram erwordfest
Takes place Third weekend in October

One of the UK's leading literature festivals. The festival includes authors' events, readings, panel events, workshops, children's activities and performances. Founded 2000.

Edinburgh International Book Festival
Edinburgh College of Arts, 74 Lauriston Place, Edinburgh EH3 9DF
tel 0131 718 5666
email admin@edbookfest.co.uk
website www.edbookfest.co.uk
Twitter @edbookfest
Takes place 14–30 August 2021

The largest public celebration of the written word in the world. In addition to a unique independent bookselling operation, around 1,000 UK and international writers appear in over 900 events for adults and children. Programme details available in June. Founded 1983.

Ennis Book Club Festival
tel +353 (0)87 9723647
email info@ennisbookclubfestival.com
website www.ennisbookclubfestival.com
Takes place First weekend in March

An annual literary weekend which brings together book club members, book lovers, writers and other artists. Includes lectures, readings, discussions, theatre, music and more.

Free the Word!
PEN International, Unit A, Koops Mill Mews, 162–164 Abbey Street, London SE1 2AN
tel 020-7405 0338
email info@pen-international.org
website www.pen-international.org/celebrating-literature/free-the-word
Twitter @pen_int

Free the Word! is PEN International's roaming event series of contemporary literature from around the world. The Free the Word! team works with PEN Centres, festivals and book fairs to develop an international network of literary events. Founded 2008.

Guildford Book Festival
c/o Tourist Information Office, 155 High Street, Guildford GU1 3AJ
tel (01483) 444334
email director@guildfordbookfestival.co.uk
website www.guildfordbookfestival.co.uk
Twitter @gfordbookfest
Co-directors Jane Beaton, Alex Andrews
Takes place 3–10 October 2021

An annual festival with a diverse programme of outstanding conversation and lively debate to inspire and entertain. Held throughout the historic town, it draws audiences from throughout London and the South East. Hosts author events, workshops and a schools programme, plus selected online events. Its aim is to further an interest and love of literature through involvement and entertainment. Founded 1989.

Raworths Harrogate Literature Festival
32 Cheltenham Parade, Harrogate HG1 1DB
tel (01423) 562303
email info@harrogate-festival.org.uk
website https://harrogateinternationalfestivals.com/raworths-literature-festival
Twitter @HarrogateFest
Takes place October

Four days of literary events designed to inspire and stimulate. Founded 1966.

The Hay Festival
The Drill Hall, 25 Lion Street,
Hay-on-Wye HR3 5AD
tel (01497) 822620
email admin@hayfestival.org
website www.hayfestival.com
Facebook www.facebook.com/hayfestival
Twitter @hayfestival
Takes place May

This annual festival of literature and the arts in Hay-on-Wye, Wales, brings together writers, musicians, film-makers, historians, politicians, environmentalists and scientists from around the world to communicate challenging ideas. Hundreds of events over ten days. Within the annual festival is a festival for families and children, HAYDAYS, which introduces children, from toddlers to teenagers, to their favourite authors and holds workshops to entertain and educate. Programme published April.

Huddersfield Literature Festival
email office@huddlitfest.org.uk
website www.huddlitfest.org.uk
Festival Director Michelle Hodgson
Takes place March

An award-winning 10-day festival held annually. Showcasing major names, new, emerging and established writers/artists, the programme includes author talks, writing and performance workshops, multi-arts performances, innovative spoken word events and family-friendly events. Includes many free and low-cost events, and several with subtitling by Stagetext. Founded 2006.

Ilkley Literature Festival
9 The Grove, Ilkley LS29 9LW
tel (01943) 601210

email info@ilkleylitfest.org.uk
website www.ilkleyliteraturefestival.org.uk
Facebook www.facebook.com/ilkleylitfest
Twitter @ilkleylitfest
Director Erica Morris, *Coordinator* Becky Wholley
Takes place 1–17 October 2021

One of the UK's longest-running and widest-ranging literature festivals with over 150 events, from author discussions to workshops, readings, literary walks, children's events and a festival fringe. Founded 1973.

Independent Bookshop Week
website www.indiebookshopweek.org.uk
Facebook www.facebook.com/booksaremybag
Twitter @booksaremybag
Instagram booksaremybag
Takes place June

An annual celebration of independent bookshops, part of the Books are My Bag campaign to promote all high street bookshops in the UK and Ireland and the idea of shopping locally and sustainably.

International Literature Festival Dublin
GEC, Taylor's Lane, Dublin 8, Republic of Ireland
tel +353 (0)1 415 1295
email info@ilfdublin.com
website https://ilfdublin.com
Twitter @ILFDublin
Takes place May

Ireland's premier literary event gathering the finest writers to debate, provoke and delight. The Festival continues to champion Dublin's position as a UNESCO City of Literature, celebrating the local alongside the global and the power of words to change the world. With readings, discussions, debates, workshops, performances and screenings, the Festival creates a hotbed of ideas for all ages. Founded 1998.

Jewish Book Week
ORT House, 126 Albert Street, London NW1 7NE
tel 020-7446 8771
email info@jewishbookweek.com
website https://jewishbookweek.com
Twitter @JewishBookWeek
Festival Director Claudia Rubenstein
Takes place February/March

A 10-day festival of writing, arts and culture, with contributors from around the world and sessions in London and nationwide. Includes events for children and teenagers. Founded 1952.

King's Lynn Festival
Fermoy Gallery, 7–9 St George's Courtyard, King Street, King's Lynn, Norfolk PE30 1EU
tel (01553) 767557
email info@kingslynnfestival.org.uk
website www.kingslynnfestival.org.uk
Twitter @KLFestival

Artistic Director Ambrose Miller
Takes place July plus year round events

An annual arts festival with a music focus, including literature events featuring leading guest writers. Founded 1951.

King's Lynn Literature Festivals
email enquiries@lynnlitfests.com
website www.lynnlitfests.com
Chairman Tony Ellis
Takes place September/March

Poetry Festival (24–26 September 2021): An annual festival which brings 12 worldwide-published poets to King's Lynn for a weekend of readings and discussions, including Kevin Crossley Holland and Pascale Pettit.

Fiction Festival (11–13 March 2022): An annual festival which brings ten published novelists to King's Lynn for a weekend of readings and discussions including Louis de Bernieres, D.J. Taylor and Rachel Hore.

Laureate na nÓg/Ireland's Children's Laureate
Children's Books Ireland,
17 North Great George's Street, Dublin 1, D01 R2F1
tel +353 (0)18 727475
email info@childrenslaureate.ie
email info@childrensbooksireland.ie
website www.childrenslaureate.ie
Laureate na nÓg Project Manager Aingeala Flannery

This is a project recognising the role and importance of literature for children in Ireland, established to engage young people with high-quality literature and to underline the importance of children's literature in Ireland's cultural and imaginative life. It was awarded for the first time in 2010. The laureate participates in selected events and activities around Ireland and internationally during their newly extended three-year term as of 2020.
   The laureate is chosen in recognition of their widely recognised high-quality children's writing or illustration and the positive impact they have had on readers as well as other writers and illustrators. Laureate na nÓg 2010–12, Siobhán Parkinson; 2012–14, Niamh Sharkey; 2014–16, Eoin Colfer; 2016–18, P.J. Lynch; 2018–20, Sarah Crossan; 2020–22, Áine Ní Ghlinn.

Ledbury Poetry Festival
The Master's House, St Katherine's, Bye Street, Ledbury HR8 1EA
tel (01531) 636232
email manager@poetry-festival.co.uk
website www.poetry-festival.co.uk
Twitter @ledburyfest
Festival Manager Phillippa Slinger
Takes place July

An annual festival featuring nationally and internationally renowned poets, together with a poet-in-residence programme, slams, competitions, workshops, community events and exhibitions. It also runs poetry events for children. An International Poetry Competition, with £1,000 prize money and a winners' reading event during the festival, launches every February.

Leeds Lit Fest
Leeds City Centre Box Office, Leeds Town Hall, The Headrow, Leeds LS1 3AD
email enquiries@leedslitfest.co.uk
website www.leedslitfest.co.uk
Facebook www.facebook.com/LeedsLitFest
Twitter @LeedsLit
Takes place March

The festival celebrates the vibrant and thriving literature scene that exists in Leeds with local writers and performers showcasing their talents along with national and international artists with an exciting programme of author talks, workshops, panels, performance, digital, poetry and spoken word events.

Listowel Writers' Week
24 The Square, Listowel, Co. Kerry V31 RD93, Republic of Ireland
tel +353 (0)68 21074
email info@writersweek.ie
website https://writersweek.ie
Facebook www.facebook.com/writersweek
Twitter @WritersWeek
Takes place June

An annual literary festival devoted to bringing together writers and audiences at unique and innovative events in the historic and intimate surroundings of Listowel, County Kerry. At its heart is a commitment to developing and promoting writing talent, underpinned by the values of partnership, inclusivity and civic responsibility. Events include workshops, readings, seminars, lectures, book launches, art exhibitions and a comprehensive children's and teenagers' programme. Founded 1971.

Litfest
The Storey, Meeting House Lane, Lancaster LA1 1TH
tel (01524) 509005
email marketing@litfest.org
website www.litfest.org
Facebook www.facebook.com/LitfestLancaster
Twitter @Litfest
Takes place March

Annual literature festival featuring local, national and international writers, poets and performers. Litfest is the literature development agency for Lancashire with a year-round programme of readings, performances and workshops.

London Literature Festival

email customer@southbankcentre.co.uk
website www.southbankcentre.co.uk
Facebook www.facebook.com/southbankcentre
Twitter @southbankcentre
Takes place 21–31 October 2021

The Southbank Centre runs a year-round programme of readings, talks, workshops and debates. The annual London Literature Festival kicks off each year with Poetry International, the Southbank Centre's longest running festival, bringing together a wide range of poets from around the world. Founded 1967.

Manchester Children's Book Festival

Manchester Metropolitan University,
All Saints Building, Manchester M15 6BH
tel 0161-247 2000
email mcbf@mmu.ac.uk
website www.mmu.ac.uk/mcbf
Facebook www.facebook.com/MCBFestival
Twitter @MCBFestival
Instagram mcbfestival

A festival of year-round activities celebrating the very best writing for children, inspiring young people to engage with literature and creativity across the curriculum and offering extended projects and training to ensure the event has an impact and legacy in classrooms. Founded 2009.

Manchester Literature Festival

The Department Store, 5 Oak Street,
Manchester M4 5JD
email office@manchesterliteraturefestival.co.uk
website www.manchesterliteraturefestival.co.uk
Twitter @McrLitFest
Co-Directors Cathy Bolton and Sarah-Jane Roberts
Takes place October

An annual two-week festival showcasing new commissions and celebrating the best literature and imaginative writing from around the world. Note that MLF only accepts a small number of submissions each year with the majority of the Festival being curated by the team.

May Festival

Festivals and Events Team, University of Aberdeen,
King's College, Aberdeen AB24 3FX
tel (01224) 273233
email festival@abdn.ac.uk
website www.abdn.ac.uk/mayfestival
Takes place May

The Festival offers more than 120 events spanning popular themes including literature, music, film, science, visual arts and sport. The University of Aberdeen offers a *Discover* strand of events which gives audiences the opportunity to gain an insight into the research going on at the university. In addition, the Festival features a tours programme and

historic exhibitions, and offers a programme of events to celebrate and showcase north east Scotland's unique cultural landscape.

National Eisteddfod of Wales

40 Parc Ty Glas, Llanisien, Cardiff CF14 5DU
tel 0845 409 0300
email gwyb@eisteddfod.org.uk
website https://eisteddfod.wales
Twitter @eisteddfod
Takes place August

Wales's largest cultural festival. Activities include competitions in all aspects of the arts, fringe performances and majestic ceremonies. In addition to activities held in the main pavilion, it houses over 250 trade stands along with a literary pavilion, arts exhibition, an outdoor performance stage and a purpose-built theatre. The event is held in a different part of Wales every year. Please refer to the website for details.

Newcastle Noir

website www.newcastlenoir.co.uk
Facebook www.facebook.com/NewcastleNoir
Twitter @NewcastleNoir

An annual crime fiction festival established to promote top-class crime writing in the region and to celebrate an intriguing and increasingly diverse genre. Founded 2014.

Noireland International Crime Fiction Festival

83 Botanic Avenue, Belfast BT7 1JL
email info@noireland.com
website www.noireland.com
Facebook www.facebook.com/noirelandfest
Twitter @NOIRELANDFest
Takes place Spring

The Festival was founded to provide a platform for the wealth of crime writing talent emerging from Ireland, showcasing it alongside some of the biggest international names in crime and thriller writing. The three-day annual festival explores crime writing from across the world and looks at the impact that Ireland has had on crime writing, from the Irish cops of New York to the sons and daughters of immigrants who have transformed the genre.

*Noir*wich Crime Writing Festival

tel (01603) 877177
email info@nationalcentreforwriting.org.uk
website https://noirwich.co.uk
Facebook www.facebook.com/noirwich
Twitter @NOIRwichFEST
Takes place 9–12 September 2021

The Festival celebrates the sharpest noir and crime writing over four days of author events, film screenings and writing masterclasses in the historic city of Norwich, UNESCO City of Literature. A collaboration between the National Centre for Writing and the University of East Anglia.

Norfolk & Norwich Festival

Festival Office, Augustine Steward House,
14 Tombland, Norwich NR3 1HF
tel (01603) 877750
email info@nnfestival.org.uk
website https://nnfestival.org.uk
Facebook www.facebook.com/NNFestival
Twitter @NNFest
Takes place May

For 17 days each year the Festival transforms public spaces, city streets, performance venues, parks, forests and beaches, bringing people together to experience a variety of events spanning music, theatre, literature, visual arts, circus, dance and free outdoor events.

Northern Short Story Festival

website www.bigbookend.co.uk/nssf
Facebook www.facebook.com/NoShoStoFest
Twitter @NoShoSto

The North's only festival dedicated to celebrating and championing the short story. Aims to bring the best in short story writing to Leeds, celebrate the many writers in the region and support independent presses working nationwide. Provides regular pop-up events, networking opportunities and workshops, and runs The Academy scheme and NoShoSto Book Club. Founded 2016.

Off the Shelf Festival of Words Sheffield

Cathedral Court, 46 Church Street, Sheffield S1 2GN
tel 0114 222 3895
email offtheshelf@sheffield.ac.uk
website www.offtheshelf.org.uk
Takes place 15–30 October 2021

See great writers, historians, poets, artists, scientists, journalists and musicians at this diverse and innovative festival. Events city-wide for all ages.

Oundle Festival of Literature

email oundlelitfestival@hotmail.co.uk
website www.oundlelitfest.org.uk
Facebook www.facebook.com/
OundleFestivalOfLiterature
Twitter @OundleLitFest
Festival Director Helen Shair

The Festival runs a programme of all-year-round events aimed at exciting, informing, entertaining and educating a wide variety of people through talks, discussions and workshops by award-winning and local authors and poets. The Festival uses a variety of venues in the beautiful market town of Oundle, plus online Zoom Webinar events.

FT Weekend Oxford Literary Festival

c/o Critchleys, Beaver House,
23–28 Hythe Bridge Street, Oxford OX1 2EP
email info@oxfordliteraryfestival.org
website https://oxfordliteraryfestival.org
Takes place March/April

An annual festival for both adults and children held in venues across the city and university. Presents topical debates, fiction and non-fiction discussion panels, and adult and children's authors who have recently published books. Topics range from contemporary fiction to discussions on politics, history, science, gardening, food, poetry, philosophy, art and crime fiction.

Richmond upon Thames Lit Fest

Orleans House Gallery, Orleans Road,
Twickenham TW1 3BL
020-8831 6000
email artsinfo@richmondandwandsworth.gov.uk
website www.richmondliterature.com
Twitter @richmondlitfest
Takes place November

An annual festival featuring a diverse programme of authors, commentators and leading figures, in a range of interesting and unique venues across the borough. The festival includes something for everyone, with an exciting programme for all ages and interests.

Rye Arts Festival

tel (01797) 462168
email secretary@ryeartsfestival.org.uk
website https://ryeartsfestival.org.uk
Facebook www.facebook.com/Ryeartsfestival
Twitter @Ryearts
Takes place Last 2 weeks of September

Annual festival of literary events featuring biographers, novelists, political and environmental writers with book signings and discussions. Runs concurrently with festival of music and visual arts.

Salisbury International Arts Festival

Wiltshire Creative, Salisbury Playhouse,
Malthouse Lane, Salisbury SP2 7RA
tel (01722) 320117
email info@wiltshirecreative.co.uk
website www.wiltshirecreative.co.uk/whats-on/festival
Facebook www.facebook.com/SalisburyFestival
Twitter @WiltsCreative
Takes place May–June

A thriving, annual multi-arts festival that delivers over 150 arts events each year, including concerts, comedy, poetry, dance, exhibitions, outdoor spectacles and commissioned works.

The Self-Publishing Conference

tel 0116 279 2299
email books@troubador.co.uk
website www.selfpublishingconference.org.uk
Twitter @Selfpubconf

The UK's only dedicated self-publishing conference. This annual event covers all aspects of self-publishing from production through to marketing and distribution. The conference offers plenty of networking opportunities and access to over 16 presentations. Founded 2013.

The Stanfords Travel Writers Festival
website www.stanfords.co.uk/stanfords-travel-writers-festival
Takes place Held late-January to early-February

Held during the Destinations: The Holiday & Travel Show in London's Olympia, the festival hosts book launches and live author events. Founded 2014.

StAnza: Scotland's International Poetry Festival
tel (01334) 475000 (box office); (01334) 474610 (programmes)
email stanza@stanzapoetry.org
website www.stanzapoetry.org
Facebook www.facebook.com/stanzapoetry
Twitter @StAnzaPoetry
Instagram stanzapoetry
Festival Director Lucy Burnett
Takes place March

The festival engages with all forms of poetry: read and spoken verse, poetry in exhibition, performance poetry, cross-media collaboration, schools work, book launches and poetry workshops, with numerous UK and international guests and weekend children's events. Founded 1997.

States of Independence
website http://leicestercentreforcreativewriting.our.dmu.ac.uk/
Facebook www.facebook.com/StatesOfIndependence/
Twitter @Statesofindie
Takes place Takes place March

An annual one-day festival celebrating independent publishing. Held at De Montfort University in Leicester. Involves independent publishers from the region and beyond. A free event with a varied programme of sessions and a book fair.

Stratford-upon-Avon Literary Festival
email info@stratfordliteraryfestival.co.uk
website www.stratlitfest.co.uk
Facebook www.facebook.com/stratfordlitfest
Twitter @StratLitFest
Takes place May with events in autumn

The main festival takes place in May plus more events in November. The Festival is a feast of workshops, panel discussions, celebrity and best-selling author events. A charity, the festival also runs a programme of educational events and projects for families and regional schools aimed at entertaining and inspiring children, as well as events in the community and bedtime story writing workshops in prisons.

Stratford-upon-Avon Poetry Festival
website www.shakespeare.org.uk
Facebook www.facebook.com/ShakespeareBT
Twitter @ShakespeareBT
Takes place June

This annual festival celebrates Shakespeare's creative genius. Organised by the Shakespeare Birthplace Trust, the festival presents an exciting line-up of readings, performances and workshops showcasing the talents of inspirational and award-winning artists from all over the world. It also includes a special programme of family-friendly events. For more information and ticket bookings visit the website.

The Summer Festival of Writing
4 Acer Walk, Oxford OX2 6EX
tel 0345 459 9560 , +1 (646)-974-9060 (US)
email info@jerichowriters.com
website https://jerichowriters.com/events/summer-festival-of-writing/
Takes place June–August 2021

A three-month online festival for all writers providing the opportunity to connect with others from across the world. Writers will have the opportunity to hear from literary agents, publishers, and professional authors. This includes pitching work to literary agents; receiving live feedback from industry professionals; and enter writing competitions.

Swindon Festival of Literature
Lower Shaw Farm, Shaw, Swindon, Wilts. SN5 5PJ
tel (01793) 771080
email swindonlitfest@lowershawfarm.co.uk
website www.swindonfestivalofliterature.co.uk
Festival Director Matt Holland
Takes place May

An annual celebration of live literature and the arts through prose, poetry, drama, dance, music, circus skills and storytelling, with readings, discussions, performances and talks in theatres, arts centres, parks and pubs. A festival of ideas and entertainment with leading authors, speakers and performers.

Theakston Old Peculier Crime Writing Festival
Old Swan Hotel, Swan Road, Harrogate HG1 2SR
tel (01423) 562303
email crime@harrogate-festival.org.uk
website www.harrogateinternationalfestivals.com/crime-writing-festival
Twitter @HarrogateFest
Takes place July

Europe's largest celebration of crime fiction, featuring over 90 authors.

The Dylan Thomas Exhibition
The Dylan Thomas Centre, Somerset Place, Swansea SA1 1RR

tel (01792) 463980
email dylanthomas.lit@swansea.gov.uk
website www.dylanthomas.com
Facebook www.facebook.com/dylanthomascentre
Twitter @DTCSwansea
Events Manager Jo Furber

A year round resource celebrating the life and work of Swansea's most famous son: performances, family friendly events, poetry, and workshops. Dylan Thomas talks and tours by arrangement.

UEA Live

Arts 3.28, Arts and Humanities Events,
University of East Anglia, Norwich NR4 7TJ
tel (01603) 593412
email uealive@uea.ac.uk
website www.uealive.com
Facebook www.facebook.com/uealitfest
Twitter @UEALitfest
Takes place February to May

An annual festival of events bringing established writers of fiction, biography and poetry to a public audience in the Eastern region. Founded 1991.

Upton Cressett Literary and History Festival

Upton Cressett Hall, Upton Cressett, Nr Bridgnorth, Shrops. WV16 6UH
email enquiries@uptoncressett.co.uk
website www.uptoncressetthall.co.uk

For over 40 years, Upton Cressett has played host to a wide variety of writers, historians, politicians and public figures. Following the success of a series of history/literary talks and concerts in the Norman church, a two-day annual festival was launched to celebrate the creative spirit of the Upton Cressett Literary Foundation, a unique writers' retreat in The Gatehouse, now in its ninth year. The festival features an array of speakers, artists and events including talks, Elizabethan costume, dancing, falconry and live music. The festival aims to celebrate the very best of heritage, books, artisan life, music and architecture.

Warwick Words History Festival

The Court House, Jury Street, Warwick CV34 4EW
tel (07944) 768607
email info@warwickwords.co.uk
website https://warwickwords.co.uk
Twitter @WarwickWords
Takes place 4–10 October 2021

Celebrate historical writing, fact and fiction, meet the authors and discuss their work. Founded 1999.

Ways With Words Festivals of Words and Ideas

Droridge Farm, Dartington, Totnes, Devon TQ9 6JG
tel (01803) 867373

email admin@wayswithwords.co.uk
website http://wayswithwords.co.uk
Facebook www.facebook.com/wayswithwords
Twitter @Ways_With_Words
Takes place July

Runs three major festivals of words and ideas in the UK each year, as well as courses based in Umbria for writers, painters and people wanting to learn a bit of Italian. Promotes both the written and spoken word and seeks to bring people together in beautiful surroundings to make contact with writers, journalists and experts in various fields. Founded 1991.

Wells Festival of Literature

email admin@wellsfestivaloliterature.org.uk
website www.wellsfestivaloliterature.org.uk
Facebook www.facebook.com/Wellslitfest
Twitter @wellslitfest
Instagram wellsfestivaloliterature
Takes place 16–23 October 2021

An eight-day hybrid festival, featuring leading writers of fiction and non-fiction, poets and performers. Live speakers and audience with live online participation and viewing available after each event until the end of November. Programme includes talks, discussions, workshops and bookclub. Poetry (first prize £1000), short story, book for children and young poets' competitions. Events in local schools and the community throughout the year. Helps fund a variety of educational projects locally to encourage young people to love literature.

Wigtown Book Festival

Wigtown Festival Company, 11 North Main Street, Wigtown DG8 9HN
tel (01988) 402036
email mail@wigtownbookfestival.com
website www.wigtownbookfestival.com
Facebook www.facebook.com/WigtownBookFestival
Twitter @WigtownBookFest
Takes place 23 September– 3 October 2021

An annual celebration of literature and the arts in Scotland's National Book Town. Includes author events, theatre, music, film and children's and young people's programmes.

Winchester Poetry Festival

c/o 41 Nuns Road, Winchester, Hampshire SO23 7EF
email hello@winchesterpoetryfestival.org
website www.winchesterpoetryfestival.org
Twitter @WinPoetryFest
Instagram winchesterpoetry
Contact Madelaine Smith
Takes place 8–10 October 2021

A biennial festival dedicated to poetry. The 2021 festival is built upon the postponed 2020 festival. Please see website for confirmed dates and activities.

Societies, prizes and festivals

World Book Day

email wbd@education.co.uk
website www.worldbookday.com
Facebook www.facebook.com/worldbookdayuk
Twitter @WorldBookDayUK
Ceo Cassie Chadderton
Takes place First Thursday in March

World Book Day changes lives through a love of books and shared reading. Its mission is to promote reading for pleasure, offering every child and young person the opportunity to have a book of their own. Reading for pleasure is the single biggest indicator of a child's future success – more than their family circumstances, their parents' educational background or their income. They want to see more children, particularly those from disadvantaged backgrounds, form a life-long habit of reading for pleasure and the improved life chances this brings them.

The Writers' Weekend

website www.writersweekend.uk
Facebook www.facebook.com/WritersWkend
Twitter @WritersWkend
Director Sara Gangai
Takes place June/July

A conference for emerging writers, working in all genres and at all levels. Attendees participate in writing workshops, informative talks and one-to-one appointments with top literary agents to pitch their manuscripts. The Weekend is full of opportunities to network with fellow writers, published authors, agents and editors, attend panels, discuss topics of interest in small groups and share writing at open mics to a supportive and friendly crowd. The keynote speakers change every year. In 2021, best-selling writer Diana Gabaldon, author of the 'Outlander' series, and award-winning children's author/illustrator, Chris Riddell, gave keynote talks. The aim of the Weekend is to help writers achieve their writing goal, whether it is to improve or get published. In addition to the Weekend, four competitions are also held. See website for details on the programme and competitions, and information on the 2022 event, which will be held either as an in-person, virtual or hybrid event.

YALC (Young Adult Literature Convention)

email yalc@showmastersevents.com
website https://londonfilmandcomiccon.com/yalc
Facebook www.facebook.com/ukYALC
Twitter @yalc_uk
Takes place Annually in July

YALC is a celebration of the best young adult books and authors. It is an interactive event where YA fans can meet their favourite authors, listen to panel discussions and take part in workshops. YALC is run by Showmasters, which runs the London Film and Comic Con. Lots of opportunities available for promotional activities. Founded 2014.

Self-publishing
Self-publishing online: the emerging template for sales success

With the self-publishing revolution rapidly transforming the industry, Harry Bingham explains how indie authors can now unlock huge sales through some simple techniques for connecting with readers online.

In a past era – not long ago in terms of years, but whole aeons in terms of the industry – self-publishing involved the creation and sale of print books. Lacking access to major national distribution chains, that activity was inevitably small-scale. If you sold 500 books and broke even in the exercise, you had done well. If you sold 1,000, you were a self-pub superstar.

That version of self-publishing still exists, and is perfectly reputable. But the rise of Amazon and the advent of the ebook have, together, utterly transformed the boundaries of the possible. You want to reach readers worldwide? Sure, no problem. You want to earn good money from every book sold? Consider it done. You want to sell tens of thousands of copies, make a prosperous living, have a close bond with thousands of readers? Of course. These things aren't easy to achieve exactly, but they're no longer remarkable. These truths, however, are weirdly invisible, in part because of the continuing cultural authority of print and the High Street. A typical traditional trade publisher today sells about 70% of its work in print. The remaining portion will be made up mostly of ebooks, together with a rapidly growing slice of audio.

But these – very familiar – figures are deeply misleading. For one thing, they ignore Amazon's own publishing activity; the firm is, after all, a publisher as well as a retailer. They also ignore all the sales generated by indie authors (or self-publishers; I use the terms interchangeably).

These two non-traditional sources, Amazon plus the indies, now account for a stonking 50% share of all adult fiction sales. And never mind format! If you look at *where* books are sold – print, digital and audio – it turns out that around 75% of all adult books – fiction and non-fiction – are sold online. The same is true of almost half of all books for children. (These stats relate to the US market only, as no comparable estimates exist for the UK. That said, although the British trajectory is broadly similar, online penetration in the US has probably proceeded further.)

These data lead us to the two rocket-fuelled propellants of the self-pub revolution:

1. Traditional publishers have a lock on high-street bookselling. Indie authors simply can't gain access to national chains without a corporate publisher on side. But *anyone* has access to Amazon. All you need is an email address. Uploading an ebook is particularly simple, but creating print books isn't much harder, and most big-selling indies will be profiting from audio too.

2. Amazon's royalties are extraordinary. If you sell £100 worth of ebooks on Amazon, the firm will pay you just a shade under £70. If you sell the same value of ebooks via a traditional

publisher and literary agent, you're likely to see less than £15. In most industries, would-be insurgents have to do something better than the incumbents in order to thrive. In this industry, the royalty gap is such that you can sell fewer books, *and* price them more cheaply, *and* still make a ton more money.

Those royalties are the golden flame that attracts self-pubbers – a commercial advantage of vast potential. But how to unlock it? Because the beauty of Amazon – its accessibility – is also its terror. Amazon currently lists over 6,000,000 ebooks for sale. Every three months, that number increases by at least 150,000. How do you compete against those millions? How will your book find its readers?

Hit and hope is not the answer. That has never worked, and never will. Equally, you can't just use social media to bellow in people's faces: 'Buy my book, it's great.' The problem isn't just that it's repellent to act that way. It's also – and mostly – that no one buys books because people are shouting at them. And OK, if you're deft enough and committed enough, if you blog and tweet and post and engage with enough people, on enough sites, and do so while making sure that no more than one in ten of your messages are sales-related – then, sure, you'll sell some books. But not many. It's not a way to succeed. So what is?

The answer is simple: you connect with readers. You get people to read your work and, if they like it, to give you their email address, so you can be in touch whenever you have a new work out. Some readers will give you an address, but forgetfully and without commitment. Many, however, will stay committed to you and your books, so that they will buy and *buy when you prompt them to*. That fact means you can, as your list builds up, create little sale tsunamis. Fifty sales in a day. Then a hundred and fifty. Then a thousand. That, in itself, doesn't sound so impressive. Sure, if you have a mailing list of 3,000 names, and a third of those buy your book within 24 hours of your email, you'll sell 1,000 books. But what comes next? You need to be selling in the tens of thousands to make a living.

The answer is Amazon. Its marketing algorithms are constantly on the lookout for books that sell. And if those data-bots encounter a surge of sales in a new title, they recognise that the product is hot. It's something that Amazon wants to market. And it does that, automatically, via marketing emails, by popping you onto bestseller lists, by elevating you on relevant searches, and much else. A small list can generate revenues out of all proportion to its size.

In 2015, I marketed my crime novel *This Thing of Darkness* in the US using what was then a very small email list of just 330 names. I was dealing with new-born twins at the time and did nothing to sell that book beyond one email to those readers. Over the next 12 (sleepless) months, I earned about $30,000 from that book and its sisters. A small list; a stunning result.

This technique lies at the heart of almost every recent indie success story. Better still: it's totally ethical. *It's how things should work*. It's word of mouth re-engineered for the digital age. So all those questions about how to market your books now narrow down to just three:

• How do you most effectively collect email addresses?
• How do you maximise the effectiveness of your email-driven sales surge?
• How do you make sure that *all* your titles get that Amazon-love, not just the one you're currently launching?

The first question is easily answered. No one likes giving away their personal data, so you don't *ask* the reader for anything. Rather, you *offer* them something: 'Get an exclusive free story to download.' You make that offer, or something along those lines, in the front- or end-material of your ebook. That call to action links to a page on your website, where your reader can give you the email address to which you'll send the story. (All that stuff can be automated, of course. You can do it yourself or pay a tech-guy, as I do.) Naturally, you disclose that readers will receive further emails from you, but that's not some kind of small-print marketing subterfuge. On the contrary: readers *like* to be in direct contact with favoured authors. This is 'permission marketing' at its truest.

In terms of maximising sales effectiveness, you need to make sure that your book's metadata is as solid as it can be. That means writing a strong book description. It means making sure that your choice of Amazon category is logical. It means making sure that your keywords are well-chosen to get you on the right sub-bestseller lists and the right thematic searches. Those things sound scary and technical, but they're not hard. It's a morning's work, no more.

As for making sure that sales success in one title bleeds over to the rest, the answer there is also simple. The moment to market another of your books to a reader is in the glow of that moment when they've just finished one. So make sure you list *all* of your titles in the back of *all* of your books. When it comes to your ebooks, don't just provide a boring, unclickable list; you need to insert links direct to the e-stores where your books are available. Those links mean that your reader doesn't have to be more than two or three clicks from making another purchase. Two or three clicks from placing more money in your pocket.

And that, in essence, is that. To be sure, a number of tricks remain. Prolific Works (www.prolificworks.com) is an extraordinary way to kick your mailing list off from scratch. Facebook lead-generation ads still work well for some authors, in some contexts. If properly used, Bookbub (www.bookbub.com) is a delightful machine whose primary purpose is to make you richer. Launch teams can ensure a flurry of great reviews when your book launches on Amazon. The sequencing of things like pre-orders, Kindle Countdown deals, email blasts, pricing changes and so on can make serious differences to how well you do overall.

And do remember that, while ebooks are likely to dominate your self-pub revenue stream (as they do mine), you can succeed in any format. 2015 was the Year of the Colouring Book, as far as the publishing industry was concerned, and indeed Amazon.com duly reported that 11 of its top 35 print sellers were adult colouring books. That much is well known, but get this: *five of those 11 top-sellers were indie-published*. The issue isn't format, it's sales channel. And, if you create great content and work hard to connect with your readers (or crayon-wielding adults), there's no reason why you can't succeed.

Likewise, while Amazon is likely to provide a clear majority of your revenues, the other e-stores can start to perform well for you too. Some indies report that Amazon represents less than 50% of their overall income, though, if you're just starting out, you should probably work with Amazon exclusively.

But all these things are refinements. They're not the strategy. The strategy is simply this: you write a great book; you find your first readers, probably via giveaways on Facebook or Prolific Works; those readers like your stuff and choose to give you their email address in return for some exclusive material; you use those email addresses to kick start your sales for the next book. Then – rinse and repeat, rinse and repeat, rinse and repeat.

The very best part about all this? The more you use this motor, the more powerful it becomes. Your mailing list increases and your sales grow. Each year, a higher income than the year before. The self-pub revolution is still young, but it's mighty. It has given authors wholly new options, a wholly new authority. I don't know what the industry will look like in ten years' time, but it's changing fast, and changing radically. And, just for once, authors are on the winning side.

Harry Bingham is the author of the *Fiona Griffiths* series of crime novels (and much else). The sixth book in the series, *The Deepest Grave*, was released by Orion in 2017. He is traditionally published in the UK and self-published in the US, and greatly relishes both routes. He also runs Jericho Writers, an online club for writers. Readers wanting more detail on the techniques mentioned in this article can get them via https://jerichowriters.com/.

See also...
• *Making waves online*, page 630

Going solo: self-publishing in the digital age

Dean Crawford explains how, thanks to digital, it is now possible to make a living as an independent author. He compares the pros and cons of traditional and indie publishing, and reveals why for many writers it makes sense to go it alone.

If, in 1995, when I was writing my first tentative lines in the hope of one day becoming a full-time author, you had told me that it would take me 15 years to get my first publishing deal, I might have believed you. Had you then told me that there would be two deals, both life-changing, I would have been sceptical. But if you'd told me that within three years of securing such deals, I would break away from the major publishing houses and become an independent author, I'd have told you that you were insane. Why, after gaining representation from a top London literary agency and after two *to-die-for* deals in a row, would I do something as daft as *that*?

The answer is, of course, digital. The world of publishing has been utterly transformed by the rise of the ebook. The way in which readers access books has been altered so dramatically that it's now those readers, not big publishing houses' marketing and PR departments, who decide what sells. The carefully guarded 'gatekeeper' model of the big publishing houses has been superseded by search engines. No longer is the reader restricted to what their local bookshop or library can fit on their shelves. A reader can now download any book, at any time, from pretty much anywhere in the world. It is in this new and fast-moving marketplace that the independent author thrives.

I loved writing for the big houses and had a tremendously exciting time; I saw my books advertised on television, met celebrities, was caught up in the whirl of deals bigger than I'd ever dared hope for and my first books were *Sunday Times* paperback bestsellers. Yet amid all of this I spotted an opportunity that most authors had not, and I began to reconsider my career path. The reason I did so is that the traditional publishing model makes it very hard for the vast majority of authors to make a living, and I realised that I was one of a *very* lucky few.

When one of my novels was turned down by publishers in 2013 due to a shift toward dark, female-orientated psychological thrillers, I knew that the manuscript didn't need to stay on my hard drive gathering digital dust. I'd been watching the rise of many 'indie' authors and, despite the disdain of the traditionally published community, I felt that digital was here to stay and that, if I wanted to remain a successful author, I needed to grab every opportunity. Writing is an art – but publishing is a business.

I published my first indie title, *Eden*, in late July 2013. The effect was immediate. The book rose close to the top of the Amazon charts on both sides of the Atlantic, outperforming all of my traditionally published books, and earned me more per month than the day job I'd left when I'd signed my first publishing deals three years before. Suddenly, I realised what indie authors were so excited about. Big advances were wonderful aspirations, but they were vanishingly rare. With independent publishing, though, thousands of unknowns were suddenly making a better living from their writing than from their day jobs and were going full-time in droves. Sadly, the reverse was happening in traditional publishing, as writers increasingly were unable to make a living doing the job that they loved.

The difference between the two methods of making a living as an author is purely down to economics. A paperback from a traditional publisher will earn the author an average royalty of 12.5% net. With net prices often a third of the RRP, the author of a £6.99 paperback will earn a measly £0.25 royalty, and only then after sales have earned out any advances already paid. No wonder, then, that so many traditionally published authors struggle to get by. In contrast, an independently published book costs perhaps £2.99, with the author receiving a royalty of just under 70% in most cases. That's around £2 per book for the indie author – a huge difference.

Of course, the independent author does not benefit from high-street sales, although in some respects that is changing, but the advantages are clear. A traditionally published author who has already earned out their advance payment, selling an average of 50 books per day, is going to earn less than £5,000 per year in royalties. Their independent counterpart selling the same number of books globally on the digital market will earn nearly £39,000 over the same period. And that figure doesn't include sales of print-on-demand paperbacks and audiobooks, all of which are available to indie authors as well as their traditionally published counterparts.

However, there are cons as well as pros. The independent author is, well, *independent*. Editing, cover design, marketing and other duties normally handled by the publishing house are shouldered by the author. This is not the terror that it may at first seem, though. Authors happily signed to traditional houses are also expected to do much of their own marketing; only the big names get big campaigns. Cover designs can be purchased for often very reasonable prices or produced by the author themselves using the many free art packages available on the internet. Only editing requires true investment, and should be sought from a reputable source, ideally from an editor who also works for the traditional houses or who can provide references from authors who have used their services.

It is often forgotten that the big names of today were forged in times when publishers had the capacity to nurture an author to success. Back then, a poorly performing debut was not necessarily the end of the line if the author displayed a strong work ethic. Today, that is no longer the case. It is sometimes said that a traditionally published debut has only two weeks of shelf time to prove itself before it's set aside to make room for the next 'new thing'. Today, publishing is littered with tales of authors whose dreams crumbled when their beloved debut failed to sell and their contracts ended. It is also increasingly filled with authors who, like me, have found that independent publishing has become the more profitable – and longer lasting – means of putting our lovingly crafted words into the hands of our readers, not to mention food on the table.

For those who harbour dreams of great fame among the traditionally published titans but find themselves unable to break through, all hope is not lost. Big houses often seek talent among the bigger-selling indies, and some authors do go on to strike deals. Quite a few independent authors have obtained literary agents and gone on to sell television and film options. Interestingly, however, many indies now actively resist offers from traditional houses, being happier where they are. I know of several authors who have regretted selling their rights, and a small few who have turned down six-figure advances from traditional houses, preferring to remain independent. That, in itself, shows how favourable being an independent author can be.

What should be noted by the newcomer, above all other considerations, is that you should never, *ever* pay for a company to publish independent novels. The modern version of the vanity press preys on the unwary. No matter what credentials they claim, no matter what publishing house they may be attached to, never pay for their services. Independent publishing should never cost the author more than their editing and their marketing. On the subject of marketing, be ready to learn as much as you can and expect to invest both time and money into it – Amazon has created a marketplace where, for the most part, advertising is a requirement, not a choice.

For those who simply cannot face the extra burdens of independent publishing, there are an increasing number of reputable digital publishing houses who take on the roles of editor and marketeer on behalf of the author. Once again, the hopeful author should select only those who do not charge an up-front fee and instead make money on commission; they should only profit from your art when you do.

For decades, authors, agents and editors lamented that it had never been harder to make a living as an author. Now the mantra is different: it has never been a better time to become an author. The road is no easier because of independent publishing, for writing a novel is not an easy task. Going solo is not easier than going with a traditional publisher – for there is much for the newcomer to learn – but to *make a living* as an independent author is, without a doubt, far easier to do than with a traditional deal. The same sales figures that would cause a traditional house to drop an author like a hot rock can be sufficient for an indie to leave their day job and forge ahead with a viable career. An indie published book can pay the mortgage, buy that new car, maybe just provide the author with extra pocket money, when before the digital revolution a writer's unpublished books would earn them nothing.

It really never has been a better time to be an author, and now you have the chance to be in full control of your career.

Dean Crawford is the author of over 30 science fiction thrillers and action-adventure novels, 18 of them independently published by Fictum, the imprint he set up in 2013. They include titles in the *Power Reads*, *Warner & Lopez*, *Old Ironsides*, *Tyler Griffin* and *Atlantia* series. Many of his traditionally published books have been *Sunday Times* bestsellers and his independent titles regularly make the Amazon Top 100 Paid lists in the UK and US. Find out more at www.deancrawfordbooks.com.

See also...
• *Self-publishing online: the emerging template for sales success*, page 607

Self-publishing

Getting your book stocked in a high-street bookshop

So you've written your book. It's finally finished, you have it printed, and you're ready to share it with readers. But how do you get your self-published novel onto the shelves of a high-street bookshop? Independent bookseller, Sheila O'Reilly, guides you on your way.

How to contact booksellers

• Ideally booksellers like to be emailed. It gives us time to think about your proposal; it gives us time to chat to our colleagues, and it gives us the opportunity to deal with the request within our normal day.

• If you do decide to show us the book in person, please don't visit unannounced. It's beneficial instead to email ahead so we can arrange a quick appointment for you with the appropriate buyer, at a time that works with the shop diary.

What booksellers need to know

To help us make our decision, you should include the following information on your proposal:

• A quick synopsis of the book - two or three sentences is perfect.

• A couple of lines about who you are.

• The sales details:

   - How much your book retails for.

   - Include a professional invoice outlining your terms of business.

   - How much you are selling it to bookshops for. [Trade terms vary between publishers.] The market research agency, Nielsen, reports that the average discount received by bookshops from publishers is just over 40% off the recommended retail price. In the UK, the publisher almost always pays for the carriage charge in getting the books to the bookshop.

   - The format (paperback/hardback). We would always recommend that the book has a spine; that the title is printed on the spine; and that there is a 13-digit EAN bar code (based on the ISBN) printed on the book.

   - Returns information. The most usual trade practice for independently published titles would be for the books to be supplied on 'consignment terms' (which means that the bookshop will pay for the stock once it has sold and can return unsold stock when it chooses). An alternative is 'sale or return', where the bookshop pays for the stock according to the payment terms of your invoice, but has the right to return unsold stock for a full refund.

   - Think about payment terms and the length of time the bookshop should have the stock for sale. If after this agreed length of time the books have not sold it is your responsibility to collect unsold stock. If the books are not collected after three months, the bookseller can dispose of the stock as they deem fit.

   - A few sample pages for us to read.

   - Why you think the book will sell in our bookshop.

   - Who the competitors – or comparable authors – are in your eyes.

   - In which section we should display the book.

- A jpg image of the book cover or jacket.
- If the book has any local ties; is it set in our area? Did you go to school around the corner?
- Do you have any local publicity lined up or in the pipeline (e.g. features, interviews or extracts in local news media)? This can have real value in improving local sales.

Tips

• Be competitive regarding the pricing of your book. A standard paperback is around £8.99.

• Look at the production quality; a well-presented finished product speaks volumes. Look at books in similar genres to your own on bookshop shelves and note the current design styles/finishes/fonts being used.

• Give important consideration to the cover or jacket design. Review the competition, check out the award-winning designs from the latest British Book Design & Production Awards (www.britishbookawards.org). If you want your book to take up space on a shelf face out (the most popular display method) the jacket must be of stunning design and quality. Book cover design is a specialist discipline, so commissioning an experienced designer is often the best way to give your book an edge alongside other publications.

• Pick your time of year carefully. The majority of new writers are launched in the beginning of the year. If you release too close to Christmas, your book will get lost on the shelves. If you come in February or March, we often have the space to display your book where it has a better chance of selling.

• Booksellers would not welcome being sent an Amazon link in your proposal. Whilst, of course, Amazon is likely to be another outlet for your book, most high-street bookshops choose to have no commercial dealings with Amazon because of the perceived negative impact they have had on Britain's high streets and physical bookshops.

• Think about how you might promote your book and direct people to the bookshop for sales. We send our sales information to Nielsen/BookScan, so if we sell a lot of copies your book will get noticed around the book industry.

• Outline what will be your marketing and publicity plan for the book if we take stock to generate interest.

• Supply: make sure your book can be distributed via the national trade wholesalers Gardners (www.gardners.com), at a standard trade discount, with returns. If in the Republic of Ireland, use either Easons (www.easons.com) or Argosy (www.argosybooks.ie).

• Ask your printer how they can help to distribute your book via the wholesalers mentioned above. Many will take care of this on your behalf. For instance, a traditional book printer like Clays will warehouse copies of your books then distribute them when wholesale orders come in, while Ingram Spark/Lightning Source will print each copy to order and distribute them to retailers via the main wholesale routes.

• Fix a realistic wholesale discount when you set up your book for distribution, whether you do this directly via the wholesalers, or via your printer. It might be tempting to keep the discount as low as possible to increase your royalties, but the lower you make it the less realistic it will be for a bookshop to stock it. Do your research – find out how much of a cut the wholesaler will take (as a very general guide, it could be in the area of 15%), and remember that the average discount bookshops receive is in the region of 40% of the cover price.

• Thinking through and planning for these elements of distribution will simplify our ordering/reordering of your book and increases your chance of being stocked by us tenfold. Whilst bookshops might from time to time agree to being supplied directly by an author, each time a separate supplier is set up for an individual book it adds greatly to the bookshop's paperwork and accounting burden and, more importantly, means that it takes longer to reorder the book once it sells. Most bookshops order every day from Gardners, Easons or Agrosy at the click of a button, and so ensuring those wholesalers have stock of your book is the best way to make it easily accessible to every bookshop in the country.

• Months before the book is due to be published, begin the social media campaign and include your local bookshops.

• Gather the email addresses of friends and contacts, and once the book is published tell them that they can order it through such-and-such a bookshop. This will show the local bookshop that there is interest and they, in turn, are more likely to say 'yes' to stocking your book.

• If you sell copies direct to all your friends and family, it is unlikely that the local bookshop will have a market to sell to. If you persist in taking this step, don't be surprised if after a month or so you get an email from them announcing they have sold none and want to return the books.

• If you have a website, please direct potential customers to any bookshops that have agreed to stock your book.

• If a bookshop does order copies of your book and agrees to be supplied by you directly, then don't forget to deliver the books along with an invoice. It is very important the latter has your contact details (for future orders) and bank details (for payment).

• Do not constantly call the bookshop to check on sales (tempting as that might be).

How a typical high-street bookshop decides on the books to stock

Every bookshop has a finite amount of space and budget to spend each month. The book buyers will go through a series of decisions before saying 'yes' or 'no' to any particular book.

For many bookshops the decision is helped by the representatives from publishers, who will brief them on the new books, why they believe it will sell in the bookshop, and what promotion the publisher is putting behind the book.

Here is an outline of some of the decisions taken by a bookseller before deciding to stock a book:

Our market: we understand what our customers like to read and what genres sell well. We tailor our stock around that (we also try and find the books they didn't know they liked).

Our tastes: if we read and love a book, you can be sure we're going to be telling our customers about it.

The subject: if a book is on a topic that we feel will be of interest to our customers, then that is a huge swaying factor for us.

The author: if we know their work and their track record, we can make a judgement on how well we think the book will sell for us. Also, if the author is local and is likely to have a local following and/or supportive friends and family, then this will influence us.

Marketing: we look at what sort of promotion the book will be getting locally, further afield and on social media (is there already a buzz around it?).

Format and price: this is a major selling point for us; it's not unusual to wait for a paperback to come out before taking a chance on a title.

Design: as with the format, we look at the jacket. Sometimes a stunning cover can be the swaying point between us taking a book or not.

After all this, the bookseller may decline to stock your book. Don't take that personally or expect an explanation; time does not allow for that for every book we decline to stock.

One thing to remember is, please don't be disheartened if we say 'no' to your book. What works for some bookshops doesn't work for others. What sells huge numbers in, say, the Edinburgh Bookshop might not sell in Bath and what sells in Bath may not sell in Oswestry. That's the beauty of high-street bookshops – they are all different. You can find lists of Britain's bookshops at www.booksellers.org.uk/bookshopsearch.aspx.

What can you expect from a bookshop?

Despite the many one-way tips above, getting a book into a reader's hands is very much a team effort between an author, a publisher and a bookseller. Here's what you can expect from a bookshop when you approach them with your book:

• In all circumstances, to be treated with the respect and consideration you'd expect any business to give to a potential business partner.

• Once the bookseller has had a chance to consider the book properly, a clear and prompt answer as to whether or not the bookshop is willing to accept the book into its stock.

• If the bookshop does take the book and the book sells, to pay you promptly in accordance with the payment terms you have specified and to give quick consideration to reordering more stock.

• If the bookshop is included in any social media campaign around a book it has agreed to stock, to participate actively in that campaign.

Extracted from the Booksellers Association *Want to get your Book stocked in a High Street Bookshop?* written by **Sheila O'Reilly**, an experienced independent bookseller, who previously owned Dulwich Books, London. For the complete Guide see https://www.booksellers.org.uk/Industry-Info/Industry-Info/Getting-your-book-stocked-in-a-high-street-bookshop.

See also...

• *Getting books to market: how books are sold*, page 110

Getting books to market: how books are sold, page 110

Self-publishing

What do self-publishing providers offer?

Jeremy Thompson presents the options for engaging an author services company.

Now that self-publishing is widely accepted and it is easier to do it than ever before, authors are presented with a broader range of opportunities to deliver their book or ebook to readers. This brings with it a greater responsibility to you, the author and publisher, to make the right choices for your publishing project. The various options for self-publishing may seem bewildering at first, and each has their pros and cons. But some relatively simple research will prove invaluable in ensuring you make the right choices for your book.

Motivation influences method

There are many reasons why authors choose to self-publish, and contrary to popular belief, the decision to do so is not always motivated by the aspiration to be a bestselling novelist. That is only one reason; others include the wish to impart knowledge to a wider audience; the desire to publish a specialist book with a relatively small target audience; the fulfilment of a hobby; publishing as part of a business or charity; and yes, vanity (a wish to see one's name on a book cover is fine, as long as you have realistic expectations of your work).

Understanding why you are self-publishing is important, as the reasons for doing so can help point to the best way in which to go about it. For example, if you are publishing simply for pleasure, and have few expectations that your book will 'set the world alight', then you'd be wise not to invest in a large number of copies; using 'print on demand' (POD) or producing an ebook could be a good way forward. If you have a book that you're publishing to give away or sell as part of your business to a relatively captive audience, then a short print run of a few hundred copies might be wise. If you want your novel to reach as many readers as possible and to sell it widely, you'll need to have physical copies to get into the retail supply chain and in front of potential readers, so opt for a longer print run of perhaps 500 or more. The more copies you print, the greater the economies of scale.

Decisions on how to self-publish are often influenced by the money you are prepared to invest in (and risk on) your project. Making a decision on what self-publishing route to take based on financial grounds alone is fine, as long as you understand the implications of that decision. For example, as the name implies, print-on-demand (POD) books are only printed when someone actually places an order for a copy; there are no physical copies available to sell. As POD books are largely sold on a 'firm sale' basis, bookshops will rarely stock them, so most POD sales will be made through online retailers. This is particularly the case when authors publish with Amazon KDP ... bookshops are very reluctant to source books from Amazon! In addition, as the POD unit print cost is higher than if a quantity of books are printed in one go, the retail price of a book is likely to be fairly high to cover the print cost and retailer's discount, and make you some profit. Authors often assume that POD is some miracle form of low-cost book publishing, but if that were so, why don't major commercial publishers distribute all of their books in this way? The disadvantages of POD include limited retail distribution and high print cost; these can work for many types of book, like specialist non-fiction titles or academic books that command high cover prices, but it can be difficult to make it cost-effective for fiction or children's books.

At the other end of the scale, printing 3,000 copies of a novel will only pay off if you can get that book onto the retailers' shelves and in front of potential readers, or if you have some other form of 'captive' readership that you can reach with your marketing. Distribution to retailers works largely on the 'sale or return' model, using distribution companies and sales teams to sell new books to bookshops (and bookshops are still the largest sellers of books in the UK). If you can't get your book into the bookshop distribution chain, you are limiting the prospect of selling your 3,000 copies, and money tied up in unsaleable stock is money wasted.

Publishing an ebook is an increasingly popular method of self-publishing, but it too has its pros and cons. On the up side, it can be done very cheaply and quickly; the flip side is that, as hundreds of new ebooks are published each day, how do you get yours noticed? Authors who publish an ebook alone need to spend a lot of time and effort on getting noticed, and sadly most will rarely sell a great number of copies.

As a self-publisher, you need to make sure you understand the limitations of each form of publishing method before you decide on the best route for your book. It can make the difference between success or failure for your book before it's even produced.

Choosing an author services company

In its truest sense, self-publishing means that you as author undertake all the processes undertaken by a commercial publisher to bring a book to market: editing, design, production, marketing, promotion and distribution. If you're multi-talented and have a lot of spare time, then you may want to do all of these things yourself, but for most authors it's a question of contracting an author services company to carry out some or all of the tasks required. From the start it should be understood that most author services companies make their money by selling their services to you as the author; very few have a lot of market knowledge and even fewer offer any real form of active marketing or have bookshop distribution. Choosing the right company to work with is crucial in ensuring that your self-publishing expectations stand a chance of being met. Author services companies come in various guises, but they can broadly be broken into three categories:

• **DIY POD services.** You upload your manuscript and cover design, and your book (or ebook) is simply published 'as is'. It's relatively cheap, and great if you are not too concerned about the design quality and POD or electronic distribution is what you want.

• **Assisted services companies.** These companies offer typesetting and cover design, and perhaps some limited distribution and marketing options. If you're looking for a better product and some basic help in selling your book then this could be right for you.

• **Full service companies.** These suppliers tend to work at the better quality end of the self-publishing market, offering authoritative advice, bespoke design, active trade and media marketing and, in a couple of cases, real bookshop distribution options.

In addition, there is a plethora of companies and individuals offering component parts of the book production and marketing process, such as copy-editing, proofreading, cover design, public relations, etc.

The key for any self-publisher in choosing a company to work with is research. Having decided why you are self-publishing and set your expectations from doing so, the next step is to see who offers what, and at what cost, and to match the right company with what you are seeking. A search on the internet for 'self-publishing' will present you with many choices, so explore the company websites, compare what is being offered, and generally get a feel for what each says they do. Are they just selling services to authors, or are they selling their authors' books? Do they offer active marketing or just 'marketing advice'? Don't take their word for it, though: seek independent advice from other authors or independent industry commentators – there are three sources of reliable, independent information on self-publishing service providers: this *Yearbook* and associated website (www.writersandartists.co.uk); ALLi (see page 515); and the Independent Publishing Magazine (www.theindependentpublishingmagazine.com), which gives authoritative reviews of self-publishing companies and an annual ranking of the best (and worst) based upon author feedback.

Having identified some companies that look as if they will help you meet your publishing expectations, you need to establish how much it will cost. Get detailed quotations from companies and compare like-for-like. Ask questions of those companies if anything is in doubt: ask to see a contract; ask for a sample of their product (many companies still produce terrible quality books!). Time spent at this stage will ensure that you get a good feel for the company you're considering working with, and that can be the difference between a happy self-publishing experience and a disastrous one.

Marketing and distribution

Authors often concentrate on producing a book or ebook and ignore the part of the equation that actually sells the book. Examine carefully what author services companies offer. Distribution includes all the processes involved in getting a book or ebook in front of potential readers, but many companies offer simply a limited, online-only service. Marketing is the process of alerting both the media (whether in print, on air or online) and potential readers that a book is available. Similarly, very few companies spend much effort to actively market their authors' work. The right choice of marketing and distribution service can make or break a book even before production has started.

As the author and self-publisher, you must decide how to get it into the hands of readers. You will need to make decisions on whether POD or wider retail distribution is required; whether the marketing services offered by an author services company are enough for your book; or if a public relations company might be the way forward. Remember, this is 'self'-publishing, so it is up to you to make the right choices for you.

A brave new world

Self-publishing offers authors a host of opportunities to make their work available to readers. Making the right decisions to meet your expectations for your book or ebook in the early stages of the publishing process will pay dividends. Understand your motivations; research the production options well; understand distribution choices; give marketing the importance it requires; and above all, enjoy your self-publishing experience.

Jeremy Thompson FRSA founded Troubador Publishing (www.troubador.co.uk) in 1996 and started the Matador (www.troubador.co.uk/matador) self-publishing imprint in 1999, which has since helped over 10,000 authors to self-publish. Troubador also runs the annual Self-Publishing Conference and holds a 'Self-Publishing Experience' Day at its offices near Leicester. Troubador also runs Indie-Go (www.indie-go.co.uk), offering component author services, and in 2015 it acquired The Book Guild Ltd, an independent partnership publisher. Jeremy was elected as a Fellow of the Royal Academy of Arts in 2019 in recognition of his work in independent publishing.

In praise of fanfic

Hari Patience uncovers the rich field of fanfiction, a world full of creative opportunities and possibilities, where prequels, sequels, crossovers, alternate universes and viewpoints, 'fix-its' and 'what ifs' provide fertile ground for writers to practise and enjoy their craft.

Recently I read an amazing reimagining of Jane Austen's *Pride and Prejudice* (1813). Unlike other versions that have appeared over the years, this one featured no zombies and no murders in need of solving at Pemberley Hall – instead it was an exquisitely plotted alternative life of Elizabeth Bennet that unfurled over about 500,000 words (the original novel is only around 120,000 words long), wherein our heroine followed the drum to the Peninsula war with her first husband. Such was the scope of the story that it had several alternate endings and an impressive cameo from the Duke of Wellington.

I'd love to recommend it to everyone I've ever met, but I suspect that more than a few of them would turn their noses up at it. You see, it wasn't a published novel but a story written by a fan, something generally referred to as fanfic or fanfiction.

What is fanfic?

There are many ways of describing fanfiction – some call it theft, others 'unoriginal drivel', still more have mocked it for being full of badly spelled porn written by teenagers. But if we're looking for a basic description, a fanfic is a story (or comic or video edit) that is based on an original work by someone else. That work could be a novel, a comic book, a television show or film – it could even be based on a podcast or cartoon strip. A particularly 'Marmite' (you love it or you hate it) area of fanfic is Real Person Fiction or RPF, in which the author conjures a story where their favourite pop star is in love with them, or possibly in love with their band mate, or maybe just running a coffee shop somewhere in the Lower East Side. You would be hard-pressed to describe RPF as being based on an original work by another creative though. Some could possibly be claimed by the public relations experts who feed stories to the tabloids.

It might be easier to say what fanfic is not. It is not profitable. It is not sellable. It is not something that any fan can claim is entirely theirs, even if the particular creative interpretation is their own, as it is grown from the seed of someone else's idea. Fanfiction is written without authorisation or permission. Sometimes an author may be approached by a copyright owner (the original author, their estate or publisher) to write an official prequel or sequel, such as Geraldine McCaughrean's *Peter Pan in Scarlet* (OUP 2006). Commissioned work is not fanfiction; it may have been written by a fan but, because that fan had permission, it doesn't meet the criteria.

So why, in this *Yearbook* designed to help struggling writers and artists find their way into paid creative work, are we talking about fanfic? Because, while we may all dream of *Sunday Times* bestseller lists, Hollywood three-picture-deals, or writing the Great British Novel, we shouldn't lose sight of what brought us here in the first place – the sheer joy of creation. Historically fanfiction has fallen into something of a grey area. In the early days of the internet author and publishers pushed back hard, sending 'cease and desist' letters, in some cases to children. Entire fanfiction archive websites disappeared overnight when faced with the wrath of a major studio or publisher. It was standard operating practice for years for fanfiction writers to include a disclaimer at the top of every chapter saying something like: 'I do not own these characters and am writing this story for my own amusement and not for any profit'.

In 2014, UK copyright law was amended to include: 'Fair dealing with a work for the purposes of caricature, parody or pastiche does not infringe copyright in the work.'[1] Many have taken this to mean that fanfiction – so long as it is not generating any money – is legal. As with many questions of legality, the enforcement of this depends upon the creativity of your legal counsel and the flexibility of the judge hearing the case. We are not legal experts here at the *Yearbook* and, should you wish to write something that could be classed as fanfiction for the purposes of profitable publication, we would advise speaking to a lawyer with expertise in copyright law first.

Fanfiction websites

The website Archive of Our Own (AO3; https://archiveofourown.org) looks to US Copyright law for protection. On their website AO3 state: '… fanworks are creative and transformative, core fair uses, and [we] will therefore be proactive in protecting and defending fanworks from commercial exploitation and legal challenge.' AO3 is an entirely non-profit, non-commercial endeavour, funded by regular donation drives that ensure the servers stay on and the site stays live; they also maintain a legal support service for fans who may need it.

Now, instead of cracking down on fanfic writers, authors are advised by publishers and lawyers not to read any of the fanfiction associated with their works. The fear is that, if an author is known to read fanfic, and if an idea first explored by a fan should surface in a future novel by the original author, then the author could be sued by the fan writer. I've seen several tweets and blogs by content creators asking people not to send them character musings or sequel ideas, as even reading someone else's take could prevent them from writing a potential sequel.

So, the legal threat to fanfiction is gone but the social stigma remains. Fanfiction is regarded as derivative, lesser, a juvenile pursuit – a reputation that I feel is entirely undeserved. It's time for us to re-evaluate the worth of fanfiction, both as readers and writers.

Fanfiction websites

Archive of Our Own (AO3)
https://archiveofourown.org

The largest fanfiction website in the world, which hosts over 7.5 million fanworks across over 43,000 fandoms. Established in 2007, this is the main home for fanfic online – especially as it has its own lawyers who work to ensure that fanfic authors are protected from legal threats. Perhaps as a result of this legal protection, AO3 has no formal restrictions on content for publication, though it does ask that all users tag any sexually explicit or potentially problematic work. Any story published with no warning tags in place is automatically placed behind a disclaimer, to prevent people from stumbling across it accidentally. In 2019 AO3 won the Hugo Award for Best Related Work.

Fanfiction.net (FF.net)
www.fanfiction.net

The second largest fanfiction website. Started in 1998, it has over 12 million registered users and hosts stories in over 40 languages. In comparison to AO3, FF.net has stricter publishing guidelines in terms of what is allowed to be published; no explicit adult fiction is permitted (though some can still be found that has yet to be removed) and anything related to works published by Anne Rice, Laurel K. Hamilton, Robin Hobb and several other authors are also banned at their request.

1 http://www.legislation.gov.uk/uksi/2014/2356/regulation/5/made

Self-publishing

Why write fanfic?

Do you remember when you were a child? If your toy box was anything like mine, you never had a full set of everything … a few My Little Ponies, a He-Man, some Barbies and one random Care Bear. Short of the full cast needed to recreate a favourite movie or story, I was forced to create crossover mash-ups: a My Little Pony might rescue Barbie from a kidnapping to thwart the evil plans of He-Man; the next day He-Man might need rescuing from the nefarious clutches of the Care Bear. Fanfic can be like that – take all your favourite characters, throw them into a scenario, and munch some popcorn while they figure it out.

There's a huge amount of freedom in not writing for publication. You get to experiment – to try out new genres or new styles. If you're someone who over-writes, you could hone your short-form writing by taking on the challenge of writing 100-word 'drabbles' or three-sentence stories. If you want to work on your dialogue, you could attempt to tell a story using only speech and see if you can still make it clear who is saying what.

Fanfiction offers many opportunities for writing and style exercises. When you're writing a story set in an established universe some of the heavy lifting is already done – you don't need to describe characters or establish the rules of the world, as your audience already knows them. That leaves you the freedom to focus in on the type of story you want to write. Author Neil Gaiman has said that fanfiction is 'a good place to write while you've still got training wheels on',[2] and it is certainly true that being able to write in someone else's universe – where your audience already knows the rules and you don't have to explain them – is a comforting place to start.

What could I write?

Have you ever wondered what Irene Adler's internal narrative might have been in *Sherlock*? Or Darth Vader's thoughts at the end of *The Empire Strikes Back*? Considering how certain events might have been seen from someone else's point of view (POV) is a standard fanfiction trope. Twisting the narrative like this can reveal hidden motivations and may even make sense of some of the apparent plot holes. This is not an approach unique to fanfiction, as many authors have revisited the stories of out-of-copyright characters, as in the re-imagining of Mrs Rochester from Charlotte Brontë's *Jane Eyre* (1847) in *Wide Sargasso Sea* (André Deutsch 1966) by Jean Rhys.

Rather than a different point of view, you could try a different universe – or rather an alternate universe (AU). Again, this is a wide-ranging trope, found in well-known creative works such as the film *Apocalypse Now*, an alternate universe re-telling of Joseph Conrad's *Heart of Darkness*, or *10 Things I Hate About You*, which brings Shakespeare's *The Taming of the Shrew* into an American high school. In an AU you might find Justice League teaming up as food truck chefs in Manhattan or facing off as coaches of rival sports teams. AUs cover a wide array of possibilities; popular recurring themes include placing all the characters in high school or running a coffee shop together. It's well known now that *Fifty Shades of Grey* (Vintage Books 2011) started life as an AU fanfic of Stephanie Meyer's *Twilight* series (Little, Brown 2005-08).

Another approach to alternate universes is to take a 'what if' approach to a canon moment … What if Sam and Dean Winchester of *Supernatural* were African-American? What if Aragorn was female? What if Veronica Mars became an FBI agent? … What changes

Self-publishing

would this make to the existing canon? Would the Winchesters have had a different reaction from the law-enforcement officers they worked with to kill monsters? Would Aragorn have still been well-received as the returning king? Would Veronica have found happiness solving federal crimes? Fanfic gives the writer, and their audience, a way of exploring these possibilities. It's something that *Marvel* comics have done for years with their *What If ...?* special issues and short runs like *1602* and *Powerless*, so it's not too surprising to find their fans exploring similar ideas in 'fic'.

A type of story which fits within alternate universes but is so common as to have its own label is the crossover. What if Buffy Summers was a Jaeger pilot (*Pacific Rim*) – who would her co-pilot be? Or what would Bilbo Baggins' daemon be? Was Eliot Spencer from *Leverage* ever a member of a Stargate team (the show runners say he was, but they couldn't get permission to mention it on screen)? It's fun to see fictional universes collide and the copyright owners have used this to great effect with team-up games such as *Super Smash Bros* or *Kingdom Hearts*, the occasional visit by Mulder and Scully to *The Simpsons'* Springfield, and the massive multi-show crossovers run each year for *Arrow*, *The Flash*, *Legends of Tomorrow* and more.

It's not unusual for fans to be dissatisfied with the twists and turns that the official narrative has taken. Marvel Cinematic Universe fans rebelled en masse, with the #CoulsonLives hashtag, after Coulson's apparent death in *The Avengers*. In time, he was resurrected to lead *Marvel's Agents of SHIELD* television show, but before that happened fanfiction writers had provided myriad examples of how Agent Coulson miraculously survived or mysteriously came back to life, as 'fix-it fics'. Sometimes fix-its are also crossovers, in which characters from one show or book turn up to help solve a problem in another. *Leverage*, featuring Robin-Hood-like criminals, is so popular as a fix-it crossover partner that its characters have helped fix fandoms from *The Avengers* to *The Walking Dead*.

These five tropes barely scratch the surface of the ocean of possibilities there are in fanfiction – it's a very open field and all contributions are welcome.

A final thought

Some people might ask why they should waste their time writing fanfiction when they could be working on an original work for publication. To that I offer three responses:

1. Any form of regular writing practice can make you a better writer.

2. Even if you never get published, writing and sharing fanfic online can connect you to a community of readers, who will generally offer incredibly positive commentary on your work (in 20 years of writing fanfic I have received a grand total of two negative comments out of thousands). That audience can help you feel pride and delight in your writing on even the most difficult day.

3. Creative hobbies are proven to make people happier[3] – and even better at their day jobs – with a 15-30% increase in positive performance reviews tracked in one study.[4] Happy people are also 12% more productive at work.[5]

3 'New research published by the Society for Personality and Social Psychology (and not the Institute of the Completely Obvious, as you may have expected), says that valuing your time more than the pursuit of money leads to feelings of greater wellbeing. And by valuing your time, they mean spending it wisely on hobbies, exercising or being with your family.' https://www.theguardian.com/commentisfree/2016/jan/11/hobbies-happier-gardening-bird-watching-stroking-cat

4 'One study from San Francisco State University found that people who often engaged in a creative activity scored 15-30 percent higher on performance rankings. They were also more likely to come up with creative solutions to on-the-job problems.' https://www.fastcompany.com/90389174/how-hobbies-benefit-your-productivity

5 'Economists carried out a number of experiments to test the idea that happy employees work harder. In the laboratory, they found happiness made people around 12% more productive.' https://warwick.ac.uk/newsandevents/pressreleases/new_study_shows

Nobody writes fanfiction to get famous; though some people have made it through the glass ceiling between fan-writer and professional author due to their fanfiction works, they are the exception, not the rule. No, we write fanfiction because it's a creative outlet, and because as fanfic writers we may even develop fans of our own who leave positive feedback on our work and increase our kudos. We write for the joy of creation, the excitement of receiving glowing comments and the accomplishment of finishing a story. We write because we have to, and we write because – although not all of us get to be published – with fanfiction we can all get to be read.

Hari Patience-Davies has been finding joy and fulfilment writing fanfiction for over 20 years, but she won't tell you her AO3 username. Hari is co-founder and Storytelling Coach for Patience Davies Consulting www.patiencedavies.com.

Building your author brand

What is an 'author brand' and why does it matter? Sam Missingham shares her tips and techniques on how self-published authors can develop their profile to attract readers to their work.

Most people I meet hate the idea that authors are brands; they seem to assume that this means the publishing industry is treating them like tins of baked beans, sports clothing or chocolate bars. I think there is a fear that this is part of a dehumanising process treating an author like a product with a logo to be packaged and sold. this reveals a lack of understanding of what is involved in building an author brand and why it is so important. The aim of a strong author brand – to put it into much more positive terms – is to build an authentic relationship with readers and, further, to encourage readers to think and feel certain emotions. It is also about establishing your uniqueness.

Most of us already have connections with the authors of our favourite books. Think for a second about, say, Ian Rankin. If you enjoy his books, you might be interested in Edinburgh, the character of Rebus, and the type of crime novels Ian writes. If you are more of a fan, you may have heard him speak at an event, you might follow him on social media, you might know that Ian likes a pint and visiting record shops, and that he loves taking photos of his walks around his home city. You can probably recognise that he has a unique voice. How have Ian and his publishers (Hachette UK) built his brand? Ian has done the most important part, which is to write consistently great books for over 20 years, and this is undoubtedly the best way to build an authentic relationship with readers and establish an author brand. His publishers have amplified his unique voice through publicity, marketing and events. They ran a week-long Rebus event in Edinburgh and reinforced Ian's brand across the city and beyond.

To help you establish your own unique brand in practical ways, here are three important elements of author branding you can focus on:

1. Design

The design elements of your author brand involve the creative choices you make for your book covers, your website, your social media and anything else that is seen by the market and potential readers (is 'outward-facing'). I think it is always useful to think in terms of 'genre signposting', which in simple terms means the colours, imagery and fonts or typography that are typically used. The use of styles that follow existing publishing standards will immediately identify the genre your book fits into – if it is sci-fi, a young adult novel, Regency romance, or a cookbook. Some people think all crime or romance books look the same, but actually they have been designed with similar elements so that readers immediately recognise them. Here's how to establish the design elements of your author brand.
• Ask a professional designer to help you. This is always my first piece of advice. Designers who have experience of working in publishing have a deep understanding of genres, of what readers expect, and of wider design trends and how they can make you look like a professional writer. A lot of self-published authors are still designing their own covers and many of them just aren't good enough. Don't forget – the aim is to attract readers of your genre; your cover will set their expectations of your book.

• Identify three or four authors who are successful in your genre; take a good, critical look at their covers, their websites, sign up to their newsletters, check out their social media accounts, and do a Google image search on their names. You should see some similarities in the design elements they have used. Then pick out elements that you like and which you think could work for you and your books. Ask yourself how you can express your *uniqueness* within this established aesthetic.

• If you are designing your own covers, ads, website and social media assets, I recommend you keep things simple: within the bounds of the genre aesthetic that you've identified above. Choose a very small number of colours, fonts and images and use them across your promotion and marketing. Consistency and repetition play a part in building your brand. Canva, www.canva.com, is an excellent design tool and can take you a long way towards looking like a professional author.

• Get feedback from readers, industry insiders, bloggers and booksellers on what you are currently doing. What do they think when they look at your book cover? And at your website? What could you do better? You will probably be quite surprised by their answers. Listen to them. Try to avoid asking partners or friends, because they will rarely give you honest, informed feedback.

These design elements should be used consistently across your website, social media, ads, point of sale, merchandise and any other touchpoints you have with your readers.

2. Voice

Your author voice refers to how and what you communicate, the tone you take, and what you make your readers think and feel. Looking at existing, successful examples is always useful, such as Marian Keyes, who has a fantastic author voice; she is incredibly funny, kind and open; she is an absolute master of social media – brilliant on Twitter, makes great videos on Instagram, and her newsletter is hilarious. Take a look at www.mariankeyes.com, Twitter @MarianKeyes, www.facebook.com/MarianKeyes and www.instagram.com/marian_keyes. You will notice that Marian talks regularly about her mum, her love of makeup, her nieces and nephews, Ireland, her travels, and occasionally her ailments. Her openness, authenticity and humour, along with her brilliant books, make her an incredibly popular and successful author. Her voice plays an important part in this. Navigate the sites and social media of authors you admire or in the genre in which your own books sit, what inspires you, what can you emulate?

A little side-note about authenticity: some authors I have worked with think that this involves revealing everything about themselves, and this is not the case. Think carefully about what you are happy to talk about – whether that is your hobbies, family or social life. We all need boundaries and privacy, so think this through. If you are working with a publicist, they will ask you about this, to find hooks to pitch your story to journalists. Be clear about how much of yourself you are willing to reveal. Once you have established these topics, make sure you talk honestly about them; maintaining an inauthentic author persona might be possible for a while, but is not sustainable long-term.

Back to author voice. What you say and how you say it will influence how your readers, agents, booksellers and publishers feel about you. What would you like them to think? That you are fun, inspiring, knowledgeable, supportive? Find a way to convey your values through your voice. LJ Ross is a very successful author, whose bestselling DCI Ryan mysteries are set in the north east of England. She shares her love of the region, supports local people and businesses, and runs several philanthropic initiatives. Her readers are incredibly engaged with her books and they know that she, in turn, is incredibly committed to them.

Your voice should be within keeping of your genre and appropriate for your audience. Never lose sight of who your readers and wider audience are; so if you write children's books, don't forget that your voice must appeal to parents, teachers and school librarians, as well as being suitable for children.

3. Consistency and repetition

Once you have established the elements of your author brand, you should use them everywhere and consistently. You want your audience to become familiar with you. Your imagery, colours, voice and covers will all help them to do that. Consider using the same author photo across all of your social media; people will recognise you and, if they enjoy you on Twitter, will probably follow you elsewhere. Add the same photo somewhere prominent on your website too.

Here are a few other tips to help you establish your author brand:

• If you already have some readers, ask for their feedback: What do they like? What do they enjoy about what you share? What do they think about your covers? Run some polls on Twitter or on your Facebook page.

• Engage with a group of your hardcore fans and use them as a sounding board. Treat them like your VIP readers. You can provide them with unique and pre-publication access to some of your content in return for their input.

• Read some of the reader or blogger reviews of your books in case these are useful to suggest how to improve what you do. If you don't want to do this yourself, consider asking someone you trust to pull out any positive points – and any constructive criticism in the negative ones (it *is* there sometimes!).

• Go into a bookshop and have a good look at where your book sits on the shelf (or where you hope it will sit, if it's not published yet); see which authors are being highlighted in your genre; take photos. If you feel confident enough, talk to a bookseller – they really are the fount of all knowledge and will probably give you insights that you simply can't get elsewhere.

Go through a similar process on Amazon (and other online booksellers) in the categories and subcategories where your book will sit. Look at the bestsellers in each category; go to their websites and look at their ads, their blurbs, and consider the tone they are using.

There is always so much to learn from other more established authors. Learn from the best – and adapt ideas to work for you. In addition to Ian Rankin, LJ Ross and Marian Keyes, I would highly recommend the following authors.

– Rob Biddulph (www.robbiddulph.com) is a children's author who has absolutely nailed his brand. Take a look at #DrawWithRob to see how he engaged with his readers during the Covid-19 pandemic and built on all of the positive elements of his approach.

– Salena Godden (www.salenagodden.co.uk) is a brilliant author and poet; take a look at how she uses social media, videos and live performances to create a very strong author identity.

– Simon Alexander Ong (www.simonalexanderong.com) is a business book author and life coach; his author brand is spot-on for the professional audience he is trying to attract. He is particularly good on Instagram (www.instagram.com/simonalexandero).

– Joanne Harris (www.joanne-harris.co.uk) is brilliant at everything; there are all kinds of ideas and tips you could pick up from her use of social media.

I hope this advice will help you nail *your* author brand and convince you just how important it is to an author's publishing strategy.

Sam Missingham is founder of The Empowered Author, a book marketing service for authors. Find out more at https://theempoweredauthor.com and follow her on Twitter @samatlounge.

See also...
- *Making waves online*, page 630
- *Getting your book stocked in a high-street bookshop*, page 614

Making waves online

Simon Appleby outlines how writers can use the internet to get noticed.

Make some noise!

Whether you're a published writer with an ongoing deal, or an aspiring writer with lots of ideas or even a finished manuscript, the challenge remains the same. How do you get your name known, your words read, your manuscripts taken on, your book bought? Whether you're looking for a traditional publishing deal, you're considering self-publishing, or have some other approach in mind, this article is intended to help you promote your work online.

The prevalence of smartphones, tablets and mobile internet means that book and author websites are, more than ever, in direct competition with every form of media, not just other websites. This includes TV-on-demand services such as Netflix, social media platforms, instant messaging and online gaming.

But it's crucial to find a way to get people's attention and build a devoted following of your own. Readers are bombarded with options and are unlikely to stumble upon your site by accident. You need to lure readers and critics to your writing, and, in turn, attract publishers.

Risk-averse publishers (and agents) look to the internet for inspiration and to gauge marketability. Much of your activity should demonstrate to a publisher that people like your work and would pay to read more of it. The E.L. James's global phenomenon *Fifty Shades of Grey* began life on an internet fan-fiction forum, the ultimate reminder that there are many ways to be discovered as a writer. Equally, Hugh Howey achieved extraordinary success – which included worldwide fame and lucrative publishing and film-rights deals – from self-publishing his books, as did paranormal romance writer Amanda Hocking.

But it didn't come easily and even those who've achieved international recognition still need to work hard. Published authors are expected to show a continued commitment to their own success – marketing, publicity, social media. Gone are the days when landing a publishing deal meant you could sit back and let the publisher do all the work. It's important to develop the skills first, because you'll have far less trouble adjusting to the work once the publishing deal is in place.

The technologies, platforms and communities involved in online promotion evolve constantly. But the concepts behind developing a manageable approach to promoting your writing on the internet – to get you closer to your readers and them closer to you – stay virtually the same. This article doesn't deliver detailed DIY instructions, but it does offer ideas for developing your internet presence in a structured and accessible fashion.

There's a lot of noise out there, and to be heard you will have to make some of your own. The technical side of things is not rocket science – there are numerous (and free) solutions which do most of the hard work for you. But it does take persistence and a good idea of what you want to accomplish and who you want to appeal to. This means setting aside some time to plan your approach. It's just like writing – you put the building blocks in place and then, once you start, you won't be able to stop!

Set up your own website and blog

Chances are you're already doing this, but if not you should be. To get started, check out authors who are selling themselves well (and badly). Websites that are easy to navigate, visually appealing, functional and up to date tend to generate the best response. Your website should reflect your style, allowing your visitors to get a sense of who you are. You can look at professional authors' websites for inspiration, but it's also possible to find great examples among lesser-known authors. A good website needn't be expensive or difficult to maintain. Many household names use basic, off-the-shelf website themes.

It's important to include as much information about your published books as your visitors can find on major retailer websites. Ideally, give them extra content they won't find anywhere else. If you can, let visitors in on little secrets or give them insight into the writing process. For example, you might include some interesting copy you wrote for your book but didn't include in the final version.

Include a blog on your website. It's a great way to impart useful or interesting information and drive users to your site. For example, you could publish some of your work to find out what people think about it, or discuss other authors' work, the writing market, or the processes you go through in your writing. Perhaps you could write about the books you liked as a child, topics you researched to write a book, or places you went while researching. Google looks for information it hasn't seen before, and a blog is a great way to update your site.

Place your blog at the centre of your online universe so that all your social media presences point to it. Also, decide what level of engagement you want to offer visitors. Do you want to allow people to comment on your blog posts, for example?

Finally, remember what you write will be available on the internet for a long time, so think carefully about how you talk about yourself, your life and other writers. And don't put anything in writing that you wouldn't want a potential reader or publisher to see.

Get discovered

Good content will only help promote your writing if people are aware of it, so make sure you have a solid understanding of search engine optimisation (SEO). Research the key terms people use to search (there are many keyword research tools available) and include them in your content, but take care to ensure they only appear in context. Search engines prioritise unique, high-quality information, which your readers find useful and interesting, so keep it relevant, fresh and clearly written.

Explore social networking and communities

To help people find your website or blog, you must be a willing participant of the social internet. There are innumerable online communities relevant to authors. But you can find them just as you would find a good book – by searching according to your tastes and listening to the recommendations of your friends. By joining these communities, you can potentially transform your online reputation. It won't happen overnight, but if you continue to engage and participate in discussions, you'll increase your friends and visitor numbers, encourage people to read your words, and boost your reputation. Here are the main categories of community that could be relevant to you:

• Writing communities – where you can get your work evaluated and rate the work of others. These are both a source of useful feedback and encouragement, and a place to get noticed by publishers (sometimes even leading to book deals).

• General book communities – where book owners, librarians, collectors and authors come together – an instant source of like-minded people. Popular communities include Goodreads and LibraryThing.

• Forums – these can be wide-ranging or focused on one subject, but if you find one you like, hang around and join in. However, don't expect to drop in, plug your work and reap the gratitude of other users if you're not prepared to stick around.

• Social networking – this is the broadest category, encompassing thousands of sites large and small. Find the ones that are right for you and that you're comfortable with. Don't set up a Twitter page if you don't want to spend time engaging with other users, for example.

Make 'friends'

There was a time when 'social media' meant Facebook and Twitter to most people. The social media landscape is now much more fragmented – you also have to consider Instagram, Tumblr, Flickr, SoundCloud and many more, as well as book-oriented networks such as Goodreads and LibraryThing. You can't work with all of them and do a great job. The key is to focus on platforms that allow you to reach your audience, and, more importantly, suit the content you want to create. Don't forget LinkedIn. While this was once the province of traditional professionals, today authors, agents and publishing people use it. And there are numerous groups for discussing topics of interest to authors. You may be able to use it to find collaborators (perhaps an illustrator or photographer), and a smartly completed LinkedIn profile is your online CV – essential if you want to be taken seriously.

Use the right tool for the job

It may not be so simple in life, but online there's a tool for almost every situation. I can't tell you every item a good toolkit should contain, but here are some general principles and a few key tools, all of which are free and easy to use.

Some quality author websites

Roald Dahl

www.roalddahl.com

A great wealth of content available, but avoids any unnecessary visual whizbanggery.

Mark Stay

witchesofwoodville.com

Mark shows how writers can extend the world they create on to their website as well – with his characters given a prominent role.

Shannon Selin

https://shannonselin.com

Shannon's focused content marketing has resulted in over 100 weekly blog posts on all things Napoleonic.

Haruki Murakami

www.harukimurakami.com

US site that embraces the aesthetic of Murakami's book cover designs.

Kay Hutchison

https://kayhutchison.com

Promoting a non-fiction title and using content from the book (the glossary, and a spare chapter) to give readers a good insight in to the contents.

Anthony Horowitz

www.anthonyhorowitz.com

A welcoming, fresh and engaging site, recently revamped.

Jonathan Coe

jonathancoewriter.com

A good example of a site which provides a definitive understanding of an author's career – every work, every edition, every cover.

Becky Chambers

otherscribbles.com

An elegant and minimalist site that really showcases the books. Sometimes, less is more.

Yuval Noah Harari

ynharari.com

A good example of the range of functions that an effective website must perform for a non-fiction author, covering events, media appearances and related interests.

• **Stay on 'brand'**: keep a standard biography and a decent photo of yourself handy when setting up your user profiles. It helps to represent yourself consistently across every platform. Always try to use the same username as well. Keep a note of the profiles you set up and update them periodically.

• **Social conversation**: use social networking sites, micro-blogging services (i.e. Twitter) and your own site to engage with your current and potential readers and fellow authors.

• **Share and enjoy**: there's a platform on which to share any type of content you create, from video (YouTube, Vimeo) and photos (Flickr, Photobucket), to audio/podcasts (SoundCloud). Research the most visited platforms in each category – there's no point targeting unpopular ones. When you share content, think about whether you need to maintain your copyright, or whether you want to grant people permission to share or use your work by choosing a Creative Commons license (http://creativecommons.org).

• **Listening and measuring tools**: it's good to know when to drop in and contribute to a conversation that's taking place about you or your work. It's also great to know when someone has just linked to your website. You can set up Google Alerts to notify you when these things happen. Or, to follow the blogs that interest you and keep track of new writers and industry trends, use Really Simple Syndication (RSS), might also provide you with topics to blog about. I suggest NewsBlur or feedly, but there are numerous feed readers available.

To understand what tools work for you, you need to measure their impact. Monitoring websites can help, as can blog statistics within packages such as Google Analytics. You can also use tools that will help you identify how often you, or your chosen genre of writing, are being discussed.

• **Cheat**: to keep the content on your social media channels flowing, use tools that suggest news articles and blog posts for you to share, based on your preferences and interests. These can be real time-savers if you want to post something every day. Similar to functionality within social media dashboards such as Hootsuite, these tools also enable you to schedule content so you can spread out your activities over a longer period.

• **Stay current**: make sure any information about you is current and detailed. Keep your Wikipedia entry up to date if you have one, taking care to stay factual. Update information about yourself on sites such as LibraryThing, and make sure your publishing company knows about your online activities so it can promote them.

Engage with your audience

As a writer spending time online, you are inevitably going to come across comments about your work at some point – sometimes positive, sometimes critical, and occasionally abusive. Keep your cool and remember, when deciding how to react to something, one of these four responses will usually be appropriate:

• **Endorse**: a positive comment, such as a good review, or someone saying they've been inspired by your work, is worth shouting about. Link to it in your own social media, tell your publisher and respond to the creator, helping to cement his or her enthusiasm. It's good to endorse others' work too. Link to the work of another author who has inspired you, or who has recently created interesting content. It's possible that the author or others may return the favour at some point.

• **Engage**: talk to fans and critics on their forums of choice. Respond to constructive criticism professionally and never take it personally.

• **Ignore**: if you can't say anything nice …
• **Enforce**: if anyone becomes abusive or infringes your rights, take measured steps to do something about it (such as contacting their forum moderator or ISP), but never descend to their level. Anything you say in anger may come back to haunt you later.

One more thing. *Never* pretend to be someone you're not, anywhere, for any reason. Always represent yourself honestly as 'the author in question'. Successful authors, who shall remain nameless here, have seriously damaged their credibility and careers through the practice of 'sock puppetry': leaving glowing reviews of their own work under false names and trashing their rivals' books. There really is such a thing as bad publicity.

Delve into some online PR

Put simply, this involves talking to people about your work to get them to write about it. If you're willing to take the time to contact bloggers and offer review copies, interviews, competition prizes or other content they can use, some of them are likely to respond positively. Understand their pressures – they want to find things to write about, but they may also be bombarded with offers every day.

Use some of the same organisational skills that you use when researching and talking to agents and publishers, and when looking through the *Writers' & Artists' Yearbook*. Do your homework on blogs too. Before you approach a blogger, read the blog thoroughly to make sure your work is right for that blog. And read any submission guidelines the site may have. Keep a record of who you contact, and when, to make sure you don't send repeated messages to the same person. And follow up any communications you've made with sites that offer to look at your work. Finally, always present yourself professionally. It's all common sense, but in my experience that doesn't mean everyone does it properly.

Promote your book on a budget

You can get creative and be noticed even with little or no money to spend. By creating content to promote your book yourself, you can save expensive marketing costs.

Ways to do this include writing blogs or articles 'in character'. Or, you could set up a Twitter feed in your character's name, or write microfiction. Enlist the services of friends and family, and their cameras, video cameras, computers and, most importantly, skills to create images or videos that you can promote yourself with. I know you're creative, or you wouldn't be reading this, so there's no doubt you can think of a way to get yourself noticed (and don't get hung up on being wholly original, or you might never get started).

Simon Appleby is the Founder and Managing Director of Bookswarm (www.bookswarm.co.uk), the only digital agency in the UK dedicated to delivering projects for publishers, authors and others in the world of books. Bookswarm has extensive experience in website design and development. It has delivered websites for a wide range of authors, including Martina Cole, Stephen King, Patrick Ness, Gerald Scarfe, Hanif Kureishi and Dorothy Koomson.

Book sites, blogs and podcasts

This is a small selection of the best book sites, blogs and podcasts recommended by the editors of the *Yearbook*.

BOOK SITES AND BLOGS

The Artist's Road
website http://artistsroad.wordpress.com
Founder Patrick Ross

Blog created to record the cross-USA road trip that the author Patrick Ross took in the summer of 2010. During his trip he interviewed over 40 artists with the aim of discussing the motivations, challenges and rewards of their lifestyles, and passing on their creative wisdom. It now details his insights into living an 'art-committed life' through writing and creativity.

Book Patrol
website https://bookpatrol.net/category/book-beat/
Founder Michael Lieberman

Founded in 2006 in the US as a blog to promote books and literacy, it is now a hub for all things book-related. Posting about book news, book reviews and technology. The site has an online shop selling a large collection of curated material.

Books & Such
website www.booksandsuch.com/blog
Founder Janel Kobobel Grant

Blog from a literary agent's perspective, advising on writing query letters and improving MSS before submitting them to agents. Also addresses how to find an agent and get published. Highlights the importance of the editing process in adding to writing quality. Discusses the various aspects of traditional publishing and self-promotion.

The Bookseller
website www.thebookseller.com/blogs

The online website of *The Bookseller*, a magazine which covers publishing industry news. Includes insights into trends and influences, interviews and articles from publishers and lists of bestsellers across a variety of genres.

Nathan Bransford
website http://blog.nathanbransford.com
Founder Nathan Bransford

This author and former literary agent blogs about the writing, editing and publishing process and includes tips on improving plots, dialogue and characters, writing a query letter and synopsis and finding a literary agent. Analyses and debates a range of topics including ebooks and their pricing, social media options, marketing, cover design and plot themes.

Collected
website www.rlf.org.uk/showcase-home/
Founder Royal Literary Fund

Weekly articles published by writers on topics related to literature and writing. Includes discussions on genre, form, research, inspiration and the perfect place to write.

Cornflower Books
website www.cornflowerbooks.co.uk
Founder Karen Howlett

Reviews a wide range of books and has a monthly online book club. Debates cover designs and includes a 'writing and publishing' section, interviews with well-known authors about their books, writing process and routine. Selects 'books of the year' in different genres, and discusses literary festivals and prizes.

The Creative Penn
website www.thecreativepenn.com
Founder Joanna Penn

Focuses on the writing process and how to market and sell your book. Advice on dealing with criticism, finding an agent and writing query letters, POD and ebook publishing, as well as online and social media marketing. Debates traditional publishing, 'hybrid' and self-publishing options and includes audio/video interviews with self-published authors.

Daily Writing Tips
website www.dailywritingtips.com
Founder Maeve Maddox

Publishing new content every week with articles covering the whole writing spectrum: from grammar and punctuation to usage and vocabulary.

Dear Author
website www.dearauthor.com
Founder Jane Litte

Focuses on romantic novels. All reviews are written in the form of a letter to the author. Includes interviews with authors about their writing style.

Fiction Notes
website www.darcypattison.com
Founder Darcy Pattison

Darcy Pattison is a published non-fiction writer and children's author, as well as an experienced speaker. Her website archives eight years of blog posts on children's writing, reviews of her work, resources for writers and information on her speaking engagements where she specialises in novel revision.

Jane Friedman

website http://janefriedman.com
Founder Jane Friedman

Focuses on digital publishing, provides tips for writers on how to beat writers' block, DIY ebook publishing, marketing your writing and publicising it online through blogs, social media and websites to create your 'author platform'. Includes guidance on copyright and securing permissions.

Goins, Writer

website http://goinswriter.com
Founder Jeff Goins

Focuses on advising authors about their writing journey, the business of writing and how to maximise productivity and profits. Highlights how authors can build a core fanbase 'tribe' through a focused approach and by adding value to social media and blogs.

Goodreads

website www.goodreads.com

Users can see what their friends and favourite authors are reading, rate books they've read, write reviews, and customise bookshelves full of books 'Read' and books 'To Read'. A regular newsletter provides book news and author interviews. Owned by Amazon.

Helping Writers Become Authors

website www.helpingwritersbecomeauthors.com
Founder K.M. Weiland

Tips on story structure, creating memorable characters and plot development. Advice about finding writing inspiration and the writing process, story revision and MS editing stages. Includes an extensive list of books for aspiring authors.

Live Write Thrive

website www.livewritethrive.com
Founder C.S. Lakin

Set up by a writer, editor and writing coach who specialises in fiction, fantasy and YA, this blog focuses on helping writers discover what kind of copy-editing and critiquing services their work will need once it is finished. Includes articles by guest bloggers and tips on grammar.

Lovereading

website www.lovereading.co.uk

Independent book recommendation site designed to inspire and inform readers, with the aim of helping them choose their next read. Features include: categories broken down by interest; downloadable opening extracts of featured books; like-for-like recommendations for discovering new authors; expert reviews and reader review panels.

A Newbie's Guide to Publishing

website http://jakonrath.blogspot.co.uk
Founder Joe Konrath

Blog by a self-published author which discusses the writing and publishing process and focuses on self-publishing ebooks, and looks at developments and trends in this area. Includes interviews with self-published authors about their books.

The Organised Writer

website http://organised-writer.com/
Founder Antony Johnston

Houses a host of resources designed to make getting organised as a writer easier, including accounting spreadsheets.

Positive Writer

website http://positivewriter.com
Founder Bryan Hutchinson

A motivational blog for creatives, particularly writers, focusing on how to overcome doubt and negativity to unlock your inner creativity. It includes handy tips on marketing and interviews with other authors.

Reading Matters

website http://readingmattersblog.com
Founder Kim Forrester

The site's main focus is Irish and Australian contemporary fiction; reviews are personable and informative. Every Tuesday the site welcomes guest bloggers to share their favourite books and promote their own blogs.

Lauren Sapala

website http://laurensapala.com
Founder Lauren Sapala

This blog gives pep talks to writers in moments of self-doubt. With posts about how to get inspired and stay focused, its aim is to nurture and empower your creative flame.

Savidge Reads

website https://savidgereads.wordpress.com
Founder Simon Savidge

Entertaining and chatty reviews of literary novels, from modern classics to contemporary fiction from a self-proclaimed bookaholic.

Soapbox

website www.publishersweekly.com/pw/by-topic/columns-and-blogs/soapbox/index.html
Founder Publishers Weekly

Discussions and interviews on all aspects of the literary world: writing, publishing and bookselling. Includes advice and insights as well as big topic debates including censorship, diversity and defunding libraries.

Terribleminds

website http://terribleminds.com/ramble/blog
Founder Chuck Wendig

Comical, easy-to-read blog about author Chuck Wendig's trials and tribulations whilst writing.

There Are No Rules

website www.writersdigest.com/editor-blogs/there-are-no-rules

Blog by the editors of Writer's Digest, focusing on the writing process, plot and character development, query letters and creating an author platform through social media and public speaking. Hosts a range of regular webinars with industry professionals including agents.

This Itch of Writing

website http://emmadarwin.typepad.com/thisitchofwriting
Founder Emma Darwin

An author's advice on the craft of authoring successful books both fiction and creative non-fiction.

Well-Storied

website www.well-storied.com
Founder Kristen Kieffer

Articles, resources and podcasts, focusing on the craft of writing, finding motivation and building a routine.

The Write Life

website http://thewritelife.com
Founder Alexis Grant

This blog is designed to encourage individuals to connect and share experiences with fellow writers during the different writing stages. Posts include advice on blogging, freelancing, finding an agent, publicity and self-publishing amongst other topics.

The Write Practice

website http://thewritepractice.com
Founder Joe Bunting

Focuses on the craft of writing, building a routine and how to get published; includes advice for writers on different stages of the writing process and submitting MSS to agents.

Writer Unboxed

website http://writerunboxed.com
Co-founders Therese Walsh (Editor-in-Chief), Kathleen Bolton

Comical tips on the art and craft of writing fiction, the writing process, and marketing your work. Includes interviews with established authors also offering advice.

Writers & Artists

website www.writersandartists.co.uk

Up-to-date news, views and advice on all aspects of writing and publishing on the site brought to you by the creators of this *Yearbook*. As well as guest blogs, videos and articles from established and debut writers across all genres, there are sections on self-publishing, a community area for sharing work, details of competitions and book-related events, including those hosted by Writers & Artists. Users can sign-up to receive special discounts on editorial services and books and to a regular newsletter.

PODCASTS

Always Take Notes

www.alwaystakenotes.com
Co-hosts Simon Akam, Rachel Lloyd

A bi-monthly podcast interviewing a diverse range of writers and publishing industry experts on a variety of topics, from the mysteries of slush piles and per-word rates, to how to pitch a book and how data are changing the ways newspapers do business.

Begin Self-Publishing Podcast

website https://beginselfpublishing.com
Host Tim Lewis

Promotes self-publishing by demystifying the whole process and gives advice on how to safely navigate all services available to self-published writers.

Books and Authors

website www.bbc.co.uk/programmes/p02nrsfl/episodes/downloads
Hosts various including Elizabeth Day, Johny Pitts and Harriett Gilbert
Provider BBC Radio 4

A weekly podcast with highlights from BBC Radio 4 programmes *Open Book*, in which hosts Elizabeth Day and Johny Pitts interview bestselling authors about their work; and *A Good Read*, in which Harriett Gilbert hosts a lively discussion with her guests about their favourite books.

The Creative Penn Podcast

website www.thecreativepenn.com/podcasts
Host Joanna Penn

Published on Mondays, this weekly podcast informs aspiring authors about available publishing options and book marketing through informative discussions and interviews.

Creative Writing Career

website http://creativewritingcareer.com
Hosts Stephan Bugaj, Justin Sloan, Kevin Tumlinson

Hosted by leading industry professionals whose credits include writing for Pixar, FOX and HBO, this US podcast provides practical advice to writers on all forms of multimedia writing. Topics covered include books and comics, video games and e-publishing, and writing screenplays for television and film.

Self-publishing

Dead Robots' Society

website http://deadrobotssociety.com
Hosts Justin Macumber, Terry Mixon, Paul E. Cooley

Created *for* aspiring writers *by* aspiring writers, this fun podcast offers advice and support by sharing anecdotes and discussing current topics of interest.

The Drunken Odyssey

website https://thedrunkenodyssey.com
Host John King

Started to create a community hub for writers, this podcast is a forum to discuss all aspects of creative writing and literature.

Grammar Girl Quick and Dirty Tips for Better Writing

website www.quickanddirtytips.com/grammar-girl
Host Mignon Fogarty
Provider QuickandDirtyTips

This award-winning weekly podcast provides a bitesize guide to the English language. Each week tackles a specific feature from style and usage, to grammar and punctuation, all in the hope of providing friendly tips on how to become a better writer.

The *Guardian* Books Podcast

website www.theguardian.com/books/series/books
Hosts Claire Armitstead, Richard Lea, Sian Cain
Provider theguardian.com

The *Guardian*'s book editor, Claire Armitstead, provides a weekly podcast that looks at the world of books, poetry and great writing, including interviews with prominent authors; recordings of *Guardian* live events; panel discussions examining current themes in contemporary writing; and readings of selected literary works.

Helping Writers Become Authors

website www.helpingwritersbecomeauthors.com/podcasts
Host K.M. Weiland

Published author, K.M. Weiland produces weekly podcasts to help guide aspiring authors on how to craft and edit a manuscript ready to be sent to a literary agent.

I Should Be Writing

website http://murverse.com/subscribe-to-podcasts/
Host Mur Lafferty

This award-winning podcast is about the process science fiction writer Mur Lafferty went through to go from a wannabe writer to a professional and published author. It documents the highs and lows of a writing career and provides comprehensive how-to tips and interviews.

The *New Yorker*: Fiction

website www.newyorker.com/podcast/fiction
Host Deborah Treisman
Provider WNYC Studios and The *New Yorker*

New Yorker fiction editor, Deborah Treisman, invites an author whose work is being published by the magazine that month to join her in this monthly podcast. Each author selects a piece of short fiction from the magazine's archive to read and analyse.

The Graham Norton Book Club

website www.audible.co.uk
Host Graham Norton, co-hosts Alex Clark, Sara Collins
Provider Audible

TV star and writer, Graham Norton, hosts a series of podcasts in conversation with well-known audiobook narrators and authors on all subjects to do with books.

The Penguin Podcast

website www.penguin.co.uk/podcasts.html
Provider Penguin Books UK

This series, published fortnightly, gives intimate access to bestselling authors through interviews where they discuss their work and give examples of five things that have inspired and shaped their writing.

Reading and Writing Podcast

website http://readingandwritingpodcast.com
Host Jeff Rutherford

This interview-style podcast encourages readers to call in and leave voicemail messages and questions ready for the host to ask the guest writer, who discusses their work and writing practices.

The Self-Publishing Podcast

website https://sterlingandstone.net/series/self-publishing-podcast
Hosts Johnny B. Truant, Sean Platt, David Wright
Provider Sterling & Stone

The hosts explore how a writer can become truly 'authorpreneurial', getting their books published and making money without resorting to agents and traditional publishing models.

Story Grid

website https://storygrid.simplecast.fm
Hosts Shawn Coyne, Tim Grahl

Hosted by a book editor with more than 25 years' experience in publishing and a struggling writer, the duo discuss what features bestselling novels have in common and how authors can utilise these to write a great story that works.

Write Now With Sarah Werner

website www.sarahwerner.com/episodes
Host Sarah Werner

A weekly podcast produced with aspiring writers in mind; provides advice, inspiration, and encouragement to writers to find a suitable work-life balance.

The Writer Files

website https://rainmaker.fm/series/writer
Host Kelton Reid

This long-running podcast explores productivity and creativity, seeing how accomplished writers tackle writer's block and keep the ink flowing and cursor moving.

The Writership Podcast

website https://writership.com/episodes
Hosts Leslie Watts, Clark Chamberlain

Provides help, support and advice to fiction writers on how they can develop the appropriate skills to self-edit their completed manuscript.

Writers Aloud

www.rlf.org.uk/showcase-home/
Provider Royal Literary Fund

This podcast invites published authors to discuss life as a writer and the influences and circumstances which have shaped their writing. Books, poetry, radio, television and theatre are all covered across a range of genres. The Royal Literary Fund also produce short films (In Focus) and bite-size podcasts only a few minutes long (Vox) covering similar topics.

Writing Coach

http://annkroeker.com/
Host Ann Kroeker

This podcast offers practical writing advice alongside tips and tricks to find inspiration and motivation. Episodes are short and concise for writers on the go. Guest authors share their experiences and insights on writing and publishing.

Writing Excuses

website www.writingexcuses.com
Hosts Maurice Broaddus, Aliette de Bodard, Amal El-Mohtar, Valynne E. Maetani Mary Robinette Kowal, Brandon Sanderson, Howard Tayler, Dan Wells

Produced by writers, this weekly podcast offers sensible and strategic advice to all who write, whether for pleasure or profit, on how they can revise and edit their work to create a better story. Each week there is a homework assignment and suggested reading.

Editorial services and self-publishing providers

This is a selection of the expanding list of companies that offer editorial, production, marketing and distribution support predominantly for authors who want to self-publish. As with all the organisations mentioned in the *Yearbook*, we recommend that you check carefully what companies offer and what they would charge. Note that in the entries below, 'POD' refers to 'print on demand'.

Amolibros
Loundshay Manor Cottage, Preston Bowyer, Milverton, Somerset TA4 1QF
tel (01823) 401527
email amolibros@aol.com
website www.amolibros.com
Director Jane Tatam

Offers print and ebook design, production, copy-editing and distribution through online retailers. Sales and marketing services include design and production of adverts, leaflets, author websites, distribution of press releases and direct mail campaigns.

A1 Book Publishing UK
Room 1, 48 Park Road, Birmingham B18 5JH
tel 0121 679 1027
email a1booksuk@gmail.com
website www.a1proofreading.co.uk
Facebook www.facebook.com/A1-Book-Publishing-UK-240624720597580/
Contact Adam Lomond

Offers a variety of services to self-publishing authors, including proofreading manuscripts (£9.99 per 1,000 words), book covers, book design and eBook conversion. KDP/Amazon publishing service available for £245. Distribution and marketing support also available. Founded 2012.

arima publishing
ASK House, Northgate Avenue, Bury St Edmunds, Suffolk IP32 6BB
tel (01284) 717885
email info@arimapublishing.com
website www.arimapublishing.co.uk

Offers POD options in hardback and paperback formats. Distributes print books through wholesalers, and to online retailers. Proofreading and image scanning also available. Also provides a typing service for handwritten manuscripts. Authors receive a royalty rate of 30% of full cover price for direct sales from the arima online bookshop, and 20% for general sales.

Art Circus Books
132 Frankwell, Shrewsbury SY3 8JX
email info@artcircusbooks.co.uk
website www.artcircusbooks.co.uk
Contact Steve Edwards

Publishing arm of www.theartcircus.com. Produces books for artists, whether for general publication or in support of artist exhibitions, concerts and events. Provides advice and support to artists wishing to self-publish across all aspects of the publishing process as well as print-management. Also works in collaboration with UKGiclee (Fine Art Printers). Founded 2013.

@YouCaxton
23 High Street, Bishops Castle, Shropshire SY9 5BE
email newbooks@youcaxton.co.uk
website www.youcaxton.co.uk
Facebook www.facebook.com/pages/YouCaxton-Publishing/133150206770479
Twitter @YouCaxton
Partners Robert Fowke, Robert Branton and Steven Edwards

Specialises in high-quality memoir and general non-fiction, selected fiction and high-end, full-colour productions and art books.

Support for self-publishers: structural editing; copy-editing; proofreading, cover design and interior layout; print and ebook production and a full distribution service. Additional services include: a range of marketing tools for self-publishing: author websites and web pages; a book packaging and design service for publishers; a publication project management service for academic and corporate clients. Also provides a fine-art printing service for photographers and artists.

The Author School
email abiolabello@theauthorschool.com
email helenlewis@theauthorschool.com
website www.theauthorschool.com
Twitter @theauthorschool
Founders Helen Lewis, Abiola Bello

Practical help for authors from experts with decades of experience in the publishing industry between them. Based in London, it runs events, workshops, online courses, mentoring and one-to-ones for new and experienced authors at any stage of their book journey. Bestselling authors, literary agents and publishers are invited to the events as special guests. In 2021, The Author School will be introducing a membership for authors who want to take their career to the next level. Founded 2015.

Authoright
71–75 Shelton Street, London WC2H 9JQ
tel 020-7993 8225
email info@authoright.com
website www.authoright.com
website www.bookpublishing.co.uk
Twitter @Authoright
Ceo & Co-founder Gareth Howard, *Coo & Co-founder* Hayley Radford

Marketing and publicity firm for new and unpublished writers, based in London and New York. Offers a range of services to traditionally published and self-published authors, including structural editing, copy-editing and proofreading, cover design, website design, press releases, blog tours and marketing and publicity campaigns in the UK and US. Case studies and testimonials available on request.

Betterwrite
107A Maas Road, Birmingham B31 2PP
tel 0121 475 5876
email robertmatthews_edit@yahoo.co.uk
website https://betterwrite.com
Contact Rob Matthews

Experienced team of twelve editors, all members of the Chartered Institute of Editing and Proofreading (formerly SfEP), working across all fiction genres: crime/thriller/mystery, adventure/fantasy/romance, sci-fi, historical, children's books, YA fiction and commercial women's fiction. Non-fiction projects also undertaken.

Once authors are matched with the most appropriate editor for their work, the text is prepared for publication or self-publication via a three-stage procedure. First, there is a developmental/structural edit, advising authors of big-picture issues like character, plot and narrative technique. Second, authors can revise their text following the guidance of a development editor, so that they remain in control of their writing. Third, the work undergoes a line and copy-edit, correcting grammar, spelling and punctuation errors and improving the overall flow.

Phone or email for a free sample edit.

Blue Ocean Publishing
16 Rayners Close, Fowlmere, Royston SG8 7TF
tel (01763) 208887
email blueoceanpublishing@btconnect.com
website www.blueoceanpublishing.biz

Professional, personal self publishing of books, ebooks, brochures, CDs, DVDs and games for individuals and organisations. Complete design and editorial services are available, as are advice on MSS and assistance with marketing, writing and distribution. Founded 2007.

Bonacia
Bonacia, Remus House, Coltsfoot Drive, Woodston, Peterborough PE2 9BF
tel (01733) 898103
email info@bonacia.co.uk
website https://bonacia.co.uk/contact
Twitter @Bonacialtd

Via its Spiderwize division offers POD self-publishing packages for several genres including fiction, autobiography and poetry. Prices start from £650, for the ebook package, but print and combined options are also available. See website for full information.

Bookollective
email hello@bookollective.com
website www.bookollective.com
Facebook www.facebook.com/bookollective
Twitter @bookollective
Contacts Esther Harris (editorial), Aimee Coveney (design), Helen McCusker (publicity)

Award-winning team offering a range of publicity, promotion and marketing options, editing services, book-cover design and website creation. Works alongside publishers, industry professionals and direct with writers. Also hosts regular networking events and literary areas within festivals.

BookPrinting UK
Remus House, Coltsfoot Drive, Woodston, Peterborough PE2 9BF
tel (01733) 898102
email info@bookprintinguk.com
website www.bookprintinguk.com
Twitter @BookPrintingUK
Contact Naz Stewart

Offers colour and b&w printing and POD books in a range of bindings. Can provide custom illustration and interior layout options, as well as typesetting. Supplies templates for formatting manuscript files before sending. Can also distribute print books direct to customers. Prints bookmarks, posters and flyers.

Cameron Publicity and Marketing Ltd
180 Piccadilly, London W1J 9HF
tel 020-7917 9812
email info@cameronpm.co.uk
website www.cameronpm.co.uk
Facebook www.facebook.com/CameronPublicity
Twitter @CameronPMtweets
Director Ben Cameron

Publicity and marketing campaigns for publishers and independent authors including media awareness, websites and social media. Founded 2006.

The Choir Press
132 Bristol Road, Gloucester GL1 5SR
tel (01452) 500016
email enquiries@thechoirpress.co.uk
website www.selfpublishingbooks.co.uk
Contacts Miles Bailey, Rachel Woodman

Self-publishing company offering print-on-demand, short-run and long-run printed books, as well as ebook conversion. Also undertakes high-quality illustrated non-fiction projects. Founded 1982.

Clink Street Publishing

71–75 Shelton Street, London WC2H 9JQ
tel 020-7993 8225
email info@clinkstreetpublishing.com
website www.bookpublishing.co.uk

Boutique self-publishing imprint from Authoright, with an experienced team of editors, project managers, designers and publicists publishing and promoting writers across all genres. Also has links with literary scouts with a view to securing foreign translation rights. Case studies and testimonials available on request.

Consulting Cops for Writers

1 Keeper Lodges, Epping, Essex CM16 5HP
tel 07968 582423
email enquiries@consultingcops.com
website www.consultingcops.com
Twitter @ConsultingCops
Ceo and Founder Lyndon Smith

Experienced team of serving and former police officers/staff, offering to match writers' crime-related work with the relevant expert and supply them with the information they need to ensure their project reads authentically. Services include: scene/chapter/whole project review; research; consultation. Website includes a variety of useful author aids, including police ranks, acronyms, phonetic alphabet and websites to assist further research.

Dissect Designs

email tim@dissectdesigns.com
website www.dissectdesigns.com
Twitter @dissectdesigns
Contact Tim Barber

Bespoke book cover design for hardbacks, paperbacks, ebooks or audiobooks by an experienced cover designer. All genres covered.

eBook Versions

27 Old Gloucester Street, London WC1N 3AX
website www.ebookversions.com

Offers ebook, paperback and hardback self-publishing and distribution through online retailers and trade wholesalers including Amazon Kindle Direct Publishing, Apple iBookstores, Kobo Books, Gardners Books, IngramSpark and more than 300 independent high street booksellers. Fees begin at £95 for ebook conversion of a manuscript of up to 100,000 words. POD paperback and hardback pre-press production is available from £295. OCR scanning of hardbacks, paperbacks and typescripts is also offered.

eBookPartnership.com

7 Bell Yard, London WC2A 2JR
email helpdesk@ebookpartnership.com
website www.ebookpartnership.com
Twitter @ebookpartners

Ebook conversion and distribution services. Conversion to standard and fixed layout ebook files. Complex conversion specialists. Worldwide distribution and management of ebook files for authors, publishers, businesses and non-profit organisations. Extensive network of retailers, libraries and subscription services. Set-up fee; clients retain 100% of royalties. Client admin system, no fees for changes to listings. Founded 2010.

Exprimez

20 St Nicholas Gardens, Rochester, Kent ME2 3NT
email matthew@exprimez.com
website https://exprimez.com
Founder Matthew Smith

Publishing consultancy offering an extensive range of bespoke support services for authors and organisations, including book coaching, writing and publishing tools, manuscript consulting, developmental book editing, ghostwriting, social media training, content development, rights, contracts and author representation. All enquiries welcome.

Frank Fahy Publishing Services

5 Barna Village Centre, Barna, Galway, H91 DF24, Republic of Ireland
tel +353 (0)86 2269330
email frank.fahy0@gmail.com
website https://frankfahypublishing.wordpress.com/

Specialises in preparing manuscripts for book production, either as printed books or digital ebooks. This can include, as required, copy-editing and/or proofreading, or preparing presentations for submission to publishers. Estimates are free of charge and authors' individual requirements discussed. Publishing projects of all kinds considered, from individuals, institutions or businesses. Founded 2007.

Fiction Atelier

email fictionatelier@gmail.com
website fictionatelier.wordpress.com
Contacts Lucy Ellmann, Todd McEwen

Novelists Lucy Ellmann and Todd McEwen offer one-to-one help to serious writers of fiction: editing, line editing, discussion and feedback. £100 an hour, paid in advance. Flat rates also available. Free initial trial edit. Reply guaranteed.

Finish Your Novel

email info@finishyournovel.org
website www.finishyournovel.org
Mentors Clare Allan, Alexandra Benedict, Jonathan Myerson

Bespoke mentoring service from the former directors of the groundbreaking Novel Writing MA at City University London. Award-winning writers Jonathan Myerson and Clare Allan have more than a decade's experience in guiding writers from first idea to finished manuscript. Taster sessions available, or book the full Ten Session Course and commit to completing that novel once and for all. Also offered: full draft readings; specialist webinars; and a range of support tailored to specific needs. See website for pricing information.

Firsty Group

Clarendon House, Unit 4, Green Lane Ind. Estate, Thatcham, Berks. RG19 3RG
tel (01635) 581185
email info@firstygroup.com
website http://firstygroup.com
Twitter @firstygroup
Instagram @firstygroup

Provides web development and e-commerce solutions for the publishing industry, from bespoke projects to bolt-on software as a service. Enables publishers to sell print, ebooks and audiobooks directly to customers through open-source content management systems, API links to distribution partners and a thorough understanding of metadata. Also provides direct-to-customer publisher support and assistance within customer service, financial accounting and marketing. Founders of Glassboxx, which enables authors, publishers and retailers to sell their ebooks and audiobooks directly to the end customer with full, frictionless DRM.

Grammar Factory Publishing

3906-25 Telegram Mews, Toronto, ON M5V 3Z1, Canada
email info@grammarfactory.com
website https://grammarfactory.com
Executive Publisher Scott MacMillan

Professional service publisher offering ghostwriting, editing and publishing services; customers include speakers, business leaders and entrepreneurs.

Grosvenor House Publishing

Link House, 140 The Broadway, Tolworth, Surrey KT6 7HT
tel 020-8339 6060
website www.grosvenorhousepublishing.co.uk
Founder Kim Cross

Publishes across a range of genres including children's and non-fiction in colour, b&w, POD, paperback, hardback and ebook formats. Offers a £795 publishing package which includes typesetting and five free print copies as well as an ISBN, and print and ebook distribution via online retailers. Marketing services include producing posters and postcards, and website set-up from template with two years' hosting. Ebook publishing costs £195 if the

print edition of the book has been produced by the company and £495 otherwise. Print costs and royalties depend on book specification. A proofreading service is offered at a rate of £5 per 1,000 words. See website for full list of costs.

iBooks Author

website www.apple.com/uk/ibooks-author

App that allows authors to create interactive e-textbooks and other types of ebooks, such as photo books, travel, or craft/cookery books for iPad. Features include video and audio, interactive diagrams, photos and 3D images. They can then be sold through the iBooks Store. Authors may choose fonts and template page layouts or design their own. Charts, tables, text, images and interactive features can also be added.

The Inkwell Group

The Old Post Office, Kilmacanogue, Co. Wicklow A98 V215, Republic of Ireland
tel +353 (0)1 2765921, +353 087 2835382
website www.inkwellwriters.ie
website www.writing.ie
Facebook www.facebook.com/TheInkwellGroup
Twitter @inkwellHQ
Contact Vanessa Fox O'Loughlin

Literary consultancy providing industry-led critique, readers reports and editing services, plus career-strategy consultancy. Inkwell also provides a full range of 'Getting Published' events and workshops for festivals and organisations, and are literary scouts working with some of Ireland and the UK's top agents.

Inkwell developed www.writing.ic, the award-winning online writing resources magazine, and the National Emerging Writer Programme with Dublin UNESCO City of Literature which includes free writing advice from experts on YouTube. Founded 2006.

Jelly Bean Self-Publishing

Candy Jar Ltd, Mackintosh House, 136 Newport Road, Cardiff CF24 1DJ
tel 029-211 57202
email submissions@jellybeanselfpublishing.co.uk
website www.jellybeanselfpublishing.co.uk
Twitter @Jelly_BeanUK
Director Shaun Russell

Self-publishing imprint of Candy Jar Books. Offers a bespoke service for new and experienced authors at any step of the publishing process, including but not limited to editing and typesetting, illustration, cover design, website design, audiobook production and marketing services. Submissions are welcomed, and meetings are available on request. Founded 2012.

Journey Books

Bradt Guides, 31A High Street, Chesham, Bucks. HP5 1BW

tel (01753) 893444
email journeybooks@bradtguides.com
website www.bradtguides.com/journeybooks/

Contract publishing imprint from award-winning travel publisher, Bradt Guides. Offers a range of publishing services, from an initial editorial report to full trade publication with professional editing, typesetting, design and worldwide distribution for print and ebooks. A particular expertise in travel-related books but will happily consider all proposals. Competitive pricing and a range of tailor-made packages. Suitable for both first-timers and previously published authors looking to publish independently without compromising on production quality or access to trade distribution.

Kindle Direct Publishing

website https://kdp.amazon.com
Facebook www.facebook.com/KindleDirectPublishing
Twitter @AmazonKDP

Ebook self-publishing and distribution platform for Kindle and Kindle Apps. Its business model offers up to a 70% royalty (on certain retail prices between $2.99–$9.99) in many countries and availability in Amazon stores worldwide. POD options are also available. Note that KDP Select makes books exclusive to Amazon (which means they cannot be sold through an author's personal website, for example), but authors can share in the Global Fund amount every time the book is borrowed from the Kindle Owners' Lending Library.

Kobo Writing Life

email writinglife@kobo.com
website www.kobo.com/gb/en/p/aboutkobo
Facebook www.facebook.com/KoboWritingLife
Twitter @kobo

Ebook self-publishing platform where authors can upload manuscripts and cover images. These files are then converted into ebooks before being distributed through the Kobo ebookstore. Authors are able to set pricing and DRM territories, as well as track sales. Royalty rates vary depending on price or territory; enquire directly. Free to join. Owned by Rakuten.

Lavender and White Publishing

Snipe Lodge, Moycullen, County Galway, Republic of Ireland
email info@lavenderandwhite.co.uk
website www.lavenderandwhite.co.uk
Facebook www.facebook.com/Lavender-and-White-Publishing-201996279902790/
Twitter @LavenderandW
Editorial Director Jacqueline Broderick, *Editor* Sarah Lewis

Offers a range of services for self-publishing authors, including: editing; proofreading; cover design; typesetting; ebook conversion; POD; marketing and sell-through services; mentoring; and ghostwriting.

Costs vary depending on services required; email for a quote. Easy payment options available.

Manuscripts & Mentoring

25 Corinne Road, London N19 5EZ
tel 07973 300276
email manuscriptmentoring@gmail.com
website www.genevievefox.com
Twitter @genevievefox21
Contact Genevieve Fox

Helps both fledgling and experienced writers of fiction, non-fiction and YA fiction get from first draft to finished manuscript. Primary services: editing; one-to-one tutoring; manuscript overviews; advice on structure, plot, themes and characterisation; submission to agents; and self-publishing. Also available: mentoring; writing plans; ghostwriting; media coaching; and creative writing courses. Genevieve Fox is a published author, journalist and creative writing tutor.

Margie's Mark

email margie@margiesmark.com
website https://margiesmark.design/index.html
Twitter @MargieMark
Contact Margie Markevicius

Supplies graphic design services, including logo design, and can apply designs to social media accounts. Also offers: book cover design and formatting for print and POD; design of ebook ePub files; website design and maintenance; content updates. US-based.

Matador

Troubador Publishing Ltd, 9 Priory Business Park, Wistow Road, Kibworth Beauchamp, Leicester LE8 0RX
tel 0116 279 2299
email books@troubador.co.uk
website www.troubador.co.uk/matador
Facebook www.facebook.com/matadorbooks
Twitter @matadorbooks
Managing Director Jeremy Thompson, *Operations Director* Jane Rowland

The self-publishing imprint of Troubador Publishing. Offers POD, short-run digital- and litho-printed books as well as audiobooks and ebook production, with distribution through high-street bookshops and online retailers. Also worldwide ebook distribution. Author services include all book, ebook and audiobook production, trade and retail marketing, plus bookshop distribution via Orca Book Services and Sales Representation by Star Book Sales.

For audiobooks, authors choose from a range of available narrators. Once studio recording has been completed and the finished audiobook approved, the author can choose to distribute themselves or through Matador. Production prices start at £1,450 for a book of up to 40,000 words, and distribution is a one-off fee of £40. Prices include audiobook artwork, and individual support and advice throughout the process. Founded 1999.

Mereo Books

2nd Floor, 6–8 Dyer Street,
Cirencester Glos. GL7 2PF
tel 020-3286 8686
email info@mereobooks.co.uk
website www.mereobooks.com
Twitter @MereoBooks
Director Antonia Tingle, *Editor-in-Chief* Chris Newton

Publishes in hardback, paperback, audio and ebook formats. Also offers ghostwriting services. Allocates ISBNs and distributes to online retailers including Amazon and Barnes & Noble, as ebooks or POD and from stock through Orca Book Services trade distribution or through their international sales network of agents. Books sold through the Mereo website as well as via trade sales representation with Harbour Publishing Services and trade distribution by Orca Book Services, and listed with wholesalers. Additional services include editing, typesetting, interior layout design, cover design, eBook production, book promotion and book marketing for both fiction and non-fiction titles, using all in-house expertise.

MiblArt

email team@miblart.com
website https://miblart.com/
Book cover design company for self-published authors. Services offered include: ebook and print cover design; illustrated book cover design; ebook and print formatting; creation of marketing materials for authors (banners for social media, logos, bookmarks, brochures, websites).

Author benefits include: unlimited number of revisions and quick turnround times. No upfront payment is required. Authors retain all copyrights. Founded 2015.

MJV Literary Author Services

71–75 Shelton Street, London WC2H 9JQ
email authors@mjvliterary.com
website www.mjvliterary.com
Contact Matt McAvoy

Offers professional proofreading, copy-editing and beta-reading services for authors of all genres, including fiction, non-fiction and children's books, as well as a popular ebook and KDP-ready Kindle-book creation service, at $69.

As part of the company's #ReturnToRealBooks campaign, KDP-formatted print-ready typesetting is offered free with all proofreading and copy-editing instructions. Other services include translation into English with full copy-editing, for non-English language authors.

Editing services start from $6.50 per 1,000 words, and include two editor passes as standard. Clients include self-published and traditionally published authors from all over the world, as well as publishers.

Senior Editor Matt McAvoy also operates a popular book-review blog (www.mattmcavoy.com), and is a member of the Chartered Institute of Editing and Proofreading (CIEP).

New Generation Publishing

51 Gower Street, London WC1E 6HJ
tel 020-8127 0793 (production queries)
tel (01234) 711956 (publishing enquiries)
email info@newgeneration-publishing.com
website www.newgeneration-publishing.com
Facebook www.facebook.com/
NewGenerationPublishing
Twitter @NGPublishing

Provides publication in paperback, hardback and ebook and audiobook with global print and retail distribution. Publishing packages range from Standard Paperback to the Bestseller options; bespoke packages are also available. Services include layout, cover design, ISBN allocation, editing, proofreading, bookselling, bookstore placement, website design and manuscript critique. Distribution provided via online retailers, high-street shops, libraries and wholesalers. Promotional materials available including distributed press releases and social media. Free marketing and promotional support service also offered. Offices in London and Buckinghamshire; author visits welcome. Free guide to publishing available on request.

Otherwise Publishing

tel (01424) 718297
email angela@otherwise-publishing.co.uk
email simon@otherwise-publishing.co.uk
website www.otherwise-publishing.co.uk
Facebook www.facebook.com/otherwisepublishing
Co-founders Angela Young, Simon Daley

Offers a range of services enabling new and experienced authors to self-publish in bespoke form, with an emphasis on quality. Authors can expect to earn a high percentage of cover price.

A specialist team provides advice and full project management, from initial idea through to delivery of printed books. Services include concept development, copywriting and ghostwriting, structural editing, proofreading, indexing, cover design, page design and typesetting, photography, illustration, printing, binding, shipping and options for warehousing, distribution, sales and publicity. Previous winner in the self-publishing category of the British Book Design and Production Awards.

Paragon Publishing

4 North Street, Rothersthorpe, Northants NN7 3JB
tel (01604) 832149

email intoprint@live.com
website www.intoprint.net
Proprietor Mark Webb

Packagers of non-fiction and fiction books for independent authors and small publishers, working regularly with schools, universities, associations and writers' groups. Provides a range of editorial, design and typesetting services to create PDFs in black and white or colour, as well as print on demand options. Publishes Kindle, and ePub on Play and Kobo, and multilingual editions. Experienced at working with new writers to help them to publish, providing ISBN, marketing consultancy and distribution to booksellers worldwide. Ghostwriting and illustration services also available. Founded 1992.

Pomegranate PA

Clavering House, Clavering Place,
Newcastle upon Tyne NE1 3NG
tel 07443 490752
email karen@pomegranatepa.co.uk
website www.pomegranatepa.co.uk
Twitter @pomegranatepa
Freelance Proofreader Karen Stubbs

Proofreading and editorial service. All subjects considered. Founded 2013.

Prepare to Publish Ltd

Blackbirds Studio, Bayliss Yard, Charlbury OX7 3RS
tel (01865) 922923
email mail@preparetopublish.com
website www.preparetopublish.com
Editor Andrew Chapman

Editorial and typesetting agency for book and magazine production. A team of more than a dozen experienced freelancers provides development-editing, copy-editing and proofreading services (fiction and non-fiction, but not poetry or children's books), plus typesetting. Clients typically include: publishers looking to outsource the editorial process; businesses planning publications; and authors who have completed a first draft.

Publishing Services

9 Curwen Road, London W12 9AF
tel 07984 585861
email susanne@susannelumsden.co.uk
website www.susannelumsden.co.uk
Twitter @SusanneLumsden
Contact Susanne Lumsden

Former non-fiction director of Faber & Faber offers consultancy and publishing services for quality non-fiction titles. Services are aimed at individuals, charities and organisations with a sales and/or marketing platform who wish to publish books to mainstream standards as well as publicise them. Project appraisal covers goals, resources and publishing requirements: format/s, pricing if applicable, editorial work, design & printing, sales &

marketing (including digital and social media marketing) and timing. Has access to a network of experienced colleagues in design, typesetting, printing, ebook conversion, websites, promotion and publicity.

PublishNation

Suite 544, Kemp House, 152 City Road,
London EC1V 2NX
email david@publishnation.co.uk
website www.publishnation.co.uk
Publisher David Morrison

Offers POD paperback and Kindle format ebooks, available through Amazon. Publication in both print and digital formats costs £250 or £150 for Kindle format. Images may be included from £2.95 each. A range of book sizes is available, as are free template book covers. Enhanced cover design costs £40. Marketing services include creation of a press release, social media accounts and author website. Standard proofreading is £7 per 1,000 words, while an 'express' option from £125 focuses on the beginning of the manuscript. Editorial critique reports range in price from £99 for manuscripts of up to 15,000 words to £219 for manuscripts of up to 120,000 words.

Reedsy

email service@reedsy.com
website https://reedsy.com
Twitter @ReedsyHQ
Founders Emmanuel Nataf, Matt Cobb, Ricardo Fayet, Vincent Durand

Curated marketplace with over 400,000 members that helps authors and publishers connect with editors, designers and marketers. Reedsy also offers free publishing courses via its Learning platform, available from the learning section of the website. Founded 2014.

The Right Book Company

c/o SRA Books, Unit 3, Spike Island,
133 Cumberland Road, Bristol BS8 4TY
tel (01789) 761345
email hello@therightbookcompany.com
website http://therightbookcompany.com
Facebook www.facebook.com/therightbookcompany
Twitter @therightbookco
Founder, Director and Publisher Sue Richardson

Publishing and book marketing consultancy and services for businesses, small publishers and non-fiction authors.

Rowanvale Books Ltd

The Gate, Keppoch Street, Roath, Cardiff CF24 3JW
email info@rowanvalebooks.com
website www.rowanvalebooks.com
Twitter @RowanvaleBooks
Managing Director Cat Charlton

Provider of publishing services such as proofreading and copy-editing, cover design and illustration, ebook conversion, paperback printing and marketing. Distribution to over 40,000 online and print retailers and libraries worldwide. Founded 2012.

The Self-Publishing Partnership
7 Green Park Station, Green Park Road,
Bath BA1 1JB
tel (01225) 478444
email enquiries@selfpublishingpartnership.co.uk
website www.selfpublishingpartnership.co.uk
Twitter @SelfPublishBath
Contacts Douglas Walker, Garry Manning

Independent providers of self-publishing services with personal guidance and support. Services include: proofreading/copy-editing; page design and typesetting; cover design (bespoke or standard); ebooks; ISBNs, trade & legal cataloguing; promotion and marketing advice; and trade-order fulfilment (invoicing & distribution).

Selfpublishbooks.ie
Springhill House, Carrigtwohill,
Co. Cork T45 NX81, Republic of Ireland
tel + 353 (0)2 14883370
email selfpublish@lettertec.com
website www.selfpublishbooks.ie
Facebook www.facebook.com/selfpublishbooks
Twitter @printbooks

Services include digital printing and binding options, including perfect binding and saddle stitching. Offers custom cover design or can include author-supplied images and artwork. Also offers editing, proofreading and formatting services. Can design promotional materials including posters and bookmarks and allocate ISBNs. Printing prices start from 100 copies but fewer can be printed on request. A division of Lettertec.

Self-Publishing Review
email editor@selfpublishingreview.com
website www.selfpublishingreview.com
Facebook www.facebook.com/selfpublishingreview
Twitter @selfpubreview
Instagram @selfpubreview

Offers professional editorial book reviews, Amazon eBook promotions, affordable editing services, and full-service publishing for authors. Services start from $29 for book marketing services, from $89 for book review services, and from $499 for editing. Amazon mailing list promotions start at $229. Founded 2008.

SilverWood Books
14 Small Street, Bristol BS1 1DE
tel 0117 910 5829
email enquiries@silverwoodbooks.co.uk
website www.silverwoodbooks.co.uk
Twitter @SilverWoodBooks
Publishing Director Helen Hart

Offers complete 'done for you'/self-publishing services, including manuscript feedback, editing and proofreading, professional cover and page design, typesetting, ebook hand-formatting and conversion, b&w and colour POD, short-run and lithographic printing, one-to-one support and coaching. Distributes to bookshops via wholesalers and to online retailers including Amazon.

Partner Member of The Alliance of Independent Authors. Lists books in its own SilverWood online bookstore. UK wholesale distribution via Central Books. Nielsen Enhanced Data Listing. Book marketing services and consultations available. VAT at the standard rate added to services but not print. See website for pricing information.

Smart Quill Editorial & Scouting
email info@smartquilleditorial.co.uk
website http://smartquilleditorial.co.uk
Literary Consultant, Editor and Scout Philippa Donovan

Structural edits and line edits, with prices from £1,200. Scouts for literary agents and film/tv producers. Fiction (all genres), narrative non-fiction, YA, middle grade and picture books. Named as a Publishing Rising Star 2014 by *The Bookseller* magazine, Unsung Publishing Hero 2016, and judge for the London Book Fair Cameo Book to Screen Awards 2019 and 2020.

Softwood Self-Publishing
email swspublishing@gmail.com
website www.swspublishing.com
Facebook www.facebook.com/swspublishing
Twitter @swspublishing
Instagram @swspublishing
Founder and Editor-in-Chief Maddy Glenn, *Creative Director* Nathan James

Supports the work of authors who are taking both traditional publishing and self-published routes to market. Editing services include manuscript critiques, copy-editing, content editing and proofreading. Also offers a pitching service for those ready to take their manuscript to an agent. For self-publishing authors, provides guidance in formatting, book design, marketing, and distribution. Self-published authors can also take advantage of a free book-listing service, which promotes their work via Softwood's dedicated library website. Founded 2017.

Spiffing Covers
6 Jolliffe's Court, 51–57 High Street, Wivenhoe, Colchester, Essex CO7 9AZ
tel (01206) 585200
email enquiries@spiffingcovers.com
website www.spiffingcovers.com
Facebook www.facebook.com/spiffingcovers
Twitter @spiffingcovers
Managing Director Stefan Proudfoot

Independent publishing agency specialising in fully bespoke services and one-to-one consultation with clients. Offers a range of services, from cover design to editing and proofreading and international multi-channel distribution. Also assists authors with brand-building for their own independent publishing. Authors retain their own copyright and all royalties. Founded 2013.

Tantamount
Coventry University Technology Park, Puma Way, Coventry CV1 2TT
tel 024-7722 0299
email hello@tantamount.com
website www.tantamount.com
website www.authorbranding.co.uk
Twitter @TantamountBooks

Specialists in enhanced digital publications and author branding. Offer an extensive range of editorial, design and publishing services to individual authors and publishing houses. Integrated online presence and self-publishing services allow writers to deal with a single supplier for all digital, design and publishing requirements and to achieve a unified and coherent brand image for their work. Specialist support for first-time professional writers through 'From Authority to Authorship' system. Founded 2002.

Michael Terence Publishing
Two Brewers House, 2A Wellington Street, Thame OX9 3BN
tel 020-3582 2002
email admin@mtp.agency
website www.mtp.agency/submissions
Founders Karolina Robinson, Keith Abbott

Publishes across a range of genres: fiction (including crime, science fiction, historical, children's, poetry) and non-fiction (including biography, true stories). Special consideration given to new and little-published authors. Open for submissions from authors worldwide: see website for full details. Founded 2016.

Try Writing
tel 07773 797 817
email traceyiceton@hotmail.co.uk
website www.trywriting.co.uk
Contact Tracey Iceton

Provides a full range of manuscript appraisal/critiquing services, editorial guidance and one-to-one mentoring programmes for emerging creative writers across all genres/forms of writing but specialising in fiction (short stories and novels). Services are tailored to authors' individual needs and offer constructive, practical advice designed to help manuscripts achieve publishable standard. Try Writing is run by Tracey Iceton PhD, author of the *Celtic Colours Trilogy* (Cinnamon Press) and creative writing tutor.

2QT Ltd (Publishing)
Settle, North Yorkshire BD24 9BZ
tel (01729) 821046
website www.2qt.co.uk
Facebook www.facebook.com/2QTPublishing
Director Catherine Cousins

Offering flexible, tailored packages. Services include editing and proofreading, manuscript critique, cover design and typesetting. Also offers ebook conversion and access to distribution, POD and other printing options. Allocates ISBNs and barcodes.

White Magic Studios
1 Brunel Way, Slough SL1 1FQ
tel 020-3475 0507
email info@whitemagicstudios.co.uk
website www.whitemagicstudios.co.uk
Facebook www.facebook.com/whitemagicstudiosuk

Offers a range of services to authors, including: book cover design; text layout and formatting; illustrations for children's books; author website set-up, and e-book conversion. Editorial support also available: see website for full range of options.

whitefox
39 Roderick Road, London NW3 2NP
email info@wearewhitefox.com
website www.wearewhitefox.com
Facebook www.facebook.com/wearewhitefox
Twitter @wearewhitefox
Instagram @whitefox_publishing
Partners Annabel Wright, John Bond

Creative agency that works with writers, publishers, agents and brands to help publish bespoke books. Specialises in non-fiction. Can provide entire publishing packages for individuals or organisations looking to self-publish as well as one-off services, depending on individual requirements. Works with a large curated network of professional freelancers providing expertise in editorial, design, marketing and PR, sales and distribution alongside an experienced in-house team. Founded 2012.

Wise Words Editorial
email info@wisewordseditorial.com
website www.wisewordseditorial.com
Twitter @WiseWordsEd

Provides proofreading services for fiction and non-fiction manuscripts and ebooks. Rate is £5/$7 per 1,000 words for proofreading documents over 50,000 words. Authors are sent a file showing edits as well as the final proofread file.

The Word Tank
2 Springfield Cottages, Bletchinglye Lane, Rotherfield TN6 3NN
email enquiries@thewordtank.com
website www.thewordtank.com
Twitter @thewordtank
Contacts Chris Brock, Victoria Brock
Professional editing and publishing services from an experienced husband-and-wife team, including:

proofreading; copy-editing; copywriting; cover design; and interior formatting. Also independent publishing and marketing support. Partner members of Alliance of Independent Authors; professional members of Chartered Institute of Editors and Proofreaders.

Wrate's Editing Services

14C Woodland Road, London SE19 1NT
tel 020-8670 0660
email danielle@wrateseditingservices.co.uk
website http://wrateseditingservices.co.uk
Twitter @WratesEditing
Instagram @wrates_editing
Contact Danielle Wrate

Helps authors with all aspects of the self-publishing process, from draft manuscript to publication. Primary services include proofreading, copy-editing, structural editing, cover design, interior layout, ebook conversion, printing, ISBN registration and marketing. Works with both novelists and non-fiction authors; free, no-obligation sample edit and publishing guide available. Founded 2013.

WRITERSWORLD

2 Bear Close Flats, Bear Close, Woodstock,
Oxon OX20 1JX
tel 0800 1214966
email enquiries@writersworld.co.uk
website www.writersworld.co.uk
Founder & Owner Graham Cook

Specialises in self-publishing, POD books and book reprints. Also issues ISBNs on behalf of authors, pays them 90% of the royalties and supplies them with copies of their books at print cost. Worldwide book distribution. Founded 2000.

The Writing Hall

33 Mount Pleasant, Ackworth, Pontefract,
West Yorkshire, WF7 7HU
tel 07983 089621
email info@thewritinghall.co.uk
website www.thewritinghall.co.uk
Facebook www.facebook.com/thewritinghall
Twitter @thewritinghall
Contact Diane Hall

Services include: developmental editing and copy-editing; proofreading; typesetting; cover design; small run printing; ebook formatting; writing workshops, book launches and literary events; marketing and social media coaching. Additional services include: writing coaching/mentoring; manuscript critique; ghostwriting; and literary consultancy and advice.
Submissions are welcome, in most genres, particularly contemporary fiction, business titles, romance, comedy. Founded 2007.

York Publishing Services

64 Hallfield Road, Layerthorpe, York YO1 7ZQ
tel (01904) 431213
email enqs@yps-publishing.co.uk
website www.yps-publishing.co.uk
Facebook www.facebook.com/
YorkPublishingServices/

Offers print and ebook publishing options, as well as distribution to bookshops and online retailers including Amazon. Services include copy-editing, proofreading, page and cover design, and printing. Provides page proofs and sample bound copy before main print run. Marketing services include: compiling a press pack with press release sent to media; social media set-up (£250 plus VAT); posters; and direct mail campaigns. Book is also listed on the YPS online bookstore. Printing and editing price dependent on specification.

Resources for writers
Editing your work

If you are publishing, via a traditional publisher or independently, editing your work is an essential part of the process. This article outlines for authors what is involved.

What is editing?

Broadly speaking, editing involves refining your writing ('copy') to make it as readable as possible and thus ready to be published. There are four main editorial stages:

• **Manuscript assessment/critique** is an initial assessment of the strengths and weaknesses of your work, with general suggestions for improvement.

• **Developmental/structural editing** gives more in-depth feedback on aspects of your work such as pace, writing style and appropriate language for your readership, and technical features such as characterisation (fiction) or reference styles (non-fiction).

• **Copy-editing** focuses on the detail, accuracy, completeness and consistency of your text, including grammar, spelling and punctuation.

• **Proofreading** is the final check of the layout and also picks up anything overlooked earlier.

Should I edit my work before submitting it to an agent or publisher?

Most fiction is not submitted direct to a publisher but will find its way to a commissioning or acquisitions editor via a literary agent (see the articles in this *Yearbook* in the *Literary agents* section, which starts on page 405). Some specialist non-fiction can be submitted directly to an appropriate publisher. The listings under *Book publishers*, starting on page 130, will indicate if a company accepts unsolicited scripts. In all cases it is important to follow the agent or publisher submission guidelines.

You should always check any submission for basic spelling and grammatical mistakes ('typos') and to ensure that there are no blatant inconsistencies or factual inaccuracies. It is up to you whether you pay a professional editor to do this for you, but you are unlikely to need a full copy-edit of your whole work at this stage. It may help, though, to have an outsider or beta-reader give you feedback.

If your manuscript is accepted for publication, it is usually the publisher who will arrange and pay for the editing of your complete work. However, in academic publishing some authors are now asked to arrange and/or pay for their own copy-editing (and index). Beware of companies who ask you to pay for publishing your novel or non-fiction book – this is not traditional publishing. There are legitimate companies who do offer paid-for self-publishing packages (see below and *What do self-publishing providers offer?* on page 618), but tread carefully. A publisher who asks you to contribute to the publishing costs is a 'vanity' publisher and should be avoided.

What if I am self-publishing?

Independent authors do not have to obtain or pay for editorial advice, but if you want to sell a book that looks as good and reads as well as a professionally produced one, you are unlikely to achieve this on your own. There are a host of individuals and companies available to review and edit your work at all stages in the writing process, and to guide you through design and layout to publication and marketing.

When engaging a professional editor, be cautious and read the small print about what services are being offered and what qualifications the provider has to do the job. Decide what type of help you require and employ people with a track record and recommendations. Importantly, agree a fair price for the work. If you seek out the cheapest offering you are unlikely to get the best result. Writers & Artists offer editorial services for authors. Look also at the advice, rates, and directory of editorial professionals provided by the Chartered Institute of Editing and Proofreading (www.ciep.uk).

What happens during editing?

While processes differ from publisher to publisher, the sequence of events from draft manuscript to published copy is roughly similar. If you are self-publishing and working direct with an editor the sequence of events will be determined by which services you buy and importantly, don't design or typeset your work before it has been edited.

• If your work needs structural or developmental editing the publisher or freelance editor will make suggestions and you will need to revise your work accordingly.

• You will then submit the finished work for copy-editing. You should make sure you follow your publisher's style and formatting guidelines or ask your freelance editor to devise a style guide for you. This will save time in the detailed copy-edit because the text will be made consistent in line with this style guide. The editor or publisher may ask you to answer queries that arise during copy-editing.

• When the text is finalised it will be sent for typesetting or layout. If you are publishing independently, unless you are very experienced, you should find a reputable professional to do your interior page layout for print and ebook and commission a professional cover designer.

• You may be sent one or more sets of proofs of the layout, or your publisher may handle this stage. Again, if you are self-publishing then checking the proofs carefully is up to you. See the handy checklist in the **Common mistakes** box.

• Your work is now ready for publication – and the all-important marketing.

What are the differences between copy-editing and proofreading?

Copy-editing and proofreading are crucial stages in the publishing process and, while the two can often be confused or referred to interchangeably, there are important differences. The copy-editing function normally takes place when your work is complete but before typesetting or design, allowing substantial revisions to be made at minimal cost. Proof-reading, on the other hand, typically takes place after your work has been copy-edited and typeset and serves to 'fine-polish' the text to ensure that it is free from editorial and layout inaccuracies.

Copy-editing

This is the essential stage for all writers and should be done after you are happy with the general structure and content of your work. As this is the detailed, line-by-line edit, if you rewrite or add material after this stage your work will need to be edited again. The aim of copy-editing is to ensure that whatever appears in public is accurate, easy to follow, fit for purpose and free of error, omission, inconsistency and repetition. This process picks up

embarrassing mistakes, ambiguities and anomalies, alerts you to possible legal problems and marks up your work for the typesetter/designer. Typically, copy-editing involves:
• checking for mistakes in spelling, grammar and punctuation;
• creating a style sheet; applying consistency in spelling, punctuation, capitalisation, etc;
• making sure the text flows well, is logically ordered and is appropriate for your target audience;
• marking up or formatting the structure for the designer – e.g. headings, tables, lists, boxed items, quotes;
• checking any illustrations and figures correspond with what's written in the text;
• checking that any bibliographical references and notes are correctly ordered and styled and that none are missing;
• making sure you have any necessary introductory pages (prelims);
• querying obvious errors of fact, misleading information or parts that are unclear.

How much editing your copy will require (and therefore how long it will take) depends on a number of factors, including:
• the complexity of the subject matter;
• how consistent you have been;
• whether you have correctly followed a publisher's house style (or your own);
• the quality of your writing.

Common mistakes to look out for when editing and proofreading

• Punctuation mistakes, especially with direct speech and quotations.
• Inadvertently repeated words, e.g. 'and and . . .'.
• Phrases used inappropriately, e.g. 'should of' instead of 'should have' or 'compare to' instead of 'compare with'.
• Apostrophe misuse, e.g. its/it's and plurals (*not* banana's).
• Words with similar spelling or pronunciation but with different meanings used incorrectly, e.g. their/they're/there and effect/affect.
• Mixed use of past and present tenses.
• Use of plural verbs with single subjects (or vice versa), e.g. 'one in five children *are*... ' instead of 'one in five children *is*...' or '[the company] *has* 100 employees and [the company] *provide* free childcare' instead of 'provides' (or 'have' and 'provide').
• Obvious factual errors, e.g. 'the Battle of Hastings in 1766'.
• Inconsistent use of abbreviations and acronyms.
• Abbreviations/acronyms that have not been defined at least once in full.
• Missing bullet points or numbers in a sequenced list.
• Typing errors, e.g. '3' instead of '£'.
• Inconsistent layout of names, addresses, telephone numbers and email/web addresses.
• Incorrect or no use of trademarks, e.g. 'blackberry' instead of 'BlackBerry™'.
• References in the text that do not correspond to footnotes.
• Inaccurate or inadequate cross-referencing.
• Index listings not found on the page given in the index.
• Text inadvertently reordered or cut during the typesetting process.
• Headings wrongly formatted as body text.
• Running heads (at the top of pages) that do not correspond to chapter headings.
• Fonts and font sizes used incorrectly.
• Formatting inconsistencies such as poorly aligned margins or uneven columns.
• Captions/headings omitted from illustrations, photographs or diagrams.
• Illustrations/photographs/diagrams without appropriate copyright references.
• Widows and orphans, i.e. text which runs over page breaks and leaves a word or a line stranded.

In the past, manuscripts were copy-edited on paper, which was labour-intensive and time-consuming. These days, nearly all copy-editing is carried out electronically, usually using Microsoft Word (or sometimes a bespoke publishing system). Suggested changes are usually made using the Track Changes function; queries for the author or publisher are often inserted using Comments. Copy-editors and publishers work in different ways. You may be asked to work through the changes and comments accepting, rejecting or answering each one; you may be sent a 'clean' edited version to approve; or you may just be sent queries to answer.

Proofreading

As this is the final check for errors and layout problems, you should not make major changes at this stage. These days you will normally receive proofs as pdf documents, which should be marked up using in-built commenting tools. Learn how to use the strikeout, insertion and commenting tools in your preferred pdf program (the free version of Adobe Reader, for example, will be sufficient). Proofs may be marked-up using proof correction marks (see below), but this is now less common – check with your publisher or editor which method you are expected to use. Some publishers still work with hard copy paper proofs, or you may prefer to work this way yourself, in which case it will be useful to learn to use the main proof correction marks.

What are proofreading symbols and why do I need to know them?

Proofreading symbols (proof correction marks) are the 'shorthand' that some copy-editors and proofreaders use for correcting written material and they are set by the British Standards Institution (BSi). Typesetters, designers and printers also sometimes use these as part of correcting page layout, style and format.

If you are sent a set of page proofs using this method it is important that you have at least a basic understanding of the main marks so that you can interpret corrections that have been made or add your own corrections quickly, uniformly and without any ambiguity. The main proof correction marks you need to know are shown in the tables which follow.

Using the marks

• When proofreading, make a mark in the text to show exactly where the correction needs to be made. The marginal mark is used to specify what needs to be done.
• If there is more than one mark in a line, mark from left to right and use both margins if you need to.
• Every marginal mark should be followed by an oblique stroke, unless it is already followed by the insert mark or the amendment is a delete symbol.
• Circle any comments or notes you write in the margins to distinguish them from the corrections.
• For copy-editing, marks are made in the text only.

Handy proofreading tips

Effective proofreading takes time and practice but by following these tips you'll be able to spot mistakes more quickly and accurately:
• Set aside adequate time for proofreading. It requires concentration and should not be rushed.

Proof-correction marks

These marks conform to BS 5261C: 2005. In the tables below, 'character' means a letter or individual mark in the text; 'matter' means the content and could be text, a table or a picture.

Marks/symbols for general instructions

INSTRUCTIONS	MARGIN	TEXT
Leave the text in its original state and ignore any marks that have been made: stet (Latin for 'let it stand')	✓	‑ ‑ ‑ ‑ under the characters to be left as they were
Query for the author/typesetter/printer/publisher	(?)	A circle should be placed around matter to be queried
Remove non-textual marks	✗	A circle should be placed around marks to be removed
End of change	/	None

Marks/symbols for inserting, deleting and replacing text

INSTRUCTIONS	MARGIN	TEXT
Matter to be inserted	New matter, followed by ⅄	⅄
Additional matter supplied separately	⅄ followed by a letter in a diamond which identifies additional matter ⟨A⟩	⅄
Delete a character (and close up)	ℰ	/ through the character
Delete text (and close up)	ℰ	⊢⊣ through text
Character to replace marked character	New character, followed by /	/ through the character
Text to replace marked text	New text, followed by /	⊢⊣ through text

Marks/symbols for grammar and punctuation

INSTRUCTIONS	MARGIN	TEXT
Full stop	⊙	⅄ at insertion point or through character /
Comma	,	As above
Semi-colon	;	As above
Colon	⊙	As above
Hyphen	⊢—⊣	As above
Single quote marks	＇ or ＇	As above
Double quote marks	＂ or ＂	As above
Apostrophe	＇	As above
Ellipses or leader dots	⟨•••⟩	As above
Insert/replace dash	ⓝ Size of dash to be stated between uprights	As above

Marks/symbols for altering the look/style/layout of text

INSTRUCTIONS	MARGIN	TEXT
Put text in italics	⌐__⌐	___ under text to be changed
Remove italics, replace with roman text	⌐_+_	Circle text to be changed
Put text in bold	∿∿∿	∿∿ under text to be changed
Remove bold	∿+∿	Circle text to be changed
Put text in capitals	≡	≡ under text to be changed
Put text in small capitals	=	= under text to be changed
Put text in lower case	≢ or ≠	Circle text to be changed
Change character to superscript	Y under character	‖ through character to be changed
Insert a superscript character	Y under character	⋏ at point of insertion
Change character to subscript	⋏ above character	‖ through character to be changed
Insert a subscript character	⋏ above character	⋏ at point of insertion
Remove bold and italics	⌐_⧻_	Circle text to be changed
Paragraph break	⌐⌐	⌐⌐
Remove paragraph break, run on text	⌒	⌒
Indent text	⊏⌐	⊏⌐
Remove indent	⊐⌐	⊐⌐
Insert or replace space between characters or words	Y	⋏ at relevant point of insertion or ‖ through character
Reduce space between characters or words	↑	‖
Insert space between lines or paragraphs	Mark extends into margin	—(or)—
Reduce space between lines or paragraphs	Mark extends into margin	→ or ←
Transpose lines	⊆	⊆
Transpose characters or words	⊔	⊔
Close space between characters	⌒	character ⌒ character
Underline words	(underline)	⌒ circle words
Take over character(s) or word(s) to next line/column/page	Mark extends into margin	⊏
Take back character(s) or word(s) to previous line/column/page	Mark extends into margin	⊐

• Before starting on a proofreading task, make sure you have easy access to a dictionary and thesaurus, and ensure that you have any relevant style guides for spellings, use of capitals and format/design.

• If possible, proofread the document several times and concentrate on different aspects each time, e.g. sense/tone, format, grammar/punctuation/use of language.

• Always double-check scientific, mathematical or medical symbols as they can often be corrupted during the typesetting process. Accented characters and currency symbols can also cause problems.

• If possible, have a version of the pre-typeset, copy-edited text to refer to while you proofread – it might help solve minor inaccuracies or inconsistencies more quickly.

Further resources

Butcher, Judith; Drake, Caroline and Leach, Maureen, *Butcher's Copy-editing: The Cambridge Handbook for Editors, Copy-editors and Proofreaders* (Cambridge University Press, 4th edn 2006)

Butterfield, J., *Fowler's Dictionary of Modern English Usage* (Oxford University Press, 4th edn 2015)

Hunter, Margaret, *Proofreading or Copyediting? A Quick Guide to Using Editorial Professionals* (CIEP 2020)

Ritter, R.M., *New Oxford Dictionary for Writers and Editors: The Essential A-Z Guide to the Written Word* (Oxford University Press, 2nd revised edn 2014)

The Chicago Manual of Style: The Essential Guide for Writers, Editors, and Publishers (University of Chicago Press, 17th edn 2017; www.chicagomanualofstyle.org/home.html)

Waddingham, Anne (ed.), *New Hart's Rules: The Oxford Style Guide* (Oxford University Press, 2nd edn 2014)

The Chartered Institute of Editing and Proofreading (CIEP) offers training, mentoring, support and advice for editors and proofreaders and a freely searchable directory of editorial professionals, www.ciep.uk (see page 526)

This article has been written by three professional editors. **Lauren Simpson** (lauren.simpson73@gmail.com) has over 20 years' experience as an editor, writer, publishing consultant and proofreader, both freelance and in-house. She is currently the Managing Editor at Globe Law and Business. **Margaret Hunter** (daisyeditorial.co.uk) offers copy-editing, proofreading and layout services to businesses, organisations and independent authors. She joined the CIEP Council in 2015. **Gerard M-F Hill** (much-better-text.com) served on the CIEP Council from 2007 to 2016 and co-led its successful bid for chartership. He has worked as a copy-editor, indexer, proofreader, consultant and ghostwriter.

Writing an award-winning blog

Successful book blogger Julia Mitchell tells how she found a creative and fulfilling outlet as well as an inspiring, supportive and productive community through blogging, and urges others to take the leap and get started.

'Hello, my name's Julia and the internet is my life.' Does that sound sad? Well, how about this: 'Hi there, my name's Julia and I'm an award-winning book blogger with thousands of followers on Instagram, and I'm making an income from being creative online'. Now that's more like it!

So how did this all begin? Back in 2016 I started my book-themed Instagram account, Julia's Bookcase, when I was fresh out of university and in need of something productive to do with my time. While lolling about in bed in the middle of the night, I spontaneously created a new Instagram account and uploaded a photo of the book that I was reading, *A Darker Shade of Magic* (Tor Books 2015) by Victoria Schwab, and an obsession was born. As my skills improved, I found myself submerged in a community of avid readers.

Fast forward to 2019 and along came my second 'child', my blog – Julia's Bookcase. As much as I loved Instagram, I'd been craving a place where I could create long-form content that was evergreen and would be discovered again and again by bookish internet wanderers. I've since filled that space with a varied mix of book recommendations, Instagram tips and details of my literary travels. To date I've written about boutique hotels, a national book-shop town, a residential library, a real-life Hobbit Hole and more. The web is where I've carved out a little space just for myself – a place to open up and pour my heart out, and where I can connect with others like me. There's no one to edit me or tell me no; I never have to ask permission or persuade others to see my point of view. It's my own little rabbit hole to escape into every evening and weekend.

So my blog was born and to my delight I found, waiting for me on the internet, a huge community of amazing, creative entrepreneurs. There were writers, photographers, artists, designers and crafters, bookworms, travellers, fashionistas, beauty experts and minimalists, all sharing their creations with the world and inspiring me to continue contributing my own. The web is a place where the playing field has been levelled, and softer, more cautious creatives (like myself!) have an equal chance of being heard. It's where the quiet people thrive. To date, I've worked with a number of high-profile brands, from National Express and Visit Scotland to Universal Pictures and *Stylist* magazine. I've created sponsored Instagram posts on both my grid and my stories, and written advertorial pieces on my blog for Bookatable.com and Fora, a wonderful flexible working space in East London. This isn't a full-time gig for me (I spend my days working in book publishing), but by night my creative projects have blossomed into a successful and fulfilling side hustle. I'm just an ordinary person who's worked hard … and if I can do it, then you can do it too.

Time to get started

So take a moment to think about a project you've always wanted to launch but never quite had the courage to begin. If you're reading this, then you're probably a writer, so perhaps you've always liked the idea of running your own blog - a place where you can write the words of your choosing and make money doing it. Or maybe you relish the idea of pairing words with images and sharing your love of sustainable fashion on a dedicated Instagram account of your own. This is the seed of an idea, and my first advice for you is simply to *begin*. Forget about producing a perfect, complete work of art and just get started, learning as you go. One of the great things about the internet is that, when you start a creative project like this, no one's going to be watching. You can experiment without consequence.

Setting up a basic blog is easy, and you won't need even a smidge of coding knowledge. There are a number of sites such as WordPress, Squarespace and Wix, which will guide you through the process of setting up your first fully functioning website, and all for free. It's a quick process, and you can easily get it up and running within the space of a Sunday afternoon. If you have the budget, then I would recommend purchasing your own URL as it looks more professional (for example, juliasbookcase.com instead of juliasbook-case.squarespace.com), although this isn't compulsory. How frequently you post is up to you, but I'd encourage you to find a schedule that you can realistically and consistently stick to. I usually post around three times a month. When it comes to finding and retaining readers, social media is your friend. I share all of my blog posts with my followers on Instagram, which is where the majority of my website traffic comes from, but I also regularly share my writing on Twitter, and always make the most of SEO. Pinterest is another blogger favourite for increasing traffic, although don't feel like you need to try all of these channels at once. I suggest you start by setting up an adjacent Instagram account – all you need to do is download the app and sign up.

Find your community

When you're creating something online, it's vital to embrace community – both fitting into one and moulding one of your own. It can be so easy to get bogged down in the technicalities of a project when you're first starting out ... like whether you should host your blog on WordPress or Squarespace (I use Squarespace) or what colour scheme you should follow on your Instagram account. But unless you find your tribe, that is, the people who are interested in what you're creating, then it's unlikely that many people will see it at all, regardless of its quality.

A blogger's jargon buster

Instagram 'grid'
There are two main ways that you can share content on Instagram, the first is on your **grid**: the collection of square images that show up on your profile page and are seen by your followers on their homepage.

Instagram 'stories'
Alternatively, content can be shared on your Instagram **story**: stories are found at the top of the homepage and expire after 24 hours.

SEO
Also known as **search engine optimisation**: this is the process of optimising/making the most of your content so that it can be found through search engines such as Google.

If you're launching a blog, I urge you to start a Twitter or Instagram account to run alongside it. That's where you will find like-minded people and create friendships with those who will read your blog posts. On Instagram, try scrolling down the 'bookstagram' hashtag, liking and commenting on the photos that catch your eye. Don't produce spam but leave meaningful comments and follow accounts that you would like to see again. Whatever project you're starting, this is how to get found on a web that is saturated with the voices of others. My favourite Instagram guru, Sara Tasker, likes to say 'there's always room at the top' and I wholeheartedly agree.

So here you are – this is your permission slip to take the leap and start something magical.

Julia Mitchell is a book editor by day and an award-winning blogger, Instagrammer and freelance writer by night. In 2020, she was named The London Book Fair UK's Book Blogger of the Year. She's obsessed with all things bookish, owns a colour-coordinated bookshelf and has a penchant for strong cups of tea.

Indexing

A good index is essential to the user of a non-fiction book; a bad index will let down an otherwise excellent book. The functions of indexes, and the skills needed to compile them, are explained here by the Society of Indexers.

An index is a detailed key to the contents of a document, unlike a contents list, which shows only the sections into which the document is divided (e.g. chapters). An index guides readers to information by providing a systematic arrangement of entries (single words, phrases, acronyms, names and so on) in a suitably organised list (usually alphabetical) that refers them to specific locations using page, column, section, frame, figure, table, paragraph, line or other appropriate numbers or hyperlinks.

Professional indexing

A well-crafted index produced by a skilled professional with appropriate subject expertise is an essential feature of almost every non-fiction book. A professional indexer has subject knowledge and considers the text from a readers' perspective, anticipating how they will approach the subject and what language they will use. The indexer analyses the content of the text and provides a carefully structured index to guide readers efficiently into the main text of the book.

A detailed, comprehensive and regularly updated Directory of Professional Indexers is on the Society of Indexers' website. Professional competence is recognised in three stages by the Society. Professional Members (MSocInd) have successfully completed initial training (see below) or have many years' continuous experience. Advanced Professional Members (MSocInd(Adv)) have demonstrated skills and experience gained since their initial training, while Fellows of the Society of Indexers (FSocInd) have been through a rigorous assessment procedure to demonstrate the quality of their work.

Indexing fees depend on many factors, particularly the complexity of the text, but for an index to a straightforward text the Society recommends £26.15 an hour, £2.95 a page, or £7.90 per 1,000 words (in 2021).

Indexing should normally be organised by the publisher, but may be left to the author to do or to arrange. It is rarely a popular task with authors, and they are often not well suited to the task, which takes objectivity, perspective, speed, patience, attention to detail and, above all, training, experience and specialist software. Moreover, authors are generally too close to the text by this stage.

Ebooks and other electronic material

An index is necessary for ebooks and other electronic material. It is a complete myth that users of ebooks can rely solely on keyword-based retrieval systems; these pick out far too much information to be usable and far too little to be reliable. Only careful analysis by the human brain creates suitable index terms for non-fiction ebooks. There are no shortcuts for judging relevance, for extracting meaning and significance from the text, for identifying complex concepts, or for recognising different ways of expressing similar ideas. Index entries must also be properly linked to the text when a printed book is converted into an ebook. Linked indexes can be achieved via the technique of embedded indexing, where index entries are anchored within the text at their precise location.

The Society of Indexers

The Society of Indexers was founded in 1957 and is the only autonomous professional body for indexers in the UK. The main objectives of the Society are to promote high standards in all types of indexing and highlight the role of indexers in the organisation of knowledge; to provide, promote and recognise facilities for both the initial and the further training of indexers; to establish criteria for assessing conformity to indexing standards; and to conduct research and publish guidance, ideas and information about indexing. It seeks to establish good relationships between indexers, librarians, publishers and authors, both to advance good indexing and to ensure that the contribution of indexers to the organisation and retrieval of knowledge is properly recognised.

Further information

Society of Indexers
Woodbourn Business Centre, 10 Jessell Street, Sheffield S9 3HY
tel 0114 453 4928
email admin@indexers.org.uk
website www.indexers.org.uk
Twitter @indexers
Membership (2021) new member £109 p.a. (including 25% discount valid for first year of membership); standard membership £145 p.a.

The Society holds an annual conference and publishes a learned journal, *The Indexer* (quarterly), a newsletter and *Occasional Papers on Indexing*. Additional resources are published on its website. The society also runs National Indexing Day (#indexday) each March, with events for publishers to learn more about indexing.

Indexing as a career

Indexing is often taken up as a second career, frequently drawing on expertise developed in some other field. Both intellectually demanding and creative, it requires considerable and sustained mental effort. Indexers need to be well-organised, flexible, disciplined and self-motivated, and resilient enough to cope with the uncertainties of freelance work. The Society of Indexers' long-established training course, which has received the CILIP Seal of Recognition (see CILIP page 531), gives a thorough grounding in indexing principles and practice on real documents. Based on the principle of open learning, it enables students to learn in their own way and at their own pace. There is access to study materials, practice exercises and quizzes, and links to a wide range of useful resources. Online tutorials are undertaken at various stages during the course. After completing the four assessed modules, which cover the core indexing skills, students undertake a book-length practical indexing assignment. Successful completion of the course leads to Accreditation, designation as a Professional Indexer (MSocInd), and entry in the Society's online *Directory of Professional Indexers*.

Further reading

Booth, P.F., *Indexing: The Manual of Good Practice* (K.G. Saur 2001)

British Standards Institution, *British Standard Recommendations for Examining Documents, Determining their Subjects and Selecting Indexing Terms* (BS6529:1984)

'Indexes' (chapter from *The Chicago Manual of Style*, 17th edn; University of Chicago Press 2017)

International Standards Organisation, *Information and Documentation – Guidelines for the Content, Organization and Presentation of Indexes* (ISO 999:1996)

Mulvany, N.C., *Indexing Books* (University of Chicago Press, 2nd edn 2005)

Stauber, D.M., *Facing the Text: Content and Structure in Book Indexing* (Cedar Row Press 2004)

ISBNs: what you need to know

The Nielsen ISBN Agency for UK & Ireland receives a large number of enquiries about the ISBN system. The most frequently asked questions are answered here; for more information visit www.nielsenisbnstore.com.

What is an ISBN?

An ISBN is an International Standard Book Number and is 13 digits long.

What is the purpose of an ISBN?

An ISBN is a product number, used by publishers, booksellers and libraries for ordering, listing and stock control purposes. It enables them to identify a particular publisher and allows the publisher to identify a specific edition of a specific title in a specific format within their output.

Contact details

Nielsen ISBN Agency for UK and Ireland
3rd Floor, Midas House, 62 Goldsworth Road, Woking GU21 6LQ
tel (01483) 712215
email isbn.agency@nielseniq.com
website www.nielsenisbnstore.com

Does an ISBN protect copyright?

A widely held belief is that an ISBN protects copyright. It doesn't, it is an identifier, a product code. The copyright belongs to the author. In general, publishers don't tend to buy copyrights for books. They license the copyrights, which the author retains.

What is a publisher?

The publisher is generally the person or organisation taking the financial and other risks in making a product available. For example, if a product goes on sale and sells no copies at all, the publisher loses money. If you get paid anyway, you are likely to be a designer, printer, author or consultant of some kind.

What is the format of an ISBN?

The ISBN is 13 digits long and is divided into five parts separated by spaces or hyphens.
• Prefix element: for the foreseeable future this will be 978 or 979
• Registration group element: identifies a geographic or national grouping. It shows where the publisher is based
• Registrant element: identifies a specific publisher or imprint
• Publication element: identifies a specific edition of a specific title in a specific format
• Check digit: the final digit which mathematically validates the rest of the number
The four parts following the prefix element can be of varying length.
Prior to 1 January 2007 ISBNs were ten digits long; any existing ten-digit ISBNs must be converted by prefixing them with '978' and the check digit must be recalculated using a Modulus 10 system with alternate weights of 1 and 3. The ISBN Agency can help you with this.

Do I *have* to have an ISBN?

There is no legal requirement in the UK and Ireland for an ISBN and it conveys no form of legal or copyright protection. It is simply a product identification number.

Why should I use an ISBN?

If you wish to sell your publication through major bookselling chains, independent book-shops or internet retailers, they will require you to have an ISBN to assist their internal processing and ordering systems.

The ISBN also provides access to bibliographic databases, such as the Nielsen Book Database, which use ISBNs as references. These databases help booksellers and libraries to provide information for customers. Nielsen Book has a range of information, electronic trading and retail sales monitoring services which use ISBNs and are vital for the dissem-ination, trading and monitoring of books in the supply chain. The ISBN therefore provides access to additional marketing opportunities which could help sales of your product.

Where can I get an ISBN?

ISBNs are assigned to publishers in the country where the publisher's main office is based. This is irrespective of the language of the publication or the intended market for the book.

The ISBN Agency is the national agency for the UK and Republic of Ireland and British Overseas Territories. A publisher based elsewhere will not be able to get numbers from the UK Agency (even if you are a British Citizen) but can contact the Nielsen ISBN Agency for details of the relevant national Agency.

If you are based in the UK and Ireland you can purchase ISBNs online from the Nielsen ISBN Store: www.nielsenisbnstore.com.

How long does it take to get an ISBN?

If you purchase your ISBNs online from the Nielsen ISBN Store you will receive your ISBN allocation within minutes. If you are purchasing ISBNs direct from the ISBN Agency via an off-line application, it can take up to five days. The processing period begins when a correctly completed application is received in the ISBN Agency and payment is received.

How much does it cost to get an ISBN?

Refer to www.nielsenisbnstore.com or email the ISBN Agency: isbn.agency@nielsen.com.

What if I only want one ISBN?

ISBNs can be bought individually or in blocks of ten or more; visit the ISBN Store to find out more.

Who is eligible for ISBNs?

Any individual or organisation who is publishing a qualifying product for general sale or distribution to the market. By publishing we mean making a work available to the public.

Which products do NOT qualify for ISBNs?

Any publication that is without a defined end should not be assigned an ISBN. For example, publications that are regularly updated and intended to continue indefinitely are not eli-gible for an ISBN.

Some examples of products that do not qualify for an ISBN are:

• Journals, periodicals, serials, newspapers in their entirety (single issues or articles, where these are made available separately, may qualify for ISBN);

• Abstract entities such as textual works and other abstract creations of intellectual or artistic content;

• Ephemeral printed materials such as advertising matter and the like;

• Customised print-on-demand publications (Publications that are available only on a limited basis, such as customised print-on-demand publications with content specifically

tailored to a user's request shall not be assigned an ISBN. If a customised publication is being made available for wider sale, e.g. as a college course pack available through a college book store, then an ISBN may be assigned);
• Printed music;
• Art prints and art folders without title page and text;
• Personal documents (such as a curriculum vitae or personal profile);
• Greetings cards;
• Music sound recordings;
• Software that is intended for any purpose other than educational or instructional;
• Electronic bulletin boards;
• Emails and other digital correspondence;
• Updating websites;
• Games.

Following a review of the UK market, it is now permissible for ISBNs to be assigned to calendars and diaries, provided that they are not intended for purely time-management purposes and that a substantial proportion of their content is textual or graphic.

What is an ISSN?

An International Standard Serial Number. This is the numbering system for journals, magazines, periodicals, newspapers and newsletters. It is administered by the British Library, *tel* (01937) 546959; *email* issn-uk@bl.uk; *website* www.bl.uk/help/Get-an-ISBN-or-ISSN-for-your-publication#

Where do I put the ISBN?

The ISBN should appear on the reverse of the title page, sometimes called the copyright page or the imprint page, and on the outside back cover of the book. If the book has a dust jacket, the ISBN should also appear on the back of this. If the publication is not a book, the ISBN should appear on the product, and on the packaging or inlay card. If the publication is a map, the ISBN should be visible when the map is folded and should also appear near the publisher statement if this is elsewhere.

I am reprinting a book with no changes – do I need a new ISBN?

No.

I am reprinting a book but adding a new chapter – do I need a new ISBN?

Yes. You are adding a significant amount of additional material, altering the content of the book.

I am reprinting a book with a new cover design – should I change the ISBN?

No. A change of cover design with no changes to the content of the book should not have a new ISBN.

I am changing the binding on the book to paperback rather than hardback. Do I need a new ISBN?

Yes. Changes in binding always require new ISBNs even if there are no changes to the content of the book.

I am changing the price – do I need a new ISBN?

No. Price changes with no other changes do not require new ISBNs and indeed must not change the ISBN.

Public Lending Right

Under the PLR system, payment is made from public funds to authors and other contributors (writers, illustrators/photographers, translators, adapters/retellers, ghostwriters, editors/compilers/abridgers/revisers, narrators and producers) whose books (print, audiobook and ebook) are lent from public libraries. Payment is annual; the amount authors receive is proportionate to the number of times that their books were borrowed during the previous year (July to June).

How the system works

From the applications received, the PLR office compiles a database of authors and books (the PLR Register). A representative sample of book issues is recorded, consisting of all loans from selected public libraries. This is then multiplied in proportion to total library lending to produce, for each book, an estimate of its total annual loans throughout the country. The estimated loans are matched against the database of registered authors and titles to discover how many loans are credited to each registered book for the calculation of PLR payments, using the ISBN printed in the book (see below).

Parliament allocates a sum each year (£6.6 million for 2019/20) for PLR. This fund pays the administrative costs of PLR and reimburses local authorities for recording loans in the sample libraries (see below). The remaining money is divided by the total estimated national loan figure for all registered books in order to work out how much can be paid for each estimated loan of every registered ISBN.

Further information

Public Lending Right
PO Box 751, Boston Spa, Wetherby,
West Yorkshire LS22 9FW
tel (01937) 546030
website www.bl.uk/plr
website www.plrinternational.com
Contact Head of PLR Operations

The UK PLR scheme is administered by the British Library from its offices in Boston Spa. The UK PLR office also provides registration for the Irish PLR scheme on behalf of the Irish Public Lending Remuneration office.

Application forms, information and publications are all obtainable from the PLR Office. See website for further information on eligibility for PLR, loans statistics and forthcoming developments.

British Library Advisory Committee for Public Lending Right
Advises the British Library Board, the PLR Head of Policy and Engagement and Head of PLR Operations on the operation and future development of the PLR scheme.

Limits on payments

If all the registered interests in an author's books score so few loans that they would earn less than £1 in a year, no payment is due. However, if the books of one registered author score so high that the author's PLR earnings for the year would exceed £6,600, then only £6,600 is paid. (No author can earn more than £6,600 in PLR in any one year.) Money that is not paid out because of these limits belongs to the fund and increases the amounts paid that year to other authors.

The sample

Because it would be expensive and impracticable to attempt to collect loans data from every library authority in the UK, a statistical sampling method is employed instead. The sample represents only public lending libraries – academic, school, private and commercial libraries are not included. Only books which are loaned from public libraries can earn PLR; consultations of books on library premises are excluded.

The sample consists of the entire loans records for a year from libraries in more than 30 public library authorities spread through England, Scotland and Wales, and whole data is collected from Northern Ireland. Sample loans represent around 20% of the national total. All the computerised sampling points in an authority contribute loans data ('multi-site' sampling). The aim is to increase the sample without any significant increase in costs. In order to ensure representative sampling, at least seven libraries are replaced every year and a library cannot stay in the sample for more than four years. Loans are totalled every 12 months for the period 1 July–30 June.

An author's entitlement to PLR depends on the loans accrued by his or her books in the sample. This figure is averaged up to produce first regional and then finally national estimated loans.

ISBNs

The PLR system uses ISBNs (International Standard Book Numbers) to identify books lent and correlate loans with entries on the PLR Register so that payments can be made. ISBNs are required for all registrations. Different editions (e.g. 1st, 2nd, hardback, paperback, large print) of the same book have different ISBNs. See *ISBNs: what you need to know* on page 662.

Authorship

In the PLR system the author of a printed book or ebook is any contributor such as the writer, illustrator, translator, compiler, editor or reviser. Authors must be named on the book's title page, or be able to prove authorship by some other means (e.g. receipt of royalties). The ownership of copyright has no bearing on PLR eligibility. Narrators, producers and abridgers are also eligible to apply for PLR shares in audiobooks and e-audiobooks.

Co-authorship/illustrators. In the PLR system the authors of a book are those writers, translators, editors, compilers and illustrators as defined above. Authors must apply for

---

Summary of the 38th year's results

Registration: authors. When registration closed for the 38th year (30 June 2020) there were 66,888 authors and assignees.

Eligible loans. The loans from UK libraries credited to registered books – approximately 33% of all library borrowings – qualify for payment. The remaining loans relate to books that are ineligible for various reasons, to books written by dead or foreign authors, and to books that have simply not been applied for.

Money and payments. PLR's administrative costs are deducted from the fund allocated to the British Library Board annually by Parliament. Total government funding for 2019/20 was £6.6 million. The amount distributed to authors was just over £6 million. The Rate per Loan for 2019/20 was 9.55 pence.

The numbers of authors in various payment categories are as follows:

*299	payments at	£5,000–6,600
356	payments between	£2,500–4,999.99
790	payments between	£1,000–2,499.99
838	payments between	£500–999.99
3,189	payments between	£100–499.99
16,225	payments between	£1–99.99
21,697	TOTAL	

* Includes 200 authors whose book loans reached the maximum threshold

registration before their books can earn PLR and this can be done via the PLR website. There is no restriction on the number of authors who can register shares in any one book as long as they satisfy the eligibility criteria.

Writers and/or illustrators. At least one contributor must be eligible and they must jointly agree what share of PLR each will take based on contribution. This agreement is necessary even if one or two are ineligible or do not wish to register for PLR. The eligible authors will receive the share(s) specified in the application.

Translators. Translators may apply for a 30% fixed share (to be shared equally between joint translators).

Editors and compilers. An editor or compiler may apply to register a 20% share if they have written at least 10% of the book's content or more than ten pages of text in addition to normal editorial work and are named on the title page. Alternatively, editors may register 20% if they have a royalty agreement with the publisher. In the case of joint editors/compilers, the total editor's share should be divided equally.

Audiobooks. PLR shares in audiobooks are fixed by the UK scheme and may not be varied. *Writers* may register a fixed 60% share in an audiobook, providing that it has not been abridged or translated. In cases where the writer has made an additional contribution (e.g. as narrator), she/he may claim both shares. *Narrators* may register a fixed 20% PLR share in an audiobook. *Producers* may register a fixed 20% share in an audiobook. *Abridgers* (in

Most borrowed authors

Children's authors

1 Daisy Meadows
2 Julia Donaldson
3 Francesca Simon
4 David Walliams
5 Adam Blade
6 Roald Dahl
7 Jeff Kinney
8 Jacqueline Wilson
9 Liz Pichon
10 J.K. Rowling
11 Fiona Watt
12 Claire Freedman
13 Lucy Cousins
14 Michael Morpurgo
15 Jeanne Willis
16 Giles Andreae
17 Kes Grey
18 Enid Blyton
19 David McKee
20 Roderick Hunt

Authors of adult fiction

1 James Patterson
2 Lee Child
3 M.C. Beaton
4 Danielle Steele
5 Anna Jacobs
6 David Baldacci
7 Nora Roberts
8 Ann Cleeves
9 Peter James
10 Michael Connelly
11 Clive Cussler
12 John Grisham
13 Alexander McCall Smith
14 Peter May
15 Agatha Christie
16 Peter Robinson
17 Dilly Court
18 Elly Griffiths
19 Val McDermid
20 J.D. Robb

These two lists are of the most borrowed authors in UK public libraries. They are based on PLR sample loans in the period July 2018–June 2019 (data for 2019–20 not available before going to press; this will be published on the PLR website in 2021). They include all writers, both registered and unregistered, but not illustrators where the book has a separate writer. Writing names are used; pseudonyms have not been combined.

Please note that these top 20 listings are based on the February 2019 UK PLR payment calculations.

cases where the writer's original text has been abridged prior to recording as an audiobook) qualify for 12% (20% of the writer's share). *Translators* (in cases where the writer's original text has been translated from another language) qualify for 18% (30% of the writer's share). If there is more than one writer, narrator, etc the appropriate shares should be divided equally.

Dead or missing co-authors. Where it is impossible to agree shares with a co-author because that person is dead or untraceable, then the surviving co-author or co-authors may submit an application to register a share which reflects their individual contribution to the book.

Transferring PLR after death. First applications may not be made by the estate of a deceased author. However, if an author registers during their lifetime the PLR in their books can be transferred to a new owner and continues for up to 70 years after the date of their death. The new owner can apply to register new titles if first published one year before, or up to ten years after, the date of the author's death. New editions of existing registered titles can also be registered posthumously.

Residential qualifications. To register for the UK PLR scheme, at the time of application authors must have their only home or principal home in the UK or in any of the other countries within the European Economic Area (i.e. EC member states plus Iceland, Norway and Liechtenstein).

Eligible books

In the PLR system each edition of a book is registered and treated as a separate book. A book is eligible for PLR registration provided that:
• it has an eligible author (or co-author);
• it is printed and bound (paperbacks count as bound);
• it has already been published;
• copies of it have been put on sale, i.e. it is not a free handout;
• the authorship is personal, i.e. not a company or association, and the book is not crown copyright;
• it has an ISBN;
• it is not wholly or mainly a musical score;
• it is not a newspaper, magazine, journal or periodical.

Audiobooks. An audiobook is defined as an 'authored text' or 'a work recorded as a sound recording and consisting mainly of spoken words'. Applications can therefore only be accepted to register audiobooks which meet these requirements and are the equivalent of a printed book. Music, dramatisations and live recordings do not qualify for registration. To qualify for UK PLR in an audiobook contributors should be named on the case in which the audiobook is held; or be able to refer to a contract with the publisher; or be named within the audiobook recording.

Ebooks. Previously only ebooks downloaded to fixed terminals in library premises and then taken away on loan on portable devices to be read elsewhere qualified for PLR payment. Information provided by libraries suggested that the vast majority of ebook and digital audio lending was carried out 'remotely' to home PCs and mobile devices, which meant the loan did not qualify for PLR.

On 27 April 2017 the Digital Economy Bill, which included provision to extend the UK PLR legislation to include remote loans of ebooks from public libraries, received Royal

Assent. The new arrangements took effect officially from 1 July 2018, and remote ebook loans data is now collected, and the first payments arising from the newly eligible loans were made in February 2020. The PLR website provides updated information on this legislation.

Statements and payment

Authors with an online account may view their statement online. Registered authors without an online account receive a statement posted to their address if a payment is due.

Sampling arrangements

To help minimise the unfairness that arises inevitably from a sampling system, the scheme specifies the eight regions within which authorities and sampling points have to be designated and includes libraries of varying size. Part of the sample drops out by rotation each year to allow fresh libraries to be included. The following library authorities were designated for the year 1 July 2020–30 June 2021 (all are multi-site authorities). This list is based on the nine government regions for England plus Northern Ireland, Scotland and Wales. The composition of the PLR library authority sample changes annually and not all regions have to be represented each year.
• East – no library authorities during 2020/21
• East Midlands – Derbyshire, Rutland
• London – Bromley, Greenwich, Hounslow, Lewisham
• North East – Durham, Northumberland
• North West & Merseyside – Bury, Lancashire, Trafford
• South East – Bracknell Forest, Isle of Wight, Oxfordshire, West Sussex
• South West – Devon, Plymouth, Shropshire, Wiltshire
• West Midlands – Dudley
• Yorkshire & The Humber – Calderdale, Wakefield
• Northern Ireland – The Northern Ireland Library Authority
• Scotland – Falkirk, Fife, Highland, South Lanarkshire
• Wales – Bridgend, Carmarthenshire, Conwy, Newport.
Participating local authorities are reimbursed on an actual cost basis for additional expenditure incurred in providing loans data to the PLR Office. The extra PLR work mostly consists of modifications to computer programs to accumulate loans data in the local authority computer and to transmit the data to the PLR Office.

Reciprocal arrangements

Reciprocal PLR arrangements now exist with the German, Dutch, Austrian and other European PLR schemes. Authors can apply for overseas PLR for most of these countries through the ALCS (Authors' Licensing and Collecting Society; see page 715). The exception to this rule is Ireland. Authors should now register for Irish PLR through the UK PLR Office. Further information on PLR schemes internationally and recent developments within the EC towards wider recognition of PLR is available from the PLR Office or on the international PLR website.

A matter of style: A mini A-Z of literary terms

Literary terms are linguistic and stylistic features that writers can employ to enhance their writing.

adage

A popular saying or expression which conveys a shared and often repeated belief. It might be a proverb or an aphorism or a maxim, but has a sense of universal truth about it.

alliteration

The repeated use of the same vowel or consonant, especially at the beginning of a series of words, to create a distinct rhythm.

allusion

A reference which is (often) subtly implied, but which assumes the reader will comprehend, based on a shared understanding or knowledge of what is being alluded to. Reference might be to a person, an event or a book.

amplification

Expanding a sentence to draw attention to or to exaggerate or intensify an aspect of a story or argument.

analogy

A comparison between two similar things used to illustrate an argument or explanation. These things might not be in any obvious sense similar, but figuratively might be drawn together to highlight a specific characteristic or sentiment.

anaphora

One or more words repeated sequentially or consecutively, especially at the beginning of a series of statements, to attract the reader's attention.

anecdote

The retelling or recounting of a personal story or experience, often to reference a specific event from which to extrapolate a broader point.

anthimeria

Swapping one part of speech in a way that is not grammatically correct, for example replacing a verb with a noun for metaphorical effect.

anthropomorphism

Animals, objects or other non-human beings given human characteristics and portrayed as though they were human.

antimetabole

When words or phrases in one part of a sentence are inverted and used in the second part.

antiphrasis

Where a word is used opposite to its actual meaning and thus is a form of irony.

aphorism

A short statement which is intended to summarise an accepted truth in a distinctively clever or witty way.

apologue

A fable or short story which is intended to teach a moral lesson, often using animals as characters.

apophasis

Asserting or emphasising something by denying it or stating that it will not be mentioned. This is also known as paralipsis.

archetype

A universal idea or image or person which serves as a common example or representation and is recognisable because of its frequent use.

assonance

The repeated use of the same vowel sounds to create a distinct rhythmic pattern, to set a mood or reiterate the meaning of words.

asyndeton

Writing stripped down to its crucial meaning and essentials, where, for example, conjunctions or pronouns are omitted.

auxesis

The listing of concepts or things in their ascending order of importance.

cacophony

A series of conflicting sounds used together to create an inharmonious rhythm.

chiasmus

Where the grammatical structure of one phrase or sentence is repeated in a second phrase or sentence where a related concept appears in reverse order.

cliché

A common phrase which has been repeated so often that it has lost any sincere or impactful meaning.

diacope

The repetition of a word or words in a sentence, with other words dropped in between; used for emphasis or to enhance a description.

dissonance

An arrangement of cacophonous or discordant sounds to create a harsh and jarring effect.

epigram

A short, often witty statement to praise, commemorate or mock, often used as an inscription at the start of a book or chapter.

epistrophe

Successive phrases or sentences where the final word is repeated.

epithet

An adjective or description used to qualify a specifically named person or thing, that captures their most admired or despised qualities and is universally the way they are referred to.

eponym

The protagonist or character whose name is also given to the title of a work.

euphemism

A seemingly harmless word or phrase with a second meaning which is considered impolite or inappropriate or might wish to convey a less literal meaning in a subtle way.

euphony

A series of complementary sounds, usually vowels or soft consonants, which flow together and create a smooth rhythm.

extended metaphor

A metaphor which is sustained throughout a piece of writing and is returned to several times in order to extend or add depth to the comparison or meaning.

hamartia

A flaw or failure in a character, that they themselves are not usually able to see, that leads to his or her downfall.

homophone

Two or more words which sound the same but are spelt differently and have different meanings, for example 'would' and 'wood', 'flower' and 'flour'.

hyperbaton

Where words are arranged in an unexpected way that upends the usual grammatical order.

hyperbole

Exaggeration intended to emphasise and highlight, and which strays into the realm of untruth, something not to be understood literally.

idiom

A common phrase whose meaning is not literal and is specific to the language it originates from, for example 'as fit as a fiddle'.

juxtaposition

Where two things are placed together to create a contrast or invite comparison.

litotes

An understated or ironic figure of speech in which an idea or thing is emphasised by rejecting its opposite, for example 'You won't be sorry' to convey satisfaction or pleasure.

malapropism

The misuse of words for humorous effect, named after Mrs Malaprop in R. B. Sheridan's *The Rivals* (1775).

metanoia

An exaggerated or extreme statement lessened or undermined by a successive statement which suggests a changed mind or a calmed emotion.

metaphor

Where one thing is said to be another to invite comparison or emphasise a similarity.

metonymy

A recognisable or inherent aspect of a thing used to represent the thing itself, for example a businessman being referred to as a 'suit', the monarchy as the 'Crown', or newspapers collectively as 'the Press'.

nemesis

The embodiment of a punishment often presented as an antagonist or enemy.

onomatopoeia

Words which imitate the sounds they represent, for example 'click' and 'clack', or the use of consonant sounds to mimic the sound they are describing, for example to create the rhythm of high heels on a wooden floor.

oxymoron

A phrase which joins contradictory words to create a paradox, for example 'pretty ugly'.

personification

An idea, or event presented as a human operation; adopting human attributes.

pleonasm

The redundant use of extra words which repeat rather than expand meaning, such as 'burning fire' or 'a really new innovation'.

polyptoton

The repetition of a word, or its root, with a different grammatical application each time.

rhetorical question

A question which is not intended to be answered but is instead used to emphasise a point.

simile

Where one thing is said to be like another to invite comparison and emphasise a similarity.

spoonerism

When the first consonant sounds of two or more words are swapped to create a new phrase for humorous effect.

syllogism

A form of logical reasoning where two propositions or ideas, which share a common element, together confirm a given conclusion.

synecdoche

Where a part may be used for the whole or the whole stand for a part.

transferred epithet

When an adjectival word or phrase is attached to a noun which it doesn't strictly describe (thus transferred), for example 'sleepless nights'.

zeugma

Where one word is used to describe two others in different contexts, for example 'she lost her keys and her temper'.

Who's who in publishing

agent

See **literary agent**.

aggregator

A company or website that gathers together related content from a range of other sources and provides various different services and resources, such as formatting and distribution, to ebook authors.

art editor

A person in charge of the layout and design of a magazine, who commissions the photographs and illustrations and is responsible for its overall appearance and style.

audio editor

A person who edits the raw audio from the recording into the final, retail-ready audiobook.

audio producer

A person who supervises the entire production process of the audiobook.

author

A person who has written a book, article, or other piece of original writing.

book packager

See **packager**.

columnist

A person who regularly writes an article for publication in a newspaper or magazine.

commissioning editor

A person who asks authors to write books for the part of the publisher's list for which he or she is responsible or who takes on an author who approaches them direct or via an agent with a proposal. Also called **acquisitions editor** or **acquiring editor** (more commonly in the US). A person who signs up writers (commissions them to write) an article for a magazine or newspaper.

contributor

A person who writes an article that is included in a magazine or paper, or who writes a chapter or section that is included in a book.

copy-editor

A person whose job is to check material ready for publication for accuracy, clarity of message, writing style and consistency of spelling, punctuation and grammar.

desk editor

Manages a list of titles, seeing them through the editorial and production processes, and works closely with authors.

distributor

Acts as a link between the publisher and retailer. The distributor can receive orders from retailers, ship books, invoice, collect revenue and deal with returns. Distributors often handle books from several publishers. Digital distributors handle ebook distribution.

editor

A person in charge of publishing a newspaper or magazine who makes the final decisions about the content and format. A person in book publishing who has responsibility for the content of a book and can be variously a senior person (editor-in-chief) or day-to-day contact for authors (copy-editor, development editor, commissioning editor, etc).

editorial assistant

A person who assists senior editorial staff at a publishing company, newspaper, or similar business with various administrative duties, as well as editorial tasks in preparing copy for publication.

illustrator

A person who designs and draws a visual rendering of the source material, such as characters or settings, in a 2D media. Using traditional or digital methods, an illustrator creates artwork manually rather than photographically.

journalist

A person who prepares and writes material for a newspaper or magazine, news website, television or radio programme, or any similar medium.

literary agent

Somebody whose job is to negotiate publishing contracts, involving royalties, advances and rights sales on behalf of an author and who earns commission on the proceeds of the sales they negotiate.

literary scout

A person who looks for unpublished manuscripts to recommend to clients for publication as books, or adaptation into film scripts, etc.

marketing department

The department that originates the sales material – catalogues, order forms, blads, samplers, posters, book proofs and advertisements – to promote published titles.

narrator

A person who reads a text aloud into a recording device to create an audiobook. This may be the author of the text, or a professional voice artist.

packager

A company that creates a finished book for a publisher.

picture researcher

A person who looks for pictures relevant to a particular topic, so that they can be used as illustrations in, for example, a book, newspaper or TV programme.

printer

A person or company whose job is to produce printed books, magazines, newspapers or similar material. The many stages in this process include establishing the product specifications, preparing the pages for print, operating the printing presses, and binding and finishing the final product.

production controller

A person in the production department of a publishing company who deals with printers and paper suppliers.

production department

The department responsible for the technical aspects of planning and producing material for publication to a schedule and as specified by the client. Their work involves liaising with editors, designers, typesetters, printers and binders.

proofreader

A person whose job is to check typeset pages and text for layout, design, spelling and grammatical errors missed at copy-editing, prior to publication.

publicity department

The department that works with the author and the media on 'free' publicity when a book is published – e.g. reviews, features, author interviews, bookshop readings and signings, festival appearances, book tours and radio and TV interviews.

publisher

A person or company that publishes books, magazines or newspapers.

rights manager

A person who negotiates and coordinates rights sales (e.g. for subsidiary, translation or foreign rights). Often travels to book fairs to negotiate rights sales.

sales department

The department responsible for selling and marketing the publications produced by a publishing company, to bring about maximum sales and profit. Its tasks include identifying physical and digital outlets, ensuring orders and supplies of stock.

self-publishing services provider

Company that provides (for a fee) the complete range of activities to support a self-publishing author get their book into print or ebook. These include editorial, design, production, marketing and selling: i.e. all tasks carried out by a traditional publisher for their authors.

sensitivity reader

Assesses a manuscript with a particular issue of representation in mind, usually one that they have personal experience of.

sub-editor

A person who corrects and checks articles in a newspaper before they are printed.

translator

A person who translates copy, such as a manuscript, from one language into another.

typesetter

A person or company that 'sets' text and prepares the final layout of the page for printing. It can also now involve XML tagging for ebook creation.

vanity publisher

A publisher who charges an author a fee in order to publish his or her work for them, and is not responsible for selling the product.

web content manager

A person who controls the type and quality of material shown on a website or blog and is responsible for how it is produced, organised, presented and updated.

wholesaler

A person or company that buys large quantities of books, magazines, etc from publishers, transports and stores them, and then sells them in smaller quantities to a range of retailers.

Glossary of publishing terms

advance

Money paid by a publisher to an author before a book is published which will be covered by future royalties. A publishing contract often allows an author an advance payment against future royalties; the author will not receive any further royalties until the amount paid in advance has been earned by sales of the book.

AI (advance information sheet)

A document that is put together by a publishing company to provide sales and marketing information about a book before publication and can be sent several months before publication to sales representatives. It typically includes details of the format and contents of the book, key selling points and information about intended readership, as well as information about promotions and reviews.

auction

An auction, usually arranged by a literary agent, takes place when multiple publishing houses are interested in acquiring a manuscript and bid against one another to secure the domestic or territorial rights.

B format

See **trade paperback**.

backlist

The range of books already published by a publisher, or indie author, that are still in print.

beta reader

A person who reads a book before it is published in order to mark errors and suggest improvements, typically without receiving payment.

BIC

A group of categories and subcategories that can be applied to a book to accurately describe it and to help place it in the market.

BISAC

Subject heading codes that categorise your book into topics and subtopics. Used by sellers to place your book in the correct section of their store or online listings.

blad (book layout and design)

A pre-publication sales and marketing tool. It is often a printed booklet that contains sample pages, images and front and back covers, which acts as a preview for promotional use or for sales and rights teams to show to potential retailers, customers or reviewers.

blurb

A short piece of writing or a paragraph that praises and promotes a book, which usually appears on the back or inside cover and may be used in sales and marketing material.

book club edition

An edition of a book specially printed and bound for a book club for sale to its members.

book proof

A bound set of uncorrected reading proofs. Traditionally publisher sales teams send pre-publication copies to reviewers.

brief

A set of instructions given to a designer about a project, such as a cover or internal design.

C format

A term most often used to describe a paperback edition published simultaneously with, and in the same format as, the hardback original.

co-edition

The publication of a book by two publishing companies in different countries, where the first company has originated the work and then sells sheets to the second publisher (or licenses the second publisher to reprint the book locally).

copy-editing

The editorial stage where an editor looks for spelling mistakes, grammatical errors and factual errors. They may rework sentences or paragraphs to add clarity to the work.

copyright

The legal right, which the creator of an original work has, to only allow copying of the work with permission and sometimes on payment of royalties or a copyright fee. An amendment to the Copyright, Designs and Patents Act (1988) states that in the UK most works are protected for 70 years from the creator's death. The copyright page (or imprint page) at the start of a book asserts copyright ownership and author identification.

crowdfunding

A publishing model that requires a book to surpass a financial goal before it can go into production. This money comes from pledges made by readers who back the project. In return, each backer usually receives a different level of acknowledgement (based on the amount pledged) from the author within the published book.

edition

A quantity of books printed without changes to the content. A 'new edition' is a reprint of an existing title that incorporates substantial textual alterations. Originally one edition meant a single print run, though today an edition may consist of several separate printings, or impressions.

endmatter

Material at the end of the main body of a book which may be useful to the reader, including references, appendices, indexes and bibliography. Also called back matter.

ePUB files

Digital book format compatible with all electronic devices and e-readers.

extent

The number of pages in a book.

first edition

The first print run of a book. It can occasionally gain secondhand value if either the book or its author become collectable.

folio

A large sheet of paper folded twice across the middle and trimmed to make four pages of a book. Also a page number.

frontlist

New books just published (generally in their first year of publication) or about to be published by a publisher. Promotion of the frontlist is heavy, and the frontlist carries most of a publisher's investment. On the other hand, a backlist which continues to sell is usually the most profitable part of a publisher's list.

HTML markup

Instructing the text that will appear on a webpage to look a certain way, such as bold (<b></b>) or italic (<i></i>). These markup indicators are often called tags.

imagery

The use of pictures, photographs, illustrations and other type of images within a book.

impression

A single print run of a book; all books in an impression are manufactured at the same time and are identical. A 'second impression' would be the second batch of copies to be printed and bound. The impression number is usually marked on the copyright/imprint page. There can be several impressions in an edition, all sharing the same ISBN.

imprint

The publisher's or printer's name which appears on the title page of a book or in the bibliographical details; a brand name under which a book is published within a larger publishing company, usually representing a specialised subject area.

inspection copy

A copy of a publication sent or given with time allowed for a decision to purchase or return it. In academic publishing, lecturers can request inspection copies to decide whether to make a book/textbook recommended reading or adopt it as a core textbook for their course.

internal(s)

Refers to the actual page design and layout of the pages that make up a book.

ISBN

International Standard Book Number. The ISBN is formed of 13 digits and is unique to a published title.

ISSN

International Standard Serial Number. An international system used on periodicals, magazines, learned journals, etc. The ISSN is formed of eight digits, which refer to the country in which the magazine is published and the title of the publication.

kill fee

A fee paid to a freelance writer for material written on assignment but not used, typically a percentage of the total payment.

manuscript

The pre-published version of an author's work, now usually submitted in electronic form.

metadata

Data that describes the content of a book to aid online discoverability – typically title, author, ISBN, key terms, description and other bibliographic information.

moral right

The right of people such as editors or illustrators to have some say in the publication of a work to which they have contributed, even if they do not own the copyright.

MS (*pl* MSS)

The abbreviation commonly used for 'manuscript'.

nom de plume

A pseudonym or 'pen-name' under which a writer may choose to publish their work instead of their real name.

out of print or o.p.

Relating to a book of which the publisher has no copies left and which is not going to be reprinted. Print-on-demand technology, however, means that a book can be kept 'in print' indefinitely.

page proofs

A set of designed and typeset pages in a book used to check the accuracy of typesetting and page layout before publication, and also as an advance promotional tool. These are provided in electronic form, such as a pdf.

paper engineering

The mechanics of creating novelty books and pop-ups.

PDF/pdf

Portable Document Format. A data file generated from PostScript that is platform-independent, application-independent and font-independent. Acrobat is Adobe's suite of software used to generate, edit and view pdf files.

point of sale

Merchandising display material provided by publishers to bookshops in order to promote particular titles.

prelims

The initial pages of a book, including the title page and table of contents, which precede the main text. Also called front matter.

pre-press

Before going to press, to be printed.

print on demand or POD

The facility to print and bind a small number of books at short notice, without the need for a large print run, using digital technology. When an order comes through, a digital file of the book can be printed individually and automatically.

print run

The quantity of a book printed at one time in an impression.

public lending right

An author's right to receive from the public purse a payment for the loan of works from public libraries in the UK.

publisher's agreement

A contract between a publisher and the copyright holder, author, agent or another publisher, which lays down the terms under which the publisher will publish the book for the copyright holder.

publishing contract

An agreement between a publisher and an author by which the author grants the publisher the right to publish the work against payment of a fee, usually in the form of a royalty.

query letter

A letter from an author to an agent pitching their book.

reading fee

Money paid to an editor for reading a manuscript and commenting on it. Reputable literary agents should never charge such a fee.

recto

Relating to the right-hand page of a book, usually given an odd number.

reprint

Copies of a book made from the original, but with a note in the publication details of the date of reprinting and possibly a new title page and cover design.

review copy

An advance copy of a book sent to magazines, newspapers and/or other media for the purposes of review. A 'book proof' may be sent out before the final book is printed or published.

revises

If any corrections are made to your typeset proofs by the proofreader, a new round of proofs will be produced which are known as revises or revised proofs.

rights

The legal right to publish something such as a book, picture or extract from a text.

royalty

Money paid to a writer for the right to use his or her property, usually a percentage of sales or an agreed amount per sale.

royalty split

The way in which a royalty is divided between several authors or between author and illustrator.

royalty statement

A printed statement from a publisher showing how much royalty is due to an author.

sale or return

An arrangement between a retailer and publisher where any unwanted or unsold books can be returned to the publisher, and the purchase costs reimbursed to the retailer. If no arrangement is in place, retailers cannot return unwanted or unsold stock to the publisher.

sans serif

A style of printing letters with all lines of equal thickness and no serifs. Sans faces are less easy to read than seriffed faces and they are rarely used for continuous text, although some magazines use them for text matter.

serialisation

Publication of a book in parts in a magazine or newspaper.

serif

A small decorative line added to letters in some fonts; a font that uses serifs, such as Times. The addition of serifs (1) keeps the letters apart while at the same time making it possible to link one letter to the next, and (2) makes the letters distinct, in particular the top parts which the reader recognises when reading.

slush pile

Unsolicited manuscripts which are sent to publishers or agents.

STM

The accepted abbreviation for the scientific, technical and medical publishing sector.

structural editing

This type of editing looks at the overall structure and content of your book. It should address story structure alongside plot, characters, and themes.

style sheet

A guide listing all the rules of house style for a publishing company which has to be followed by authors and editors.

submission guidelines

Instructions given by agents or publishers on how they wish to receive submissions from authors.

subscription sale or 'sub'

Sales of a title to booksellers in advance of publication, and orders taken from wholesalers and retailers to be supplied by the publisher shortly before the publication date.

subsidiary rights

Rights other than the right to publish a book in its first form, e.g. paperback rights; rights to adapt the book; rights to serialise it in a magazine; film and TV rights; audio, ebook, foreign and translation rights.

sub-title

A secondary or subordinate title of a published work providing additional information about its content. More commonly found in works of non-fiction.

synopsis

A concise plot summary of a manuscript (usually one side of A4) that covers the major plot points, narrative arcs and characters.

territory

Areas of the world where the publisher has the rights to publish or can make foreign rights deals.

Thema

A globally applicable subject classification system for books to aid the merchandising and discoverability of the title. This type of classification can be used alongside BIC.

trade discount

A reduction in price given to a customer in the same trade, as by a publisher to another publisher or to a bookseller.

trade paperback (B format)

A paperback edition of a book that is superior in production quality to, and larger than, a mass-market paperback edition, size 198x129mm.

trim size or trimmed size

The measurements of a page of a book after it has been cut, or of a sheet of paper after it has been cut to size.

type specification or 'spec'

A brief created by the design department of a publishing house for how a book should be typeset.

typeface

A set of characters that share a distinctive and consistent design. Typefaces come in families of different weights, e.g. Helvetica Roman, Helvetica Italic, Bold, Bold Italic, etc. Hundreds of typefaces exist and new ones are still being designed. Today, 'font' is often used synonymously with 'typeface' though originally font meant the characters were all the same size, e.g. Helvetica Italic 11 point.

typescript or manuscript

The final draft of a book. This unedited text is usually an electronic Word file. The term 'typescript' (abbreviated TS or ts) is synonymous with 'manuscript' (abbreviated MS or ms; plural is MSS or mss).

typographic error or typo

A mistake made when keying text or typesetting.

typography

The art and technique of arranging type.

unsolicited manuscript

An unpublished manuscript sent to a publisher without having been commissioned or requested.

See also...
● *Who's who in publishing,* page 673

USP

Unique selling point. A distinctive quality or feature of a book that distinguishes it within the market.

verso

The left-hand page of a book, usually given an even number.

voice casting

The process of finding a suitable voice artist to narrate audiobooks.

volume rights

The right to publish the work in hardback, paperback or ebook.

XML tagging

Inserting tags into the text that can allow it to be converted for ebooks or for use in electronic formats.

YA

A term used within children's publishing to refer to books written to appeal to an audience of teenagers or young adults.

Resources for writers

Software for writers

This is a selection of software programmes and applications designed to enhance your writing experience and aid productivity. Each product has its own selection of features; we recommend you check the cost carefully, as many involve a fixed-term subscription or licence fee but do also offer free trials.

WRITING SOFTWARE

Aeon Timeline

www.aeontimeline.com
£42 one-off fee

Includes tools and features to help you understand characters, avoid plot holes and inconsistencies, and visualise your story in new ways.

Bibisco

https://bibisco.com
Community edition: Free; Supporters edition: Pay what you want

Designed to allow a writer to focus on their characters and develop rounded and complex narratives, with particular emphasis on the manuscript's geographical, temporal and social context.

Dabble

www.dabblewriter.com
From $48 p.a.

Gives writers the freedom to plot, write and edit on a desktop, in a browser or offline, and automatically syncs all versions across your devices. Features include plot grids, progress tracking and goal setting.

FocusWriter

https://gottcode.org/focuswriter
Free

Provides a simple and distraction-free writing environment with a hide-away interface, so you can focus solely on your writing.

FreeWriter

www.freewritersoftware.com
Free

Contains all the functionality you need to format and organise documents, including spell-checking, full dictionary, extensive thesaurus, global search and replace, automatic voice read-back and speech recognition. There are facilities to help build robust story elements, so that you can profile characters, places, ideas and plot themes. There are also helpful tools to enable you to set productivity targets and plot your progress against these.

Novelize

www.getnovelize.com
$65 p.a.

Developed for fiction writers, this web-based writing app means you can work on your book anywhere on any device. Keep your research in one place in the notebook displayed on the writing screen and track your progress.

Novel Factory

www.novel-software.com
From $75 p.a

Plan your book with confidence by using the Roadmap feature which provides tools and structures to suit your needs. Includes detailed character overviews including biographies and images, as well as scene tabs and writing statistics about your work.

Novel Suite

www.novelsuite.com/novel-writing-software
$99 p.a.

An all-in-one novel writing application that can be used across all devices. Manage multiple books using character profiles, scene outlines and writing template tools.

Scrivener

www.literatureandlatte.com/scrivener/overview
From £47 one-off fee

Tailored for long writing projects with everything you need housed in one place; it is a typewriter, ring binder and scrapbook, allowing you to optimise your digital workspace.

SmartEdit Writer

www.smart-edit.com/Writer
Free

Organically build your book one scene or one chapter at a time, then drag and drop to arrange these on your document tree. Store your research images, URLs and notes alongside work for easy access, then export your manuscript into a single Word document when ready.

Ulysses

https://ulysses.app
£48.99 p.a.

Document management for all writing projects, with flexible export options including pdf, Word, ebook and HTML which are appropriately formatted and styled.

WriteItNow

www.ravensheadservices.com
$59.95 one-off fee

Includes sophisticated worldbuilding features to create detailed and complex settings and characters. Recommends suitable names for your characters based on the historical period and geographical setting of your story.

EDITING SOFTWARE

After the Deadline

www.afterthedeadline.com
Free

A context-driven grammar and spelling checker, it underlines potential issues and gives a suggestion with an explanation of how you can rectify the error.

AutoCrit

www.autocrit.com
Free

Analyses your entire manuscript and suggests insightful improvements in the form of an individual summary report, showing where your strengths and weaknesses lie.

Grammarly

www.grammarly.com
Free

Provides accurate and context-specific suggestions when the application detects grammar, spelling,

punctuation, word choice and style mistakes in your writing.

Hemingway Editor

www.hemingwayapp.com
$19.99 one-off fee

Helps you write with clarity and confidence. This application is like a spellchecker, but for style. It will highlight any areas that need tightening up by identifying: adverbs, passive voice, and uninspiring or over-complicated words.

ProWritingAid

https://prowritingaid.com
£79 p.a.

For use via the web, or as an add-on to word processing software, it interrogates your work for a multitude of potential issues such as passive voice, clichés, missing dialogue tags and pace, and suggests how you can rectify any errors or make style improvements.

SmartEdit

www.smart-edit.com
$77 one-off fee

Sits inside Microsoft Word and runs 25 individual checks whilst you work, flagging areas that need attention, including: highlighting repeated words, listing adverbs and foreign phrases used and identifying possible misused words.

WordRake

www.wordrake.com
$129 p.a.

When you click the 'rake' button in Microsoft Word, the text editor will read your document and suggest edits to tighten and add clarity to your work.

Libraries

Libraries are not just repositories for books and a source of reference. They provide an increasing range of different services, using a multitude of media to reach more diverse audiences. Opening times might vary or be temporarily suspended due to coronavirus restrictions.

TYPES OF LIBRARIES

• **Public libraries** are accessible to the general population and are usually funded by a local or district council. They typically offer a mix of lending and reference facilities. Public libraries are distinct from research libraries, subscription libraries and other specialist libraries in terms of their funding and access, but may offer some of the same facilities to visitors. Public library services are facing financial challenges and cuts to funding so many library authorities are looking for new approaches to working with communities in order to build sustainable library services for the future.
• A list of **community libraries** in the UK can be found at www.publiclibrariesnews.com.
• An **academic library** is usually affiliated to an educational institution and primarily serves the students and faculty of that institution. Some are accessible to the public.
• A **subscription library** is one that is funded via membership or endowments. Access is often restricted to members but membership is sometimes extended to groups who are non-members, such as students.
• Many libraries belong to the Association of Independent Libraries and a list of members can be found on the Association's website (see below).
• This website is a tool to find your nearest and local UK public libraries: www.gov.uk/local-library-services.

SOME OF THE BEST

Britain has such a wealth of comprehensive and historic libraries that a full list of them is not possible in this publication. Here is just a small selection of popular public libraries in the UK.

Barbican Library

Barbican Centre, Silk Street, London EC2Y 8DS
tel 020-7638 0569
email barbicanlib@cityoflondon.gov.uk
website www.barbican.org.uk/your-visit/during-your-visit/library
Facebook www.facebook.com/Barbicanlibrary
Twitter @barbicanlib

The largest of the City of London's lending libraries with a strong arts and music section, a London collection, literature events programme and reading groups.

Belfast Central Library

Royal Avenue, Belfast BT1 1EA
tel 028-9050 9150
email belfast.central@librariesni.org.uk
website www.librariesni.org.uk/Libraries/Pages/Belfast-Central-Library.aspx
Facebook www.facebook.com/BelfastCentralLibrary
Twitter @BelfastCentLib

The library's reference library is the largest in stock terms in Northern Ireland. The library houses a number of special collections including a digital film archive and the Northern Ireland Music Archive.

Library of Birmingham

Centenary Square, Broad Street, Birmingham B1 2ND
tel 0121 242 4242
email enquiries@libraryofbirmingham.com
website www.libraryofbirmingham.com
Facebook www.facebook.com/libraryofbirmingham
Twitter @LibraryofBham

The Library of Birmingham replaced Birmingham Central Library in September 2013 and is the largest public library in the UK and the largest regional library in Europe.

Bristol Central Library

College Green, City Centre, Bristol BS1 5TL
tel 0117 9037250
email bristol.library.service@bristol.gov.uk
website www.bristol.gov.uk/libraries-archives/central-library

Bristol's main library. It includes collections related to Bristol's slave trade, 19th-century travel and art. An appointment must be made five working days in advance to view rare items. Appointments can be made by email or phone.

Canterbury Library

18 High Street, Canterbury, Kent CT1 2RA
tel 03000 413131
email canterburylibrary@kent.gov.uk
website www.kent.gov.uk/leisure-and-community/libraries

The main library for the city of Canterbury. For services see website.

Cardiff Central Library

The Hayes, Cardiff CF10 1FL
tel 029-2038 2116

email centrallibrary@cardiff.gov.uk
website www.cardiff.gov.uk/ENG/resident/Libraries-and-archives/Find-a-library/Pages/Central Library.aspx

The largest public library in Wales, opened in 2009, houses 90,000 books, 10,000 of which are in Welsh.

Leeds Library

18 Commercial Street, Leeds LS1 6AL
tel 0113 245 3071
email enquiries@theleedslibrary.org.uk
website www.theleedslibrary.org.uk
Facebook www.facebook.com/leedslibrary
Twitter @theleedslibrary

Founded in 1768 as a proprietary subscription library and is now the oldest surviving example of this sort of library in the UK. It includes specialist collections in travel, topography, biography, history and literature. There are long runs of periodicals, popular novels, children's books, and Civil War pamphlets and Reformation Tracts. About 1,500 new books and audio/visual items are added every year.

Liverpool Central Library

William Brown Street, Liverpool L3 8EW
tel 0151 233 3069
email refbt.central.library@liverpool.gov.uk
website https://liverpool.gov.uk/libraries/find-a-library/central-library/

A few years ago Liverpool Central Library underwent major refurbishment. It reopened in May 2013. The collection includes 15,000 rare books.

London Library

14 St James's Square, London SW1Y 4LG
tel 020-7766 4700
email reception@londonlibrary.co.uk
website www.londonlibrary.co.uk
Facebook www.facebook.com/thelondonlibrary
Twitter @thelondonlib

A subscription lending library containing more than one million books and periodicals in over 50 languages, the collection includes works from the 16th century to the latest publications in print and electronic form. Membership is open to all.

Manchester Central Library

St Peter's Square, Manchester M2 5PD
tel 0161 234 1983
email libraries@manchester.gov.uk
website www.manchester.gov.uk/centrallibrary

Manchester's main library, the second biggest public lending library in the UK, reopened in March 2014 after major refurbishment.

Mitchell Library

North Street, Glasgow G3 7DN
tel 0141 287 2999

email libraries@glasgowlife.org.uk
website www.glasgowlife.org.uk/libraries/venues/the-mitchell-library
Facebook www.facebook.com/GlasgowLibraries
Twitter @GlasgowLib

The largest public reference library in Europe housing almost two million volumes. Holds an unrivalled collection of material relating to the city of Glasgow.

Newcastle City Library

Charles Avison Building, 33 Newbridge Street West, Newcastle upon Tyne NE1 8AX
tel 0191 277 4100
email information@newcastle.gov.uk
website www.newcastle.gov.uk/services/libraries-culture/your-libraries/city-library-community-hub
Facebook www.facebook.com/NewcastleLibraries
Twitter @ToonLibraries

Newcastle's main public library includes a café, exhibition spaces, a rare books and watercolours collection, a viewing deck and six floors of books.

Norfolk and Norwich Millennium Library

The Forum, Millennium Plain, Norwich NR2 1AW
email libraries@norfolk.gov.uk
website www.norfolk.gov.uk/libraries-local-history-and-archives/libraries/

Recently substantially refurbished, as well as holding tens of thousands of books, the Norfolk and Norwich Millennium Library hosts regular events with the aim of engaging the local community, including board-games afternoons and expert-advice sessions.

Nottingham Central Library

Nottingham Central Library, Angel Row, Nottingham NG1 6HP
tel 0115 915 2828
email enquiryline@nottinghamcity.gov.uk
website www.nottinghamcity.gov.uk/centrallib

The main library for the city of Nottingham, with books on four floors.

Westminster Reference Library

35 St Martin's Street, London WC2H 7HP
tel 020-7641 6200 (press 2)
email referencelibrarywc2@westminster.gov.uk
website www.westminster.gov.uk/westminster-reference-library

Specialist public reference library with collections in performing arts and art and design. Hosts regular and varied events, includes an exhibition space and a Business Information Point. Also has a range of business resources including market research, company and legal databases.

LIBRARIES OF LEGAL DEPOSIT IN THE UK AND IRELAND

A library of legal deposit is a library that has the power to request (at no charge) a copy of anything published in the UK. There are six legal deposit libraries in the UK and Ireland. To obtain a copy of a book, five out of the six legal deposit libraries must make a request in writing to a publisher within one year of publication of a book, newspaper or journal. Different rules apply to the British Library in that all UK libraries and Republic of Ireland publishers have a legal responsibility to send a copy of each of their publications to the library, without a written request being made. The British Library is the only legal deposit library with its own Legal Deposit Office. Since April 2013, legal deposit also covers material published digitally and online, so that the legal deposit libraries can provide a national archive of the UK's non-print published material, such as websites, blogs, e-journals and CDROMs.

Agency for the Legal Deposit Libraries (ALDL)

Unit 21 Marnin Way, Edinburgh EH12 9GD
tel 0131 334 2833
email publisher.enquiries@legaldeposit.org.uk
website www.legaldeposit.org.uk

The ALDL requests and receives copies of publications for distribution to five major libraries (not the British Library). It is maintained by five legal deposit libraries and ensures that they receive legal deposit copies of British and Irish publications. The agency must request copies on behalf of the libraries within 12 months of the date of publication. On receiving such a request, a publisher must supply a copy for each of the requesting libraries under the terms of the Legal Deposit Libraries Act 2003 (UK) and the Copyright and Related Rights Act 2000 (Ireland).

Bodleian Libraries of the University of Oxford

Broad Street, Oxford OX1 3BG
tel (01865) 277162
email reader.services@bodleian.ox.ac.uk
website www.bodleian.ox.ac.uk
Facebook www.facebook.com/bodleianlibraries
Twitter @bodleianlibs

With over 13 million items and including 80,000 e-journals and vast quantities of materials in many other formats, the Bodleian Libraries together form the second-largest library in the UK after the British Library, and is the main reference library of Oxford University. It is one of the oldest libraries in Europe.

The British Library

St Pancras Building, 96 Euston Road,
London NW1 2DB
tel 0330 333 1144 (switchboard)
Legal Deposit Office: The British Library, Boston Spa, Wetherby, West Yorkshire LS23 7BQ
tel (01937) 546268
email legal-deposit-books@bl.uk
website www.bl.uk
Facebook www.facebook.com/britishlibrary
Twitter @britishlibrary

The British Library holds books, journals, newspapers, sound recordings, patents, original manuscripts, maps, online images and texts, plays, digital books, and poet and author recordings. The collection holds over 170 million published items from across the globe, including 3.5 million printed books and e-books, 310,000 manuscript volumes, 60 million patents, 60 million newspapers, over four million maps, over 260,000 journal titles, many of them digital, seven million sound recordings and eight million stamps.

Cambridge University Library

West Road, Cambridge CB3 9DR
tel (01223) 333000
email library@lib.cam.ac.uk
website www.lib.cam.ac.uk

Cambridge University Library houses its own collection and also comprises four other libraries within the university. The library dates back to the 15th century and now has a collection of over nine million books. It is the only legal deposit library that keeps a large percentage of its books on open access.

National Library of Scotland

George IV Bridge, Edinburgh EH1 1EW
tel 0131 623 3700
email enquiries@nls.uk
website www.nls.uk
Facebook www.facebook.com/NationalLibraryOfScotland
Twitter @natlibscot

The National Library of Scotland holds over 20 million printed and electronic items. It is the world's central source for research relating to Scotland and the Scots. The library also holds a copy of the Gutenberg Bible, a First Folio of Shakespeare, and the last letter written by Mary Queen of Scots. In 2005 the library bought the John Murray Archive for £31 million; it contains important items relating to Jane Austen, Lord Byron and Sir Arthur Conan Doyle.

National Library of Wales

Aberystwyth, Ceredigion SY23 3BU
tel (01970) 632800
email gofyn@llgc.org.uk
website www.library.wales
Facebook www.facebook.com/llgcymranlwales/
Twitter @nlwales

The National Library of Wales was established in 1907 and holds over six million books and newspapers, including many important works such as the first book printed in Welsh and the first Welsh translation of the Bible.

Trinity College Library Dublin

College Green, Dublin 2, Republic of Ireland
tel +353 (0)1 896 1127
email library@tcd.ie
website www.tcd.ie/library
Facebook www.facebook.com/tcdlibrary
Twitter @tcdlibrary

Trinity College Library is the largest library in Ireland and is home to the *Book of Kells* – two of the four volumes are on permanent public display. The library houses sound recordings, maps, databases, and a digital collection. Currently it has over seven million printed volumes with extensive collections of journals, manuscripts, maps and music reflecting over 400 years of academic development.

DESIGNATED OUTSTANDING COLLECTIONS

The Designated Outstanding Collections scheme was established in 1997 by the Museums and Galleries Commission to identify collections of national and international importance in non-national museums and galleries. In 2005 the scheme was extended to include libraries and archives. The scheme is now administered by Arts Council England and there are currently 154 Designated Outstanding Collections in England. To find out if there is a Designated Outstanding Collection library near you, visit the Designation section of the Arts Council website (www.artscouncil.org.uk).

SPECIALIST LIBRARIES IN THE UK

Writers often need access to specialised information sources in order to research their work. The following are a sample of specialist libraries in the UK. In addition to the libraries listed below, many university libraries hold special collections which are accessible to the public, usually by appointment. For example, the University of Exeter library's special collection includes the Agatha Christie Archive, the Du Maurier Collection and the Gale Morant Archive. Check individual university library websites for details.

BBC Written Archives Centre

Peppard Road, Caversham Park, Reading RG4 8TS
tel 020-8008 5661
email heritage@bbc.co.uk
website www.bbc.co.uk/archive/written-archives-centre-visiting-the-archive/zfqpwty

Home of the BBC's written records. Holds thousands of files, scripts and working papers, dating from the BBC's formation in 1922 to the 1980s together with information about past programmes and the history

of broadcasting. Does not have recordings or information about current programmes. Accredited students or staff members at a higher education institution, writers commissioned for a publication or those working towards commercial projects can arrange a visit to the BBC Written Archives Centre for research purposes. Visits are by appointment only, between 9.45am to 5.00pm, Wednesday to Friday.

BFI National Archive and Reuben Library

Belvedere Road, South Bank, London SE1 8XT
tel 020-7255 1444
email library@bfi.org.uk
website www.bfi.org.uk/archive-collections
Facebook www.facebook.com/BritishFilmInstitute
Twitter @BFI

Established in 1933, the BFI National Archive is one of the largest film and television collections anywhere. Dating from the earliest days of film to the 21st century, it contains nearly a million titles. The archive holds over 800,000 film titles – including television programmes, documentaries, newsreels, as well as educational and training films – and is updated daily. The majority of the collection is British material but it also features internationally significant holdings from around the world. The Archive also collects films which feature key British actors and the work of British directors. Using the latest preservation methods, the BFI cares for a variety of often obsolete formats. The BFI Reuben Library at BFI Southbank is home to a huge collection of books, journals, documents and audio recordings about the world of film and television.

British Library for Development Studies (BLDS)

Institute of Development Studies at the University of Sussex, Brighton BN1 9RE
tel (01273) 678163
email blds@ids.ac.uk
website www.ids.ac.uk/about/

Europe's largest research collection on economic and social change in developing countries.

British Newspaper Archive

tel (01382) 210100
website www.britishnewspaperarchive.co.uk
Facebook www.facebook.com/TheBritishNewspaperArchive
Twitter @BNArchive

The British Newspaper Archive gives access to over three million historical local, national and regional newspaper pages from across the UK and Ireland. The Archive is currently in partnership with the British Library and findmypast to digitise up to 40 million newspaper pages from the British Library's vast collection.

Caird Library and Archive

Greenwich, London SE10 9NF
tel 020-8312 6516
email library@rmg.co.uk
website www.rmg.co.uk/collections/caird-library

Specialist maritime research library at the National
Maritime Museum in Greenwich.

Catholic National Library

Centre for Catholic Studies, University of Durham,
Stockton Road, Durham DH1 3LE
tel 0191 334 1656
email ccs.admin@durham.ac.uk
website www.dur.ac.uk/theology.religion/ccs

Holds over 70,000 books, pamphlets and periodicals
on theology, spirituality and related subjects,
biography and history.

Chained Library

Hereford Cathedral Library and Archives,
Hereford Cathedral, 5 College Cloisters,
Cathedral Close, Hereford HR1 2NG
tel (01432) 374225
email library@herefordcatherdral.org
website www.herefordcathedral.org/chained-library

Hereford Cathedral has housed a collection of books
accessible to the public from the 12th century. The
chaining of books was a widespread security system
in European libraries from the Middle Ages to the
18th century; this is the largest to survive with all its
chains, rods and locks intact. The library is open
Tuesday, Wednesday and Thursday 10am to 4pm
and the first Saturday in each month 10am until
1pm.

Chawton House Library

Chawton, Alton, Hants GU34 1SJ
tel (01420) 541010
email info@chawton.net
website www.chawtonhouse.org
Facebook www.facebook.com/ChawtonHouse
Twitter @ChawtonHouse

A collection of over 15,000 items focusing on
women's writing in English from 1600 to 1830
including some manuscripts. The library also houses
the Knight Collection, which is the private library
belonging to the Knight family, the owners of
Chawton House for over 400 years.

Chetham's Library

Long Milgate, Manchester M3 1SB
tel 0161 834 7961
email fwilde@chethams.org.uk
website https://library.chethams.com

Founded in 1653, this is the oldest public library in
the English-speaking world. In addition to a
collection of early printed books, it includes
manuscript diaries, letters and deeds, prints, paintings
and glass lantern slides. Use of the library is free, no
membership or reader's ticket is required.
Researchers need a prior appointment by phone or
email (above) at least one working day in advance to
consult library material.

City Business Library

Aldermanbury, London EC2V 7HH
tel 020-7332 1812
email cbl@cityoflondon.gov.uk
website www.cityoflondon.gov.uk/business/economic-
research-and-information/city-business-library/
Facebook www.facebook.com/CityBusinessLibrary
Twitter @CBL_London

One of the leading business information sources in
the UK.

Commonwealth Library and Archives

Commonwealth Secretariat, Marlborough House,
Pall Mall, London SW1Y 5HX
tel 020-7747 6164 (librarian) / 020-7747 6167
(archivist)
email library@commonwealth.int
website http://thecommonwealth.org/contact
Facebook www.facebook.com/commonwealthsec
Twitter @commonwealthsec

Collection covers politics and international relations,
economics, education, health, gender, environment
and management. Holds a comprehensive collection
of Commonwealth Secretariat publications and its
archives.

Crafts Council Research Library

Crafts Council, 44A Pentonville Road,
London N1 9BY
tel 020-7806 2500
email reception@craftscouncil.org.uk
website www.craftscouncil.org.uk
Facebook www.facebook.com/CraftsCouncilUK/
Twitter @CraftsCouncilUK

This is a reference library which normally opens to
the public two days a week by appointment. Houses a
large collection of contemporary craft books and
catalogues as well as journals. Covers ceramics,
textiles, jewellery, fashion accessories and paper.

Feminist Library

The Sojourner Truth Community Centre,
161 Sumner Rd, Peckham, London SE15 6JL
tel 020-7261 0879
email admin@feministlibrary.co.uk
website www.feministlibrary.co.uk
Facebook www.facebook.co/feministlibrary
Twitter @feministlibrary

The Feminist Library holds a large archive collection
of women's liberation movement literature,
particularly second-wave materials dating from the
late 1960s to the 1990s.

Gladstone's Library

Church Lane, Hawarden, Flintshire CH5 3DF
tel (01244) 532350
email enquiries@gladlib.org
website www.gladstoneslibrary.org

Britain's first residential library, the building houses 20,000 of Gladstone's books. Since the library opened in 1902, it has continued to acquire books specialising in those subjects that were of most interest to Gladstone: theology, history, philosophy, classics, art and literature. Researchers seeking an extended period of quiet study can stay in one of 26 rooms in the Gothic stone building.

Goethe-Institut London Library

50 Princes Gate, Exhibition Road, London SW7 2PH
tel 020-7596 4000
email library@london.goethe.org
email info-london@goethe.org
website www.goethe.de/london
Facebook www.facebook.com/goethe.institut.london
Twitter @GI_London1

Specialises in German literature, especially contemporary fiction and drama, film DVDs and books/audiovisual material on German culture and recent history. E-library gives access to Goethe Institut libraries in the UK, Ireland and the Netherlands and allows electronic downloading of ebooks, e-audiobooks and electronic newspapers for a predetermined period of time.

Guildhall Library

Aldermanbury, London EC2V 7HH
tel 020-7332 1868/1870
email guildhall.library@cityoflondon.gov.uk
website www.cityoflondon.gov.uk/guildhalllibrary
Twitter @GuildhallLib

Books collection comprises over 200,000 titles dating from the 15th century to the 21st century and includes books, pamphlets, periodicals, trade directories and poll books. Covers all aspects of life in London, past and present.

Imperial War Museum Library

IWM London, Lambeth Road, London SE1 6HZ
website www.iwm.org.uk
Facebook www.facebook.com/iwm.london
Twitter @I_W_M

Houses a unique collection of books and reports on 20th- and 21st-century conflict, including unit histories, technical manuals, biographies, autobiographies and publications. Includes newspapers, trench journals, propaganda leaflets, ephemeral literature and pamphlets. Viewing is by appointment only: https://customerportal.iwm.org.uk/booking-iwm/. There are two sessions per day for visiting the library Monday to Thursday: 10am to 1pm and 2pm to 5pm.

Lambeth Palace Library

Lambeth Palace Road, South Bank, London SE1 7JU
tel 020-7898 1400
email archives@churchofengland.org
website www.lambethpalacelibrary.org
Facebook www.facebook.com/LambethPalaceLibrary
Twitter @lampallib

The historic library of the Archbishops of Canterbury and the principal library and record office for the Church of England.

The Library of the Society of Friends

Friends House, 173–177 Euston Road,
London NW1 2BJ
tel 020-7663 1135
email library@quaker.org.uk
website www.quaker.org.uk/resources/library

The library has over 80,000 books and pamphlets, including a unique collection of 17th-century Quaker and anti-Quaker material.

Linen Hall Library

17 Donegall Square North, Belfast BT1 5GB
tel 028-9032 1707
email info@linenhall.com
website www.linenhall.com
Facebook www.facebook.com/LinenHallLibraryBelfast
Twitter @thelinenhall

Renowned for its Irish and Local Studies Collection, including early Belfast and Ulster printed books and 350,000 items in the Northern Ireland Political Collection (NIPC). Also large General Lending Collection.

National Art Library

Victoria & Albert Museum, Cromwell Road,
London SW7 2RL
tel 020-7942 2000
email hello@vam.ac.uk
website www.vam.ac.uk
Facebook www.facebook.com/victoriaandalbertmuseum
Twitter @V_and_A

Open from Tuesday to Saturday, anyone can register to visit its collection, which focuses on the decorative arts in the museum's collection. It houses around one million books but also holds prints, drawings, paintings, photographs, ceramics and glass, textiles and fashion, furniture, design, metalwork and sculpture. The collections range from medieval manuscripts to contemporary artists' books and armorial bindings to comics and graphic novels.

Natural History Museum Library and Information Services

Cromwell Road, London SW7 5BD
tel 020-7942 5000 (switchboard)/ 020-7942 5460 (archives/general library) / 020-7942 6156 (ornithology library, Tring)

email library@nhm.ac.uk
website www.nhm.ac.uk/research-curation/science-facilities/library
Facebook www.facebook.com/naturalhistorymuseum
Twitter @NHM_Library

Online catalogue contains all library material acquired since 1989 and about 80% of earlier items. The library collection contains more than one million items, including almost 400,000 books, 22,000 ongoing journal titles, 350,000 artworks and over 100,000 catalogued archival items. Contact via the website.

RNIB National Library Service
105 Judd Street, London WC1H 9NE
tel 020-7391 2052
email heritageservices@rnib.org.uk
website www.rnib.org.uk/professionals/knowledge-and-research-hub/heritage-services/research-library
Facebook www.facebook.com/rnibuk
Twitter @RNIB

The library holds over 60,000 items on all aspects of sight loss. Short abstracts are provided for many items, including journal articles.

John Rylands Research Institute and Library
150 Deansgate, Manchester M3 3EH
tel 0161 306 0555
email uml.special-collections@manchester.ac.uk
website www.library.manchester.ac.uk/rylands/

The library is part of the University of Manchester but is open to the public. Home to 1.4 million items, including books, manuscripts, maps, artworks and objects.

Science Museum Library
The Dana Research Centre and Library, 165 Queens Gate, London SW7 5HD
tel 020-7942 4242
email smlinfo@sciencemuseum.ac.uk
website www.sciencemuseum.org.uk/researchers/dana-research-centre-and-library
Facebook www.facebook.com/sciencemuseumlondon
Twitter @sciencemuseum

Allows access to around 500,000 items covering museum studies, the history and biography of science technology and medicine and the philosophical and social aspects of these subjects.

Tate Library & Archive
Tate Britain, Millbank, London SW1P 4RG
tel 020-7887 8838
email reading.rooms@tate.org.uk
website www.tate.org.uk/research/library

Broadly covers those areas in which the Tate collects. The library includes British art from the Renaissance to the present day and international modern art from 1900. The archive covers British art from 1900 and contains a wealth of unpublished material on artists, art world figures and organisations.

Wellcome Library
Wellcome Collection, 183 Euston Road, London NW1 2BE
tel 020-7611 8722
email library@wellcome.ac.uk
website http://wellcomelibrary.org/
Facebook www.facebook.com/Wellcomelibrary/
Twitter @WellcomeLibrary

One of the world's major resources for the study of medical history. Also houses an expanding collection of material relating to contemporary medicine and biomedical science in society.

Moving Image and Sound Collections
tel 020-7611 8899
email collections@wellcome.ac.uk
website https://wellcomelibrary.org/collections/about-the-collections/moving-image-and-sound-collection/

Physical materials in the collection are held in closed stores, and can be requested through the catalogue to view or listen to in the Library.

Wellcome Images
tel 020-7611 8348
email images@wellcome.ac.uk
website https://wellcomecollection.org/works
Facebook www.facebook.com/WellcomeImages
Twitter @wellcomeimages

Collection of images, including artworks and photographs, from the library of the Wellcome Collection which have been collected over several decades.

Westminster Music Library
Victoria Library, 160 Buckingham Palace Road, London SW1W 9UD
tel 020-7641 6200
email musiclibrary@westminster.gov.uk
website www.westminster.gov.uk/libraries

Holds a wide range of scores, orchestral sets, books on music, music journals and a collection of Mozart sound recordings, formerly the GLASS collection.

Women's Library @ LSE
Lionel Robbins Building,
The London School of Economics and Political Science, 10 Portugal Street, Westminster, London WC2A 2HD
tel 020-7955 7229
email library.enquiries@lse.ac.uk
website www.lse.ac.uk/library/collections/featuredCollections/womensLibraryLSE.aspx
Twitter @LSELibrary

Houses the most extensive collection of women's history in the UK. Part of the London School of Economics.

Wordsworth Library

Dove Cottage, Grasmere, Cumbria LA22 9SH
tel (015394) 35544
website https://wordsworth.org.uk/
Facebook www.facebook.com/WordsworthTrust/

William Wordsworth's home, Dove Cottage, houses a small library which is situated in a two-storey converted coach house adjacent to the cottage museum. It contains treasures of all kinds related to the Romantic movement, from books to paintings and Wordsworth's manuscripts.

Working Class Movement Library

Jubilee House, 51 The Crescent, Salford M5 4WX
tel 0161 736 3601
email enquiries@wcml.org.uk
website www.wcml.org.uk
Facebook www.facebook.com/wcmlibrary
Twitter @wcmlibrary

Records over 200 years of organising and campaigning by ordinary men and women. The collection provides an insight into working people's daily lives. Collection contains: books, pamphlets, archives, photographs, plays, poetry, songs, banners, posters, badges, cartoons, journals, biographies, reports.

Wren Library

Trinity College Cambridge, Cambridge CB2 1TJ
email wren.library@trin.cam.ac.uk
email archives@trin.cam.ac.uk
website www.trin.cam.ac.uk/library/wren-library

This library houses the manuscript of Winnie-the-Pooh and the papers of philosopher Ludwig Wittgenstein. As an academic library it's only open to the public for two hours each day during term time. To view rare books and manuscripts use the first email above. To view the college archive and modern manuscripts use the second email above.

Zoological Society of London Library

Outer Circle, Regent's Park, London NW1 4RY
tel 020-7449 6293
email library@zsl.org
website www.zsl.org/about-us/library
Facebook www.facebook.com/officialzsl
Twitter @officialzsl

Contains a unique collection of journals and books on zoology and animal conservation.

ORGANISATIONS THAT SUPPORT LIBRARIES

There are many organisations which are affiliated to, and champion the use of libraries in the UK. These include:

Arts Council England

website www.artscouncil.org.uk

Arts Council England is the developmental agency for libraries in England and has responsibility for supporting and developing libraries. See also page 343.

Association of Independent Libraries

Church Lane, Doncaster DN5 7AU
email emma.marigliano@gmail.com
website http://independentlibraries.co.uk

Aims to develop the conservation, restoration and public awareness of independent libraries in the UK. Together, its members possess over two million books and have many listed buildings in their care. Founded 1989.

Association of Senior and Children's Education Librarians (ASCEL)

website www.ascel.org.uk

A national membership network of Senior Children's and Education Librarians. It aims to stimulate developments and share initiatives relating to children and young people using public libraries and educational services.

BookTrust

website www.booktrust.org.uk

Aims to give everyone access to books and the chance to benefit from reading. See also page 529.

Chartered Institute of Library and Information Professionals (CILIP)

7 Ridgmount Street, London WC1E 7AE
tel 020-7255 0500
email info@cilip.org.uk
website www.cilip.org.uk

The leading professional body for librarians, information specialists and knowledge managers. Aims for a fair and economically prosperous society underpinned by literacy, access to information and the transfer of knowledge. CILIP is a registered charity. Offices in London, Wales, Scotland and Northern Ireland.

The Community Knowledge Hub for Libraries

website http://libraries.communityknowledgehub.org.uk

Unites expert guidance and resources with an interactive community of organisations and local authorities involved with community-managed and supported libraries.

Friends of Libraries

Many libraries in the UK have Friends of Libraries organisations affiliated to them which support library use through charitable means. Sometimes Friends groups are set up to campaign against a potential council closures of libraries or reductions in budgets. They have been known to set up their own community libraries.

Friends of National Libraries
website www.friendsofnationallibraries.org.uk

A registered charity founded in 1931. Helps libraries in the UK acquire books, manuscripts and archives, in particular those that might otherwise leave the UK.

Internet Library for Librarians
email info@itcompany.com
website www.itcompany.com/inforetriever/index.htm

Internet Library for Librarians has been one of the most popular information resource sites for librarians since 1994. It is an information portal specifically designed for librarians to locate internet resources related to their profession.

Libraries All Party Parliamentary Group (APPG)

The goal of the Libraries APPG is to provide information and opportunities for debate about the important role libraries play in society and their future; to highlight the contribution that a wide variety of library and information services make, including those in public, school, government, health sector, colleges, private companies and university libraries; and to promote and discuss themes in the wider information and knowledge sector including the impact of technology, skills and training, professional standards and broader issues.

Libraries Connected
email info@librariesconnected.org.uk
website www.librariesconnected.org.uk

Libraries Connected is a charity, previously known as the Society of Chief Librarians (SCL). Partly funded by Arts Council England as the Sector Support Organisation for libraries. This funding provides increased capacity with a new team of staff and trustees to work alongside our members. Remains a membership organisation, made up of every library service in England, Wales and Northern Ireland.

Libraries Week
website www.librariesweek.org.uk

The first Libraries Day took place in February 2012 and is now a week-long annual event in the UK dedicated to the celebration of libraries and librarians. Author talks and competitions are arranged by local authorities, universities, library services and local community groups.

The Library Campaign
website www.librarycampaign.com

Aims to advance the lifelong education of the public by the promotion, support, assistance and improvement of libraries through the activities of friends and user groups.

Library Planet
website https://libraryplanet.net/

A crowdsourced travel guide for libraries of the world. The intention is to inspire library travellers.

National Literacy Trust
website www.literacytrust.org.uk

Aims to improve reading, writing, speaking and listening skills in disadvantaged communities, in part through access to libraries. See also page 530.

Private Libraries Association
email info@plabooks.org
website www.plabooks.org

An international society of book collectors and lovers of books. Membership: £30 p.a. Publications include *The Private Library* (quarterly), annual *Private Press Books*, and other books on book collecting. Founded 1956.

Public Library News
website www.publiclibrariesnews.com

Promotes knowledge about libraries in the UK.

The Reading Agency
website https://readingagency.org.uk

Aims to give everyone an equal chance in life by helping people become confident and enthusiastic readers, and that includes supporting library use.

School Library Association (SLA)
1 Pine Court, Kembrey Park, Swindon SN2 8AD
tel (01793) 530166
email info@sla.org.uk
website www.sla.org.uk

The main goal of the SLA is to support people involved with school libraries, promoting high-quality reading and learning opportunities for all. Founded 1937.

Voices for the Library
website www.voicesforthelibrary.org.uk/blog/

Provides information about the public library service in the UK and the role of professional librarians. Library users can share their stories about the difference public libraries have made to their lives on the website.

Writers' retreats and creative writing courses

The following list of creative writing courses and writers' retreats is not exhaustive but is intended to give readers a flavour of the many options available. Some offer bursaries. Details of postgraduate courses are on page 698.

⚠ Readers should note that face-to-face courses and retreats may not go ahead in their usual way due to coronavirus restrictions. Please check websites for details.

Resources for writers

Anam Cara

tel +353 277 4441
email anamcararetreat@gmail.com
website www.anamcararetreat.com
Facebook www.facebook.com/anamcararetreat
Contact Sue Booth-Forbes

An all-inclusive residential retreat offering private and common working rooms and sanctuary for people who seriously want to enhance their craft. Whether writers and artists want to work by themselves or as part of a workshop, or special interest group, Anam Cara provides support, creature comforts and peace to help everyone produce their best work.

Arvon

Postal address The John Osborne Arvon Centre, Clunton, Craven Arms, Shropshire SY7 0JA
tel 020-7324 2554
email national@arvon.org
website www.arvon.org
Facebook www.facebook.com/arvonfoundation
Twitter @arvonfoundation
Chief Executive and Artistic Director Andrew Kidd

See individual entries for Arvon's writing houses: The Hurst – The John Osborne Arvon Centre (see page 694), Lumb Bank – The Ted Hughes Arvon Centre (see page 695), Totleigh Barton (see page 697) and Writers Retreat at The Clockhouse (opposite). Arvon hosts five-day residential creative writing courses and retreats in beautiful writing houses, set in inspiring countryside locations. Courses include morning workshops, one-to-one tutorials with leading authors and plenty of time and space to write. Courses cover a range of genres including fiction, poetry, theatre, creative non-fiction, writing for children and many more. Arvon also has an online programme of courses and events, 'Arvon at Home', which includes masterclasses, live guest readings and online writing weeks. Arvon runs a grants system for those who are not able to afford the full course fee.

Arvon Writers Retreat at the Clockhouse

Arvon Writers Retreat at the Clockhouse, Clunton, Craven Arms, Shropshire SY7 0JA
tel (01588) 640658
email thehurst@arvon.org
website www.arvon.org
Director Natasha Carlish, *Senior Administrator* Dan Pavitt

The Clockhouse has four apartments, each with a bedroom, study and en suite bathroom, and all food provided, for six-day and four-day writing retreats.

Anne Aylor Creative Writing Courses

46 Beversbrook Road, London N19 4QH
tel 020-7263 0669
email admin2020@anneaylor.co.uk
website www.anneaylor.co.uk
Contact Anne Aylor

Offers a range of short, weekend and overseas courses, as well as customised courses for all levels of ability.

The Book Doctor and Creativity Coach

email philippa_pride@yahoo.co.uk
website www.thebookdoctor.co.uk
Twitter @the_book_doctor
Contact Philippa Pride

Masterclasses (Free Your Creativity, Get Started on Your Book and Develop Your Book and Get it Published), one-to-one coaching and consultancy.

University of Cambridge Institute of Continuing Education

Madingley Hall, Madingley, Cambridge CB23 8AQ
tel (01223) 746222
email enquiries@ice.cam.ac.uk
website www.ice.cam.ac.uk
Facebook www.facebook.com/CambridgeICE
Twitter @litandcw_ice

Home to the University of Cambridge Centre for Creative Writing. A wide range of short and part-time courses at introductory and advanced levels on creative writing, literature, and art history.

Casa Ana Creative Writing Retreats

Calle Artesa 7, Ferreirola, 18414 La Taha, Granada, Spain
tel +34 678 298 497
email info@casa-ana.com
website www.casa-ana.com/creative-writing-retreats
Programme directors Anne Hunt and Mary-Jane Holmes

Mentored writing retreats and courses. Casa Ana is a 400-year old house in the Alpujarra, the southern slopes of the Sierra Nevada mountains in Andalusia. Offers four residential writers' retreats each year in spring, summer and autumn. There are nine places available in each retreat and they last for two weeks. The retreats include a one-to-one mentoring service and optional reading/critiquing sessions. Also hosts week-long novel writing retreat in July with experienced tutors at various times during the year. All retreats and courses conducted in English.

Central St Martins College of Arts & Design, Short Course Office

Granary Square, 1 Granary Building, King's Cross, London N1C 4AA
website www.arts.ac.uk/colleges/central-saint-martins/courses/short-courses
Twitter @CSMShortCourses

Central St Martins offers an annual programme of courses in a variety of subjects taught by expert practitioners.

Chalk the Sun Creative Writing

tel 07852 483001
email creativewriting@chalkthesun.co.uk
website www.chalkthesun.co.uk
Facebook www.facebook.com/CreativeWritingChalktheSun
Twitter @ChalktheSun
Programme Director Ardella Jones

Offers monthly creative writing workshops for new writers and for novelists plus occasional specialist sessions for children's writers and scriptwriters, one-to-one development tutorials, personalised distance learning and manuscript editing services. Tutors include ex-CBBC producer, commissioning editor Jonathan Wolfman, playwright Danusia Iwaszko, thriller novelist and screenwriter Simon Lewis, and children's publisher and editor Simona Sideri. London Writers' Room workshops are taught in small groups in a relaxed venue near Colliers Wood tube station in SW19. Also runs writing holidays and weekly workshops in Andalusia, Spain.

Château de Lavigny International Writers' Residence

Le Château, Route d'Etoy 10, 1175 Lavigny, Switzerland
tel +41 21 808 6143
email chlavigny@hotmail.com
website www.chateaudelavigny.ch

An international residence for writers in the canton of Vaud in Switzerland, welcoming each summer 20 or more writers from around the world. Writers come for four weeks, in groups of up to six, from May to October. They are housed in the former home of German publisher Heinrich Maria Ledig-Rowohlt and his wife Jane, an 18th-century manor house among vineyards and hills overlooking Lake Geneva. There is a fee for the full board during four weeks; lodging for the duration is free. Sessions are in English or French and writers must be published. It is still possible to apply for a full-grant fellowship including full bed and board, but only a few full-grant fellowships are offered each year.

City Lit

1–10 Keeley Street, London WC2B 4BA
tel 020-7831 7831
email writing@citylit.ac.uk
website www.citylit.ac.uk/courses/history-culture-and-writing/writing

Situated in the heart of London, the writing department at City Lit offers affordable courses on approaching agents, impressing publishers and writing fiction, poetry, short stories, memoir and non-fiction. Courses are also available in stage and screenwriting.

The Complete Creative Writing Course

email jamie@writingcourses.org.uk
website www.writingcourses.org.uk
Contact Jamie Winter

Inspiring creative writing courses held at the Groucho Club in Soho and nearby locations, starting in January, May and October. Offers beginner, intermediate and advanced courses, and runs weekend classes, summer school and online courses. Tutors are all published writers and experienced teachers. Courses of six three-hour sessions include stimulating exercises, feedback, discussion and homework. Cost ranges from £125 to £425.

Cove Park

Peaton Hill, Cove, Argyll and Bute G84 0PE
tel (01436) 850500
email information@covepark.org
website www.covepark.org
Ceo Francesca Bertolotti-Bailey

Cove Park is Scotland's international artist residency centre and offers a year-round programme of residencies for writers, translators and artists from all disciplines. For details of the funded residency programme, visit the website and subscribe to the newsletter.

The Creative Writer's Workshop

Kinvara, Co. Galway, Republic of Ireland
tel +353 (0)86 2523428

email office@thecreativewritersworkshop.com
website www.thecreativewritersworkshop.com
Facebook www.facebook.com/
IreneGrahamWritingCourses
Founder Irene Graham

The Creative Writer's Workshop provides:

• live fiction writing retreat online;
• 12-week memoir writing course online with workbook;
• fiction and memoir writing retreats in the west of Ireland;
• one-on-one private coaching in fiction and memoir writing;
• writing for marketing course.

Irene Graham is the founder of the Creative Writer's Workshop (1991) and the Memoir Writing Club. She is also author of *The Memoir Writing Workbook*. Her fiction and memoir writing workshops are accredited by George Mason University in the USA as part of its undergraduate and graduate degree programmes.

Curtis Brown Creative

28–29 Haymarket, London SW1Y 4SP
tel 020-7393 4201
email cbccourses@curtisbrown.co.uk
website www.curtisbrowncreative.co.uk
Facebook www.facebook.com/CurtisBrownCreative
Twitter @cbcreative
Instagram curtisbrowncreative

The writing school led by one of the UK's leading talent agencies, offering writing classes in London and online. With 110+ students going on to get publishing deals so far, alumni include Jessie Burton, Jane Harper, Nicholas Searle and Laura Marshall. As well as offering courses on the novel, Curtis Brown Creative have an expanding roster of online courses, covering memoirs, short stories, screenwriting, children's picture books and more. They also run the Breakthrough Writers' Programme, which offers fully funded courses, mentoring and scholarships for under-represented writers.

Emerson College

Emerson College, Forest Row, East Sussex RH18 5JX
tel (01342) 822238
email bookings@emerson.org.uk
website www.emerson.org.uk
Facebook www.facebook.com/emersoncollegeuk
Twitter @EmersonCollege

A centre for adult education based on the works of Rudolf Steiner. Emerson is a rich environment for personal, professional, artistic and spiritual growth. Visual and performing arts courses, trainings in caring professions and regenerative cultivation are held throughout the year; full-time and modular programmes available. Founded 1962.

Faber Academy

74–77 Great Russell Street, London WC1B 3DA
tel 020-7927 3827
email academy@faber.co.uk
website www.faberacademy.co.uk
Facebook www.facebook.com/faberacademy
Twitter @faberacademy
Instagram faber_academy

Creative writing courses with character – online and in London. Fiction, memoir and poetry courses run by award-winning tutors and industry experts.

Fictionfire Literary Consultancy

110 Oxford Road, Old Marston, Oxford OX3 0RD
tel 07827 455723
email info@fictionfire.co.uk
website www.fictionfire.co.uk
Facebook www.facebook.com/
FictionfireLiteraryConsultancy
Twitter @LornaFergusson
Contact Lorna Fergusson

Offers in-person and online creative writing courses, retreats and workshops. Guest talks and workshops can be arranged for writers' groups, libraries, conferences and festivals. Manuscript appraisal, editing, mentoring and consultation also available. Founded 2009.

Fire in the Head

email roselle@fire-in-the-head.co.uk
website www.roselle-angwin.co.uk
website www.thewildways.co.uk
Twitter @Qualiabird
Contact Roselle Angwin

Courses and mentoring in poetry, novels, life writing, creative, reflective, psychospiritual and therapeutic writing, outdoor eco-writing, journaling and personal development. Retreats, short courses, online/distance learning courses, tuition and appraisals.

Maria Frankland Creative Writing Courses

tel 07464 310998
email maria@mariafrankland.co.uk
website www.mariafrankland.co.uk
Contact Maria Frankland

Creative writing teacher, author and poet Maria Frankland offers the following courses: Write a Novel, Write a Collection of Poetry, Write your Life Story and Write a Collection of Short Stories. The courses support all stages from planning to publication and follow a progressive 26-session online programme over a year. Visit the website to receive a free booklet: *The 7 S.E.C.R.E.T.S. to Achieving your Writing Dreams*.

The French House Party, Carcassonne

tel (01299) 896819
website www.frenchhouseparty.eu
Twitter @FrenchHousePart
Director Moira Martingale

Creative courses in south west France cover literature, drama, song-writing, performance, film-making and art and mixed media.

Garsdale Retreat
tel (01539) 234184
email garsdaleretreat@gmail.com
website www.thegarsdaleretreat.co.uk
Contact Rebecca Nouchette

A creative writing centre in the remote and beautiful setting of the Yorkshire Dales National Park. It provides untutored retreats and inspirational residential courses tutored by professional writers, enabling participants to develop their individual creativity in a place of peace and tranquility. All levels of ability are welcomed and a high level of individual tuition is offered in classes with a maximum of eight. All courses and retreats are fully catered with locally sourced food, allowing participants to focus entirely on their writing.

The Grange
9 Eastcliff Road, Shanklin, Isle of Wight PO37 6AA
tel (01983) 867644
email stay@thegrangebythesea.com
website www.thegrangebythesea.com

An offshoot of Skyros with its renowned Writers' Lab that has attracted some very well-respected authors. The Grange hosts weekend residential creative writing workshops in a 4-star B&B in the old village of Shanklin on the south coast of the Isle of Wight. Nestled in greenery, it is very secluded, yet only moments from thatched pubs, cosy tearooms, the local train station, shops, restaurants and the long sandy beach. A beautiful and peaceful place to write.

Green Ink Writers' Gym
tel 07870 630788
email info@greeninkwritersgym.com
website www.greeninkwritersgym.com
Contact Dr Rachel Knightley

Practical and inspiring creative writing courses, coaching and editorial support. Sessions provide the skills, motivation and sense of fun to guide authors from work-in-progress to 'the end'. All sessions currently running on Zoom.

Hawthornden Castle
International Retreat for Writers, Lasswade, Midlothian EH18 1EG
tel 0131 440 2180
email office@hawthornden.org
Contact The Director

Exists to provide a peaceful setting where published writers can work without disturbance. The retreat houses up to six writers at a time, who are known as Hawthornden Fellows. Writers from any part of the world may apply for the fellowships. No monetary assistance is given, nor any contribution to travelling

expenses, but fellows board as guests of the retreat. Application forms are available from January for the following calendar year. Deadline for applications: 30 June.

The Hurst – The John Osborne Arvon Centre
Arvon, The Hurst, Clunton, Craven Arms, Shropshire SY7 0JA
tel (01588) 640658
email thehurst@arvon.org
website www.arvon.org
Director Natasha Carlish, *Senior Administrator* Dan Pavitt

Offers residential writing courses from April to December. Grants available. The Hurst is situated in the beautiful Clun Valley in Shropshire, 12 miles from Ludlow, and is set in 30 acres of woodland, with gardens and a lake.

Irish Writers Centre – Áras Scríbhneoirí na hÉireann
19 Parnell Square, Dublin D01 E102, Republic of Ireland
tel +353 (0)1 872 1302
email info@writerscentre.ie
website https://irishwriterscentre.ie
Facebook www.facebook.com/IrishWritersCtr
Twitter @IrishWritersCtr
Instagram irishwriterscentre

The national resource centre for Irish writers. It runs workshops, seminars and events related to the art of writing, hosts professional development seminars for writers and provides space for writers, writing groups and other literary organisations. It also provides information to writers and the general public.

Isle of Wight Writing Courses and Workshops
F&F Productions, 39 Ranelagh Road, Sandown, Isle of Wight PO36 8NT
tel (01983) 407772
email felicity@writeplot.co.uk
website www.felicityfairthompson.co.uk
website www.wightdiamondpress.com
Contact Felicity Fair Thompson

Residential and non-residential occasional weekends for beginners and experienced writers. Individual advice and workshops. Guests have time to write and enjoy the beautiful Isle of Wight in comfortable and roomy B&B accommodation two minutes from beach path and coastal walks to Sandown and Shanklin. Also offers email and postal MS critiques and editing, plus one-to-one advice on film scripts and fiction.

Jericho Writers
4 Acer Walk, Oxford OX2 6EX
tel 0345 459 9560 , +1 646-974-9060 (US)

email info@jerichowriters.com
website https://jerichowriters.com
Twitter @JerichoWriters
Instagram JerichoWriters
Founder Harry Bingham

An inclusive online writing organisation that offers editorial services for all genres, tutored courses, and events for all genres. Jericho Writers also offer guidance for self-publishers; masterclasses; AgentMatch (a database of over 1,000 literary agents); a free Community for writers to connect; and expert guides to writing and publishing (Jericho Writers Publishing).

Knuston Hall

Irchester, Wellingborough, Northants NN29 7EU
tel (01604) 362200
email enquiries@knustonhall.org.uk
website www.knustonhall.org.uk/index.jspx
Facebook www.facebook.com/pages/KnustonHall
Twitter @knustonhall

Offers an extensive programme of courses and events which can be attended on a residential or non-residential basis.

Le Verger

Savignac-Lédrier, Dordogne 24270, France
tel (01223) 316539 (UK)
email info@retreatfrance.co.uk
website www.retreatfrance.co.uk
Contact David Lambert

Offers residential writers' retreats or tutored courses (poetry, fiction, screenwriting, writing for the stage and life writing) from May to October with experienced tutors. Guests stay in a comfortable stone house outside a picturesque village in the Dordogne countryside of southwest France. Shared or individual accommodation in the main house, the Piggery or writers' cabins, full board (with local wines) for up to 10 writers. As well as creative and academic writers, Le Verger welcomes artists, photographers and anyone working on a creative project. Also offers yoga, meditation and creativity, and French at all levels. Transfers to/from Limoges and Brive. Listed with the National Association of Writers in Education (NAWE).

Limnisa Centre for Writers

Agios Georgios, Methana 18030, Greece
tel +31 681 027701, 07906 730450
email mariel@limnisa.com
website www.limnisa.com

International retreats and workshops for writers. Two hours by ferry from Piraeus, Limnisa stands in its own shaded garden with access to a tranquil beach, in a stunning position on the Methana Peninsula with views to Epidavros and the island of Aegina. Offers single rooms, studios or tents and all-vegetarian meals. Check website for details and dates.

Lumb Bank – The Ted Hughes Arvon Centre

Arvon, Lumb Bank, Heptonstall, Hebden Bridge, West Yorkshire HX7 6DF
tel (01422) 843714
email lumbbank@arvon.org
website www.arvon.org
Directors Rosie Scott, Helen Meller, *Deputy Director* Jill Penny, *Administrator* Becky Liddell

Offers online and residential writing courses. Grants available. Lumb Bank is an 18th-century former mill-owner's house set in 20 acres of steep pasture land.

Marlborough College Summer School

Marlborough, Wilts. SN8 1PA
tel (01672) 892388
email admin@summerschool.co.uk
website https://summerschool.co.uk
Facebook www.facebook.com/MarlboroughCollegeSummerSchool
Twitter @MCol_Summer
Instagram @marlboroughsummerschool

Runs from mid-July to mid-August each year. This multi-generational event plays host to over 400 courses, many of which specialise in the creative arts, including poetry, scriptwriting and writing memoir. Residential options available. Founded 1974.

Missenden School of Creative Arts

c/o Missenden Abbey, Great Missenden, Bucks. HP16 0BD
tel 07955 484605
email info@missendenschoolofcreativearts.co.uk
website www.missendenschoolofcreativearts.co.uk

Weekend and summer school art, craft and general interest courses for all abilities.

Moniack Mhor

Teavarran, Kiltarlity, Beauly, Inverness-shire IV4 7HT
tel (01463) 741675
email info@moniackmhor.org.uk
website www.moniackmhor.org.uk
Centre Director Rachel Humphries

Scotland's Creative Writing Centre, running residential creative writing courses, retreats and residencies throughout the year. In addition, the centre offers a programme of awards, residencies and retreats for writing groups and organisations. Tuition is by established writers, and the range of courses is designed to suit writers at all stages. Grants are available on all courses. High on a hill close to Loch Ness, the centre is an inspirational, inclusive and nurturing setting for writers to spend an intensive period focusing on their work. Founded 1993.

Monkton Wyld Court

Elsdon's Lane, Monkton Wyld, Dorset DT6 6DQ
tel (01297) 560342

email info@monktonwyldcourt.org
website https://monktonwyldcourt.co.uk/writers-retreats/

A neo-gothic mansion in a secluded valley on the Dorset/Devon border. Monkton Wyld Court is an educational charity offering affordable, full board, short- and long-term accommodation to writers of all sorts. Email or call to discuss availability.

Morley College
61 Westminster Bridge Road, London SE1 7HT
tel 020-7450 1889
website www.morleycollege.ac.uk
Facebook www.facebook.com/morleycollegewaterloo
Twitter @morleycollege

Offers a number of creative writing courses throughout the year.

Open College of the Arts
The Michael Young Arts Centre, Room 201, DMC02, County Way, Barnsley S70 2JW
email enquiries@oca.ac.uk
website www.oca.ac.uk

Distance learning arts courses. Study part-time foundation, degree or master's courses from home, at a pace that suits you which includes creative writing, scriptwriting, writing skills and 'Starting your novel'.

Oxford University Summer School for Adults
Department for Continuing Education, 1 Wellington Square, Oxford OX1 2JA
email oussa@conted.ox.ac.uk
website www.conted.ox.ac.uk/oussa

Offers a choice of 60 one-week accredited courses in a variety of subjects, including creative writing. No prior knowledge is required and classes are pitched at an introductory level. Participants are taught in small seminar groups by experienced tutors with a proven background in adult education.

Pitch to Publication
tel 07952 724299
email pitchtopublication@gmail.com
Twitter @glyniskoz
Twitter @liathughesjoshi
Contacts Glynis Kozma, Liat Hughes Joshi

Pitch to Publication is an eight-week online course with telephone tuition and coaching. It is designed to take prospective non-fiction authors to the point where they are ready to submit a well-honed pitch to agents and publishers. Taught by two experienced, published non-fiction writers. Open to all. Courses run every eight to 10 weeks.

SCBWI-BI Writers' Events
email araevents@britishscbwi.org
website https://britishisles.scbwi.org/events
Twitter @scbwi
Instagram scbwi_british_isles

See website for latest information about retreats and other writing and literary events organised by SCBWI-BI.

Scottish Universities' International Summer School
21 Buccleuch Place, Edinburgh EH8 9LN
tel 0131 650 4369
email suiss@ed.ac.uk
website www.suiss.ed.ac.uk
Facebook www.facebook.com/ScottishUniversitiesInternationalSummerSchool/
Twitter @suiss_EDI

See the website for full details of the creative writing and theatre and performance programmes.

Skyros Writers' Lab
9 Eastcliff Road, Shanklin, Isle of Wight PO37 6AA
tel (01983) 865566
email holidays@skyros.com
website www.skyros.com
Facebook www.facebook.com/skyroshols
Twitter @SkyrosHolidays

The Skyros Writers' Lab, situated on the Greek island of Skyros, offers writers of all levels the opportunity to learn from distinguished writers, share the joys and struggles of the creative process, discover their strengths and polish their skills. Courses are open to novices with a passion for writing as well as writers with a book under their belt. Arrive with work in progress or just an empty page; all are welcome. Visiting authors who have included Steven Berkoff, Mez Packer, Leigh Russell, Sophie Hannah, Rachel Billington, Margaret Drabble, Hanif Kureishi, D.M. Thomas, Sue Townsend, Marina Warner, Hugo Williams, Hilary Mantel, James Kelman, Barry Unsworth, Bernice Rubens and Alison Lurie.

Stiwdio Maelor
Maelor, Corris, Machynlleth SY20 9SP
tel 07480 231003
email stiwdiomaelor@gmail.com
website https://stiwdiomaelor.com
Contact Veronica Calarco

Provides residencies with individual studios and accommodation for writers and artists in a stunning area in North Wales, allowing them to refocus on their work and find new inspiration. Maelor has a bursary programme and a competition every year to enable creatives to complete residencies fee-free; see the website for further details. Founded 2014.

Swanwick, The Writers' Summer School
Hayes Conference Centre, Swanwick, Derbyshire DE55 1AU
tel (01290) 552248
email secretary@swanwickwritersschool.org.uk
website www.swanwickwritersschool.org.uk
Facebook www.facebook.com/SwanwickWriters

Twitter @swanwickwriters
Takes place 7–13 August 2021

Operating for over 70 years, Swanwick offers the opportunity to learn new skills and hone existing ones. There is an extensive choice of courses, talks and workshops. Offers several highly subsidised places for writers aged between 18 and 30, and assistance for writers unable to afford the full course fee. Full details of the programme and information on how to apply for the TopWrite Programme and Assisted Places Scheme are available on the website.

TLC Literary Adventures

East Side, Kings Cross Station, London N1C 4AX
tel 020-7324 2563
email info@literaryconsultancy.co.uk
website www.literaryconsultancy.co.uk
website https://literaryconsultancy.co.uk/literary-adventures
Facebook www.facebook.com/pages/The-Literary-Consultancy/331088000235106
Twitter @TLCUK
Director Aki Schilz

TLC's annual writing retreat is held at the idyllic Casa Ana in Andalusia, Spain. Workshops are led by award-winning novelist Paul McVeigh. TLC Literary Adventures offers an environment where inspiration and improvisation meet. Guests have access to world-class teaching and get a chance to work, read, listen and relax in a stunning setting which opens the mind and the senses. The retreat is open to writers of fiction, memoir and general non-fiction. Groups are limited to a maximum of 12.

Totleigh Barton

Arvon, Totleigh Barton, Sheepwash, Beaworthy, Devon EX21 5NS
tel (01409) 231338
email totleighbarton@arvon.org
website www.arvon.org
Twitter @TotleighBarton
Centre Director Mary Morris, *Centre Administrator* Kerensa Wilton

Offers residential writing courses all year round. Grants available. Totleigh Barton is a thatched, 16th-century manor house surrounded by farmland in Devon, two miles from the village of Sheepwash.

Travellers' Tales

58 Summerlee Avenue, London N2 9QH
email info@travellerstales.org
website www.travellerstales.org
Director Jonathan Lorie

UK's leading training agency for travel writers at all levels. Offers vocational courses with the UK's top travel photographers and travel writers in London, including beginners' weekends, masterclasses and creative retreats. Online tuition also available. Founded 2004.

Tŷ Newydd Writing Centre

Tŷ Newydd, Llanystumdwy, Cricieth, Gwynedd LL52 0LW
tel (01766) 522811
email tynewydd@literaturewales.org
website www.tynewydd.wales
Twitter @ty_newydd

Tŷ Newydd, the former home of Prime Minister David Lloyd George, has hosted residential creative writing courses for writers of all abilities for over 30 years. Open to everyone over the age of 16. Courses cover everything from poetry and popular fiction to writing for the theatre and developing a novel for young adults. No qualifications are necessary; staff can advise on the suitability of courses. Also offers courses for schools, corporate courses and awaydays for companies. Tŷ Newydd is also home to Nant, the writers' retreat cottage located on site. Run by Literature Wales, the national company for the development of literature in Wales.

Upton Cressett Foundation

Upton Cressett Hall, Upton Cressett, Nr Bridgnorth, Shrops. WV16 6UH
tel (01746) 714373
email laura@uptoncressett.co.uk
website https://uptoncressetthall.co.uk

Guest fellows are invited to stay and write in the Foundation's historic Elizabethan gatehouse or Moat House for up to three weeks (off season) to make progress with a literary project. The idea is to give established writers an opportunity to make headway with a work-in-progress in a remote and beautiful creative environment away from domestic or second career distractions. Since 2019 one of the stays awarded is the Philip Kerr Fellowship named after the bestselling author who died in 2018. This is for a writer of commercial or crime fiction. Previous fellows include artist Adam Dant, biographer Lara Feigel, historian Juliet Gardiner and the playwright Ella Hickson.

Urban Writers' Retreat

email hello@urbanwritersretreat.co.uk
website www.urbanwritersretreat.co.uk
Facebook www.facebook.com/UrbanWritersRetreat
Twitter @urbanwriters
Contact Charlie Haynes

Urban Writers' Retreat creates time and space so you can focus and just write. Escape the real world and all its distractions at one-day retreats in London and blissful residential retreats in the countryside, or get online courses and support to help you kick procrastination into touch.

Writers & Artists

Bloomsbury Publishing plc, 50 Bedford Square, London WC1B 3DP
tel 020-7631 5985

email writersandartists@bloomsbury.com
website www.writersandartists.co.uk
Facebook www.facebook.com/WritersArtistsYearbook
Twitter @Writers_Artists
Contacts James Rennoldson, Clare Povey

Writers & Artists (W&A) run online and offline masterclasses, conferences and writing courses throughout the year. These are run independently or in collaboration with literary festivals, universities and charities such as Book Aid International, Literature Works and the Open University. An annual How to Write for Children & Young Adults conference is held in February, while writing courses – which cover a variety of genres – take place on weekday evenings. W&A also offers a range of editing services, and works regularly with literary agents to provide guidance on the submission process. The W&A platform is free to join, contains hundreds of writing and publishing advice articles, and offers a lively community area and personalisation features.

The Writers Bureau

8–10 Dutton Street, Manchester M3 1LE
tel 0161 819 9922
email studentservices@writersbureau.com
website www.writersbureau.com
Facebook www.facebook.com/thewritersbureau
Twitter @writersbureau

The Writers Bureau offers a wide range of writing-related distance-learning courses including: Creative Writing, Freelance Journalism, Proofreading and Copy-Editing, Writing for Children, Copywriting, Poetry, How to Market Your Book, Non-Fiction Writing, Article Writing, Fiction Writing, Novel and Short Story Writing, Biographies, Memoirs and Family Histories, How to Write for Competitions, Writing for the Internet, Report Writing, Business Writing and Effective Time Management. The courses are suitable for both beginners and writers wanting to brush up on their skills. Also holds annual writing competitions with cash and free courses as prizes. See www.wbcompetition.com.

POSTGRADUATE COURSES

Aberystwyth University

Department of English and Creative Writing, Hugh Owen Building, Penglais Campus, Aberystwyth, Ceredigion SY23 3DY
tel (01970) 621537
email english@aber.ac.uk
website www.aber.ac.uk/en/english

MA Creative Writing, MA Literary Studies, PhD Creative Writing, PhD English and PhD in Creative Writing for international students.

Bath Spa University

Bath Spa University, Newton Park, Newton St Loe, Bath BA2 9BN

tel (01225) 875875
email admissions@bathspa.ac.uk
website www.bathspa.ac.uk/schools/school-of-creative-industries

Offers a variety of postgraduate courses on subjects including Creative Writing, Writing for Young People, Travel and Nature Writing, Scriptwriting, and Children's Publishing.

Birkbeck College, University of London

Malet Street, London WC1E 7HX
tel 020-7631 6000
website www.bbk.ac.uk/schools/arts
website http://mironline.org/
Facebook www.facebook.com/BirkbeckUniversityofLondon
Twitter @BirkbeckUoL
Twitter @mironlinebbk

MA Creative Writing, MFA Creative Writing, MA Creative Industries, MA Creative and Critical Writing, MSc Management with Creative Industries, MA Journalism and MA Screenwriting.

University of Bolton

Deane Road Campus, Bolton BL3 5AB
tel (01204) 900600
email enquiries@bolton.ac.uk
website www.bolton.ac.uk/subject-areas/english-and-creative-writing
Facebook www.facebook.com/UniversityofBolton
Twitter @BoltonUni

Creative Writing specialisms.

University of Brighton

School of Humanities, Village Way, Falmer, Brighton BN1 9PH
tel (01273) 643359
email jsm@brighton.ac.uk
website www.brighton.ac.uk/courses/study/Creative-Writing-MA-PGCert-PGDip.aspx
Contact Dr Jess Moriarty

Creative Writing MA (PGCert PGDip). Working with professional writers, students develop skills to produce and share stories in a variety of genres. Provides links with local publishers, writers and creative companies and offers a unique salon series where industry experts offer practical advice and insights. Students have the opportunity to share their work through established student-led anthologies and open mic nights. Undergraduate and postgraduate courses available.

Brunel University London

Uxbridge, Middlesex UB8 3PH
tel (01895) 274000
website www.brunel.ac.uk/creative-writing
Twitter @Bruneluni

MA Creative Writing.

Cardiff University

Cardiff School of English and Philosophy,
John Percival Building, Colum Drive,
Cardiff CF10 3EU
tel 029-2087 6049
email encap@cardiff.ac.uk
website www.cardiff.ac.uk

MA Creative Writing, MA News Journalism and
Magazines, PhD Creative and Critical Writing.

University of Chichester

Bishop Otter Campus, College Lane, Chichester,
West Sussex PO19 6PE
tel (01243) 816000
email h.frey@chi.ac.uk
email h.dunkerley@chi.ac.uk
website www.chi.ac.uk
Contacts Prof. Hugo Frey (Head of Department), Dr
Hugh Dunkerley (MA in Creative Writing
Programme Coordinator)

BA Creative Writing, MA Creative Writing, PhD
Creative Writing. Students work with practising
writers. Specialisms include: novels, short stories,
creative non-fiction, writing for children,
screenwriting and poetry. Hosts regular visits by
high-profile writers, editors and agents. Visiting
Professors: Kate Mosse and Alison MacLeod. Many
students go on to publish and win prizes.

City, University of London

School of Arts and Social Sciences,
Northampton Square, London EC1V 0HB
email SASS-Enquiries@city.ac.uk
website www.city.ac.uk
Facebook www.facebook.com/cityuniversitylondon
Twitter @CityUniLondon

Postgraduate courses in creative writing, English,
journalism and publishing.

University of Cumbria

tel 0808 291 6578
email enquirycentre@cumbria.ac.uk
website www.cumbria.ac.uk
Facebook www.facebook.com/universityofcumbria
Twitter @CumbriaUni

MA Creative Writing, MA Literature, Romanticism
and the English Lake District, MA Graphic Novel and
Children's Book Illustration

De Montfort University

The Gateway, Leicester LE1 9BH
tel 0116 255 1551
email enquiry@dmu.ac.uk
website www.dmu.ac.uk

MA Creative Writing, MA English Literature, MA
English Language.

University of East Anglia

Admissions Office, School of Literature,
Drama and Creative Writing,
Faculty of Arts and Humanities,
Norwich Research Park, Norwich NR4 7TJ
tel (01603) 591515
email admissions@uea.ac.uk
website www.uea.ac.uk/about/school-of-literature-
drama-and-creative-writing

MA Creative Writing: Poetry, MA Creative Writing:
Prose Fiction, MA Creative Writing: Scriptwriting,
MA Biography and Creative Non-Fiction, MA
Creative Writing: Crime Fiction, MA Literary
Translation, MA Modern and Contemporary
Writing. Master's by research, MPhil and PhD.

Edge Hill University

Department of English,
History and Creative Writing, St Helens Road,
Ormskirk L39 4QP
tel (01695) 579997
email coxa@edgehill.ac.uk
website www.edgehill.ac.uk/
englishhistorycreativewriting

MA in Creative Writing (full- and part-time,
established 1989) and PhD programmes in creative
writing.

University of Edinburgh

Old College, South Bridge, Edinburgh EH8 9YL
tel 0131 650 1000
website www.ed.ac.uk
website www.eca.ed.ac.uk
Twitter @UniofEdinburgh
Interim Ceo Nicola Ramsey

Postgraduate courses include Creative Writing, Film
Studies, Film Directing and Illustration.

University of Essex

Wivenhoe Park, Colchester CO4 3SQ
tel (01206) 872626
email pgadmit@essex.ac.uk
website www.essex.ac.uk/literature-film-and-theatre-
studies
Facebook www.facebook.com/uniofessex
Twitter @Uni_of_Essex
Twitter @LiFTS_at_essex

Postgraduate courses include Creative Writing,
English Language, Film Studies, Theatre Practice and
Scriptwriting.

Falmouth University

Falmouth Campus, Woodlane, Falmouth,
Cornwall TR11 4RH
tel (01326) 211077
website www.falmouth.ac.uk

MA Film & Television, MA Fine Art (online), MA
Comedy Writing (online) MA Game Art, MA
Illustration (online), MA Illustration: Authorial
Practice, MA Professional Writing, MA Writing for
Script and Screen (online), Communication Design
MA, Creative Advertising MA, Graphic Design MA

(online), MA Journalism (online), MA Marketing and Digital Communications (online), MA Photography (online).

University of Glasgow

Creative Writing, School of Critical Studies,
5 Lilybank Gardens, Glasgow G12 8QQ
tel 0141 330 8372
email critstudies-pgenquiries@glasglow.ac.uk
website www.gla.ac.uk/subjects/creativewriting
Twitter @UoGWriting

MLitt, MFA and DFA in Creative Writing, MLitt by distance learning, low residency MFA/DFA.

University of Hull

Cottingham Road, Hull HU6 7RX
tel (01482) 346311
website www.hull.ac.uk/faculties/subjects/english
Facebook www.facebook.com/UniversityOfHull
Twitter @UniOfHull

Postgraduate courses include Creative Writing, Digital Media, Theatre Making.

Kingston University

Penrhyn Road, Kingston upon Thames,
Surrey KT1 2EE
tel 020-3510 0106
website www.kingston.ac.uk
Facebook www.facebook.com/kingstonuni
Twitter @KingstonUni

Postgraduate courses in Creative Writing, Journalism, Publishing.

Lancaster University

Department of English Literature and Creative Writing, County College, Lancaster University, Lancaster LA1 4YD
tel (01524) 593089
email eclwteaching@lancaster.ac.uk
website www.lancaster.ac.uk/english-literature-and-creative-writing
Contact The Teaching Office

MA Creative Writing by Distance Learning, MA Creative Writing (Modular), MA Creative Writing with English Literary Studies, MA English Literary Studies with Creative Writing, MA English Literary Studies, MA English Literary Research, PhD Creative Writing, PhD English Literature and Creative Writing, PhD English Literature.

University of Leeds

Faculty of Arts, Humanities and Cultures, University of Leeds, Leeds LS2 9JJ
website ahc.leeds.ac.uk
Facebook www.facebook.com/universityofleeds
Twitter @UniversityLeeds

Master's courses include Writing for Performance and Publication, Creative Writing and Critical Life, Media Industries, and Film, Photography and Media.

Leeds Beckett University

City Campus, Woodhouse Lane, Leeds, LS1 3HE
tel 0113 812 0000
email admissionsenquiries@leedsbeckett.ac.uk
website www.leedsbeckett.ac.uk
Facebook www.facebook.com/leedsbeckett
Twitter @leedsbeckett

MA Documentary Filmmaking, MA Drama and Creative Writing in Education.

Liverpool John Moores University

Tithebarn Street, Liverpool L2 2QP
tel 0151 231 2121
email courses@ljmu.ac.uk
website www.ljmu.ac.uk

MA Screenwriting and MA Writing.

University of London, Goldsmiths

Goldsmiths, University of London,
London SE14 6NW
tel 020-7919 7171
website www.gold.ac.uk
Facebook www.facebook.com/GoldsmithsUoL
Twitter @GoldsmithsUoL
Instagram goldsmithsuol

Postgraduate courses include Art and Ecology, Artists' Film and Moving Image, Art Psychotherapy, Arts and Learning, Black British Literature, Children's Literature, Children's Illustration, Computational Arts, Computer Games Art and Design, Creative and Life Writing, Creative Writing and Education, Curating, Digital Media, Dramaturgy and Writing for Performance, Film and Screen Studies, Filmmaking, Fine Art, Journalism, Performance Making, Radio, Script Writing, Translation.

University of London, Royal Holloway

Egham, Surrey TW20 0EX
tel (01784) 434455
website www.royalholloway.ac.uk
Facebook www.facebook.com/royalholloway
Twitter @RoyalHolloway

Postgraduate courses include Creative Writing, Playwriting, Screenwriting for Television and Film, Producing Film and Television.

London College of Communication

tel 020-7514 6500
website www.arts.ac.uk/colleges/london-college-of-communication
Facebook www.facebook.com/londoncollegeofcommunication
Twitter @LCCLondon

Postgraduate courses include Publishing, Screenwriting, Television, Photography, Games Design, Virtual Reality, Illustration, Film.

The London Film School
24 Shelton Street, London WC2H 9UB
tel 020-7836 9642
email info@lfs.org.uk
website https://lfs.org.uk

MA Screenwriting, MA Filmmaking.

University of Manchester
University of Manchester, Oxford Road,
Manchester M13 9PL
tel 0161 275 3107
website www.alc.manchester.ac.uk/
centrefornewwriting
Twitter ECW_UoM

Master's courses in Creative Writing, Playwriting and
Screenwriting.

The Manchester Writing School at Manchester Metropolitan University
Arts & Humanities Building, Cavendish Street,
Manchester, M15 6BG
tel 0161 247 1787
email writingschool@mmu.ac.uk
website www.mmu.ac.uk/english/mcr-writing-school
Twitter @McrWritingSchl
Contact (admission and general enquiries) James
Draper, Manager

Master of Fine Arts (MFA) and Master of Arts (MA)
in Creative Writing with specialist routes in Novel,
Poetry, Writing for Children & Young Adults,
Scriptwriting and Creative Non-Fiction. Campus-
based and international online distance learning,
available to study full-time (MA: one year, MFA: two
years) or part-time (MA: two years; MFA: three
years). September and January enrolment.
Scholarships available (including Joyce Nield Fund
for non-UK Commonwealth students). Evening
taught, with strong industry links. MFA students
complete a full-length book/script. MA in Publishing
presented in collaboration with the iSchool at
Manchester Met and industry partners. PhD in
Creative Writing, including PhD by practice.

Middlesex University
The Burroughts, Hendon, London NW4 4BT
tel 020-8411 5555
website www.mdx.ac.uk/courses/creative-media-and-
writing
Facebook www.facebook.com/MiddlesexUniversity
Twitter @MiddlesexUni

MA Novel Writing, MA Scriptwriting, MA Digital
Journalism. Research degrees and journalism courses.

National Film and Television School
Beaconsfield Studios, Station Road, Beaconsfield,
Bucks. HP9 1LG
tel (01494) 671234

email info@nfts.co.uk
website https://nfts.co.uk
Facebook www.facebook.comNFTSFilmTV
Twitter @NFTSFilmTV

MA, diploma, certificate and short courses covering a
wide range of disciplines relating to television and
film.

Newcastle University
Newcastle upon Tyne NE1 7RU
tel 0191 208 6000
website www.ncl.ac.uk
Facebook www.facebook.com/newcastleuniversity
Twitter @UniofNewcastle

Degree and short courses include Creative Writing,
Media and Journalism.

Northumbria University
Faculty of Arts, Design and Social Sciences,
Lipman Building, Newcastle upon Tyne NE1 8ST
tel 0191 227 4444
email laura.fish@northumbria.ac.uk
website www.northumbria.ac.uk
Programme Leader Laura Fish

MA Creative Writing.

Nottingham Trent University
School of Arts and Humanities, Clifton Lane,
Nottingham NG11 8NS
tel 0115 848 4200
email rory.waterman@ntu.ac.uk
email hum.enquiries@ntu.ac.uk
website www.ntu.ac.uk/course/english-linguistics-
creative-writing
Twitter @ntuhum
Contact Dr Rory Waterman, Programme Leader

MA Creative Writing. A practice-based course in
Nottingham UNESCO City of Literature, and one of
the longest-established and successful programmes of
its kind in the UK (currently celebrating 27 years),
with close links to the writing industry, an annual
anthology, a programme of guest talks and
workshops and many highly successful graduate
writers. Diverse module options include: Fiction,
Poetry, Writing for Stage, Radio and Screen, and
Children's and Young Adult Fiction.

Oxford University
Department for Continuing Education,
Rewley House, 1 Wellington Square,
Oxford OX1 2JA
tel (01865) 270360
website www.conted.ox.ac.uk

MSt in Creative Writing: a two-year part-time
master's degree covering prose fiction, narrative non-
fiction, poetry, radio and TV drama, stage drama and
screenwriting. Offers high contact hours, genre
specialization and critical and creative breadth. *Email*:
mstcreativewriting@conted.ox.ac.uk.

Undergraduate Diploma in Creative Writing: a two-year part-time course covering prose, poetry, drama and analytical reading. Two study options available: online study with a three-week residential summer school; face-to-face study in Oxford structured around Saturday day schools (four per term) and a six-day summer school. *Email*: undergraduate@conted.ox.ac.uk

Short online courses and virtual classes in creative writing and literature - multiple intakes per year. *Email*: onlinecourses@conted.ox.ac.uk.

University of Plymouth
Drake Circus, Plymouth PL4 8AA
tel (01752) 600600
email admissions@plymouth.ac.uk
website www.plymouth.ac.uk
Facebook www.facebook.com/plymouthuni
Twitter @PlymUni

MA courses include Creative Writing, English Literature, Illustration and Publishing.

Queen's University, Belfast
University Road, Belfast BT7 1NN
tel 028-9024 5133
website www.qub.ac.uk
Facebook www.facebook.com/
QueensUniversityBelfast
Twitter @QueensUBelfast

MA/Postgraduate Diploma Creative Writing, PhD Creative Writing.

University of Roehampton
Grove House, Roehampton Lane, London SW15 5PJ
tel 020-8392 3000
website www.roehampton.ac.uk
Facebook www.facebook.com/roehamptonuni
Twitter @RoehamptonUni
Instagram uni_roehampton

Postgraduate courses include Children's Literature, Journalism, Creative Writing, Screenwriting, Publishing, Film Practices.

The Royal Central School of Speech and Drama
Embassy Theatre, Eton Avenue, London NW3 3HY
tel 020-7722 8183
email sarah.grochala@cssd.ac.uk
website www.cssd.ac.uk
Twitter @CSSDLondon

MA/MFA Writing for Stage and Broadcast Media.

University of St Andrews
School of English, St Andrews, Fife KY16 9AR
tel (01334) 462668

email pgeng@st-andrews.ac.uk
website www.st-andrews.ac.uk/english/postgraduate
Contact Alexandra Wallace, PG Administrator

MFA or MLitt in Creative Writing: Poetry or Prose; PhD, MFA or MLitt in Playwriting and Screenwriting.

University of Salford
The Crescent, Salford M5 4WT
tel 0161 295 5000
website www.salford.ac.uk
Facebook www.facebook.com/salforduni
Twitter @SalfordUni

Courses include Journalism, Screen Media Industries and Media Production.

Sheffield Hallam University
City Campus, Howard Street, Sheffield S1 1WB
tel 0114 225 5555
email enquiries@shu.ac.uk
website www.shu.ac.uk
Facebook www.facebook.com/
sheffieldhallamuniversity
Twitter @sheffhallumuni

Postgraduate courses include Creative Writing, Sports Journalism, Multimedia Journalism.

University of South Wales
Treforest, Pontypridd CF37 1DL
tel (01443) 760101
website www.southwales.ac.uk/courses/mphil-in-writing
Twitter @UniSouthWales

MPhil Writing.

University of Wales Trinity Saint David
tel (01570) 422351
email fhpadmissions@uwtsd.ac.uk
website www.uwtsd.ac.uk/ma-creative-writing
Facebook www.facebook.com/trinitysaintdavid
Twitter @UWTSD

MA Creative Writing.

University of Warwick
Department of English and Comparative Literary Studies, Humanities Building, Coventry CV4 7AL
tel 024-7652 3665
email pgenglish@warwick.ac.uk
website www.warwick.ac.uk/fac/arts/scapvc/wwp/
study/postgraduate

MA in Writing.

Law and copyright
UK copyright law and publishing rights

Publisher Lynette Owen outlines the basic principles of copyright and how UK copyright law provides a framework for the protection of creative works, with particular reference to publishing.

Creators including writers and artists are dependent on copyright to protect their works and to underpin the arrangements they make with the publishers who bring their works to market. The United Kingdom has the oldest tradition of copyright legislation, starting with the Statute of Anne which came into force in 1710. The last full revision of UK copyright law resulted in the Copyright, Designs and Patents Act 1988 (CPDA); this replaced the 1956 Copyright Act, which in turn replaced the 1911 Copyright Act. Since the 1988 Act, there have been a number of revisions, usually undertaken via Statutory Instrument.

What is copyright?

Copyright is one aspect of intellectual property rights (IPR), which are often defined as relating to 'works of the mind'. Other aspects include design and patent rights. Copyright has both positive and negative aspects – it enables rightsholders to authorise the use of their work in a variety of ways and also to take action against unauthorised use. It is worth flagging here that there are different philosophies of copyright; the UK, in common with other Anglophone countries, operates under common law, based on factual case law, and views copyright works as property which can be traded and transferred. By contrast, countries which operate under civil law, based on civil codes, (e.g. the countries of mainland Europe) view copyright (referred to as *droit d'auteur*) more as a human right belonging to the creator, with far more restrictive regulations on how it can be exploited.

How does it work?

Each country has its own national copyright legislation which normally covers works created by citizens of that country, creators normally resident in that country and works first published in that country. There is also normally an obligation to respect the creative works originating in other countries which belong to the same international copyright conventions; this is normally undertaken in the form of 'national treatment', i.e. each member country provides to the creative works from other member states the same standard of protection it would grant to the works of its own citizens. This means that there may be varying standards of protection from country to country, for example in terms of the duration of copyright protection; there may also be differing exceptions to copyright from country to country. Most countries in the world now belong to one or more of the international copyright conventions: the Berne Convention (1886), the Universal Copyright Convention (1952) and the World Intellectual Property Organization (WIPO) Copyright Treaty (1996, but in force from 2002 – this convention reinforces the concept of copyright in the digital age). Membership of a convention requires member states to observe certain minimum standards of copyright protection.

What types of work are protected by copyright?

The CDPA (Copyright, Designs and Patents Act 1988) provides copyright protection to three main categories of creative works:

1. Original literary, dramatic, musical and artistic works

'Literary works' includes any work which is written, including tables, graphs, compilations and computer programs. It also includes databases which involve creativity in terms of selection by the compiler. Dramatic and musical works include performable works such as plays and dances, with the lyrics of musical works protected separately. Artistic works include graphic works (paintings, drawings, maps, engravings or similar works), sculptures, collages, works of architecture and works of artistic craftsmanship (although these can also be protected under design rights). All works must be original and in written or other fixed form.

2. Sound recordings, films and broadcasts

These are also protected and may involve the many different copyrights of performers, producers and broadcasters. Broadcasts traditionally covered transmission by radio and television, but now include satellite broadcasts and transmissions via the internet.

3. Copyright in typographical arrangements

This is a specific right under UK copyright law which does not appear in the legislation of many other countries. This right covers the design and layout of text and, as such, is a right quite separate from that of the creative content of the text; it belongs to the publisher in recognition of their skill and investment in the layout of a work and lasts for 25 years from the date of first publication of that version of the text.

Who owns the copyright?

The first owner of copyright is normally the creator, e.g. the writer, artist, composer, etc. The major exception to this, in UK copyright law, is if a work is created as part of the creator's regular employment, in which case copyright belongs to the employer. A good example of this would be when a publisher employs a team of lexicographers in-house to compile dictionary entries. US copyright law has a provision for 'works for hire' where content (text, illustrations, etc) may be commissioned by a publisher, usually on the basis of an outright fee, with copyright then belonging to the commissioning entity.

In the case of copyright controlled by the creator, he or she will then have a choice on how to deal with the question of copyright when dealing with a publisher. For an author or illustrator seeking a contract with a publisher, there are two possibilities:

i) They may retain ownership of the copyright and grant an exclusive licence or licences to one or more publishers for publication of the work in an agreed language, in agreed format/s, within agreed sales territories and for an agreed period of time. For example, an author could grant an exclusive licence to a UK publisher for the UK and Commonwealth markets, and a separate licence to a US publisher for the American market. This is a common scenario in trade (general) publishing.

ii) In educational, academic and professional publishing, the scenario may be different. The author may be asked to assign copyright to the publishing house – this is often a requirement for academic journal articles but may also be requested for books, even when the author is receiving an advance and ongoing royalties; it is particularly logical for multi-author works where individual contributors may each be paid an outright fee. There is often much misunderstanding of copyright assignment and publishers should always be prepared to explain to authors and illustrators their reasons for requesting it. One particularly powerful reason is that it is often much simpler to take action against piracy if copyright is in the name of the publishing house.

With the rise of the internet, there is a need for protection of internet transmissions and for user-generated works; these are covered under provisions for 'communication to the public' and 'making available to the public'. However, the question of copyright ownership in user-generated works is complex, given the scale of material which is uploaded to social media sites such as YouTube, Facebook, Twitter, Instagram and others. If the material uploaded is original to the person undertaking the uploading, then copyright will belong to them, but a lot of such material may belong to other parties and may have been uploaded without their knowledge or consent.

What are moral rights?

Moral rights are personal to the creator and were introduced into UK copyright legislation for the first time in the CDPA 1988; they had long been a feature of civil law. They are quite separate from the economic rights of the creator and in the UK they last for the same period as copyright protection; in some other legislations they are inalienable and perpetual. They include the right of paternity (the right to be recognised as the creator), the right of integrity (the right to object to derogatory or damaging treatment of the work) and the right to object to false attribution of a work. UK legislation is unusual in that it requires the creator to assert his or her right of paternity (this is often done via a notice on the title verso page of a book); it also allows for the creator to waive his or her moral rights, something which may be necessary for certain forms of publication or when a book is used as the basis for film or television exploitation.

How long does copyright last?

In the case of the UK, the period of protection is now 70 years from the end of the year in which the creator dies – in the case of works of collaborative authorship, from the end of the year in which the last author dies. The term of protection was extended from 50 to 70 years for all works still in copyright as at 1 July 1995, as a result of an EU directive to harmonise the term of copyright within the European Union. Works published in the USA since 1 January 1978 also now have a similar period of protection. However, many countries in the world still have a shorter period of protection (e.g. Japan and China have a period of 50 years *post mortem auctoris*).

What does copyright enable the owner to do?

It enables the owner to undertake or authorise reproduction and distribution of the work to the public, as well as a range of other methods of exploiting the work, including performance, broadcasting and adaptations (which would include translations). It is normally an infringement of copyright for anyone to undertake any of these activities without authorisation from the copyright holder.

What action can be taken against copyright infringement?

UK copyright legislation permits action to be taken under civil or criminal law, depending on the nature of the infringement; penalties are decided by the courts. By contrast, the legislation of some countries defines the penalties in terms of maximum financial fines or terms of imprisonment. There are many possible categories of infringement – these could include unauthorised reproduction, unauthorised adaptation, plagiarism and passing off. In the internet age, unauthorised use of copyright content has increased; some is undertaken for commercial purposes via torrent sites, whilst other cases may be file sharing (e.g. of textbooks amongst students). The Publishers Association has a website which enables its members to issue 'notice and takedown' to infringing sites (see www.copyrightinfringementportal.com).

Are there exceptions to copyright?

Most national copyright laws list a number of uses of copyright material which can be undertaken without permission from or payment to the copyright owner, subject to certain conditions. The CDPA 1988 provides for a number of these:
• Fair dealing with a literary, dramatic, musical or artistic work for the purposes of research or study;
• Fair dealing for the purposes of criticism or review;
• Fair dealing with a work (other than a photograph) for the purpose or reporting current events.

These uses are permitted subject to due acknowledgement to the creator and the source, provided they do not adversely affect the normal interests of the copyright holder. There is no statutory definition of *fair dealing*, but most publishers would consider that fair dealing does not apply to use in the context of a commercial publication, so an author wishing to include copyright text or illustrations from outside sources in his or her own book should not assume that this is covered by fair dealing, however short the material may be.

The CDPA also provides for the copying of material for educational purposes, provided this is not undertaken by a reprographic process; thus, for example, displaying a passage of text on an interactive whiteboard is permitted. Large-scale copying of limited amounts of copyright material via photocopying or scanning (e.g. for course-packs for schools or universities, or on a company intranet) is covered under collective licences issued by the Copyright Licensing Agency (CLA) which negotiates licences to schools, colleges, universities, government departments and private businesses for such use; a share of licence revenue is paid to authors via the Authors Licensing and Collecting Society (ALCS), to visual artists via the

Useful websites

Authors Licensing and Collecting Society (ALCS): www.alcs.co.uk

Copyright Licensing Agency (CLA): www.cla.co.uk

Design and Artists Copyright Society (DACS): www.dacs.org.uk

Intellectual Property Office (IPO): www.gov.uk/government/organisations/intellectual-property-office

Picture Industry Collecting Society for Effective Licensing (PICSEL): www.picsel.org.uk

Publishers' Licensing Services (PLS): www.pls.org.uk

Publishers Association: www.publishers.org.uk

Society of Authors: www.societyofauthors.org

World Intellectual Property Organisation (WIPO): www.wipo.int/portal/en/index.html

Design and Artists Collecting Society (DACS) or the Picture Industry Collecting Society for Effective Licensing (PICSEL), and to publishers via Publishers' Licensing Services (PLS). Organisations similar to CLA exist in many overseas countries and revenue from the copying of extracts from UK copyright works abroad is channelled to CLA via bilateral agreements with those organisations.

There are also provisions for the inclusion of short passages of published literary and dramatic works in educational anthologies, provided this does not affect the interests of the copyright holders and that such material does not represent the majority of the anthology.

The CDPA 1988 permits the making of a single copy of a copyright work by a library on behalf of a person undertaking research or private study, and it also permits libraries to make copies for the purposes of preservation or replacement of a damaged item.

There has been a copyright exception for visually impaired people since the Copyright (Visually Impaired Persons) Act 2002, giving them the right to accessible versions of copyright content (e.g. in Braille, audio or text-to-speech versions).

2014 saw the introduction of a number of amendments to existing copyright exceptions and some new exceptions, introduced via statutory instruments. Among them was an exception for copying for private use; fair dealing for non-commercial research or private study; a fair dealing exception for criticism or review or otherwise (the latter term undefined); a new exception for caricature, parody or pastiche; a new exception for text and data analysis for non-commercial research; and an extension of the exception for visually impaired persons to cover persons whose ability to read is affected by their disability (either physical or e.g. dyslexia). It remains the case that any fair dealing use must acknowledge the source and must not affect the normal interests of the rightsholder.

> ### Copyright acts
>
> - Copyright, Designs and Patents Act 1988 (but it is vital to use an up-to-date amended version). See www.gov.uk/government/organisations/intellectual-property-office.
> - Duration of Copyright and Rights in Performances Regulations 1995 (SI 1995 No. 3297)
> - Copyright and Rights in Database Regulations 1997 (SI 1997/3032) amended by the Copyright and Rights in Databases (Amendment) Regulations 2003 (SI 2003/2501)
> - Copyright and Related Rights Regulations 2003 (SI 2003 No. 2498)
> - Intellectual Property (Enforcement, etc) Regulations 2006 (SI 2006 No. 1028)
> - Performances (Moral Rights, etc) Regulations 2006 (SI 2006 No. 18)
> - Copyright and Rights in Performances (Quotation and Parody) Regulations 2014
> - Copyright and Rights in Performances (Personal Copies for Private Use) Regulations 2014

How has UK copyright law changed?

In particular, UK copyright law has been influenced by a number of EU directives over the years, which have normally been implemented via statutory instruments. The most significant have been: the 1993 Directive on the Duration of Copyright and Authors' Rights (93/98/EEC), implemented via the Duration of Copyright and Rights in Performance Regulations 1995 (SI 1995 No 3297); the EC Database Directive 96/9 EC which was implemented via the Copyright and Rights in Databases Regulations 1997; and the EU Directive 2001/29/EC on the Harmonisation of Certain Aspects of Copyright and Related Rights in the Information Society, which included a transmission right and the right for copyright holders to use encryption and identifier systems to protect their works (implemented by SI 2003 No. 2498, the Copyright and Related Rights Regulations). The EC is currently considering a major copyright review, but with the lack of clarity following the UK's departure from the EU in January 2020 and on-going Brexit negotiations, it is unclear what effect that might have on UK copyright legislation.

Copyright under the microscope?

The last 20 years have seen a plethora of reviews of copyright – at international, multi-national and national level – raising the question of the balance of interest between rights-holders and users, and questioning whether copyright remains fit for purpose. The rise of the internet has raised expectations amongst many users that content should be instantly available and preferably free of charge. The dangers of this have been seen all too clearly, in particular with the adverse impact on the music, film and computer software industries and their creators. On the other hand, some creators have been happy to make their work available under a range of Creative Commons licences, some more restrictive than others. There is an ongoing move towards Open Access in the academic sector, with its impact being felt particularly in the area of academic journals.

Copyright has had a long history of adapting to developments in technology and to changing market needs; hence it remains fit for purpose and is a necessary framework that enables creators to receive a just reward for the use of their work and to recognise the skills and investment of those who, like publishers, bring their works to market.

Further reading

Cornish, William et al., *Intellectual Property, Patents, Copyrights, Trademarks and Allied Rights* (Sweet & Maxwell, 9th edn 2019)

Bently, Lionel and Sherman, Brad, *Intellectual Property Law* (OUP, 4th edn 2014)

Caddick, Nicholas et al., *Copinger and Skone James on Copyright* (Sweet & Maxwell, 17th edn 2016)

Jones, Hugh and Benson, Christopher, *Publishing Law* (Routledge, 5th edn 2016)

Haggart Davies, Gillian, *Copyright for Artists, Photographers and Designers* (A&C Black 2010)

Haggart Davies, Gillian, *Copyright for Writers, Editors and Publishers* (A&C Black 2011)

Owen, Lynette (Gen. Ed.), *Clark's Publishing Agreements: A Book of Precedents* (Bloomsbury Professional, 10th edn 2017)

For a view of copyright from the US perspective:

Netanel, Neil Weinstock, *Copyright: What Everyone Needs to Know* (OUP New York 2018)

Lynette Owen OBE, has worked at Cambridge University Press, Pitman Publishing, Marshall Cavendish and Pearson Education, and is now a freelance copyright and rights consultant at Lynette Owen Consulting. Her book, *Selling Rights*, is published by Routledge (8th edition 2019).

See also...

• *Copyright Licensing Agency Ltd*, page 713

A legal lexicon

data protection

You have a duty to protect the privacy of your readers if they share their personal information with you (name, D.O.B., gender, email or home address, etc.). This might be through a newsletter sign up, survey or book order on your website. The Data Protection Act 2018 insists that recipients of this kind of personal information must store it safely, use it only for the purpose communicated to the individual and only store data for as long as is necessary.

defamation

To defame someone is to damage their reputation and can result in legal action taken against the author or publisher if the case is serious enough. Defamatory content might include mocking and ridicule or making a false statement about a person or company. In fiction a character could be considered defamatory if they bear resemblance to a real person or body of people. Defamation court cases can be extremely expensive, meaning that publishers will often cease publication if there is even a possibility of being sued and will include clauses in their contracts stating the author is responsible (legally and financially) for any defamatory content found in their work.

intellectual property (IP)

An idea or creation which is not tangible or material but is sellable and ownable. This includes trademarks, copyrights and patents of character names, plot devices and fictional places; text, photographs and illustrations; databases and software.

libel

Defamatory statements which are written or published. This can now include social media posts and comments – the authors of which have been successfully sued in court.

moral rights

There are two key moral rights which an author should be aware of, they apply even after an author has assigned their copyright to another party. The right to paternity gives an author the right to assert themselves as the creator of a work and prevents false attribution. The right to integrity prevents a work being edited or changed without the author's permission.

permissions

If someone wants to use part or the whole of your work, they must first receive your permission to do so (or the permission of the copyright or licence holder). As an author you must do the same if you want to use someone else's work, for example an illustration or quotation. Permissions are granted in a contract and usually in return for payment. Permissions must be cleared before publication to avoid contravening copyright.

privacy and confidentiality

A breach of privacy occurs when confidential information is shared beyond the person or people for whom it was intended and can be met with legal action. A duty of confidence exists between an author and their publisher which prevents confidential information, such as ideas and manuscripts as well as commercial information about the publisher, from being shared. An author must also respect the right to privacy – in either fiction or non-fiction – if their work is inspired by real people or events. For example, if you are writing about your former line of work, avoid sharing confidential or sensitive information, or if you are writing a romance novel, avoid basing your lead character on an ex.

slander

Defamatory statements which are spoken aloud. For an author this could include statements made during a book tour or promotional interview.

subsidiary rights

Also known as ancillary rights, i.e. secondary to volume rights (see below), these are rights which are licensed to a publisher which then licenses them to a third party. These might be a foreign publisher with whom a translation is negotiated or a newspaper or magazine that wishes to print an extract from a book. A literary agent will often not assign copyright in some subsidiary rights to a publisher and will manage them for an author. These include those rights that might be exploited in areas beyond the page, such as film or TV and merchandising rights.

trademark

A sign, design or expression can be protected by a trademark which identifies the individuality of these symbols and their distinction from those used by others in a similar business and protects them from copying. For example, J.K. Rowling has copyrighted various character names and features of her *Harry Potter* series, such as Hogwarts School of Witchcraft and Wizardry and Gryffindor House.

volume rights

The rights for a publisher to publish a book in its main editions: print, audio and ebook.

Law and copyright

Author–Publisher contracts

Publishing contracts can be lengthy, it's helpful to know what types of clauses they are likely to include and why they are there.

If you have an agent, he or she will negotiate your publishing contract on your behalf. Organisations such as the of the Society of Authors (see page 509) and WGGB (see page 512) offer contract review services. A contract is a legal agreement between two parties and exists to protect both author and publisher. It includes clauses on rights and obligations to avoid ambiguity as to the responsibilities of both parties. The clauses in your publishing contract are likely to include those listed below.

Definitions used throughout the contract will often be included at the beginning or in an appendix, and might include terms such as 'Net receipts', 'Hybrid Product', 'First Serial', 'Territory', and 'Electronic Book'.

Legal operation and enforcement of the contract is covered by a few standard clauses, such as those relating to 'Interpretation', 'Arbitration', 'Confidentiality', 'Notices' and 'Entire Agreement'.

Free to publish

The author confirms that she is able to enter into the agreement and that the book she is writing is a unique, new property, her own work and will not contain any legally compromising material. Note that the first example below indicates the style of legalese in which your contract is likely to be couched:

Exclusivity 'The Author hereby grants to the Publishers during the legal term of copyright the sole and exclusive licence to publish the said work in volume form.'

Warranty and indemnity are confirmed, meaning the author states that she is freely able to enter into the agreement, is the sole author, owns the rights in the 'work' and that it is unique, i.e. has not been published elsewhere previously and does not contain any libellous or defamatory material or content that isn't hers to include, i.e. that is someone else's copyright and that the author has cleared permissions with the copyright holder for any part of somebody else's work being reproduced in the book. The author agrees to cover any legal costs, other fees or losses if she is in any way in breach of the warranty.

Territory

This is the geographical areas where the book can be sold, for example UK and Europe, or North American, or World territories.

Rights

Legal Term is the period that the contract covers, from date of signature of the contract by both parties or until rights are reverted to the author.

Granting and Reversion An author agrees that the publisher is allowed to publish their Work during the legal term. Rights might revert (back to the author) automatically when sales dip below a minimum annual level, of say fifty copies. An author may negotiate to have rights in their book reverted and will be able to purchase any remaining stock. At that stage the contract is also formally terminated.

Termination might also occur if either party breaches any of the terms of the contract, for example if the author fails to deliver a manuscript of the quality expected on time and if it is found to be plagiarised. Late delivery alone would not usually be grounds for termination, but an author should always inform the agent or publisher if a contracted delivery date cannot be fulfilled.

Copyright Notice and Infringement This covers how the author's name will appear in the book, i.e. © name of author, 20XX. These clauses confirm that copyright in the Work is the property of the author. They will also make it clear that, if the publisher decides to protect the copyright of a book insofar as it threatens the value of the rights sold to a publisher, the author will assist the publisher (at the publisher's expense).

Subsidiary rights include:
• Anthology and quotation rights
• Broadcast reading and audiobook rights
• Digital and electronic rights
• Dramatisation, film, documentary, television sound broadcasting video or other mechanical reproduction rights
• English language rights (royalty exclusive)
• First serial rights (first place e.g. in a magazine where an extract from an original Work is serialised or published)
• Large print, educational, reprint or paperback rights licensed to a book club or to another publisher
• Micrography reprography, merchandising and manufacturing rights
• Second serial rights (rights sold subsequent to the first serial rights, see above)
• Single-extract or digest or book condensation rights
• Translation rights (royalty exclusive)
• US rights (royalty exclusive)

Each set of rights will be subject to a royalty percentage, payable to the author when these rights have been exercised. Some rights are held back or retained by an agent or author, so they might be exploited at another time and be subject to negotiation with a third party after publication. These tend to be the potentially more lucrative rights if exploited, such as dramatisation and film, translation or audio. Some 'hybrid' authors will license print rights to a publisher but retain digital book rights to allow them to self-publish in that format; a contract would make clear in which territories each edition might be sold.

Practicalities

Delivery – this will include a realistic delivery date and the specifications as to what will be delivered in what format (e.g. complete digital manuscript), to what extent (70,000 words including any endmatter) and accompanied by any material (extracts, quotations) for which copyright might need to be cleared.

Payments

Advances The advance is an example of financial goodwill, a pact that author and editor have cemented through the contract to agree to work together and to make money from the activity. It is usually paid in two or three equal tranches, payable on signature of the contract, on delivery and approval of the final manuscript, and on first publication. The advance against royalties means a payment made before any actual revenue from sales of your book have been received.

Royalties are the fees paid to an author on the sale of copies of their book and are subject to sliding scales, so that as a book becomes more successful an author benefits more. As more and more copies are sold the investment the publisher made in producing the first print run will be recouped; subsequent runs might become very profitable for the publisher and rightly an agent will argue for an author to profit from this success too. Such rising royalty rates for a published price contract might look something like this:

• **on home sales**: 7.5 per cent of the published price on the first ten thousand (10,000) copies sold; 10 per cent of the published price up to twenty thousand (20,000) copies sold and 12.5 per cent of the published price on all copies sold thereafter, such royalty not to be deemed a precedent between the Publishers and Author or agent;

• **on home sales where the discount is 52.5 per cent or more**: four-fifths (4/5ths) of the prevailing royalty; on home sales where the discount is 60 per cent or more: three-fifths (3/5ths) of the prevailing rate.

Free and presentation copies will be provided to the author (anywhere between six and fifteen free copies) on publication and to potential reviewers as part of a promotional campaign; royalty payments are not made against these gratis copies. Authors may purchase copies of their own book at discount.

Payment process, accounting periods and other details about how and when the publisher will remunerate the author (or their agent on the author's behalf) will be included.

Publishing process

Author corrections and their proofreading responsibilities might be clearly laid out, covering what checking tasks an author will be expected to undertake and when and which might be carried out and paid for by the publisher, such as having an index prepared or clearing permissions for images or quotations. It might also include a clause in which the publisher 'reserves the right to charge the Author' for the cost of author corrections to page proofs if these are over and above the usual level of alterations. Such costs might be debited against the author's royalty account.

Promotion clauses advise that a publisher shall advertise, promote and market the Work as they deem appropriate 'in their sole discretion'. If you feel strongly as an author that you wish to be consulted about any aspect of promotion or cover design you could ask for such clauses to be modified. The most you are likely to get is an amendment that agrees an author will be 'consulted' and asked to 'agree' to the publisher's plan and that their agreement 'will not be unreasonably withheld'.

Publication date might not be firmly set when the contract is signed but the publisher's commissioning editor should have a clear idea of what quarter they would like the book to appear in. An agreement would usually stipulate that the book should be published within twelve months of date of delivery and acceptance 'unless prevented by circumstances over which they have no control or unless mutually agreed'.

New and updated editions for non-fiction titles might be referred to, defining what would constitute a 'new' rather than a 'revised' edition and how much new content it might include, say at least 10 per cent new material. The author would be offered first refusal on preparing a new edition, but the publisher would want to include a clause to allow them to ask another writer to complete such a project if they perceived there was a market for it, but the original author was unable or unwilling to take on the commission.

The contract should not daunt an author. It is supposed to be a joint declaration and not biased in favour of one party or the other.

By **Alysoun Owen**, Editor of the *Writers' & Artists' Yearbook* and author of the *Writers' & Artists' Guide to Getting Published* (Bloomsbury 2019).

Copyright Licensing Agency Ltd

The Copyright Licensing Agency (CLA) is a non-profit body established to help organisations to legally copy and share extracts from published works.

It is recognised by the government (www.gov.uk/copyright-licensing-agency-licence) as the collective licensing body for the reuse of text and images from books, journals and magazines.More information on collective licensing bodies can be found at: www.gov.uk/guidance/licensing-bodies-and-collective-management-organisations.

It licenses on behalf of its four members: ALCS (the Authors' Licensing and Collecting Society), PLS (Publishers' Licensing Services), DACS (The Design and Copyright Society) and PICSEL (Picture Industry Collecting Society for Effective Licensing).

CLA's licences permit limited copying, including photocopying, scanning and emailing of articles and extracts from books, journals and magazines, as well as digital copying from electronic publications, online titles and websites. CLA issues its licences to schools, further and higher education, businesses and government bodies. The money collected is distributed to the copyright owners to ensure that they are fairly rewarded for the use of their intellectual property. It gives licensees protection against the risk of copyright infringement and includes an indemnity against legal action, offering a simple solution to copyright compliance.

Why was CLA established?

CLA was set up in 1983 by its founding members, the ALCS (see page 715) and PLS (see page 719). CLA represents creators and publishers by licensing the copying of their work and promoting the role and value of copyright. It also collects money for visual artists and has two other collective management organisation members who represent visual artists; DACS (Design and Artists Copyright Society; page 717) and PICSEL (Picture Industry Collecting Society for Effective Licensing) distribute money from CLA licence fees to visual artists such as illustrators and photographers. By championing copyright it is helping to sustain creativity and maintain the incentive to produce new work.

> ### Further information
>
> **The Copyright Licensing Agency Ltd**
> 5th Floor, Shackleton House,
> 4 Battle Bridge Lane, London SE1 2HX
> *tel* 020-7400 3100
> *email* cla@cla.co.uk
> *website* www.cla.co.uk

How CLA helps creators and users of copyright work

CLA provides content users with access to millions of titles worldwide. In return, CLA ensures that creators, artists, photographers and writers, along with publishers, are paid royalties for the copying, sharing and re-use of limited extracts of their published work.

Through this collective licensing system CLA provides users with the simplest and most cost-effective means of obtaining authorisation for the use of their work.

CLA has licences which enable digitisation of existing print material, enabling users to scan and electronically send extracts from print copyright works as well as copy digital electronic and online publications, including websites.

Who is licensed?

CLA offers licences to three principal sectors:
• education (schools, further and higher education);
• government (central departments, local authorities, public bodies); and
• business (businesses, industry and the professions).

The licences meet the specific needs of each sector and user groups within each sector. Depending upon the requirement, there are both blanket and transactional licences available. Every licence allows copying from most print and digital books, journals, magazines and periodicals published in the UK.

The international dimension

Many countries have established equivalents to CLA and the number of such agencies is set to grow. Nearly all these agencies, including CLA, are members of the International Federation of Reproduction Rights Organisations (IFRRO).

Through reciprocal arrangements covering 38 overseas territories, including the USA, Canada and most EU countries, CLA's licences allow copying from an expanding list of international publications. CLA receives monies from these territories for the copying of UK material abroad, passing it on to UK rights holders.

Distribution of licence fees

The fees collected from licensees are forwarded to ALCS, PLS, DACS and PISCEL for distribution to publishers, writers and visual artists. The allocation of fees is based on subscriptions, library holdings and detailed surveys of copying activity (see www.cla.co.uk/who-we-represent and read the 'Distribution Model Report'). CLA has collected and distributed over £1.45 billion as royalties to copyright owners since 1983. For the year 2019/20, £76.8 million was paid to creators and publishers in the UK and abroad.

Copyright. Made simple

The CLA exists to simplify copyright for content users and copyright owners. They help their customers to legally access, copy and share published content while making sure copyright owners are paid royalties for the use of their work.

Their rights, licences and innovative digital services (including the Digital Content Store for Higher Education; and the Education Platform for UK schools) make it easy for content users to use and manage digitalised content and digital versions of books. By doing so they simplify access to the work of 100,000 authors, 25,000 visual artists and 3,500 publishers and play an important part in supporting the creative industries.

Authors' Licensing and Collecting Society

ALCS is the rights management society for UK writers.

ALCS is the largest writers' organisation in the UK with a membership of over 100,000. In the financial year of 2019/20, it paid 110,000 writers over £36.8 million (net) in royalties. Once you've paid your £36 lifetime membership fee, whatever you've earned in secondary royalties is paid into your bank account during twice yearly distributions. You can be part of this organisation which is committed to ensuring that writers' intellectual and moral rights are fully respected and fairly rewarded. ALCS represents all types of writers and includes educational, research and academic authors drawn from the professions - scriptwriters, adapters, playwrights, poets, editors and freelance journalists, across the print and broadcast media.

Established in 1977, ALCS (a non-profit company) was set up in the wake of the campaign to establish a Public Lending Right (see page 665) to help writers protect and exploit their collective rights. The organisation now represents the interests of all UK writers and aims to ensure that they are fairly compensated for any works that are copied, broadcast or recorded.

Internationally recognised as a leading authority on copyright matters and authors' interests, ALCS is committed to fostering an awareness of intellectual property issues among the writing community. It maintains a close watching brief on all matters affecting copyright, both in the UK and internationally, and makes regular representations to the UK government and the European Union.

ALCS collects fees that are difficult, time-consuming or legally impossible for writers and their representatives to claim on an individual basis, money that is nonetheless due to them. To date, it has distributed over £500 million in secondary royalties to writers. Over the years, ALCS has developed highly specialised knowledge and sophisticated systems that can track writers and their works against any secondary use for which they are due payment. A network of international contacts and reciprocal agreements with foreign collecting societies also ensures that UK writers are compensated for any similar use overseas.

The primary sources of fees due to writers are secondary royalties from the following:

Membership

Authors' Licensing and Collecting Society Ltd
5th Floor, Shackleton House,
4 Battle Bridge Lane, London SE1 2HX
tel 020-7264 5700
email alcs@alcs.co.uk
website www.alcs.co.uk
Chief Executive Owen Atkinson

Membership is open to all writers and successors to their estates at a one-off fee of £36. Members of the Society of Authors, the Writers' Guild of Great Britain, National Union of Journalists, Chartered Institute of Journalists and British Association of Journalists have free membership of ALCS. Operations are primarily funded through a commission levied on distributions and membership fees. The commission on funds generated for Ordinary members is currently 9.5%. Most writers will find that this, together with a number of other membership benefits, provides good value.

Law and copyright

Photocopying and scanning

The single largest source of income, this is administered by the Copyright Licensing Agency (CLA; see page 713). Created in 1982 by ALCS and the Publishers' Licensing Services (PLS), CLA grants licences to users for copying books and serials. This includes schools, colleges, universities, central and local government departments, as well as the British Library, businesses and other institutions. Licence fees are based on the number of people who benefit and the number of copies made. The revenue from this is then split between the rights holders: authors, publishers and artists. Money due to authors is transferred to ALCS for distribution. ALCS also receives photocopying payments from foreign sources.

Foreign Public Lending Right

The Public Lending Right (PLR) system pays authors whose books are borrowed from public libraries. Through reciprocal agreements, ALCS members receive payment through a number of overseas Public Lending Right (PLR) schemes, currently from Germany, Belgium, the Netherlands, France, Austria, Estonia and Ireland. Please note that ALCS does not administer the UK Public Lending Right; this is managed directly by the UK PLR Office (see page 665).

Simultaneous cable retransmission

This involves the simultaneous showing of one country's television signals in another country, via a cable network. Cable companies pay a central collecting organisation a percentage of their subscription fees, which must be collectively administered. This sum is then divided by the rights holders. ALCS receives the writers' share for British programmes containing literary and dramatic material and distributes it to them.

Educational recording

ALCS, together with the main broadcasters and rights holders, set up the Educational Recording Agency (ERA) in 1989 to offer licences to educational establishments. ERA collects fees from the licensees and pays ALCS the amount due to writers for their literary works.

Other sources of income include a blank tape levy and small, miscellaneous literary rights.

Tracing authors

ALCS is dedicated to protecting and promoting authors' rights and enabling writers to maximise their income. It is committed to ensuring that royalties due to writers are efficiently collected and speedily distributed to them. One of its greatest challenges is finding some of the writers for whom it holds funds and ensuring that they claim their money.

Any published author or broadcast writer could have some funds held by ALCS for them. It may be a nominal sum or it could run into several thousand pounds. Either call or visit the ALCS website – see **Membership** box for contact details.

DACS (Design and Artists Copyright Society)

Established by artists for artists, DACS is the UK's leading visual artists' rights management organisation.

As a not-for-profit organisation, DACS translates rights into revenues and recognition for a wide spectrum of visual artists. It collects and distributes royalties to visual artists and their estates through its different services, including Payback, Artist's Resale Right, Copyright Licensing and Artimage – in addition to lobbying, advocacy and legal advice for visual artists.

Contact details

DACS
33 Old Bethnal Green Road, London E2 6AA
tel 020-7336 8811
email info@dacs.org.uk
website www.dacs.org.uk

DACS is part of an international network of rights management organisations. Today DACS acts as a trusted broker for over 100,000 artists worldwide and in 2018 it distributed £18 million in royalties to artists and estates. See website for more information about DACS and its services.

Payback

Each year DACS pays a share of royalties to visual artists whose work has been reproduced in UK magazines and books or broadcast on UK television channels. DACS operates this service for situations where it would be impractical or near impossible for an artist to license their rights on an individual basis, for example when a university student wants to photocopy pages from a book that features their work.

Artist's Resale Right

The Artist's Resale Right entitles artists to a royalty each time their work is resold for €1,000 or more by an auction house, gallery or dealer. DACS ensures artists receive their royalties from qualifying sales not just in the UK but also from other countries in the European Economic Area (EEA). Since 1 January 2012 in the UK, artists' heirs and beneficiaries can now benefit from these royalties. (See website for details of eligibility criteria.)

Copyright Licensing

This service benefits artists and their estates when their work is reproduced for commercial purposes, for example on t-shirts or greetings cards, in a book or on a website. DACS can take care of everything on behalf of the artist, ensuring terms, fees and contractual arrangements are all in order and in their best interests. Artists who use this service are also represented globally through the DACS international network of rights management organisations.

Copyright facts

• Copyright is a right granted to visual artists under law.
• Copyright in all artistic works is established from the moment of creation – the only qualification is that the work must be original.

Law and copyright

• There is no registration system in the UK; copyright comes into operation automatically and lasts the lifetime of the visual artist plus a period of 70 years after their death.
• After death, copyright is usually transferred to the visual artist's heirs or beneficiaries. When the 70-year period has expired, the work then enters the public domain and no longer benefits from copyright protection.
• The copyright owner has the exclusive right to authorise the reproduction (or copy) of a work in any medium by any other party.
• Any reproduction can only take place with the copyright owner's consent.
• Permission is usually granted in return for a fee, which enables the visual artist to derive some income from other people using his or her work.
• If a visual artist is commissioned to produce a work, he or she will usually retain the copyright unless an agreement is signed which specifically assigns the copyright. When visual creators are employees and create work during the course of their employment, the employer retains the copyright in those works.

See also...
• *Freelancing for beginners*, page 475

Law and copyright

Publishers' Licensing Services

Publishers' Licensing Services' (PLS) mission is to provide efficient and effective copyright and licensing services to support publishers in providing access to their content.

PLS manages the interests of publishers in licensing the copying of extracts from books, journals, magazines and websites. PLS provides various other services, including PLS® Permissions, which streamlines the process of seeking and managing permissions, and Access to Research, which enables free access in public libraries to academic journal articles.

A not-for-profit organisation, PLS has been serving the collective interests of publishers since 1981. It is owned and governed by four publisher trade associations.

Key activities
• Collective licensing

Collective licensing offers a simple and cost-effective solution for those who wish to copy from published materials without breaking the law, and for rights-holders where direct licensing is inefficient and not cost-effective.

PLS licenses the rights granted to it by publishersthrough two licensing organisations. Copyright Licensing Agency (CLA) licenses organisations in the education, public and business sectors, allowing them to copy extracts from a broad range of titles in return for a licence fee. CLA also has reciprocal agreements with equivalent organisations around the world. CLA is able, therefore, to collect licensing revenue for the use of UK publications abroad. PLS licenses some magazine publishers' rights to businesses and government through NLA media access. PLS distributes the resulting licensing revenue to publishers according to the usage data collected from users. PLS made over £36m distributable to publishers in 2020/21.

> **Contact details**
>
> **PLS**
> 5th Floor, Shackleton House, Hay's Galleria,
> London SE1 2HX
> *tel* 020-7079 5930
> *email* pls@pls.org.uk
> *website* www.pls.org.uk

• Permissions

PLS Permissions is a suite of services designed to improve response times for permission requests, decrease the administrative burden of permissions, and reach new markets. The suite comprises:

PermissionsDirect, which enables publishers to manage their permissions more efficiently using PLSclear;

PermissionsAssist, a service by which publishers outsource their permissions management to PLS;

PLSclear, a free service that enables editors and authors seeking to reuse published content to request permission from publishers quickly and easily.

PLS Permissions was launched in 2017. The service is now a firmly established part of the permissions landscape with increasing numbers of permissions-seekers bookmarking PLSclear.com as their first port of call and a steady flow of publishers signing up to the service over the course of the year. PLS has an example of a publisher fully engaged with the service reducing permissions processing time from six months to two weeks, with clear benefits for both the publisher and requestors.

Find out more at www.PLS-Permissions.com.

• Access to research

The Access to Research service provides free access to over 30 million academic articles in public libraries across the UK. More than 98% of UK local authorities have signed up.

Access to Research was launched in response to a key recommendation of the Finch Group, namely that the major journal publishers should grant public libraries a licence to provide free walk-in access to their academic articles. Access to Research is the result of a unique collaboration between publishers, who have made their journal content available for free to UK libraries and librarians. The content is searchable through the Summon discovery service, generously provided by ProQuest.

Find out more at www.accesstoresearch.org.uk.

See also...
- *Authors' Licensing and Collecting Society*, page 715
- *Copyright Licensing Agency Ltd*, page 713
- *UK copyright law and publishing rights*, page 703

Money, tax and benefits
Managing your finances: a guide for writers

Chartered accountants Jonathan and Louise Ford of Writers Tax Limited set out a clear view of the various financial issues that a writer needs to understand and consider at each stage of their writing career, with helpful links and valuable advice.

In some ways the financial issues of being a writer are no different to pursuing any other occupation. You earn money for your skill, you deduct the costs you have incurred earning your money, and you pay tax on what's left. However, there are several factors that, in combination, make the situation of a writer unique; many writers have income from multiple sources, as well as overseas tax issues and matters concerning copyright.

We'll look at the different stages of a writer's career and the financial aspects s/he may need to consider as their career develops: 1) getting started – unpaid writing done for love not money; 2) paid writing often running alongside traditional employed income; 3) paid writing as main source of income; 4) lifelong considerations.

Stage 1: getting started

When you're at an early stage of your writing career and not earning any money from it, there is little you need to do to stay compliant. However, there are still some important things you can consider.

Setting up a dormant limited company

If you are planning to write a book and you would like the royalty income of that book to be held in a limited company, then consider setting up a company even before you start writing. This will allow you to write the book on behalf of your company. If you wait to set the company up until the book is complete, and publishers are interested, then you would have to transfer the copyright of the book to the company at market value; this could cause issues in terms of valuing the copyright and can create a tax problem that

Do I need an accountant?

If your financial situation is straightforward, there may be no need for you to appoint an accountant. If you are employed, then PAYE usually does a reasonable job of collecting the right amount of tax. Your writing income may be quite modest so it should be straightforward to deal with and – if the numbers are not very big – it may not cause too many issues if you get things wrong. To help you as your career develops, a good accountant can do the following:

- Deal with HMRC on your behalf;
- Submit your tax returns on time, so you don't get penalties for being late;
- Make sure you are claiming for the things you can claim for (and not claiming for things you shouldn't);
- Advise you on ways of saving tax legitimately;
- Help you to keep your records accurately;
- Help you to avoid nasty surprises and unexpected tax bills;
- Be on hand for all your tax related questions.

Anybody can call themselves an accountant, even if they have no qualifications or experience. Try to choose someone who is a member of a professional accountancy body, such as ICAEW, ICAS, AAT, ACCA or CIOT. It is also worth getting recommendations from other writers. Social media groups can be a useful source when looking for accountants who act for lots of writers and understand their needs.

could have been avoided. To decide whether this is right for you, you need to weigh up the cost and hassle of having a dormant limited company against the possible future advantages.

Creative averaging

There are a number of conditions you need to satisfy to be eligible for creative averaging; more details are available on HMRC Helpsheet HS234. One such condition is that you cannot use your first year of trading as part of any creative averaging calculation. Using the example given in the box, Theo would need to be submitting information to HMRC about his writing business from the 2018/19 tax year to be able to claim Creative Averaging in 2020/21.

Loss relief against other income

It is possible for a sole trader to make a loss and to set that loss against other income. This can be beneficial for tax reasons. For example, if an author makes a loss of £5,000 and they also have *employed income* of £30,000, they could offset the £5,000 loss against their employed income so that they only have to pay tax on £25,0-00. To be able to offset losses against other income, you need to be able to show HMRC that the loss has been incurred on a commercial basis with a view to making a profit. A vague idea that one day you might write a book on Greece would not be sufficient evidence to get a tax deduction on the costs of your holiday.

Creative averaging example

Theo earns nothing in the tax year 2019/20 while he is writing his novel.

In 2020/21 his book is published and he makes a profit of £25,000. Without creative averaging his tax bill in 2019/20 would be nothing, but in 2020/21 he would owe £2,500 income tax and £1,553.60 in National Insurance – a total of £4,053.60.

If he elects to use creative averaging, his £25,000 profit would be split across both tax years, giving him a National Insurance bill of £507.12 in 2019/20 and of £428.60 in 2020/21. By choosing to use creative averaging, Theo would have saved £3,117.88 over the two tax years.

Pre-trading expenses

If you haven't been reporting expenditure to HMRC as losses, then it is still possible to get tax relief for 'pre-trading expenditure'. The relief allows you to claim for expenditure incurred within seven years of starting to trade and, in effect, gives tax relief as if it was incurred on the first day of trading. The 'wholly and exclusive' rule will still apply, so it is important to be able to link the expenditure you are claiming to the income you are receiving. The stronger the link, the more likely HMRC are to accept it. In order to maximise any possible pre-trading expenditure claim, it is important to try and keep records and receipts *just in case* you might need them in the future.

Stage 2: paid writing as additional income

Most writers at this stage will still be running their writing business as a sole trader (or freelancer – there is no difference in terms of tax). Legally you don't need to do anything to set up as a sole trader. As soon as you start writing with a view to making a profit, you've become a sole trader. The tax system is very flexible. You can have a part-time employed job, be a partner in a bookshop and be a published author, all at the same time. Important things to consider at this stage are:

Registering with HMRC

If you earn more than £1,000 from self-employment you need to register as a sole trader with HMRC. You can do this at www.gov.uk/register-for-self-assessment/self-employed. You need to register by 5 October in your second tax year (tax years run from 6 April to 5 April).

For example, if you started on 20 November 2020 (tax year 2020/21) then you would need to register with HMRC by 5 October 2021 (tax year 2021/22). You would then get sent a tax return to complete by 31 January 2022 if filing online or 31 October 2021 if filing by paper.

Submitting a tax return

The tax system is called Self Assessment and this means that it is necessary for you to assess what rules and regulations apply to your tax position. There are a range of penalties that HMRC levy and, although it is possible in certain circumstances to appeal the penalties, it is well worth doing all you can to avoid them in the first place.

Keeping records

A self-employed person needs to keep records for at least 5 years from 31 January following the tax year they relate to. For example, if you have transactions in the tax year to 5 April 2021, you need to keep your records until 31 January 2027. You can keep records digitally or on paper. You should keep copies of bank statements, contracts, receipts for expenditure you are claiming for and any invoices you have raised. It is also worth keeping a note of any unusual non-business transactions. If you win £1,000 at the races or get a generous gift from Aunt Ethel, you want to be able to prove this wasn't undeclared income from writing.

It is usually a good idea to have a separate business bank account that you use just for your writing income. This will help to keep things organised and could give you a little more privacy, as your accountant – and possibly HMRC – don't have to look through all your private outgoings.

HMRC Self Assessment penalties

Late filing

Up to 3 months late £100, plus

after 3 months £10 per day for 90 days, plus

after 3 months penalties accrue at regular intervals based on 5% of the tax due or £300 – whichever is the greater.

You can estimate your penalty at www.gov.uk/estimate-self-assessment-penalties.

Late payment of tax

5% of tax due if not paid within 30 days with further 5% penalties every 6 months.

Interest is also charged (currently 2.7%).

Incorrect returns

Penalties are charged for tax returns that HMRC consider to be incorrect. There is an appeals process. The penalties are all behaviour based and are as follows:

• Careless errors – 0% to 30% of the additional tax due.

• Deliberate errors – 20% to 70% of the additional tax due.

• Deliberate and concealed errors – 30% to 100% of the additional tax due.

Money, tax and benefits

Claiming expenses

A writer pays tax on their profit. Profit is income less allowable costs, often referred to as 'expenses'. Sometimes people talk about things being 'tax deductible', which means they can be deducted from your profit before calculating the tax bill, rather than being deducted from your tax bill. For example, if a higher-rate tax payer spends £100 on stationery, this is tax deductible and so it will reduce her profits by £100 and save income tax at 40%, i.e. £40.

Trading allowance

You can claim a £1,000 Trading Allowance against your self-employed income instead of claiming for expenses you have incurred. You cannot claim the Trading Allowance and expenses at the same time. Claiming the Trading Allowance would be suitable when the Trading Allowance is more than the expenses incurred. However, you can't use the Trading Allowance to turn your profit into a loss. There are also restrictions to prevent you from using the Trading Allowance if the income is received from a business controlled by you, or by someone connected to you.

What can you claim for?

The rule is that an expense must be 'wholly and exclusively' for the purpose of your business. Typical costs are:
- Accountancy
- Advertising costs
- Agent commission
- Bank charges
- Computing and IT costs
- Printing, postage and stationery
- Professional subscriptions
- Internet and telephone
- Software subscriptions
- Research costs
- Travel

Some costs may have an element of private use. In this case, HMRC will allow the cost to be apportioned provided you can justify the calculation. For example:
- Motor expenses – may be apportioned according to business use.
- Home as office – apportioned according to rooms and time spent in use.

Alternatively, you may be able to use HMRC Simplified Expenses. You can find more details at www.gov.uk/simpler-income-tax-simplified-expenses.

Cloud bookkeeping

Recent years have seen the development of relatively cheap, simple bookkeeping packages like Xero and Quickbooks. These allow you to link up your business bank account to your accounting records, so you can quickly and accurately keep track of your income and expenditure. They have the advantage of being regularly backed up, less prone to error, and easy to use. You can also store your receipts and paperwork digitally. As the UK moves towards a new system of reporting called Making Tax Digital from April 2023, it will become more important to be able to easily record and report your income.

Prizes and bursaries

There are many prizes and awards open to authors and other creatives, and entering competitions or seeking awards is a normal part of these professions and a good way for them to obtain extra income from their work. Such prizes are usually taxable. However, there are exceptions. When a prize is unsolicited, and awarded as a mark of honour, distinction or public esteem in recognition of outstanding achievement in a particular field, it won't be taxable. For example, if your publisher or agent enters you for a competition without your knowledge or consent, any prize money received should not be taxable.

Payments on account

For self-employed people the tax system can require payments on account of tax to be made every six months. Each payment on account is half of the previous year's tax bill.

For example: Jo's first year of trading is the tax year 2020/21; she owes tax of £4,000 for the 2020/21 tax year which is due for payment by 31 January 2022. Also, on 31 January 2022 she'll need to pay a payment on account of £2,000 towards her 2021/22 tax bill. She'll have to make a further payment of £2,000 in July 2022. Her actual tax bill for 2021/22 is £5,000. In January 2023 her payments will be:

	£
Tax due for tax year 2021/22	5,000
Less:	
Payment on account - paid 31 January 2022	2,000
Payment on account - paid 31 July 2022	2,000
Balance for 2021/22	1,000
Add:	
Payment on account for 2022/23 (50% of £5,000)	2,500
Total due 31 January 2023	3,500

When income is rising, payments on account can catch out the unwary, as each January there is both a shortfall of tax and a new, higher payment on account to pay. A sensible approach is to save for your tax throughout the year and to complete your tax return early in the tax year, so you have plenty of notice if the bill is higher than expected.

When income is falling (or ceasing) then it is possible to make a claim to HMRC to reduce payments on account so that you don't pay tax in advance that is more than necessary. If the payments on account you make are more than your tax bill, these will be offset against your next payments on account or refunded to you.

Setting up a limited company as a 'money box'

If you already have a paid job, then it's possible that your additional income from writing may take your total income into a higher tax band. If you don't need the money now, setting up a limited company could mean that the company pays corporation tax at a lower rate.

For example, Jamie earns £50,000 through his employment; he also receives £1,820 in Child Benefit in respect of his two children. He earns a further £10,000 in profit as a writer. He doesn't need to access the additional money now and is happy to leave it in his company. His tax liability as a sole trader can be compared with that of the limited company as follows:

Sole trader	£
Income tax on £10,000 @ 40%	4,000
High Income Child Benefit Tax Charge	1,820
Total due	5,820

Limited company	£
Corporation tax on £10,000 @ 19%	1,900
Total due	1,900

Although this is an extreme example, it shows that through using a limited company Jamie has saved £3,920 of tax on £10,000 of income. Once Jamie wants to take the money out of the company, it will be taxable on him personally, but he can control the amount paid so that it is covered by his personal allowance entirely or subject to a lower rate of tax than he is paying now. If Jamie's plans are to build up a savings buffer, so that one day he can take the plunge and become a full-time writer, then this could be of real benefit.

Stage 3: writing as main source of income

Typically, a writer at this stage will either be self-employed or trade through a limited company. A limited company has to be 'incorporated' at Companies House and, once it is set up, it exists as a legal entity. It can enter into contracts, have a bank account, and exist without you. It is possible to trade both as a sole trader and through a limited company. It may even be the case that an author has some of their books taxed as a sole trader and other titles taxed within a limited company.

Issues on incorporation

If you do trade through a limited company, it is important to ensure that the underlying paperwork is correct. Here are some issues to bear in mind:
• For a company to receive copyright income, it must be legally entitled to the income. This can be achieved by ensuring the company exists before the book has been written and a service contract is in place between the director (i.e. the author) and the company.
• It isn't sufficient to simply 'bank' any proceeds into your company. All contracts need to be properly drawn up in the company's name.

IR35

IR35 was introduced in April 2000 to stop the practice of employees setting up a limited company (a 'personal service company') and invoicing their employer for their work rather than being paid as an employee. This practice led to a large tax saving for both the employer and the employee.

IR35 only applies to limited companies, so a writer who is trading as a sole trader can ignore it. From April 2021 both public entities and larger private companies will have to look at the status of people working through personal service companies and, if necessary, deduct tax and National Insurance.

For most writers operating through a personal service company, it will be clear that they are not working for anyone as disguised employment. For other writers the situation may be more uncertain. For example, a copywriter with their own company providing weekly content for a client who describes them as their 'Content Manager', pays them a regular salary, expects them to attend meetings on site and doesn't allow a substitute, may be caught by the IR35 rules.

The IR35 rules are complex and, if caught by the rules, your limited company has to pay out most of the money it receives as a salary to the employee – together with Employers National Insurance.

Specialist help should be sought if you think your company may be affected by IR35.

• If you simply give your copyright to your company, it can create a tax issue; HMRC will expect you to pay income tax on the market value of the gift and will also expect the company to pay tax on the income it receives. In effect, the same income could be taxed twice.

• It is possible to sell the copyright to the company. This results in a better tax position, as the company would be able to get some tax relief for the cost of the copyright, but it will require a valuation of the copyright which brings with it costs and some uncertainty.

Sole trader or limited company – the key differences

Sole trader	Limited company
Starting up	
Nothing legal required	Must be incorporated at Companies House
Closing down	
Nothing legal required	Must be formally struck off at Companies House
Legal protection	
None – you and the business are one and the same	Limited liability (but watch out for contracts that pass on liabilities to directors)
If you are sued, then all your assets are at stake	If the company is sued, then only the assets of the company are at stake
Tax on profits	
Income tax paid depending on total earnings from all sources in the year; rates may be 0%, 20%, 40% or 45% depending on income	Corporation tax paid. Rate is currently 19%, although this is due to rise in 2023
Tax on profits extracted	
Not applicable – you pay tax on profit whether extracted or not	Dividend tax due at rates of 0%, 7.5%, 32.5% or 38.1% depending on income
National Insurance	
Pay Class 2 National Insurance and Class 4 National Insurance	Only pay National Insurance on salaries paid to employees if they earn over the limit
Reporting	
Must complete an individual Self Assessment tax return each year	Must file accounts each year with Companies House. Must submit a Confirmation Statement each year to Companies House. Must file a corporation tax return each year with HMRC. May have to run a payroll and report to HMRC. Likely that director/shareholder will have to complete an individual Self Assessment tax return each year
Separate business bank account	
Advisable	Essential
VAT	
Can be VAT registered; it is a person that is VAT registered, not a business, which may have unintended consequences	Can be VAT registered
Creative averaging	
Can be used	Cannot be used
Why choose this one?	
Simple; cheap; you want to take all the money out of business when it's earned, not concerned about legal liability	Save tax if you don't require all the money or are able to take advantage of splitting income; provides legal liability protection

Money, tax and benefits

• Once your company owns the copyright, royalty income is 'locked' into being paid to the company. If you wished to own the copyright personally, it would need to be transferred out of the company at a fair value. You may find you have a company for a much longer time than you first anticipate, because it may not be practical to close it down until the copyright has a negligible value.

VAT

VAT (Value Added Tax) is a tax that businesses are required to charge their customers for goods or services. A writer is no different from any other business and therefore must charge VAT when supplying writing services. The standard UK rate of VAT is currently 20%. VAT is a complicated subject and much of it is beyond the scope of this book. However, there are some key things a writer should be aware of.

A VAT-registered business usually submits a quarterly VAT return within one month and seven days of the end of the VAT quarter. Any VAT due is then paid by the same deadline. Being VAT-registered is not entirely bad news; a VAT-registered business has to charge VAT on their relevant services, but they can also claim back VAT on things they buy for their business. For example, in the VAT quarter ending 31 December 2020 a writer gets a publishing deal for £10,000 plus £2,000 of VAT. Their agent charges them £1,500 plus £300 VAT, and they buy a computer for writing for £500 plus £100 VAT. They would submit a VAT return to HMRC by 7 February 2021 and pay over £1,600, as follows:

	£
VAT charged	2,000
Less:	
VAT on agent's fees	300
VAT on computer	100
Paid to HMRC	1,600

Although this may make you feel worse off, especially when you are paying £1,600 to HMRC, you are in fact better off by £400 – this being the difference between the VAT you have been paid and the VAT you have paid out.

VAT registration threshold

A business needs to register for VAT when the level of sales exceeds the VAT threshold. The VAT threshold is currently £85,000 and it applies to the last 12 months. To know whether you need to register or not, you have to look back at your cumulative sales over the last 12 months and, if these exceed the VAT threshold, you must register. You are also required to register if you believe your sales in the next 30 days alone will be more than the VAT threshold – for example if you bag a big publishing deal.

Some writers will make an early 'protective' VAT registration, so that they know they are registered and don't have to worry about tripping over the VAT threshold. It is important to remember that the turnover figure is not necessarily the amount you receive. For example, a writer gets an advance of £10,000; their agent deducts 15% plus their VAT and so the writer only receives £8,200. The figure that counts towards the VAT threshold is £10,000.

Finally, you do not need to include employment income in your turnover calculation or non-UK income (such as royalties from Amazon).

Voluntary registration

You can voluntarily register for VAT even if your sales are under the VAT registration threshold. The reason you may want to do this is to recover the VAT you are being charged – typically by your agent. For example, a writer gets a publishing deal for £25,000; their agent charges 15% commission plus VAT. If they are not VAT-registered, they'll lose the agent VAT of £750 but, if they are VAT-registered, they'd be able to recover this.

Being in the 'VAT club' will allow you to recover VAT on all your other business expenditure, such as computer costs and accountancy fees. Whether it is a good idea to register early depends on your circumstances. If you're not incurring much VAT, then it may not be worth the hassle.

What to include in your sales for VAT

You need to include all your UK sales and any foreign sales collected by your UK publisher. You can exclude any direct foreign sales (such as Amazon self-publishing or sales you or your agent have agreed with a foreign publisher). If you're a sole trader, you can exclude any employed income. But, if you are self-employed as something else too (e.g. you're both a plumber and a writer), you need to aggregate both sets of income. The VAT registration belongs to the *person* not the *business*.

Claiming back VAT

When you first register for VAT, you can reclaim VAT on goods purchased up to four years prior to registration provided those goods are still held when registration takes place. VAT on services supplied in the six months prior to registration may also be reclaimed. To claim VAT you'll need a valid VAT receipt; a credit card receipt isn't enough, and a VAT inspector will disallow any expenditure that you can't produce a valid VAT receipt for – even if it's obvious that you would have paid VAT.

Not all expenditure has VAT charged on it:

Usually has VAT	Usually has no VAT
Agent commission	Trains, planes and taxis
Accountancy fees	Software subscriptions from overseas
Stationery	Postage
Computers and UK software	Entertainment
Internet and mobile phone	Insurance

Withholding tax and double taxation relief

Writers will often receive some or, in the case of an author selling via Amazon Kindle Direct Publishing (KDP), most of their income from an overseas source. Many foreign

Money, tax and benefits

Coronavirus

There is a substantial amount of help and advice through the government website, www.gov.uk/coronavirus. Due to the rapidly changing situation, this should be the place to refer to for up-to-date information.

Government support falls broadly into two categories:
- **Direct grants** – grants (like the Self-Employment Income Support Scheme) are taxable as if they are normal trading income. The grant should be recognised as income in the year it is received.
- **Deferring payment** – many people have struggled to pay their tax bills on time. Various schemes are in place to help and it is best to address the problem with HMRC.

countries will charge a 'withholding tax' on such royalty payments, for example 30% in the case of the USA. Once withholding tax is paid, it is often not cost effective to try to recover it from the country in question, as doing so may require local professional advice and tax returns to be submitted to the country in question.

It is often possible to avoid any withholding tax being deducted in the first instance by completing the information required by the overseas publisher, so they don't have to apply withholding tax. Amazon KDP has an online tax interview to make it as easy as possible for you to comply. Other publishers in other countries will have to follow their own rules and will often ask for a Certificate of Residence to prove you are a UK tax payer. There are more details on applying for a Certificate of Residence at www.gov.uk/guidance/get-a-certificate-of-residence.

If you do suffer withholding tax, then it may be possible to use the foreign tax you have paid to offset against your tax liability on the same income when you complete your tax return. This may give you a worse result, though, as you will pay tax at the highest rate between the two countries. For example, if you are a UK basic rate tax payer and suffer 30% in the US, that will cover the 20% tax you would have to pay in the UK. You would not get a refund of the additional 10%. But, if you are a higher rate tax payer paying 40% tax, you would have to pay the additional 10% tax in the UK.

Stage 4: Lifelong considerations

As a writer's career becomes more established, there are other financial considerations.

Pensions

State Pension

To qualify for the new State Pension, you need a minimum of 10 qualifying years and at least 35 qualifying years to receive the maximum payments. You can check your pension entitlement online at www.gov.uk/check-state-pension. If you have gaps in your pension contribution history, then you can consider making voluntary contributions.

Writers' Guild Pension Fund

For their members writing for TV, radio and film, WGGB (Writers' Guild of Great Britain) have negotiated agreements with the BBC, ITV and PACT so that pension contributions are made to the Writers' Guild Pension Fund. In return for the writer making a contribution to the fund, the production company will also make a contribution, in addition to the writer's fee. More details are available from WGGB (see page 512 for contact details).

Private pensions

If you have been employed, you may have an occupational pension from your employment in place. Most writers who have been self-employed will depend upon their own pension arrangements using 'defined contribution' schemes. Contributions to a private pension by an individual are made net of basic rate income tax. This means that a contribution of £80 actually means the amount invested is £100, with £20 being claimed by the pension company from the Government. A higher-rate tax payer would save another £20 in income tax, making the cost of putting £100 into a pension just £60. There are rules regarding how much you can invest each year and many people will need professional advice as to what scheme they invest in.

Insurances

Being a self-employed writer does mean that you don't have the same safety net that many employees may have. It is sensible to think about how you and your family would manage if you died or, through injury or illness, were unable to continue to earn a living. There are insurance policies that are available to help.

- **Life insurance** can provide a lump sum or a monthly income for a period of time if you die.
- **Critical illness insurance** can provide a lump sum or a monthly income for a period of time if you are diagnosed with a critical illness.
- **Income protection insurance** can provide a monthly income if you are unable to work due to ill health.

Wills

Making a will is important for a number of reasons. Amongst other things, you can specify who inherits your assets, make tax efficient choices, and provide instructions as to who looks after your minor children. A writer also needs to consider what happens with any copyright they hold as part of their estate. Copyright can last up to 70 years after death, so it may represent a valuable asset. You may also have particular instructions as to what happens to your personal papers and unpublished works. It is also worth thinking about what happens with digital assets such as blogs, social media accounts, online videos, and access to cloud storage services like Dropbox. A bit of forward planning may save a lot of trouble for the people dealing with your estate.

Further advice: useful websites

HMRC
www.gov.uk/government/organisations/hm-revenue-customs

Institute of Chartered Accountants in England and Wales
www.icaew.com

Institute of Chartered Accountants Scotland
www.icas.com

These author associations offer support and advice on financial matters to their members.

National Union of Journalists
www.nuj.org.uk (see page 528)

Society of Authors
www.societyofauthors.org (see page 509)

Writers' Guild of Great Britain
https://writersguild.org.uk (see page 512)

Accountancy and business software tools include:

Sage
www.sage.com/en-gb/cp/accounting

Quickbooks
https://quickbooks.intuit.com/uk

Xero
www.xero.com/uk

Jonathan Ford BSC FCA MSWW and **Louise Ford** BA FCA are the directors of Writers Tax Ltd, a firm of chartered accountants that specialises in helping authors, scriptwriters and other professional writers with their tax and accountancy needs, which they established in 2020. They both qualified as chartered accountants with Price Waterhouse in Liverpool. Jonathan worked at Grant Thornton and later as Financial Controller at Mersey TV before setting up his own company. See their website https://writers.tax for more information.

Money, tax and benefits

National Insurance contributions

Sarah Bradford sets out the facts about National Insurance, explaining the principle that underlies it, the various classes of contribution payable by workers, both employed and self-employed, the related benefit entitlements, and information on current rates and earnings thresholds.

Nature of National Insurance contributions

The payment of National Insurance contributions secures access to the state pension and to contributory benefits. This is the contributory principle of National Insurance. National Insurance contributions are payable by employed earners and their employers and also by self-employed earners. People who do not have any earnings or whose earnings are not sufficient to trigger a liability to pay National Insurance contributions can choose to pay National Insurance contributions voluntarily to maintain their contributions record.

If sufficient National Insurance contributions of the right type are paid for a tax year, the year will be a qualifying year for National Insurance purposes. A person needs 35 qualifying years in order to receive the full state pension when they reach state pension age. Where a person has at least ten qualifying years, they will receive a reduced state pension.

Classes of National Insurance

There are various different classes of National Insurance contribution. The class (or classes) that you pay will depend on whether you are an employed earner, a self-employed earner, an employer or a voluntary contributor. Contributions may be earnings-related, payable on profits or payable at a flat rate, depending on the class.

The different classes of contribution are shown in the box below. Class 1, 2 and 4 contributions are only payable once earnings exceed certain thresholds and limits. The rates and thresholds applying for 2021/22 are set out in the box on page 736.

Contributions payable by writers and artists

As for other earners, the class of National Insurance payable by writers and artists depends on whether they are a self-employed earner or an employed earner. This is not something

Classes of National Insurance

Nature of contribution	Payable by
Class 1 Earnings-related	Employed earners (primary Class 1 contributions) Employer (secondary Class 1 contributions)
Class 1A Earnings-related	Employer on taxable benefits in kind and taxable termination payments and sporting testimonials
Class 1B Earnings-related	Employer on items included within a PAYE Settlement Agreement and on the tax due under that agreement
Class 2 Flat rate	Self-employed earners
Class 3 Flat rate	Voluntary contributions
Class 3A Variable amount	Payable between 12 October 2015 and 5 April 2017 voluntarily by those who reached state pension age before 6 April 2016 to boost their state pension
Class 4 Profits-related	Self-employed earners

that they can choose – it will depend on the facts of the engagement. It is important that the employment status of the writer or artist is categorised correctly as this will affect not only what class (and therefore how) they pay, but also what benefits they are entitled to.

Categorisation – employed earner v self-employed earner

To ensure that writers and artists pay the correct class of National Insurance contributions, it is important they are correctly categorised. Employed earners will pay Class 1 National Insurance contributions, whereas self-employed earners will pay Class 2 and Class 4 contributions.

A worker's categorisation depends on the characteristics of the engagement. In many cases, it will be clear whether a worker is an employed earner or a self-employed earner. For example, a writer who is employed by a publishing firm and has a contract of employment will be an employed earner and will pay Class 1 National Insurance contributions on their earnings, whereas a freelance writer who undertakes commissions for a variety of people and is paid a fee for each commission will be a self-employed earner and will pay Class 2 and Class 4 contributions.

Characteristics of employment

The following characteristics apply to an engagement where the worker is an employee:
• the person is required to work regularly unless they are unwell or on leave;
• they are expected to work a minimum number of hours a week and expect to be paid for the time that they work;
• a manager or supervisor is responsible for their workload, and will say when a job should be finished or how it should be done;
• they must do the work themselves – they can't send someone else to do it instead;
• the business deducts tax and National Insurance from their pay;
• they are entitled to paid holiday;
• they are entitled to statutory payments;
• they can join the business' pensions scheme;
• they are subject to grievance and disciplinary procedures;
• the contract sets out the procedure applying in the event of redundancy;
• they work at the business premises or at a location specified by the business;
• they only work for that business or, if they have another job, it is completely separate;
• the offer letter and contract refer to the 'employee' and the 'employer'.

For example, a staff writer who is paid a salary and contracted to work 35 hours a week would be an employed earner.

Characteristics of self-employment

The following characteristics indicate that the writer or artist is a self-employed earner:
• they are in business for themselves and are responsible for the success or failure of the business and can make a profit or a loss;
• they decide what work they take on and where and how they do it;
• they can hire someone else to do the work;
• they are responsible for fixing unsatisfactory work in their own time;
• they agree a fixed price for a job – the fee is the same regardless of how long it takes them to do the work;

• they use their own money to buy any equipment needed and to cover the running costs of the business;

• they work for more than one client.

A writer who is commissioned to write specific articles for different publications and who works for a number of publishers, being paid a fee for each article, would be a self-employed earner.

Marginal cases

It will not always be clear whether a writer or artist is an employed earner or a self-employed earner. In this situation, it is necessary to look at the overall picture and see whether, on balance, the writer or artist is employed or self-employed. It should be noted that there is not one single definitive test, rather a question of seeing what characteristics of employment and what characteristics of self-employment are present.

In reaching a decision, the following factors need to be considered:

• The nature of the contract and the written terms – a contract for *services* indicates employment and a contract of *service* indicates self-employment.

• The nature of the engager's business and the nature of the job.

• Right of substitution – a right to send a substitute indicates self-employment.

• Mutuality of obligation – for a contract for services there must be minimum mutual obligations; the employer is obliged to offer work and the employee is obliged to do that work.

• Right of control – a high degree of control (on the part of the employer) over how and where the worker performs the work suggests employment.

• Provision of equipment – the provision by the worker of their own equipment suggests self-employment.

• Financial risk – a person who is self-employed bears a higher degree of financial risk than an employee.

• Opportunity to profit – a person who is self-employed has the opportunity to profit if they do the job quicker or under-budget.

• Length of engagement – while this is not a decisive factor, an open-ended contract is more likely to indicate employment.

• Part and parcel of the organisation – a worker who is seen as 'part and parcel' of the organisation is likely to be an employee.

• Entitlement to benefits – a worker who is entitled to employee-type benefits, such as a pension, is more likely to be an employee.

• Personal factors – a highly skilled worker may not need supervising but may still be an employee.

• Intention – while intention alone cannot determine status, it can be useful in forming an opinion on whether the worker is employed or self-employed.

Check Employment Status for Tax (CEST) tool

HMRC have produced a tool – the Check Employment Status for Tax (CEST) tool – which can be used to reach a decision on whether a writer or artist is employed or self-employed. The tool asks a series of questions on the engagement, which must be answered honestly, in order to reach a decision. As long as the information provided is accurate and represents the reality of the engagement, HMRC will stand by the decision that is reached. The CEST tool is available on the Gov.uk website at www.gov.uk/guidance/check-employment-status-for-tax.

Workers providing their services through a personal service company

Anti-avoidance rules apply where services are provided through a personal limited company or another intermediary to an end client. There are two sets of rules to consider – the off-payroll working rules and the IR35 rules. The rules that apply depend on the nature of the end client.

• Off-payroll working rules

The off-payroll working rules were introduced from 6 April 2017. They apply from the date when services were provided through an intermediary to a private sector body. The rules were extended from 6 April 2021, and from that date they also apply when the end client is a medium or large private sector organisation.

The end client must carry out a status determination to ascertain whether the worker would be an employee of the end client if they provided their services to them directly. Where this is the case, the end client must deduct tax and National Insurance from payments made to the worker's personal company (after adjusting the bill for VAT and the cost of any materials), and report this to HMRC. The worker receives credit for the tax and National Insurance on payment made to them by their personal limited company. They do not need to consider the IR35 rules because the off-payroll working rules apply instead.

• IR35

From 6 April 2021 onwards, the IR35 rules only apply where a worker provides their services to a small private sector organisation through an intermediary, such as a personal service company. The worker's personal service company must determine whether the worker would be an employee of the small private sector organisation if they provided their services directly. If the answer is 'yes' the IR35 rules apply. The intermediary must calculate the deemed employment payment at the end of the tax year, and account for tax and National Insurance on that payment to HMRC.

Employed earners – Class 1 National Insurance

Class 1 National Insurance is payable on the earnings of an employed earner. The employed earner pays primary contributions and the secondary contributor (which is generally the employer) pays secondary contributions. The payment of primary Class 1 National Insurance contributions by the employed earner is the mechanism by which the employed earner earns the right to the state pension and contributory benefits. Secondary Class 1 contributions, payable by the employer, do not earn benefit entitlement – they are akin to a tax on the employee's earnings.

Contributions are calculated by reference to earnings for the earnings period on a non-cumulative basis; no account is taken of earnings previously in the tax year, only those for the earnings period. The earnings period will normally correspond to the pay interval. However, directors have an annual earnings period, regardless of their actual pay frequency. The employer must deduct primary contributions from the employee's pay and pay them over to HMRC together with tax deducted under PAYE and the employer's secondary contributions.

• Primary Class 1 National Insurance

Primary Class 1 National Insurance contributions are payable by employees aged 16 and over until they reach state pension age (which depends on their date of birth). No contributions are payable until earnings reach the *lower earnings limit* (set at £120 per week, £520 per month, £6,240 per year for 2021/22). They are then payable at a notional zero rate until earnings reach the primary threshold. This is important as it secures the year as a qualifying year for National Insurance purposes (as long as earnings are paid above the lower earnings limit for each earnings period in the tax year). Where earnings are below the lower earnings limit, the year is not a qualifying year (although may become one if the worker receives National Insurance credits or pays voluntary contributions).

National Insurance rates and thresholds 2021/22

National Insurance class	Rate or threshold
Class 1	
Lower earnings limit	£120 per week
	£520 per month
	£6,240 per year
Primary threshold	£184 per week
	£797 per month
	£9,568 per year
Secondary threshold	£170 per week
	£737 per month
	£8,840 per year
Upper earnings limit	£967 per week
	£4,189 per month
	£50,270 per year
Upper secondary threshold for under 21s	£967 per week
	£4,189 per month
	£50,270 per year
Apprentice upper secondary threshold	£967 per week
	£4,189 per month
	£50,270 per year
Primary (employee) contributions	
On earnings between the primary threshold and the upper earnings limit	12%
On earnings above the upper earnings limit	2%
Secondary (employer) contributions	
On earnings above the relevant secondary threshold	13.8%
Class 1A and Class 1B	
Contribution rate (employer only)	13.8%
Class 2	
Flat rate contribution	£3.05 per week
Small profits threshold	£6,515 a year
Class 3	
Flat rate contribution	£15.40 per week
Class 4	
Lower profits limit	£9,568 a year
Upper profits limit	£50,270 a year

Contributions are payable on earnings above the *primary threshold* (set at £184 per week, £797 per month, £9,568 per year for 2021/22) at the main primary rate of 12% until earnings reach the *upper earnings limit* (set at £967 per week, £4,189 per month, £50,270 per year for 2021/22). Contributions are payable at the additional primary rate of 2% on earnings above the upper earnings limit.

• Secondary Class 1 contributions

Secondary contributions are payable by the secondary contributor, which in most cases is the employed earner's employer. They are payable on the earnings of an employee aged 16 and above; unlike primary contributions, the secondary liability does not stop when the employed earner reaches state pension age.

Contributions are payable at the secondary rate of 13.8% on earnings in excess of the *secondary threshold* (set at £170 per week, £737 per month, £8,840 per year for 2021/22). A higher threshold applies to the earnings of employees under the age of 21 (the upper secondary threshold for under 21s) and to those of apprentices under the age of 25 (the apprentice upper secondary threshold). Both of these thresholds are aligned with the *upper earnings limit* for primary Class 1 purposes (set at £967 per week, £4,189 per month and £50,270 per year for 2021/22). These thresholds only apply for secondary Class 1 purposes; the employee or apprentice pays the usual primary contributions.

• Earnings for Class 1 purposes

Class 1 contributions are calculated on the earnings for the earnings period. The definition of 'earnings' includes any remuneration or profits derived from the employment. This will include payments of wages and salary, but will also include other items such as statutory sick pay, statutory payments, and certain share-based remuneration. Comprehensive guidance on what to include in earnings for National Insurance purposes can be found in the HMRC guidance CWG2 *Employer further guide to PAYE and National Insurance contributions*. The 2021/22 edition is available on the Gov.uk website at www.gov.uk/government/publications/cwg2-further-guide-to-paye-and-national-insurance-contributions.

• Class 1A National Insurance contributions

Class 1A National Insurance contributions are employer-only contributions payable on taxable benefits in kind and also on taxable termination payments in excess of the £30,000 tax-free threshold and taxable sporting testimonials in excess of the £100,000 tax-free threshold. They are payable at the Class 1A rate of 13.8%.

• Class 1B National Insurance

Class 1B National Insurance contributions are employer-only contributions payable in place of the Class 1 or Class 1A liability that would otherwise arise on items included within a PAYE Settlement Agreement (PSA), and also on the tax due under the PSA.

Self-employed earners – Class 2 and Class 4 National Insurance contributions

Where a writer or artist is a self-employed earner, they will pay Class 2 contributions, and also Class 4 contributions on their profits. Class 2 and Class 4 National Insurance contributions are payable via the Self Assessment system and must be paid by 31 January after the end of the tax year to which they relate (i.e. by 31 January 2023 for 2021/22 contributions).

Money, tax and benefits

• Class 2 National Insurance contributions

Class 2 National Insurance contributions are flat-rate contributions payable by self-employed earners whose profits exceed the *small profits threshold*, set at £6,515 for 2021/22. Class 2 National Insurance contributions are payable at the rate of £3.05 per week for 2021/22. The payment of Class 2 contributions is the mechanism by which a self-employed earner earns entitlement to the state pension and contributory benefits. Contributions must be paid for the full year for the year to be a qualifying year. A person whose profits from self-employment are below the small profits threshold can pay Class 2 National Insurance contributions voluntarily. This is a cheap way to build up pension entitlement.

• Class 4 National Insurance contributions

Class 4 National Insurance contributions are payable by self-employed earners on their profits. They do not provide any benefit entitlement, and in effect are a tax on profits. No contributions are payable on profits below the *lower profits threshold*, set at £9,568 for 2021/22. Class 4 contributions are payable at the rate of 9% on profits between the lower profits limit and the *upper profits limit*, set at £50,270 for 2021/22, and on profits in excess of the upper profits limit, at the additional Class 4 rate of 2%.

Voluntary contributions – Class 3

A person can pay voluntary Class 3 contributions to plug gaps in their contributions record. For 2021/22, Class 3 contributions are payable at the rate of £15.40 per week. Where a person has profits from self-employment below the *small profits threshold* (set at £6,515 for 2021/22), they can instead pay Class 2 contributions voluntarily; at £3.05 per week for 2021/22 this is a much cheaper option.

Maximum contributions

Where a person has more than one job, or is both employed and self-employed, there is a cap on the contributions that are payable for the year. The calculations are complex.

National Insurance credits

National Insurance credits are available in certain circumstances where people are unable to work or because they are ill. There are two types of credit. Class 1 credits count towards state pension and contributory benefits, while Class 3 credits only count towards the state pension. Further detail on National Insurance credits can be found on the Gov.uk website at www.gov.uk/national-insurance-credits.

Benefit entitlement

The payment of National Insurance contributions (and the award of National Insurance credits) earns entitlement to the state pension and certain contributory benefits. Only the payment of primary Class 1, Class 2 and Class 3 contributions confer benefit entitlement. Benefit entitlement depends on the class of contribution paid.

Benefit entitlement

Class of contributions	Benefit entitlement
Primary Class 1 (employed earner)	State Pension, contribution-based Jobseeker's Allowance, contribution-based Employment and Support Allowance, Maternity Allowance and Bereavement Payment, Bereavement Allowance, Widowed Parent's Allowance, Bereavement Support Payment.
Class 2 (self-employed earners)	State Pension, contribution-based Employment and Support Allowance, Maternity Allowance and Bereavement Allowance.
Class 3 (voluntary contributions)	State Pension and Bereavement Payment, Bereavement Allowance, Widowed Parent's Allowance.

Sarah Bradford BA (Hons), FCA CTA (Fellow) is the director of Writetax Ltd and WriteTax Consultancy Services Ltd, and the author of *National Insurance Contributions 2021/22* (and earlier editions) published by Bloomsbury Professional. She writes widely on tax and National Insurance contributions.

Indexes

Subject indexes
Magazines by subject area

These lists provide a broad classification and pointer to possible markets. Contacts for *Magazines UK and Ireland* start on page 36.

Advertising, design, printing and publishing

BFS Journal   42
British Journalism Review   44
Campaign   46
Greetings Today   60
PR Week   78
Press Gazette   78
Slightly Foxed   85

Agriculture, farming and horticulture

Country Life   49
Country Smallholding   49
The Countryman   50
Farmers Weekly   56
The Field   56
Irish Farmers Journal   65
Poultry World   77
The Scottish Farmer   83

Architecture and building

The Architects' Journal   38
Architectural Design   38
The Architectural Review   38
Architecture Today   38
Building   45
Building Design   45
Country Homes and Interiors   49
Country Life   49
Homes & Gardens   62
Housebuilder   63
SelfBuild & Design   84
Wallpaper*   91

Art and collecting

Apollo   38
Art + Framing Today   38
Art Monthly   38
The Art Newspaper   39
Art Quarterly   39
ArtReview and ArtReview Asia   39
The Artist   39
Artists & Illustrators   39
The Book Collector   43
The Burlington Magazine   45
Ceramic Review   47

Coin News   48
Country Life   49
Crafts Magazine   50
Eastern Art Report   54
Embroidery   54
Gibbons Stamp Monthly   59
Irish Arts Review   65
Leisure Painter   67
Medal News   70
RA Magazine   80
Stamp Magazine   86
TATE ETC   88

Aviation

Aeroplane Monthly   36
AIR International   37
Aviation News   40

Business, industry and management

Director   52
FIRE   56
Fishing News   57
Governance and Compliance   59
Management Today   69
MoneyWeek   71
People Management   76
Spear's Magazine   86
The Woodworker   93

Cinema and films

Campaign   46
Empire   54
The Face   55
Little White Lies   68
Screen International   84
Sight and Sound   85
Total Film   90

Computers

Computer Weekly   48
Computeractive   48
Custom PC   51
PC Pro   75
Scientific Computing World   83

Economics, accountancy and finance

Accountancy Age   36
Accountancy Daily   36

Accounting & Business   36
Africa Confidential   37
African Business   37
The Banker   41
Economica   54
The Economist   54
Financial Adviser   56
Insurance Age   64
Insurance Post   64
Investors Chronicle   65
MoneyWeek   71
Spear's Magazine   86
Taxation   88

Education

Educate   54
The Linguist   68
Modern Language Review   71
Music Teacher   72
Nursery World   74
Reality   81
The School Librarian   83

Engineering and mechanics

Car Mechanics   46
Electrical Review   54
Energy Engineering   55
The Engineer   55
Engineering in Miniature   55
FIRE   56
Model Engineer   71
RAIL   80
Railway Gazette International   80
The Railway Magazine   80

Fiction

Aesthetica Magazine   36
Ambit   37
Ash Tales   39
Bandit Fiction   40
Banipal   41
BFS Horizons   42
Black Static   43
Brittle Star   45
Chat   47
Crannóg   50
Critical Quarterly   50
Crystal Magazine   50
Cyphers   51
Diva   52
Dream Catcher   53
The Dublin Review   53
Erotic Review   55
Firewords   57
Flash: The International Short-Short Story
    Magazine   57
Granta   60

Gutter   60
Horla   62
The Interpreter's House   65
Interzone   65
Ireland's Own   65
Irish Pages: A Journal of Contemporary Writing   66
Kent Life   66
The Lady   67
Lighthouse Literary Journal   68
Litro   68
The London Magazine: A Review of Literature and
    the Arts   69
Lothian Life   69
Magma Poetry   69
The Moth   71
Mslexia   72
My Weekly   72
Neon   73
The North   74
Orbis International Literary Journal   75
The People's Friend   76
Planet: The Welsh Internationalist   76
Popshot Quarterly   77
Pride   79
Prospect Magazine   79
Riggwelter   82
Riptide Journal   82
Sarasvati   83
The Scots Magazine   83
Shooter Literary Magazine   85
Shoreline of Infinity   85
Stand Magazine   87
Structo   87
Take a Break   88
Tears in the Fence   88
that's life!   89
Time Out London   89
walk   91
Wasafiri   92
The Weekly News   92
The White Review   92
woman&home   93
Woman's Own   93
Woman's Weekly   93
Your Cat Magazine   95
Yours   95
Yours Fiction   95

Food and drink

BBC Good Food   41
Bella   42
The Caterer   46
Condé Nast Traveller   49
Country Smallholding   49
Decanter   51
delicious.   52
Good Housekeeping   59
Healthy   61
House & Garden   63

LandScape Magazine   67
Living Plantfully   69
The National Trust Magazine   73
Olive   75
Prima   79
Sainsbury's Magazine   83
Scottish Field   84
Speciality Food   86
The Vegan   90
Vegan Food & Living   91
Vegan Life   91
Waitrose Food   91
Women Together   93

Gardening

Amateur Gardening   37
BBC Gardeners' World Magazine   41
Country Life   49
The English Garden   55
The Field   56
Flora   57
Garden Answers   58
Garden News   58
Grow Your Own   60
Hortus   62
House & Garden   63
Kitchen Garden   67
woman&home   93

Health and home

Asylum   40
Black Beauty & Hair   43
Breathe   44
Candis   46
Country Homes and Interiors   49
Country Living   49
H&E naturist   60
Homes & Gardens   62
House & Garden   63
House Beautiful   63
Ideal Home   63
Period Living   76
Saga Magazine   83
Sainsbury's Magazine   83
Style at Home   87
25 Beautiful Homes   90
The Vegan   90
Women Together   93
The World of Interiors   94
Yours   95

History and archaeology

BBC History Magazine   41
Coin News   48
Geographical   59
History Today   62
The National Trust Magazine   73
Picture Postcard Collecting   76

Hotel, catering and leisure

The Caterer   46
HCM   61

Humour and satire

Private Eye   79
Viz   91

Legal and police

Family Law journal   56
The Lawyer   67
Legal Week   67
New Law Journal   73
The Police Journal: Theory, Practice and
     Principles   77
Seen and Heard   84

Leisure interests, pets

Astronomy Now   39
BBC Sky at Night Magazine   42
Bird Watching   43
Birdwatch   43
Caravan Magazine   46
Climber   48
Country Walking   49
Dogs Today   53
Family Tree   56
The Field   56
Flora   57
Gibbons Stamp Monthly   59
Mixmag   70
MMM (The Motorhomers' Magazine)   70
Model Boats   71
Our Dogs   75
Practical Caravan   78
Practical Fishkeeping   78
Scottish Field   84
The Sewing Directory   84
Stamp Magazine   86
TGO (The Great Outdoors) Magazine   89
Time Out London   89
Wasafiri   92
The Woodworker   93
Your Cat Magazine   95
Your Dog Magazine   95
Your Horse Magazine   95

Literary (see also Poetry)

Acumen Literary Journal   36
Aesthetica Magazine   36
ARTEMISpoetry   39
Ash Tales   39
The Author   40
Bandit Fiction   40
Banipal   41
Black Static   43

Blithe Spirit   43
The Book Collector   43
Books Ireland   44
The Bookseller   44
British Journalism Review   44
Brittle Star   45
Crannóg   50
Critical Quarterly   50
Crystal Magazine   50
The Dickensian   52
Dream Catcher   53
The Dublin Review   53
Fenland Poetry Journal   56
Firewords   57
Flash: The International Short-Short Story
    Magazine   57
The Frogmore Papers   58
Granta   60
Gutter   60
Here Comes Everyone   61
Horla   62
The Independent Publishing Magazine   63
Index on Censorship   64
Ink Sweat & Tears   64
International Affairs   64
The Interpreter's House   65
Irish Pages: A Journal of Contemporary Writing   66
Lighthouse Literary Journal   68
Literary Review   68
Litro   68
The London Magazine: A Review of Literature and
    the Arts   69
London Review of Books   69
Magma Poetry   69
Modern Language Review   71
Modern Poetry in Translation   71
The Moth   71
Mslexia   72
Neon   73
New Welsh Reader   74
The North   74
The Oldie   75
Orbis International Literary Journal   75
Oxford Poetry   75
Planet: The Welsh Internationalist   76
Popshot Quarterly   77
Prole   79
Prospect Magazine   79
Pushing Out the Boat   79
Reality   81
Riggwelter   82
Riptide Journal   82
Shooter Literary Magazine   85
Slightly Foxed   85
SOUTH Poetry Magazine   86
The Spectator   86
Stand Magazine   87
Strong Words   87
Structo   87
Tears in the Fence   88

Wasafiri   92
The White Review   92
Writing Magazine   94

Local government and civil service

Community Care   48
LGC (Local Government Chronicle)   68

Marketing and retailing

Accountancy Daily   36
Campaign   46
Drapers   53
Greetings Today   60
The Grocer   60
Marketing Week   70
Retail Week   81

Medicine and nursing

British Medical Journal   45
Irish Journal of Medical Science   65
Irish Medical Times   65
The Lancet   67
Nursery World   74
Nursing Times   74
The Practising Midwife   78
The Practitioner   78
Pulse   79

Magazines aimed at Men

Attitude   40
Esquire   55
Gay Times   59
GQ   60
Men's Fitness   70
Men's Health   70
square mile   86

Military

Jane's Defence Weekly   66
RUSI Journal   82

Motor transport and cycling

Auto Express   40
BBC Top Gear   42
Bike   43
Buses   45
Car   46
Car Mechanics   46
Classic Cars   48
Commercial Motor   48
Custom Car   50
Cycling Weekly   51
MCN (Motor Cycle News)   70
MMM (The Motorhomers' Magazine)   70

Truck & Driver 90
Trucking 90
What Car? 92

Music and recording

BBC Music Magazine 41
Classical Music 48
Early Music 53
The Face 55
Hi-Fi News 61
Kerrang! 67
Mojo 71
Music Teacher 72
Music Week 72
Musical Opinion 72
Musical Times 72
NME (New Musical Express) 74
Opera 75
Opera Now 75
Record Collector 81
The Songwriter 86
Songwriting and Composing 86
The Strad 87
Tempo 89

Natural history

BBC Wildlife Magazine 42
Bird Watching 43
Birdwatch 43
British Birds 44
Geographical 59
LandScape Magazine 67
The National Trust Magazine 73
Nature 73
Our Dogs 75
Resurgence & Ecologist 81

Nautical and marine

Boat International 43
Classic Boat Magazine 47
Diver 53
Maritime Journal 70
Motor Boat and Yachting 72
The Motorship 72
Practical Boat Owner 78
Sea Breezes 84
Ships Monthly 84
Waterways World 92
Yachting Monthly 94
Yachting World 94
Yachts and Yachting 94

Photography

Amateur Photographer 37
British Journal of Photography 44

Poetry

Acumen Literary Journal 36
Aesthetica Magazine 36

Agenda 37
Allegro Poetry 37
Ambit 37
ARTEMISpoetry 39
Banipal 41
BFS Horizons 42
Blithe Spirit 43
Brittle Star 45
Butcher's Dog 46
Crannóg 50
Critical Quarterly 50
Crystal Magazine 50
Cumbria Magazine 50
Cyphers 51
The Dawntreader 51
Dream Catcher 53
Fenland Poetry Journal 56
Fireworks 57
The Frogmore Papers 58
Gutter 60
hedgerow: a journal of small poems 61
Here Comes Everyone 61
Ink Sweat & Tears 64
The Interpreter's House 65
Irish Pages: A Journal of Contemporary Writing 66
Lighthouse Literary Journal 68
Literary Review 68
The London Magazine: A Review of Literature and the Arts 69
London Review of Books 69
Long Poem Magazine 69
Magma Poetry 69
Modern Poetry in Translation 71
The Moth 71
Mslexia 72
Neon 73
New Welsh Reader 74
The North 74
Orbis International Literary Journal 75
Oxford Poetry 75
Planet: The Welsh Internationalist 76
PN Review 76
Poetry Ireland Review/Iris Éigse Éireann 77
Poetry London 77
The Poetry Review 77
Poetry Wales 77
Popshot Quarterly 77
Pride 79
Prole 79
Pushing Out the Boat 79
Reach Poetry 80
The Rialto 82
Riggwelter 82
Riptide Journal 82
Sarasvati 83
Shooter Literary Magazine 85
Shoreline of Infinity 85
SOUTH Poetry Magazine 86
Stand Magazine 87
Structo 87

Tears in the Fence 88
Wasafiri 92
The White Review 92

Politics

Africa Confidential 37
The Critic 50
gal-dem 58
Hot Press 62
Inspire Magazine 64
International Affairs 64
The Mace 69
MoneyWeek 71
New Internationalist 73
New Statesman 74
Peace News 76
The Political Quarterly 77
Prospect Magazine 79
Red Pepper 81
The Spectator 86
The Week 92
The World Today 94

Radio and TV

Broadcast 45
Campaign 46
Empire 54
Hi-Fi News 61
InterMedia 64
Opera Now 75
Practical Wireless 78
Radio Times 80
The Stage 86
Television 89
TV Times Magazine 90
What's On TV 92

Religion, philosophy and New Age

Africa: St Patrick's Missions 36
Baptist Times 41
The Catholic Herald 47
Catholic Pictorial 47
The Catholic Universe 47
Church of England Newspaper 47
Church Times 47
The Dawntreader 51
Fortean Times 57
The Friend 58
The Furrow 58
Inspire Magazine 64
Jewish Chronicle 66
Jewish Telegraph 66
Life and Work: The Magazine of the Church of
    Scotland 68
Methodist Recorder 70
New Humanist 73
Reality 81

Reform 81
The Tablet 88
The War Cry 92
Woman Alive 93

Rural life and country

BBC Countryfile Magazine 41
Cotswold Life 49
Country Life 49
The Countryman 50
Cumbria Magazine 50
Dalesman 51
Derbyshire Life 52
Devon Life 52
Dorset Life – The Dorset Magazine 53
East Lothian Life 53
Essex Life 55
Evergreen 55
The Field 56
Kent Life 66
Lincolnshire Life 68
Lothian Life 69
The National Trust Magazine 73
The Scots Magazine 83
Scottish Field 84
Shooting Times and Country Magazine 85
Suffolk Norfolk Life 88
Surrey Life 88
This England 89
Women Together 93
Yorkshire Life 95

Sciences

BBC Science Focus 41
BBC Sky at Night Magazine 42
Nature 73
New Scientist 73
Scientific Computing World 83

Sports and games

Angling Times 38
Athletics Weekly 40
Bowls International 44
Darts World 51
Descent 52
The Field 56
Fly Fishing & Fly Tying 57
FourFourTwo 57
Golf Monthly 59
Horse & Hound 62
Horse & Rider 62
MBUK (Mountain Biking UK) 70
Men's Fitness 70
Our Dogs 75
Racing Post 80
Rugby World 82
Runner's World 82

Indexes

Sea Angler   84
Shooting Times and Country Magazine   85
Skier and Snowboarder Magazine   85
TGO (The Great Outdoors) Magazine   89
Today's Golfer   89
Trail   90
Trout & Salmon   90
World Fishing & Aquaculture   94
World Soccer   94

Theatre, drama and dancing

Dancing Times   51
Radio Times   80
The Stage   86
TV Times Magazine   90

Travel and geography

Caravan Magazine   46
Condé Nast Traveller   49
France   58
Geographical   59
The Geographical Journal   59
Wallpaper*   91
Wanderlust   91

Magazines aimed at Women

Bella   42
Best   42
Black Beauty & Hair   43
Breathe   44
Candis   46
Chat   47

Cosmopolitan   49
Dare   51
Diva   52
ELLE (UK)   54
Glamour   59
Good Housekeeping   59
Harper's Bazaar   61
Heat   61
Hello!   61
Inside Soap   64
Irish Tatler   66
The Lady   67
Mslexia   72
My Weekly   72
Nursery World   74
OK!   74
The People's Friend   76
Pride   79
Prima   79
Psychologies   79
Real People   81
Red   81
Take a Break   88
Tatler   88
that's life!   89
Vanity Fair   90
Vogue   91
WI Life   92
Woman   93
Woman Alive   93
woman&home   93
Woman's Own   93
Woman's Way   93
Woman's Weekly   93
Yours Fiction   95

Publishers of fiction (UK)

Contacts for *Book publishers UK and Ireland* start on page 130.

Adventure/westerns

4th Estate   155
Blackstaff Press Ltd   135
Bloomsbury Publishing Plc   136
Chatto & Windus/Hogarth   193
Faber and Faber Ltd   148
Hachette UK   154
Robert Hale Ltd   154
Harlequin (UK) Ltd   154
Headline Publishing Group   157
Honno Ltd (Welsh Women's Press)   197
Little, Brown Book Group   164
Mentor Books   167
John Murray Press   168
The Orion Publishing Group Ltd   173
Pan Macmillan   174
Penguin Random House UK   176
Piatkus Constable & Robinson   164
Saffron Books   181
Transworld Publishers   190
Vintage   192
Virago   164

BAME

Allison & Busby Ltd   131
Cassava Republic Press   140
Chapman Publishing   140
Honno Ltd (Welsh Women's Press)   197
HopeRoad   158
Mango Books   167
Peepal Tree Press   175
Quartet Books (The Women's Press)   179

Comedy/humour

Allison & Busby Ltd   131
Authentic Media Ltd   133
Everyman's Library   148
Little, Brown Book Group   164
Methuen & Co Ltd   168
The Oleander Press   172
Michael O'Mara Books Ltd   172
The Orion Publishing Group Ltd   173
Piccadilly Press   177
Quartet Books (The Women's Press)   179
Transworld Publishers   190

Crime/detective/mystery

4th Estate   155
Allison & Busby Ltd   131
Bad Press Ink   133

Bitter Lemon Press   135
Blackstaff Press Ltd   135
Bloodhound Books Ltd   136
Bloomsbury Publishing Plc   136
Bonnier Books UK   137
Cloud Lodge Books Ltd   141
Cornerstone   142
Cranthorpe Millner Publishers   143
Ebury Publishing   146
Everyman's Library   148
Faber and Faber Ltd   148
Hachette UK   154
Robert Hale Ltd   154
Hamish Hamilton   154
HarperCollins Publishers   155
HarperFiction   155
Hera Books   157
Hobeck Books   158
Holland House Books   158
Honno Ltd (Welsh Women's Press)   197
Joffe Books   161
Michael Joseph   161
Little, Brown Book Group   164
Macmillan Children's Books   174
Mentor Books   167
Northodox Press   170
Michael O'Mara Books Ltd   172
Orenda Books   172
The Orion Publishing Group Ltd   173
Pan Macmillan   174
Penguin Random House UK   176
Piatkus Constable & Robinson   164
Quartet Books (The Women's Press)   179
Rat's Tales Ltd   180
Red Rattle Books   180
Red Dog Press   180
Sapere Books   182
Sceptre   183
Seren   184
Serpent's Tail   178
Severn House Publishers   184
SRL Publishing Ltd   187
Transworld Publishers   190
Vintage   192
Virago   164
Zaffre   195

Erotica

Honno Ltd (Welsh Women's Press)   197
Nexus   170
Quartet Books (The Women's Press)   179

LGBTQI+

4th Estate   155
Bold Strokes Books, Inc.   208

Marion Boyars Publishers Ltd/Prospect Books   137
Chapman Publishing   140
Hamish Hamilton   154
HarperCollins Publishers   155
Hodder & Stoughton   158
Little, Brown Book Group   164
Michael O'Mara Books Ltd   172
Pan Macmillan   174
Penguin Random House UK   176
Quartet Books (The Women's Press)   179
Sceptre   183
Serpent's Tail   178
Vintage   192
Virago   164

General

4th Estate   155
Abacus   130
Agora Books   130
Allison & Busby Ltd   131
Amazon Publishing   131
Authentic Media Ltd   133
Blackstaff Press Ltd   135
Bloomsbury Publishing Plc   136
Bold Strokes Books, Inc.   208
Bonnier Books UK   137
Bookouture   137
Marion Boyars Publishers Ltd/Prospect Books   137
Jonathan Cape   193
Century & Arrow   140
Chapman Publishing   140
Cicada Books   141
Cló Iar-Chonnachta Teo   141
Cornerstone   142
Crescent Moon Publishing   143
Dahlia Publishing   144
Eyewear Publishing Ltd   197
Faber and Faber Ltd   148
The Gallery Press   151
Garnet Publishing Ltd   151
Guppy Publishing Ltd   153
Halban Publishers   154
Robert Hale Ltd   154
Hamish Hamilton   154
Harlequin (UK) Ltd   154
HarperCollins Publishers   155
Head of Zeus   157
Hera Books   157
Hodder & Stoughton   158
Honno Ltd (Welsh Women's Press)   197
Michael Joseph   161
Legend Press Ltd   163
Little, Brown Book Group   164
Macmillan Children's Books   174
Manilla Press   167
Mentor Books   167
Methuen & Co Ltd   168
Mirror Books   168
New Island Books   169

Old Barn Books   171
The Oleander Press   172
Michael O'Mara Books Ltd   172
The Orion Publishing Group Ltd   173
Pan Macmillan   174
Peepal Tree Press   175
Piatkus Constable & Robinson   164
Poolbeg Press Ltd   177
Quartet Books (The Women's Press)   179
Route   181
Sandstone Press Ltd   182
Sceptre   183
Scribe   184
Seren   184
Serpent's Tail   178
Severn House Publishers   184
Silvertail Books   185
Simon & Schuster UK Ltd   185
Studio Press   187
Thistle Publishing   189
Three Hares Publishing   190
Transworld Publishers   190
Troubador Publishing Ltd   191
Unbound   196
Valley Press   192
Velocity Press   192
Virago   164
Y Lolfa Cyf   195

Graphic/cartoons

Jonathan Cape   193
Guppy Publishing Ltd   153
Nobrow Books   170
SelfMadeHero   184
Titan Books   190

Historical

4th Estate   155
Allison & Busby Ltd   131
Birlinn Ltd   134
Blackstaff Press Ltd   135
Chapman Publishing   140
Cranachan Publishing   143
Cranthorpe Millner Publishers   143
Darf Publishers Ltd   144
Everyman's Library   148
Robert Hale Ltd   154
Harlequin (UK) Ltd   154
HarperCollins Publishers   155
Holland House Books   158
Honno Ltd (Welsh Women's Press)   197
John Hunt Publishing Ltd   159
Impress Books Ltd   197
Indigo Dreams Publishing Ltd   160
IWM (Imperial War Museums) Publishing   160
Michael Joseph   161
The Lilliput Press Ltd   163

Little, Brown Book Group   164
Mentor Books   167
The Oleander Press   172
Pan Macmillan   174
Penguin Random House UK   176
Piatkus Constable & Robinson   164
Quartet Books (The Women's Press)   179
Sapere Books   182
Sceptre   183
Severn House Publishers   184
Sparsile Books   186
Transworld Publishers   190
Vintage   192
Virago   164

Horror

Bad Press Ink   133
Mentor Books   167
Red Rattle Books   180
Snowbooks Ltd   185
Titan Books   190

Literary

4th Estate   155
Abacus   130
Allison & Busby Ltd   131
Alma Books   131
And Other Stories   196
Arkbound   196
Atlantic Books   133
Authentic Media Ltd   133
Banshee Press Ltd   134
Bearded Badger Publishing Ltd   134
Blackstaff Press Ltd   135
Bloomsbury Publishing Plc   136
Bluemoose Books   136
Bonnier Books UK   137
Marion Boyars Publishers Ltd/Prospect Books   137
Jonathan Cape   193
Capuchin Classics   187
Chapman Publishing   140
Chatto & Windus/Hogarth   193
Cloud Lodge Books Ltd   141
Cranthorpe Millner Publishers   143
Crescent Moon Publishing   143
Darf Publishers Ltd   144
Daunt Books   144
Dead Ink Books   196
Dedalus Ltd   145
Dodo Ink   145
Dogberry Ltd   145
Enitharmon Editions   148
Everyman's Library   148
Faber and Faber Ltd   148
Flipped Eye Publishing   150
404 Ink   151
Granta Books   152
Halban Publishers   154

Robert Hale Ltd   154
Hamish Hamilton   154
HarperCollins Publishers   155
Harvill Secker   156
Head of Zeus   157
Headline Publishing Group   157
Hodder & Stoughton   158
Holland House Books   158
Honno Ltd (Welsh Women's Press)   197
Indigo Dreams Publishing Ltd   160
Influx Press   160
Lightning Books   163
The Lilliput Press Ltd   163
Little, Brown Book Group   164
Mentor Books   167
The Mercier Press   167
Methuen & Co Ltd   168
John Murray Press   168
Muswell Press   169
Myriad Editions   169
New Welsh Rarebyte   170
Nordisk Books Ltd   170
The Oleander Press   172
Orenda Books   172
Peter Owen Publishers   173
Pan Macmillan   174
Penguin Random House UK   176
Piatkus Constable & Robinson   164
Picador   174
Quercus Publishing Plc   179
Renard Press Ltd   180
Sandstone Press Ltd   182
Saraband   183
Sceptre   183
Scotland Street Press   183
Seren   184
Serpent's Tail   178
Simon & Schuster UK Ltd   185
Skyhorse Publishing   220
Sparsile Books   186
Stewed Rhubarb Press   187
Tramp Press DAC   190
Transworld Publishers   190
Tuskar Rock   178
Vintage   192

New/experimental

Chapman Publishing   140
Crescent Moon Publishing   143
Faber and Faber Ltd   148
Honno Ltd (Welsh Women's Press)   197
Revenge Ink   180
Seren   184
Serpent's Tail   178

Romantic/chick-lit/women's

Avon   155
Blackstaff Press Ltd   135

Bonnier Books UK   137
Ebury Publishing   146
Gill   152
Hachette UK   154
Harlequin (UK) Ltd   154
HarperFiction   155
Harpeth Road Press   212
Hera Books   157
Honno Ltd (Welsh Women's Press)   197
Joffe Books   161
Michael Joseph   161
Little, Brown Book Group   164
Macmillan Children's Books   174
Mentor Books   167
Mills & Boon Historical   154
Mills & Boon Medical   154
Mills & Boon Modern Romance   154
Pan Macmillan   174
Piatkus Constable & Robinson   164
Sapere Books   182
Severn House Publishers   184
Transworld Publishers   190
Zaffre   195

Sci-fi/fantasy

Angry Robot Books   132
Bad Press Ink   133
Burning Chair Publishing   138
Cloud Lodge Books Ltd   141
Cranthorpe Millner Publishers   143
Ebury Publishing   146
Galley Beggar Press   151
Gollancz   173
Hachette UK   154
HarperCollinsIreland   155
HarperCollins Publishers   155
Honno Ltd (Welsh Women's Press)   197
Little, Brown Book Group   164
Luna Press Publishing   166
Orbit   172
The Orion Publishing Group Ltd   173
Pan Macmillan   174
Penguin Random House UK   176
Quartet Books (The Women's Press)   179
Simon & Schuster UK Ltd   185
Snowbooks Ltd   185
Transworld Publishers   190

Short stories

4th Estate   155
Ad Hoc Fiction   130
Chapman Publishing   140
Cló Iar-Chonnachta Teo   141
Comma Press   196
Dahlia Publishing   144
Everyman's Library   148
Faber and Faber Ltd   148
Fly on the Wall Press   197

Galley Beggar Press   151
Granta Books   152
Hamish Hamilton   154
Honno Ltd (Welsh Women's Press)   197
ISF Publishing   160
The Lilliput Press Ltd   163
Methuen & Co Ltd   168
Pan Macmillan   174
Penguin Random House UK   176
Quartet Books (The Women's Press)   179
Route   181
Seren   184
Stewed Rhubarb Press   187
Stonewood Press   187
Three Hares Publishing   190
Transworld Publishers   190
Valley Press   192
Y Lolfa Cyf   195

Teen/YA

Andersen Press Ltd   132
Burning Chair Publishing   138
Chicken House   140
Dogberry Ltd   145
Dref Wen   146
Everything With Words Ltd   148
Faber and Faber Ltd   148
David Fickling Books   149
Firefly Press Ltd   149
Floris Books   150
Guppy Publishing Ltd   153
Hachette Children's Group   153
HarperCollins Children's Books   155
HopeRoad   158
Mantra Lingua Ltd   167
Mentor Books   167
Piccadilly Press   177
Poolbeg Press Ltd   177
Scholastic Children's Books   183
SRL Publishing Ltd   187
Walker Books Ltd   193

Translation/international

Alma Books   131
Barbican Press Ltd   134
Chapman Publishing   140
Cló Iar-Chonnachta Teo   141
Darf Publishers Ltd   144
Dedalus Ltd   145
Enitharmon Editions   148
Everyman's Library   148
Faber and Faber Ltd   148
Halban Publishers   154
Harvill Secker   156
Honno Ltd (Welsh Women's Press)   197
HopeRoad   158
Nordisk Books Ltd   170
The Oleander Press   172

Orenda Books 172
The Orion Publishing Group Ltd 173
Parthian Books 174
Pushkin Press 178
Quartet Books (The Women's Press) 179
Seren 184
Serpent's Tail 178

War

Little, Brown Book Group 164
The Orion Publishing Group Ltd 173
Severn House Publishers 184
Transworld Publishers 190
Ulric Publishing 191

Publishers of non-fiction (UK)

Contacts for *Book publishers UK and Ireland* start on page 130.

Academic and professional

Allyn & Bacon   175
Arena Publishing   132
Arena Sport   135
Brilliant Publications Ltd   138
Cambridge University Press   139
James Clarke & Co. Ltd   141
Cork University Press   142
Council for British Archaeology   143
CRC Press   189
University College Dublin Press   146
Duckworth Books Ltd   146
Dunedin Academic Press   146
Earthscan   146
Edinburgh University Press   147
The Educational Company of Ireland   147
Elsevier Ltd   147
University of Exeter Press   148
Four Courts Press   150
FT Prentice Hall   175
Garland Science   189
Gingko   152
Harcourt   175
Hart Publishing   156
ICSA Publishing Ltd   159
Institute of Public Administration   160
Irish Academic Press Ltd   160
Ithaca Press   151
Jane's   161
Peter Lang Ltd   162
Liverpool University Press   165
The Lutterworth Press   166
McGraw-Hill Education   166
Management Books 2000 Ltd   166
Manchester University Press   166
New Riders   175
Oxford University Press   173
Palgrave Macmillan   187
Penguin Press   176
Policy Studies Institute (PSI)   177
Polity Press   177
Portland Press Ltd   177
Prentice Hall   175
Psychology Press   178
Routledge   189
Saffron Books   181
SAGE Publishing   182
SAMS Publishing   175
Scholastic Educational Resources   183
SCM Press   159
Silvertail Books   185
Siri Scientific Press   185
Sussex Academic Press   188

Taylor & Francis Group   189
TSO (The Stationery Office)   191
Veritas Publications   192
Virtue Books Ltd   193
University of Wales Press   193
Welsh Academic Press   194
John Wiley & Sons Ltd   194
Yale University Press London   195

Agriculture, farming and horticulture

Henley Hall Press   157
Think Books   189
Whittet Books Ltd   194

Animals and birds

J.A. Allen   131
The Crowood Press   144
David & Charles Ltd   144
Kenilworth Press   179
New Holland Publishers (UK) Ltd   199
Open Gate Press   172
Think Books   189
Whittet Books Ltd   194

Archaeology

Ashmolean Museum Publications   133
Birlinn Ltd   134
Boydell & Brewer Ltd   137
The British Museum Press   138
Cambridge University Press   139
Council for British Archaeology   143
University of Exeter Press   148
Logaston Press   165
Routledge   189
Shire Books   185
Souvenir Press   178
I.B. Tauris   189
Thames & Hudson Ltd   189

Architecture and building

ACC Art Books Ltd   130
Giles de la Mare Publishers Ltd   145
The Dovecote Press Ltd   145
Garnet Publishing Ltd   151
Laurence King Publishing Ltd   162
Frances Lincoln   163
Manchester University Press   166
Merrell Publishers Ltd   167
Oxford University Press   173
Prestel Publishing Ltd   178

Quiller   179
Reaktion Books   180
Saffron Books   181
Sheldrake Press   184
Spon Press   189
Taschen UK Ltd   188
Thames & Hudson Ltd   189
Yale University Press London   195

Art and craft

Anness Publishing   132
Mitchell Beazley   171
Black Dog Press   135
Cico Books   181
Collins   155
The Crowood Press   144
David & Charles Ltd   144
Floris Books   150
Guild of Master Craftsman Publications Ltd   153
Halsgrove Publishing   154
Frances Lincoln   163
Murdoch Books   168
New Holland Publishers (UK) Ltd   199
Pimpernel Press Ltd   177
Quadrille   179
The Quarto Group, Inc.   179
Quarto Group Publishing UK   179
Saffron Books   181
Search Press Ltd   184
September Publishing   184

Astronomy

Canopus Publishing Ltd   139

Aviation

Ian Allan Publishing Ltd   131
The Crowood Press   144
Fonthill Media Ltd   150
Grub Street Publishing   153
Jane's   161
Osprey Publishing Ltd   173
Pen & Sword Books Ltd   175

Bibliography

British Library Publishing   138
Impress Books Ltd   197
September Publishing   184

Biography, autobiography and memoir

4th Estate   155
Amberley Publishing   131
Atlantic Books   133
Atrium and Attic Press   142
Aureus Publishing Ltd   133
Barbican Press Ltd   134

Black & White Publishing Ltd   135
Blackstaff Press Ltd   135
John Blake Publishing   135
Blink Publishing   135
The Bodley Head   193
Canbury Press Ltd   139
Canongate Books Ltd   139
Jonathan Cape   193
Chatto & Windus/Hogarth   193
James Clarke & Co. Ltd   141
Cornerstone   142
Cranthorpe Millner Publishers   143
Giles de la Mare Publishers Ltd   145
André Deutsch   194
Dogberry Ltd   145
Ebury Publishing   146
Ebury Self   147
Fleming Publications   150
Fonthill Media Ltd   150
Gibson Square   152
Gill   152
Gill Books   152
Granta Books   152
Halban Publishers   154
Hamish Hamilton   176
Harper NonFiction   155
Harper Voyager   156
Harper360   156
Haus Publishing Ltd   156
Headline Publishing Group   157
Henley Hall Press   157
Hodder & Stoughton   158
Hutchinson Heinemann   142
Indigo Dreams Publishing Ltd   160
Michael Joseph   161
The Lilliput Press Ltd   163
Little, Brown   164
The Lutterworth Press   166
Mandrake of Oxford   167
Manilla Press   167
Mentor Books   167
Methuen & Co Ltd   168
Mirror Books   168
Morrigan Book Company   168
Murdoch Books   168
John Murray Press   168
New Island Books   169
The O'Brien Press Ltd   171
Michael O'Mara Books Ltd   172
Omnibus Press/Wise Music Group   172
Peter Owen Publishers   173
Oxford University Press   173
Penguin General   175
Penguin Press   176
Pimlico   193
Plexus Publishing Ltd   177
Politico's Publishing   168
Profile Books Ltd   178
Quartet Books (The Women's Press)   179
Quarto Group Publishing UK   179

Indexes

Quiller   179
Rider   180
Salt Publishing   182
Saraband   183
September Publishing   184
Serpent's Tail   178
Shepheard-Walwyn (Publishers) Ltd   184
Sigma Press   185
Souvenir Press   178
Sparsile Books   186
Square Peg   193
SRL Publishing Ltd   187
I.B. Tauris   189
Veritas Publications   192
Welsh Academic Press   194
Yale University Press London   195

Business, industry and management

Bennion Kearny Ltd   134
Nicholas Brealey Publishing   169
Crown House Publishing Ltd   143
Edward Elgar Publishing Ltd   147
FT Prentice Hall   175
Gower Books   189
Jordan Publishing Ltd   161
Kogan Page Ltd   162
McGraw-Hill Education   166
Management Books 2000 Ltd   166
Oak Tree Press   171
Profile Books Ltd   178
Penguin Random House UK   176
Routledge   189
Spon Press   189
TSO (The Stationery Office)   191
Wharton   175

Cartography/maps

AA Publishing   130
Bodleian Library Publishing   137
British Library Publishing   138
Collins   155
Discovery Walking Guides Ltd   145
Everyman's Library   148
HarperCollins Publishers   155
Michelin Travel Partners UK Ltd   168
Myriad Editions   169

Comedy, humour

4th Estate   155
Birlinn Ltd   134
Black & White Publishing Ltd   135
Blackstaff Press Ltd   135
Blink Publishing   135
Cassell   171
Century   754
André Deutsch   194
Ebury Publishing   146

Ebury Self   147
Hardie Grant UK   154
Hodder & Stoughton   158
Mentor Books   167
The Mercier Press   167
Methuen & Co Ltd   168
New Holland Publishers (UK) Ltd   199
New Island Books   169
The O'Brien Press Ltd   171
Michael O'Mara Books Ltd   172
Profile Books Ltd   178
Quadrille   179
Quiller   179
September Publishing   184
Souvenir Press   178
Square Peg   193
Studio Press   187
Summersdale Publishers Ltd   188

Computers and computing

McGraw-Hill Education   166
P8tech   174
Peachpit Press   175
Pelagic Publishing   175
QUE Publishing   175
SAMS Publishing   175
Springer Nature Group Ltd   186

Cookery, food and drink

Anness Publishing   132
Atrium and Attic Press   142
Mitchell Beazley   171
Black & White Publishing Ltd   135
Blackstaff Press Ltd   135
John Blake Publishing   135
Blink Publishing   135
Marion Boyars Publishers Ltd/Prospect Books   137
Collins   155
Conran Octopus   171
André Deutsch   194
DK   145
Ebury Self   147
Elliott & Thompson   147
Flame Tree Publishing   149
W. Foulsham & Co. Ltd   150
Gill   152
Gill Books   152
Grub Street Publishing   153
Hamlyn   171
Hardie Grant UK   154
Harper NonFiction   155
Headline Publishing Group   157
Hodder & Stoughton   158
Igloo Books Ltd   159
Michael Joseph   161
Kitchen Press   162
Kyle Books   162
Murdoch Books   168

New Holland Publishers (UK) Ltd   199
Nourish Books   170
On Stream Publications   172
Quadrille   179
The Quarto Group, Inc.   179
Quiller   179
Ryland Peters & Small   181
Sheldrake Press   184
Square Peg   193
SRL Publishing Ltd   187
Virtue Books Ltd   193
Watkins Media   193

Crime

Black & White Publishing Ltd   135
John Blake Publishing   135
Cornerstone   142
Mandrake of Oxford   167
Mentor Books   167
Milo Books Ltd   168
Mirror Books   168
The O'Brien Press Ltd   171
Routledge   189

Cultural studies

Atrium and Attic Press   142
Bitter Lemon Press   135
Marion Boyars Publishers Ltd/Prospect Books   137
Nicholas Brealey Publishing   169
The British Museum Press   138
Cornerstone   142
Crescent Moon Publishing   143
Edinburgh University Press   147
Free Association Books   151
Gibson Square   152
Lawrence & Wishart Ltd   162
Manchester University Press   166
Phaidon Press Ltd   176
Pluto Press   177
Polity Press   177
Prestel Publishing Ltd   178
Reaktion Books   180
Repeater Books   180
I.B. Tauris   189
Thames & Hudson Ltd   189
Verso Ltd   192

Current affairs

4th Estate   155
Atlantic Books   133
Basic Books   208
The Bodley Head   193
Jonathan Cape   193
Chatto & Windus/Hogarth   193
André Deutsch   194
Fabian Society   149
Gibson Square   152

Gill   152
Hamish Hamilton   176
Harvill Secker   193
Lawrence & Wishart Ltd   162
The Mercier Press   167
Milo Books Ltd   168
New Island Books   169
Oneworld Publications   172
Oxford University Press   173
Penguin Press   176
Poolbeg Press Ltd   177
Politico's Publishing   168
Profile Books Ltd   178
Repeater Books   180
Rider   180
Serpent's Tail   178
I.B. Tauris   189
TSO (The Stationery Office)   191
Verso Ltd   192
Yale University Press London   195

Design

ACC Art Books Ltd   130
The Bright Press   138
Flame Tree Publishing   149
Laurence King Publishing Ltd   162
Kyle Books   162
Frances Lincoln   163
Manchester University Press   166
Merrell Publishers Ltd   167
New Riders   175
Prestel Publishing Ltd   178
Reaktion Books   180
Taschen UK Ltd   188
Thames & Hudson Ltd   189

Economics, accountancy and finance

The Bodley Head   193
Nicholas Brealey Publishing   169
Butterworths   163
Cornerstone   142
Edward Elgar Publishing Ltd   147
Fabian Society   149
Institute of Public Administration   160
Kogan Page Ltd   162
LexisNexis   163
McGraw-Hill Education   166
W.W. Norton & Company   170
Oxford University Press   173
Penguin Press   176
Pluto Press   177
Routledge   189
Rowman & Littlefield   181
Tolley   163
Verso Ltd   192
Yale University Press London   195

Education

BBC Active   175
Brilliant Publications Ltd   138

Cambridge University Press   139
Colourpoint Creative Ltd   141
Cranachan Publishing   143
Crown House Publishing Ltd   143
Benjamin Cummings   175
Dref Wen   146
The Educational Company of Ireland   147
Educational Explorers (Publishers)   147
Fabian Society   149
CJ Fallon   149
Flame Tree Publishing   149
Folens Publishers   150
Gill   152
Gill Education   152
GL Assessment   152
Goldsmiths Press   152
Harcourt   175
Hodder Education   158
Hodder Gibson   158
Hopscotch   158
Jessica Kingsley Publishers   169
Kogan Page Ltd   162
Longman   175
McGraw-Hill Education   166
Macmillan Education   186
Mentor Books   167
Northcote House Publishers Ltd   170
Oxford University Press   173
Pearson UK   175
Practical Pre-School Books   158
Prentice Hall   175
Scholastic Educational Resources   183
Souvenir Press   178
Welsh Academic Press   194
ZigZag Education   195

Engineering and mechanics
Bernard Babani (publishing) Ltd   133
Cambridge University Press   139
CRC Press   189
Spon Press   189
Springer Nature Group Ltd   186

Environment and development
Arkbound   196
Canbury Press Ltd   139
Earthscan   146
Green Print   167
Henley Hall Press   157
Frances Lincoln   163
Oneworld Publications   172
Open Gate Press   172
Pelagic Publishing   175
Pluto Press   177
Routledge   189
Sawday's   183
Zed Books Ltd   195

Fashion
ACC Art Books Ltd   130
Laurence King Publishing Ltd   162

Quarto Group Publishing UK   179
Thames & Hudson Ltd   189

Film and cinema
Batsford   756
BFI Publishing   134
Marion Boyars Publishers Ltd/Prospect Books   137
Crescent Moon Publishing   143
DK   145
University of Exeter Press   148
Faber and Faber Ltd   148
Methuen & Co Ltd   168
Plexus Publishing Ltd   177
Quarto Group Publishing UK   179
Reaktion Books   180
Roundhouse Group   181
Studio Press   187
Taschen UK Ltd   188
I.B. Tauris   189
Titan Books   190

Fine art and antiques
ACC Art Books Ltd   130
Ashmolean Museum Publications   133
Mitchell Beazley   171
Bodleian Library Publishing   137
Boydell & Brewer Ltd   137
The British Museum Press   138
Cambridge University Press   139
Giles de la Mare Publishers Ltd   145
Richard Dennis Publications   145
André Deutsch   194
Flame Tree Publishing   149
Four Courts Press   150
Garnet Publishing Ltd   151
Gibson Square   152
Laurence King Publishing Ltd   162
Frances Lincoln   163
Liverpool University Press   165
Manchester University Press   166
Mandrake of Oxford   167
Merrell Publishers Ltd   167
Miller's   171
Peter Owen Publishers   173
Phaidon Press Ltd   176
Prestel Publishing Ltd   178
Reaktion Books   180
Royal Collection Trust   181
Stacey Publishing Ltd   187
Taschen UK Ltd   188
Tate Enterprises Ltd   188
I.B. Tauris   189
Thames & Hudson Ltd   189
Unicorn Publishing Group LLP   191
Philip Wilson Publishers   195
Yale University Press London   195

Gardening
ACC Art Books Ltd   130
Anness Publishing   132

Mitchell Beazley   171
Cassell   171
Collins   155
Conran Octopus   171
The Crowood Press   144
David & Charles Ltd   144
DK   145
W. Foulsham & Co. Ltd   150
Hamlyn   171
Hardie Grant UK   154
Headline Publishing Group   157
Kyle Books   162
Frances Lincoln   163
Murdoch Books   168
New Holland Publishers (UK) Ltd   199
Quadrille   179
Quiller   179
Ryland Peters & Small   181
Thames & Hudson Ltd   189
Think Books   189

Gender studies and gay and lesbian and LGBTQI+

Atrium and Attic Press   142
Crescent Moon Publishing   143
Polity Press   177
Quartet Books (The Women's Press)   179
Routledge   189
Serpent's Tail   178
Virago   164
Zed Books Ltd   195

General non-fiction

Allison & Busby Ltd   131
Alma Books   131
Amazon Publishing   131
And Other Stories   196
Aurora Metro   133
Birlinn Ltd   134
Black & White Publishing Ltd   135
Canongate Books Ltd   139
Colourpoint Creative Ltd   141
Cornerstone   142
Cressrelles Publishing Co. Ltd   143
Crux Publishing   144
Doubleday (UK)   190
Faber and Faber Ltd   148
Fig Tree   176
404 Ink   151
Halban Publishers   154
Robert Hale Ltd   154
HarperCollins Publishers   155
Hashtag Press   156
Haus Publishing Ltd   156
Headline Publishing Group   157
Hodder & Stoughton   158
Michael Joseph   161
Little, Brown Book Group   164

LOM ART   165
Myriad Editions   169
Octopus Publishing Group   171
Orion Fiction   173
The Orion Publishing Group Ltd   173
Peter Owen Publishers   173
Penguin Random House UK   176
Piatkus Constable & Robinson   164
Picador   174
Poolbeg Press Ltd   177
Quercus Publishing Plc   179
Renard Press Ltd   180
Royal National Institute of Blind People
   (RNIB)   181
Sandstone Press Ltd   182
Scribe   184
Short Books Ltd   185
Simon & Schuster UK Ltd   185
Snowbooks Ltd   185
Souvenir Press   178
Sphere   164
Thistle Publishing   189
Three Hares Publishing   190
Tramp Press DAC   190
Transworld Ireland   190
Transworld Publishers   190
Troubador Publishing Ltd   191
Ulverscroft Ltd   191
Unbound   196
Windmill Books   143

Health

Anness Publishing   132
John Blake Publishing   135
Cassell   171
DK   145
W. Foulsham & Co. Ltd   150
Gaia Books   171
Hamlyn   171
Hardie Grant UK   154
Kyle Books   162
The Mercier Press   167
New Holland Publishers (UK) Ltd   199
Nourish Books   170
Quadrille   179
Quartet Books (The Women's Press)   179
Routledge   189
Sheldon Press   169
Trigger Publishing   190
Vermilion   192
Watkins Media   193

Heritage

Cassell   171
Country Books   143
Countryside Books   143
DB Publishing   145
Irish Academic Press Ltd   160

Pimpernel Press Ltd   177
Sigma Press   185

History

Ian Allan Publishing Ltd   131
The Alpha Press   188
Amberley Publishing   131
Amgueddfa Cymru – National Museum Wales   131
Appletree Press Ltd   132
Arena Publishing   132
Ashmolean Museum Publications   133
Atlantic Books   133
Basic Books   208
Birlinn Ltd   134
Blackstaff Press Ltd   135
Bodleian Library Publishing   137
The Bodley Head   193
Boydell & Brewer Ltd   137
British Library Publishing   138
The British Museum Press   138
Cambridge University Press   139
Canongate Books Ltd   139
Jonathan Cape   193
Cassell   171
Chatto & Windus/Hogarth   193
James Clarke & Co. Ltd   141
Cló Iar-Chonnachta Teo   141
Cork University Press   142
Cornerstone   142
Country Books   143
Cranthorpe Millner Publishers   143
Giles de la Mare Publishers Ltd   145
André Deutsch   194
DK   145
The Dovecote Press Ltd   145
University College Dublin Press   146
Ebury Self   147
Edinburgh University Press   147
University of Exeter Press   148
Fleming Publications   150
Four Courts Press   150
Gibson Square   152
Gill   152
Gill Books   152
Goldsmiths Press   152
Halban Publishers   154
Hamish Hamilton   176
Harvill Secker   193
Headline Publishing Group   157
Henley Hall Press   157
Hodder & Stoughton   158
Hutchinson Heinemann   142
Impress Books Ltd   197
Irish Academic Press Ltd   160
IWM (Imperial War Museums) Publishing   160
Lawrence & Wishart Ltd   162
The Lilliput Press Ltd   163
Liverpool University Press   165
Logaston Press   165

The Lutterworth Press   166
Manchester University Press   166
Mentor Books   167
The Mercier Press   167
Merlin Press Ltd   167
Methuen & Co Ltd   168
Morrigan Book Company   168
Murdoch Books   168
John Murray Press   168
The O'Brien Press Ltd   171
The Oleander Press   172
Michael O'Mara Books Ltd   172
Oneworld Publications   172
Peter Owen Publishers   173
Oxford University Press   173
Pen & Sword Books Ltd   175
Penguin Press   176
Pimlico   193
Pimpernel Press Ltd   177
Pluto Press   177
Polity Press   177
Profile Books Ltd   178
Reaktion Books   180
Rider   180
Routledge   189
Saraband   183
Sheldrake Press   184
Shepheard-Walwyn (Publishers) Ltd   184
Shire Books   185
Skyhorse Publishing   220
Society of Genealogists Enterprises Ltd   186
Sussex Academic Press   188
I.B. Tauris   189
Vallentine Mitchell   192
Verso Ltd   192
Welsh Academic Press   194

Illustrated books

Mitchell Beazley   171
Cassell   171
Conran Octopus   171
DK   145
Gaia Books   171
Godsfield Press   171
Hamlyn   171
Hardie Grant UK   154
Laurence King Publishing Ltd   162
Frances Lincoln   163
Merrell Publishers Ltd   167
Miller's   171
New Holland Publishers (UK) Ltd   199
Osprey Publishing Ltd   173
Quadrille   179
The Quarto Group, Inc.   179
Ryland Peters & Small   181
Square Peg   193
Stacey Publishing Ltd   187

International issues

Earthscan   146
Edinburgh University Press   147

Fabian Society   149
Pluto Press   177
Rider   180
Rowman & Littlefield   181
Stacey Publishing Ltd   187
I.B. Tauris   189
University of Wales Press   193
Zed Books Ltd   195

Irish interest

Appletree Press Ltd   132
Atrium and Attic Press   142
Cló Iar-Chonnachta Teo   141
Colourpoint Creative Ltd   141
Cork University Press   142
University College Dublin Press   146
The Educational Company of Ireland   147
Flyleaf Press   150
Folens Publishers   150
Four Courts Press   150
Gill   152
The Lilliput Press Ltd   163
The Mercier Press   167
Morrigan Book Company   168
On Stream Publications   172
Pluto Press   177
Colin Smythe Ltd   185

Languages and ELT

Cambridge University Press   139
Longman   175
Macmillan Education   186
The Oleander Press   172
Oxford University Press   173
Penguin Longman   175

Law

Butterworths   163
Cambridge University Press   139
Edinburgh University Press   147
Edward Elgar Publishing Ltd   147
Hart Publishing   156
Institute of Public Administration   160
Jordan Publishing Ltd   161
Jessica Kingsley Publishers   169
Charles Knight   163
LexisNexis   163
Manchester University Press   166
Oxford University Press   173
Sweet & Maxwell   188
Thomson Reuters – Round Hall   190
Tolley   163

Leisure interests and hobbies

Collins   155
Countryside Books   143

David & Charles Ltd   144
W. Foulsham & Co. Ltd   150
Guild of Master Craftsman Publications Ltd   153
Search Press Ltd   184

Lifestyle, home and DIY

Anness Publishing   132
Mitchell Beazley   171
Blink Publishing   135
Cico Books   181
Collins   155
Conran Octopus   171
The Crowood Press   144
David & Charles Ltd   144
Elliott & Thompson   147
W. Foulsham & Co. Ltd   150
Gill Books   152
Hamlyn   171
Haynes Publishing   157
Murdoch Books   168
New Holland Publishers (UK) Ltd   199
Quadrille   179
Quarto Group Publishing UK   179
Quiller   179

Literary criticism and essays

Bodleian Library Publishing   137
Boydell & Brewer Ltd   137
British Library Publishing   138
James Clarke & Co. Ltd   141
University College Dublin Press   146
Edinburgh University Press   147
Enitharmon Editions   148
Hamish Hamilton   176
Harvill Secker   193
The Lilliput Press Ltd   163
Liverpool University Press   165
Manchester University Press   166
Northcote House Publishers Ltd   170
Out-Spoken Press   594
Pimlico   193
Polity Press   177
Quartet Books (The Women's Press)   179
Routledge   189
Salt Publishing   182
Colin Smythe Ltd   185
University of Wales Press   193
York Notes   175

Local government and civil service

Edward Elgar Publishing Ltd   147
Institute of Public Administration   160

Local interest

Amberley Publishing   131
Halsgrove Publishing   154

Logaston Press   165
Lonely Planet Publications Ltd   165
Metro Publications Ltd   168
Stenlake Publishing Ltd   187
Two Rivers Press Ltd   191

Medicine and nursing

Cambridge University Press   139
DK   145
Elsevier Ltd   147
F100 Group   148
Hodder Education   158
McGraw-Hill Education   166
Oxford University Press   173
Routledge   189
SAGE Publishing   182
Springer Nature Group Ltd   186
John Wiley & Sons Ltd   194

Military

Ian Allan Publishing Ltd   131
Birlinn Ltd   134
Blink Publishing   135
Collins   155
The Crowood Press   144
David & Charles Ltd   144
Fonthill Media Ltd   150
Grub Street Publishing   153
IWM (Imperial War Museums) Publishing   160
Jane's   161
Michael Joseph   161
Osprey Publishing Ltd   173
Pen & Sword Books Ltd   175
Quarto Group Publishing UK   179
Ulric Publishing   191

Mind, body & spirit (MBS)

Bonnier Books UK   137
Cico Books   181
Crown House Publishing Ltd   143
Findhorn Press Ltd   149
Floris Books   150
Gaia Books   171
Gill Books   152
Godsfield Press   171
Hardie Grant UK   154
Hay House Publishers   156
Hodder & Stoughton   158
John Hunt Publishing Ltd   159
Kyle Books   162
The Mercier Press   167
Piatkus Constable & Robinson   164
Quadrille   179
Quantum   150
Watkins Media   193

Music

Aureus Publishing Ltd   133
Black Dog Press   135

Marion Boyars Publishers Ltd/Prospect Books   137
Boydell & Brewer Ltd   137
British Library Publishing   138
Cambridge University Press   139
Cork University Press   142
Giles de la Mare Publishers Ltd   145
Ebury Self   147
Elliott & Thompson   147
Faber and Faber Ltd   148
Flame Tree Publishing   149
Harvill Secker   193
The Lutterworth Press   166
W.W. Norton & Company   170
Omnibus Press/Wise Music Group   172
Oxford University Press   173
Plexus Publishing Ltd   177
Serpent's Tail   178
Sheldrake Press   184
Stainer & Bell Ltd   187
Velocity Press   192
Yale University Press London   195

Natural history

Blackstaff Press Ltd   135
Bodleian Library Publishing   137
Collins   155
The Crowood Press   144
David & Charles Ltd   144
DK   145
The Dovecote Press Ltd   145
Granta Books   152
Little Toller Books   165
Natural History Museum Publishing   169
New Holland Publishers (UK) Ltd   199
Saraband   183
Siri Scientific Press   185
Square Peg   193
Think Books   189
Whittet Books Ltd   194

Nautical and marine

Ian Allan Publishing Ltd   131
Boydell & Brewer Ltd   137
Brown, Son & Ferguson Ltd   138
University of Exeter Press   148
Fonthill Media Ltd   150
Jane's   161
Pen & Sword Books Ltd   175

Novelty, gift books

Appletree Press Ltd   132
Helen Exley   148
Igloo Books Ltd   159
Frances Lincoln   163
New Holland Publishers (UK) Ltd   199
Quadrille   179
Ryland Peters & Small   181

Shepheard-Walwyn (Publishers) Ltd 184
Square Peg 193
Summersdale Publishers Ltd 188

Parenting, relationships and self-help

Nicholas Brealey Publishing 169
Columba Books 142
Free Association Books 151
Hamlyn 171
Ryland Peters & Small 181
Sheldon Press 169
Square Peg 193
Vermilion 192

Performing arts

The Bright Press 138
The Crowood Press 144
University of Exeter Press 148
Faber and Faber Ltd 148
J. Garnet Miller 143
Kenyon-Deane 143
Methuen & Co Ltd 168
New Playwrights' Network 143
Northcote House Publishers Ltd 170
Oberon Books 171
Peter Owen Publishers 173
Oxford University Press 173
Roundhouse Group 181
Routledge 189

Photography

Appletree Press Ltd 132
Black Dog Press 135
The Bright Press 138
Jonathan Cape 193
David & Charles Ltd 144
DK 145
Fleming Publications 150
Merrell Publishers Ltd 167
Prestel Publishing Ltd 178
Reaktion Books 180
Taschen UK Ltd 188
Thames & Hudson Ltd 189

Politics

Arena Publishing 132
Atlantic Books 133
Basic Books 208
Blackstaff Press Ltd 135
The Bodley Head 193
Cambridge University Press 139
Canbury Press Ltd 139
Canongate Books Ltd 139
Jonathan Cape 193
Chatto & Windus/Hogarth 193
University College Dublin Press 146

Edinburgh University Press 147
Gibson Square 152
Goldsmiths Press 152
Green Print 167
Hamish Hamilton 176
Henley Hall Press 157
Imprint Academic Ltd 160
Institute of Public Administration 160
Lawrence & Wishart Ltd 162
Little, Brown 164
Manchester University Press 166
Mentor Books 167
The Mercier Press 167
The O'Brien Press Ltd 171
Oneworld Publications 172
Penguin General 175
Pluto Press 177
Polity Press 177
Politico's Publishing 168
Profile Books Ltd 178
Quartet Books (The Women's Press) 179
Repeater Books 180
Routledge 189
Rowman & Littlefield 181
Serpent's Tail 178
Shepheard-Walwyn (Publishers) Ltd 184
Verso Ltd 192
Welsh Academic Press 194
Zed Books Ltd 195

Popular culture

Ian Allan Publishing Ltd 131
Bello 174
Blink Publishing 135
Bonnier Books UK 137
Canongate Books Ltd 139
Ebury Publishing 146
Henley Hall Press 157
Michael Joseph 161
Lawrence & Wishart Ltd 162
Muswell Press 169
Penguin Random House UK 176
Plexus Publishing Ltd 177
Repeater Books 180
Serpent's Tail 178
Taschen UK Ltd 188
Two Hoots 174

Popular reference

Collins 155
The Crowood Press 144
Ebury Self 147
W. Foulsham & Co. Ltd 150
Gaia Books 171
Geddes & Grosset 151
Hamlyn 171
HarperCollins Publishers 155
Headline Publishing Group 157

Icon Books Ltd   159
Infinite Ideas   160
The Quarto Group, Inc.   179
Quiller   179
Shire Books   185
Thames & Hudson Ltd   189

Reference

Anness Publishing   132
Atlantic Books   133
Bloomsbury Digital Resources   136
British Library Publishing   138
Cambridge University Press   139
James Clarke & Co. Ltd   141
Cornerstone   142
DK   145
Elsevier Ltd   147
Encyclopaedia Britannica (UK) Ltd   148
Flame Tree Publishing   149
Fly on the Wall Press   197
Gill Books   152
Guinness World Records   153
HarperCollins Publishers   155
Hodder Education   158
Kyle Books   162
John Murray Press   168
The O'Brien Press Ltd   171
The Oleander Press   172
Oxford University Press   173
Penguin General   175
Prentice Hall   175
Routledge   189
Stacey Publishing Ltd   187
Taylor & Francis Group   189
Unicorn Publishing Group LLP   191

Religion, philosophy and New Age

The Alpha Press   188
Authentic Media Ltd   133
Bryntirion Press   138
Cambridge University Press   139
Canterbury Press   159
Catholic Truth Society   140
Chatto & Windus/Hogarth   193
Christian Education   140
James Clarke & Co. Ltd   141
Columba Books   142
Darton, Longman and Todd Ltd   144
Edinburgh University Press   147
Floris Books   150
W. Foulsham & Co. Ltd   150
Four Courts Press   150
Garnet Publishing Ltd   151
Gresham Books Ltd   153
Hodder Faith   169
John Hunt Publishing Ltd   159
Hymns Ancient and Modern Ltd   159
Imprint Academic Ltd   160

ISF Publishing   160
Jessica Kingsley Publishers   169
Kube Publishing Ltd   162
Lion Hudson Ltd   163
The Lutterworth Press   166
Mandrake of Oxford   167
Kevin Mayhew Ltd   167
Mud Pie   168
Oneworld Publications   172
Open Gate Press   172
Oxford University Press   173
Rider   180
George Ronald   180
Routledge   189
St Pauls Publishing   182
SCM Press   159
Scripture Union   184
SPCK   186
Stainer & Bell Ltd   187
Sussex Academic Press   188
I.B. Tauris   189
Thames & Hudson Ltd   189
Vallentine Mitchell   192
Veritas Publications   192
Verso Ltd   192
Wooden Books   195

Rural life and country

The Crowood Press   144
Quiller   179
Merlin Unwin Books Ltd   192
Whittet Books Ltd   194

Science

The Bodley Head   193
Canopus Publishing Ltd   139
CRC Press   189
Benjamin Cummings   175
Dunedin Academic Press   146
Ebury Self   147
Elsevier Ltd   147
F100 Group   148
Floris Books   150
Garland Science   189
Goldsmiths Press   152
Hutchinson Heinemann   142
IOP Publishing   160
Frances Lincoln   163
McGraw-Hill Education   166
Natural History Museum Publishing   169
W.W. Norton & Company   170
Oneworld Publications   172
Oxford University Press   173
Portland Press Ltd   177
Profile Books Ltd   178
Routledge   189
SAGE Publishing   182
Science Museum Group   183

Sparsile Books   186
Spon Press   189
Springer Nature Group Ltd   186
John Wiley & Sons Ltd   194
Yale University Press London   195

Scottish interest

Appletree Press Ltd   132
Arena Sport   135
Birlinn Ltd   134
Edinburgh University Press   147
Floris Books   150
House of Lochar   159
Shepheard-Walwyn (Publishers) Ltd   184
Stewed Rhubarb Press   187

Social sciences

Allyn & Bacon   175
Bristol University Press/Policy Press   138
Cambridge University Press   139
University College Dublin Press   146
Fonthill Media Ltd   150
Free Association Books   151
Goldsmiths Press   152
Jessica Kingsley Publishers   169
Peter Lang Ltd   162
Liverpool University Press   165
McGraw-Hill Education   166
W.W. Norton & Company   170
Open Gate Press   172
Open University Press   172
Policy Studies Institute (PSI)   177
Polity Press   177
Psychology Press   178
Routledge   189
SAGE Publishing   182
Souvenir Press   178
University of Wales Press   193
Zed Books Ltd   195

Sports and games

Ian Allan Publishing Ltd   131
J.A. Allen   131
The Alpha Press   188
Appletree Press Ltd   132
Aureus Publishing Ltd   133
Bennion Kearny Ltd   134
Birlinn Ltd   134
Black & White Publishing Ltd   135
Blackstaff Press Ltd   135
Chase My Snail   226
The Crowood Press   144
DB Publishing   145
Ebury Publishing   146
Ebury Self   147
Elliott & Thompson   147
W. Foulsham & Co. Ltd   150

Hamlyn   171
Harper NonFiction   155
Methuen & Co Ltd   168
Milo Books Ltd   168
New Holland Publishers (UK) Ltd   199
The O'Brien Press Ltd   171
Quarto Group Publishing UK   179
Quiller   179
St. David's Press   182
Sigma Press   185
Skyhorse Publishing   220
Souvenir Press   178
Spon Press   189
SportBooks Ltd   186
Yellow Jersey Press   193

The media

Pluto Press   177

Transport, including cycling

AA Publishing   130
Ian Allan Publishing Ltd   131
Amberley Publishing   131
The Crowood Press   144
Haynes Publishing   157
Stenlake Publishing Ltd   187
Ulric Publishing   191

Travel and geography

4th Estate   155
AA Publishing   130
Apa Publications   132
Appletree Press Ltd   132
Arena Publishing   132
Bennion Kearny Ltd   134
Blackstaff Press Ltd   135
Blue Guides Ltd   136
Bradt Travel Guides Ltd   138
Nicholas Brealey Publishing   169
Canongate Books Ltd   139
Jonathan Cape   193
Chase My Snail   226
Chatto & Windus/Hogarth   193
Cicerone Press   141
Countryside Books   143
Giles de la Mare Publishers Ltd   145
Discovery Walking Guides Ltd   145
DK   145
Ebury Publishing   146
Ebury Self   147
Eland Publishing Ltd   147
Eye Books   148
W. Foulsham & Co. Ltd   150
Garnet Publishing Ltd   151
Gibson Square   152
Granta Books   152
Hamish Hamilton   176

Hodder & Stoughton   158
ISF Publishing   160
Lonely Planet Publications Ltd   165
Methuen & Co Ltd   168
Michelin Travel Partners UK Ltd   168
Murdoch Books   168
John Murray Press   168
New Holland Publishers (UK) Ltd   199
The Oleander Press   172
On Stream Publications   172
Penguin General   175
Penguin Random House UK   176
Prestel Publishing Ltd   178
Quarto Group Publishing UK   179
Quiller   179
Reaktion Books   180
Rider   180
Sawday's   183
September Publishing   184
Sheldrake Press   184
Souvenir Press   178
Square Peg   193
Stacey Publishing Ltd   187
Summersdale Publishers Ltd   188
Sunflower Books   188
I.B. Tauris   189

TV, TV tie-ins and radio

Bello   174
BFI Publishing   134
DK   145
Ebury Publishing   146
Ebury Self   147
Harper Voyager   156
Titan Books   190

Welsh interest

Amgueddfa Cymru – National Museum Wales   131
Dref Wen   146
Honno Ltd (Welsh Women's Press)   197
Seren   184
University of Wales Press   193
Welsh Academic Press   194
Y Lolfa Cyf   195

Writers' guides

Barbican Press Ltd   134
Bloomsbury Publishing Plc   143
Country Books   143
David & Charles Ltd   144
Fly on the Wall Press   197

Children's book publishers and packagers (UK)

Listings for *Book publishers UK and Ireland* start on page 130 and listings for *Book packagers* start on page 226.

Audiobooks
Book publishers
Child's Play (International) Ltd   140
Dref Wen   146
HarperCollins Publishers   155
Mantra Lingua Ltd   167
The Orion Publishing Group Ltd   173
St Pauls Publishing   182
Scripture Union   184

Children's fiction
Book publishers
Andersen Press Ltd   132
Bloomsbury Publishing Plc   136
Bonnier Books UK   137
Burning Chair Publishing   138
Child's Play (International) Ltd   140
Cicada Books   141
Cló Iar-Chonnachta Teo   141
Cranachan Publishing   143
Dref Wen   146
Everyman's Library   148
Everything With Words Ltd   148
Faber and Faber Ltd   148
David Fickling Books   149
Fircone Books Ltd   149
Firefly Press Ltd   149
Fisherton Press   149
Floris Books   150
Guppy Publishing Ltd   153
Hachette Children's Group   153
Happy Yak   154
HarperCollins Publishers   155
Hot Key Books   158
House of Lochar   159
Lion Hudson Ltd   163
Little Tiger Group   164
Luna Press Publishing   166
Mabecron Books Ltd   166
Mantra Lingua Ltd   167
Kevin Mayhew Ltd   167
Mentor Books   167
The Mercier Press   167
Nobrow Books   170
The O'Brien Press Ltd   171
Old Barn Books   171
Orchard Books   172

The Orion Publishing Group Ltd   173
Oxford University Press   173
Patrician Press   174
Penguin Random House Children's UK   176
Piccadilly Press   177
Puffin   178
Pure Indigo Ltd   178
Ransom Publishing Ltd   179
Ruby Tuesday Books Ltd   181
Scripture Union   184
Simon & Schuster UK Ltd   185
Studio Press   187
Templar Books   189
Three Hares Publishing   190
Tiny Owl Publishing Ltd   190
Troika   191
Usborne Publishing Ltd   192
Walker Books Ltd   193
Wide Eyed Editions   194
Y Lolfa Cyf   195

Book packagers
Graham-Cameron Publishing & Illustration   227
Working Partners Ltd   228

Children's non-fiction
Book publishers
Amber Books Ltd   131
Anness Publishing   132
Authentic Media Ltd   133
Award Publications Ltd   133
The British Museum Press   138
Child's Play (International) Ltd   140
Cranachan Publishing   143
Dref Wen   146
Encyclopaedia Britannica (UK) Ltd   148
Faber and Faber Ltd   148
Fircone Books Ltd   149
Geddes & Grosset   151
GL Assessment   152
Hachette Children's Group   153
Happy Yak   154
HarperCollins Publishers   155
Igloo Books Ltd   159
IWM (Imperial War Museums) Publishing   160
Lion Hudson Ltd   163
LOM ART   165
Mantra Lingua Ltd   167

Mentor Books   167
Nobrow Books   170
Nosy Crow   170
The O'Brien Press Ltd   171
Michael O'Mara Books Ltd   172
The Orion Publishing Group Ltd   173
Oxford University Press   173
Pavilion Children's Books   174
Penguin Random House Children's UK   176
Piccadilly Press   177
Portland Press Ltd   177
Puffin   178
Ransom Publishing Ltd   179
Salariya Book Company Ltd   182
Schofield & Sims Ltd   183
Science Museum Group   183
Scripture Union   184
Simon & Schuster UK Ltd   185
Ulric Publishing   191
Usborne Publishing Ltd   192
Walker Books Ltd   193
Wide Eyed Editions   194
Y Lolfa Cyf   195
ZigZag Education   195

Book packagers

Aladdin Books Ltd   226
Bender Richardson White   226
Brown Bear Books Ltd   226
John Brown Group – Children's Division   226
Graham-Cameron Publishing & Illustration   227
Hart McLeod Ltd   227
Orpheus Books Ltd   227
Toucan Books Ltd   228
Windmill Books Ltd   228

Multimedia
Book publishers
Authentic Media Ltd   133
GL Assessment   152
HarperCollins Publishers   155
Mantra Lingua Ltd   167
Oxford University Press   173
Puffin   178
Ransom Publishing Ltd   179
St Pauls Publishing   182

Book packagers
John Brown Group – Children's Division   226

Novelty and activity books
Book publishers
Award Publications Ltd   133
Bloomsbury Publishing Plc   136
Child's Play (International) Ltd   140
Dref Wen   146

Fircone Books Ltd   149
Flame Tree Publishing   149
Floris Books   150
Hachette Children's Group   153
Happy Yak   154
Igloo Books Ltd   159
Kings Road Publishing   162
Frances Lincoln   163
Lion Hudson Ltd   163
Little Tiger Group   164
Mabecron Books   166
Kevin Mayhew Ltd   167
Mentor Books   167
Michael O'Mara Books Ltd   172
Orchard Books   172
Oxford University Press   173
Pavilion Children's Books   174
Penguin Random House Children's UK   176
Puffin   178
Ransom Publishing Ltd   179
Scripture Union   184
Tango Books Ltd   188
Tarquin Publications   188
Usborne Publishing Ltd   192
Walker Books Ltd   193

Book packagers
Aladdin Books Ltd   226
John Brown Group – Children's Division   226

Picture books
Book publishers
Andersen Press Ltd   132
Authentic Media Ltd   133
Award Publications Ltd   133
Bloomsbury Publishing Plc   136
Child's Play (International) Ltd   140
Cló Iar-Chonnachta Teo   141
Dref Wen   146
Everyman's Library   148
Faber and Faber Ltd   148
Fisherton Press   149
Floris Books   150
Guppy Publishing Ltd   153
Hachette Children's Group   153
HarperCollins Publishers   155
Igloo Books Ltd   159
Kings Road Publishing   162
Frances Lincoln   163
Lion Hudson Ltd   163
Little Tiger Group   164
Mantra Lingua Ltd   167
Nobrow Books   170
Nosy Crow   170
The O'Brien Press Ltd   171
Michael O'Mara Books Ltd   172

Orchard Books 172
The Orion Publishing Group Ltd 173
Oxford University Press 173
Pavilion Children's Books 174
Piccadilly Press 177
Puffin 178
Scripture Union 184
Studio Press 187
Troika 191
Usborne Publishing Ltd 192
Walker Books Ltd 193

Book packagers

Aladdin Books Ltd 226
John Brown Group – Children's Division 226
Graham-Cameron Publishing & Illustration 227
Heart of Albion 227

Poetry
Book publishers

Authentic Media Ltd 133
Bloomsbury Publishing Plc 136
Cló Iar-Chonnachta Teo 141
Dref Wen 146
Everyman's Library 148
Faber and Faber Ltd 148
HarperCollins Publishers 155
Frances Lincoln 163
Orchard Books 172
Out-Spoken Press 594
Oxford University Press 173

Puffin 178
Walker Books Ltd 193

Book packagers

Heart of Albion 227

Religion
Book publishers

Authentic Media Ltd 133
Catholic Truth Society 140
Christian Education 140
Dref Wen 146
Gresham Books Ltd 153
HarperCollins Publishers 155
Kube Publishing Ltd 162
Frances Lincoln 163
Lion Hudson Ltd 163
Mantra Lingua Ltd 167
Kevin Mayhew Ltd 167
Oxford University Press 173
George Ronald 180
St Pauls Publishing 182
Scripture Union 184
Society for Promoting Christian Knowledge 186
Stacey Publishing Ltd 187
Usborne Publishing Ltd 192
Veritas Publications 192

Book packagers

Heart of Albion 227

Publishers of plays (UK)

Barbican Press Ltd   134
Brown, Son & Ferguson Ltd   138
Chapman Publishing   140
Cló Iar-Chonnachta Teo   141
Concord Theatricals   142
Cressrelles Publishing Co. Ltd   143
Everyman's Library   148
Faber and Faber Ltd   148
The Gallery Press   151
J. Garnet Miller   151
Nick Hern Books Ltd   157

Kenyon-Deane   161
The Lilliput Press Ltd   163
Kevin Mayhew Ltd   167
New Playwrights' Network   169
Oberon Books   171
The Oleander Press   172
The Playwrights Publishing Company   177
Renard Press Ltd   180
Seren   184
Colin Smythe Ltd   185
Josef Weinberger Plays Ltd   194

Publishers of poetry (UK)

Arc Publications   132
Barbican Press Ltd   134
Blackstaff Press Ltd   135
Bloodaxe Books Ltd   135
Canongate Books Ltd   139
Jonathan Cape   193
Carcanet Press Ltd   140
Chapman Publishing   140
Chatto & Windus/Hogarth   193
Cló Iar-Chonnachta Teo   141
Crescent Moon Publishing   143
The Emma Press Ltd   148
Enitharmon Editions   148
Everyman's Library   148
Eyewear Publishing Ltd   197
Faber and Faber Ltd   148
Flipped Eye Publishing   150
Fly on the Wall Press   197
404 Ink   151

The Gallery Press   151
Hippopotamus Press   157
Honno Ltd (Welsh Women's Press)   197
The Lilliput Press Ltd   163
Liverpool University Press   165
Luath Press Ltd   165
Mango Books   167
New Island Books   169
The Oleander Press   172
Oversteps Books Ltd   173
Parthian Books   174
Penguin Press   176
Penguin Random House UK   176
Picador   174
Renard Press Ltd   180
Route   181
Seren   184
Stonewood Press   187
Two Rivers Press Ltd   191
Valley Press   192

Literary agents for children's books

The following literary agents will consider work suitable for children's books, from authors and/or illustrators of children's books. Listings start on page 430. See also *Art agents and commercial art studios* on page 492.

3 Seas Literary Agency   464
The Agency (London) Ltd   430
Aitken Alexander Associates Ltd   430
Darley Anderson Literary, TV and Film Agency   431
ANDLYN   431
The Authors' Agent   461
Bath Literary Agency   432
The Bell Lomax Moreton Agency   432
The Bent Agency   464
The Bent Agency   432
The Blair Partnership   433
Jenny Brown Associates   434
Felicity Bryan Associates   434
C&W Agency   435
Georgina Capel Associates Ltd   435
The Catchpole Agency   436
The Chudney Agency   466
Anne Clark Literary Agency   436
CookeMcDermid   462
Creative Authors Ltd   437
Rupert Crew Ltd   437
Curtis Brown   437
Liza Dawson Associates   467
DHH Literary Agency   438
Diamond Kahn & Woods Literary Agency   438
Sandra Dijkstra & Associates   467
Dunham Literary Inc.   467
Dystel, Goderich & Bourret LLC   467
Eddison Pearson Ltd   439
The Ethan Ellenberg Literary Agency   467
Folio Literary Management   468
Fraser Ross Associates   440
Golvan Arts Management   461
The Good Literary Agency   440
Greene & Heaton Ltd   441
The Greenhouse Literary Agency   441
Marianne Gunn O'Connor Literary, Film/TV Agency   442
Hardman & Swainson   443
Antony Harwood Ltd   443
A.M. Heath & Co. Ltd   443
Sophie Hicks Agency   443
David Higham Associates Ltd   444
Kate Hordern Literary Agency Ltd   444
Janklow & Nesbit (UK) Ltd   445

Johnson & Alcock Ltd   445
Kane Literary Agency   446
Margaret Kennedy Agency   461
Harvey Klinger Inc.   470
kt literary   470
LBA Books   447
Levine Greenberg Rostan Literary Agency   471
Lindsay Literary Agency   447
Luithlen Agency   448
McIntosh & Otis Inc.   471
Eunice McMullen Ltd   448
Andrew Mann Ltd   448
Marjacq Scripts Ltd   448
MBA Literary and Script Agents Ltd   449
Sarah McKenzie Literary Management   462
Madeleine Milburn Literary, TV & Film Agency   449
MMB Creative (Mulcahy Sweeney Associates Ltd)   450
Jean V. Naggar Literary Agency Inc.   472
Kate Nash Literary Agency   450
Northbank Talent Management   451
Andrew Nurnberg Associates Ltd   451
P.S. Literary Agency   463
Paper Lion Ltd   451
Peters Fraser & Dunlop Ltd   452
Alison Picard, Literary Agent   472
Frances Plumpton Literary Agency   464
Redhammer Management Ltd   452
Rogers, Coleridge & White Ltd   453
Elizabeth Roy Literary Agency   454
Susan Schulman Literary Agency LLC   472
Scovil Galen Ghosh Literary Agency, Inc.   473
Caroline Sheldon Literary Agency Ltd   455
Skylark Literary Limited   455
The Soho Agency Ltd (previously LAW/Lucas Alexander Whitley Ltd)   456
Abner Stein   456
The Strothman Agency   473
Sarah Such Literary Agency   457
TFS Literary Agency   464
United Agents LLP   458
Jo Unwin Literary Agency   458
Watson, Little Ltd   458
Whispering Buffalo Literary Agency Ltd   459
Eve White Literary Agency Limited   459
Susan Yearwood Agency   460

Literary agents for television, film, radio and theatre

Listings for these and other literary agents start on page 430.

The Agency (London) Ltd 430
Aitken Alexander Associates Ltd 430
Berlin Associates Ltd 433
Blake Friedmann Literary, TV & Film Agency
    Ltd 433
Alan Brodie Representation 434
Georgina Capel Associates Ltd 435
Casarotto Ramsay & Associates Ltd 435
Jonathan Clowes Ltd 436
Rosica Colin Ltd 436
Concord Theatricals 466
Richard Curtis Associates Inc. 466
Curtis Brown 437
Curtis Brown Ltd 467
Judy Daish Associates Ltd 437
Dalzell & Beresford Ltd 438
Felix de Wolfe 438
Fillingham Weston Associates 439
Film Rights Ltd 439
Laurence Fitch Ltd 439
FRA 440
Jüri Gabriel 440
Global Lion Intellectual Property Management
    Inc. 468
Golvan Arts Management 461
Bill Goodall Literary Agency 441
Sanford J. Greenburger Associates Inc. 469
David Higham Associates Ltd 444
Valerie Hoskins Associates Ltd 444

Independent Talent Group Ltd 445
JFL Agency Ltd 445
Robin Jones Literary Agency (RJLA) 445
Michelle Kass Associates Ltd 446
Knight Hall Agency Ltd 446
LBA Books 447
Limelight Celebrity Management Ltd 447
MBA Literary and Script Agents Ltd 449
Madeleine Milburn Literary, TV & Film Agency 449
PBJ & KBJ Management 451
Peters Fraser & Dunlop Ltd 452
Playmarket 464
Sayle Screen Ltd 454
Susan Schulman Literary Agency LLC 472
The Sharland Organisation Ltd 455
Sheil Land Associates Ltd 455
Elaine Steel Writers' Agent 456
Micheline Steinberg Associates 456
Rochelle Stevens & Co 456
Sarah Such Literary Agency 457
The Tennyson Agency 457
Trident Media Group 473
Nick Turner Management Ltd 457
Josef Weinberger Plays Ltd 458
WGM Atlantic Talent and Literary Group 458
Eve White Literary Agency Limited 459
WME 459
WME 473
WordLink Incorporated 473
Zeitgeist Agency 462

Indexes

Prizes and awards by subject area

This index gives the major subject area of each entry in the main listing which begins on page 556.

BAME

The James Berry Poetry Prize   558
FAB Prize for Undiscovered Talent   567
Fresh Ink Award   568
Jhalak Prize   571
Killing It: The Killer Reads Competition for Undiscovered Writers   572
Owned Voices Novel Award   578
Mo Siewcharran Prize   592

Biography

The Australian/Vogel's Literary Award   557
The Biographers' Club Slightly Foxed Best First Biography Prize   558
The Biographers' Club Tony Lothian Prize   558
The Pol Roger Duff Cooper Prize   563
Costa Book Awards   563
East Anglian Book Awards   565
The Elizabeth Longford Prize for Historical Biography   573
The PEN Ackerley Prize for Autobiography and Memoir   578
The Samuel Pepys Award   579
Runciman Award   581
The James Tait Black Memorial Prizes   584

Children

The Hans Christian Andersen Awards   556
Blue Peter Book Awards   559
Bookbug Picture Book Prize   559
BookTrust Storytime Prize   560
Cheltenham Illustration Awards   562
The Children's Book Award   562
The KPMG Children's Books Ireland Awards   562
The Children's Laureate   562
The CILIP Carnegie and Kate Greenaway Children's Book Awards   562
English Association English 4–11 Children's Book Awards   566
FAB Prize for Undiscovered Talent   567
The Eleanor Farjeon Award   567
Indie Book Awards   570
Jhalak Prize   571
The Macmillan Prize for Illustration   574
New Zealand Book Awards for Children and Young Adults   577
The People's Book Prize   578
The Queen's Knickers Award   580
The Times/Chicken House Children's Fiction Competition   585

Tir na n-Og Awards   585
Wildlife Photographer of the Year   587
YouWriteOncom Book Awards   588

Drama – theatre, TV and radio

ARIAS (Audio & Radio Industry Awards)   557
Verity Bargate Award   557
The David Cohen Prize for Literature   563
FOCAL International Awards   567
The Imison Award   570
The Peggy Ramsay Foundation   591
RTÉ Radio, Drama On One, P.J. O'Connor Awards for Radio Drama   581
RTÉ Radio 1 Short Story Competition in Honour of Francis MacManus   581
Segora International Writing Competitions   582
Swansea University Dylan Thomas Prize   584
The Tinniswood Award   585

Essays

The David Cohen Prize for Literature   563
Copyright Essay Prize   563
Reginald Taylor and Lord Fletcher Essay Competition   585

Fiction

The Aeon Award   556
Arts Council England   588
The Australian/Vogel's Literary Award   557
Authors' Club Awards   557
The Bath Novel Award   558
Blue Pencil Agency First Novel Award   559
The Boardman Tasker Prize   559
The Bollinger Everyman Wodehouse Prize for Comic Fiction   559
The Booker Prize   559
The International Booker Prize   559
British Czech and Slovak Association Writing Competition   560
British Fantasy Awards   561
British Science Fiction Association Awards   561
Gordon Burn Prize   561
Caledonia Novel Award   561
Peggy Chapman-Andrews First Novel Award   561
Arthur C. Clarke Award   563
The David Cohen Prize for Literature   563
Comedy Women in Print Awards   563
Commonwealth Short Story Prize   563
Costa Book Awards   563

Creative Future Writers' Award 564
Creative Scotland 589
The Curtis Brown Prize for Prose Fiction (University of East Anglia) 564
CWA Dagger Awards 564
The DSC Prize for South Asian Literature 565
East Anglian Book Awards 565
The Desmond Elliott Prize 566
Encore Award 566
English Association English 4–11 Children's Book Awards 566
European Union Prize for Literature 566
FAB Prize for Undiscovered Talent 567
The Geoffrey Faber Memorial Prize 567
First Novel Prize 567
Rathbones Folio Prize 568
The Franco-British Society's Literary Prize 568
Fresh Ink Award 568
The Goldsmiths Prize 569
The Hawthornden Prize 569
The Impress Prize for New Writers 570
Indie Book Awards 570
International Dublin Literary Award 571
International Prize for Arabic Fiction 571
An Post Irish Book Awards 571
Jhalak Prize 571
Kerry Group Irish Novel of the Year Award 572
Kindle Storyteller Award 572
The Kitschies 572
Laxfield Literary Launch Prize 572
The Lindisfarne Prize for Crime Fiction 573
Little, Brown Award for Crime Fiction (University of East Anglia) 573
The London Hellenic Prize 573
McIlvanney Prize for the Scottish Crime Novel of the Year and The Bloody Scotland Debut of the Year 574
The McKitterick Prize 574
The Manchester Prizes for Fiction and Poetry 575
The Somerset Maugham Awards 575
The Mythopoeic Fantasy Award for Adult Literature 576
New Angle Prize for East Anglian Literature 576
New Anglia Manuscript Prize 576
The Nobel Prize in Literature 577
Ockham New Zealand Book Awards 578
Owned Voices Novel Award 578
Page Turner Awards 773
The People's Book Prize 578
Polari Book Prize 579
The Portico Prize 579
Queen Mary Wasafiri New Writing Prize 579
Republic of Consciousness Prize for Small Presses 580
The Romantic Novel of the Year Awards 580
RSL Christopher Bland Prize 580
RSL Ondaatje Prize 581
Rubery Book Award 581
Runciman Award 581
The Saltire Society Literary Awards 581

Walter Scott Prize for Historical Fiction 582
Mo Siewcharran Prize 592
Wilbur Smith Adventure Writing Prize 583
Staunch Book Prize 583
The Sunday Times/University of Warwick Young Writer of the Year Award 584
Swansea University Dylan Thomas Prize 584
The James Tait Black Memorial Prizes 584
The Paul Torday Memorial Prize 586
The Betty Trask Prize and Awards 586
The Wainwright Prize 586
Wales Book of the Year Award 586
The Warwick Prize for Women in Translation 587
Wellcome Book Prize 587
Wingate Literary Prize 587
Women's Prize for Fiction 588
David T.K. Wong Fellowship 591
Writers' & Artists' Working-Class Writers' Prize 593
YouWriteOncom Book Awards 588
Zooker Award 588

Grants, bursaries and fellowships

Arts Council England 588
The Arts Council/An Chomhairle Ealaíon 588
The Authors' Contingency Fund 589
The Authors' Foundation 589
Carole Blake Open Doors Project 589
The K. Blundell Trust 589
Alfred Bradley Bursary Award 589
Creative Scotland 589
The Julia Darling Travel Fellowship 589
E.M. Forster Award 590
The Eric Gregory Awards 590
Hawthornden Fellowships 590
Francis Head Bequest 590
The P.D. James Memorial Fund 590
Leverhulme Research Fellowships 590
The John Masefield Memorial Trust 591
Northern Writers' Awards 591
The Peggy Ramsay Foundation 591
Deborah Rogers Foundation Writers Award and David Miller Bursary 580
The Royal Literary Fund 591
TLC/Arts Council England Free Reads Scheme 591
The Travelling Scholarships 591
David T.K. Wong Fellowship 591
Writers & Artists bursaries 593

Illustration

Academy of British Cover Design: Annual Cover Design Competition 556
The Hans Christian Andersen Awards 556
British Science Fiction Association Awards 561
Cheltenham Illustration Awards 562
The KPMG Children's Books Ireland Awards 562
Derwent Art Prize 565
FAB Prize for Undiscovered Talent 567

The Eleanor Farjeon Award   567
FOCAL International Awards   567
The Macmillan Prize for Illustration   574
The Moth Art Prize   575
The Queen's Knickers Award   580
The Jill Smythies Award   583
Tir na n-Og Awards   585
The V&A Illustration Awards   586
World Illustration Awards   588

Journalism

London Press Club Awards   573
The Orwell Prizes   578
The Press Awards   579

LGBTQI+

The James Berry Poetry Prize   558
Polari Book Prize   579

New Media/Digital

New Media Writing Prize   577

Non-fiction

ALCS Educational Writers' Award   556
The Australian/Vogel's Literary Award   557
Authors' Club Awards   557
The Baillie Gifford Prize for Non-Fiction   557
The David Berry Prize   558
The Boardman Tasker Prize   559
British Academy Medals and Prizes   560
British Czech and Slovak Association Writing
   Competition   560
British Science Fiction Association Awards   561
The Pol Roger Duff Cooper Prize   563
The Rose Mary Crawshay Prize   564
Creative Scotland   589
Cundill History Prize   564
CWA Dagger Awards   564
East Anglian Book Awards   565
English Association English 4–11 Children's Book
   Awards   566
Financial Times and McKinsey Business Book of the
   Year Award   567
The Franco-British Society's Literary Prize   568
Gladstone History Book Prize   568
The Gourmand World Cookbook Awards   569
Jane Grigson Trust Award   569
William Hill Sports Book of the Year Award   570
The Calvin and Rose G. Hoffman Memorial Prize for
   Distinguished Scholarly Essay on Christopher
   Marlowe   570
The Impress Prize for New Writers   570
Jhalak Prize   571
The K&IM Information Resources Awards   571
Kraszna-Krausz Book Awards   572
The London Hellenic Prize   573

Longman-History Today Book Prize   574
McIlvanney Prize for the Scottish Crime Novel of the
   Year and The Bloody Scotland Debut of the
   Year   574
The Somerset Maugham Awards   575
The Mythopoeic Scholarship Award in Inklings
   Studies   576
The Mythopoeic Scholarship Award in Myth and
   Fantasy Studies   576
The Nature Writing Prize for Working Class
   Writers   592
Ockham New Zealand Book Awards   578
The People's Book Prize   578
The Portico Prize   579
RSL Christopher Bland Prize   580
RSL Giles St Aubyn Awards for Non-Fiction   581
RSL Ondaatje Prize   581
The Royal Society Young People's Book Prize   581
Runciman Award   581
The Saltire Society Literary Awards   581
The André Simon Memorial Fund Book
   Awards   583
The Telegraph Sports Book Awards   583
The Sunday Times/University of Warwick Young
   Writer of the Year Award   584
The Royal Society Science Book Prize   585
The Wainwright Prize   586
Wales Book of the Year Award   586
The Warwick Prize for Women in Translation   587
Wellcome Book Prize   587
The Whitfield Prize   587
Wingate Literary Prize   587
The Wolfson History Prize   587
Writers & Artists Working-Class Writer's Prize   593

Photography

Deutsche Börse Photography Foundation Prize   565
FOCAL International Awards   567
RSPCA Young Photographer Awards   581
Wildlife Photographer of the Year   587

Poetry

Arts Council England   588
The Arts Council/An Chomhairle Ealaíon   588
The James Berry Poetry Prize   558
The Boardman Tasker Prize   559
The Bridport Prize   560
Canterbury Festival Poet of the Year   561
Cholmondeley Awards   562
The David Cohen Prize for Literature   563
Costa Book Awards   563
Creative Future Writers' Award   564
Creative Scotland   589
East Anglian Book Awards   565
The T.S. Eliot Prize   566
The Geoffrey Faber Memorial Prize   567
Fish Publishing Writing Prizes   567
Fool for Poetry Chapbook Competition   568

Forward Prizes for Poetry   568
Foyle Young Poets of the Year Award   349
The Ginkgo Prize for Ecopoetry   568
The Ted Hughes Award for New Work in
    Poetry   570
The International Poetry Business Book & Pamphlet
    Competition   571
Jerwood Compton Poetry Fellowships   590
Jhalak Prize   571
Kent and Sussex Poetry Society Open Poetry
    Competition   572
Laurel Prize for Ecopoetry   572
Listowel Writers' Week Poetry Competitions   573
The Sarah Maguire Prize   574
The Michael Marks Awards for Poetry
    Pamphlets   575
The Somerset Maugham Awards   575
The Moth Poetry Prize   576
Michael Murphy Memorial Poetry Prize   576
National Poetry Competition   576
New Angle Prize for East Anglian Literature   576
The New Poets Prize   577
Ockham New Zealand Book Awards   578
The Plough Prize   579
Polari Book Prize   579
Queen Mary Wasafiri New Writing Prize   579
The Rialto Nature and Place Poetry
    Competition   580
Runciman Award   581
The Saltire Society Literary Awards   581
Segora International Writing Competitions   582
The Stephen Spender Prize   583
The Sunday Times/University of Warwick Young
    Writer of the Year Award   584
Swansea University Dylan Thomas Prize   584
Ver Poets Open Competition   586
Wales Book of the Year Award   586
The Warwick Prize for Women in Translation   587
Winchester Poetry Prize   587
Women Poets' Prize at the Rebecca Swift
    Foundation   588
YouWriteOncom Book Awards   588

Short stories

The ALCS Tom-Gallon Trust Award   556
Dinesh Allirajah Prize for Short Fiction   556
Bath Flash Fiction Awards   557
BBC National Short Story Award   558
The Bridport Prize   560
The David Cohen Prize for Literature   563
CWA Dagger Awards   564
Desperate Literature Short Fiction Prize   565
Edge Hill Short Story Prize   566
Fish Publishing Writing Prizes   567
Jhalak Prize   571
The London Magazine Short Story, Poetry and Essay
    Competitions   573
Bryan MacMahon Short Story Award   574
The Mogford Prize for Food and Drink Short Story
    Writing   575
The Moth Short Story Prize   576
New Welsh Writing Awards   577
The Observer/Jonathan Cape/Comica Graphic Short
    Story Prize   578
Polari Book Prize   579
V.S. Pritchett Short Story Prize   579
RTÉ Radio 1 Short Story Competition in Honour of
    Francis MacManus   581
Rubery Book Award   581
Segora International Writing Competitions   582
The Sunday Times Audible Short Story Award   584
Swansea University Dylan Thomas Prize   584
The White Review Short Story Prize   587
Writers' & Artists' Yearbook 2022 Short Story
    Competition   588
YouWriteOn.com Book Awards   588

Translation

The Goethe-Institut Award for New
    Translation   569
Harvill Secker Young Translators' Prize   569
International Prize for Arabic Fiction   571
Kindle Storyteller Award   572
The Sarah Maguire Prize   574
The Stephen Spender Prize   583
The Translation Prizes   586
The Warwick Prize for Women in Translation   587

General index

Key topics and terms that appear in the articles within this *Yearbook* are listed here.

accountants 482
adaptation process 354
adapting a novel 354
adapting books for stage and screen 354
advance 407
advertising 301
advertising agencies 478
advice for new writers 239, 244
advice for non-fiction authors 415
advice for television writers 357
agent-author trust 415
agents 257, 410
Alliance of Independent Authors 515
Amazon 102
art buyers 478
artists 488
aspiring authors 265
aspiring writers 127, 241
attracting a non-fiction agent or publisher 423
Audible 370
audio drama 365
audiobook market 369
audiobooks 102, 369
audiobooks, producing your own 369
author earnings 109
author services, choosing a company 619
author services companies 618
author-publishers 515
authorial voice 250
Authors' Licensing and Collecting Society 510, 669, 715
authors, tracing 716
authorship 666
awards 506

BBC 365
BBC (radio) 383
BBC Writersroom 358
becoming a poet 329, 336
becoming a screenwriter 351
becoming an author 244
bestsellers 107, 232
biography 241, 295
blog writing 303
blogging 658
blogs 631
blogs, travel 311
book blogs 635
book deal 406
Book Fairs 407, 411, 428, 484
book sales 110
book trade 102
books, illustrations 475

booksellers, promoting your work to 614
bookshops, getting your book in 614
bursaries 506, 593

cable retransmission, simultaneous 716
cancellation fees 481
career, writing 117
character development 248
character-led novels 268
characterisation 233, 268
characters 268, 275
characters, romantic 272
children's books, illustrating for 476
collective licensing 719
comedy, romantic 284
comics 280
commercial radio 383
commission, literary agents 419
commissioning for radio 383
commissions, pricing 481
contracts 480
copies sold 107
copy writing 13
copying 716
copyright 480, 666, 703, 713
copyright law 703
Copyright Licensing Agency 713
copyright ownership 704
copyright protection 704
copywriting 301
courses, writing 506
creating a brand 303
creative writing courses 247
crime fiction 124, 231, 247
crime writing 265
crowdfunding 114, 490
cultivating your talent 117

DACS 717
debut novel 105, 121, 246
debut novelists 405
design companies 476
dialogue 242
dialogue, videogames 375
digital publishing 611
discovering talent 427
distribution 111, 620
diversity 106, 248
drama 366
dramatist 365

ebooks 102, 611, 660
editing 242, 406, 651
editing a magazine 11

editing advice   651
editing tips   651
editing your work   651
editors, magazines   7
editors, newspapers   7
electronic adaptation rights   420
elevator pitch   410

facts, non-fiction   305
fake news   3
fanfiction   621
fantastical fiction   277
fantasy   125, 277
feedback   248
feedback on your writing   336, 506
festivals   507
fees   480
    chasing   482
    fixed *v* negotiable   481
festivals, literary   501
film, writing for   351
financial difficulties   488
finding a publisher   419
finding an agent   257
first chapter   233
fledgling writers   244
food science   320
freelance illustrators   475
freelance indexing   661
freelance writer   301
freelance writers   7

genre   277
genre fiction   124
genre-bending literature   296
genres   124, 262
getting noticed   630
getting published   427
getting published, poetry   330, 336
getting your play published   385
ghostwriting   298
glossary, publishing roles   673
grants   488
graphic novel writing courses   280
graphic novels   280
greeting cards   476

health   320
health and wellness writing   320
high-street bookshops   614
historical fiction   288
historical, non-fiction   292
history   292
hooking your reader   233
horror writing   231
how to write a how-to book   253
how-to books   253

illustration, non-fiction   483
illustrations, illustrators   475
illustrators   488
independent authors   611

independent publishing   611
indexers, professional   660
indexing   660
indie publishers and debut novels   121
internet   334
internet, as a networking tool   630
interviews, with potential clients   478
ISBNs   111, 666, 668
    FAQs about   662
ISSNs   664

journalism   11

legal risks of writing   296
libraries   241, 507
licence   480
licence to copy   714
literary agent, role of   408
literary agents   99, 230, 251, 257, 259, 405, 410, 415, 427
literary agents, multimedia   419
literary festivals   501
literary festivals, preparing for   502
literary prize winners   594
literary scouts   407
literature festivals   101–2, 241, 246
location, sagas   276
location, videogames   375
love stories   271

magazines   11
magazines and newspapers, illustrations   475
making money   488
managing permissions management   719
managing your writing career   117
market knowledge   118
marketing   13, 104, 107, 111, 251, 620
memoir   241, 295
memoir writing, legal risks   296
mentoring   127, 241
mentoring schemes   127
metadata   111, 609
mini-genres   124
moral rights   705
multimedia   419
mystery fiction   124

narrative design   375
natural world   317
nature writing   317
negotiating deals   420
networking   101, 630
new writers   239
news writing   2
newspapers and magazines   1
non-disclosure agreements   299
non-fiction   292, 305
non-fiction authors   415
non-fiction, book proposals   423
non-fiction, illustration   483

novel writing   233, 246
novels, crowdfunding   114

offer of representation   405
online networking   630
online portfolio   484
online, self-publishing   607
online, writing for   2
opportunities for writers   505
oral traditions   334

performance poetry   339
performance poets   334
photocopying and scanning   716
pitch   410
pitch-to-print   7
pitching   5, 7, 374
plays   367, 385
podcast   367
podcasting   361
podcasting, commercial opportunities   361
poet, how to become a   329
poetry   332, 336
    getting published   334
    performance   334
poetry competitions   339
poetry in times of change   332
poetry organisations   342
poetry, performing   339
poetry, reaching your audience   336
poetry, writing   329
popular fiction   124
popular history   292
portfolio   303
POV   242, 367
preparing for literary festivals   502
presentation   99
print on demand   618
print, writing for   2
prize winners   594
professionalism   118
promoting your book   615
promoting your work   507
promoting yourself online   630
promotion   251
proofreading symbols   654
proposal, non-fiction   423
proposals   324
Public Lending Right   665, 668, 716
public relations   634
publicity   104, 111, 246
publisher revenue   108
publishers
    and ISBNs   663
    approaching   100
Publishers' Licensing Services   719
publishing agreements   420
publishing contract   406
publishing contracts, illustrators   484
publishing deals   428

publishing process   421
publishing roles glossary   673

radio   365
radio, BBC   383
radio broadcasting   383
radio, commercial   383
reading as a writer   241
reading poetry   332
reciprocal arrangements, PLR   669
rejection fees   481
rejections   334
research   231
research, non-fiction   305
rights, authors'   716
romance   126, 271
romantic characters   272
romantic comedy, writing   284
romantic fiction   271
romcoms   284
royalties   488

saga writing   274
sagas   274
sale-or-return   112
sales figures   107
sales team   112
sampling arrangements, PLR   669
science fiction   125, 277
science writing   314
screenwriting   351
self-employed artists and illustrators   488
self-promotion   479
self-publishing   369, 611, 618
self-publishing, online   607
self-publishing providers   618
self-publishing tips   614
setting up a blog   659
setting up a magazine   11
social media   112, 237, 301, 630
Society of Authors   509
Society of Indexers   660–1
speculative fiction   277
sponsorship   490
sports books   324
sports nutrition   321
sports writing   324
starting a blog   658
sub-genres   124
submission process   406
submissions   100, 651
submissions to agents   410
submissions to publishers   427
submitting poetry   338
subsidiary rights   407
syndicates   1
synopsis   411, 484

talent, cultivating your   117
talent, developing   505
technical subjects   314

technical writing   314
television and film, writing for   351
television, film and radio   512
television, writing for   357
theatre   385
theatre critic, career as   389
theatre critics   389
theatre for children   513
theatre, writing about   389
thrillers   265
travel articles   312
travel blogging and advertising revenue   311
travel blogs   311
travel books   312
travel writing   309

under-represented writers   105, 506, 592–4

videogames   373
videogames, writing   373
voice-over   366

websites   630
what do literary agents do?   408, 427
winning awards   248, 250
world-building, videogames   376
writers, freelance   7

Writers' Guild of Great Britain   512
writers, opportunities for   505
writing a blog   658
writing career   117, 230, 250
writing character-led novels   268
writing courses   506
writing different genres   262
writing dream   237
writing fanfiction   621, 623
writing for children   259
writing for different audiences   262
writing for television   357
writing for television and film   351
writing for the health and wellness market   320
writing historical fiction   288
writing how-to books   253
writing, online   2
writing poetry   332
writing, print   2
writing romantic comedy   284
writing romantic fiction   271
writing sagas   274
writing, sports books   324
writing techniques   242, 247
writing, travel   309
writing workshops   246

Listings index

All companies, public and commercial organisations, societies, festivals and prize-giving bodies, that have a listing in the *Yearbook* are included in this index.

AA Publishing   130
Abacus *see* Little, Brown Book Group
Abbey Theatre Amharclann na Mainistreach   396
ABC-CLIO   207
Aberystwyth University   698
Abingdon Press   207
Harry N. Abrams, Inc.   207
Acacia House Publishing Services Ltd   462
Academic File Information Services   96
Academic Press *see* Elsevier Ltd
Academy of British Cover Design: Annual Cover
    Design Competition   556
ACC Art Books Ltd   130
Accidental Agency, The   430
Accountancy Age   36
Accountancy Daily   36
Accounting & Business   36
ACER Press   198
Actors Touring Company   401
Acumen Literary Journal   36
Ad Donker *see* Jonathan Ball Publishers
Ad Hoc Fiction   130
Ad Lib Publishers   130
Advertising Standards Authority   377
Advocate Art Ltd   492
Aeon Award, The   556
Aeroplane Monthly   36
Aesthetica Magazine   36
Aevitas Creative Management   464
Aevitas Creative Management UK Limited   430
Africa Confidential   37
Africa: St Patrick's Missions   36
African Business   37
Agency for the Legal Deposit Libraries (ALDL)   684
Agency (London) Ltd, The   430
Agenda   37
Agora Books   130
AIR International   37
Airlife Publishing *see* Crowood Press, The
AITA/IATA asbl International Amateur Theatre
    Association   544
Aitken Alexander Associates Ltd   430
Akashic Books Ltd   207
University of Alabama Press, The   207
Aladdin Books Ltd   226
ALCS Educational Writers' Award   556
ALCS Tom-Gallon Trust Award, The   556
Aldeburgh Poetry Festival   596
All Party Parliamentary Writers Group   547
Ian Allan Publishing Ltd   131
Allegro Poetry   37

J.A. Allen   131
Allen & Unwin Pty Ltd   198
Alliance of Literary Societies   532
Alliance of Literary Societies (ALS)   343
Allied Artists/Artistic License   492
Dinesh Allirajah Prize for Short Fiction   556
Allison & Busby Ltd   131
Allographic   345
Allyn & Bacon *see* Pearson UK
ALM: Australian Literary Management   461
Alma Books   131
Almanac Gallery, The   497
Alpha Press, The *see* Sussex Academic Press
Amateur Gardening   37
Amateur Photographer   37
Amazon Prime/Amazon Studios   381
Amazon Publishing   131
Amber Books Ltd   131
Amberley Publishing   131
Ambit   37
American Booksellers Association   516
American Literary Translators Association   545
American Society for Indexing   525
American Society of Composers, Authors and
    Publishers   555
Amgueddfa Cymru – National Museum Wales   131
Amolibros   640
AMP Literary   430
Ampersand Agency Ltd, The   431
Anam Cara   691
And Other Stories   196
Hans Christian Andersen Awards, The   556
Andersen Press Ltd   132
Darley Anderson Literary, TV and Film Agency   431
ANDLYN   431
Angels' Share, The *see* Neil Wilson Publishing Ltd
Angling Times   38
Angry Robot Books   132
Anness Publishing   132
Annick Press Ltd   201
Anubis Literary Agency   431
A1 Book Publishing UK   640
Apa Publications   132
Apollo   38
Applause Theatre and Cinema Book Publishers   208
Apple TV+   381
Appledore Book Festival   596
Apples and Snakes   346
Appletree Press Ltd   132
Arc Publications   132
Arcade Publishing   208

Architects' Journal, The 38
Architectural Design 38
Architectural Press *see* Elsevier Ltd
Architectural Review, The 38
Architecture Today 38
Arena Illustration Ltd 492
Arena Publishing 132
Argus, The 30
ARIAS (Audio & Radio Industry Awards) 557
arima publishing 640
University of Arkansas Press, The 208
Arkbound 196
Yvonne Arnaud Theatre Management Ltd 396
Art + Framing Today 38
Art Agency, The 492
Art Circus Books 640
Art Market, The 492
Art Monthly 38
Art Newspaper, The 39
Art Quarterly 39
ArtReview and ArtReview Asia 39
Artellus Ltd 431
ARTEMISpoetry 39
Artist, The 39
Artist Partners Ltd 492
Artistique International 492
Artists & Illustrators 39
Arts Club, The 547
Arts Council/An Chomhairle Ealaíon 520
Arts Council England 343, 520, 588, 689
Arts Council/An Chomhairle Ealaíon, The 588
Arts Council of Northern Ireland 520
Arts Council of Wales 343
Artworks, The 492
Arvon 691 347
Arvon Writers Retreat at the Clockhouse 691
Ash Tales 39
Ashgate Publishing Ltd *see* Taylor & Francis Group
Ashmolean Museum Publications 133
Asia House Bagri Literature Festival 596
Asian Today, The 33
Aspects Irish Literature Festival 596
Association for Scottish Literary Studies 532
Association of American Literary Agents 516
Association of American Publishers 516
Association of Authors' Agents, The 516
Association of British Science Writers 547
Association of Canadian Publishers 516
Association of Christian Writers 547
Association of Freelance Editors, Proofreaders and
    Indexers of Ireland 526
Association of Freelance Writers 526
Association of Illustrators, The 539
Association of Independent Libraries 689
Association of Learned and Professional Society
    Publishers, The 546
Association of Photographers, The 539
Association of Senior and Children's Education
    Librarians (ASCEL) 689
Astronomy Now 39

Asylum 40
Athletics Weekly 40
Atlantic Books 133
Atlantic Monthly Press *see* Grove Atlantic, Inc.
Atrium *see* Cork University Press
Attic Press *see* Cork University Press
Attitude 40
@YouCaxton 640
Auckland University Press 203
Audible 223
Audio Factory 223
Audiobook Creation Exchange (ACX) 223
Audiobooks.com 223
Aureus Publishing Ltd 133
Aurora Metro 133
Jane Austen Society, The 532
Australia Council 521
Australian Copyright Council 525
Australian Publishers Association 516
Australian Society of Authors, The 516
Australian Writers' Guild 516
Australian/Vogel's Literary Award, The 557
Authentic Media Ltd 133
Author, The 40
Author School, The 640
Authoright 641
Authority Guides, The 133
Authors' Agent, The 461
Authors Aloud UK 548
Authors' Club 547
Authors' Club Awards 557
Authors' Contingency Fund, The 589
Authors' Foundation, The 589
Author's Republic 223
Auto Express 40
Avery *see* Penguin Publishing Group
Aviation News 40
Avon *see* HarperCollins Publishers
Award Publications Ltd 133
Axelrod Agency, The 464
Axisweb 539
Aye Write! Glasgow's Book Festival 596
Anne Aylor Creative Writing Courses 691

Bernard Babani (publishing) Ltd 133
BackTrack 40
Bad Press Ink 133
BAFTA (British Academy of Film and Television
    Arts) 544
Baillie Gifford Borders Book Festival 596
Baillie Gifford Prize for Non-Fiction, The 557
Bailliere Tindall *see* Elsevier Ltd
Jonathan Ball Publishers 205
Banbury Guardian 30
Bandit Fiction 40
Bang Said the Gun 346
Banipal 41
Banker, The 41
Banshee Press Ltd 134
BAPLA (British Association of Picture Libraries and
    Agencies) 539

Baptist Times   41
BARB   382
Barbican Library   682
Barbican Press Ltd   134
Bardd Plant Cymru (Welsh-Language Children's
      Poet Laureate)   557
Barefoot Books   208
Verity Bargate Award   557
Tassy Barham Associates   432
Kate Barker Literary Agency   432
Barrington Stoke   134
Basic Books   208
David Bateman Ltd   203
Bath Festival, The   596
Bath Flash Fiction Awards   557
Bath Literary Agency   432
Bath Novel Award, The   558
Bath Spa University   698
Nicola Baxter   226
BBC, The   377
BBC Books see Ebury Publishing
BBC Countryfile Magazine   41
BBC Gardeners' World Magazine   41
BBC Good Food   41
BBC History Magazine   41
BBC Music Magazine   41
BBC National Short Story Award   558
BBC News   15
BBC Radio   383
BBC Science Focus   41
BBC Sky at Night Magazine   42
BBC Top Gear   42
BBC Wildlife Magazine   42
BBC Written Archives Centre   685
BBC Young Writers' Award   558
Beacon Press   208
Bearded Badger Publishing Ltd   134
Beckford Society, The   532
BECTU (Broadcasting Entertainment
      Communications and Theatre Union)   544
Beehive Illustration   493
Belfast Central Library   682
Belfast Telegraph   24
Belgrade Theatre, The   396
Bell Lomax Moreton Agency, The   432
Bella   42
Bella Books   208
Lorella Belli Literary Agency Ltd (LBLA)   432
Bender Richardson White   226
Arnold Bennett Society   532
Bennion Kearny Ltd   134
E.F. Benson Society, The   533
Bent Agency, The   432, 464
Berkley Books see Penguin Publishing Group
Berlin Associates Ltd   433
Berlitz Publishing see Apa Publications
David Berry Prize, The   558
James Berry Poetry Prize, The   558
Berwick Advertiser   26
Best   42

Besterman/McColvin Medals see K&IM Information
      Resources Awards, The
Betterwrite   641
BFI (British Film Institute)   544
BFI National Archive and Reuben Library   685
BFI Publishing   134
BFS Horizons   42
BFS Journal   42
Bibliographical Society   546
Big Issue, The   42
Big Red Illustration Agency, The   493
Bike   43
Bindery Agency, The   465
Biographers' Club Slightly Foxed Best First Biography
      Prize, The   558
Biographers' Club Tony Lothian Prize, The   558
Bird Watching   43
Birdwatch   43
Birkbeck College, University of London   698
Birlinn Ltd   134
Library of Birmingham   682
Birmingham Literature Festival   597
Birmingham Repertory Theatre Ltd   396
Bitter Lemon Press   135
bks Agency, The   433
Black & White Publishing Ltd   135
Black Beauty & Hair   43
Black Dog Press   135
Black Static   43
Blackpool Art Society, The   539
Blackpool Gazette   27
Blackstaff Press Ltd   135
Blair Partnership, The   433
Blake Friedmann Literary, TV & Film Agency
      Ltd   433
Carole Blake Open Doors Project   589
John Blake Publishing   135
Blink Publishing   135
Blithe Spirit   43
Bloodaxe Books Ltd   135
Bloodhound Books Ltd   136
Bloody Scotland Festival   597
Bloomsbury Publishing Plc   136
Bloomsbury Publishing Pty Ltd   198
Bloomsbury Publishing USA   208
Blue Guides Ltd   136
Blue Heron Literary   465
Blue Ocean Publishing   641
Blue Pencil Agency First Novel Award   559
Blue Peter Book Awards   559
Bluemoose Books   136
K. Blundell Trust, The   589
Boardman Tasker Prize, The   559
Boat International   43
Bodleian Libraries of the University of Oxford   684
Bodleian Library Publishing   137
Bodley Head, The see Vintage
Bold Strokes Books, Inc.   208
Bollinger Everyman Wodehouse Prize for Comic
      Fiction, The   559

Bolton News   27
University of Bolton   698
Bonacia   641
Bonnier Books UK   137
Bonnier Publishing Australia   198
Book Aid International   548
Book Bureau Literary Agency, The   433
Book Collector, The   43
Book Doctor and Creativity Coach, The   691
Book Guild Ltd, The   137
Book Marketing Society   548
Book Slam   346
BookBeat   223
BookBlast® Ltd   434
Bookbug Picture Book Prize   559
Booker Prize, The   559
International Booker Prize, The   559
Bookollective   641
Bookouture   137
BookPrinting UK   641
Books Are My Bag Readers Awards   559
Books Council of Wales/Cyngor Llyfrau
    Cymru   521
Books Ireland   44
Bookseller, The   44
Booksellers Association of the United Kingdom &
    Ireland Ltd, The   517
BookTrust   529, 689
BookTrust Represents   548
BookTrust Storytime Prize   560
Bootleg Theatre Company, The   396
Georges Borchardt Inc.   465
George Borrow Society, The   533
Boundless Theatre   401
Bournemouth Echo   31
R.R. Bowker   209
Bowls International   44
Marion Boyars Publishers Ltd/Prospect Books   137
Boydell & Brewer Ltd   137
Boyds Mills & Kane   209
Bradford Literary Agency   465
Alfred Bradley Bursary Award   589
Bradt Travel Guides Ltd   138
Brainwarp   96
Brandt & Hochman Literary Agents Inc.   465
Branford Boase Award, The   560
Brattle Agency, The   465
Barbara Braun Associates Inc.   465
Bravo Blue Agency, The   434
Bread and Roses   597
Nicholas Brealey *see* John Murray Press
Breathe   44
Bridge Theatre, The   393
Bridport Prize, The   560
Bright Press, The   138
University of Brighton   698
Brighton Festival   597
Brilliant Publications Ltd   138
Bristol Central Library   682
Bristol Old Vic   396

Bristol University Press/Policy Press   138
British Academy   521
British Academy Medals and Prizes   560
British Association of Journalists   526
British Birds   44
British Book Awards, The   560
British Centre for Literary Translation   545
British Chess Magazine   44
British Copyright Council   525
British Council, The   345, 521
British Czech and Slovak Association Writing
    Competition   560
British Fantasy Awards   561
British Fantasy Society, The   548
British Guild of Agricultural Journalists   526
British Guild of Beer Writers   548
British Guild of Travel Writers, The   548
British Haiku Society, The   342, 549
British Institute of Professional Photography   539
British Interactive Media Association   540
British Journal of Photography   44
British Journalism Review   44
British Library, The   684
British Library for Development Studies
    (BLDS)   685
British Library Publishing   138
British Medical Journal   45
British Museum Press, The   138
British Newspaper Archive   685
British Science Fiction Association Awards   561
British Science Fiction Association Ltd   549
British Society of Comedy Writers   549
British Society of Magazine Editors   526
Brittle Star   45
Broadcast   45
Rick Broadhead & Associates   462
Alan Brodie Representation   434
Brontë Society, The   533
Brotherstone Creative Management   434
Jenny Brown Associates   434
Brown Bear Books Ltd   226
John Brown Group – Children's Division   226
Brown, Son & Ferguson Ltd   138
Browne & Miller Literary Associates   465
Browning Society, The   533
Brunel University London   698
Felicity Bryan Associates   434
Bryntirion Press   138
BT   381
John Buchan Society, The   533
Building   45
Building Design   45
Bukowski Agency Ltd, The   462
Bulls Presstjänst AB   96
Burford Books, Inc.   209
Burlington Magazine, The   45
Gordon Burn Prize   561
Burnet Media   205
Burning Chair Publishing   138
Juliet Burton Literary Agency   435

Burton Mail 25
Buses 45
Bush Theatre 393
Business Traveller 45
Buster Books *see* Michael O'Mara Books Ltd
Butcher's Dog 46
Butterworth-Heinemann *see* Elsevier Ltd
Butterworths *see* LexisNexis
Buxton International Festival 597
Byron Society (Newstead Abbey) 533

Café Writers Norwich 346
AKO Caine Prize for African Writing, The 561
Caird Library and Archive 686
Caledonia Novel Award 561
Cambrian News 33
Cambridge Bibliographical Society 546
Cambridge Literary Festival 597
Cambridge News 25
Cambridge University Library 684
University of Cambridge Institute of Continuing
    Education 691
Cambridge University Press 139, 209
Cambridge University Press, Africa 205
Cambridge University Press 198
Cameron Creswell Agency/Cameron's Management,
    The 461
Cameron Publicity and Marketing Ltd 641
Campaign 46
Campaign for Freedom of Information 531
Campbell *see* Pan Macmillan
Charlie Campbell Literary Agents 435
Canadian Authors Association 517
Canadian Publishers' Council 517
Canadian Society of Children's Authors, Illustrators
    & Performers (CANSCAIP) 517
Canbury Press Ltd 139
Candis 46
Candlewick Press 209
C&W Agency 435
Candy Jar Books 139
Canelo Digital Publishing Ltd 139
Cannon Poets 347
Canongate Audio Books 223
Canongate Books Ltd 139
Canopus Publishing Ltd 139
Canterbury Festival 345, 597
Canterbury Festival Poet of the Year 561
Canterbury Library 682
Canterbury Press *see* Hymns Ancient and Modern
    Ltd
Jonathan Cape *see* Vintage
Georgina Capel Associates Ltd 435
Capital Crime Festival 597
Capuchin Classics *see* Stacey Publishing Ltd
Car 46
Car Mechanics 46
Caravan Magazine 46
Carcanet Press Ltd 140
Card Connection Ltd 497
Cardiff Central Library 682

Cardiff University 699
CardsWorld Ltd t/a 4C For Charity 497
Carlisle News and Star 28
Carnegie Medal *see* CILIP Carnegie and Kate
    Greenaway Children's Book Awards, The
Lewis Carroll Society, The 533
Cartoonists Club of Great Britain 540
Maria Carvainis Agency Inc. 466
Casa Ana Creative Writing Retreats 692
Casarotto Ramsay & Associates Ltd 435
Robert Caskie Ltd 435
Caspari Ltd 497
Cassava Republic Press 140
Catchpole Agency, The 436
Caterer, The 46
Caterpillar Books *see* Little Tiger Group
Catholic Herald, The 47
Catholic National Library 686
Catholic Pictorial 47
Catholic Truth Society 140
Catholic Universe, The 47
Caxton Press, The 203
CB1 Poetry 346
Cengage 140
Cengage Learning Australia 198
Cengage Learning New Zealand 203
Center Street 209
Central Illustration Agency 493
Central St Martins College of Arts & Design, Short
    Course Office 692
Century & Arrow *see* Cornerstone
Ceramic Review 47
Château de Lavigny International Writers'
    Residence 692
Chained Library 686
Chalk the Sun Creative Writing 692
Channel 4 379
Channel 5 380
Chapman & Vincent 436
Chapman Publishing 140
Peggy Chapman-Andrews First Novel Award 561
Charleston Festival 597
Charlton Press, The 201
Chartered Institute of Editing and
    Proofreading 526
Chartered Institute of Journalists, The 526
Chartered Institute of Library and Information
    Professionals (CILIP) 689
Chartered Institute of Linguists 545
Chartered Society of Designers, The 540
Chase My Snail 226
Chat 47
Chatto & Windus *see* Vintage
Chawton House Library 686
Cheltenham Illustration Awards 562
Times and The Sunday Times Cheltenham Literature
    Festival, The 598
Chester Chronicle, The 28
Chetham's Library 686
University of Chicago Press 209

Chichester Festival Theatre 396
University of Chichester 699
Chicken House 140
Children's Book Award, The 562
Children's Book Circle, The 529
KPMG Children's Books Ireland Awards, The 562
Children's Books Ireland 529
Children's Laureate, The 562
Child's Play (International) Ltd 140
Chiswick Playhouse 393
Choir Press, The 641
Cholmondeley Awards 562
Teresa Chris Literary Agency Ltd 436
Christian Education 140
Chronicle, The 26
Chronicle & Echo, Northampton 25
Chronicle Books 209
Chudney Agency, The 466
Church of England Newspaper 47
Church Times 47
Churchill Livingstone see Elsevier Ltd
Churchwarden Publications Ltd 141
Cicada Books 141
Cicerone Press 141
Cico Books see Ryland Peters & Small
CILIP Carnegie and Kate Greenaway Children's Book
    Awards, The 562
CILIP (The Library and Information
    Association) 531
Circle of Wine Writers 549
Cisco Press see Pearson UK
City Business Library 686
City Lit 348, 692
City, University of London 699
City AM Ltd 15
John Clare Society, The 533
Claret Press 141
Anne Clark Literary Agency 436
James Clarke & Co. Ltd 141
Arthur C. Clarke Award 563
Classic Boat Magazine 47
Classic Cars 48
Classical Association 546
Classical Music 48
Mary Clemmey Literary Agency 436
Climber 48
Clink Street Publishing 642
Cliveden Literary Festival 598
Cló Iar-Chonnachta Teo 141, 223
Closer 48
Cloud Lodge Books Ltd 141
Jonathan Clowes Ltd 436
Michael Codron Plays Ltd 393
Coffee House Poetry at The Troubadour 346
Coffee House Press 210
David Cohen Prize for Literature, The 563
Coin News 48
Rosica Colin Ltd 436
Collaborate Agency 493
Frances Collin Literary Agency 466

Wilkie Collins Society, The 533
Colneis Marketing Ltd 497
Colourpoint Creative Ltd 141
Columba Books 142
Columbia University Press 210
Column Arts Agency 493
Comedy Women in Print Awards 563
Comic Creators' Prize 592
Comma Press 196
Commercial Motor 48
Commercial radio 383
Commonwealth Library and Archives 686
Commonwealth Short Story Prize 563
Community Care 48
Community Knowledge Hub for Libraries, The 689
Complete Creative Writing Course, The 692
Computer Weekly 48
Computeractive 48
Concord Theatricals 142, 466
Concordia Publishing House 210
Condé Nast Traveller 49
Don Congdon Associates Inc. 466
Joseph Conrad Society (UK), The 534
Conran Octopus see Octopus Publishing Group
Conservation, The 15
Constable & Robinson Ltd see Little, Brown Book
    Group
Consulting Cops for Writers 642
Contact Theatre Company 396
Contemporary Books 210
Jane Conway-Gordon Ltd 436
CookeMcDermid 462
Coombs Moylett Maclean Literary Agency 437
Pol Roger Duff Cooper Prize, The 563
Cooper Square Publishing 210
Doe Coover Agency, The 466
Copyright Clearance Center Inc. 525
Copyright Essay Prize 563
Cork International Short Story Festival and Poetry
    Festival 598
Cork University Press 142
Cornell University Press 210
Cornerstone 142
Cornish Guardian 31
Cornishman 31
Cosmopolitan 49
Costa Book Awards 563
Cotswold Life 49
Council for British Archaeology 143
Country Books 143
Country Homes and Interiors 49
Country Life 49
Country Living 49
Country Smallholding 49
Country Walking 49
Countryman, The 50
Countryman Press, The 210
Countryside Books 143
Courier, The 28
Cove Park 692

Coventry Telegraph   33
Crafts Council Research Library   686
Crafts Magazine   50
Cranachan Publishing   143
Crannóg   50
Cranthorpe Millner Publishers   143
Rose Mary Crawshay Prize, The   564
CRC Press *see* Taylor & Francis Group
Creation Theatre Company   397
Creative Access   517
Creative Authors Ltd   437
Creative Content Ltd   224
Creative Coverage   493
Creative Future Writers' Award   564
Creative Industries Federation   517
Creative Scotland   521, 589
Creative Writer's Workshop, The   692
Crescent Moon Publishing   143
Cressrelles Publishing Co. Ltd   143
Rupert Crew Ltd   437
Crime Readers' Association   549
Crime Writers' Association   549
CrimeFest   598
Critic, The   50
Critical Quarterly   50
Critics' Circle, The   550
Crown House Publishing Ltd   143
Crown Publishing Group *see* Penguin Random
    House.
Crowood Press, The   144
Crux Publishing   144
Crystal Magazine   50
Cúirt International Festival of Literature   598
Cullen Stanley International   466
Cumbria Magazine   50
University of Cumbria   699
Benjamin Cummings *see* Pearson UK
Cundill History Prize   564
James Currey *see* Boydell & Brewer Ltd
Curtis Brown Prize for Prose Fiction (University of
    East Anglia), The   564
Richard Curtis Associates Inc.   466
Curtis Brown   437
Curtis Brown (Australia) Pty Ltd   461
Curtis Brown Creative   693
Curtis Brown Ltd   467
Curve   397
Custom Car   50
Custom PC   51
CWA Dagger Awards   564
Cwlwm Cyhoeddwyr Cymru   517
Cycling Weekly   51
Cyphers   51

Dahlia Publishing   144
Daily Express   15
Daily Mail   15
Daily Mirror   16
Daily Post   33
Daily Record   16
Daily Star   16

Daily Star Sunday   16
Daily Telegraph   16
Judy Daish Associates Ltd   437
Dalesman   51
Dalkey Creates   598
Dalzell & Beresford Ltd   438
Dancing Times   51
Dare   51
Darf Publishers Ltd   144
Darley Anderson Illustration Agency   493
Jenny Darling & Associates   461
Julia Darling Travel Fellowship, The   589
Darlington and Stockton Times   26
Darton, Longman and Todd Ltd   144
Darts World   51
Daunt Books   144
Daunt Books Festival, The   598
David & Charles Ltd   144
David Lewis Agency   493
Caroline Davidson Literary Agency   438
DAW Books, Inc.   210
Dawntreader, The   51
Liza Dawson Associates   467
DB Publishing   145
Giles de la Mare Publishers Ltd   145
Walter de la Mare Society   534
De Montfort University   699
Felix de Wolfe   438
Dead Ink Books   196
Début Art & The Coningsby Gallery   494
Decanter   51
Dedalus Ltd   145
delicious.   52
Delta Books *see* Jonathan Ball Publishers
Richard Dennis Publications   145
Derby Book Festival   599
Derby Telegraph   25
Derby Theatre   397
Derbyshire Life   52
Derwent Art Prize   565
Descent   52
Desperate Literature Short Fiction Prize   565
André Deutsch *see* Welbeck Publishing Group
Deutsche Börse Photography Foundation Prize   565
Devon Life   52
DGA Ltd   438
DHH Literary Agency   438
Diagram Visual Information Ltd   226
Diamond Kahn & Woods Literary Agency   438
Dickens Fellowship   534
Dickensian, The   52
Digital Camera   52
Digital Press *see* Elsevier Ltd
Sandra Dijkstra & Associates   467
Elise Dillsworth Agency   439
Director   52
Discovery Walking Guides Ltd   145
Disney+   381
Dissect Designs   642
Diva   52

Diver 53
DK 145
DMG Media Licensing 96
Dodo Ink 145
Dogberry Ltd 145
Dogs Today 53
Tom Doherty Associates, LLC 210
Donaghy Literary Group 463
John Donald *see* Birlinn Ltd
Dorling Kindersley *see* DK
Dorset Echo 31
Dorset Life – The Dorset Magazine 53
Douglas & McIntyre (2013) Ltd 201
Dovecote Press Ltd, The 145
Dover Publications, Inc. 211
Drapers 53
Dream Catcher 53
Dref Wen 146
Druid 397
Drummond Agency 461
Dry Red Press 497
DSC Prize for South Asian Literature, The 565
Dublin Book Festival 599
University College Dublin Press 146
Dublin Review, The 53
Duckworth Books Ltd 146
Robert Dudley Agency 439
Dukes, The 397
Dundee Evening Telegraph and Post 29
Dundee Rep and Scottish Dance Theatre
    Limited 397
Dundurn Press 201
Dunedin Academic Press 146
Dunham Literary Inc. 467
Dunmore Publishing Ltd 203
Dunow, Carlson & Lerner 467
Durham Advertiser 26
Durham Book Festival 599
Dutch Uncle 494
Dutton *see* Penguin Publishing Group
Dynasty Press 146
Dystel, Goderich & Bourret LLC 467

Early English Text Society 546
Early Music 53
Earthscan 146
University of East Anglia 699
East Anglian Book Awards 565
East Anglian Daily Times 25
East Lothian Life 53
East Riding Festival of Words 599
Eastern Angles 402
Eastern Art Report 54
Eastern Daily Press 25
Eastwing 494
eBook Versions 642
eBookPartnership.com 642
Ebury Press *see* Ebury Publishing
Ebury Publishing 146
Echo 30
Economica 54

Economist, The 54
ECW Press Ltd 201
Eddison Pearson Ltd 439
Edge Hill Short Story Prize 566
Edge Hill University 699
Edify Ltd 204
Edinburgh Bibliographical Society 547
Edinburgh International Book Festival 599
University of Edinburgh 699
Edinburgh University Press 147
Editors' and Proofreaders' Alliance of Northern
    Ireland 526
Educate 54
Educational Company of Ireland, The 147
Educational Explorers (Publishers) 147
Edwards Fuglewicz Literary Agency 439
Eland Publishing Ltd 147
Electric Monkey *see* HarperCollins Publishers
Electrical Review 54
Elevate Mentoring Scheme 593
11:9 *see* Neil Wilson Publishing Ltd
Edward Elgar Publishing Ltd 147
George Eliot Fellowship, The 534
T.S. Eliot Prize, The 566
ELK Publishing 198
ELLE (UK) 54
Ethan Ellenberg Literary Agency, The 467
Elliott & Thompson 147
Desmond Elliott Prize, The 566
Elsevier Australia 198
Elsevier (Clinical Solutions) 211
Elsevier Ltd 147
Simon Elvin Ltd 497
Elwin Street Productions Ltd 226
Embroidery 54
Emerging Writers Programme 593
Emerson College 693
Emma Press Ltd, The 148
Empire 54
Encore Award 566
Encyclopaedia Britannica (UK) Ltd 148
Energy Engineering 55
Engineer, The 55
Engineering in Miniature 55
English Association 531
English Association English 4–11 Children's Book
    Awards 566
English Garden, The 55
English Speaking Board (International) 531
English-Speaking Union, The 531
Enitharmon Editions 148
Ennis Book Club Festival 599
Erotic Review 55
Esquire 55
Essex Chronicle 30
Essex Life 55
University of Essex 699
European Broadcasting Union 527
European Union Prize for Literature 566
Europress Features (UK) 96

Faith Evans Associates   439
Evening Echo   24
Evening Express (Aberdeen)   29
Evening News (Edinburgh)   29
Event & Visual Communication Association   540
Evergreen   55
Everyman Theatre Cheltenham   397
Everyman's Library   148
Everything With Words Ltd   148
Exeter Northcott Theatre   397
University of Exeter Press   148
Helen Exley   148
Express & Echo   31
Express & Star   33
Exprimez   642
Eye Books   148
Eye Candy Illustration   494
Eyewear Publishing Ltd   197

F100 Group   148
FAB Prize for Undiscovered Talent   567
Faber Academy   693
Faber and Faber Ltd   148
Geoffrey Faber Memorial Prize, The   567
Fabian Society   149
Face, The   55
Facebook Watch   382
FACT   525
Alfred Fagon Award, The   567
Frank Fahy Publishing Services   642
Fairchild Books see Bloomsbury Publishing Plc
CJ Fallon   149
Falmouth University   699
Family Law journal   56
Family Tree   56
Eleanor Farjeon Award, The   567
Farmers Weekly   56
Farrar, Straus and Giroux, LLC   211
Farshore Books see HarperCollins Publishers
TheFED – A Network of Writing and Community
    Publishers   550
Federation of British Artists   540
Federation of European Publishers   517
Feminist Library   686
Feminist Review   56
Fenland Poetry Journal   56
David Fickling Books   149
Fiction Atelier   642
Fictionfire Literary Consultancy   693
Field, The   56
Fig Tree see Penguin General
Fillingham Weston Associates   439
Film Rights Ltd   439
Financial Adviser   56
Financial Times   17
Financial Times and McKinsey Business Book of the
    Year Award   567
Finborough Theatre   393
Diana Finch Literary Agency   467
Find the Right Words   346
Findaway Voices   224

Findhorn Press Ltd   149
Fine Art Trade Guild   540
FinePrint Literary Management   468
Finish Your Novel   642
Fircone Books Ltd   149
FIRE   56
Fire in the Head   693
Firefly Press Ltd   149
Fireworks   57
First Novel Prize   567
Firsty Group   643
Fish Publishing Writing Prizes   567
Fisherton Press   149
Fishing News   57
Laurence Fitch Ltd   439
Fitzhenry & Whiteside Ltd   201
Fitzrovia Press Ltd   149
Flame Tree Publishing   149
Flash: The International Short-Short Story
    Magazine   57
Ian Fleming Associates see Phosphor Art Ltd
Fleming Publications   150
Flint & Pitch Productions   346
Flipped Eye Publishing   150
Flora   57
Floris Books   150
Fly Fishing & Fly Tying   57
Flyaway Books   211
Flyleaf Press   150
Fly on the Wall Press   197
FOCAL International Awards   567
FOCAL International Ltd (Federation of Commercial
    AudioVisual Libraries International Ltd)   540
Folens Publishers   150
Rathbones Folio Prize   568
Folio Illustration Agency   494
Folio Literary Management   468
Folklore Society, The   534
Fonthill Media LLC   211
Fonthill Media Ltd   150
Fool for Poetry Chapbook Competition   568
Foreign Press Association in London   527
Foresight News   96
E.M. Forster Award   590
Fortean Times   57
Forward Prizes for Poetry   568
W. Foulsham & Co. Ltd   150
Four Courts Press   150
404 Ink   151
FourFourTwo   57
4th Estate see HarperCollins Publishers
Fox & Howard Literary Agency   440
Robert Fox Ltd   394
Foyle Young Poets of the Year Award   349
FRA   440
France   58
Franco-British Society's Literary Prize, The   568
Maria Frankland Creative Writing Courses   693
Fraser Ross Associates   440
Jeanne Fredericks Literary Agency Inc.   468

Free Association Books   151
Free Painters & Sculptors London   541
Free the Word!   599
Free Word   529
Freesat   382
French House Party, Carcassonne, The   693
Fresh Ink Award   568
Sarah Jane Freymann Literary Agency   468
Friedrich Agency, The   468
Friend, The   58
Friends of Libraries   689
Friends of National Libraries   690
Frieze   58
Frogmore Papers, The   58
Frontline *see* Pen & Sword Books Ltd
FT Prentice Hall *see* Pearson UK
Fulcrum Publishing   211
Furrow, The   58
Future Bookshelf   593

Jüri Gabriel   440
Gaelic Books Council/Comhairle nan Leabhraichean, The   521
Gaia Books *see* Octopus Publishing Group
gal-dem   58
Galago Publishing (Pty) Ltd   205
Gallery Press, The   151
Galley Beggar Press   151
Gallic Books   151
Garden Answers   58
Garden Media Guild, The   550
Garden News   58
Garland Science *see* Taylor & Francis Group
J. Garnet Miller *see* Cressrelles Publishing Co. Ltd
Garnet Publishing Ltd   151
Garsdale Retreat   694
Gaskell Society, The   534
Gay Authors Workshop   550
Gay Times   59
Gazette, The   26
Geddes & Grosset   151
Gelfman Schneider ICM Partners   468
Geographical   59
Geographical Journal, The   59
Getty Publications   211
Gibbons Stamp Monthly   59
Gibbs Smith   211
Gibson Square   152
Gill   152
Gingko   152
Ginkgo Prize for Ecopoetry, The   568
GL Assessment   152
Gladstone History Book Prize   568
Gladstone's Library   687
Glamour   59
Glasgow Evening Times   29
University of Glasgow   700
Gleam Titles   440
Global Blended Learning Ltd   226
Global Lion Intellectual Property Management Inc.   468

Gloucester Citizen   32
Gloucestershire Echo   32
David R. Godine, Publisher, Inc.   212
Godsfield Press *see* Octopus Publishing Group
Goethe-Institut Award for New Translation, The   569
Goethe-Institut London Library   687
Barry Goldblatt Literary LLC   469
Frances Goldin Literary Agency   469
Goldsmiths Press   152
Goldsmiths Prize, The   569
Golf Monthly   59
Golvan Arts Management   461
Good Housekeeping   59
Good Illustration Ltd   494
Good Literary Agency, The   440
Bill Goodall Literary Agency   441
Gourmand World Cookbook Awards, The   569
Governance and Compliance   59
Gower Books *see* Taylor & Francis Group
GQ   60
Graeae Theatre Company   402
Graham Maw Christie   441
Graham-Cameron Illustration   494
Graham-Cameron Publishing & Illustration   227
Grammar Factory Publishing   643
Grand Central Publishing   212
Grange, The   694
Granta   60
Granta Books   152
Graphic Humour Ltd   497
Grazia   60
Great British Card Company, The   498
Annette Green Authors' Agency   441
Christine Green Authors' Agent   441
Green Ink Writers' Gym   694
Green Pebble   498
Green Print *see* Merlin Press Ltd
Kate Greenaway Medal *see* CILIP Carnegie and Kate Greenaway Children's Book Awards, The
Louise Greenberg Books Ltd   441
Sanford J. Greenburger Associates Inc.   469
Greene & Heaton Ltd   441
Graham Greene Birthplace Trust   534
Greenhouse Literary Agency, The   441
Greenock Telegraph   29
Greeting Card Association, The   541
Greetings Today   60
Gregory & Company Authors' Agents   442
Eric Gregory Awards, The   590
Gresham Books Ltd   153
Gresham Publishing Company Ltd, The   153
Griffin Poetry Prize, The   569
Jane Grigson Trust Award   569
Grimsby Telegraph   34
Grocer, The   60
David Grossman Literary Agency Ltd   442
Grosvenor House Publishing   643
Grove Atlantic, Inc.   212
Grow Your Own   60

Grub Street Publishing 153
Guardian, The 17
Guardian Syndication 96
Guernsey Arts Commission 522
Guild of Aviation Artists, The 541
Guild of Food Writers 550
Guild of Health Writers 550
Guild of International Songwriters & Composers, The 555
Guild of Master Craftsman Publications Ltd 153
Guild of Motoring Writers, The 551
Guild of Railway Artists 541
Guildford Book Festival 599
Guildhall Library 687
Guinness World Records 153
Guitarist 60
Gulf Professional Press see Elsevier Ltd
Marianne Gunn O'Connor Literary, Film/TV Agency 442
Guppy Publishing Ltd 153
Gutter 60
Gwyn Palmer Associates (Literary Agents) Ltd 442

Hachette Audio 224
Hachette Australia Pty Ltd 199
Hachette Book Group 212
Hachette Children's Group 153
Hachette New Zealand Ltd 204
Hachette UK 154
Hakluyt Society 551
Halban Publishers 154
Halcyon Publishing Ltd 204
Robert Hale Ltd 154
Halifax Courier 34
Hallmark Cards Plc 498
Halsgrove Publishing 154
Hamilton Agency, The 442
Hamish Hamilton see Penguin General
Hamlyn see Octopus Publishing Group
Hammer and Tongue 346
Hampshire Chronicle 30
Hampstead Theatre 394
Hanbury Agency Ltd, Literary Agents, The 442
H&E naturist 60
Happy Yak 154
Hardie Grant UK 154
Hardman & Swainson 443
Patrick Hardy Books see Lutterworth Press, The
Thomas Hardy Society, The 535
Harleian Society 551
Harlequin Enterprises Ltd 201
Harlequin (UK) Ltd 154
HarperCollins Publishers 155, 212, 224
HarperCollins Publishers (Australia) Pty Ltd Group 199
HarperCollins Publishers Ltd 201
HarperCollins Publishers (New Zealand) Ltd 204
Harper's Bazaar 61
Harpeth Road Press 212
Harriman House 156
Joy Harris Literary Agency Inc., The 469

Raworths Harrogate Literature Festival 600
Harrogate Theatre 397
Hart McLeod Ltd 227
Hart Publishing 156
Hartlepool Mail 27
Hartline Agency 469
Harvard University Press 212
Harvill Secker see Vintage
Harvill Secker Young Translators' Prize 569
Antony Harwood Ltd 443
Hashtag Press 156
Haus Publishing Ltd 156
John Hawkins & Associates Inc. 469
Hawthorn Press 156
Hawthornden Castle 694
Hawthornden Fellowships 590
Hawthornden Prize, The 569
Hay Festival, The 600
Hay House Publishers 156
Haynes Publishing 157
Hayters Teamwork 96
HCM 61
Francis Head Bequest 590
Head of Zeus 157
Headline Publishing Group 157
Headliners 97
Headlong Theatre 402
Healthy 61
Heart of Albion 227
Heat 61
A.M. Heath & Co. Ltd 443
hedgerow: a journal of small poems 61
Hello! 61
Sinead Heneghan Literary Agency 443
Henley Hall Press 157
Hera Books 157
Herald 17, 24, 32
Herald Express 32
Herald on Sunday 17
Here Comes Everyone 61
Hereford Times 32
Jeff Herman Agency LLC, The 469
Hermes House see Anness Publishing
Nick Hern Books Ltd 157
Hesketh Hubbard Art Society 541
Hesperus Press Ltd 157
PEN Hessell-Tiltman Prize for History, The 570
hhb agency ltd 443
Hi-Fi News 61
Sophie Hicks Agency 443
High Life 62
High Spot Literary 464
David Higham Associates Ltd 444
Hill and Wang see Farrar, Straus and Giroux, LLC
Hill Nadell Literary Agency 469
William Hill Sports Book of the Year Award 570
Hilliard Society of Miniaturists, The 541
James Hilton Society, The 535
Hippocrene Books, Inc. 212
Hippopotamus Press 157

Historical Novel Society   551
Historical Writers' Association   551
History Press Ltd, The   157
History Today   62
Hobeck Books   158
Hodder & Stoughton   158
Hodder & Stoughton Audiobooks   224
Hodder Children's Books *see* Hachette Children's Group
Hodder Education   158
Hodder Faith *see* John Murray Press
Hodder Gibson   158
Calvin and Rose G. Hoffman Memorial Prize for Distinguished Scholarly Essay on Christopher Marlowe, The   570
Holiday House, Inc.   212
Holland House Books   158
Sherlock Holmes Society of London, The   535
Holroyde Cartey Ltd   444
Henry Holt and Company LLC   213
Vanessa Holt Ltd   444
Holroyde Cartey   494
HOME: Theatre   398
Homes & Gardens   62
Honno Ltd (Welsh Women's Press)   197
HopeRoad   158
Johns Hopkins University Press   213
Hopscotch   158
Kate Hordern Literary Agency Ltd   444
Horla   62
Horror Writers Association   551
Horse & Hound   62
Horse & Rider   62
Hortus   62
Valerie Hoskins Associates Ltd   444
Hot Key Books   158
Hot Press   62
Houghton Mifflin Harcourt   213
House & Garden   63
House Beautiful   63
House of Lochar   159
Housebuilder   63
Housman Society   535
W. F. Howes Ltd   224
Huddersfield Daily Examiner   34
Huddersfield Literature Festival   600
Ted Hughes Award for New Work in Poetry, The   570
Hull Daily Mail   34
Hull Truck Theatre Co. Ltd   402
University of Hull   700
Clare Hulton Literary Agency   444
Hulu   382
John Hunt Publishing Ltd   159
Hurst – The John Osborne Arvon Centre, The   694
Hutchinson Heinemann *see* Cornerstone
Hymns Ancient and Modern Ltd   159

i   17
i Weekend   18
iBooks Author   643

ICM Partners   470
Icon Books Ltd   159
Icon Magazine   63
ICSA Publishing Ltd   159
Ideal Home   63
Idler, The   63
Igloo Books Ltd   159
Ilkley Literature Festival   600
University of Illinois Press   213
IllustrationX   494
Image by Design Art Licensing   495
Imaginative Book Illustration Society   541
Imagine That Publishing Ltd   159
IMG UK Ltd   444
Imison Award, The   570
Imperial War Museum Library   687
Impress Books Ltd   197
Impress Prize for New Writers, The   570
Imprint Academic Ltd   160
Improve Your Coarse Fishing   63
In Pinn *see* Neil Wilson Publishing Ltd
Incorporated Society of Musicians   555
Independent   18
Independent Bookshop Week   600
Independent Press Standards Organisation   527
Independent Publishers Guild   517
Independent Publishing Magazine, The   63
Independent Radio News (IRN)   97
Independent Talent Group Ltd   445
Independent Theatre Council   544
Independent   32
Index on Censorship   64
Indiana University Press   213
Indie Book Awards   570
Indiegogo   196
Indigo Dreams Publishing Ltd   160
Infinite Ideas   160
Influx Press   160
Infobase Publishing   213
Ink Sweat & Tears   64
Inkshares   196, 213
Inkwell Group, The   643
InkWell Management   470
Inky Illustration   495
Inner Traditions Bear & Company   213
Inscribe   593
Inside Soap   64
Inspire Magazine   64
Institute of Designers in Ireland   541
Institute of Internal Communication   532
Institute of Public Administration   160
Institute of Translation and Interpreting, The   546
Insurance Age   64
Insurance Post   64
Intercontinental Literary Agency Ltd   445
InterMedia   64
International Affairs   64
International Authors Forum   518
International Dublin Literary Award   571
International Literature Festival Dublin   600

International Poetry Business Book & Pamphlet
    Competition, The   571
International Prize for Arabic Fiction   571
International Publishers Association   518
International Society of Typographic Designers   541
Internet Library for Librarians   690
Interpreter's House, The   65
Interzone   65
Inverness Courier   29
Investors Chronicle   65
IOP Publishing   160
Ipsos MORI   383
Ipswich Star   25
Ireland's Own   65
Irish Academic Press Ltd   160
Irish Arts Review   65
An Post Irish Book Awards   571
Irish Copyright Licensing Agency, The   525
Irish Examiner   18
Irish Farmers Journal   65
Irish Independent   18
Irish Journal of Medical Science   65
Irish Medical Times   65
Irish News   24
Irish Pages: A Journal of Contemporary Writing   66
Irish Post, The   66
Irish Tatler   66
Irish Times, The   18
Irish Writers Centre   518
Irish Writers Centre – Áras Scríbhneoirí na
    hÉireann   694
Irish Writers' Union/Comhar na Scríbhneoirí   518
ISF Publishing   160
Isis/Soundings   224
Isle of Wight Writing Courses and Workshops   694
Isle of Wight County Press   30
Ithaca Press see Garnet Publishing Ltd
ITV Plc   380
Ivors Academy of Music Creators, The   555
Ivy Press Ltd   227
IWM (Imperial War Museums) Publishing   160

JABberwocky Literary Agency Inc.   470
Jacaranda Books Art Music Ltd   161
Heather Jackson Literary Agent   470
JAI see Elsevier Ltd
P.D. James Memorial Fund, The   590
Jane's   161
Jane's Defence Weekly   66
Janklow & Nesbit Associates   470
Janklow & Nesbit (UK) Ltd   445
Jawdance   346
Jelly Bean Self-Publishing   643
Jericho Writers   694
Jersey Evening Post   24
Jerwood Compton Poetry Fellowships   590
Jewish Book Week   600
Jewish Chronicle   66
Jewish Telegraph   66
JFL Agency Ltd   445
Jhalak Prize   571

Joffe Books   161
Joffe Books Prize for Crime Fiction Writers of
    Colour   592
Johnson & Alcock Ltd   445
Johnson Society, The   535
Johnson Society of London   535
Jolly Fish Press   213
Tibor Jones & Associates   445
Robin Jones Literary Agency (RJLA)   445
Jordan Publishing Ltd   161
Michael Joseph   161
Journal, The   27
Journalists' Charity   527
Journey Books   643
JSR   495
Jane Judd Literary Agency   445
Juta and Company (Pty) Ltd   205

K&IM Information Resources Awards, The   571
Kane Literary Agency   446
University Press of Kansas   213
Michelle Kass Associates Ltd   446
Keane Kataria Literary Agency   446
B.L. Kearley Art & Antiques   495
Keats-Shelley Memorial Association   535
Keller Media Inc.   470
Kelpies see Floris Books
Kenilworth Press see Quiller Publishing Ltd
Margaret Kennedy Agency   461
Kent and Sussex Courier   30
Kent & Sussex Poetry Society   346
Kent and Sussex Poetry Society Open Poetry
    Competition   572
Kent Life   66
Bill Kenwright Ltd   394
Kenyon-Deane see Cressrelles Publishing Co. Ltd
Kerrang!   67
Kerry Group Irish Novel of the Year Award   572
Ki Agency Ltd   446
Kickstarter   196
Kids Can Press Ltd   202
Kids Corner   495
Killing It: The Killer Reads Competition for
    Undiscovered Writers   572
Kiln Theatre   394
Kindle Direct Publishing   644
Kindle Storyteller Award   572
Laurence King Publishing Ltd   162
King's Head Theatre   394
King's Lynn Festival   600
King's Lynn Literature Festivals   601
Kings Road Publishing   162
Jessica Kingsley Publishers see John Murray Press
Kingston University   700
Kipling Society, The   535
Kitchen Garden   67
Kitchen Press   162
Kitschies, The   572
Harvey Klinger Inc.   470
Knight Agency, The   470
Charles Knight see LexisNexis

Knight Features Ltd 97, 446
Knight Hall Agency Ltd 446
Knopf Canada *see* Penguin Random House Canada
    Ltd
Knopf Doubleday Publishing Group 214
Knuston Hall 695
Kobo 224
Kobo Writing Life 644
Kogan Page Ltd 162
Kraszna-Krausz Book Awards 572
Krause Publications 214
kt literary 470
Kube Publishing Ltd 162
University of KwaZulu-Natal Press 205
Kyle Books 162

Lady, The 67
Charles Lamb Society, The 536
Lambeth Palace Library 687
Lancashire Post 28
Lancashire Telegraph 28
Lancaster University 700
Lancet, The 67
LandScape Magazine 67
Peter Lang Ltd 162
Lantana Publishing 197
Laureate na nÓg/Ireland's Children's Laureate 601
Laurel Prize for Ecopoetry 572
Lavender and White Publishing 644
Lawbook Co. 199
Lawrence & Wishart Ltd 162
D.H. Lawrence Society, The 536
T.E. Lawrence Society, The 536
Lawyer, The 67
Laxfield Literary Associates 446
Laxfield Literary Launch Prize 572
LBA Books 447
Le Verger 695
Susanna Lea Associates 471
Susanna Lea Associates Ltd 447
Leader, The 33
Ledbury Poetry Festival 345, 601
Leeds Beckett University 700
Leeds Library 683
Leeds Lit Fest 601
Leeds Playhouse 398
Leeds Postcards 498
University of Leeds 700
Left Bank Literary 462
Legal Week 67
Legend Press Ltd 163
Leicester Mercury 25
Leisure Painter 67
Lemonade Illustration Agency 495
Leverhulme Research Fellowships 590
Levine Greenberg Rostan Literary Agency 471
Barbara Levy Literary Agency 447
Lewis Mason *see* Ian Allan Publishing Ltd
LexisNexis 163
LexisNexis Butterworths Australia 199
LexisNexis Canada, Inc. 202

LexisNexis NZ Ltd 204
Lexus Ltd 227
LGC (Local Government Chronicle) 68
Libraries All Party Parliamentary Group
    (APPG) 690
Libraries Connected 690
Libraries Week 690
Library Campaign, The 690
Library of the Society of Friends, The 687
Library Planet 690
Life and Work: The Magazine of the Church of
    Scotland 68
Lighthouse Literary Journal 68
Lightning Books 163
Lilliput Press Ltd, The 163
Limelight Celebrity Management Ltd 447
Limnisa Centre for Writers 695
Frances Lincoln 163
Lincolnshire Echo 34
Lincolnshire Life 68
Lindisfarne Prize for Crime Fiction, The 573
Lindsay Literary Agency 447
Linen Hall Library 687
Ling Design Ltd 498
Linguist, The 68
Lion Hudson Ltd 163
Lipstick of London 495
Listowel Writers' Week 601
Listowel Writers' Week Poetry Competitions 573
Literary Review 68
Literature Wales 342, 522
Literature Works 522
Litfest 601
Litro 68
Little, Brown & Company 214
Little, Brown Award for Crime Fiction (University of
    East Anglia) 573
Little, Brown Book Group 164
Little People Books 227
Little Theatre Guild of Great Britain 544
Little Tiger Group 164
Little Toller Books 165
Little White Lies 68
Live Theatre 398
Liverpool Central Library 683
Liverpool Echo 28
Liverpool Everyman and Playhouse 398
Liverpool John Moores University 700
Liverpool Literary Agency, The 447
Liverpool University Press 165
Living Plantfully 69
Llewellyn Worldwide 214
Logaston Press 165
LOM ART 165
London Magazine Short Story, Poetry and Essay
    Competitions, The 573
London Bubble, The 402
London College of Communication 700
London Evening Standard 26
London Film School, The 701

University of London, Goldsmiths   700
London Hellenic Prize, The   573
London Library   683
London Literature Festival   602
London Magazine: A Review of Literature and the Arts, The   69
London Press Club Awards   573
London Review of Books   69
University of London, Royal Holloway   700
Lone Pine Publishing   202
Lonely Planet   214
Lonely Planet Publications Ltd   165
Long Poem Magazine   69
Elizabeth Longford Prize for Historical Biography, The   573
Longman see Pearson UK
Longman-History Today Book Prize   574
Julia Lord Literary Management   471
Lorenz Books see Anness Publishing
Lothian Life   69
LoveReading4Kids   529
LoveReading4Schools   530
Andrew Lownie Literary Agency   448
Luath Press Ltd   165
Luithlen Agency   448
Lumb Bank – The Ted Hughes Arvon Centre   695
Luna Press Publishing   166
Lund Humphries   166
Lutterworth Press, The   166
Lutyens & Rubinstein   448
David Luxton Associates Ltd   448
Sir William Lyons Award, The   574
Lyons Press, The   214
Lyric Hammersmith   394

M6 Theatre Company   402
Donald Maass Literary Agency   471
Mabecron Books ltd   166
Duncan McAra   448
Margret McBride Literary Agency   471
Mace, The   69
McGill-Queen's University Press   202
McGraw-Hill Book Company New Zealand Ltd   204
McGraw-Hill Education   166, 199
McGraw-Hill Professional   214
McGraw-Hill Ryerson Ltd   202
McIlvanney Prize for the Scottish Crime Novel of the Year and The Bloody Scotland Debut of the Year   574
McIntosh & Otis Inc.   471
Frances McKay Illustration   495
MacKenzie Wolf   471
McKitterick Prize, The   574
Bryan MacMahon Short Story Award   574
Macmillan Digital Audio   225
Macmillan Education see Springer Nature Group Ltd
Macmillan Education South Africa   206
Macmillan Prize for Illustration, The   574
Macmillan Publishers, Inc.   215
Eunice McMullen Ltd   448

McPherson & Company   215
Made Simple Books see Elsevier Ltd
Magazines Canada   527
Magma Poetry   69
Sarah Maguire Prize, The   574
Mail, The   28
Mail on Sunday   18
Management Books 2000 Ltd   166
Management Today   69
Manchester Central Library   683
Manchester Children's Book Festival   602
Manchester Evening News   28
Manchester Literature Festival   602
Manchester Poetry Library   344
Manchester Prizes for Fiction and Poetry, The   575
University of Manchester   701
Manchester University Press   166
Manchester Writing School at Manchester Metropolitan University, The   701
Mandrake of Oxford   167
Mango Books   167
Manilla Press   167
Carol Mann Agency   471
Andrew Mann Ltd   448
Mantra Lingua Ltd   167
Manuscripts & Mentoring   644
Margie's Mark   644
Maritime Journal   70
Marjacq Scripts Ltd   448
Market House Books Ltd   227
Marketing Week   70
Michael Marks Awards for Poetry Pamphlets, The   575
Marlborough College Summer School   695
Marlowe Society, The   536
Marsh Agency Ltd, The   449
Evan Marshall Agency, The   472
John Masefield Memorial Trust, The   591
John Masefield Society, The   536
University of Massachusetts Press, The   215
Master Photographers Association   542
Matador   644
Somerset Maugham Awards, The   575
May Festival   602
Kevin Mayhew Ltd   167
MBA Literary and Script Agents Ltd   449
MBUK (Mountain Biking UK)   70
Sarah McKenzie Literary Management   462
MCN (Motor Cycle News)   70
Medal News   70
Media Music Now   225
Media Society, The   527
Media.info   384
Medici Cards   498
Medway Messenger   30
Megaphone Writers Development Scheme   593
Meiklejohn Illustration   496
Melbourne University Press   199
Men's Fitness   70
Men's Health   70

Mentor Books   167
Mercier Press, The   167
Mercury Theatre Colchester   398
Mereo Books   645
Merky Books New Writers' Prize   592
Merlin Press Ltd   167
Merrell Publishers Ltd   167
Methodist Recorder   70
Methuen & Co Ltd   168
Metro Publications Ltd   168
MiblArt   645
Michelin Travel Partners UK Ltd   168
University of Michigan Press, The   215
Microsoft Press   215
Middlesex University   701
Miko Greetings   498
Madeleine Milburn Literary, TV & Film
    Agency   449
Milkweed Editions   215
Miller's *see* Octopus Publishing Group
Mills & Boon *see* Harlequin (UK) Ltd
Rachel Mills Literary Ltd   449
Milo Books Ltd   168
Mirror Books   168
Missenden School of Creative Arts   695
University of Missouri Press   215
MIT Press, The   215
Mitchell Beazley *see* Octopus Publishing Group
Mitchell Library   683
Mixmag   70
MJV Literary Author Services   645
MMB Creative (Mulcahy Sweeney Associates
    Ltd)   450
MMM (The Motorhomers' Magazine)   70
Mobius *see* Hodder & Stoughton
Model Boats   71
Model Engineer   71
Modern Language Review   71
Modern Poetry in Translation   71
Mogford Prize for Food and Drink Short Story
    Writing, The   575
Mojo   71
MoneyWeek   71
Moniack Mhor   695
Monkey Feet Illustration Agency, The   496
Monkton Wyld Court   695
Moonpig   498
Morgan Green Creatives Ltd   450
Morgan Kauffman *see* Elsevier Ltd
Morley College   696
Morning Star   19
Morrigan Book Company   168
William Morris Society   536
Moth, The   71
Moth Art Prize, The   575
Moth Poetry Prize, The   576
Moth Short Story Prize, The   576
Motor Boat and Yachting   72
Motorship, The   72
Mslexia   72

Mud Pie   168
Murdoch Books   168
Judith Murdoch Literary Agency   450
Michael Murphy Memorial Poetry Prize   576
John Murray Press   168
Mushens Entertainment   450
Music Publishers Association   555
Music Teacher   72
Music Week   72
Musical Opinion   72
Musical Times   72
Muswell Press   169
My Weekly   72
Myriad Editions   169
Mythopoeic Fantasy Award for Adult Literature,
    The   576
Mythopoeic Scholarship Award in Inklings Studies,
    The   576
Mythopoeic Scholarship Award in Myth and Fantasy
    Studies, The   576
Mythopoeic Society, The   551

Jean V. Naggar Literary Agency Inc.   472
Kate Nash Literary Agency   450
National, The   19
National Acrylic Painters' Association   542
National Art Library   687
National Association of Writers' Groups   344   552
National Association of Writers in Education
    (NAWE)   348
National Centre for Writing   552
National Council for the Training of
    Journalists   527
National Eisteddfod of Wales   602
National Film and Television School   701
National Library of Scotland   684
National Library of Wales   684
National Literacy Trust   530, 690
National Poetry Competition   576
National Poetry Library   344
National Society for Education in Art and
    Design   542
National Trust Magazine, The   73
National Union of Journalists   528
Natural History Museum Library and Information
    Services   687
Natural History Museum Publishing   169
Nature   73
The Nature Writing Prize for Working Class
    Writers'   592
Naxos AudioBooks   225
NB Illustration   496
NB magazine   73
NB Publishers (Pty) Ltd   206
Neal Street Productions Ltd   394
Neil Bradley Studio   97
Nelson Education   202
Thomas Nelson Publisher   215
Neon   73
Edith Nesbit Society, The   536
Netflix   382

New Africa Books (Pty) Ltd   206
New Angle Prize for East Anglian Literature   576
New Anglia Manuscript Prize   576
New Blitz Literary and Editorial TV Agency   97
New English Art Club   547
New European, The   19
New Generation Publishing   645
New Harbinger Publications   216
New Holland Publishers (UK) Ltd   199
New Humanist   73
New Internationalist   73
New Island Books   169
New Law Journal   73
New Media Writing Prize   577
University of New Mexico Press   216
New Perspectives Theatre Company   402
New Playwrights' Network   169
New Poets Prize, The   577
New Riders see Pearson UK
New Scientist   73
New Statesman   74
New Theatre: Dublin, The   398
New Vic Theatre   398
New Welsh Reader   74
New Welsh Writing Awards   577
New Wolsey Theatre, The   398
New Writing North   552
New Writing South   552
New Zealand Association of Literary Agents   518
New Zealand Book Awards for Children and Young
    Adults   577
New Zealand Council for Educational Research   204
New Zealand Writers Guild   518
Newcastle City Library   683
Newcastle Noir   602
Newcastle University   701
NeWest Press   202
Newnes see Elsevier Ltd
News Letter   24
News Media Association   528
News, Portsmouth, The   30
New Welsh Rarebyte   170
Nexus see Ebury Publishing
Nielsen Bestseller Awards in association with
    Coutts   577
NME (New Musical Express)   74
Nobel Prize in Literature, The   577
Nobrow Books   170
Noireland International Crime Fiction Festival   602
Noirwich Crime Writing Festival   602
Nordisk Books Ltd   170
Norfolk & Norwich Festival   603
Norfolk and Norwich Millennium Library   683
North, The   74
University of North Carolina Press, The   216
North Literary Agency, The   450
North Point Press see Farrar, Straus and Giroux, LLC
North-Holland see Elsevier Ltd
Northbank Talent Management   451
Northcote House Publishers Ltd   170

Northern Echo, The   27
Northern Poetry Library   344
Northern Short Story Festival   603
Northern Stage (Theatrical Productions) Ltd   399
Northern Writers' Awards   591
Northodox Press   170
Northumbria University   701
W.W. Norton & Company, Inc.   216
W.W. Norton & Company   170
Norwich Evening News   25
Nosy Crow   170
Nottingham Central Library   683
Nottingham Playhouse   399
Nottingham Post   26
Nottingham Trent University   701
Nourish Books   170
Jane Novak Literary Agency   462
Andrew Nurnberg Associates Ltd   451
Nursery World   74
Nursing Times   74
NWP see Neil Wilson Publishing Ltd

Oak Tree Press   171
Oberon Books see Bloomsbury Publishing Plc
Oberon Press   202
O'Brien Press Ltd, The   171
Observer, The   19
Observer/Jonathan Cape/Comica Graphic Short Story
    Prize, The   578
Ockham New Zealand Book Awards   578
OCM Bocas Prize for Caribbean Literature   578
Octagon Theatre   399
Octopus Publishing Group   171
Ofcom   377
Off the Shelf Festival of Words Sheffield   603
OK!   74
University of Oklahoma Press   216
Old Barn Books   171
Old Pond Publishing   171
Old Red Lion Theatre, The   394
Oldham Coliseum Theatre   399
Oldie, The   75
Oleander Press, The   172
Olive   75
Michael O'Mara Books Ltd   172
Omnibus Press/Wise Music Group   172
On Stream Publications   172
Oneworld Publications   172
Open College of the Arts   696
Open Gate Press   172
Open University Press see McGraw-Hill Education
Opera   75
Opera Now   75
OR Books   216
Orange Tree Theatre   394
Orbis International Literary Journal   75
Orbit see Little, Brown Book Group
Orchard Books see Hachette Children's Group
Orenda Books   172
Orion Publishing Group Ltd, The   173, 225
Orpheus Books Ltd   227

Orwell Prizes, The   578
Osprey Publishing Ltd   173
Otago University Press   204
Otherwise Publishing   645
Oundle Festival of Literature   603
Our Dogs   75
Out of Joint   402
Out-Spoken   346
Out-Spoken Press   594
Outdoor Writers and Photographers Guild   552
Outline Artists   496
Overlook Press, The   216
Oversteps Books Ltd   173
Wilfred Owen Association   536
Deborah Owen   451
Peter Owen Publishers   173
Owned Voices   552
Owned Voices Novel Award   578
Oxford Bibliographical Society   547
FT Weekend Oxford Literary Festival   603
Oxford Mail   30
Oxford Poetry   75
Oxford Times, The   31
Oxford University   701
Oxford University Press   173, 216
Oxford University Press, Canada   202
Oxford University Press Southern Africa   206
Oxford University Summer School for Adults   696

P8tech   174
PA Media   97
Pact (Producers Alliance for Cinema and
   Television)   383, 545
Paines Plough   402
Paisley Daily Express   29
Palgrave Macmillan *see* Springer Nature Group Ltd
Pan Macmillan   174
Pan Macmillan Australia Pty Ltd   199
Pan Macmillan SA (Pty) Ltd   206
Paper House   498
Paper Lion Ltd   451
Paper Nations   552
Paperlink Ltd   499
Paragon House Publishers   216
Paragon Publishing   645
Parthian Books   174
Pastel Society, The   542
Patrician Press   174
Pavilion Children's Books   174
PBJ & KBJ Management   451
PC Pro   75
Peace News   76
Peachpit Press *see* Pearson UK
Maggie Pearlstine Associates   451
Pearson Canada   202
Pearson South Africa   206
Pearson UK   175
Kay Peddle Literary   451
Peepal Tree Press   175
Jonathan Pegg Literary Agency   452
Pelagic Publishing   175

Pelican Publishing   217
PEN Ackerley Prize for Autobiography and Memoir,
   The   578
Pen & Sword Books Ltd   175
PEN International   552
Pen to Print   553
Penguin General   175
Penguin Longman *see* Pearson UK
Penguin Press   176
Penguin Publishing Group   217
Penguin Random House   217
Penguin Random House Australia Pty Ltd   199
Penguin Random House Canada Ltd   202
Penguin Random House Children's UK   176
Penguin Random House New Zealand Ltd   204
Penguin Random House (Pty) Ltd   206
Penguin Random House UK   176
Penguin Random House UK Audio   225
Penguin Young Readers   217
University of Pennsylvania Press   217
Pennsylvania State University Press   217
People Management   76
People's Book Prize, The   578
People's Friend, The   76
Samuel Pepys Award, The   579
Pergamon *see* Elsevier (Clinical Solutions)
Period Living   76
Permanent Press, The   217
Persephone Books   176
Personal Managers' Association Ltd, The   518
Peterborough Telegraph   26
PEW Literary   452
Peters Fraser & Dunlop Ltd   452
Phaidon Press Ltd   176
Philip's *see* Octopus Publishing Group
Phosphor Art Ltd   496
Photographer, The   76
Piatkus *see* Little, Brown Book Group
Alison Picard, Literary Agent   472
Piccadilly Press   177
PICSEL (Picture Industry Collecting Society for
   Effective Licensing)   525
Picture Postcard Collecting   76
Picture Research Association, The   542
Pimlico *see* Vintage
Pimpernel Press Ltd   177
Pineapple Park   499
Pippin Properties Inc.   472
Pippin Publishing Corporation   203
Pitch to Publication   696
Planet: The Welsh Internationalist   76
Player–Playwrights   545
Playmarket   464
Playwrights Publishing Company, The   177
Plexus Publishing Ltd   177
Plough Prize, The   579
Plum Pudding Illustration   496
Plume *see* Penguin Publishing Group
Frances Plumpton Literary Agency   464
Pluto Press   177

University of Plymouth 702
PN Review 76
Poetry Archive, The 344
Poetry Book Society, The 342
Poetry Business, The 342
Poetry Ireland 342
Poetry Ireland Review/Iris Éigse Éireann 77
Poetry Kit, The 344
Poetry Library 348
Poetry London 77
Poetry Review, The 77
Poetry School, The 348
Poetry Society, The 342
Poetry Society Education 348
Poetry Space 345
Poetry Unplugged at the Poetry Café 347
Poetry Wales 77
Poets and Writers 345
Poets' Café 347
Sylvie Poggio Artists Agency 496
Poke, The 19
Polari 347
Polari Book Prize 579
Police Journal: Theory, Practice and Principles,
    The 77
Policy Press see Bristol University Press/Policy Press
Policy Studies Institute (PSI) 177
Political Quarterly, The 77
Politico's Publishing see Methuen & Co Ltd
politics.co.uk 20
Polity Press 177
Polygon see Birlinn Ltd
Pomegranate PA 646
Poolbeg Press Ltd 177
Popshot Quarterly 77
Portico Prize, The 579
Portland Press Ltd 177
Post 32
Potomac Books, Inc. 218
Beatrix Potter Society, The 536
Poultry World 77
powerHouse Books 218
Shelley Power Literary Agency Ltd 452
Powys Society, The 536
PR Week 78
Practical Boat Owner 78
Practical Caravan 78
Practical Fishkeeping 78
Practical Wireless 78
Practising Midwife, The 78
Practitioner, The 78
Prepare to Publish Ltd 646
Press, The 35
Press and Journal 29
Press Awards, The 579
Press Gazette 78
Prestel Publishing Ltd 178
Pride 79
J.B. Priestley Society, The 537
Prima 79

Princeton University Press 218
Princeton University Press – Europe 178
Printmakers Council 542
V.S. Pritchett Short Story Prize 579
Private Eye 79
Private Libraries Association 532, 690
Professional Cartoonists' Organisation 542
Professional Publishers Association 519
Profile Books Ltd 178
Prole 79
Prospect Magazine 79
Proteus Theatre Company 403
PRS for Music 555
P.S. Literary Agency 463
Psychologies 79
Psychology Press 178
Public Library News 690
Public Media Alliance 383
Publishers Association, The 519
Publishers Association of New Zealand 519
Publishers' Association of South Africa 519
Publishers' Publicity Circle 519
Publishing Ireland/Foilsiú Éireann 519
Publishing Scotland 519
Publishing Services 646
Publishizer 196
PublishNation 646
Puffin see Penguin Random House Children's UK
Puffin see Penguin Young Readers
Pulse 79
Pure Indigo Ltd 178
Pushing Out the Boat 79
Pushkin Press 178
Puzzle House, The 97
Pyramid see Octopus Publishing Group

Quadrille 179
Quantum see W. Foulsham & Co. Ltd
Quartet Books (The Women's Press) 179
Quarto Group, Inc., The 179
Quarto Group Publishing UK 179
Quarto Publishing Group USA 218
QUE Publishing see Pearson UK
Queen Mary Wasafiri New Writing Prize 579
Queen's Knickers Award, The 580
Queen's Theatre, Hornchurch 399
Queen's University, Belfast 702
University of Queensland Press 200
Quercus Publishing Plc 179
Questors Theatre, The 395
Quiller Publishing Ltd 179
Joey Quincey Literary Agency 452
Nigel Quiney Publications Ltd 499

RA Magazine 80
Racing Post 80
Radio Academy, The 384
Radio Times 80
Radiocentre 384
RAIL 80
Railway Gazette International 80

Railway Magazine, The   80
Rainbow Poetry Recitals   347
RAJAR   384
Peggy Ramsay Foundation, The   591
Rand McNally   218
Random House Children's Books   218
Random House Publishing Group   218
Rann Media   97
Ransom Publishing Ltd   179
Rat's Tales Ltd   180
Razorbill *see* Penguin Young Readers
Reach Poetry   80
Read for Good   530
Reader's Digest   80
Reading Agency, The   530, 690
Reading Chronicle   31
Reaktion Books   180
Real People   81
Reality   81
Record Collector   81
Red   81
Red Ladder Theatre Company   403
Red Pepper   81
Red Rattle Books   180
Red Dog Press   180
Redhammer Management Ltd   452
Reedsy   646
Rees Literary Agency   472
Reform   81
Renard Press Ltd   180
Repeater Books   180
Reporters Without Borders   528
Republic of Consciousness Prize for Small
    Presses   580
Resurgence & Ecologist   81
Retail Week   81
Revenge Ink   180
Rhiza Edge   200
Rialto, The   82
Rialto Nature and Place Poetry Competition,
    The   580
Lisa Richards Agency, The   453
Richford Becklow Agency   453
Richmond upon Thames Lit Fest   603
Rider *see* Ebury Publishing
Riggwelter   82
Right Book Company, The   646
Angela Rinaldi Literary Agency, The   472
Riptide Journal   82
Rizzoli International Publications, Inc.   218
RNIB National Library Service   688
Robertson Murray Literary Agency   453
Rocking Chair Books Literary Agency   453
Rodale Book Group   219
University of Roehampton   702
Rogers, Coleridge & White Ltd   453
Deborah Rogers Foundation Writers Award and
    David Miller Bursary   580
Romantic Novel of the Year Awards, The   580
Romantic Novelists' Association, The   553

George Ronald   180
Ronsdale Press   203
Root Literary   472
Felix Rosenstiels Widow & Son Ltd   499
Jane Rotrosen Agency   472
Roundhouse Group   181
Route   181
Routledge   219
Routledge *see* Taylor & Francis Group
Rowanvale Books Ltd   646
Rowman & Littlefield   219   181
Elizabeth Roy Literary Agency   454
Royal Academy of Arts   522
Royal Birmingham Society of Artists   522
Royal Central School of Speech and Drama,
    The   702
Royal Collection Trust   181
Royal Court Theatre   395
Royal Exchange Theatre Company Ltd   399
Royal Institute of Oil Painters   522
Royal Institute of Painters in Water Colours   522
Royal Literary Fund, The   591
Royal Lyceum Theatre Company   399
Royal Musical Association, The   523
Royal National Institute of Blind People
    (RNIB)   181   82
Royal National Theatre   395
Royal Photographic Society, The   523
Royal Scottish Academy of Art and Architecture,
    The   523
Royal Shakespeare Company   399
Royal Society, The   523
RSA (Royal Society for the Encouragement of Arts,
    Manufactures and Commerce)   523
Royal Society of British Artists   523
Royal Society of Literature   524
RSL Christopher Bland Prize   580
RSL Giles St Aubyn Awards for Non-Fiction   581
RSL Ondaatje Prize   581
Royal Society of Marine Artists   524
Royal Society of Miniature Painters, Sculptors and
    Gravers, The   524
Royal Society of Painter-Printmakers   524
Royal Society of Portrait Painters   524
Royal Society of Sculptors   524
Royal Society Young People's Book Prize, The   581
Royal Television Society   383
Royal Watercolour Society   524
Royal West of England Academy   524
RSPCA Young Photographer Awards   581
RTÉ   381
RTÉ Radio 1 Short Story Competition in Honour of
    Francis MacManus   581
RTÉ Radio, Drama On One, P.J. O'Connor Awards
    for Radio Drama   581
Rubery Book Award   581
Ruby Tuesday Books Ltd   181
Rugby World   82
Runciman Award   581
Runner's World   82

Running Press Book Publishers 219
Ruppin Agency, The 454
RUSI Journal 82
Ruskin Society, The 537
Rutgers University Press 219
Rye Arts Festival 603
Ryland Peters & Small 181
John Rylands Research Institute and Library 688

S4C 381
SAA 542
Sabotage Reviews 345
Saffron Books 181
Saga Magazine 83
SAGE Publishing 182
Sainsbury's Magazine 83
University of St Andrews 702
St. David's Press 182
St Martin's Press, Inc. 219
St Pauls Publishing 182
Salariya Book Company Ltd 182
University of Salford 702
Salisbury International Arts Festival 603
Salisbury Playhouse 400
Salt Publishing 182
Saltire Society Literary Awards, The 581
SAMS Publishing see Pearson UK
Sandstone Press Ltd 182
Santa Monica Press 219
Santoro London 499
Sapere Books 182
Saqi Books 182
Saraband 183
Sarasvati 83
Sasquatch Books 219
Saunders see Elsevier (Clinical Solutions)
Malcolm Saville Society, The 537
Sawday's 183
Dorothy L. Sayers Society, The 537
Sayle Literary Agency, The 454
Sayle Screen Ltd 454
Scarborough News 35
Scattered Authors' Society 553
SCBWI-BI Writers' Events 696
Sceptre see Hodder & Stoughton
Schofield & Sims Ltd 183
Scholastic Australia Pty Ltd 200
Scholastic, Inc. 219
Scholastic Ltd 183
School Librarian, The 83
School Libraries in View 83
School Library Association (SLA) 690
Susan Schulman Literary Agency LLC 472
Science Factory Ltd, The 454
Science Museum Group 183
Science Museum Library 688
Scientific Computing World 83
SCM Press see Hymns Ancient and Modern Ltd
Scotland on Sunday 20
Scotland Street Press 183
Scots Magazine, The 83

Scotsman 20
Walter Scott Prize for Historical Fiction 582
Scott Meredith Literary Agency 473
Kim Scott Walwyn Prize, The 582
Scottish Arts Club 547
Scottish Association of Writers 553
Scottish Book of the Year see Saltire Society Literary
    Awards, The
Scottish Book Trust 530
Scottish Farmer, The 83
Scottish Fellowship of Christian Writers 553
Scottish Field 84
Scottish First Book of the Year see Saltire Society
    Literary Awards, The
Scottish Newspaper Society 528
Scottish Poetry Library 344
Scottish Research Book Award see Saltire Society
    Literary Awards, The
Scottish Sun 20
Scottish Universities' International Summer
    School 696
Scovil Galen Ghosh Literary Agency, Inc. 473
Screen International 84
Scribe 184
Scripture Union 184
Scunthorpe Telegraph 35
Sea Angler 84
Sea Breezes 84
Seal Press 220
Seamus Heaney Centre at Queen's, The 343
Search Press Ltd 184
Second Nature Ltd 499
Seen and Heard 84
Segora International Writing Competitions 582
Linda Seifert Management Ltd 454
Self-Publishing Conference, The 603
Self-Publishing Partnership, The 647
SelfBuild & Design 84
SelfMadeHero 184
Selfpublishbooks.ie 647
Self-Publishing Review 647
Sentinel 34, 220
September Publishing 184
Seren 184
Seven Stories – The National Centre for Children's
    Books 530
Seventh Avenue Literary Management 463
Severn House Publishers 184
Sewing Directory, The 84
SFX Magazine 84
Sharland Organisation Ltd, The 455
Shaw Society, The 537
Shearsman Books 184
Sheffield Hallam University 702
Sheffield Theatres 400
Sheil Land Associates Ltd 455
Caroline Sheldon Literary Agency Ltd 455
Sheldon Press see John Murray Press
Sheldrake Press 184
Shepheard-Walwyn (Publishers) Ltd 184

Sherman Theatre   400
Shields Gazette, The   27
Ships Monthly   84
Shire Books   185
Shooter Literary Magazine   85
Shooting Times and Country Magazine   85
Shoreline of Infinity   85
Short Books Ltd   185
Shortlands Poetry Circle   343
Show of Strength Theatre Company Ltd   400
Shropshire Star   34
Shuter and Shooter Publishers (Pty) Ltd   206
Shuttle, The   34
Mo Siewcharran Prize   592
Sight and Sound   85
Sigma Press   185
Silvertail Books   185
SilverWood Books   647
Simon & Schuster Audio   225
Simon & Schuster (Australia) Pty Ltd   200
Simon & Schuster Children's Publishing
    Division   220
Simon & Schuster, Inc.   220
Simon & Schuster UK Ltd   185
André Simon Memorial Fund Book Awards,
    The   583
Sinclair-Stevenson   455
Siri Scientific Press   185
Sirius Media Services Ltd   97
Skier and Snowboarder Magazine   85
Sky   382
Sky Arts RSL Writers Awards   593
Skyhorse Publishing   220
Skylark Literary Limited   455
Skyros Writers' Lab   696
Slightly Foxed   85
Slimming World Magazine   85
Beverley Slopen   463
Smart Quill Editorial & Scouting   647
Wilbur Smith Adventure Writing Prize   583
Robert Smith Literary Agency Ltd   455
Colin Smythe Ltd   185
Jill Smythies Award, The   583
Snowbooks Ltd   185
SoapBox   347
Socialist Worker   20
Society for Promoting Christian Knowledge   186
Society for Theatre Research, The   545
Society of Artists Agents   519
Society of Authors, The   519
Society of Botanical Artists, The   543
Society of Children's Book Writers and Illustrators
    (SCBWI)   553
Society of Civil and Public Service Writers, The   554
Society of Editors   528
Society of Genealogists Enterprises Ltd   186
Society of Graphic Fine Art   543
Society of Heraldic Arts   543
Society of Medical Writers, The   554
Society of Scribes and Illuminators   543

Society of Wildlife Artists   543
Society of Women Artists, The   543
Society of Women Writers & Journalists   528
Society of Young Publishers   519
Softwood Self-Publishing   647
Soho Agency Ltd (previously LAW/Lucas Alexander
    Whitley Ltd), The   456
Soho Press, Inc.   220
Soho Theatre   395
Somerville Press Ltd   186
Songwriter, The   86
Songwriting and Composing   86
Sourcebooks, Inc.   220
South African Writers' Circle   554
SOUTH Poetry Magazine   86
South Wales Argus   33
South Wales Echo   33
South Wales Evening Post   33
University of South Wales   702
Southern Daily Echo   31
Southport Reporter   28
Southwater see Anness Publishing
Southwest Scriptwriters   554
SP Literary Agency   456
Sparsile Books   186
SPCK see Society for Promoting Christian Knowledge
Spear's Magazine   86
Speciality Food   86
Spectator, The   86
Speechmark Publishing Ltd   186
Stephen Spender Prize, The   583
Sphere see Little, Brown Book Group
Sphinx Theatre Company   403
Spiffing Covers   647
Spinifex Press   200
Philip G. Spitzer Literary Agency Inc.   473
Spon see Taylor & Francis Group
SportBooks Ltd   186
Telegraph Sports Book Awards, The   583
Sports Journalists' Association   528
Spread the Word   554
Springer Nature Group Ltd   186
Spruce see Octopus Publishing Group
square mile   86
SRL Publishing Ltd   187
Stacey Publishing Ltd   187
Stage, The   86
Stainer & Bell Ltd   187
Stamp Magazine   86
Stand Magazine   87
Stanford University Press   221
Stanfords Travel Writers Festival, The   604
StAnza: Scotland's International Poetry Festival   604
States of Independence   604
Staunch Book Prize   583
Elaine Steel Writers' Agent   456
Abner Stein   456
Micheline Steinberg Associates   456
Stenlake Publishing Ltd   187
Stephen Joseph Theatre   400

Rochelle Stevens & Co   456
Robert Louis Stevenson Club, The   537
Stewed Rhubarb Press   187
Stiwdio Maelor   696
Stonewood Press   187
Story Therapy CIC   531
Strad, The   87
Stratford-upon-Avon Literary Festival   604
Stratford-upon-Avon Poetry Festival   604
Stripes see Little Tiger Group
Strong Words   87
Strothman Agency, The   473
Structo   87
Studio Press   187
Stuff   87
Style at Home   87
Stylist   87
Sarah Such Literary Agency   457
Suffolk Norfolk Life   88
Summer Festival of Writing, The   604
Summersdale Publishers Ltd   188
Sun   20
Sun on Sunday   20
Sunbird Publishers see Jonathan Ball Publishers
Sunday Business Post   21
Sunday Express   21
Sunday Independent   21
Sunday Life   24
Sunday Mail   21
Sunday Mercury   34
Sunday Mirror   21
Sunday National   21
Sunday People   21
Sunday Post   22
Sunday Sun, The   27
Sunday Telegraph   22
Sunday Times, The   22
Sunday Times Audible Short Story Award, The   584
Sunday Times/University of Warwick Young Writer
    of the Year Award, The   584
Sunderland Echo   27
Sunflower Books   188
Surrey Life   88
Survivors' Poetry   343
Susijn Agency Ltd, The   457
Sussex Academic Press   188
Swansea Grand Theatre   400
Swansea University Dylan Thomas Prize   584
Swanwick, The Writers' Summer School   696
Carolyn Swayze Literary Agency Ltd   463
Sweet & Maxwell   188
Emily Sweet Associates   457
Sweet Cherry Publishing   188
Swindon Advertiser   31
Swindon Festival of Literature   604

Tablet, The   88
James Tait Black Memorial Prizes, The   584
Take a Break   88
Take a Break's Take a Puzzle   88
Talawa Theatre Company   403

Tallbean   496
Tango Books Ltd   188
Tantamount   648
Tarquin Publications   188
Taschen UK Ltd   188
Tate Enterprises Ltd   188
TATE ETC   88
Tate Library & Archive   688
Tatler   88
Noel Tatt Group/Impress Publishing   499
I.B. Tauris   189
Taxation   88
Taylor & Francis Group   189
Reginald Taylor and Lord Fletcher Essay
    Competition   585
Tears in the Fence   88
Telegraph & Argus   35
Telegraph – Content Licensing & Syndication,
    The   97
Television   89
Templar Books   189
Tempo   89
Ten Speed Press   221
University of Tennessee Press   221
Tennyson Agency, The   457
Tennyson Society, The   537
Michael Terence Publishing   648
TES (The Times Educational Supplement)   22
TESS (The Times Educational Supplement
    Scotland)   22
University of Texas Press   221
TFS Literary Agency   464
TGO (The Great Outdoors) Magazine   89
Thames & Hudson Ltd   189
that's life!   89
THE (Times Higher Education)   22
Royal Society Science Book Prize, The   585
Theakston Old Peculier Crime Writing Festival   604
Theatr Clwyd   400
Theatre Absolute   403
Theatre Centre   403
Theatre Royal Bath   401
Theatre Royal Plymouth   401
Theatre Royal, Stratford East   395
Theatre Royal Windsor   401
Think Books   189
Thinkwell Books   189
This England   89
Thistle Publishing   189
Vicki Thomas Associates   496
Dylan Thomas Exhibition, The   604
Edward Thomas Fellowship, The   537
Dylan Thomas Society   538
Thompson Educational Publishing   203
Thomson Reuters – Round Hall   190
Three Hares Publishing   190
Time Out London   89
Times, The   23
Times/Chicken House Children's Fiction
    Competition, The   585

Tinniswood Award, The   585
Tiny Owl Publishing Ltd   190
Tir na n-Og Awards   585
Titan Books   190
TLC Literary Adventures   697
TLC/Arts Council England Free Reads Scheme   591
TLS (The Times Literary Supplement)   23
Today's Golfer   89
Tolkien Society, The   538
Tolley *see* LexisNexis
Top Santé   89
Paul Torday Memorial Prize, The   586
University of Toronto Press   203
Tortoise   23
Total Film   90
Totleigh Barton   697
Toucan Books Ltd   228
Tower Poetry   343
Christopher Tower Poetry Prize   349
Trail   90
Tramp Press DAC   190
Translation Prizes, The   586
Translators Association   546
Transworld Publishers   190
Betty Trask Prize and Awards, The   586
Travellers' Tales   697
Travelling Scholarships, The   591
Traverse Theatre   401
Simon Trewin Literary and Media Rights
      Agency   457
Trident Media Group   473
Trigger Publishing   190
Trinity College Library Dublin   685
Troika   191
Trollope Society, The   538
Troubador Publishing Ltd   191
Trout & Salmon   90
Truck & Driver   90
Trucking   90
Try Writing   648
TSO (The Stationery Office)   191
Tundra Books   203
Jane Turnbull Agency   457
Nick Turner Management Ltd   457
Turner Society, The   543
Tuttle Publishing/Periplus Editions   221
TV Times Magazine   90
25 Beautiful Homes   90
Two Piers Literary Agency   458
Two Rivers Press Ltd   191
2QT Ltd (Publishing)   648
Tŷ Newydd Writing Centre   348, 697

UEA Live   605
UK Greetings Ltd   499
Ulric Publishing   191
Ulverscroft Ltd   191, 225
Unbound   196
Unicorn Publishing Group LLP   191
Unicorn Theatre   395
Unisa Press   207

United Agents LLP   458
UNSW Press   200
Merlin Unwin Books Ltd   192
Jo Unwin Literary Agency   458
Upton Cressett Foundation   697
Upton Cressett Literary and History Festival   605
Urban Writers' Retreat   697
Usborne Publishing Ltd   192
UWA Publishing   200

Vallentine Mitchell   192
Valley Press   192
Van Schaik Publishers   207
V&A Illustration Awards, The   586
Vanity Fair   90
Vegan, The   90
Vegan Food & Living   91
Vegan Life   91
Velocity Press   192
Ver Poets   343
Ver Poets Open Competition   586
Veritas Publications   192
Vermilion *see* Ebury Publishing
Verso Ltd   192
Victoria University Press   204
Viking *see* Penguin General
Viking Press *see* Penguin Publishing Group
Viking Sevenseas NZ Ltd   205
Vintage   192
Virgin Media   382
Virtue Books Ltd   193
Visible Fictions   401
Vital Spark, The *see* Neil Wilson Publishing Ltd
Viz   91
Vogue   91
Voice, The   23
Voice of the Listener & Viewer   528
Voices for the Library   690

Wade and Co. Literary Agency Ltd   458
Wainwright Prize, The   586
Waitrose Food   91
Wales Book of the Year Award   586
Wales on Sunday   23
University of Wales Press   193
University of Wales Trinity Saint David   702
walk   91
Walker Books Ltd   193
Walker Books US   221
Wallpaper*   91
Walmsley Society, The   538
Wanderlust   91
War Cry, The   92
Warwick Prize for Women in Translation, The   587
University of Warwick   702
Warwick Words History Festival   605
Wasafiri   92
University of Washington Press   221
WaterBrook Multnomah Publishing Group   222
Waterways World   92
Watford Palace Theatre   401

Watkins Media   193
Watkins Publishing   194
Watkins/Loomis Agency Inc.   473
Watson, Little Ltd   458
Watson-Guptill Publications   222
Franklin Watts *see* Hachette Children's Group
Wayland *see* Hachette Children's Group
Ways With Words Festivals of Words and
    Ideas   605
Mary Webb Society   538
Week, The   92
Weekly News, The   92
Josef Weinberger Plays Ltd   194, 458
Welbeck Publishing Group   194
Wellcome Book Prize   587
Wellcome Library   688
Wells Festival of Literature   605
H.G. Wells Society, The   538
Welsh Academic Press   194
WENN   97
Wessex News, Features and Photos Agency   98
Western Daily Press   32
Western Morning News   32
Westminster Music Library   688
Westminster Reference Library   683
Westwood Creative Artists   463
Wey Poets (Surrey Poetry Centre)   348
WGM Atlantic Talent and Literary Group   458
What Car?   92
What's On TV   92
Whispering Buffalo Literary Agency Ltd   459
White Bear Theatre Club   395
Eve White Literary Agency Limited   459
White Magic Studios   648
White Review, The   92, 587
whitefox   648
Whitfield Prize, The   587
Whittet Books Ltd   194
WI Life   92
Wide Eyed Editions   194
Dinah Wiener Ltd   459
Wigtown Book Festival   605
Oscar Wilde Society, The   538
Wildlife Photographer of the Year   587
John Wiley & Sons Australia Ltd   200
John Wiley & Sons Ltd   194
John Wiley & Sons, Inc.   222
Alice Williams Literary   459
Henry Williamson Society, The   538
Neil Wilson Publishing Ltd   195
Philip Wilson Publishers   195
Winchester Poetry Festival   605
Winchester Poetry Prize   587
Windmill Books *see* Cornerstone
Windmill Books Ltd   228
Wingate Literary Prize   587
Wise Words Editorial   648
Wishing Well Studios   499
Wits University Press   207
WME   459, 473

P.G. Wodehouse Society (UK), The   539
Wolfson History Prize, The   587
Woman   93
Woman Alive   93
woman&home   93
Woman's Own   93
Woman's Way   93
Woman's Weekly   93
Wombat Books   201
Women Poets' Prize at the Rebecca Swift
    Foundation   588
Women Together   93
Women Who Draw   543
Women's Library @ LSE   688
Women's Prize for Fiction   588
David T.K. Wong Fellowship   591
Wooden Books   195
Woodmansterne Publications Ltd   499
Woodworker, The   93
Virginia Woolf Society of Great Britain   539
Worcester News   34
Word Tank, The   648
WordLink Incorporated   473
Wordsworth Library   689
Working Class Movement Library   689
Working Class Writers Festival   593
Working Partners Ltd   228
Workman Publishing Company   222
World Book Day   606
World Fishing & Aquaculture   94
World Illustration Awards   588
World of Interiors, The   94
World Soccer   94
World Today, The   94
Worshipful Company of Stationers and Newspaper
    Makers, The   554
Wrate's Editing Services   649
Wren Library   689
WriteNow Programme   594
Write Out Loud   345
Writers Advice Centre for Children's Books   554
Writers & Artists   594, 697
Writers' & Artists' Yearbook 2022 Short Story
    Competition   588
Writers & Artists Working-Class Writers' Prize   593
Writers Bureau, The   698
Writer's Digest Books   222
Writers Guild of America, East Inc.   520
Writers Guild of America, West Inc.   520
Writers Guild of Canada   520
WGGB (Writers' Guild of Great Britain)   520
Writers Guild of Ireland   520
Writers House LLC   473
Writers' Practice, The   459
Writers' Union of Canada, The   520
Writers' Weekend, The   606
WRITERSWORLD   649
Writing Hall, The   649
Writing Magazine   94

Wylie Agency Inc., The   473
Wylie Agency (UK) Ltd, The   460

Y Lolfa Cyf   195
Yachting Journalists' Association   529
Yachting Monthly   94
Yachting World   94
Yachts and Yachting   94
YALC (Young Adult Literature Convention)   606
Yale University Press   222
Yale University Press London   195
Susan Yearwood Agency   460
Yellow Jersey Press *see* Vintage
Yen Press   222
York Theatre Royal   401
York Publishing Services   649
Yorkshire Life   95
Yorkshire Post   35
Young Poets Network   349
Francis Brett Young Society   539

Young Vic Theatre Company   395
A Younger Theatre   396
Your Cat Magazine   95
Your Dog Magazine   95
Your Horse Magazine   95
Yours   95
Yours Fiction   95
YouTube Originals   382
YouView   382
YouWriteOn.com Book Awards   588

Zaffre   195
Zambezi Publishing Ltd   195
Zed Books Ltd   195
Zeitgeist Agency   462
Zeno Agency Ltd   460
ZigZag Education   195
Zooker Award   588
Zoological Society of London Library   689